2006

YEARBOOK OF CHINA AGRICULTURAL PRODUCTS PROCESSING INDUSTRIES

中国农产品加工业年鉴

科学技术部农村科技司
中国农业机械化科学研究院 编
中国包装和食品机械总公司

中国农业出版社
CHINA AGRICULTURE PRESS

内 容 简 介

本年鉴较系统地记述了我国有关农产品加工业发展的方针、政策、法律、法规和规划等贯彻执行情况；有关领导、专家对发展我国农产品加工业的论述；本领域内相关行业的发展综述；简介了相关行业经济运行情况及名、优、特、新产品；全面介绍了我国各省、自治区、直辖市农产品加工业发展现状；登载了农产品加工业的国内外统计资料；记载了相关的国家标准、行业标准、专利以及本行业的大事记。本年鉴资料新颖、准确、科学、翔实，内容丰富，可供政府管理部门、协会、学会、中介组织、生产企业、科研教学单位的管理人员、策划人员、教育工作者和科技工作者参考。

《中国农产品加工业年鉴》编辑委员会

编　辑　部

地　　址：北京市德胜门外北沙滩 1 号 82 信箱

邮　　编：100083

电　　话：010 - 64882617

传　　真：010 - 64878271　64862459

E - mail：cpfmchy@caams. org. cn

编辑出版说明

一、为紧跟我国农产品加工业发展的时代脉搏和大力宣传主旋律，在各级领导和行业专家的支持与帮助下，我们组织编辑出版的《中国农产品加工业年鉴》(2006) 与广大读者见面了，其宗旨是为我国农产品加工业的发展起到桥梁和促进作用。

二、《中国农产品加工业年鉴》由科学技术部、国家发展和改革委员会、农业部、国家林业局、国家粮食局、中华全国供销合作总社、中国机械工业联合会、中国轻工业联合会的有关主管部门及农产品加工业相关协会、学会、科研院所、大专院校等，与中国农业机械化科学研究院、中国包装和食品机械总公司联合编辑出版。

三、《中国农产品加工业年鉴》(2006) 安排了8个部分的框架内容，每个栏目名称基本未变，其中的内容和数据均以2005年的基本情况为主，但根据资料的获取难易程度也有部分2005年前后的情况，并保持每卷年鉴的连续性。其中的政策法规及重要文件、大事记均以2006年的基本情况为主。

四、《中国农产品加工业年鉴》记述了相关方针、政策、法律、法规和规划等贯彻执行情况；记述了有关领导、专家对发展我国农产品加工业的论述；记述了本领域相关行业的发展综述；介绍了农产品加工业行业经济运行情况及名、优、特、新产品；介绍了我国各省、自治区、直辖市农产品加工业发展现状；登载了农产品加工业国内外统计资料；记载了相关的国家标准、行业标准、专利以及本行业的大事记。年鉴既述事，也记人，每年编辑、出版一卷。若干年后，不但可以见证我国每年的农产品加工业发展情况，而且将是系统、全面、可靠、翔实的史册和工具书。由于年鉴的权威性和正式的连续出版发行，将有益于国内外各界了解和研究我国农产品加工业现状与发展等情况，促进相互交流与合作；有益于各部门借鉴现实和历史经验，掌握全局，运筹帷幄，制定政策和发展规划，指导本行业健康发展；有益于社会各界沟通行业信息、产品信息，互相学习，取长补短，推动我国农产品加工业的发展和国民经济的腾飞。

五、本年鉴各部分所列数据，因来源渠道不同，不尽一致。全面的数据均以国家统计局提供的为准。本年鉴全国性统计数据均不包括香港、澳门两个特别行政区和台湾省。两区一省的相关数据，在年鉴的附录中列出。

六、为系统、准确、科学、翔实地反映我国农产品加工业现状，并力争办出本年鉴的特色，我们在编辑中继续突出了综述文章以当年国家重点抓的农产品加工业中的有关行业为主，全书内容以推动产业发展为主，国家标准、行业标准与专利以加工工艺、设备和相应的产品为主，统计数据以国家统计局经济行业分类为主，国外的统计数据以特点显著的部分发达国家和少数发展中国家为主等。

七、本年鉴的编辑、出版、发行等工作，得到了中央及各级有关部门、协会、学会、科研院所、高等院校、生产企业、社会团体的大力支持和帮助，谨此表示衷心的感谢。

目 录

编辑出版说明

第一部分 专题论述

积极发展农产品加工业 构筑新农村与和谐社会的产业支撑 …… 3
努力实施"双百市场工程" 大力推进农产品现代流通体系建设 …… 8
加强食品药品监管 当好人民健康的保卫者 …… 11
全面建设小康社会 加快推进粮食科技创新体系建设 …… 14
继承发展 改革创新 全面开创食品安全监管工作新局面 …… 19
"十一五"期间我国纺织工业的发展 …… 30
加强体系队伍能力建设 推动无公害农产品事业快速发展 …… 33
食品工业承前启后 继续保持良好快速发展态势 …… 40
我国肉类工业的经济运行状况与发展特点 …… 45
我国造纸工业的发展与"十一五"展望 …… 47
我国印刷及设备器材工业的回顾与展望 …… 51
落实"十一五"规划精神 开创皮革行业发展新局面 …… 53
我国橡胶工业现状及"十一五"目标 …… 56

第二部分 相关行业发展概况

粮油食品加工业 …… 61
油料加工业 …… 66
大豆加工业 …… 69
淀粉加工业 …… 75
制糖工业 …… 78
乳制品制造业 …… 81
果品加工业 …… 86
蔬菜加工业 …… 92
茶叶加工业 …… 97
蜂产品加工业 …… 100
食用菌加工业 …… 105
烟草加工业 …… 108
酿酒工业 …… 112
蚕丝加工业 …… 115
饲料加工业 …… 118
水产品加工业 …… 123
林产品加工业 …… 128
农作物秸秆加工业 …… 132
机械工业系统农产品加工机械制造业 …… 135
食品与包装机械制造业 …… 137
棉花加工机械制造业 …… 140

第三部分 政策法规及重要文件

关于进一步加强流通环节食品安全监管工作的意见 …… 145
重大活动食品卫生监督规范 …… 148
国家重大食品安全事故应急预案 …… 150
出入境口岸食品卫生监督管理规定 …… 154
中华人民共和国农产品质量安全法 …… 157
农产品包装和标识管理办法 …… 161
关于加强农产品质量安全监管能力建设的意见 …… 162
关于"十一五"粮食科技发展的指导意见 …… 164
农产品出口"十一五"发展规划 …… 169
全国食品工业"十一五"发展纲要 …… 177
农产品加工业"十一五"发展规划 …… 189

第四部分 国内综合统计资料

农林牧渔业主要产品产量统计 …… 203
表 1 我国主要农产品产量（2001—2005 年） …… 203
表 2 各地区主要农产品产量（2005 年） …… 204
表 3 我国玉米主产区生产情况（2005 年） …… 209
表 4 各地区水果产量（2005 年） …… 209
表 5 各地区茶叶产量（2005 年） …… 211
表 6 我国农垦系统主要农产品产量（2004—2005 年） …… 212
表 7 各地区农垦系统主要农产品产量

(2005 年) …………………………… 213
表 8 我国农垦系统茶、蚕、果、林生产情况（2004—2005 年）………………… 214
表 9 我国热带、亚热带作物产量（2005 年） …………………………… 214
表 10 我国棉花主产区生产情况（2004—2005 年）…………………… 214
表 11 我国主要蔬菜产量增减情况（2004—2005 年）…………………… 215
表 12 我国主要林产品产量（2001—2005 年）…………………… 215
表 13 各地区主要林产品产量（2005 年）… 216
表 14 我国主要牲畜饲养情况（2001—2005 年）…………………… 217
表 15 我国主要畜产品产量（2001—2005 年）…………………… 217
表 16 各地区奶类产量（2004—2005 年） … 218
表 17 我国农垦系统主要畜产品产量（2004—2005 年）…………………… 218
表 18 我国水产品产量（2001—2005 年） … 219
表 19 各地区水产品产量（2005 年） ……… 219
表 20 我国沿海地区海洋捕捞水产品产量（2005 年）…………………………… 220
表 21 我国沿海地区海水养殖水产品产量（2005 年）…………………………… 220
表 22 各地区农垦系统水产品产量（2005 年）…………………………… 221
表 23 轻工业系统食品工业所需农牧业原料生产量（2003—2004 年） …………… 222
表 24 我国各地区主要中药材产量（2005 年）…………………………… 223
表 25 我国按人口平均的主要农畜产品产量（2001—2005 年）…………………… 223
农产品加工机械拥有量及农产品加工行业固定资产投资情况…………………… 224
表 26 农业部系统农产品加工机械年末拥有量（2005 年） …………………… 224
表 27 我国农产品加工行业固定资产投资情况（2005 年） ………………… 225
表 28 我国农产品加工行业新增固定资产后主要产品新增生产能力（2004—2005 年）…………………… 225
表 29 我国农产品加工行业 50 万元以上施工、投产项目个数（2005 年） …… 226
表 30 林业系统森工固定资产投资（2005 年） …………………………… 226
表 31 林业系统各地区森工固定资产投资（2005 年） …………………………… 226
表 32 我国农垦系统固定资产投资（2004—2005 年） ………………………… 227
表 33 我国食品工业完成固定资产投资后新增主要产品生产能力（2003—2004 年）……………………………………… 227
表 34 我国水产行业固定资产投资（2004—2005 年） ………………………… 227
按国民经济行业分类统计农产品加工业现状…… 228
表 35 我国农产品加工业全部国有及规模以上非国有工业企业主要指标（2005 年） …………………………… 228
表 36 我国农产品加工业全部国有及规模以上非国有工业企业主要经济效益指标（2005 年） …………………………… 228
表 37 我国农产品加工业国有及国有控股工业企业主要指标（2005 年） …………… 229
表 38 我国农产品加工业国有及国有控股工业企业主要经济效益指标（2005 年）… 229
表 39 我国农产品加工业“三资”工业企业主要指标（2005 年） ………………… 230
表 40 我国农产品加工业“三资”工业企业主要经济效益指标（2005 年） ……… 230
表 41 我国农产品加工业私营工业企业主要指标（2005 年） ………………… 231
表 42 我国农产品加工业私营工业企业主要经济效益指标（2005 年） ……… 231
表 43 我国农产品加工业大中型工业企业主要指标（2005 年） ………………… 231
表 44 我国农产品加工业大中型工业企业主要经济效益指标（2005 年） ……… 232
表 45 2005/2006 年制糖期全国制糖行业主要经济技术指标 ………………… 232
表 46 我国食品和包装机械生产、经营、销售情况（2005 年） ………………… 232
表 47 林业系统农产品加工业总产值及销售产值（2004—2005 年） ………… 233
表 48 林业系统各地区农产品加工业总产值（2005 年） …………………………… 233
表 49 林业系统各地区农产品加工业销售产值（2005 年） ……………………… 235
表 50 林业系统农产品加工业国有独立核算大中型工业企业主要经济效益指标（2005 年） …………………………… 236
表 51 林业系统农产品加工业各地区国有

独立核算大中型工业企业主要经济效益指标（2005 年） …………………… 237
表 52 我国水产品加工业发展情况（2004—2005 年） ……………………… 238
表 53 我国水产品加工业加工能力、产量及产值（2002—2005 年） ………………… 238
表 54 我国沿海省、自治区、直辖市水产品加工业生产情况（2005 年） ………… 239
表 55 我国乡镇集体企业农产品加工业现状（2004 年） ……………………………… 239
表 56 我国乡镇规模以上农产品加工业企业基本情况（2004—2005 年） …… 240
表 57 轻工业系统农产品加工业分行业主要经济指标（2004 年） …………… 240
表 58 轻工业系统食品工业分行业主要经济指标（2004 年） …………… 240
表 59 我国食品工业焙烤糖制食品行业主要经济指标（2004 年） …………… 241
表 60 我国饮料行业主要经济指标（2003—2004 年） ……………………… 242
表 61 我国乳制品行业主要经济指标（2004—2005 年） ……………………… 242
表 62 轻工业系统机械行业重点企业分类（涉及农产品加工部分）主要经济指标（2004 年） ………………… 242
表 63 我国烟草工业主要经济指标（2003—2004 年） ……………………… 242
表 64 我国纺织工业主要经济指标（2005 年） ……………………………… 243
表 65 纺织工业国有及国有控股企业主要经济指标（2005 年） …………… 243
表 66 纺织工业棉纺行业规模以上企业主要经济指标（2005 年） …………… 244
表 67 纺织工业毛纺行业规模以上企业主要经济指标（2005 年） …………… 244
表 68 纺织工业丝绸行业规模以上企业主要经济指标（2005 年） ……… 245
表 69 纺织工业麻纺织行业主要经济指标（2005 年） …………………… 245
表 70 纺织工业印染行业规模以上企业主要经济指标（2005 年） …………… 246
表 71 纺织工业针织行业规模以上企业主要经济指标（2005 年） …………… 246
表 72 纺织工业服装制造业主要经济指标（2005 年） ………………………… 246
表 73 纺织工业纺机行业主要经济指标（2005 年） ……………………………… 247
表 74 我国皮革工业经济运行情况（2003—2004 年） ……………………… 247
表 75 我国家具行业经济运行情况（2003—2004 年） ……………………… 247
表 76 我国造纸工业各地区主要经济指标（2004 年） ……………………………… 247
表 77 我国新闻出版业产业基本情况（2004 年） ……………………………… 248
表 78 我国 120 个书刊印刷企业（含其他印刷）主要经济指标（2004 年） …… 249
表 79 我国 120 个包装印刷企业主要经济指标（2003—2004 年） ……………… 249
表 80 我国 58 个印刷机械企业主要经济指标（2004 年） …………………… 249
表 81 我国橡胶工业主要经济指标（2005 年） ……………………………… 250
表 82 我国橡胶工业全部独立核算工业企业主要经济指标（2001—2003 年） …… 250
表 83 我国中药行业经济效益情况（2004—2005 年） ……………………… 251
表 84 我国农产品加工业能源消费总量和主要能源品种消费量（2004 年） …… 251
农产品加工业主要产品产量 ………………………… 252
表 85 我国农产品加工业主要产品产量（2004—2005 年） ……………………… 252
表 86 轻工业系统农产品加工业主要产品产量（2004 年） …………………… 252
表 87 我国粮油工业主要产品产量（2003—2004 年） ……………………… 253
表 88 我国淀粉产量及品种情况（2005 年） ……………………………… 253
表 89 我国淀粉深加工品产量（2005 年） … 254
表 90 我国淀粉产量分布及生产规模情况（2005 年） ……………………………… 254
表 91 我国玉米淀粉生产规模情况（2005 年） ……………………………… 254
表 92 我国部分淀粉深加工品生产规模情况（2004—2005 年） ……………… 255
表 93 我国食品添加剂主要产品产量（2003—2004 年） ……………………… 256
表 94 我国饮料行业软饮料各地区主要产品产量（2004 年） …………………… 256
表 95 我国罐头工业各地区产品产量（2003—2004 年） ……………………… 257
表 96 我国烟草工业主要产品产量

（2002—2004 年）……………………… 257
表 97 我国酒精工业产品产量（2003—2004 年）……………………… 258
表 98 我国各地区白酒产量（2003—2004 年）……………………… 258
表 99 我国饲料工业产品产量（2002—2005 年）……………………… 259
表 100 2005/2006 年制糖期糖料与食糖生产情况 ……………………………… 259
表 101 我国食用菌产量、产值、出口情况（2005 年） ………………………… 260
表 102 我国农垦系统农产品加工业主要产品产量（2004—2005 年）……………… 262
表 103 农垦系统各地区农产品加工业主要产品产量（2005 年）………………… 263
表 104 我国森林工业主要产品产量（2004—2005 年） …………………… 264
表 105 林业系统森林工业主要产品产量（2004—2005 年） …………………… 264
表 106 各地区森林工业主要产品产量（2005 年） ………………………… 266
表 107 林业系统各地区森林工业主要产品产量（2005 年）……………………… 267
表 108 我国水产品加工产品的主要种类与产量（2002—2005 年）……………… 268
表 109 纺织工业主要产品产量（规模以上企业）（2004—2005 年） …………… 269
表 110 纺织工业丝绸行业主要产品产量（2004—2005 年） …………………… 269
表 111 纺织工业麻纺织行业主要产品产量（2004—2005 年）……………………… 270
表 112 我国皮革行业主要产品产量（2003—2004 年）……………………… 270
表 113 我国家具工业主要产品产量（2004—2005 年） …………………… 270
表 114 我国造纸工业纸浆消耗情况（2003—2004 年）……………………… 270
表 115 我国各类造纸纤维原料所占比重（2004 年） ………………………… 271
表 116 我国机制纸及纸板主要品种产量（2003—2004 年） …………………… 271
表 117 各地区重点纸品产量（2004 年） …… 271
表 118 我国纸和纸板消费结构情况（2003—2004 年） …………………… 272
表 119 我国造纸工业主要产品生产及消费情况（2003—2004 年） …………… 273
表 120 我国纸和纸板生产、消费及进口量与人均消费量（2001—2004 年） …… 273
表 121 我国 120 个重点书刊印刷（含其他印刷)企业主要产品产量（2004 年） …… 273
表 122 我国纸和纸板人均消费量与美国的比较（2001—2004 年）…………… 273
表 123 我国橡胶工业主要产品产量（2004—2005 年） …………………… 274
表 124 我国人均主要工农业产品产量（2001—2005 年） …………………… 274

农产品加工业主要产品出口创汇情况………… 275
表 125 我国海关出口农产品及加工品数量与金额（2004—2005 年）…………… 275
表 126 我国海关进口农产品及加工品数量与金额（2004—2005 年）…………… 277
表 127 我国乡镇企业主要农产品加工业产品出口创汇情况（2004—2005 年）…… 277
表 128 我国林产品进出口数量（2004—2005 年） …………………… 278
表 129 我国林产品进出口金额（2004—2005 年） …………………… 279
表 130 我国食用菌产品出口情况（2005 年） ……………………………… 281
表 131 轻工业系统农产品加工业主要出口产品创汇情况（2004 年）…………… 282
表 132 轻工业系统农产品加工业主要进口产品情况（2004 年）………………… 282
表 133 我国乳制品进口情况（2005 年）…… 283
表 134 我国乳制品出口情况（2005 年）…… 283
表 135 我国罐头产品出口情况（2004 年） …………………………… 284
表 136 我国罐头产品出口的主要国家或地区（2003—2004 年） …………………… 285
表 137 我国卷烟出口的主要国家或地区（2003—2004 年） …………………… 285
表 138 我国进口卷烟的国家或地区（2003—2004 年）……………………… 286
表 139 我国蜂蜜生产及出口情况（2002—2005 年） …………………… 286
表 140 我国蜂产品出口情况（2004—2005 年）……………………… 286
表 141 我国蜂产品出口的主要国家或地区（2005 年） …………………………… 286
表 142 我国水产品进出口贸易情况（2002—2005 年） …………………… 287
表 143 我国食品和包装机械进出口情况

(2004—2005 年) …………………… 287
表 144 纺织工业纺织原料及制品进出口额统计(2005 年) …………………… 288
表 145 纺织工业纺织品服装进出口额(2005 年) …………………… 289
表 146 我国纺织品服装进出口贸易情况(2001—2005 年) …………………… 290
表 147 纺织工业主要毛纺产品进出口数量比较(2004—2005 年) …………………… 290
表 148 纺织工业针织物及针织服装出口情况(2005 年) …………………… 291
表 149 纺织工业真丝产品分类出口情况(2005 年) …………………… 291
表 150 纺织工业印染六大类产品进出口情况(2005 年) …………………… 292
表 151 纺织工业主要家纺产品出口数量和金额情况(2005 年) …………………… 292
表 152 纺织工业纺织机械进出口情况(2004—2005 年) …………………… 292
表 153 纺织工业纺织机械产品各类企业出口所占比重(2005 年) …………………… 293
表 154 我国皮革工业主要产品进出口情况(2005 年) …………………… 293
表 155 我国家具工业主要产品进出口情况(2005 年) …………………… 294
表 156 我国纸浆及废纸进出口情况(2003—2004 年) …………………… 294
表 157 我国纸、纸板、纸浆及废纸进口情况(2001—2004 年) …………………… 295
表 158 我国印刷机械进出口统计(2004 年) …………………… 295
表 159 我国中药行业进出口情况(2004—2005 年) …………………… 296
表 160 我国橡胶工业制品出口量与出口额(2001—2003 年) …………………… 296
表 161 我国橡胶工业制品进口量与进口额(2001—2003 年) …………………… 297
表 162 我国橡胶工业中轮胎细分产品进出口情况(2004 年) …………………… 297
表 163 我国橡胶工业橡胶机械进出口情况(2004 年) …………………… 298
表 164 我国天然橡胶、合成橡胶进口情况(2001—2003 年) …………………… 298
农产品加工业部分行业与企业排序 …………………… 298
表 165 2004 年轻工业系统农产品加工业分行业主要经济指标 …………………… 298
表 166 2004 年轻工业系统农产品加工业分行业进出口总额 …………………… 299
表 167 2004 年我国白酒制造业销售收入前 10 名企业 …………………… 300
表 168 2004 年我国白酒行业创利税前 10 名企业 …………………… 300
表 169 2004 年我国白酒行业白酒产量前 10 名企业 …………………… 300
表 170 2004 年我国啤酒企业自产麦芽和专业麦芽企业产品销售情况 …………………… 301
表 171 2004 年我国啤酒产量 20 万千升以上企业 …………………… 301
表 172 2004 年我国啤酒销售收入 3 亿元以上企业 …………………… 301
表 173 2004 年我国啤酒创利税总额亿元以上企业 …………………… 302
表 174 2004 年我国葡萄酒产量居行业中前 10 名的省、自治区、直辖市 …………………… 302
表 175 2004 年我国葡萄酒行业产量、效益名列前茅的省 …………………… 302
表 176 2004 年我国饮料行业按产量排序前 9 名企业 …………………… 302
表 177 2005/2006 年度我国纺织工业各行业“企业竞争力”前 10 名企业 …………………… 303
表 178 2005/2006 年度我国纺织工业出口前 100 名企业 …………………… 304
表 179 2005 年度我国纺织工业主营业务收入前 100 名企业 …………………… 306
表 180 2005 年度我国纺织工业毛纺织毛针织行业主营业务收入前 50 名企业 …………………… 307
表 181 2005 年度我国纺织工业针织行业主营业务收入前 50 名企业 …………………… 307
表 182 2005 年度我国纺织工业丝绸行业主营业务收入前 30 名企业 …………………… 308
表 183 2005 年度我国纺织工业棉纺(色)织行业主营业务收入前 50 名企业 …………………… 308
表 184 2005 年度我国纺织工业化纤行业主营业务收入前 50 名企业 …………………… 309
表 185 2005 年度我国纺织工业麻纺织行业主营业务收入前 30 名企业 …………………… 310
表 186 2005 年度我国纺织工业印染行业主营业务收入前 50 名企业 …………………… 310
表 187 2004 年我国被认定为“真皮标志生态皮革”的企业 …………………… 311
表 188 2004 年我国皮革工业荣获“中国真皮名鞋品牌”与“中国真皮名装品牌”

的企业 …………………………………… 311
表 189 2004 年我国重点造纸企业销售收入排名前 30 名企业 …………………… 312
表 190 2004 年我国重点造纸企业创利税总额排名前 30 名企业 …………………… 312
表 191 2004 年我国重点造纸企业产量排名前 30 名企业 …………………… 313
表 192 2002—2004 年我国纸及纸板产量 100 万 t 以上的省 …………………… 313
表 193 2004 年我国印刷企业实现利税前 20 名企业 …………………… 313
表 194 2004 年我国印刷企业胶印产量百万以上对开色令企业 …………………… 314
表 195 2004 年我国包装印刷企业销售收入亿元以上的主要企业 ………………… 314
表 196 2004 年我国包装印刷企业实现利税总额千万元以上前 20 名企业 ……… 314
表 197 2004 年我国重点造纸机械企业实现销售收入 5 000 万元以上的企业 …… 315
表 198 2004 年我国重点造纸机械企业实现利税总额 500 万元以上的企业 ……… 315
表 199 2004 年劳动生产率在 10 万元以上的重点造纸机械企业 ………………… 315
表 200 2003 年我国橡胶工业协会会员企业按销售收入排序 ……………………… 315
表 201 2004 年我国橡胶机械行业前 20 名企业主要经济指标 …………………… 316
表 202 2004 年我国中成药独立核算企业按资产总额前 50 名企业 ……………… 317
表 203 2004 年我国中成药独立核算企业销售收入前 50 名企业 ………………… 317
表 204 2005 年我国中成药按出口金额前 10 名企业 ……………………………… 318
我国西部地区综合统计…………………………… 318
表 205 我国西部地区主要农产品产量（2004—2005 年） …………………… 318
表 206 我国西部地区主要农产品单位面积产量（2004—2005 年） ……………… 319
表 207 我国西部地区茶叶产量（2005 年） ……………………………… 320
表 208 我国西部地区水果产量（2004—2005 年） …………………… 320
表 209 我国西部地区森林工业主要产品产量（2005 年） ……………………… 321
表 210 我国西部地区热带、亚热带作物面积和产量（2005 年） ………………… 321
表 211 我国西部地区主要畜产品产量（2004—2005 年） …………………… 322
表 212 我国西部地区水产品产量（2004—2005 年） …………………… 322
表 213 我国西部地区人均主要农产品、畜产品、水产品产量（2004—2005 年） ……… 322
表 214 我国西部地区农林牧渔业总产值、增加值及构成（2004—2005 年） ……… 323
表 215 我国西部地区林业产业总产值（2005 年） ……………………………… 324
表 216 我国西部地区林业系统森林工业固定资产投资（2005 年） ……………… 324
表 217 我国西部地区林业系统农产品加工业总产值（2005 年） ………………… 325
表 218 我国西部地区林业系统农产品加工业销售产值（2005 年） ……………… 326
表 219 我国西部地区林业系统农产品加工业国有独立核算大中型企业主要经济指标（2005 年） ……………………………… 327
表 220 我国西部地区乡镇规模以上农产品加工企业主要经济指标（2005 年） …………………………… 327
表 221 我国西部地区食品工业分行业工业总产值（2004 年） …………………… 328
表 222 我国西部地区纺织工业主要经济指标（2005 年） ……………………… 328
表 223 我国西部地区纺织工业（国有及国有控股企业）主要经济指标（2005 年） ………………………… 329
表 224 我国西部地区森林工业主要产品产量（2005 年） ………………………… 329
表 225 我国西部地区农垦系统主要农产品加工企业产品产量（2005 年） ……… 330
表 226 我国西部地区轻工业系统农产品加工业产品产量（2004 年） ………… 331
表 227 我国西部地区纺织工业纺织品、服装进出口额（2005 年） ……………… 332
其他………………………………………… 333
表 228 农业部批准的第十二批定点农产品批发市场（2006 年） ………………… 333
表 229 2004 年度我国食品工业最具成长性民营企业（100 个） ………………… 334
表 230 2004 年度我国食品工业百强企业…… 335
表 231 我国轻工业系统中列入国家 500 强企业的农产品加工企业（2004 年） ……………………………… 337

第五部分 各省、自治区、直辖市农产品加工业

北京京郊农产品加工业…………………………… 341
天津市农产品加工业……………………………… 343
河北省农产品加工业……………………………… 345
山西省农产品加工业……………………………… 347
内蒙古自治区农畜产品加工业…………………… 349
辽宁省农产品加工业……………………………… 352
吉林省农产品加工业……………………………… 355
黑龙江省农产品加工业…………………………… 357
上海市农产品加工业……………………………… 359
江苏省农产品加工业……………………………… 362
浙江省农产品加工业……………………………… 364
安徽省农产品加工业……………………………… 366
福建省农产品加工业……………………………… 368
江西省农产品加工业……………………………… 372
山东省农产品加工业……………………………… 375
河南省农产品加工业……………………………… 378
湖北省农产品加工业……………………………… 380
湖南省农产品加工业……………………………… 382
广东省农产品加工业……………………………… 386
广西壮族自治区农产品加工业…………………… 389
海南省农产品加工业……………………………… 392
重庆市农产品加工业……………………………… 395
四川省农产品加工业……………………………… 398
贵州省农产品加工业……………………………… 400
云南省农产品加工业……………………………… 402
西藏自治区农畜产品加工业……………………… 405
陕西省农产品加工业……………………………… 407
甘肃省农产品加工业……………………………… 409
青海省农畜产品加工业…………………………… 412
宁夏回族自治区农产品加工业…………………… 415
新疆维吾尔自治区农产品加工业………………… 420

第六部分 标准、专利

农产品加工业部分国家标准（2006 年） ……… 427
农产品加工业机械行业标准（2006 年） ……… 435
农产品加工业轻工行业标准（2006 年） ……… 436
农产品加工业纺织行业标准（2006 年） ……… 437
农产品加工业水产行业标准（2006 年） ……… 439
农产品加工业烟草行业标准（2006 年） ……… 440
农产品加工业包装行业标准（2006 年） ……… 440
农产品加工业发明专利（2005 年） ………………… 441

第七部分 大 事 记

第八部分 附 录

表 1 部分国家（地区）农业生产指数（2005 年） …………………………………… 471
表 2 我国台湾省农业生产指数（2002—2004 年） ……………………………… 471
表 3 部分国家（地区）主要粮食收获面积、单产、总产量（2005 年） ……………… 471
表 4 部分国家（地区）马铃薯收获面积、单产、总产量（2005 年） ……………… 472
表 5 部分国家（地区）甘薯收获面积、单产、总产量（2005 年） ……………… 473
表 6 部分国家（地区）木薯收获面积、单产、总产量（2005 年） ……………… 473
表 7 部分国家（地区）主要油料收获面积、单产、总产量（2005 年） ……………… 474
表 8 部分国家（地区）籽棉、黄麻收获面积、单产、总产量（2005 年） ……… 475
表 9 部分国家（地区）烟叶、茶叶收获面积、单产、总产量（2005 年） ……… 475
表 10 部分国家（地区）甘蔗、甜菜收获面积、单产、总产量（2005 年） …… 476
表 11 部分国家（地区）蔬菜、水果和坚果产量（2005 年） ………………………… 476
表 12 部分国家（地区）甘蓝、番茄收获面积、单产、总产量（2005 年） …… 477
表 13 部分国家（地区）茄子、青辣椒和青胡椒收获面积、单产、总产量（2005 年） …………………………………… 477
表 14 部分国家（地区）西葫芦和南瓜、黄瓜收获面积、单产、总产量（2005 年） …………………………………………… 478
表 15 部分国家（地区）干洋葱、大蒜收获面积、单产、总产量（2005 年） …… 478
表 16 部分国家（地区）西瓜、胡萝卜收获面积、单产、总产量（2005 年） …… 479
表 17 部分国家（地区）樱桃、葡萄收获面积、单产、总产量（2005 年） …… 479
表 18 部分国家（地区）橙、杧果等产量（2005 年） …………………………………… 480
表 19 部分国家（地区）苹果、草莓等产量（2005 年） …………………………………… 480

表 20 部分国家（地区）生咖啡、可可豆收获面积、单产、总产量（2005 年） …… 481
表 21 我国台湾省主要农产品产量（2002—2004 年） …… 481
表 22 部分国家（地区）肉类产量（2004—2005 年） …… 481
表 23 部分国家（地区）牛奶产量（2004—2005 年） …… 482
表 24 部分国家（地区）鸡蛋产量（2004—2005 年） …… 482
表 25 部分国家（地区）蜂蜜产量（2004—2005 年） …… 483
表 26 部分国家（地区）羊毛产量（2004—2005 年） …… 484
表 27 部分国家（地区）人均每天食物热值、蛋白质和脂肪含量（2003 年） …… 484
表 28 我国农业主要产品产量居世界位次（1949—2005 年） …… 485
表 29 世界主要国家天然橡胶生产情况（2003—2005 年） …… 485
表 30 世界主要农畜产品最大生产国（2005 年） …… 485
表 31 香港特别行政区工业生产指数（2002—2005 年） …… 486
表 32 我国台湾省农产品加工业主要产品产量（2001—2005 年） …… 486
表 33 美国农产品加工业主要经济指标（2000—2001 年） …… 487
表 34 日本农产品加工业主要经济指标（2001 年） …… 487
表 35 德国农产品加工业主要经济指标（2000 年） …… 488
表 36 英国农产品加工业主要经济指标（2000 年） …… 488
表 37 法国农产品加工业主要经济指标（2000 年） …… 489
表 38 意大利农产品加工业主要经济指标（1999—2000 年） …… 489
表 39 加拿大农产品加工业主要经济指标（2000—2001 年） …… 490
表 40 澳大利亚农产品加工业主要经济指标（2001 年） …… 490
表 41 印度农产品加工业主要经济指标（2001 年） …… 491
表 42 韩国农产品加工业主要经济指标（2000—2001 年） …… 491
表 43 我国台湾省出口与进口商品分类（2002—2005 年） …… 491
表 44 部分国家（地区）农产品进口额和出口额（2002—2003 年） …… 491
表 45 部分国家（地区）牛肉、绵羊肉、猪肉进出口数量（2004 年） …… 491
表 46 部分国家（地区）牛肉、绵羊肉、猪肉进出口金额（2004 年） …… 492
表 47 部分国家（地区）鸡肉、鸭肉、火鸡肉进出口数量（2004 年） …… 492
表 48 部分国家（地区）鸡肉、鸭肉、火鸡肉进出口金额（2004 年） …… 494
表 49 我国纺织服装出口到各国和地区贸易额前 10 名国家和地区（2005 年） …… 494
表 50 世界和中国纺织纤维产量（含 PP 纤维）（2002—2004 年） …… 495
表 51 世界主要国家（地区）合成纤维产量（含 PP 纤维）（2002—2004 年） …… 495
表 52 世界主要国家（地区）棉花产量（2002—2004 年） …… 495
表 53 世界主要国家棉花耗用量（2002—2004 年） …… 495
表 54 全球人均纤维消费量（1990—2004 年） …… 496
表 55 世界纸浆分类产量（2003—2004 年） …… 496
表 56 世界与中国纸浆、纸及纸板生产与消费情况（2002—2004 年） …… 496
表 57 我国台湾省主要纸品产销量情况（2004 年） …… 497
表 58 我国台湾省纸业在全球的地位（2004 年） …… 497
表 59 世界纸和纸板产量排名前 10 名的国家（2004 年） …… 497
表 60 世界纸和纸浆产量排名前 10 名的国家（2004 年） …… 498
表 61 世界纸浆主要净进口和净出口前 5 名的国家（2004 年） …… 498
表 62 世界纸和纸浆消费量与人均消费量前 5 名的国家（2004 年） …… 498
表 63 世界纸和纸板产品三大净进口国（2002—2004 年） …… 498
表 64 世界天然橡胶和合成橡胶产量、消费量（2001—2004 年） …… 499
表 65 世界主要国家（地区）合成橡胶产量（2002—2004 年） …… 499

表 66　世界主要国家（地区）天然橡胶产量（2002—2004 年）…………………………… 499
表 67　我国台湾省天然橡胶和合成橡胶消费量（2001—2003 年）…………………………… 500
表 68　世界橡胶机械生产厂商前 10 名排序（2003 年）…………………………………… 500
表 69　按营业额排序的世界最大 500 家企业中相关农产品加工企业（2004 年）…… 500

Contents

Editor's Notes

Part Ⅰ Special Subjects Exposition

Active Development of Agricultural Products Processing Industry, Construct Industria Sustain of the New Countryside and the Harmonious Society …… 3
Making Great Efforts to Enforce Two - hundred Markets Project, Devote Major Efforts to Promote the System Development of Modern Circulation of Agricultural Products …… 8
Strengthen Supervisory and Management of Food and Medicines, Working as the Safeguarder of People's Health …… 11
Overall Development of Well - to - do Society, Quicken Advance the System Development of Innovate by Science and Technology for Grain …… 14
Carry on and Develop, Reform and Innovate, Overall Create a New Situation of Supervisory and Management of Food Safety …… 19
Development of Textile Industry of Our Country in 11th Five Year Period …… 30
Strengthen the System Development of Ranks Ability, To Promote the Quick Development of the Undertaking of No - public - harm Agricultural Products …… 33
Serve as a Link Between Past and Future of Food Industry, Continue to Keep Situation Well of the Quick Development …… 40
Economic Situation and Development Characteristic of Meat Industry of Our Country …… 45
Development of Paper Industry and Look Forward to the Future in 11th Five Year Period of Our Country …… 47
Review the Past and Look Forward to the Future of Printing and Equipment Industry of Our Country …… 51
Carry out Project Spirit in 11th Five Year Period, Create a New Situation of Development of Leather Trades …… 53
Present Situation and Aim in 11th Five Year Period of Rubber Industry of Our Country …… 56

Part Ⅱ Development Situation of Related Trades

Grain, oil and food Processing Industries …… 61
Oil Processing Industry …… 66
Soy - bean Processing Industry …… 69
Starch Processing Industry …… 75
Sugar - making Industry …… 78
Dairy Products Processing Industry …… 81
Fruits Processing Industry …… 86
Vegetable Processing Industry …… 92
Tea Processing Industry …… 97
Honeybee Products Processing Industry …… 100
Edible Mushroom Processing Industry …… 105
Tobacco Processing Industry …… 108

Brewery Industry …… 112
Natural Silk Processing Industry …… 115
Feed Processing Industry …… 118
Aquatic Products Processing Industry …… 123
Forestry Products Processing Industry …… 128
Crop - stalk Processing Industry …… 132
Agricultural Products Processing Machine Building Industry in the System of Machine Building Industry …… 135
Food Processing and Packing Machine Building Industry …… 137
Cotton Processing Machine Building Industry …… 140

Part Ⅲ Policies, Regulations and Important Documents

Suggestions on Further Strengthen of Supervisory and Management of Food Safety in Intermediate Links …… 145
Supervisory Standard of Food Hygiene in Important Activities …… 148
Preventive Plan of Emergency for Major Accident of Food Safety in Our Country …… 150
Stipulation of Supervisory and Management of Food Hygiene at the Port of Entry and Exit …… 154
Law of Quality and Safety of Agricultural Products …… 157
Management Means of Packing and Identification of Agricultural Products …… 161
Suggestion in Regard to Strengthen the Development of Supervisory and Management Ability of Quality and Safety of Agricultural Products …… 162
Guidance Ideas on Scientific and Technical Development of Grain in 11th Five Year Period …… 164
Program of Developing Agricultural Products Export in 11th Five Year Period …… 169
Program of Developing China's Food Industry in 11th Five Year Period …… 177
Program of Developing Agricultural Products Processing Industries in 11th Five Year Period …… 189

Part Ⅳ Domestic Comprehensive Statistics Materials

Statistics of Production of Main Products of Agriculture, Forest, Livestock and Fishery …… 203
Table 1 Yield of Main Agricultural Products of Our Country (2001—2005) …… 203
Table 2 Yield of Main Agricultural Products in Various Regions (2005) …… 204
Table 3 Situation of Production of Major Corn Production Areas of Our Country (2005) …… 209
Table 4 Yield of Fruits in Various Regions (2005) …… 209
Table 5 Yield of Tea in Various Regions (2005) …… 211
Table 6 Yield of Main Agricultural Products in the System of Land Reclamation and Cultivation (2004—2005) …… 212
Table 7 Yield of Main Agricultural Products of Land Reclamation and Cultivation System in Various Regions (2005) …… 213
Table 8 Production of Tea, Silkworm, Fruit and Forest Products in the Land Reclamation and Cultivation System of Our Country (2004—2005) …… 214
Table 9 Yield of tropical and Sub - tropical Crops of Our country (2005) …… 214
Table 10 Situation of Production of Major Cotton Production Areas of Our Country (2004—2005) …… 214
Table 11 Increase and Decrease of Production of Main Vegetables of Our Country (2004—2005) …… 215
Table 12 Yield of Main Forestry Products of our Country (2001—2005) …… 215

Table 13 Yield of Main Forestry Products in Various Regions (2005) ······ 216
Table 14 Situation of Livestock Raising of Our Country (2001—2005) ······ 217
Table 15 Yield of Main Livestock Products of Our Country (2001—2005) ······ 217
Table 16 Yield of Dairy Products in Various Regions of the Country (2004—2005) ······ 218
Table 17 Yield of Main Animal Products of Land Reclamation and Cultivation system (2004—2005) ······ 218
Table 18 Yield of Aquatic Products of Our Country (2001—2005) ······ 219
Table 19 Yield of Aquatic Products in Various Regions of the Country (2005) ······ 219
Table 20 Yield of Sea and Ocean Fishery along the Coast of our Country (2005) ······ 220
Table 21 Output of Aquatic Products Along Sea Shore of Our Country (2005) ······ 220
Table 22 Yield of Aquatic Products in Various Regions of the Land Reclamation and Cultivation system (2005) ······ 221
Table 23 Quantity of Agricultural and Animal Products Used as Raw Materials by the Food Enterprises in the Light Industry (2003—2004) ······ 222
Table 24 Production of Main Chinese Medical Herbs in Various Regions of our Country (2005) ······ 223
Table 25 Average Yield per capita of Main Agricultural and Livestock Products of our Country (2001—2005) ······ 223

Holding Quantity of Agricultural Products Processing Machines and the Situation of Fixed Assets Investment of Agriculture Products Processing Trade ······ 224

Table 26 Holding Quantity of Processing Machines of Some Agricultural Products in the System of the Ministry of Agriculture at the End of the yesr (2005) ······ 224
Table 27 Situation of Fixed Asset Investment of Agricultural Product Processing Trade of Our Country (2005) ······ 225
Table 28 New Increase of Production Capability after Increased Fixed Assets of Agricultural Product Processing Trade (2004—2005) ······ 225
Table 29 Number of Agricultural Product Processing Trades with 500 000 yuan, Constructed and Put into Production (2005) ······ 226
Table 30 Investment of Fixed Assets of Forestry Processing Industry in the Forestry System (2005) ······ 226
Table 31 Investment of Fixed Assets in Various Region of Forestry Processing Industry in the Forestry System (2005) ······ 226
Table 32 Investment of Fixed Assets of the System of Land Reclamation and Cultivation of our Country (2004—2005) ······ 227
Table 33 The Newly Increased Production Capacity of Main Products of Food Industry of our Country After Investment in Fixed Assets (2003—2004) ······ 227
Table 34 Investment in Fixed Assets of Aquatic Industry of our Country (2004—2005) ······ 227

Present Situation of Agricultural Products Processing Industry Based on the Classified Trade Statistics of National Economy ······ 228

Table 35 Main Targets of Entirely State - owned and Above - scale Non - state - owned Enterprises of Agricultural Products Processing Industry of our Country (2005) ······ 228
Table 36 Main Economic Performance Targets of Entirely State - owned and Above - scale Non - state - owned Enterprises of Agricultural Products Processing Industry of our Country (2005) ······ 228
Table 37 Main Targets of State - owned and State Holding Enterprises of Agricultural Products Processing Industry of our Country (2005) ······ 229
Table 38 Main Economic Performance Targets of State - owned and State Holding Enterprises of Agricultural products Processing Industry of our Country (2005) ······ 229

Table 39 Main Targets of Three Capital Enterprises of Agricultural Products Processing Industry of our Country (2005) …… 230
Table 40 Main Economic Performance Targets of Three - Capital Enterprises of Agricultural Products Processing Industry of Our Country (2005) …… 230
Table 41 Main Targets of Private Enterprises of Agricultural Products Processing Industry of Our Country (2005) …… 231
Table 42 Main Economic Performance Targets of Private Enterprises of Agricultural Products Processing Industry of Our Country (2005) …… 231
Table 43 Main Targets of Agricultural Product Processing Industry of Large and Medium Scale of Our Country (2005) …… 231
Table 44 Main Economic Performance Targets of Agricultural Product Processing Industry of Large and Medium Scale of Our Country (2005) …… 232
Table 45 Main Economic and Technical Targets of Sugar Making Enterprises of our Country During the Sugar Making Period 2005/2006 …… 232
Table 46 Situation of Production, Management and Sales of Food and Packing Machines of our Country (2005) …… 232
Table 47 Gross Output and Sales Value of Agricultural Products Processing Industry in Forestry System (2004—2005) …… 233
Table 48 Gross Output of Agricultural Products Processing Industry in Various Regions of the Forestry System (2005) …… 233
Table 49 Gross Sales Value of Agricultural Products Processing Industry in Various Regions of the Forestry System (2005) …… 235
Table 50 Main Economic Performance Targets of State - owned, Independent Accounting, Large and Medium Trades of Agricultural Product processing Industry of Forestry System (2005) …… 236
Table 51 Main Economic Performance Targets of State - owned, Independent Accounting, Large and Medium Trades of Agricultural Product Processing Industry in Various Regions of Forestry System (2005) …… 237
Table 52 Develop the Status Quo of Aquatic Products Processing Industry of our Country (2004—2005) …… 238
Table 53 Processing Capability, Output and Output Value of Aquatic Products Processing of our Country (2002—2005) …… 238
Table 54 The Situation of Aquatic Products Processing in Provinces along the Coast of our Country (2005) …… 239
Table 55 Present Situation of Agricultural Products Processing Industry of Collective Village and Township Enterprises (2004) …… 239
Table 56 Basic Condition of Agricultural Products Processing Industry Over the Village and Township Scale of Our country (2004—2005) …… 240
Table 57 Main Economic Targets of Classified Trades of Agricultural Products Processing Industry in the Light Industry System (2004) …… 240
Table 58 Main Economic Targets of Classified Food Industries in the Light Industry System (2004) …… 240
Table 59 Main Economic Targets of Baking Food and Sugar - made Product Industries of Our Country (2004) …… 241
Table 60 Main Economic Targets of Beverage Trade of Our Country (2003—2004) …… 242
Table 61 Main Economic Targets of Dairy Product Trade of the Country (2004—2005) …… 242

Table 62 Main Economic Targets of Classified Key Trades of Machine Building Enterprises (Related to the Part of Agricultural Products Processing) in the system of Light Industry (2004) ······ 242
Table 63 Main Economic Targets of Tobacco Industry of Whole Country (2003—2004) ······ 242
Table 64 Main Economic Targets of Textile Industry of Whole country (2005) ······ 243
Table 65 Main Economic Target of Textile Industry of the Country (Entirely State-owned and State Holding Enterprises) (2005) ······ 243
Table 66 Main Economic Targets Above-scale Enterprises of Cotton Spinning Trades of Textile Industry (2005) ······ 244
Table 67 Main Economic Targets Above-scale Enterprises of Wool Spinning Trades of Textile Industry (2005) ······ 244
Table 68 Main Economic Targets Above-scale Enterprises of Silk Trades of Textile Industry (2005) ······ 245
Table 69 Main Economic Targets of hemp and Flax Spinning Trades of Textile Industry (2005) ······ 245
Table 70 Main Economic Targets Above-scale Enterprises of Printing and Dyeing Trades of Textile Industry (2005) ······ 246
Table 71 Main Economic Targets Above-scale Enterprises of Knit Goods Trades of Textile Industry (2005) ······ 246
Table 72 Main Economic Target of Dress Making Trade of Textile Industry (2005) ······ 246
Table 73 Main Economic Targets of Textile Machine Building Trades of Textile Industry (2005) ······ 247
Table 74 Status of Economic Operation of Leather Industry of our Country (2003—2004) ······ 247
Table 75 Status of Economic Operation of Furniture Trade of our Country (2003—2004) ······ 247
Table 76 Main Economic Targets in Various Regions of Our Paper Making Industry (2004) ······ 247
Table 77 Basic Condition of Journalism Industry of our Country (2004) ······ 248
Table 78 Main Economic Targets by 120 Enterprises Printing Books and Periodicals (Including Other Printings) of the Country (2004) ······ 249
Table 79 Main Economic Targets of 120 Enterprises Packing and Printing of the Country (2003—2004) ······ 249
Table 80 Main Economic Targets of 58 Printing Machine Enterprises of the Country (2004) ······ 249
Table 81 Main Economic Target of Rubber Industry of Our Country (2005) ······ 250
Table 82 Main Economic Targets of Whole-independent Accounting Enterprises of Rubber Industry of Our Country (2001—2003) ······ 250
Table 83 Status of Economic Benefit of Traditional Chinese Medicine Trades (2004—2005) ······ 251
Table 84 Total Consumption of Energy and Consumption of Main Energy Variety of Agricultural Products Processing Industry of Our Country (2004) ······ 251
Output of Main Products of Agricultural Products Production Industry ······ 252
Table 85 Output of Main Products of Agricultural Products Processing Industry of Our country (2004—2005) ······ 252
Table 86 Output of Main Products of Agricultural Products Processing Industry in the Light Industry (2004) ······ 252
Table 87 Output of Main Products of Grain and Oil Processing Industry of Our Country (2003—2004) ······ 253
Table 88 Output and Stains of Starch of Our Country (2005) ······ 253
Table 89 Output of Deep Processed Starch Products of Our Country (2005) ······ 254

Table 90 Output Distribution and Production Scale of Starch of our Country (2005) ······ 254
Table 91 Situation of Production Scale of Corn Starch of Our Country (2005) ······ 254
Table 92 Production Scale of Partial Starch and Deep Processed Products of Our Country (2004—2005) ······ 255
Table 93 Output of Main Products of Food Additives of Our Country (2003—2004) ······ 256
Table 94 Output of Main Products of Beverage Making Industry in Various Regions of Our Country (2004) ······ 256
Table 95 Main Output of Canned Food Industry in Various Regions of Our Country (2003—2004) ······ 257
Table 96 Output of Main Products of Tobacco Industry of Our Country (2002—2004) ······ 257
Table 97 Output of Products of Alcohol Industry of Our Country (2003—2004) ······ 258
Table 98 Output of White Spirit in Various Areas of Our Country (2003—2004) ······ 258
Table 99 Output of Main Products of Feed Industry of Our Country (2002—2005) ······ 259
Table 100 Output of Sugar Crops and Sugar during Sugar Production Period 2005/2006 ······ 259
Table 101 Output, Output Value and Export of Edible Mushroom of Our Country (2005) ······ 260
Table 102 Output of Main Products of Agricultural Products Processing Enterprises in the System of Land Reclamation and Cultivation of Our Country (2004—2005) ······ 262
Table 103 Output of Main Products of Agricultural Products Processing Industry in Various Areas in the System of Land Reclamation and Cultivation of Our Country (2005) ······ 263
Table 104 Output of Main Products in Forestry Industry of Our Country (2004—2005) ······ 264
Table 105 Output of Main Industrial Products in Forestry System (2004—2005) ······ 264
Table 106 Output of Main Products in Various Areas of Forestry Industry (2005) ······ 266
Table 107 Output of Main Industrial Products in Various Areas of Forestry System (2005) ······ 267
Table 108 Major Varieties and Output of Main Processed Aquatic products of Our Country (2002—2005) ······ 268
Table 109 Output of Main Products in Textile Industry (Above - scale Enterprises) (2004—2005) ······ 269
Table 110 Output of Main Products of Silk Trade of Textile Industry (2004—2005) ······ 269
Table 111 Output of Main Products of Hemp Textile of Textile Industry of Our Country (2004—2005) ······ 270
Table 112 Output of Main Products of Leather Industry of Our Country (2003—2004) ······ 270
Table 113 Output of Main Products of Furniture Industry of Our Country (2004—2005) ······ 270
Table 114 Situation of Pulp Consumption of Paper Making Industry of Our Country (2003—2004) ······ 270
Table 115 The proportion of Every Variety of Raw Materia of Paper - making Fibre (2004) ······ 271
Table 116 Output of Main Varieties of Machine - made Paper and Paper Board of Our Country (2003—2004) ······ 271
Table 117 Output of Major Paper Products in Various Areas (2004) ······ 271
Table 118 Situation of Consumption Structure of Paper and Paper Board of Our Country (2003—2004) ······ 272
Table 119 Consumption and Production of Main Products of Paper Making Industry of Our Country (2003—2004) ······ 273
Table 120 Average Consumption of Per Capita, Amount of Exported, Consumption and Production of Paper and Paper Board of Our Country (2001—2004) ······ 273
Table 121 Output of Main Products of by 120 Enterprises Printing Books and Periodicals (Including Other Printings) of the Country (2004) ······ 273
Table 122 Compare with Average Consumption of Per Capita of Our Paper and Paper Board of the Country and the United States (2001—2004) ······ 273

Table 123 Output of Main Products of Rubber Industry of Our Country (2004—2005) ········ 274
Table 124 Output per capita of Main Industrial and Agricultural Products of Our Country (2001—2005) ········ 274

Situation of Export and Foreign Exchange Earned of Main Products of Agricultural Products Processing Industry ········ 275

Table 125 Quantity and Amount of Money of Exported Agricultural Products and Processed Products Through Customs of Our Country (2004—2005) ········ 275
Table 126 Quantity and Amount of Money of Imported Agricultural Products and Processed Products Through Customs of Our Country (2004—2005) ········ 277
Table 127 Foreign Exchange Earned by Exporting Main Processed Agricultural Products of Village and Township Enterprises (2004—2005) ········ 277
Table 128 Amount of Forestry Products Imported and Exported of Our Country (2004—2005) ········ 278
Table 129 Amount of Money Earned and Spent Through Exporting and Importing Forestry Products (2004—2005) ········ 279
Table 130 Situation of Exporting Edible Mushroom of Our Country (2005) ········ 281
Table 131 Foreign Exchange Earned through Exporting Main Products of Light Industry (2004) ········ 282
Table 132 Foreign Exchange Spent through Importing Main Products in Light Industry (2004) ········ 282
Table 133 Situation of Imported Dairy Products of Our Country (2005) ········ 283
Table 134 Situation of Exported Dairy Products of Our Country (2005) ········ 283
Table 135 Situation of Exporting Canned Goods of Our Country (2004) ········ 284
Table 136 Main Countries and Regions Whereto the Canned Goods of Our Country are Exported (2003—2004) ········ 285
Table 137 Main Countries and Regions Whereto Cigarettes of Our Country are Exported (2003—2004) ········ 285
Table 138 Main Countries and Regions Wherefrom Cigarettes are Imported to Our Country (2003—2004) ········ 286
Table 139 Situation of Production and Export of Honey Bee of Our Country (2002—2005) ········ 286
Table 140 Situation of Exported Honeybee Products of Our Country (2004—2005) ········ 286
Table 141 Main Countries and Regions of Exported Honeybee Products of Our Country (2005) ········ 286
Table 142 Situation of Import and Export of Aquatic Products of Our Country (2002—2005) ········ 287
Table 143 Situation of Import and Export of Food Processing and Packing Machines of Our Country (2004—2005) ········ 287
Table 144 Statistics of Import and Export of Raw Textile Materials and Products of Textile Industry (2005) ········ 288
Table 145 Amount of Import and Export of Textile products and clothes of Textile Industry (2005) ········ 289
Table 146 Situation of Import and Export of Textile products and clothes of Our Country (2001—2005) ········ 290
Table 147 Comparison of Import and Export of Main Wool Textile Products of Textile Industry (2004—2005) ········ 290
Table 148 Situation of Export of Knit Products and Knit Clothes of Textile Industry (2005) ········ 291
Table 149 Situation of Export of Classified Real Silk Products of Textile Industry (2005) ········ 291
Table 150 Situation of Import and Export of Major Printing and dying Products of Textile Industry (2005) ········ 292
Table 151 Situation of Amount and Quantity from Export of Products of Main Household Weave of Textile Industry (2005) ········ 292

Table 152 Situation of Import and Export of Textile Machines of Textile Industry (2004—2005) ········ 292
Table 153 Proportion of Various Trades of Textile Industry on Exporting Textile Machines (2005) ········ 293
Table 154 Situation of Import and Export of Major Products of Our Leather Industry (2005) ········ 293
Table 155 Situation of Import and Export of Major Products of Furniture Industry of Our Country (2005) ········ 294
Table 156 Situation of Import and Export of Pulp and Waste Paper of Our Country (2003—2004) ········ 294
Table 157 Situation of Import of Paper, Pulp and Waste Paper of Our Country (2001—2004) ········ 295
Table 158 Statistics of Import and Export of Printing Machines of Our Country (2004) ········ 295
Table 159 Situation of Import and Export of Chinese Medicine Trade (2004—2005) ········ 296
Table 160 Quantity of Export and Amount of Money Earned of Products from Rubber Industry of Our Country (2001—2003) ········ 296
Table 161 Quantity of Import and Amount of Money Spent on Products from Rubber Industry of China (2001—2003) ········ 297
Table 162 Situation of Import and Export of Shoe Products of Classify from Rubber Industry of China (2004) ········ 297
Table 163 Situation of Import and Export of Rubber Machines from Rubber Industry of China (2004) ········ 298
Table 164 Situation of Import of Natural Rubber and Synthetic Rubber of Our Country (2001—2003) ········ 298
Sequence of Trades and Enterprises of Agricultural Products Processing Industry ········ 298
Table 165 Main Economic Targets of Classified Trades of Agricultural Products Processing Enterprises of Light Industry (2004) ········ 298
Table 166 Total Amount of Import and Export of Classified Agricultural Product Processing Trades of Light Industry (2004) ········ 299
Table 167 The Front 10 Enterprises Earning High Sales Income of the White Spirit Production Trades of Our Country (2004) ········ 300
Table 168 The Front 10 Enterprises Making High Profit Tax from Selling White Spirit Trades of Our Country (2004) ········ 300
Table 169 The Front 10 Enterprises with High Production of White Spirit Trades of Our Country (2004) ········ 300
Table 170 Sales Situation of Self-production and Specialized Malt from Beer Enterprises of Our Country (2004) ········ 301
Table 171 The Enterprises with Annual Production of Beer Over 200 000 kl of Our Country (2004) ··· 301
Table 172 The Enterprises with Sales Revenue of Beer Over 300 000 000 yuan of Our Country (2004) ········ 301
Table 173 The Enterprises Making High Profit Tax of Beer Over 100 000 000 yuan of Our Country (2004) ········ 302
Table 174 The Provinces, Autonomous Regions and Municipals of Front 10 Enterprises with High Production of Best Wine in the Trades (2004) ········ 302
Table 175 The Best Wine Producing Provinces of Our Country with High Production and Beneficial Result (2004) ········ 302
Table 176 The Front 9 Enterprises with High Production of Beverage Trades of Our Country (2004) ········ 302
Table 177 The Front 10 Enterprises of Various Trades of Textile Industry with Strong Competitive Capacity of Our Country 2005/2006 ········ 303

Table 178 The Front 100 Enterprises of Textile Industry with High Export of Our Country 2005/2006 ······ 304
Table 179 The Front 100 Enterprises of Textile Industry with High Revenue from Principal Business (2005) ······ 306
Table 180 The First 50 Enterprises of Wool Spinning and Wool Knitting Product Industry with High Revenue from Principal Business (2005) ······ 307
Table 181 The Front 50 Knitting Enterprises of Textile Industry of Our Country with High Revenue from Principal Business (2005) ······ 307
Table 182 The First 30 Enterprises of Silk Spinning and Weaving Trades of Textile Industry of Our Country with High Revenue from Principal Business (2005) ······ 308
Table 183 The Front 50 Cotton Spinning Enterprises of Textile Industry of Our Country with High Revenue from Principal Business (2005) ······ 308
Table 184 The Front 50 Chemical Fiber Enterprises of Textile Industry of Our Country with High Revenue from Principal Business (2005) ······ 309
Table 185 The First 30 Enterprises of Hemp Spinning and Weaving Trades of Textile Industry of Our Country with High Revenue from Principal Business (2005) ······ 310
Table 186 The Front 50 Printing and Dying Enterprises of Textile Industry of Our Country with High Revenue from Principal Business (2005) ······ 310
Table 187 The Leather Enterprises Considered asGenuine Leather Marking Ecologic Leather of Our Country (2004) ······ 311
Table 188 Enterprises and Brands Honored as Genuine Leather Shoes and Genuine Leather Clothes of Leather Industry of Our Country (2004) ······ 311
Table 189 The First 30 Enterprises of Key Paper Making Trade with High Amount of Sales Income of Our Country (2004) ······ 312
Table 190 The First 30 Enterprises of Key Paper Making Trade Achieving High Amount of Profit Tax of Our Country (2004) ······ 312
Table 191 The Front 30 Key Paper Making Enterprises of Our Country with High Total Profit (2004) ······ 313
Table 192 Provinces with Output of Paper and Paper Board Over One Million ton (2002—2004) ······ 313
Table 193 The First 20 Book and Periodical Printing Enterprises Realizing Industrial Profit Tax (2004) ······ 313
Table 194 Output of Offset Printing Over One Million Folio Kinds of Printing Enterprises of Our Country (2004) ······ 314
Table 195 Main Enterprises with Sales Income Over One Hundred Million yuan of Printing and Packing Enterprises of Our Country (2004) ······ 314
Table 196 The Front 20 Packing and Printing Enterprises of Our Country with Total Profit and Tax Over 10 Million yuan (2004) ······ 314
Table 197 Enterprises of Pulp and Paper Making Machine Manufacturing Industry of Our Country with Sales Income Over 50 Million Yuan (2004) ······ 315
Table 198 Enterprises of Pulp and Paper Making Machine Manufacturing Industry of Our Country Realizing Profit Tax Over 5 Million Yuan (2004) ······ 315
Table 199 Enterprises of Pulp and Paper Making Machine Manufacturing Industry of Our Country with Labor Productivity Over 100 000 Yuan (2004) ······ 315
Table 200 Order of Sales Income of Enterprises of Association Members of Rubber Industry of Our Country (2003) ······ 315

Table 201 Main Economic Targets of the Front 20 Rubber Machine Enterprises of Our Country (2004) …… 316
Table 202 The First 50 Enterprises of Whole - independent Accounting Enterprises with General Assets of Chinese Medicine Industry (2004) …… 317
Table 203 The First 50 Enterprises of Whole - independent Accounting Enterprises with Sales Income of Chinese Medicine Industry (2004) …… 317
Table 204 The First 10 Enterprises of Export Amount of Chinese Medicine Industry (2005) …… 318
Comprehensive Statistics of the Western Area of Our Country …… 318
Table 205 Output of Production of Main Agricultural Products in Western Area of Our Country (2004—2005) …… 318
Table 206 Yield per Unit Area of Main Agricultural Products in Western Area of Our Country (2004—2005) …… 319
Table 207 Yield of Tea in Western Area of Our Country (2005) …… 320
Table 208 Yield of Fruits in Western Area of Our Country (2004—2005) …… 320
Table 209 Yield of Main Forestry Products in Western Area of Our Country (2005) …… 321
Table 210 Area and Yield of Tropic and Sub - tropic Crops in Western Part of Our Country (2005) …… 321
Table 211 Output of Main Animal Products in Western Area of Our Country (2004—2005) …… 322
Table 212 Output of Aquatic Products in Western Area of Our Country (2004—2005) …… 322
Table 213 Average Output per capita of Main Agricultural Products, Livestock Products and Aquatic Products in Western Area of Our Country (2004—2005) …… 322
Table 214 Total Production Value, Increased Value and Components of Agriculture, Animal Husbandry and Fishery in Western Area of Our Country (2004—2005) …… 323
Table 215 Total Production Value of Forestry in Western Area of Our Country (2005) …… 324
Table 216 Situation of Fixed Assets Investment of Forestry Industry of Forestry System in Western Area of Our Country (2005) …… 324
Table 217 Total Production Value of Agricultural Product Processing Trades of Forestry System in Western Area of Our Country (2005) …… 325
Table 218 Sales Value of Agricultural Products Processing Trades of Forestry System in Western Area of Our country (2005) …… 326
Table 219 Main Economic Targets of State - owned, Independent Accounting, Large and Medium Size Industrial Enterprises of Agriculturol Products Processing of Forestry System in Western Part of Our Country (2005) …… 327
Table 220 Main Economic Targets of Above - scale Agricultural Products Processing Enterprises of Village and Township in Western Area of Our Country (2005) …… 327
Table 221 Total Industrial Production Value of Classified Food Industry in Western Area of Our Country (2004) …… 328
Table 222 Main Economic Targets of Textile Industry in Western Area of Our Country (2005) …… 328
Table 223 Main economic Targets of Textile Industry (state owned and state - owned holding) in Western Area of Our Country (2005) …… 329
Table 224 Volume of Production of Main Products of Forestry Industry in Western Area of Our Country (2005) …… 329
Table 225 Output of Major Products of Agricultural Products Processing Enterprises of Agricultural Land Reclamation and Cultivation System in Western Area of Our Country (2005) …… 330
Table 226 Output of Agricultural Products Processing Trades of Light Industry in Western Area of Our Country (2004) …… 331

Table 227 Amount of Import and Export of Textiles and Clothes in Western Area of Our Country (2005) …… 332
Others …… 333
Table 228 Terminal Market of Fixed Point of Agricultural Product of the Twelfth Batch by Agriculture Ministry Validation (2006) …… 333
Table 229 Private Enterprises (a hundred) of Best Growth of Food Industry of Our Country (2004) …… 334
Table 230 Food Industry Enterprises Enlisted in 100 National Strong Enterprises of Our Country (2004) …… 335
Table 231 Agricultural Product Processing Enterprises Enlisted in 500 National Strong Enterprises of Light Industry (2004) …… 337

Part V Agricultural Products Processing Industries in Various Provinces, Autonomous Regions and Cities of Our Country

Agricultural Products Processing Industry of suburbs in Beijing City …… 341
Agricultural Products Processing Industry in Tianjin city …… 343
Agricultural Products Processing Industry in Hebei Province …… 345
Agricultural Products Processing Industry in Shanxi Province …… 347
Agricultural and Livestock Products Processing Industry in Inner Mongo Autonomous Region …… 349
Agricultural Products Processing Industry in Liaoning Province …… 352
Agricultural Products Processing Industry in Jilin Province …… 355
Agricultural Products Processing Industry in Heilongjiang Province …… 357
Agricultural Products Processing Industry in Shanghai City …… 359
Agricultural Products Processing Industry in Jiangsu Province …… 362
Agricultural Products Processing Industry in Zhejiang Province …… 364
Agricultural Products Processing Industry in Anhui Province …… 366
Agricultural Products Processing Industry in Fujian Province …… 368
Agricultural Products Processing Industry in Jiangxi Province …… 372
Agricultural Products Processing Industry in Shandong Province …… 375
Agricultural Products Processing Industry in Henan Province …… 378
Agricultural Products Processing Industry in Hubei Province …… 380
Agricultural Products Processing Industry in Hunan Province …… 382
Agricultural Products Processing Industry in Guangdong Province …… 386
Agricultural Products Processing Industry in Guangxi Autonomous Region …… 389
Agricultural Products Processing Industry in Hainan Province …… 395
Agricultural Products Processing Industry in Chongqing City …… 398
Agricultural Products Processing Industry in Sichuan Province …… 400
Agricultural Products Processing Industry in Guizhou Province …… 402
Agricultural Products Processing Industry in Yunnan Province …… 405
Agricultural and Livestock Products Processing Industry in Tibet Autonomous Region …… 407
Agricultural Products Processing Industry in Shanxi Province …… 409
Agricultural Products Processing Industry in Gansu Province …… 412
Agricultural Products Processing Industry in Qinghai Province
Agricultural Products Processing Industry in Ningxia Autonomous Region …… 415
Agricultural Products Processing Industry in Xinjiang Autonomous Region …… 420

Part Ⅵ Standards and Patents

National Standards of Agricultural Products Processing Industry (2006) ········· 427
Machine Trade Standards of Agricultural Products Processing Industry (2006) ········· 435
Light Industry Trade Standards of Agricultural Products Processing Industry (2006) ········· 436
Textile Industry Trade Standards of Agricultural Products Processing Industry (2006) ········· 437
Aquatic Trade Standards of Agricultural Products Processing Industry (2006) ········· 439
Tobacco Trade Standards of Agricultural Products Processing Industry (2006) ········· 440
Packing Trade Standards of Agricultural Products Processing Industry (2006) ········· 440
Invention Patents of Agricultural Products Processing Industry (2005) ········· 441

Part Ⅶ Chronicle of Events

Part Ⅷ Appendix

Table 1 Agricultural Production Index of Some Countries (Regions) (2005) ········· 471
Table 2 Agricultural Production Index of Taiwan Province of Our Country (2002—2004) ········· 471
Table 3 Harvesting Area of Main Gains, Unit Yield and Total Yield of some Countries (Districts) (2005) ········· 471
Table 4 Harvesting Area , Unit Yield and Total Yield of Potato of Some Counties (Districts) (2005) ········· 472
Table 5 Harvesting Area , Unit Yield and Total Yield of Sweet Potato of Some Countries (Districts) (2005) ········· 473
Table 6 Harvesting Area, Unit Yield and Total Yield of Cassava of Some Countries (Districts) (2005) ········· 473
Table 7 Harvesting Area, Unit Yield and Gross Yield of Main Oil - bearing Seeds of Some Countries (Districts) (2005) ········· 474
Table 8 Harvesting Area, Unit Yield and Gross Yield of Unginned Cotton and Jute of Some Countries (Districts) (2005) ········· 475
Table 9 Harvesting Area, Unit Yield and Gross Yield of Tobacco and Tea of Some Countries (Districts) (2005) ········· 475
Table 10 Harvesting Area, Unit Yield and Gross Yield of Sugar Cane and Sugar Beet of Some Countries (Districts) (2005) ········· 476
Table 11 Gross Yield of Vegetable, Fruit and Hard Nut of Some Countries (Districts) (2005) ········· 476
Table 12 Harvesting Area, Unit Yield and Gross Yield of Wild Cabbage and Tomato of Some Countries (Districts) (2005) ········· 477
Table 13 Harvesting Area, Unit Yield and Gross Yield of Egg plant, Green Pepper and Hot pepper of Some Countries (Districts) (2005) ········· 477
Table 14 Harvesting Area, Unit Yield and Gross Yield of Pumpkin, Summer Squash and Cucumber of Some Countries (Districts) (2005) ········· 478
Table 15 Harvesting Area, Unit Yield and Gross Yield of Dry Onion and Garlic of Some Countries (Districts) (2005) ········· 478
Table 16 Harvesting Area, Unit Yield and Gross Yield of Water Melon and Carrot of Some Countries (Districts) (2005) ········· 479

Table 17 Harvesting Area, Unit Yield and Gross Yield of Cherry and Grape of Some Countries (Districts) (2005) …… 479
Table 18 Gross Yield of Orange, Mango and etc., of Some Countries (Districts) (2005) …… 480
Table 19 Total Yield of Apple, Straw Berry and etc. of Some Countries (Districts) (2005) …… 480
Table 20 Harvesting Area, Unit Yield and Gross Yield of Raw Cafe and Coconut of Some Countries (Districts) (2005) …… 481
Table 21 Gross Yield of Main Agricultural Products of Taiwan Province of Our Country (2002—2004) …… 481
Table 22 Total Production of Meat of Some Countries (Districts) (2004—2005) …… 481
Table 23 Gross Production of Milk of Some Countries (Districts) (2004—2005) …… 482
Table 24 Gross Production of Eggs of Some Countries (Districts) (2004—2005) …… 482
Table 25 Gross Production of Honey Bee of Some Countries (Districts) (2004—2005) …… 483
Table 26 Gross Production of Wool of Some Countries (Districts) (2004—2005) …… 484
Table 27 Amount of Heat, Protein and Fat from Daily Food of Some Countries (Districts) (2003) …… 484
Table 28 Rank in the World About the Output of Main Agricultural Products of Our country (1949—2005) …… 485
Table 29 Situation of Natural Rubber Production Among Main Rubber Production Coutries of the World (2003—2005) …… 485
Table 30 Major Production Countries Producing Main Agricultural and Livestock Products (2005) …… 485
Table 31 Industrial Production Index of Hong Kong Special Administration region (2002—2005) …… 486
Table 32 Gross Production of Main Products of Agricultural Products Processing Industries of Taiwan Province of Our Country (2001—2005) …… 486
Table 33 Main Economic Targets of Agricultural Products Processing Industries of USA (2000—2001) …… 487
Table 34 Main Economic Targets of Agricultural Products Processing Industries of Japan (2001) …… 487
Table 35 Main Economic Targets of Agricultural Products Processing Industries of German (2000) … 488
Table 36 Main Economic Targets of Agricultural Products Processing Industries of England (2000) … 488
Table 37 Main Economic Targets of Agricultural Products Processing Industries of France (2000) …… 489
Table 38 Main Economic Targets of Agricultural Products Processing Industries of Italy (1999—2000) …… 489
Table 39 Main Economic Targets of Agricultural Products Processing Industries of Canada (2000—2001) …… 490
Table 40 Main Economic Targets of Agricultural Products Processing Industries of Australia (2001) …… 490
Table 41 Main Economic Targets of Agricultural Products Processing Industries of India (2001) …… 491
Table 42 Main Economic Targets of Agricultural Products Processing Industries of The Republic of Korea (2000—2001) …… 491
Table 43 Classified Imported and Exported Commercial Products of Taiwan Province of Our Country (2002—2005) …… 491
Table 44 Volume of Import and Export of Agricultural Products of Some Countries (Regions) (2002—2003) …… 491
Table 45 Number of Import and Export of Livestock of Some Countries (Regions) (2004) …… 491
Table 46 Amount of Money Spent and Earned for Importing and Exporting Livestock of Some Countries (Regions) (2004) …… 492
Table 47 Amount of Import and Export of Birds of Some Countries (Regions) (2004) …… 492

Table 48 Amount of Money Spent and Earned for Importing and Exporting Birds of Some Countries (Regions) (2004) …… 494
Table 49 The First 10 Countries and Regions with Total Sum of Export of Textile and Clothes of Whole Globe (2005) …… 494
Table 50 Production Volume of Textile Fiber of China and the World (Including PP Fiber) (2002—2004) …… 495
Table 51 Production Volume of Synthetic Fiber (Including PP Fiber) of Some Main Countries (Regions) of the World (2002—2004) …… 495
Table 52 Production Volume of Cotton of Main Countries (Regions) of the World (2002—2004) …… 495
Table 53 Consumption Volume of Cotton of Main Countries of the World (2002—2004) …… 495
Table 54 Consumption Volume of Fiber per Capital of the Glob (1990—2004) …… 496
Table 55 Output of Classified Pulp of the World (2003—2004) …… 496
Table 56 Situation of Production and Consumption of Paper Pulp, Paper and Paper Board of the World and China (2002—2004) …… 496
Table 57 Situation of Production and Consumption of Paper Products of Taiwan Province of Our Country (2004) …… 497
Table 58 Situation of Requirement of Industrial Paper of Taiwan Province of Our Country (2004) …… 497
Table 59 The First 10 Countries of Production Volume of Paper and Paper Board in the World (2004) …… 497
Table 60 The First 10 Countries of Production Volume of Paper and Paper Pulp in the World (2004) …… 498
Table 61 The First 5 Countries of Net-importing and Net-exporting Paper Pulp in the World (2004) …… 498
Table 62 The First 5 Countries of Consumption Volume and Average Consumption of Per Capita of Paper and Paper Pulp in the World (2004) …… 498
Table 63 The First 3 Countries of Net-importing of Paper and Paper Board in the World (2002—2004) …… 498
Table 64 Output and Amount of Consumption of Natural Rubber and Synthetic Rubber of the World (2001—2004) …… 499
Table 65 Output of Synthetic Rubber of Major Countries (Regions) of the World (2002—2004) …… 499
Table 66 Output of Natural Rubber of Major Countries (Regions) of the World (2002—2004) …… 499
Table 67 Consumption volume of Natural and Synthetic Rubber of Taiwan Province of Our Country (2001—2003) …… 500
Table 68 Order of the First 10 Countries of Rubber Engineering Works in the World (2003) …… 500
Table 69 The Agricultural Products Processing Enterprises Within The Major 500 Enterprises (Based on Turnover) of the World (2004) …… 500

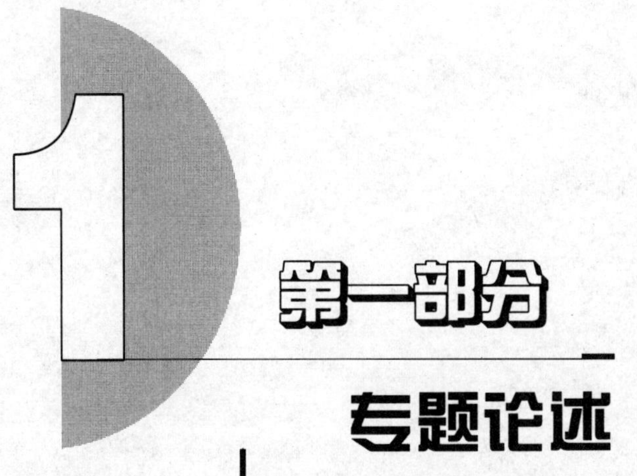

第一部分

专题论述

积极发展农产品加工业 构筑新农村与和谐社会的产业支撑

农业部副部长　危朝安

党中央、国务院非常重视农产品加工业的发展。2005年的中央1号文件明确指出，要“以发展农产品加工业为突破口，走新型工业化道路，促进农业增效、农民增收和地区经济发展。”2006年的中央1号文件进一步强调，“要着力培育一批竞争力、带动力强的龙头企业和企业集群示范基地。”温家宝总理在2006年的政府工作报告中指出，要“推进农业产业化，大力发展农村二、三产业特别是农产品加工业，壮大县域经济”。回良玉副总理在2006年中央党校建设社会主义新农村专题研讨班上强调，“要着力发展农产品精深加工，延长农业产业链，提高农业比较效益，提升农产品档次，促进农民增收”。中央文件精神和领导同志重要讲话，为做好农产品加工业工作指明了方向，一定要认真学习，切实贯彻，抓紧落实。

一、近几年我国农产品加工业发展的成效和主要经验

进入新阶段尤其是党的十六大以来，我国农产品加工业快速发展。据统计，2005年我国规模以上农产品加工企业7万多个，完成产值达到4.2万亿元，“十五”期间年均增长近15%，从业人数1 785万人，占全部工业从业人员的28%。农产品加工业已经成为国民经济发展中总量最大、发展最快、对“三农”带动最大的支柱产业之一。

（一）主要成效

1. *有力促进了农产品的增值增效*　各地按照农业产业化经营的思路发展农产品加工业，不断拓展产业链，向农业生产的深度和广度进军，实现农产品的多次增值。以吉林省为例：该省玉米加工实现了三次升级三重增值，从传统的粮食粗加工产品到肉禽蛋奶转化，再到生产赖氨酸、燃料乙醇等化工产品，进一步生产塑料、服装等产品。2004年吉林省玉米加工量仅420万t，2005年增加到696万t，2006年达到约800万t。通过发展精深加工，农民种植玉米的经济效益成倍增长，玉米价格出现了与产量同步增长的局面。2005年，吉林省以玉米为主的农产品加工业产值突破1 000亿元，2006年达到约1 150亿元，与化工、汽车两大产业一起成为该省国民经济发展的三大支柱产业。其他一些省和一些地区这样的局面也在逐步形成。

2. *真正带动了农民就业增收*　发展农产品加工业，可以更广泛、更充分地吸收农民就业，同时带动农业综合效益提高，增加农民收入。据测算，我国农产品加工业与农业的比值，每增加0.1个百分点，就可以带动230万人就业，带动农民人均增收193元。目前，国家级农业产业化龙头企业580多个，带动农户8 726万户，占全国农户总数的35.2%，参与产业化经营的农户比普通农户每户年平均增收1 300多元。

3. *切实提升了农业整体素质和竞争力*　主要表现在两个方面：一是提升了科技和技术装备水平。根据对187家国家重点龙头企业调查，有124个企业拥有独立的研发机构，大量的企业引进了国际最先进的生产工艺和设备，引进和推广了一批成熟的高新科技成果，如生物工程技术、超高温灭菌、冷冻保鲜、分子蒸馏等。二是提升了我国农产品质量安全水平。一大批农产品加工企业广泛采用国际先进标准、获得国际认可，通过无公害食品、绿色食品和有机食品等认证。

4. *加快发展了一大批带动力和竞争力强的农产品加工龙头企业*　近年来，涌现出一大批起点高、成长快、规模大的领军企业。全国共有农业产业化龙头企业6.1万多个，其中国家级的龙头企业580多个，省级重点龙头企业3 750多个。双汇、得利斯、金锣、皓月、雨润、德大、龙大、蒙牛、三元、伊利、三鹿、汇源、大成、华龙等一大批农产品加工龙头企业不仅规模大、效益好，而且带动能力强、辐射面广。目前，全国农产品加工业增加值的20%以上是由固定资产5 000万元以上的企业创造的，并有效带动了关联企业的发展。

5. *较好地推动了优势产业集群的初步形成*　各

地根据资源禀赋和区位优势，建设了一批特色鲜明的农产品加工产业带，如黄淮海地区优质专用小麦加工产业带，东北及内蒙古东部玉米、大豆加工产业带，长江流域优质油菜加工产业带，中原地区牛羊肉加工产业带，东北、华北、西北地区奶业加工产业带，环渤海湾地区和西北黄土高原苹果加工产业带，中南、西南地区柑橘加工产业带，沿海及重点江河湖泊流域优质水产品加工产业带，茶叶主产区优质茶叶加工产业带。产业带的发展带动了龙头企业集聚和优势产业集群。

（二）主要经验

近几年来，各级农业部门，包括乡镇企业部门和农产品加工部门，按照中央的要求，从当地实际出发，加大了农产品加工业的推进力度，积累了丰富经验。

1. *明确工作职能，强化工作要求*　为履行好农业部对农产品加工业的指导管理服务职能，形成推进农产品加工业发展的合力，根据国务院领导同志的批示精神，农业部在2001年成立农产品加工业领导小组，制定发展规划，完善扶持政策，搞好综合服务，加强工作指导，开展农产品加工推进行动，取得明显成效。2005年11月中编办正式批复同意在农业部增设农产品加工局。中央进一步明确农业部的农产品加工业行政管理职能，这既是对农业部推动农产品加工业工作的充分肯定，更是对今后工作的更高要求。

2. *制定发展规划，加强对农产品加工业的宏观指导*　“十五”期间，为指导农产品加工业持续健康发展，农业部制定并组织实施了《重点农产品加工业发展规划》，吉林、内蒙古、江苏、山东、河北、北京、大连等地政府也根据实际情况，分别制定了本地的农产品加工业发展规划。农业部按照《中共中央关于制定国民经济和社会发展第十一个五年规划的建议》的总体部署和《农业农村经济发展“十一五”规划》的统一要求，又编制了《农产品加工业“十一五”发展规划》，即将发布实施，必将指导和促进农产品加工业快速健康发展。

3. *培育和扶持骨干企业，提升企业技术水平*　近年来，农业部积极培育和扶持农产品加工骨干企业，确定584个农产品加工业示范企业，促进了农产品加工业核心竞争力的提升。为提高企业的技术水平，2004年以来，农业部在粮油、果蔬、畜产品、水产品四个领域，筛选推广一批对我国农产品（食品）加工业发展产生重大影响的攻关技术、引进技术、推广技术和高新技术，在北京、吉林、江苏、湖南、贵州、四川、西藏等地举办了农产品加工科技成果对接活动。

4. *启动和开展标准化生产和质量检测工作，完善质量标准体系*　组织编制了《农产品加工业标准制修订指南（2003—2005年）》，组织制订了70多项农产品加工及检验的农业行业标准。为帮助农产品加工企业及时了解WTO、CAC、ISO等国际组织和美国、日本、韩国、欧盟等主要贸易国农产品标准及进出口政策，农业部启动了国际农产品加工标准跟踪信息平台建设项目。建立了112个部级农产品质量检测中心，开展粮油、果蔬、畜产品、水产品及其加工品的质量检测工作，不断完善农产品及加工品质量检测体系。

5. *建立服务平台，加强服务体系建设*　2004年，农业部建设并开通中国国家农产品加工信息网，2006年以来在网上发布各类信息3万条，每日访问量6万余次，其中国外访问量为30%左右。大力加强农产品加工业职业技能培训体系建设和考核鉴定工作，目前已有27个省份建立了以农产品加工为主的职业技能培训基地和技能鉴定站，进行了包括米面油制作、畜禽屠宰、畜禽加工等32个工种的培训及考核鉴定工作。以中国农业科学院农产品加工研究所、农业部规划设计研究院农副产品加工研究所为依托，逐步建立并完善科技服务体系。积极推动农产品加工市场体系建设，举办农产品加工贸易博览会、农产品加工业名品精品展等活动，为企业开拓市场提供服务。

（三）问题与不足

在总结农产品加工业发展成效和经验的同时，也应清醒地看到存在的一些问题和不足。

1. *加工规模和整体水平还比较低*　总体上看，中小企业和家庭作坊较多，产业集中度不高，处于低水平循环。目前，发达国家农产品加工率在90%左右，我国只有45%左右（粗加工以上）；发达国家农产品深加工（二次以上加工）占80%，我国只有30%左右；发达国家农产品加工产值与农业产值之比为2～4：1，我国仅为1.1：1。

2. *加工技术装备差距还比较大*　我国农产品加工的技术装备水平80%还处于20世纪70～80年代的世界平均水平，15%左右处于20世纪90年代水平，只有5%左右达到国际先进水平。

3. *加工标准和质量控制体系不完善*　尽管我国制订了不少农产品加工设备、过程及产品标准，但普遍存在标准陈旧，体系不健全，不适应行业发展与国际接轨的需要，甚至有些重要领域严重存在标准空白现象。

4. *服务体系建设滞后*　农民专业合作经济组织和行业协会发展滞后，公益性社会化服务平台尚未形成。

5. 管理体制不完善，政策不配套，特别是企业贷款比较困难，市场封锁现象依然存在 这些与建立完善的市场经济体制和中央关于支持“三农”的要求尚有一定差距，需要认真加以解决。

二、农产品加工业发展面临的形势和发展思路

农产品加工水平是衡量一个国家农业现代化程度的重要标志，是提升农业整体素质和效益的关键环节。实践证明，发展农产品加工业，有利于优化农业和农村经济结构，推动农业产业升级，引领农业向着标准化、规模化、产业化发展，加快现代农业建设步伐；有利于农产品的深度开发，丰富农产品内容，满足消费者的多样化需求，开拓农产品市场，扩大内需；有利于拓展农产品产业链，扩大农民就业，增加农民收入，提高农村购买力；有利于增强农业的综合素质，增强农业适应市场变化的能力，提高农产品的竞争力；有利于发挥农业资源优势，培育主导产业，形成新农村建设的产业基础。要从全局和战略的高度，充分认识发展农产品加工业的重大意义，按照科学发展观的要求，牢牢把握发展这个执政兴国的第一要务和解决一切问题的关键，抓住新机遇，增强责任感和紧迫感，积极推进农产品加工业持续健康发展。

1. 用科学发展观指导农产品加工业发展 科学发展观是我们党对经济社会发展规律的新认识，是统领农业和农村经济发展全局的重要指导思想。发展农产品加工，必须以科学发展观为统领，拓宽发展思路，创新发展理念，实现又快又好的发展。要坚持以人为本，把促进农业发展、农村繁荣、农民富裕作为农产品加工业发展的出发点和落脚点。通过农产品加工业的带动，建设专业化、标准化、规模化生产基地，形成加工企业与农户风险共担、利益均沾的利益连接机制，使农民分享到加工环节利益。要坚持市场导向，充分发挥市场对资源配置的主导作用，通过优化资源配置，提高行业的整体效益。要坚持质量安全，建立健全农产品加工标准体系和“从农田到餐桌”的全程质量控制体系；严格执行农产品（食品）卫生标准和产品标准，大力发展无公害食品、绿色食品和有机食品，确保农产品加工质量安全。要坚持科技创新，整合科技资源，加强国外先进技术的引进、消化和吸收，加大技术集成和原始创新，加强企业技术创新。要坚持因地制宜，分类指导，充分发挥资源、经济、市场和技术优势，依托优势农产品生产区域，发展特色农产品加工业，将资源优势、区位优势转变为经济优势。要实施可持续发展战略，积极发展环境友好型和资源节约型农产品加工业；重视清洁生产和循环利用，走可持续发展道路。

2. 围绕社会主义新农村建设谋划农产品加工业发展 推进新农村建设是一项长期而繁重的历史任务。要积极发挥农产品加工业在现代农业建设中的重要作用，鼓励和引导农产品加工企业通过多种形式参与新农村建设。一是产业带动。要发挥农产品加工企业的带动优势，帮助一个村或几个村积极发展“一村一品”，大力培育主导产业，建设规模化、专业化的原料生产基地，培植不同类型的专业村、特色村。二是村企联动。要发挥农产品加工企业的组织优势，采取股份合作或村企合一的形式，建立“以企兴村、以村促企、村企共赢”的新机制。三是投资推动。要发挥农产品加工企业资本优势，因地制宜，量力而行，采取多种形式参与新农村建设。四是科技驱动。要发挥农产品加工企业科技创新优势，积极推进科技成果转化为现实生产力，变技术优势为产业优势，进而形成经济优势。五是服务拉动。要发挥农产品加工企业技术、信息优势，建立农村经济信息网站，提供生产技术、市场信息等服务，带领农民开拓市场、增收致富。六是外向牵动。要发挥农产品加工企业品牌优势，利用国际营销网络，在国外建基地、办工厂，积极开拓国际市场，带动农村富余劳动力输出。

3. 按照城乡统筹发展方略推进农产品加工业发展 贯彻工业反哺农业、城市支持农村和多予少取放活的方针，从根本上打破城乡分割的二元结构的体制机制，有利于促进农业不断增效、农村加快发展、农民持续增收，为农产品加工业发展提供有利的体制和机制保障；强化支农惠农政策，增加国家对农业和农村投入，完善农村金融服务体系，有利于吸引各类投资主体投资农产品加工，为农产品加工业发展提供有利的资金环境；坚持农村基本经营制度，保障农民土地承包经营的各项权利，发展农民专业合作组织，增强农村集体组织服务功能，有利于提高农民的组织化程度，为农产品加工业发展提供有利的组织保障；加快农业科技进步，推进现代农业建设，有利于提升农业科技含量和装备水平，为农产品加工业发展提供有利的科技支撑；调整优化农业结构，推进城镇化，发展县域经济，有利于优势资源向优势产业聚集，进一步优化农产品加工业的发展环境；加快培训新型农民，鼓励农民工回乡创业，有利于提高农村劳动力整体素质，为农产品加工业发展提供各类人才。总之，统筹城乡发展方略，为农产品加工业发展带来了新的机遇。对此，一定要深刻领会，紧紧抓住难得机遇，

加快发展步伐。

4. *通过实施可持续发展战略提升农产品加工发展质量* 增长方式粗放是我国经济社会发展的突出问题，由此导致效率不高、效益低下和环境压力明显加大。必须加快转变增长方式，走可持续发展的路子。要发展绿色经济，把基地建设与改善农业生态环境有机结合起来，加大农业污染防治力度，建设符合现代农业要求的农产品加工基地；发展集约经济，提高农业的有机构成，集约利用资源和土地；发展生物质经济，推动农产品初加工后的副产品及其有机废弃物的系列开发，实现增值增效；发展循环经济，引导龙头企业努力实现低消耗、低排放、高效率，促进再生资源的循环利用和非再生资源的节约利用。

5. *利用国内国际两个市场全面提高农产品加工业发展水平* 当前，世界多极化和经济全球化的趋势深入发展，科技进步日新月异，特别是随着我国入世过渡期的结束，经济市场化和国际化进程加快，农产品加工业发展面临更为激烈的市场竞争。从国际市场看，进口农产品关税水平进一步降低，对国内农产品生产压力加大；农产品出口"门槛"提高，贸易摩擦增多，出口难度增加；外资进入和并购我国农产品加工龙头企业的势头加快。从国内市场看，随着生活水平的提高和消费结构的变化，人们对大宗农产品和初级农产品的需求增长逐步减缓，但对加工农产品的需求逐步增加，对农产品质量安全生态的要求越来越高。发展农产品加工，必须面向市场，实施以质取胜、多元化发展战略，增强农产品市场竞争力。既要立足于国内市场，又要实施"走出去"战略，引导和支持龙头企业在更大范围、更高层次上参与国际合作与竞争；既要做大做强传统产业和主导产品，又要不断开发新产品，开拓新市场；既要依托资源优势，大力发展劳动密集型产业，又要采用先进技术装备，大力发展农产品精深加工。

三、"十一五"农产品加工业发展的目标和主要任务

"十一五"是我国农业和农村经济发展的关键时期，也是建设社会主义新农村和构建社会主义和谐社会的重要时期，加快发展农产品加工有着重要意义。当前和今后一个时期，农产品加工业发展要坚持以邓小平理论和"三个代表"重要思想为指导，以科学发展观为统领，全面贯彻党的十六届五中、六中全会精神，按照"转变、拓展、提升"三大战略的总体部署，围绕现代农业建设、农民就业增收、社会主义新农村建设及农村和谐社会建设，以科学规划为先导，以科技创新为支撑，切实转变经济增长方式，重点发展精深加工，逐步实现由初级加工向精深加工的转变、由数量增长向质量和效益提高转变。在结构调整和产业不断升级、质量和效益明显提高、显著降低加工能耗的前提下，力争实现年均增长12%的发展速度，2010年农产品加工业产值突破7万亿元，到"十一五"末农产品加工业产值与农业产值之比超过1.5：1。

（一）具体目标

1. *农产品加工水平要有较大提高* 到2010年我国主要农产品加工转化率（初加工以上）达到60%，精深加工比重明显增加，主要农产品深加工比例（两次以上加工的产品占其产量的比例）达到40%以上。

2. *产品质量水平要有较大提升* 绿色食品和有机食品生产得到更快发展，60%左右规模以上的农产品加工企业通过ISO、HACCP体系认证，培育一批在国内外市场具有较大潜力和市场占有率的名牌产品。

3. *技术装备水平要有较大提升* 农产品加工新技术得到推广和较广泛应用，农产品加工关键装备国产化率达到60%以上，总体技术与装备水平达到21世纪初的国际先进水平，部分领域达到同期国际先进水平。

4. *龙头企业集群要有较大发展* 培育一大批年销售收入超过100亿元和超过50亿元的龙头企业，做大做强一批农产品加工示范企业和国际竞争力强的出口企业。

5. *基地建设布局要更加优化* 根据《农产品优势布局规划》和《特色农产品布局规划》以及农产品出口需要，建设一大批高标准农产品生产和加工基地，带动农户进行标准化生产。

6. *产业化经营带动能力要有较大提升* 扶持发展一批农民专业合作经济组织和中介服务组织，力争使更多农户进入农业产业化经营领域，农户来自产业化经营的收入明显增加。

（二）主要任务

为了实现上述目标，必须统筹规划，抓住关键，突出重点，切实抓好以下工作：

1. *进一步完善和落实扶持政策* 继续落实好2004年以来中央三个1号文件关于加快发展农产品加工业的要求和国务院办公厅《关于促进农产品加工业发展的意见》。加强与有关部门的协调工作，全面落实已有的优惠政策。积极争取财政部门设立农产品加工发展专项资金，加大对农产品加工业的财政支持，加强对重点优势农产品加工业的基础设施建设、关键技术研发、引进和推广的扶持，加强对农产品加

工业创业的扶持，加强对农产品加工综合利用的扶持。积极配合税务部门做好农产品加工业增值税改革，争取对农产品加工企业开展综合利用、建设加工专用原料基地的税收优惠政策。积极协调金融部门推行积极的金融政策，通过探索仓单质押等办法，不断扩大对企业流动资金的支持；争取政策性银行加大对农产品加工业支持的力度，增加中长期贷款；争取扩大农业政策性保险的试点范围。

2. 认真组织实施《农产品加工业“十一五”规划》 为加强对农产品加工业发展的宏观指导，农业部编制了《农产品加工业“十一五”发展规划》，确定了“十一五”期间农产品加工业发展的指导思想、发展原则和工作目标，明确了重点领域和区域布局，提出了一批重点项目和政策措施。《农产品加工业“十一五”发展规划》突出优势农产品加工，主要对粮油加工、果蔬加工、畜产品加工、水产品加工和传统农产品加工等五个重点领域的发展进行了部署。各地要按照全国规划的统一部署，结合实际制订本地区的农产品加工发展规划，分类指导，加强服务，切实推进规划的实施。

3. 加强重点工程建设 积极实施《农业产业化和农产品加工推进行动》，加快六大重点项目建设：一是农产品加工示范基地建设工程，选择资源和市场配套性强、可以形成产业集聚和经济优势的农产品加工区域及大城市郊区，进行重点建设。二是农产品加工专用原料基地建设工程，在《农业部优势农产品区域布局规划》确定的13种优势农产品、41个优势产区内，选育加工专用品种，进行重点建设。三是农产品加工技术创新工程，有效整合大专院校、科研单位和企业的力量，主攻公共关键技术。四是农产品加工质量安全保障工程，完善农产品加工质量标准和检测体系，加强全过程标准化管理和质量控制。五是农产品加工信息化建设工程，为政府、企业、农户提供及时准确的信息，提供技术和贸易等各方面的服务。六是农产品加工创业工程，加强对新办中小型农产品加工企业创业的扶持和服务。

4. 建立和完善社会化服务体系 一是技术创新服务。整合农产品加工业科研资源，实行产学研结合的机制，加快建立以企业为主体、科研院所和大型骨干加工企业为支撑的农产品加工业技术创新平台，开展联合攻关，争取在关键设备和新技术、新工艺、新产品研发方面有所突破。建设国家农产品加工研究中心，以中央或地方大专院校、科研单位为依托建设50个专业性的农产品加工研发分中心。二是质量标准服务。发布实施《“十一五”农产品加工标准制修订指南》，进一步完善农产品加工国际标准跟踪平台，指导企业加强农产品加工全程质量控制体系建设，加强对已认证企业的后续监管。三是信息服务。健全完善中国国家农产品加工信息网，构筑县、市、省和国家多层次的农产品加工信息网络。积极探索开展电子商务以及物流信息化试点，建立农产品加工市场信息预警机制。四是人才培训服务。发挥乡镇企业培训体系和各类社会教育资源的作用，加强人才培养和技术培训。继续开展蓝色证书培训，重点围绕粮油、果蔬、畜产品、水产品和传统农产品加工等行业的需求，开展多种形式的职业培训和重点工种的职业技能培训与鉴定工作。努力搞好农产品加工创业培训，引导农产品优势产区的农民围绕发展加工业创业和就业。五是指导行业协会服务。鼓励各类农产品加工业协会等服务组织，围绕农产品加工业的需要，积极发挥中介组织作用，促进我国农产品加工业的行业管理和服务逐步规范化。

5. 加强领导和工作指导 各级农业部门要按照中央的要求，切实履行起对职责范围内农产品加工业的宏观管理和指导工作。按照农产品加工业的发展规律，转变工作职能，创新工作方式，完善工作机制，提高工作水平。力争做到“四个到位”：一是组织领导到位。按照科学规划、合理布局、统筹协调、突出重点的总要求，加强农业部门职能范围内的农产品加工业行政管理职能建设，建立统一、协调、高效的工作体系。二是整合各种要素落实到位。选择重点区域、重点产业、重点产品和重点企业，在不改变现有计划、资金、项目运行方式及隶属关系的条件下，列出专项，给予重点支持。三是环境创造落实到位。加强部门合作与沟通，进一步完善和落实各项政策和扶持措施；加强典型宣传，营造良好的外部环境；加强服务，切实了解和解决农产品加工业发展遇到的实际困难和问题。四是合力推进落实到位。各级农业部门内部要积极配合，通力协作，明确分工，落实责任，形成推进农产品加工业发展的工作合力。

总之，积极发展农产品加工业，是农业和农村经济进入新阶段的必然选择，是建设现代农业的客观要求，是时代赋予的历史责任。一定要紧密团结在以胡锦涛为总书记的党中央周围，坚持科学发展观，全面贯彻落实十六届五中、六中全会精神，脚踏实地，开拓创新，扎扎实实推进农产品加工业持续健康发展，为社会主义新农村建设和社会主义和谐社会建设做出新的更大贡献。

（本文为作者于2006年11月在全国农产品加工业工作会议上的讲话，略有删改）

努力实施“双百市场工程”大力推进农产品现代流通体系建设

商务部部长助理 黄 海

“双百市场工程”自2006年2月实施以来，经过各级商务主管部门、有关市场和企业的共同努力，开局良好。为进一步推进“双百市场工程”，商务部决定分别召开农产品批发市场和流通企业建设现场会，进一步统一思想，提高认识，交流经验，解读政策，对下一步工作做出部署。

一、充分认识构建农产品现代流通体系的重要意义

当前，我国农产品流通体系薄弱，流通不畅，农民卖难问题突出，不仅直接影响农民增收和农村消费，而且成为扩大内需的一大瓶颈。从全国情况看，相当多的农村地区之所以贫困，很大程度上是由于农产品流通方式落后、标准化程度低、流通环节损耗率高、流通效率低造成的。

1. *构建农产品现代流通体系是解决农产品卖难、促进农民增收的客观要求* 2005年7月，商务部委托有关单位对全国20个省555个村1万个农户问卷调查显示：42%的农户自己销售农产品，45%的农户将农产品卖给个体商贩，只有2.7%的农户通过订单销售农产品。2006年，山西、河南一些地方出现种西瓜亏本、桃子卖难的情况，国务院领导高度重视。这也说明，我国农产品流通体系确实存在着比较大的问题，农产品流通的市场化水平还比较低，农民很难从流通环节分享增值带来的收益，农产品卖难问题长期存在，农民收入也难以增加。

2. *构建农产品现代流通体系是提高农产品流通标准化程度、提高流通效率的有效途径* 改革开放20多年来，我国农产品批发市场已具有相当规模，已经成为我国农产品流通的主渠道。全国现有4 300个农产品批发市场，虽然只占农产品市场总数的16%左右，却承担着70%以上农产品的流通，在满足城乡消费、扩大农产品流通、促进农民增收、推动农业产业化方面，发挥了积极的作用。但也必须看到，大多数农产品批发市场基础设施差，装备水平低，经营秩序不规范，服务功能单一，流通成本高、效率低、效益差，难以发挥引导农业生产和保证农产品安全的作用，不利于扩大农产品流通规模、提高农产品流通效率和国际竞争力。因此，推进农产品批发市场升级改造，提高农产品流通的标准化、规范化水平，是构建农产品现代流通体系的一个重要组成部分。

3. *构建农产品现代流通体系是发展新型流通方式、减少农产品在流通中损耗的重要举措* 我国农产品物流发展滞后，信息传递不畅，标准化水平低，保鲜、包装等关键技术水平难以满足农产品流通发展的需要。发达国家农产品超市销售比例在70%以上，而我国平均只有6%左右。农产品冷链系统建设方面差距更为明显，目前我国只有10%的肉类、20%的水产品、少量的牛奶和豆制品进入冷链系统，而欧美国家进入冷链系统的农产品比例为85%。由于农产品流通中损耗十分严重，我国生鲜产品物流费用占总成本的70%，远远高于国际平均水平。构建农产品现代流通体系，促进专业化分工，可以大大减少农产品流通中的价值损失，达到降低损耗的目的。

4. *构建农产品现代流通体系是强化农产品质量管理、保障农产品流通安全的重要手段* 农产品流通关系到亿万农民切身利益和广大消费者的身体健康，需要政府部门高度重视和严格管理。我国农产品供给已经实现总量基本平衡，农产品消费安全问题越来越受到社会各界的重视。我国农业生产过于分散，小生产与大市场的矛盾短期内难以解决，必须一手抓生产源头，发展优质高效农业和品质优良、特色明显、附加值高的优势农产品；一手抓市场流通，建立农产品质量安全可追溯系统，阻止品质差、不安全的农产品进入流通领域。推进农产品批发市场标准化建设，是规范农产品流通秩序和保障农产品流通安全的重要基础和前提。

二、“双百市场工程”主要任务和工作目标

为培育一批面向国内外市场的大型农产品批发市场和流通企业，构建与国际市场接轨的农产品现代流

通体系，促进农民增收和保障农产品流通安全，商务部启动了“双百市场工程”。这是商务部为推动“三农”问题解决、促进社会主义新农村建设而采取的又一项重大举措。

1.“双百市场工程”的主要任务　重点改造100个大型农产品批发市场，重点加强仓储、物流配送等基础设施和检验检测中心等准公益性设施建设，发挥标准化市场的示范作用和辐射效应，引导农产品批发市场全面改造提升、完善服务功能。着力培育100个大型农产品流通企业，重点加强农产品冷链系统与配送中心建设，推动农产品流通规模化和现代化，提高优势农产品市场营销水平，探索和推广贸工农一体化、内外贸相结合的经营模式。

2.“双百市场工程”的工作目标　力争用三年时间，通过政府引导及重点市场、重点企业示范带动，培育一批符合国家标准、面向国内外市场、现代化的大型农产品批发市场和能够带动农产品出口的大型农产品流通企业，带动全国一半左右（约2 000个）农产品批发市场的升级改造，使农产品流通成本明显降低，流通环节损耗大幅减少；全国约300个大型农产品流通企业经超市销售农产品的比例达到30%以上，更多优势农产品进入跨国公司的国际营销网络，初步构建与国际市场接轨的农产品现代流通体系。

三、“双百市场工程”实施进展顺利

各级商务主管部门收到商务部关于开展“双百市场工程”的通知后，主动向政府领导同志汇报，积极争取财政等有关部门的支持，各项工作进展顺利。

1. 认真开展项目推荐工作　各地商务主管部门在全面摸清本地农产品批发市场及流通企业发展情况基础上，制定了本地区“双百市场工程”实施规划，并按照公开、公平、公正原则，择优推荐市场和企业。全国37个省、自治区、直辖市（包括计划单列市、新疆生产建设兵团）共推荐了207个大型农产品批发市场的692个建设和改造项目，其中准公益性项目341个，基础设施建设项目351个，计划投资总额111.5亿元；推荐了174个大型农产品流通企业，申报项目450个，其中冷链系统项目155个，配送中心项目295个，计划总投资69.4亿元。

2. 积极争取有关部门和地方政府部门支持　商务部加强与财政等部门的沟通，争取相关政策支持。国家开发银行与商务部联合发文，安排专项贷款支持“双百市场工程”等农村市场体系建设，并给予利率下浮优惠。各地商务主管部门主动向地方政府汇报，争取相关的配套政策。北京从商业流通发展资金中安排近3 000万元支持农产品批发市场建设；天津对投资额超过5 000万元的“双百市场工程”项目直接补助200万元；陕西安排2 000万元农村现代流通体系建设专项资金，用于配套支持“双百市场工程”；深圳安排1 000万元对“双百市场工程”项目提供3年的全额贴息；安徽从中部发展资金（500万元）和流通业发展资金（1 000万元）中安排部分资金对“双百市场工程”项目进行直接补助；辽宁准备从省政府安排的财政贴息资金中划出500万～600万元用于支持纳入“双百市场工程”的市场和企业；吉林从省外贸发展资金中安排160万元对10个农产品批发市场和流通企业予以直接补助。

3. 制定资金管理办法　商务部决定从中央贸易发展基金中安排5亿元，采取直补和贴息相结合的方式，支持大型农产品批发市场和大型农产品流通企业承担的建设和改造项目。其中，农产品批发市场改造资金3亿元，农产品流通企业发展资金2亿元。商务部会同财政部联合下发了《关于做好2006年度农产品现代流通体系建设资金管理工作的通知》，对资金支持方式、标准、原则等做出了规定。对于批发市场建设和改造质量安全可追溯系统等准公益性设施，以及流通企业冷链系统项目，国家将给予直接补贴。对于批发市场建设仓储、配送等基础设施以及流通企业建设生鲜农产品配送中心所取得的金融机构中长期固定资产贷款，国家将通过贴息方式予以支持。按照《通知》要求，商务部已向财政部申请拨付各地2006年度农产品现代流通体系建设项目资金。

4. 完成2006年度农产品现代流通体系建设项目核准工作　商务部市场建设司对申报材料进行了严格审核，组织召开了大型农产品批发市场和流通企业专家评审会。国务院有关部门和行业组织的负责同志参加评审。与会专家本着公开、公平、公正的精神，按照扶优扶强、适当向中西部地区和东北等老工业基地倾斜的原则，优选出100个辐射面广、带动能力强的大型农产品批发市场和100个有实力的大型农产品流通企业，总计263个直补项目和151个贴息项目。其中，批发市场准公益性项目172个、基础设施项目81个；流通企业冷链系统项目90个、配送中心项目71个。商务部已经下发2006年度农产品现代流通体系建设项目的通知。

5. 加强项目管理工作　为加强农产品现代流通体系建设项目管理工作，一是开通了“双百市场工程”管理信息系统，发挥社会监督作用。包括大型农产品批发市场子系统和大型农产品流通企业子系统。二是制定并印发了农产品现代流通体系建设项目建设标准与验收规范。经征求有关部门和企业意见，商务部组织制定了大型农产品批发市场质量安全可追溯系统、安全监控中心、检验检测中心及废弃物处理中心等4个准公益性项目建设标准及大型农产品流通企业项目建设标准以及农产品现代流通体系建设项目验收规范。建设标准对项目功能、设施设备配置等方面提出了明确要求；验收规范从原则、对象、时间、程序等方面做出了规定。

6. 预期效果良好 商务部确定支持的100个市场总体上是辐射面广、对主要农产品产销影响较大的全国性和跨区域农产品批发市场。2005年交易额累计达到2 453亿元，占全国1 268个亿元以上农产品市场交易总额7 083亿元的35%。其中，中西部地区的专业市场大多具有鲜明的地方特色。预计项目全部建成后，可以新增年交易额500亿元，带动增加就业人数150万人，并逐步使2亿城市居民吃上放心菜。100个大型农产品流通企业普遍具有较强的实力，2005年食用农产品销售额为384亿元。预计全部项目建成后，试点企业可以新增年销售额35亿元，农产品经超市销售的比例提高到30%以上。

在肯定成绩的同时，也要看到当前工作中还存在一定问题。一是少数省市对“双百市场工程”不重视，至今未出台相应的配套政策。二是各地工作进度参差不齐，一些省市尚未制定资金审核和拨付程序。三是部分省市商务主管部门与相关部门的沟通协调工作不够，有待进一步加强。

四、进一步推进农产品现代流通体系建设

农产品流通体系建设是一项长期而艰巨的任务，工作开头难，保质保量地进行下去更难。各地商务主管部门和参加“双百市场工程”的市场、企业，一定要高度重视，落实责任，努力做好各项工作。

1. 加快项目落实工作 根据商务部、财政部关于2006年度农产品现代流通体系建设资金管理的通知，申请资金支持的项目应当符合商务部确定的项目建设标准及验收规范，在2006年内竣工，并经省级商务及财政主管部门验收合格的建设和改造项目，省级商务主管部门要加强组织领导，督促承办单位抓紧做好项目落实工作，确保项目在年底前完成。承办单位务必要加快项目工作进度，正在实施的项目要争取早日竣工，尚未实施的项目要尽快启动，已经竣工的项目要尽快申请验收。涉及基础设施建设项目的单位要格外注意进度，尤其是北方地区要考虑气候对施工的影响。对2006年不能如期完成的项目，商务部将采取批准顺延或者取消实施项目等方式予以调整。

2. 确保项目建设质量 省级商务主管部门要严格按照商务部制定的农产品现代流通体系建设项目建设标准与验收规范，结合本地项目实际情况，抓紧对相关建设标准与验收规范进行完善。要会同财政等相关部门，按照完善后的项目建设标准与验收规范，于2007年1月31日前做好项目验收工作。为了使项目更加符合各地实际，允许各地对项目建设标准与验收规范做适当修改和补充。各地不要盲目提高标准，也不能随意降低项目建设标准和要求。各承办单位要严格按照商务部及省级商务主管部门提出的项目建设标准和验收规范，组织项目建设与改造工作。既要有的放矢，保证达到基本功能要求，也要着眼于长远，确保建设项目符合市场竞争和企业发展的需要。在改善市场经营环境、配置设施设备方面，要真抓实干、真材实料，不要搞花架子、样子货。

3. 认真做好资金拨付及管理工作 一是抓紧制定资金审核和拨付程序。根据商务部、财政部的要求，各省级商务主管部门应会同财政主管部门，制定本地区的资金审核和拨付程序，并于2006年9月15日前向商务部、财政部有关司局备案。截至目前，只有辽宁、陕西、新疆、内蒙古、四川、山西、河北、河南、宁夏、甘肃、天津、浙江、大连、青海共14个省、自治区、直辖市及计划单列市完成，还有23个省份至今未向商务部和财政部报备资金审核和拨付程序。这些省份必须加快工作进度，务必于11月6日前完成报备工作。如果因逾期不报影响资金预拨，将追究有关单位的责任。二是切实加强与财政部门的沟通协调工作。商务主管部门要主动向当地财政部门通报“双百市场工程”工作进展情况，积极争取支持，努力形成分工合作、协调配合的工作局面。三是严格资金使用管理。任何单位不得骗取、挪用或者截留农产品现代流通体系建设专项资金，对违反规定、弄虚作假、存在严重问题的单位，商务部、财政部不仅要全额收回资金，而且将取消其以后年度申请资格。触犯法律的，依法追究有关单位和个人的责任。四是加强项目审计和资金使用监督工作，确保补助资金真正用在农产品现代流通体系建设上。

4. 切实加强项目管理 各地商务主管部门要加强对项目的管理工作，建立健全动态跟踪、定期评估、监督检查和信息上报制度。省级商务主管部门、承办单位，要及时向商务部报送项目进展情况和本地农产品现代流通体系建设工作情况。省级商务主管部门要指定专人负责与商务部的日常联系工作，并于每月8日前向商务部报送上月工作进展情况。试点市场和企业也要通过“双百市场工程”管理信息系统同步报送所承办项目进展及后续运行情况。

商务部市场建设司要进一步加强项目管理工作，充分发挥“双百市场工程”管理信息系统的作用。对试点市场和企业，要实行动态管理和优胜劣汰。商务部将会同有关部门，对验收通过的建设项目进行抽查。2007年上半年，将对2006年农产品现代流通体系建设项目实施情况进行一次总体评估。各地商务主管部门要加强与财政等部门的沟通协调，积极争取地方政府的配套政策，加强对试点单位的指导。工作中出现的新情况、新问题，要及时向商务部报告。

5. 发挥项目引导和示范作用　项目承办单位要自觉增强社会责任意识，搞好项目设施设备运行及日常维护工作，使检验检测中心、废弃物处理中心、质量安全可追溯系统、安全监控中心等设施真正运转起来，并切实发挥作用。承办同类项目的单位，要相互借鉴，取长补短，不断提高项目建设质量和水平。省级商务主管部门要树立典型、推广经验，发挥标准化市场和重点建设项目的示范与带动作用，促进农产品批发市场整体改造提升，提高农产品流通的标准化、规范化和现代化水平。要引导市场完善加工配送、统一结算、价格发布等功能，发展网上交易、拍卖等新型流通方式。市场建设司要结合农产品批发市场标准化改造工作，抓紧做好大型农产品批发市场与流通企业授牌工作。要广泛宣传实施“双百市场工程”的意义和作用，总结推广好的经验，使全社会都来关注农产品流通的发展，吸引更多的社会资金投入农产品流通基础设施建设。

（本文为作者于2006年10月在全国大型农产品批发市场建设现场会上的讲话，略有删改）

加强食品药品监管
当好人民健康的保卫者

国家食品药品监督管理局局长　邵明立

食品药品监管系统贯彻落实党的十六届五中全会精神，就是要抓住“十一五”时期的发展机遇，全面落实科学发展观，把工作重心转向满足人民群众的食品药品安全需求上来，努力加强自身建设，不断加强对食品药品监管，确保人民群众饮食用药安全，为社会主义和谐社会和全面小康社会建设提供保障。

一、把保障群众饮食用药安全作为中心任务

党的十六大把提高全民族的健康素质作为全面建设小康社会的奋斗目标之一，要求在发展经济的同时，更加关注人和社会的全面发展。十六届五中全会又进一步提出，要把“认真解决人民群众最关心、最直接、最现实的利益问题”摆在突出位置。因此，食品药品监管系统必须把保障群众饮食用药安全作为中心任务，切实抓紧抓好。

1. 把保障群众饮食用药安全作为中心任务，是坚持以人为本的需要　天地之间，莫贵于民。人的需求和全面发展，是经济社会发展的起点和归宿。在人的多层次需求中，生命安全需要和身体健康需要是人的最基本需要。改革开放以来，我国人民群众的食品药品需求已经由单纯追求数量上的满足，转变为追求质量的提高。据统计，目前我国食品、医药工业总产值已超过2万亿元，食品和医疗保健的消费已成为居民消费支出的最大部分，占消费总支出的40%以上。与此同时，由于种种原因，我国食品药品安全仍呈现出高风险的趋势。在食品安全方面，农产品的源头污染，食品生产加工领域的假冒伪劣，食品流通环节的不规范等，屡屡造成一些重大食品安全事故，如劣质奶粉、苏丹红、瘦肉精和频繁曝光的各种假劣食品等。在药品安全方面，部分农村和贫困地区假劣药品问题突出，药品生产经营秩序不规范，虚假违法广告屡禁不止，不合理用药导致的药源性疾病增加。可以说，食品药品安全已成为党中央高度重视、群众普遍关心的重大社会问题。

2. 把保障群众饮食用药安全作为中心任务，是坚持立党为公、执政为民的需要　食品药品安全是体现我们党立党为公、执政为民的一个窗口。党中央、国务院历来高度重视食品药品的安全问题，在食品药品监管体制改革、法制建设、执法体系建设等方面做

出了重要部署，采取了一系列有力措施。这主要表现在：建立了集中统一的药品监管体制，完善了与社会主义市场经济相适应的药品监管法规体系，深入实施食品放心工程，持续大力整顿食品药品市场秩序，查处了一批大案要案和重大食品安全事故，有效遏制了制售假劣食品药品的违法犯罪行为。中央的这些政策措施关注民生、反映民意，得到了群众的衷心拥护。各级食品药品监督管理部门，要坚持把维护群众的饮食用药权益和生命健康作为根本而长远的目标，把群众利益高于一切的理念贯穿始终，大力加强监管，为人民群众把好安全关。

3. *把保障群众饮食用药安全作为中心任务，是促进社会全面发展的需要* 坚持科学发展观，必须从经济增长与全面发展的辩证关系出发，准确理解食品药品监管工作的性质，大力促进社会全面发展。经济增长可以为公众提供更多、更丰富的产品，但是仅有经济增长是远远不够的，因为经济增长并不等于全面发展。那些认为经济增长可以解决发展中的全部问题，经济增长可以自然而然实现其他社会发展目标的观念，是片面的。“十一五”期间，要努力实现全面、协调、可持续发展，让发展成果惠及广大群众，而不是单纯追求经济增长。食品药品这样的特殊商品，由于直接关系公众身体健康和生命安全，其生产经营必须置于科学、高效的监管之下，确保行业发展和企业获益不以牺牲公共利益和群众健康为代价，必须维护社会的公平与正义。要充分认识到，食品药品行业一旦缺乏监管，或者监管部门偏离人民的立场，不能科学、公正地依法履行监管职责，各种各样损害公众生命健康的情形就可能发生。

4. *把保障群众饮食用药安全作为中心任务，是促进社会和谐的需要* 食品药品安全是公共安全的重要组成部分。建设民主法制、公平正义、诚信友爱、充满活力、安定有序、人与自然和谐相处的社会主义和谐社会，食品药品安全是最基本的保障之一。当前，我国已经进入“黄金发展期”与“矛盾凸现期”并存的特殊发展时期，食品药品安全问题日益突出。一旦发生食品药品安全问题，如不能得到迅速有效的解决，不仅会威胁到群众生命安全和社会安全，给群众和社会造成不可挽回的损失，甚至会引发种种社会不稳定因素。因此，加强食品药品监管，减少和防范食品药品安全事故，必须作为构建和谐社会的重要内容。要努力让群众身体健康和生命安全得到最基本的保障，不再为日常饮食用药担惊受怕，共享经济社会发展的成果。要坚持依法行政，维护市场秩序，让广大食品药品从业者在法制框架内，守法经营，诚信经营，为社会创造更多更好的财富。

二、加强食品药品监管应注意的几个问题

我国食品药品监管工作正处在转型发展的重要时期，地区和城乡发展不平衡、技术监督体系和监督执法队伍不适应发展需要的问题比较突出。当前，加强食品药品监管应着力解决好以下问题：

1. *注重城乡及地区间监管工作的协调发展，着力加强农村监督* 我国经济社会发展的城乡及地区不平衡，客观上造成了食品药品监管的城乡及地区不平衡。在中西部欠发达地区尤其是广大农村，食品药品监管力量薄弱，监管的基础设施、执法装备和技术水平落后，检验检测设备严重不足，加上人员不足，使监管面临很大的实际困难。“十一五”期间，要大力改善不发达地区尤其是广大农村的执法条件，突出抓好农村监管能力建设，特别是要围绕农村新型合作医疗制度改革，不断加强农村药品供应网络和监督网络建设，保障农民用药安全有效、价格合理、方便及时。

2. *注重基础设施和技术支撑体系建设，着力加强技术监督* 要积极争取国家和地方财政支持，加大对食品药品监管的基础设施和执法装备投入，为基层监管部门的监督执法创造基本条件。要进一步提高监管信息化水平，逐步实现各级食品药品监管部门信息共享、协同执法，为公众提供优质服务。要不断提高我国食品药品标准、食品药品生产经营规范以及食品药品检验检测技术水平，按照统筹规划、统一标准、合理适用、资源共享、分清责任的原则，建设既符合中国国情又符合国际贸易要求的技术支撑体系。

3. *注重日常监管和应急处理能力建设，着力加强监督执法* 监管工作不可能毕其功于一役。要按照整顿规范与促进发展、深化改革、扩大开放相结合的原则，坚持整顿与规范并重，打击与建设同步，近期与长远结合，标本兼治、重在治本的工作思路，从薄弱环节入手，整顿药品生产经营秩序，强化食品药品安全监管，加大查处大案要案的力度，严厉打击制售假劣食品药品的行为。同时，要充分估计到食品药品安全可能出现的各种问题，对公共安全可能造成的严重威胁，坚持“健全体制、明确责任，居安思危、预防为主，强化法治、依靠科技，协同应对、快速反应，加强基层、全民参与”的工作要求，建立健全应对重大突发食品药品安全事故的应急体系，确保一旦有事，能够有效组织、快速反应、高效运转、处理得当，预防和减少突发事件及其造成的损失，最大限度地保障人民群众的生命财产安全。

4. 注重依法行政和执法队伍建设，着力加强执法监督 国务院出台的《全面推进依法行政实施纲要》明确提出，“经过十年左右坚持不懈的努力，基本实现建设法治政府的目标”。“十一五”期间，要进一步健全食品药品法规体系，构建比较完备的食品药品监管法律体系。要不断规范行政权力和行政行为，严格按照法定程序和权限行使权力、履行职责。要加强执法监督，加强对行政行为的监督检查，逐步建立以执法有依据、行为有规范、权力有制约、过程有监控、违法有追究为主要内容的行政执法责任制度。依法行政，人是最关键的因素。要大力实施人才战略，着力建设行政管理人才、食品药品专业技术人才两支队伍，全面提高全系统工作人员的素质，以人力资源开发推动食品药品监管工作的发展。

三、加强食品药品监管工作的主要目标

党的十六届五中全会明确提出：要“强化对食品、药品、餐饮卫生等的监管”。“十一五”期间，食品药品监管部门作为公众健康的保护者，必须坚持用科学发展观分析判断工作中的问题和矛盾，将群众的根本利益放到首要位置，把保障群众饮食用药安全作为一切工作的出发点和落脚点，努力提高监管水平，保证食品药品监管全面覆盖，不断促进社会和谐。

1. 提高食品安全综合监督水平 要健全食品安全综合监督体系，充分发挥食品安全综合协调职能的积极作用，推进以《食品安全法》为基础的食品安全法规体系的建立和完善。大力推进食品安全标准体系建设，健全保健食品市场准入和安全监管体系。全面推进食品放心工程，建立科学、规范的食品安全评估和“食品放心工程”评价制度。完善食品安全信息发布制度，构建食品安全信用体系的基本框架和运行机制。全面落实食品安全重大事故应急预案，建立食品安全重大事件预警机制和应急救援体系，力争到2010年使食品安全信息监测网络体系覆盖90%以上的县（市），食品安全信息监测率达到80%，重大食品安全事故处理率达到100%。配合有关部门，继续加强对农业投入品监管，提高蔬菜农药残留合格率，基本解决畜产品含“瘦肉精”的问题；遏制滥用食品添加剂行为，继续在餐饮业和学校食堂中扩大实施食品卫生量化分级管理；提高食品市场中的索证索票率，逐步建立食品监管部门间协同工作和联合执法制度。

2. 提高药品安全保障水平 要积极落实《药品管理法》、《药品管理法实施条例》和《医疗器械监督管理条例》，规范行政审批，不断完善药品监管法规体系，使药品监管工作做到有法可依、有法必依。推进药物非临床研究管理规范（GLP）和药物临床试验管理规范（GCP）认证，基本满足我国新药注册的药物临床试验和国际多中心临床试验要求。建立相对完善的药品、医疗器械经营质量管理规范（GSP），对中药饮片、医用氧、体外诊断试剂、药用辅料等全面实施药品生产质量管理规范（GMP），逐步实施中药材生产质量管理规范（GAP）。医疗机构要按照制剂配制质量管理规范（GPP）进行制剂配制。实行处方药和非处方药分类管理，防止药物滥用。加强药品、医疗器械技术审评体系建设，提高产品国家标准，参与国际标准制定。继续推进执业药师制度建设，提高从业人员素质。建立较为规范的药品不良反应和再评价制度，从整体上提高我国对药品不良反应的发现、报告、预警和应急控制能力，淘汰部分有严重安全隐患的药品，减少药源性疾病和其他不良事件的发生。建立覆盖全国的医药生产经营企业、医疗卫生机构和监管部门的药品不良反应监测报告体系，50%以上的报告质量要达到世界卫生组织要求的2级水平。扩大农村药品监督网和供应网的覆盖面，力争到“十一五”末农村药品监督网覆盖率达到100%，农村药品供应网覆盖率达到90%，县以上医疗机构药房、80%乡镇卫生院药房和60%村卫生室、个体诊所达到规范药房标准。要加强市场监督，“十一五”期间药品监督抽验覆盖面要由现在的30%提高到80%，伪劣药品阳性检出率要从现在的5%～10%提高到30%～40%。口岸药品检验所对所有进口药品、生物制品及国家药典等药品品种的独立全项检验能力基本达到100%，省级药检所对所有国家药品标准的独立全项检验能力基本达到100%；地市药检所对所有国家药品标准的独立全项检验能力由20%提高到80%；国家级医疗器械检验机构对归口产品的检验能力达到100%，全系统对进口新产品、国产高新技术产品及高风险产品的检验能力达到90%以上。

3. 推进食品药品监管系统建设 一是提高队伍素质。积极探索建立与食品药品监督管理体制相匹配的人才培养、培训机制，进一步提高队伍素质，优化队伍结构。通过引进人才和加大在职培训力度，力争到“十一五”末，全系统公务员和各类专业技术人员中，具有食品、药品（含医疗器械）、医学、法律或相关专业的人员占70%以上，本科以上学历人员占50%以上。大力推进省、市、县局领导班子专业化、年轻化，在各级药品检验机构中，专业技术人员要不低于70%，业务负责人员应具备高级专业技术职称。二是加强基础设施建设。对国家口岸药品检验机构和

省地两级药品检验机构的部分实验室进行改造，增补部分仪器设备。建立和完善医疗器械检验检测体系，配备相关仪器设备。以基层为重点，加强省、地、县三级行政执法机构建设，配备必要的执法装备。力争到“十一五”末，全系统基础设施、执法装备与检验检测设备基本满足监管任务需要。三是加强信息化建设。全系统要把信息化建设作为提高监管效能的重要措施，力争到“十一五”末，建立起食品药品监管电子政务体系框架，建成国家食品药品信息网络平台和监管数据中心，实现跨部门、跨区域、高性能的信息快速传输、交换和使用，基本实现全国食品药品监管系统信息资源共享。

全面建设小康社会 加快推进粮食科技创新体系建设

国家粮食局副局长　郄建伟

这次全国粮食科技大会，是在认真贯彻落实全国科技大会精神，坚持走中国特色自主创新道路的形势下召开的。下面我就粮食科技工作中如何落实《国家中长期科学和技术发展规划纲要》精神，完成《“十一五”粮食科技发展指导意见》提出的各项工作，谈几点意见。

一、“十五”粮食科技工作取得了显著成绩

“十五”期间，粮食科技工作呈现良好的发展局面。以绿色储粮技术、深加工综合利用技术为标志的粮食科技进步，对保障国家粮食安全，促进粮食产业化发展，满足城乡居民日益增长的需求起到了重要的支撑作用。国家粮食科技项目和资金投入显著增加，粮食科技产生的经济社会效益明显增长，行业科技总体水平有较大幅度提高。粮食科技体制改革取得了新的成效，粮食企业技术创新能力显著增强。通过国家重大项目的实施，取得了一批具有产业化前景的科技成果，培养和锻炼了科技人才队伍。

（一）粮食科技投入显著增长，人才队伍不断成长壮大

“十五”期间，国家粮食局组织的国家科技攻关、社会公益研究专项、科技基础性工作专项、农业科技成果转化资金项目、国家高技术产业化示范工程等重点项目约130项，总投资超过10亿元。“十五”粮食科技投入的主要特点：一是科研项目投入资金来源多元化。除国拨经费外，银行贷款、自筹资金和其他资金也成为科研经费的重要来源。二是科技攻关项目经费投入的份额较大。科技攻关项目经费的投入高于高技术产业化、科技成果转化项目的投入。三是粮食科技投入的两大重点领域是加工和仓储。这两个领域的投入高于物流、质量检测方面的投入。四是原部属科研单位承担的项目比例较大。国家粮食科技项目中，原部属科研单位承担的项目和资金的份额均为60%左右，这反映出原部属科研院所的主力军作用。粮食科技投入的增加和项目的实施，有力地促进了科研事业的发展，锻炼了科研队伍，培养了科技人才。到2005年底，全国粮食系统专业技术人员约11.6万人，其中具有高级专业技术职称的近3 000人，具有中级专业技术职称的近3.7万人。中青年学科带头人和技术骨干迅速成长，45岁以下的技术人员占75%。2004年、2005年国家粮食局评审出研究员及研究员待遇的高级工程师24人，享受政府特殊津贴的专家5人。

（二）粮食科技总体水平明显提高，科技成果广泛应用

1. 一批自主开发先进实用的粮食流通技术，得到全面的推广和产业化应用　在国家粮库建设中，普遍应用了自主研究开发的机械通风、环流熏蒸、计算机粮情检测和谷物冷却等四项新技术，大幅度提高了仓储技术水平。郑州粮食科学研究设计院等单位研究开发的“散粮储运装备技术与应用”，为区域化散粮流通提供了技术支撑；局科研院、河南工业大学等单位开发的低温储粮技术、成都粮食储藏科学研究所等单位开发的二氧化碳气调储粮等技术得到了示范应用；郑州粮科院、北京中谷润粮科技公司等单位自主开发的玉米低温真空干燥技术、浅圆仓装仓防破碎装置、粮仓气密技术等成果解决了粮食流通实际工作中的诸多技术瓶颈。粮库建设设计水平有了很

大的提高，由国家粮食局组织编制的《国家储备粮库通用仓型设计选用图集》获2004年国家优秀标准设计金奖。

2. 粮油加工技术和装备的引进和消化吸收再创新，使我国粮食技术和装备水平迈上新台阶　武汉工业学院研究开发的油料挤压膨化、“双低”菜籽脱皮冷榨等制油技术，西安油脂科学研究设计院完成的“超滤膜法由油茶饼粕中提取精制油茶皂甙”，黑龙江粮食科学研究所开发的大豆异黄酮与皂甙，江南大学开发的稻米及副产品加工利用增值技术，山东怡康集团的无水葡萄糖高技术生产线，丰原集团玉米液发酵生产柠檬酸技术，大成集团以玉米为原料生产化工醇等自主创新技术，都促进了传统粮油加工业的升级改造，带动了粮食深加工产业化和农村经济发展。江苏牧羊集团、武汉皇冠友谊油脂工程公司、湖北省永祥粮食机械有限公司、天津圣昌达机械有限公司等自主开发设计的加工成套设备和工程设计达到国际国内先进水平。

3. 粮油质量标准检测技术及计算机信息技术得到广泛应用　局科研院组织研发的电子式粉质仪和拉伸仪替代了进口产品，深受用户好评。无锡粮食科学设计研究院、局标准质量中心等单位研究开发的粮食品质测报技术体系及数据共享技术等为全国粮食产后质量调查和优质粮食品质测报提供了技术服务。局科研院、江南大学承担完成的“食品功能因子作用机理、分类及标准研究”、武汉粮食科学研究设计院完成的“饲料显微镜检查图谱及识别系统”等为保障粮油、饲料加工产品质量安全提供了有力的技术支撑。中国科学院遥感应用研究所、国家粮食局信息中心承担的国家“863”计划中“粮食预警遥感辅助决策系统”项目，河南工业大学组织开发的“国家储备粮库建设智能决策系统”等，为国家粮食宏观调控与决策提供了技术支持。

4. 农户科学储粮示范工程取得良好社会经济效益　由科技部、农业部、财政部和国家粮食局共同组织的“粮食丰产科技工程”重大科技项目，在河北、辽宁、吉林、黑龙江、江苏、江西、山东、河南、湖北、湖南、四川、安徽、陕西等省粮食局的积极组织配合下，由成都粮食储藏科学研究所、河南工业大学、辽宁粮食科学研究所、湖南粮食科学设计研究院等单位承担的“减少三大粮食作物农户储粮损失技术集成与示范”课题，经过对粮食主产区上万户农民的技术宣传和培训，先后建立了农户科学储粮技术示范点3 644个，有力地指导了农村科学储粮，取得了良好的社会经济效益，受到了广大农民群众的好评，在社会引起了强烈反响。这项工作对降低粮食储藏损失，保障粮食安全，增加农民收入，促进社会主义新农村的建设起到了重要示范作用。温家宝总理对这项工作曾做出了重要批示：“我国农户储粮数量巨大，推广科学储粮技术，改善储粮条件，减少损失，对于保障国家粮食安全有着重要意义。国家粮食局要继续抓好这项工作，有关部门要予以支持和配合”。将按照总理的批示精神，加大工作力度继续抓好这项工作。

“十五”期间，由国家粮食局组织的130多项各类国家科技项目中，达到国际先进水平的12项，国内领先水平的49项，国内先进水平的9项，填补国内空白的13项。“十五”期间，在国家科技进步奖项中，有4项粮食科技成果获得国家科技进步二等奖。这些项目是：由郑州粮科院等单位承担完成的“散粮储运装备技术与应用”，江南大学等单位完成的“稻米及其副产品加工利用增值技术”，北京化工大学等单位完成的“大豆精深加工成套技术及关键设备”，中国农业科学院油料作物研究所等单位完成的“‘双低’油菜芥酸硫甙定量速测技术及仪器的研制与应用”。这4项科技成果标志着我国粮食流通、粮油深加工和质量检测技术水平跨上了一个新台阶。另外，国家粮食局成功组织举办了以“粮油食品安全与农村科学储粮”为主题的2006年粮食科技活动周。全国20个省、自治区、直辖市粮食局、中储粮总公司、中粮集团、中谷集团、地方粮食科研院所和院校、粮油质检中心、粮油学会和协会、有关企业等数百家单位参加了活动。这次科技周在全国40多个大中城市和200多个县（市）、乡共举办了500多场次形式多样、内容丰富、气氛热烈的群众性粮食科普活动。这次活动成为全面展示粮食行业科技创新体系的窗口，是对粮食行业科技力量的一次检阅，展示了成果，振奋了精神，收到了良好的社会效果。

（三）粮食科技体制改革取得新的成效，科技创新环境逐步改善

1. 粮食行业公益性基础性科研力量得到加强　局科研院改制为公益性科研院后，更新了科研设施，改善了科研基础条件，增强了承担国家及行业重大公益性科技项目的能力。通过改革，优化了学科结构和人才结构，加强了粮食质量安全检测、粮食资源综合利用等新技术的研究。通过改革完善了用人制度，引入了竞争机制，全面推行了岗位聘用制，中青年科技队伍加速成长和壮大。

2. 原部属院所转制后市场意识和科研成果产业化能力加强　无锡、郑州、武汉、西安、成都等5个科研院所转制为科技型企业，进入中谷粮油集团组成了科技总公司。它们转变观念，树立服务行业、服务市场、服务社会的意识，不断拓宽工程设计和技术开发的业务范围。国家粮食局投入专项资金用于这些院所的仪器设备更新及基础设施改造，增强了这些院所的新技术新产品的自主开发能力和科技成果转化能力。2004年局里批准组建了国家粮食局粮食物流、粮油食品、储藏物保护等10个工程研究中心，总投入约1亿元，加强了粮食行业科技成果转化中试平台的建设。

3. 省级粮食科研机构基本完成了转制工作，进入快速发展时期　湖南、黑龙江、辽宁、内蒙古、陕西、浙江、江西、福建、广东等省级粮食科研院所面向市场，服务企业取得了较好的社会经济效益，在促进地方粮食科技发展中发挥了重要作用。国家粮食局利用国债资金对37个省级粮油质检中心的检测仪器进行更新配置，大大改善了地方粮油质检工作的装备水平。

4. 一批大型企业为了适应市场竞争和产品性能质量提高的要求，采取产学研相结合的方式，相继建立了研究与开发机构，使企业的研发队伍和研发力量得到了加强，创新成果不断涌现　“十五”期间，中国储备粮管理总公司投入科研经费约1亿元，取得21项专利；山东鲁花集团投入科研经费约0.8亿元，取得8项专利技术；江苏牧羊集团投入科研经费约0.6亿元，取得167项专利技术。企业成为科技投入主体的作用已经初步显现。

“十五”期间，粮食科技发展还存在一些问题，一是粮食科技投入仍然偏少，并缺乏长期稳定的增长机制；二是粮食科技支撑发展能力不能适应产业发展的需求；三是粮食科技自主创新能力不强，具有自主知识产权的核心技术缺乏；四是科技队伍中创新型人才、学科带头人和跨学科人才比较缺乏，科研院所的人才结构和学科结构有待调整完善；五是粮食科技管理体制需进一步改革，科研院所的分配机制、竞争机制、人才流动机制尚需完善。

二、全面提高粮食科技的整体实力和水平

（一）“十一五”粮食科技面临良好的发展环境

1. 党中央、国务院对粮食工作和粮食科技自主创新高度重视　粮食是关系国计民生的重要战略物资，是农民收入的重要来源。党中央、国务院对粮食的生产和流通工作历来高度重视，胡锦涛总书记和温家宝总理多次对粮食工作做出重要批示。《国家中长期科学和技术发展规划纲要》中将许多粮食生产和流通的科技课题列为科技发展的重点领域和优先主题，中共中央、国务院《关于实施科技规划纲要增强自主创新能力的决定》，确定了我国科技发展的大政方针和基本战略。这些都为粮食科技工作的发展指明了前进的方向。

2. 新科技革命和经济全球化为粮食科技的发展带来新契机　进入21世纪以来，以信息技术、生命科学和生物技术、新材料新能源不断取得重大突破为主要标志的科学技术发展日新月异，由此，推动了世界范围内生产力、生产方式、生活方式发生了前所未有的深刻变化，也促进了生产要素流动和产业结构升级，推动了经济全球化的进程。新科技革命和经济全球化必将对粮食科技的发展产生深刻的影响。新技术革命将使粮食流通信息的获取、处理、交换效率大大提高，将使粮食生产、储藏、加工、物流的技术发展空间不断拓展，使国家粮食安全的保障能力大大加强。

3. 经济的发展和人民生活水平的提高需要粮食科技提供有力支撑　未来15年是全面建设小康社会、实现我国人均GDP达到3 000美元的重要阶段。在工业化和城镇化不断加速的双重作用下，我国城乡居民收入快速增长，生活水平不断提高，消费结构迅速升级。公众对粮油食品营养化、方便化、多样化、健康化的要求日益增强，从而要求粮油食品加工业加快产业结构调整，提供更加丰富多样的食品，要求加快研发大量的新技术、新产品、新设备满足粮食生产、储存、运输、加工等方面的需求。必须大力推进粮食科技进步，依靠科技创新向人民群众提供日益丰富的产品。同时，转变经济增长方式、建设社会主义新农村、构建资源节约型和环境友好型社会的历史任务，也将对粮食科技事业发展提出更高的要求。

4. 粮食流通体制改革的不断深化促进粮食科技工作的发展　“十五”期间，我国粮食流通改革工作取得了丰硕成果，科技管理体制改革也取得了显著进展，这将为“十一五”粮食科技奠定良好的发展基础。粮食流通体制改革工作的重要目标，就是坚持市场化改革的方向，不断提高粮食综合生产能力，发展现代粮食流通，促进粮食产业化发展，这就要求粮食科技在粮食产后减损、品质快速检测、保证储存质量、发展现代物流、提高加工深度、延长产业链条、带动其他相关产业的发展等方面提供现代化的技术和装备的支撑。

（二）“十一五”粮食科技发展的战略目标和主要任务

“十一五”期间是落实科学发展观，全面建设小康社会的关键时期。必须以科学发展观为统领，以国家粮食安全和市场需求为导向，以可持续发展战略为

重点，坚持“自主创新、重点跨越、支撑发展、引领未来”的指导方针，建立符合建设社会主义新农村和构建资源节约型、环境友好型社会要求的安全、环保、节约和高效的粮食流通技术体系。

1. 战略目标　“到2020年使我国粮食科技自主创新能力显著增强，科技促进粮食流通产业发展和保障国家粮食安全的能力大幅度提高，粮食科技整体实力进入世界前列”。“十一五”期间粮食科技发展要力争在重点产品、重点工艺、重点技术、重点装备上实现重大技术突破。粮食储藏技术达到同期国际先进水平，粮食物流和加工技术与装备得到优化升级，粮食质量标准检测技术不断完善，农村传统的粮食流通方式得到改造，建设一支结构合理、研发能力强的基础科研队伍。完善粮食科技创新机制，形成以企业为主体、产学研相结合、科技资源共享、技术优势互补的粮食科技创新体系。

2. 重点领域　《国家中长期科学和技术发展规划纲要》中，将主要农产品和农林特产资源精深及清洁生态型加工技术与设备，粮油产后减损及绿色储运技术与设施，鲜活农产品保鲜与物流配送，食品安全监测技术，生物质能源以及生物质新材料和化工产品等生产关键技术都列入了国家科技重点领域及优先主题。根据《纲要》的精神，结合粮食科技的实际，“十一五”期间我国粮食科技发展的重点领域：一是以生态理论为指导，发展绿色、高效、实用的仓储技术。通过改善储藏环境、保持储粮品质、降低储藏损耗、提高监管手段的各项技术措施，促进储粮技术方式由传统型向绿色生态型转变。二是以成套高技术设备和生物（工程）技术为重点的粮食深加工技术。通过生物技术、精细化工技术、智能化设备制造等高技术在粮油加工业应用，促进高效、节约和清洁生产技术的发展。三是以发展散粮运输为重点推进传统粮食物流业的改造。重点发展实用、高效、经济的散粮接收、发放、运输的设施和装备，研究集装单元化散粮运输技术，建设物流信息平台，完善物流技术标准，构建高效、便捷、安全的粮食物流体系。四是以应用基础研究为平台，发展粮食质量快速检测技术和仪器设备，加速粮食质量检测仪器的升级换代，带动国产仪器的研发和推广。五是以预警、监测为重点的粮食流通现代化的信息技术。主要是推进信息技术在粮食储藏、加工、物流、质量标准仪器、品质测报等领域的研究开发与应用。

3. 主要任务　“十一五”期间，粮食科技要在以下五个方面持续加大自主创新的力度：

（1）注重应用基础研究和边缘学科的高新技术的结合，培育粮食科技持续创新能力　组织开展粮食物质信息学与储藏品质变化机理、谷物油脂化学及生物活性物质功能、转基因粮油食品检测等多方面应用基础研究。组织粮食行业公益性、基础性重点技术标准研究，把重大科学研究成果与粮食应用科学相结合，培育和发展粮食科技新兴学科、交叉学科，注重粮食科技的前瞻性，鼓励前沿技术领域的研究探索。加强产学研结合和组织多学科的合作攻关，提升我国粮食科学的研究水平和参与国际合作研究与竞争的能力。

（2）加大信息技术和生物技术在粮食流通领域的研究和应用，带动和促进粮食科技跨越式发展　重点开展数字粮食流通、信息采集预警预报、信息控制技术和基于3S技术的管理决策系统的研究开发，推进粮食流通电子商务的发展，在重点地区、重点领域实现粮食预警、监测和动态信息化管理。开展粮食生物工程高新技术研究与产业化示范，加强生物技术在粮油食品加工领域中的应用研究，不断开发新型食品；加强生物技术在以粮食及其副产品（废弃物）为原料的生物质能源和生物材料方面的应用，对粮食在能源、医药、材料、化工、纺织、造纸等行业的各类深加工关键技术进行攻关及产业化示范。

（3）组织和实施科技攻关，重点突破一批重大关键技术　集中优势力量，组织跨行业、跨部门的联合攻关，重点研发粮食质量快速检测仪器、监测应用技术和相关的传感器技术。以信息化带动高效便捷的粮食物流关键技术和装备的研发，开发粮食散运和集装箱运输的技术和装备。开展生态环保储粮技术研究，组织对低温储粮、生物防治、化学熏蒸药剂替代等关键技术的攻关。对有利于降低能耗，保护环境和提高综合利用率的酶技术、发酵技术、膜分离技术、超临界萃取、超微粉碎、质构重组及机电一体化等高技术进行攻关，拓展各种高技术在粮油深加工和产业化中的应用。加强相关技术集成化创新，促进粮食技术产品的优化升级，提高产业的国际竞争力。引进国外先进的粮食流通与加工重大关键技术与装备，并联合制造企业、高等院校、科研机构进行消化吸收再创新。

（4）搭建粮食科技公共基础条件平台，为推动粮食科技创新活动提供支撑　重点组织开展粮食科学仪器、设备、技术标准、科学数据共享、科技信息公共服务平台与实验基地建设，推进国家、行业标准和检测技术体系建设。以粮食科研机构、科技型企业为主，积极争取组建国家级粮食储藏、物流、深加工等工程技术研究中心；在不同地区以省级粮食科研院所为依托，组建具有地域资源特征、具有不同专业特色、不同优势产品的国家粮食局工程技术研究中心；

以重点产品为依托，积极组织大型粮食龙头企业申请国家认定的企业技术研发中心。按照“整合、共享、完善、提高”的原则，克服条块分割、区域分散、相互封闭、重复建设的弊端，使分散在各部门各行业各单位的科技资源发挥出最大效益。

（5）加快先进适用技术的推广应用，促进产业技术升级　开展粮食流通先进适用新技术、新产品、新装备的成果转化工作。继续推广4项储粮新技术，保证储粮安全；加强粮食四散技术（即：散存、散装、散运、散卸）的推广，提升粮食物流的现代化水平；改造传统落后的农村粮食产后流通技术方式，以粮食主产区的收纳库为依托，推广农村粮食集中处理的干燥技术与装备；通过储藏、加工、物流、信息及标准化等技术的集成，建立农村粮食产后整理、干燥、储藏、加工、运输等集约化处理技术服务体系与示范；开发适用于农户储粮的新型技术及装具，开展农村粮食产后减损及安全保障关键技术的研究和集成示范。

三、努力奋斗，提高粮食行业科技创新能力

为落实《国家中长期科学和技术发展规划纲要》的精神，完成《“十一五”粮食科技发展指导意见》提出的各项工作任务，“十一五”期间，粮食科技重点抓好以下几个方面的工作：

1. 多渠道增加粮食科技投入，建立投入稳定增长的长效机制　稳定的科技投入是粮食科技发展的重要条件。一是各级粮食行政管理部门要积极争取财政等部门对粮食科技的资金投入，主动协调增加省级粮食科研经费预算，积极落实本地区粮食科技项目的配套政策。主产区的粮食行政管理部门，要配合即将启动实施的“十一五”粮食丰产科技工程项目，落实农户科学储粮技术集成示范项目的配套资金，并积极探索建立农村科学储粮资金投入增长的长效机制。二是“十一五”期间，国家财政将大幅度增加科技投入，重点支持基础研究、前沿技术和公益研究，支持重大战略产品和重大科技工程，科技基础条件平台建设等。各地、各单位要依据《国家中长期科学和技术发展规划纲要》，紧密结合行业和区域经济发展的需要，提出粮食科技重大项目建议，积极争取国家财政资金对粮食科技的支持，组织和落实好各类国家粮食重大科技项目和重点任务。三是公益类科研院所、转制科研院所要以建立院所长科研基金等方式，对基础性、公益性、交叉学科和前沿高技术研究给予资金支持，并逐渐形成长期稳定的投入和激励机制。四是大型龙头企业要积极组建技术研发机构，建立与科研院所、高校的良好合作机制，力争从每年的利润中拿出较多的资金，稳定投入到新技术新产品的研发上，并搞好技术和人才的储备。中小型粮食企业，也要依靠技术进步，重视新产品开发，以一定经费投入技术改造和技术创新，不断提高市场竞争力。

2. 深化科研院所体制改革，推进创新体系建设　建立面向市场的现代科研制度是深化科研院所体制改革的重要任务。要不断优化粮食科技结构，建立激发科研创新活力的制度环境，完善市场配置科技资源的管理方式，逐步建立符合市场经济规律和科学技术发展规律的科技运行机制。为此，一是要继续稳步推进社会公益类科研机构改革，转变运行机制，建立激励机制，突出以人为本，吸引国内外高层研究人才，集中力量建设有学科特色和学科优势的研究领域，不断提高粮食科技的基础研究和应用基础研究的能力。要把粮食公益类院所和大学建设成培养学科带头人才的重要基地。二是转制院所要紧紧围绕行业和市场需要，加强新技术、新产品的研发，拓宽服务范围，提高服务能力和科技成果转化能力。三是建设以地方粮食科研院所为主的区域科研创新体系，进一步突出省级粮食科研院所学科优势和区域特色。省级科研机构、质量检测机构要发挥在应用研究、新技术新产品推广、基层技术服务方面的骨干作用。地县粮食科研机构、质量检测机构要加强对地区粮食经济和农村产后的技术服务，结合农村技术推广体系的建设，不断推广先进适用的新技术。要通过加强地区间、部门（行业）间的科研人员交流和技术项目合作，发展和强化技术优势，不断提高市场竞争力。四是建设中介机构有效参与的科技服务体系。“十一五”期间要通过加强中介组织的社会化网络服务体系建设，发挥各级粮食协会、粮油学会联系各创新主体的桥梁纽带作用，为粮食科技发展，为企业技术创新不断提供技术咨询、信息指导和市场调研等服务。加强与政府管理部门的沟通，通过网络化服务推广技术成果，使之成为创新体系的重要组成部分。

3. 优化政策环境，充分发挥企业技术创新的主体作用　建立以企业为主体、市场为导向、产学研相结合的技术创新体系，一是要创造良好的政策环境，促进企业真正成为技术创新的主体。要消除长期以来对企业（特别是民营企业）的偏见和体制上运行的障碍，打破行业和部门的界线，创造对不同类型、不同规模、不同性质的企业之间公平竞争的环境，营造良好的运行机制和政策环境，增强企业技术创新的积极性，使企业成为科技创新资金的主要投入者，成为科技成果转化和产业化技术开发的主体。要采取有力政策措施，促进人才、资金、技术等要素向企业的转

移。二是加大对企业、转制院所技术创新的支持力度，在课题立项前听取企业对粮食科技项目意见，吸收企业参与粮食科技项目的申报和实施，优先支持有条件的企业集团牵头或由企业与高校、科研院所联合承担有产业化前景的重大项目和技术攻关项目，如农业科技成果转化项目、科技支撑项目、高技术产业化项目等，建立以企业为主体、产学研相结合的项目实施机制。加大对大型骨干企业技术创新基地建设的支持，支持有条件的企业独立或联合科研院所及高校建立国家级、省部级工程技术研究中心、国家认定的企业技术中心。引导有自主知识产权、自主品牌的企业尽快成为有持续创新能力的创新型企业。各级粮食部门要积极帮助企业在技术创新和高技术产业化发展方面获取政策支持。三是支持企业建设研发中心，鼓励企业与科研部门、高校联合共建工程实验室、共性技术研发和工程化平台。建设一批企业研发中心，打造企业技术创新和产业化平台。四是发挥中小企业在技术创新中的作用。中小企业特别是科技型中小企业是科技创新的不可忽视的力量，要通过科技政策和经济政策的扶持，使粮食中小企业的创新能力不断提高。

4. 建立和完善创新人才的培养和成长机制 “十一五”期间，要紧紧围绕粮食科技创新需要，把粮食科技人才队伍建设摆到重要的战略位置。一是要努力建立一支高素质的人才队伍。要尽快改变粮食科研中缺乏领军人物的状况，加快中青年为主体的创新型学科带头人的培养，要给他们创造条件，通过国家科技项目的实施培养和锻炼他们，使他们尽快成长壮大。要抓好专业技术人才队伍建设，制订专业技术人才的培养规划，落实培训措施，使专业技术人才队伍的学科结构、知识结构和年龄结构适应发展的需要。要重视科研管理人才队伍的建设，培养和造就出敢于向世界领先技术挑战的科技管理人才。要利用国际国内人才资源市场，引进粮食科技发展急需的科研技术人才。二是要完善粮食行业科技人才的培养体系。要充分发挥高等院校、科研院所、粮食教育培训机构的重要作用，加快各类专业技术人才的培养。要通过国际科技合作研究、人才交流、专项培训等多种渠道，使在职科技人员更新知识，跟踪前沿技术，提高创新能力。三是要大力营造尊重劳动、尊重知识、尊重人才、尊重创造的氛围，努力把优秀科研人才聚集到粮食科技创新的实践中来。树立科研诚信，抑制学术不端行为，努力营造讲科学、用科学、学科学的新风气，形成鼓励探索、敢于突破、潜心钻研、宽容失败的创新环境，摒弃浮躁浮夸和急功近利的不良学风。四是要建立有利于发现人才、培养人才、激励人才的机制。要建立科学严谨的科技成果评价体系和公平公正的技术创新奖励制度。要进一步完善高素质创新人才和管理人才公开招聘制度，形成跨部门、跨领域的人才流动和竞争的机制，不断吸引社会优秀科技人才、海外留学人员加入粮食科技队伍，为推动粮食科技进步和创新贡献智慧和力量。

5. 加强国际合作，扩大我国粮食科技在国际交流中的地位和影响 充分利用各方面的有利条件，不断扩大多种形式的国际科技合作与交流。要站在科技发展前沿，及时掌握国际粮食科技发展的最新动态。要加强和国外粮食科技机构的联系和合作，突出重点，改进合作方式，拓宽合作领域和渠道，提高合作成效。支持各级各类粮食科研机构、高等院校、企业研发机构积极加入有关国际粮食科技的学术团体和组织，积极参与各种双边或多边的国际交流活动，并在其中增长知识，获取经验，扩大影响，发挥作用。鼓励科研院所、高等院校与海外研究开发机构建立联合实验室和研究开发中心。鼓励企业扩大高新技术及其产品的出口。要创造有利条件，吸引更多的国际粮食方面学术团体、专家、学者到中国来举办学术会议、进行讲学和合作研究，使我国的粮食科技工作更好地适应国际经济一体化的需要。

（本文为作者于2006年8月在“全国粮食科学技术大会”上的工作报告）

继承发展 改革创新
全面开创食品安全监管工作新局面

国家质量监督检验检疫总局食品生产监管司司长 邬建平

这次会议的主要任务是：回顾近年来食品安全监管工作取得的成绩，总结经验，分析形势，动员全国食品安全监管战线，坚持以科学发展观为统领，统一思想，提高认识，继承发展，改革创新，健全和完善食品安全监管体系，不断提高食品安全监管工作服务经济、促进发展的有效性。

一、总局成立以来，食品安全监管工作的突出成绩和经验

2001年以来，按照党中央、国务院关于从源头抓质量的战略部署，在总局的统一指挥下，将食品质量安全监管作为各项工作的重中之重，狠抓不懈，创建并有效地实施了以食品质量安全市场准入制度为主要内容的一系列食品安全监管制度，大力整顿了食品生产加工业。

1. *开拓了产品质量监督工作新机制，食品质量安全市场准入制度取得显著成效* 自2001年下半年起，总局在对米、面、油、酱油、醋等五类食品生产加工企业进行产品质量监督抽查和企业保证产品质量安全必备条件调查的基础上，遵循适应市场经济规律、符合世贸规则、借鉴国外成功经验、结合我国国情的原则，集中全系统智慧，探索建立了以食品生产许可、强制检验、市场准入（QS）标志为主要内容的食品质量安全市场准入制度。5年来，经过全系统上下共同努力，按照分步实施的原则，已经对28大类食品全部启动了食品质量安全市场准入制度。截至目前，国家标准中规定的28大类525种食品中已有370种食品纳入了市场准入制度管理，覆盖面达到70%以上，共发放食品生产许可证63 000余张。

实践证明，食品质量安全市场准入工作创建了产品质量监督工作新机制，实施几年来取得了实实在在的成效。一是建立了一套崭新的食品质量安全监管制度。在国务院的菜篮子工程、全国整顿和规范市场经济秩序专项整治工程、《关于进一步加强食品安全工作的决定》等一系列重大政策性文件中均明确把食品质量安全市场准入制度作为国家实施食品安全监管的重要制度之一。二是建立了一套比较完整的食品安全监管法律法规体系。2005年国务院颁布了《中华人民共和国工业生产许可证管理条例》，总局也先后发布了《食品生产加工企业质量安全监督管理实施细则（试行）》、《食品质量安全市场准入审查通则》、28类食品的生产许可证审查细则、《关于加强对获得食品生产许可证企业后续监管工作的意见》以及相关的规范性文件，并从2005年9月1日起，通过依法授权，实现了总局和省局的两级生产许可，“两级发证、三级操作”的新机制在全系统稳步推行。三是规范了食品生产加工领域秩序，促进了食品行业的产业结构调整，提高了食品生产加工企业保证产品质量安全的保障能力，提升了食品质量安全的整体水平。四是建设了一支业务精湛、科学求实、认真负责的专业队伍。共培训了食品质量安全市场准入师资460名，注册审查员5 768名，其中高级审查员108名。五是我们的工作受到了各方肯定和广泛好评。食品质量安全市场准入制度作为实施食品安全监管工作的有效手段得到了国务院领导的充分肯定。广大人民群众认为这是党和政府为老百姓抓了一件实实在在的“民心工程”。已经形成了在大中城市的商场、超市无QS标志的食品不上货架，消费者无QS标志的食品不购买的良好氛围。

2. *妥善应对食品安全突发事件，应急处理能力和水平显著提高* 食品安全突发事件发生频率高是近年来食品安全问题的一个显著特点。同志们对2004年阜阳奶粉事件应该记忆犹新，2005年则更为突出，连续发生了苏丹红、孔雀石绿、阪岐氏杆菌、丙烯酰胺、雀巢奶粉碘超标、“甲醛”啤酒、猪链球菌、食品保鲜膜中DEHA等多起事件，几乎是每个月都有一个食品质量安全卫生问题成为社会各界广泛关注的热点。在总局的统一领导下，我们的队伍总是在第一时间积极应对，采取组织专项抽查、及时发布检查结果、紧急出台相关标准等应急措施，有效控制和减少了可能产生的不利影响，最大限度地减少了食品安全事件造成的危害，保障了广大人民群众的身体健康和生命安全，有效维护了社会稳定和市场经济秩序，有效维护了国家形象和食品出口贸易。总局和各级质检部门对一系列食品安全突发事件的积极应对、果断举措和妥善处理，获得了良好效果，充分体现了我们的队伍关键时刻靠得住、冲得上、打得赢的顽强作风，得到了社会各界的广泛好评。在妥善处理一系列突发食品安全事件的工作实践中，总结出特事特办、快速反应、紧急处置、应急检验、引导宣传等一系列宝贵经验，并制定实施了《食品安全突发事件应急反应预案》，为今后有效应对突发食品安全事件和建立长效机制打下了良好基础。

3. *加强食品安全监管体系建设，各地初步建立了食品安全区域监管责任制* 近年来，在总结基层食品生产企业监管经验的基础上，按照总局统一部署，各省质量技术监督部门普遍推广建立了以“三员四定、三进四图、两书一报告”为主要内容的食品安全区域监管责任制。同时，进一步加强和改进对食品生产加工企业巡查、回访、监督抽查、强制检验、年度检查等日常监管措施，及时掌握食品企业生产条件的变化情况，及时发现不安全隐患，实现对食品安全问题的早发现、早控制和早处理。食品质量安全卫生的

日常监管工作正朝着目标明确、任务清晰、措施具体、责任到人、监管到位的方向努力。另外，为认真落实国务院《关于进一步加强食品安全工作的决定》中的各项要求，各级质监部门集思广益，改变工作模式，主动争取政府的支持，较好地完成了总局部署的“四个一”的工作要求。

全国31个省、自治区、直辖市食品安全区域监管责任制均得到了较好的落实。一是实行辖区责任制，明确了监管责任。全国31个省份都建立了食品安全区域监管责任制，共有食品安全监管区域16 030个。二是加强队伍建设，保证了人员到位。食品安全专职监督员25 346人，聘请政府协管员72 474人，社会信息员106 573人。三是加大巡查力度，提高了监管威慑力。2005年，全年实施企业巡查713 062次，查处无证企业25 596个，建立308 735个食品生产企业的信息化管理企业档案。四是推行安全承诺制，强化了企业责任。截止到2005年底，共调查到全国食品生产企业357 436个，其中，签订食品安全承诺书的食品生产企业244 987个，占总数的69%。五是推动地方政府负总责，有效发挥了监管主力军作用。截至目前，全国有13个省份专门成立了由省政府领导任组长的食品生产加工业整顿领导小组，有10个省份成立了由省质量技术监督局一把手任组长的食品生产加工业整顿领导小组；有384个地级市、2 525个行政县成立了由政府领导任组长的食品生产加工业整顿工作领导小组。同时，有23个省份以政府名义召开了整顿食品生产加工业专项会议，23个省份以政府名义印发了专项整顿方案；地市级、县级人民政府分别以政府名义制定下发食品生产加工业整顿工作方案415个、2 756个，地市级、县级人民政府分别以政府名义召开的食品生产加工业整顿工作会议782次、4 188次。六是推行一级抓一级，实现了层层抓落实。目前，全国市（地）级政府与所辖县（市）级政府签订责任书1 772份，县级政府与所辖乡（镇）政府签订责任书25 131份。

4. **不断深化食品相关产品及化妆品监督管理，为全面实施食品相关产品和化妆品市场准入打下了坚实基础** 5年来，在集中精力推进食品质量安全市场准入工作的同时，对食品相关产品及化妆品的生产许可证管理工作也加大了实施力度。一是大力推进食品添加剂生产许可证管理工作。截至目前，已对具有国家标准、行业标准的169种食品添加剂全部启动了发证工作，并于2005年年底公告开展了无证查处工作。二是加大了食用酒精、工业和商业用电热加工设备等5种食品相关产品的生产许可证管理工作。截至目前，已对食用酒精、餐具洗涤剂、压力锅、食品用香精、工业和商业用电热加工设备等5种产品发布实施了生产许可证实施细则，组建了相关审查部，共确认发证检验机构52家，对1 810家企业发放了生产许可证。三是严格实施化妆品生产许可证管理。已对洗发、护肤用品等几十类化妆品实施了许可证管理，目前已颁发化妆品生产许可证3 609张。

5. **强化质检机构食品检验能力和水平建设，食品安全监管的技术保障能力大幅提升** 检验机构的检验能力和检验水平高低，直接影响着食品安全监管工作的科学性和权威性。几年来，全国质量技术监督系统围绕从源头抓质量，以抓食品安全为突破口，重点加强了检验机构食品检验能力的建设，并以实施食品质量安全市场制度为契机，大力加强了国家级食品类质检中心和省级质检机构的检验能力与检验水平建设，全系统的食品实验室条件有了较大改善。5年来，23个省份新组建了34个国家级食品质检中心，基本实现了每个省都有国家级的食品类质检中心。31个省份建立了173个省级食品检测机构，全系统依法设置和授权了3 000多个食品质量检验机构。经过近几年来的努力，质检系统的部分国家级食品检验检构的检验能力接近或达到了国际先进水平，省级检验机构拥有一批高精尖仪器设备和高素质专业技术队伍，地市级检验机构检测能力有所完善，食品生产加工集中地的县级检验机构基本具备了食品理化、微生物、感官等常规检验能力。几年来，通过实施食品市场准入制度，国家和省局批准了一大批发证检验机构和实施日常监督、定期检验的食品检验机构。目前，全系统正在加快形成一个以国家中心为龙头、省级质检机构为重点、市（地）级质检机构为骨干、县级质检机构为基础的食品检验检测体系，为有效实施食品质量安全监管工作提供强有力的技术保障。

6. **突出加强食品质量国家监督抽查工作，不断提高食品安全监管工作的有效性和权威性** 近年来，由总局组织的国家监督抽查和省局组织的地方监督抽查工作都把食品作为重点，按照突出重点产品、重点项目、重点企业、重点区域的要求，加大了对产品质量不稳定的中小型食品企业的监督抽查力度。2001—2005年，共对17 000余个企业的20 000多批次食品进行了国家监督抽查。其中，还多次组织全国范围内的较大规模的食品专项抽查，如奶粉专项、辣味食品专项、第一批实施市场准入的米、面、油、酱油、醋五类食品专项、大桶水专项、肉制品专项、淡水鱼制品专项、啤酒专项、液态奶专项、食品相关塑料制品专项等等。5年来，实实在在地将食品作为监督抽查工作的第一重点，无论是抽查企业数量，还是抽查食品种类，所占全年监督抽查总量的比例之大，都是开展产品质量监督抽查工作20年来所从未有过的。通过加大抽查覆盖面，重点检查安全、卫生等强制性指标，及时公布抽查信息，以合格产品引导消费，同时做好监督抽查不合格产品的整改工作。对监督抽查中发现的质量安全卫生存在严重问题的食品，通过不同方式责令企业收回。5年来，以食品为重点的国家监督抽查工作紧紧围绕经济建设和社会发展，观念不断创新，制度不断完善，有效性不断提高，在规范市场、引导消费、服务经济、促进发展等诸多方面发挥了重要作用。

7. 开展复原乳专项监管工作，进一步规范液态奶生产秩序，促进奶业及奶制品行业健康发展 为保护广大奶农的切身利益，促进奶业及乳制品行业健康发展，2005年9月，国务院办公厅印发了《关于加强液态奶生产经营管理的通知》。为落实国务院的要求，国家质检总局会同国家发展和改革委员会、农业部、海关总署、国家工商行政管理总局等部门，立即指导督促各地食品安全监管部门，实施了液态奶生产企业驻厂检查，建立了复原乳生产备案制度，进一步明确了复原乳标识标注的相关规定，加强了液态奶生产经营企业的监督管理。在实施驻厂检查工作中，北京、天津、上海、内蒙古、黑龙江、河北等24个省、自治区、直辖市积极抽调各部门监管人员、执法人员及食品专家共近400人，组成液态奶驻厂监管小组。自2005年12月5日至12月20日，各地区克服时间紧、人员少等困难，对《通知》确定的120家液态奶生产企业全部实施了驻厂监管。各监管小组恪尽职守、兢兢业业，确保监管工作的有效性。经过半年时间的液态奶专项监管工作，液态奶生产经营秩序得到了进一步的规范，原料奶价格明显回升，进口奶粉数量明显下降。

8. 忠实履行食品卫生监管新职责，认真发挥生产加工环节食品安全监管主力军作用 2004年9月，国务院印发了《关于进一步加强食品安全工作的决定》，明确规定质检部门负责食品生产加工环节的监管，并将原由卫生部门承担的食品生产加工环节的卫生监管职责划归质检部门。从2004年9～12月，总局领导分赴25个省、直辖市，与省政府联合召开质量技术监督系统干部大会，贯彻国务院的决定，统一思想、统一行动，并把2005年作为全国质检系统的食品安全年，号召全系统全力打好食品安全攻坚战，充分发挥食品生产加工环节监管的主力军作用。2005年5月，总局成立食品安全监管领导小组，紧接着全国31个省份质检部门也先后成立了领导小组。一年多来，全国质量技术监督系统认真贯彻落实国务院的重大决定，围绕“大力整顿食品生产加工业，切实提高食品工业水平”的重要任务，采取措施，扎实工作，严格实施食品质量安全市场准入制度，建立食品安全区域监管责任制，加大食品监督抽查，严厉打击制售假冒伪劣食品违法行为，打了一场漂亮的食品安全监管攻坚战，得到了国务院领导的充分肯定。吴仪副总理在总局呈报的关于落实食品生产加工环节监管职责情况的报告上批示：“实行一个监管环节由一个部门监管是国务院加强食品安全监管做出的一项重要决定，质检部门在加强食品生产加工环节的监管方面做了大量工作，取得了明显成效，应予表扬”。让全系统感到更加鼓舞的是，在党中央、国务院的关心支持下，2005年11月23日，中编办正式批复总局增设食品生产监管司，全面负责食品生产加工环节的质量安全卫生日常监管工作。

5年来，在总局的统一指挥和统一部署下，全国质量监督战线的同志们开拓创新，顽强拼搏，真抓实干，奋发有为，在以食品质量安全市场准入制度为主要内容的食品安全监管工作中夺取了一个又一个胜利，创建了质量监督工作新机制，开创了质检事业新天地，全系统食品安全监管工作取得了可喜成绩。这些成绩的取得，得益于党中央、国务院的英明决策，得益于总局党组的高度重视、正确决策和亲切关怀，得益于全国质量监督战线广大干部职工的众志成城和艰苦奋斗。5年来全国质量监督战线同志们的艰辛努力，为建立健全食品安全监管长效机制奠定了扎实的基础，使全面构筑食品安全监管体系有了良好的开端。

在总结成绩的同时，还必须清醒地看到，当前食品安全监管工作仍然面临着诸多挑战：一是食品行业生产力水平较低。调查结果显示，全国食品企业72%左右是10人以下小作坊，产品质量存在着严重的安全隐患。二是食品整体质量水平仍较差。几年来抽查结果表明，食品平均抽样合格率始终徘徊在75%上下，食品中微生物超标、农药兽药残留超标、重金属超标现象比较突出。三是一些地区的监管工作还不够扎实，措施不落实、监管不到位的情况仍然存在，一些同志还存在畏难、畏责的思想。四是食品生产加工企业市场准入的工作量很大，突发事件、小作坊、食品添加剂以及包装材料等方面的监管难题需要破解。五是食品安全监管保障条件和措施还不到位。全国还有8个省局没有成立食品安全监管机构，现有人员中能满足当前食品卫生监管工作需要的专业人员少，部分检验机构的检验能力需要进一步加强。六是食品安全监管制度的有效性还需要不断提高，建立一个食品安全监管长效机制仍然任重道远。对面临的这些问题，都要高度重视，冷静思考，深入研究，要把这些问题作为当前和今后一段时期食品安全监管工作的主攻方向，作为食品安全监管工作下一步改革和创新的着力点，放宽视野，开拓创新，采取切实可行的措施认真加以解决。

二、开拓新思路，构建新格局，建立健全食品安全监管体系

当前，建立和完善我国生产加工领域食品安全监管体系的指导思想是：紧紧围绕国民经济和社会发展“十一五”规划的整体部署，以科学发展观统领食品安全监管各项工作，以服务经济、促进发展为目标，立足以人为本，着眼长治久安，继承发展，开拓创新，尽快建立和完善适应我国国情的生产加工环节食品安全监管体系，促进我国食品工业有序发展，切实维护广大人民群众健康安全。按照这一指导思想和总体要求，建立和完善我国生产加工领域食品安全监管体系需重点把握以下几个方面：

（一）围绕三条主线，确立食品安全监管工作思路

1. 围绕贯彻落实科学发展观这条主线，不断提升食品安全工作服务大局促进发展的有效性　科学发展观强调要把经济社会全面、协调、可持续发展统一起来，强调要按照“五个统筹”的要求推进改革和发展。在工作中贯彻落实科学发展观，就是要求不断提高、不断开拓、不断创新。目前我们国家正处在经济高速发展的时候，一味地墨守成规，没有新的思路去适应社会的发展变化，食品安全监管制度就没有生命力。食品安全的科学发展观一方面要牢牢抓住食品安全，利用生产许可、市场准入、监督抽查、强制检验、日常监管等各项措施，严格质量把关，确保食品质量安全，实实在在地维护广大人民群众的切身利益，让广大人民群众吃得放心，喝得安心。另一方面要有计划、有目标、有措施地推进“四个一批”，即扶持一批优秀企业、优质产品和优良品牌；帮促一批小规模的加工企业；关闭一批不符合食品卫生条件的黑窝点；打击一批食品制假售假的犯罪分子。通过大力实施“四个一批”，实现食品行业全面、协调和可持续发展，大力促进食品产业结构调整，提升企业和产品的竞争力，促进经济和社会协调发展。

2. 围绕建设社会主义新农村这条主线，不断推动食品行业整体生产力水平全面提升　近3年来中央连续发了3个有关“三农”工作的1号文件，从增加农民收入到提高农业综合生产能力，再到建设社会主义新农村。中央的着眼点已经不仅仅在于解决农民的生计，现在更多的是放在统筹城乡经济社会发展的这一重大方略。“十一五”期间的工作能否取得重大突破，很大程度上取决于能否抓住这个重要的历史机遇，将大力整顿食品生产加工业，全面提升食品行业整体生产力水平这个大战略，更好地融入到党和国家建设社会主义新农村的伟大历史任务中去。近年来的5次食品企业专项调查表明，全国17.7万个食品企业中，10人以下的小企业占到72%左右，而这些小企业是农村经济的一个重要组成，大部分都分布在城乡结合部和农村。现在，要牢牢抓住建设社会主义新农村这个历史机遇，充分发挥地方政府的组织领导作用，充分调动农村基层组织的积极性，充分发挥质检系统干部群众的创新能力，集中全社会的智慧，制定适应小企业、小作坊的食品安全监管措施，引导规范农村小企业、小作坊，提高食品生产卫生保障能力，提高食品安全水平，促进农村经济发展和农民致富，为建设社会主义新农村做出应有的贡献。

3. 围绕立足以人为本，构筑社会主义和谐社会这条主线，努力实现食品安全长治久安　食品安全问题不仅是经济发展问题，也是重大的社会问题，是一项关系到人民群众生命安全和身体健康，关系到经济健康发展和社会稳定，关系到党和政府在人民群众中形象和威信的“民心工程”。5年来，集中全系统的力量，集中全系统的资源，重点开展食品安全监管工作，取得了阶段性胜利。但是，必须充分认识到食品安全工作的长期性、艰巨性和复杂性，不能企望毕其功于一役、一蹴而就。必须树立打持久战的思想，把食品安全工作作为一项关系国计民生、关乎社会稳定的长期历史任务，统一部署，从全局上整体把握。思想上要沉下心来，冷静思考，迎难而上；战略上要把握大局，全面推进，立足长治久安；战术上要步步为营，稳扎稳打，全面构筑长治久安的食品安全长城。具体而言，就是要以维护食品安全为目标，以全面提升食品企业生产力水平和管理水平为根本，以建立食品质量安全信用体系为方向，以完善食品标准和检测技术为基础，以落实各项监管制度为手段，强化扶优与治劣、监督与服务相结合，促进政府监管、市场调节、企业自律三方面发挥作用，不断提高食品质量安全总体水平，为国家和地方发展大局服好务、把好关，促进质检事业更大发展。

（二）坚持四条宝贵经验，不断提高食品安全监管工作有效性

回顾几年来食品安全监管工作的奋斗历程，有许多宝贵的经验需要在今后工作中继续坚持，其中最重要的经验有四点：

1. 立足国情，实事求是　几年来的食品安全监管工作实践充分证明：分析和解决我国的食品安全问

题，必须立足当前我国国情和整体生产力水平，从实际出发，这是工作的基础。发达国家采取的食品安全监管思路、模式、制度，拿到国内来行不行得通，关键的关键，是能否根据国内的具体情况，有针对性地加以取舍和改革。现行的有效监管制度都是在立足国情的基础上借鉴和吸收世界上发达国家的做法或者自己创建的。今后对现有制度的改革完善、创建新的监管制度，都必须坚持这个原则，否则可能就是空中楼阁。

2. *立足当前，着眼长远* 俗语说人无远虑，必有近忧。能否有效保障食品质量安全，关键是能不能准确分析食品安全监管工作中的突出问题，措施得当，应对有效，牢牢抓住当前食品安全监管工作的关键点，同时也要根据社会的发展进步和人民群众对食品安全逐步提高的要求，对食品安全监管工作的发展做出有效规划，在围绕国家建设大局，不断适应政府职能转变，确立不同时期食品安全工作发展定位的基础上，明确长远发展目标，提出前瞻性对策措施。否则，工作方向、工作政策就有可能摇摆，甚至有可能走弯路。

3. *立足发展，开拓创新* 过去几年来食品安全监管工作取得显著成效的根本原因之一就是始终坚持观念创新、机制创新、制度创新和工作创新。当前，生产加工领域的食品安全形势仍然严峻，食品安全监管工作还面临着许多新任务、新要求和新问题，这就要求必须在观念上更多地发挥生产企业、地方政府、社会力量等各方协同配合的作用，将食品安全重心放在建立预防机制上；更多地统筹谋略，走科学化、法制化和规范化的发展道路；制度上更多地借鉴国际上先进经验，创造性地建立适合我们实际情况的监管制度；工作上更多地运用电子化、信息化、网络化等现代科学技术手段，大力推进电子政务建设，不断提高工作效率。

4. *立足尽职，权责一致* 当前，我国正在加快建立健全政府行为“有权必有责、用权受监督、侵权要赔偿、违规要追究”的权责一致新机制，总局也出台了一系列文件，加强行政执法工作的责任制和过错责任追究制建设。这些制度的根本目的是引导同志们忠实履行职责，避免不作为和乱作为。在食品安全监管工作中更好地做好本职工作，需要切实将“地方政府负总责，一把手负全责，企业负首责”的“三个责任”落到实处。一是多争取多推动地方政府贯彻落实国务院《关于进一步加强食品安全工作的决定》中要求地方政府对食品安全负总责的责任，二是必须把食品安全监管工作作为“一把手”工程，三是强化食品生产加工企业法人作为食品安全第一责任人的责任。此外，也要充分发挥相关职能部门既要各管一段又要加强协作的作用。现在，国务院已明确食品生产监管司负责食品生产环节安全卫生的监管工作，给全系统上下增设了机构，配置了人员，这就要求尽职尽责，管好自己的分工环节，谁的职责没有尽到位出了问题，谁就必须承担责任。

（三）构建食品安全监管工作新格局，实现食品安全监管科学化、规范化、制度化

食品生产监管司成立后，就如何开展当前和今后较长一段时间的食品安全监管工作进行了深入研究，并组织了一些省局的同志进行了专题讨论，结合目前我国食品生产加工行业的实际状况和存在的主要问题，应该按照以下总体思路开展食品安全监管工作：

1. *坚持“统一管理，分类监管，重心下移，层级负责”的食品安全监管新机制* 统一管理的重点是由总局统筹规划全国食品安全监管工作，统一制修订食品、食品相关产品及化妆品的监管政策和技术法规。分类监管主要包括两个方面，一是按照食品风险水平、技术含量高低、行业规范程度、检验和监管难易程度等情况进行分类，二是根据食品生产加工企业的生产条件、管理水平、质量状况、人员素质和遵纪守法等情况对企业对产品进行分类。分类监管可以提高监管效率，有效利用监管资源。重心下移主要是总局下放行政许可审批权限，将更多的行政许可工作交由地方局承担；地方局下沉监管重心，更多地发挥基层质检部门的作用，基层质检部门将更多的精力放到城乡结合部和农村地区。层级负责就是各级质量技术监督部门既要各司其职，各负其责，又要一级抓一级，层层抓落实。实践中注重明确各方权力和责任，做到权责明晰，确保有效监管。

2. *加强食品安全监管体系建设，在“狠抓源头，重点突破，齐抓共管，全面推进”上多下工夫*

（1）狠抓源头 源头抓质量是履行职能的基本定位，从生产加工环节抓好食品安全监管是党中央、国务院赋予的重要职责，也是全系统几年来取得成果的法宝。食品安全问题是个系统工程，鉴于我国的国情，这更是一个长期的、复杂的、艰巨的任务。要努力再用2～3年的时间，狠抓源头，重打基础，全面掌握食品生产加工领域质量安全卫生状况，为健全和完善食品安全监管体系做好基础保障工作：一是完成全国普查，基本完成所有食品、食品相关产品及化妆品地毯式的普查工作，坚持“政府组织、全员出动、横向到边、纵向到底、不留死角”。二是全面建立企业档案。要在全国普查的基础上，建立所有企业的重要信息档案。三是全部实施分类监管，加快建立企业诚信记录。按照企业的生产条件和违法违规记录，对辖区内所有企业全部实施分类监管，加快建立企业质量安全诚信记录。四是实现全部动态跟踪管理。各地质量技术监督部门要确保对辖区内的每一个生产企业一年内至少有一次检查记录，对重点监管的企业要加大检查力度，实现动态跟踪、有效管理。五是区域监管责任全部落实到人。要求各级质量技术监督部门对本辖区内的所有食品、食品相关产品及化妆品生产加工企业的监管责任全部分解到具体工作人员，确保责任到人，监管到位。

（2）重点突破　在食品安全监管各项工作全面推进的同时，更要优先服务于当前最紧迫的任务，重点监管安全风险高且安全事故频发的重点产品，集中力量整顿农村与城乡结合部等监管薄弱地带，努力实现“四个重点突破”：第一，重点突破小作坊有效监管难题，坚决克服食品生产加工业整顿的最大障碍。第二，重点突破使用非食品原料生产加工食品、超范围滥用食品添加剂等违法行为难以遏制的问题，确保食品安全不出大的问题。第三，重点突破市场准入“重许可、轻监管”的突出问题，达不到准入条件的坚决不允许准入；获得准入后，凡是不能保持准入条件的，坚决吊销生产许可证。第四，重点突破食品安全监管工作被动局面，提高食品安全风险监测和突发事件应急处理能力和水平，实现早发现、早预防、早控制、早处理。

（3）齐抓共管　在生产加工领域建设食品安全有效监管体系，仅靠质量技术监督部门自己的力量是远远不够的。在今后的工作中，一方面全系统要继续坚持举全系统之力，抓好食品安全工作，发挥主导作用，另一方面在坚持以服务于工作的现实需要为出发点，更多地发挥关注食品安全的各方力量，实现食品安全监管工作多方参与，多管齐下，齐抓共管。一是充分发挥市场机制基础调节作用，强化企业第一责任人意识，督促和引导企业加强自律，这是解决食品安全问题的关键所在。二是充分落实地方政府对食品安全负总责的要求。积极与其他有关职能部门一道，在地方政府的统一领导下，既各司其职，各负其责，把好各自关口，又通力协作，加强配合，形成合力，在发挥主力军作用的同时，共同把好食品质量安全关。三是充分发挥地方基层组织的作用，加快基层行政执法人员和专业监督员、政府协管员和社会信息员等社会力量组合搭配，更大地发挥地方基层组织的协管作用。四是充分发挥各种技术机构的作用。要鼓励和支持技术机构从技术上为确保食品安全奠定基础，研究并解决食品生产加工中的问题。五是充分发挥行业协会、学会、高校等社会团体及科研机构的作用。要积极地以成立食品安全专家委员会、专业技术委员会等为载体，更多地吸纳社团界、学术界力量，促进与其更多地协作配合。

（4）全面推进　第一，全面推进质量安全市场准入制度。在全面推进加工食品市场准入工作的同时，要尽快实现食品添加剂、食品容器、包装材料和食品用工具、设备、洗涤剂、消毒剂等七大类食品相关产品全面实施质量安全市场准入制度。第二，全面推进食品安全全方位监管。今后，在加强食品最终产品质量安全监管的同时，还要加强对食品原料、食品添加剂、食品接触材料和食品标签等的全方位监管。第三，全面推进法律法规体系的建设。总局将会全力关注《食品安全法》的制定工作，并在充分调研的基础上提出并逐步完善食品安全监管法律法规框架。第四，完善食品安全监管长效机制，建立健全以下几项制度，逐渐完善生产加工领域食品安全监管体系。一是食品安全风险评价制度，二是不安全食品召回制度，三是食品安全应急处理制度，四是食品强制检验制度，五是产品溯源制度，六是日常巡查制度。要在工作中改革创新，不断完善这些制度，全面构筑食品安全防线。

三、开拓创新，扎实工作，确保“十一五”食品安全监管工作开局良好

吴仪副总理在全国质检系统先进集体先进工作者表彰大会上指出：5 年来质检工作取得了显著成绩，在保障食品安全方面功不可没。保障食品安全的难点和重点都在生产环节，这些年你们坚决贯彻国务院的决定，切实承担起了生产加工环节的食品卫生监管任务，一方面，严厉打击非食品原料生产食品、违规使用药物和添加剂等不法行为，查处了苏丹红、孔雀石绿等一大批违法案件，打了不少漂亮仗；另一方面，在开展全国食品企业普查的基础上，实行了市场准入制度，建立了区域监管责任制。应该说，这几年我国食品安全形式逐年好转，与你们的辛勤工作是密不可分的。吴仪副总理的讲话，既是鼓励，也是要求；既肯定了成绩，也寄予了更高的希望。绝不能辜负吴仪副总理的期望，继续努力，做好食品安全监管工作。2006 年是国家“十一五”计划的开局之年，也是食品生产监管司成立的第一年，要继承发展，改革创新，扎实工作，再接再厉，为 2006 食品安全年交上一个合格的答卷，并重点在以下 12 个方面取得积极进展：

（一）加快食品质量安全市场准入制度实施进程，确保 28 大类食品年内全部实行市场准入制度管理

2006 年食品质量安全市场准入工作的首要任务

就是要按照总局的统一部署，实现28大类525种食品全部纳入市场准入制度管理。在市场准入工作中，要以贯彻落实《中华人民共和国工业产品生产许可证管理条例》为契机，严格按照行政审批制度改革的要求，全面实现食品市场准入工作“审查、批准、监管”三分离，坚持“八公开”制度，即食品生产许可制度的项目名称、依据、申请条件、受理单位、许可程序、许可期限、收费标准、许可结果公开，并具体抓好六项任务：

1. 完成全部28大类食品的市场准入工作　在已实施370种食品市场准入的基础上，将28大类525种食品中剩余的155种食品，年底前全部启动市场准入工作。计划在6月初发布7个实施细则，对糕点、豆制品、蜂产品、果冻、挂面、鸡精和酱类产品等32种食品开展发证工作。并抓紧开展这7个实施细则的宣贯、培训工作，做好发证检验机构的指定和审查员培训，完成审查员的统一考试注册。这7个细则的实施将使市场准入食品的品种达到402种。同时，总局将组织专家对其余的123种食品进行研究，将原料、工艺、产品性质相似的食品纳入一个细则，提高准入工作的有效性和可操作性。例如，可以将小米、高粱米、大麦米、黍米等米类，以及籼米粉、粳米粉、糯米粉、玉米粉等粉类共19种产品纳入一个细则来审查发证。计划再用12个左右的细则，完成对全部食品的全面覆盖。

2. 根据食品监管需要，完成对食品分类的调整　食品质量安全市场准入制度所用的食品分类是基于原来的食品分类标准进行的，食品分类标准进行修改以后，包含了大量的农产品以及初级加工品等和食品生产监管工作不相关的产品，从市场准入长远的发展来看，必须将现有的分类进行调整，以适应食品生产监管的需要。将组织专家来完成这项工作，原则上还是保留28大类食品。

3. 加快糖果等13类食品发证速度，尽快开展无证查处工作　2004年12月总局组织开展了糖果制品等13类食品市场准入工作。截止到2006年4月底，全国共发放了约4 000张生产许可证，通过对一些省市的了解，获证企业数量与调查摸底数量相差较大，一些大中型企业还没有取得食品生产许可证。各地务必要采取有效的措施加快发证进程，在2006年年底前完成发证并开始无证查处工作。特别是要高度重视边销茶的发证工作，生产边销茶的重点省份要积极采取措施，通过督促、帮扶等手段保证有足够数量的边销茶生产企业取得食品生产许可证，保障边销茶的供给。鉴于边销茶的特殊性，总局将对茶叶细则进行修改，加强对边销茶的监督管理。

4. 做好食品生产许可证延续及换证工作，加强获证企业后续监管　总局自2003年1月9日起批准发放的食品生产许可证书已陆续到期，为做好食品生产许可延续及换证工作，各省应高度重视并严格按照总局印发的《关于做好食品生产许可证期满延续及换证工作规定》要求，做好许可证延续及换证工作。依法由省级质量技术监督部门实施食品生产许可的，各省要统筹规划，充分发挥地市局和检验机构的作用，加快换发生产许可证工作进度，确保企业及时完成换证。属于总局负责实施的食品生产许可，各地应加快对换证企业的现场审查和产品检验，及时将初审材料上报总局食品监管司。总局将对不按时进行换证的企业，注销其生产许可证。

5. 做好白酒、婴幼儿配方乳粉的许可证过渡工作　白酒、婴幼儿配方乳粉过去实行工业产品生产许可证管理，现在已纳入到食品质量安全市场准入制度管理，需要总局和各省局共同做好这两种产品的许可制度过渡工作，保证工作的连续性。在没有明确如何交接之前，先要按原来的工作程序开展工作，具体交接事宜，总局将另外行文规范。但有两点需要明确，一是要发放食品生产许可证，按食品生产许可证的编号规则进行编号；二是有效期由原来的5年改为3年。总局拟对这两种食品的审查细则进行修订，保持与其他食品的统一。2006年白酒生产许可证也进入换证期，总局印发了《关于白酒产品生产许可证到期换证的通知》。目前已批准了81家企业换发食品生产许可证，但仍有661家企业到期需换证。

6. 严格责任追究，规范市场准入工作　食品质量安全市场准入，是一项严肃的行政许可工作，必须按照准入制度规定，严格发证范围，严格发证条件，严格行政审批时限，严格各岗位人员职责，严格行政许可责任追究，保证食品质量安全市场准入工作的质量。

总局将组织对各地的市场准入工作进行检查，加强对食品生产许可工作的规范，保证市场准入的标准、程序、时限、操作规程的统一。各级市场准入部门工作的进度、质量、社会反响将直接印证这项工作的成败，不可等闲视之，必须要下大力气抓紧、抓好、抓出成效。

(二) 开拓市场准入工作新领域，迅速推进实施食品相关产品和化妆品市场准入制度

食品相关产品市场准入是一项新任务，也是一项重点任务。在生产加工环节的食品监管职责划归质检部门负责之前，对食用化工产品、食用酒精等一些食品相关产品已实施了生产许可证管理，但是并没有将关系食品安全的相关产品作为一个大类来专门管理。

2006年，按照“立足当前，突出重点，分期分批，稳步推进”的原则，加快实施食品相关产品和化妆品的市场准入管理。

1. *明确食品相关产品目录，进一步加快实施市场准入制度的步伐* 根据《中华人民共和国食品卫生法》、《中华人民共和国工业产品生产许可证管理条例》和国务院办公厅《2006年全国食品安全专项整治行动方案》的规定，食品相关产品分别是：食品添加剂，食品容器、包装材料和食品用工具、设备、洗涤剂、消毒剂等七大类。计划用两年时间对目前明确的所有食品相关产品启动生产许可证管理，加快制定生产许可证审查通则和审查细则。2006年的重点是食品包装、容器和工具的发证工作。食品包装要按照塑料包装、纸质包装和金属包装三步走计划，在2006年年底前全部启动。

2. *做好食用化工产品等六类食品相关产品生产许可证管理的过渡工作* 食用化工产品、食品用香精、压力锅、工业和商业用食品电热加工设备、食用酒精、餐具洗涤剂等六类产品过去实行工业产品生产许可证管理，现在已纳入到食品质量安全市场准入制度管理。目前，总局正组织专家对这六类产品的细则进行制修订。在新的细则公布之前，各地要按原来的工作程序开展工作。新的细则公布之后，按照新的要求做好发证工作。具体事项将专门发文明确。

3. *切实做好化妆品产品生产许可证换发证工作* 2006年是化妆品产品的换发证年，化妆品产品生产企业量大面广、花色品种众多，换证工作繁杂。鉴此，以下三点工作迫在眉睫。一是根据《工业产品生产许可证管理条例》和国标、行标的变化，做好化妆品产品生产许可证细则的修订工作，保证换证质量。二是加强化妆品产品的技术规范和功效验证研究，为细则修订和换发证工作的开展做好技术支撑。三是各省局要强化对化妆品产品换发证工作的督导，确保平稳过渡。同时，2006年食品生产监管司将启动牙膏产品生产许可证发证工作。

4. *对食品相关产品和化妆品生产企业进行普查，摸清监管底数* 要通过普查，建立企业档案，全面掌握各类产品生产企业数量、分布、规模和以往质量状况等基本信息，做到“管理一类产品，摸清一个行业”，在此基础上，实施分类监管。

（三）建立食品添加剂使用备案管理制度，全面加大食品添加剂监管力度

2006年，食品添加剂是食品安全监管工作的重中之重，将探索建立更严格、更有效的食品添加剂监管制度，制定食品添加剂监督管理办法，坚决遏制滥用食品添加剂的多发态势。一要掌握食品添加剂生产企业状况；二要严格实施食品添加剂市场准入制度，努力在2006年年底实现所有国标、行标的食品添加剂全部纳入市场准入制度管理；三要建立食品添加剂使用备案管理制度，掌握企业使用食品添加剂的基本情况和添加剂来源，监督企业严格按规定使用添加剂；四要检查是否超范围、超限量使用添加剂；五要检查使用的添加剂是否存在质量安全卫生问题。

食品添加剂是食品安全监管工作的难点，要在以下几个方面加大工作力度，一是针对食品添加剂的产品标准和检验方法标准不完善的问题，将配合标准委有系统、分步骤的完善食品添加的产品标准。指导检验机构加强对食品添加剂检验方法的研究，逐步完善食品添加剂的检验方法标准，为食品添加剂的监管提供有力的技术保障。二是更充分地发挥食品安全监管专业监督员、政府协管员和社会信息员的作用，及时发现添加剂生产、尤其是使用中的各种问题，提高日常监管的有效性。三是坚持从重从严的原则，凡是存在故意使用非食品用原料生产加工食品行为的，一律移送公安机关处理。四是加大惩戒力度，对于有使用非食品用原料生产加工食品违法行为的，3年内不得申请食品及食品相关产品生产许可证。已经取得食品生产许可证的，立即吊证。

（四）抓住建设社会主义新农村战略机遇，将食品小作坊监管更好地融入到这个历史任务中去，探索新思路，寻求新突破

农村食品由于其数量多、规模小、分布散、条件差，一直是监管难点，但是小作坊的监管效果直接关系到食品安全监管的全盘工作能否取得实效。当前，食品小作坊问题已经成为规范食品生产加工领域生产经营秩序不可逾越的障碍，已经成为我国提高食品安全整体水平和推进社会主义新农村建设的瓶颈之一。当前，建设社会主义新农村是党和国家的重要历史任务，也是全民的历史任务，要充分利用这个战略机遇，将解决食品小作坊问题智慧地融入建设社会主义新农村历史大潮，正视国情，探索和研究更加可行有效的监管措施。

“十一五”期间，小作坊监管要始终坚持“既要管好、又要便民”原则，要在摸清底数、落实质量安全承诺制、鼓励小作坊联营发展和严厉查处违法行为的基础上，进一步加强宣传引导，实行分类监管，并探索建立小作坊质量安全控制体系。一是加强宣传引导。就是从建设社会主义新农村的高度，确保一方平安的角度，促进地方政府提高对加强小作坊监管重要意义的认识。没有地方政府的支持，就无法破解小作坊监管的难题。同时，要从守法诚信、扩大生产、增加收入的角度，引导小作坊经营者提高食品安全自律意识，掌握食品安全基本知识。二是实行分类监管。就是对于已实施准入制度管理的食品，要依法组织开展无证查处。但是，对于当地人民群众日常生活离不开，地处偏远地区的、很少量的食品生产加工小作坊，可以允许有条件地存在。同时，县级质量技术监督部门要登记造册、加强监管，并报当地人民政府和上级质量技术监督部门备案。对于尚未纳入准入制度管理或未开始实施无证查处的食品，要引导生产加工小作坊完善条件，规范经营。三是积极探索建立小作坊质量安全控制体系。就是针对我国还没有一个适用于食品生产小型企业的安全卫生控制体系的现状，研究制定农村小型食品加工企业质量控制体系。对食品小作坊、小企业的监管措施，原则就是逐步提高其控制能力、降低风险、消除隐患、减少危害、确保安全，不能苛求他们按照 HACCP、GMP 等要求规范生产。但是，必须引导小作坊满足最基本安全卫生条件和管理要求，确保其产品的安全卫生。计划 2006 年探索建立小作坊食品安全问题的控制体系，并选择山东、广东、浙江、吉林、河南、陕西等 6 省开始农村小作坊监管示范工程建设。

（五）进一步提升突发食品安全事件应急处理能力和水平，促进应急处理工作的科学化、规范化和制度化

食品安全突发事件由于其突发性和非常规性的特点，影响的范围广，规律难以掌握，如果没有高效的应急机制和果断的处理措施，局势将难以控制。2006 年将建立和完善食品安全应急反应机制，锻炼和提高整个质监队伍应对食品安全突发事件的能力和水平。一是完善突发食品安全事件应急反应预案。健全组织机构，明确快速反应程序，落实工作职责和责任，组织编制《食品安全突发事件应急处理工作手册》，组织相关培训和演练，加快建立实施食品安全快速反应联动机制，使一线工作人员面对突发事件能够做到掌握主动，反应迅速，处置果敢。二是建立突发事件紧急报告制度。对发生区域性的食品安全事件或者重大食品安全事故时，省级质量技术监督部门必须及时就有关情况向总局汇报。三是实行定期食品安全专家咨询制度和突发食品安全公共事件专家评估制度。通过评估了解潜在的食品安全隐患，准确掌握突发事件的危害程度和发生原因，提高突发事件应急处理的科学性、权威性和准确性。四是加强应急处理电子化、信息化和网络化建设，提高处理突发食品安全事件的能力。

（六）改革和完善食品专项抽查制度，加大实施不安全产品召回，强化溯源管理，提高食品安全监管工作的执行力、威慑力和有效性

监督抽查一直都是质量技术监督工作的一个重要制度，是体现质量监督工作执行力、威慑力的有效措施，更是做好食品安全监管工作的一个重要手段，监督抽查结果也是反映食品安全监管工作成效的重要指标。食品专项抽查是食品监督抽查的一种重要形式，主要是积极应对食品安全突发事件。在突发事件发生的第一时间，组织专家和技术机构对突发事件危害性进行分析，并委托相关技术机构按统一检验标准，统一检验项目，统一检验方法，对食品实施专项抽查，及时了解到实际情况，采取有效应对措施，正确引导舆论。加大实施不安全产品召回，强化溯源管理是今后我们工作的一个重点。将尽快组织制订《不安全食品召回管理办法》，同时，将通过整合全国食品抽查资源，了解各级质量技术监督部门和质检技术机构在日常工作中发现的食品安全问题，收集国际国内各种渠道发布的不安全食品信息，从而分析我国食品安全存在的主要问题，有针对性地采取措施。对行业性、区域性质量问题，开展食品专项整治工作；对部分存在安全卫生问题的食品，进行跟踪抽查，对确实存在不安全隐患的食品实施召回，并通过加强对企业的产品溯源管理，加大后处理力度，查找问题，消除隐患，切实提高监管工作的权威性和有效性。

（七）严格履行卫生监督职责，大力实行强制检验制度

《中华人民共和国产品质量法》规定，产品质量必须检验合格，不得以不合格产品冒充合格产品，这是法律规定的强制检验，执行强制检验制度是企业的法定义务。2002 年《国务院关于加强新阶段“菜篮子”工作的通知》第一次明确提出要建立实施强制检验制度，2004 年国务院《关于进一步加强食品安全工作的决定》和中编办有关食品监管职能调整的《通知》等重要文件均将强制检验作为从源头抓质量的有效措施，给予了充分肯定，并对质检部门实施强制检验、确保食品质量安全提出了明确要求。总局《食品生产加工企业质量安全监督管理实施细则（试行）》第 39 条明确规定对食品生产加工企业的产品实施强制检验制度。质量技术监督部门负责确定强制检验的频次，并组织实施。当前，要在忠实履行生产加工环节日常卫生监管职责、全面强化食品安全监管的新形势下，以新的思路、新的模式、新的目标，对强制检验制度进行进一步的改革、规范和完善。一是在实施市场准入制度中，严格执行市场准入强制检验，确保获证企业产品质量不出问题。市场准入的强制检验主要包括发证前和获证后两个方面的内容。二是落实食品生产加工企业的日常卫生监管职责，制定定期强制检验工作计划，加大日常检验力度，确保少出问题。三是对监督检查安全卫生项目不合格的企业，实行加严或批批强制检验，直至企业能够确保其产品质量安全。具体实施中注意以下三点：第一，要合理确定强制检验的项目和指标，重点检验安全卫生指标。第二，要合理确定检验周期，根据分类监管的原则确定强制检验频次。第三，要严格执行检验收费管理规定，严格按照财政和物价部门制定发布的文件进行收费。各省要结合本省实际，制定切实有效的实施办法，大力推进强制检验制度，切实发挥强制检验制度督促企业严格自律，从源头确保食品质量卫生安全的有效作用，努力将其建设成为食品安全监管机制中的一项基本制度。

（八）加强对地方日常监管工作的督导力度，促进各地进一步落实食品安全区域监管责任制

2006年，各地要进一步完善食品安全区域监管责任制，切实落实食品安全区域监管责任制中的“三员四定、三进四图、两书一报告”等各项具体要求。各省局要想方设法为基层提供必要的监管装备和监管经费，努力解决基层监管工作中的实际困难。各省局要在监管实践中，积极探索新的监管方法和模式，进一步加强对食品生产加工环节安全卫生的日常监管工作。总局对地方开展食品安全监管工作会建立督导制度。总局将组织有关专家和各省从事食品安全监管工作骨干力量，采取不同的方式，定期或不定期对地方质量技术监督部门落实巡查、回访、监督抽查、强制检验、年检、各种备案管理等的工作情况，进行全方位的督促检查。并建立督导情况信息通报制度，及时介绍和推广各地在监管工作中创造的好经验、好做法，及时通报批评监管措施落实不到位的单位。2006年，各地质量技术监督部门要继续深入抓好复原乳的日常监管工作，防止反弹。复原乳的监管直接关系到“三农”问题，各地质量技术监督部门要从讲政治的高度重视复原乳的监管工作，切实落实国务院和总局关于复原乳监管的各项要求。

（九）建立健全食品安全风险监测分析与预警制度，实现食品安全监管早发现、早控制、早处理

近年来，我国食品生产加工企业暴露出了许多问题，较为突出的是，一些企业在利益的驱使下，在食品加工过程中大量使用非食品原料，如在面粉中添加滑石粉，在鱼丸、鲜虾等食物中添加硼砂，而这些非法行为往往能够隐蔽较长时间，引起广泛关注的苏丹红事件、孔雀石绿等事件等均是此类非法行为。2006年，将重点选择5个省份，确定监测城市、监测对象和监测项目开展工作，以国家级食品质检机构和食品安全专家为专业技术支持，对监测结果进行对比分析，对可能造成的危害进行评估、预测、预报，并提供有针对性的控制措施，形成风险评估报告，作为我国非食品用原料控制监管和预防重大食品安全事件决策的技术依据，提高国内生产加工环节食品安全风险监测、分析与风险预警的能力和水平。

（十）积极推进中国产品质量电子监管网建设，加快网上行政审批步伐，大力提升食品安全监管工作的电子化、信息化和网络化水平

按照总局提出的统一要求，将配合有关司局加快推进中国产品质量电子监管网建设，大力提升食品安全监管工作有效性。同时，积极探索建立食品电子标签身份证制度，建立食品安全溯源体系。从高风险食品入手，指导企业采用产品电子标签，建立产品原料、添加剂使用、生产批次、厂名厂址等重要信息可溯源管理，加强企业动态监管。推广实施电子政务是质检工作实现技术创新、管理创新、体制创新的重点工程，将为食品安全监管工作带来深刻的变革。要按照总局质检信息化发展“十一五”专项规划的部署，以“金质工程”为主线，将信息化建设贯穿到食品安全监管各项工作中。食品安全监管工作的信息化就是要把企业普查、风险检测与预警、市场准入、后续监管、监督抽查、人员和机构监管等六个主要方面工作实现整体的信息化、网络化，整合全国的质检资源和监管信息，形成一个全国联动的食品安全监管网。2006年要重点完善食品生产许可证网上申报审批系统，并按照总局规定，在2006年年底前，实现部分食品生产许可证网上审批。

（十一）加强管理队伍和技术队伍建设，做好食品安全监管保障工作

高素质的管理人才和专家队伍是做好食品安全监管工作的重要保障，2006年将重点加强五个方面建设。一是促进地方食品安全监管机构和专职人员的尽快到位。截至目前，全国已有17个省经省编办批准成立了专门的食品安全监管机构，6个省成立了食品安全监管临时机构，配备了专门人员。各省应充分利用国务院《决定》中明确要求地方政府做好食品安全监管的机构、编制、人员、经费等保障工作的契机，积极借鉴兄弟省的模式和经验，加快争取地方政府对食品安全监管工作的大力支持，确保在2006年底，基本上都设立专门的食品安全监管机构，有专门的一支队伍负责食品安全工作。二是建立食品安全监督员队伍。计划制定食品质量安全监督员管理规定，从2006年开始，对从事食品生产加工环节监管工作的人员实行教育、培训制度，提高基层人员素质和整体水平，逐渐建设一支业务过硬的食品安全监督员队伍。三是加强发证检验机构的考核和审查员培训注册，重点是加强新实施市场准入制度的食品注册审查员的培训和考核。四是提高食品检验机构人员的能力和素质，重点是加强研究型人才的培养。五是结合生产加工领域食品安全监管工作需要，组建食品安全专家咨询委员会。另外，按照总局的统一部署，积极开展治理商业贿赂专项工作。重点是在食品许可工作机构、发证检验机构和审查员队伍中，开展以摸底调查、自查自纠、处理违法案件、建立防范长效机制为主要内容的专项活动。这次工作总局食品生产监管司还要专门发文进行部署。

（十二）加强食品安全科技研究，认真落实食品科技“十一五”规划及立项工作，不断提升食品质量安全技术保障的能力和水平

近年来，在食品安全检验能力提升方面做了许多工作，特别是检验机构投入了大量人力、财力和物力加强了相关研究工作。但是，在食品毒理评价能力、新资源食品卫生学评价能力、潜在的风险性研究能力等方面与国际水平相比、与食品安全监管工作实际需要相比，还有很大差距。“十一五”期间国家重大科技专项课题中，与食品安全有关的问题占到了很突出的位置。近几个月，在科技司和食品生产监管司的精心组织下，全国40多个食品检验机构共申报了127个与食品生产加工环节监管相关的科研课题。在科技司的直接领导下，食品生产监管司又组织专家按照国家“十一五”重大科技专项的要求，对这些课题进行了分类归并，最后专题申报了4个课题的11个专项。目前，总局正在加强和科技部的沟通，在“十一五”国家重大科技专项食品安全关键技术研究课题中已经列入或正在考虑列入的重大课题包括：食品接触材料安全性检测、食品中掺假物识别、农村小型食品加工企业质量安全控制体系、食品溯源与原产地保护、食品添加剂安全性评价与安全使用标准、食品中有害物多残留检测设备的研发、重大活动食品安全预警与应急处理技术研究等。所有这些课题都与工作密切相关，有些是工作中直接使用的。今后的工作中，要继续把与食品安全有关的科研工作放到十分重要的位置上抓，做好技术保障储备，不断提升食品安全监管工作的科学化水平。

（本文为作者于2006年5月在全国食品生产监管工作会议上的工作报告）

“十一五”期间我国纺织工业的发展

国家发展和改革委员会工业司副司长　贺燕丽

“十一五”是我国纺织工业发展中最重要的转型时期，为贯彻落实《国民经济和社会发展第十一个五年规划纲要》的精神，以科学发展观统领纺织工业发展的全局，做好纺织工业发展的指导工作，推动纺织工业结构调整和产业升级，积极转变经济增长方式，国家发展和改革委员会同有关部门和中国纺织工业协会编制了《纺织工业“十一五”发展纲要》（以下简称《发展纲要》）。《发展纲要》全面总结了我国纺织工业“十五”取得的成就和发展中存在的问题，深入分析了国内外环境变化和行业发展趋势，从全局和战略的高度对我国纺织工业未来五年的发展进行了总体部署，是国家指导“十一五”纺织工业健康发展的纲领性文件。

一、认真总结“十五”纺织工业的发展，是做好“十一五”各项工作的基础

纺织工业是我国国民经济的重要产业之一，也是具有国际竞争优势的产业。对扩大就业、增加农民收入、积累资金、出口创汇、繁荣市场、提高城镇化水平、带动相关产业和促进区域经济发展发挥了重要的作用。纺织工业虽然是一个市场化程度较高的行业，但它的发展直接关系到国民经济的稳定，关系到推进工业结构优化升级的战略大局。“十五”期间是我国纺织工业历史上发展速度最快、效益最好的5年，纺织工业的市场活力得到充分发挥，国际竞争力和可持续发展能力进一步增强，为“十一五”纺织工业健康发展奠定了坚实的基础。《发展纲要》从行业的规模增长、产业结构调整以及产业竞争力等方面对纺织工业“十五”的发展情况进行了全面总结。

1. 行业保持快速、稳定增长，经济运行质量和效益稳步提高　2005年，全国规模以上纺织工业企业产品销售收入达到19 794亿元，“十五”期间年均增长18.9%；全社会口径纺织纤维加工量2 690万t，“十五”期间年均增长14.6%。规模以上纺织企业利税总额、利润总额分别为1 231.42亿元、689.72亿元，比2000年增长104.6%和133.5%。

2. 自主创新能力得到明显增强，工艺技术和装

备水平得到较快提升　“十五”期间，国产纺机装备技术取得重大突破，大型聚酯和化纤成套装置的单位投资大幅下降；精梳纱、无结头纱、无梭布的比重从“十五”初期的20.2%、40%、21.4%分别提高到23.3%、58%和50%；自主开发的新型纤维品种在实现产业化生产方面取得重大进展。

3. 产业结构调整继续深入，纺织工业技术结构、产品结构、区域结构、资产结构得到明显改善　服装、家用、产业用三大类终端产品纤维消费量的比重由“十五”初期的68：19：13转变为54：33：13；规模以上企业中，非国有企业销售收入由71.7%上升为90.8%，纺织行业的多元化竞争格局已经形成。纺织工业布局形成向大企业集中、向沿海地区集中和向产业集群集中的格局。纺织行业前100位企业的销售收入占规模以上企业销售收入的21.9%。全国80%的规模以上纺织企业集中在江苏、浙江、广东、上海、山东、福建东部沿海五省一市。以民营中小企业为主体、具有专业特色的产业集群、专业城镇逐步形成。

4. 出口继续保持持续、较快增长，出口结构不断优化　“十五”期间，我国纺织品服装出口额年均增长17.2%，2005年达到1 175亿美元，占全球纺织品服装贸易额的比例从2000年的15%上升到24%。其中，纺织品出口比重上升，由2000年的30.8%上升到2005年的37.4%；一般贸易比重也由2000年的55.7%提高到69.7%。

5. 利用外资成效显著，外资企业发挥重要作用　2004年，我国纺织工业新设立外商投资企业5 969个，合同外资金额55.9亿美元，同比增长25.7%。浙江、江苏、山东、福建和广东省纺织工业合同利用外资金额占全国的84%。外商投资企业出口交货值占全行业的34.3%。

总结“十五”发展取得的成就，纺织工业实现快速发展的动因主要有四个方面：一是国内市场化进程加快，市场配置资源起到了关键作用，大大增强了纺织工业的市场活力。二是坚持依靠科技进步，纺织工业自主创新能力得到明显增强。三是随着国民经济的持续快速增长，国内需求不断扩大是纺织工业快速发展的第一拉动力。四是经济全球化加快和我国加入WTO，促进了纺织工业国际竞争优势的发挥。这几方面仍将是纺织工业“十一五”发展的主要动力。

“十五”期间纺织工业虽然取得了前所未有的成绩，但在经济转型过程中长期积累的矛盾和问题依然很多，技术、管理、创新、国际化水平与发达国家相比还存在很大差距，目前在全球产业分工中尚处于加工制造环节，制约着我国建设纺织强国的进程。一是在纺织工业快速发展中，粗放型增长方式没有得到根本转变。一些地区和企业片面追求规模、产值的高增长，盲目铺摊子，“同构性”发展，而人才、技术和管理水平的提升滞后，高投入、高消耗、高排放、低效率的状况还没有得到根本改善，企业持续发展能力不足。二是纺织工业的自主创新能力还有待提高，研发资金投入低，研发能力不足。根据2004年经济普查数据，规模以上纺织工业企业研发投入比例仅为销售收入的0.25%，与发达国家平均5%的投入水平差距很大。行业整体技术装备水平、纺织加工工艺技术、产品开发创新能力以及对全球化市场的快速反应能力落后于世界先进水平。三是在品牌培育和品牌创新方面还缺乏经验和准备。世界纺织品服装已完全进入买方市场，传统的大规模、大批量、低成本生产、低价竞销已经不能适应新的需求。国内高档和中高档消费市场被大量的国际知名品牌和二线品牌所占据，国内品牌却难以进入。生产企业的出口产品以贴牌加工为主，多数企业缺乏对出口营销渠道的控制力，由于多道中间环节，使附加值大量流失。

二、认真分析纺织工业面临的形势，是把握纺织工业“十一五”发展的前提

随着全球经济一体化进程不断深入，世界纺织产业结构调整和产业转移步伐正在加快，由于我国纺织工业具有较显著的国际比较优势，吸引了越来越多的国际资本和跨国采购商，为我国纺织工业提供了新的发展空间。内需增长仍将是我国纺织工业发展最主要的拉动力，我国国民经济及相关产业的发展，将促进纺织品服装消费持续增长，为纺织工业带来了很大的发展机遇。根据2010年人均国内生产总值比2000年翻一番的预期目标，未来5年我国人均衣着类纤维消费仍将保持较快增长。随着“十一五”我国城镇化建设加快，城市化水平每提高1个百分点，新增城市人口约为1 500万人，家用纺织品需求总量将大幅增长。我国汽车、建筑、卫生、水利、农业、交通、能源等相关产业的发展，必将带动产业用纺织品消费的快速增长。同时，也要清醒地看到，纺织工业的发展还面临着严峻的挑战。国际纺织品贸易中的不确定因素增加，市场竞争日趋激烈，今后相当长的时期内，纺织品贸易摩擦和各种形式的贸易保护将不可避免并有加剧的趋势，一些新兴的纺织工业国家，凭借更加低廉的劳动力成本和欧美区域性的贸易保护等有利条件，正在逐步挤占全球纺织品贸易一体化后的国际市场份额。纺织工业在发展中也面临着日益突出的环

境、资源、制造成本上升的制约，以及国际石油价格、人民币汇率等许多不确定因素的考验。未来5年，纺织工业发展面临的机遇与挑战并存，只有把握好国际国内纺织工业发展的趋势，才能促进纺织工业全面、协调和可持续发展。

三、坚持科学发展观，是贯彻落实纺织工业“十一五”发展纲要的基本点

针对纺织工业发展的现状和面临的形势，以及“十一五”国民经济和社会发展的要求，纺织工业将进入一个以增强自主创新能力为中心环节，大力推进结构调整和产业升级的新时期。坚持科学发展观，加快产业结构调整，切实转变经济增长方式，实现纺织工业的全面、协调和可持续发展，是我国从纺织大国向纺织强国迈进的必然选择。《发展纲要》确立的“十一五”纺织工业发展的指导思想是：认真贯彻落实《国民经济和社会发展第十一个五年规划纲要》精神，紧紧围绕建设纺织强国的发展战略目标，坚持科学发展观，按照走新型工业化道路要求，充分发挥市场配置资源的基础性作用和产业政策的导向作用，依靠科技进步和自主创新，积极转变增长方式，优化进出口结构，着力创建自主品牌，加快纺织产业升级；提高资源利用效率，大力发展节能环保和生态纺织技术；引导纺织产业集群升级，推进产业梯度转移，加快中西部地区纺织工业发展；加强国际经济技术合作，充分利用国际国内两个市场、两种资源；建立健全纺织企业社会责任体系，规范行业市场竞争秩序，促进纺织工业实现全面、协调、可持续发展，为全面建设小康社会和满足人民日益丰富的纺织品服装消费需求做出贡献。

《发展纲要》把纺织工业“十一五”发展的目标体系分为预期性和约束性两大类。主要的规模和经济指标属于预期性目标，是通过对大量历史数据资料的整理分析，并综合考虑“十一五”时期我国国民经济增长、城镇化建设、纺织品服装消费结构变化，以及全球经济发展、纺织品贸易格局变化趋势、我国出口纺织品结构变化等因素后做出的预测。预计到2010年，纺织纤维加工总量将从2005年的2 690万t增长到3 600万t，年均增长6%。其中国内纤维消费量约占纤维加工总量的75%。全行业销售产值从2005年的33 000亿元增长到60 000亿元，年均增长12.7%。纺织品服装出口额将从2005年的1 175亿美元增长到1 800亿美元，年均增长9%。从这些规模类指标来看，“十一五”期间的增速都大大低于“十五”期间的增速。这是由于“十五”时期纺织工业的增长既有经济发展的规律性，也有一定的特殊性，多种因素结合造成了纺织工业的快速增长。“十一五”时期，随着环境、资源制约日益显著，国际贸易摩擦频发，企业面临的市场竞争更加激烈，粗放型的增长模式将难以为继，纺织工业将转到以调整产业结构、提高运行效益为主的发展道路上来，形成以质量、创新和快速反应为主体的产业竞争优势，构筑起符合走新型工业化道路要求的产业发展模式。

《国民经济和社会发展第十一个五年规划纲要》中，对经济社会提出了提高资源利用效率、降低污染物排放的目标要求，到“十一五”末，单位国内生产总值能源消耗降低20%左右，单位工业增加值用水量降低30%，工业固体废物综合利用率提高到60%，主要污染物排放总量减少10%。结合纺织工业的实际情况，《发展纲要》也提出了节能降耗和环境保护等方面的约束性目标。到“十一五”末，吨纤维耗电量降低10%，单位产值的纤维使用量降低20%，单位产值的污水排放量降低22%，吨纤维耗水量降低20%。《发展纲要》明确了实现这些目标主要是通过行业的科技进步和结构调整，限制和淘汰低效率、高能耗、高污染的低水平产能，加快自主创新的步伐，大力推进节能、清洁生产和环境保护技术的推广和应用，降低能耗和污染物排放水平。

四、扎扎实实落实好“十一五”纺织工业发展的重点任务

为切实推进我国纺织工业产业升级和结构调整，转变经济增长方式，实现“十一五”发展目标，结合《国民经济和社会发展第十一个五年规划纲要》中确立的纺织工业发展重点，《发展纲要》从纺织各分行业的结构调整、自主创新、利用外资、区域布局、品牌建设、原料供应、标准化建设及应对贸易摩擦等方面提出了“十一五”纺织工业发展的重点任务。下面着重谈几个方面的任务：

1. 坚持自主创新　要认真贯彻全国科技大会提出的“自主创新、重点跨越、支撑发展、引领未来”的方针，不断加强纺织技术、装备创新和管理创新，推进纺织工业科技进步和产业升级。《发展纲要》提出要以《纺织工业科技进步发展纲要》中确定的28项关键技术和10项重点新型纺织机械技术装备国产化的攻关与产业化为突破口，大力开展纺织技术和装备创新，提高产业科技含量，推进行业的科技进步和产业升级。要以企业为主体，形成以市场为导向，技术与生产实现良性循环的技术进步和创新体系。强化技术自主开发的力度，加速培育有自主知识产权的主

导产品和核心技术，提高产品的科技含量。加快提高纺织机械机电一体化水平和信息技术水平，提高产品的先进性和稳定性，为纺织工业走新型工业化道路，打好纺机装备基础。另一方面，要不断加强企业管理创新，提高企业管理水平，增强参与国际竞争的能力。

2. 优化产业区域布局　要充分发挥市场配置资源的基础性作用，积极推进纺织工业梯度转移，促进东部沿海和中西部地区产业链衔接，逐步形成东西互动、分工协作、优势互补、协调发展的产业梯度格局，提升我国纺织工业的整体竞争力。产业集群是广大中小企业适应社会化生产要求的主要存在方式，集群产业的升级对全行业转变增长方式意义重大。因此，“十一五”期间要继续推进和发展新型产业集群，在产业集聚地区建立纺织创新平台，并以此为基点构筑行业性公共服务体系，提高集群企业的生产力水平和实力。

3. 大力加强品牌建设　着力打造自主品牌，提高纺织工业技术含量和自主品牌比重，增强我国自主品牌的国际竞争力，扭转我国纺织工业在全球产业链中的不利地位。强化企业的品牌意识，加大产品开发、市场开拓的力度；重点扶持一批在品牌设计、技术研发、市场营销网络建设方面的优势企业；鼓励纺织各行业、重点区域通过建立并发挥产业创新公共服务平台的作用，创建行业性、区域性公共品牌。

4. 积极推进国际化经营　面对经济全球化形势，充分利用两种资源、两个市场，积极参与国际分工，发展跨国生产和经营，推进产业结构升级，拓展行业发展空间，真正实现从“封闭经济”向“开放经济”的转变。全球经济一体化发展趋势为我国纺织产业实施“走出去”战略创造了有利条件，这将有利于提高产业的国际化经营水平，并以此带动和扩大国内的技术、装备的出口，实现就地发展、就地销售和向第三国销售。

5. 要立足扩大内需　“十一五”期间，纺织工业应注重调整“重出口、轻内需”的倾向，把产业发展的重心放在立足扩大内需上，逐步调整纺织纤维加工量的内需和出口的比例，在满足人民群众日益增长的衣着类消费的同时，注重发展市场潜力巨大的家用纺织品和产业用纺织品，改善家用纺织品和产业用纺织品比重偏小的产业结构。

五、认真贯彻落实《发展纲要》的几点要求

1. 各地发改委系统要认真学习和贯彻《发展纲要》确定的“十一五”纺织工业发展的指导思想和发展目标，提高认识，把握大局，统一思想，根据本地区比较优势，制定本地区的纺织工业发展纲要，落实好《发展纲要》提出的重点任务。

2. 政府管理部门要认真贯彻好《发展纲要》，根据纲要的精神，提出相应的投资政策、土地政策、金融政策、财税政策、贸易政策等，搞好宏观调控，建立纺织工业发展的良好环境，促进我国纺织工业健康有序发展。

3. 中国纺织工业协会和各地行业协会要根据《发展纲要》的精神尽快制定本行业的发展规划，积极做好《发展纲要》的宣传和指导工作，积极发挥桥梁和纽带作用，不断提高行业服务水平，分析市场变化，加强组织协调和行业自律，引导行业发展。

4. 广大纺织企业要切实转变发展观念，以《发展纲要》为指导，不断提高自主创新能力，增强行业全局意识和全球化竞争意识，积极落实企业社会责任，为建设纺织强国做出贡献。

（本文为作者于 2006 年 6 月在纺织工业“十一五”发展纲要发布会上的讲话，略有删改）

加强体系队伍能力建设 推动无公害农产品事业快速发展

中国绿色食品发展中心主任　马爱国

这次会议的主要任务是全面总结无公害农产品工作推动三年来的成功经验和做法，认真贯彻全国农产品市场信息质量工作座谈会精神，围绕无公害农产品“全面加快发展、全力打造品牌”的目标任务，进一步转变工作思路、创新工作方式，加强体系队伍和能力建设，充分发挥整个系统的职能作用和整体优势，

推动无公害农产品事业持续健康地加快发展。

一、无公害农产品工作推动三年来的总结与回顾

全国统一无公害农产品认证从2003年4月启动开始，到现在正好三年。这三年，应当说是无公害农产品事业发展的关键时期，处于起步和打基础的阶段。工作的基本任务是建立统一、规范的工作制度，积极创造条件，打开工作局面，全力推进事业发展。回顾三年来的工作，每年都有一个工作重心和突破口，2003年重点是构建基本制度和工作体系，启动全国统一认证；2004年重点是完善运行机制，推进地方认证向全国统一认证的转换；2005年积极创造政策环境，拓宽事业发展空间，推动无公害农产品全面加快发展。三年来，在农业部党组的正确领导下，在各级政府和农业部门的重视、支持下，在质检、工商、卫生等相关部门的积极配合推动下，通过整个系统上上下下的努力探索、开拓创新、扎实工作，无公害农产品认证及管理工作取得了显著的成效，总体上看工作制度基本建立，体系队伍逐步健全，认证规模快速增长，社会影响不断扩大，工作得到了方方面面的认可。总结起来，成绩来之不易，凝聚了整个工作系统的心血。从业绩层面，主要表现在以下几个方面：

（一）制度基本建立，程序日趋规范

无公害农产品认证是一项全新的工作，在实际工作中不断地加以探索和完善，已初步建立起了一套“统一规范、简便快捷”的规章制度和工作程序。

1、*在基本制度方面* 2002年4月29日农业部会同国家质量监督检验检疫总局联合颁布了《无公害农产品管理办法》，为无公害农产品管理奠定了制度基础。2003年，农业部会同国家认证认可监督管理委员会相继联合颁布了《无公害农产品标志管理办法》、《无公害农产品认证程序》和《无公害农产品产地认定程序》。这些办法和程序，是无公害农产品事业发展特别是无公害农产品认证工作的重要依据。

2. *在宏观政策方面* 为推动无公害农产品迅速启动和快速发展，2003年，农业部先后印发了关于做好无公害农产品认证工作和关于进一步规范无公害农产品产地认定产品认证工作两个部发文件；2005年，农业部提出了《关于发展无公害农产品绿色食品有机农产品的意见》，给出了明确的政策导向，极大地推动了无公害农产品事业健康发展。

3. *在产品目录技术标准方面* 农业部从2001年开始，已分五批共制定发布无公害农产品行业标准379项，其中种植业标准210个，畜牧业标准75个，渔业标准94个。标准规范包括产地环境标准、生产技术规范和产品质量安全标准以及认证检测、评审规范。目前已纳入无公害农产品认证目录的农产品种类达535个，其中种植业产品344个，畜牧业产品62个，渔业产品129个。约有80%以上的“菜篮子”和“米袋子”产品已实施无公害农产品认证。

4. *在技术规范方面* 农业部农产品质量安全中心作为无公害农产品认证、监督与管理的职能机构，根据工作需要，按照总的制度框架和程序规定，先后制定了一大批行之有效的操作层面措施和办法。包括无公害农产品认证委托检测机构管理办法、产地环境检测管理办法、产品认证复查换证规范、产地认定复查换证规范等，其中产品抽样、产地检测等技术规范以农业行业标准形式发布。部中心还组织编制了符合无公害农产品认证与管理需要的《质量手册》和相应的内部工作程序文件。工作规范和程序文件的建立，协调了方方面面的关系，统一了全国上下的工作行为，提高了工作质量和效率。

（二）工作队伍基本建立，支撑体系日趋完善

1. *工作机构体系基本建立并向地县两级延伸* 全国除农业部农产品质量安全中心及所属的3个专业分中心外，31个省、自治区、直辖市已设立或明确68个相关行业的无公害农产品省级工作机构，专门负责本地区、本行业的无公害农产品产地认定、产品认证及相关的监督管理工作。其中，1/3以上的厅局成立了专门的农产品质量安全中心，超过2/3的地市和1/2的市县明确了无公害农产品工作机构。

2. *产地认定、产品认证检测体系基本建立* 按照“合理布局、择优委托”的原则，已在全国范围内选择、考核、认可了无公害农产品产地环境检测机构191个，无公害农产品认证检测机构132个，其中80%为农业系统的专业质检机构和检测中心。

3. *现场检查员队伍已有一定规模* 截至目前，全国已培训注册无公害农产品检查员1 229名，省级工作机构的业务骨干已经基本轮训一遍，部分地市业务骨干也得到培训，与此同时，各地也陆续培训了一大批无公害农产品产地认定检查员。

4. *专家评审队伍不断充实完善* 绝大部分省（自治区、直辖市）都成立了无公害农产品产地认定专家评审委员会，全国无公害农产品认证专家评审委员会的专家也从最初的81人增加到了283人，同时建立了定期聘请专家对产地认定和产品认证工作进行技术把关和终审的制度。

（三）产地认定全面推进，产品认证快速发展

1. *地方认证向全国统一认证转换顺畅* 在全国

统一标志的认证工作正式实施之前，各地在无公害农产品认证方面做了大量有益的尝试。为尽快将各地的认证纳入到全国统一的无公害农产品认证上来，按照农业部领导的指示精神，经过近一年的时间，全国共有21个省、自治区、直辖市的地方认证成功向全国统一认证转换，有8 950个产品通过认证转换。地方认证向全国统一认证转换的完成，标志着无公害农产品认证“全国一盘棋”的工作格局基本形成，正式步入了“统一标准、统一标志、统一认证、统一管理、统一监督”的发展轨道。

2. *产地认定全面推进*　无公害农产品产地认定自2002年开展以来，认定产地规模快速增长。截至2006年3月底，全国已累计认定无公害农产品产地23 853个，其中种植业产地17 031个，面积1 982.4万hm^2，占全国耕地面积的15.2%（总面积按1.3亿hm^2计算）；畜牧业产地4 196个，合计23.7亿头（只）；渔业产地2 626个，面积189.1万hm^2。

3. *产品认证快速增长*　三年来，无公害农产品认证数量每年以成倍的速度递增。截至2006年3月底，全国统一认证的无公害农产品累计已达18 829个，获证单位10 583个。其中种植业产品14 345个，畜牧业产品1 929个，渔业产品2 555个，产品总量达到11 702万t，约占食用农产品商品量的28%。

4. *证后监管工作全面启动*　从2004年开始，部中心已连续三年对16个省份的1 300多个获证产品实施了监督抽检。从2006年开始，无公害农产品获证产品已纳入到了农业部的农产品质量安全例行监测计划，各地也已将无公害农产品监管纳入到本地区、本行业的农产品质量安全例行监测范围。

（四）功能作用日益显现，认证绩效全面发挥

随着无公害农产品产地认定和产品认证工作的不断深入，数量规模的快速增长，无公害农产品认证在促进农业和农村经济发展，特别是在促进农业“三增”方面的作用日益显现。

1. *通过无公害农产品发展，有力地推进了农产品质量安全水平的提高*　无公害农产品产地认定和产品认证的快速推进，认定基地和认证企业在推动农产品生产全程控制管理、提高农产品质量安全水平方面发挥了重要的示范、带动作用。同时，全国已经有26个省份将发展无公害农产品与各类农业项目建设紧密结合，将通过产品认证作为项目验收的基本条件。通过发展无公害农产品，不仅提高项目建设水平，更重要的是示范辐射周边，促进农产品质量安全整体水平的提高。

2. *通过产地认定，有力地带动了农业标准化和规模化发展*　目前全国已有1 982.4万hm^2的耕地通过无公害农产品产地认定，约占耕地总面积的15.2%。这些产地都比较好地推行了标准化生产和全程质量安全控制措施，有效控制了产地环境和产品污染。近一半的产地实行连片认定、基地化生产，有力地带动了农业标准化和规模化发展，提升了农业产业素质。

3. *通过产品认证，有力地推动了农业产业化发展和市场准入制度的建立*　据统计，2003年各类龙头企业、行业协会和技术推广（服务）机构仅占无公害农产品认证申报单位总数的27%，到2005年已上升到55%，在申报主体中已占据主导地位，认证工作有力促进了农业产业化发展。2005年，全国农业产业化工作会议要求，各级农业部门要按照标准创建无公害农产品、优势产品生产基地，打造名牌产品。农业部已经把通过无公害农产品认证作为申报专业合作经济组织项目的基本条件。同时无公害农产品已经被西安等20多个大中城市作为农产品上市销售的基本条件，认证工作有力促进了农产品市场准入制度的建立。

4. *通过无公害农产品品牌拉动，有力地促进了农业“三增”*　从各地情况看，通过认证的无公害农产品在销路和销售价格方面普遍得到改善，一部分产品加贴标志以后从批发市场转向了超市，销售价格也明显上升，部分产品还进入了国际市场。据不完全统计，2005年无公害农产品出口量突破400万t，出口额达到13.7亿美元。

通过三年来各级农业部门的不断探索和实践，无公害农产品工作步入“统一规范、快速发展”的轨道，事业发展的方向也更加明确、工作思路更加清晰、工作推进措施更加有力。

1. *无公害农产品作为市场准入的基本条件依法实施标志管理的走向已基本明确*　2006年，南京的全国工作会议和即将颁布实施的《农产品质量安全法》，对无公害农产品水平定位和发展方向都已非常明确。从农产品质量安全管理工作的发展趋势看，推动和发展无公害农产品将是一项长期的经常性任务。无公害农产品作为农产品市场准入的基本条件，目的是满足大众消费需要，保证基本安全，在产地认定和产品认证的基础上，将逐步从阶段性认证走向强制性要求，依法实施标志管理。

2. *无公害农产品作为公益事业依靠政府推动的机制已基本形成*　发展无公害农产品是解决农产品质量安全问题的根本措施，是实现农民生产性收入增加的重要举措，对维护公众健康和公共安全具有十分重要的作用。各级政府和农业部门将发展无公害农产品事业纳入本地区农业和农村经济工作的重要议事日程，采取了一系列行之有效的政策措施，进一步加大了政府推动的力度。湖南省将发展无公害农产品列入省政府为民办实事范畴，湖北、江西、江苏等省将无公害农产品发展列入各级农业部门的年度业绩考核指标，绝大多数地方政府和农业部门安排了规模不小的财政专项资金，对获证产品和基地进行奖励和补贴。山东省农、财两厅还就推进无公害农产品、绿色食品、有机食品出台了具体政策意见和补贴奖励办法，有力地推动了事业加快发展。

3. 无公害农产品产地认定与产品认证相结合的工作模式已基本确立　从制度设计的初衷看，产地认定重点解决千家万户分散农户生产过程的控制，产品认证主要解决农产品的市场准入问题，二者是有机的统一。产地认定由省里负责，有利于推动生产的标准化，产品认证的审批发证由部里统一管理，有利于全国的互认和市场流通。对农产品质量安全的控制而言，产地认定和产品认证是一个整体，是不可分割的两个部分。产地认定是产品认证的基础和前提，产品认证是产地认定结果的升华和后续。在整个无公害农产品产地认定和产品认证的链条中，产地认定的责任更重，工作量更大，要占整个工作量的70%～80%。在实际工作中，不断地调整工作方式方法，尽可能地使产地认定和产品认证紧密结合。在产地认定产品认证申请受理时，主张产地认定与产品认证工作放到一个部门，融为一体开展工作；在现场检查和技术审查环节，鼓励同步进行，资料信息共享互认；在证书发放方面，尽可能缩短间隔周期，以满足申请者的市场营销需要。

二、积极推进改革创新，无公害农产品事业发展潜力巨大

总的来说，无公害农产品发展形势较好，市场需求旺盛，具备了诸多有利的条件。但是从推动工作更上一个台阶的角度看，目前也还存在一些薄弱环节，特别是《农产品质量安全法》出台以后，需要从制度、机制和体制等方面进一步加强。归纳起来，主要有四个方面：

1. 体系队伍尚不够健全，发展能力有待进一步增强　主要表现在三个方面。第一，在工作机构方面，虽然全国的省级工作机构已经搭建起来了，但类型各异，形式多样，有的是行政处室，有的是事业单位，多数是加挂牌子或在现有机构建制内增加职能来开展工作，已不适应形势的变化和发展的要求。有将近一半的省级工作机构分散在不同行业，地区发展协调成本高、难度大。而且还有将近1/3的地市和一半的区县没有相应的无公害农产品工作机构。第二，在工作队伍方面，省级工作机构的专职人员少，总人数不到600人，其中兼职人员超过一半，工作始终处于比较紧张的状态。地县两级差距更大，绝大部分是兼职人员，而且还在频繁地变动。第三，在能力建设方面，接受过专门培训的人员较少，全国经过培训注册的检查员只有1 200多人，平均每个省不到40人，每个地市不到4人，县一级几乎没有经过培训注册的检查员。工作人手和专业技能的缺乏以及工作经费等方面的条件不足影响制约了无公害农产品事业的加快发展。

2. 产地认定与产品认证结合不够紧密，工作效率有待全面提升　通过近几年的不断实践，在整个系统的共同努力下，产地认定与产品认证的结合能达到目前的程度已经相当不容易了。但客观地看，目前的认证程序还比较繁琐，特别是产地认定与产品认证的结合不够紧密，存在着明显的重复和脱节现象。有一组数据是一个例证，目前全国已认定无公害农产品产地23 845个，认证的产品是18 829个，产品数占产地认定数的78.9%，至少有20%多已认定的产地未能申请产品认证，这还不包括同一产地生产多个产品的实际情况。从规模看，种植业认定产地面积已达1 982.4万 hm^2，但通过认证的种植业产品生产规模只有733.4万 hm^2，仅占认定产地面积规模的37%，有将近2/3的产地认定未能发挥应有的产品认证作用。从表象上看，产地认定与产品认证工作的脱节表现在产地认定和产品认证数量规模的不相称，但背后的实质是产地认定和产品认证按两套程序设计，环节多、重复劳动、时效性差。非常可惜的是投入了大量的人力、财力做了产地认定，却未后续进行产品认证，起不到应有的作用和效果，无法实现工作推动的真正目的。再一个就是产地认定与产品认证发展很不平衡。截至目前，全国认定产地和认证产品主要集中在江苏、浙江、山东等少数省份，认定认证数量排名前5位的省份产地规模和产品数量分别占到了全国总量的63.4%和45.8%，排名后10位的省份所占的比例尚不到总数的5%，其中畜牧业和渔业还各有2个省份产地认定是空白，有4个省畜产品和6个省水产品认证为空白。对绝大部分地方来说，平均每个县市认证的产品也就3～5个，规模太小了，难以发挥无公害农产品的示范带动作用和市场准入功能。

3. 认证认定工作规范性不够，整个系统工作质量有待尽快提高　无公害农产品这几年的发展速度总的来说是比较快的，总体的运行质量在逐年提升，但也存在着一定的薄弱环节。主要表现在四个方面：一是认证周期偏长，一般产品认证从申报受理到发证要

5～8个月，最短也要3个月，这还不包括产地认定的时间；二是申报材料质量不高，产品认证文审一次通过率只有80%左右，其中畜牧业产品不到30%；三是关键环节现场核查率低，种植业和渔业产品的现场核查几乎未开展，畜牧业产品的现场核查率也不足10%；四是各地在标准运用、检测参数确定、审核重点方面尺度把握不一，特别是产地认定主要侧重对产地环境的检测评价，对于标准化生产和生产过程控制没有作为关键环节，将生产过程中的技术把关工作后移到了产品认证环节，影响了整个工作系统的运行质量，需要从制度和程序环节层面做出相应的调整。

4. 品牌宣传推广不够，消费认知度有待迅速扩大　无公害农产品虽然有了一定的知名度，部分获证产品也借助无公害农产品的公共品牌提升了品牌知名度，实现了优质优价。但总体上看，无公害农产品现在的知名度与其市场定位以及总量规模是不相适应的。标志加贴率不到15%，市场贴标产品少，消费者对无公害农产品的选择空间非常小。据调查，北京市场消费者对无公害农产品的认知度仅为18%；上海市用户评价显示，无公害农产品的品牌认知度在整个农产品认证行业中也处于偏低位置。出现这种情况的原因是多方面的，但主要是宣传以及品牌打造工作滞后。

以上这些问题是在发展过程中出现的，从自身角度看，有一定的共性和普遍性，是当前影响制约事业发展的主要因素，因此，在充分肯定成绩的同时，应始终保持清醒的头脑，要居安思危，增强忧患意识、紧迫感和责任感，大家一道共同思考，积极探索，转变工作思路，创新工作方式，全面加强体系队伍建设，充分调动和发挥整个工作系统的积极性和能动性，努力推动无公害农产品事业加快发展。从立足固本和强化能力的角度出发，要在当前和今后相当长一个时期着力抓好以下几个方面的能力建设和改革创新：

（一）加快健全体系队伍，强化系统能力建设

健全体系、强化能力建设是无公害农产品事业健康发展的重要组织保证，也是当前面临的最紧迫的任务。

一要健全机构　从工作推动的主体看，当前重中之重是要加快健全省级工作机构，明确地县两级工作依托机构。就省级工作机构而言，行政与事业各有侧重共同推动的模式是比较成功的做法。从行政推动的角度，重点是将无公害农产品发展纳入到整个农产品质量安全管理大局，统筹谋划、全力支持；从具体工作的推进看，成立专门的无公害农产品工作机构，将产地认定与产品认证合二为一，有利于推动无公害农产品事业加快发展。同时，要加强行业之间的统筹协调和沟通，形成农业系统的工作合力，充分发挥产地认定、产品认证专家评审委员会的技术把关作用，确保产地认定产品认证工作的科学性。地县两级要充分依托农业行政与技术推广机构的现有人力资源，尽快把工作推动起来，要做到无公害农产品工作在部、省、地、县四级层层有人管，事事有人抓。

二要强化职能　从无公害农产品的工作内涵和即将颁布的《农产品质量安全法》的规定看，各级工作机构的工作职能要进一步明确细化，尽快从单一的产品认证向无公害农产品产前、产中、产后全过程拓展，包括投入品使用管理、标准化生产、产品检测、包装标识、监督检查等。部中心包括三个分中心，重点抓好规划计划、组织协调、审批发证、标志管理、监督检查；省一级重点是要抓好产地认定、产品检测、认证初审、标志推广、监督抽查；地县两级重点是要抓好宣传动员、组织申报、技术指导、技术培训，具体承担实施现场检查与证后的日常监督管理。

三要理顺关系　无公害农产品认证是一项政府推动的公益性农产品质量安全管理措施，涉及到方方面面的资源整合和优势互补，如何尽快实现从目前的多头管理转变为统一行动，是当前无公害农产品工作的一个重点。要正确处理好各个方面的关系和协调配合，降低运行成本，提高工作效率，包括处理好产地认定与产品认证的衔接，无公害农产品与绿色食品、有机食品的摆布，种植业、畜牧业、渔业三者之间，行政与事业，中央与地方，以及农业系统主体地位与外部门支持推动的关系。要充分发挥各相关方面的力量，共同推进无公害农产品事业发展，加快建立起全国上下、系统内外分工明确、责任具体、协调统一、共同支持的良好工作局面和氛围。

四要规范管理　无公害农产品产地认定产品认证是一项政府推动的公益性事业，具有很强的专业性和技术性。工作是否规范直接关系到政府部门的权威性和公信力。要按照整个工作过程“行有据、查有迹、追有踪”的原则，加强技术标准、检验检测、现场检查、专家评审、证后监督等各个环节的规范和管理，提高整个无公害农产品工作的质量和效率。

五要建立激励机制　无公害农产品工作推动三年多来，系统上下做了大量艰苦扎实的工作，涌现了一批典型和先进，需要及时加以鼓励和激励。部中心计划从2006年开始，每两年以中心名义、每五年提请以农业部名义对在无公害农产品事业推进中涌现出的先进集体和先进个人进行表彰和奖励。

（二）推进产地认定产品认证一体化运行，加快完善工作程序

简化无公害农产品产地认定产品认证程序，实施产地认定与产品认证一体化推进，是各级无公害农产品工作机构和申请人的共同心愿和呼声。这一点，在部中心为筹备开好这次会议召开的三个层面的座谈会上，各级工作机构、农业部门以及企业的意见都非常集中，说明大家都想到一块了。如何解决好产地认定和产品认证脱节问题，部中心也做了一些调研和试点，也有了一些基本的考虑。初步想法是，在遵循现有基本制度框架的前提下，对现有的业务分工、工作流程及有关要求作适当的调整，通过试点探索规律，逐步推行无公害农产品产地认定产品认证一体化运作，从根本上解决产地认定与产品认证脱节的问题。具体来说，从操作层面主要有以下五个方面的调整：一是将产地认定与产品认证在程序上合二为一，即申请人向县级工作机构提交一次申请，即可完成产地认定和产品认证申请，不需要重复申请；二是将产地认定与产品认证申报材料合为一套，各有侧重，一套申报材料满足两个方面的认定认证需要；三是将产地认定和产品认证审查合并进行，整个认定认证过程中需要现场检查和技术审查的，同步安排，技术审查和现场检查的结果在产地认定和产品认证审批发证时共享；四是改单品种独立申报为同一产地、同一申请人多品种一次性申报，一个申请书和一套附报材料覆盖全部产品，减轻申请人和各级工作机构的工作量、申报成本、审查成本；五是打破申请人资格条件的人为限制，鉴于国情和农情，从有利于推动工作和农产品质量安全管理的角度出发，凡是具有一定组织能力和责任追溯能力的单位和个人，都可以作为无公害农产品产地认定和产品认证申报的主体，包括部分地方基层政府及其所属的各种产销联合体、协会等服务农民和拓展农产品市场的服务组织。

通过调整，可以从操作层面弥补现有制度的缺陷和不足，有效解决产地认定与产品认证脱节问题，避免重复，提高有效性和时效性，充分发挥省地县三级农业部门的技术优势和工作积极性。在工作调研中部分同志也提出了一些担心，比如产地认定和与产品认证申请主体不一问题，产地认定与产品认证受理机构不同等。对此做了一些分析，在申请主体方面，产地认定与产品认证申请主体的重合度是比较高的，其中畜牧业达到90%以上。在工作机构方面，目前全国68个无公害农产品省级工作机构中，有61个工作机构既承担产地认定又承担产品认证工作。从申请主体和工作机制看，产地认定产品认证一体化的条件是成熟的，也是非常有利的。对现实工作中存在的一些不一致问题，各地要结合实际情况，大胆创新，整合力量，逐步克服、解决体制和技术上的障碍。

（三）改革完善标志管理，全力打造公共品牌

无公害农产品认证要发挥市场准入和引导消费的作用，必须要打造公共品牌形象，要通过树立品牌促进消费，引导消费，方便市场准入，促进优质优价。无公害农产品品牌的打造，最主要的还是要依托宣传和推广标志来实现。但目前无公害农产品标志的知名度还远远不够，在公众消费和市场准入过程中的作用远远没有发挥。下一步，要以标志宣传推广和标志管理改革为重点，努力打造无公害农产品公共品牌。

1. *加大标志宣传推广力度* 各级工作机构要充分利用《农产品质量安全法》出台的大好时机，强化对无公害农产品标志的普及宣传；要充分利用报纸、杂志、互联网等媒体，加强无公害农产品标志宣传；要结合金农工程、农产品营销等财政专项以及农交会、绿博会等公共平台，加大无公害农产品的推介，提升无公害农产品品牌形象。

2. *改革创新标志使用方式* 标志是无公害农产品的身份证明，推广标志是无公害农产品认证工作的重要组成部分，也是打造无公害农产品品牌的关键。标志推广工作的好坏直接关系品牌打造的成败，也关系到社会认知程度。对此，各级无公害农产品工作机构要高度重视标志推广工作，将其作为工作重点。2006年部中心也将采取两项改革措施推进标志推广工作，一是启动无公害农产品标志推广试点工作，2006年3月份已经对12个省份的试点工作做了部署，总的想法是要充分利用现有的一切资源和手段，调动企业用标的积极性，力争通过试点使标志推广在发展基础较好的省份有所突破；二是改革标志使用方式，改变原来单一加贴标志方式，试点探索标志加贴与标志图案统一标准印刷相结合的模式。对于标志推广工作成绩突出的省级工作机构中心将给予适当的工作补助经费，要采取多种措施千方百计推动标志使用，提高标志的加贴率和知名度。关于标志印制问题，因涉及到制度层面的调整，农业部市场与经济信息司和国家认监委也很关注，希望能够得到更多的支持，以扭转现在标志加贴率低、认证难以发挥作用的被动局面。

（四）加强监督管理，提高认证质量和水平

南京全国工作会议上明确提出要正确处理好加快发展与强化监督的关系。当前，加快发展、扩大总量规模是无公害农产品的工作重点，监督管理也必须及时跟进。只有监管工作到位了，才能保证认证工作及其结果的质量，才能树立品牌的公信力，才能推动事业更健康快速地发展。某省无公害猪肉和绿色食品蔬菜事件的一个主要原因就是证后监管没跟上，出了问题。对这一点，整个系统的认识高度一致，要引以为鉴。在监督管理方面，要着重加强三个方面的检查：

1. 加强获证产地产品跟踪检验　各级工作机构要按照《无公害农产品管理办法》要求，加强对获证产地产品的监督检查，督促获证企业和基地严格按照无公害农产品生产技术规范组织生产，确保获证产品符合无公害农产品标准要求。

2. 加强标识标志使用监督检查　要严格按照《无公害农产品标志管理办法》，加强对无公害农产品标志使用情况的检查，特别要加大对上市产品标志使用的监督检查，确保无公害农产品标志正确规范使用，防止假冒无公害农产品标志的违法行为，保护获证企业和消费者的合法权益，维护无公害农产品标志的权威性。

3. 加强产地产品现场检查　现场检查是无公害农产品产地认定与产品认证的关键环节。产地认定的重点是要加强生产过程的监督检查，包括产地环境、农业投入品、生产过程的检查。产品认证要在产地认定的基础上，突出生产过程控制有效性的监督抽查。原则上，产地认定应当全部实施现场检查，产品认证的现场抽查（核查、督查）也应当落实到位，确保产地认定和产品认证的工作质量。

三、关于推进 2006 年工作的几点意见

2006 年是“十一五”的开局之年，也是全面推进社会主义新农村建设的第一年。农业部启动实施了“三大战略、九大行动”。各地按照农业部关于农产品质量安全工作的总体部署，紧紧围绕“农产品质量安全绿色行动”，积极制定好“十一五”期间本地区、本行业无公害农产品发展规划，开创性地做好 2006 年的各项工作。关于 2006 年无公害农产品工作，年初印发了工作要点，对全年的工作进行了部署。希望结合各地的实际，认真贯彻落实。在这里，再着重强调五个方面：

（一）加快产地认定和产品认证，确保全年工作目标的实现

产地认定，要继续围绕优势农产品产业带建设以及各类农产品生产基地和示范区建设，特别是要围绕农产品标准化示范县的创建，加快产地认定进程，有条件的地方要继续坚持产地认定整体推进的有益经验和做法，迅速扩大产地规模。力争全年新认定无公害农产品产地 7 000 个，种植业产地 5 000 个，畜牧业产地 1 000 个，渔业产地 1 000 个，产地认定面积累计达到全国生产面积 18%左右。

产品认证，要进一步发挥龙头企业、合作经济组织、行业协会以及各类技术服务机构的组织带动和示范作用，重点抓好优势产业带、优粮工程和已认定基地的产品申报，以具备市场竞争优势的园艺、畜禽、水产品等劳动密集型产品为主导，积极扩大认证规模，推动农业结构调整深化和农产品品牌创建，促进农业增效、农民增收、农产品市场竞争力增强。力争全年完成无公害农产品认证 5 000 个，其中种植业产品 3 500 个，畜牧业产品 750 个，渔业产品 750 个。

复查换证，要充分借鉴地方认证向全国统一认证转换工作的经验，以省为单位统一部署、统一组织、统一安排，实行分期分批集中换证，尽可能简化手续，提高效率，减轻获证单位负担。对于到期产地和产品，要提前做好预警，及时跟进服务。要根据无公害农产品产地认定和产品认证复查换证技术规范要求，把握好审查和检查重点，确保到期产地和产品的复查换证率。

（二）要建立资质考核认可制度，推进工作体系能力建设

加强整个工作系统能力建设是无公害农产品事业加快发展的基础，也是整个系统今后一个时期的重要任务。2006 年部中心制定《无公害农产品工作机构管理办法》，明确各级工作机构的职责范围、工作任务、考核内容、考核方式，启动业绩和能力考核制度，推动体系队伍能力建设。对工作机构的资质认可，重点是拟定工作机构的资质条件，包括机构的职能、编制、人员及工作条件等方面。通过验收考核，推动各级政府和农业部门加快建立健全无公害农产品工作机构。

（三）要改革创新标志管理，提升标志知名度

2006 年，标志管理改革是无公害农产品工作的一个重点。问题的关键是要从制度和技术两个层面入手推动标志管理改革，方便标志使用，提高标志使用率。在总结试点经验的基础上，完善《无公害农产品包装物标志印刷管理办法》和相应的技术规范，明确包装物印刷标志图案要求，推行标志加贴与标志图案印刷相结合的模式。积极开发研制形式多样符合无公害农产品特点的标志加贴、印制方式，包括启用锁扣标志和长条标志，增加标识内容，在标志外围增加发证机关全称、证书编号以及防伪查询信息，提高标志的权威性。在中国农产品质量安全网上开辟申领无公害农产品标志专栏，为获证单位提供多种选择，使标志申领工作更加方便快捷。

（四）要积极推进产地认定与产品认证一体化试点

推进无公害农产品产地认定与产品认证一体化进

程已经势在必行，各省级工作机构要高度重视，积极谋划。2006年部中心将在黑龙江试点的基础上，研究制定推进产地认定与产品认证一体化实施意见，扩大试点范围。各省、自治区、直辖市也可以结合当地的实际情况，在本地区、本行业范围内试点。试点工作要把握三个基本原则，一是要遵循现有的基本制度框架，对现行的基本制度不作大的调整；二是要确保产地认定和产品认证质量，关键环节不能省略；三是要实现信息资源充分共享，对于产地认定和产品认证共同需要的信息，要尽量简化申报材料，合并审查程序。

（五）要加大宣传，积极培育消费市场

无公害农产品认证的目的是服务生产者和消费者，让申请者的产品更方便地进入市场，让消费者买得明白，吃得放心。无公害农产品工作在做好认证的同时，要借助市场准入机制完善的大环境抓好市场培育工作，充分发挥市场机制作用，实现无公害农产品的市场价值。要积极探索在农产品大型批发市场建立形象统一、标识醒目的无公害农产品专销区，积极推动无公害农产品进超市，支持无公害农产品生产基地与各类农产品销售市场建立产销合作机制，促进无公害农产品市场贸易和品牌增值。

总之，发展无公害农产品，是建设现代农业的重要内容，是社会主义新农村建设的重要方面，是一项服务农民、惠及百姓的德政工程。各级无公害农产品工作机构，要从农业和农村经济发展的大局出发，积极转变工作思路，努力改进工作方式，大力推进无公害农产品加快发展，不断提高工作质量和效率，以实际行动参与和推进农业部“三大战略、九大行动”的实施，不断提高我国农产品质量安全水平，为推进社会主义新农村建设和实现小康社会的宏伟目标做出积极的贡献。

（本文为作者于2006年4月在全国无公害农产品工作座谈会上的讲话）

食品工业承前启后 继续保持良好快速发展态势

中国食品工业协会会长　王文哲

2005年，全国规模以上食品企业累计完成工业总产值20 344.83亿元，占全国工业份额的8.15%，比上年同期增长26.85%；食品企业完成工业增加值6 299.95亿元，比上年同期增长18.08%，增速高出全国工业平均水平1.64个百分点，占全国工业经济份额的9.48%。同时，全行业完成销售收入19 899.94亿元，比上年增长26.78%，产品销售率98.55%，产销衔接良好；全行业实现利税总额3 365.26亿元，占全国工业的13.29%，其中实现利润1 234.68亿元，比上年同期增长三成。食品工业继续发挥国民经济支柱产业的重要作用，顺利完成了“十五”计划的预期目标，为实现“十一五”规划的良好开局奠定了基础。

一、2005年食品工业总体回顾

（一）市场繁荣，供需平衡，主要食品产销量快速提高

2005年，全国食品工业销售产值20 049.71亿元，同比增长27.30%；完成产品销售收入19 899.94亿元，同比增长26.78%。2005年食品市场特征表现在：一是消费者对安全、营养、优质名牌食品的认可程度和需求量显著提高；二是与日常生活密切相关的粮、油、肉、蛋、乳等基础食品，销售数量大增；三是时尚、假日食品（如糖果巧克力、葡萄酒、白酒、咖啡）消费需求增加；四是食品消费价格呈略有增长。由于人民生活水平不断提高，方便、快捷、营养、健康食品产量大幅度提高，速冻食品、液体乳、果汁及果汁饮料，市场销售表现突出；与人民生活密切相关的日常消费食品（如鲜冻肉、大米、面粉等产品）销售有显著增长；受时尚消费、假日经济（包括婚庆等）的拉动，糖果、葡萄酒等产品品种增加，产量提高。受国家宏观调控影响，卷烟产量增长幅度不高，比上年同期增长4个百分点，机制糖产量比上年下降12.60%。2005年我国主要食品产量见表1。

表 1 2005 年我国主要食品产量情况 单位：万 t、万 kl

名 称	产 量	同比增长（%）	名 称	产 量	同比增长（%）
速冻米面食品	130.67	40.22	方便面	327.92	20.52
鲜冷藏冻肉	688.90	36.29	碳酸饮料	771.94	19.17
发酵酒精	368.13	35.65	酱油	198.72	18.42
大米	1 766.24	33.42	糕点	42.95	18.26
小麦粉	3 992.29	31.89	味精	135.97	17.93
液体乳	1 145.79	29.37	食用植物油	1 612.21	17.74
果汁及果汁饮料	634.56	29.17	原盐	4 454.73	16.35
乳制品	1 310.42	27.97	罐头	360.06	16.27
冷冻饮品	144.57	25.71	白酒	349.37	15.04
葡萄酒	43.44	25.42	糖果	78.93	12.91
软饮料	3 380.42	24.08	饮料酒	3 565.81	11.00
瓶（罐）装饮用水	1 386.28	23.75	啤酒	3 061.55	10.35
饼干	136.75	23.68	卷烟（亿支）	19 560.12	4.40
精制茶	52.41	21.09	成品糖	903.99	−12.60

注：①按产量增长幅度排序。

②乳制品产量包括液体乳，软饮料产量包括果汁及果汁饮料、瓶（罐）装饮用水。

（二）食品工业经济效益有效改善

2005 年，食品工业总体经营水平进一步优化和改善，全行业总资产贡献率、产品销售利润率和资本保值增值率，分别比上年同期提高 1.47%、0.38% 和 1.30%；食品工业人均利税为 7.43 万元，比上年增加 0.84 万元，人均工业总产值 44.90 万元，比上年增加 6.69 万元。食品行业面对原辅材料和交通能源价格上涨，禽流感疫情等多方不利影响，通过企业内部挖潜和提高劳动生产率，加强销售网络建设、建立科学合理的物流和分销体系，以及发展连锁经营和品牌专卖店（场）等方式，减少中间环节，在加工生产管理上注重节约能耗等措施，努力消化了价格上涨造成的不利影响，实现了较好的经济效益水平。

（三）全国分区域食品工业发展概况

2005 年，我国食品工业经济发展的一个明显特点是经济发展的协调性明显增强，各级政府将发展食品产业作为解决“三农”问题、拉动地方经济增长的重要手段。从全国分区域食品工业分布情况分析，东部地区食品工业在优化结构的基础上取得较快发展，东部食品工业产业基础雄厚，基本上代表了全国食品工业生产水平，2005 年继续保持在全国的先进水平。中部地区六省的国土面积仅占我国国土面积的 10%，但为国家提供了 1/3 的粮食、41%的油料、28%的肉类，外出农村劳动力占全国劳动力的 43%。西部地区在国家西部大开发等政策扶持下，积极、有序推进食品工业较快发展，烟草加工业、饮料酒制造业在全国占有重要地位。2005 年，全国完成食品销售收入前 10 个省、直辖市分别是山东、广东、河南、江苏、四川、浙江、河北、上海、云南和辽宁省，这 10 个省、直辖市共实现销售收入 13 468.82 亿元，占全国食品工业比重的 67.68%。

（四）食品工业重点行业发展各具特色

1. 粮食加工行业 近年来我国小麦粉产量持续增长，2005 年比 2001 年增产 1 664.84 万 t，平均年增产 333 万 t。2005 年谷物磨制业生产形势良好，全行业实现工业总产值 1 303 亿元，工业销售收入 1 259 亿元，增速在三成以上。实现利税和利润总额分别比上年增长 71.35%和 72.05%。粮食行业高速发展的主要原因：一是近年来各级政府高度重视农业和农产品发展，对粮食和农业经济在政策、税收和投入上实施各项积极政策，保证了粮食生产连年丰收。二是借助国家对“三农”问题的关注和各地大力发展区域经济对包括粮食企业在内的农产品加工业予以鼓励和扶持的机会，粮食加工企业的产量和效益得到较大提高，米、面等产品的品牌化培育和市场化建设取得显著成效，产品质量和特色更加突出，企业整体生产规模和经营水平得到进一步提高，改变了过去米面加工业规模小、布局分散、装备落后的现象，使国家统计口径内的规模以上企业数量大大增加，因而从统计数据上反映出粮食加工业较为全面的变化情况。

2. 食用植物油加工业 近年来，我国食用油消费量不断增加，但油料供应远远不能满足日益增长的加工需要，对食用植物油供应造成影响。2005 年，我国食用油和油料进口大量增加，食用油进口总额达 31.52 亿美元，保障了生产加工所需原料，满足了生产发展需要和供给增加。2005 年，全行业完成工业总产值 2 107 亿元，实现产品销售收入 2 090 亿元，食用植物油产量 1 612 万 t，同比增长 17.7%。同时，食用油的消费突出了安全、健康概念，人均食用油消费达到 12kg/人年，供需总量不断增加，促进了植物油加工骨干企业生产能力和规模得到较大提高。2005 年，全行业销售额 10 亿元以上的企业达 46 个，年产量 10 万 t 以上的企业 36 个。

3. 肉及肉制品加工业　2005 年，肉类加工行业克服禽流感疫情、原辅材料和运费价格上涨等多重困难，共完成工业总产值 1 061 亿元，同比增长超过三成，生产肉类产品 689 万 t，比上年同期增长 36.3%。实现工业产品销售收入 1 116 亿元，同比增长 34.8%；利税增长超过四成，利润增长 58.6%。我国肉类生产企业日臻成熟，生产集中度水平不断提高，2005 年，肉类企业销售额 100 亿元以上的生产企业有 2 个，销售额在 10 亿元以上的企业 25 个，肉制品行业拥有自主品牌、较高的研发能力和核心竞争力的企业集团发展速度加快，其产品产量和经济效益在全行业占据主导地位。

4. 制糖业　食糖既是人民群众生活必需品，也是食品工业的主要原料，因此制糖业是食品工业的重点行业之一。2005 年，全国共有制糖生产企业 212 个，生产成品糖 903.99 万 t，比上年下降 12.06%。由于产量下滑，需求增加，造成 2005 年食糖价格增幅较大。特别是我国食糖消费总量中，工业消费比重约占总供应量的七成，民用消费约占三成，食糖价格上涨，使糖果、烘焙、饮料等制造业成本压力增大，并带动了淀粉糖浆的价格上扬。由于供需关系原因，近期食糖供应仍然偏紧，工业用食糖价格基本保持在 5 000 元/t 左右。

5. 饮料工业　2005 年，全国累计生产各类软饮料 3 380 万 t，同比增长 24.08%，瓶装饮用水 1 386 万 t，同比增长 23.75%。由于竞争激烈，近年来传统饮料（碳酸饮料和饮用水）价格普遍下降，无论淡旺季，饮料产品打折和卖赠促销活动十分频繁，新产品推出频率加快。茶饮料发展速度迅猛，市场份额不断扩大。2005 年，南方一些知名凉茶品牌迅速崛起，受到消费者追捧。除碳酸饮料和瓶装水依然占据统治地位以外，果汁饮料销量增幅较大，2005 年，共生产果汁及果汁饮料 635 万 t，比上年增长 29.17%，同时含乳（乳酸菌）饮料和富含营养补充剂的配方饮品成为市场的新宠。

6. 饮料酒工业　2005 年是我国饮料酒制造业得到全面发展，取得较好成绩的一年，白酒、啤酒、葡萄酒、黄酒等主要酒种的产量、销售和利税三项经济指标均实现较大幅度增长。

（1）白酒行业　2005 年，全国白酒总产量 349.37 万 kl，同比增长 15.04%，实现了自 20 世纪 90 年代中期以来最大的增长幅度。全国共销售白酒 358.10 万 kl，销售多于生产量，产销率 103.10%，期末库存比年初减少 1.20%。白酒行业生产集中度继续提高，拥有市场知名品牌的白酒骨干企业生产量同比均有所增加，产量较大的 10 个知名企业完成产量 53.29 万 kl，占全行业总产量 15.27%。2005 年，规模以上白酒企业销售收入 722.65 亿元，同比增加 22.34%。实现利税 190.77 亿元，同比增长 20.59%。其中，完成税金 117.57 亿元，同比增加 17.62%；实现利润 73.19 亿元，同比增长 25.69%。2005 年，白酒行业产量和经济效益的同比增长，主要源于企业产品结构的调整和市场消费需求稳定。由于白酒行业税收负担过重，原本生产中低档产品微利或亏损，2005 年企业又受到能源、运输和原辅材料价格上涨的压力，为消化涨价因素和税收影响，企业加大了产品结构调整力度，许多企业新开发了中高档产品投放市场，或加大了原有中高价位产品的营销投入，一些供需旺盛的名优产品出厂价格先后上调了十几至五六十元不等，使白酒骨干企业的销售收入和实现利税出现较大幅度增长。

（2）啤酒行业　2005 年，我国啤酒行业以 3 061 万 kl 的总产量，继续保持世界第一大生产国地位。2005 年，啤酒行业的全球性品牌、全国品牌、区域优势品牌之间竞争激烈，啤酒行业在资本竞争和营销竞争中，逐步向大品牌相对控制和相对垄断市场的趋势发展。同时，啤酒行业的市场细分速度加快，消费需求的多元化和科技创新的有利条件催生了如无醇啤酒、高浓低醇啤酒、果味啤酒、苦瓜啤酒等新口味产品，啤酒的浓度、颜色和口味呈多样性发展。此外，2005 年，城市啤酒市场趋于稳定，餐饮、娱乐、夜店市场销量比重提高，农村市场大幅增长。过去几年，啤酒行业的增长主要集中在城市和家庭的低档酒，为谋求新的增长点，越来越多的企业把目光瞄准了广大农村市场。2005 年，啤酒业还承受了原材料和运费上涨以及啤酒“甲醛”风波的不利影响，使全行业产销量和经济效益保持稳定增长。2005 年，啤酒价格较以前有所稳定，5～6 元/瓶和 10～12 元/瓶的销售量有所增长，面向普通大众的餐饮店和农村市场以 2～2.5 元/瓶的低档产品为主。

（3）葡萄酒行业　我国现有规模以上企业 150 多家，2005 年总产量 43.44 万 kl，同比增长 25.42%。葡萄酒总量不大，但多年来增幅较高，是食品工业各门类中保持连续快速增长水平的行业之一。同时，葡萄酒行业通过加大投入、注重品牌建设和大力提高产品质量，改善产品风格，近年来行业生产集中度逐年提高，如张裕集团和中粮酒业（沙城、昌黎、烟台长城酒厂）2005年产量都达到7万多kl；中法合营王朝葡萄酿酒公司产量达3.5万多kl；山东威龙葡萄酒公司产量达3.4万多kl。这4家企业的销量约占全行业产量的一半，实现经济效益也居行业前列。此外，我国葡萄酒行业的工艺技术和生产设备水平与国际先进水平逐渐接轨，产品质量稳定提高。

7. 乳制品工业　2005年，液体乳和乳制品产量继续保持较快增长，增长幅度分别为29%和28%。但由于竞争激烈，特别是在大、中型城市等鲜奶重点消费地区，乳业巨头价格战更为激烈，造成企业销售成本居高不下，盈利能力没有明显回升。2005年，由于国家出台鲜奶标识强制规定，以及汇率变化和国内企业奶粉生产设备增加等因素，进口奶粉总量比上年大幅下降。2005年，乳品行业规模以上企业销售收入同比增长38%，但由于受城市消费总量限制、产品差异化不易实现和原料不易保存等因素制约，液体乳产品生产企业通过流通渠道和产品价格竞争，争取消费市场，整合行业资源的态势仍将继续，同时，奶粉、配方奶粉和乳制品品种、规格、产量将有所增加，相关进口产品将面临更大的竞争压力。

8. 调味品工业　2005年，我国调味品工业运行平稳，酱油产量增长18%；发酵制品中味精增长17%；其他复合调味料产量也有所增加。近年来，随着人民生活水平的提高，调味品的生产一直呈现较快增长局面，随着生产工艺的不断完善和技术装备的更新，产量大幅提高，产品结构调整成效显著，品种规格更加丰富；骨干企业和名牌产品的扩张加快，调味品行业生产集中度逐年提高，一批大型企业创造的全国知名品牌和区域优势品牌，成为居民和餐饮消费的主导产品，日、韩、香港和东南亚等地进口和合资企业的产品，虽然售价偏高，但由于质量较高和风味突出，其市场占有率和销售量也在稳步提高。

9. 水产品加工业　2005年，全年水产品总产量达5 100万t，渔业经济总产值达7 200亿元，渔业产值4 070亿元，渔民人均收入有所增加，实现了“十五”计划的主要目标。水产品加工能力和水平明显提高，形成了以龙头企业为主体、以优势产品为重点、以出口贸易为导向的水产加工业发展格局。水产品出口达80亿美元，占农产品出口总额的30%，连续六年居我国农产品出口首位，连续4年居世界水产品出口首位。休闲渔业成为发展亮点，年产值达100亿元。远洋渔业产量达135万t，产值105亿元，初步实现了开拓大洋性渔业的战略目标。

10. 糖果制造业　2005年，糖果产量增幅为12.91%，大大低于2003—2004年度增长12%的幅度。增长减少的主要原因是糖果的主要原料砂糖大幅涨价，极大地提高生产成本，很多中小企业出现大幅度亏损，不得不控制生产，甚至有些小型企业被迫在旺季停产，否则即会造成生产越多亏损越大的情况。2005年，糖果企业继续大力调整产品结构的力度，巧克力、软糖、酥糖、奶糖的比例继续上升，分别达9.5%、16.0%、9%和23.5%，中高档产品的比例持续上升。糖果行业的突出问题表现在：由于砂糖涨价幅度过高，整个行业的利润大幅下滑；企业规模两极分化的状况更为突出；产品质量参差不齐，相差悬殊，历次检测中质量较差的产品以小型企业居多，质监部门的监督难度仍然很大；市场竞争进一步加剧，外资品牌继续扩张，其市场份额不断增加。

（五）食品工业固定资产投资活跃

2005年，食品行业全年完成固定资产投资额1 835.54亿元，比上年同期增长51.32%；全行业新增固定资产1 064.46亿元，同比增长59.11%；新增固定资产交付使用率57.99%。从食品工业固定资产投资额的主要来源分析，国家预算内资金占投资额比重0.50%；国内贷款占9.07%；食品行业利用外资占7.90%；企业自筹资金占投资额77.31%。2005年全国食品工业固定资产投资情况见表2。

表2　2005年全国食品工业固定资产投资情况

名　称	已完成固定资产投资额（亿元）	新增固定资产（亿元）	施工项目个数（个）	本年新开工项目（个）	本年完成项目（个）
全国总计	1 835.54	1 064.46	8 229	5 945	3 565
采盐	29.12	14.67	86	70	32
农副食品加工	847.90	504.16	4 120	3 124	1 869
食品制造业	525.67	306.60	2 291	1 610	915
饮料制造业	338.11	192.72	1 472	1 028	642
烟草制品业	94.74	46.31	260	113	107

（六）食品进出口贸易持续增长

2005年，我国食品企业克服重重贸易壁垒，取得食品进出口贸易较大增长的成绩。全年食品进出口总值449.66亿美元，占全国商品进出口总额的3.16%，比上年同期增长13.74%。其中，出口创汇243.80亿美元，同比增长24.84%；进口205.87亿美元，同比增长2.90%。在各类出口食品中，出口量大、换汇额高的主要有以下几类产品：水产品（出口金额71.82亿美元，贸易顺差额42.79亿美元）、肉及肉制品（出口金额24.44亿美元，贸易顺差额17.62亿美元）、水果及制品（出口金额14.44亿美元，贸易顺差额5.77亿美元）、谷物原粮（出口金额14.13亿美元，贸易顺差额0.18亿美元）、软饮料（出口金额9.40亿美元，贸易顺差额8.49亿美元）、罐头等食品等，以上食品出口创汇在亿元以上，除食用油脂外，上述产品对外贸易中出现较高顺差。在各类进口食品中，进口数量大用汇额高的主要有以下几类食品：食用油脂（进口金额31.52亿美元，贸易逆差额29.24亿美元）、水产品、肉及肉制品、乳制品（进口金额4.59亿美元，贸易逆差额3.77亿美元）。其中贸易逆差较高的产品有食用油脂、乳制品等产品。

二、2006年食品工业发展趋势

2006年是国家实施国民经济和社会发展“十一五”总体规划的第一年，也是食品工业“十一五”规划开局之年，我国食品工业面临更为有利的发展环境。首先，食品工业发展受益于良好的宏观经济和产业政策影响，具备快速发展的有利条件。作为化解“三农”问题的重要产业和拉动区域经济发展的支柱产业，随着西部大开发，振兴东北老工业基地和中部崛起政策的实施，在落实党的十六届五中全会精神，构建和谐社会的事业中，食品工业将进一步得到全社会的重视和扶持。其次，随着综合国力不断加强，人们生活水平继续提高，生活方式和消费理念发生深刻转变等诸多因素，食品市场将更为广阔。与人民生活密切相关的米、面、油、肉类及产品、乳及乳制品、禽蛋、水产品和饮料、调味品、方便食品等食物消费需求进一步增加。从回顾“十五”期间我国食品工业各行业发展情况分析，2006年，我国食品工业销售额继续保持20%以上的增长速度，主要食品产量实现15%～30%左右的不同幅度增长，产业集中度继续增加，品牌、质量、风格成为影响购买力的主要因素。2006年，食品工业主要行业呈现各具特色的发展形势：

1. 肉和肉制品供应稳步增长，鲜牛、羊肉消费量增加，质量、卫生、安全成为影响肉和肉制品消费的重要因素。随着禽流感、疯牛病、口蹄疫等全球性疫情得到控制，人们对肉制品消费信心增加，猪、牛、羊和禽类的消费量将逐渐上升；由于生活节奏加快和生活习惯变化，市场对肉制品需求旺盛，肉制品企业采用先进工艺技术和优良设备，加大优质营养高档肉制品生产的能力显著增强，肉制品的品种、花色、质量和风味更为全面和丰富。

2. 乳品工业产品竞争依然剧烈，产品结构的转化、升级步伐加快，乳品企业掀起以资本和市场为纽带的兼并、重组浪潮，挟品牌优势的产业巨头，对占有区域市场和局部奶源优势的中小企业进行整合，“啤酒收购大战”的烽烟，在奶业继续重演。由于液态奶行业竞争加剧致使企业盈利低下乃至亏损，乳粉、酸奶、奶酪和含乳饮料等利润率相对较高的产品受到企业高度重视，产业巨头对牛初乳和婴幼儿配方奶粉等高端产品更为青睐，以价格和服务优势与长期占据我国市场的国际乳业巨头和“洋品牌”争夺市场。

3. 软饮料中的果汁和果粒饮料、营养补充饮料市场份额显著扩大，各类茶饮料市场稳步增加，碳酸饮料和瓶装饮用水市场稳定，饮料工业采用新工艺、新技术、新包装的速度加快，健康、营养、天然、洁净成为引导饮料消费的主题。

4. 饮料酒制造业呈现较为强劲的发展趋势。由于国家决定将白酒从量消费税降低5个百分点，可在一定程度上缓解白酒企业税负过重的压力，使大型骨干企业盈利能力略有增加，对于企业合理调整产品结构，扩大市场优质白酒产品供应总量将有所促进。啤酒业将继续保持稳定增长，啤酒行业技术创新和新产品研发步伐加快，品种将更加丰富，纯生啤酒、无醇啤酒、鲜酿啤酒、黑色啤酒、果蔬味啤酒等特色产品比重加大，消费选择更加丰富，罐装啤酒比例下降，普通啤酒的价格竞争依然激烈，平均吨酒利润增幅不大，企业继续重视规模效益化的发展方式。葡萄酒和黄酒仍呈现较快增长，产品产量保持20%以上的增幅，庄园酒、酒龄酒继续作为中、高档葡萄酒的热点，受到企业和消费者的追捧，葡萄酒行业继续保持较好的盈利水平。黄酒总产量和生产集中度继续提高，消费区域逐渐扩大，黄酒企业对传统营销模式的创新，对开发黄酒消费市场和塑造品牌形象，发挥越来越积极的重要作用。

5. 受消费理念日益成熟和消费水平不断提高的影响，调味品系列化和高档化趋势明显，调味品企业质量改进和品牌建设意识空前高涨，产品包装和宣传推广的专业化、精细化程度会有很大提高。调味品企业正在改变传统作坊式、分散式的陈旧生产模式，企业集团化、规模化发展迅速，管理模式和营销手段也更加科学、规范。产品结构的调整和完善，不仅使居民日常消费质量显著提高，也使餐饮行业、食品企业的原料供应更为丰富，对提高和改善方便食品、肉制品、休闲食品、罐头、速冻调理食品的质量风格，促进产品的升级换代提供很大的帮助。

6. 糖制品、糕点、饼干等烘焙食品、方便食品、休闲食品的机遇与挑战并存。由于食糖价格高涨，以食糖为原料的食品企业在工艺技术上着力转化以淀粉糖替代食糖，以减轻成本压力，淀粉糖生产企业面临有利发展时机，同时，对促进玉米等农产品的加工转化极为有利。糕点、饼干、方便食品等产量呈强劲增长态势，企业工艺技术进步和技术装备的改革提高速度加快，产品品种日益丰富，市场细分化趋势明显；企业适应市场的能力进一步增强，根据市场导向和消费需求的变化，不断推陈出新，调整产品的市场定位和营销策略，产品呈系列化、多样化方向发展。糖果产量预计有小幅增长，中高档产品比率继续提高，特别是巧克力仍会大幅增加，由于市场准入制度的实施，生产企业总数有所减少，致使生产更趋集中。

7. 随着人民生活水平的提高，水产品需求总量继续扩大，2006 年我国水产品价格仍处于走强趋势，但增长幅度不会高于上年。水产加工业中远洋海产品需求量增幅略大于淡水养殖类，水产品精细加工产品产量增加，质量提高，在扩大出口和满足内需两个方面，都将呈现良好发展态势。

我国肉类工业的经济运行状况与发展特点

中国肉类协会

2005 年，肉类食品业（涵指肉类禽蛋）经历了几波安全性撞击，如 6～8 月的猪链球菌感染、10 月末的禽高致病流感，这些接踵而来的突发性撞击给全行业或局部地域无论在生产上、加工上还是在市场上都形成了较大振荡，价格一直低迷，市场供需难以预测，给企业运行带来许多困难，对社会效益和经济效益都带来一定的影响和损失。但由于企业成熟度不断提高，集约化程度快速成长，因而，2005 年行业在推进中仍然稳步发展，企业取得了良好运作和成绩。表现出三增长态势：一是肉类产业对社会仍具吸引力、投资量增加；二是市场继续扩容，销售量增加；三是企业运作趋向平稳，经济效益增加。这一成绩的取得为新的一年发展，为“十一五”开局创造了一个良好的基础和开端。

一、生产规模与区域布局

据资料显示，2005 年全国国有及规模以上肉类食品加工企业（包括肉类罐头制造）为 2 544 个，其中畜禽屠宰加工为 1 476 个、肉制品加工 990 个、肉类罐头制造 78 个。企业总数比上年增加 312 个，其中屠宰增加 359 个，制品加工减缩 48 个，罐头制造增加 1 个。2005 年，工业资产总额达到 1 174.58 亿元，比上年增加 160.1 亿元，增长 15.78％。其中畜禽屠宰加工形成资产额为 557.41 亿元，增加 149.28 亿元，增长 36.58％；肉制品及副产品加工资产额为 586.49 亿元，增加 26.2 亿元，增长 4.68％；肉类罐头制造资产额 30.68 亿元，减少 15.33 亿元，负增长 33.32％。数据表明，畜禽屠宰加工对社会保持了强劲吸引力。近年来，其投资量呈现出较大幅度增长，而肉制品加工投资量有些放慢，甚至一些中小企业被兼并或转产。

在肉类工业投资形成资产量的分布上，明显地形成了梯次。第一梯次即前 10 位的地域有山东、河南、内蒙古、辽宁、四川、吉林、江苏、黑龙江、河北、北京等，工业资产总额达到 914.26 亿元，占全国规模以上企业总额 80％，比上年提高 1 个百分点。其中山东、河南两地突显出工业集约性力量，其资产量占第一梯次的 52.7％，占到全国规模以上企业总额的 42％。2001—2005 年的 5 年来，肉类工业资产总额由 2000 年的 624.88 亿元增加到 1 143.9 亿元，增加 519.02 亿元，增长 83.06％。

二、主要经济指标

2005 年，肉类加工业销售总收入达到 2 289.73 亿元，比上年增加 633.15 亿元，增长 38.22％。其中畜禽屠宰加工肉销售为 1 139.63 亿元，增加 395.09 亿元，增长 53.06％；肉制品及副产品加工销售为 1 115.92亿元，增加 239.88 亿元，增长 27.38％；肉禽类罐头制造销售为34.17亿元，减少1.82亿元，负增长5.06%。数据表明，畜禽屠宰加工生鲜肉销售收入量和增长幅度均明显大于和快于肉制品销售量增加和幅度增长。在全国行业中，肉类工业销售收入也同样形成明显的地域梯次。第一梯次的地域是山东、河南、四川、辽宁、内蒙古、江苏、河北、吉林、黑龙江、北京等10个省、自治区、直辖市，其销售总收入达到1 911.59亿元，占全国规模以上企业销售总额的85%，比上年提高2个百分点。其中山东、河南、四川、辽宁4省销售收入最为突出，其销售量占第一梯次的73.8%，占全国总销售量的62.55%。2001—2005年5年来，肉类工业销售总额由2000年的733.43亿元增加到2 255.55亿元，增加1 522.12亿元，增长207.5%。

2005年，肉类工业规模以上企业实现利润总额79.41亿元，比上年增加29.93亿元，增长60.48%。其中畜禽屠宰加工实现利润为30.8亿元，增加14.15亿元，增长85.01%；肉类制品及副产品加工实现利润为47.57亿元，增加15.55亿元，增长48.53%；肉禽类罐头制造实现利润为1.04亿元，增加0.23亿元，增长29.2%。在全行业实现利润中，畜禽屠宰加工利润虽比肉制品加工利润的绝对增量少一些，但是其增长幅度明显升高。全行业中地域的企业效益水平出现明显差异，排在第一梯次即前10位的省、自治区有山东、河南、内蒙古、四川、河北、辽宁、江苏、黑龙江、浙江、吉林，实现利润为70.27亿元，占全国肉类工业规模以上企业总利润90%。其中山东、河南、内蒙古三地实现利润占第一梯次的77.2%，占全国肉类工业总利润的69.22%。2001—2005年5年来，全国肉类工业规模以上企业实现利润由2000年的17.99亿元增加到79.41亿元，增加61.42亿元，增长341.4%。

三、发展特点

2005年，全国肉类加工业发展能有这样好的态势，其中有几点值得总结。

1. “三农”问题成为国家农业产业政策倾斜的重点，农牧业结构调整力度加大，畜禽业发展成为调整的重要支点　2005年，虽然畜禽业受到动物疫病冲击，但是由于政府高度重视和支持，增强了农牧养殖业的信心，据资料显示，2005年全国肉类总产量达到7 743万t，比上年增加498万t，增长6.9%。其中猪肉为5 010万t，增加309万t，增长6.6%；牛肉为711万t，增加35.6万t，增长5.3%；羊肉435万t，增加36万t，增长9.1%；禽肉1 464万t，增加112.8万t，增长8.3%。禽蛋产量2 879万t，增加155.8万t，增长5.7%。畜牧业的发展，肉类资源稳定扩大，给肉类加工业发展提供了原料基础和可支配货源，给肉类市场提供了可支配的商品量。

2. 粮食增产为畜禽产业发展提供了物质保障，粮食生产与畜禽生产发展呈现在同步而平稳的良性循环中　2005年，我国粮食产量达到48 400万t，比上年增产3.1%。畜禽肉类蛋品增加值初步核算约为10 000亿元，占国内生产总值的5.5%，占第一产业增加值的44%。

3. 畜禽产业带逐步形成，区域化管理加强，产业形成相应联动　从肉类产业区域经济看，已逐步形成以长江中下游为中心向南北两翼扩散的生猪生产带；以中原和东北为主的肉牛生产带；以西北牧区和中原及西南为主的肉羊生产带；以东部省份为主的禽肉和以中原省份为主的禽蛋生产带；以东北、华北及京津沪等为主的奶业生产带。肉类工业生产随着畜禽生产集约及市场拓展而调整组合，形成了有机联动，产生了社会和经济效应。上述山东、河南、内蒙古、四川及东北等地肉类工业的资产、销售及效益的增加值迅速扩大，既拉动了地域畜禽产业发展，又带动了全国肉类工业的全面提升。

4. 肉类结构随着市场需求在发展中调整　2005年，我国肉类结构处于稳步调整。猪肉、禽肉、牛肉、羊肉、杂畜肉的比重依次为65∶19∶9∶5∶2，这一结构总体上符合我国国情，即在发展进程中适应形成的消费习惯、民族性特点和动物生物体生长周期以及市场变化。特别值得一提的是我国猪肉由过去占肉类总量85%以上比重调整到现在占65%，既保障了肉类市场总需求的平衡，又保障了肉类结构在调整中的替代。我国的肉类结构与世界肉类结构的变化过程基本是符合的，世界肉类结构比重中，猪肉、禽肉、牛肉、羊肉、杂畜肉分别为40∶30∶24∶5∶1。所以，我国在肉类发展中依然坚持了猪肉业稳定发展，禽业积极发展，牛羊业加快发展的原则，推进肉类品种合理结构。

2005年，我国肉类人均占有量达到59.2kg，其中猪肉38.3kg、禽肉11.2kg、牛肉5.4kg、羊肉3.3kg；鲜蛋22kg，分别比上年增加3.5kg、2.1kg、0.8kg、0.2kg、0.2kg和1kg。与2000年相比，肉类人均占有量增加10.9kg，其中猪肉、禽肉、牛肉、羊肉及鲜蛋分别增加6.5kg、1.7kg、1.2kg、1.1kg和4.5kg。

5. 肉类工业企业的集约化、规模化、现代化水平稳步提高　从2005年对肉类行业评估的50强企业就彰显了这一现象，2002年的50强规模企业销售额截档为10 000万元，2005年截档线达到40 000万元，提高3倍。50强企业仅占全行业规模以上企业的3%，资产总额占到71%，销售总额占到69%，创造利润占90%。强势企业规模化突出，有力地推进了行业集约化、现代化水平的提高。2005年，规模以上企业畜禽屠宰和肉类加工产能比由上年1∶1.67提高到1∶1.98，增长18.6%，其中畜禽屠宰产能比由上年1∶1.82提高到1∶2.04，增长12%；肉制品加工产能比由上年1∶1.56提高到1∶1.90，增长21.7%；肉禽罐头制造产能比由上年1∶0.78提高到1∶1.11，增长42.3%。随着产能比的提高，企业竞争力和经济效益明显提升，企业走向良性循环。2005年，肉类行业规模以上企业综合利润率仍低于全国工业规模以上企业平均5.9%的利润率，整体行业还处于低利运行中，属低利产业，但是其利润率达到历史最高水平，由上年的3%提高到3.47%，增长15.7%，其中屠宰加工利润率由上年的2.23%提高到2.7%，增长21.1%；肉制品及副产品加工利润率由上年的3.65%提高4.26%，增长16.7%。肉类罐头制造利润率由上年的2.22%提高到3.73%，增长68%。

6. *产品结构随着市场需求在同步调整* 2005年，肉类制品及副产品加工产量达到850万t，比上年增加150万t，增长21.4%，其中中西式制品结构约为45∶55，西式技术制作制品中，高温制品约占到20%，低温制品约占35%，中式制品数量在技术的改进中不断提升。从2001—2005年的5年中，肉制品产量比2000年增加500万t，增长142.8%。肉制品加工量占我国肉类总产量的比重由2000年的5.7%上升到2005年的11%。

7. *品牌战略成为提升企业形象的有力杠杆，成为推动地域经济的支持力量* 2005年止，肉类行业共获得中国名牌产品28个24家企业。如高温制品（高温火腿肠）有：河南双汇、山东金锣、江苏雨润、河南邦杰、四川美好、吉林德大（以上为2002年初评，2005年复评）、河南汇通（2005年初评）。低温肉制品有：河南双汇、河南众品、山东金锣、江苏雨润、湖南唐人神、山东德利斯、烟台喜旺（以上为2004年初评）。速冻调理禽肉熟制品有：山东诸城尽美、秦皇岛正大、山东凤祥、河南华英、吉林德大、大连大成、河南大用、河南永达、青岛九联、北京双大、山东新昌、北京华都（以上为2005年初评）。肉类罐头制造有：上海梅林、厦门古龙（以上为2005年初评）。2005年止，获肉类蛋品中国驰名商标品牌15个：河南“双汇”、山东“得利斯”、内蒙古“草原兴发”、山东“龙大”、内蒙古“塞飞亚”、湖南“唐人神”、大连“喀咯嗒”、内蒙古“小肥羊”、山东“金锣”、四川“高金”、黑龙江“希波”、山西“冠云”、内蒙古“科尔沁”、厦门“古龙”、中国“中粮”。2005年，获国家产品质量免检的肉类食品企业为：河南双汇、河南邦杰、吉林德大、江苏旺润、山东金锣、四川美好、山东江泉、河南汇通。在食品安全质量凸现的今天，品牌战略昭示了企业技术水平和素质水平的提升，是企业持续发展和科学发展结合的体现，在推动地方经济和规范市场中起到了良好的效应。

8. *努力构筑合作交流平台，使企业更加透明、开放* 到2005年，肉类食品行业与世界肉类组织联合成功的连续举办了三届高层技术的、管理的及安全的多元研讨会和中国国际肉类工业展览会，在把中国的肉类企业及其产品推向世界同行，推向国内外公众的同时，吸引了众多国家对我国肉类发展和市场潜在的极大关注，来华考察、合作交流、贸易洽谈明显增多，美国、澳大利亚、加拿大、德国、法国、新西兰、爱尔兰等都派出大型代表团来华参观考察、交流研讨。由于影响的扩大，使我国成功地争取到2006年国际天然肠衣大会在中国北京举办，申请到2007年世界肉类科技大会在中国北京举办和世界猪肉大会在中国南京举办。

我国造纸工业的发展与“十一五”展望

中国造纸学会顾问 胡宗渊

造纸工业是一个与国民经济发展和社会文明建设息息相关的重要产业。目前，国家已将我国造纸工业确定为国民经济重要的基础原材料工业。纸和纸板消费量的增长速度与国内生产总值的增长度同步。它与国民经济的林业、农业、机械制造、化工、热电动力以及交通运输等相关部门和行业的关联大，同时它又是为新闻、出版、印刷和商业等部门服务的。是作为衡量一个国家现代化水平和文明程度的重要标志之一，在加工制造业生产能力普遍过剩的现阶段，造纸工业是属典型的需求拉动型行业。因此，造纸工业是一个“永不衰竭”的朝阳工业。

一、我国造纸工业取得的成就

回眸“十五”，我国造纸工业高速发展。“十五”计划的发展目标，可以说是进行很顺利。归纳起来有以下几方面的成就：

1. *全国纸和纸板的生产量已居世界第二位，年消费量也居世界第二位，举世瞩目* 2005 年，我国纸和纸板的生产量约 5 500 万 t，远远超过“十五”计划预测的 3 920 万 t。2005 年，我国消费量已达到 6 000万 t，超过原计划预测的 5 000 万 t。由于国内纸张产量增加，这两年进口纸张数量在减少。

2. *我国造纸工业在原料结构调整方面，有了很大变化* 在原计划中希望提高木浆纤维和废纸的比重。在实际生产中，造纸企业为提高纸张产品档次和减少污染，木浆用量大量增加，但因国内木浆供应不足，近几年我国就进口大量的商品木浆，同时，废纸浆用量的增长速度最惊人，2005 年，废纸用量达到 3 624万 t，利用率在 60%以上，大大超过原计划的 45%，因此非木纤维的比重相对地在降低。

3. *我国造纸企业结构调整也有较大变化* 造纸企业总数已由“十五”初期的 5 000 多个，减少为 3 500个左右，这主要是为减少造纸给环境所造成的严重污染，各地许多小草浆造纸厂纷纷关停。同时，企业生产规模开始向大型化发展，大型企业向集团化发展。

4. *我国造纸企业的现代化水平有很大的提高* 实现了“十五”计划中要求“推进重点企业实现大型化和生产现代化”的发展目标。近年来新建和改建的一大批造纸企业先后从国外引进先进的装备和技术，大大提高了我国纸张产品的质量和档次。有些企业如山东华泰纸业集团最近引进的新闻纸机和海南金海浆厂的整套技术和装备，不仅是当今世界第一流的水平，而且在生产规模上也是世界上最大的。这些企业不仅设备先进，而且管理水平也很高，因此，纸张产品不仅替代了进口，满足了国内市场的需求，每年还不断增加向国外的出口量。

5. *产品质量大幅度提高，出口产品数量增加* 近年来，由于我国造纸企业的纸张产品质量大幅度提高，出口产品数量逐年增加，现在纸张出口趋势正在明显增长。可是，出口数量还很少，2004 年总出口量仅有 125 万 t，占全国纸张总产量的 2.5%。

6. *我国造纸工业国际化、集中化、专业化的格局初步形成* 在设备现代化程度上，近年来，国内许多造纸企业引进了数量很多的国外技术装备，同时，由于我国造纸原料短缺，每年又在不断从国外购进商品木浆和废纸，也还有些企业在向国外出口纸张，因此，国内许多大的造纸企业已经完全与国际接轨。这都是我国造纸工业国际化的趋势。我国造纸产业集聚度越来越高，基本上形成了三大块：珠江三角洲，主要是以生产包装纸为主；长江三角洲，主要是外企为主，主要生产高档纸张，如铜版纸和高档文化用纸；环渤海集群的核心地带——山东半岛，现在是纸张产量最高的区域，主要生产各种品种纸张。这三大区域是我国纸张集中生产地。另外，随着纸张的不断整合，我国造纸企业专业化的趋势越来越明显。几个大的造纸企业都有各自的拳头产品。金东纸业的高档铜版纸，山东华泰纸业的新闻纸，晨鸣集团的铜版纸、文化用纸有很强的竞争力，宁波中华纸业、山东的太阳、博汇纸业和广东东莞的玖龙、理文纸业的板纸和卡纸都很有名。造纸企业都在向生产名牌专业产品而努力。

7. *造纸业开放的力度进一步加大* 面对中国造纸业巨大的发展空间，在我国修订的《外商投资产业指导目录》中，放开了除钞票纸和邮票纸等少数品种的纸业领域以后，世界纸业巨头加快了在中国的投资步伐，他们投资项目都集中在高档纸品领域。同时，在国内市场激烈的竞争中，许多国内纸业巨头和国外纸业巨头都有合作要求，而在进行“强强联合”。

8. *污染治理初见成效* 我国造纸工业对生态环境造成的破坏情况有很大改善，污染情况有所减轻，我国造纸行业污染防治工作已初见成效，环境污染问题初步得到缓解。全国各地原有大批给环境造成严重污染的小草浆厂纷纷关停，而近年来新建和改建的一大批现代化制浆造纸工厂，技术装备新，建有完善的治污措施，走循环经济道路，实施清洁生产，废水及排放 COD 指标都大大低于国家标准。

9. *技术装备水平明显提高* 近年来，我国造纸设备的制造业也在迅速崛起，已形成了具有相当规模和技术水平的专业设备制造体系。“十五”期间，国家为支持造纸设备制造业的发展，使用国债贷款引进国外先进造纸设备的制造技术，极大地推进了我国造纸设备的国产化进程。先后和国外几个著名的造纸设备制造厂家签订了包括废纸处理、双盘磨浆机、浆料流送系统、水力流浆箱、可控中高辊、机内涂布机、软压光机、复卷机和切纸机等项技术转让合同，这些关键设备的制造技术都是我国造纸企业的急需，因此，由于这些技术的引进，不仅对我国造纸设备企业的技术进步起了很大作用，而且也大大推动了我国造纸工业的飞跃发展。

10. 我国造纸科学技术研究工作也取得很大成绩 “十五”期间，我国的大专院校、科研单位和许多造纸企业的科技工作人员，发挥了自己的聪明智慧，在造纸、制浆的各个领域都研究开发出许多很有价值的科研成果，使我国造纸企业在生产上的应用取得了很好的成效。

二、我国造纸工业存在的问题

在“十五”期间，我国的造纸工业虽然取得了不小的成绩，但是也还应清醒地看到，在前进的道路上还有不少的困难、问题和矛盾。其中比较突出的是：

1. 我国已是世界一个造纸大国，但并不是一个造纸强国 当今国际造纸工业是向高速、高效、高质量、低消耗、生产连续化、自动化，并且是与环境相协调、走循环经济道路，朝着新型现代化大工业的方向发展。而从我国造纸行业整体来看，无论是生产水平、技术水平，还是管理水平，和世界造纸发达国家比，还有很大差距。

2. 我国造纸工业的经济结构仍不够合理 不管是原料结构、企业规模结构都还不是在短时期内可以解决的。

3. 我国绝大多数的造纸企业的增长方式还是粗放式的 在资源消耗、动力能源消耗方面，都有很大的节约潜力。

4. 我国造纸工业对环境造成的污染程度还是很严重 2004 年，全国工业废水排放量为 221.1 亿 t，其中造纸行业废水排放量高达 31.8 亿 t，占总量的 14.4%，仅次于化工行业，位居第二。从废水中最主要的化学耗氧量指标（COD）来看，全国工业 COD 总排放量为 509.7 万 t，其中造纸行业就占 33.0%，高居第一。因此，我国造纸工业的环保工作压力相当大。

5. 总体水平落后 由于历史原因，我国造纸工业绝大多数企业的规模偏小技术和装备落后，生产和管理水平低，再加上原料结构的不合理，以及其他一些客观原因的影响，纸张产品质量差，档次低，原材物料消耗大，成本高，在国内外市场上缺乏竞争力，因此，许多造纸工厂因经济效益差，经常处于亏损边缘，严重危及着工厂的生存和发展。

6. 经济效益依然不高 国内有些纸张品种的产能扩张暂时过快，加上近年来进口纸张关税下调，纸业市场竞争激烈，国内原材物料、能源、运输价格上涨，纸厂产品制造成本明显上升，纸产品毛利率呈下降趋势，不少造纸企业经济效益已不太好。

7. 竞争能力不强 改革开放以来，我国经济取得显著成就，但整个造纸行业对国民经济的贡献率仅为 2.2%。在 2005 年中国企业 500 强中，造纸企业仅有 3 家。晨鸣纸业集团排名第 141 位，金东纸业排名第 383 位，华泰集团排名第 429 位。三家造纸企业的平均销售额为 69.4 亿元，为 500 强平均水平 34.9 亿元的 29.5%。企业入选总数占 0.6%，销售额占总额不足 0.2%。

8. 部分科研成果不能转化为生产力 这些年虽然经过我国造纸工作者的不断努力，在科学技术研究方面，取得了很大成绩，但有些科研成果还不能顺利有效地转化为生产力。也还有些科技成果在技术上可行，但在经济上却不可行，因此也就无法在实际生产上应用。更有些科技难题，还未能突破。

三、“十一五”展望

1. 我国造纸工业有广阔的发展空间 据有关部门预测，2010 年我国纸和纸板的消费量将达到 8 000 万 t。随着我国国民经济快速发展趋势，国内纸张市场需求仍将继续增加，在“十一五”期间，我国造纸行业仍处于高速成长期，纸和纸板的消费量还有很大的上升空间，这是我国造纸工业发展的极好机遇。随着近年来新技术的发展，一些传统的纸张产品的消费会受到一定影响而出现萎缩，但总的来说，纸制品还是有其广阔的应用市场。预测未来几年，我国纸张生产量的增长速度将继续在 10%以上，仍将高于国家国民经济的增长速度。特别是新闻纸、包装纸和纸板及生活用纸等几个主要纸张产品都仍将大幅度增长。当然纸张的增长还必须要看今后我国造纸原料的供给情况，笔者认为，若没有足够造纸原料的支撑，我国造纸工业的可持续发展将受到极大影响。

2. 造纸原料的短缺问题必须认真重视和对待 随着我国造纸工业的快速发展，造纸总产量的迅速增长，造纸纤维原料的供给不足已成为我国造纸工业发展的重要因素。造纸原料短缺问题，今后会是越来越严重。因我国木材资源缺乏，致使我国造纸原料结构长期的不合理，木浆比重小。现在国家虽将林纸一体化已作为国家的发展战略，为缓解纸浆原料的短缺，2001 年国家颁布《加快造纸工业原料林基地建设的若干意见》及 2004 年《全国林纸一体化工程建设“十五”及 2010 年专项规划》出台，要求造纸行业到 2010 年，建设速生林基地 550 万 hm^2，新增木浆产量550万t，将国产木浆比重由目前的6%提高到15%。但林纸一体化的一些工程项目，当前在实施过程中困难很多，并不是短期间内所能实现的。即或就是实现了这一指标，但国产木浆量也不够。因此，每年还不得不大量进口商品木浆，进口数量逐年还得大幅度增加。2004年已达731.8万t，年增长在15%左右。在大量进口木浆的同时，现在每年还大量进口废纸，以代替一部分木浆。另外，因国内草浆造纸厂的污染不容易解决，许多小草浆厂也改用废纸为原料，由于废纸用量大增，所以我国造纸工业的原料比重中，废纸浆的比重逐年上升。据有关部门提供的数据，2005年已达到60%以上，大大超过"十五"预测55%指标。但因国内废纸的回收工作跟不上，国内废纸回收率一直只有30%左右。据海关提供数据，2005年我国从国外进口的废纸数量已高达1 704万t，大大超过了预测。为解决我国造纸工业原料结构的不合理和造纸原料的严重短缺，目前我国执行的造纸工业原料方针是："造纸原料结构是转向以木材为主要原料，要逐步形成以木材纤维为主，扩大废纸回收利用，科学合理使用非木材纤维的多元化原料结构"。这个原料方针是完全正确的，同时这几年，在执行中也取得了很好成绩。但应该看到，造纸业属资源性行业，不可能完全依赖进口，否则等于将使我国的经济安全受制于人。如果再不认真加快努力去解决的话，不仅会严重制约我国造纸工业的可持续发展，也将会对我国国民的经济发展产生一定影响。因此，造纸原料的短缺问题，是我国造纸工业今后发展的重要瓶颈，必须认真对待。

3. 构建环境友好型社会，这是国家今后发展的要求　不可否认，造纸工业是传统工业中的环境污染大户。造纸工业在世界上曾被认为是一个污染严重、破坏环境的行业。20世纪60年代国外造纸工业也曾对环境造成过严重污染。但是，从60年代后期，由于制浆造纸污染治理技术的研究、开发取得成效，特别是走循环经济道路，它们已经实现了清洁生产，不再对生态环境造成破坏。我国造纸工业是能耗、水耗大户，但应该看到，这是由于历史原因所造成。因为许多造纸厂，特别是那些小草浆造纸厂，它们的生产规模比较小、装备又比较落后，又没有治污措施，因此给环境造成了严重的破坏。近年来新建和改建的一大批现代化制浆造纸工厂，技术装备新，管理的好，投入大量资金用于环保治理，建有完善的治污措施，走循环经济道路，实施清洁生产，情况就大不一样。这些企业的废水及排放COD指标都大大低于国家标准。因此，加快推进循环经济、实施可持续发展战略，"应用企业生产过程清洁化的生产技术"，从源头上治理污染，应该是当务之急。面对环保压力，我国造纸工业在"十一五"期间，一定要扎扎实实地努力工作，在治理污染方面做出成绩，这也是落实科学发展观、构建环境友好型社会的真正体现。

4. 把节约放在首位　中央在全国建设节约型社会会议上，要求"十一五"坚持开发与节约并重，把节约放在首位。依靠技术创新，全面推进节能、节水、节材的资源节约和资源综合利用。造纸工业的发展与资源的关系极为密切，但我国造纸行业从总体来说，还没有摆脱粗放式的经营方式，表现是资源利用率普遍低。大多数中小型造纸企业的管理落后，浪费大，生产中各项原材物料消耗、能源消耗都很高。资料表明，我国纸和纸板的能耗比国际先进水平高达120%，我国一般纸张产品的电耗和汽耗都高于世界的先进水平，而水耗尤为突出。我国造纸用水量比国外纸厂高很多。我国纸厂吨纸水耗高达100m^3，吨浆纸综合水耗高达300m^3 以上。而国外纸厂吨纸水耗仅为10～20m^3，甚至低于10m^3。吨浆纸水耗为35～50m^3，水重复利用率为40%。因此，我国造纸节约用水的潜力很大。近年来，我国新建和改建的许多造纸企业，它们的用水量能达到世界先进水平，有的甚至还低于世界水平。如山东华泰纸业是我国最大的新闻纸生产企业，重视工厂的节约用水，水循环利用率达到96%以上。该厂2005年新投产的新闻纸机，吨纸水耗仅8m^3。金东纸业节约工厂用水，2004年该厂水循环利用率达95%。新建成投产的年产100万t金海纸浆厂，吨浆补充新水量仅为30m^3，低于国家标准90m^3。工厂的生产用水量增加，必然也增加了工厂的排水量，也就增加了工厂废水的治理难度。因此，加强节水防污是我国造纸工业可持续发展的很重要条件。必须切切实实地采取一切措施，来实现合理用水。构建资源型社会必须注意各种资源的节约、回收和再利用。造纸企业必须严格遵循循环经济和清洁生产理念，在生产中尽快地改变"消耗多、污染大、效率低"的状况。最大限度地实现废物的减量化和资源化，积极开展"减少资源和能源消耗技术、工农业生产排放物的再利用技术、再生资源化利用技术等等循环支撑技术的研究和推广应用"。使用最少的原料生产出最多的产品，将每道工序产生的废弃物尽量在企业内部消化，大大提高资源利用率，使其形成生产循环链，从而实现资源综合利用和循环利用，大大节约资源，使我国造纸工业走循环经济的发展道路，为加快建设资源节约型的中国造纸工业而努力。

5. 坚持走自主创新的道路　中央在全国科学技术大会上提出了坚持走中国特色自主创新道路、建设

创新型国家的战略任务。坚持自主创新，加速科技进步，就是依靠自己的力量来发展现代科学技术。我国造纸工业是一个传统工业，近年来虽然发展很快，也取得了辉煌成绩，但还面临着许许多多的困难和问题。因此，必须把握着我国造纸工业发展的重点瓶颈，努力突破，来完成技术革命的伟大历史使命。例如我国造纸工业的节约资源，在生产工艺上如何进行改革；对待造纸原料的短缺问题，研究如何合理利用现有的造纸资源和开辟新原料的应用；对待我国造纸行业要解决严重的治污问题，如何从源头上、技术上来攻关突破；为适应我国国民经济的发展和市场需求，优化我国造纸工业的纸张产品结构，如何尽快研制开发出高档次、高技术含量、高附加值的新品种，来填补国内空白，满足市场需求，并替代进口；在造纸设备制造方面，在消化吸收国外先进技术的基础上，如何自主创新、开发研制出低投入、高产出，节能、节水、节气、降耗、少污染而又是高质量、高性能、高效率、自动化程度高，具有中国特色的新技术装备。

我国印刷及设备器材工业的回顾与展望

中国印刷及设备器材工业协会

一、2005 年发展状况

根据中国印刷及设备器材工业协会统计，2005 年，我国印刷国内产值为 3 100 亿元，出口（为海外加工）约 38 亿美元，进口很少；印刷设备国内产值为 110 亿元，进口 16.5 亿美元，出口 3.8 亿美元，进口大于出口，大于国内产值；印刷器材（版材、油墨、胶片）国内产值为 1 110 亿元，进口 6.55 亿美元，出口 2.33 亿美元。2005 年，印刷用纸和纸板国内产量为 5 500 万 t，进口 527 万 t，出口 194 万 t，全国年消耗约 6 000 万 t。全国印刷设备年购置费 210 多亿元，全国印刷耗材每年（纸和纸板、版材、油墨、胶片等）达 2 500 亿元。

1. 印刷行业　印刷行业作为人类传播知识和文明的重要而独特的产业，历来受到党和政府的重视，特别是改革开放以来，我国印刷工业持续、快速、稳定发展，已形成了包括书刊印刷、包装印刷、报纸印刷、商业印刷和特种印刷等门类齐全，基本满足国民经济各行各业的需求的一个产业部门。2005 年，在我国印刷产值中，印前产值为 185 亿元，同比增长 9.5%；书刊印刷 750 亿元，同比增长 6.1%；报业印刷 505 亿元，同比增长 10%；包装装潢印刷 1 080 亿元，同比增长 10%；外贸印刷 290 亿元，同比增长 31.8%；其他 290 亿元，同比增长 10%。主要发展特点为：一是区域性印刷产业带正在形成，“泛珠三角”、“长三角”、“环渤海”经济区初步形成了各具特色的区域印刷中心。二是印刷业产业结构和产品结构的调整加快，低水平重复和盲目扩张受到抑制，用高新技术和装备改造印刷产业，形成了一批装备先进、质量上乘、竞争力强的印刷企业集团，特别是包装印刷行业发展较快。三是以数字技术为主体的新一轮技术创新已经到来，计算机直接制版技术正在逐步推广、普及；高效一体化印刷流程正在不断开发完善，推动了印刷企业的技术进步和设备升级。四是对外合作与交流不断扩大，合资、独资印刷企业已发展到 3 000 多家，印刷企业的竞争更加激烈，地区发展的不平衡性愈加突出。印刷制品走向国际市场，已成为行业十分关注的问题。五是印刷企业的改制、改革不断深化，市场机制在资源配置中发挥基础性作用愈加明显。

2. 印刷设备及印刷器材行业　印刷设备及印刷器材是印刷工业发展必不可少的物质和技术基础，现代印刷技术的发展，对印刷设备和印刷器材提出了更高的要求，印刷设备的高效多色化、印后设备多样自动化和印刷器材的高质系列化是近 10 年来印刷设备与器材的技术发展方向。随着改革开放的不断深入，该行业经历了引进技术、消化吸收、再创新的阶段以及合资合作、企业整合和资本重组，加速了我国印刷设备及印刷器材的升级换代，同时在生产能力与产品水平方面得到较快提升。例如，在 2005 年的印刷器材产值中，纸和纸板产值为 1 000 亿元，油墨产值为 60 亿元，印刷版材产值为 40 亿元，其他材料为 10 亿元。印刷设备及印刷器材在基本满足国内市场需求的同时，逐年扩大对外出口，开拓国际市场初见成效。主要发展特点为：一是产品技术水平和质量有了较大幅度的提高，质量和服务意识大大加强，基本满足了国内市场的需求。二是面向国内国际两个市场，积极开拓国际市场，扩大了产品出口，但对高档产品而言，依赖进口的局面没有得到根本改变。三是我国印刷设备与印刷器材水平质量取得较大提高，但总体上说与国外先进水平相比仍有一定差距。特别是在印前、印刷高端产品方面差距较大，印后加工设备与国际先进水平的差距越来越小。关键是企业自主开发创新能力较弱，研发的投入不足，没有形成能与世界著名厂商竞争的研发能力。

二、"十五"主要进展

回顾"十五"期间，我国印刷工业与其他行业一样，在深化改革、扩大开放方针指引下，在我国经济建设高速发展的促进下发生了巨大变化，得到了长足的发展。主要表现在：

1. 管理体制发生了历史性的变革　"十五"期间，从国家新闻出版总署到各省、自治区、直辖市新闻出版局，先后将归属新闻出版总署、省局的出版社、新华书店、印刷厂与其脱钩，使以往新闻出版、发行、印刷政企不分、政社不分、企事业不分的管理体制发生了历史性的变革。使国有印刷企业从计划经济和行业保护的环境中脱离出来，走向了市场。激发了广大印刷企业自主经营、自负盈亏、自我约束、自我发展的主观能动性。

2. 管理制度更加完善科学　"十五"期间，国家新闻出版总署和有关部门先后修订或制订了《印刷业管理条例》、《印刷品承印管理规定》、《印刷业经营者资格条件的暂行规定》以及《设立外商投资印刷业的暂行规定》等管理法规制度。特别是《印刷业管理条例》，第一次明确规定了国务院出版行政机构主管全国印刷业监督管理工作。改变了以往新闻出版署管出版物印刷，轻工部门管包装装潢印刷，其他印刷品由工商、公安部门监督管理的模式，避免了政出多门、管理分散、权责不明的混乱情况。此外，上述规章制度经过多次修订比过去更加完善、科学，更加切合实际，促进我国印刷工业健康、有序地发展。

3. 企业所有制多种多样　以往印刷企业国有、集体占统治地位，"十五"期间，股份制、民营、外资等各种经济成分的印刷企业得到快速发展。尤其是民营、股份制印刷企业迅速增加，几乎占全国印刷行业总数的80%以上。形成了多种经济成分的印刷企业互相补充、互相竞争、互相促进、健康向上的局面。

4. 印刷技术有了新的提高　"十五"期间，为了提高生产效率和印刷质量以及企业的竞争能力，全国大多数印刷企业不同程度地进行技术改造，更新设备，其规模和深度都是空前的。"十五"前印刷制版的主要设备是电子分色机，"十五"计划中，直接制版系统CTP逐步取代了电子分色机。至2005年全国进口CTP装置514台，使制版的技术和生产效率有了进一步提高。胶印在全国普及的基础上，向高速、精印方向发展。进口胶印机数量大幅度增加。"十五"期间，5年共进口单张纸胶印机4 550台，其中2005年进口1 135台，是2001年的1.76倍。在胶印机进口大幅度上升的同时，国产印刷设备产销也大幅度增长。此外，印刷技术的进步，提高了产品的印刷质量，提高了生产效率，有的开辟了新的印刷领域，有力地促进印刷业的发展。

5. 印刷总量大幅度增长　"十五"期间，是我国印刷业持续发展的时期。深化改革激发了企业的活力，加强管理促进了印刷的健康有序发展，技术进步提高了生产效率和印刷质量，我国经济建设的高速发展为印刷业的发展提供了广大市场和强大动力。因此，使印刷业在"十五"期间得到了良好的发展，印刷总量大幅度增长。据统计，2000年全国书报刊的印刷总量为1 276亿印张，2005年则达2 231.67亿印张，6年中增长了75%；用纸量从2000年的296万t增加到2005年的524.45万t，6年中增长了77%。其中图书总印量由2000年的376.21亿印张到2005年493.29亿印张，增长31.12%；学生课本由2000年的194.65亿印张增加到2005年的253.93亿印张，增长30.45%；期刊由2000年的100.04亿印张增加到2005年的125.26亿印张，增长25.2%；报纸由2000年的799.83亿印张增加到2005年的1 613.14亿印张，增长101.68%。

三、存在主要问题

通过对当前市场情况分析，我国印刷及设备器材工业存在以下几个问题，值得认真探索与解决。

1. 行业结构仍需大力调整　当前，无论是印刷企业或印刷装备器材业，由于资金、装备、技术力量相对悬殊，起点亦有高低，总的是高起点的少，大多数企业在低水平上徘徊。例如，小胶印机、切纸机，在一个地区或全国就有几十家在生产，规模都不大，此类现象十几年来没有发生根本性的变化。由于大量重复生产，也使低价竞争日益激烈。

2. 大型企业少　在10多万家印刷企业中产值销售额超过10亿元以上的厂家屈指可数。最好的企业也是在20亿元左右。至今上市公司在印刷装备业也寥寥无几。在公布的印刷行业百强榜中，也是以1亿元为入榜起点，但与印刷行业总体相比，所占比例很低。这说明印刷行业生产集中度很低。

3. 标准严重滞后　印刷企业及印刷装备器材标准滞后，严重阻碍了高新技术的进步与产品质量的提高。这一点在2006年9月召开的首届全国印刷机械标准化论坛上，已得到了与会专家和代表们的共识。现行印刷机械的标准虽然多年来几经修订，并颁布了一些新的技术标准，但基本上还是20世纪80年代的传统标准。

4. 品牌效应仍未得到应有的重视　除北人的胶印机、上海申威达的切纸机、南阳二胶的PS版及长春印机公司的切纸机被评为省市名牌外，印刷工业至今还没有被评为中国名牌的产品。知名品牌除具有各项技术经济的可比性指标外，主要还是看市场销售占有率。知名品牌的缺乏，直接制约着企业竞争力的提升。除了缺乏核心技术及资金投入不足及设计、工艺高级技术人才缺乏外，关键是印刷工业企业的决策者只注重产品的经济价值，而没有重视品牌的战略价值。

四、“十一五”发展前景

我国“十五”期间国民经济持续快速协调发展，人民生活水平不断提高，为我国印刷业的持续发展奠定了良好的基础。一是我国已确立了全面建设小康社会的宏伟目标，到2020年国内生产总值比2000年翻两番，这为我国印刷及设备器材工业提供了新的发展机遇。二是对外开放进一步扩大，对外交流与合作进一步加强必将为我国印刷及设备器材工业的发展提供广阔的市场空间。三是印刷品作为信息服务产品，仍是当今世界的主流传媒产品，与互联网、电子媒体等互为补充，共同发展。四是印刷技术已向数字化、网络化全面发展，认真实施“印前数字、网络化；印刷多色、高效化；印后多样、自动化；器材高质、系列化”的二十八字技术发展方针，必将推动我国印刷及设备器材工业的新发展。基于上述有利条件，我国印刷及设备器材工业在今后10年将持续、快速、协调发展，具体目标为：一是以科学发展观为指导，既要有较快的发展速度，更要注重提高经济增长的质量和效益，预计“十一五”期间我国印刷及设备器材工业总产值年均增长速度为8%左右。到2010年，我国印刷工业总产值预计达到4 400亿元。二是发挥区域经济的优势与特色，将泛珠三角地区、长三角地区和环渤海经济区建成各具特色的印刷基地。三是推进印刷数字化、网络化进程，研制先进、高效的印刷技术装备，培育一批具有国际竞争力的大型骨干企业。四是印刷设备重点提高多色高速胶印机的质量和可靠性；发展柔性版及凹版印刷机品种；实现印后设备多样、自动化，积极开发数字、网络化和直接制版先进设备。五是印刷器材实现高质、系列化，满足印刷工业发展的需要。纸和纸版的生产将以9%的速度增长，高质纸产品的比例将超过60%；油墨要重点发展水基油墨、无水胶印油墨、无芳基胶印油墨及各种特种油墨；PS版材要提高质量，在满足国内市场的同时，扩大出口。热敏CTP和紫激光CTP版材要尽快形成批量生产能力。

落实“十一五”规划精神
开创皮革行业发展新局面

中国皮革协会理事长　徐　永

我国皮革行业是轻工业的重要组成部分，在新的历史时期将继续承担着丰富轻工市场、扩大内需、增加积累、出口创汇、吸纳城乡劳动力，以及促进农牧业持续稳定发展和构建和谐社会的重要任务。

一、皮革行业“十一五”期间发展的五个要点

1. 按照走新型工业化道路的要求，把皮革工业“十一五”期间的发展作为促进皮革行业“二次创业”、实现从皮革大国跨入皮革强国行列的新起点。

2. 把提高皮革工业自主创新能力、调整产品结构、转变增长方式、促进产业升级作为中心环节，并把提高产业创新能力、发展自主知识产权的技术和提高自主品牌的竞争力作为转变增长方式的重要环节。

3. 遵循产业发展的客观规律，推进区域布局的调整，实现梯度转移，加快中西部和东北老工业基地皮革工业的发展，与东部产业提升形成协调发展的

格局。

4. 充分利用国际国内的两个市场和两种资源，适应内需发展为主和转变外贸增长方式的要求，提高企业走出去和跨国配置资源的能力。

5. 按照以人为本，建设和谐社会的要求，更加注重经济社会协调发展，进一步加强行业自律，重视环保和社会责任，努力规范行业市场的竞争秩序。

二、未来五年皮革行业发展的指导思想和战略目标

(一)“十五”期间皮革行业取得的显著成绩

1. 皮革行业主要产品的产量和产值名列世界前茅，进一步确立了皮革生产大国的位置。

2. 皮革行业出口增长较快，国际竞争力有了一定的提高，为跨入皮革强国行列奠定了基础。

3. 皮革行业提供大量城乡劳动就业岗位，为建设社会主义新农村和构建和谐社会做出了贡献。

4. 皮革行业结构调整步伐加快，特色区域建设成效显著，拉动了当地经济社会的发展。

5. 以“真皮标志”和“生态皮革”为平台，实施质量和品牌战略取得初步成果。

6. 运用高新技术改造传统产业成效显著，技术装备及配套产业水平大幅提高。

7. 民营经济得到快速发展，皮革行业整体竞争力显著提升。

8. 竞争意识不断增强，皮革行业自律进一步规范和加强。

在发展的过程中，也存在着一些问题，主要是：粗放的增长方式及低水平扩张的倾向影响了行业的核心竞争力；行业自主创新能力较弱，产品质量和品牌建设方面与世界先进国家尚有较大差距；制革作为皮革产业的基础，原料皮质量差、数量不足，环境污染治理任务艰巨；在“十五”期间发展速度过快，出口依存度偏高，也加大了行业的经营风险等等。

(二)“十一五”皮革行业发展的指导思想和战略目标

1. 指导思想　全面贯彻落实科学发展观，坚持可持续发展战略，发展绿色皮革产业，走资源节约型、环境友好型的新型工业化发展道路，加快产业结构调整和升级，加强自主创新，转变增长方式，使全行业从数量主导型过渡到以质量、品种、出口、效益型为主导的“二次创业”发展新阶段。

2. 战略目标　一是控制产量增长，鼓励提高产品附加值，保持行业总产值（或销售收入）年均增长10%；二是控制出口数量增长，鼓励出口价格提高，保持行业出口创汇年均增长10%；三是提高资源利用率，单位国内生产总值能源消耗比“十五”末期降低20%；四是更加有效控制环境污染，实现增产不增污；五是倡导自主品牌，到2010年或更长一点时间争创3～5个世界知名品牌，为从皮革生产大国跨入皮革强国行列打好基础。

三、几项引导性措施和建议

1. 原料皮的数量及质量保证是皮革产业可持续发展的基础　“十一五”期间，皮革、毛皮工业所需的原料皮仍将立足国内，但尚需继续进口部分原料皮，才能保证皮革工业的平稳较快发展。畜牧业和皮革行业相互依存，相互推动。没有畜牧养殖业的发展，就没有皮革行业的发展，因此，“十一五”期间要充分发挥我国原料皮资源优势，积极推动畜牧养殖业、制革、毛皮及其加工业联合发展的进程。促进猪、牛、羊养殖基地建设国际化，做到优化良种，皮肉兼顾，不断提高存栏量，从管理及市场方面引导逐年提高出栏开剥率，逐年改善原料皮资源不足及质量差的现状。加快毛皮经济动物的繁育发展，推动毛皮经济动物的养殖基地建设，努力培育中国的貂、狐、貉优良品种，保证毛皮加工业的数量及质量需求。建立完善原料皮收购、防腐、销售的原料皮经销队伍，倡导貂、狐、貉等细杂皮在销售中引入拍卖机制，进一步规范原料皮市场运营机制。提高生皮开剥、加工、防腐技术，确保开剥、保存、运输中不损害原料皮质量，推进我国原料皮市场国际化。配合政府主管部门进一步完善包括经济动物福利、饲养技术管理等标准和法规，促进我国畜牧养殖业与国际接轨。

2. 合理布局，调整结构，促进产业升级，形成东中西部优势互补、良性互动的区域协调发展格局　在东部沿海地区要着力增强自主创新能力，推进产业结构的优化升级，重点发展高附加值、高技术含量产品，提高高档产品的比例，增加自主品牌出口，增强国际竞争力，并在节能、环保、降耗、品牌等方面走在行业前面；中部地区将发挥“承东启西”的作用，一方面注意吸纳东部的技术，另一方面发挥现有皮革工业基础，提高现有皮革工业综合水平，促进中部皮革产业崛起；在西部、东北部地区将根据皮革资源丰富的特点，以市场为导向，加快东西部“携手工程”，引导东部沿海名牌产品和优势企业向西部、东北部和内地梯度转移，发展具有地区特色的皮革加工业，推动西部大开发和东北老工业基地振兴。

3. 把增强自主创新能力作为产业发展的战略基点和调整产业结构、转变增长方式的中心环节　建立

以企业为主体、市场为导向、产学研相结合的技术创新体系，形成自主创新的基本体制架构。依靠科技进步，不断提高皮革产品质量及花色品种，加大清洁化制革的研发和推广力度，全面提高制革行业整体水平。以皮鞋、皮革服装、箱包等皮革制品为龙头，大力推动产业信息化建设，用信息化带动工业化，全面提高开发设计水平。大力研究开发生产优质皮革需要的皮化材料，皮化产品向低污染、多品种、多性能、系列化方向发展。加强对皮革机械设备的研究与开发，在引进、消化、吸收国外先进技术和设备的基础上提高再创新能力。鞋用材料及部件和皮革五金要向多品种、优质化发展，提高专业化配套的质量和水平。建立产品标准体系，制定和修订行业有关标准，促进标准工作与国际接轨，为企业参与国际竞争打好基础。引导企业提高专利和知识产权保护意识，加大知识产权保护力度，依靠自主的知识产权不断提高核心竞争力。努力探索将公共的技术中心、国家（行业）研究中心、重点实验室及主要专业研究所和大专院校结合起来，建立具有行业特色的产学研相结合的创新体系。通过不同途径和多种形式，加强对皮革技术、设计、管理人才的培养以及对技术工人的技能培训，不断提高全行业整体素质。

4. 发展自主品牌是调整产业结构、转变增长方式的先导，真皮标志和生态皮革是培育行业品牌的平台，也是行业质量自律的载体　企业则是打造自主品牌和落实走出去方针的主体。名牌是竞争力、是生命力。它不仅是一个企业经济实力和市场信誉的重要标志，拥有品牌的多少，还是行业经济实力的象征，是建成皮革强国的标志。因此，“十一五”期间，要大力实施品牌战略，坚持“企业创、协会推、政府帮”的联动创牌机制，在发展自主品牌上下功夫。以真皮标志和生态皮革为平台，着力做好品牌培育工作。在加强真皮标志工作的基础上，培育主要产品的排头企业，将龙头企业做大做强。通过真皮标志的推荐，优秀设计产品评选以及市场竞争的优胜劣汰，引导企业注重产品的精工细做及功能研究、款式设计，提高出口及内销产品的综合质量水平。以真皮标志为培育行业品牌的平台，继续培育自主品牌及行业名牌，即中国真皮鞋王、衣王等，推动创建皮革特色区域名牌，推动争创中国名牌、中国驰名商标、中国出口名牌、国家免检产品等项工作，形成向世界名牌进军的企业团队，为争创世界名牌打下坚实基础。

5. 鼓励有条件的地区从自身实际出发，发挥产业的聚集效应，以优势企业为龙头，影响和带动其他相关企业合作配套，共同发展，形成皮革特色产业区域　使皮革特色区域成为产业调整结构、转变增长方式的主力军和主战场。以企业高度聚集为特征的皮革特色区域经济是行业发展的亮点，是整合生产要素的重要阵地。具有“聚集效应”、“分工协作效应”、“竞争自强化效应”、“服务网络化效应”、“区域品牌效应”、“持续化发展效应”等优势。因此，“十一五”期间，要规范、培育、支持皮革特色区域的发展，促进皮革特色区域之间良性互动、错落有序、差异竞争、协调发展。要引领皮革特色区域以科学发展观统领经济发展，走新型工业化道路，推动现有产业优化升级，发挥特色区域的示范带动作用，实施精品化、品牌化、生态化、国际化的战略，成为行业调整结构，转变增长方式的中流砥柱。全行业要认真执行《关于授予中国皮革行业特色区域荣誉称号行业规范》，作为对皮革特色区域扶优限劣的行业规范。坚持对已授予荣誉称号的特色区域，进行 3 年自我评价，5 年复评，滚动提升，不搞终身制。

6. 推进节能降耗，强化环境保护，探索制革、毛皮集中加工新模式，致力于建立环境友好型、资源节约型皮革产业，走循环经济的发展道路　大力推进节能降耗，提高资源利用率，节约水资源。依靠科技进步，加强清洁制革和毛皮加工工艺研究，不断推进绿色产业的步伐。接受委托编制《制革及毛皮加工工业污染物排放标准》及《皮革制品工业污染物排放标准》，有效规范和指导污染治理工作，要加强对皮革产业环境治理的监察力度，对于环境污染治理资金应给予扶持政策。大力提倡真皮标志生态皮革，引导行业走循环经济的发展道路，努力创造条件，争取选择 2～3 个区域建立我国的绿色制革生产基地，推动资源节约型、环境友好型皮革绿色产业的形成和发展。

7. 立足扩大内需寻求皮革产业发展的新增长点，实现产业发展由依靠出口拉动向内需与外需协调带动转变　积极培育国内外多元化专业市场，为跨入皮革强国行列打好基础，积极培育国内外多元化专业市场。温家宝总理在 2005 年 9 月 6 日 21 世纪经济论坛的讲话中强调，经济发展首先要扩大内需，要确立以国内需求为主的方针。中国是一个大国，大国经济促进因素应以国内消费占主导地位，但现实是我国的外贸依存度已达 70％～80％，依存度过高会带来一定风险，特别是容易引发连锁反应式的贸易摩擦。全行业要积极调整依赖出口拉动产业发展的增长方式，调整出口产品结构，扩大在中高档市场的占有份额；努力拓展多元化国际市场，避免出口地区过于集中，减少出口贸易风险。选择国际上有影响的皮革专业展览，继续组建具有规模的中国馆，扩大对外影响，进一步拓展国外市场。在国内举办的国际皮革展览要逐渐规范化，明确分工，各有侧重，优胜劣汰。逐步培育现有规模大、有发展前途的传统专业展览成为国际知名专业大展，促进国内外技贸交流。以创新的精神，努力拓展国内市场，鼓励加工企业与现有市场营销企业嫁接，营造市场流通的新模式，加强信息反馈，降低营销成本，提高服务质量，拓展内销市场。行业、企业要加强与各大中城市皮革批发专业市场的沟通与互动，使其成为拓展国内市场的重要集散站及信息反馈渠道。鼓励企业学习国际贸易规则，尊重所在国文化，以多种形式“走出去”，积极融入当地加工及营销渠道，创造双赢的贸易合作模式。完善行业预警机制，维护产业安全。继续以中国皮革协会紧急应对小组牵头，全国各地方皮革协会相配合的预警体系为核心，做好行业预警工作，确保产业安全。

（本文为作者于 2006 年 9 月在中国皮革协会第五届理事会第四次扩大会议上的讲话，略有删改）

我国橡胶工业现状及“十一五”目标

中国橡胶工业协会

综观 2005 年我国橡胶工业的经济运行情况，行业在国民经济持续稳定增长的大环境下，实现了全面协调发展。2005 年，橡胶全行业团结协作，共同努力，克服了诸多困难，继续保持了快速增长的发展态势。

一、经济运行情况

根据中国橡胶工业协会 376 家会员单位经济指标的统计资料显示，2005 年，我国橡胶工业累计完成工业总产值 1 077.3 亿元，完成工业增加值 271.4 亿元，比 2004 年分别增长了 24.14%和 16.23%；实现销售收入 1 028.04 亿元，比 2004 年增长 24%。在出口方面，2005 年虽然遭遇国际贸易壁垒，但通过协会企业的共同积极应对，仍出现了各项经济指标均创历史新高的可喜局面，全年累计实现出口交货值 311.7 亿元，同比增长 47.14%。在消耗方面，2005 年橡胶总消耗量达到 198.3 万 t，同比增长 12%。2005 年我国橡胶行业主要经济效益指标情况见表 1。

表 1　2005 年中国橡胶行业主要经济效益指标　　单位：亿元

产品名称	工业总产值	销售收入	出口交货值	实现利税总额	实现利润总额	销售税金及附加
轮胎制造业	1 025.6	967.5	263.5	82.5	48.0	13.5
力车胎制造业	50.0	50.6	11.1	2.8	1.1	0.8
胶板管带制造业	244.9	236.4	26.1	22.2	12.6	1.5
胶鞋制造业	363.6	358.9	135.1	21.8	12.1	2.4
乳胶日用及医用品业	133.3	130.2	47.9	8.8	5.9	0.3
橡胶制品制造业	321.4	312.7	83.3	31.6	21.2	1.4
再生胶制造业	50.4	44.9	1.4	3.0	1.7	1.9
合　计	2 189.3	2 101.23	568.6	172.7	102.6	20.1

二、主要产品产量

根据中国橡胶工业协会各专业分会提供的数据，测算出 2005 年我国生胶消耗量约为 400 万 t。表 2 中所列橡胶主导产品产量除轮胎及胶鞋为国家有关部门统计数据外，其他产品产量均根据各专业分会比例和统计数据的测算得出。

表 2　2004—2005 年我国橡胶行业分产品产量

产品名称	2004 年	2005 年	同比增长（%）
轮胎（万条）	24 801	31 820	28.3
子午线轮胎（万条）	10 464	14 262	36.3
力车胎（万条）	41 210	41 165	−0.1
输送带（万 m^2）	11 349	13 702	20.7
V 带（万 Am）	76 347	86 600	13.4
胶管（万标 m）	35 057	37 827	7.9
胶鞋（万双）	100 798	123 579	22.6

（续）

产品名称	2004年	2005年	同比增长（%）
炭黑（万 t）	149	174	16.6
助剂（万 t）	32	38	18.8
帘子布（万 t）	34	35	2.9
再生胶胶粉（万 t）	152	167	9.9

1. 轮胎 2005年，来自45个会员轮胎企业的统计显示，综合外胎产量1.6亿条，比2004年同期增长16.2%。其中，子午胎产量突破1亿条，同比增长29.26%，轮胎子午化率达到66%。全钢载重子午胎产量达2 411.77万条，增幅为44.49%。轮胎出口依旧保持强势，全年累计出口轮胎6 591.43万条，实现出口交货值238.67亿元，分别增长22.08%和49.6%。轮胎企业实现产品销售收入703.5亿元，比2004年同期增长24.12%。其中子午胎销售收入达到450.2亿元，同比增长38.16%。据43个轮胎企业统计，全年累计实现利润总额达到30.4亿元，比2004年净增7.3亿元，增幅31.5%。

2. 力车胎 据21个会员企业统计，2005年共完成工业总产值54.96亿元，同比增长14.3%。实现销售收入51.73亿元，同比增长12.9%。在力车胎的3种产品中，摩托车胎增长迅速，产量达5 831万条，同比增长40.43%；手推车胎产量为1 124万条，同比增长20.6%；只有自行车胎产量略有下降，下降幅度0.1%，说明自行车胎市场相对饱和。但出口持续攀升，实现出口交货值比2004年同期增长26.8%。行业经济效益明显好转，实现利润2.6亿元，同比增长18.3%。

3. 胶管胶带 2005年统计51个会员企业，输送带产量8 256万 m^2，同比增长20.73%。其中，钢丝绳输送带同比增长30.79%，尼龙带增长35.67%，各类难燃输送带增长50.74%。胶管产量为4 268万标m，增长7.9%。V带产量增长13.43%。汽车专用胶管和汽车专用V带产量分别下降18.39%和10.99%。胶管胶带行业全年实现销售收入31.5亿元，比2004年同期增长3.18%；完成出口交货值5.68亿元，比2004年同期增长27.66%。

4. 胶鞋 2005年，胶鞋行业生产经营形势看好。据46个会员企业统计，全年产量累计达4.4亿双，同比增长3.62%；实现销售收入47.1亿元，同比增长11.51%。出口形势因受国际环境影响有所下降，但出口创汇却有所增长，全年胶鞋出口量为7 844万双，同比下降4.2%；出口创汇30 534.28美元，同比增长27.16%。鞋业共完成出口交货值27.6亿元，同比增长27.66%，利润增长44.35%。

5. 橡胶制品 从30个会员情况看，2005年累计完成工业总产值41.93亿元、工业增加值8.8亿元，分别比2004年同期增长63.43%、16.12%；实现销售收入30.28亿元，比2004年同期增长19.4%。在产品产量中，O型密封圈产量达3.6亿个，汽车制动皮碗3 049万个，纯胶密封条972t，复合密封条736万m，同比分别增长17.94%、9%、32.64%和798%。但骨架油封、矿用导风筒等产品产量有所下降，尤其抗菌素瓶塞下降幅度较大，降幅达64.97%。完成出口交货值5.1亿元。比2004年同期增长30.81%。

6. 乳胶 据17个会员企业的统计，2005年完成工业总产值13.4亿元，同比增长12.4%；实现销售收入14.68亿元，同比增长2.16%。主要产品中，安全套产量36.05亿只，增长11.84%；医用乳胶手套2.17亿双，增长26.19%；家用乳胶手套1.13亿双，增长5.68%；输血胶管417万m，增长6.58%。完成出口交货值5.6亿元，比2004年同期增长15.85%。

7. 炭黑 从40个会员企业运行情况看，2005年炭黑行业生产发展形势良好，产量111.6万t，同比增长16.56%，其中湿法造粒炭黑产量为92.7万t，比2004年增长27.24%；干法造粒炭黑生产量18.7万t，比2004年降低16.98%，适用于子午线轮胎的湿法造粒炭黑的比例越来越高。全年实现销售收入47.2亿元，比2004年同期增长32.69%。销售炭黑113.61万t，同比增长21.42%，其中湿法造粒炭黑销售了84.7万t，同比增长32.81%。由于炭黑行业抓住市场，适时调整经营战略，实现了持续稳定增长，全年共出口炭黑69 220t，同比增长22.5%，创近年来新高。

8. 废橡胶综合利用 从61个会员企业的统计资料反映看，2005年全年再生胶总产量达57.87万t，比2004年同期增长26.22%。其中，胶粉6.06万t，同比增长33%。完成销售量54.1万t，产品销售率达93.53%，比上年同期上升1.09个百分点。全行业累计实现销售收入14.5亿元，同比增长34.06%。实现利润总额8 147.33万元，同比增长52.05%。全年完成出口交货值6 124.69万元，同比增长27.39%。

9. 轮胎模具 据12个会员企业的统计，2005年全年轮胎模具行业共完成工业总产值9.1亿元，同比增长23.03%，实现销售收入8.47亿元。主要产品子午线活络模具产量完成4 614套，比2004年增长75%。完成出口交货值1 561.6万元，同比增长177.93%。

11. 助剂 从2005年53个企业各项经济指标

看，剔除不可比因素，工业总产值和销售收入与2004年同期粗略比，分别增长45.62%和50.52%，出口交货值增长近100%。助剂总产量达到29.8万t，比上年增长21.13%。

12. 骨架材料　从20个钢丝帘线和30家帘子布会员企业生产情况看，2005年钢丝帘线产量总计45.9万t，同比增长48.88%。帘子布产量总计为34.8万t，同比增长2.39%。

三、“十一五”目标

我国橡胶工业已步入发展成熟期，“十一五”期间发展重点是全面提升橡胶产品水平。发展方针是实施科学发展、循环经济和名牌战略，转变增长方式；技术创新、产品创新、效益创新，以节能、安全、环保新产品替代现有老产品，求得企业效益最大化；为走向橡胶强国奠定更加坚实的基础。据《中国橡胶工业发展战略研究》预测，“十一五”末即2010年，市场对橡胶工业的要求为：

1. 轮胎　总产量要达到3亿条，比“十五”末增长30%；子午化率达70%，子午胎总量比“十五”末增长66%。生产安全、节能、环保轮胎，继续限制斜交胎以及65、70以上系列普通轿车子午胎、内胎全钢胎，并将实行不合格产品召回制度。

2. 非轮胎橡胶制品　汽车用橡胶制品重点是培育品牌，满足各类汽车对配套产品的需求；高性能新品的研发、生产、供应争取立足国内，替代进口。建筑工程等橡胶制品，重点发展防水、减震产品，为市政建设、高层建筑、公路、桥梁、涵洞等配套，提高建筑质量。为电子、家电配套的橡胶制品，也要作为重点，搞好高档产品的配套服务。国防橡胶产品，要能满足国防建设的需要。

3. 乳胶制品　重点发展节育、防病和提高生活质量的安全套，提高医用手套等医疗用产品的质量性能。

4. 炭黑　重点发展为子午胎、汽车橡胶配件等配套的专用产品，发展子午胎用白炭黑，同时解决好原料油的质量和供应。预计2010年，炭黑总需求量将达到210万t左右。

5. 橡胶助剂　重点发展环保助剂，禁止有毒有害产品的生产和使用。“十一五”末，助剂总需求量将达到32万t～33万t，既要满足国内配套和出口增长的需求，又要从源头上解决环保问题。

6. 骨架材料　发展重点是对现有产品进行结构性调整。2010年总需求量约71万t。其中，钢丝帘线54万t，涤纶帘线5万t，尼龙帘线12万t。

7. 废橡胶综合利用　重点是再生胶及胶粉清洁生产和后加工利用。“十一五”末，再生胶总产量争取达到150万t～160万t，胶粉产量达到50万t～80万t，同时开展废橡胶作为热能利用的研发和试点。轮胎行业要进军翻胎业，重点是子午胎翻胎工艺、预硫化胎面和中垫胶制造技术攻关，翻胎设备国产化，促使轮胎翻新率增长5%～10%。输送带要加强修复利用工作。

8. 橡胶　橡胶总需求将达到500万t，其中天然胶230万t，合成胶270万t。合成胶比例加大，争取发展异戊胶、卤化丁基胶等短缺品种。

“十一五”是橡胶工业全面实施产品更新换代的转型期，其发展要建立在优化结构、提高效益和降低消耗的基础上，重点是自主研发、上水平、创品牌，不是单纯增加老产品的生产能力，更不是布新点、单纯追求产量增长，不能再走高投入、低产出、高消耗的老路，力争发展速度保持在8%～10%，出口总值要占到1/3左右。

第二部分

相关行业发展概况

粮油食品加工业

一、基本情况

据统计，2005年全国纳入统计范围的粮油加工企业有11 118个，比上年增长2 572个，同比增长30.1%。全部入统企业中，国有及国有控股企业1 454个，占13.1%；外商及港澳台商投资企业120个，占1.1%；民营企业9 544个，占85.8%。入统企业工业总产值3 011.2亿元，产品销售收入2 995.3亿元，出口交货值32.5亿元，利润总额42亿元，年末从业人数37.8万人，分别比上年增长22.5%、22.5%、－35.2%、140.8%和8.7%。按工业总产值排序前10位的省、自治区、直辖市，依次为山东、江苏、河南、广东、黑龙江、河北、安徽、湖北、福建、广西。工业总产值超过100亿元的有9个省，其中山东省506.4亿元，江苏省418.8亿元，河南省230.7亿元，详情见表1和表2，具体发展情况分述如下：

1. 大米加工业　2005年入统大米加工企业7 260个，年生产能力12 447.6万t，大米总产量2 914.6万t。其中特等大米984万t，占33.8%；标准一等米1 646.5万t，占56.5%；标准二等米239.7万t，占8.2%。产量超过100万t的有江西、黑龙江、江苏、湖北、安徽、湖南、福建、广西、四川、辽宁等10个省、自治区，其中江西省358万t、黑龙江省327万t、湖北省309.5万t。

表1　2005年粮油加工业生产经营情况

名　称	企业单位数（个）	年生产能力（万t）		产品销售收入（万元）	利润总额（万元）	年末从业人数（人）
合　计	11 118			29 952 921	420 289	378 260
其中：国有企业	1 454			3 496 061	17 121	63 626
外商及港澳台商	120			6 872 528	96 804	22 822
1. 大米加工业	7 260	12 448		7 515 652	131 202	136 550
其中：国有企业	978	2 051		1 294 712	5 909	24 249
外商及港澳台商	27	127		97 365	111	1 317
2. 小麦粉加工业	2 815	8 090		7 967 774	98 455	142 237
其中：国有企业	326	1 037		717 221	－4 187	22 836
外商及港澳台商	35	393		496 352	4 500	5 391
		油料处理	精炼			
3. 食用植物油加工业	1 043	5 732	1 761	14 469 495	190 633	99 474
其中：国有企业	150	935	208	1 484 129	15 400	16 541
外商及港澳台商	58	1 145	631	6 278 810	92 193	19 114

注：表中数据来自中国粮食行业协会《2005年度粮油加工业统计年报汇编》。

表2　2005年各省、自治区、直辖市粮油加工业主要经济指标

地　区	企业单位数（个）	工业总产值（万元）	产品销售收入（万元）	出口交货值（万元）	利润总额（万元）	资产总计（万元）	负债合计（万元）	年末从业人数（人）
合　计	11 118	30 112 475	29 952 921	325 174	420 289	17 370 480	11 902 335	378 260
北　京	23	144 991	428 463	981	1 385	72 681	28 159	2 156
天　津	79	447 612	582 018	1 011	1 025	301 854	183 174	3 693
河　北	346	1 758 016	1 828 357	49 848	44 631	668 502	516 037	13 049
山　西	46	59 666	41 848		－950	66 361	62 738	3 374
内蒙古	23	151 730	189 870		2 663	83 786	14 089	1 313
辽　宁	310	750 123	739 559	4 993	－537	717 624	635 807	8 663
吉　林	333	448 241	467 038		5 037	419 155	423 721	9 621

（续）

地　区	企业单位数（个）	工业总产值（万元）	产品销售收入（万元）	出口交货值（万元）	利润总额（万元）	资产总计（万元）	负债合计（万元）	年末从业人数（人）
黑龙江	660	1 931 019	1 886 337	62 945	20 837	1 589 907	1 200 518	30 286
上　海	90	777 804	850 096	112	16 533	402 189	248 038	4 162
江　苏	737	4 187 683	4 081 988	29 044	49 810	1 771 215	1 175 883	33 963
浙　江	201	846 018	835 104	350	−9 112	498 969	385 770	6 649
安　徽	541	1 410 199	1 416 013	1 031	27 536	770 774	483 847	24 200
福　建	338	1 163 154	1 131 374	241	1 247	753 459	681 817	7 823
江　西	1 707	867 220	882 081	9 946	14 259	345 737	166 695	22 945
山　东	440	5 064 006	5 128 325	88 440	117 313	3 267 262	2 305 516	50 577
河　南	520	2 307 013	1 996 777	1 923	33 045	996 809	689 967	40 063
湖　北	857	1 297 107	1 245 677	3 087	18 166	802 907	421 846	21 795
湖　南	460	722 583	765 038	411	20 602	669 065	340 217	12 334
广　东	246	1 992 501	1 682 840	68 838	33 496	777 543	482 991	9 831
广　西	596	982 467	1 031 066	1 757	11 402	298 704	188 391	6 758
海　南	66	19 767	18 860		−1 071	27 430	6 541	541
重　庆	387	190 741	186 009		1 933	148 207	117 829	6 876
四　川	542	736 557	704 874	46	5 733	324 130	201 985	13 933
贵　州	181	162 885	166 961		−2 733	87 271	57 533	3 503
云　南	219	160 215	151 642	64	−794	175 929	116 026	4 483
西　藏	8	926	1 083		−137	11 464	6 331	180
陕　西	227	463 160	560 396	79	6 863	366 941	254 351	10 738
甘　肃	256	168 926	170 713		−35	136 004	77 380	6 065
青　海	72	44 876	42 079		−4 791	78 934	31 962	1 797
宁　夏	189	204 308	209 773		6 748	83 366	44 477	3 291
新　疆	418	623 963	530 661	27	187	656 301	402 702	13 599

注：表中数据来自中国粮食行业协会《2005年度粮油加工统计年报汇编》。

2. 小麦粉加工业　2005年入统小麦粉加工企业2 815个，年生产能力8 090万t，小麦粉总产量3 480.4万t。其中，特制一等粉1 481.1万t，占42.6%；特制二等粉916.5万t，占26.3%；标准粉408.4万t，占11.7%；专用粉432.6万t，占12.4%。总产量超过100万t的有山东、河南、江苏、河北、安徽、陕西、广东、新疆、湖北等9个省、自治区，其中山东省736.8万t，河南省717万t，江苏省372.5万t，河北省305.6万t。

3. 食用植物油加工业　2005年入统食用植物油加工企业1 043个，年处理油料能力5 731.5万t，精炼能力1 761.2万t，食用植物油总产量1 384.1万t。其中大豆油709.6万t，占51.3%；菜籽油278.2万t，占20.1%；花生油80.2万t，占5.8%；棉籽油49.8万t，占3.6%。在总量中一级油723.3万t，占52.3%；二级油118.3万t，占8.6%；三级油79.7万t，占5.8%；四级油298.2万t，占21.6%。总产量超过50万t的有山东、江苏、河北、广东、黑龙江、上海、浙江、福建、湖北、河南等10个省、直辖市，其中山东省220.8万t、江苏省217.9万t、河北省120.9万t、广东省107.8万t。

二、主要特点

1. 民营企业经济迅速发展，所占比重进一步提高　随着市场经济的发展和粮食流通体制改革的深化以及国有企业改制重组步伐的加快，国有及国有控股企业进一步减少，民营企业快速增加，已成为粮油加工业的主导力量。2005年全国入统的粮油加工企业中，民营企业占85.8%，比上年增加9.8个百分点。其中大米民营企业占86.1%，增加8.2个百分点；小麦粉民营企业占87.2%，增加15.1个百分点；食用植物油民营企业占80%，增加8.2个百分点。民营企业与国有企业相比，除机制灵活外，还具有职工人数少，资产负债率低等优势。虽然民营企业占企业总数的85.8%，但职工人数只占77.1%；民营企业资产负债率为62.5%，而国有企业为82.8%，两者相差20个百分点。

2. 企业规模继续扩大，生产集中度进一步提高　在2005年入统企业中，日生产能力400t以上的大型企业达365个，比上年增加86个。其中1 000t以上的企业达101个，比上年增加29个。从产品产量来看，年产量达10万t以上的企业达103个，比上年增加29个。其中年产量10万t以上的大米加工企业28个，总产量达468.7万t，占入统大米企业总产量的16.1%；年产量10万t以上的小麦粉加工企业47个，总产量1 217.8万t，占入统小麦粉加工企业总产量的35%；年产量10万t以上的食用植物油加工企业28个，总产量821.4万t，占入统食用油加工企业总产量59.3%；前10个加工企业总产量占本行业入统加工企业总产量的比重分别是：大米8.5%、小麦粉17.8%、食用植物油42.3%。这些数字清楚地显现了我国大米、小麦粉、食用植物油的生产集中度又有了新提高。

3. 产品质量和档次进一步提高，名牌产品销售量扩大，效益显著 几年来，通过大力培育宣传知名企业的产品品牌，普遍增加了企业的质量意识和品牌意识，推动了经营管理水平和产品产量水平的提高，名牌产品越来越受消费者欢迎，市场占有率越来越高，优势越来越明显。2004年被国家质量监督检验检疫总局和中国名牌战略推进委员会授予“中国名牌产品”称号的大米、小麦粉企业产品销售量和经济效益都有大幅度提高。“北大荒”、“五常”、“梧桐”、“东南香”、“全佳”、“玉珠”、“金健”等7个名牌大米销售量平均比上年提高39.3%；“古船”、“五得利”、“甲家”、“廊雪”、“福临门”等13个名牌小麦粉的销售量平均比上年提高11.3%，利润增长15.6%。黑龙江北大荒米业有限公司年产量达55.8万t，比上年增长37%；河北五得利面粉集团年产量达157.3万t，比上年增长56%，利润总额增长222.9%。

4. 粮油加工企业经济效益大幅度提高，创近年来最高好水平 2005年，粮油加工入统企业实现利润总额42亿元，比上年提高140.8%。其中，大米企业实现利润13.1亿元，比上年提高42.3%；小麦粉企业实现利润总额9.8亿元，比上年提高116.3%；食用植物油企业实现利润总额19.1亿元，比上年增长417.6%。由于食用植物油企业利润大幅度提高，使得大部分食用植物油企业开始走出困境。这些企业中，出现了国有企业扭亏为盈，获得利润2.2亿元；外商及港、澳、台商投资企业利润增长998.9%；民营企业利润增长137%。

5. 资产负债率有所下降 2005年，入统粮油加工企业总资产负债率为68.5%，比上年降低4.7%。其中，大米加工企业资产负债率为63.6%，比上年降低8.3%；小麦粉加工企业资产负债率为62.6%，比上年降低8.1%；食用植物油加工企业资产负债率为73.7%，比上年降低1.1%。按所有制划分，民营企业资产负债率为62.5%，比上年降低4%；国有企业资产负债率82.8%，比上年降低7.7%；外商及港、澳、台商投资企业资产负债率为71.1%，比上年降低1.4%。企业资产负债率的降低，进一步提高了各类企业抗风险能力。

2005年，我国粮食系统各类粮油加工企业发展中，除显现以上特点外，还有10%左右的企业未开工或基本未开工，还有部分企业开工不足。据行业测算，我国大米加工企业年生产能力利用率平均为34%；小麦粉加工企业年生产能力利用率平均为61%；食用植物油加工企业生产能力过剩现象也很严重。为此，进一步提高粮油加工企业年生产能力利用率的问题，已成为业内人士十分关注的课题。

三、科研、新产品、新技术

“十五”期间，粮食系统科研院所、大专院校和相关企业共承担国家和部门各类研究课题37项，其中国家科技攻关计划项目11项，国家农业科技成果转化资金课题4项，国家科研院所社会公益研究专项资金、科技基础性工作专项资金课题11项，国家重大基础研究前期研究专项课题1项，国家科技发展软科学研究课题1项和11项国家标准制修订任务。这些项目的实施，大大增强了粮油行业发展的科技支撑和服务能力。通过“我国粮油储藏、加工重要科技基础标准研究”、“食品功能因子作用机理、分类及其标准研究”、“我国储粮真菌毒素污染防控与消减技术研究”、“食用油脂质量安全保障研究”、“谷物冷却机与机械制冷低温储粮技术的研究”等重大科技任务、专项资金重点项目以及社会公益研究专项和应用性研究项目的开展，使粮食系统科技总体水平取得了明显提高，进一步增强了我国粮食行业在国际市场上的竞争力。由国家粮食局粮食科学研究院研制开发的粉质仪和拉伸仪，在粮食行业已经得到广泛使用，两年来已生产销售50多台，销售收入达750万元；国家“十五”科技攻关子课题“饲料谷物资源开发利用产业化关键技术研究”已通过验收，并已在湖南、吉林等主产地得到广泛应用，已达到工业化生产年产50万t的规模；国家重点新产品计划项目“改进制油工艺生产新型高效低毒饲用棉籽粕”，已在湖南、河南等省多个油厂推广应用。棉籽粕粗蛋白从38%～40%，提高到46%～48%，已在湖南、河南、广西等省、自治区推广应用20万t以上。上述科研成果的转化，新产品、新技术在行业中的推广应用，有力地推动了我国粮油加工业的发展。粮食系统科研院所，相关高等院校和企业，为此做出了突出贡献。

四、质量标准与监管

为保证党中央、国务院关于加强社会信用体系建设，实现食品、药品放心工程重大部署的贯彻实施，确保广大人民吃到“放心粮油”产品，2005 年，粮食系统在粮油标准的制定、粮油标准体系建设、粮油食品质量监管等方面做了大量工作，有力地提高了我国粮油产品标准和质量以及产品质量监管水平。

1. *粮油质量标准的制定* 为进一步提高我国粮油产品的质量，2005 年，国家标准化委员会颁布和实施了 GB/T 14614.4—2005《小麦粉面团流变特性测定 吹泡仪法》、GB/T 19878—2005《动植物油脂酸值和酸度测定》等 4 项国家粮油标准。由国家粮食局颁布和实施了 LS 1206—2005《粮食仓库安全操作规程》等 3 项行业标准。废止了《高级烹调油通用技术条件》等 7 项国家标准，并将《糙米》等 6 项国家标准转化为行业标准。国家粮食局全年安排标准制修订任务 104 项，2005 年完成标准报批稿 14 项、送审稿 14 项、讨论稿 8 项。2005 年，早籼稻最低收购价预案启动后，国家发展和改革委员会、国家粮食局和国家标准化委员会三个部门联合下发了《关于适当调整 2005 年早籼稻收购整精米率控制指标的通知》，对当年收购预案的整精米率控制指标进行了调整。同时通过调查和对样品的检验，摸清了稻谷生产省份整精米率的实际情况，为国家制定相关政策和《稻谷》国家标准的贯彻执行提供了重要依据。为保证粮食安全，维护消费者的利益提供技术保障，为粮食宏观调控和稳定粮油食品市场提供技术依据，全国粮油标准化技术委员会对《小麦粉》、《大米》、《营养强化粉》、《食用调和油》、《芝麻油》等主要粮油产品国家标准的指标设置、检测方法等举办了 16 次研讨会，广泛征求业内专家和相关企业的意见，以保证新标准的客观性、先进性、可操作性；成立了《小麦粉中溴酸钾测定方法》国家标准起草小组，为小麦粉的市场监管提供了技术支撑。此外，对宁夏稻谷整精米率有关问题给予指导；对 2006 年度大米、小麦粉加工精度标准样品进行了审定；同意了卫生部在 GB 2760《食用添加剂使用卫生标准》中取消溴酸钾作为面粉处理剂的意见，并在行业中执行了禁止在小麦粉中使用溴酸钾作为处理剂的意见。这些活动进一步加大了本行业中有关标准的制定、发布、废止、转化的力度。

2. *加快了粮油标准体系建设步伐* 为了进一步推动粮食系统标准化工作，2005 年底全国粮油标准化技术委员会正式成立了粮食及制品、油料及油脂、粮油储藏及物流、粮油机械及仪器设备 4 个技术工作组，分别由国家粮食局科学研究院、武汉工学院、河南工业大学和国家粮食储备局武汉科学研究设计院为组长单位。随后国家粮食局在北京举办了标准制修订培训班，对来自行业内标准化工作单位和质检机构 90 余人进行了业务培训，进一步提高了行业内标准化工作人员的业务素质和管理水平。国家粮食局在不断完善业内标准体系建设的同时，积极参加国际标准化活动。首先组织参加了对国际标准化组织 ISO 和国际法典委员会制定的 42 项国际标准的审议工作，组织国内 7 个实验室参加了《谷物与豆类 谷物脂肪含量测定方法》、《谷物与豆类 谷物扦样》、《谷物与豆类 大米中直链淀粉测定方法》3 项国际标准方法的验证。随后组团于 2005 年 10 月参加了国际标准化组织食品委员会谷物与豆类分委员会在阿根廷召开的第 31 次会议。由于我国代表团积极争取，会议同意在国际标准 ISO 5527《谷物 词汇》中增补中文词汇和定义，并发布中文的新标准；在国际标准 ISO 2171《谷物、豆类及其副产品 灰化法测定灰分含量》中采纳我国国家标准的相关内容；在大米直链淀粉测定方法、干面筋测定、脂肪含量测定等几个国际标准中提出了我国意见并被会议所采纳。同时第一次争取到 ISO/TC34/SC4 下次年会的主办权。2005 年 11 月份国家粮食局和国家标准化委员会组团参加了国际标准化组织食品委员会动植物油脂分委员会 ISO/TC34/SC11 在德国召开的第 18 次会议，这次会议上我国正成为参与委员国。会议对国际标准 ISO 3960《动植物油脂 过氧化值的测定》等 18 项国际标准草案进行了讨论，并就部分问题形成了意见。粮食系统在积极参加国际标准化有关活动的同时，还积极开展了标准基础研究工作。在这期间，开展了“粉碎小麦粒度大小及分布的基础研究”，开发了具有自主知识产权的小麦硬度仪，并为制定“小麦硬度仪及抗粉碎硬度指数”标准和修改《小麦》国家标准提供了依据。完成了“十五”国家重大专项课题“主要食品安全标准的基础研究及技术措施”中“粮油食品安全标准体系研究与体系建议”子课题的研究，分析了国内外现状，提出了我国粮油食品安全标准体系框架，并通过了科学技术部的验收。根据国家标准化委员会的要求，粮食系统启动了粮油标准化“十一五”规划编制工作，初步确定了“十一五”期间粮油标准化工作的指导思想、主要目标和主要任务，并提出了“十一五”期间粮油标准的重大项目建议。

3. *加大了粮食质量监管力度* 为了更好地贯彻实施《粮食流通管理条例》和国家发改委、国家粮食局等7部门联合制定下发的《粮食质量监管实施办法（试行）》，粮食系统加强了相关制度、检测手段建设，加大了库存粮食质量和原粮卫生的抽查力度。截止到2005年底，粮食部门具有相关资质（通过计量认证并在有效期内），可以开展检验工作的省、市、县三级粮食检验机构已有374个，比2004年增加了50个。2005年据对199个粮食质量检验机构初步统计，新增检验仪器设备3 663.5万元。据17个省、自治区、直辖市统计，已培训粮食检验人员16 776人。为了验证这些检验人员的水平与存在的差异，以利进一步统一规范检验仪器设备，加强粮油标准制修订和促进培训交流工作。国家粮食局组织开展了由12个小麦产区和17个稻谷产区的29个省级粮食质量检验机构参加的小麦、稻谷品质测报部分检测指标的比对检验工作，在此基础上提出了指导建议。2005年，国家发改委、国家粮食局等6部门联合对天津、山西、内蒙古等15个省、自治区、直辖市国有粮食购销企业库存粮食质量和粮食卫生状况进行了抽查，抽查库点153个，共扦取和检验样品1 543份。质量检验结果为：中央储备粮的质量合格率为92.5%，宜存率95.6%，质量总体状况良好，但有个别样品杂质超标；地方储备粮的质量合格率71.6%，宜存率91.3%。其中山西、内蒙古、河南、湖南、陕西、新疆等省、自治区粮食质量状况比较好，个别省份质量合格率和宜存率水平偏低，不合格样品主要是杂质和不完善粒等指标超标，稻谷整精米率偏低。卫生检验结果：在484份样品中检出10份卫生指标不符合国家卫生标准要求，其中8份样品有机磷农药残留超标，1份黄曲霉毒素B1超标，1份霉变粒超标。在粮食质量监管工作中，各地粮食质检机构充分发挥了技术服务作用，积极配合质检、工商、食品、药品监管等部门开展了一系列抽查检测工作。据全国31个省、自治区、直辖市统计，2005年共检测样品234 595份。其中粮食部门监督检查任务占56%。工商、质检等部门委托监督检查任务占12%，社会、企业委托检验任务占32%。

五、行业工作

1. 积极开展国际交流与合作活动　2005年，国家粮食局为广泛学习国外粮食先进管理经验，先后接待了阿根廷、匈牙利、俄罗斯等30多个外国政府和企业的粮农代表团组，双方广泛交流了意见，进一步探讨了加强合作与交流的方式与途径，这些交流活动使我国受益匪浅。为进一步深化我国粮食流通体制改革，借鉴国外在粮食管理、流通、储存、加工方面的经验和先进技术，国家粮食局2005年组织了出国考察培训。其中赴美的社会粮食统计和宏观调控培训、赴澳大利亚的粮食流通市场体系与法制建设培训、赴德国的粮食流通监管体系和执法建设培训等国家外国专家局资助培训项目和7个审核类培训项目都取得了良好收效。通过出国考察和培训，使粮食管理部门、企业干部和技术人员了解国外粮食管理经验和先进技术，开阔了视野，增加了知识，为提高我国粮食管理水平和储粮技术水平发挥了积极的促进作用。为了提高我国粮食储藏、监测和加工等科技水平，国家粮食局和国家外国专家局申请引进国外智力资助，分别邀请了美国、加拿大、澳大利亚、日本等国家15位专家，来华介绍粮食储藏、检验和深加工方面的先进技术；邀请了加拿大专家来华介绍关于谷物国际标准制修订程序和加拿大粮食标准体系，为我国粮油标准制定与国际接轨提供参考。聘请2位日本专家参加在我国举办了国际粮食企业管理及深加工技术研讨会，介绍日本最新的稻米加工新技术和新产品开发情况。聘请了美国和加拿大5位专家指导我国“粮食生态储藏研究实验基地建设”项目的实施。通过引进外国专家和技术，为提高我国粮食储藏、检验和加工等科技水平发挥了积极的促进作用。为了借鉴国外发展粮食物流经验，国家粮食局会同浙江省粮食局于2005年6月在杭州召开了粮食现代物流国际研讨会，美国、加拿大、日本、新加坡等国家的专家参会，在会上介绍了国外发展粮食现代物流情况和经验。随后召开的中加粮食流通政策与管理培训研讨班、强化营养面粉国际研讨会、中国—东盟粮油企业论坛等活动也都取得了很好的收效。

2. 进一步推动了“放心粮油工程”的实施　2005年，中国粮食行业协会评审推出了第五批“放心粮油”，并对第一批、第二批“放心粮油”进行复审。据中国粮食行业协会初步统计，几年来全国共评出“放心粮油”5批，1 157个企业生产的2 155个产品命名为“放心粮油”，加上省、自治区、直辖市评定的共涉及企业1 578个，产品2 819个，还评出365个“放心店”。粮食系统开展的“放心粮油工程”规模不断扩大，质量不断提高，已开始向农村推进。据不完全统计，2005年“放心粮油”进农村活动的省、直辖市已达23个，销往农村或兑换给农民的放心米面达589万t，占全国评出的放心米面3 200万t的18.4%，比上年增加1.7倍，其中20%的企业销往农村或兑换给农民的放心粮油，在农村市场的占有率达到80%以上。据不完全统计，参与放心粮油进农村活动的骨干企业由2004年的40个，增加到132个，增加2倍多。有的企业为适应农村市场的需要，

相继开发出安全廉价的放心粮油、增加营养性粮油产品推向农村市场，受到了广大农牧民的欢迎。放心粮油进农村适应了粮食购销市场化的新形势，成为当前促进粮油企业和行业发展的新经济增长点。放心粮油进农村活动，促进了农村粮油产业链、流通链的形成。为此，涌现了一批先进典型省、自治区，通过两代一换（代农加工、代农储存、品种兑换）连锁经营有效形式，将放心粮油推向农村。据不完全统计，2005年代农加工已达338万t，比上年增长50%；代农储存297万t，比上年增长77%；品种兑换已达230万t，比上年增加1倍多。龙头企业和农村网点，已成为放心粮油进农村的主要载体。据23个省、自治区、直辖市不完全统计，2005年全国已建县级配送中心16个，农村销售服务网点4.6万个，比上年增加1.4倍。一些地方采取工商联手、工农联手等方式，建立一批以经营放心粮油食品为主的“农家店”。天津、山东、河南、安徽、陕西等省、直辖市正在建设的“农家店”有1 663个，有5个省的农村粮油服务网点纳入商务部开展的“万村千乡市场工程”，使“放心粮油工程”开始在我国农村逐步得以推广。

3. 举办展会和开展“世界粮油日”活动 2005年，粮食系统在全国举办各类综合专业性展览会、交易会8个，其中有4月份在无锡举办的国际粮油产业交易暨研讨会；6月份在南宁举办的2005中国（南宁）东南亚粮农产品绿色食品展览会暨粮农加工技术设备展示会；8月份在昆明举办的全国第二届杂粮豆类粮油食品及设备（昆明）展示交易会；10月份在四川举办的2005中国（四川）粮油精品展示交易会以及黑龙江金秋粮食交易会、中国·湖州粮油经贸洽谈会、第七届湖北粮油精品展示交易会和第四届中国优质稻米博览交易会。以上参展活动展览总面积约30 400m^2，展位总数1 355个，参加展示、交易的企业3 391个，参观人数131 900人次。粮油交易总量达1 092.2万t，交易总额202.7亿元（含意向交易），其中机械设备交易总量166台套，总金额达3 308万元。这些会展活动为衔接粮油产销促进交流和贸易发挥了应有的作用。世界粮食日是世界各国政府每年10月16日围绕发展粮食和农业生产举行纪念活动的日子。2005年，我国世界粮食日纪念活动宣传主会场设在由国家粮食局和四川省人民政府共同主办的2005中国（四川）粮油精品展示交易会开幕式现场。这次开展的纪念世界粮食日，宣传爱粮、节粮宣传周活动，气势宏大，隆重热烈。开幕式上，联合国粮农组织总干事发来贺词，四川省、国家粮食局有关领导都发表了讲话。四川省利用展会在成都举办的有利条件，在展会的中心位置设置了爱粮节粮宣传栏，并在省粮食局办公地点附近设点发放爱粮节粮宣传材料。其他地区的粮食系统也开展了形式多样的宣传活动。

（此文由中国粮油学会提供相关资料，由本编辑部汇总整理）

油料加工业

一、基本情况

2005年，我国油料作物的总产量为5 799.5万t，与2004年相比，在国产油料中，扣除大豆、花生、葵花籽和芝麻的直接食用部分后的总折油为1 014.0万t。2005年的进口油料再创历史新高，我国大豆进口量为创纪录的2 659万t，进口大豆油169.4万t，进口棕榈油433万t，进口油菜籽29.6万t，进口菜籽油17.8万t，进口油脂油料总折油达1 109.5万t。2005年出口花生果41.7万t，花生仁33.6万t，折油27.6万t，2005年扣除出口折油27.6万t，净进口折油达1 081.9万t。因此，2005年我国食用油的总供给量（国产油料折油量和净进口折油量之和）为2 095.9万t。2005年，我国食用油的总消费量为1 850万t～1 900万t，人均年消费量为14.2～14.6kg。在总供给量中国产油脂比进口油脂少了67.9万t，国产油脂占总供给量的48.4%。2005年，植物油厂的效益有所好转，全年实现利润19.06亿元，出现了一些效益好的企业，其中以花生为主要原料的山东莱阳鲁花浓香花生油有限公司，2005年全年生产花生油18.6万t，生产调和油10.3万t，实现利润高达2.65亿元，上缴税收8 900万元，可以说是全国油脂行业的佼佼者。2005年，油脂工业企业的经营状况虽然有所好转，但效益尚未恢复到2003年的水平，尤其是大豆加工企业效益仍然不够理想。造成这种状况的主要原因：一是从进口大豆价格走势看，自2005年3月下旬起，进口大豆的价格（平均到岸价）一路小幅攀升，这无疑给依靠进口大豆生产的企业造成经营的困难。二是进口大豆的榨油毛利较低，来自大连、山东、江苏和广东的资料反映，2005年只有2、3两月每吨进口大豆的榨油毛利能达到200～300元，其余都在盈、亏100元左右徘徊。同样使用国产大豆榨油的毛利也很低，有的甚至出现了亏损。2005年，全国规模以上食用植物油加工企业920个，资产总额为750.8亿元，负债合计为553.4亿元，资产负债率为74.8%。

二、科研、新产品与新技术

1. 山东鲁花集团有限公司于2006年3月27日，在内蒙古巴彦淖尔市临河区投资1.5亿元，建设10万t葵花籽油项目，主要生产葵花籽油、葵花籽调和油、葵花籽粕和葵花籽制品等。葵花籽油采用鲁花独特的压榨工艺生产，原料来自天然无污染的河套油葵，富含人体必需的营养成分，是天然的绿色保健食品。

2. 由湖北省碧山粮油机械设备有限公司完成的科技项目“棕榈油制取成套设备”于2006年3月14日在湖北安陆市通过专家鉴定。会议由湖北省科技厅主持，来自中国粮油学会、国家粮食储备局西安油脂科学研究设计院、武汉工业学院、湖北省粮食局和中国地质大学等单位的专家听取了湖北省碧山粮油机械设备有限公司棕榈油制取成套设备研制报告。该项目的工艺和设备设计及制造全部由我国自主创新完成，其中双螺旋棕榈油榨油机、离心机波纹剥壳机和热风发生炉是我国实用新型专利产品。经测试，该成套设备的技术指标已达到国际先进水平。

3. 国家粮食局油脂工程技术中心、国家粮食储备局西安油脂科学研究设计院科研中试基地于2006年5月建在陕西省渭南市高新技术开发区内，占地5 000m²，建筑面积近2 000m²，建设投资600万元。该科研中试基地建成后，将成为我国油脂行业最大的科研中试基地。中试基地以承担油脂、蛋白提取和资源深加工的中试为主要内容，瞄准国内外前沿新技术进行技术成果开发，以科研成果的工程化、产业化为目标。

4. 上海良友（集团）有限公司技术中心于2006年5月成立，该中心主要承担集团重大科研项目和新产品开发，研究开发涉及粮油食品加工及其衍生物等领域。技术中心设油脂、食品、储藏三个专业研究室和科技情报室。承担了由上海市科委批准立项的“转基因大豆的检测方法研究”项目，均通过了上海市科委的验收，部分项目实现了产业化，基因检测通过有关部门评审并取得扩项认证许可。

三、质量管理与标准化工作

（一）质量管理

1. 卫生部于2006年1月5日组织部分省市对市售的食用植物油产品进行国家卫生监督抽检，结果发现餐饮业的食用植物油产品的食品卫生问题比较突出，食用植物油的合格率仅为87.2%。卫生部在全国15个省、自治区、直辖市分别对集贸市场、餐饮单位和学校食堂经营或使用的植物油进行监督抽检，抽查指标为酸值、过氧化值、溶剂残留等，共抽查292份植物油，合格率为93.2%。抽检结果显示：过氧化值超过国家标准是食用植物油不合格的主要原因，本次抽检不合格的20份食用植物油中有13份过氧化值指标超标。

2. 国家质检总局于2006年12月公布了2006年芝麻油产品质量抽查结果，共抽查了安徽、河南、湖北、山东、上海、陕西、山西、辽宁、四川等9省、直辖市40个企业生产的46种产品，产品抽样合格率为87%。抽查结果表明，市场占有率较高的大中型企业产品质量较好，小型企业产品质量问题存在较多。本次抽查中发现的主要质量问题：一是色泽不合格。色泽是体现芝麻油感官品质的一个重要指标，色泽的好坏直接影响到芝麻油的品质。国家标准GB/T 8233—1987《芝麻油》中根据产品等级规定了产品色泽的黄色值和红色值，本次抽查中有个别产品色泽的红色值不符合标准要求。二是苯并芘含量超标。苯并芘是一种多环芳烃，在芝麻油产品中超过标准限定值对人体有害。国家强制性标准GB 2716—2005《食用植物油卫生标准》规定苯并芘的含量为≤10μg/kg。本次抽查中有个别产品苯并芘含量超标。其中有1种产品苯并芘含量实测值为20μg/kg，是标准限定值的2倍。针对本次抽查中反映出的质量问题，国家质检总局已责成各地质量技术监督部门严格按照产品质量法等有关法律法规的规定，对本次抽查中产品质量不合格的企业进行处理，限期整改。同时公布抽查中质量较好的产品及生产企业，引导消费。国家质检总局将继续对该类产品质量进行跟踪抽查，促使芝麻油产品整体质量水平的提高，为消费者创造放心满意的消费环境。

（二）标准化工作

1. 全国粮油标准化委员会油脂油料工作组第一次会议于2006年3月1日在武汉工业学院召开，来自全国粮油标准化委员会、国家粮食局标准质量中心、国家粮食局科学研究院、国家粮食储备局西安油脂科学研究设计院、国家粮食储备局无锡科学研究设计院、国家粮食储备局武汉科学研究设计院、江南大学、河南工业大学、嘉里粮油（中国）有限公司、上海福临门食品有限公司、山东鲁花集团有限公司和黑龙江九三油脂有限公司等部门和企业的代表参加了会议。

2. 根据国家标准计划要求，于 2006 年 5 月 15 日在北京组织召开了营养强化食用油和油橄榄油国家标准《征求意见稿》讨论会。会议邀请国家粮食局标准质量中心、公众营养与发展中心、国家公众营养改善项目办公室、国家粮食局科学研究院、中国疾病控制中心营养与食品安全所、江南大学、武汉工业学院、国家粮油质量监督检验中心、中国粮油学会油脂分会、中国植物油行业协会的领导和专家，中粮集团公司及所属的上海福临门食品有限公司、东海粮油（张家港）工业有限公司、北海粮油（天津）工业有限公司以及中盛粮油控股有限公司、北京古船油脂有限责任公司、上海良友海狮油脂公司、嘉里粮油（中国）有限公司和金光食品（宁波）有限公司等近 10 家国内大型油脂企业的代表参会。营养强化食用油和油橄榄油标准起草组在广泛听取各界意见的基础上，出台了营养强化食用油和油橄榄油国家标准的征求意见稿。会上，专家们提出了许多建设性的宝贵意见，使该标准更加符合我国油脂生产和贸易的实际情况，更具有较强的前瞻性和操作性。

3. 全国粮油标准化技术委员会一届五次工作会议于 2006 年 8 月 2～3 日在北京召开，参会代表有全国粮油标委会委员、各标准工作组成员、起草单位代表，并特邀国标委农轻地方部、国家标准技术审查部、标准出版社等单位的代表共 80 多人出席会议。会议由国家粮食局标准质量中心唐瑞明副主任主持；受国家粮食局副局长、全国粮油标准化技术委员会主任委员任正晓的委托，国家粮食局标准质量中心主任、全国粮油标准化技术委员会副主任委员杜政作工作报告。杜政在报告中总结回顾了一年来粮标委在国家粮食局和国家标准化管理委员会的领导下，在加强粮油标准化工作制度和工作体系建设、开展标准制修订工作、积极参与国际交流、组织编制粮油标准化“十一五”发展规划、积极开展标准研究和人员培训等方面所取得的成绩，并就粮标委下一步的工作重点进行了部署。

4. 国家质量监督检验检疫总局、国家标准化管理委员会于 2006 年 11 月 1 日在人民大会堂隆重举行了首届“中国标准创新贡献奖”颁奖大会。国家粮食局西安油脂食品及饲料质量监督检验测试中心、上海福临门食品有限公司等单位负责起草的 GB 1534—2003《花生油》、GB 1535—2003《大豆油》、GB 1536—2004《菜籽油》、GB 1537—2003《棉籽油》、GB 10464—2003《葵花籽油》、GB 11765—2003《油茶籽油》、GB 19111—2003《玉米油》、GB 19112—2003《米糠油》等 8 项国家标准获三等奖。

四、行业工作

1. 国家粮油信息中心举办的 2006 年冬之春中国粮油饲料期货市场展望会于 2006 年 1 月 14～15 日在上海召开，600 余位国内外粮油饲料期货界的代表参加了此次盛会。国家粮食局曾丽瑛副局长出席大会，并做了题为《2005 年我国粮食宏观调控工作回顾和 2006 年粮食供求形势分析》的报告，受到了与会代表的高度评价。中国粮油学会朱长国理事长、国家粮油信息中心尚强民主任等 20 多位业内专家就 2005 年国际国内粮油饲料期货市场格局进行了分析，并对 2006 年我国粮油饲料期货市场前景做出了前瞻性预测。

2. 中国粮油学会油脂专业分会 2006 年会长办公扩大会议于 2006 年 3 月 4～5 日在广东省深圳市召开，中国粮油学会油脂分会的会长、副会长、秘书长及部分特邀代表参加了会议。嘉里粮油（中国）有限公司总经理李福官，副总经理伍翔飞及深圳市发展与改革局杨加慎处长等参加了会议并发表了致词。王瑞元会长为会议作了题为《2005 年中国油脂工业》的主题发言。常务副会长姚专作了油脂专业分会 2005 年工作总结及 2006 年工作计划的报告。

3. 中国粮食行业协会举办的全国放心粮油进农村工作会议于 2006 年 4 月 10～11 日在济南召开。全国各省市粮食行业协会和放心粮油进农村先进单位的代表共 260 多人参加了会议。国家粮食局局长聂振邦和副局长张桂凤、中国粮食行业协会会长白美清、山东省政府副省长张昭福等有关领导出席了会议，商务部等有关部门也派员参加了会议。会上，白美清会长作了《让放心粮油进入农村千家万户，为建设新农村做出贡献》的报告，商务部市场建设司调研员陈素红介绍了“万村千乡市场工程”试点工作情况，中国粮食行业协会副会长赵凌云、王瑞元分别作了“放心粮油进农村”和争创中国名牌的报告，山东省粮食行业协会、山西省粮食行业协会、山东省广饶县粮食局、河南省偃师市粮食局、江苏省镇江市粮食局介绍了开展“放心粮油进农村”工作的经验，江苏省粮食行业协会、广东省粮食行业协会介绍了“放心粮油”评审监管工作经验。会议表彰了山东半球集团等 56 家先进单位，并颁发了“全国放心粮油进农村先进单位”证书和标牌。

4. 中国食品科技学会大豆食品学会主办的第二届大豆食品产业圆桌峰会于2006年5月在上海召开，会议针对我国大豆产业的发展发布了《上海宣言》，这是大豆产业首次以宣言形式对大豆产业的发展战略提出共同意见。宣言提倡产业将发展牛奶蛋白加大豆蛋白的双蛋白奶作为切入点，开发大豆食品。

5. 中国粮油学会成立20周年庆典大会于2006年6月28～30日在北京举行。大会由中国粮油学会理事长朱长国主持，到会领导有中国科协副主席、书记处书记冯长根，国家粮食局副局长张桂凤，中国粮食行业协会会长白美清以及国家粮食局流通与科技发展司司长何毅等，与会的粮油科技界代表300余人参加了庆典大会。宣读了“2005年度中国粮油学会科学技术奖”获奖名单，“中国粮油学会第一届优秀团体会员奖”名单，“中国粮油学会第一届优秀粮油科技工作者”名单，“中国粮油学会第五届优秀论文”名单。与会的有关领导和企业代表分别向获奖单位和个人颁发了奖励证书。油脂专业分会在会长王瑞元的主持下，进行了相关专题的学术研讨并召开了油脂专业分会工作会议，研究确定了油脂专业分会下半年的工作。

6. 由农业部、辽宁省农委、大连商品交易所共同主办的2006年全国大豆暨优质油料油脂交易博览会于2006年7月23～24日在大连举办。农业部副部长范小建、辽宁省副省长胡晓华等出席开幕式并为交易博览会剪彩。全国油料油脂行业的代表、受到农业部表彰的100多位全国种粮大户参加了本届交易博览会。交易博览会在总结前几届全国油料交易会成功经验的基础上，将展区设为“十五”回顾展区、综合展区及销售区，设置标准展位200个以上，展销面积近万平方米。业内100多个有代表性、有影响的企业展示了大豆及油料油脂行业的名、特、优、新产品。

7. 第六届中国粮油精品展示交易会于2006年10月16～18日在郑州国际会展中心隆重召开。河南省省委书记徐春光、国家粮食局局长聂振邦、河南省省长李成玉、联合国粮农组织代表等有关领导出席开幕式并作重要讲话，并为世界粮食日揭牌。中国粮油精品展示交易会是由国家粮食局长期举办的国内粮油精品交易会。本次交易会有来自全国26个省、自治区、直辖市的代表团参会，参会人数达3 000多人。河南省18个省辖市组成政府代表团参加会议，参展人数3 200余人。国外参展代表近百人。

（武汉工业学院食品学院　何东平）

大豆加工业

一、基本情况

（一）资源概况

1. 世界大豆生产情况　2005年，世界大豆收获面积91 390khm²，与上年相比基本持平；平均单产2 293kg/hm²，同比增长0.03%；总产量20 935万t，同比增长0.02%。世界大豆主产国有美国、巴西、阿根廷、中国和印度等（表1）。表1中5个国家的大豆总产量，占世界总产量的92.5%，构成世界大豆产量的主要市场份额。

表1　2005年世界大豆主产国生产情况

国　别	收获面积（khm²）	单　产（kg/hm²）	总产量（万t）	同比增长（%）	占世界比例（%）
美　国	28 840	2 872	8 282	－2.6	39.6
巴　西	22 900	2 192	5 020	0.8	24.0
阿根廷	14 040	2 729	3 830	21.6	18.3
中　国	9 591	1 705	1 635	－6.0	7.8
印　度	7 000	857	600	9.1	2.9

注：表中数据来自于《2006年中国农村统计年鉴》。

2. 我国大豆生产情况　2005年，我国大豆播种面积9 591khm²，与上年相比基本持平；单产1 705kg/hm²，同比增长－6.1%；总产量1 635万t，同比增长－6.0%。产量较大的省份为黑龙江、内蒙古、吉林、安徽、山东、河南、四川等地，约占全国总产量的70.7%（表2）。

表2　2005年我国大豆主产区生产情况

主产区	播种面积（khm²）	单　产（kg/hm²）	总产量（万t）	同比增长（%）	占全国比例（%）
黑龙江	3 548.4	1 774	629.5	－1.4	38.5
内蒙古	797.0	1 642	130.9	27.0	8.0
吉　林	504.8	2 579	130.2	－14.4	8.0
安　徽	917.0	968	88.8	－21.1	5.4
山　东	238.7	2 727	65.1	－9.2	4.0
河　南	533.6	1 089	58.1	－43.9	3.6
四　川	212.7	2 473	52.6	7.1	3.2

注：表中数据来自于《2005年中国农业统计资料》。

（二）加工业概况

1. 世界大豆加工概况　根据美国农业部2006年

公布的世界大豆供需平衡和豆油、豆粕主产国产量报告显示，2005/2006年度世界大豆压榨量为18 265万t，同比增长5.5%；世界豆油总产量为3 431万t，同比增长2.7%；世界豆粕总产量为14 470万t，同比增长0.5%。其中，世界各主要大豆加工国2005/2006年度大豆压榨量、豆油和豆粕产量见表3。

表3　2005/2006年世界豆油、豆粕主要生产国加工情况

主要加工国	压榨量		豆　油		豆　粕	
	产量（万t）	同比增长（%）	产量（万t）	同比增长（%）	产量（万t）	同比增长（%）
美　国	4 681	1.8	925	10.3	3 741	5.3
巴　西	2 750	－6.4	539	－19.3	2 166	－21.6
阿根廷	3 040	19.0	600	24.0	2 502	20.9
中　国	3 461	16.2	615	18.7	2 730	16.6

2. *我国大豆加工概况*　据中国植物油行业协会、国家粮油信息中心等相关粮油机构调查统计，2005年，我国采用浸出工艺压榨大豆的企业共596个。其中常年停产企业为359个，占企业总数的60.2%；常年生产及间断性生产的企业237个，占总数的39.8%。我国采用浸出工艺加工大豆的企业日压榨大豆能力为29.7万t，其中常年停产企业压榨大豆能力为7.3万t，占压榨能力总量的24.6%；常年生产及间断性生产的企业日压榨大豆能力为22.4万t，占压榨能力总量的75.4%。按大豆加工企业压榨量规模进行分类统计，日加工能力1 000t以上的大豆压榨企业为95个，日压榨能力为22.5万t。日压榨大豆500t以下的大豆加工企业为462个，日压榨大豆能力为7.8万t。其中停产企业335个，日压榨能力为5.4万t；常年生产及间断性生产的企业127个，日压榨大豆能力为2.5万t。日压榨大豆500t以上的大豆油脂加工企业134个，日压榨大豆能力为21.9万t。其中停产企业24个，日压榨能为2.0万t；常年生产及间断性生产的企业110个，日压榨大豆能力为19.9万t。另外，我国还有小型机榨油厂、油坊约2 000个以上，日压榨大豆能力约在3 000t以上。截止到2005年年底，我国大豆设计压榨能力达到8 300万t，较年初增加了1 000万t左右，而实际开工率只有40%～45%。各地间断性生产的大豆压榨企业，设备完好，不能连续生产的主要原因是资金、经营、市场问题。关于有效大豆压榨能力的确定标准很难把握，根据我国目前大豆压榨企业的实际情况，在全国常年生产及间断性生产的压榨总量中，应减除部分企业间歇性停产数量，再减除部分企业其他油籽压榨量。分析认为，把我国全年有效大豆压榨能力确定在6 500万t左右较为合理。调查统计情况表明，我国近几年新建的大型油厂已占据大豆压榨行业的主导地位，大部分中小型大豆油厂将被彻底淘汰出局。

黑龙江省是我国大豆主产省，也是我国豆油的主产省。黑龙江省生产豆油所使用的原料基本上都为国产大豆，该省生产的豆油以国标四级豆油为主，因此黑龙江省豆油市场具有一定的独特性。2005年，黑龙江省有大豆油厂160个，设计日压榨能力为3.8万t。但2005年黑龙江省有100个油厂处于停产、半停产状态，只有60个维持生产。维持生产的油厂设计日压榨能力为1.9万t，占总压榨能力的50.5%。黑龙江省的油厂大多数为100～400t的中小企业，该省压榨能力在1 000t以上的油厂只有5个。其中九三油脂集团独占4个，分别是嫩江九三分公司、北安赵光分公司、鹤岗宝泉岭分公司和哈尔滨惠民分公司。2005年，黑龙江省维持生产的油厂压榨大豆200万t，生产豆油33万t，占国产大豆生产豆油总量的23%。黑龙江省生产的豆油大部分用于省内消费，一部分销往吉林、内蒙古、辽宁，还有一小部分出口朝鲜、韩国等国。

山东省是我国豆油生产加工能力最大的省之一，设计压榨能力居全国之最。2005年，山东省有大豆油厂135个，日设计压榨量达到5.7万t。在山东省这些油厂中有102个是日压榨能力在500t以下的中小企业，1 000t以上的企业只有18个。到2005年底，山东省有117个油厂处于停产、半停产状态。主要是由于近年来我国沿海地区大豆压榨企业迅速建设和扩张，国内豆油及豆粕市场竞争十分激烈，鲁西南、鲁西北的很多中小型油厂在原料采购、产品销售、生产技术和资金等方面处于劣势，逐渐被市场所淘汰。2005年全年，山东省有18个豆油生产企业维持生产，主要是沿海地区的日压榨能力1 000t以上的大型油脂企业以及临沂和博兴等地交通便利、地理位置优越的日压榨能力500t以上的大中型企业。沿海地区的企业基本使用进口大豆加工，内陆企业则既使用进口大豆又使用国产大豆。这些企业2005年压榨产出豆油103.6万t左右。山东省生产的豆油主要在本省消费，省外的销售区域有冀南、豫北、皖北、苏北，有一小部分销售到山西部分地区。山东省大豆压榨企业主要集中在山东沿海地区，如日照新良油脂、日照邦基三维、日照黄海、龙口新龙、烟台益海、青岛华粮等。

二、科研、新产品、新技术

1. 由中国农业大学完成的“大豆专用型调节剂80%胺鲜酯·甲哌鎓粉剂研制及应用”课题，于

2005年3月7日通过教育部组织的专家鉴定。专家们一致认为，该项研究成果的总体水平达到国际先进，在胺鲜酯与甲哌鎓复配与生理机制的研究和应用达到国际领先水平，具有重大的推广应用价值。该研究项目针对当前大豆生产中存在产量低、品质差、抗逆差等问题，成功开发研制了植物生长调节剂新产品80%胺鲜酯·甲哌鎓粉剂，获得农药临时登记证、农药生产批准证书，制定了产品标准并已备案；建立了产品生产工艺和生产线，具备年产500t的生产规模，实现产业化生产；建立了生产应用技术体系，增产效果显著、稳定，防倒伏作用明显，取得了明显的经济、社会和生态效益。在东北春大豆地区和黄淮海夏大豆地区建立示范区，通过对8个点、22个品种示范应用，平均增产13.7%，品质不降低。产品及其应用技术安全、环境友好，经毒理学试验产品为低毒，未检测到使用后的种子和土壤中有残效。课题组研究还表明，80%胺鲜酯·甲哌鎓粉剂增产的生理机制在于通过改善大豆主要器官的激素系统，协调了大豆营养生长与生殖生长的关系，促进了碳、氮同化物的合成、积累及合理分配。该成果研制和产业化的产品和技术安全高效、成熟稳定，有效解决了我国大豆生产难题，增产增收、抗逆防倒伏效果突出，为我国大豆丰产优质高产提供了关键技术，为建立和优化大豆节耗增效生产体系提供了新的思路和途径，对于我国大豆生产、粮食和食品安全建设具有重要意义。

2. 由黑龙江省鸡西市北方大豆良种研究所与国家大豆工程技术研究中心承担的省重点科技攻关项目“大豆超高产技术研究”，在超高产研究上创造了国内大豆超高产的最新纪录，于2005年10月16日通过了由省科技厅组织的产量验收。验收认为，位于鸡西市滴道区兰岭乡的高产田，实打实收面积为0.088hm^2，实产549.25kg，折合每公顷产量6 241.48kg，创造国内大豆单产的最新纪录。这样，该课题在“十五”的5年中有4年获得了每公顷产6 000kg以上的高产纪录。该项研究课题之所以取得这么好的成绩，主要是采取了“三良五精”高产栽培技术。一是“三良”技术。即良种、良方和良法。其中良种就是选用在高产当家品种中株选出来的龙选一号（目前在进行生产试验，表现突出）。该品种植株适中（90cm左右），节间短，结荚均匀，荚密，在高水肥条件下不倒伏，具有强的增产潜力。良方就是根据试验地的具体情况（自然肥力、土质等），施用金丰KCS高效复合肥20kg，K_2SO_4 4kg，尿素2kg，石灰5kg，降草剂为乙草胺+2,4-D丁酯+氯嘧磺隆。良法即“五精”技术，包括精选种子、精细整地、精确施肥、精量播种和精心管理。

3. 由哈高科大豆食品有限责任公司、国家大豆技术工程中心、华南理工大学等单位共同承担的国家“十五”重大专项“大豆深加工关键技术及设备研究与开发”课题，于2005年12月8日在北京通过科技部组织的专家验收。该课题筛选出一批专业大豆新品种，在专用大豆分离蛋白生产技术上取得重要突破，开发出多种大豆分离蛋白新产品，满足了市场需求；课题组注重科技成果的转化，通过科技示范，有效地推动了大豆分离蛋白行业的快速发展。重点解决了大豆蛋白组分分离、大豆蛋白功能基团的修饰、大豆蛋白膜分离提取、大豆制品腥味快速检测、大豆蛋白定向控酶解、高纯度皂甙和异黄酮的提取和纯化、大豆磷脂的超临界萃取分离、动态膜处理大豆乳清废水提取乳清蛋白、异黄酮水解、功能肽提取等关键技术，开发出专用（乳、肉和面制品等专用）分离蛋白、异黄酮、大豆功能肽、大豆乳清蛋白等24种新产品，实现销售收入1.5亿元，利税2 280万元，出口创汇1 016万美元。该课题选育和筛选出高蛋白、高异黄酮、无腥味等特用型大豆品种13个，优质专用大豆平均亩产达150kg，比传统大豆增产15%左右。该课题建成了年产6 000t专用分离蛋白生产线，已生产乳品专用、肉制品专用、面制品专用等专用大豆分离蛋白6种；并开发以大豆异黄酮、大豆皂甙和大豆磷脂为主要原料的冲剂、胶囊、糖衣片剂等保健品，建立了日产3t膜分离连续反应器系统中试生产线，建立了一条日产50kg的大豆肽中试生产线。

三、国内外市场概况

（一）国内市场

1. 大豆供需平衡分析　据国家粮油信息中心资料显示，2005/2006年度，我国大豆总供给量为4 435万t，同比增长15.5%；总需求量为4 290万t，同比增长12.0%（表4）。由于2005/2006年度我国大豆供需有145万t的结转库存，所以该年度供给环境仍相对宽松。

表4　2005/2006年度我国大豆市场供需平衡情况

单位：万t

名　称	2004/2005年度	2005/2006年度	同比增长（%）
产　量	1 740	1 635	−6.0
进口量	2 100	2 800	33.3
总供给量	3 840	4 435	15.5
压榨量	2 900	3 330	14.8
食品与其他用量	880	920	4.5
出口量	50	40	−20.0
总需求量	3 830	4 290	12.0

2. 豆油供需平衡分析　根据国家粮油信息中心统计数据分析，2005/2006 年度，我国豆油总供给量为 753 万 t，同比增长 3.3%；总需求量为 823 万 t，同比增长 9.0%；总需求量大于总供给量 70 万 t，则该年度供给环境仍相对偏紧（表 5）。

表 5　2005/2006 年度我国豆油市场供需平衡情况

单位：万 t

名　称	2004/2005 年度	2005/2006 年度	同比增长（%）
产　量	499	593	18.8
进口量	230	160	−30.4
年度供给量	729	753	3.3
食用消费量	680	740	8.8
年度国内消费	750	820	9.3
出口量	5	3	−40.0
年度需求量	755	823	9.0

3. 豆粕供需平衡分析　根据国家粮油信息中心统计数据分析，2005/2006 年度，我国豆粕总供给量为 2 696 万 t，同比增长 20.2%；总需求量为 2 610 万 t，同比增长 20.4%；总需求量小于总供给量 86 万 t，则该年度供给环境仍相对宽松（表 6）。

表 6　2005/2006 年度我国豆粕市场供需平衡情况

单位：万 t

名　称	2004/2005 年度	2005/2006 年度	同比增长（%）
生产量	2 237	2 616	16.9
进口量	6	80	1 233.3
年度供给量	2 243	2 696	20.2
饲用消费量	2 000	2 460	19.0
年度国内消费量	2 068	2 560	23.8
出口量	100	50	−50.0
年度需求量	2 168	2 610	20.4

（二）国际市场

1. 世界大豆供需平衡分析　据美国农业部公布的供需报告显示，2005/2006 年度世界大豆总供应量（包括产量和进口量）为 27 414 万 t，同比增长 −6.4%；总需求量（包括国内消费量和出口量）为 27 813万 t，同比增长 3.4%（表 7）。其中主要出口国家有美国、阿根廷和巴西，大豆供需平衡情况见表 8；主要进口国家除中国外还有欧盟、日本和墨西哥，其大豆供需平衡情况见表 9。

表 7　2005/2006 年度世界大豆供需平衡情况

单位：万 t

名　称	2004/2005 年度	2005/2006 年度	同比增长（%）
产　量	23 077	21 949	−4.9
进口量	6 222	6 465	3.9
总供给量	29 299	27 414	−6.4
压榨量	17 872	18 265	2.2
国内消费量	20 613	21 266	3.2
出口量	6 274	6 547	4.4
总需求量	26 887	27 813	3.4

表 8　2005/2006 年度美国、阿根廷和巴西大豆供需平衡情况

单位：万 t

名　称	美　国	同比增长（%）	阿根廷	同比增长（%）	巴　西	同比增长（%）
产　量	8 400	−1.2	4 050	3.8	5 500	3.8
进　口	11	−26.7	70	1.4	20	−62.3
压榨量	4 681	1.4	3 040	11.3	2 750	−5.1
国内消费量	5 162	0.7	3 203	10.7	3 014	−5.5
出　口	2 463	−17.9	1 010	6.2	2 530	23.2

表 9　2005/2006 年度欧盟、日本和墨西哥大豆供需平衡情况

单位：万 t

名　称	欧　盟	同比增长（%）	日　本	同比增长（%）	墨西哥	同比增长（%）
产　量	86	8.9	23	35.3	15	15.4
进　口	1 415	−8.1	410	−4.7	373	6.6
压榨量	1 368	−7.1	290	−7.9	384	7.0
国内消费量	1 500	−7.0	429	−4.7	388	6.9
出　口	1	0	0	0	0	0

2. 世界豆油供需平衡分析　据美国农业部公布的供需报告显示，2005/2006 年度世界豆油总供应量（包括产量和进口量）为 4 316 万 t，同比增长 3.7%；总需求量（包括国内需求量和出口量）为 4 271 万 t，同比增长 3.3%（表 10）。其中，主要进出口国家豆油供需平衡情况见表 11。

表 10　2005/2006 年度世界豆油供需平衡情况

单位：万 t

名　称	产　量	进　口	国内需求	出　口
2004/2005 年度	3 246	916	3 201	935
2005/2006 年度	3 431	885	3 342	929
同比增长（%）	5.7	−3.4	4.4	−0.6

表 11 2005/2006 年度世界豆油主要进出口国家供需平衡情况

单位：万 t

名 称	产 量	进 口	国内需求	出 口
主要出口国	1 375	70	641	790
阿根廷	600	0	43	560
巴 西	539	2	320	206
欧 盟	236	68	279	25
主要进口国	713	322	1 053	11
印 度	97	168	288	1

3. 世界豆粕供需平衡分析 据美国农业部公布的供需报告显示，2005/2006 年度世界豆粕总供应量（包括产量和进口量）为 19 567 万 t，同比增长 6.3%；总需求量（包括国内需求量和出口量）为 19 705万 t，同比增长 7.3%（表 12）。其中，主要进出口国家豆粕供需平衡情况见表 13。

表 12 2005/2006 年度世界豆粕供需平衡情况

单位：万 t

名 称	产 量	进 口	国内需求	出 口
2004/2005 年度	13 834	4 573	13 753	4 615
2005/2006 年度	14 470	5 097	14 559	5 146
同比增长（%）	4.6	11.5	5.9	11.5

表 13 2005/2006 年度世界豆粕主要进出口国家供需平衡情况

单位：万 t

名 称	产 量	进 口	国内需求	出 口
主要出口国	5 100	19	1 158	4 091
阿根廷	2 502	0	58	2 434
巴 西	2 166	19	960	1 290
印 度	433	0	141	368
主要进口国	3 937	3 002	6 847	103
欧 盟	1 037	2 290	3 261	65

四、质量管理与标准化工作

（一）质量管理

1. 酱油、酱产品国家监督抽查 为维护消费者的合法权益，促进酱油、酱调味品行业健康发展，国家质检总局组织对 2005 年酱油、酱产品质量进行了国家监督抽查，共抽查了北京、天津、河北、黑龙江、吉林、上海、江苏、浙江、广东、江西、湖南、四川等 12 个省、直辖市 88 家企业生产的 133 种产品，合格 99 种，产品抽样合格率为 74.4%。本次抽查结果表明，市场占有率较高的大型企业产品质量较好，产品抽样合格率为 91.7%，而小型企业产品质量仍存在问题。本次抽查中发现的主要质量问题：一是氨基酸态氮含量不符合标准要求。氨基酸态氮是表明酿造酱油中大豆蛋白水解率高低的特征性指标，氨基酸态氮含量越高，酱油的质量越好，鲜味越浓。本次抽查中有 10 种产品的氨基酸态氮项目不合格。其中有 1 种酱油的氨基酸态氮含量为 0.11g/100ml（标准规定不得低于 0.4g/100ml）。二是全氮和可溶性无盐固形物的含量低。全氮和可溶性无盐固形物含量的高低，是直接反映酿造酱油的品质好坏。本次抽查中分别有 8 种产品的全氮含量和 7 种产品的无盐固形物含量不符合标准要求，其中有 1 种酱油产品全氮含量为 0.12g/100ml（标准规定≥0.8g/100ml），不到标准要求的 1/6；无盐固形物的含量为 2.53g/100ml（标准规定≥10.0g/100ml），也只有标准要求的 1/4。造成这两项指标不合格的原因主要是由于原料中蛋白质含量不足、发酵工艺控制不当等。三是酱油产品标签标注不规范。按标准要求酱油产品应在标签上标明酿造酱油或配制酱油、氨基酸态氮含量、质量等级、用于“佐餐或烹调”、产品标准号（生产工艺）。本次抽查中有 10 种产品的标签项目不符合标准要求，主要是未标明产品的质量等级、生产工艺、用途等。四是酱产品防腐剂苯甲酸含量超标。苯甲酸是一种防腐剂，添加至食品中可用于抑制微生物的生长。强制性国家标准规定苯甲酸是限量添加的（酱类标准规定≤0.5g/kg）。本次抽查有 5 种产品苯甲酸含量超标，其中 1 种产品苯甲酸含量高达 4.9g/kg，是标准规定的 9.8 倍。

2. 豆制品产品国家监督抽查 为了维护广大消费者的合法权益，促进豆制品行业健康发展，国家质检总局组织对 2005 年豆制品产品质量进行了国家监督抽查。共抽查了北京、河北、山西、上海、重庆、广东、福建、四川、安徽、湖南、湖北、陕西等 12 个省、直辖市 32 个企业生产的 40 种产品，合格 28 种，产品抽样合格率为 70%。从抽查结果看，多数大型企业产品质量比较稳定，市场占有率较高。部分小型企业的产品质量仍存在一些质量问题。一是微生物指标超标。本次抽查中有 7 种产品的大肠菌群超标。最严重的大肠菌群为 280MPN/100g（标准规定大肠菌群应小于或等于 40MPN/100g），超过标准限值的7倍。二是超范围使用食品添加剂。强制性国家标准中明确规定：豆制品生产中不得使用苯甲酸、不得使用糖精钠。本次抽查中有1种产品同时检出苯甲酸和糖精钠。三是产品标签标注不规范。本次抽查中有3种产品的标签标注不规范，主要是产品检出山梨酸而没有在标签配料表中明示。针对本次抽查中反映出的质量问题，国家质检总局责成各地质量技术监督部门按照产品质量法等有关法律法规的规定，对本次抽查的不合格生产企业依法进行处理，并限期整改，重点对食品生产中微生物超标、超范围、超量使用食品添加剂等质量问题进行监督。对抽查中产品质量较好的企业进行表扬，加大宣传力度。同时，加强对标准的宣传贯彻，督促企业按照标准组织生产，严格产品的标识标注，切实提高豆制品整体质量水平。

3. 非发酵性豆制品产品国家监督抽查　为了维护广大消费者的合法权益，保障消费者的身体健康，国家质检总局对2005年非发酵性豆制品产品质量进行了国家监督抽查。共抽查了四川、重庆、贵州等3个省、直辖市48个企业的50种产品，合格28种，产品抽样合格率为56.0%。本次抽查结果表明：一是重金属指标均在允许范围内。本次对50种豆制品涉及的总砷、铅两项金属指标进行了检验，检验结果均在允许范围内。二是菌落总数超标。豆制品营养丰富，很容易滋生微生物，本次抽查中有12种产品的菌落总数超标，经检测最严重的达230 000个/g，是标准规定限量（≤750个/g）的近307倍。有些企业工艺简单，设备陈旧简陋，环境极差，生产人员卫生意识淡薄，是造成菌落总数超标的主要原因。三是违反国家标准添加苯甲酸。苯甲酸是一种防腐剂，添加到食品中可以抑制微生物的产生。国家标准规定在豆制品中不允许添加苯甲酸。本次抽查中有5种产品检出苯甲酸。四是标签标识不规范、标注内容不完整。本次抽查中有13种产品标签不合格，主要是添加了防腐剂山梨酸，而没有在产品上标注。国家强制性标准GB 7718—1994《食品标签通用标准》明确规定了食品必须标注产品名称、配料表、净含量、制造者（经销者）名称和地址、批号、生产日期、保质期（或保存期）、产品标准号与质量等级。添加了防腐剂、甜味剂、色素等食品添加剂，必须在标签上明示，让消费者进行选择，明明白白消费。针对本次抽查中发现的问题，国家质检总局要求各地质量技术监督部门要对产品质量较好的企业大力宣传，扶优扶强；对质量较差的产品及其生产企业要予以曝光，要进行整改，到期严格复查，对复查仍不合格的要责令停产整顿，坚决不允许不合格产品出厂销售。同时各级质量技术监督部门要切实从源头抓质量，加强监管力度，组织本次不合格的生产企业集中学习宣传贯彻相关产品标准，大力宣传《产品质量法》、《标准化法》、《消费者权益保护法》，让这些企业树立起质量第一的观念，严格按国家相关产品标准进行产品生产和正确标注标签标识。并且应督促和帮助企业提高检验水平，完善和增强检测手段，培训合格的检测人员，把握质量关键控制点，加强工作人员的责任心，尽快提高产品质量。

（二）标准化工作

1. 2005年农业部颁布了《无公害食品　大豆》（NY 5310—2005）行业标准，本标准规定了无公害食品大豆的术语和定义、要求、试验方法、检验规则、标志、标签、包装、运输和贮存。本标准适用于无公害食品大豆。该标准于2005年1月19日发布，于2005年3月1日实施。

2. 2005年农业部颁布了《无公害食品　食用植物油》（NY 5306—2005）行业标准，本标准规定了无公害食品食用植物油的要求、试验方法、、检验规则、标志、标签、包装、运输和贮存。本标准适用于压榨、浸出工艺生产的无公害食品食用植物油，包括大豆油、菜籽油、花生油、棉籽油、芝麻油、葵花籽油、玉米油、油茶籽油、米糠油等，其他食用植物油可参照执行。该标准于2005年1月19日发布，于2005年3月1日实施。

3. 2005年卫生部和国家标准化管理委员会联合发布了《食用植物油卫生标准》（GB 2716—2005）国家标准，本标准规定了植物原油、食用植物油的卫生指标和检验方法以及食品添加剂、包装、标识、贮存、运输的卫生要求。本标准适用于植物原油、食用植物油，不适用于氢化油和人造奶油。该标准于2005年1月25日发布，于2005年10月1日实施。

五、行业管理

1. 国家食物与营养咨询委员会于2005年1月在北京启动了国家“大豆行动计划”标志商标许可使用工作，目的是规范实施国家“大豆行动计划”，促进我国大豆产业健康快速发展。国家“大豆行动计划”标志商标已向国家工商行政管理总局商标局申请注册，用以证明大豆制品或相关产品具有营养、安全、优质的品质，标志可以用在大豆类食品或相关产品上。国家食物与营养咨询委员会有关负责人指出，国家“大豆行动计划”标志商标是受法律保护的无形资产，未经允许或不按规定使用、仿冒等行为都是违法行为，将受到法律制裁。国家“大豆行动计划”产品标志的许可工作，由国家食物与营养咨询委员会“大豆行动计划”推广中心负责具体实施。凡从事大豆食品加工的企业或相关产品的企业均可申请、使用标志。申请使用标志为企业的自主行为，自愿申请，不受强制。对允许使用标志的产品在有效期内实行监督管理，包括抽查、检测、市场调研和受理投诉等。证明商标许可使用属市场行为，因此许可使用为有偿使用。按照国家食物与营养咨询委员会的要求，所收费用主要用于国家“大豆行动计划”产品标志、计划推广、大豆营养膳食的宣传工作和标志许可的本身运作费用。收费根据申报产品的品种、效益确定合理标准。

2. 由中国食品科学技术学会主办，中国食品发酵工业研究院、国家大豆工程技术研究中心协办的第二届大豆食品发展论坛暨中国食品科学技术学会大豆食品分会成立大会于2005年5月在北京召开，会议的中心目的是成立中国食品科学技术学会大豆食品分会，旨在“发挥学会的跨部门、跨地区、跨行业、跨学科，包容社会各界的优势，以及与国际食品科技组织联系广泛的特点，通过开展大豆食品方面国内外学术交流合作，倡导科学发展观，有效应用现代先进科技手段，提升研发水平，促进传统大豆食品推陈出新，创新产品层出不穷，不断满足人民营养健康的需求”。会议由中国食品科学技术学会孟素荷秘书长主持，著名营养学家中国学生营养促进会名誉会长于若木、中国食品科学技术学会名誉副理事长尹宗伦教授、中国食品科学技术学会副理事长刘兴信教授、中国食品发酵工业研究院院长陈学忠、民政部民间组织管理中心主任乔申乾、全国政协常委任玉岭研究员等到会并讲话。

3. 由中国作物学会大豆专业委员会主办、云南省农业科学院粮食作物研究所承办的第八届全国大豆学术讨论会于2005年8月在云南省昆明市举行。来自全国26个省（自治区、直辖市）、香港特别行政区和海外的273位代表参加了会议。大会开幕式由大豆专业委员会副理事长刘忠堂主持，常汝镇理事长作理事会工作报告。常汝镇理事长指出，大豆专业委员会定期举办全国性大豆学术讨论会和大豆科研生产研讨会，成为全国大豆科技工作者开展交流合作的重要渠道。大豆专业委员会积极促成全国大豆科技工作者的合作，组织专家参与农业部大豆振兴计划、科技入户工程等科技推广活动，向政府有关部门提出关于大豆生产和科研的建议，为我国大豆生产的发展发挥了积极作用。他希望全国大豆科技工作者齐心协力，提升我国大豆生产的科技水平，为立足国内解决我国大豆的基本需求做出贡献。这次会议共收录论文228篇，有68位代表做了学术报告，内容涉及大豆育种、栽培、生理、种质资源、基因组学、分子生物学、加工利用、宏观政策、经济信息等。

4. 由中国植物油行业协会和大连商品交易所联合举办的全国油脂油料市场展望会暨企业避险增利论坛于2005年11月在海南省三亚市召开，高秀山会长参加了会议，林永清常务副会长、矫庆丰副会长、董朝永副会长参加会议并分别主持了大会，到会代表200多人。大会围绕“分析油脂市场形势、研讨贸易避险问题”的主题，分别举行了报告会和专题论坛。会上，国家发改委经贸司王兆阳副处长作了《关于促进我国大豆产业发展的有关政策问题》的报告；商务部外贸司朱俊处长作了《关于我国明年植物油进口管理政策的走向问题》的报告；国家粮食局原副局长、中国粮油学会理事长、中国植物油行业协会名誉会长朱长国作了《全国粮油供求形势与市场价格走向》的报告；郑州粮食批发市场信息部高级分析师陈艳军作了《我国大宗油脂油料市场价格走势分析》的报告；上海嘉吉投资（中国）有限公司任燕萍经理作了《国际油脂油料市场的现状与展望》的报告；国家粮油信息中心曹智副处长作了《今年国内油脂油料市场特点及明年市场趋势展望》的报告；大连商品交易所曲立峰副总经理作了《完善大豆期货品种体系，构建油脂油料企业经营避风港》的报告等等。会议期间，中国植物油行业协会还召集部分油脂企业，举行了植物油进口企业资质研讨会，讨论了今后我国在植物油进口方面的行业自律等有关问题。

（中国包装和食品机械总公司行业办公室
王国扣）

淀 粉 加 工 业

2005年，由于我国玉米继续高产，加之各行各业对淀粉及其深加工产品需求的不断增加，以及农业部“农产品加工推进行动”的有效实施，使我国淀粉工业又呈现出快速发展的良好态势。

一、基本情况

（一）资源概况

根据有关资料报道，2005 年我国玉米总产量达到 13 936.5 万 t，比 2004 年增长 5.82%。2005 年我国玉米消费比重为：食用 6%，饲用 70%，工业用 17%，出口 4%。另据有关资料显示，2005 年世界玉米产量为 68 884 万 t，比 2004 年减少 1 939 万 t，减幅为 2.74%，其中主要生产国家的玉米产量见表 1。

表 1　2005 年主要国家玉米产量

单位：万 t

国家	2004 年	2005 年	同比增长（%）
美　国	29 992	28 224	−5.90
中　国	13 170	13 936	5.82
阿根廷	1 950	1 678	−13.95
巴　西	3 550	4 249	19.69
墨西哥	2 200	2 049	−6.90
欧盟 25 国	5 335	4 747	−11.02
总　计	70 823	68 884	−2.74

（二）加工业概况

根据中国淀粉工业协会不完全统计，2005 年我国淀粉总产量达 1 106.61 万 t，比 2004 年增加 173 万 t，增长 18.54%。其中，玉米淀粉 1 016.65 万 t，比 2004 年增长 17.90%；木薯淀粉 54.42 万 t，比 2004 年增长 29.44%；马铃薯淀粉由于受自然灾害影响，原料歉收，所以产量下降，仅为 13.74 万 t；甘薯淀粉 2.30 万 t；小麦淀粉 19.50 万 t。

1. *我国淀粉及深加工品产量和品种情况*　2005 年，我国淀粉总产量的增长幅度仍然较高，达到了 18.54%，稳居世界第二位。在深加工品种方面，我国淀粉糖生产由于技术进步，收率和质量提高，消耗不断下降；加之企业集约化经营，成本大幅下降，出现了淀粉糖单价低于蔗糖的新情况，因此市场逐渐扩大。尤其是结晶葡萄糖，增长幅度达到 58.32%，因而使淀粉糖成为食糖市场的重要补充。目前，我国淀粉糖产量仅次于美国（表 2、表 3）。

表 2　2005 年我国淀粉产量和品种情况

品　种	产量（万 t）	占总淀粉（%）	同比增长（%）
玉米淀粉	1 016.65	91.88	17.90
木薯淀粉	54.42	4.92	29.44
马铃薯淀粉	13.74	1.24	−43.85
甘薯淀粉	2.30	0.20	−42.50
小麦淀粉	19.50	1.76	大幅增长
合　计	1 106.61	100.00	18.54

2. *淀粉产量分布及生产规模情况*　从我国地区生产情况统计，山东省仍然占据着我国淀粉总产量的首位（38.17%）；其次是河北省和吉林省，分别占全国淀粉总产量的 17.58%和 17.11%。这三个省的淀粉总产量占全国淀粉总产量的 72.85%（表 4）。淀粉总产量 30 万 t 的省、自治区有山西、陕西、广西、河南四省、自治区，这四省、自治区淀粉总产量为 219.15 万 t，占全国淀粉总产量的 19.80%。其余的 13 个省、自治区、直辖市淀粉总产量仅为 81 万 t（表 4）。

表 3　2005 年我国淀粉深加工品产量与品种情况

主要品种	产量（万 t）	占深加工（%）	同比增长（%）
变性淀粉	55.86	11.72	69.84
结晶葡萄糖	112.98	23.70	58.35
液体淀粉糖	257.76	54.07	13.30
糖　醇	50.12	10.51	27.43
合　计	476.72	100.00	43.69

表 4　2005 年我国淀粉产量分布及生产规模情况

地区	淀粉产量（万 t）	占总产量（%）	生产规模情况	
			企业数（个）（10 万 t/年）	企业最大淀粉产量（万 t/年）
山　东	422.41	38.17	7	150.31
河　北	194.49	17.58	7	36.47
吉　林	189.35	17.11	3	118.96
陕　西	52.27	4.72	1	50.00
广　西	44.65	4.03		
山　西	56.15	5.07	1	20.00
河　南	66.09	5.97	3	15.02
其余 13 省、自治区、直辖市	81.20	7.35	2	12.01
合　计	1 106.61	100.00	24	

注：其他 13 省、自治区、直辖市为北京、内蒙古、辽宁、黑龙江、江苏、浙江、四川、贵州、云南、广东、海南、甘肃、新疆。

3. *淀粉加工业的特点*　一是淀粉深加工产品规模明显增大；二是淀粉深加工产品出口量不断增加；三是淀粉糖发展势头良好；四是随着变性淀粉应用领域的拓宽，产量大幅增长。

二、市场及进出口情况

2005 年，我国淀粉及其深加工品市场好于往年，各类产品都很畅销。与 2004 年相比，2005 年玉米淀粉和口服葡萄糖等售价均有较大幅度上涨。2005 年，我国玉米淀粉进出口量比 2004 年均有增加，木薯淀粉进口量比 2004 年有较大幅度下降。由于欧盟马铃薯淀粉大量低价倾销，以致2005年马铃薯淀粉进口量比前几年增加了几倍。商务部于2006年2月6日发布2006年第4号公告，决定对原产于欧盟的进口马铃薯淀粉进行反倾销调查，并于2006年8月18日发布2006年第60号公告，做出了初裁决定，自2006年8月18日起，进口经营者在进口原产于欧盟的马铃薯淀粉时，应依据初裁决定所规定的各公司的倾销幅度（35%～57.1%）向中华人民共和国海关提供相应的保证金。山梨醇由于国内产量增加，近几年进口量逐年下降；糊精及变性淀粉进出口量比2004年均有增长，特别是出口量增长109.62%，说明我国变性淀粉的发展空间很大。2005年我国淀粉及深加工品进出口情况见表5。

表5　2005年我国淀粉及部分深加工品进出口情况

品　种	进口量(t)	同比增长(%)	出口量(t)	同比增长(%)
玉米淀粉	6 711	116.83	139 391	32.14
木薯淀粉	467 279	-35.53	364	持平
马铃薯淀粉	75 574	279.62	8 873	16.81
小麦淀粉	2 809	1.84	14 582	-25.14
化学纯果糖	1 561	-29.08	6 725	增加近10倍
山梨醇	13 696	-33.07	7 901	95.91
甘露糖醇	739	33.87	1 422	持平
肌醇	11	134.54	1 970	-3.19
糊精及变性淀粉	199 810	12.00	74 885	109.62

三、生产技术发展情况

（一）生产规模

我国淀粉工业与我国工业发展的基本特征是一致的，即企业发展呈现规模扩大（表6、表7）。

表6　2005年我国玉米淀粉生产规模

项　目	2004年	2005年	同比增长(%)
年产100万t以上企业（个）	1	2	100.00
总产量（万t）	126.82	269.27	112.32
占全国玉米淀粉总产量（%）	14.71	26.49	80.08
年产40万t以上企业（个）	5	5	持平
总产量（万t）	297.86	293.10	-1.60
占全国玉米淀粉总产量（%）	34.54	28.83	-16.53
年产30万t以上企业（个）	5	3	-40
总产量（万t）	166.20	97.78	-41.17
占全国玉米淀粉总产量（%）	19.27	9.62	-50.08
年产10万t以上企业（个）	10	14	40.00
总产量（万t）	139.41	197.57	41.72
占全国玉米淀粉总产量（%）	16.17	19.43	20.16

表7　2005年我国部分淀粉深加工品生产规模

	项　目	2004年	2005年	同比增长(%)
变性淀粉	年产5万t以上企业（个）	1	2	100.00
	总产量（万t）	5.10	19.69	286.08
	占全国总产量（%）	15.51	35.25	127.27
	年产3万t以上企业（个）	2	4	100.00
	总产量（万t）	7.90	16.88	113.67
	占全国总产量（%）	24.02	30.22	25.81
	年产1万t以上企业（个）	6	6	持平
	总产量（万t）	9.83	11.54	17.40
	占全国总产量（%）	29.89	20.66	-30.88
结晶葡萄糖	年产20万t以上企业（个）	0	1	100.00
	总产量（万t）		21.72	
	占全国总产量（%）		19.22	
	年产10万t以上企业（个）	3	4	33.33
	总产量（万t）	38.20	49.47	29.50
	占全国总产量（%）	53.53	43.79	-18.20
	年产5万t以上企业（个）	3	4	33.33
	总产量（万t）	19.94	30.54	53.16
	占全国总产量（%）	27.94	27.03	-3.26
	年产2万t以上企业（个）	3	3	持平
	总产量（万t）	8.00	7.73	-3.37
	占全国总产量（%）	11.21	6.84	-38.98
液体葡萄糖	年产50万t以上企业（个）	1	2	100.00
	总产量（万t）	72.50	130.22	79.61
	占全国总产量（%）	31.87	46.88	47.10
	年产10万t以上企业（个）	7	4	-42.86
	总产量（万t）	93.96	63.70	-32.21
	占全国总产量（%）	41.30	22.93	-44.48
	年产5万t以上企业（个）	4	8	100.00
	总产量（万t）	29.59	54.70	84.86
	占全国总产量（%）	13.01	16.69	28.29

（二）新技术与新装备

吉林省轻工业设计研究院承担的科技部“十五”攻关项目“玉米变性淀粉与酒精加工技术研究与开发”两项课题通过了吉林省科技厅组织的专家鉴定，专家一致认为该两项课题已达到国内领先水平。科技部农产品深加工重大科技专项“普通玉米淀粉深加工产品开发”课题经过联合攻关，成功研制出干法变性淀粉生产关键设备——高效湍流式真空干法变性淀粉反应装置，解决了目前制约干法反应技术中的混料不均、水分不可调、体系不均匀、反应条件难以控制、反应温度高、产品色泽深、出料不彻底、产品细度不高和档次低等一系列难题。重庆江北机械有限责任公司研制的世界上最大规格的GKH1800-N虹吸刮刀离心机，已成功用于年产15万t玉米淀粉生产线。华东理工大学承担的“直接缩聚合成高分子量聚乳酸”项目通过上海市教委和科委的鉴定，该工艺简单、合理、技术具有独创性，工业化应用前景广阔。

四、值得关注的问题

（一）重复建设问题

在中央三个 1 号文件的指导和促进下，我国粮食连年丰收，但同时也出现了一些新动向值得关注，主要是玉米加工建设遍地开花，缺乏统一规划，重复建设、重复投资的苗头有所抬头，特别是大批玉米加工业迅速上马，很多大型玉米加工业投资超亿元，但是有的企业在建设时缺乏充分论证，治理措施跟不上，这样势必会付出巨大的资源和环境代价。建议各地要在科学发展观的指导下，慎重投资和决策，减少盲目建设，把量的扩张转变到质的增长上来，在产品的技术创新上下功夫，开发具有知识产权的品牌产品。

（二）淀粉糖发展问题

“十五”期间，面对我国食糖的缺口和价格不断上涨的局面，我国淀粉糖发展迅猛，产量已仅次于美国，居世界第二位。但从长远看，淀粉糖不会成为食糖市场的主角，只能是食糖市场的重要补充。因此，淀粉糖行业要努力创新和利用成熟的新工艺和新设备，进一步提高产品质量、产品回收率和原料利用率，不断增加新品种。

五、“十一五”发展展望

“十一五”淀粉工业发展的指导思想是贯彻落实国家“十一五”规划建议的精神，在科学发展观的指导下，大力发展循环经济，在技术创新、产品创新、机制创新、管理创新的基础上，把淀粉工业建成资源利用率高、物质消耗低、保护生态环境、坚持节约发展和清洁发展的可持续发展的工业。到 2010 年，我国淀粉工业主要产品的产量都还会有较大幅度的增长，其中总淀粉比 2005 年增加 700 万 t，结晶葡萄糖增加 140 万 t，液体淀粉糖（包括果葡糖浆）增加 500 万 t，变性淀粉增加 80 万 t，糖醇增加 20 万 t。

（中国淀粉工业协会　董延丰）

制　糖　工　业

我国有 18 个省、自治区产糖，沿边境地区分布，主产糖区集中在北部、西北部和西南部。其中，甘蔗糖产区主要分布在广西、云南、广东、海南及邻近省、自治区；甜菜糖主要分布在新疆、黑龙江、内蒙古及邻近省、自治区。

一、制糖期基本情况

（一）资源状况

2005/2006 年度，全国糖料种植面积 1 405.03 khm^2，同比增长 3.12%。其中，甘蔗种植 1 214.36 khm^2，同比增长 0.81%；甜菜种植 190.67khm^2，同比增长 20.74%。甘蔗主要种植省、自治区依次为：广西 766.67 khm^2，云南 244.86 khm^2，广东 126.37 khm^2，海南 60.00 khm^2，四川 5.68 khm^2，福建 5.46 khm^2，其他 5.33 khm^2。甜菜主要种植省、自治区依次为：新疆 78.00 khm^2，黑龙江 70.00 khm^2，内蒙古 34.67 khm^2，其他 8.00 khm^2。与糖料种植相关的人员近 4 000 万人。

甘蔗品种目前主要以台糖系列、桂糖系列和粤糖系列为主，三大系列品种占总种植面积的 81.7%；其他品种约占总种植面积的 18.3%。甜菜品种在各地区的种植情况差异较大，品种繁育和推广工作正在逐步加强，目前仍以原种引进为主。甜菜品种主要以德国 KWS 系列、双丰系列、瑞士先正达系列为主，占甜菜总种植面积的 72%。2005/2006 年制糖期，随着食糖价格的高位运行，糖料收购价比上年有很大幅度的提高，甘蔗平均价格为 280 元/t，甜菜平均价格为 264 元/t。全国制糖行业主要技术指标：甘蔗平均单产 54.0t/hm^2，甜菜平均单产 33.6t/hm^2。甘蔗平均含糖分 13.95%，甜菜平均含糖分 14.35%。

（二）加工业概况

我国的食糖生产销售年度为 10 月 1 日至翌年的 9 月 30 日，开榨时间由北向南各不相同。甜菜糖厂一般在 9 月底或 10 月初开机生产；甘蔗糖厂中，江西、湖南省 10 月底或 11 月初开榨，广西、广东、海南等省、自治区于 11 月中旬或 12 月初开榨，云南省 12 月底或次年 1 月初开榨。2005/2006 年制糖期制糖生产已顺利结束。自 2005 年 9 月 26 日新疆维吾尔自治区屯河投资股份有限公司焉耆糖业公司开机生产标志着本制糖期开始，至 2006 年 5 月 20 日云南省中云投资有限公司勐腊糖厂最后一个停机。2005/2006 年制糖期历时238天。

2005/2006年制糖期，受连续两年干旱影响，全国共生产食糖881.5万t，比上个制糖期下降3.91%。全国食糖总产量中甘蔗糖占90.8%，甜菜糖占9.2%。甘蔗糖产糖率12.15%，甜菜糖产糖率12.57%。食糖生产品种为白砂糖814.47万t，绵白糖31.8万t，精制糖2.67万t，赤砂糖和红糖28.50万t，原糖4.17万t。截止到2006年底，全国共有制糖生产企业（集团）139个，开工糖厂289个，其中甜菜糖生产企业（集团）24个，糖厂38个；甘蔗糖生产企业（集团）115个，糖厂251个；炼糖企业7个。2005/2006年制糖期，全国产糖量超过10万t的糖业集团已有19个，产糖580.7万t，占全国产糖总量的65.88%；糖业生产地区性优势越来越明显，广西、云南、广东、海南和新疆五大产区产糖量为833.10万t，占全国产糖总量的94.50%。全国糖料入榨量7 231.52万t，其中甘蔗入榨量6 589.69万t，甜菜入榨量641.83万t。2005/2006年制糖期，我国食糖生产情况见表1。

表1　2005/2006年制糖期我国食糖生产情况

地　区	糖料入榨量（万t）	产糖量（万t）	开工厂数（个）
全国合计	7 231.52	881.5	289
甘蔗合计	6 589.69	800.8	251
广　东	877.00	92.2	41
其中：湛江	729.60	76.7	22
广　西	4 322.00	537.7	94
云　南	1 139.00	141.3	78
海　南	151.77	17.8	19
福　建	37.07	3.7	4
四　川	34.11	3.6	6
其　他	28.73	4.5	9
甜菜合计	641.83	80.7	38
黑龙江	151.00	18.4	12
新　疆	363.00	44.1	14
内蒙古	97.83	12.5	8
其　他	30.00	5.7	4

二、市场概况

（一）国内食糖市场

2005/2006年制糖期，我国食糖价格高位运行，全国食糖综合平均价格在4 523元/t左右，工业累计销售平均价格为4 265元/t，全国制糖行业销售收入407亿元（其中综合利用产品销售收入26亿元），实现利税总额98.6亿元。农民种植糖料收入同比增加65亿元。2005/2006年制糖期，食糖消费量较上制糖期略有增加，消费量1 070万t，比上制糖期增加近20万t，同比增长1.9%。食糖消费总量中，工业消费比重70%，民用消费30%。2005/2006年制糖期我国制糖行业的运行特征为：

1. 制糖行业结构调整工作取得新的进展，甜菜糖产区的企业重组全面启动，企业规模不断扩大、经济效益连续好转，全行业已经密切关注行业发展的战略性问题，对稳定行业发展等重大问题开展了研究，特别是加大了对糖料种植的支持力度，加快了设备更新和技术进步的步伐，许多企业已经在规模种植、良种繁育推广及基地建设等方面，进行了非常有意义的尝试，并取得了可喜的成绩。

2. 本制糖期甜菜糖产量增加20万t，取得较大幅度的增产，但是由于甘蔗主产区干旱的影响，特别是海南、云南减产幅度较大，甘蔗糖比上制糖期减产57万t，因此全国食糖产量继续下降，同比减少3.9%。

3. 国际食糖期货市场创下25年来的新高，加之年初国内食糖期货上市交易，对国内食糖市场价格产生重要影响。

4. 国家有关部门对食糖市场的宏观调控力度加大且透明度增加，对稳定市场价格起到重要作用。

5. 随着糖价的全面回升和市场的稳定运行，本制糖期出现了财政收入增加，企业效益增加和农民收入大幅度提高的局面。

6. 糖价的高位运行增加了农民种植糖料的积极性，增加了企业的生产成本和经营难度，为其他甜味剂提供了发展机遇。

（二）国际食糖市场

2005/2006年制糖期国际食糖市场自年初创下25年高点后，市场内部因素正在发生实质性的变化，同时影响市场发展的外部因素也处于不断变化中。

1. *欧盟糖业改革对国际食糖市场的影响*　2005年11月，历经40年不变的欧盟糖业政策终于迎来重大改革和调整。为履行欧盟对WTO的承诺，欧盟25国最终决定改革糖业制度，调整制糖工业结构。糖业政策改革主要包括：一是价格削减。欧盟将在今后4年内对食糖保护价格进行大副削减，目前白糖保护价为631.90欧元/t，至2009/2010年制糖期结束时，保护价将削减至404.40欧元/t，削减幅度高达36%。同时，欧盟将负责向甜菜种植者补偿其64.2%的收入损失。二是结构改革。欧盟将在今后4年对制糖工业进行结构改革，主要举措是：鼓励缺乏竞争力的食糖生产商退出该行业，并对关闭的糖厂提供资金支持，以缓解社会和外部环境带来的压力。重组资金由欧盟各国财政承担，但最终将会转嫁给消费者。三是简化配额。政策改革后，A和B配额将合并成为单一配额，同时，110万tC配额也转换至合并后的配额内。四是贸易控制。自2009年起进口市场将逐步放开，同时，根据欧盟对WTO有关承诺，欧盟食糖出口将采取出口许可证制度。自2006/2007年制糖期起，原欧盟15国年总出口量将限制在127.3万t。从长期看，由于糖业改革，保护价削减，农民种植甜菜积极性受到打击，欧盟食糖产量将呈下降趋势。而食糖出口受WTO限制将比目前的年平均出口量至少减少400万t，这将直接导致世界白糖供应减少，而欧盟在国际食糖市场的地位也将由出口国变为进口国。

2. 巴西食糖生产呈增长趋势　巴西作为世界最大食糖生产国，食糖生产对世界糖价起着举足轻重的作用。造成年初国际糖价上涨的主要原因之一，就是巴西2005/2006年制糖期（2005年5月至2006年4月）食糖产量低于预期。2005/2006年制糖期，巴西共产甘蔗3.85亿t，共生产食糖2 770万t，出口1 740万t。虽然产量和出口量都略有增加，但增幅低于制糖期开始前的预期，因此导致国际糖价上涨。巴西作为世界上最具竞争力的食糖生产国，甘蔗种植面积为600万hm^2，仅占全国可耕种面积的0.6%，巴西甘蔗种植面积有扩大20倍的潜力。制糖业的丰厚利润已经吸引了国内外的投资，至2010年将有约40个新糖厂陆续开工。对于已经开始的2006/2007年制糖期，巴西圣保罗甘蔗糖业酒精协会预计：中南部可产甘蔗3.75亿t，产糖2 550万t（增产350万t），可出口1 750万t；预计产酒精156亿升，出口19亿升。如巴西北部食糖生产保持不变，则新制糖期全巴西食糖产量将高达3 000万t，这将在很大程度上填补欧盟白糖出口减少带来的缺口。

3. 石油、酒精、食糖价格的关联性日趋加强　自2003年产5月起，国际原油价格一路攀升，由每桶25美元涨至70美元以上。由于石油的不可再生性，其替代品的生产显得尤为重要。目前世界主要甘蔗生产国均已开始或正在研究利用甘蔗生产燃料酒精，而巴西每年约有50%的甘蔗用于生产燃料酒精。由于甘蔗用途的双重性，在国际油价备受关注的情况下，食糖也被冠以“能源产品”的称号。因此，国际食糖市场与油价的关联性趋于加强。在国内需求和出口需求的双重作用下，巴西势必在扩大食糖生产的同时，积极扩大酒精的生产和出口。因此，国际油价、糖价和酒精价格将在较大程度上相互关联，彼此影响。

4. 基金对食糖市场的影响力　纽约原糖期货市场一路攀升，其中几次大的上涨都是基金炒买带动的。而在年初基金多头持仓曾高达20万手合约，折合1 000万t原糖，占世界食糖贸易量的20%。由于股票市场低迷，基金近年来增大了对国际商品市场尤其是对能源市场的投入。虽然基金对食糖期货市场投入资金相对值较低，但对食糖市场本身的未平仓量而言，绝对值又较高，因此基金的操作策略对国际食糖期货价格有很大影响。

5. 国际食糖市场供求的变化　随着欧盟白糖出口的大幅减少，国际食糖市场贸易格局也会发生显著变化。首先，欧盟白糖的出口地位将逐步被巴西、泰国等传统白糖出口国取代。其次，随着中东、非洲、东南亚等国炼糖能力的增加和新建炼糖厂的逐步投产，原来的白糖进口国如沙特、阿联酋、印度等国已正在发生重要转变：即转变为原糖净进口国和白糖净出口国，与其他国家一起弥补欧盟白糖出口减少留下的空缺。该制糖期初的糖价升高，已经对国际食糖市场未来发展带来影响。高糖价使各食糖生产国加大制糖工业投入，扩大种植面积，同时也在某种程度上刺激了替代品生产，抑制了食糖消费，这种现象在发展中的国家尤为明显。2005/2006年制糖期的供求缺口使国际食糖库存进一步下降，许多消费大国的期末库存将达到历史低水平，同时该制糖期大部分生产国将增加产量，如气候的条件正常，新榨季全球食糖将会出现供大于求的局面。

（三）食糖进出口贸易

2006年我国食糖进口配额总量为194.5万t，配额内关税为15%。据海关统计，2005/2006年制糖期，我国食糖进出口贸易情况分别见表2、表3。

表2　2001—2005年我国食糖进口与贸易方式统计情况　单位：万t

年份	合计	一般贸易	来料加工	进料加工	边贸	其他
2001	119.87	85.07	3.52	30.86	0.11	0.31
2002	118.31	80.77	1.12	35.24		1.18
2003	77.51	61.74	1.30	14.17		0.30
2004	121.43	99.26	1.19	18.63		2.35
2005	138.97	85.04	5.67	41.29		6.97
总计	576.09	411.88	12.80	140.19	0.11	11.11

表3　2001—2005年全国食糖出口与贸易方式统计情况　单位：万t

年份	合计	一般贸易	来料加工	进料加工	边贸	其他
2001	19.56	1.25	2.96	15.31		0.04
2002	32.58	1.77	0.87	29.82		0.12
2003	10.32	2.15	0.88	5.71	1.29	0.29
2004	8.52	1.92	0.87	5.26		0.48
2005	35.83	2.21	4.16	29.11		0.35
总计	106.81	9.30	9.74	85.21	1.29	1.28

三、行业工作

1. 中国糖业协会于2005年11月1～3日在南京市召开了2005/2006年制糖期全国食糖产销工作会议暨全国食糖、糖蜜酒精订货会。会议研究了2005/2006年制糖期全国糖料生产及食糖产销形势。会议同期举办了中国糖业发展高层论坛。就糖料基地建设、工业发展、结构调整、规模制糖、循环经济、经贸流通、市场调控、配额管理等热点问题进行了研讨。

2.《食糖制造工》国家职业标准于2005年11月正式发布。该标准在劳动和社会保障部以及轻工业联合会相关部门的指导下，由中国糖业协会负责组织编写和审定，经劳动和社会保障部批准，自2005年1月28日施行。同时，中国糖业协会设计、印制全国统一的“食糖制造工职业培训证书”，证书在全国制糖行业通用。

3. 中国糖业技术进步大会暨2006昆明·国际糖业新技术、新装备交流展示会于2006年4月19～21日在昆明隆重召开。大会以推动糖业技术进步，促进行业稳定发展为主题。通过主题论坛、大会交流和现场展示等多种形式，全面展现了我国糖业近年来在糖料生产、制糖工艺、技术装备、节能降耗、综合利用、废物治理等方面的成就。会议期间还组建了中国糖业专家组，首聘19名中国糖业专家。同时还评出5个优秀糖机产品。

4. 中国糖业协会理事长工作会议于2006年5月13～16日在湖南衡山召开。中国糖业协会理事长、副理事长及部分特邀代表出席了会议。会议听取了秘书处一年来的工作汇报和下一步工作设想；研究分析了有关行业发展的若干重大问题，对中国糖业协会秘书处内部建设提出了若干意见。会议做出了《关于加强糖料优良品种繁育和推广工作的决议》、《关于开展甘蔗生产燃料乙醇试点推广工作的决议》、《关于改善协会秘书处办公条件和提高工作人员待遇的决议》等有关决议。

5. 由中国糖业协会主办的全国糖料工作会议暨湛江农垦糖料生产现场经验交流会于2006年7月14～16日在湛江举行。大会通过经验交流和糖料生产现场参观等方式，展示了广东湛江农垦在糖料生产机械化、引进国外先进灌溉技术以及与科研单位合作改良甘蔗品种、依靠科技进步提高生产力的成功经验。

6. 由德国F.O.Licht公司主办、中国糖业协会协办的2006北京世界糖业与酒精大会于2006年9月18～20日在北京举行。来自英国、德国、法国、巴西、俄罗斯、印度、澳大利亚、巴基斯坦、中国等国家的政府官员、专家学者和产业界代表共180余人参加了此次会议。会上，各国代表分别就世界糖业的发展形势、欧盟糖业政策对世界食糖市场的影响、全球甜味剂市场以及燃料乙醇的发展等问题，进行了广泛而深入的讨论和交流。本次会议为各国同行了解中国糖业，提升中国糖业在国际糖业界的影响力起到了很好的宣传作用，极大的推动了全球糖业界的交流与合作。

7.《白砂糖》(GB 317—2006)、《原糖》(GB 15108—2006) 两项国家标准于2006年3月31日发布，于2006年10月1日起正式实施。

(中国糖业协会　胡志江　王让梅)

乳制品制造业

一、基本情况

2005年是我国乳制品行业持续快速发展的一年，乳制品生产、销售取得了良好的业绩；乳制品市场得到了进一步开拓，更加趋于成熟。2005年，我国奶牛存栏达1 216.1万头，奶类总产量达到2 864.8万t，比上年增长21.0%，净增496万t，全国人均占有量达21.7kg。其中牛奶产量达2 735.4万t，同比增长21.0%。奶类产量前6位的省、自治区是：内蒙古696.9万t，占全国总产量的24.3%；黑龙江省444.2万t，占全国总产量的15.5%；河北省348.6万t，占全国总产量的12.2%；山东省221.0万t，占全国总产量的7.7%；新疆159.8万t，占全国总产量的5.6%；陕西省141.7万t，占全国总产量的5.0%。2005年，全国规模以上企业工业总产值达891.2亿元，同比增长27.18%。乳制品工业总产值前5位的省、自治区、直辖市是：内蒙古204.7亿元，占全国的27.7%；河北省127.1亿元，占全国的14.3%；黑龙江省110.7亿元，占全国的12.4%；

山东省85.8亿元，占全国的9.6%；上海市43.4亿元，占全国的4.9%。2005年，全国规模以上企业乳制品销售收入866.3亿元，同比增长28.29%。全国规模以上企业乳制品产量达1 204.4万t，同比增长27.97%。其中液体乳产量1 044.6万t，同比增长29.37%。乳制品产量前5位的省、自治区是：内蒙古307.53万t，其中液体乳293.5万t；河北省151.71万t，其中液体乳130.01万t；黑龙江省92.85万t，其中液体乳57.89万t；山东省89.67万t，其中液体乳78.78万t；陕西省59.72万t，其中液体乳41.23万t。工业产品销售率为97.21%。2005年，全国有规模以上企业698个，其中内资企业626个，港澳台商投资企业17个，外商投资企业55个。全部从业人员年平均人数192 265人，全员劳动生产率为138 005元。全年完成利税总额84.72亿元，其中利润48.16亿元。规模以上企业中亏损企业196个，占企业总数的28.1%，亏损总额达7.43亿元。2005年，大型骨干企业的规模、市场占有率进一步扩大，行业的集中度进一步提高。据中国乳制品工业协会统计，销售收入前10位的企业，占全国规模以上企业销售收入的56.6%；液体乳产量10万t以上的企业18个，产量占全国规模以上企业液体乳总产量的62.1%；乳粉产量万吨以上企业16个，产量约占全国乳粉总产量的63%。

二、市场概况

近年来，我国乳业一直处于高速的“超常规”发展态势。全国奶类产量2001年为1 122.9万t，比上年增加203.8万t，增长22.2%；2002年为1 400.4万t，增加277.5万t，增长24.7%；2003年为1 848.6万t，增加448.2万t，增长32.0%；2004年为2 368.4万t，增加519.8万t，增长28.1%；2005年为2 864.8万t，增加496.4万t，增长21.0%。而乳制品消费市场，特别是城镇居民乳制品消费增长趋缓，大中城市乳制品市场出现区域性的相对饱和，北京、上海、重庆三大城市的乳制品消费支出首次出现负增长，乳制品企业也逐渐将销售的重点转向富裕的农村市场，乳制品市场竞争十分激烈。价格大战、概念炒作、“自曝内幕”式的揭短等，就是激烈竞争的具体表现，如“无抗奶”、“生态奶”、“草原奶”、“新鲜奶”等。还有的企业制售伪劣假冒产品、搞虚假广告宣传、利用标签欺骗消费者。这些行为不仅损害了行业的整体利益，而且也损害了广大消费者的利益，成为影响行业发展、消费增长的一大“公害”。

由于奶牛饲养业的快速发展与消费市场培育缓慢的矛盾，出现了奶农卖奶难、倒奶等现象。2005年7月和8月份，河北省石家庄周边县、安徽省部分地区、浙江省乐清市、宁夏贺兰县等地出现了奶农倒奶现象，一些媒体从不同的角度给予了报道，引起社会各界的重视。同时在一些地方，乳制品加工厂重复建设的情况严重，造成奶源不足。有的地方，一个开发区就有几个乳品厂，有的几家工厂竟是邻居，造成生产能力过剩。有的项目竟是在没有奶源的情况下上马的。重复建设、盲目扩大加工规模，造成奶源大战。

三、国务院加强对液态奶的生产管理

由于奶牛饲养业的快速发展与消费市场培育缓慢的矛盾，出现了奶农卖奶难、倒奶等现象，引起政府有关部门和国家领导的高度重视。2005年9月27日，国务院办公厅发出《关于加强液态奶生产经营管理的通知》。《通知》指出，近一个时期，一些企业使用复原乳生产加工液态奶，在产品标识上误导消费，严重损害了广大消费者和农牧民的合法权益，影响了我国奶业健康发展。党中央、国务院领导同志对此高度重视，要求采取有效措施，加强对液态奶生产经营的管理。通知要求：一是完善液态奶标准并严格按标准组织生产。巴氏杀菌乳生产不允许添加复原乳，大力提倡和鼓励灭菌乳生产全部使用生鲜乳。二是实行生产备案制度。使用复原乳的企业，必须在产品正式投产前如实向当地质检部门备案。备案内容包括：乳粉的进口数量，进货数量、质量、产地及其生产企业；使用复原乳生产加工液态奶的投产时间和生产周期；使用复原乳生产加工液态奶的产量，每批液态奶成品中复原乳所占比例；使用复原乳生产加工的液态奶的销售区域等信息。备案信息发生变化的，应自变化之日起15日之内向原备案部门书面报告。凡是未经备案的，依照有关法律、行政法规的规定，不予颁发生产许可证；已获得生产许可证的，应于本通知下发之日起30日内向当地质检部门补办备案手续。三是严格产品标识管理。凡使用复原乳的，不论数量多少，自2005年10月15日起，必须在其产品包装主要展示面上近邻产品名称的位置，使用不小于产品名称字号且字体高度不小于主要展示面高度1/5的汉字醒目标注“复原乳”，并在产品配料表中如实标注复原乳所占原料的比例。四是加大执法力度。质检、工商等有关部门要加强对液态奶生产经营企业和市场的监督检查，严格实行强制检验制度和市场准入制度。五是认真做好宣传工作，要广泛、深入地宣传复原乳、巴氏杀菌乳、灭菌乳等科普知识，保证消费者在选择液态奶产品时能够获得客观真实的信息，切实维护消费者合法权益。

为了认真贯彻执行国办通知，国家质检总局会同国家发改委、农业部、海关总署、国家工商总局等部门，联合印发了《关于加强液态奶监督检查工作的通知》，五部委组成联合调查组，北京、上海、天津、内蒙古等24个省、自治区、直辖市积极抽调各部门监管人员、执法人员、食品专家共近400人，组成驻厂监管小组，于2005年12月5～20日，对12家龙头企业的120个工厂全部实施驻厂监管。2005年12月至2006年春节期间，各地监管部门对实施驻厂监管以外的液态奶生产企业和所有液态奶产品的市场销售企业开展了联合执法检查。通过联合执法和对使用复原乳生产液态奶企业的备案登记，全国共有液态奶生产企业1 332个，其中使用复原乳并备案的企业91个。

四、进出口贸易

2005年，我国共进口乳制品32.0万t，同比增长－7.81%；金额4.59亿美元，同比增长3.25%。进口的乳制品中以乳粉和乳清粉为主。全年共进口乳粉10.69万t，同比增长－26.2%。其中，脱脂乳粉42 646t，同比下降23.00%，货值金额9 492万美元，平均单价2 225.8美元/t；全脂乳粉61 649t，同比下降23.04%，货值金额13 176万美元，平均单价2 137.3美元/t；民用乳粉2 579t，同比下降72.60%，货值金额607万美元，平均单价2 353.6美元/t。乳清粉18.76万t，同比增长5.4%，货值金额15 764万美元，平均单价840.1美元/t。干酪7 177t,同比基本持平。2005年我国乳制品出口7.0万t，金额0.82亿美元，同比分别增长16.24%和45.43%。其中乳粉出口1.8万t，炼乳出口1.6万t。2005年乳制品贸易逆差3.77亿美元。

五、产品质量状况

2005年第一季度，国家质检总局对乳粉产品质量进行了国家监督抽查，共抽检了北京、河北、内蒙古、黑龙江、山东、山西、陕西、甘肃、宁夏等9省、自治区、直辖市64个企业生产的72种产品，合格66种，产品抽样合格率为91.7%。抽查结果表明，乳粉总体产品质量较好，特别是大中型企业的产品质量较高。本次共抽查了33个大中型企业的41种产品，合格40种，产品抽样合格率为97.6%。本次抽查，不合格产品存在的主要问题：一是蛋白质、脂肪达不到标准要求。本次抽查中有2种产品蛋白质不合格，1种产品脂肪不合格，其中1种全脂乳粉的蛋白质、脂肪两项指标均不合格。二是硝酸盐、亚硝酸盐超标。国家标准规定，硝酸盐及亚硝酸盐含量分别不超过100mg/kg和2mg/kg。本次抽查中硝酸盐和亚硝酸盐均有2种产品超标，其中一种全脂乳粉中亚硝酸盐为8.4mg/kg，是国家标准的4倍多。三是微生物指标超标。有一种产品的酵母和霉菌超标。

2005年2月2日，国家质检总局通报了2004年度制假制劣食品生产企业“黑名单”。2004年，国家质检总局按照国务院开展食品专项整治工作的部署，全国质检系统以大米、小麦粉、食用植物油、酱油、食醋、婴幼儿配方乳粉和白酒等7类食品为重点，集中开展了打假治劣和无证查处专项行动，整治和规范了一批食品生产质量安全问题严重的区域，查获了一批生产假冒伪劣食品的违法案件，查处了一批假劣食品的生产企业及加工场点。本次通报的制假制劣企业及加工场点共38家，其中劣质奶粉生产企业12个。38个违法者中，有的既无生产许可证又无卫生许可证和工商营业执照，有的存在制假制劣严重违法行为。无证企业已被责令停产，制假制劣的设备、制假原料及劣质产品全部被查封。

2005年第一季度，北京市质检局对北京市企业生产的乳粉、液体乳制品、乳酸菌饮料三类产品进行了质量监督抽查。乳粉共抽查了3家企业的5种产品，其中婴幼儿乳粉2种、其他乳粉3种全都合格，抽样合格率100%。液体乳制品抽查的产品包括酸牛乳、巴氏杀菌乳、灭菌乳等产品，抽查了24个企业的29种产品，合格的25种，抽样合格率86.2%。不合格的原因，有2种产品大肠菌群数超标，有2种产品标签标注不合格。含乳饮料共抽检10个企业的10种产品，合格的7种，抽样合格率为70%。不合格产品的主要质量问题是2种产品乳酸菌数量不达标，1种产品大肠菌数超标。

2005年4月19日，卫生部发布关于查处“正蒙牌黄金搭档婴儿奶粉”的公告。公告如下：一是消费者不要购买和给婴儿使用上述标识的产品，一旦发现该标识的产品，要立即向当地卫生监督部门举报。二是各地卫生部门要加强监督检查，一经发现上述标识的产品，要立即就地封存，并依法进行处理。同时加强与质检、工商等部门的协调配合，彻底清查劣质奶粉，严厉打击制售伪劣奶粉的行为。

2005年2季度，国家质检总局对含乳饮料进行了国家监督抽查，共抽检了广东、浙江、江苏、湖南、湖北、内蒙古、河北、山东、宁夏、上海等10个省、自治区、直辖市的30个企业的42种产品，合格的36种，产品抽样合格率为85.7%。存在的主要问题：一是部分产品名称标注不规范。如把“牛奶”

二字打得很大，而在很不显眼的位置写上“饮料”。二是部分产品标签上未标注蛋白质的含量。三是部分产品食品添加剂标注不规范。如有 4 种产品添加了甜蜜素，而标签上却没有如实标注。

2005 年 10 月，江西省质检局对婴幼儿配方乳粉进行了监督抽查，共抽查了 40 个企业的 40 种产品，合格的 36 种，抽检产品合格率为 87.5%。不合格产品存在的问题：一是卫生指标超标；二是个别产品脂肪含量不达标；三是微量元素不达标。本次抽检不合格的 5 种产品，2 种铁元素不达标，3 种锌元素不达标。

2005 年 8 月 26 日，中国名牌战略推进委员会发布本年度中国名牌产品公告。公告说，按照《中国名牌产品管理办法》规定程序，在企业自愿申请的基础上，各省、自治区、直辖市初审公示并审核推荐，中国名牌战略推进委员会专业委员会综合评价，中国名牌战略推进委员会全体委员会议审议，确认 461 个企业生产的 501 个产品为 2005 年中国名牌产品。其中有 10 个乳粉品牌、15 个液体乳品牌、5 个豆奶粉品牌获得中国名牌称号（表 1）。

表 1　2005 年乳制品制造业中国名牌产品

产品	注册商标	生产企业	备注
乳粉	三鹿	石家庄三鹿集团股份有限公司	复评
	古城	山西古城乳业集团有限公司	复评
	圣元	青岛圣元乳业有限公司	复评
	龙丹	黑龙江龙丹乳业科技股份有限公司	复评
	伊利	内蒙古伊利实业集团股份有限公司	复评
	完达山	黑龙江省完达山乳业股份有限公司	复评
	金星	哈尔滨金星乳业有限责任公司	复评
	秦俑	西安银桥生物科技有限责任公司	复评
	飞鹤	黑龙江飞鹤乳业有限责任公司	新增
	摇篮	黑龙江摇篮乳业股份有限公司	新增
液体乳	三元	北京三元食品股份有限公司	复评
	三鹿	石家庄三鹿集团股份有限公司	复评
	伊利	内蒙古伊利实业集团股份有限公司	复评
	光明	光明乳业股份有限公司（2002 年底前企业）	复评
	蒙牛	内蒙古蒙牛乳业集团股份有限公司	复评
	天山雪	维维集团股份有限公司	新增
	古城	山西古城乳业集团有限公司	新增
	龙丹	黑龙江龙丹乳业科技股份有限公司	新增
	完达山	黑龙江省完达山乳业股份有限公司	新增
	李子园	浙江李子园牛奶食品有限公司	新增
	麦趣尔	新疆麦趣尔乳业有限公司	新增
	佳宝	济南佳宝乳业有限公司	新增
	夏进	宁夏新华百货夏进乳业集团有限公司	新增
	得益	山东得益乳业有限公司	新增
	银桥	陕西银桥生物科技有限责任公司	新增
豆奶粉	大磨	黑龙江农垦壮元食品有限责任公司	新增
	龙王	黑龙江农垦龙王食品有限责任公司	新增
	维维	维维集团股份有限公司	新增
	雅士利	广东雅士利集团有限公司	新增
	黑牛	广东黑牛食品工业有限公司	新增

六、新产品新技术

“十五”国家奶业科技专项研究项目——共轭亚油酸牛奶，由中国农科院畜牧研究所历经 4 年攻关取得成功，并投入生产。共轭亚油酸是一种具有生理活性的多不饱和脂肪酸，主要存在于乳制品与反刍动物肉制品中，具有增强免疫力、调节血脂、预防糖尿病等多种生物学功效，颇具有食品开发价值。通常牛羊等反刍动物的乳及肉是人类摄取共轭亚油酸的主要来源，但含量却很低，即使在以乳、肉制品为主食的西方国家，共轭亚油酸的摄入量也达不到推荐量的 1/3。

因此，共轭亚油酸的研究与开发成为近年来国际研究的一项热门课题。该项课题，是以研究奶牛合成共轭亚油酸机理为核心，研究建立共轭亚油酸牛奶生产技术体系和开发共轭亚油酸牛奶产品，对提高牛奶营养价值和功能、促进乳品消费具有重要意义。该项目采取奶牛个体筛选、饲料营养平衡和瘤胃发酵调控等现代生物技术，建立起共轭亚油酸原料奶生产技术体系，使产出的牛奶共轭亚油酸含量由 10mg/100g 提升到 40～90mg/100g。专家认为，该项研究成果在整体上处于世界领先水平。据悉，该项目已经推广到企业，开始商业性生产。

七、行业重大事件及活动

1. 中国乳制品工业协会成立十周年庆典暨第十一次年会于 2005 年 8 月 27～29 日在“中国乳业之都”呼和浩特市举行，全国乳制品行业的企业家、专家以及同乳制品行业密切相关企业的代表，政府有关部门的领导，来自国外乳制品行业的协会、企业代表 2 000 余人出席。会议期间，同期举办了第五届乳品技术精品展示会，参展企业有 128 个，摊位近 300 个，汇聚了国内外的知名企业，展出的产品有乳品加工机械设备、检测仪器、包装材料及印刷、食品配料及添加剂等。同期举行了技术交流和讲座，有 41 位专家做技术报告。8 月 28 日上午，中国乳制品工业协会十年庆典暨第十一次年会正式开幕。会议由协会常务副理事长牟静君主持，宋崑岡理事长致大会开幕辞。全国政协常委、中国轻工业联合会副会长、国际乳联中国国家委员会主席潘蓓蕾出席会议并作重要讲话。内蒙古自治区人民政府雷·额尔德尼副主席、呼和浩特市政府汤爱军市长、中共呼和浩特市委郭健副书记、高炜明副市长出席会议。汤爱军市长代表中共呼和浩特市市委、市人民政府致欢迎辞。澳大利亚驻华公使何伟德先生、澳大利亚乳品局主席麦克吉利文博士、美国乳品协会主席卡麦罗先生、欧洲乳品协会主席马里威先生、法国农业部中国事务特派员多米尼克吉冈先生、法国乳品协会主席让保罗雅梅先生、法国驻华使馆农业参赞雷海娜女士、欧洲乳清协会主席韦勒等贵宾，专程前来出席会议并致词。开幕式上，中国轻工业联合会副秘书长、综合业务部主任杨立宣读了关于授予呼和浩特市“中国乳业之都”的通知。全国政协常委、中国轻工业联合会副会长、国际乳联中国国家委员会主席潘蓓蕾向呼和浩特市人民政府颁发“中国乳业之都”匾牌和荣誉证书。会议还向荣获乳制品行业“优秀企业”的 21 家企业颁发了奖牌，参观了伊利和蒙牛两大企业。

2. 中国乳制品工业协会于 2005 年 6 月组织了第二次乳品评鉴师考评工作，有来自天津、河北、北京、内蒙古、山东、陕西、云南、新疆的近百名乳品技术人员参加了考评，经专业知识考试、感官技能测试，有 57 位优秀者获得中国乳制品工业协会颁发的“乳品评鉴师”职称。为了规范、推动乳品评鉴师考评工作的开展，提高乳制品感官质量的提升，中国乳制品工业协会于 2005 年 3 月正式发布《乳制品感官质量评鉴师管理办法（试行）》，《办法》共分九部分，包括乳品评鉴师定义、等级区分、考评条件、培训与考试、考试管理、考试单位及考试内容等。

3. 2005 年，黑龙江省完达山乳业股份有限公司与台湾省统一集团正式成立合资公司。完达山乳业有限公司是我国乳制品行业的大型骨干企业，2005 年乳制品销售收入行业排名第 7 位，乳粉产量行业排位第 3 位，完达山牌乳粉、液体乳为中国名牌产品、免检产品、中国驰名商标。统一公司是台湾省三大乳品公司之一，1992 年进入内地市场以来，累计在内地投资 30 亿美元，建了 50 多个工厂，虽然也有乳品厂，但知名度远不及方便面、饼干、软饮料。统一集团与完达山合资，认购完达山集团在增资后的 15%的股权，认购金额总计 3 亿元。与统一集团同时认购的还有一家境外投资机构 Rich Keen Limited，该机构共认购完达山增资后 35%的股权。至此，完达山由北大荒农垦集团全资子公司转成一家合资公司，北大荒集团控股 50%。

4. 蒙牛乳业（集团）股份有限公司与丹麦阿拉·福兹公司组建合资公司，于 2005 年 8 月 26 日正式签订合资协议。蒙牛集团创建仅有 6 年的时间，2005 年乳制品销售收入在行业排名第 2 位，但奶粉销量尚未形成强势，仅占其乳制品销售额的 5%左右。丹麦阿拉·福兹公司为欧洲最大的乳品企业，世界排名第 6 位，技术力量雄厚，特别是配方奶粉技术处于领先地位。蒙牛以品牌、市场网络和厂房为基础，阿拉·福兹公司以技术、研发、管理为依托，两家共同投资 5.4 亿元，组建一个注册资本为 1.8 亿元的奶粉厂。其中蒙牛占 51%的股份，阿拉·福兹公司占 49%的股份。

5. 石家庄三鹿集团股份有限公司与新西兰恒天然集团共同成立合资公司。石家庄三鹿集团股份有限公司是我国乳制品行业的大型骨干企业，2005 年乳制品销售收入行业排名第三位，乳粉产量行业排位第一，三鹿牌乳粉、液体乳为中国名牌产品，免检产品、中国驰名商标。新西兰恒天然公司是新西兰最大的乳业公司，2004 年乳制品销售收入 79 亿美元，世界排名第6位。2005年12月1日，双方于北京正式签订合资协议，宣布双方将成立一家合资企业，恒天然集团认购三鹿集团43%的股份，约8.64亿元(1.07亿美元)。是迄今为止，我国乳制品行业对外合资，外商一次性注入资本最多的项目。

（中国乳制品工业协会　宋昆冈）

果品加工业

一、基本情况

(一) 资源概况

据《中国农业统计资料》显示，2005年我国果品产量为8 835.5万t，同比增长5.26%。其中，苹果产量为2 401.1万t，同比增长1.42%；梨产量为1 132.4万t，同比增长6.40%；柑橘产量为1 591.9万t，同比增长6.42%；热带亚热带果品产量为1 105.7万t，同比增长6.89%；其他果品（桃、猕猴桃、葡萄、枣、柿）产量为2 604.4万t，同比增长7.08%。2005年我国果品产量排名前10位的省、自治区情况见表1。随着果品业的专业化生产和区域化布局，我国果品的发展逐步向优势产区集中。例如，柑橘区域分布主要位于长江上中游、赣南湘南桂北和浙南闽西粤东三大优势产区，主要布局在四川、重庆、湖北、江西、湖南、广西等6个省、自治区、直辖市。苹果区域分布主要位于渤海湾、西北黄土高原两个苹果优势产区，其中渤海湾苹果优势区主要布局在山东、辽宁、河北等3个省，西北黄土高原苹果优势区主要布局在陕西、山西、河南、甘肃等4个省。葡萄区域分布主要布局在渤海湾葡萄产区、晋北和冀北（羊河流域）产区、黄土高原葡萄生产区、新疆及河西走廊产区。其中，渤海湾葡萄产区包括辽东半岛、河北秦皇岛、北京市、胶东半岛等为主的酿造葡萄和优质鲜食葡萄区；晋北和冀北（羊河流域）产区包括山西、河北涿鹿、怀来等地的优质酿酒品种及优良鲜食品种产区；黄土高原葡萄生产区包括山西、陕西北部、宁夏南部、甘肃北部的优质酿造品种生产区；新疆及河西走廊产区主要是优质葡萄产区，也是我国最大的葡萄干生产基地。

表1　2005年我国果品产量排名前10位的省、自治区情况

地　区	产量（万t）	同比增长（%）
山　东	1 201.5	3.97
河　北	918.5	4.74
广　东	831.7	5.56
陕　西	765.7	4.10
广　西	571.6	8.57
河　南	555.7	9.59
福　建	479.4	2.23
四　川	415.8	7.86
辽　宁	329.3	7.03
新　疆	291.3	10.23

(二) 加工业状况

2005年，我国果品加工业向优势果品加工产业带进行布局。其中脱水果品加工主要分布在东南沿海省份及宁夏、甘肃等西北地区；果品罐头、冷冻加工果品主要分布在东部及东南沿海地区，其中果品罐头主要集中在浙江、福建、北京、天津、河北等地生产；葡萄酒生产主要集中在山东（张裕）、河北（长城）和天津（王朝）。从基地建设看，建立了以环渤海地区（山东、辽宁、河北）和西北黄土高原（陕西、山西、河南）两大浓缩苹果汁加工基地，以华北地区为主的桃浆加工基地及以热带地区（海南、云南等）为主的热带水果（菠萝、杧果和香蕉）浓缩汁与浓缩浆加工基地，以新疆为主的浓缩葡萄汁加工基地，以河北、天津、安徽等地为主的桃浆、浓缩梨汁加工基地，以重庆、湖北等地为主的柑橘浓缩汁与非还原柑橘汁加工基地，而直饮型果蔬及其饮料加工则形成了以北京、上海、浙江、天津和广州等省、直辖市为主的加工基地。陕西省是我国目前最大的苹果浓缩汁加工基地。2005年，我国果品加工制品主要有果品罐头、浓缩果汁及果汁饮料、葡萄酒、脱水果品、冷冻水果及坚果等，形成产业规模的产品主要有果品罐头、果汁及葡萄酒等。

1. 果品罐头　据中国罐头工业协会数据显示，2005年，我国果品罐头产量为120.0万t，占全部罐头总产量的30%。果品罐头产业的发展不仅体现在数量的增长上，而且反映在品种、技术、企业和市场等方面的变化中。其中橘子罐头等一批出口强势品种，在国际市场上具有明显的比较优势。罐头企业积极适应市场，开发出许多新品种和新包装，推动了果品罐头出口的增长。而在国内市场，果品罐头方便、营养、安全的特点已被广大消费者认可。2005 年，我国罐头行业市场集中度较高，其中位居行业前 10 位的企业，占据了 30%的市场份额。据资料显示，我国果品罐头在产品质量、技术、工艺等方面取得了明显的进步，并在橘子罐头中体现得最为充分。具体表现为：一是普遍使用低温杀菌工艺。果品罐头的杀菌温度从 100℃降到了 80℃，有助于提高果品罐头的口感和品质。二是机械化、连续化生产程度大幅提高。我国果品罐头加工企业的加工过程，已基本实现了原材料进厂、自动脱皮、自动分瓣、自动分级、人工挑选、灌糖水、封口等连续自动的生产过程，从而大大提高了产量、品质和劳动效率。根据出口要求，产品不使用任何添加剂，只以糖作甜味剂，保持了果品的原汁原味。

2. 果汁及其饮料　据中国饮料工业协会数据显示，2005 年，我国累计生产软饮料（不含酒精饮料）3 380 万 t，同比增长 24.08%。其中含糖饮料 1 994 万 t，同比增长 24.31%。果汁在我国已经成为第三大饮料种类，仅次于碳酸饮料和瓶装水。2005 年，我国果汁及果汁饮料产量为 643.56 万 t，全国果汁销售量接近 18 亿 L，同比增长 16%。2005 年，我国有近 60 个苹果浓缩汁加工厂，总规模为每小时产1 500 t 苹果浓缩汁，其中陕西省苹果浓缩汁年设计生产能力达到 63 万 t，成为我国最大的苹果浓缩汁集中产区，产品 90%实现出口，2005 年生产浓缩苹果汁 46.6 万 t。目前，陕西拥有海升、恒兴、通达、富安、安德利等果汁加工企业 17 个、35 个加工厂，共有 43 条生产线。

3. 葡萄酒　据中国酿酒工业协会数据显示，2005 年，我国葡萄酒产量为 43.43 万 t，同比增长 25.40%；销售收入达 102.3 亿元，同比增长 42.46%；利润总额 12.56 亿元，同比增长 58.68%；上缴税金 12.07 亿元，同比增长 30.21%。张裕、王朝、长城、通化、威龙、华东 6 大品牌占据了市场总额的 78.69%，余下 20%左右的份额由大约 500 个左右的中小型企业分担。葡萄酒行业前 10 家企业的利润总额占行业利润总额的比重达到 83.75%，在 2005 年比 2004 年的 24 亿元增加额中，张裕和长城占了将近 10 亿元。2005 年，张裕公司实现主营业务收入 18 亿元，同比增长 34.81%，其中葡萄酒销售收入 13.4 亿元，同比增长 45%。长城葡萄酒 2005 年销量 7.77 万 t，同比增长 36.6%；销售收入 15.27 亿元，同比增长 31.2%。2005 年，我国葡萄酒的主销区仍然集中在沿海一带，中西部在葡萄酒销售收入中所占比例较低。以张裕为例，张裕的增长主要来自于沿海区域，中西部省份仅占张裕销售收入的 10%。

二、科研、新产品与新技术

1. 由科技部联合农业部、教育部、国家粮食局、国家林业局、中华全国供销总社和国家质检总局等有关部门启动的“农产品深加工技术与设备研究开发”国家“十五”重大科技专项中，与果品加工有关的课题有“苹果深加工关键技术与设备研究开发”、“优质鲜榨苹果汁和浑浊型苹果汁加工关键技术与产业化开发”、“特色果品贮藏保鲜技术及设备研究与开发”等。这些课题于 2005 年年底全面结束，于 2006 年 1 月全部通过验收。通过攻关，突破了浓缩苹果汁防褐变、二次浑浊、棒曲霉素控制、定向吸附、芳香物回收等关键技术；攻克了鲜榨苹果汁加工中表面清洗、陶瓷膜过滤、高压脉冲电场等非热杀菌以及非热打浆等工艺技术，开发出鲜榨苹果汁新产品；解决了苹果酒防褐变、发酵等关键技术，开发出一级苹果白兰地；研制出橙汁脱苦专用设备，开发出 NFC 橙汁新产品等等。

2. 由陕西出入境检验检疫局组织的“中国浓缩苹果汁质量安全检测控制体系的建立”课题组工作会议于 2005 年 4 月 16 日在西安召开。该科研课题组是 2004 年经国家质检总局批准成立的，由陕西出入境检验检疫局负责，课题组成员单位包括中国饮料工业协会、国家检验检疫科学研究院、济南果品研究院、部分地方检验检疫局、陕西海升果业公司和山东国投中鲁果汁公司。“中国浓缩苹果汁质量安全检测控制体系的建立”包含三个子体系的建立：一是生产加工过程的质量监控体系的建立；二是苹果汁品质检测体系的建立；三是苹果产品检测信息和技术标准体系的建立。此次课题组工作会议主要针对以上三个方面，明确了工作进度，进行了分工安排，并且对该体系建立过程中将会遇到的问题进行了分析。因该项工作任务艰巨，资金有限，课题组一致认为应抓住行业亟待解决的问题开展工作，内容包括“影响苹果汁质量安全的因素（农残因素、重金属因素、棒曲霉因素等）和特征性指标的建立等”。课题组下一阶段主要围绕苹果汁产品检测信息和技术标准体系开展工作，搜集国内外果汁方面的标准和检测方法，储备信息资源，加速课题进展。

三、国内外市场状况

（一）进口贸易

2005 年，全国累计进口果品数量（含鲜冷冻果品、果汁、果品罐头和其他加工果品等，下同）为

114.54万t，同比增长7.86%；进口金额为6.6亿美元，同比增长12.66%。进口的主要果品品种是：香蕉进口量为35.57万t，进口金额为9 997万美元；猕猴桃进口量为8.21万t，进口金额为5 372万美元；葡萄进口量为5.75万t，进口金额为8 239万美元。果品进口金额居前5位的省、直辖市是广东(32 850万美元)、上海（8 249万美元)、辽宁(7 387万美元)、北京（2 996万美元）和广西（2 926万美元)。进口果品主要来自于泰国、美国、菲律宾、智利、巴西、越南和新西兰。具体情况是：从泰国进口25.31万t，同比下降7.64%；进口金额18 396万美元，同比下降0.15%。从美国进口10.94万t，同比增长8.21%；进口金额10 835万美元，同比增长10.74%。从智利进口5.06万t，同比下降8.44%；进口金额6 174万美元，同比增长10.81%。从菲律宾进口30.77万t，同比增长4%；进口金额9 315万美元，同比增长7%。从巴西进口5.06万t，同比增长29.48%；进口金额5 015万美元，同比增长21.84%。从越南进口25.32万t，同比增长44.68%；进口金额4 723万美元，同比增长81.03%。从新西兰进口2.93万t，同比下降22.22%；进口金额2 771万美元，同比下降7.29%。此外，来自东盟的进口果品仍在进口总量中保持很高比例。2005年从东盟进口果品82.81万t，占进口总量的72.31%，同比增长9.96%；进口金额3.38亿美元，占进口总额的51.21%，同比增长11.19%。

(二）出口贸易

2005年，全国累计出口果品数量（含鲜冷冻果品、果汁、果品罐头和其他加工果品等，下同）为364.57万t，同比增长16.63%；出口金额为20.33亿美元，同比增长23.45%。从果品及加工制品出口的数量结构看，鲜冷冻果品和加工制品各占一半，主要品种仍是鲜苹果、果汁和柑橘。2005年，果品出口的具体情况是：鲜冷冻果品出口量为203.64万t，同比增长15.61%，占果品出口总量的55.86%；其他加工果品出口量为40.23万t，同比增长12.72%，占11.04%；果品罐头出口量为50.55万t，同比增长5.45%，占13.87%；果汁出口量为70.15万t，同比增长32.8%，占19.24%。山东、陕西、浙江、广东和福建是我国果品出口的主要省份。2005年，上述5省果品出口金额分别为66 163万美元、22 024万美元、20 485万美元、16 919万美元和11 453万美元。日本、美国、俄罗斯、德国是我国果品出口的主要贸易伙伴。2005年，我国出口到上述4国的水果货值分别占同期果品出口总额的20.72%、17.64%、7.53%和5.53%。我国果品对日本出口量为39.98万t，同比增长15.24%；出口额42 117万美元，同比增长23.86%。对美国出口量为48.61万t，同比增长5.17%；出口额35 854万美元，同比增长9.21%。对俄罗斯出口量为35.48万t，同比增长21.88%；出口额15 313万美元，同比增长39.32%。对德国出口量为17.09万t，同比增长66.07%；出口额11 235万美元，同比增长75.45%。此外，我国与东盟果品贸易发展较快，出口到东盟的果品占全部出口的份额有所增加。2005年，出口东盟的果品为104.91万t，占出口总量28.78%，同比增长15.75%；出口金额3.92亿美元，占出口总额的19.26%，同比增长24.16%。

(三）典型产品进出口贸易

2005年，我国果品进出口贸易顺差达到13.73亿美元，同比增长26.2%。我国果品进出口典型产品主要有果品干制品、果汁、果酱、罐头、果酒等，其进出口贸易情况见表2。

表2 2005年我国果品典型产品进出口贸易情况

名称	出口贸易		进口贸易	
	数量（t）	金额（千美元）	数量（t）	金额（千美元）
冷冻水果及坚果	156 721	116 960	18 787	31 262
椰子干	86	13	326	375
鲜或干香蕉	23 550	7 492	355 698	99 675
葡萄干	13 392	21 762	11 274	15 747
其他干制水果	29 803	48 447	45 056	27 907
冷冻橙汁	2 282	2 404	57 279	58 251
非冷冻橙汁（Brix≤20)	102	44	1 804	1 380
其他橙汁	1 273	1 300	213	258
苹果汁（Brix≤20)	1 145	1 037	285	237
其他苹果汁	647 318	457 131	176	175
混合果汁	3 049	2 509	657	1 112

（续）

名　　称	出口贸易		进口贸易	
	数量（t）	金额（千美元）	数量（t）	金额（千美元）
果酱、果冻等	60 251	46 634	1 698	3 417
菠萝罐头	72 084	37 003	2 833	1 781
柑橘罐头	299 050	198 388	570	942
梨罐头	34 511	18 701	4	4
桃罐头	76 797	61 843	2 111	1 740
荔枝罐头	23 072	15 575		
龙眼罐头	1 868	1 503	113	0
鲜葡萄酿酒	3 080	4 726	53 972	75 136
味美思等葡萄酿酒	875	1 266	21	51

数据来源：中国海关统计年鉴（2005 年）。

四、质量管理与标准化工作

（一）质量管理

1. *罐头产品质量监督抽查*　国家工商行政管理总局于 2005 年 9 月 5 日发布的流通领域罐头食品质量监测报告称，国家工商行政管理总局日前对南宁、桂林、柳州、北海、玉林、九江、南昌、鹰潭、抚州、赣州、哈尔滨、楚雄、大理、丽江、乌鲁木齐等 15 个城市的 68 家经销单位销售的罐头食品进行了质量监测。共抽取 205 组样品的罐头食品。对罐头食品中的无菌、山梨酸、苯甲酸、着色剂、亚硝酸盐、复合磷酸盐、甜味剂等项目进行了检测。经检测，168 组合格，37 组不合格，监测合格率为 82%。68 个经销单位中，共有 39 个经销单位销售的罐头商品全部合格，合格率为 57.4%。这次罐头食品质量监测发现的主要问题是防腐剂、甜味剂和着色剂在内的添加剂含量超标。防腐剂超标主要是由于一些违法企业为遮掩其在食品加工过程中卫生环境管理不当，大量添加防腐剂来抑制食品中微生物的繁殖，以延长食品的保质期所致，长期食用添加防腐剂的食品会对消费者身体造成危害。而高甜度的甜味剂的过量使用同样会损害消费者的身体健康。糖精钠是有机化工合成产品，除了在味觉上引起甜的感觉外，对人体无任何营养价值。国家工商总局提醒消费者在购买时应按其品种特点和对原料的要求进行选购，应尽量在信誉良好的商场选购正规企业生产的产品，并仔细核对生产日期、保质期，察看外包装的完整性；对玻璃瓶包装的产品，可观察其内容物块形，应完整，无异物，无混浊现象，正常产品应有一定的真空度；对金属罐包装的产品，观察有无胖听、漏听现象。

2. *葡萄酒产品质量监督抽查*　国家质检总局组织对 2005 年生产的葡萄酒进行了产品质量监督抽查。共抽查了北京、河北、天津、山东、山西、吉林、上海、甘肃、江苏、宁夏、云南、四川、新疆、广东等 14 个省、自治区、直辖市 79 个企业生产的 93 种产品，合格 82 种，产品抽样合格率为 88.2%。本次抽查的卫生指标（包括细菌总数、大肠菌群）全部合格，但在抽查中也发现一些产品质量问题：一是酒精度不符合标准要求。本次抽查中有 2 种产品酒精度不符合标准要求。二是标签标识不规范。本次抽查中有 10 种产品标签标注不规范。三是违规使用食品添加剂。本次抽查中有 1 种产品检出微量安赛蜜。安赛蜜是食品添加剂的一种，标准规定不得检出。针对本次抽查结果，国家质检总局将责成有关省级质量技术监督部门严格按照产品质量法等有关法律法规的规定，对产品质量好的企业，加大宣传力度，对产品质量不合格的企业，要督促其积极整改，及时复查。同时，组织不合格企业认真学习相关标准，严格按标准中规定的质量指标、食品标签及食品添加剂限量的要求组织生产，确保产品质量，为消费者创造放心的消费环境。

3. *果汁及果汁饮料产品质量监督抽查*　国家质检总局组织对 2005 年生产的果汁及果汁饮料进行了产品质量监督抽查。共抽查了北京、天津、河北、河南、湖北、四川、山东、江西、福建、广东、浙江等 11 个省、直辖市的果汁及果汁饮料产品，产品抽样合格率为 81.4%。本次抽查结果表明，市场占有率较高的大型企业产品质量较好，产品抽样合格率为 100%，而小型企业的产品质量存在一些质量问题。本次抽查中发现的主要质量问题：一是超量使用合成甜味剂。本次抽查中有 1 种产品检出的糖精钠含量值超标。二是可溶性固形物含量低。可溶性固形物是果汁饮料的特性指标。本次抽查中有 1 种产品检出的可溶性固形物含量为 4.1%（标准规定大于或等于 5.0%）。三是标签标注不规范。本次抽查中有 18 种产品标签标注不规范，主要是产品中检出甜味剂、防腐剂、着色剂等食品添加剂而未标注。针对本次抽查中反映出的质量问题，国家质检总局将责成各地质量技术监督部门严格按照产品质量法等有关法律法规的规定，对本次抽查中产品质量不合格的企业依法进行处理，并责令限期整改。同时，公布一批抽查中质量较好的产品及其生产企业，引导消费者选购。

（二）标准化工作

1. 标准制（修）订 2005 年，我国组织制（修）订了多项有关果品及其加工方面的标准，既有国家标准也有行业标准，既有加工原料标准也有加工制品标准及其卫生标准。其标准主要有《果冻》(GB 19883—2005)、《黄岩蜜橘》(GB 19697—2005)、《发酵酒卫生标准》(GB 2758—2005)、《干果食品卫生标准》(GB 16325—2005)、《坚果食品卫生标准》(GB 16326—2005)、《食品工业用浓缩果蔬汁（浆）卫生标准》(GB 17325—2005)、《无公害食品 柑果类果品》(NY 5014—2005)、《无公害食品 常绿果树核果类果品》(NY 5024—2005)、《无公害食品 落叶浆果类果品》(NY 5086—2005)、《无公害食品 落叶核果类果品》(NY 5112—2005)、《无公害食品 常绿果树浆果类果品》(NY 5182—2005)、《无公害食品 落叶果树坚果》(NY 5307—2005)、《罐头食品代号的标示要求》(QB 2683—2005) 等。

2.《饮料通则》国家标准顺利通过审定 由中国饮料工业协会和全国食品工业标准化技术委员会饮料分技术委员会共同组织的《饮料通则》国家标准审定会于 2005 年 12 月 21 日在北京召开。《饮料通则》国家标准是对《软饮料的分类》(GB 10789—1996) 标准的修订。中国轻工业联合会副会长、全国食品工业标准化技术委员会主任委员、中国饮料工业协会名誉理事长潘蓓蕾到会指导并对送审稿提出具体修改意见。中国饮料工业协会副理事长、全国食品工业标准化技术委员会饮料分委会顾问高级工程师史其禄主持了标准审定会。审定委员会由中国轻工业联合会综合业务部、中国饮料工业协会、全国食品工业标准化技术委员会、中国疾病预防控制中心营养与食品安全所、国家标准管理委员会标准审查部、中国食品发酵工业研究院、国家食品质量监督检验中心、中国标准出版社、中国农业大学、天津科技大学以及可口可乐、娃哈哈、汇源、康师傅、太子奶企业代表的 17 位专家组成。审定会由赵晋府教授代表起草工作组对标准编制说明进行了介绍，与会专家对标准送审稿进行了认真、细致的讨论和审议。审定委员会达成审查意见和结论认为：《饮料通则》修订标准的基础工作扎实，所提供的资料完整，制标依据充分，文本编写规范，符合制标程序；标准参考了国际标准、国外先进标准及有关规定，结合了我国实际情况，标准达到了国际水平；作为饮料行业的基础标准，明确了饮料定义、分类及技术要求；该标准的发布实施，将进一步规范饮料行业的生产及销售，有利于国家执法监督部门对饮料产品的监管、建立公平贸易和有序竞争的良好环境、促进产品质量的提高和行业的科技进步、饮料新产品的开发及饮料行业的健康发展。通过与会专家认真审议，一致通过对该标准的审定，并且责成标准起草工作组按审定会意见修改后，尽快形成标准报批稿按程序上报。

3. 罐头分技术委员会（TC64/SC2）2005 年年会暨标准预审会在北京召开 由全国食品工业标准化技术委员会罐头分技术委员会、中国罐头工业协会联合召开的罐头分技术委员会（TC64/SC2）2005 年年会暨标准预审会于 2005 年 12 月 15～16 日在北京召开，中国轻工联合会、全国食品工业标准化技术委员会、卫生部、商务部等有关领导、专家和企业代表应邀参加。会上，罐头分技术委员会主任委员梁仲康理事长就近几年来罐头行业的发展状况作了介绍；分技术委员会王柏琴秘书长就秘书处一年来所做的工作向参会代表进行了汇报。会议还对“罐头食品分析方法”等 6 项罐头食品相关标准进行了审议。并认真听取了专家和企业代表的意见，基本通过了 6 项标准的送审稿内容，后续再加以补充和完善，并提交有关部门批准。

五、行业工作

1. 中国酿酒工业协会第三次会员代表大会暨三届一次理事（扩大）会于 2005 年 3 月 18 日在北京召开，王延才当选为理事长，王琦当选为秘书长。会议期间，300 多个酿酒生产企业的代表济济一堂，我国知名的酒类品牌代表悉数到场，商务部、财政部、国资委、国家发改委、民政部、国家质检总局、中轻联的有关领导到会祝贺并致辞。大会对过去 5 年我国酿酒工业的发展概况作了汇报。中国酿酒工业协会理事长王延才指出，我国酿酒工业取得的成绩，主要表现在：一是酒类产品质量普遍提高，先进企业已基本与世界先进水平同步；二是国家和省级技术研究中心普遍建立，技术进步推动酿酒行业上了新台阶；三是经济效益有了显著增长，酒类利税总额已突破 300 亿元大关；四是产品结构、产业结构进一步调整，企业在市场经济中逐步走向成熟；五是集团化、规模化向纵深发展，强强联合已是资产重组的重要手段，各大集团加快了整合力度；六是啤酒、葡萄酒、黄酒三类酒种的16个品牌被推荐为中国名牌产品，品牌成为酒类企业增加竞争力的有力手段；七是食品安全工作得到全面重视，有力地保障消费者的安全健康；八是许可证发放制度，整顿酒类生产、销售秩序，保证了酒类健康有序地发展；九是产品进出口贸易形势较好，饮料酒出口量增大；十是酒类产品国家和行业标准的制（修）订工作全面开展，加快与国际接轨的速度。此外，通过职业技能培训、鉴定工作和行业交流活动，极大地促进了行业技术水平和职工素质的提高；在酿酒行业涌现一大批先进企业和先进个人，激励和带动了全行业的健康发展。

2. 2005年中国红酒年度流行趋势发布会于2005年3月22日在成都召开，这是我国葡萄酒行业首次对年度流行趋势的预测和发布，发布的内容包括葡萄酒的产区、口感、风格、消费理念等。这场中国葡萄酒酒界的盛会由新天国际酒业创意发起，中国酒类商业协会、香港国际知名酒文化研究会等机构联合推出，来自中国酒协、中糖集团以及上海、广东等省、直辖市酒类专卖局的领导出席了会议，我国葡萄酒业奠基人郭其昌老人也专程从北京赶到成都参加会议。会议经过多方收集各种资料，咨询国家权威部门，并与国际葡萄与葡萄酒组织、法国食品协会、意大利酿酒协会等进行专题咨询，得出2005年我国葡萄酒的流行趋势体现在八个方面：一是我国本土红酒将凸现出“西部沙地”与“东部海岸”的主流风格；二是2005年品饮白葡萄酒将成为强势流行，则销量同比上升150%以上；三是城市化进程加速消费族群的分化；四是红酒消费显露成熟标志，2005年流行的评判指标包括品牌知信度、品种基准口感、产区（最小产区）、年份、酿酒师等；五是2005年定向消费指数并不会因为红酒的品种增多而下降，而是更稳定地归集于特定品牌和特定品种；六是我国红酒消费归回本源的一个重要行为指标是以品带饮，开始采用“一餐多酒、酒菜匹配”的系统品饮方式；七是消费者以时尚元素的对称和谐作为时尚追求的法则，我国本土主流品牌会推出女士专用红酒；八是我国红酒消费市场进一步成熟并走向与国际接轨，同时还会衍生出一些红酒时尚消费，导出全新的商机。与会代表纷纷表示，如果我国葡萄酒企业能联合起来形成有规律的分布，那么势必会推动我国葡萄酒业朝着健康、快速、有序的方向发展。

3. 由中国酿酒工业协会、国家食品质量监督检验中心和蓬莱市人民政府联合举办的中国蓬莱·国际葡萄酒周于2005年8月在蓬莱举行，来自美国、法国、意大利、智利、南非、澳大利亚和中国等世界七大葡萄海岸的50多名葡萄酒专家、30多家世界知名葡萄酒企业领导参加了会议。此次会议活动包括2005中国葡萄酒产业发展论坛、葡萄酒质量鉴定报告、世界七大葡萄海岸发展高峰论坛、蓬莱产区重点葡萄展示活动，旨在弘扬葡萄酒文化，促进国际间技术交流与合作，推动葡萄酒产业共同发展。在举行的中国葡萄酒产业发展论坛上，与会葡萄酒专家和企业领导就国家质量政策、行业动态趋势、标准发布等内容展开了讨论，国家质检总局产品质量监督司纪正昆司长就国家食品质量安全市场准入相关政策法规做了解释说明。与会人员一致认为，我国葡萄酒产业正处于快速发展期，葡萄酒普及率低是阻碍产业发展的瓶颈，葡萄酒协会应注重葡萄酒文化宣传，引导群众了解葡萄酒文化，参与葡萄酒消费，葡萄酒企业则应在打品牌、提升质量上下功夫，努力拓展国外市场，将我国葡萄酒市场做大，让葡萄美酒走进寻常百姓家。在世界七大葡萄海岸发展论坛上，来自法国波尔多、意大利拖斯卡纳、美国纳帕山谷、智利卡萨布兰卡谷、澳大利亚布鲁萨山谷、南非开普敦和中国蓬莱的60多名世界顶级葡萄酒专家学者和企业代表参加了会议。会议期间，与会各方还将共同签署《世界七大葡萄海岸组织蓬莱宣言》。

4. 2005中国国际饮料科技报告会于2005年8月16日在北京召开。来自国内外饮料界专家、学者、科技工作者以及著名企业的领导和管理人员参加了会议，并作了精彩演讲。为配合2005中国国际饮料科技报告会的召开，中国饮料工业协会于2005年3月印发了《2005中国国际饮料科技报告会征集论文的通知》，受到广大饮料及其相关行业科技工作者的热烈响应，积极撰写论文。共收到国内外论文74篇（其中国内论文62篇，国外论文12篇）以及第十四届IFU大会提供的论文摘要13篇。国外论文及IFU大会提供的论文摘要已全部收入论文集。国内62篇论文经评审，入选论文56篇，这些论文内容包括有关饮料现状、发展前景及国际贸易的综述；加工工艺及新产品研发；产品质量安全与控制；饮料成分的检测；工厂设计及机械等。入选论文中不少是科研单位、大专院校的研究课题，有的已投入生产，也有的是企业科技人员生产实践经验的结晶，是理论和实践结合的产物。这些论文对科研教学和指导企业的生产、技术创新具有非常现实的意义。

5. 中国罐头工业协会2005年年会于2005年10月在厦门召开，本次年会也是中国罐头工业协会成立十周年的纪念活动。全国罐头企业相聚一堂，共同回顾10年来行业发展历程，展望未来发展愿景。会上，中国罐头工业协会理事长梁仲康在报告中指出，10年来我国罐头产业发生了深刻的变化，全国罐头行业正面临难得的发展机遇，罐头出口连年增长，国内市场也表现出较好的发展前景。这10年来，我国罐头行业逐步完成了体制转变，形成多元化的结构，行业注入新的活力；我国罐头产品质优价廉的特点，逐步使许多品种占据了国际市场主导地位；企业真正成为市场的主体，企业经营意识、管理方式和综合素质有了极大的提高，行业日趋成熟和不断进步。柑橘罐头已成为我国最大的出口罐头品种，菠萝罐头、桃罐头的出口量也呈现出较强的增长势头。主要出口市场是日本、美国、欧盟成员国。近年来，俄罗斯、中东地区、东盟国家每年从我国进口的罐头量也在增加。随着人们对技术进步和食品安全的逐步重视，我国罐头食品的质量将进一步提高，罐头产品的技术附加值也将同步提高。

（中国包装和食品机械总公司行业办公室　王国扣　中国农业科学院蔬菜花卉研究所　张学杰）

蔬菜加工业

一、基本情况

（一）资源情况

据《中国农业统计资料》显示，2005年，我国蔬菜种植面积为1 7720.7khm^2，比2004年增加160.1khm^2，同比增长0.91%；蔬菜总产量为56 451万t，比2004年增加1 387万t，同比增长2.52%。其中，全国蔬菜产量排名前5位的省份为：山东产量为8 607万t，占全国总产量的15.2%；河北产量为6 467万t，占全国总产量的11.5%；河南产量为5 880万t，占全国总产量的10.4%；江苏产量为3 605万t，占全国总产量的6.4%；湖北产量为2 917万t，占全国总产量的5.17%。主要发展特点：一是蔬菜生产向多样化发展，名、特、优型高附加值蔬菜成为2005年蔬菜生产的新亮点。二是蔬菜温室栽培技术得到大面积推广应用，蔬菜种植的季节性、地域性限制越来越小，外来蔬菜品种得到迅速国产化栽培而为大众所接受。三是在许多地区蔬菜产业已成为促进农业结构调整、增加农民收入的一个重要增长点。四是蔬菜生产在经过多年大幅增长后，供给充足，市场稳定。

（二）加工业概况

2005年，我国蔬菜加工业在蔬菜产品加工与物流、清洁生产与全程控制、产品溯源与安全检测、风险评估与技术标准等方面取得了重大进展。随着农业产业结构的调整，产业资金不断投入，我国蔬菜保鲜贮藏加工能力已达商品量的25%。全国“三绿工程”取得了良好的效果，放心菜、无公害蔬菜已大量进入市场，蔬菜加工量已达到全国蔬菜总量的10%。蔬菜加工趋向方便、洁净、营养、安全。净菜上市适应了居民快节奏、高效率的需求。速冻菜、真空保鲜菜便于贮藏和运输，附加值高，外销潜力大，市场广阔，成为我国蔬菜加工企业出口创汇优选产品。2005年，全国具有一定规模的蔬菜加工企业有12 900多个。其中，番茄酱产量达到72万t，比2004年增长3.2%；发酵型泡菜的总产量突破100万t，产值突破50亿元。为适应国际、国内市场不断提高的质量要求，许多蔬菜加工企业建起了规模化、集约化的蔬菜基地，采取“企业＋基地＋农户”的运作方式，以合同、订单形式确定企业与基地、农户的利益分配关系，控制蔬菜生产、加工、流通的全过程。加强蔬菜生产的标准化管理和环保意识，推行无公害、绿色食品和有机蔬菜成为当前蔬菜生产的发展趋势。2005年，我国包括蔬菜加工在内的绿色食品新认证企业1 839个，产品5 077个，全国有效使用绿色食品标志企业总数达到3 695个，产品总数达到9 728个；产品实物总量6 300万t，年销售1 030亿元，出口额16.2亿元；绿色食品产品质量抽查合格率达98.3%，企业年检率达92%。目前我国加工出口的蔬菜品种中鲜冷冻菜是主要品种，但利润却不及脱水蔬菜，而真空冷冻干燥蔬菜在我国蔬菜出口中的比重越来越大。虽然我国脱水蔬菜产量逐年增加，但国际市场和国内市场对脱水蔬菜的需求缺口均在5万t以上。2005年，我国许多蔬菜加工企业把开发高技术含量产品作为结构调整的着力点，使高附加值、高创汇的真空冷冻干燥蔬菜加工得到快速发展。2005年，仅在山东省就已形成了临沂、莱阳两大真空冷冻干燥蔬菜加工区，拥有年产成品300t以上真空冷冻干燥食品生产线近60条，年加工成品总量1万t以上，生产能力、出口量均居全国首位。

2005年，我国蔬菜加工业在引进外资、引进技术等方面也取得了很好的成绩。2005年11月美国康斯雷汀（中国）食品有限公司与云南大理市政府签订协议，在大理独资建设一个速冻保鲜蔬菜加工中心。根据协议，这家公司首期将投入2 000万美元，建设一座年加工5万t冻干蔬菜的加工中心，2～3个10万t冷藏保鲜净菜加工分厂，建设1 333.3hm²无公害蔬菜种植基地，对时鲜蔬菜进行科学完整的开发加工，并逐步向野菜、水果、菌类等农产品加工方面发展。产品计划销往欧洲、北美、日本、东南亚等国家和地区，该项目在5年内总投资1亿美元，建成后将成为亚洲最大的综合性农业深加工企业。2005年8月，具有百年历史的日本可果美公司在杭州组建可果美（杭州）食品有限公司，总投资金额及注册资本额分别为2 250万美元及900万美元，其中可美果、康师傅及伊藤忠各持61%、29%及10%新公司的股权。公司将生产“可果美”（Kagome）品牌的蔬菜饮料、复合蔬果饮料，董事长及总经理由可果美推派出任。日本纯果蔬饮料生产商可果美株式会社，作为2005年销售额15亿美元的专业果蔬饮料生产商，将提供该领域的经营资源和专有技术。

二、科研、新产品与新技术

1. 2005年，我国农产品深加工技术与设备研究开发重大专项“蔬菜汁产业化关键工艺技术研究与产品开发”课题，经过新疆屯河股份投资有限公司、中国农业大学、江南大学的科研人员的协同攻关，在胡萝卜汁和南瓜汁的加工品种和关键工艺技术以及番茄红素的分离提取方面取得突破性进展。加工品种方面获得了适宜的加工品种H-12，其类胡萝卜素含量达13mg/100g，高出目前胡萝卜主要加工品种黑田五寸类胡萝卜素含量（6 mg/100g）2倍多。通过生物酶解技术胡萝卜和南瓜的出汁率可以提高20%以上，有效解决了胡萝卜和南瓜出汁率低的难题，同时产品的稳定性得到了显著提高。通过酶解、溶剂提取与冷却结晶技术突破了传统的番茄红素的提取工艺。

2. 自从日本肯定列表制度实施以来，日本提高了对我国农产品出口的门槛，在此过程中我国不断提高农产品质量。2005年，快速检测蔬菜农药残留技术在上海问世，给检测蔬菜农药残留提供了重要依据。检测蔬菜农药残留技术是由上海理工大学华泽钊教授发明的。这项技术在检测时，是通过生物敏感元件——待测和参比的两根酶柱在反应腔中的温差对比，就可以检测出蔬菜中是否存在农药残留。整个过程只要9min，检测蔬菜农药残留技术与我国现行的农药残留检测方法比较，有着成本低、快速、携带方便（检测蔬菜农药残留技术的探测仪仅为3kg）等特点。这项技术已通过上海农药检测中心的鉴定，其探测仪已在企业中生产。试验表明，这项技术的检测仪依蔬菜农药含量为5‰作为参照，检测合格率为100%。

3. 科技部于2005年12月8日在北京组织召开了“十五”重大科技专项“农产品深加工技术与设备研究开发”项目验收会。专家组对中国农业大学食品科学与营养工程学院承担的“农产品质量快速检测技术及设备研究与开发”课题进行了验收。课题围绕粮、棉、油、菜等大宗农产品流通和加工中质量检测的需要，建立了农产品品质快速检测技术平台；围绕广泛被关注的食品安全热点问题，开发了粮油中生物霉素和果蔬中农药残留（有机磷与氨基甲酸酯类农药残留）的快速检测仪器或试剂盒；围绕我国农产品加工业迫切需要解决的装备核心技术问题，开发了基于VIS/SW—NIR、机器视觉和DSP（数字信号处理器）等在线无损伤探测分级生产线。

三、国内外市场概况

（一）国内市场

2005年，我国蔬菜价格总体水平高于2004年同期，呈现出季节性变化趋势。2005年第一季度，蔬菜价格处于季节性上涨末期，受冻害的影响，蔬菜的收获期延后，产量偏低，大部分蔬菜价格同比有所上升（只有胡萝卜价格同比下降）。第二季度是多种蔬菜大量上市的季节，北方大部分地区天气晴好，降水也较往年充沛；随着气温不断升高，地产蔬菜长势旺盛。而南方大部分地区暴雨较多，局部地区的雷雨大风或冰雹等强对流天气，使蔬菜的生长、运输、贮藏均受到影响，导致蔬菜各品种价格涨跌互现，价格波动比较频繁。第三季度，蔬菜价格进入季节性下跌末期，全国大部地区气温比常年同期略偏高，降水量总体偏少，蔬菜病虫害进入多发期，供应量相对减少，南方蔬菜价格略高于2004年同期水平。第四季度，部分蔬菜主产省受冻害、干旱等灾害气候影响，蔬菜供应量相对减少，全国蔬菜价格高于2004年同期水平（表1）。

表1　2005年第四季度我国蔬菜批发（平均）价格

品　种	批发价（元/kg）	环比增减（%）	同比增减（%）
芹菜	1.584	18.42	116.27
甘蓝	0.972	23.98	108.53
大白菜	0.626	−27.04	79.43
大蒜	3.197	7.57	54.85
番茄	1.85	47.82	49.31
茄子	1.947	102.16	38.65
青椒	2.166	63.78	32.10

（续）

品　种	批发价（元/kg）	环比增减（%）	同比增减（%）
胡萝卜	0.892	−23.79	26.06
黄瓜	1.936	85.57	25.78
马铃薯	1.030	3.4	21.74
豆角	2.847	71.14	10.58
洋葱	0.874	29.05	1.46
姜	4.603	−2.13	−20.42

（二）国际市场

2005年，我国累计出口蔬菜（含鲜冷冻蔬菜、加工保藏蔬菜和干蔬菜，下同）680万t，同比增长12.96%；出口创汇金额44.83亿美元，同比增长18.07%。进口9.7万t，同比下降9.2%；进口额0.82亿美元，同比下降10.6%。全年蔬菜的出口数量和金额均呈稳步增长态势。具体情况是：鲜冷冻蔬菜出口408.39万t，同比增长12.63%，占蔬菜出口总量的60.06%；出口创汇17.73亿美元，同比增长22.92%，占蔬菜出口金额的39.55%。加工保藏蔬菜出口237.88万t，同比增长15.38%，占蔬菜出口总量的34.98%；出口创汇18.66亿美元，同比增长15.19%，占蔬菜出口金额的41.63%。干蔬菜出口33.72万t，同比增长1.5%，占蔬菜出口总量的4.96%；出口创汇8.44亿美元，同比增长14.9%，占蔬菜出口金额的18.8%。山东、福建、浙江、新疆、江苏、广东是我国蔬菜出口的主要省、自治区。2005年，上述6省、自治区蔬菜出口金额分别为15.36亿美元、7.21亿美元、2.86亿美元、2.7亿美元、2.14亿美元和2.3亿美元，前5省、自治区同比增长23.03%、14.12%、5.51%、51.65%和26.82%，广东同比下降9.33%。在其他省、自治区、直辖市中，2005年，蔬菜出口同比增幅较大的有河南（增幅104%）、吉林（增幅85%）、内蒙古（增幅54%）和山西（增幅47%）；同比下降的有湖北（降幅5%）和重庆（降幅3%）。2005年，我国蔬菜典型产品进出口贸易情况见表2。

表2　2005年我国蔬菜典型产品进出口贸易情况

名　称	出口贸易		进口贸易	
	数量（t）	金额（千美元）	数量（t）	金额（千美元）
冷冻蔬菜	555 054	445 695	20 205	18 106
干制蔬菜	242 406	701 981	1 790	5 775
咸榨菜	19 786	12 407	20	0
咸蕨菜	2 494	3 530	143	177
番茄罐头	5 938	3 572	860	568
番茄酱罐头	601 302	299 989	205	178
小白蘑菇罐头	276 426	221 137	16	12
其他伞菌属蘑菇罐头	34 896	52 919	6	19
其他蘑菇罐头	11 443	18 757	2	6
脱荚豇豆及菜豆罐头	7 621	4 606	82	79
未脱荚豇豆及菜豆罐头	13 570	9 524	103	76
芦笋罐头	106 041	126 425	33	50
清水马蹄罐头	57 943	32 647	2	2
蚕豆罐头	21 229	8 638	5	0
水煮竹笋罐头	96 364	88 774	9	6
其他竹笋罐头	98 244	72 565	44	31

2005年，我国蔬菜对日本出口170.58万t，同比增长5.65%；创汇16.27亿美元，同比增长6.33%。对美国出口33.66万t，同比增长7.71%；创汇3.35亿美元，同比增长14.57%。对韩国出口58.04万t，同比增长10.01%；创汇2.95亿美元，同比增长11.33%。对马来西亚出口50.25万t，同

比增长 19.81%；创汇 2.36 亿美元，同比增长 32.32%。对俄罗斯出口 47.34 万 t，同比增长 29.94%；创汇 1.61 亿美元，同比增长 46.2%。我国出口东盟的蔬菜数量以及出口金额，与 2004 年同期相比呈量价齐增趋势。其中，蔬菜出口数量为 133.13 万 t，同比上升 15.5%，占全国出口总量的 19.58%；出口金额 5.81 亿美元，同比增加 24.05%，占全国出口总额的 12.96%。在东盟各成员国中，我国蔬菜主要输往马来西亚和印度尼西亚，分别占我国对东盟出口蔬菜金额的 40.69% 和 24.63%。我国和泰国自 2003 年 10 月 1 日起正式实施两国间蔬菜及水果产品贸易“零关税”以来，我国蔬菜出口持续增长。2005 年，我国蔬菜对泰出口 7 680万美元，同比增长 31.48%。2005 年，我国蔬菜产品年出口量在 10 万 t 以上的品种有大蒜、洋葱、番茄、干辣椒、蘑菇、芦笋、莲藕、生姜、萝卜等。受气候的影响，2005 年，世界许多番茄生产国的产量都低于 2004 年。因此，2005 年我国番茄产品出口量增加 37%，达到 60.28 万 t。

从总体上看，我国蔬菜出口的主要国家是日本、韩国等，国内蔬菜生产的比较优势主要表现在：一是我国有丰富的劳动力资源，蔬菜生产成本较低，国内菜价约为国际市场的 1/8～1/5，这使我国蔬菜出口具有极强的价格竞争力。二是对日、韩蔬菜出口存在运输时间短、成本低的运输比较优势。但我国出口蔬菜的品种仍然较少，出口的地区市场主要集中在亚洲，这种单一的市场结构难以抵御市场风险。此外，蔬菜生产规模小，无法形成规模经济，不利于形成大市场、大流通格局。我国蔬菜加工企业必须大力引进先进农业科学技术，培育、引进、推广普及农产品新品种、新技术，充分发挥我国和东盟国家农产品比较优势的互补性，突破性地发展具有比较优势的蔬菜深加工产业，依靠科技进步提升蔬菜产品国际市场竞争力，实现蔬菜出口市场多元化。努力提高绿色、有机蔬菜生产覆盖面，提高蔬菜产品的质量和档次。加大贮运技术攻关，开拓多地域国际市场，增强我国蔬菜出口企业在国际市场上的竞争能力。

四、质量管理与标准化工作

2005 年，我国蔬菜加工业的质量管理和标准化工作又取得了很大的进展。产品质量安全水平有了明显提高，蔬菜产品作为农产品质量安全认证三种基本类型的无公害农产品、绿色食品和有机食品获得了快速、健康发展。蔬菜产品安全认证、绿色食品认证、原产地认证，如 HACCP、ISO、EUROGAP 等方面已与国际接轨。

1. 我国第一个专业蔬菜质量检验机构——国家蔬菜质量监督检验中心，于 2005 年 6 月 5 日在山东潍坊市正式挂牌成立。该国家蔬菜质量监督检验中心是经国家质检总局批准，以潍坊市产品质量监督检验所为依托筹建的。2004 年 12 月，中心通过了国家认证认可监督管理委员会组织的计量认证、审查认可和实验室认可的“三合一”评审，2005 年 3 月 10 日国家认监委对国家蔬菜质量监督检验中心正式授权。过去潍坊蔬菜出口要经过多道检测关，除了有关部门在生产、加工环节上层层检测外，每批产品出口还要经过商检部门的逐一“把关”检验，即便出国后也要被抽检，手续环节较多。而国家蔬菜质量监督检验中心成立后，山东乃至全国的蔬菜有了国际水准的检验，蔬菜基地的产品只要通过中心的检验即可直接出口，免除到岸抽检，相当于开辟了一条出口的绿色通道。该中心是我国第一个专门的蔬菜类检验机构，按国际标准建设，其与世界上 50 多个国家相互承认，可大大提高我国蔬菜出口的质量安全。该中心之所以设在潍坊，是因为潍坊有寿光这个全国最大的蔬菜生产基地和集散市场，全国 30 多个省、自治区、直辖市的蔬菜在这里交易。

2. 经国家批准授权，由江西省产品质量监督检测院筹建的国家果蔬产品及加工食品质量监督检验中心，于 2005 年 10 月 12 日在江西成立。该中心具备 300 多个品种的食品质量指标的检测能力，拥有世界一流水平的检测设备，具备对农药残留、兽药残留、食品添加剂、微生物等有毒有害成分的检测能力，可承担监督检验、仲裁检验、新产品鉴定检验、生产许可证发证检验、产品认证检验及各类委托检验，可承担或参与果蔬产品及加工食品的国家标准、行业标准的制（修）订和有关标准的试验验证。

3. 2005 年，农业部继续实施“无公害食品行动计划”，提高农产品质量安全水平，全面加强农产品质量安全各项工作。一是立足治本，加强农业投入品监管。二是立足制度建设，大力推行农业标准化，积极推进农产品质量安全认证工作，加强质量安全追溯和信息发布制度，深入推进农产品质量安全监管。三是立足保障体系建设，加快农产品质量安全立法进程，努力将农产品质量安全监管工作纳入法制化、规范化管理轨道。根据 2005 年农产品质量安全例行监测结果，参照国际标准判定。37 城市蔬菜中农药残留监测全年平均合格率为 94.3%，2005 年与 2001 年相比，蔬菜中农药残留监测合格率提高了近 29 个百分点，蔬菜中农药残留超标的情况已经得到有效控制，质量安全水平有了大幅度提高。2005 年，农业部组织制定了多项无公害蔬菜标准，如《无公害食品 瓜类蔬菜》（NY 5074—2005）、《无公害食品 豆类蔬菜》（NY 5078—2005）、《无公害食品 根菜类蔬菜》（NY 5082—2005）、《无公害食品 绿叶类蔬菜》（NY 5089—2005）、《无公害食品 多年生蔬菜》（NY 5230—2005）、《无公害食品 水生蔬菜》（NY 5238—2005）等。

五、行业管理

1. 上海市食用农产品生产领域质量安全信用体系建设于2005年1月正式启动，上海蔬菜加工与出口行业协会积极响应，发动会员企业积极开展了面向社会的“诚信、守诺”活动。首批参加“诚信、守诺”活动的企业共有20家，当年已有10家企业完成了“诚信、守诺”的评估，并向社会公示第一批上海蔬菜生产质量诚信企业。该协会专门委托第三方征信评估机构，并聘请了相关农业专家。评估机构和农业专家根据《上海蔬菜生产质量安全信用行为规范》、《上海蔬菜生产质量安全信用行为规范实施办法》和《上海蔬菜生产质量安全信用档案》等相关规定，拟定了《上海蔬菜生产质量安全信用评价指标体系》，然后根据“评价指标体系”实地进行评估。评估专家每到一个企业，认真查看蔬菜生产基地，化肥、农药等农用物资仓库和整理、加工、包装车间；仔细查阅各项管理制度、田间档案制度和岗位责任制度的落实执行情况；审阅蔬菜产品质量检测报告等，并着重就产地环境条件、农业投入品的使用和管理、田间档案管理制度的建立和执行、标准化生产操作规程和产品卫生质量合格检验及企业和产品的认证情况等逐一进行评估。在评估过程中，各受评企业一致认为在本行业开展“诚信、守诺”活动是及时的，也是必要的。开展此项活动，不仅能规范生产者的行为，有利于企业做大做强，而且有利于提高蔬菜产品质量安全水平，确保广大消费者利益。

2. 第六届中国（寿光）国际蔬菜科技博览会于2005年4月20日在山东省寿光市国际会展中心隆重开幕。本届菜博会以服务“三农”为宗旨，以“绿色·科技·未来”为主题，集中反映了我国现代农业的发展方向和大众消费趋势，这对引领农民积极生产绿色优质农产品，大力发展现代农业，加快农业和农村经济发展，增加农民收入，具有重要的促进作用。与往届相比，本次菜博会的展示规模大，展示内容更丰富，技术含量更高。据悉，本届菜博会共展示品种1 000多个，其中国外先进品种占到20%以上。在1 000个展位中，韩国、以色列、瑞士、荷兰等20多个国家的展位占到25%以上。

3. 由中国绿色食品发展中心支持、中国绿色食品协会主办的2005中国国际绿色食品市场高峰论坛于2005年8月29日在北京召开。原全国人大常委会副委员长布赫出席了论坛开幕式，中国名牌战略推进委员会主任林宗棠、农业部原副部长张延喜、原轻工业部副部长杜子端、国家发改委公众营养与发展中心主任于小东、国家食品检测中心主任程劲松等出席了高峰论坛会。本次高峰论坛结合当前我国农业和农村经济新阶段的新任务和新形势，按照农业部关于加快发展绿色食品促进农民增收和农产品竞争力增强的有关部署，紧扣加强绿色食品市场建设的主题，以绿色食品企业关注的产品营销、品牌经营、市场开拓和贸易扩展为核心内容，旨在通过论坛的学习、交流形式，传播绿色营销思想，锻造绿色品牌理念，拓展国内、国际市场，帮助企业提高核心竞争力。

4. 第七届国际果蔬·食品博览会于2005年9月23～27日在山东烟台市举行，本次博览会的主题是“让绿色永恒”。商务部、科技部、农业部、国家外国专家局、中国工程院等有关领导以及有关国际组织官员、海外政要和企业界人士出席了会议。共有来自韩国、日本、印度尼西亚、新加坡、澳大利亚、美国、德国、法国、意大利、荷兰、中国香港等30多个国家和地区，以及北京、上海、天津、辽宁、江苏、新疆、内蒙古、宁夏等28个省、自治区、直辖市的有关政府机构、中介组织和果蔬食品企业参会参展。展位总数达1 370个，其中主会场870个；参展企业达1 000多个，其中海外企业160多个；参会海外客商3 000多人。

5. 由中国果品流通协会、中国蔬菜流通协会共同主办的2005第二届中国国际果蔬展览会于2005年11月10日在深圳举行。本次展会的主题是“绿色·精品·合作·发展”。展会将以果蔬产品为主，兼顾整个产业链，向国内外客商展示我国名、优、新、特果蔬产品及相关技术和成果。展会吸引了包括果蔬培植、保鲜、物流、深加工等果蔬产业链的众多知名企业，国内大型果蔬产品批发市场及果蔬经销商、进出口贸易商等参会，现场开展洽谈采购。国际果蔬流通会议、中国果蔬产业发展高层论坛、2005果蔬检验检疫暨国际贸易论坛三大专业论坛与展会同期举办，业内人士将共商中国果蔬产业在贸易流通方面的热点问题。

（山东省农业机械科学研究所　孙众沛）

茶 叶 加 工 业

一、全国茶叶生产情况

根据《中国农业统计资料》提供的数据，2005 年全国茶园面积和茶叶产量如表 1 所示。

（一）茶园面积增长情况分析

近年来，在茶叶良好经济效益带动下，加上茶文化宣传活动深入和茶叶销路不断扩展，我国各茶区茶叶生产积极性高涨。同时，茶叶又是一种适宜于贫困山区种植、促进农民脱贫致富的经济作物，尤其西部茶区发展速度较快。2005 年，我国茶园总面积达到 1 352.1khm²，比 2004 年的 1 262.3khm² 增长 7.1%。

表 1　2005 年全国茶园面积和茶叶产量

地区	茶园面积（khm²）	采摘面积（khm²）	茶叶产量（t）						
			总产量	比上年增减	其中				
					红毛茶	绿毛茶	乌龙毛茶	紧压茶原料	其他茶
全国	1 352.1	1 041.5	934 857	99 627	47 941	691 020	103 820	27 653	64 423
江苏	23.9	19.5	12 068	825	1 335	10 105			628
浙江	154.7	133.6	144 370	5 670	145	142 926	130	307	862
安徽	117.6	105.4	59 619	3 859	2 484	54 890			2 245
福建	155.2	132.6	184 826	20 430	1 652	88 923	85 924	10	8 317
江西	38.2	31.1	16 691	3 240	2 587	12 503	1 501		
山东	14.5	9.7	6 645	1 689		6 645			
河南	33.1	28.2	16 902	4 770		16 902			
湖北	138.4	101.6	84 976	8 741	6 546	67 221		9 432	1 777
湖南	80.1	67.0	71 978	5 346	15 399	35 912	625	9 497	10 545
广东	36.0	28.8	44 465	4 065	1 562	20 586	15 493	6	6 718
广西	36.9	31.2	26 181	2 830	440	20 695			5 046
海南	15.0		950	−388	1	894			55
重庆	25.8	19.0	16 545	481	3 211	10 215			3 119
四川	152.0	98.0	97 941	11 477	996	73 817	134	8 199	14 795
贵州	59.7	40.1	22 915	3 552	61	14 123	1	95	8 635
云南	218.5	164.5	115 880	20 800	11 422	102 661	12	107	1 678
西藏	0.2	0.1	3	3					3
陕西	59.5	29.2	11 382	1 143		11 382			
甘肃	6.3	1.9	520	94		520			

（二）茶叶产量增长情况分析

2005 年春季，我国茶区遭受到较严重的倒春寒冻害影响，福建、浙江两个主要产茶省的春茶产量较上年同期下降 10%以上。除云南省外，其他茶区春茶采摘期也推迟了 10～15 天。但是，由于四川、云南、广西等茶区春茶产量出现较大幅度增长，从一定程度抵消了闽、浙茶区春茶的减产，加上全国各茶区茶园投产面积的增加和夏秋茶生产状况良好，使 2005 年全国茶叶总产量达到创记录的 93.5 万 t（国家统计局统计 92 万 t），比上年的 83.5 万 t 增长 12%。现将各类茶叶增长具体状况分析如下：

1. 绿茶　我国是世界上主要绿茶生产国。如上所述，春茶期间冻害对我国绿茶产区影响较大，但由于茶农对茶园的投入增加和新茶园投产面积增大，2005 年我国绿茶产量又出现大幅度的增加，达到 69.1 万 t，比上年增长 12.7%。

2. 红茶　近年来，我国红茶生产一直不景气，但 2005 年有小幅度回升，总产量为 4.8 万 t，比上年的 4.4 万 t 增长 9%。

3. 乌龙茶　乌龙茶是我国的特有茶类。经过十余年的努力，国内乌龙茶销售，已从市场引入期进入快速上升期，销售量不断增加。近来虽出口呈下降趋势，但在国内市场推动下，乌龙茶产量仍继续快速增长。2005 年，全国乌龙茶总产量达到 10.4 万 t，比上年的 9.0 万 t 增长 15.6%。

4. 紧压茶　紧压茶是我国少数民族地区所必需

消费的茶类，经过几年调整，生产趋于稳定，消费市场变化不大，加上原料价格上涨，也制约了产量增加。2005年，紧压茶产量为2.8万t，与上年基本持平。值得说明的是，目前对紧压茶的统计，由于对边销茶的理解不一样，有些将整个边销茶统计在紧压茶中，有些则将一部分边销茶统计在绿茶中，一部分紧压茶如普洱茶则统计在其他茶类中，故上述产量数字与实际生产数可能有出入。

5. 其他茶类　国内茶叶消费近年来趋向于多元化，故统计在其他茶类中的普洱茶，近两年已成为市场销售的热点之一。云南省的一些主要茶叶企业，近两年都把生产的重点放在普洱茶上，同时也吸引了一大批有实力的企业投资于普洱茶的加工和销售，促进了其他茶类总产量的快速增加。2005年，全国其他茶类总产量为6.4万t，比上年的5.7万t增长12.3%。

6. 花茶　花茶原料茶主要是绿茶，2005年，由于花茶原料主要产区的福建闽东冻害严重，云南又因普洱茶热销，花茶原料茶产量急剧下降，造成花茶原料茶供应紧张，加之花茶窨制季节，广西横县雨水过多，使得花茶加工总量减少。2005年，全国花茶生产总量为9.0万t，比上年的9.5万t下降了5.3%。

7. 名优茶　名优茶生产已形成我国茶叶生产的主体，自20世纪90年代以来，一直呈快速增长势态。2005年，名优茶生产因受春季冻害影响和采茶劳力不足，造成一些省份名优茶产量出现下降，全国名优茶的增幅也比前几年趋缓。2005年，全国名优茶总产量为23.0万t，比上年的21.8万t增长5.5%。

二、茶叶销售情况

（一）国内销售

2005年，我国国内茶叶销售继续保持上升势头，绿茶销售继续增加，名优茶价格上升，乌龙茶、普洱茶销售增幅明显。2005年，全国茶叶销售总量为60万t，销售金额170亿元，全年茶叶平均单价为18元/kg。各茶类国内具体销售状况如下：

1. 绿茶　2005年，全国名优绿茶销售增幅放缓，但中低档绿茶销售继续增加，促使整个绿茶销售继续增加。2005年，国内绿茶销售总量为35万t，比上年的30万t增长16.7%。

2. 红茶　由于云南红茶产量下降，市场红茶供应不足，价格上升，影响了红茶的消费量。2005年，全国红茶销售总量为1.4万t，比上年的1.6万t下降了12.5%。

3. 乌龙茶　乌龙茶的消费群体在不断扩大，2004年开始，以绿茶、花茶和紧压茶消费为主的西北市场，乌龙茶销售快速增长，说明该茶类市场营销的成功。2005年，全国乌龙茶销售总量为6.8万t，比上年的5.5万t增长23.6%。

4. 其他茶类（含紧压茶）　2005年，由于紧压茶消费稳定，虽然普洱茶消费主要市场的广东有不利于普洱茶销售的报道，但云南举办普洱茶叶节和组织普洱茶马帮进京等活动，还是有效促进了普洱茶销售的增长。2005年，全国其他茶类销售总量为8.8万t，比上年的7.45万t增长18%。

5. 花茶　由于茶叶原料和茉莉花价格上涨，其结果是茉莉花茶质量下滑，价格上升，影响了花茶的销售，尤其在销区农村表现更为明显。2005年，全国花茶销售总量为8.5万t，比上年的9.4万t下降9.6%。

（二）茶叶出口

据海关统计，2005年，我国茶叶共出口到113个国家和地区，茶叶出口总量为28.7万t，比上年的27.9万t增长2.9%；出口金额4.85亿美元，比上年增长10.9%，平均价比上年增长8.4%。总起来讲出口量和出口价格稳中有升，再创历史新高。我国茶叶出口前20位国家和地区的出口状况如表2所示。

表2　我国茶叶出口前20位国家和地区的出口状况

序号	国家和地区	出口量（t）	同比增长（%）	金额（万美元）	同比增长（%）
1	摩洛哥	52 644.24	6.24	9 847.86	14.42
2	日本	34 586.34	−7.53	7 978.14	−4.93
3	乌兹别克斯坦	19 286.92	9.26	1 014.19	6.11
4	美国	18 259.54	5.62	2 950.04	21.74
5	俄罗斯	14 896.78	0.51	2 054.13	21.90
6	香港	13 867.41	8.32	3 465.73	25.58
7	加纳	13 113.04	44.47	2 503.69	70.30
8	阿尔及利亚	11 364.19	38.99	2 106.50	34.52

（续）

序号	国家和地区	出口量（t）	同比增长（%）	金额（万美元）	同比增长（%）
9	塞内加尔	8 981.28	21.29	1 666.47	44.11
10	毛里塔尼亚	8 614.91	−3.44	1 815.19	−7.38
11	巴基斯坦	8 369.50	21.34	585.21	23.80
12	利比亚	5 915.80	38.96	810.23	58.16
13	阿富汗	5 742.29	3.20	468.70	28.70
14	土库曼斯坦	5 209.51	88.69	298.90	97.77
15	德国	4 702.74	−14.54	1 113.00	3.79
16	斯里兰卡	3 572.05	26.38	578.33	23.85
17	突尼斯	3 291.32	3.03	310.60	7.67
18	冈比亚	2 957.58	−20.86	506.90	−19.86
19	波兰	2 943.60	−40.16	444.49	−33.40
20	贝宁	2 852.99	−10.01	275.02	12.19
出口总计		286 616.60	2.29	48 453.19	10.91

2005 年我国各茶类具体出口状况如下：

1. 绿茶出口　2005 年我国绿茶出口达 105 个国家和地区，出口总量为 20.6 万 t，出口金额 3.3 亿美元，分别比上年增长 5.1%和 12.4%。我国对北非、西北非、独联体国家市场绿茶出口增势强劲；对美国、加拿大出口亦有小幅上升；对欧盟出口呈小幅下降趋势；我国对日本绿茶尤其是浙江生产蒸青绿茶出口下降幅度较大。

2. 红茶出口　2005 年，我国出口红茶 3.6 万 t，出口金额 4 000 万美元，同上年相比分别下降 9%和 3%。我国对欧盟、美国、俄罗斯等市场的红茶出口均呈下降趋势。

3. 特种茶出口　2005 年，我国出口特种茶 4.5 万 t，与上年基本持平，出口金额 1.14 亿美元，同上年相比增长 12.3%。特种茶是我国独有出口商品，出口市场集中在日本、香港、美国、东南亚等，消费区域较为稳定。2005 年，我国对日本乌龙茶出口呈下降趋势。

三、我国茶叶在世界上的地位

2005 年，我国茶园面积 135.2 万 hm^2，约占世界茶园面积的 45%，自 1966 年超过印度后，一直处于世界第一位。2004 年，我国茶叶产量达到 83.5 万 t，占世界茶叶总产量 325 万 t 的 25.7%，首次超过印度，为世界茶叶产量最多的国家。2004 年我国茶叶出口 27.9 万 t，占世界茶叶总出口量 149.6 万 t 的 18.65%。仅次于肯尼亚（33.3 万 t）和斯里兰卡（30 万 t），处于世界第三位。

四、茶叶生产、贸易和科技动态

1. 1999 年以来，欧盟开始执行“零风险”计划，不断增加茶叶中农药残留的检验种类，同时严格农药残留标准。到 2005 年，茶叶中的农药残留标准已从 1999 年的 7 种增加到 2005 年的 189 种，其中 93.6%的农药标准都按仪器最小检出量（LOD）来执行。2005 年 6 月 21 日日本发布了《食品中农业化学品肯定列表制度》，2006 年 6 月 1 日起实行，标准中包括制订有临时标准的农药 263 种，还有 517 种农药按一律标准即均按 0.01mg/kg 标准执行。这对我国茶叶出口欧盟、日本将产生重大影响。

2. 为应对国际市场壁垒和确保茶叶品质，2005 年 1 月 25 日卫生部和国家标准化管理委员会联合发布《食品中污染物限量》（GB 2762—2005）和《食品中农药残留最大限量》（GB 2763—2005）国家标准，两种标准规定茶叶中铅的限量标准指标为 5mg/kg，并规定 9 种农药最大残留限量，于 10 月 1 日起实施。继 2001 年 11 月国家质检总局批准对龙井茶实施原产地域产品保护后，2004 年 7 月 8 日又批准对安溪铁观音实施原产地域产品保护，11 月 4 日国家质检总局、国家标准化管理委员会批准发布《原产地域产品—安溪铁观音》（GB 19598—2004）国家标准，于 2005 年 1 月 1 日起实施。

3. 2005 年 4 月，贵州省质监局在当地查封了浙江茶商用铅铬绿生产染色茶加工窝点，各地质监部门开始在全国市场追查铅铬绿染色茶。2005 年 7 月，北京警方与工商执法人员联合，一举端掉一个非法传销茶叶的网络组织，传销的所谓名茶均是该团伙从福建、云南等地买进的劣质茶叶，设案金额达 1 200 余万元。

4. 云南马帮普洱茶文化北京行活动，2005 年 4 月 28 日从云南省思茅市首发，这次由 99 匹马组成的马帮驮茶进京活动，历时半年，途经云南、四川、陕西、山西、河北，最后抵达北京，沿途开展普洱茶文化交流和为希望工程筹资拍卖活动，目的在于进一步掀起普洱茶市场热潮。

5. 由中国农业科学院茶叶研究所、中国茶叶学会和联合利华（中国）有限公司共同举办的2005年茶业科技创新与产业可持续发展国际研讨会于11月11～15日在杭州举行。来自联合国粮农组织、孟加拉国、德国、印度、印度尼西亚、日本、尼日利亚、斯里兰卡、南非、英国、美国、越南、中国及台湾省、香港特别行政区等17个国家、地区及国际组织的200余名专家、学者参加了会议。

五、2006年茶叶产销展望

1. 2006年我国茶叶产量将会继续增长，因为近几年发展的新茶园将陆续投产，部分将进入丰产期以四川为例，1999—2004年茶园面积增长72.7%，年平均增长14.5%；茶叶总产量增长87.8%，年平均增长17.6%。同时，从2005年世界茶叶生产实际情况看，2006年世界茶叶产量也将再创新高，这将给世界茶叶市场带来更大的压力。

2. 纵观近几年我国茶叶的出口状况，增长幅度总起来讲上升不明显，并且以出口中低档茶为主 因此，2006年的茶叶销售，将会继续遵循积极拓展国际市场、把扩大国内需求作为工作重点的原则。预计2006年我国的茶叶出口将保持稳中有升状态。国内销售市场，绿茶、乌龙茶、普洱茶将会继续增长，并且竞争将会向着更为有序的方向发展；花茶、边销茶、红茶市场变化不大。

（中国农业科学院茶叶研究所　权启爱）

蜂产品加工业

一、基本情况

蜂产品是人类重要的营养源。它以其纯天然、富含多种神奇的生理活性物质、无毒副作用、食用方便、价格适宜、食疗功效明显等特点成为人们喜爱的营养保健佳品。2005年6月23日，国家工商行政管理总局通过官方网站正式公布新近认定的驰名商标，江西汪氏蜜蜂园有限公司注册的“汪氏及图案商标”被认定为“中国驰名商标”，汪氏也是此次唯一当选的蜂产品企业。在中国蜂产品协会的500多个团体会员中，有100多个涉外经营企业。近年来，这些企业的生产、经营和管理水平有了很大的提高，产品质量和安全得到很大提升，市场竞争力不断增强，在应对国外反倾销、贸易技术壁垒、提高蜂产品质量和安全方面做出了积极贡献。

据资料表明，荣获全国蜂产品行业龙头企业的13家企业，呈现出六个特点：一是覆盖面较广。13个龙头企业覆盖华北、东北、华东、中南、西南五大区，北京、吉林、浙江、江苏、安徽、江西、广东、河南、四川9省、直辖市，其中北京、浙江各3个。二是经营规模较大。13个龙头企业年销售收入均在1 300万元以上。三是经济效益较好。13个龙头企业年实现利税均在150万元以上。四是带动能力较强。13个龙头企业共带动3.12万户蜂农、饲养蜜蜂121.53万群，13个企业带动蜂农均在500户以上，饲养蜂群均在1.8万群以上。并通过合同、契约、股份制等形式形成比较紧密的联系，其中有的企业在基地建设和带动蜂农方面已形成制度，发展比较规范。五是质量较稳定。13个龙头企业普遍建立健全了质量管理、质量监控体系。六是知名度较高。13个龙头企业均被地方主管部门或行业推荐认定为龙头企业，其中6个企业荣获省（市）级农业产业化龙头企业，7个企业荣获全国蜂产品行业优秀企业，还有一家企业荣获农业产业化国家龙头企业称号。

二、生产与出口情况

（一）蜂产品

我国蜂产品出口不是很集中，出口额较大的省份有江苏、湖北、浙江、安徽和河南。1995—2005年，上述5个省合计出口额占全国蜂产品出口总额的比重平均为53.95%；比重逐年增大，由1995年的39.98%增加到2005年的62.73%，5个省比重差别不大。其中，江苏比重逐渐减小；湖北比重逐渐增大，2000年以后出口额位居全国首位。2004—2005年我国蜂产品出口贸易情况见表1。

表1 2004—2005年我国蜂产品出口贸易情况

产品名称		2004年	2005年	同比增长（%）
蜂蜜	数量（t）	81 325.00	88 499.00	8.82
	金额（万美元）	8 900.87	8 762.89	−1.55
	平均单价（美元/kg）	1.09	0.99	−9.51
鲜蜂王浆	数量（t）	664.92	794.78	19.53
	金额（万美元）	979.45	1 224.18	24.99
	平均单价（美元/kg）	14.73	15.40	4.55
蜂王浆冻干粉	数量（t）	205.13	168.01	−18.10
	金额（万美元）	868.63	733.77	−15.53
	平均单价（美元/kg）	42.34	43.67	3.14
出口蜂产品金额总计（万美元）		10 748.95	10 720.85	−0.26

（二）蜂蜜

蜂蜜是一种营养丰富的天然绿色食品和医疗保健用品，在国际和国内都具有良好的市场。目前，我国蜂蜜生产量居世界首位，全国现有蜂群数量约700万群，年产蜂蜜20万t左右。我国蜂蜜年出口量占世界蜂蜜年出口总量的20%左右，多年居世界首位。2005年我国蜂蜜出口49个国家和地区，比上年增加13个国家；共出口蜂蜜8.85万t，比上年增长8.8%；出口金额为8 762.9万美元，比上年下降1.6%；平均单价0.99美元/kg，比上年下降9.5%。2005年，我国蜂蜜出口前10国家和地区情况见表2。

表2 2005年我国蜂蜜出口前10国家和地区情况

排名	国家和地区	出口数量（t）	出口金额（万美元）	单价（美元/kg）	数量百分比（%）	金额百分比（%）
1	日本	41 396.9	4 369.4	1.06	46.78	49.86
2	美国	28 264.5	2 390.9	0.85	31.94	27.29
3	加拿大	3 115.7	293.8	0.94	3.52	3.35
4	西班牙	2 602.9	272.0	1.04	2.94	3.10
5	韩国	2 101.0	187.8	0.89	2.37	2.14
6	新加坡	1 711.4	214.3	1.25	1.93	2.45
7	英国	1 268.2	123.3	0.97	1.43	1.41
8	德国	1 265.5	133.7	1.06	1.43	1.53
9	马来西亚	1 225.6	125.4	1.02	1.39	1.43
10	香港	1 060.2	137.6	1.30	1.20	1.57
49个国家和地区合计		88 499.0	8 762.9	0.99	100.00	100.00

（三）蜂王浆

我国是蜂王浆生产大国，也是蜂王浆主要出口国。2005年，全国蜂王浆年产量约3 000t左右，达到历史最高水平。比2004年的2 800t增加200t，增幅7.14%。2005年，全国蜂王浆市场的特点是内销、外销两旺，国内市场销售量超过国际市场，大中城市销售继续扩大，小城镇的市场也开始启动，外销量与外销产值均有小幅增长。据行家估测，2005年，全国蜂王浆内销量至少在1 500t以上。这是自2001年全国蜂王浆销售突破1 000t以来连续第5年快速增长。国内市场不仅集中在南京、北京、广州、大连、武汉等大城市，一些中小城市的王浆销售也异常火暴。价位一般在140～500元之间，其中小城镇为140～200元，中等城市为200～300元，大城市为200～500元，最高可达800元以上。以平均每千克300元计，内贸销售额应在4.5亿元以上，接近外贸销售额的3倍。内外贸蜂王浆销售总产值达6亿元以上。据海关统计，2005年，鲜王浆出口794.78t，比上年的665t增加129.78t，增幅达19.52%。蜂王浆干粉出口168t，比上年的205t减少37t，减幅达18.05%。鲜浆和干粉累计出口折算成鲜蜂王浆共计1 298.80t，比上年的1 280t增加了18.80t，增幅为

1.47%；鲜蜂王浆出口创汇 1 224.19 万美元，平均每千克 15.40 美元，比上年的 14.73 美元上升 10.46%；蜂王浆干粉出口创汇 733.77 万美元，平均每千克 43.68 美元，比上年的 42.34 美元上升 3.17%。浆粉总出口产值 1 957.96 万美元（约合 1.59 亿元人民币），比上年的 1 848 万美元增长 5.95%。从浆粉出口增长幅度（1.47%）小于出口创汇增长幅度（5.95%）看，也说明 2005 年度我国蜂王浆出口价位有所上升。

我国蜂王浆出口的主要市场相对集中，主要分布在日本、美国、瑞士、香港、法国和澳大利亚等六大市场。这六大市场年出口量均在 40t 以上，总出口量达 1 097.43t，占出口总量的 84.50%。其中日本市场超过 800t，美国市场接近 100t，瑞士市场超过 50t，香港、法国和澳大利亚市场均超过 40t。超过 50t 的 3 个主力市场总体上看比较稳定，但均有下降。其中出口日本 812.54t，比 2004 年的 815t 减少 2.46t；对美国出口 94.86t，比 2004 年的 101t 减少 6.14t；对瑞士出口 55.69t，比 2004 年的 58t 减少 2.31t。2005 年对法国出口鲜蜂王浆 41.97t，比 2004 年的 2t 增加了近 20 倍，出口蜂王浆干粉 1t，填补了 2004 年没有出口的空白，两项合计 44.97t，超过出口澳大利亚的 43.25t。由 2004 年的 2t 迅猛增长了 21 倍，使得法国市场成为我国蜂王浆出口的第五大市场。生产型企业已成为王浆出口的主力。一些具有自营进出口权的生产型企业加入到蜂王浆出口经营队伍中，并由于价格、服务等优势，正成为我国蜂王浆出口的主力。在前 20 位鲜蜂王浆出口企业中，有 13 家是王浆加工企业，占 65%；在前 10 位鲜蜂王浆干粉出口企业中，有 6 家是王浆加工企业，占 60%。2005 年，我国蜂王浆出口前 10 国家和地区情况见表 3。

表 3　2005 年我国蜂王浆出口前 10 国家和地区情况

排名	国家和地区	出口数量（t）	出口金额（万美元）	单　价（美元/kg）	数量百分比（%）	金额百分比（%）
1	日　本	812.54	824.81	16.31	63.62	67.38
2	法　国	44.97	62.17	14.81	5.28	5.08
3	香　港	42.89	53.86	12.56	5.40	4.40
4	美　国	94.86	40.36	13.26	3.83	3.30
5	德　国	22.31	35.09	15.73	2.81	2.87
6	土耳其	25.50	29.71	11.65	3.21	2.43
7	沙特阿拉伯	23.26	27.32	11.75	2.93	2.23
8	瑞　士	55.69	23.23	15.86	1.84	1.90
9	西班牙	10.53	16.23	15.41	1.32	1.33
10	韩　国	11.60	15.84	13.65	1.46	1.29
出口总计		1 097.43	1 224.18	15.40	16.31	63.62

注：表中出口数量，为鲜蜂王浆与干蜂王浆折合为鲜蜂王浆后合计数量。

三、质量管理、标准化工作

1. 我国是蜂产品出口大国，产品种类繁多，质量上存在的问题主要表现在三个方面：一是兽药残留问题，如氯霉素；二是掺假问题；三是采集不成熟蜂蜜问题。其中兽药残留问题和掺假问题，随着国际市场对蜂产品的安全、卫生项目要求越来越严格，而我们又缺乏具体检测和解决问题的方法，此问题表现的尤为突出。

2. 2005 年 3 月 28 日，在北京召开的 2004 年度全国科学技术奖励大会上，秦皇岛检验检疫局研究员庞国芳带领的课题组完成的《中国蜂产品质量评价新技术研究与应用》课题，攻克了国外蜂产品检验技术壁垒，提升了我国蜂产品的质量，促进了出口，荣获了 2004 年度国家科技进步二等奖。从 1997 年开始至 2004 年，庞国芳研究员和他的助手们费时 8 年，从碳同位素技术入手，研究建立了蜂产品质量评价检验方法标准体系。该体系荟萃了当代固相萃取、离子交换、液液分配、柱层析、衍生化、微波消解以及酶化学等 14 种样品前处理新技术；集成气相色谱、液相色谱、薄层色谱、有机质谱、无机质谱、吸收光谱、发射光谱、酶联免疫和生物鉴定等 15 种测试新技术。制定了化学和微生物学联合研究方案，攻克了蜂产品中八大类兽药、五大类农药等共计 370 种微量化学物质的检测技术，普查了碳同位素的分布，揭示了我国 25 个省、自治区、直辖市的 27 种蜂蜜碳同位素的分布规律，制定了用于蜂产品检测的 30 项国家标准。成功建立了一个完整的、系统的、与国际先进标准接轨的蜂产品质量技术标准体系，填补了国内空白。这些标准达到或超过当前蜂产品检验的国际先进技术水平，攻克了我国蜂产品在国际市场的技术壁垒，破解了我国蜂产品在欧盟、美国和日本世界三大主销市场所有贸易技术壁垒，使我国的蜂产品检验技术实现了跨越式发展，彻底摆脱了我国蜂产品出口受制于人的局面，也为我国争得了在蜂产品进出口贸易中检验检疫工作的主动权，有力地促进蜂产品的出口，维护了国家的经济利益。同时，这项研究也满足了我国蜂产品生产、加工过程质量控制的迫切要求，对促进我国蜂业发展、提高蜂产品质量具有重要意义。

3. 由全国供销合作总社蜜蜂产品标准化技术委员会秘书处、南京老山药业股份有限公司、中国蜂产品协会蜂蜜专业委员会起草的 GB18796—2005《蜂蜜》强制性国家标准已于 2005 年 10 月 26 日由国家质检总局和国家标准委批准。生产领域自 2006 年 3 月 1 日起实施，流通领域自 2006 年 11 月 1 日起实施。GB18796—2005《蜂蜜》强制性国家标准是对 2002 年版推荐性国家标准的修订，适用于所有的蜂蜜，包括各种直接食用的蜂蜜。除了巢脾蜂蜜（巢蜜）以外，其他以蜂蜜作为产品名称或产品名称主词的产品均应符合这个标准。GB18796—2005《蜂蜜》的强制性国家标准要求主要包括：一是等级要求：依理化品质不同，分为一级品和二级品两个等级。取消了 2002 年版中分为优级品与合格品的规定。二是对蜂蜜中水分含量、果糖和葡萄糖含量、蔗糖含量指标做了强制性要求。把酸度、羟甲基糠醛、淀粉酶活性、灰分作为推荐性指标。三是扩展了安全卫生要求。2005 年版标准规定，蜂蜜应符合 GB 14963 标准和法律、法规、规章及有关标准要求。四是明确了真实性要求：蜂蜜中不得添加或混入任何淀粉类、糖类、代糖类物质。不得添加或混入任何防腐剂、澄清剂、增稠剂等异物。五是规范了产品名称。符合本标准定义的产品方可称为“蜂蜜”或简称为“蜜”。六是对包装和标志做了强制性要求。

四、科研成果及开发

1. 由中国农业科学院蜜蜂研究所主持的农业部农业结构调整重大技术研究专项《蜂王浆及蜂胶中功能因子的分离提取技术及深加工产业化的研究》课题，于 2005 年 10 月通过验收，该课题完成了蜂胶和蜂王浆中功能因子的分离提取工艺的研究，研制出改善睡眠和辅助调节血糖保健食品配方各 1 个，形成产业化生产技术各 1 套，并制定了产品的质量标准；2 个产品均顺利通过国家指定机构进行的安全性毒理学、功能学、稳定性和卫生学试验，制定了产品的功效成分检测方法和企业标准；申请国家专利 2 项，其中已获授权 1 项；发表论文 15 篇，出版专著 2 部；培养硕士研究生 1 名；研发的产品有市场开发前景，对蜜蜂养殖和加工产业的发展，以及蜂农增收和农业结构调整具有促进作用。超额完成课题任务。

2. 1996—2005 年，全国共有国药准字批准文号和卫食健字与国食健字批准文号的蜂产品 411 个。其中具有国药准字批准文号的蜂产品 82 个，占总数的 20%，具有卫食健字与国食健字批准文号的蜂产品 329 个，占总数的 80%，说明蜂产品类药品，尤其是保健食品日益受到广大消费者的青睐；蜂产品类药品、保健食品开发日益受到广大企业的高度重视。

3. 1996—2005 年 10 年间共有保健食品批号的蜂产品 329 个，其中卫食健字 178 个，国食健字 151 个，分别占总数的 54.1% 和 45.9%。国食健字 2004 年开始审批，2 年间就达 151 个，说明 2004—2005 年间具有保健食品批准文号的蜂产品得到企业的高度重视和较快发展。企业取得保健食品批号是企业的无形资产，有利于引导消费，扩大销售，有利于提高企业的知名度影响力，有利于提高企业品牌的技术含量、附加值和国际、国内市场竞争力。

4. 已获批准的蜂王浆保健食品具有免疫调节、抗疲劳、延缓衰老、调节血脂、调节血糖、抗辐射、抗氧化、耐缺氧、改善胃肠道功能（润肠通便）、改善记忆、改善睡眠、美容（祛黄褐斑）和对化学性肝损伤有辅助保护作用等 13 项功效，经济较发达地区和行业重点骨干企业对这项工作的重视，也说明蜂王浆类保健食品具有广阔市场前景。

5. 已获批准的蜂胶类保健食品具有免疫调节和增强免疫力、调节血脂和辅助降血脂、调节血糖和辅助降血糖、延缓衰老、美容（祛黄褐斑）、改善胃肠道功能（润肠通便）和对胃黏膜有辅助保护功能、清咽润喉、抗疲劳、辅助抑制肿瘤、对化学性肝损伤有一定保护作用、改善睡眠、抗氧化、抗辐射、抗突变等 14 项功效。经近百家企业的科学实验和临床试验证明蜂胶类保健食品具有上述多种功效，尤其是免疫调节、调节血脂、调节血糖等功效。蜂胶类保健食品集中在大中城市和具有较大规模、较高管理水平的行业龙头企业生产，有较强的生命力和巨大的发展潜力。

6. 蜂花粉类保健食品有 40 个，蜂蜜类保健食品有 3 个。蜂蜜、蜂花粉类食品对增进人们营养，保障人体健康作用显著，在国际、国内市场深受消费者欢迎。

五、行业管理

1. 中国蜂产品协会第五届会员代表大会于 2005

年3月10日在上海市召开，来自全国蜂产品行业的286名会员单位代表参加了会议。大会由中国蜂产品协会常务副会长金文存主持。罗梦传会长代表中国蜂产品协会四届理事会向大会作工作报告；徐逢贤副会长向大会作中国蜂产品协会章程修改的说明和四届理事会财务收支情况的报告；管春华副会长宣读协会资产管理制度；杨寒冰副会长宣读表彰四届理事会期间（2001—2004年）对全国蜂产品行业做出突出贡献的先进单位、先进个人名单；程文显、王振山副会长分别宣读协会理事会理事、常务理事建议名单；赵小川秘书长宣读中华全国供销合作总社党组、总社人事部《关于中国蜂产品协会第五届理事会负责人人选安排的批复》文件和中国蜂产品协会第五届理事会负责人人选建议名单。大会采用举手表决的形式，一致通过《工作报告》、《章程》、《资产管理制度》；大会按照中国蜂产品协会章程，一致同意选举罗梦传同志为第五届理事会会长，金文存同志为常务副会长兼法人代表以及其他人选。

2. 中国蜂产品协会改革发展座谈会于2005年8月16日在北京召开，会议主要内容是座谈、讨论今后协会改革发展的思路。会议由中国蜂产品协会会长罗梦传主持，协会的副会长、秘书长和在北京的部分常务理事、理事、会员单位的董事长、总经理及协会秘书处的人员参加了会议。在座谈会上，与会代表对协会近年来所做的工作和取得的成绩给予充分肯定，并对协会今后工作提出了许多宝贵意见和建议。如建议协会进一步加强标准化建设、强化市场规范、建立数字蜂产品体系、制定行业生产技术规范、发挥协会的桥梁纽带作用等等。罗会长在总结发言中指出，今后协会改革发展思路要体现四性：一是科学性。既要考虑协会当前工作，又要考虑长远发展；既要考虑经济发展，又要考虑职工队伍素质的提高；既要考虑提高蜂产品生产、经营企业经济效益，又要兼顾社会效益和养蜂生产者及蜂产品消费者能够得到更多的实惠。二是针对性。要紧密联系本行业、本协会的实际，具有较强的针对性、指导性使成功经验更好地得到推广应用，使问题更快地得以解决。三是连续性。新一届改革发展思路要与协会前几届，尤其是上一届的思路相衔接，承上启下，继往开来。四是前瞻性。要有较强的时代感，要与时俱进，要大胆试大胆创，要有所突破，有所创新。

3. 中华全国供销合作总社于2005年9月20～22日在南京召开《蜂蜜》国家标准审定会。这次审定会邀请了国家质检总局食品局、执法司，国家标准委、农业部、中国蜂产品协会、中国养蜂学会等代表在内的专家参加。此次《蜂蜜》国家标准修订非等效采用了国际食品法典委员会（CAC）《蜂蜜法规标准》（CODEXSTAN 12：2001 REV. 2），进一步缩小了与国际先进标准的差距。本次审定的《蜂蜜》国家标准与原《蜂蜜》国家标准（GB/T18796—2002）相比主要调整了以下内容：一是由推荐性标准改为条文强制性标准，鼓励生产和经营成熟蜜。二是对蜂蜜的名称做了明确界定，对不同的品种提出不同的蔗糖含量要求。三是增加了蜂蜜的真实性要求，不得在蜂蜜中添加任何非蜂蜜物质。四是规定了仲裁试验方法。五是修改、增补了常见单一花种蜂蜜的感官特性，作为标准的规范性附录。这些内容的修订对于解决长期以来困扰我国蜂蜜市场的蜂蜜成熟度、药物残留与重金属残留、掺假等问题将起到积极作用。同时，新标准将成为我国技术监督、工商管理部门开展蜂蜜市场执法检查的有利工具；也是行业协会和蜂产品生产、经营企业加强行业自律、规范市场秩序、维护广大蜂产品消费者合法权益的重要依据。对于促进我国蜂产品健康发展，提高市场竞争能力意义重大。

4. 由中国蜂产品协会、江山市人民政府联合主办，中国食文化研究会、中国食品土畜进出口商会、中国医药保健品进出口商会、中国连锁经营协会、浙江省农业厅、浙江省供销社、浙江省蜜蜂产业协会、浙江省蜂业协会等单位协办的首届中国（江山）蜜蜂文化节暨中国国际蜂产品经贸洽谈会于2005年10月28～30日在"中国蜜蜂之乡"浙江省江山市隆重举行。本次蜜蜂文化节与经贸洽谈会是中国蜂业界有史以来第一次举办，其活动内容之丰富，参加对象范围之广、档次之高都是我国蜂业界之最。围绕"健康·和谐·发展"为主题，成功地举办了五大板块、共11项活动。一是高峰论坛。600多人参加蜜蜂文化与蜂企业文化、蜜蜂产品与人类健康高峰论坛，邀请了浙江大学、国家质量监督检验检疫总局、国家标准化管理委员会、中国蜂产品协会等中央单位、科研单位、院校的领导、学者、教授介绍了蜂业研究成就，共同探讨了蜜蜂文化与企业文化、蜜蜂产品与人类健康。二是经贸洽谈。举办了来自全国蜂业企业80多个柜台蜂产品展示展销、经贸洽谈和签约仪式、企业返利蜂农大会等。三是技能大赛。来自全国25个省、自治区、直辖市82个企业101名蜂业技术能手参加了全国蜂产品质量感官技能大赛，比赛分为两部分，蜂产品的理论知识笔试和感官技能操作测试。四是文化活动。举办了"蜂之韵"全国摄影大赛，共收到全国19个省、自治区、直辖市137位摄影爱好者的474件摄影参加比赛稿件，经过专家评选，选出一等奖1名、二等奖3名、三等奖5名、人选奖40名，并对优秀作品进行了现场展示。五是表彰奖励。在

2005年度全国蜂王浆产品市场质量调查中，符合国家标准的产品生产企业63家；表彰2005年荣获“全国蜂产品行业质量工作先进单位”称号的企业35家；评选表彰首届中国（江山）蜜蜂文化节暨中国国际蜂产品经贸洽谈会参展企业的优秀包装设计奖1名、包装设计奖2名、优秀新产品奖2名、新产品奖5名、特别奖2名。

（中国农业科学院蜜蜂研究所 闫继红）

食用菌加工业

一、基本情况

2005年，我国食用菌产业又取得了持续、健康发展，小小蘑菇继续做出了大文章，为增加农民收入、改善城乡居民生活质量、为社会主义新农村建设做出了新的贡献。据全国25个省、自治区、直辖市统计，2005年，全国食用菌产量已达到1 334万t，比2004年增长14.96%；总产值达585亿元，比2004年增长21.44%；出口食用菌产品62.8万t，创汇9.6亿美元，分别比2004年增长7.96%和6.43%。从全国食用菌发展来看，2005年，全国食用菌鲜菇产量超过100万t的有河南、福建、山东和江苏4个省，其中山东省与2004年相比增长21.65%，从原居全国第四位而进入第三位；生产鲜菇30万～80万t的有河北、四川、浙江、湖北、湖南、黑龙江、辽宁、陕西、吉林、广东、江西、广西、安徽等13个省、自治区；生产鲜菇10万t以下的有上海、重庆、天津、云南、山西、北京、新疆、宁夏等8个省、自治区、直辖市。从食用菌产值来看，河南、福建、山东三省已超过50亿元；产值为20亿～40亿元的有河北、广东、浙江、湖南、黑龙江、四川、陕西、江苏、吉林、湖北等10个省；产值为10亿～20亿元的有辽宁、江西、广西、安徽、云南等5个省、自治区。与2004年相比，广东省和吉林省产值分别增长141.62%和91%，增产幅度较大，从而踏入第二梯队，而广西和安徽也因比2004年分别增长71.5%和52.78%，也进入第三梯队；其他省、自治区、直辖市均在1亿～10亿元或1亿元以下，但这些省、自治区、直辖市的食用菌年产值与2004年相比普遍都有提高。从品种发展来看，年产量超过100万t的有平菇、香菇、双孢菇、毛木耳4个品种；年产量20万～90万t的有黑木耳、金针菇、姬菇、鸡腿菇、草菇、滑菇等6个品种；年产量5万～19万t的有银耳、白灵菇、茯苓、杏鲍菇、秀珍菇、灵芝、小平菇、天麻等8个品种；年产量超过1万t的有猴头菇、姬松茸、竹荪、牛肝菌等4个品种；年产量1万t以下的有灰树菇、松茸、羊肚菌等3个品种。在众多食用菌品种中以平菇、香菇、双孢菇、毛木耳的产量居首位，4个品种的产量约占2005年总产量的65.67%。我国食用菌产量按品种划分增长情况见表1。

表1 2005年我国食用菌产量按品种划分增长情况

品 种	2004年产量（万t）	2005年产量（万t）	同比增长（%）	品 种	2004年产量（万t）	2005年产量（万t）	同比增长（%）
全国总计	**1 160.4**	**1 334**	**14.96**	茯 苓	15.9	17	6.92
平 菇	298.6	370	25.91	杏鲍菇	6.1	13	113.11
香 菇	246.9	242	−1.98	秀珍菇	5.7	9.5	66.67
双孢菇	156.4	152	−2.81	灵 芝	6.0	8.6	43.33
毛木耳	90.9	112	23.21	小平菇	8.0	6.8	−15.00
黑木耳	77.4	97	25.32	天 麻	11.6	5.0	−56.90
金针菇	72.7	83	14.17	猴头菇	1.5	4.5	200.00
姬 菇	22.3	34	52.47	姬松茸	2.7	4.3	59.26
鸡腿菇	22.7	28	23.35	竹 荪	3.4	3.7	8.82
草 菇	22.8	27	18.42	牛肝菌	1.74	1.7	−2.30
滑 菇	17.4	20	14.94	灰树菇	5.0	0.4	−92.00
茶树菇	12.2	19	55.74	松 茸	0.13	0.16	23.00
银 耳	17.4	18	3.45	羊肚菌	0.10	0.08	−20.00
白灵菇	8.2	17	107.32	其 他	19.70	27	37.06

据中国食用菌商务网调查，2004年全国食用菌的餐饮消费量比2001年以前有了明显提升，仅北京地区日消费食用菌鲜品总量就达20万kg以上，全国年食用菌餐饮消费总额在300亿元以上。消费量的扩大，促进了食用菌流通市场的良性发展，为食用菌产业持续发展创造了良好条件。现在全国已建起了食用菌主产县（年产值超过1亿元）100个；已建大型产地批发市场10多个，食用菌产业队伍已发展到2 000多万人，已成为我国农村脱贫致富的又一支生力军。由于我国食用菌产量持续高速增长，现在食用菌产量已占世界总产量的70%以上，在数量上已成为世界食用菌生产大国和出口大国。从全国各省、自治区、直辖市食用菌产量、产值、出口创汇、国内国际市场的开拓等节节攀升的势头来看，再次印证了这一新兴产业所具有的久盛不衰的巨大潜力。

二、科研、新产品、新技术

中国食用菌协会高度重视食用菌的科研、新产品、新技术的研发工作，坚持科学发展观，把依靠科学技术、促进生产发展作为行业内长期的战略任务。2005年，协会参与制定了“十一五”食用菌行业发展规划，组织专家参加了科技项目的研究攻关，组织专家审定了河北康宝甜味口蘑、香杵口蘑两个新品种，组织评审了“浙江聚宝灵芝菌种培育与产业化”、“北京白灵菇和杏孢菇优良品种选育及栽培技术”、“江苏富硒金针菇、平菇技术开发”、“山东阿魏菇、杏孢菇的研究与产业化”、“辽宁全禾液体菌种培育器与生产工艺”、“浙江香菇栽培基质资源开发利用研究”、“河南食用菌产业化研究与应用”、“云南野生食用菌保鲜、加工、储运关键技术研究”、“江西食用菌及山野菜保鲜技术研究”、“北京食用菌有害生物调查及主要有害生物防治技术与应用”等科研成果。此外，在协会的大力推动下，2005年全行业已安排的43项“星火计划”项目，分别取得了不少成效。一年中，由于“食用菌产品竞争力科技提升工程”的继续实施，标准化生产活动、菌种年活动、国际间技术交流与合作、全行业技术培训等各项活动的全面开展，以及“科研攻关项目”、“星火计划”项目紧张有序地进行，从而在食用菌行业创造了依靠科技进步、推进产业继续快速发展的大好局面。

三、出口创汇

据海关统计，2005年，我国食用、药用菌产品出口量为62.8万t，比2004年增长8.04%；出口金额为9.6亿美元，比2004年增长6.81%，继续保持了出口创汇连年增长的势头，但与2004年相比增速有所放慢。2005年，食、药用菌产品出口仍呈现以蘑菇罐头为主的加工品、鲜品和干品三足鼎立的格局。其中，出口金额5 000万美元以上的食、药用菌产品品种有6个，分别是鲜松茸、鲜香菇、干香菇、小白菇罐头、其他伞菌属蘑菇罐头和药用菌品种（含灵芝）。出口金额分别达到5 856万美元、5 590万美元、1.76亿美元、2.2亿美元、5 292万美元和1.46亿美元。6个品种合计出口额占全年食、药用菌出口总额的73.64%。除上述出口的6个产品外，还有干木耳、干银耳、干金针菇、干牛肝菌等，出口金额一般在1 000万～3 500万美元之间，表现出强劲的出口增长势头（表2）。

从食、药用菌产品品种出口趋势看，出现部分品种小幅度下降、野生药用菌前景看好的态势。我国的蘑菇罐头、盐水菇、速冻菇等产品出口金额之所以有所下降，一是因为遇到了澳大利亚和墨西哥对这类产品进行了反倾销调查；二是由于欧盟一直对上述产品实施严格的配额限制所至。产品中的鲜松茸、鲜金针菇等产品仍继续保持良好的出口势头，以松茸、块菌、牛肝菌为代表的野生菌出口将保持稳定，但由于加拿大、美国、墨西哥、摩洛哥等国家也出口这类产品，为此将会增加新的竞争对手。以灵芝、虫草为代表的药用菌出口形势继续乐观。以白灵菇、杏孢菇、灰树菇、茶树菇、姬松茸为代表的珍稀食用菌市场发展潜力很大，这类品种产品今后将继续走俏国内外市场。

从产品出口的地理发展趋势看，东亚地区是食、药用菌生产和销售的主要地区，也是我国食、药用菌产品最主要的主销市场。近年来，我国向日本、韩国以及香港、台湾省出口食、药用菌产品已占我国出口市场份额的一半。因此，短期内我国食、药用菌产品在这一地区第一主销市场的地位还不会动摇。但是几年来，由于日本、韩国和台湾省都具备很强的食用菌生产实力，他们除向本地区提供产品外，还向欧美等一些发达国家出口高档食、药用菌产品。加之该地区食、药用菌消费市场已陷入相对饱和状态，因此未来这一地区食、药用菌产品市场竞争将越演越烈。南亚地区是我国传统的食、药用菌产品出口地区，这一地区华人数量最多，饮食习惯与我国比较接近，对食、药用菌产品需求量很大，应加大对这一地区市场的开发力度，大力推介一些食、药用菌新品种，尤其是当地难以生产的品种，扩大我国对该地区的出口。北美地区的美国和加拿大是我国食、药用菌产品出口的另一个重要市场，也是极具潜力的新兴市场。各类蘑菇罐头、干鲜香菇是我国对北美地区的主销产品。由于该地区亚裔人口数量快速增长，传统的食用菌产品需求越来越旺盛，而且产品利润空间很丰厚。只要进一步提高保鲜技术，进一步提升产品质量，通过海运降低运输成本，则在该地区获得的产品利润将更可观。意大利、法国、德国和荷兰也是我国食、药用菌产品的主要进口国家，虽然他们在进口中一直实施严格的配额限制和严格的检验、检疫指标及农药残留、重金属的检测指标，稍有不慎就会被挤出欧洲市场。但是，由于欧盟珍稀菇类产品仍有不小的市场空间，而且2006年我国正在与欧盟进行贸易谈判，只需在谈判中适当增加从中国进口蘑菇罐头配额，那么今后我国对欧盟蘑菇罐头的出口将会有所增长。俄罗斯和独联体国家一直都是我国蘑菇罐头的主要销售市场之一，俄罗斯食用菌生产技术水平与欧美国家有很大的差距，而且产量仅占本国市场需求量的20%，因此这一地区将是我国今后重点考虑开拓的国际市场之一。

表2　2005年全国食用菌产品出口创汇情况

商品名称	数量（t）	同比增长（%）	金额（万美元）	同比增长（%）
合计	**628 413**	**8.04**	**96 382**	**6.81**
蘑菇菌丝	9 091	50.00	236	20.20
伞菌属蘑菇	2 761	99.46	828	125.31
鲜或冷藏的块菌	1 148	40.07	168	−14.32
鲜或冷藏的松茸	1 429	23.58	5 856	9.89
鲜或冷藏的香菇	26 412	−18.17	5 590	−9.09
鲜或冷藏的金针菇	1 047	1.55	103	8.36
鲜或冷藏的草菇	5 229	54.48	65	52.43
鲜或冷藏的口蘑	39	−10.11	0.75	9.58
其他鲜或冷藏的蘑菇	6 515	−17.84	1 372	3.05
冷冻松茸	658	26.19	1 118	18.62
盐水小白蘑菇	15 622	8.52	1 399	7.93
盐水的其他伞菌属蘑菇	19 348	13.90	2 273	8.45
其他暂时保藏的伞菌属蘑菇	1 400	15.98	138	17.25
盐水松茸	350	−39.08	535	−21.34
盐水的其他蘑菇及块菌	7 035	4.94	932	69.56
其他暂时保藏的蘑菇及块菌	16 159	25.87	1 669	30.64
干伞菌属蘑菇	700	−53.33	937	−55.20
干木耳	7 936	−4.84	3 486	15.47
干银耳	2 384	24.60	1 178	29.17
干香菇	24 267	−1.84	17 556	15.33
干金针菇	20	117.20	7.4	120.18
干草菇	9.8	80.65	3.8	82.92
干口蘑	2.2	12.20	3.9	321.11
干牛肝菌	1 062		1 669	
未列名干蘑菇及块菌	1 877	−3.98	1 949	−4.06
冬虫夏草	3.6	−25.90	1 338	−14.98
天麻	88	96.50	35	13.16
茯苓	5 103	33.03	557	3.64
未列名药用植物及其他部分	139 020	20.17	14 571	20.80
小白蘑菇（洋蘑菇）罐头	276 410	3.52	22 114	3.15
其他伞菌属蘑菇罐头	34 894	40.55	5 292	−29.64
其他制作或保藏的伞菌属蘑菇	4 209	14.09	732	6.55
制作或保藏的块菌	3 911	−69.91	487	−58.37
其他蘑菇罐头	11 443	72.26	1 876	133.39
其他制作或保藏的蘑菇	828	−26.65	307	−30.85

四、行业工作

1. 加大宣传力度，促进社会消费创造新的商机

从2003年起，中国食用菌协会连续组织了食用菌餐饮（烹饪）大赛。前后三届大赛共推出食用菌名店、特色店25个，全国食用菌烹饪名师15人，食用菌金牌菜67个，新开发的菌菜360个。中国食用菌协会和中央电视台“天天饮食”栏目联手举办了食用菌饮食周，用15种食用菌产品做15道菜，制成15集电视专题片，在中央电视台1、2、4频道宣传了食用菌烹饪方法及其营养价值。北京电视台在“八方食圣”节目中也举办了食用菌烹饪擂台赛，同时还举办了食用菌餐饮业发展战略研讨会。这些活动，向消费者普及了食用菌知识、烹饪方法与技巧，使广大消费者深入了解食用菌的营养价值和保健作用，促进了全社会消费食用菌，为食用菌产业创造了良好的商机。

2. 组织大型行业活动，为企业提供多方位服务 中国食用菌协会以组织大型行业活动为平台，为会员单位提供了多方位服务。2005 年，继续举办了多次全国性的技术交流会、贸易洽谈会、高峰论谈会、展览展销会以及全行业的评比选优活动，以利沟通思路、交流信息、介绍经验、树立样板、发展生产、促进贸易。其中全国第四届食用菌新产品新技术展销会暨保健品开发及产业项目推介交流会；首届食用菌烹饪大赛；第四届中国食用菌会员代表大会；第六届中国（庆元）香菇节暨全国食用菌生产区、县（市）论坛，都是对全行业产生影响的重要活动。

3. 积极参与不断拓展国际交流与合作 中国食用菌协会始终高度重视食用菌领域的国际交流与合作，积极参与食用菌界国际事务活动。2005 年 4 月，国际蘑菇学会在上海召开了新一届委员会执委会，会后新一届执委会主席和执委安东应邀来北京访问了中国食用菌协会并与协会进行了工作交流。随后 2005 年 6 月经国际蘑菇协会批准成立了中国办事处，办事处受委托代理国际蘑菇学会在中国的事务。2005 年 4 月，协会在上海举办了第五届世界食用菌生物学与产品大会。2005 年 9 月协会在承德举办了中国、澳大利亚、和韩国三国食用菌协会会长三方会谈，并就相互支持与合作达成一致意见。

4. 积极向政府部门汇报工作，发挥中介组织的作用 中国食用菌协会一直把积极向政府反映行业协会意见与要求、争取政府重视与支持、发挥中介组织作用等，作为协会的日常重点工作来抓。近三年来，协会分别向政府高层领导及财政部、农业部、科技部、国家发改委、国家标准化管理委员会进行了多次工作汇报。一方面汇报了这一行业发展现状，对我国农村经济发展中的作用、对农民增收的作用以及发展态势和特点，另一方面也提出了需要帮助解决的困难和问题。协会的多次工作汇报引起了我国党、政高层领导的极大关注，他们在外地视察工作时，也分别视察了食用菌生产基地并参加了相关活动，对食用菌产业的发展做出了重要批示。2005 年 9 月，中国食用菌协会向国务院副总理回良玉呈报了“恳请高度重视食用菌在农业循环经济中的独特作用”的报告后，回良玉副总理当天就给予了批复。协会向有关政府部门汇报后，也很快得到了他们的理解和支持。如科技部听取汇报后，很快在科技部所在各类计划中充分考虑了食用菌项目，列在国家“星火计划”中的食用菌项目每年都以二位数字以上增速递增。为引起各级科技部门对食用菌产业更多的关注，科技部特邀中国食用菌协会参加了由科技部主持的食用菌有关会议。向农业部汇报后，他们已表示将在对制定食用菌标准、加强食用菌菌种管理、菌种知识产权保护、建立示范基地方面给予必要的支持；向财政部汇报后，他们很快帮助解决了协会参加国际组织的费用问题；向国家质检总局汇报后，他们对食用菌原产地保护问题将适当给予解决。由于协会的频繁活动，使食用菌产业发展中的有关问题得到了政府有关部门乃至高层领导的重视，从而为这一产业继续快速发展创造了良好条件。

（中国食用菌协会　林彩民）

烟草加工业

2005 年是“十五”时期的最后一年，全国烟草行业在党中央、国务院及国家发改委的正确领导下，在各有关部门和地方政府的大力支持下，按照年初的工作部署，继续抓好“四个推进”，正确处理“五个关系”，依靠全行业干部职工的不懈努力和扎实工作，圆满完成了各项工作任务，保持了行业平稳健康发展。

一、基本情况

2005 年我国烟草行业实现税利比 2000 年增长 124.3%，年均增长 17.5%，是实行烟草专卖制度以来发展比较好的一个时期。2005 年，全行业累计生产卷烟 19 420 亿支（3 884 万箱），同比增长 3.67%；销售卷烟 19 470 亿支（3 894 万箱），同比增长 3.7%；年末卷烟工商库存 1 287 亿支（257 万箱），保持正常库存水平。全年卷烟生产牌号为 325 个，比上年减少 169 个；前 10 个牌号生产集中度为 26.4%；百牌号生产比重为 84.7%；名优卷烟生产比重为 39.5%。烟叶、卷烟出口总量与上年基本持平，全年实现出口创汇 5.7 亿美元，同比增长 8.6%。全年共有 13 个卷烟工业企业完成了组织结构调整，具有法人资格的卷烟工业企业已调整减少到44个。全年共有202个县级公司取消法人资格，到2005年底全行业已累计取消县级烟草公司法人资格1 317个。完成了7个打叶复烤企业的公司制改造工作，全行业已有44个打叶复烤企业按照公司制进行改制。全国持证卷烟零售客户中实行电话订货的达到430万户，占零售客户总数的97%；实行电子结算的195万户，占零售客户总数的43.97%。全行业有近50%的地市级公司完成了对配送部门的整合，实现了"一库式"配送，直接分拣到户的达到296万户。全年共查处制售假冒商标卷烟案件34.7万起，查获假冒卷烟73万件、制假烟叶1.2万t，捣毁制假窝点2 908个，查缴制假烟机1 608台，打掉销售假烟网络23个，依法拘留制假不法人员5 336人，判刑1 697人、劳教82人。全行业已建立7个国家级、10个行业级企业技术中心，其中8个企业技术中心被人事部认定为博士后科研工作站。卷烟焦油量平均降至13.5mg/支。

二、科研、新产品与新技术

（一）四大战略性课题进展顺利

国家烟草专卖局提出以"烟草育种、卷烟调香、特色工艺、减害降焦"四大战略性课题为突破口，全面推动烟草科技进步。

1. 烟草育种课题　制定了《烟草育种工程方案》，组织了"抗病毒病优质烟草新品种选育"、"抗旱优质烤烟新品种选育"两个重点项目招标工作；进行了全国烟草品种审定委员会专家库成员推荐工作和品种审定委员会章程、审定办法等文件的修改完善工作；制定并起草了《烟草种质资源平台建设实施方案》、《中国烟草基因组计划工作思路》、《烟草新品种选育"后补助"实施办法》。

2. 卷烟调香课题　制定了《卷烟调香工程方案》，在技术、品控、人才三大体系建设方面已形成工作思路。在调香技术、品控技术研究方面实施项目带动战略；制定了《卷烟调香人才培养实施方案》。

3. 特色工艺课题　进一步完善了《特色工艺工作方案》，在分组加工原料特性研究方面取得技术突破，红河卷烟厂等8家试点企业已应用分组加工技术生产卷烟产品。提出了以"三化加工技术"分组加工技术、均质化加工技术、数字化加工技术为核心的特色工艺技术研究内容。实现卷烟产品设计系统化、加工精细化、控制智能化、生产集约化，初步形成中式卷烟特色工艺技术体系。

4. 降焦减害课题　进一步完善了《减害降焦工作方案》，按照"稳步降焦，重在减害"工作思路，通过实施项目带动战略，以品牌为载体，积极推进减害技术的深层次研究和低危害卷烟产品的开发。

（二）烟草区划研究工作深入展开

明确了"统一方法、统一标准、统一平台"的工作原则，加强了"组织保障、技术支撑和工作落实"三大体系，形成了中国烟草种植区划工作的"1＋7"运作模式。

1. 落实了区划研究相关工作　完成了我国烟叶主产区评价工作及烟叶生产相关历史资料的收集整理和普查工作，完成了2004年度我国烤烟、白肋烟、香料烟样品分析检测和2005年度烟叶、土壤样品取样工作，初步建立了烟叶质量评价指标体系、植烟土壤适宜性评价指标体系、气候适生性评价指标体系。

2. 优质烟叶生产科技示范基地建设发挥了科技创新平台作用　较好地落实科研开发、技术推广和规模化生产三大任务。解决一批影响烟区可持续发展和烟叶质量进一步提高的关键技术。

三、国内外市场概况

（一）烟叶市场

1. 烟叶生产、销售　2005年，全世界预计可生产烟叶503.9万t，其中烤烟387.34万t，占总产量的77%；白肋烟79.98万t，占16%；香料烟预计达36.58万t，占7%。各地区的大致比例为亚洲54%（其中我国占36.5%），南美洲22%，非洲9%，欧洲8%，北美洲7%，大洋洲（澳大利亚）很少。2005年世界烟叶总产量比2004年增加3.44万t，增幅为0.69%。其中，烤烟比2004年多11.21万t，增幅为2.98%；白肋烟比2004年减少8.41万t，降幅为9.51%；香料烟预计比2004年多0.64万t，增幅为1.78%。也就是说，2005年烤烟和香料烟的产量有所增加，而白肋烟产量稍有下降。烤烟增加主要来自于中国，香料烟增加主要来自于土耳其和保加利亚等香料烟主要出口国，白肋烟减少主要是因为美国、马拉维和巴西等主要出口国产量下降所致。巴西是近几年世界烟叶生产最引人注目的国家，其总产量已经占世界的16.9%（2004年值）。巴西烟叶大部分用于出口，有报道说巴西烟叶已占世界出口烟叶总量的70%。美国烟叶近年来一直呈下滑趋势。2005年，美国取消了生产配额限制，但是烟叶产量不仅没有增加，反而有所下降。配额补贴取消以后，烟叶价格明显下降（烤烟和白肋烟价格分别从2003年的4.07美元/kg和4.39美元/kg下降到2004年的3.20美元/kg和3.31美元/kg），但是与巴西（烤烟和白肋烟售价分别为 1.76 美元/kg 和 1.56 美元/kg）和非洲国家烟叶价格相比仍然相差 1 倍甚至几倍，因此在国际烟草市场的竞争力依然有限。与之相比。印度近年来烟叶生产发展迅速，热量丰富，雨量充沛，土地面积大，增产的潜力很大。津巴布韦作为非洲传统的烟叶生产大国，近年来由于政府推行土地改革，烟叶生产受到影响，至今产量仍然较低。2005 年产量（7.33 万 t）虽然较 2004 年产量（6.99 万 t）稍有增加，但尚不足 2000 年产量（23.69 万 t）的 1/3。津巴布韦烟叶生产恢复到历史最高水平尚需时日，因此跨国烟草公司积极帮助坦桑尼亚、赞比亚、乌干达、莫桑比克等国发展烟叶生产，近年来这些国家烟叶产量增长迅速。

2. 主要烟叶供应商　一是环球烟叶公司。2005 年，该公司克服了巴西和非洲烟草运输延误、欧盟罚款导致利润下降等诸多不利因素，在烟草、木材、建筑产品、农产品等方面都得到了较好的发展，全年营业收入 32.8 亿美元，其中烟草收入 16.7 亿美元，比 2004 年同期增长 2%。二是联一国际公司。该公司是由世界第二大烟叶公司——德孟公司和第三大烟叶公司——标准商业公司于 2005 年正式合并而成。德孟公司的股东拥有新公司 52%的股权，标准商业公司的股东则拥有新公司 48%的股权。两大跨国烟叶公司的合并，意味着全球烟叶市场竞争将更加激烈。

（二）卷烟市场

1. 卷烟生产、销售　世界卷烟市场近年来总体上保持小幅增长态势，但发达国家在持续收缩，发展中国家在不断扩张。综合有关资料，2005 年全球卷烟产量约 5.91 万亿支，比 2004 年增长 1.5%。除中国之外，2005 年卷烟产量超过 1 000 亿支的国家还有美国、俄罗斯、日本、印度尼西亚、德国、巴西、韩国、土耳其、荷兰和乌克兰 10 个国家。从卷烟产量排名居前 20 位的国家来看，绝大多数发达国家卷烟产量在下降，其中西班牙、英国和美国分别下降了 24.4%、20.9%和 17.1%，也是下降最快的 3 个国家。而绝大多数发展中国家卷烟产量均在增加，其中乌克兰、越南和巴基斯坦分别增长了 88.1%、61.5%和 48.0%，也是增长最快的 3 个国家。世界卷烟市场目前主要存在三大公司类型。其一是实行国家专卖制度的中国烟草总公司，卷烟产销规模占世界总量的 1/3，但对外贸易依存度很低。其二是以奥驰亚集团、英美烟草公司为代表的跨国烟草公司，其生产经营几乎遍及世界各国，许多国家的卷烟市场均被这些跨国烟草公司所控制。其三是以本地化生产经营为主的中小型烟草公司，这些公司大多数为民营企业，但在埃及、土耳其、越南、泰国和保加利亚等少数国家也实行国家垄断经营。当前世界卷烟市场已日益向垄断化方向发展，中小烟草公司市场份额逐步被跨国烟草公司所挤占。

2. 主要跨国烟草公司发展动态　一是奥驰亚集团。该集团是除中国烟草总公司外（下同）的世界第一大跨国烟草公司，由菲莫美国烟草公司、菲莫国际烟草公司、卡夫食品公司和菲莫资产经营公司 4 家公司构成。2005 年，集团总资产为 1 079.5 亿美元，营业收入为 978.5 亿美元，营业利润为 165.9 亿美元，全球雇员达 19.9 万人。奥驰亚集团拥有全球第一大卷烟品牌“万宝路”，2005 年销量达 4 705 亿支，是中国第一大卷烟品牌“白沙”的 6.2 倍。2005 年“万宝路”在美国的市场份额达 40%，创造了历史最高水平。二是日本烟草公司。该公司是世界第三大跨国烟草公司，2005 年继续在国内市场重点加强产品创新、渠道控制和终端促销。在产品创新方面，针对成长性市场如 1mg 焦油含量、薄荷型以及每包在 300 日元以上的产品市场，从研发、设计、市场推广等方面投入更多的资源，推动这部分市场全面增长。2005 年，创历史性记录地推出 18 个新产品，到 2005 年底，1mg 焦油含量、薄荷类产品以及每包 300 日元以上的产品市场份额分别为 8.6%、3.7%和 2.3%。三是帝国烟草公司。该公司是一个业务遍及 130 多个国家和地区、经营规模居世界第四位的大型跨国烟草公司，2005 年销售卷烟 1 725 亿支，销售自制烟 26 600t，与 2004 年基本持平。英国和德国是其两个主要市场，2005 年帝国烟草公司在英国销售卷烟 239 亿支，销售自制烟 2 100t；在德国销售卷烟 209 亿支，销售自制烟 7 100t。从主要财务指标看，2005 年帝国烟草公司营业收入为 112.6 亿英镑，营业利润为 10.4 亿英镑，资产总额为 62.6 亿英镑。

3. 国际卷烟市场发展态势分析　企业并购重组继续推进，跨国烟草公司对发展中国家的市场扩张力度持续加大，亚洲市场将成为市场竞争的焦点，奥驰亚集团的竞争优势将更加明显。欧洲市场卷烟销量继续下降，企业竞争格局将发生重大变化，帝国烟草公司、加莱赫烟草集团、阿塔迪斯公司、瑞典火柴公司等处于第二梯队（奥驰亚集团、英美烟草公司、日本烟草公司为第一梯队）的跨国烟草公司将成为引发市场变动的主要力量。总体来看，全球卷烟市场日趋集中是必然趋势。在推进企业并购的同时，各大跨国烟草公司会更加重视其卷烟品牌的整合扩张。《烟草控制框架公约》生效后，直接和间接的卷烟品牌广告将受到前所未有的严格限制，卷烟品牌成长主要依托于消费者的重复购买，因此现有规模将成为下一阶段品牌生存与发展的关键因素。在这种情况下，各大公司将会不遗余力地谋求尽快做大自己的战略主导品牌。目前各大公司的"战略主导品牌"大都是4～10个。可以预见，随着竞争的加剧和各大跨国烟草公司进一步加大品牌扩张整合力度，"万宝路"、"柔和七星"、"健牌"等国际性品牌的市场占有率将持续提高。卷烟走私和手卷烟市场的扩大，将对全球烟草产业造成更加严峻的威胁和挑战，越来越多的烟草企业会选择开发低价卷烟品牌和进军手卷烟市场。在各国政府烟草管制不断加强和跨国烟草公司市场扩张力度不断加大的共同影响下，发达国家烟叶和卷烟产销量将持续下降，发展中国家烟叶和卷烟产销量将继续增长，全球烟草市场总体上将保持基本稳定。

四、质量管理与标准化工作

2005年，我国烟草行业开展的质量管理和标准化工作如下：

（一）质量管理

1. 进一步加强行业质量监督体系建设　已有23个省级烟草质检站通过审查认可和授权，云南、上海质检站确定为行业重点质检站，进一步明确了省级质检机构的职能定位，启动了质检实验室管理信息化工作，形成了由国家质检中心、行业重点质检站和省级质检站组成的行业质量监督检验体系。

2. 进行了产品质量监督市场抽检和统检　共检查了国内47家卷烟企业生产的167个牌号、380个规格的卷烟产品，检验牌次约为900牌次。所查380个规格的卷烟产品产量约占总产量70%左右。2005年行业卷烟焦油量加权平均值已降到13.5mg/支，较2004年13.6mg/支降低0.1mg/支。按计划完成了滤棒、卷烟纸、接装纸、丝束、香精香料产品的质量监督工作。共抽查了17个滤棒产品、17个卷烟纸产品、94个接装纸产品、20个丝束产品，其中2个醋纤产品、18个接装纸产品、3个丝束产品不合格。

3. 积极开展了假冒伪劣产品鉴别工作　共受理15个地区假冒伪劣烟机的质量鉴别，对51台套假冒伪劣烟机及4批450余件烟机零配件进行了假冒伪劣质量鉴别。同时对4批丝束，12批滤棒和3批烟叶进行真伪鉴别。全行业共计鉴别检验假冒卷烟75 756批次。

4. 烟叶工商交接工作日趋规范性和公正性　从近100万担工商交接烟叶中随即抽检656个批次、33 438把烟叶，计24个等级。抽检的烟叶涉及17个省（直辖市）、66个地（市）级烟叶产区和43个卷烟企业及3个有工商交接烟叶业务的复烤企业。烟叶工商交接平均等级合格率为65%。

5. 组织参加了中国名牌产品评比活动　全行业共有16个品牌被国家质检总局评为中国名牌卷烟，即：白沙、中华、云烟、红梅、红河、红双喜、玉溪、芙蓉王、利群、红塔山、黄果树、双喜、南京、大红鹰、红金龙、哈德门。

（二）标准化工作

1. 加强了标准化组织机构建设　完成了行业标准化技术委员会所属8个分标委的换届工作。组织制定了《烟草行业标准化制修订项目经费管理办法》和《烟草行业标准化制修订项目管理办法》。

2. 完成了对第三批国家级烟叶标准化生产示范县建设项目的验收与考核工作　表彰和奖励了国家级烟叶标准化生产示范县中的10个示范县和42位先进个人；浏阳等6个烟叶标准化生产示范县和冯国桢等9位先进个人受到了国家标准委的表彰和奖励。

3. 完成了《卷烟》国标发布与宣贯工作　配合国家标准委完成了新《卷烟》国标的审核、WTO/TBT通报和发布工作。组织举办了3期《卷烟》国标培训班（培训850多人次）。

4. 完成了行业标准制修订工作　批准制修订71项行业（国家）标准，发布国家标准9项，行业标准10项，卷烟感官标准样品20个，卷烟烟气标准样品4个。另有23个行业标准已通过审定即将发布。组织了《卷烟品牌许可生产》、《卷烟企业清洁生产通则》等行业重要标准起草与评审工作。

五、行业管理

1. 完善烟草行业管理体制，进一步深化行业改革　2005年4月18日，《国务院关于2005年深化经济体制改革的意见》全文公开发表，《意见》明确提出要"完善烟草行业管理体制"。烟草行业要进一步理顺资产管理体制，中国烟草总公司依法对所属工商企业的国有资产行使出资人权利，经营和管理国有资产，承担保值增值责任。国家烟草专卖局在工商企业中选取部分试点单位，对建立具有行业特点的现代产权制度进行探索。

2. 克服非市场因素，国家烟草专卖局宏观调控准确及时　2005年3～4月，行业经济运行出现"三偏"（进度偏快、结构偏高、增长偏热），多个省份卷烟销量同比下降，结构性矛盾突出。国家烟草专卖局于3～5月连续两次召开全行业电视电话会议，及时提出一系列加强和改善宏观调控的措施，消除经济运行中的非市场因素和结构性矛盾，有效地保持了全行业的平稳发展。

3. 内部管理监督工作扎实推进，重在长效　国家烟草专卖局党组于2005年5月30日在北京召开了全国烟草行业加强内部管理监督工作会议。会议从加强财务管理和审计监督，加强专卖监督管理和整顿规范，加强党风廉政建设特别是建立健全教育、制度、监督并重的惩治和预防腐败体系三个方面，对全面加强行业内部管理监督工作进行了具体部署，并提出明确要求。此后，国家烟草专卖局又分别召开加强内部管理监督工作进展情况电视电话汇报会、整顿规范领导小组会议和全国烟草行业加强内部管理监督工作汇报会，着力将这项工作深入、持久、扎实地推进下去。

4. 烟叶生产“防止过热、稳定规模”，努力保持可持续发展　2005 年 10 月 26 日召开的全国烟叶工作座谈会明确指出，2006 年的烟叶生产收购计划维持 2005 年的水平，不开口子，不做调整，各地必须坚决按照国家计划严格执行；2006 年的烟叶扶持政策保持 2005 年的水平不变。2005 年，烟叶工作实现了自 1998 年以来连续 8 年的稳定生产，但部分产区出现过热倾向，为了“防止过热，稳定规模”，国家烟草专卖局果断采取措施，保持烟叶生产的可持续发展。

5.《烟草控制框架公约》获人大常委会批准，烟草行业积极履约　2005 年 8 月 28 日，第十届全国人大常委会第十七次会议决定：批准世界卫生组织《烟草控制框架公约》。国家烟草专卖局作为国务院烟草专卖行政主管部门，坚决拥护中国政府在烟草控制方面的立场和态度；烟草行业将继续坚持依法组织生产经营活动，以积极的态度履行《公约》。

6.“6·18”打假战果辉煌，重点打击假烟制售网络　2005 年 6 月 18 日，在国家烟草专卖局和公安部的统一组织下，京冀两地烟草、公安部门联合行动，成功打掉了一个辐射河北、北京部分地区的囤积、运输、批发、销售假烟的犯罪网络。“6·18”特大跨省贩卖假烟网络案的成功破获，标志着该行业在加大打击假烟生产力度的同时，将打击销售假烟网络作为解决售假问题的治本之策，从制假源头和销售两个环节遏制假烟的反弹。

7. 行业项目获国家科技进步二等奖，自主创新能力增强　“降低卷烟烟气中有害成分的技术研究”项目于 2005 年 3 月 28 日获国家科学技术进步奖二等奖，标志着该行业在减害降焦和增强自主创新能力方面所做的不懈努力得到了肯定，在科技创新中取得了突破性进展。

8. 行业劳动模范受表彰，职工素质全面提高　第四届全国烟草行业先进集体、劳动模范暨第七届烟草行业技术能手表彰大会于 2005 年 7 月 7 日在北京召开，64 个先进集体、79 名劳动模范、58 名技术能手受到表彰。2005 年，烟草行业共有 37 人获全国劳动模范称号，是行业历史上获此称号人数最多的一年。国家烟草专卖局号召在全行业广泛掀起学习先进的活动热潮，全面推动烟草行业精神文明建设。

（郑州烟草研究院　王英元）

酿 酒 工 业

一、基本情况

2005 年，是酿酒行业持续健康发展的一年。从经济环境看，商务部出台了 3 个有关酒类流通管理的标准和办法，全面展开了规范酒类流通秩序工作，为保护酒类生产者、经营者、消费者的合法权益提供了可靠的保障；全国白酒生产许可证发放工作基本完成，已安排全国查处工作；财政部多次召开调整白酒消费税的会议，广大企业的意见得到了国家的关注和采纳。从企业内部看，通过不断的改革、改制，企业活力日益旺盛，经营理念日趋科学，结构调整已见成效，产品质量和经济效益明显提高。据国家质检总局产品质量监督司抽查，2005 年白酒产品抽样合格率为 88.8%，啤酒产品抽样合格率为 87.5%，黄酒产品抽样合格率为 90.9%，葡萄酒产品抽样合格率为 88.2%。全行业的发展速度、效益指标的增长都超过两位数，分酒种看，除果露酒的税收增幅是一位数外，其他指标的增长也都达到了两位数。

2005 年，规模以上企业饮料酒总产量达 3 822.46万 kl，同比增长 7.84%。其中，啤酒产量 3 061.56万 kl，同比增长 10.30%；白酒产量 349.34 万 kl，同比增长 15.00%；葡萄酒产量 43.43 万 kl，同比增长 11.5%；酒精产量 368.13 万 kl，同比增长 35.60%；黄酒产量 200 万 kl，同比增长 30%。规模以上企业实现利润 133.46 亿元，同比增长 33.35%。其中，啤酒企业实现利润 35.63 亿元，同比增长 24.98%；白酒企业实现利润 73.19 亿元，同比增长 25.69%；葡萄酒企业实现利润 12.56 亿元，同比增长 58.78%；酒精企业实现利润 6.25 亿元，同比增长141.31%；黄酒企业实现利润3.38亿元，同比增长18.60%；果露酒企业实现利润2.45亿元，同比增长11.36%。上缴税金267.33亿元，同比增长14.51%。其中，啤酒企业上缴税金120.57亿元，同比增长11.38%；白酒企业上缴税金117.58亿元，同比增长17.62%；葡萄酒企业上缴税金12.07亿元，同比增长30.21%；酒精企业上缴税金9.16亿元，同比增长47.29%；黄酒企业上缴税金4.26亿元，同比增长12.70%；果露酒企业上缴税金3.68亿元，同比增长6.23%。税利合计400.80亿元，同比增长20.17%。

二、发展特点

综观一年来的行业动态，经过近几年的调整改革，大部分企业适应市场经济的能力愈来愈强，行业发展日趋健康合理。表现在：

1. 啤酒行业　2005年，虽然面对啤酒进口关税降为零、啤酒原料和能源大幅提价、“甲醛”风波等不利因素，但经过全行业的努力，行业所面临的难题已得到化解。啤酒产量稳步增长，产品销售收入稳中有升，关税降低对进出口并未构成影响。2005年，共出口啤酒14.69万kl，比上年同期增长4.04%；进口啤酒2.1万kl，比上年同期降低了21.28%。质量、品种的影响力越来越明显，装备国产化发展较快，营销逐渐步入现代化管理的轨道。

2. 白酒行业　经过几年的调整，首次呈现速度效益同步增长。2005年，我国白酒产量达349.34万kl，同比增长15.00%，净增34.64万kl；销售收入达722.65亿元，同比增长22.34%，净增110亿元；利润达73.19亿元，同比增长25.69%，净增14.53亿元；税金达117.58亿元，同比增长17.62%，净增17.58亿元。销售费用的增长率与销售收入增长率和利润、税金增长率基本同步。从销售收入看，前5名企业的销售收入达351.28亿元（即茅台、五粮液、剑南春、泸州老窖、汾酒），占全行业的48.60%；前26名企业的销售收入达485.83亿元，占全行业的67.22%。在这前26家企业中，过去的老名酒企业、优质酒企业占到了70%，产量和销售收入占到近90%。这说明随着我国市场经济的日益发展和成熟，白酒行业的生产和流通领域日趋理性、健康。老名牌的品牌优势、装备优势、质量优势、管理优势、资金优势，已经充分显现并得到市场和消费者的认可。

3. 黄酒行业　加大了广告投入，提升了生产能力，更新了产品结构，增多了黄酒人才，加大了行业整合的力度，获得的奖项也增多了。2005年，古越龙山绍兴酒有限公司和东风绍兴酒有限公司，斥资近亿元投入央视广告，其他企业广告的投入量均比上年有较大的增加。一年中，黄酒行业有22个企业的25个品牌的28个产品，获得了全国酒类产品安全诚信推荐品牌。有8个企业获得了国家质检总局授予的免检产品证书。

4. 葡萄酒行业　葡萄酒消费明显上升，形成酒类消费热点，在产量、产品结构、产品质量、生产工艺装备、产品品牌等方面都得到健康发展。从产量的发展看，2005年葡萄酒的发展在饮料酒中是增长速度最快的酒种，平均年增长率在10%以上。2005年葡萄酒产量为43.43万kl，增长11.5%，如再加上年上报外企的产量，全年接近50万kl。2005年与2000年比利润总额提高到12.5亿元，增长212.5%；税金总额提高到12亿元，增长140%；销售收入提高到102亿元，增长140%；资产总计提高到139亿元，增长96%。葡萄酒行业总资产贡献率、流动资产周转率、产品销售利润率等主要经济指标高于其他酒种的平均水平，行业优势明显。

5. 酒精行业　在上年高速发展的基础上，2005年酒精实现利润6.25亿元，同比增长141.31%；税金9.16亿元，同比增长47.29%。2005年11月份，国家发改委召集有关专家研讨生物能源生产代替品问题，建议全国生产车用乙醇150万t，相信随着国际原油价格的大幅飙升以及国内燃料酒精的逐步推广，我国燃料酒精市场化进程会进一步加快。

三、存在主要问题

2005年，虽然酿酒工业发展很快，但从宏观上还有不少问题需要解决，科学发展的任务依然很重。一是啤酒行业。我国啤酒产量虽然连续3年实现产量世界第一，但产量不能代表盈利水平、装备和管理水平。与欧美等发达国家相比，还存在较大差距，特别是盈利水平较低，出口量少，国际市场竞争力不强。要真正实现“世界啤酒强国”，还有很长的路要走。二是白酒行业。虽然近两年产量有所回升，但大部分企业的经济效益不容乐观，结构不合理的问题仍需下大力气解决。三是酒精行业。盲目扩建和新建的现象仍然很严重。在这些新增产能中，以玉米为原料的很少，大部分都是用木薯为原料，而国内木薯产量很少，只能依靠进口，原料来源将是很大问题。四是葡萄酒行业。葡萄原料减产，价格上涨幅度很大，抢原料风重新刮起，对原料质量有所影响。进口葡萄酒攻势很猛，意大利、西班牙等葡萄酒生产国以团队组合的形式向我国推介产品。进口酒愈来愈多，2005年进口量为5.31万kl，比上年同期增长21.23%左右。

四、行业活动

（一）开展职业技能鉴定工作，举办全国首届评酒师技能大赛

1. 在中国轻工业职业技能鉴定指导中心的指导下，中国酿酒工业协会全面开展了职业技能鉴定工作。已建立了20个酿酒行业职业技能鉴定站，涉及17个省、自治区、直辖市，有3 543人通过了鉴定，领到了由劳动和社会保障部颁发的职业资格证书。其中，高级技师807人、技师845人、高级酿造工747人、中级酿造工523人，初级酿造工621人。

2. 全国总工会、中国酿酒工业协会、中国轻纺烟草财贸工会、劳动和社会保障部就业指导中心、中国轻工业职业技能鉴定指导中心共同举办了“枝江杯”全国首届品酒技能（白酒）大赛。多数企业结合比赛开展岗位培训、技术练兵、技术比武，对参赛选手给予有力支持。据统计，共有27个省组织了省级竞赛，华北、东北、西北地区还组织了跨省竞赛。派出选手的企业达2 600余个，仅省级比赛的参赛选手就达到了近万名，充分体现了大赛的广泛性、群众性和代表性。2005年11月15～17日，来自28个省、自治区、直辖市89个企业的101名选手在湖北省宜昌市进行了决赛。通过决赛，为指导企业技术革新、提升产品质量奠定了基础。

（二）召开全国酒类产品质量安全诚信推荐品牌表彰大会与2005中国国际酿酒技术及包装设备展览会

1. 中国酿酒工业协会于2005年10月24～26日在上海举行了全国酒类产品质量安全诚信推荐品牌表彰大会，向221个企业品牌颁发了证书和铜牌。大会宣读了《诚信宣言》，300多名代表在大会诚信宣言上签名，做中国酒业诚信体系最坚定的执行者和捍卫者。会议肯定了酿酒企业，特别是一些大中型酿酒企业在抓质量、创品牌、重安全方面做出的不懈努力。这批企业将作为国家市场秩序整顿诚信体系建设的重点企业。

2. 召开全国酒类产品质量安全诚信推荐品牌表彰大会期间，由中国酿酒工业协会主办了2005中国国际酿酒技术及包装设备展览会。展览会期间，协会召开了葡萄酒分会、果露酒分会、白酒分会、黄酒分会、酒精分会、中国酿酒工业协会科教设计装备专业委员会2005年工作会议。安排有代表性的国内外参展商分别在各分会的专业会议上，以酿酒工业新工艺、新装备以及现代科技在酿酒工业的应用为主题，举办专题技术讲座和专题研讨会。

（三）及时应对甲醛风波，建立啤酒行业突发事件的预警和应急机制

1. 我国啤酒行业于2003年曾出现过一次“甲醛风波”，经过正面宣传，甲醛风波逐步平息。2005年，由于一些别有用心的人恶意炒作，再次掀起“甲醛风波”。不但影响了国内的啤酒消费市场，还影响了中国啤酒的国际形象。为迅速制止媒体恶意炒作，协会一方面及时向社会说明了啤酒生产使用甲醛的现状及安全性，另一方面积极向国家质检总局反映情况，申请啤酒质量检查。经查，国家质检总局产品质量监督司发布了“我国啤酒甲醛含量符合世卫规定”的新闻稿，使人为炒作的“甲醛风波”得到平息。

2. 中国酿酒工业协会于2005年7月组织召开了啤酒生产与消费安全座谈会，以啤酒生产与消费安全为主题进行了研讨，就建立快速反应机制、加强与主流媒体的信息沟通、建立与政府机构和执法机关的良好工作关系、统一行业舆论等问题形成共识，并成立啤酒产业安全协调小组。随后，啤酒分会又组织一些大企业代表参加了国家标准化委员会召开的啤酒中甲醛限量有关问题研讨会，充分反映了啤酒行业的意见。

（四）积极参加税制改革，反映行业企业要求

1. 在2005年两会期间，数位全国人大代表、政协委员代表提交了关于加快酒类立法方面的建议案，希望国家尽快研究酒类立法、酒税调整问题。提案转到协会后，迅速提出了《关于加快酒类立法和加强酒类管理的意见》，要求国家加强酒类立法统一管理酒行业，同时降低酒税、取消白酒从量消费税。

2. 中国酿酒工业协会于2005年3月10日收到财政部办公厅《关于调整和完善白酒消费税政策征求意见的函》后，组织了90多个全国重点白酒企业和26个省级地方酒协会负责人对文件内容进行了认真的讨论，并于3月22日给财政部税政司提交了《关于对白酒消费税政策调整的建议报告》，建议把企业依法纳税作为换发生产许可证和许可证年检的一项重要指标，赞成合并粮食白酒和薯类白酒的消费税税率，白酒贴标工作应选择有代表性的地区试点，应取消白酒从量消费税。

3. 根据国家税务总局对个别行业广告费税前扣除比例进行了调整（食品为8%，制药行业为25%），而葡萄酒企业的广告费税前扣除比例一直是2%的问题，协会向国家税务总局和财政部提出报告，反映葡萄酒企业税赋过重的问题，希望将其扣除比例提高到10%。2005年11月，税务总局和财政部专门组织石家庄国税局、青岛国税局、长城公司、协会召开了座谈会，就葡萄酒企业的税费问题进行了研讨。

（五）积极推动我国酒类产品质量认证工作

国家认证认可监督管理委员会、商务部于2005年9月发布了《食品质量认证实施规则 酒类》公告，中国酿酒工业协会在酿酒行业开展了“质量认证工程”。2006年1月18日，国家认监委、商务部在北京联合召开了中国酒类质量认证首批获证企业颁证大会，向茅台、五粮液、燕京、青岛、张裕、长城、古越龙山等首批29个企业共计115个单元产品颁发了中国酒类质量认证证书。获证产品总产量达212.9万t，占全国酒类企业生产总量的6.2%；产值为205.9亿元，占全国酒类总产值的15.3%。这标志着我国酒类质量等级认证取得突破性进展。实施酒类质量认证，揭示企业产品信息，帮助消费者区分优质酒产品、普通酒产品和劣质酒产品，满足消费者安全、健康、高品质的消费需求和产品质量识别。有助于减少流通环节中假酒、劣酒生存的空间，维护酒类生产流通的健康秩序，有利于提高企业效益和行业利益。

（中国酿酒工业协会 王耀荣）

蚕丝加工业

一、基本情况

2005年，中国蚕丝行业继续保持了较快发展势头。无论在蚕茧产量、丝的产量上，还是在蚕、丝内销和出口价格上，保持着良好的运行态势。

（一）蚕茧生产

1. 产量 根据对20个省、自治区、直辖市的统计，2005年全国的桑园面积为774khm²，与2004年相比减少0.95%；发种量为1 705.76万张，同比增长8.93%；蚕茧产量为61.61万t，同比增长12.00%；收购量为50.57万t，同比增长18.13%；收购综合均价为19 554元/t，同比增长22.64%。

2. 资源分布 2005年，茧丝行情较好，加上政策引导和相关部门的大力推动，全国和部分主产区“东桑西移”，保持了桑园面积和蚕茧生产的基本稳定，蚕茧生产部门和蚕农的生产积极性普遍有所提高，注重加强桑园管理，提高生产能力，取得了一定的效果。尤其是春茧的生产总体形势好于往年，取得了丰产增收的良好成效。东部一些主产区在夏秋季受灾害性气候和桑园病虫害等影响，造成蚕茧产量下降。但是以广西为代表的西部产区迅速崛起，生产量大幅增加，使2005年全国蚕茧产量与上年相比增长12%。增产幅度较大的省、自治区、直辖市有广西（产量14.01万t，增幅52%）、广东（产量3.43万t，增幅27%）、安徽（产量3.38万t，增幅25%）、陕西（产量2.03万t，增幅24%）、重庆（产量3.10万t，增幅21%）。2005年，广西的桑园面积和蚕茧产量已跃居全国第一，四川、重庆、陕西、宁夏等中西部省、自治区、直辖市桑蚕业发展也呈现迅速增长势头。中西部地区蚕茧产量占全国总产量的比例逐年增加，已占全国产量的一半以上。

随着“东桑西移”工程成功实施，促进了蚕桑生产的梯度转移，更使蚕桑生产朝着规模化、基地化、产业化方向发展，形成了东部（如江苏海安、东台等）蚕桑基地优质化、西部地区（如广西、云南、甘肃等）蚕桑基地规模化、东西中部协调发展的格局。江苏东台首家被授予“中国茧丝绸基地”称号。丝绸生产逐步朝区域特色产业集群化方向发展，嵊州领带城不断做大做强，杭州余杭及湖州周边地区形成了分工明细、协调合作、成本较低的丝织加工产业带，浙江凯喜雅丝绸加工园区、嘉欣丝绸加工园区技术水平和产品档次不断提高，以四川南充为代表的西部丝绸生产正在重新崛起，南充市、桐乡市被授予“中国绸都”和“中国蚕丝被、真丝毯生产基地”称号。

（二）加工量、产值、利税

由2005年底的缫丝企业生产准产证复审情况表明，随着我国市场经济改革的深化以及丝绸行业结构调整的进行，缫丝行业的基本面发生了根本性改变，一批企业被市场所淘汰，一批企业在市场竞争中脱颖而出。通过企业改革、兼并重组以及优胜劣汰的市场调整，缫丝企业结构调整得到进一步优化；通过企业技术改造与技术更新，自动缫丝机的大量使用，使缫丝行业的整体面貌焕然一新，缫丝行业整体实力更加巩固，整体竞争力得到了进一步加强，生丝产量和质量得到了提高。2005年，我国规模以上丝绸工业企业数2 558个，丝绸加工业总产值1 300亿元，产品销售收入完成1 322亿元，同比增长17.5%；实现利润32亿元，同比增长17%；资产负债率为65%。丝产量13万t，同比增长22.9%；丝织品75亿m，同比增长9.7%；丝绸产品销售收入完成1 250亿元，同比增长17.3%。丝绸出口继续增长，2005年真丝绸类产品出口37亿美元，同比增长18%。丝绸印染业销售收入214亿元，同比增长5%，实现利润5.1亿元，同比增长13%；丝绸复制品业销售收入64亿元，同比增长31%，实现利润3.8亿元，同比增长20%；丝绸针织业销售收入106亿元，同比增长14%，实现利润4.8亿元，同比增长30%。各行业都实现了较大幅度的增长，其中以缫丝和丝绸复制品两个行业的增幅较大。

2005年，丝绸行业亏损状况继续得到改善，据统计，亏损企业数下降至432个，亏损面下降至16.9%，同比减少4个百分点，亏损企业亏损总额为5.88亿元，同比下降5.6%。

二、国内外市场概况

(一) 出口贸易

2005年是我国真丝绸出口年景最好的一年。在2003年及2004年连续两年出口有较大增长的基础上，2005年出口又进一步增长了15.6%，达到37.52亿美元，创造了我国真丝绸出口的历史最高记录。

1. 蚕丝类商品出口量价齐升，出口金额大幅增加　全年蚕丝类商品出口3.05万t，同比增长10.59%；平均单价为20.18美元/kg，同比上升15.87%；全年蚕丝类商品出口金额达6.15亿美元，同比增长28.3%。蚕丝类商品中主要出口产品依次为绢纺纱线、厂丝、捻线丝，3种商品累计出口额占丝类商品出口的比重为78.42%。其中绢纺纱线出口1.24万t，金额2.3亿美元，同比分别增长了28.22%和49.67%；厂丝出口继续大幅增长，出口量为6 722t，金额达1.54亿美元，同比分别增长了89%和120.92%。

2. 真丝绸缎出口稳定增长　全年真丝绸缎商品出口2.9亿m，金额7.33亿美元，平均单价2.52美元/m，同比分别增长15.04%、23.98%、7.77%。其中，坯绸出口2.36亿m，金额5.21亿美元，同比数量增长14.53%，金额增长25.52%；印染绸出口5 261万m，金额2亿美元，同比数量增长16.16%，金额增长19.37%。

3. 丝绸制成品出口以丝绸服装为主，出口额增幅放缓　丝绸制成品出口24.04亿美元，同比增长10.53%，略低于丝绸商品出口整体增幅。其中，服装出口20 487.69万件套、19.11亿美元，同比数量仅增长1.04%，金额增长6.82%。

4. 对主要市场的出口总体增加　在对我国丝绸商品5个出口额最大的主销市场中，对美国绸缎出口量增长9.62%，出口额增长21.67%；丝绸服装出口量增长7.09%，出口额增长8.27%。对印度蚕丝类商品出口量增长1.42%，出口额增长22.60%；绸缎出口量下降1.8%，但是出口金额增长13.95%。对日本蚕丝类出口增幅较大，出口量和出口额分别增长25.63%和45.55%；真丝绸缎的出口量和出口额也增长16.05%和27.50%。对意大利的各类丝绸商品出口均有较大的增幅，其中蚕丝类商品出口量和出口金额分别增长18.94%、34.04%，真丝绸缎的出口量和出口额分别增长34.93%和33.91%。主销市场中对香港各类丝绸商品的出口量和出口金额都有所下降。

5. 各大类丝绸商品出口都普遍获得增长　丝类出口6.45亿美元，同比增长28.5%；绸类出口7.33亿美元，同比增长24%；服装及制品出口24亿美元，同比增长10.5%。

值得一提的是各类商品金额的增长幅度都高于数量的增长幅度。这反映出单价普遍上升，已完全走出前几年的“出口量增价跌的怪圈”。出口产品结构也进一步优化。服装制品及印染绸的出口已占出口总值的70%，改变了过去以原料出口为主的局面。这些情况说明了在科学发展观的指导下，丝绸出口正在转变增长模式，由数量增长型逐渐向效益增长型转变。

(二) 国内需求情况

随着国内经济的发展和人民生活水平的提高，人们对丝绸需求日益增加，真丝产品的内销比例有所增加，床上用品如蚕丝被、真丝内衣等丝绸产品受到广大消费者的青睐。蚕丝被等床上用品的耗丝量较大，其在国内市场的热销带动了丝绸原料的消费。据估算，2005年国内丝绸消费量增幅达到20%以上。

(三) 进口贸易

蚕丝类商品和蚕丝织物类商品进口的折丝量为0.89万t，其中茧、丝、绸累计折丝量约6 810t，同比减少约41.69%。进口蚕茧（折丝）58t，同比减少10.91%；进口蚕丝类4 028t，同比减少55.46%，这里主要是废丝进口（2 873t）减少62.22%；进口蚕丝织物约2 724t，同比增长5.99%。

三、新产品、新技术

1. 丝绸新品不断涌现　2005年，我国传统丝绸面料品质有了大幅度提高，各种功能的蚕丝被层出不穷，床上用品日益朝着高档化、时尚化、系列化方向发展，利用高科技和传统工艺相结合的丝绸艺术品档次不断提高，彩色茧丝研究与开发取得突破性进展，安徽丝绸公司、江苏鑫缘丝绸集团已具备彩色茧丝深加工和市场销售的能力。桑蚕茧丝资源综合利用不断向深层次、高技术化方向发展，已被广泛应用到医药、食品、化工、农产品等多种行业。江苏苏豪的“人造皮肤”已进入实质性开发生产阶段，江苏无锡的“医药缝纫线”已进入了产业化生产，形成了较好的经济效益，四川郎中蚕研所的雄蚕醋具有一定药用效果已得到市场认可。特别是我国家蚕基因组研究取得重大突破性进展，已列为科技部“973”国家重大科技攻关项目，并获得3 000万元政策支持，这将为我国茧丝绸行业今后的发展带来更新的变化。

2. *名牌产品不断增加* 一批在国内具有一定知名度的企业，除了推出品牌产品外，品牌意识也在增强。这些企业代表了我国丝绸业的总体形象和发展方向，具备了参与国际市场竞争的能力，成为带动丝绸行业发展的骨干企业。与此同时，一批在产品品种、科研开发中以“专、精、特、新”见长的中小企业的品牌不断涌现，特别是鑫缘茧丝绸集团股份有限公司、江苏华佳投资集团有限公司、浙江凯喜雅国际股份有限公司、江苏苏豪国际集团股份有限公司等企业获得了2005年度桑蚕生丝产品“中国名牌”企业品牌；浙江金鹰股份有限公司、富润控股集团有限公司获得2005年度桑蚕绢丝产品“中国名牌”企业品牌。目前丝绸行业已有浙江凯喜雅国际股份有限公司、万事利集团公司、达利丝绸（浙江）有限公司，获得了北京2008奥运会特许经营资格。特别是高档丝绸标志的推出，迅速推动了我国丝绸行业的发展。

3. *纳米级再生蚕丝纤维制品的研制与开发* 以茧丝绸加工中的废弃蚕丝为原料，将丝素纤维再生为具有良好可纺性的丝素蛋白溶液，采用静电纺工艺制成再生丝素纤维和纳米再生丝素/尼龙复合纤维，纤维相互交络成为具有多孔结构的非织造织物。可用做生物医用材料、防护材料以及精密过滤材料等，如分别对涤纶织物、棉织物、黏胶人造丝织物等进行纳米丝纤维的涂覆加工，可开发出医用防护口罩、保健三角内裤等抗菌内衣产品。

4. *桑蚕干茧自动缫丝检测设备通过鉴定* 该项目由中国纤维检验局牵头，杭州纺织机械有限公司负责研制，浙江省第三茧质检定所、山东省茧丝检验所等单位具体负责试样验证并共同联合开发。桑蚕干茧自动缫丝检测设备样机外观良好，结构完整，全机自动控制程度高，实现了自动索理绪、自动纤度控制、自动添绪执行、自动接绪卷绕、落绪茧自动捕集和分离；在缫丝检验自动化核心领域，攻克了关键的自动计数技术，创造性地研制了自动计长、添绪、吊糙计数装置，大大提高了生产效率和稳定性；计数装置实现了三个自动检测计数：自动计测添绪次数，自动计测生丝长度，自动计测吊糙次数。索绪汤温、缫丝汤温实现了自动控制；样机能快速、准确、全面地检验蚕茧质量指标，工效比立缫提高1.5倍，用工比立缫节约60%；计量测长等仪器仪表精度较高，工艺参数的波动性较小，适用性、重复性、稳定性较为理想。

四、质量管理与标准化工作

1. *桑蚕干茧国家新标准出台* 为进一步促进和提高桑蚕干茧的质量，适应缫丝生产的发展，由中国纤维检验局提出，中国纤维检验局、山东省茧丝检验所、浙江省第三茧质检定所等单位起草的GB9176—2006《桑蚕干茧》送审稿在北京进行审定。在各位专家共同努力下，桑蚕干茧国标送审稿的修改工作顺利完成，正在按有关程序报批。桑蚕茧干茧的国家标准GB9176—1988发布实施已经18年，对促进我国的桑蚕品种改良、提高桑蚕茧质量、方便贸易结算等方面发挥了重要作用。但是随着我国种桑养蚕事业的发展，这个标准亟待修订和完善。《桑蚕干茧》国标的主要修订内容是：解舒检验的试验设备由原来的立缫机变更为茧检定自动试样机，有关试验条件作了相应的修改；解舒试验由定粒式改为定纤式，每个检验批次的试验样本由5区改为3区，绪数由10绪改为5绪；清洁、洁净检验将按GB1798—2001《生丝试验方法》进行，增加了万米吊糙指标的检验；桑蚕干茧的质量要求与质量标识摒弃了现行标准中的茧级概念，取而代之的是质量标识的概念，其目的是直接标明桑蚕干茧的主要质量指标。

2. *《茧丝质量监督管理办法》开始施行* 为了加强对茧丝质量的监督管理，明确茧丝质量责任，促进茧丝质量的提高，维护茧丝市场秩序和茧丝交易各方的合法权益，国家质量监督检验检疫总局局务会议审议通过了《茧丝质量监督管理办法》，并于2005年3月1日开始施行。《办法》要求茧丝经营者从事收购桑蚕鲜茧或者加工桑蚕干茧活动的，必须在设施和环境、设备和仪器、从业人员、质量检验标准、内部质量保证制度等方面具备规定的条件，并经过专业纤维检验机构的审核。桑蚕鲜茧收购、桑蚕干茧加工质量保证条件的基本要求由国家质检总局会同国家发改委制定；各地区的具体要求由省级质量技术监督部门会同同级发展改革管理部门制定。地方质量保证条件不得低于国家质量保证基本条件。

3. 四项农业行业（蚕桑）标准通过专家审定 由中国农业科学院蚕业研究所及农业部蚕桑产业产品质量监督检验测试中心（镇江）等主持起草的《桑蚕一杂交种繁育技术规程》、《桑园用药技术规程》、《养蚕用药技术规程》和《柞蚕一代杂交种》四项农业行业（蚕桑）标准，于2005年11月27日在镇江市通过了来自全国科研、教育、生产、推广和检测等单位的专家审定。《桑蚕一杂交种繁育技术规程》等四项农业行业（蚕桑）标准具有充分的理论依据和广泛的实践基础，体现了科学性、先进性、适用性和前瞻性的统一，具有国际先进水平。其中《桑园用药技术规程》、《养蚕用药技术规程》标准文本的制定填补了国内空白。四项农业行业（蚕桑）标准颁布实施后，将对我国茧丝绸生产起到积极作用。

4. 制定生丝电子检测国家标准 以我国生丝标准为代表形成国际生丝标准，是我国由丝绸大国向丝绸强国转变的重要方面。生丝电子检测是当今世界生丝检测的方向。近两年来，中国丝绸协会、全国纺织品标准化技术委员会丝绸分会、浙江丝绸科技有限公司和浙江省检验检疫局丝类检验中心在生丝电子检测方面分别做了大量的工作，都取得初步进展。

五、行业管理

1. 坚持资格准入制度 各省级商务主管部门（茧丝办）制定了《鲜茧收购资格认定实施细则》，进一步规范蚕茧收烘管理，完善鲜茧收购制度，维护正常的鲜茧收购秩序。严格资格准入制度，做好《鲜茧收购资格证书》的复审和公示工作。既要打破区域封锁，引入竞争机制，避免损害蚕农利益，又要防止发证过多而造成抢购、哄抬茧价、大量收购毛脚茧的现象。

2. 加大执法力度 各级工商行政管理机关严格按照蚕茧收购资格进行核准登记，从源头上严把市场主体准入关。严禁已取得资格认定的经营者以挂靠、租赁和承包等方式为未取得资格认定的经营者从事蚕茧收购提供渠道。进一步加大执法力度，严厉查处未经资格认定和核准登记擅自从事蚕茧收购等违法违规行为，切实做到把不合格的收购主体清除出蚕茧收购市场，维护蚕茧收购市场秩序。

3. 落实收购资金，做到优质优价 蚕茧收购有关单位结合当年产销形势和当地实际情况，提早做好准备工作，积极做好省际、市县之间的协调工作。提前筹措收购资金，保证资金及时、足额到位，对蚕农要做好收茧服务工作，不打“白条”。有关质量检验机构切实加强对蚕茧收购质量的监督，保证优质优价。

4. 出台了一系列宏观调控措施 在蚕茧生产收烘工作中，各部委对收烘工作中能够预见的和已出现的一些问题进行了及时的控制，商务部、农业部《2005年度全国桑蚕种桑蚕茧桑蚕丝生产指导性计划》，国家发改委、商务部、国家工商行政管理总局《关于做好2005年蚕茧收购价格及加强收购管理工作的通知》和《关于做好2005年秋茧生产与收购工作的通知》，对保护蚕农利益、稳定蚕茧生产和收购价格，促进行业健康发展进行了积极的引导。各省、自治区、直辖市主管委、厅对春茧收烘工作十分重视，根据以上文件精神和各地的具体情况，下发了相应的政策指导性文件。各级行政管理部门的重视和正确引导，对蚕桑生产的适度发展和维护良好的收购秩序发挥了积极的作用。

（中国农业科学院蚕业研究所 梁培生）

饲料加工业

一、发展概况

（一）产量继续大幅增长

根据各省、自治区、直辖市提供的数据分析，2005年全国饲料加工业产值达2 742亿元，工业饲料总产量达1.07亿t，分别比上年增长12.9%和11.04%。全国配合饲料产量为7 762万t，同比增长10.4%；浓缩饲料2 498万t，同比增长12.32%；添加剂预混合饲料472万t，同比增长16.31%。添加剂预混合饲料、浓缩饲料和配合饲料三者的比例由上年的1∶5.5∶17.3调整为1∶5.3∶16.4，产品结构更加符合养殖业结构的需求。

（二）结构调整幅度较大

2005年，我国饲料工业生产结构发生明显变化。配合饲料产量增幅较大，超过1996年以来年均增长率5.49%，但所占比重略微有所下降，占饲料总产量的72.31%。配合饲料增幅创10年来的新高，是近些年发展的最好时期，特别是高价乳猪配合饲料增长最快。浓缩饲料生产呈下降的走势，增长幅度和上年相比下降 1.3 个百分点，占饲料总产量的 23.29%；添加剂预混合饲料增速放缓，但增幅最高，超过近 5 年来年均增长率的 9.86 百分点，占饲料总产量的 4.4%，这主要是自配料快速增长等因素的作用。

从饲料产品类别看，配合饲料中，猪配合饲料总产量 2 561 万 t，比上年增长 9.8%；蛋禽配合饲料 1 429万 t，增长 3.24%；肉禽配合饲料 2 427 万 t，增长 9.36%；水产配合饲料 984 万 t，增长 25.03%；反刍动物精料补充料 236 万 t，增长 25.79%；其他配合饲料 124 万 t，增长 4.24%。浓缩饲料中，猪浓缩饲料产量 1 434 万 t，增长 15.74%；蛋禽浓缩饲料产量 516 万 t，增长 16.14%；肉禽浓缩饲料产量 345 万 t，增长 3.29%；反刍动物浓缩饲料产量 131 万 t，增长 8.67%；水产浓缩饲料 34 万 t，增长 13.4%；其他浓缩饲料产量 38 万 t，增长 18.87%。预混合饲料中，猪预混合饲料产量 254 万 t，同比增长 15.18%；蛋禽预混合饲料产量 96 万 t，增长 27.56%；肉禽预混合饲料产量 53 万 t，下降 3.2%；水产预混合饲料产量 17.9 万 t，增长 25.57%；反刍动物预混合饲料产量 19.5 万 t，增长 7.44%；其他预混合饲料产量 30 万 t，增长 40.17%。

（三）品种结构合理

2005 年，猪料、蛋禽料、肉禽料、水产料、反刍料及其他料总产量分别为 4 250 万 t、2 041 万 t、2 826万 t、1 036 万 t、387 万 t 和 192 万 t，同比分别增长 5.66%、5.54%、7.68%、19.76%、15.57%、10.29%。符合稳定猪禽生产，大力发展反刍和水产动物饲料生产的产业政策。

（四）区域差距缩小

2005 年，东部 10 省（直辖市）总产量为 4 861 万 t，占全国总产量的 45%；中部 6 省总产量为2 458 万 t，占全国总产量的 23%；东北 3 省总产量为1 476 万 t，占全国总产量 14%；西部 12 省（西藏没有统计数字）总产量为 1 938 万 t，占全国总产量的 18%。从区域发展速度来看，东部 10 省（直辖市）和中部 6 省发展势头依旧迅猛，东北 3 省增速较为强劲，西部 12 省（自治区、直辖市）虽然增速相对缓慢，但与上年相比也保持着较高的增长速度。东部 10 省（直辖市）、中部 6 省、东北 3 省、西部 12 省（自治区、直辖市）的工业饲料产量增幅分别为 12.25%、11.69%、10.10%和 8.05%。

（五）原料生产稳定

1. 玉米　2005 年，全国玉米产量为 1.34 亿 t，比上年增长 4.69%。据海关统计，全年玉米出口量为 861 万 t，比上年增长 272.73%。

2. 大豆　2005 年，国内大豆产量达到1 830万 t，比上年增长 1.67%。据海关统计，进口大豆 2 659 万 t，比上年增长 31.44%，国内大豆总供应量在4 500 万 t 左右。

3. 鱼粉　2005 年，国内鱼粉总产量为 39.5 万 t，比上年增长 19.6%。据海关统计，全年进口量约达 158 万 t，是近年来进口鱼粉数量较多的年份。全年鱼粉总供应量达到近 200 万 t，鱼粉总消费量约 180 万 t 以上。

4. 添加剂　2005 年，赖氨酸产量达 33.6 万 t（含 65%赖氨酸），比上年增长 93.6%。赖氨酸进口量为 5.46 万 t，比上年下降 28.76%；2005 年，我国赖氨酸出口量增幅明显，为历年最高，全年出口量在 6.46 万 t 左右。这主要得益于我国赖氨酸产能的扩大和产品质量的提高。2005 年赖氨酸市场需求量约 20 万 t，比上年增长约 15%以上。市场供应过剩，库存量较大，是该年度的市场供需特点。2005 年蛋氨酸进口数量达到了 6.67 万 t，比上年下降 22.26%。

（六）产业结构优化

2005 年，全国饲料企业按经济类型统计总数为 15 518 个，比上年增加 989 个，增长 6.81%。其中，国有企业 488 个，集体企业 527 个，私营企业 8 880 个，联营企业 407 个，股份制企业 3 797 个，港澳台资企业 157 个，外商企业 307 个，其他类型企业 955 个。与 2004 年相比，国有企业、集体企业的企业数继续呈现明显下降趋势，分别减少 109 和 105 个，降幅分别为 18.26%、16.61%。私营企业增加 553 个，增长 6.6%；联营企业下降 32 个，降幅为 7.3%；股份制企业增加 368 个，增长 10.7%；港澳台企业增加 7 个，增长 4.7%；外商企业数增加 20 个，增长 6.9%；其他类型企业增加 199 个，增长 26.32%。

（七）从业人数增长

2005 年，饲料企业年末职工人数为 50.5 万人，比上年增长 6.81%；大专以上技术人员 13 万人，占职工总人数的 25.82%，比上年提高 2 个百分点。其中，博士 1 185 人，占职工总人数的 0.2%；硕士 3 349人，占职工总人数的 0.66%；大学本科 47 390 人，占职工总人数的 9.3%；大学专科 78 586 个，占职工总人数的 15.6%；技术工种共 57 860 人，占职工总人数的 11.49%。

（八）机械设备增加

2005 年，饲料加工机械设备共 26 789 台套，比上年增加 2 611 台套。其中，成套机组为 4 405 套，比上年增加 1 158 套，增长 35.66%；单机 22 384

台，比上年增加 1 453 台，增长 6.94%。在成套设备中，时产 10 t 以上设备 827 台套，比上年增加 514 台套；时产 5～10 t 的设备 839 台套，增加 248 台套；时产 1～5t 的设备 2 739 台套，比上年增加 396 台套。在单机设备中，粉碎机 10 143 台，增加 5 552 台；混合机 4 689 台，增加 988 台；制粒机 1 717 台，增加 249 台；其他类型设备 5 835 台，下降 5 331 台。

二、主要特点

1. *饲料企业抗风险能力明显增强* 2005 年是我国养殖业的多事之年。生猪养殖受到了四川猪链球菌事件的严重影响，水产养殖受孔雀石绿事件拖累，养禽业受到高致病性禽流感蔓延的沉重打击，奶牛养殖受到进口还原奶的巨大冲击。这些事件的发生不仅直接影响了养殖业，还给饲料生产企业带来严重影响。但由于饲料企业特别是大型企业集团经历了上年 SARS、高致病性禽流感和原料大幅涨价等的冲击后，纷纷采取了风险控制措施，通过多元化经营、产业链延伸、开发替代资源、开拓国外市场等多种手段，使企业的抗风险能力明显增强。在 2005 年极端不利的情况下，饲料工业仍取得了饲料产量、产值和效益的同步增长。

2. *产能迅速增加* 自从改革开放以来，我国工业饲料产量一直保持较高的发展速度，饲料企业产能迅速增加，2005 年仅黑龙江、辽宁和山东 3 个省就新增产能（双班）500 多万 t，超过了我国自 1991 年饲料产量跃居世界第二位之后 15 年饲料产量年均增加 467 万 t 的增速。这主要是由于出于对未来饲料工业发展前景的良好预期，一方面大型饲料企业集团不断加大兼并重组速度，企业规模迅速扩大，如新希望集团与山东六和集团成功联合重组后集团的饲料产能已突破 1 000 万 t；另一方面有大量新企业加入，如北京 2005 年新增饲料生产企业 75 个，天津新增企业 50 个。此外，许多老企业纷纷加大了技术和设备改造力度，产能迅速提高。预计 2005 年全国饲料工业产能（双班）将突破 1.4 亿 t。

3. *科技含量和产品附加值不断增加* 饲料是动物营养科技的载体，是现代饲料加工工艺设备的终端产品。近几年，随着饲料行业从业人员素质的不断提高和大量饲料新技术得到应用，饲料产品的科技含量和附加值不断增加。2005 年，大专以上学历的专业技术人员占到从业人员总数的 1/4；饲料产品中附加值高的添加剂和添加剂预混合饲料的增长幅度比浓缩饲料高 4 个百分点，是配合饲料的 1.6 倍。科技对饲料工业发展的贡献率已超过 40%。随着科技水平的提高，饲料对养殖业提高生产水平发挥着越来越关键作用。我国肉鸡配合饲料的转化率已由“八五”时期的 2.5∶1 提高到目前的 1.8∶1，出栏缩短 18 天左右；肥育猪由 3.3∶1 提高到 3.0∶1，出栏缩短 40 天左右；养殖水产品由 2.0∶1 提高到 1.8∶1，养殖效益明显提高。

4. *饲料产品在高质量水平上趋于稳定* 2005 年，随着各地开始换发生产许可证和出台饲料企业设置（审查）办法，提高了饲料企业的进入门槛，许多设备设施落后的企业被淘汰，现有企业加工设备现代化水平明显提高。同时，饲料企业科学管理水平不断提高。2005 年，全国约有 120 多个企业通过 HACCP 认证，380 多个企业通过了 ISO9001 等认证，另外还有 70 多个企业饲料通过产品认证。同时，各级饲料主管部门对饲料产品的监管力度也不断加大。2005 年，仅农业部就组织在全国开展了 5 次饲料监督抽查。这些措施的实施，使饲料产品质量稳定在较好水平上。2005 年，全国饲料产品质量检测平均合格率为 92.4%。其中，配合饲料合格率 97.9%，与上年持平；动物源性饲料合格率 84%，比上年提高 3.7 个百分点；饲料生产经营环节“瘦肉精”等违禁药品检出率为 0。全国饲料质量的平均合格率比 1987 年第一次国家饲料产品质量抽查提高了 4.6 倍。

5. *集团化和产业化程度进一步提高* 2005 年以来，一批优秀的大中型企业通过资产重组、联营并购、延长产业链等方式，加快了产业化、集团化发展步伐，逐步呈现出强者更强的趋势，规模化优势显现。如新希望集团与山东六和集团实现成功联合，两个集团拥有下属公司 170 多个。其中包括 5 个国家级农业产业化龙头企业，重组后集团的饲料产量全年有望达到 600 万 t，进入全球饲料行业 10 强。大型集团企业跨区建厂的速度也进一步加快，2005 年仅黑龙江省、江苏、浙江和陕西等 4 个省就新建 230 多个企业，其中绝大多数为大北农、恒兴、通威、正虹等企业集团的分厂。在国内企业扩张的同时，国外跨国饲料企业集团扩张步伐加快。美国嘉吉公司收购普瑞纳公司，美国泰森食品股份有限公司兼并福建圣农集团。国内中小型饲料企业也纷纷结盟，努力做大做强。如先后成立了绿色伟农联合体、广盟经济合作组织、“7＋1”高科技饲料企业联合体、外资企业联谊会、中大型饲料企业技术总监联谊会、河南中大型企业联合体等等。为了增强抵抗市场风险的能力，国内的饲料企业加速了向农、工、贸，产、供、销一条龙产业化经营方向转变的速度，取得了显著成效。2005 年，仅辽宁一省就有禾丰和大成 2 个饲料企业被列为农业产业化国家重点龙头企业，10 个饲料企业被列为省级龙头企业。以饲料企业为“龙头”，向产前、产中、产后延伸的产业化经营的发展，不仅延长了产业链，提高了产品附加值，而且带动了相关产业发展，增强了企业竞争力，还减少了中间环节，降低了饲料成本，对带动农民致富、增加农民收入、发展农村经济发挥了积极作用。

6. 产业结构调整步伐加快，产品结构更趋合理 随着饲料企业集团化和产业化步伐的加快，饲料产业结构调整的步伐随之加快，饲料产品结构更趋合理。一是科技含量高、产品附加值高的饲料比例进一步增加。二是畜禽产品结构随着养殖业生产结构的调整迅速调整。2005 年猪、禽、水产和反刍家畜饲料的比例为 40∶46∶9.8∶3.6。同时由于特种养殖和宠物饲养数量的增加，特种饲料的产量也出现快速增长，如黑龙江 2005 年狐等饲料产量增加 8 万多 t。三是饲料产品结构更加符合地方特点。养殖水平发达的地区由于规模化养殖水平和科学养殖水平较高，对配合饲料的需求加大，如 2005 年山东、浙江和江苏等省的配合饲料增长比例都高于其他饲料。而有些省份，由于受养殖水平较低，更多采用浓缩饲料和预混合饲料，配合饲料增长速度远低于其他饲料，部分省份甚至出现负增长，如甘肃、青海。四是生产企业比例增加，经营企业比例下降。由于越来越多的企业采取直销方式和产业化模式销售饲料产品，以降低饲料价格，提高竞争力，使饲料经营企业数量逐渐减少，如北京市 2005 年饲料经营企业减少 26 个，同比减少 12.3 个百分点。

7. 企业分化程度进一步加剧 饲料行业经过不断的兼并、重组和整合，企业分化程度也进一步加剧，饲料企业呈现强者更强的趋势。根据 2005 年农业部重点跟踪企业生产情况分析，饲料企业集团优势更加明显，小型企业的劣势更加显现。1～5 月份，55%的饲料企业产量增长，29.5%的企业产量下降，15.5%的饲料企业产量持平。预计 2005 年山东排名前 10 位饲料生产企业的饲料产量将占到全省饲料总产量的 40%左右，辽宁省排名前 10 位的饲料企业饲料产量也将占到全省饲料产量的 30%。而华北地区的不少小企业却面临倒闭。

8. 饲料行业监管日趋规范，服务意识进一步增强 为了加强对饲料行业发展的管理，各地纷纷出台措施，规范饲料管理行为。一是大力推行政务公开。农业部已将进口饲料登记和生产证申办纳入行政综合审批大厅，同时将申报条件、办理时限和申办程序等有关内容在审批大厅和网上公开，以方便企业申办。许多省级饲料主管部门，如北京等省、直辖市也采取了类似的措施。二是对动物源性饲料生产企业实行生产许可证管理。《动物源性饲料产品安全卫生管理办法》2004 年 10 月 1 日开始正式实施以后，各地饲料主管部门严格规范审批行为，对不合格的动物源性饲料生产企业坚决不发放安全卫生合格证。三是加强对设立饲料企业的管理办法。目前的《饲料和饲料添加剂管理条例》仅规定了对添加剂和添加剂预混合饲料的管理，而对浓缩饲料和配合饲料监管缺乏依据，导致饲料企业良莠不齐。为了加大对这些企业的管理，各地纷纷根据当地情况，出台了饲料企业资格审查办法，如黑龙江的《饲料资质审查合格证》，安徽的《安徽省饲料生产企业审查合格证管理办法》。四是建立网上审批系统。北京、辽宁和上海等省、直辖市按照“规范、高效、便民”的原则建立了网上申报、受理、审批系统，大大提高了工作效率，为企业提供了经济、便捷的服务。五是加强了行业信息指导工作。如上海、江苏、山西等省、直辖市饲料主管部门定期把政策法规、管理规定、行业动态、市场供求等信息发给下级管理部门和生产企业。

9. 饲料企业国际竞争力进一步加强 饲料企业实施“走出去”战略的优势日渐突现。一是已形成了较为完备的现代饲料工业生产体系。饲料行业从机械加工、原料生产、添加剂生产和成品生产水平已显著提高，形成了门类比较齐全的饲料工业体系。二是部分饲料产品在国际市场占有一定优势。我国氯化胆碱、饲料级维生素 A、D、E、K、C 及 B 族维生素全部实现国产化，产品质量好，价格合理；维生素 A、E、C 等饲料级维生素已占国际市场 30%～50%的市场份额。赖氨酸已摆脱完全依赖进口的情况，并实现了部分出口。三是我国的饲料机械生产技术和设备已达到国际先进水平，饲料加工设备出口量逐年增加，加上优质的售后服务，深受东南亚地区的欢迎。四是一批饲料企业已走出国门，在朝鲜、东南亚等地区投资兴办饲料企业，已经具备了在海外投资办企业的实力和经验。黑龙江的饲料已出口到俄罗斯、韩国等 5 个国家。

三、存在的问题

2005 年，饲料工业虽然克服了众多困难，取得了可喜的成绩，但依然受到原料资源短缺，经营和养殖环节饲料监管困难，饲料法律法规体系滞后于饲料业发展，科研投入不足，基础研究薄弱等老问题的困扰。除此之外，饲料工业的发展还面临着一些新问题，主要表现为疫病对饲料工业的影响越来越大，饲料原料中的有毒有害物质对饲料安全的威胁越来越严重，饲料监管的服务水平还有待进一步提高，饲料工业产能出现过剩等。

1. *畜禽疫病对饲料工业的影响日趋加剧* 2005年，疫病对饲料工业的影响日趋加剧，7月份，虽然只是四川局部地区发生人感染猪链球菌病，却使全国猪价持续普遍下滑，饲料工业受到严重打击，工业饲料产量由上半年的同比增长16.3%急剧下降至第三季度的同比增长1.4%；进入10月份，高致病性禽流感疫情在全国的蔓延，造成养禽业生产受阻和消费急剧下降，部分地区活禽交易被禁止，许多省鸡苗有价无市，活鸡价格大幅下降，种禽场纷纷宰杀种鸡或将种鸡蛋当普通鸡蛋销售。如江苏省肉鸡价格已降至每千克不足3.0元，浙江省疫情发生前需要2.8元/只的蛋鸭苗现在卖1元3只，送上门还无人敢要。养禽业的下滑，使家禽饲料生产企业几乎陷于停滞。

2. *饲料原料中的有毒有害物质严重威胁饲料安全* 随着饲料监管体系的完善和监管力度的加大，在饲料中违法违规添加"瘦肉精"等违禁药品的现象出现明显减少，但饲料卫生指标不合格特别是有毒有害物质超标对饲料安全的威胁越来越严重。突出表现为：一是霉菌毒素严重超标，不仅造成直接经济损失，还造成饲料原料供应紧张。据预测，我国大宗饲料原料有近1/3霉菌毒素超标，每年仅此一项造成的经济损失达20亿元。由于霉菌毒素超标造成饲料原料不能使用导致的损失更大，如河南省2005年1 100万t饲料用玉米约有20%～30%因阴雨天气霉变，而不能直接作为饲料使用，不得不从外地大量调入玉米。二是铅、镉、铬和砷等重金属超标，不仅导致饲料不合格，还造成重金属在动物性食品和水等环境中的蓄积，严重威胁人类健康。2005年，全国饲料检测结果显示配合饲料合格率97.9%，导致配合饲料不合格的主要因素就是重金属超标。

3. *饲料监管的服务水平还有待进一步提高* 随着饲料监管法规体系的完善和《行政许可法》的实施，各级饲料主管部门依法行政的管理水平和服务水平不断提高，但也暴露出一些新的问题。一是出现地方保护主义抬头现象。在2005年猪链球菌和高致病性禽流感疫情发生期间，有些县市以防控疫病为由限制或禁止外地企业的饲料进入流通，饲料企业反映强烈。二是生产许可证换发滞后。2005年我国最早一批生产许可证到期，需要集中换发新证，由于工作量大，部分省饲料主管部门上报工作滞后，导致一些企业不能及时拿到新证。遭到其他饲料主管部门的查封，给饲料企业造成了损失。三是人员少，且变动频繁。部分省份饲料主管部门专职管理人员少，人员变动频繁，导致饲料管理工作连续性差，对企业和行业情况不了解，管理不到位，工作力度小等。

4. *饲料工业产能开始出现过剩* 饲料业在我国是一个市场化程度较高、进入门槛较低的行业。由于饲料工业的高速发展和稳定的利润空间，吸引了大量企业和个人投资饲料业，导致饲料工业产能迅速增加。如仅辽宁一省2005年就新增产能（双班）200万t。随着饲料企业产能的迅速增加，饲料也出现一个值得警惕的现象，即企业开工不足，生产设备闲置。估计2005年全国饲料工业产能（双班）达到1.4亿t，产能超过实际产量40%。个别省份产能过剩更为严重，如辽宁省2005年实际产能（双班）达到1 600万t，而实际饲料产量仅有620多万t，产能是实际产量的2.57倍，吉林省的产能也比实际产量高近1倍。如何引导和整合现有资源，实现资源的最优化利用成为一个值得思考的问题。

四、保障措施

1. *进一步完善饲料法规和标准体系* 不断完善饲料管理法规，修改完善并颁布实施《饲料生产企业审查办法》等法规。配合立法机关积极推进《饲料法》的起草，进一步完善饲料安全监管制度。建立健全饲料安全标准体系，包括饲料和饲料添加剂质量安全标准、动物性饲料检测方法标准、禁止在饲料和动物饮用水中使用的药物检测方法标准、各类违禁药品和限量使用的各种抗生素的速测方法标准等。

2. *继续加大政策扶持和资金投入力度* 加大政策扶持，继续执行国家对饲料行业的现行税收优惠政策。"十五"期间，国家已对饲料产品（单一饲料、混合饲料、配合饲料、浓缩饲料、复合预混合饲料）实行免征增值税的优惠，在"十一五"期间应当继续执行这一优惠政策；鼓励和支持有条件的饲料企业跨区域收购所需的饲料原料。各级财政要加大对饲料业的资金投入力度，重点用于饲料高新技术的开发和推广以及市场信息体系、监测检验体系和优质饲料基地建设。金融部门要充分发挥信贷的扶持作用，努力提高金融服务水平，积极扶持多种经济成分的饲料企业。积极引导社会资本投资饲料业，加快饲料业利用外资的步伐。

3. *加强饲料安全监管* 加强饲料安全监管，实行生产、经营和使用全方位质量安全检测，强化源头管理和生产监控。加大饲料和畜产品中"瘦肉精"等违禁药品专项整治工作力度，对危及饲料安全的各类生产、经营企业和产品予以曝光。稳定饲料执法队伍，提高执法人员素质，更新执法手段，提高执法水平，加大对假冒伪劣饲料的打击力度。加强饲料安全的舆论宣传，大力宣传普及科学饲料配方和健康养殖技术，提高饲料从业人员的能力和信心，为饲料工业的健康发展创造良好的环境。

4. 大力推进饲料工业科技进步 “十一五”期间，我国饲料工业的增长要转移到依靠科技进步、提高质量和效益的轨道上来，加大对国家级公益性饲料科研机构的建设投入。加快饲料科技创新特别是自主创新的步伐，加强饲料科技攻关，积极研制开发安全高效、无残留、无污染的饲料和饲料添加剂新产品。在争取政府加大投入的同时，鼓励大中型饲料企业建立和完善企业技术研发中心，增加研究和开发投入，增强技术创新能力。鼓励科研单位、院校和企业共同开展多种形式的合作，推动科技成果商品化、产业化。

5. 充分发挥行业协会的作用 建立健全各级饲料行业协会，充分发挥饲料行业协会联系政府和企业的桥梁和纽带作用，协助政府加强行业管理，积极开展行业指导，帮助企业提高质量安全管理水平，增强企业竞争力。组织开展饲料工业标准化、科技推广、对外交流和职业技能培训等工作。加强行业自律，逐步建立企业诚信制度，保障公平、公正、公开、有序的市场秩序，促进产业发展。协助企业遵循国际市场规则，拓展国际市场。充分利用 WTO 的保障条款，维护饲料行业权益。

6. 提高饲料产业化经营水平 进一步培育具有国际竞争力的名牌企业，通过兼并、联合、重组等形式，形成一批拥有自主知识产权、竞争能力强的大公司和企业集团，提高产业集中度和产品开发潜力，支持饲料工业在更大的范围内和更深的程度上参与国际合作与竞争。总结推广以饲料企业为龙头，饲料、饲养、加工一体化和部分中间环节专业化的模式，带动农户进入市场。充分发挥饲料企业与农户联系紧密的特点，鼓励饲料企业采取“订单农业”、“公司＋农户”等方式，把原料生产、加工、销售、养殖等环节有机联系起来，形成较为稳定的产销关系和利益关系。支持饲料企业、专业大户和经纪人牵头组建农村专业化合作经济组织，提高生产经营的组织化程度。各地区和有关部门要将符合条件的饲料企业列为农业产业化龙头企业，优先予以扶持。通过各种优惠政策，鼓励和支持内地饲料企业到西部边远地区投资建厂，发挥龙头企业作用，带动当地饲料工业的发展，促进养殖业发展，增加农民收入。

（农业部畜牧业司 李大鹏 刘继业）

水产品加工业

一、水产品生产状况

据《中国农业统计资料》显示，2005 年我国水产品总产量为 5 101.7 万 t，占世界水产品总产量的 1/3 以上，比 2004 年增加 199.9 万 t，同比增长 4.1%。其中，海洋捕捞产量为 1 453.3 万 t，比上年增加 2.2 万 t，同比增长 0.2%；海水养殖产量为 1 384.8万t，比上年增加 68.1 万 t，同比增长 5.2%。内陆捕捞产量为 255.1 万 t，比上年增加 13.1 万 t，同比增长 5.4%；内陆养殖产量为 2 008.5 万 t，比上年增加 116.4 万 t，同比增长 6.2%。总产量中，捕捞产量 1 708.4 万 t，占总产量的 33.5%；养殖产量 3 393.7 万 t，占总产量的 66.5%。按生长环境分，海水产品产量为 2 838.1 万 t，占总产量的 55.6%，同比增长 2.5%；内陆水产品产量为 2 263.6 万 t，占总产量的 44.4%，同比增长 6.1%。水产品人均占有量逐年提高，从 1995 年的 20.9kg 提高到 2005 年的 37.1kg，年平均增幅为 9.0%。2005 年，我国水产品产量超过百万吨的省、自治区有 12 个（表 1)。

表 1 2005 年我国水产品产量超过百万吨的地区情况

序 号	地 区	产量（万 t)	同比增长（%）
1	山 东	736.14	2.50
2	广 东	695.23	4.62
3	福 建	602.22	1.86
4	浙 江	483.77	−1.98
5	辽 宁	425.34	5.67
6	江 苏	388.66	6.15
7	湖 北	318.03	5.26
8	广 西	283.94	5.60
9	安 徽	177.57	3.65
10	湖 南	173.52	4.46
11	江 西	168.36	7.69
12	海 南	150.01	10.43

二、水产品加工状况

（一）生产规模状况

2005年，我国水产品加工企业数为9 128个，比2004年增加383个，同比增长4.38%；年加工能力为1 426.63万t，同比增长18.89%。年加工能力超过百万吨的省份有6个（表2）。2005年，我国水产品加工业冷库数为6 328座，同比增长6.10%；冻结能力为26.45万t/d，同比增长5.21%；冷藏能力为256.69万t/次，同比增长17.65%；制冰能力为12.96万t/d，同比增长27.56%；冷藏总量为9 903.87万t/d，同比增长－45.70%；制冰总量为809.44万t，同比增长5.68%。其中，冷藏总量超过100万t/d的省、直辖市有7个（表3）。

表2　2005年水产品年加工能力超过百万吨的地区情况

序号	地　区	企业数（个）	同比增长（%）	加工能力（万t/年）	同比增长（%）
1	山　东	1 855	3.98	583.77	43.43
2	广　东	1 139	－1.04	192.99	7.37
3	江　苏	765	4.65	192.51	2.66
4	辽　宁	717	10.48	182.27	11.93
5	浙　江	1 962	1.76	173.52	4.79
6	福　建	1 475	1.86	151.51	7.42

表3　2005年我国水产品冷藏总量超过100万t/d的地区情况

序号	地　区	冷库数（座）	冻结能力（万t/d）	冷藏能力（万t/次）	制冰能力（万t/d）	冷藏总量（万t/d）	制冰总量（万t）
1	山　东	1 698	11.05	81.04	3.55	4 881.95	161.83
2	浙　江	1 176	2.29	40.22	2.42	2 764.96	267.26
3	天　津	24	0.25	3.17	0.03	632.29	1.02
4	广　东	493	1.09	14.49	1.25	509.44	118.13
5	福　建	613	1.15	18.32	1.40	534.57	106.50
6	河　北	231	2.93	5.07	0.34	287.39	1.76
7	江　苏	583	1.63	33.32	0.99	175.16	47.84

（二）水产加工品状况

2005年，我国水产加工品总量为1 195.48万t，同比增长15.84%。其中淡水加工产品为112.28万t，同比增长22.12%。水产加工品总量超过50万t的省份有6个（表4）。2005年，我国冷冻水产品产量为725.87万t，同比增长21.12%。其中冷冻品为377.95万t，同比增长24.31%；冷冻加工品为293.43万t，同比增长29.40%。冷冻水产品产量超过10万t的省、自治区有9个（表5）。2005年，我国鱼糜制品及干腌制品产量为194.56万t，同比增长14.15%。其中鱼糜制品为44.63万t，同比增长35.32%；干制品为76.00万t，同比增长7.85%；藻类加工制品为51.56万t，同比增长15.48%。罐制品产量为17.74万t，同比增长23.37%。鱼糜制品及干腌制品、罐制品产量排序前5名的省份有辽宁、浙江、福建、山东、广东（表6）。

表4　2005年水产加工品总量超过50万t的地区情况

序号	地　区	水产加工品总量（万t）	同比增长（%）	淡水加工产品（万t）	同比增长（%）
1	山　东	443.19	32.10	5.30	18.57
2	福　建	176.71	6.97	7.17	49.38
3	浙　江	173.35	5.86	7.37	−8.33
4	广　东	119.47	4.65	24.32	21.97
5	辽　宁	111.58	13.75	1.75	127.27
6	江　苏	58.31	14.92	15.09	57.41

表5　2005年我国冷冻水产品产量超过10万t的地区情况

序号	地区	冷冻水产品（万t）	同比增长（%）	其中	
				冷冻品（万t）	冷冻加工品（万t）
1	山　东	266.81	48.04	149.28	102.50
2	浙　江	136.03	5.84	66.40	36.05
3	广　东	81.30	4.98	24.79	56.51
4	福　建	79.27	16.71	58.26	18.92
5	辽　宁	64.07	12.60	24.89	37.90
6	江　苏	36.72	17.32	13.90	22.73
7	海　南	25.88	1.73	17.20	6.47
8	广　西	11.03	－24.09	9.83	1.20
9	湖　北	10.17	88.33	5.67	4.50

表 6　2005 年鱼糜制品及干腌制品、罐制品产量排序前 5 位的地区情况

序号	地　区	鱼糜制品及干腌制品（万 t）	其　中			罐制品（万 t）
			鱼糜制品（万 t）	干制品（万 t）	藻类加工（万 t）	
1	山　东	52.97	20.87	21.33	3.98	6.79
2	福　建	40.88	6.69	12.80	21.18	1.24
3	辽　宁	37.39	2.52	7.13	24.09	0.86
4	广　东	18.69	4.78	6.21	0.15	4.15
5	浙　江	17.87	3.62	12.12	0.83	1.50

三、水产品进出口贸易

据农业部渔业局的统计显示，2005 年，我国水产品进出口贸易继续保持稳步增长，但出口增长势头减缓。全年进出口总量为 623 万 t，进出口总额为 120.1 亿美元。其中，出口量为 257 万 t，出口额 78.9 亿美元，分别比上年增长 6%和 13%，出口量增幅回落 9 个百分点，出口额增幅回落 14 个百分点；进口量为 366 万 t，进口额为 41.2 亿美元，分别比上年增长 24%和 27%；贸易顺差 37.7 亿美元，与上年持平。水产品出口额占农产品出口总额的 28.6%，继续位居大宗农产品出口首位。

（一）主要贸易结构

1. *贸易方式*　国内自产水产品出口占出口总额的 64%，进口原料加工再出口占出口总额的 36%。其中，国内自产水产品出口量为 165.7 万 t，与上年出口量持平。出口额为 50.5 亿美元，比上年增长 5.4%；加工贸易出口量为 91.3 万 t，出口额 28.4 亿美元，分别同比增长 20%和 30%。

2. *出口品种*　从加工方式上比较，初级冷冻水产品占出口总额的 59%，深加工品占 41%。从具体品种上比较，国内自产资源以对虾、鳗鱼、罗非鱼、大黄鱼、贝类等养殖品种出口为主；来进口原料加工再出口主要品种为鳕鱼片、鲭鱼片和鱿鱼产品。

3. *出口市场*　出口市场格局变化不大，日本、韩国、美国和欧盟仍是我国水产品出口的主要市场，占水产品出口总额的 79.2%，与上年持平。

4. *出口省份*　山东、广东、辽宁、浙江和福建 5 个沿海省继续排列出口前 5 位，5 省出口额占水产品出口总额的 90%。其中山东省占 35%，主要是来进料加工鱼片和贝类出口；广东省依靠对虾、罗非鱼等优势养殖水产品出口继续位居第二。内陆水产品出口前 3 名依次为江西、湖北和吉林。

5. *进口情况*　2005 年我国进口水产品为 366 万 t，扣除来进料加工原料 143 万 t 和鱼粉 158 万 t，我国实际进口供居民食用的水产品为 65 万 t（不含远洋自捕鱼运回），比 2004 年增加近 10 万 t。

6. *进出口价格*　2005 年，出口水产品综合平均价格为 3 071 美元/t，同比上涨 6.7%。其中，活鱼、冰鲜、冷冻鱼、贝类、藻类等价格涨幅在 10%～30%之间，虾蟹类产品价格稳中略降，干腌制品价格呈下降趋势，降幅 10%。进口水产品综合平均价格为1 126 美元/t，比上年上涨 3.8%。其中，鱼粉价格基本稳定，来进料加工原料进口价格大幅度上涨，平均提高了 12%；供国内食用的进口水产品价格上涨 7%。

（二）主要发展特点

1. *应对反倾销挑战，深加工能力逐步提高*　2005 年初，美国对我国初级冷冻虾产品开始征收高额反倾销税，我国冷冻虾出口严重受阻，全年出口量为 3.9 万 t，出口额为 2.1 亿美元，同比分别下降 26%和 23%。贸易壁垒虽然造成一定影响，但同时也成为一种动力，推动企业重视产品结构的调整，致力加工技术革新，部分企业用不到半年时间完成了加工设备和工艺改造，面包虾、蒸煮虾、调味虾生产能力大幅度提高，产品颇受国际市场欢迎，企业收益不降反升，有效抵御了贸易壁垒风险。在虾深加工带动下，鱼类、藻类、贝类深加工也正蓬勃发展。据调查，加工近海捕捞低值鱼出口，附加值可以提高 5～6 倍。2005 年，全国深加工水产品出口比重达到 43%，比 2004 年提高了近 6 个百分点。

2. *珍惜重新开放，欧盟成为我国水产品出口第三大市场*　因 2002 年初氯霉素事件致使欧盟对我国动物源性食品实施封关，直到 2004 年下半年才全部解禁。2005 年，我国政府和企业格外重视和珍惜来之不易的市场开放，加强质量安全管理，确保水产品符合欧盟标准，杜绝含氯霉素产品流入欧盟。2005 年对欧盟出口额达到 10.7 亿美元，实现历史最高水平。比 2002 年欧盟封关当年的 2.8 亿美元出口额（为有可比性，按欧盟 25 国计算）增加 3 倍，比封关前 2001 年 4.9 亿美元的出口额增加 1.2 倍。其中，我国自有水产品资源（淡水小龙虾、对虾、冻鱼等）出口总量为 10.6 万 t，出口总额为 3.6 亿美元，分别比上年增长 45%和 86%。2005 年欧盟超过韩国成为

我国水产品出口第三大市场。对韩国出口由于初级水产品较多，出口价值相对较低。

3. *加快产业带建设，特色水产品出口渐成规模* 对虾、鳗鱼、罗非鱼、大黄鱼、贝类、河蟹等六大优势养殖品种出口仍是主力军，2005年出口量为69万t，出口额为30.5亿美元，占水产品出口总量额的27%和39%，占国内自有渔业资源出口额的60%。除了六大品种外，各地根据自身的渔业资源特点，积极培育具有本地区特色的水产品出口，加快特色产品产业带建设。江苏省的淡水小龙虾、紫菜、珍珠出口占全国水产品出口额的70%以上；山东省活鱼面向韩国，广东省活鱼主攻香港；浙江省依靠天然资源，捕捞虾仁出口大量销往欧盟；内陆省份斑点叉尾鮰等各种鱼类、淡水小龙虾出口成为主力。

4. *发挥区位优势，来进料加工势头不减* 尽管国际捕捞水产品原料价格持续上升，但是山东、辽宁两省凭借劳动力资源优势和区位优势，继续发展水产品来进料加工，加工规模较上年有了进一步扩展。其中，山东省水产品来进料加工出口量为60万t，出口额为19亿美元，分别同比增长17%和31%；辽宁省水产品来进料加工出口量为23万t，出口额为6.3亿美元，分别同比增长36%和43%。经过近10年的努力，上述两省已形成了世界上最大的鱼片加工基地，提高了我国水产品的国际影响力，并带动了部分内陆地区水产品来进料加工业的发展。

5. *政府高度重视，各项措施支持有力* 促进水产品出口，走外向型渔业发展道路，充分利用“两个市场、两种资源”，推动渔业持续健康发展，已成为各级政府渔业政策的一项重要内容。2005年，农业部加大了对优势出口水产品养殖区域扶持力度，命名了水产品加工业园区和加工示范企业；针对出现的食品安全问题，加强了对内专项整治和对外沟通谈判，力争减轻渔民和企业损失，促进出口稳定发展；支持中国国际渔业博览会扩大规模、办出水平，组织近百家企业走出国门参加世界渔业展览，宣传中国渔业，扩大企业视野。各地渔业行政主管部门也实施了不同形式的出口支持措施。广东省从“重大科技兴海”、“一条鱼工程”、“出口示范基地建设”等项目中每年筹措1 000多万元支持水产品加工出口业。辽宁省根据渔业发展规划，有重点地编制一批渔业对外招商项目。湖北省召开全省促进水产品出口现场会，组织推广面向出口的淡水小龙虾和罗氏沼虾的健康养殖。

四、标准化工作

1. 农业部于2005年1月4日以第450号公告发布了《罗非鱼配合饲料》等15项水产行业标准，标准名称及代号如下：《罗非鱼配合饲料》（SC/T 1025—2004）、《大银鱼》（SC 1067—2004）、《暗纹东方鲀》（SC 1068—2004）、《暗纹东方鲀养殖技术规范 第1部分：亲鱼》（SC/T 1069.1—2004）、《暗纹东方鲀养殖技术规范 第2部分：人工繁育技术》（SC/T 1069.2—2004）、《暗纹东方鲀养殖技术规范 第3部分：鱼苗鱼种培育技术》（SC/T1069.3—2004）、《暗纹东方鲀养殖技术规范 第4部分：养成技术》（SC/T 1069.4—2004）、《青鱼配合饲料》（SC/T 1073—2004）、《团头鲂配合饲料》（SC/T 1074—2004）、《鲫鱼配合饲料》（SC/T 1076—2004）、《渔用配合饲料通用技术要求》（SC/T 1077—2004）、《中华绒螯蟹配合饲料》（SC/T 1078—2004）、《皱纹盘鲍》（SC 2011—2004）、《大菱鲆配合饲料》（SC/T 2031—2004）、《甲壳质与壳聚糖》（SC/T 3403—2004）。这批标准自2005年2月1日起实施。

2. 农业部于2005年1月19日以第455号公告发布了《无公害食品 鲷》等10项无公害水产品标准。这10项无公害水产品标准依据无公害食品标准体系框架编制，替代了部分原有标准，体现了归类原则，适用范围更加广泛，内容上更加完善。标准名称及代号如下：《无公害食品 鲷》（NY 5311—2005）、《无公害食品 石斑鱼》（NY 5312—2005）、《无公害食品 鲍》（NY 5313—2005）、《无公害食品 蛏》（NY 5314—2005）、《无公害食品 蚶》（NY 5315—2005）、《无公害食品 普通淡水鱼》（NY 5053—2005）、《无公害食品 海藻》（NY 5056—2005）、《无公害食品 石首鱼》（NY 5060—2005）、《无公害食品 淡水蟹》（NY 5064—2005）、《无公害食品 淡水虾》（NY 5158—2005）。这批标准自2005年3月1日起实施。

3. 由农业部渔业局主办、中国渔业协会鳗业工作委员会承办的冻烤鳗国家标准听证活动于2005年4月11日在北京举办。来自生产、管理、科研、质检、标准化、出入境检验、社会团体等单位的专家和代表共计40余人参加了听证活动。农业部渔业局陈毅德副局长到会并做了讲话。陈毅德副局长指出，举办冻烤鳗标准听证活动是农业部渔业局采取新形式、新方法开展渔业标准化工作的一次有益尝试，是贯彻党的十六大和十六届四中全会精神的一次具体行动，是推进决策科学化、民主化的需要，对加强水产品质量安全管理、扩大水产品出口有着积极的意义。活动期间，标准起草单位介绍了标准起草过程及主要技术内容的确定依据，同时接受了有关单位和人员的质询。专家组在广泛听取生产、管理、科研、质检、标准化、出入境检验、社会团体等单位和个人意见的基础上，对标准的技术内容特别是安全限量指标进行了充分研讨，形成了听证与审定意见，会议达到了预期目的。既宣传了渔业标准化工作，增加了标准制定工作的透明度，体现了标准制定协商一致和公开、公平、公正的原则，又为进一步完善标准内容提供了依据，确保了标准的科学性、先进性、合理性和可行性。

4. 农业部渔业局于2005年7月20～21日在吉林省延吉市召开了渔业水域环境标准研讨会，来自科研、环境监测、标准化等单位的专家和标准起草人参加了会议，农业部市场与经济信息司派员莅会指导。会议期间，交流了《渔业水质标准》等8项标准起草情况，讨论确定了渔业水域环境标准制修订原则，研究讨论了渔业水域环境标准体系表，对每项渔业水域环境标准草案提出了具体修改意见和建议，并对下一步工作提出了意见和建议。会议认为，近几年来，在渔业科研、环境监测、标准化、管理等单位的共同努力和积极配合下，渔业水域环境标准体系建设工作取得了一定成效。先后制修订了10项渔业水域环境标准，其中的《无公害食品 海水养殖用水水质》、《无公害食品 淡水养殖用水水质》标准已批准发布，在各地开展的无公害水产品产地认证工作中发挥了重要作用，成为现行行业标准、地方标准广为引用的标准，其他养殖用水与废水排放标准、环境监测技术规范、渔业污染事故损失计算方法等8项标准进展情况良好，有5项完成了送审，还有3项正在起草中。会议认为，今后要围绕行业发展需求，结合渔业水域环境保护工作的迫切需要，本着重点抓住“两头”（即用水和排水）、兼顾个别需求的原则来规划渔业水域环境标准体系。要重点做好渔业用水和排水标准的制（修）订，同时抓紧制（修）订相关检测方法和技术规范。技术内容上，既要协调好与相关法律、法规、标准之间的关系，又要参考国内外的有关规定，同时考虑中国的国情，从有利于行业和产业发展，有利于渔业生态环境保护的角度去制定和完善标准。

五、行业工作

1. 中国水产学会第八次全国会员代表大会于2005年6月22日在江苏省无锡市召开。来自全国34个省、自治区、直辖市及计划单列市水产学会和有关科研教育及企事业单位所推荐的139名代表出席了会议。代表们围绕此次会议议程，审议并通过了七届理事会工作报告、财务报告，选举产生了新一届理事会，审议通过了中国水产学会八届理事会分支机构主要负责人。农业部副部长牛盾、中国科协书记处书记冯长根分别代表农业部和中国科协出席大会，并做了重要讲话，对学会的工作都给予了充分的肯定，同时也对水产科技工作者和水产学会工作提出了明确要求。唐启升理事长代表七届理事会向大会做了题为《创新理念，锐意进取，为创建适应社会发展充满生机活力的现代化科技团体而奋斗》的工作报告。江苏省政府副省长黄莉新，农业部渔业局副局长、中国渔政指挥中心主任李健华，无锡市副市长黄继鹏等出席了大会。中国水产学会秘书长张铭羽主持开幕式。会议认为，中国水产学会“七大”以来，按照树立科学发展观的要求，紧密结合学会工作实际，积极探索社会主义市场经济条件下的学会工作规律，充分发挥学术交流主渠道、科普工作主力军、国际民间科技交流与合作主要代表的作用，努力推进学会改革，各项工作取得了新的进展。会议选举产生了由103人组成的中国水产学会第八届理事会，唐启升院士当选为理事长。会议提出，学会要坚持以人为本，竭诚为科技工作者服务，充分调动科技工作者的积极性、主动性和创造性，努力构建为科技工作者服务体系，把学会建成“科技工作者之家”。

2. 农业部渔业局于2005年6月26～28日在北京召开了全国渔业“十一五”时期发展规划提纲讨论工作会。会议由农业部渔业局副局长、中国渔政指挥中心主任李健华主持。本次会议是2004年吉林延吉全国渔业“十一五”发展规划会后的又一次例会，本次会议的主题是讨论近期拟订的规划提纲。会议期间，农业部渔业局计划处刘新中就新拟订的规划提纲作了说明；中国水产科学研究院院长王衍亮、全国水产技术推广总站站长魏宝振以及浙江省、江苏省、江西省渔业厅局的负责人在充分肯定提纲框架结构的基础上提出了修改意见，并对“十一五”时期渔业发展的新亮点、管理与科技创新提出了建议，为进一步修改规划提纲提供了有益的思路；李健华副局长作了总结发言并要求规划编制组对会议发言进行整理，拟订更加细化、更能准确反映“十五”渔业发展成果、问题与“十一五”时期渔业发展理念、方向、目标、工作重点的提纲，在渔业局内部征求意见，把规划工作建立在更加科学化、民主化的基础上。

3. 全国水产技术推广协作研讨会于2005年11月11日在广州召开。这次研讨会，在加强全国各地水产技术推广协作方面，共商推进水产技术推广工作的发展，共同开创水产技术推广工作新局面。全国水产技术推广总站站长魏宝振、副站长居礼和全国各省（自治区、直辖市）水产技术推广站站长、水科院系统研究所和大专院校的领导及专家50余人出席了研讨会。会议由居礼副站长主持，广东省海洋与渔业局局长李珠江代表广东作题为《开创水产技术推广工作新局面》的讲话。江苏、上海、四川、山西、湖南、黑龙江等省、直辖市的站长作了交流发言。最后，魏宝振站长作了总结讲话。研讨会就技术推广、体系建设、水生动物防疫检疫、病害防治、水产品质量安全等问题以及目前全国水产技术推广系统共同面临的一些难题进行了深入研讨和交流，达成了统一的认识。会议期间，代表们还参观了在广州举办的第十届中国国际渔业博览会和中国国际水产养殖展览会，并赴深圳市水产技术推广总站参观考察，与该站的领导及同志进行了广泛的交流座谈。

4. 全国渔业科技工作座谈会于 2005 年 11 月 12～13 日在广西南宁召开。会议总结交流了“十五”期间我国渔业科技发展经验和成就，深入分析了目前困扰渔业科技工作的突出问题，研究探讨了渔业科技“十一五”乃至中长期的发展思路。农业部渔业局副局长陈毅德、中国水产科学研究院院长王衍亮、全国水产技术推广总站副站长孙喜模，以及各省级渔业行政主管部门的有关领导和科技处处长 60 余人出席了会议。陈毅德在座谈会上作了重要讲话，王衍亮作了题为《中长期渔业科技发展规划战略研究》的报告。陈毅德强调，要进一步明确今后一段时期渔业科技工作的思路和重点，扎实推进科研工作，力争在以下重点领域取得突破：第一，水产养殖业可持续发展领域，主攻品种培育、养殖模式和集约化养殖技术，提高水产养殖良种化水平，发展“资源节约、环境友好”型健康养殖模式。第二，水产品综合利用领域，主攻水产品加工和产物资源综合利用，提高水产品加工率和产品附加值，开发水产产物新资源。第三，资源与环境领域，主攻远洋渔业资源开发和近海渔业资源养护，强化渔业资源和环境监测与评估。第四，水产品质量安全领域，主攻水产品质量安全和风险评估，为建立和完善水产品质量安全标准体系和管理体系提供技术支撑。第五，渔业装备与工程领域，主攻水产养殖、加工设施和远洋渔业装备，加强新技术和新材料在渔业领域的开发应用。第六，渔业信息化领域，主攻数字渔业技术，实现信息共享。同时，要深入开展渔业科技体制改革，稳妥推进基层水产技术推广体系改革工作。与会代表就新时期渔业科技管理工作的定位、工作重点及措施等有关问题进行了热烈研讨。

（中国海洋大学教授　林洪　中国水产流通与加工协会副秘书长　于斌）

林产品加工业

一、经济林、竹及花卉产业

2005 年，经济林造林面积增长速度下降，但经济林产品产量增幅较大。新造经济林面积 337.80khm^2，比 2004 年减少 118.90khm^2，下降 26.03%。经济林产品总产量 9 228.72 万 t，比 2004 年增长 17.26%。其中，水果 8 251.55 万 t，同比增长 18.58%；干果 349.57 万 t；林产饮料产品 93.67 万 t，同比增长 27.07%；林产调料产品 36.07 万 t，同比增长 22.67%；森林食品 422.85 万 t，同比减少 6.54%；木本药材 75.04 万 t，同比增长 30.29%。

2005 年，主要竹产品继续保持增长势头，竹材产量 11.52 亿根，比 2004 年增长 4.92%。其中，毛竹 7.23 亿根，与 2004 年基本持平；篙竹 4.29 亿根，比 2004 年增长 17.86%。村及村以下各级组织和农民是竹材生产的主要力量，所生产的竹材达到 9.06 亿根，占全部竹材产量的 78.64%。竹胶合板 167.32 万 m^3，竹刨花板 0.31 万 m^3，竹木复合地板1 565.94 万 m^3，分别比 2004 年增长 42.42%、72.22% 和 186.93%。

2005 年，花卉产业仍保持发展态势，花卉产业总产值 386.36 亿元，与 2004 年相比增加 41.77 亿元。从产量看，鲜切花 66.36 亿支，鲜切叶 4.59 亿支，干花 0.55 万支；盆栽植物 19.29 亿盆，其中盆花 14.79 亿盆，盆景 2.62 亿盆，盆栽观叶植物 1.87 亿盆；观赏苗木 51.35 亿株；草坪 1.85 亿 m^2。从生产、经营规模看，我国现有成规模的花卉市场 4 467 个，大中型花卉企业 4 942 个；花卉从业人员 272 万人，其中专业技术人员 21 万人；控温温室面积和日光温室面积分别为 1 355 万 m^2 和 5 777 万 m^2。

二、木材生产及林产工业

1. 木材产量继续回升　由于天然林资源保护工

程区人工商品林采伐试点和农田防护林采伐更新试点扩大，全国木材产量继续保持回升势头。2005年共生产木材5 560.31万m^3，比2004年增加362.98万m^3，增长6.98%。其中，原木5 022.86万m^3，比2004年增加310.77万m^3，同比增长6.60%；薪材产量537.45万m^3，比2004年增加52.21万m^3，同比增长10.76%。

木材产量按生产单位分，林业系统内生产的木材为2 389.78万m^3，占全部木材产量的42.98%。其中，系统内国有林场、事业单位生产木材1 027.89万m^3；系统外企、事业单位采伐自营林地的木材170.25万m^3，占全部木材产量的3.06%；乡（镇）集体企业及单位生产木材323.89万m^3，占5.83%；村及村以下各级组织和农民个人生产的木材2 676.39万m^3，占48.13%，比2004年增加435.06万m^3，同比增长19.41%。

2. *锯材产量继续增长* 2005年，全部锯材产量1 790.29万m^3，比2004年增长16.82%。其中，热带锯材产量57.31万m^3，占全部锯材产量的3.20%，比2004年降低3.65个百分点。

3. *人造板产量增速不减* 2005年，我国人造板产量达到6 392.89万m^3，比2004年增长17.38%。其中，热带材人造板产量152.28万m^3，占全部人造板产量的2.38%。在全部人造板产量中，胶合板2 514.97万m^3，比2004年增长19.84%，占全部人造板产量的39.34%；纤维板2 060.56万m^3，比2004年增长32.05%，占全部人造板产量的32.23%。其中，中密度纤维板1 854.14万m^3；刨花板576.08万m^3，比2004年减少10.40%，占全部人造板产量的9.01%；其他人造板1 241.28万m^3（细木工板占79.09%），比2004年增长8.46%，占全部人造板产量的19.42%。

从人造板生产布局看，非重点林区的山东、江苏、河北、浙江4省，已经成为我国人造板的主要产地。2005年，4省人造板产量达3 762.12万m^3，占全国人造板总产量的58.85%，山东和江苏两省人造板产量都已突破1 000万m^3。

4. *木地板产量快速增长* 2005年，全部木地板产量达17 322.79万m^2，比2004年增长40.83%。其中，实木地板7 743.72万m^2，比2004年增长51.54%，占全部木地板产量的44.70%；实木复合木地板1 278.24万m^2，下降53.74%，占全部木地板产量的7.38%；强化木地板5 126.25万m^2，增长91.29%，占全部木地板产量的29.59%。

5. *木制家具产量大幅增长* 2005年，全国木制家具总产量11 328万件，与2004年的8 350.70万件（中国家具协会数据）相比，增长35.65%。

6. *国内木浆产量增幅较大* 2005年，纸和纸板总产量5 600万t，比2004年增长13.13%；纸浆产量4 446万t，比2004年增长19.42%，其中木浆产量370.8万t，比2004年增长55.80%。

7. *林化产品生产有涨有降* 2005年，全国松香类产品产量67.19万t，比2004年增长24.92%。其中，松香产量为60.66万t，增长24.85%；松节油产量6.53万t，增长23.16%；栲胶7 668t，紫胶产量779t，分别比2004年下降36.70%和30.26%。

三、木材产品市场供需状况

（一）木材供给

木材产品市场供给由国内供给和进口两部分构成。国内供给包括商品材、农民自用材和农民烧柴、木质纤维板和刨花板；进口包括进口原木、锯材、单板、人造板、家具、木浆、木片、纸和纸制品、废纸及其他木质林产品。2005年木材产品市场总供给为32 597.75万m^3。

1. *商品材* 2005年，全部商品材的产量为5 560.31万m^3，比2004年增长6.98%。其中，原木产量为5 022.87万m^3，薪材（不符合原木标准的木材）537.44万m^3。

2. *农民自用材和烧柴* 根据测算，农民自用材和烧柴折合木材量为6 598.05万m^3。其中，农民自用材为2 236.11万m^3，农民烧柴为4 361.94万m^3。

3. *木质纤维板和刨花板* 2005年，全国木质纤维板产量为2 060.56万m^3，比2004年增长32.05%；刨花板（普通刨花板和定向刨花板）产量为576.08万m^3，比2004年减少10.40%；木质纤维板和刨花板折合木材供给4 573.13万m^3，扣除与薪材产量的重复计算部分，木质纤维板和刨花板相当于净增加木材供给4 492.51万m^3。

4. *进口* 2005年，我国进口原木2 936.80万m^3，除原木外的其他木质林产品进口折合木材9 210.08万m^3。扣除出口木材及木质林产品折合木材4 900.37万m^3，2005年，我国实际净进口木材量为7 246.51万m^3。

5. *其他* 2005年超限额采伐、上年库存等形式形成的木材供给约为3 800万m^3。

（二）木材消费

木材产品市场消费由国内消费和出口两部分构成。国内消费包括工业与建筑用材消费、农民自用材和烧柴消费；出口包括出口原木、锯材、单板、人造板、家具、木浆、木片、纸和纸制品、废纸及其他木质林产品。2005年，木材产品市场总消耗量为32 576.10万m^3。

1. 工业与建筑用材消费　据国家统计局和有关部门统计及相关产品木材消耗系数推算，2005年我国建筑业与工业用材折合木材消耗量为23 090.18万m^3。其中，建筑业用材（包括装修与装饰）9 438.48万m^3，家具用材（指家具的国内消费部分，出口家具耗材包括在出口项目中）3 478.32万m^3，造纸业用材8 477.28万m^3，煤炭业用材927.29万m^3，车船制造、铁路、化工等其他部门用材768.81万m^3。

2. 农民自用材和烧柴　根据测算，农民自用材消耗量为2 236.11万m^3，农民烧柴消耗量为4 361.94万m^3。由于农民自用材消耗中90%左右用于农民建房等，约合2 012.50万m^3，扣除这部分与建筑用材消耗的重复计算后，农民自用材和烧柴消耗量为4 585.55万m^3。

3. 出口　2005年，我国原木出口0.69万m^3，除原木外的其他木质林产品出口折合木材4 899.68万m^3。

（三）木材产品市场供需特点

2005年，我国木材市场总体运行状况供求平衡，行情尚好，价格稳中有升。经过天然林资源保护工程实施7年来的不断努力，我国国内商品材的供应量已略高于天然林资源保护工程启动前的水平，国内木材产品产量约占木材产品市场总供应量的3/4，并且2005年木材市场表现出以下特点：

1. 国内供给稳步复苏，供给能力明显增加　从北方来看，一是林木资源较天然林资源保护工程实施初期有了明显增加；二是木材加工综合利用率有了根本性的提高，增加了木材的有效供给。具体看，传统的东北针叶木材的市场占有率在逐步提高，不仅在华北地区收回了俄罗斯进口材挤占的市场份额、进入了南方和西部市场，而且销售价格高于进口材，特别是加工后的板材，深受国内市场的欢迎。另外，随着东北林区木材加工业的发展，木材综合利用率进一步提高，使一向销路不好的次、小、薪材也得到了有效利用；以往畅销的水曲柳、榆、桦、杨等材种，依然旺销，价格坚挺。

南方产区需求旺盛、价格上扬，木材加工发展势头迅猛，木材附加值与综合利用率都有大幅度提高。2005年，我国南方地区自然灾害频繁发生，影响了木材生产，进入第四季度以后木材产量和市场供给增加。在南方地区国内资源市场供给中约1/2为人工林木材。人工林木材资源的大量供给为木材加工业发展提供了重要的资源保证。

2. 资源快速增长，传统销区变产区　随着中原、苏北地区、华东、华北以至西北地区等地速生丰产林快速发展，大量杨木、桐木等木材资源进入市场，木材加工相应快速发展，规模不断扩大。特别是苏北、鲁南、豫中、冀东、河西走廊等地的木材加工、家具制作、人造板生产已经成为当地经济发展的重要支柱产业。传统木材销区的平原省份，如江苏、山东、河北、河南等先后完成了从销区到产区的根本改变。

3. 木材进口减缓，出口明显增加　我国在木材及其制品方面，木材进口总体减缓，增速下降，但出口明显增加。我国木材产品在对外贸易方面的市场成熟度有了较大程度的提高，贸易收支状况得到进一步改善。

四、主要林产品价格

据国家统计局农调队的统计资料显示，2005年林业产品价格指数为104.79%，木材产品出厂价格指数为103.17%。

伴随着我国基础建设材料如钢铁、塑料、石材等价格行情的持续上涨，作为基建、装饰装修、家具制造主要原材料的木材及其森林工业产品的综合价格不断提高，致使林产品出厂价格总体呈上涨态势。根据国家统计局农调队的统计，2005年全国林产品生产价格平均上涨4.79%，其中一季度上涨2.58%，二季度上涨2.45%，三季度上涨4.42%，四季度上涨7.2%。2005年，全国木材生产价格平均上涨3.17%，其中一季度上涨2.92%，二季度上涨4.54%，三季度上涨5.06%，四季度上涨1.64%。

1. 原木　据国家统计局城调队调查的月度数据，2005年除云南松有小幅波动外，各种原木的购进价格基本保持稳定。红松原木的购进价格从年初的730元/m^3左右一直保持上升态势，到5、6月份突破了900元/m^3，之后又略降到873元/m^3；落叶松原木的价格从年初的700元/m^3呈略降态势，到7月份出现大幅下降，跌至550元/m^3，之后价格持续上涨，到12月份达到722元/m^3以上；马尾松原木的价格稳定在450元/m^3左右；杉木原木的价格小幅上升，从年初的590元/m^3左右上升到12月份的722元/m^3；云南松原木的价格在2005年波动较大，分别在1月份的价格最低，为678元/m^3，7月份价格又大幅度提升，达到了价格的最高点850元/m^3的水平，随之稳定在850元/m^3左右的水平；其他等内原木的购进价格也有小幅的上扬，从年初的560元/m^3增加到12月份的600元/m^3左右。

2. 锯材　2005年，普通锯材的全年平均购进价格为920元/m^3，比2004年降低2.88%。从全年来看，普通锯材的价格一年内呈稳定上升，从年初的950元/m^3左右上升到了年末的1 050元/m^3。其中，落叶松厚板从1月份的1 200元/m^3下跌到3月份的1 100元/m^3，随后价格开始回升，并保持在1 150元/m^3波动；杉木厚板价格起伏也比较大，从年初最低点不到1 000元/m^3开始上升，5月份达到了1 066元/m^3，然后价格开始稳步小幅上扬，到12月份上升到1 162.4元/m^3；马尾松厚板在前半年一直保持在630元/m^3左右，从7月份开始微幅上扬增加到9月份的660元/m^3，9月份到10月份增幅最大，达到了16%以上，然后价格基本稳定，维持在790元/m^3的水平。

3. 人造板　2005年，胶合板、纤维板和刨花板的平均出厂价格分别为1 622.2元/m^3、816.2元/m^3和618.6元/m^3。从各月出厂价格走势看，胶合板价格变动表现出以2、5月和8月分别为价格的低点和最高点的循环波动过程；纤维板价格在8月份为价格最高点，全年其他月份的价格基本保持稳定；从全年来看，刨花板价格基本保持平稳。

4. 木浆　2005年，机械木浆和化学木浆的平均出厂价格分别为3 966.4元/t和3 496.9元/t，比2004年分别提高26.68%和5.14%。从各月的出厂价格走势看，全国木浆的出厂价格变化表现出波动较大，机械木浆出厂价格的波动幅度大于化学木浆。从购进价格来看，机械木浆和化学木浆的年均价格分别为4 488.8元/t和4 372.8元/t，化学木浆年中价格波动较大，从2月份开始大幅度上扬，之后的月份有所波动，到8月份达到最高点4 527.7元/t，以后价格有小幅回落，机械木浆各月购进价格变化呈现出波动中基本稳定的态势。

5. 其他林产品　2005年，橡胶、椰子油、柑橘和苹果的平均购进价格分别为11 020.1元/t、7 488.20元/t、1 175.0元/t、538.9元/t。与2004年相比，橡胶和椰子油分别上升0.23%和6.31%，柑橘和苹果的购进价格分别上升19.61%和1.07%。从各月价格变化看，橡胶价格波动较大，从1月份价格下跌到2月份的最低点9 789.8元/t，之后价格保持平稳，但从6月份开始呈现出波动中大幅上涨，年末达到12 600元/t的水平；椰子油价格在波动中呈现略微下降的趋势；柑橘和苹果的价格波动基本同步，两者在8月份之前都是比较平稳，从8月份开始价格有所提升，在12月份分别达到了价格的最高点。

五、主要林产品进出口

（一）基本态势

1. 林产品进出口贸易高速增长，但增幅明显回落，出口增速高于进口，贸易逆差大幅缩小；在全国商品进出口贸易中所占比重略有下降　2005年林产品进出口贸易总额为412.90亿美元，比2004年增长18.14%。其中，林产品出口额205.74亿美元，比2004增长26.21%，增幅回落7.01个百分点，占全国商品出口额的2.70%，比2004年下降了0.05个百分点；林产品进口额207.15亿美元，比2004年增长11.09%，增幅回落9.20个百分点，占全国商品进口额的3.14%，比2004年下降了0.18个百分点。2005年林产品进出口贸易逆差为1.41亿美元，比2004年缩小93.98%。

2. 林产品进出口以木质林产品为主，木质林产品在林产品出口中的比重进一步提高，但在林产品进口中的比重继续下降　2005年林产品进出口贸易总额中，木质林产品占71.94%，比2004年下降了0.37个百分点，非木质林产品占29.06%；在林产品出口额中，木质林产品和非木质林产品所占比重分别为71.26%和28.74%，木质林产品所占比重比2004年提高了1.94个百分点；在林产品进口额中，木质林产品和非木质林产品所占比重分别为72.62%和27.38%，木质林产品所占比重比2004年下降2.31百分点。

3. 林产品进出口中，亚洲和北美市场份额下降，欧洲市场份额进一步提高　2005年，林产品出口总额中各洲所占份额分别为：亚洲41.19%，北美洲33.81%，欧洲19.31%，大洋洲2.37%，非洲2.18%，拉丁美洲1.15%。与2004年相比，亚洲和北美的市场份额分别下降了2.62个百分点和0.18个百分点，欧洲市场份额提高了2.26个百分点；林产品进口总额中各洲所占份额分别为：亚洲47.40%，欧洲21.72%，北美洲17.30%，拉丁美洲5.76%，大洋洲4.71%，非洲3.11%。与2004年相比，亚洲和北美的市场份额分别下降了1.27个百分点和0.15个百分点，欧洲市场份额提高了1.36个百分点。

从主要贸易伙伴看，前5位贸易伙伴集中了63.94%的林产品出口市场份额和54.83%的林产品进口市场份额。基本的市场格局变化不大，主要变化是出口市场中日本的份额减少了2.37个百分点，进口市场中马来西亚的份额减少了1.49个百分点。

（二）木质林产品进出口

木质林产品进出口贸易快速增长，但增幅明显回落，出口增速远高于进口增速，贸易逆差大幅缩减。2005年，木质林产品进出口贸易总额为297.04亿美元，比2004年增长17.54%。其中，出口146.61亿美元，同比增长29.75%，比2004年回落9.79个百分点；进口 150.43 亿美元，同比增长 7.66%，比 2004 年回落 9.76 个百分点。木质林产品贸易逆差为 3.82 亿美元，比 2004 年缩减了 22.92 亿美元。

从产品结构看，2005 木质林产品出口额中，家具、木制品、人造板及单板所占比重接近 85%。进口额中，纸及纸浆、原木和锯材（含特形材）的比重超过 93%。与 2004 年相比，进出口产品结构变化不大，但在木质林产品出口额中，人造板和单板所占比重提高了 3.02 个百分点，木制品所占比重下降了 4.56 个百分点；在木质林产品进口额中，原木所占比重提高了 1.49 个百分点，而人造板及单板所占比重下降了 1.44 个百分点。

从地区结构看，美国、日本和香港虽仍集中了我国 60%以上的木质林产品出口份额，但市场集中度总体上表现出明显的下降趋势；木质林产品进口以俄罗斯、美国和印度尼西亚市场为主，并由印度尼西亚等亚洲市场向俄美市场集中，市场集中度总体表现出上升趋势。2005 年按贸易额排序，前 5 位出口贸易伙伴依次为：美国占 37.67%，日本 13.11%，香港 10.17%，英国 5.17%，加拿大 3.17%。与 2004 年相比，美国、日本和香港所占份额分别下降了 0.80、2.17 和 1.70 个百分点；前 5 位进口贸易伙伴依次为：俄罗斯占 15.58%，美国 14.85%，印度尼西亚 8.49%，加拿大 7.63%，日本 6.51%。与 2004 年相比，俄罗斯和美国所占份额分别提高了 1.57 和 0.92 个百分点，印度尼西亚的份额减少了 1.18 个百分点。

（三）非木质林产品进出口

非木质林产品进出口高速增长，进口增幅高于出口增幅，贸易顺差进一步缩小。2005 年，非木质林产品出口 59.13 亿美元，进口 56.72 亿美元，比 2004 年分别增长 18.22%和 21.34%。非木质林产品进出口贸易顺差为 2.41 亿美元，比 2004 年减少 0.86 亿美元。非木质林产品出口额中，果类所占份额最大，进口额中 70%以上为林化产品。

（国家林业局发展计划与资金管理司
刘建杰　于百川）

农作物秸秆加工业

一、基本情况

2005 年，我国农作物秸秆得到了进一步综合利用，在生物质能源、秸秆饲料化加工等方面取得新进展。秸秆综合利用比较好的地区，秸秆的多功能性发挥得比较充分，产生了良好的经济、社会、生态和环境效益。秸秆青贮饲料促进了奶业的发展，秸秆氨化促进了肉牛业的发展，一些地方的秸秆发电正在规划实施，还有些地方秸秆环保建材发展迅速。通过对秸秆的综合利用，在促进农业发展、繁荣农村经济、增加农民收入等方面发挥着重要作用。

2005 年，全国青贮秸秆 1.75 亿 t，氨化秸秆 5 300万 t，两项折算节约饲料粮 4 700 多万 t。全国机械化秸秆还田面积达到 19 341khm^2，比 2004 年增加 978.7khm^2，增长 5.33%。全国秸秆粉碎还田机拥有量达到 47.32 万台。据中国农业机械工业协会统计，2005 年我国秸秆粉碎还田机产、销量均增长 30%以上，这也反映出秸秆利用率的上升态势。全国农作物秸秆处理利用率由 2000 年的 15.8%提高到 2005 年的 17.7%。但是也应该看到，我国焚烧秸秆的现象仍十分突出，不仅造成严重的资源浪费，而且还严重污染环境，影响人们正常生活和身体健康，影响飞机起降和交通干线及高压输电线路安全。据统计资料显示，我国焚烧秸秆重点区有安徽、江苏、四川、陕西、河南、河北、山西、山东等省。2005 年夏季通过卫星遥感监测到火点 3 902 个，影响 78 个地区、346 个县，高于 2004 年火点 2 481 个，影响 61 个地区、208 个县的同期监测。秋季共监测到火点数 502 个，影响 55 个地区、135 个县，略低于 2004 年火点 697 个，影响 62 个地区、144 个县的同期监测。为了加强秸秆禁烧和综合利用，在中央的统一指导下，全国各地加大了秸秆禁烧和综合利用工作的力度，秸秆利用水平普遍得到提高。主要表现在：

1. 北京市　2005 年基本实现了小麦秸秆全面禁烧，小麦秸秆综合利用率达到了 100%。实现小麦秸秆全面禁烧，提高秸秆的综合利用，是北京市农机化发展的一项重点工作。为做好这项工作，北京市农业局和市农委联合印发了《关于做好 2005 年小麦秸秆禁烧工作的通知》；北京市农业局与 13 个区（县）政府签订了禁烧责任书；针对 2005 年小麦种植面积比上年增加较多的情况，加强了机具调配能力，制订了“三夏”农机生产应急预案，确保机具足够到位。“三夏”期间加强了禁烧工作大检查，市农业局组织了4个检查小组，对13个区、县的禁烧工作分片进行拉网式检查。经过上下共同努力，2005年完成机收小麦68.5khm²，小麦秸秆再次实现了全面禁烧。秸秆综合利用也有了较大的发展，机械捡拾打捆面积8.79 khm²。

2. 天津市 2005年，继续开展秸秆粉碎还田技术推广，同时加强了秸秆饲料化加工技术推广，分别推广应用了玉米秸秆收割机、玉米饲料收获机。棉花拔秆机得到广泛的应用。此外，还在农村秸秆气化工程建设上取得了较大的进展，在政府资金扶持下，当年全市共建成秸秆气化炉24座。

3. 河北省 随着秸秆综合利用途径的增多，2005年河北省秸秆综合利用率达到了65%。由于河北省的秸秆利用工作不断深化，所以实现了从最初的单纯禁烧到如今的多渠道综合利用的转变。该省的秸秆综合利用以秸秆还田、青贮、压块饲料为主，其中秸秆粉碎还田在全省快速普及，占到秸秆综合利用的55%。在扩大秸秆还田面积的基础上，加大了玉米联合收获的力度，推进玉米机械化收获进程，积极开发推广秸秆青贮、打捆、揉丝、压块饲料等技术途径，实现了向秸秆综合利用的深度进军。

4. 山东省 2005年，山东农机部门把小麦秸秆综合利用与小麦跨区机收工作一起抓，大力推广秸秆综合利用技术，将秸秆变“废”为“宝”。全省小麦秸秆综合利用面积达2 418.7khm²，秸秆利用率达到74.3%。青岛、烟台、潍坊、枣庄、东营、滨州等市大力推广小麦秸秆打捆机械，实行小麦机收、秸秆机械打捆“一条龙”服务，在收割小麦的同时将麦秸进行捡拾打捆，成为造纸原料，麦茬则就地还田成为肥料。淄博市周村区农机部门协调龙头企业同森木业公司，分别在本区的4个乡镇选择农机大户或农机服务组织，成立秸秆收获打捆示范服务队，每个服务队购置打捆机1台套（财政补贴30%、同森木业公司筹集40%、服务队自筹30%），并达成小麦秸秆收购协议，三年内企业按市场价敞开收购机手所收的麦秸。2005年，该区共收集小麦秸秆4 500t，为农民增收135万元。滕州市采取半喂入式收割，将小麦收割后保留完好的秸秆外销，每亩秸秆可卖120元。

5. 陕西省 2005年秸秆综合利用机械拥有量达到14.08万台，全省秸秆综合利用实施规模达到1 000 khm²，约占小麦、玉米和水稻种植面积的40%。与2002年相比，2005年秸秆机械化综合利用水平提高22%。

6. 沈阳市 该市于2005年11月21日被列为当年为城乡百姓办的22件实事之一的“农村秸秆气化站建设”工作基本结束，这项工作使全市新建秸秆气化站10个，分布在于洪、东陵等地区，在当地居住的5 000多户农民用上了秸秆燃气，告别了他们一直烧柴火的传统历史。

二、科研、新产品、新技术

1. 由农业部规划设计研究院承担的“甜高粱茎秆制取乙醇技术”课题，于2005年12月2日通过了国家“863”计划能源技术领域办公室的验收。“甜高粱茎秆制取乙醇技术”课题完成了年产400t甜高粱茎秆汁液液态固定化酵母流化床快速发酵技术与工艺装备的开发，该项技术适合糖质原料液态发酵工艺规模化燃料乙醇生产。在“九五”研究工作的基础上，课题在甜高粱茎秆固体发酵工艺方面又取得了较大进展，优化了原料处理、菌种制备、发酵过程控制、蒸馏等工艺参数，有效地降低了过程的能耗，缩短了发酵时间，操作简便，残糖低，能源转换效率高。课题还完成了对甜高粱茎秆制取乙醇的技术、经济、环保和农业产业调整等方面的分析和评价。课题成果已荣获2005年联合国工发组织颁发的“全球可再生能源领域最具投资价值十大领先技术蓝天奖”。课题在山东省安丘市建设了年产400t乙醇的甜高粱茎秆液态发酵生产性中试示范工程，在黑龙江省桦川县建设了具备年产5 000t乙醇能力的甜高粱茎秆固体发酵工业化生产示范工程。课题成果的推广应用，不仅可以形成具有中国特色的燃料乙醇发展模式，还可以开辟具有战略性的能源农业和生物能源产业，对我国实现可持续发展具有重要意义。

2. 我国首个“秸秆与煤粉混烧发电”项目于2005年12月16日在山东省枣庄市十里泉发电厂（华电国际电力股份有限公司的主力电厂之一）竣工投产，标志着我国生物质发电技术取得了新的重大进展。该项目的秸秆混烧发电技术是国际上比较先进的发电技术之一，由山东省工程咨询院编制可研报告和初步设计，2004年10月经山东省发展改革委核准，2005年5月开工建设，11月底经调试进入试运期。通过近一个月的带料运行试验，实现了秸秆混烧发电项目从理论到实践的突破，为秸秆掺烧发电改造技术在我国的推广应用奠定了坚实的基础。秸秆混烧发电从锅炉加热蒸汽之后的工艺技术与常规火力发电基本相同，只是在燃料输送、锅炉燃烧器设计与制造方面有所不同。按丹麦BWE公司提供的技术经验，现有火电厂改为秸秆混烧电厂，秸秆掺烧按热值计算一般不超过20%，关键问题要解决秸秆粉末透气性，防止引起输送管道堵塞的问题。十里泉秸秆混烧技术改造项目，总投资 8 000 多万元。增加了 1 套秸秆收购、储存、粉碎和输送设备，2 台从丹麦 BWE 公司进口的输入热负荷为 3 万 kW 的秸秆专用燃烧器，并对供风系统及相关控制系统进行了优化。锅炉改造后原有系统和参数不变，既可实现秸秆与煤粉混烧，也仍可单独烧煤。预计年消耗秸秆 10.5 万 t，可替代原煤约 7.56 万 t。据统计，十里泉发电厂秸秆混烧发电项目投产后，可以使周边地区 3 万多农户受益，年可增加农民收入约 3 000 多万元。

3. 中国林业科学研究院木材工业研究所承担的科技部“863 计划”课题“麦秸中密度板成套生产工艺技术”和“玉米秸秆均质复合板制造技术”，于 2005 年 12 月 18 日通过了山东省科技厅组织的成果鉴定。山东省科技厅、中纪委扶贫办、国家发改委木材节约中心、山东省林业局、山东省环保局以及淄博市的主要领导参加了项目鉴定和生产线开工仪式，来自中国科学院、国家林业局林产工业设计院、北京林业机械研究所和山东理工大学等 6 个单位的知名专家应邀作为鉴定专家委员会进行了该项目的成果鉴定。与会专家认真听取了课题组的课题工作汇报，审核了鉴定资料，进行了现场质疑答辩。课题鉴定认为，“麦秸中密度板成套生产工艺技术”和“玉米秸秆均质复合板制造技术”两项成果，紧密配合目前农业剩余物资源开发利用的形势需要，符合国家有关环保政策，能够追踪国际前沿科技领域与研究方向。对我国人造板工业开拓原料来源，为林业“六大工程”提供了基础支持，有效解决了麦秸、玉米秸秆综合处理的技术问题，具有十分重要的现实意义和应用价值。两项成果的研究成功填补了国内该领域的研究空白，特别是在“麦秸碎料单元联合制备系统”、“单层压机连续铺装周期性脱模技术”、“玉米秸秆全生物量利用制造板材和饲料技术”和“玉米秸秆纤维制备和分离技术”方面有创新性，达到了国际先进水平。“麦秸中密度板成套生产工艺技术”和“玉米秸秆均质复合板制造技术”两项成果顺利通过鉴定，标志着我国在该领域的研究方面又取得了突破性进展，可为我国建设节约型社会和发展循环经济提供技术支持。

三、行业管理

1. 农业部科技教育司于 2005 年 5 月 10 日在郑州市河南农业大学组织召开了全国秸秆固化成型技术研讨会，其目的是为了总结近年来我国各地出现的各种秸秆固化成型技术成果，分析评价秸秆固化成型燃料的应用前景，研讨有利于秸秆固化成型技术大规模推广应用的机制，从而促进农作物秸秆的资源化利用。出席研讨会的有来自全国各地从事秸秆固化成型燃料与相关设备开发利用的科研单位、大专院校、管理推广部门和生产企业的代表。研讨会期间，全体与会代表还赴新乡和新郑参观了河南农业大学秸秆固化成型燃料生产示范基地，并到周边的农户考察了秸秆固化成型燃料及其配套炉具的现场使用情况。会议通过研讨交流，就今后我国秸秆固化成型技术达成四点共识：一是秸秆固化成型技术经过多年的开发与应用，已经取得了阶段性成果，应该及时进行总结，向国务院有关领导和有关部门提出建议报告，争取多方面的政策和财政支持。二是尽快组织有关专家针对我国秸秆固化成型技术开发应用现状以及整个能源市场发展趋势，认真研究和分析我国秸秆固化成型技术所面临的障碍以及需要解决的问题，编制出秸秆固化成型技术中长期发展规划，从而促进其持续发展。三是秸秆固化成型技术不仅是技术问题，更多的是管理问题，因此在实施秸秆固化成型技术推广应用初期，就要走产业化的道路。要同时关注农村、城市和工业，也要根据不同用户的需要，开发系列化、多样化产品。四是要在各部门、各单位和各企业之间建立起一种协作的长效机制，鼓励大家互相交流，信息共享。争取每年定期组织一次研讨活动，努力为大家提供一个交流的平台，使这项技术能够高效、快速和健康地发展。

2. 黑龙江省秸秆综合利用协会于 2005 年 6 月 12 日成立。来自全省各地的会员参加了省秸秆综合利用协会成立暨秸秆生产饲草新产品推广大会，这标志着黑龙江省在秸秆综合利用方面有了专业协会。新成立的省秸秆综合利用协会将组织全省农业、农机、畜牧、环保、科技、科研教学、生产单位，研制、开发、推广秸秆综合利用的现代新技术，促进秸秆综合利用产业化的快速发展，指导秸秆综合利用的经营者和使用者，合理有效地开发利用秸秆的使用和制作功能，提高秸秆使用的有效率，加强秸秆资源优化配置的作用。

3. 国家发改委、科技部、国家环保总局于 2005 年 10 月 28 日联合发布了《国家鼓励发展的资源节约综合利用和环境保护技术》，该文件有多条涉及秸秆综合利用的技术。其中，第 35 条为“农作物秸秆无废料综合利用技术”，该技术包括秸秆就地高密度压缩、好氧发酵纤维分离及制品成型和生物有机肥制造。主要是以各种农作物秸秆为原料，采用生物技术分离、提取植物纤维，制造出各类工业包装材料、密度板等轻型建筑材料，利用剩余物质制造有机肥，实现秸秆的 100% 利用。第 81 条为“生物质气化技术”，该技术是将农作物秸秆等生物质在控氧下燃烧反应的能量转换过程。当其被点燃，只供给适量的空气，控制反应，使碳、氢、氧元素转化为可燃的一氧化碳、氢气、甲烷、丙烷等气体，秸秆中大部分能量转移到气体中；当气体再燃烧时，能量就释放出来。采用该技术可有效地利用了农业废弃物，且秸秆通过气化利用，与直接燃烧相比，1t 燃料可减少排放 SO_2 140kg 及烟尘 20kg。该技术适用于天然林资源保护工程、移民新村、自然遗产保护区、中心村、小集镇等。

4. 由天津市农业机械推广总站负责起草的天津市地方标准《玉米秸秆压块袋装微贮技术规范》，于 2005 年 12 月 14 日通过了天津市质量技术监督局组织的专家组审查。《玉米秸秆压块袋装微贮技术规范》的制定，对提高天津市秸秆饲料加工技术水平和机械化程度，促进秸秆资源有效利用，提高农业综合效益，提升农业产业化水平，实现农民增收、农业增效和农村可持续发展，将起到积极的推动作用。

（天津市农业机械学会　胡　伟）

机械工业系统农产品加工机械制造业

一、基本情况

据机械工业信息中心统计，2005 年我国机械工业系统农产品加工机械制造业主要生产企业 274 家，全年从业人员平均人数为 46 247 人。固定资产 246 756万元，流动资产平均余额 441 880 万元。全年完成工业总产值为 97.99 亿元，比上年同期增长约 33.4%；完成工业销售产值为 88.80 亿元，同比增长 33.97%；实现产品销售收入 84.85 亿元，同比增长 35.11%。出口交货值 6.68 亿元，同比增长 26.01%；新产品产值为 4.22 亿元，同比下降 22.21%。流动资产平均余额 36.28 亿元，同比增长 17.54%；固定资产净值平均余额 21.43 亿元，同比增长 10.9%。资产总计 69.4 亿元，同比增长 17.37%。

二、市场情况

1. 粮食加工机械　我国粮食加工机械产品正在进行结构调整，逐步向高效、大中型、成套化方向发展，以适合市场的要求。2005 年，粮食加工机械产量为 960 757 台套，同比增长 6.16%。其中，碾米机械主要生产企业山东同泰集团股份有限公司 2005 年完成产品销售收入 10 157 万元、同比增长 11.78%；江苏晶谷米机集团公司完成产品销售收入 41 128 万元，同比增长 61.79%；广西绿珠股份有限公司完成产品销售收入 1 062.8 万元，同比增长 57.1%；山东省汶上县北大机械有限公司完成产品销售收入 6 969 万元，同比增长 8.24%；湖北安陆碧山粮机设备有限公司完成产品销售收入 4 782 万元，同比下降 7.72%。原来一些有规模的老企业由于产品结构和企业改革等方面的原因，生产销售出现了萎缩。面粉加工机械行业也出现了好的回升局面。河北苹乐面粉机械集团有限公司 2005 年完成产品销售收入 14 440 万元，同比增长 85.31%；无锡布勒机械制造有限公司完成产品销售收入 18 209 万元，同比增长 23.27%；山东恒力虎山机械设备有限公司完成产品销售收入 61 368 万元，同比增长 23.77%；河南漯河面粉机械有限公司完成产品销售收入 10 722 万元，同比增长 36.82%；河北皇牌机械公司完成产品销售收入 7 253 万元，同比下降 6%；漯河市雪城面粉机械有限公司完成产品销售收入 5 302 万元，同比增长 36.47%；修武县永乐粮机有限责任公司 6 967 万元，同比增长 17.39%，河南郾城县中原粮食机械厂完成产品销售收入 3 321 万元，同比增长 24.56%；陕西渭南农科股份有限公司完成产品销售收入 2 009 万元，同比下降 29.9%。一些面粉机械配件企业也出现了热销的形势，如漯河市民生粮机轧辊有限公司完成轧辊销售 4 696 万元，同比增长 33.03%；漯河市轧辊厂完成轧辊销售 2 488 万元，同比增长 16.37%。面粉加工机械行业加快对产品结构进行调整，一些及时调整的企业适应了市场的需求，出现了产销两旺的好形势。

2. 油料加工机械　2005 年，油料加工机械行业多年来缺乏对新产品的科研投入，产品维持原来的技术水平，质量及技术没有出现大的提升，产品单一，产销继续下降。如河北南皮机械制造有限责任公司完成产品销售收入 3 259 万元，同比下降 8.66%；四川青江机器有限公司完成产品销售收入 2 717 万元，同比下降 16.75%。

3. 棉花加工机械 2005年，我国棉花加工机械产品生产厂家约300个左右，棉花加工机械产量约25 068台套，同比增长0.31%。工业总产值企业排序前10名的企业有：山东天鹅棉业机械股份有限公司工业总产值为22 000万元，南通棉花机械有限公司工业总产值为11 434万元，河北邯郸棉机有限公司工业总产值为8 054万元，江苏省启东供销机械有限公司工业总产值为6 003万元，济南天辰棉麻机械制造有限公司工业总产值为3 700万元，河北南皮机械制造有限责任公司工业总产值为3 600万元，山东华棉机械有限公司工业总产值为3 600万元，江苏省大丰供销机械厂有限公司工业总产值为3 178万元，南通越江棉花机械有限公司工业总产值为2 796万元，河北邯武棉机厂工业总产值为2 600万元。

4. 茶叶加工机械 我国茶叶机械制造企业主要分布在浙江、福建等省，其中2005年浙江省有各类茶叶机械制造企业300多个，经工商登记的180个左右，获得质检标准备案的110个，获得农机产品推广鉴定证书的33个，主要集中在杭州、绍兴、金华和衢州等地区。比较规范和较健全规章制度的企业约100个左右。年产值在1 000万元以上的企业10个，年产值在5 000万元以上的有5个。2005年浙江茶叶机械销售额达10亿元，浙江衢州上洋机械有限公司、衢州市绿峰茶机有限公司、富阳金鑫集团公司、绍兴茶机总厂、新昌恒峰名茶机械厂等，年产量超万台(套)，产值均在5 000万元以上。浙江的茶叶机械制造业在全国市场占有率达70%以上，在江苏、安徽、河南、湖南、湖北、重庆、四川、云南、贵州、福建和山东等省、自治区、直辖市均有销售，销售数量逐年呈上升趋势。

三、新产品开发情况

2005年，粮油加工机械完成新产品产值为4.22亿元，同比下降22.21%。农产品加工机械全行业普遍缺乏了对新产品的投入，新产品产值在总产值中的比例减少，不能根据市场的变化调整产品机构，企业缺乏自主创新意识，开放程度不够，产品不能很好适应市场的需求。整个行业总体上发展缓慢，特别是小型榨油机等产品不能根据人民生活水平的提高改进工艺结构，提升食用油的档次和质量，因此市场销售不畅。但是，前几年投入的一批科研、新产品开发项目于2005年完成了验收或鉴定。

1. 受科技部委托，国家粮食局粮食行政管理司于2005年1月13日在武汉工业学院主持召开了农业科技成果转化资金——“板栗深加工技术及产品开发中试”项目验收会。专家组认真听取了项目组工作汇报，审查了有关文件资料，部分专家进行了现场考察，经过质疑、讨论，专家组建议项目验收合格。“板栗深加工技术及产品开发中试”项目实现了板栗保鲜技术、板栗机械剥壳及同时保鲜护色技术、板栗膏（酱、蓉）生产技术和板栗壳提取色素技术的中试成果转化，并建成了板栗保鲜护色灭菌速冻的中试生产线、产量为360kg/h和410kg/h板栗壳及保鲜护色生产线、板栗食品（如膏、酱、蓉、休闲板栗果、板栗蜜饯等）中试生产线。完成了合同规定的任务，达到了合同的考核指标。科技成果成熟度高，有利于推广。产品市场开发前景大，具有较强的竞争力。板栗是大别山区重要经济作物，板栗产业已经成为罗田等县市的支柱产业。该项技术成果的成功转化和推广应用对带动地方经济发展、改善生态环境和提高农民收入具有重要的现实意义。

2. 受科技部委托，国家粮食局粮食行政管理司于2005年5月13日在河北省新乐市主持召开了“低温储粮综合技术中试”农业科技成果转化资金项目验收会。专家组认真听取了项目组工作汇报，审查了有关文件资料，考察了有关现场（中储粮新乐直属库），经过质疑、讨论，专家组建议项目验收合格。“低温储粮综合技术中试”项目采用了太阳热反射涂料的应用技术、仓内环流调节粮堆温度因子技术、提高仓房气密性技术。三项技术的集成已达到较高的熟化程度，具备了广泛推广应用的条件。研究提出了低温储粮综合技术规范（草案），申报了国家发明专利。低温储粮综合技术的运用，能充分利用自然冷源，提高储粮安全性，降低储粮作业成本，延缓储粮陈化，实现生态储粮，具有广阔的市场应用前景。专家建议进一步加大推广力度，对南方的稻谷、北方的玉米进一步进行示范，完善技术规程；对储粮品质的变化规律作有针对性的测试分析。

3. 根据科技部有关验收要求，国家粮食局粮食行政管理司于2005年6月24日对国家粮食局科学研究院等单位承担的“糙米加工副产品增值开发技术”项目进行了验收。专家组通过认真审阅验收材料，对课题组进行了质疑，经过讨论专家组认为项目完成了预期目标，验收材料符合验收要求，一致同意项目验收合格。“糙米加工副产品增值开发技术”以米糠、碎米等为原料，围绕米糠灭酶稳定化、米糠油分子(短程)蒸馏脱酸（脱臭）、米糠营养素和米糠营养纤维工程化、糠腊提取二十八烷醇、三十烷醇及籼米碎米生产低聚异麦芽糖、米蛋白等工艺技术进行了系统性的科技攻关，达到了米糠的综合利用，对糙米和碎米的深加工具有指导意义，对推进我国大米副产品的增值利用有着积极意义。

4. 由中国农业科学院茶叶研究所承担的“茶叶安全加工技术规范集成与应用”课题于2005年12月3日通过了浙江省科技厅组织的专家验收评审会。验收专家分别来自浙江大学、浙江省科技厅、浙江省农业厅、浙江省出入境检验检疫局、浙江省食品药品监督管理局、浙江省海洋与渔业局、浙江省疾病预防控制中心和浙江省海洋水产研究所等单位。专家组听取了课题执行情况总结报告后，一致认为该课题完成的《绿色安全茶叶加工技术规程》在杭州市有关茶叶企业进行示范应用针对性强、先进、合理、可行；根据茶叶安全包装材料的具体指标，筛选出适合茶叶包装的材料品种；专题实施期间，组织举办无公害茶叶生产技术培训和咨询活动10余次，在示范推广的茶叶安全加工技术中，生产绿色安全茶叶4 000余t，取得了明显的社会效益和经济效益。

（中国农业机械工业协会 洪暹国）

食品与包装机械制造业

一、行业发展状况

截止到2005年底，我国食品和包装机械行业企业总数约6 000个，但年销售额超过500万元的不到2 000个，还有约2 000个企业时隐时现，很不稳定，有订货就做，无订货就停；全行业产品总量超过400万台套，可基本满足国内市场需求。在整个行业中，前30位的企业累计销售额108亿元，占行业总销售额的16.05%。销售额最高的企业是湖北京山轻工机械公司，约为18亿元。此外，行业企业区域分布很不均匀，江苏、浙江、广东、河北、山东较多，西部地区明显偏少，直辖市中上海最多，天津次之。2005年，全行业销售额已达673.7亿元，较2004年增长20.5%，与2000年相比增长90.85%，5年平均增长率为17.53%，形成了第二个高速增长期（20世纪80年代曾达到30%的增速）。产品销售率96.09%，产品销售收入同比增长20.82%，销售费用增长17.07%，销售税金及附加同比增长92.04%，管理费用同比增长13.3%，新产品产值率14.73%，财务费用同比增长10.54%，利息支出同比增长20.08%，资产同比增长10.51%，负债增长12.92%，销售收入利润率5.84%，总资产贡献率9.99%，资本保值增值率107.23%，资产负债率58.78%，流动资产周转次数1.45次/年，成本费用利润率6.17%。2005年，我国食品和包装机械出口总额60 734.65万美元，与2004年相比增长70%。其中，食品机械出口额17 491.21万美元，同比增长122%；包装机械出口额43 243.44万美元，同比增长55.5%。2005年食品和包装机械进口总额199 959.03万美元，较2004年下降11%。其中，食品机械进口额40 007.85万美元，同比增长68%；包装机械进口额159 951.18万美元，同比下降21.8%。进口的食品机械主要来自德国、日本、意大利、芬兰和台湾省，包装机械主要来自德国、日本、意大利、美国和瑞士。食品和包装机械出口地区主要是亚洲（东盟10国、中东、中亚5国及俄罗斯）占52.38%，其他为欧洲和北美地区。

二、市场态势分析

1. 行业新产品开发步伐较快　全行业近5年累计开发新产品1 000余种，除部分新产品是老产品的更新换代，大部分都是自动化程度高、技术含量高的产品，少数产品已进入世界先进行列，参与世界强手竞争。如广州达意隆包装机械公司的24 000瓶/h的PET吹瓶机，含气及不含气液体灌装生产线已进入可口可乐、达能、生力等世界知名企业；张家港新美星的24 000瓶/h的无菌冷灌装机已出口到日本的大冢企业4条整线，合同金额为11 400万元；杭州中亚机械有限公司的乳品包装机已成法国达能企业的定点供应商；汕头粤东机械厂、安平食品机械公司、杭州永创机械公司、温州中国华联机械公司的产品已是批量出口，山东赛信机械的膨化玉米片生产线也打开了出口市场。中国包装和食品机械总公司的土豆片生产线出口好于内销，他们研制的果蔬汁饮料高压(6 000atm)杀菌中试线已正常运行。应世界知名的瑞典利乐拉伐公司的要求，杭州中亚机械有限公司、广州达意隆包装机械公司、乐惠集团都在为其生产相关设备，既出口又内销。达意隆包装机械公司最大的一单灌装线出口合同金额达到1 340万美元（人民币升值前）。在世界知名的食品机械及包装机械展览会上都可以看到中国企业参展，其参展设备的技术水平及外观质量与世界知名企业与国际知名品牌并肩竞争。

2. *行业（产业、产品）结构调整步伐加快* 如温州地区已形成产业链，这样有利于降低生产成本，提高零部件加工质量，提高区域性的竞争力。一批新型的企业集团脱颖而出，如瑞安市的吴泰集团共由28家企业组成，28个企业的产品不重复，避免了内部竞争，联合打造市场，互为配套，可为客户提供整线设备，提高了为客户服务的能力，提高了自身的市场竞争力。集团内各企业仍然独立核算，取得了集团内各企业共赢的效果。河北省东光县是包装行业的基地之一，过去的机械产品形象是低档次、低价格，现在各企业联合起来组织了县级协会，制订了行业自律，提倡差异化竞争，企业进行了自我约束，逐步走出了低品质、低价位的低端怪圈，各企业的产品档次已拉开，中高档产品已开始出现，区域性竞争力逐步提升。

3. *产品竞争非常激烈，利润空间不大* 一是在技术含量低的小型设备方面，几乎没有自己知识产权，谁都可以做，大都作坊式生产，价格低廉，这样的企业往往依傍于中等规模的企业群生存，拾遗补缺，以捡漏为主，竞争可以用“惨烈”来形容。二是在中档规模的企业有一定的加工能力，但缺乏技术力量，基本没有自主知识产权，其产品在同行业中大同小异，竞争激烈；一小部分靠质量取得了声誉，但面对低水平竞争对手，他们做企业显得很艰难，利润不高。三是做高端产品的大企业，都是技术力量雄厚，装备水平较高，企业管理较好，售后服务到位。他们的产品在国内竞争并不算激烈，主要面临着与国际同行的竞争，这种竞争已逐步延伸到国际市场。这一类企业已把触角伸到国外，国际知名的行业展会已有他们的产品参展，而且表现不俗，引起了国外同行的关注。但也有个别企业仿制了国外的设备又将这种设备拿到国外参展，引起了知识产权纠纷，以致国外有的展会对中国的参展商进行审查，有的干脆不允许某种侵权产品参展。

三、科研、新产品、新技术

1. 由福建安溪韵和机械有限公司研制的“茶叶微波冷冻干燥杀菌成套设备”于2005年5月正式批量生产。利用这套设备对茶叶进行杀青、烘干，不仅能有效去除乌龙茶的苦、涩、杂味，最大限度地保存了茶叶的原汁、原味，并保留维生素和叶绿素等营养物质，茶叶的保存期限可延长到1年左右。微波杀青的优点是快速、高效，由于时间短，茶叶的有机质流失少，使茶叶的质量有了保证。试验表明，采用微波杀青的速度和效能是常规加热方法的4～20倍。具体地说，将发酵后的茶叶用微波杀青，一般在3min内就可以完成，目前还没有发现有其他的相关设备能达到这个速度。而将冷冻干燥与微波干燥相结合，不仅速度快，还能达到低温脱水的作用。冷冻干燥技术的利用，使茶叶加工过程中只存在物理反应。由于固体成分被其位置上的坚冰支持着，当冰升华时，在干燥的剩余物质里会留下孔隙，这样就保留了茶叶的生物和化学结构以及其活性的完整性，也就能最大限度地保存茶叶原有的色、香、味等化学成分。这套茶叶微波冷冻干燥杀菌设备由于采用了可调微波，所以能适应不同茶叶加工阶段使用，一机多用，大大改善了茶叶生产的卫生环境，有效地控制加工过程中的污染问题，与目前提倡的清洁生产不谋而合。

2. 由乐惠集团惠州市乐惠实业有限公司与中国农业大学食品科学与营养工程学院共同研制开发的国内首条PET无菌冷灌装生产线，于2005年4月26日通过了由中国轻工业联合会组织的国家级新产品技术鉴定。来自中国饮料工业协会、中国无菌包装协会、国家食品质量检测中心、中国轻工机械协会、中国食品发酵研究院、中国农业大学、天津科技大学、北京工商大学的顶级权威专家，组成鉴定委员会。经过缜密的资料审查、现场观摩、技术讨论和用户调查后，专家们一致认为：该条生产线符合国际PET无菌冷灌装通行标准的技术要求和典型配置模式，填补了国内在该领域的空白，整体技术指标达到了国际先进水平。该生产线的开发成功，显示乐惠集团已掌握了PET瓶无菌冷灌装生产线的核心技术，具备在PET瓶无菌冷灌装设备生产这一高端领域的技术实力。据悉，PET瓶无菌冷灌装生产线技术含量较高，除保障优秀的机械运行稳定性外，还综合运用隔离密封技术、微生物控制与检验技术、清洗杀菌技术和空气净化技术，并具有很高的自动化控制水平。该生产线集成了物料UHT设备、无菌罐、消毒液配制系统、无菌水设备、无菌压缩空气单元、空瓶灌注消毒机、理盖及盖消毒设备、洁净空气单元、尾气洗涤设备、灌装线CIP设备以及西帕、吹瓶机，艺康泡沫清洗机等，并采取一系列完善措施，保证产品的无菌效果，已应用于橙汁、草莓汁、桃汁、山楂汁、猕猴桃汁、蔓越莓汁等多种产品的生产。据用户反映，该生产线结构布局合理，实用性好，设备故障率低，更重要的是无菌性能可靠，生产自动化程度高，设有过程全自动控制、数据报表记录和故障预警追查系统，可以确保各个关键工序得到有效监控，使用起来非常放心。PET瓶是目前全球最流行的饮料包装形式，适用于PET瓶的无菌冷灌装是继热灌装技术后，在饮料包装领域的又一重大工艺技术升级。无菌冷灌装不会损害饮料的营养成分，可以生产出色香味俱全的高质量产品，故特别适合热敏性强的产品，如果汁饮料、茶饮料或含乳饮料。产品适用范围广，许多无法应用热灌装工艺的饮料，可以通过无菌冷灌装而采用PET包装。乐惠PET瓶无菌冷灌装生产线的推出，适应国内饮料行业高速发展的需要，可代替同类进口产品，具有很高的性价比，对促进民族饮料包装设备制造业的发展具有重要意义。

3. 由南京轻机集团研制的24 000瓶/h纯生啤酒灌装生产线于2005年8月在燕京啤酒集团湖北仙桃啤酒有限公司顺利投入运行，使啤酒厂家真正拥有了自己的国产纯生啤酒生产线，这在我国纯生啤酒装备制造领域具有划时代的意义。纯生啤酒的生产是采用低温膜过滤技术，去除啤酒中残留的酵母等微生物，使其具有清爽、新鲜的口味。纯生啤酒生产经无菌酿造、无菌过滤、无菌灌装，使整个生产过程中均需严格无菌。该生产线自卸箱至装箱（除膜过滤、贴标机等配套设备外）各单机、瓶箱输送、终端过滤系统、控制系统均由南京轻机集团提供，全线应用了多项高新技术。主要特点：一是洗瓶机为双端式，传动采用主传动与进、出瓶分离传动，出瓶端为不锈钢结构，碱液浸泡时间达15min以上，并配置碱液自动检测及添加系统。二是灌装系统采用冲瓶、灌装、压盖三位一体形式。其中，冲瓶机喷冲机构为双通道，喷嘴可沿瓶中心轴线移动，保证冲瓶效果；灌装阀采用外置式流体机械灌装阀（专利号：ZL01263284.8），整机具有两次抽真空能力，且有无瓶不抽真空功能，传动采用模块化设计和变频无级调速，灌装缸内物料液位高度由电探针控制，物料背压实现自动控制，灌装稳定可靠；压盖系统的瓶盖滑道配置紫外线杀菌装置，为开放式设计，可进行热水及消毒液喷冲、清洗，便于清洁。三是全系统配有完善的四罐全自动CIP系统、泡沫清洗系统及热水外部冲洗系统，保证灌装系统在无菌状态下生产。四是杀菌机为温瓶/杀菌两用机。载瓶输送带为网栅式不锈钢链网，其强度高，耐高温，透水性好，输送平稳；配置PU值自动控制，温度控制精度高。因此，该生产线具有技术先进、结构紧凑、配置合理、运行平稳、节能降耗等优点。

四、行业工作

1. 中国食品和包装机械工业协会于2005年4月8日在云南省昆明市召开了第三届第四次理事会，同期召开了新的中国食品和包装机械行业专家委员会成立会议。来自17个省、自治区、直辖市的53名代表共聚一堂，回顾在第三届理事会的领导下行业各项工作取得的成绩和进步。大会由何南至秘书长主持，昆明市副市长、中国食品和包装机械工业协会副会长王奇英到会并发表重要讲话。他指出：随着我国社会主义市场经济的不断完善，行业协会的作用越来越重要，担负的任务越来越重。他对中国食品和包装机械工业协会多年来在这一新兴工业领域中所取得的长足进步表示祝贺，并对协会的工作给予了充分的肯定。大会听取了岳书学会长关于中国食品和包装机械工业协会第三届第四次理事会工作报告。岳会长详细地介绍了中国食品和包装机械工业行业的成就及所面临的问题，指出了近几年行业出口的走向，对业内近几年出现的低价劣质产品现象提出了批评，提倡差异化竞争，以新技术、新产品为先导，以质量取胜，以技术开发为突破口，向行业的世界水平进军。岳会长在报告中总结了协会2004年的工作，并提出了2005年的工作设想。最后，李树君副理事长（现为理事长）做了总结报告。他对协会工作提出了希望与建设性意见。

2. 由中国食品和包装机械工业协会、中国包装和食品机械总公司与法国爱博展览集团共同主办的第五届中国上海国际包装和食品加工技术展览会于2005年5月18～20日在上海新国际博览中心隆重举行，此次展会承接与中国国际食品饮料展览会，同期同地举办，两大展会强强携手，并以22 000m^{2}的超大规模亮相，可成为国内同行业中参观选购设备、了解国内外食品机械和包装机械及相关产品发展趋势的首选展会。中央电视台、上海电视台、中国食品报、中国包装报、中国食品质量报等多家媒体合作伙伴对本次盛会做展前、展中、展后的全面跟踪报道，此外，国外相关媒体也同步关注、宣传本次展会。

3. 第九届中国国际食品加工和包装机械展览会于2005年10月26～29日在北京中国国际展览中心举行，全国政协副主席郝建秀、阿不来提·阿不都热西提、中国机械工业联合会会长于珍及主办单位的领导和部分驻华使节出席了开幕式并剪彩。展出面积约15 000m^2，展出内容有食品加工机械、烹煮设备、食品包装机械、包装印刷机械、包装容器制造机械、包装材料加工机械以及药品包装机械等。该展会已成为国内包装和食品机械行业中规模最大、档次最高的大型国际化专业展，在国际上也享有一定的知名度。本届展会有来自意大利、德国、西班牙、美国、法国、英国、日本、韩国等10多个国家和香港、台湾省的

90多家海外企业及来自北京、上海、天津、广东、浙江、江苏等15个省、直辖市的230家国内厂商参展。意大利对外贸易协会、意大利食品生产加工和保鲜机械与设备制造商协会、意大利自动包装机械制造协会、韩国包装机械协会、日本食品机械工业协会都组团参加了展会。这次展览会是我国包装和食品机械行业的一次盛会，在展会期间还同期举办了数次技术交流活动，同步介绍本行业国内外的发展动态和趋势。

4. 由中国食品和包装机械工业协会、中国肉类协会共同组建的肉类加工机械专业委员会于2005年12月22日在北京正式成立，并同时召开了第一届会员代表大会。来自我国肉类机械的大学、科研院所、专业媒体和专业生产厂家等参加了会议。肉类加工机械专业委员会的成立，是中国食品和包装机械工业协会、中国肉类协会这两个协会从行业发展和市场需要出发，为更好地推动肉类加工机械和我国肉类加工行业的发展，打破部门界限和系统阻隔，共同致力使肉类加工机械行业使之导入良性的、健康的发展轨道的重要举措。肉类加工机械专业委员会成立后将发挥以下作用：一是组织行业企业与国外同行进行国际间的技术交流，引进先进的生产技术、材料、生产工艺和生产管理理念，有计划地组织新产品开发和合资合作。二是组织企业间的技术交流，促进国内肉类加工机械企业的发展。达到相互促进，共同发展，努力提高我国肉类加工机械的技术水平。三是组织制定行业规范和标准。推广好产品，带动一般产品，淘汰那些质量差的劣质产品。促进肉类加工机械的健康发展。四是组织专业展览会，为企业在信息上创造与外界和关联产业之间的沟通和交流。五是为企业提供信息服务、咨询服务。包括提供国内外行业发展的技术信息和开拓国际市场信息，我国肉类加工机械不仅要适应和满足人们日益高涨的生产和生活需求，还要争取设备出口创汇。六是组织行业企业共同应对国际贸易争端，维护企业的合法权益。

（中国食品和包装机械工业协会　何南至）

棉花加工机械制造业

一、生产情况

据不完全统计，2005年全国棉花加工机械产品生产厂家已发展到近300个。其中上报统计数据的有21个，占获得棉花加工机械生产许可证企业的50%。这21家棉机制造企业总人数为5 386人，其中工程技术人员622人。固定资产净值2.63亿元，全年完成工业总产值7.8亿元，实现利税0.74亿元。2005年，这21家棉花加工机械企业生产轧花机1 644台，打包机512台，400型打包机242台，皮棉清理机1 977台，籽棉清理机439台，锯齿剥绒机1 030台。2005年，全国棉机制造企业排序前10名的基本情况见表1。

表1　2005年全国棉机制造企业排序前10名的基本情况

单位名称	工业总产值（万元）	销售额（万元）	利税总额（万元）	固定资产净值（万元）	职工人数（人）	轧花机（台）	打包机（台）	400型打包机（台）
山东天鹅棉业机械股份有限公司	22 000	18 172	1 860	1 994	498	360	42	42
南通棉花机械有限公司	11 434	10 195	1 897	1 487	479		203	95
河北邯郸棉机有限公司	8 054	12 316	1 246	6 265	1 128	147	13	13
江苏省启东供销机械有限公司	6 003	3 986	451	1 257	238		16	16
济南天辰棉麻机械制造有限公司	3 700	2 100	225	3 200	130	120		
河北南皮机械制造有限责任公司	3 600	3 206	596	1 860	360		5	5
山东华棉机械有限公司	3 600	3 280	210	381	121	155		
江苏省大丰供销机械厂有限公司	3 178	2 808	205	930	400	67	0	0
南通越江棉花机械有限公司	2 796	2 680	126	1 112	116	874	58	38
河北邯武棉机厂	2 600	2 000	280	0	200	0		

注：本表数据来自中国棉花协会棉花加工分会。

二、体制改革

1. 对棉花加工机械产品实行生产许可证制度 自从2002年国家质量监督检验检疫总局下发国质检监函[2002]39号《关于对部分棉花加工机械产品实行生产许可证制度的通知》以来，全国工业产品生产许可证办公室棉花加工机械产品生产许可证审查部抓紧开展工作。截止到2005年底获得棉花加工机械生产许可证的企业共有42个，锯齿轧花机发证25个，200型液压棉花打包机发证23个，400型液压棉花打包机8个。

2. 棉花质量检验体制改革 2005棉花加工年度，是棉花质量检验体制改革的第一个推广年。国家发展和改革委员会对天津、河北、山东、上海、江苏、安徽、河南、湖北、湖南、四川、山西、陕西、甘肃、新疆等14个产棉大省、自治区、直辖市和新疆生产建设兵团的322家（含2004年14个试点棉花加工企业）已按照改革规定完成技术改造的加工企业进行了贷款贴息。改革规定，凡参与棉花质量检验体制改革的棉花加工企业，必须采用压力为400t的大型打包机进行加工，并于2005年7月11日棉花质量检验体制改革工作协调指导小组正式批准棉花质量检验体制改革加工设备更新改造的主要设备，由南通棉机有限公司、邯郸棉机有限公司、山东天鹅棉业机械股份有限公司、湖北省供销合作社棉花机械厂、南通越江棉花机械有限公司、启东市供销机械有限公司、河北南皮机械制造有限公司、上海兴棉机械有限公司等8家企业提供，从而确保了这项改革的顺利实施。

三、市场情况

（一）棉花加工的市场特点

1. 2004年2月之后，由于棉价的大幅回落，使得棉花加工企业和流通企业发生了大规模的亏损。2005年，我国的棉花市场逐渐趋于冷静，农民的种棉意向锐减，河南、山东、河北等地往年留着种棉的耕地许多都种上了小麦，预期产量的减少使得棉花价格逐渐回暖。此外，2005年纺织总体形势转好，且原油涨价拉高了化纤的价格，有关部门纷纷预测棉花产需缺口将继续扩大，从而带动了棉价上涨。

2. 2005年，我国皮棉产量为570万t，棉花质量检验体制改革已进入正式推广的第一年。国家发展和改革委员会经过层层审批，对322个有收购加工资格的、完成更新改造的棉花加工企业给予了贷款贴息。按照改革之初设计的每个厂年加工能力5 000t计算，由这322个企业加工出的227kg大包型棉花约为161万t，占2005年棉花产量的28%。改革之前的市场统计认为，我国的棉花加工企业有近20 000个，按我国棉花年产量570万t计算，每个企业的年平均加工量仅为285t。而改革后的加工企业，年平均加工能力将提高16倍之多。通过一年的试点和推广，棉花质量检验体制改革的先进性逐步体现出来，越来越多的企业认识到改革是必然趋势，并积极参与到改革的大潮中来。

（二）棉机制造业的市场特点

棉机制造业产品结构，主要围绕棉花质量检验体制改革进行调整，市场竞争已趋向白热化，行业利润大幅下降。

1. 2005年是国家棉花质量检验体制改革推广工作的第一年，各地参与改革的棉花加工企业积极性十分高涨，更新改造企业的数量有300多个，对与改革相关的棉机产品如400t打包机、大型成套轧花设备等的需求量明显增加。改革文件中批准的8个大型打包机的提供厂商，都在不同程度上提高了400型打包机及其附属设备的生产和销售数量。例如，业内较有影响力的南通棉机有限公司和山东天鹅棉业机械股份有限公司的400型打包机的销售数量，均有了20余台套的增长。

2. 棉机市场的竞争愈加激烈，行业利润大幅下降。据全国工业产品生产许可证办公室棉机生产许可证审查部统计，我国仅生产轧花机和打包机的主机生产厂家有64个，算上辅机和配件生产厂家有上百个。而取得棉机生产许可证的企业却不多，很多企业并不具备生产条件，但由于价格便宜，有市场需求，所以产品供不应求。相当多的劣质产品进入了棉机市场，对我国棉机制造业的技术进步以及棉花加工业的发展产生了不利的影响。按照棉花质量检验体制改革的规划，未来我国棉花加工企业要由现在的近20 000个，压缩到2 400个左右。在这样的背景下，各棉机制造企业在地方市场、全国市场展开了激烈竞争，价格战、分期付款、赊销等竞争方式层出不穷。无序的、激烈的市场竞争，导致了棉机制造企业的利润急剧下降。

从对近3年棉机制造行业工业总产值排名前10位的企业进行统计来看，2003年10个企业的工业总产值为6.8亿元，2004年为11.7亿元，2005年为6.7亿元；2003年10个企业的利税总额为0.98亿元，2004年为1.14亿元，2005年为0.71亿元。工业总产值和利税总额在近3年内达到最低水平，工业总产值较上年下降42.7%，利税总额较上年下降

37.1%。与改革相关的产品数量增大，但工业总产值降低，可见棉机制造行业在2005年是获利甚微的一年。

四、科研与新产品开发

在棉花质量检验体制改革的影响下，新的棉机产品和工艺的研发主要集中在改革相关技术项目的开发上。从2004年改革伊始便着手研究的几项重要技术，如在线测量回潮率装置、异型纤维挑拣机等，逐步在更新改造企业的使用中加以完善。异型纤维挑拣技术仍是较难以完全攻克的、市场关注较高的技术热点。2005年中华全国供销合作总社组织研制的新产品项目，即南通棉花机械有限公司研制的“MFBK型自动搭扣装置”和“MQHY型籽棉异性纤维清理机”，均为目前企业改造中急需的产品，因此颇受欢迎。

五、行业管理

1. 协助国家发改委检查了322个棉花加工企业更新改造贷款和贴息执行情况，并及时向主管部门汇报，推动了棉花质量检验体制改革工作的顺利进行。

2. 2005年12月28日，中国棉花协会棉花加工分会正式召开成立大会，初步制定了分会2006年工作计划，选举产生了分会的会长、副会长、秘书长等领导班子成员；继续参与棉花加工行业的改革、技术研发与推广、国外考察等行业管理工作。

（中国棉花协会棉花加工分会　尹青云）

3 第三部分

政策法规及重要文件

关于进一步加强流通环节食品安全监管工作的意见

（国家工商行政管理总局　2006年1月9日）

为认真贯彻落实党的十六届五中全会、中央经济工作会议和全国工商行政管理工作会议精神，充分发挥工商行政管理机关职能作用，切实加强流通环节食品安全监管工作，维护食品市场秩序和消费者合法权益，根据《国务院关于进一步加强食品安全工作的决定》和全国整顿和规范市场经济秩序领导小组的要求，现就进一步加强流通环节食品安全监管工作，提出如下意见：

1. 深入开展食品安全专项执法检查，切实维护食品市场消费安全　各级工商行政管理机关要在巩固发展食品安全专项整治成果的基础上，深入开展食品安全专项执法检查，加大工作力度，严格规范食品经营行为，切实维护食品市场消费安全。围绕粮、肉、蔬菜、水产品、奶制品、豆制品、酒、饮料、儿童食品、保健食品等与广大人民群众生活密切相关、消费者投诉多的食品开展重点品种专项执法检查；围绕城市社区、城乡结合部、农村市场开展重点区域专项执法检查；围绕商场、超市、集贸市场、批发市场、经营门店等开展重点场所和落实经营者自律制度的专项执法检查；围绕“五一”、“十一”、中秋、元旦、春节和夏季、秋冬季开展节日食品和季节性食品专项执法检查。主要解决流通环节食品质量和销售假冒伪劣食品问题，以及规范食品经营主体资格和经营行为，落实经营者自律，依法取缔无照经营，努力确保食品市场消费安全。各地还可结合本地区实际，选择重点，认真适时组织好专项检查。

2. 加大对食品违法案件的查处力度，严厉打击制售假冒伪劣食品违法行为　要集中执法力量，强化案件查办工作，重点查处制售假冒伪劣食品、无证无照生产经营食品、经销不合格食品和有毒有害食品、食品中使用非食品添加剂、虚假食品广告、商标侵权和食品的假包装、假标识、假商标印制品等违法案件，特别要抓好对大要案件的排查和查处工作，认真清理积案。要严格规范办案程序，切实做到事实清楚、证据充分、定性准确、适用法律准确、处罚适当、程序合法，经得起司法行政诉讼的监督。要健全食品违法案件受理、查办、督办责任制和错案追究制，严格办案纪律，提高办案质量和效率。要建立健全重大食品违法案件逐级报告制度和案件协查与协作机制，对流通环节食品违法案件涉及生产环节的食品质量问题，既要依法查处销售不合格食品及其他质量违法行为，又要将有关情况通报质检、卫生等部门。对涉嫌犯罪案件，要依法及时移交公安机关。对举报食品违法案件的有功人员，要按照财政部、工商总局、质检总局《举报制售假冒伪劣产品违法犯罪活动有功人员奖励办法》给予奖励。

3. 严格把好食品经营主体准入关，依法清理和规范经营主体资格　要坚持依法登记注册，严格注册程序，对食品生产经营涉及前置审批事项的，坚持先证后照，对未取得食品卫生许可证的，不得受理办理登记注册。对取得食品卫生许可证后申办企业和个体工商户的，在核定经营范围时应注明食品生产销售或经营项目。要结合企业年检、个体工商户验照和日常市场检查，按照“谁登记、谁负责”的原则，每年对食品经营主体资格进行逐户清理和规范，重点核查食品卫生许可证是否合法有效、登记事项是否发生变化。对许可证失效或登记事项发生变化的，要责令其限期办理变更登记或依法办理注销登记，否则，依法吊销营业执照。要会同有关部门严格按照《无照经营查处取缔办法》的规定，依法取缔食品无照经营。对查处中遇到的实际困难和政策性问题，要及时向当地政府报告。要与质检、卫生等部门互相通报证照监管信息，及时将食品经营主体的营业执照发放、注销、吊销等情况抄告质检、卫生等部门。

4. 切实加强食品经营主体经济户口管理，大力推行食品经营主体信用分类监管　要进一步完善食品生产经营主体经济户口管理制度，严格食品经营主体登记档案管理。各级工商行政管理注册登记机关要通过计算机网络或书面文书将食品生产经营主体登记注册的基本情况通知所在区域基层工商所，工商所要落实人员及时认领，并结合市场巡查对本辖区所有食品生产经营主体纳入经济户口管理。要结合金信工程的建设，建立和完善食品经营主体注册登记电子档案和经济户口数据库，并逐步实现各级工商行政管理机关及工商所食品经营主体经济户口管理联网。基层工商所要对本辖区食品生产经营主体实行一户一账一卡制度，即对每户食品生产经营主体建立登记台账和经济户口卡片，做到底数清、情况明，食品生产经营主体经济户口管理规范有序。严格实行食品经营主体信用分类监管制度，积极推进食品经营企业和个体工商户信用体系建设。要结合全国工商系统企业信用分类监管和个体工商户分层分类登记监管制度的实施，根据食品监管法律法规及制度要求，研究制定食品经营主体信用分类监管的方案，认真组织实施。要结合市场巡查，依据食品经营者诚信守法情况，将本辖区食品经营主体划分为A、B、C、D四个类别，有针对性地加强对失信、严重失信食品经营企业和个体工商户的重点监管。要尽快建立食品经营主体信用分类数据库，逐步建立省级范围内的食品经营主体信用分类监管计算机网络系统，最终实现与总局联网和省际之间信息共享。

5. *充分发挥基层工商所职能作用，不断强化食品安全日常监管*　各级工商行政管理机关要将食品安全监管重心下移，将监管任务和责任层层落实到基层工商所。基层工商所要严格按照国家工商总局制定下发的《工商行政管理所食品安全监督管理工作规范》的要求，落实监管人员、监管任务、监管责任和监管措施，重点监管食品经营主体资格、经营行为和食品质量。以基层工商所为单位将其所管辖区域划分为若干监管责任区，落实具体监管责任人，实施“两图一书”管理模式，即：工商所辖区食品经营布局图、监管人员责任区分布图、工商所与食品经营者签订的《食品安全责任书》。要加大基层工商所对食品市场的巡查力度，坚持“六查六看”，即：查经营资格，看食品经营者证照是否齐全和按要求悬挂，是否出租出借证照，是否超范围经营；查进货票证，看食品经营者在进货时是否履行了检查验收责任，是否索取了供货方有关资质、发货票等票证；查经销食品，看是否有质量合格证明、检验检疫证明，是否掺杂使假、以假充真、以次充好、以不合格食品冒充合格食品，是否为国家明令淘汰、失效、变质的食品；查包装标识，看食品标识内容是否虚假，是否有产品名称、厂名、厂址，是否标明食品主要成分和含量，是否标明生产日期和有效期限；查商标广告，看食品商标是否有侵权和违法使用行为，食品广告是否有虚假和误导宣传的内容；查市场开办者责任，看食品市场开办者是否履行了对进场经营者资格审查的义务，经营场所内部质量管理制度是否健全和落实。要引导和监督食品经营者建立和落实各项自律制度，及时查处违法经营，规范经营行为，严格登记对每户经营者的巡查记录，按户健全市场巡查监管档案，并与食品经营主体经济户口管理和信用分类监管有机结合，全面地反映每户食品经营者诚信守法的真实情况。要不断创新基层监管方式方法，借助信息化网络、现代办公设备和快速检测等技术手段，进一步提高基层日常监管的科技含量和现代化水平。各级工商行政管理机关要根据《工商行政管理所食品安全监督管理工作规范》的要求，加强对工商所食品安全监管工作的指导、督查和考核，充实基层执法力量，加强法律法规和食品安全知识培训，改善执法装备，提供监管经费和人员的保障，确保基层工商所履行食品安全监管职责落实到位。

6. *加强对农村食品市场的监管，确保农村食品消费安全*　要把加强农村食品安全工作作为建设社会主义新农村的重要任务，努力建立农村食品市场质量安全防控体系，在农村大力推行12315维权联络站、消费者投诉站建设和食品安全监督站、义务监督员制度，加强农村食品安全宣传和监督工作，不断提高农村消费者的自我保护意识和识假辨假及依法维权能力。要加强对农村中小城市、县城、乡镇等区域和农村食品批发市场、集贸市场、批发企业及送货上门经营活动的重点监管，严厉打击以降价促销等名义面向农村销售假冒伪劣食品等违法行为。要重点加强对农村小食品店、小商贩、小摊点、小作坊、小集市的监管，特别要抓好城乡结合部、城中村、旅游景区和农村消费比较集中的场所经营食品的日常巡查和集中整治。要严厉打击和查处农村食品市场的无证无照经营、掺杂使假和经营过期霉变、有毒有害食品及不合格食品的违法行为，确保农村食品消费安全。积极支持商务部门推行农村连锁超市、便利店等现代流通网络的建设，引导游商小贩进店、入市或定点经营，不断完善和规范农村食品销售的设施和条件，促进农村食品市场的繁荣稳定与安全。

7. *严格食品市场准入和经营者自律管理，严把食品入市质量关*　各地要建立健全食品质量市场准入体系，引导和监督食品经营者建立和落实进货查验、索证索票、购销台账、质量承诺、不合格食品主动退市等制度，确保入市食品质量合格；鼓励食品批发市场、集贸市场、商场、超市与农产品、水产品、畜产品养殖、种植基地及加工包装食品的重点企业实行“场厂挂钩”、“场地挂钩”等协议准入制度；监督食品市场开办者、柜台出租者、展销会举办者落实对入场经营者的食品质量管理制度，切实从源头上确保食品质量。要把食品经营者落实自律制度的重点放在商场、超市和食品批发市场、食品批发企业，监督其内部经营各环节的食品质量管理，强化食品经营者的质量责任意识，不断提高其自查自纠、自检自管的能力，切实对消费者负责。要积极会同和配合有关部门开展“百城万店无假货”和“三绿工程”等活动。要在当地政府的领导和协调下，会同有关部门开展食品“放心示范店”、“放心示范超市”、“放心示范市场”和“放心消费城市”等创建活动，积极推进食品市场准入体系建设。

8. **建立和完善食品质量监测体系，积极推行食品质量分类监管**　各级工商行政管理机关要在严格食品入市监管的同时，加强对食品交易、食品退市的全程监管。一是严格食品质量监测。要认真贯彻执行《流通领域商品质量监测办法》，把监测作为对食品质量监管的重要手段，逐步形成工商行政管理机关抽检、消费者送检、经营者自检相结合的流通环节食品质量监测体系。各级工商行政管理机关特别是基层工商所要健全食品质量监测机制，配备快速检测车、检测箱等设备，有针对性地加强食品质量日常监测和快速检测，并严格按照有关规定发布食品安全信息，及时发布消费警示和提示。各级工商行政管理机关要建立健全食品安全监测数据直报点制度，加强对重点区域和食品交易场所的定点监测。积极引导和督促批发市场、超市、大中型食品经营企业配备设施和人员，建立质量自检制度，切实对其经营的食品质量负责。二是严格实施食品分类监管。各级工商行政管理机关要针对流通环节食品的不同来源和不同生产方式的特点，区别情况，分类监管。对经加工制作的定型包装食品，重点检查包装标识是否符合法律法规及标准的规定，是否有厂名、厂址、合格证、生产日期、保质期等；对质检部门实施市场准入的 28 类 525 种食品，重点检查是否加贴了“QS”标志及是否伪造或者冒用“QS”标志；对农产品、水产品和畜产品及大宗鲜活食品，利用快速检测等方法，重点检测农药残留、甲醛、氯霉素等有毒有害项目；对冷冻食品，要会同相关部门严格标准和规范，加强从车间速冻、冷藏运输到冷柜销售各环节的监管；对散装、裸装食品，监督经营者制作食品标签，重点加强对食品名称、产地、保质期等的管理；对流通环节现场制作食品，要重点检查经营条件和用料质量，督促经营者明示生产日期、保质期等内容。同时，要探索和推行食品按风险度监管的机制，对消费安全危害大的食品，省级工商行政管理机关要组织力量进行食品风险评估，确定本辖区内高风险、一般风险、低风险的食品品种，实行对风险食品按名录监管，并创造条件逐步实现网上监管，确保对高风险食品监管到位。三是严格对食品退市的监管。各地要把不合格食品退市作为食品质量监管的重要环节，建立健全行政监管强制退市和经营者主动退市、协议退市相结合的管理机制，各省级工商行政管理机关要结合本地实际制定食品退市制度和办法。要对市场巡查、质量监测、快速检测中发现和消费者申诉举报经依法确认的不合格食品，区别不同情况，依法采取责令经营者停止销售、退回供货方、追回或销毁等退市措施，并及时向不合格食品涉及范围内的工商行政管理机关通报。对退市的同种类、批次、型号的食品必须经依法检验合格后方可重新入市。对不主动退市和责令退市后仍不退市，或名义上退市实际改头换面继续销售的，依法从重处罚。

9. **全面推进食品安全监管法规和制度建设，积极构建食品安全长效监管体系**　要通过加强法律法规和制度建设，着力构建工商监管、经营者自律、社会监督“三位一体”的流通环节食品安全长效监管体系。一是建立健全食品安全监管法制体系。要积极参与《食品安全法》的起草工作，加快制定《流通领域商品质量监督管理条例》，进一步清理和完善流通环节食品安全监管配套规章，积极推进流通环节食品安全监管的地方法规建设。要围绕严格食品市场主体准入、监管食品质量、规范食品经营行为和取缔食品无照经营等方面，建立和完善市场监管制度，重点是食品市场经营主体准入制度、食品市场巡查制度、食品经营主体信用分类监管制度、食品分类管理制度、不合格食品退市制度、食品安全信息公示制度等，努力提高食品市场监管制度化、规范化水平。二是建立健全食品安全监管执法网络体系。要以 12315 行政执法网络体系为依托，通过 12315 网络进社区、进村镇、进商家、进市场等办法，充分发挥“一会两站”的作用，形成食品安全监管的受理投诉、跟踪督办和案件查处相结合的行政执法网络，不断提高监管的能力和水平。要结合金信工程和 12315 网络建设，整合资源，建立全系统五级贯通的食品安全监管信息网络，逐步实现食品安全网上受理投诉申诉、网上报送反馈信息、网上查询、网上发布、网上督办和网上指挥调度，不断提高食品市场监管现代化水平。三是建立健全食品安全监管预警和应急处置体系。要按照国务院制定的《国家重大食品事故应急预案》、国家工商总局下发的《工商行政管理系统市场监管应急预案》和《工商行政管理系统重大食品安全事件应急预案》的要求，层层制定和落实食品安全应急预案，及时妥善处置食品安全突发事件，形成全系统上下贯通的食品安全预警防范和应急处置机制。各级工商行政管理机关要建立健全食品安全重大事项报告制度，畅通信息，严禁迟报、漏报和瞒报。四是建立健全食品安全监管社会监督体系。要通过与各级消费者协会、食品行业组织建立沟通协作机制，充分发挥消协组织的社会监督和行业组织的自律作用；通过贯彻落实中宣部会同工商总局等七个部门下发的《关于进一步做好食品安全报道工作的意见》精神，充分发挥新闻媒体的舆论监督和宣传引导作用；通过扩大12315网络和聘请食品安全监督员等办法，鼓励引导广大消费者积极参与社会监督，努力营造食品安全社会监督氛围。

10. *加强组织领导，严格责任制度，狠抓检查落实* 各级工商行政管理机关要在当地党委、政府的统一领导下，结合当地实际研究制定和实施流通环节食品安全“十一五”规划，切实加强组织领导，密切与相关职能部门协作配合，认真履行市场监管职责。要建立健全属地监管领导责任制，一把手负总责，主管领导负直接领导责任；要建立健全指导监督责任制，各级工商行政管理机关的消费者权益保护、市场、企业、个体私营、公平交易、商标、广告等机构分别按职能各负其责，对职责范围内的食品安全工作进行指导监督；要建立健全岗位责任制，基层工商所实行分片划段，岗位责任到人，工商所和监管人员对其管辖区的食品安全负责。要建立健全食品安全监管考核机制，强化食品安全责任追究制度。要充分发挥全系统各级纪检、监察机构的职能作用，对执法人员履行食品安全监管职责和执法是否到位及是否依法行政进行效能监察，对食品安全监管中失察、失职、渎职造成严重后果的，要依法依纪追究有关单位、领导和责任人的责任。要采取重点督查、交叉检查、明察暗访等办法，一级抓一级，层层抓落实，切实做到食品安全监管工作组织领导、工作任务、工作措施、工作责任、经费保障、人员力量逐一落实到位，保障流通环节食品安全，促进经济社会又快又好发展。

重大活动食品卫生监督规范

（卫生部　卫监督发〔2006〕56号　2006年2月13日）

第一章　总　　则

第一条　为规范重大活动食品卫生监督工作，防止食品污染和有害因素对人体健康的危害，保障食品卫生安全，依据《中华人民共和国食品卫生法》、《突发公共卫生事件应急条例》、《餐饮业食品卫生管理办法》等法律法规制定本规范。

第二条　本规范适用于省级以上人民政府要求卫生行政部门对具有特定规模的政治、经济、文化、体育及其他重大社会活动（以下简称重大活动）实施的专项食品卫生监督工作。

第三条　重大活动食品卫生监督，坚持预防为主、属地管理、分级监督的原则。

第四条　重大活动食品卫生监督分为全程卫生监督和重点卫生监督两种方式。卫生行政部门依据重大活动具体内容，确定实施重大活动食品卫生监督的方式。

第五条　重大活动的主办单位应当对重大活动食品卫生安全负责，主办单位与接待单位应按照本规范的要求，配合卫生行政部门做好重大活动食品卫生监督工作。

第二章　工作程序与内容

第六条　重大活动主办单位应于活动举办前20日将以下相关信息及资料，通报省级卫生行政部门登记备案：

（一）重大活动名称、举办时间、举办地点、参加人数；

（二）主办单位名称、联系人、通讯方式；

（三）接待单位名称、数量、地址、联系人及通讯方式；

（四）参与活动人员驻地分布和餐饮、住宿情况；

（五）供餐单位、供餐形式、供餐地点及重要宴会、旅游活动、重大活动期间指定或赞助食品等相关情况。

第七条　省级卫生行政部门应根据重大活动相关信息及资料，开展以下工作：

（一）制定重大活动食品卫生监督工作预案，主要内容包括组织领导、工作任务、职责分工、监督监测计划及经费预算；

（二）制定重大活动食品污染及食物中毒事件应急处理预案；

（三）对接待单位开展食品卫生监督监测和食品卫生状况评估；

（四）做好卫生监督人员、物资、车辆、通讯等后勤保障工作。

第八条 省级卫生行政部门应当将重大活动食品卫生监督工作预案、重大活动食品污染及食物中毒事件应急处理预案报同级人民政府并通知重大活动主办单位。

第九条 重大活动接待单位必须具备下列基本条件：

（一）持有效的食品卫生许可证；

（二）具备与重大活动供餐人数、规模相适应的接待服务能力；

（三）食品卫生监督量化分级管理达到A级标准（或具备与A级标准相当的卫生条件）；

（四）食品从业人员持有效健康检查证明，健康档案记录完备；

（五）食品及原料供应渠道符合卫生要求，相关证件资料完备；

（六）生活饮用水水质符合国家生活饮用水卫生标准；

（七）省级卫生行政部门根据重大活动情况提出的其他条件。

第十条 卫生行政部门对接待单位进行食品卫生监督评估应包括以下内容：

（一）接待单位卫生管理组织、管理人员、卫生管理制度设立情况；

（二）食品生产经营场所布局设置、卫生设备设施运行情况；

（三）食品生产加工制作过程卫生监督检查情况；

（四）直接入口食品及食品工具、用具、容器卫生监测情况；

（五）食品从业人员身体健康检查证明及健康状况；

（六）接待单位存在的食品卫生隐患问题及卫生监督意见；

（七）省级卫生行政部门根据重大活动情况规定的其他内容。对接待单位食品卫生监督评估的方式包括卫生管理资料审查和现场食品卫生监督检查。

第十一条 卫生行政部门应在评估工作结束后3日内撰写《重大活动接待单位食品卫生监督评估报告》并送交活动主办单位、接待单位签收。接待单位应依照卫生监督意见内容进行整改，主办单位应当督促检查整改情况。

第十二条 重大活动全程食品卫生监督主要包括：

（一）审查食谱、食品采购、食品库房、从业人员健康、加工环境、加工程序、冷菜制作、餐具清洗消毒、备餐与供餐时间、食品中心温度、食品留样、自带食品和赞助食品等内容；

（二）卫生行政部门选派专职卫生监督人员进驻重大活动现场，对食品生产加工制作环节进行动态卫生监督，填写卫生监督笔录和卫生监督意见书；

（三）实施食品卫生计划监测和现场食品卫生快速监测。

第十三条 重大活动重点食品卫生监督主要包括：

（一）审查食谱、食品采购、从业人员健康、冷菜制作、餐具清洗消毒、食品留样等内容；

（二）根据重大活动规模、人数确定是否选派卫生监督人员进驻重大活动现场；

（三）对食品生产加工制作重点环节进行动态卫生监督，填写卫生监督笔录和卫生监督意见书，必要时进行食品卫生监测。

第十四条 有下列情形之一的食品，接待单位应停止使用：

（一）食谱审查认定可能引发食物中毒的食品；

（二）卫生检验可疑阳性的生活饮用水和食品；

（三）未能出示有效食品卫生许可证的直接入口食品；

（四）超过保质期限的食品、食品原料、半成品和成品；

（五）外购散装直接入口熟食制品；

（六）省级卫生行政部门为预防食物中毒而规定禁止食用的食品；

（七）国家、地方法律法规规定的其他禁止生产经营的食品。

第十五条 发生可疑食品污染、食物中毒等突发公共卫生事件时，重大活动接待单位应向所在地区卫生行政部门和重大活动主办单位报告并采取以下相应措施：

（一）配合医疗卫生机构抢救治疗病人；

（二）立即停止食品生产加工和供餐活动；

（三）保留造成或者可能导致食品污染、食物中毒的食品及其原料、工具、设备和现场；

（四）配合卫生行政部门现场调查取证，如实提供食品留样及相关证据和材料；

（五）依照卫生行政部门提出的卫生监督意见立即整改。卫生行政部门应立即启动应急处理预案，组织对中毒人员进行救治，对可疑中毒或污染食物及有关工具、设备和现场采取临时控制措施，开展现场卫生学和流行病学调查及采取其他处置措施。

第三章 组织管理

第十六条 省级卫生行政部门根据重大活动食品卫生监督工作要求，负责组织落实重大活动食品卫生监督任务。主办单位应保障重大活动食品卫生监督监测所需的工作条件，提供相应工作支持。

第十七条 重大活动期间，卫生行政部门、活动主办单位、活动接待单位应建立有效的食品卫生监督信息沟通机制。

第十八条 省级卫生行政部门应将重大活动期间的食品卫生监督监测结果、食物中毒等突发公共卫生事件向同级人民政府报告，同时告知重大活动主办单位，涉及保密内容的应遵守有关规定。

第十九条 省级卫生行政部门应建立管辖区域内重大活动接待单位基础信息数据库，包括接待单位卫生资质、条件设施、安全标准、操作规范、卫生培训、实验室设置等内容。

第四章 附 则

第二十条 省级以下卫生行政部门重大活动食品卫生监督参照本规范执行。

第二十一条 本规范由卫生部负责解释。

第二十二条 本规范自公布之日起实施。

国家重大食品安全事故应急预案

（国务院 2006年2月26日）

一、总 则

1. 工作目的 建立健全应对突发重大食品安全事故的救助体系和运行机制，规范和指导应急处理工作，有效预防、积极应对、及时控制重大食品安全事故，高效组织应急救援工作，最大限度地减少重大食品安全事故的危害，保障公众身体健康与生命安全，维护正常的社会秩序。

2. 编制依据 依据《中华人民共和国食品卫生法》、《中华人民共和国产品质量法》、《突发公共卫生事件应急条例》、《国家突发公共事件总体应急预案》和《国务院关于进一步加强食品安全工作的决定》，制定本预案。

3. 事故分级 按食品安全事故的性质、危害程度和涉及范围，将重大食品安全事故分为特别重大食品安全事故（Ⅰ级）、重大食品安全事故（Ⅱ级）、较大食品安全事故（Ⅲ级）和一般食品安全事故（Ⅳ级）四级。

4. 适用范围 在食物（食品）种植、养殖、生产加工、包装、仓储、运输、流通、消费等环节中发生食源性疾患，造成社会公众大量病亡或者可能对人体健康构成潜在的重大危害，并造成严重社会影响的重大食品安全事故适用本预案。

5. 工作原则 按照“全国统一领导、地方政府负责、部门指导协调、各方联合行动”的食品安全工作原则，根据食品安全事故的范围、性质和危害程度，对重大食品安全事故实行分级管理；有关部门按照本预案规定，落实各自的职责。坚持群防群控，加强日常监测，及时分析、评估和预警。对可能引发的重大食品安全事故，要做到早发现、早报告、早控制。采用先进科学技术，充分发挥专家作用，实行科学民主决策，依法规范应急救援工作，确保应急预案的科学性、权威性和可操作性。对重大食品安全事故要作出快速反应，及时启动应急预案，严格控制事故发展，有效开展应急救援工作，做好重大食品安全事故的善后处理及整改督查工作。

二、应急处理指挥机构

1. 国家重大食品安全事故应急指挥部 特别重大食品安全事故发生后，根据需要成立国家重大食品安全事故应急指挥部（以下简称“国家应急指挥部”），负责对全国重大食品安全事故应急处理工作的统一领导和指挥。国家应急指挥部办公室设在食品药品监管局。国家应急指挥部成员单位根据重大食品安全事故的性质和应急处理工作的需要确定。

2. 地方各级应急指挥部 重大食品安全事故发生后，事故发生地县级以上地方人民政府应当按事故级别成立重大食品安全事故应急指挥部，在上级应急指挥机构的指导和本级人民政府的领导下，组织和指挥本地区的重大食品安全事故应急救援工作。重大食品安全事故应急指挥部由本级政府有关部门组成，其日常办事机构设在食品安全综合监管部门。

3. 重大食品安全事故日常管理机构　食品药品监管局负责国家重大食品安全事故的日常监管工作。地方各级食品安全综合监管部门，要结合本地实际，负责本行政区域内重大食品安全事故应急救援的组织、协调以及管理工作。

4. 专家咨询委员会　各级食品安全综合监管部门建立重大食品安全事故专家库，在重大食品安全事故发生后，从专家库中确定相关专业专家，组建重大食品安全事故专家咨询委员会对重大食品安全事故应急工作提出咨询和建议，进行技术指导。

三、监测、预警与报告

（一）监测系统

国家建立统一的重大食品安全事故监测、报告网络体系，加强食品安全信息管理和综合利用，构建各部门间信息沟通平台，实现互联互通和资源共享。建立畅通的信息监测和通报网络体系，形成统一、科学的食品安全信息评估和预警指标体系，及时研究分析食品安全形势，对食品安全问题做到早发现、早预防、早整治、早解决。设立全国统一的举报电话。加强对监测工作的管理和监督，保证监测质量。

（二）预警系统

1. 加强日常监管　卫生、工商、质检、农业、商务、海关、环保、教育等部门应当按照各自职责，加强对重点品种、重点环节、重点场所，尤其是高风险食品种植、养殖、生产、加工、包装、贮藏、经营、消费等环节的食品安全日常监管；建立健全重大食品安全信息数据库和信息报告系统，及时分析对公众健康的危害程度、可能的发展趋势，及时作出预警，并保障系统的有效运行。

2. 建立通报制度

（1）通报范围：a. 对公众健康造成或者可能造成严重损害的重大食品安全事故；b. 涉及人数较多的群体性食物中毒或者出现死亡病例的重大食品安全事故。

（2）通报方式：a. 接到重大食品安全事故报告后，应当在2小时内向与事故有关地区的食品安全综合监管部门和国务院有关部门通报，有蔓延趋势的还应向地方各级食品安全综合监管部门通报，加强预警预防工作。b. 根据重大食品安全事故危险源监控信息，对可能引发的重大食品安全事故的险情，食品药品监管部门应当及时通报，必要时及时上报。

涉及港、澳、台地区人员或者外国公民，或者事故可能影响到境外，及时向香港、澳门、台湾地区有关机构或者有关国家通报。

3. 建立举报制度　任何单位和个人有权向国务院有关部门举报重大食品安全事故和隐患，以及相关责任部门、单位、人员不履行或者不按规定履行食品安全事故监管职责的行为。国务院有关部门接到举报后，应当及时组织或者通报有关部门，对举报事项进行调查处理。

4. 应急准备和预防　及时对可能导致重大食品安全事故信息进行分析，按照应急预案的程序及时研究确定应对措施。接到可能导致重大食品安全事故的信息后，应密切关注事态发展，并按照预案做好应急准备和预防工作；事态严重时及时上报，做好应急准备工作。做好可能引发重大食品安全事故信息的分析、预警工作。

（三）报告制度

食品药品监管部门会同有关部门建立、健全重大食品安全事故报告系统。县级以上地方人民政府食品安全综合监管部门应当按照重大食品安全事故报告的有关规定，主动监测，按规定报告。

1. 重大食品安全事故发生（发现）单位报告　重大食品安全事故发生（发现）后，事故现场有关人员应当立即报告单位负责人，单位负责人接到报告后，应当立即向当地政府、食品安全综合监管部门及有关部门报告，也可以直接向食品药品监管局或者省级食品安全综合监管部门报告。

2. 报告范围

（1）对公众健康造成或者可能造成严重损害的重大食品安全事故；

（2）涉及人数较多的群体性食物中毒或者出现死亡病例的重大食品安全事故。

3. 下级向上级报告　地方人民政府和食品安全综合监管部门接到重大食品安全事故报告后，应当立即向上级人民政府和上级食品安全综合监管部门报告，并在2小时内报告至省（自治区、直辖市）人民政府。地方人民政府和食品安全综合监管部门也可以直接向国务院和食品药品监管局以及相关部门报告。食品药品监管局和相关部门、事故发生地的省（自治区、直辖市）人民政府在接到重大食品安全事故报告后，应当在2小时内向国务院报告。

4. 责任报告单位

（1）食品种植、养殖、生产、加工、流通企业及餐饮单位；

（2）食品检验机构、科研院所以及与食品安全有关的单位；

(3) 重大食品安全事故发生（发现）单位；

(4) 地方各级食品安全综合监管部门和有关部门。

5. 责任报告人

(1) 行使职责的地方各级食品安全综合监管部门和相关部门的工作人员；

(2) 从事食品行业的工作人员；

(3) 消费者。

任何单位和个人对重大食品安全事故不得瞒报、迟报、谎报或者授意他人瞒报、迟报、谎报，不得阻碍他人报告。

6. 报告时限要求　事故发生地人民政府或有关部门应在知悉重大食品安全事故后1小时内作出初次报告；根据事故处理的进程或者上级的要求随时作出阶段报告；在事故处理结束后10日内作出总结报告。

7. 初次报告　应尽可能报告事故发生的时间、地点、单位、危害程度、死亡人数、事故报告单位及报告时间、报告单位联系人员及联系方式、事故发生原因的初步判断、事故发生后采取的措施及事故控制情况等，如有可能应当报告事故的简要经过。

8. 阶段报告　既要报告新发生的情况，也要对初次报告的情况进行补充和修正，包括事故的发展与变化、处置进程、事故原因等。

9. 总结报告　包括重大食品安全事故鉴定结论，对事故的处理工作进行总结，分析事故原因和影响因素，提出今后对类似事故的防范和处置建议。

四、重大食品安全事故的应急响应

(一) 分级响应

Ⅰ级应急响应由国家应急指挥部或办公室组织实施。其中，重大食物中毒的应急响应与处置按《国家突发公共卫生事件应急预案》实施。当组织实施Ⅰ级应急响应行动时，事发地人民政府应当按照相应的预案全力以赴地组织救援，并及时报告救援工作进展情况。

Ⅱ级以下应急响应行动的组织实施由省级人民政府决定。各省（自治区、直辖市）人民政府在国家应急指挥部的统一领导和指挥下，结合本地区的实际情况，组织协调市（地）、县（区）人民政府开展重大食品安全事故的应急处理工作。地方各级人民政府根据事故的严重程度启动相应的应急预案，超出本级应急救援处置能力时，及时报请上一级政府和有关部门启动相应的应急预案。

重大食品安全事故发生后，地方各级人民政府及有关部门应当根据事故发生情况，及时采取必要的应急措施，做好应急处理工作。

1. 特别重大食品安全事故的应急响应（Ⅰ级）

(1) 特别重大食品安全事故发生后，国家应急指挥部办公室应当及时向国家应急指挥部报告基本情况、事态发展和救援进展等。

(2) 向指挥部成员单位通报事故情况，组织有关成员单位立即进行调查确认，对事故进行评估，根据评估确认的结果，启动国家重大食品安全事故应急预案，组织应急救援。

(3) 组织指挥部成员单位迅速到位，立即启动事故处理机构的工作；迅速开展应急救援和组织新闻发布工作，并部署省（自治区、直辖市）相关部门开展应急救援工作。

(4) 开通与事故发生地的省级应急救援指挥机构、现场应急救援指挥部、相关专业应急救援指挥机构的通信联系，随时掌握事故发展动态。

(5) 根据有关部门和专家的建议，通知有关应急救援机构随时待命，为地方或专业应急救援指挥机构提供技术支持。

(6) 派出有关人员和专家赶赴现场参加、指导现场应急救援，必要时协调专业应急力量救援。

(7) 组织协调事故应急救援工作，必要时召集国家应急指挥部有关成员和专家一同协调指挥。

2. 重大食品安全事故的应急响应（Ⅱ级）

(1) 省级人民政府应急响应　省级人民政府根据省级食品安全综合监管部门的建议和食品安全事故应急处理的需要，成立食品安全事故应急处理指挥部，负责行政区域内重大食品安全事故应急处理的统一领导和指挥；决定启动重大食品安全事故应急处置工作。

(2) 省级食品安全综合监管部门应急响应接到重大食品安全事故报告后，省级食品安全综合监管部门应当立即进行调查确认，对事故进行评估，根据评估确认的结果，按规定向上级报告事故情况；提出启动省级重大食品安全事故应急指挥部工作程序，提出应急处理工作建议；及时向其他有关部门、毗邻或可能涉及的省（自治区、直辖市）相关部门通报情况；有关工作小组立即启动，组织、协调、落实各项应急措施；指导、部署市（地）相关部门开展应急救援工作。

(3) 省级以下地方人民政府应急响应　重大食品安全事故发生地人民政府及有关部门在省级人民政府或者省级应急指挥部的统一指挥下，按照要求认真履行职责，落实有关工作。

(4) 食品药品监管局应急响应　加强对省级食品

安全综合监管部门的督导，根据需要会同国务院有关部门赴事发地指导督办应急处理工作。

3. 较大食品安全事故的应急响应（Ⅲ级）

（1）市（地）级人民政府应急响应 市（地）级人民政府负责组织发生在本行政区域内的较大食品安全事故的统一领导和指挥，根据食品安全综合监管部门的报告和建议，决定启动较大食品安全事故的应急处置工作。

（2）市（地）级食品安全综合监管部门应急响应 接到较大食品安全事故报告后，市（地）级食品安全综合监管部门应当立即进行调查确认，对事故进行评估，根据评估确认的结果，按规定向上级报告事故情况；提出启动市（地）级较大食品安全事故应急救援工作，提出应急处理工作建议，及时向其他有关部门、毗邻或可能涉及的市（地）相关部门通报有关情况；相应工作小组立即启动工作，组织、协调、落实各项应急措施；指导、部署相关部门开展应急救援工作。

（3）省级食品安全综合监管部门应急响应 加强对市（地）级食品安全综合监管部门应急救援工作的指导、监督，协助解决应急救援工作中的困难。

4. 一般食品安全事故的应急响应（Ⅳ级） 一般食品安全事故发生后，县级人民政府负责组织有关部门开展应急救援工作。县级食品安全综合监管部门接到事故报告后，应当立即组织调查、确认和评估，及时采取措施控制事态发展；按规定向同级人民政府报告，提出是否启动应急救援预案，有关事故情况应当立即向相关部门报告、通报。市（地）级食品安全综合监管部门应当对事故应急处理工作给予指导、监督和有关方面的支持。

5. 响应的升级与降级 当重大食品安全事故随时间发展进一步加重，食品安全事故危害特别严重，并有蔓延扩大的趋势，情况复杂难以控制时，应当上报指挥部审定，及时提升预警和反应级别；对事故危害已迅速消除，并不会进一步扩散的，应当上报指挥部审定，相应降低反应级别或者撤销预警。

（二）指挥协调

进入Ⅰ级响应后，国家应急指挥部办公室及有关专业应急救援机构立即按照预案组织相关应急救援力量，配合地方政府组织实施应急救援。国家应急指挥部办公室根据重大食品安全事故的情况协调有关部门及其应急机构、救援队伍和事发地毗邻省（自治区、直辖市）人民政府应急救援指挥机构，相关机构按照各自应急预案提供增援或保障，有关应急队伍在现场应急救援指挥部统一指挥下，密切配合，共同实施救援和紧急处理行动。事发地省级人民政府负责成立现场应急指挥机构，在国家应急指挥部或者指挥部工作组的指挥或指导下，负责现场应急处置工作；现场应急指挥机构成立前，先期到达的各应急救援队伍和事故单位的救援力量必须迅速、有效地实施先期处置；事故发生地人民政府负责协调，全力控制事态发展，防止次生、衍生和耦合事故（事件）发生，果断控制或切断事故危害链。重大食品安全事故应急预案启动后，上一级应急指挥部办公室应当指导事故发生地人民政府实施重大食品安全事故应急处理工作。

（三）紧急处置

现场处置主要依靠本行政区域内的应急处置力量。重大食品安全事故发生后，发生事故的单位和当地人民政府按照应急预案迅速采取措施。事态出现急剧恶化的情况时，现场应急救援指挥部在充分考虑专家和有关方面意见的基础上，及时制定紧急处置方案，依法采取紧急处置措施。

（四）响应终结

重大食品安全事故隐患或相关危险因素消除后，重大食品安全事故应急救援终结，应急救援队伍撤离现场。应急指挥部办公室组织有关专家进行分析论证，经现场检测评价确无危害和风险后，提出终止应急响应的建议，报应急指挥部批准宣布应急响应结束。

五、后期处置

1. 善后处置 省级人民政府负责组织重大食品安全事故的善后处置工作，包括人员安置、补偿，征用物资补偿，污染物收集、清理与处理等事项。尽快消除事故影响，妥善安置和慰问受害和受影响人员，尽快恢复正常秩序，保证社会稳定。重大食品安全事故发生后，保险机构及时开展应急救援人员保险受理和受灾人员保险理赔工作。造成重大食品安全事故的责任单位和责任人应当按照有关规定对受害人给予赔偿。

2. 责任追究 对在重大食品安全事故的预防、通报、报告、调查、控制和处理过程中，有玩忽职守、失职、渎职等行为的，依据有关法律法规追究有关责任人的责任。

3. 总结报告 重大食品安全事故善后处置工作结束后，地方应急救援指挥部总结分析应急救援经验教训，提出改进应急救援工作的建议，完成应急救援总结报告并及时上报。

六、应急保障

1. 信息保障 食品安全综合监管部门建立重大

食品安全事故的专项信息报告系统。重大食品安全事故发生后，应急指挥部应当及时向社会发布食品安全事故信息。

2. 医疗保障　重大食品安全事故造成人员伤害的，卫生系统应急救援工作应当立即启动，救治人员应当立即赶赴现场，开展医疗救治工作。

3. 人员保障　应急指挥部办公室负责组织食品安全监察专员及相关部门人员、专家参加事故处理。

4. 技术保障　重大食品安全事故的技术鉴定工作必须由有资质的检测机构承担。当发生重大食品安全事故时，受重大食品安全事故指挥部或者食品安全综合监管部门委托，立即采集样本，按有关标准要求实施检测，为重大食品安全事故定性提供科学依据。

5. 物资保障　各级人民政府应当保障重大食品安全事故应急处理所需设施、设备和物资，保障应急物资储备，提供应急救援资金，所需经费列入同级人民政府财政预算。

6. 演习演练　各级人民政府及有关部门要按照“统一规划、分类实施、分级负责、突出重点、适应需求”的原则，采取定期和不定期相结合形式，组织开展突发重大食品安全事故的应急演习演练。食品药品监管局会同国务院有关部门指导突发重大食品安全事故的应急救援演习演练工作。组织全国性和区域性突发重大食品安全事故的应急演习演练，以检验和强化应急准备、协调和应急响应能力，并对演习演练结果进行总结和评估，进一步完善应急预案。省级食品安全综合监管部门要根据本地区实际情况和工作需要，结合应急预案，统一组织突发重大食品安全事故的应急演习演练。有关企事业单位应当根据自身特点，定期或不定期组织本单位的应急救援演习演练。

7. 宣教培训　各级人民政府及其相关部门应当加强对广大消费者进行食品安全知识的教育，提高消费者的风险和责任意识，正确引导消费。

七、附　则

（一）名词术语

食品安全：是指食品中不应包含有可能损害或威胁人体健康的有毒、有害物质或不安全因素，不可导致消费者急性、慢性中毒或感染疾病，不能产生危及消费者及其后代健康的隐患。

食品安全的范围：包括食品数量安全、食品质量安全、食品卫生安全。本预案涉及到的食品安全主要是指食品质量卫生安全。

食源性疾患：亦称食源性疾病。凡是致病因素通过食物进入人体，使人体罹患感染性或中毒性疾病的，都称之为食源性疾患。

高风险食品：可能发生较高程度污染和危害的食品。

本预案有关数量的表述中，“以上”含本数，“以下”不含本数。

（二）预案实施时间

本预案自印发之日起实施。

出入境口岸食品卫生监督管理规定

（国家质量监督检验检疫总局　2006 年 3 月 1 日）

第一章　总　则

第一条　为加强出入境口岸食品卫生监督管理，保证出入境口岸食品卫生安全，保障公众健康，根据《中华人民共和国国境卫生检疫法》及其实施细则、《中华人民共和国食品卫生法》等有关法律法规的规定，制定本规定。

第二条　本规定适用于对在出入境口岸从事食品生产经营单位以及为出入境交通工具提供食品、饮用水服务的口岸食品生产经营单位（以下简称食品生产经营单位）的卫生监督管理。

第三条　国家质量监督检验检疫总局（以下简称国家质检总局）主管全国出入境口岸食品卫生监督管理工作。

国家质检总局设在各地的出入境检验检疫机构（以下简称检验检疫机构）负责本辖区出入境口岸食品卫生监督管理工作。

第四条　检验检疫机构对食品生产经营单位实行卫生许可管理；对在出入境口岸内以及出入境交通工具上的食品、饮用水从业人员（以下简称从业人员）实行健康许可管理。

检验检疫机构对口岸食品卫生监督管理实行风险分析和分级管理。

第五条　检验检疫机构按照国家有关食品卫生标准对出入境口岸食品进行卫生监督管理。尚未制定国家标准的，可以按照国家质检总局指定的相关标准进行卫生监督管理。

第二章　食品生产经营单位的许可管理

第六条　食品生产经营单位在新建、扩建、改建时应当接受其所在地检验检疫机构的卫生监督。

第七条　食品生产经营单位从事口岸食品生产经营活动前，应当向其所在地检验检疫机构申请办理《中华人民共和国国境口岸食品生产经营单位卫生许可证》（以下简称《卫生许可证》，见附件1）。

第八条　申请《卫生许可证》的食品生产经营单位应当具备以下卫生条件：

（一）具备与食品生产经营活动相适应的经营场所、卫生环境、卫生设施及设备；

（二）餐饮业应当制定符合餐饮加工、经营过程卫生安全要求的操作规范以及保证所加工、经营餐饮质量的管理制度和责任制度；

（三）具有健全的卫生管理组织和制度；

（四）从业人员未患有有碍食品卫生安全的传染病；

（五）从业人员具备与所从事的食品生产经营工作相适应的食品卫生安全常识。

第九条　食品生产经营单位在申请办理《卫生许可证》时，须向检验检疫机构提交以下材料：

（一）《卫生许可证》申请书；

（二）《营业执照》复印件（取得后补交）；

（三）内部卫生管理组织、制度和机构资料；

（四）从业人员《健康证明书》和卫生知识培训合格证明；

（五）生产经营场所平面图和生产工艺流程图；

（六）生产原料组成成分、生产设备资料、卫生设施和产品包装材料说明；

（七）食品生产单位提交生产用水卫生检验报告；

（八）产品卫生标准、产品标识，生产产品的卫生检验结果以及安全卫生控制措施；

（九）其他需要提交的有关资料。

第十条　检验检疫机构按规定要求对申请材料进行审核，确定材料是否齐全、是否符合有关规定要求，作出受理或者不受理的决定，并出具书面凭证。对提交的材料不齐全或者不规范的，应当当场或者在受理后5日内一次告知申请人补正。逾期不告知的，自收到申请材料之日起即为受理。检验检疫机构受理食品生产经营单位申请后，对申请材料进行审核，并按照国家质检总局的规定进行现场卫生许可考核及量化评分。检验检疫机构根据材料审核、现场考核及评分的结果，自受理之日起20日内，对食品生产经营单位作出准予许可或者不予许可的决定（现场考核时间除外，现场考核时间最长不超过1个月），并应当自作出决定之日起10日内向申请人颁发或者送达卫生许可证件。《卫生许可证》有效期为1年。食品生产经营单位需要延续《卫生许可证》有效期的，应当在《卫生许可证》期满前30日内向检验检疫机构提出申请。

第十一条　在《卫生许可证》有效期内，食品生产经营单位变更生产经营项目、变更法人、变更单位名称、迁移厂址、改建、扩建、新建项目时，应当向作出卫生许可决定的检验检疫机构申报。

第十二条　食品生产经营单位在停业时，应当到作出卫生许可决定的检验检疫机构办理注销手续，缴销《卫生许可证》。

第十三条　食品生产经营单位在向异地食品生产经营单位提供食品及食品用产品时，可凭有效的《卫生许可证》到该地的检验检疫机构备案。

第三章　从业人员卫生管理

第十四条　检验检疫机构对从业人员实行健康许可管理。从业人员每年必须到检验检疫机构认可的医疗卫生机构进行健康检查，新参加工作和临时参加工作的从业人员上岗前必须进行健康检查。

第十五条　从业人员应当向检验检疫机构申请《健康证明书》。申请办理《健康证明书》时，应当提交以下材料：

（一）《健康证》申请书；

（二）有效的身份证明；

（三）检验检疫机构认可的医疗卫生机构出具的体检报告。

检验检疫机构按照国家质检总局的有关规定对上述材料进行审查，对经审查合格的从业人员，颁发《健康证明书》。《健康证明书》有效期为1年。取得《健康证明书》的人员，方可从事口岸食品生产经营工作。

第十六条　检验检疫机构负责监督、指导和协助本口岸食品生产经营单位的人员培训和考核工作。从业人员应当具备食品卫生常识和食品法律、法规知识。

第十七条　检验检疫机构将健康检查合格和卫生

知识培训合格的结果制作成胸卡（见附件2）。从业人员工作时应当佩带胸卡以备检查。

第四章 食品卫生监督管理

第十八条 食品生产经营单位应当健全本单位的食品卫生管理制度，配备专职或者兼职的食品卫生管理人员，加强对所生产经营食品的检验工作。

第十九条 食品生产经营单位应当建立进货检查验收制度。采购食品及原料时，应当按照国家有关规定索取检验合格证或者化验单，查阅卫生许可证。向出入境交通工具提供食品的单位应当建立进货检查验收制度，同时应当建立销售食品及原料单位的卫生档案。检验检疫机构定期对采购的食品及原料进行抽查，并对其卫生档案进行审核。

卫生档案应当包括下列资料：

（一）营业执照（复印件）；

（二）生产许可证（复印件）；

（三）卫生许可证（复印件）；

（四）使用进口原材料者，需提供进口食品卫生证书（复印件）；

（五）供货合同或者意向书；

（六）相关批次的检验合格证或者化验单；

（七）产品清单及其他需要的有关资料。

第二十条 检验检疫机构根据法律、法规、规章以及卫生规范的要求对食品生产经营单位进行监督检查，监督检查主要包括：

（一）卫生许可证、从业人员健康证及卫生知识培训情况；

（二）卫生管理组织和管理制度情况；

（三）环境卫生、个人卫生、卫生设施、设备布局和工艺流程情况；

（四）食品生产、采集、收购、加工、贮存、运输、陈列、供应、销售等情况；

（五）食品原料、半成品、成品等的感官性状及食品添加剂使用情况以及索证情况；

（六）食品卫生检验情况；

（七）对食品的卫生质量、餐具、饮具及盛放直接入口食品的容器进行现场检查，进行必要的采样检验；

（八）供水的卫生情况；

（九）使用洗涤剂和消毒剂的卫生情况；

（十）医学媒介生物防治情况。

第二十一条 检验检疫机构对食品生产经营单位进行日常卫生监督，应当由2名以上口岸卫生监督员根据现场检查情况，规范填写评分表。评分表须经被监督单位负责人或者有关人员核实无误后，由口岸卫生监督员和被监督单位负责人或者有关人员共同签字，修改之处由被监督单位负责人或者有关人员签名或者印章覆盖。被监督单位负责人或者有关人员拒绝签字的，口岸卫生监督员应当在评分表上注明拒签事由。

第二十二条 检验检疫机构应当根据食品卫生检验的有关规定采集样品，并及时送检。采样时应当向被采样单位或者个人出具采样凭证（见附件3）。

第二十三条 向出入境交通工具供应食品、饮用水的食品生产经营单位，供应食品、饮用水前应当向检验检疫机构申报，经检验检疫机构对供货产品登记记录、相关批次的检疫合格证和检验报告以及其他必要的有关资料等审核无误后，方可供应食品和饮用水。

第二十四条 航空食品生产经营单位应当积极推行生产企业良好操作规范（GMP）、危害分析与关键控制点（HACCP）等质量控制与保证体系，提高食品卫生安全水平。

第五章 风险分析与分级管理

第二十五条 检验检疫机构依照有关法律、行政法规和标准的规定，结合现场监督情况，对出入境口岸食品实行风险分析和分级管理。

第二十六条 检验检疫机构应当组织技术力量，对口岸食源性疾病发生、流行以及分布进行监测，对口岸食源性疾病流行趋势进行预测，并提出预防控制对策，开展风险分析。

第二十七条 检验检疫机构根据对口岸食品生产经营单位进行卫生许可审查和日常卫生监督检查的结果，对不同类型的食品生产经营单位实施分级管理。

（一）卫生许可审查和日常卫生监督检查均为良好的单位，评为A级单位。检验检疫机构对A级单位每月监督1次；

（二）卫生许可审查和日常卫生监督检查有一个良好的，评为B级单位，检验检疫机构对B级单位每月监督2次；

（三）卫生许可审查和日常卫生监督检查均为一般的，评为C级单位，检验检疫机构对C级单位每月监督4次；

（四）卫生许可审查结论为差，或者卫生许可审查结论为良好，但是日常卫生监督较差的，评为D级单位，检验检疫机构对D级单位不予卫生许可，或者次年不予续延卫生许可。

第二十八条 检验检疫机构对不同级别的单位进

行动态监督管理，根据风险分析和日常监督情况，每年1次进行必要的升级或者降级调整（见附件4）。

第二十九条 检验检疫机构应当根据国家质检总局发布的食品预警通报，及时采取有效的措施，防止相关食品向出入境口岸及出入境交通工具供应。

第三十条 出入境口岸发生食物中毒、食品污染、食源性疾患等事故时，检验检疫机构应当启动《出入境口岸食物中毒应急处理预案》，及时处置，并根据预案要求向相关部门通报。

第六章 罚 则

第三十一条 口岸食品生产经营单位有下列情况之一的，检验检疫机构依照《中华人民共和国国境卫生检疫法》及其实施细则等法律法规的相关规定予以行政处罚：

（一）未取得《卫生许可证》或者伪造《卫生许可证》从事食品生产经营活动的；

（二）涂改、出借《卫生许可证》的；

（三）允许未获得《健康证明书》的从业人员上岗的，或者对患有有碍食品卫生安全的传染病的从业人员不按规定调离的；

（四）拒不接受检验检疫机构卫生监督的；

（五）其他违反法律法规或者有关规定的。

第三十二条 从业人员有下列情况之一的，由检验检疫机构依照《中华人民共和国国境卫生检疫法》及其实施细则等法律法规的相关规定予以行政处罚：

（一）未取得《健康证明书》而从事食品生产经营活动的；

（二）伪造体检报告的；

（三）其他违反法律法规或者有关规定的。

第三十三条 检验检疫机构工作人员滥用职权，徇私舞弊，玩忽职守的，根据情节轻重，给予行政处分或者依法追究刑事责任。

第七章 附 则

第三十四条 本规定由国家质检总局负责解释。

第三十五条 本规定自2006年4月1日起施行。

（注：附件略）

中华人民共和国农产品质量安全法

（2006年4月29日第十届全国人民代表大会常务委员会第二十一次会议通过）

第一章 总 则

第一条 为保障农产品质量安全，维护公众健康，促进农业和农村经济发展，制定本法。

第二条 本法所称农产品，是指来源于农业的初级产品，即在农业活动中获得的植物、动物、微生物及其产品。本法所称农产品质量安全，是指农产品质量符合保障人的健康、安全的要求。

第三条 县级以上人民政府农业行政主管部门负责农产品质量安全的监督管理工作；县级以上人民政府有关部门按照职责分工，负责农产品质量安全的有关工作。

第四条 县级以上人民政府应当将农产品质量安全管理工作纳入本级国民经济和社会发展规划，并安排农产品质量安全经费，用于开展农产品质量安全工作。

第五条 县级以上地方人民政府统一领导、协调本行政区域内的农产品质量安全工作，并采取措施，建立健全农产品质量安全服务体系，提高农产品质量安全水平。

第六条 国务院农业行政主管部门应当设立由有关方面专家组成的农产品质量安全风险评估专家委员会，对可能影响农产品质量安全的潜在危害进行风险分析和评估。国务院农业行政主管部门应当根据农产品质量安全风险评估结果采取相应的管理措施，并将农产品质量安全风险评估结果及时通报国务院有关部门。

第七条 国务院农业行政主管部门和省、自治区、直辖市人民政府农业行政主管部门应当按照职责权限，发布有关农产品质量安全状况信息。

第八条 国家引导、推广农产品标准化生产，鼓励和支持生产优质农产品，禁止生产、销售不符合国家规定的农产品质量安全标准的农产品。

第九条 国家支持农产品质量安全科学技术研究，推行科学的质量安全管理方法，推广先进安全的生产技术。

第十条 各级人民政府及有关部门应当加强农产品质量安全知识的宣传，提高公众的农产品质量安全意识，引导农产品生产者、销售者加强质量安全管理，保障农产品消费安全。

第二章 农产品质量安全标准

第十一条 国家建立健全农产品质量安全标准体系。农产品质量安全标准是强制性的技术规范。农产品质量安全标准的制定和发布，依照有关法律、行政法规的规定执行。

第十二条 制定农产品质量安全标准应当充分考虑农产品质量安全风险评估结果，并听取农产品生产者、销售者和消费者的意见，保障消费安全。

第十三条 农产品质量安全标准应当根据科学技术发展水平以及农产品质量安全的需要，及时修订。

第十四条 农产品质量安全标准由农业行政主管部门商有关部门组织实施。

第三章 农产品产地

第十五条 县级以上地方人民政府农业行政主管部门按照保障农产品质量安全的要求，根据农产品品种特性和生产区域大气、土壤、水体中有毒有害物质状况等因素，认为不适宜特定农产品生产的，提出禁止生产的区域，报本级人民政府批准后公布。具体办法由国务院农业行政主管部门商国务院环境保护行政主管部门制定。农产品禁止生产区域的调整，依照前款规定的程序办理。

第十六条 县级以上人民政府应当采取措施，加强农产品基地建设，改善农产品的生产条件。县级以上人民政府农业行政主管部门应当采取措施，推进保障农产品质量安全的标准化生产综合示范区、示范农场、养殖小区和无规定动植物疫病区的建设。

第十七条 禁止在有毒有害物质超过规定标准的区域生产、捕捞、采集食用农产品和建立农产品生产基地。

第十八条 禁止违反法律、法规的规定向农产品产地排放或者倾倒废水、废气、固体废物或者其他有毒有害物质。农业生产用水和用作肥料的固体废物，应当符合国家规定的标准。

第十九条 农产品生产者应当合理使用化肥、农药、兽药、农用薄膜等化工产品，防止对农产品产地造成污染。

第四章 农产品生产

第二十条 国务院农业行政主管部门和省、自治区、直辖市人民政府农业行政主管部门应当制定保障农产品质量安全的生产技术要求和操作规程。县级以上人民政府农业行政主管部门应当加强对农产品生产的指导。

第二十一条 对可能影响农产品质量安全的农药、兽药、饲料和饲料添加剂、肥料、兽医器械，依照有关法律、行政法规的规定实行许可制度。国务院农业行政主管部门和省、自治区、直辖市人民政府农业行政主管部门应当定期对可能危及农产品质量安全的农药、兽药、饲料和饲料添加剂、肥料等农业投入品进行监督抽查，并公布抽查结果。

第二十二条 县级以上人民政府农业行政主管部门应当加强对农业投入品使用的管理和指导，建立健全农业投入品的安全使用制度。

第二十三条 农业科研教育机构和农业技术推广机构应当加强对农产品生产者质量安全知识和技能的培训。

第二十四条 农产品生产企业和农民专业合作经济组织应当建立农产品生产记录，如实记载下列事项：

（一）使用农业投入品的名称、来源、用法、用量和使用、停用的日期；

（二）动物疫病、植物病虫草害的发生和防治情况；

（三）收获、屠宰或者捕捞的日期。

农产品生产记录应当保存二年。禁止伪造农产品生产记录。国家鼓励其他农产品生产者建立农产品生产记录。

第二十五条 农产品生产者应当按照法律、行政法规和国务院农业行政主管部门的规定，合理使用农业投入品，严格执行农业投入品使用安全间隔期或者休药期的规定，防止危及农产品质量安全。禁止在农产品生产过程中使用国家明令禁止使用的农业投入品。

第二十六条 农产品生产企业和农民专业合作经济组织，应当自行或者委托检测机构对农产品质量安全状况进行检测；经检测不符合农产品质量安全标准的农产品，不得销售。

第二十七条 农民专业合作经济组织和农产品行业协会对其成员应当及时提供生产技术服务，建立农产品质量安全管理制度，健全农产品质量安全控制体系，加强自律管理。

第五章 农产品包装和标识

第二十八条 农产品生产企业、农民专业合作经济组织以及从事农产品收购的单位或者个人销售的农产品，按照规定应当包装或者附加标识的，须经包装或者附加标识后方可销售。包装物或者标识上应当按照规定标明产品的品名、产地、生产者、生产日期、保质期、产品质量等级等内容；使用添加剂的，还应当按照规定标明添加剂的名称。具体办法由国务院农业行政主管部门制定。

第二十九条 农产品在包装、保鲜、贮存、运输中所使用的保鲜剂、防腐剂、添加剂等材料，应当符合国家有关强制性的技术规范。

第三十条 属于农业转基因生物的农产品，应当按照农业转基因生物安全管理的有关规定进行标识。

第三十一条 依法需要实施检疫的动植物及其产品，应当附具检疫合格标志、检疫合格证明。

第三十二条 销售的农产品必须符合农产品质量安全标准，生产者可以申请使用无公害农产品标志。农产品质量符合国家规定的有关优质农产品标准的，生产者可以申请使用相应的农产品质量标志。禁止冒用前款规定的农产品质量标志。

第六章 监督检查

第三十三条 有下列情形之一的农产品，不得销售：

（一）含有国家禁止使用的农药、兽药或者其他化学物质的；

（二）农药、兽药等化学物质残留或者含有的重金属等有毒有害物质不符合农产品质量安全标准的；

（三）含有的致病性寄生虫、微生物或者生物毒素不符合农产品质量安全标准的；

（四）使用的保鲜剂、防腐剂、添加剂等材料不符合国家有关强制性的技术规范的；

（五）其他不符合农产品质量安全标准的。

第三十四条 国家建立农产品质量安全监测制度。县级以上人民政府农业行政主管部门应当按照保障农产品质量安全的要求，制定并组织实施农产品质量安全监测计划，对生产中或者市场上销售的农产品进行监督抽查。监督抽查结果由国务院农业行政主管部门或者省、自治区、直辖市人民政府农业行政主管部门按照权限予以公布。监督抽查检测应当委托符合本法第三十五条规定条件的农产品质量安全检测机构进行，不得向被抽查人收取费用，抽取的样品不得超过国务院农业行政主管部门规定的数量。上级农业行政主管部门监督抽查的农产品，下级农业行政主管部门不得另行重复抽查。

第三十五条 农产品质量安全检测应当充分利用现有的符合条件的检测机构。从事农产品质量安全检测的机构，必须具备相应的检测条件和能力，由省级以上人民政府农业行政主管部门或者其授权的部门考核合格。具体办法由国务院农业行政主管部门制定。农产品质量安全检测机构应当依法经计量认证合格。

第三十六条 农产品生产者、销售者对监督抽查检测结果有异议的，可以自收到检测结果之日起5日内，向组织实施农产品质量安全监督抽查的农业行政主管部门或者其上级农业行政主管部门申请复检。采用国务院农业行政主管部门会同有关部门认定的快速检测方法进行农产品质量安全监督抽查检测，被抽查人对检测结果有异议的，可以自收到检测结果时起4小时内申请复检。复检不得采用快速检测方法。因检测结果错误给当事人造成损害的，依法承担赔偿责任。

第三十七条 农产品批发市场应当设立或者委托农产品质量安全检测机构，对进场销售的农产品质量安全状况进行抽查检测；发现不符合农产品质量安全标准的，应当要求销售者立即停止销售，并向农业行政主管部门报告。农产品销售企业对其销售的农产品，应当建立健全进货检查验收制度；经查验不符合农产品质量安全标准的，不得销售。

第三十八条 国家鼓励单位和个人对农产品质量安全进行社会监督。任何单位和个人都有权对违反本法的行为进行检举、揭发和控告。有关部门收到相关的检举、揭发和控告后，应当及时处理。

第三十九条 县级以上人民政府农业行政主管部门在农产品质量安全监督检查中，可以对生产、销售的农产品进行现场检查，调查了解农产品质量安全的有关情况，查阅、复制与农产品质量安全有关的记录和其他资料；对经检测不符合农产品质量安全标准的农产品，有权查封、扣押。

第四十条 发生农产品质量安全事故时，有关单位和个人应当采取控制措施，及时向所在地乡级人民政府和县级人民政府农业行政主管部门报告；收到报告的机关应当及时处理并报上一级人民政府和有关部门。发生重大农产品质量安全事故时，农业行政主管部门应当及时通报同级食品药品监督管理部门。

第四十一条 县级以上人民政府农业行政主管部

门在农产品质量安全监督管理中，发现有本法第三十三条所列情形之一的农产品，应当按照农产品质量安全责任追究制度的要求，查明责任人，依法予以处理或者提出处理建议。

第四十二条 进口的农产品必须按照国家规定的农产品质量安全标准进行检验；尚未制定有关农产品质量安全标准的，应当依法及时制定，未制定之前，可以参照国家有关部门指定的国外有关标准进行检验。

第七章 法律责任

第四十三条 农产品质量安全监督管理人员不依法履行监督职责，或者滥用职权的，依法给予行政处分。

第四十四条 农产品质量安全检测机构伪造检测结果的，责令改正，没收违法所得，并处5万元以上10万元以下罚款，对直接负责的主管人员和其他直接责任人员处1万元以上5万元以下罚款；情节严重的，撤销其检测资格；造成损害的，依法承担赔偿责任。农产品质量安全检测机构出具检测结果不实，造成损害的，依法承担赔偿责任；造成重大损害的，并撤销其检测资格。

第四十五条 违反法律、法规规定，向农产品产地排放或者倾倒废水、废气、固体废物或者其他有毒有害物质的，依照有关环境保护法律、法规的规定处罚；造成损害的，依法承担赔偿责任。

第四十六条 使用农业投入品违反法律、行政法规和国务院农业行政主管部门的规定的，依照有关法律、行政法规的规定处罚。

第四十七条 农产品生产企业、农民专业合作经济组织未建立或者未按照规定保存农产品生产记录的，或者伪造农产品生产记录的，责令限期改正；逾期不改正的，可以处2 000元以下罚款。

第四十八条 违反本法第二十八条规定，销售的农产品未按照规定进行包装、标识的，责令限期改正；逾期不改正的，可以处2 000元以下罚款。

第四十九条 有本法第三十三条第四项规定情形，使用的保鲜剂、防腐剂、添加剂等材料不符合国家有关强制性的技术规范的，责令停止销售，对被污染的农产品进行无害化处理，对不能进行无害化处理的予以监督销毁；没收违法所得，并处2 000元以上2万元以下罚款。

第五十条 农产品生产企业、农民专业合作经济组织销售的农产品有本法第三十三条第一项至第三项或者第五项所列情形之一的，责令停止销售，追回已经销售的农产品，对违法销售的农产品进行无害化处理或者予以监督销毁；没收违法所得，并处2 000元以上2万元以下罚款。农产品销售企业销售的农产品有前款所列情形的，依照前款规定处理、处罚。农产品批发市场中销售的农产品有第一款所列情形的对违法销售的农产品依照第一款规定处理，对农产品销售者依照第一款规定处罚。农产品批发市场违反本法第三十七条第一款规定的，责令改正，处2 000元以上2万元以下罚款。

第五十一条 违反本法第三十二条规定，冒用农产品质量标志的，责令改正，没收违法所得，并处2 000元以上2万元以下罚款。

第五十二条 本法第四十四条、第四十七条至第四十九条、第五十条第一款、第四款和第五十一条规定的处理、处罚，由县级以上人民政府农业行政主管部门决定；第五十条第二款、第三款规定的处理、处罚，由工商行政管理部门决定。法律对行政处罚及处罚机关有其他规定的，从其规定。但是，对同一违法行为不得重复处罚。

第五十三条 违反本法规定，构成犯罪的，依法追究刑事责任。

第五十四条 生产、销售本法第三十三条所列农产品，给消费者造成损害的，依法承担赔偿责任。农产品批发市场中销售的农产品有前款规定情形的，消费者可以向农产品批发市场要求赔偿；属于生产者、销售者责任的，农产品批发市场有权追偿。消费者也可以直接向农产品生产者、销售者要求赔偿。

第八章 附 则

第五十五条 生猪屠宰的管理按照国家有关规定执行。

第五十六条 本法自2006年11月1日起施行。

农产品包装和标识管理办法

（农业部　2006 年 10 月 17 日）

第一章　总　则

第一条　为规范农产品生产经营行为，加强农产品包装和标识管理，建立健全农产品可追溯制度，保障农产品质量安全，依据《中华人民共和国农产品质量安全法》，制定本办法。

第二条　农产品的包装和标识活动应当符合本办法规定。

第三条　农业部负责全国农产品包装和标识的监督管理工作。县级以上地方人民政府农业行政主管部门负责本行政区域内农产品包装和标识的监督管理工作。

第四条　国家支持农产品包装和标识科学研究，推行科学的包装方法，推广先进的标识技术。

第五条　县级以上人民政府农业行政主管部门应当将农产品包装和标识管理经费纳入年度预算。

第六条　县级以上人民政府农业行政主管部门对在农产品包装和标识工作中做出突出贡献的单位和个人，予以表彰和奖励。

第二章　农产品包装

第七条　农产品生产企业、农民专业合作经济组织以及从事农产品收购的单位或者个人，用于销售的下列农产品必须包装：

（一）获得无公害农产品、绿色食品、有机农产品等认证的农产品，但鲜活畜、禽、水产品除外。

（二）省级以上人民政府农业行政主管部门规定的其他需要包装销售的农产品。

符合规定包装的农产品拆包后直接向消费者销售的，可以不再另行包装。

第八条　农产品包装应当符合农产品储藏、运输、销售及保障安全的要求，便于拆卸和搬运。

第九条　包装农产品的材料和使用的保鲜剂、防腐剂、添加剂等物质必须符合国家强制性技术规范要求。包装农产品应当防止机械损伤和二次污染。

第三章　农产品标识

第十条　农产品生产企业、农民专业合作经济组织以及从事农产品收购的单位或者个人包装销售的农产品，应当在包装物上标注或者附加标识标明品名、产地、生产者或者销售者名称、生产日期。有分级标准或者使用添加剂的，还应当标明产品质量等级或者添加剂名称。未包装的农产品，应当采取附加标签、标识牌、标识带、说明书等形式标明农产品的品名、生产地、生产者或者销售者名称等内容。

第十一条　农产品标识所用文字应当使用规范的中文。标识标注的内容应当准确、清晰、显著。

第十二条　销售获得无公害农产品、绿色食品、有机农产品等质量标志使用权的农产品，应当标注相应标志和发证机构。禁止冒用无公害农产品、绿色食品、有机农产品等质量标志。

第十三条　畜禽及其产品、属于农业转基因生物的农产品，还应当按照有关规定进行标识。

第四章　监督检查

第十四条　农产品生产企业、农民专业合作经济组织以及从事农产品收购的单位或者个人，应当对其销售农产品的包装质量和标识内容负责。

第十五条　县级以上人民政府农业行政主管部门依照《中华人民共和国农产品质量安全法》对农产品包装和标识进行监督检查。

第十六条　有下列情形之一的，由县级以上人民政府农业行政主管部门按照《中华人民共和国农产品质量安全法》第四十八条、四十九条、五十一条、五十二条的规定处理、处罚：

（一）使用的农产品包装材料不符合强制性技术规范要求的；

（二）农产品包装过程中使用的保鲜剂、防腐剂、添加剂等材料不符合强制性技术规范要求的；

（三）应当包装的农产品未经包装销售的；

（四）冒用无公害农产品、绿色食品等质量标志的；

（五）农产品未按照规定标识的。

第五章 附 则

第十七条 本办法下列用语的含义：

（一）农产品包装：是指对农产品实施装箱、装盒、装袋、包裹、捆扎等。

（二）保鲜剂：是指保持农产品新鲜品质，减少流通损失，延长贮存时间的人工合成化学物质或者天然物质。

（三）防腐剂：是指防止农产品腐烂变质的人工合成化学物质或者天然物质。

（四）添加剂：是指为改善农产品品质和色、香、味以及加工性能加入的人工合成化学物质或者天然物质。

（五）生产日期：植物产品是指收获日期；畜禽产品是指屠宰或者产出日期；水产品是指起捕日期；其他产品是指包装或者销售时的日期。

第十八条 本办法自2006年11月1日起施行。

关于加强农产品质量安全监管能力建设的意见

（农业部 农市发［2006］17号 2006年11月7日）

各省、自治区、直辖市、计划单列市农业（农林、农牧、农林渔业）、农机、畜牧、兽医、农垦、乡镇企业、渔业厅（局、委、办），新疆生产建设兵团农业局：

农产品质量安全监管能力建设是实施农产品质量安全管理的重要保障。随着《农产品质量安全法》的颁布和实施，农产品质量安全监管工作进入了新阶段。为尽快构建与《农产品质量安全法》相适应的农产品质量安全监管体系，全面提升我国农产品质量安全监管能力，现提出以下意见。

一、充分认识农产品质量安全监管能力建设的必要性和紧迫性

（一）加强农产品质量安全监管能力建设是各级农业部门履行法律职责、确保农产品质量安全的紧迫任务

《农产品质量安全法》赋予农业部门实施农产品质量安全监管的新职能，迫切要求各级农业行政主管部门尽快实现从以生产领域监管为主，向产前、产中、产后全程监管转变；从以行政推动为主，向行政管理与行政执法并重转变。现有的农产品质量安全监管机构队伍不健全、监管制度不完善、监管手段落后，已明显不适应新形势、新任务的要求。全面加强农产品质量安全监管能力建设，创新监管机制、监管制度，强化监管力量，已成为当前农业部门转变政府职能，推进依法行政的一项刻不容缓的重要任务。

（二）加强农产品质量安全监管能力建设是提高农产品竞争力、发展现代农业的客观要求

随着经济全球化进程的加快和我国加入WTO，我国农产品在国内和国际两个市场的竞争日趋激烈，农产品质量安全水平已经成为农产品市场竞争的主要因素。加强农产品质量安全监管能力建设，依法加强监管，保障农产品质量安全，是提高农产品竞争力，促进现代农业发展的客观要求。

（三）加强农产品质量安全监管能力建设是确保农产品消费安全、构建和谐社会的有力保障

依法加强农产品质量安全监管能力建设，是贯彻科学发展观，落实“以人为本”和对人民群众高度负责的具体体现，是提高政府公信力、维护社会稳定的重要措施，也是全面建设小康社会、努力创建和谐社会的重要举措。

二、农产品质量安全监管能力建设的指导思想、原则和目标

（四）指导思想

以邓小平理论和“三个代表”重要思想为指导，全面落实科学发展观，以我国现行农业行政管理体制为基本框架，以保障《农产品质量安全法》的有效实施为基本目标，按照政府全面履行经济调节、市场监管、社会管理、公共服务的要求，转变政府职能，增

强依法行政能力。充分发挥和调动各方面的力量，整合资源，形成合力，加强农产品质量安全监管能力建设，促进农业增长方式的转变，实现数量与质量、安全与效益的有机统一和整体提升。

（五）基本原则

一是统筹规划、合理布局。以保障《农产品质量安全法》的有效实施为目标，确保权责统一。既要着眼于长远，统筹规划，建立全程监管的长效工作机制，也要结合各地、各行业管理工作实际，因地制宜，科学筹划，合理布局、稳妥推进。二是依法监管、严格把关。依法监管必须做到有法必依、违法必究。以事实为依据，以法律为准绳，制定和完善相关监管制度和规定、严格实施责任追究制度。三是整合资源、开拓创新。要根据农产品质量安全监管工作的客观要求，解放思想，不断创新，加强分工与协调，发扬互助合作精神，推进农产品质量安全监管资源有效整合，构建合力推进的监管机制。四是强化服务，促进发展。以良好的作风，推进农产品质量安全监管能力建设。结合我国农业生产实际，把法的各项要求落到实处，对农户重在引导、教育和技术指导，对农民专业合作经济组织、生产企业、批发市场等组织化程度较高的主体，重在健全制度，规范行为。

（六）主要目标

力争用5年左右的时间，明确职责，充实人员，完善法规，逐步建立起科学、公正、高效和保障有力的农产品质量安全监管体系，尽快提升农产品质量安全监管能力，促进农业和农村经济可持续发展。

三、全面加强农产品质量安全监管能力建设

（七）切实履行农产品质量安全管理职责

各级农业行政主管部门要根据农产品质量安全监管面临的新形势和新任务，切实履行农产品质量安全管理职责，适应依法实施农产品质量安全行政管理的要求。各级农业行政主管部门应明确一个归口管理机构，综合协调农产品质量安全工作，认真实施农产品质量安全法律法规和方针政策，制定并实施农产品质量安全工作规划或计划，依法监督和管理农业标准化、农产品产地环境、包装和标识、检测机构考核认定、农产品质量安全监测、监督检查等工作，并依据职责权限发布农产品质量安全信息和推行农产品市场准入工作，依法对下级农产品质量安全工作进行指导和监督，确保农产品质量安全各项工作落实到位。

（八）不断提高农产品质量安全监管执法水平

各级农业行政主管部门要根据《农产品质量安全法》的规定，结合各地实际，抓紧制定和完善农业标准化、农产品质量安全检测机构资质认定、农产品质量安全监测、农产品包装与标识、农产品产地安全管理、农产品生产档案管理、农产品市场准入管理、农业投入品安全使用、农业投入品监督抽查结果公布、快速检测方法认定、农产品质量安全信息发布、农产品质量安全责任追究等相关办法，形成一套比较完善的农产品质量安全监管工作制度，并认真加以实施。要将农产品质量安全执法作为农业行政执法的重要内容，加强执法力量，完善手段，规范执法行为，加大执法力度，切实履行法律赋予各级农业行政主管部门的行政处罚、行政许可、行政强制等执法职权，已经推行综合执法的省、市、县，要进一步充实力量，提高农产品质量安全监管的执法水平。没有推行综合执法的地区，要尽快整合执法力量，明确执法机构，适应农产品质量安全行政执法工作的要求，不断提高农产品质量安全监管执法水平。

（九）加快农产品质量安全检验检测体系建设

要按照统筹规划、资源整合、布局合理、专业齐全、运行高效的原则，充分利用现有机构，整合现有资源，建立健全国家、省、县农产品质量安全检验检测机构。各检验检测机构的业务范围以行政管理部门考核的授权为限。农业部建立国家级综合研究中心、部级专业性及区域性检测中心，主要承担农产品质量安全风险评估，例行监测和监督抽查及国家、行业标准研制等工作；省级农业行政主管部门建立综合性农产品质量安全检验检测中心，主要承担省级农产品质量安全监督抽查、地方标准研制等工作；县级农业行政主管部门建立农产品质量安全检验检测机构，主要承担农产品质量安全日常监督检验检测和相关的技术咨询服务。各地要按照全国农产品质量安全检验检测体系建设的总体规划，抓紧编制本地区农产品质量安全检验检测体系建设规划，并认真组织实施。督促农产品批发市场、农产品生产基地建立自律性农产品质量安全检测机构。鼓励和引导农产品生产企业、批发市场、重点产地等建立速测站（点），并开展相应的检验检测工作。

（十）增强农产品质量安全技术服务能力

各级农业行政主管部门，要充分利用现有农业高等院校、科研机构、农业企业、社会团体等科研资源，强化农产品质量安全的风险评估研究，加强对农产品质量安全技术标准的研究，加速农产品质量安全生产技术、农产品质量安全检测仪器和技术方法的研发，积极参与国际交流与合作，加快先进的农产品质量安全科学技术的引进、消化、吸收和自主创新步伐，加强农业信息化的建设，实现农产品生产经营档

案的电子化管理。各级农业技术推广机构，要将贯彻实施《农产品质量安全法》作为一项重要任务，将农产品质量安全技术服务作为农业技术推广的重要内容，组织农业科技人员深入农村，广泛开展农产品质量安全服务指导，推行标准化生产，推广生态、安全的农业生产技术和农业投入品，净化产地环境，强化源头控制，规范生产过程，加强生产档案管理，确保农产品质量安全。

（十一）加强农产品质量安全监管队伍建设

根据农产品质量安全监管工作需要，各地要切实加强农产品质量安全行政管理、行政执法、检验检测、技术服务队伍建设，通过引进、培训等多种途径，充实技术力量和人员。加强对农产品质量安全监管工作人员的管理，牢固树立法律意识和责任意识，努力提高监管人员的业务能力和综合素质，逐步形成一支结构合理、作风优良、业务过硬的监管工作队伍。既要培养一批在风险评估、标准制定、检验检测、质量认证等方面与国际接轨、具有较高专业水准的专家型人才，又要培养一批通晓行政执法等专业知识和法律法规的管理型人才，更要培养一批面向基层、面向实践、面向生产第一线的实用型人才。

四、加强对农产品质量安全监管能力建设的组织领导

（十二）切实加强组织领导

各级农业行政主管部门要从树立和落实科学发展观、推动现代农业发展、加快建设社会主义新农村的高度，加强领导，依法行政，切实加强农产品质量安全监管能力建设。正确处理好行政管理和行政执法的关系，政府监管和行业自律的关系，依法监管和引导服务的关系，尽快形成政府主导、部门配合、上下联动、社会各方面共同参与的农产品质量安全监管工作机制，努力营造良好的政策环境和工作环境。确保农产品质量安全监管工作机构健全、责任明确、运转高效、行动统一。

（十三）建立正常的经费保障机制

各级农业行政主管部门要抓紧制定本地区农产品质量安全管理工作规划和年度计划，积极争取纳入当地国民经济和社会发展规划。统筹调整现有农业资金使用结构，保证农产品质量安全管理工作所需经费，加强农产品质量安全经费的监督管理。要鼓励和引导企业和社会资金投入农产品质量安全事业，逐步建立多元化的投入机制。加大对农产品质量安全的基础设施、监督网络、检验检测、信息手段、科技研发等方面的资金投入与支持，增强农产品质量安全监管保障能力。

（十四）创新工作方法

各级农业行政主管部门要把贯彻《农产品质量安全法》作为当前农业和农村经济工作的重要任务来抓。在采取有效措施，确保农产品质量安全监管工作积极稳妥推进的同时，要及时总结经验，不断改革创新思路，大胆探索新的监管模式和工作方法，不断提高监管效率。

关于"十一五"粮食科技发展的指导意见

（国家粮食局　国粮展〔2006〕63号　2006年4月29日）

各省、自治区、直辖市、计划单列市粮食局，各级粮食科研院所、院校，中国储备粮管理总公司，中国粮油食品（集团）有限公司，国家粮食局有关直属、联系单位，大型粮油企业：

为增强粮食科技自主创新能力，充分利用粮食科技资源，发挥粮食行政管理部门、科研院所、高等院校和企业的作用，按照全国科学技术大会精神和《国家中长期科学和技术发展规划纲要（2006—2020年）》（以下简称《规划纲要》）各项工作任务，现提出以下指导意见。

一、"十五"粮食科技工作取得显著成效

"十五"以绿色储粮技术、深加工综合利用技术为标志的科技进步，对保障国家粮食安全，促进粮食产业化发展起到了重要的支撑作用。粮食科技项目和经费投入显著增长，粮食科技项目经济社会效益显著提升，行业科技总体水平明显提高。由国家科技项目带动，一批自主开发、适合国情的先进、实用的储粮

新技术，随着“十五”国家粮食基础设施建设，得到了全面推广和产业化应用，有效地提升了粮食储运技术现代化水平；粮油加工技术装备的引进消化吸收再创新，使我国粮油加工技术和装备水平迈上了一个新台阶，部分粮食深加工产品进入国际市场并参与竞争；以适应市场发展需求的粮油质量标准检测技术及计算机信息等技术得到广泛应用；以企业为主体，产学研相结合的发展模式，成为粮食技术创新的主流趋势。粮食科技体制改革取得了初步成效。

二、“十一五”粮食科技面临的国内外环境和重大需求

（一）国内外环境

“十一五”期间，科学技术和自主创新能力日益成为国家间竞争的焦点和决定性因素。随着WTO后过渡期的结束，我国粮食产业将置身于更加激烈的国际竞争之中，发达国家以控制核心技术为特征将继续保持优势地位，标准和知识产权构成的技术壁垒日益成为各国间贸易保护的重要手段。同期，随着国内人口、资源、环境压力的不断加大，特别是到2010年，我国人口将达到13.6亿人，粮食供需紧平衡的状态将长期存在。因此，要抓住技术进步和经济全球化给我国粮食产业和技术发展带来的后发优势和跨越式发展的历史机遇，依靠科技进步，充分利用两个市场、两种资源，积极参与国际合作，在激烈的国际市场竞争中，提高我国粮食技术创新能力，加快高新技术产业化进程，以保障国家粮食安全，提高国家粮食宏观调控能力，增强我国粮食科技和产品的国际竞争力。

（二）重大科技需求

1. 保障粮食安全，建立更加完善的粮食产后技术支撑体系 保证粮食的可供应数量是国家粮食安全的物质基础。随着粮食生产成本的不断提高，减少粮食产后流通过程中的损失，保持粮食储存、运输中品质，是提高粮食综合生产能力和粮食资源利用率的有效途径。“十一五”期间，要以满足市场需求和国家粮食宏观调控为目标，实现便捷、高效、安全的粮食流通方式，增强粮食应对突发事件的快速反应能力，满足粮油检测技术市场需求和维护公众食物质量安全，建立更加完善的粮食流通技术支撑体系。

2. 为建设社会主义新农村，亟待改造传统的粮食流通技术 目前，集中分布在粮食产区的农村小型粮油加工企业，其加工质量差，效益低，资源浪费严重，能源消耗高出大型加工业企业约30%～50%；农村粮食产后收购、处理环节中，还存在着传统落后的晾晒、储存等方式；农户储粮的虫、霉、鼠害严重，在源头上影响粮食质量安全。因此，通过继续推广新型适用的农户储粮、农村干燥处理技术和设备，改造传统落后的粮食流通技术，建立农村粮食产后安全技术服务体系，进一步提高农村粮食流通与加工的技术水平。

3. 为建设资源节约型、环境友好型社会，发展环保、安全、节约、高效的粮食流通技术 长期以来，我国粮食资源利用效率低，高成本、高消耗、高污染的增长方式阻碍了粮食流通产业的高效增长。“十一五”期间，推动以行业的技术进步带动粮食经济运行方式的转变，在粮食储藏、加工、物流等环节，积极采用环保、安全、节约、高效技术，研究开发适合粮食生产经营活动的各种新型技术，逐步淘汰落后的生产工艺、设备和技术，加强粮食综合利用和增值转化，发展循环经济，促进粮食流通产业走新型工业化道路。

4. 以发展高技术带动产业结构优化升级，不断增加粮食加工产品的市场竞争力 “十一五”期间，面对国外资本、产品、成熟技术和过剩生产能力不断涌入的国际竞争压力，粮食科技发展方向也要适时调整，要将信息技术、生物（工程）技术、智能化技术等高技术抓紧引入粮食流通领域，不断带动粮食产业结构调整和产品优化升级，充分提高粮食产品附加值和延长产业链。通过应用高新技术，降低粮食加工、储藏、流通环节的生产成本，不断将高技术产品投入市场参与国际竞争。

三、“十一五”粮食科技发展的指导思想、发展目标和基本原则

（一）指导思想

以科学发展观为统领，以国家粮食安全和市场需求为导向，以支撑粮食流通产业可持续发展为重点，坚持“自主创新、重点跨越、支撑发展、引领未来”的科技发展指导方针，建立符合建设社会主义新农村和构建资源节约型、环境友好型社会要求的，安全、环保、节约和高效的粮食流通技术体系，促进粮食行业循环经济的发展。

（二）发展目标

按照《规划纲要》提出的我国科学技术发展的总体目标要求，为把我国建设成为创新型国家，到2020年，我国粮食科技发展的总体战略目标为：粮食科技自主创新能力显著增强，科技促进粮食流通产业发展和保障国家粮食安全的能力大幅度提高，粮食科技整体实力进入世界前列。

为实现上述总体目标，“十一五”期间，粮食科

技要形成较完善的粮食流通技术支撑体系，粮食科技总体水平有较大提高；力争对粮食产后减损、绿色高效储运和深加工技术装备等重大技术瓶颈有所突破，在重点产品、重点工艺、重点技术、重点装备上实现关键技术创新；粮食储藏技术达到同期国际先进水平，粮食物流和加工技术装备得到优化升级，粮食质量标准检测技术不断完善，农村传统的粮食流通技术方式得到改造；建设一支结构合理、持续研发能力强的粮食基础科研队伍，完善粮食科技创新机制，形成以企业为主体、产学研相结合、科技资源共享、技术优势互补的粮食科技创新体系。

（三）基本原则

1. 创新引领的原则 以科技创新引导技术发展方向，不断带动产业进步，促进粮食产业结构调整和产品优化升级，培育产业发展的经济增长点，通过扶持基于自主创新的知识产权和核心技术，鼓励原始创新、集成创新和消化吸收再创新。把创新作为促进粮食产业可持续发展的动力。

2. 统筹协调的原则 坚持“有所为，有所不为”，统筹兼顾，协调发展。强调突出科技创新，同时兼顾技术普及；突出发展高新技术，同时兼顾常规技术的改造；强调关键技术攻关，同时兼顾重大成果的推广应用。全面提高粮食科技的整体现代化水平。

3. 优化机制的原则 以体制创新和完善机制作为粮食科技创新体系建设的基础，积极探索和建立竞争、流动、开放的科技运行机制。优化人才队伍的学科结构和布局结构，逐步建立以市场配置为基础，政府投入引导社会各类资源相互补充的有效机制。

四、“十一五”粮食科技优先发展的领域和重点工作

按照发展目标和基本原则，提出“十一五”粮食科技优先发展的技术领域和重点工作。

（一）优先发展的技术领域

1. 以生态理论为指导的绿色、高效、实用的仓储技术 促进储粮技术方式由传统向绿色生态型转变。以改善储藏环境、降低储藏成本、提高监管手段为主要技术取向。

2. 以成套高技术设备和生物（工程）技术为重点的粮食深加工技术 通过生物技术、精细化工技术、智能化设备制造等高技术在粮油加工业应用，促进高效、节约、增值和清洁生产技术的发展。

3. 以新型散粮装运方式为带动的高效快速的粮食物流技术 发展散粮物流技术、集装化装备、现代物流信息技术和标准化，构建高效、便捷、安全的粮食物流体系。

4. 以应用基础研究和国产仪器为支撑的粮食质量快速检测技术 主要发展快速检测技术和仪器设备，加速粮食质量检测仪器的升级换代，促进检测技术及国产仪器迈上新的台阶。

5. 以预警、监测为重点的粮食流通现代化的信息技术 主要是推进信息技术在粮食宏观调控及储藏、加工、物流、质量标准仪器、品质测报等领域的全面开发应用。

（二）重点工作

按照我国粮食科技工作的实际情况和粮食流通产业发展方向，“十一五”重点攻克一批重大关键共性技术和技术装备，结合国家科技计划的结构框架，从六个层面部署重点工作：

1. 加快信息技术和生物技术在粮食流通领域的全面应用，带动和促进粮食科技向高技术领域的跨越式发展 重点开展“数字粮食流通”、信息采集、预警、预报、控制技术和基于3S技术的管理决策技术的研究开发，推进粮食流通电子商务的发展。在重点地区、重点方面实现粮食预警、监测和动态信息管理。

开展粮食生物工程高新技术研究与产业化，重点对生物技术在以粮食及其副产品（废弃物）为原料的生物质能源和生物材料方面的应用；对粮食在营养食品、造纸、医药、材料、化工、纺织、能源等方面的各类深加工技术和产品关键技术进行攻关及产业化示范，形成具有自主知识产权的粮食深加工、生物质材料、生物质能源新技术和机电一体化成套设备。

2. 实施科技攻关，重点突破一批制约粮食流通发展的重大关键技术 集中行业优势力量，组织跨行业、跨部门的联合攻关。重点研发粮食快速检测仪器、监测应用技术和相关的传感器技术；以信息化带动高效便捷的粮食物流关键技术和装备，开发粮食散装化和集装化运输技术装备；开展生态环保储粮、生物防治、化学熏蒸药剂替代、低温储粮等关键技术的攻关；对高效利用、清洁生产、提高产品附加值、降低能耗，提高综合利用率和环境保护的酶技术、发酵技术、膜分离技术、超临界萃取、超微粉碎、质构重组及机电一体化等高技术进行攻关和产业化；继续组织开展“粮食丰产科技工程”，针对农村和粮食流通过程的产后减损增效技术开展研究和集成示范，形成一批具有自主知识产权的技术、产品和装备。

3. 注重交叉学科和应用基础研究，培育粮食科技持续创新能力 组织开展粮食物质信息学与储存品质变化机理、谷物油脂化学及生物活性物质功能、转基因粮食食品检测等多方面应用基础研究，粮食行业

公益性、基础性重点技术标准研究，把重大科学研究成果与粮食应用科学相结合，培育和发展粮食科技新兴学科、交叉学科，注重粮食科技的前瞻性，鼓励前沿技术领域的研究探索。

4. 支持集成创新和引进消化吸收再创新，推动粮食传统产业的优化升级　通过技术集成创新、引进消化吸收再创新，逐步改造和淘汰粮油食品加工落后的生产技术和工艺。引进国外先进的粮食流通与加工重大关键技术与装备，要联合制造企业、高等院校、科研机构进行消化吸收再创新，限制盲目和重复引进。加强相关技术集成化创新。提高粮食技术产品的优化升级和产业的国际市场竞争力。

5. 推广先进适用的技术和设备，改造传统落后的农村粮食产后流通技术方式　开展粮食流通先进、适用的新技术、新产品、新装备科技成果转化、推广应用和科学普及等工作，以粮食主产区的收纳库为依托，推广适用农户储粮的新型技术设备和农村粮食集中处理的干燥技术，通过储藏、物流、加工、信息及标准化等技术的集成，探索建立农村粮食产后存储、整理、干燥、加工、运输等集约化处理技术服务体系与示范。开展农村粮食产后安全保障关键技术集成与示范。

6. 搭建粮食科技公共基础条件平台，为推动粮食科技创新活动提供支撑　重点组织开展粮食科学仪器、设备、技术标准、科学数据共享、科技信息公共服务平台与实验基地建设。加大粮食流通公益性、基础性技术标准研究，推进国家、行业标准和检测技术体系建设。加强基础研究和科技成果转化能力建设，在不同的粮食技术应用领域、不同的地区建立若干个国家工程技术（研究）中心、企业工程技术中心和国家（部门）重点实验室。

五、粮食行业科技创新体系建设

按照《规划纲要》提出的到2020年把我国建设成科技创新型国家的目标要求，为确保“十一五”粮食科技对产业发展的支撑，完成“十一五”粮食科技发展各项目标任务，需调动各方面积极性和广大科技人员的创造性，形成环境条件优良、机制运行良好、组织措施完善的国家粮食科技创新体系。

（一）粮食科技创新体系

按照粮食行业科技发展的体系框架，结合粮食行业的实际情况和发展要求，“十一五”着力从五个方面建立粮食科技创新体系。

1. 完善粮食科技协调管理体系　全面指导行业科技发展方向，统筹、协调、管理行业科技资源，通过组织实施重大科技项目，推进粮食科学技术进步和技术创新。各级粮食行政主管部门通过管理协调，组织和引导社会科技资源向粮食行业配置，营造上下结合的政策环境。

2. 建设以龙头企业和科技型企业为主体，产学研互动的技术创新体系　粮食龙头企业在粮食经济和产业发展中的重要作用，决定了其在粮食科技创新体系中的主体地位。“十一五”重点突出建立以企业为主体、产学研互动的机制，在企业形成吸引人才、创新技术的研发平台，不断培育企业竞争的后发优势。通过增强企业自身的人才集聚和研发能力，使企业成为创新人才和资金的主要投入者、科技成果转化的主体、新技术的创造者和产业发展先导技术的引领者。

转制科研院所是粮食行业科技创新体系的优良资源，是行业应用技术研发的主体力量。发挥以转制科研院所和大型粮食科技型企业为主体，市场经济为导向，建立粮食行业产学研相结合的创新机制，实现创新主体与经营主体最紧密的结合。促进企业与科研单位和高校之间的知识流动和技术转让。在以高新技术为先导，转变企业经济增长方式的同时，不断提高企业高技术产品的市场竞争能力和抗风险能力。

3. 建设以公益科研机构和大学为主的科研创新体系　发挥社会公益科研机构和大学新科学创造和引领技术持续创新的作用。通过建立稳定的投入和激励机制，形成优良的科研环境，突出以人为本，把社会公益科研机构和大学建成粮食学科带头人才的主要培养基地，不断提高粮食科技的原始创新能力。吸引国内外高层研究人才，为粮食科学发展贡献聪明才智。

4. 建设以地方粮食科研院所为主的区域科研创新体系　进一步突出省级粮食科研院所学科优势和服务特色。各级粮食科研机构、质量检测机构要加强对地区粮食经济和农村粮食产后的技术服务。联合农村技术推广体系，建立国家与区域农村粮食产后技术服务中心。不断推广先进、适用的粮食新技术，改变农村传统落后的粮食流通技术方式。通过成果转化和高技术产业化，为区域经济发展和产业结构调整，粮食主产区产业化，培育新的经济增长点给予技术支撑。通过加强国家与地方，以及地区间、部门（行业）间的科研人员交流和技术项目合作，发展和强化技术优势，不断提高市场竞争力。

5. 建设中介机构有效参与的科技服务体系　“十一五”通过加强中介组织的社会化网络服务体系建设，发挥各级粮食行业协会、粮油学会联系各创新主体的桥梁纽带作用，为粮食科技发展，为企业技术创新不断提供信息指导和市场服务。加强与政府管理部门的沟通，通过网络化服务推广技术成果，使之成为创新体系的重要组成部分。

(二)粮食科技创新体系的建设重点

针对粮食行业发展长期存在的问题，“十一五”为建立“层次清晰、结构合理、运行高效、支撑有力”的粮食科技创新体系，要重点抓好以下工作。

1. 加强粮食科技运行机制的建设　深化粮食科研院所体制改革，研究解决粮食科技创新体系中的结构性和机制性问题，在适应市场经济和科学自身发展规律的前提下，针对科研院所转制后仍存在传统体制的薄弱环节，加快建立既能够发挥市场配置科技资源，又能提高政府协调能力；既能激发创新主体的内在活力，又能实现体系协同发展的管理体制。大型粮食科技型企业，更要注重体制机制建设，形成稳定的技术研发经费投入，在不断创造企业效益的同时，注重发挥粮食科技优良资源在粮食产业和社会经济中的作用。

“十一五”积极引导社会科技资源参与粮食科技创新活动，鼓励跨部门、跨行业、跨领域的科技合作与竞争，鼓励人才流动，形成“竞争、协作、流动、开放”的运行机制，建立合理、有效的技术创新奖励制度，吸引社会优秀科技人才，推动粮食科技进步和创新。

2. 抓好自主创新能力的建设　自主创新的核心技术和知识产权是我国粮食产业突破发达国家及其跨国公司技术垄断，获得国际贸易有利地位和保护国家粮食安全的战略基点。在借鉴国外先进技术同时，广泛学习和引入其他行业的先进技术成果，加强基础研究，发展交叉学科和前沿技术，以发展生物技术及应用作为突破口，在粮食储藏、加工等环节提高自主创新能力；以信息技术和先进制造等技术集成为核心，提高重大技术装备的自主创新能力。

3. 加强基础条件及成果转化平台建设　“十一五”要体现为粮食科技创新成果和产业化等科技活动提供有效的转化平台。紧紧围绕国家粮食安全以及粮食重大产业化工程，如粮食流通通道建设、粮食深加工产业化工程示范、粮食安全储藏等的重大技术问题，在公益科研机构和大学组建国家粮食局重点开放实验室，并争取创建国家级粮食重点实验室；以粮食科研机构为主组建国家级粮食工程技术研究中心；在不同地区以优势技术领域、优势技术产品为重点组建国家粮食局(省级)粮食工程技术研究中心；以重点粮食产品和特色资源型产品为依托，在粮食主产区的大型龙头企业，建立国家级粮食企业工程技术研发中心。加快重大科技成果工程化、集成化和产业化，构建支撑有力、机制灵活、分工明确、运行高效的粮食工程技术转化平台。

六、组织措施

为落实《规划纲要》的各项战略部署，确保粮食科技在“十一五”有较快的发展，各级粮食行政管理部门要充分认识新时期粮食科技对粮食产业化发展和全面建设小康社会的支撑作用，切实加强粮食科技的指导管理工作。为充分激发创新主体的创新活力，调动广大粮食科技工作者的积极性和创造性，把粮食科技创新体系建成政府部门引导，市场配置资源，发挥行业优势、吸引社会力量的协调互动开放式格局，要不断调整工作思路、组织方式和工作方法，形成有力的组织措施和政策保障。

1. 逐步改变粮食科技的管理方式　粮食科技管理部门要改变单纯的以项目支持和单项技术研发的科技管理模式，根据市场发展的需求，通过科学的安排项目和有效的管理方式，强化和引导粮食科技发展方向，将项目安排与基地建设和人才队伍培养结合起来。在科技攻关过程中，既要注意发挥行业优势，也要加强与其他行业及农村科技推广体系的联合。通过对重点技术领域的扶持，形成项目、基地、人才互相协调的科技发展新局面。积极研究探讨有利于引导和推动从跟踪模仿研发向自主创新研发转变的管理方式。

2. 加大对公益类科研院所的科研投入　在国家不断加大对公益基础研究投入的同时，公益类院所要继续完善管理和运行机制，逐步建立现代科研院所制度，探索以院所长基金等方式，建立对基础研究、交叉学科和前沿高技术研究的稳定投入和激励机制。把粮食应用基础研究与人才战略紧密联系起来，为公益类院所的发展创造一流的研发环境。

3. 积极争取对粮食科技的政策支持　各级粮食管理部门、各类粮食科研单位，要按照《国务院关于实施科技发展纲要若干配套政策的通知》(国发〔2006〕6号)的要求，积极组织和促进《规划纲要》及其配套政策的落实，积极争取各级财政、金融、税务等部门对粮食科研和高技术项目的优惠政策和资金投入，逐步增加省级粮食科研经费预算。各级粮食部门应积极争取粮食产后处理技术、设备享受同等农机的政策性补贴。

4. 为企业创造发展科技的政策环境　各级粮食部门要积极帮助企业在技术创新和高技术产业化发展方面获取政策支持；对企业重大技术和设备引进项目，要组织科研单位、设备企业进行消化吸收和再创新，并争取享受政策性扶持；对于带动主产区粮食生产、产业结构调整作用较大的重大粮食深加工技术、设备的项目，也要积极争取国家政策性扶持。鼓励设立粮食科技型中小企业风险基金，形成有利于科技型企业扩大规模、产品、技术升级的资金扶持机制。

农产品出口“十一五”发展规划

（商务部 2006年8月24日）

前 言

我国是农业大国，解决好“三农”问题是今后相当长一个时期我们党和政府的重要工作。制定农产品出口“十一五”发展规划，分析国际农产品贸易形势，明确发展目标和战略措施，是提升我国农产品出口国际竞争力，扩大农产品出口，解决农村就业和农民增收的重要举措，是落实科学发展观，统筹城乡发展、统筹区域发展、统筹经济社会发展、统筹人与自然和谐发展、统筹国内发展和对外开放的重要体现，也是全面建设小康社会的必然要求。

“十五”期间，随着我国农产品国际竞争力不断增强，农产品出口取得长足发展，出口规模不断扩大，从“十五”初期的160亿美元增长到2005年的271.8亿美元，增长70%，占当年全国出口总额（7 620亿美元)的3.6%，占当年农业增加值（22 718亿元人民币）的9.6%。在世界农产品贸易中的排名也不断上升，根据WTO（世界贸易组织）统计显示，2004年我国农产品出口排在世界第5位，占世界农产品贸易的比重为3.2%，比“十五”初期有所提高。

“十五”期间，我国农产品出口发生了四大变化：一是商品结构发生变化，有比较优势的劳动密集型产品在出口中逐步占据主导地位。2005年园艺、畜禽、水海等几类优势产品合计出口183.6亿美元，占农产品出口总额的67.5%。农产品出口品种迅速增加，由900多种发展到1 300多种，许多小商品成为骨干出口品种。大蒜、花生、烤鳗、蘑菇罐头、苹果汁、香菇、蜂蜜等农产品出口量已位居世界第一，茶叶、番茄酱罐头、肠衣、烟草、玉米等出口量居世界第二。从产业布局来看，各地已逐步形成一批特色农产品的生产、加工基地，如山东的蔬菜出口基地、云南的花卉出口基地、福建的烤鳗加工、浙江、福建和河南的香菇、陕西和山东的苹果及苹果汁等等。农产品加工水平不断提高，从种养、加工、包装、运输到营销、新产品开发，部分产品已初步形成了一条成熟、完整的产业链。二是经营主体发生变化，外资、民营企业成为出口主力军。农产品出口已从改革开放初期由少数外贸公司专营、以创汇为目的，发展到以1.76万家企业为主体、利用比较优势积极参与国际竞争的局面，贸工农一体化的企业已成为出口主导力量。2005年外资企业农产品出口达117亿美元，占农产品出口总额的43%，已超过国有企业，跃居第一。民营企业出口农产品出口总额中的比重从“十五”初期的7%增长到25%，增速迅猛。三是出口模式发生变化，“公司＋基地”、“公司＋基地＋农户”的经营模式正逐步普及，出口企业质量安全意识明显提高。大部分农产品出口企业已拥有自己的生产基地，实现了标准化生产，并逐步建立起科学、有效的质量监控体系，出口企业质量安全意识提高，突破技术壁垒效果显著。部分企业实行了贸工农一体化，向“优质、高产、高效、生态、安全”的现代农业迈进。出口企业获得国际通行认证明显增长，目前全国获得有机认证企业近1 000家，通过危害分析与关键控制点（HACCP）认证企业2 000多家。四是市场格局有所改善，市场多元化格局正逐步形成。多年来，我国农产品出口的传统市场集中在日本、香港、欧盟、美国、韩国、东盟六大市场，尽管目前对六大市场的出口比重仍保持在80%以上，但近年来对新兴市场的出口增幅远远高于传统市场，截至2005年，我国农产品已远销到200多个国家和地区。

“十五”期间，一些商品已经形成多元化的市场格局，率先打入发达国家和新兴市场：大宗粮食产品首次实现对台湾省出口，还远销到非洲、西亚等地区的市场，突破了原来以日、韩、东南亚为主的市场格局；水果对北美、欧洲、拉美出口实现新突破；中断8年后，重新恢复对中东的活畜出口。

长期以来，农产品出口对带动农村就业、增加农民收入、优化农业产业结构、提高农产品国际竞争力、提升国内相关产业水平发挥了重要作用，对解决“三农”问题意义重大。一是增加农民收入。在当前国内大部分农产品供过于求的情况下，农产品出口效益普遍好于国内销售，在一些主产区，出口农产品已经成为当地农民收入的主要来源。二是带动农村就业。农产品出口带动了农业、制造业、其他服务业的发展，为这些部门创造了大量的就业岗位。据专家测算，每1万美元的农产品出口，能直接和间接创造约20个就业岗位，以2005年的出口额计算，农产品出口共创造了5 400多万个就业岗位。三是促进农业发展。为了适应国际市场的“高标准，严要求”，我出口农产品在基地建设、品种、品质、包装、储运、品牌等方面标准不断优化，在农业对外开放过程中，我国也引进了大量的国外品种、资金、技术和先进的管理经验。各地发展外向型农业，形成了一些优势农产品生产和出口基地，如山东的蔬菜出口基地，云南的花卉、松茸出口基地，福建的烤鳗加工，陕西的苹果和果汁，新疆的番茄等等。

目前，我国农产品出口仍然存在着质量安全水平有待提高、受国外技术壁垒影响较大、促进农产品出口和发展的政策体系尚未建立健全，农产品出口企业缺乏核心竞争力等问题。如果不加快解决，将严重制约农产品出口的增长和可持续发展。目前，中国已步入入世“后过渡期”，农业面临的国际化竞争压力全面增加，中国小规模分散经营的传统农业与国外大规模现代化农业难以竞争的局面，在较长时期内不会出现逆转；发达国家对农业高补贴、高保护所形成的不公正国际农产品贸易环境，在短期内也不会得到根本的改变。因此，“十一五”期间，应着重解决影响农产品出口的一系列重大政策问题，创造良好的政策环境和贸易环境，健全出口促进机制，全面提升产品的质量安全水平，着力扶持农产品出口企业，提高我国农产品的国际竞争力，为调整农业生产结构，推进现代农业建设发挥积极作用。

一、指导思想和原则

（一）指导思想

以邓小平理论和“三个代表”重要思想为指导，全面贯彻党的十六大和十六届五中全会精神，紧密围绕建设社会主义新农村奋斗目标，树立和落实科学发展观，千方百计扩大农产品出口，促进农产品出口增长方式转变和出口结构调整，改善农产品质量和卫生安全状况，发展高产、优质、高效、生态、安全农业，促进农产品加工转化增值，提高农产品出口竞争力，培育农产品出口企业，推动农产品出口的可持续发展，进而提高我国农业的对外开放水平，为带动农民增收、优化农业生产结构、促进农业产业化经营、推进农业现代化进程做出贡献。

（二）基本原则

1. 坚持科学的发展观，促进农村就业和农民增收　促进“三农”问题的解决是现阶段扩大农产品出口的根本任务。农产品出口发展要立足服务经济社会发展大局，充分发挥其增加农民就业、促进农民增收和推动农业产业结构调整、提高农业竞争力的重要作用。

2. 坚持从实际出发，充分发挥比较优势　我国农产品出口还处于初级阶段，远远落后于我国的整体外贸发展水平，企业规模和实力较弱，产品质量和加工水平还不高，农产品出口的质量和效益还不高，对农民就业增收和农业产业结构调整的带动作用还有待进一步增强。扩大和发展农产品出口，必须根据中国农业资源禀赋的特征充分发挥劳动力资源丰富的优势，避开土地、水资源短缺的劣势，从实际出发，科学合理地制订发展目标、战略措施，并组织实施。

3. 坚持技术创新，着力培育核心竞争力　今后国际农产品竞争的实质是技术的竞争，技术创新是未来农产品竞争的方向。“十一五”期间，要着力实施科技兴贸战略，通过引进和自主研发新产品、新技术，加快技术创新、结构升级，提高农产品加工程度，优化出口产品结构，努力提高出口农产品的技术含量和附加值。

4. 坚持市场化方向，积极培育出口经营主体　充分发挥市场配置资源的基础性作用，重点是为市场主体创造良好的运行环境，协调国家宏观目标和市场主体的微观行为，促进农产品出口的可持续发展。

5. 坚持重点突出、统筹兼顾的发展原则　“十一五”期间，要重点支持农产品出口优势明显、条件较好的地区积极扩大出口；重点扶持蔬菜、水果、茶叶、水海产品、禽肉等具有竞争优势的出口农产品；重点扶持贸工农一体化，拥有自有生产基地，产品质量安全有保障，加工能力强、出口竞争优势明显的企业。同时，兼顾不同地区、不同行业、不同企业类型、不同产品和不同市场间的协调发展，统筹考虑近期和远期目标。

（三）发展战略

根据上述指导思想和基本原则，“十一五”期间，我国农产品扩大出口的总体战略思路是，确立以低成本为基础的劳动密集型农产品出口比较优势战略，提高以质量安全为核心的出口农产品国际竞争力，建立以市场多元化为特征的全球农产品出口体系。完善促进农产品出口的政策措施，积极应对复杂的国际竞争环境，提升我国农业的对外开放程度，优化产业结构，增加农村就业，带动农民增收。

1. 确立以低成本为基础的劳动密集型农产品出口比较优势战略 我国在今后相当长的时期内，水产品、畜产品、园艺产品和加工品等劳动密集型农产品，在国际市场分工和竞争中具有较强的比较优势。确立比较优势出口发展战略，一是立足于促进农业结构战略性调整，提高资源配置效率；二是以缓解农村就业压力为战略出发点，由出口的"外汇贡献"向"就业贡献"转变。这不仅是中国农业发挥优势、参与国际竞争的需要，也是建设现代农业，发展农村经济，增加农民收入的战略选择。

2. 提高以质量安全为核心的出口农产品国际竞争力 目前我国出口农产品因疫病、农兽药残留和环境污染等质量安全卫生问题，极易引发国外技术壁垒的限制，已经在很大程度上限制水产品、畜产品、水果和蔬菜等出口优势的发挥。扩大农产品出口，占领国际竞争的制高点，不仅要发挥劳动密集型农产品的竞争优势，更需要通过提高产品的质量安全水平，结合技术创新与结构升级，学习、引进发达国家和地区的优良品种、食品加工技术、营销模式、国际经营的先进经验，全面提升我国农产品的核心竞争力，在国际市场树立良好声誉。

3. 建立以市场多元化为特征的农产品出口市场体系 近年来，我国对大洋洲、南美的农产品出口逐步扩大，但出口高度依赖日本、韩国、东盟、欧盟等传统市场的格局仍未改变。由于农产品贸易是国际贸易摩擦高发领域，出口市场的过度集中，易遭受进口国技术壁垒、反倾销以及其他非关税壁垒的限制，也不利于规避国际市场风险，影响建立农产品出口的稳定增长机制。逐步调整农产品出口市场结构，建立以"市场多元化"为特征的全球农产品出口市场体系，要稳定和扩大日韩、东盟等传统市场，深度开拓欧盟、美国等潜力巨大的市场，积极发展中东、独联体等新兴市场。

二、农产品出口竞争力分析

（一）中国农产品出口的国际环境

1. 全球农产品贸易稳步增长 全球农产品贸易在经历了从1997—1999年三年的负增长以来，从2000年开始稳步增长，特别是2003年和2004年均保持着10%以上的增幅。根据WTO统计，2000—2004年全球农产品贸易年均增长9%，与全球货物贸易的增长率持平。

2. 发达国家在农产品贸易中的比例逐步增加 与20世纪60年代相比，发达国家在国际农产品贸易中的比重从不到60%增长到70%以上，发展中国家目前所占比重不到30%，这一方面是因为发达国家农业竞争力强，购买力充足，有能力出口和进口更多的农产品，另一方面是因为发展中国家主要出口的初级农产品价格持续下降。

3. 消费结构发生变化，加工制成品比重上升 谷物占食品消费的比例不断下降，水海产品、蔬菜、水果所占比例稳步增长。目前美国消费者每年消费的蔬菜和水果的数量比20年前增长了25%，对有机食品的需求高速增长。可直接消费的最终制品的比例从1980年的不足20%上升至目前的30%以上。

4. 国际农业竞争环境依然不公平 美国、欧盟等发达国家仍然保留了大量农业补贴，并继续使用出口补贴和出口信贷等出口支持政策。巨额补贴极大地扭曲了农产品的国际贸易，一方面提高了发达国家自身的农业竞争力，抵消了包括中国在内的发展中国家的农产品的竞争优势；另一方面，对发展中国家的农业产业带来冲击，对没有能力补贴农业的发展中国家造成巨大损害，不利于中国农产品进入发达国家市场。此外，在国际农产品贸易中，传统的关税配额以及关税高峰、关税升级、季节性关税，以技术性贸易壁垒为代表的非关税壁垒也普遍存在，成为我农产品出口的巨大障碍。

5. WTO新一轮农业谈判进展缓慢 由于各种利益关系错综复杂，谈判难度很大，建立国际农业贸易新规则和新秩序步履维艰。在今后相当长的一段时期内，中国农产品出口将面临极其复杂的国际竞争环境。国际农产品市场的准入条件没有得到有效改善，不仅农产品关税高峰、关税升级问题严重，而且针对中国农产品的"反倾销"、"特保条款"也有可能不断升级。

（二）中国农产品出口的比较优势

我国耕地面积1.3亿hm^2，仅占国土面积的10.4%，人均占有耕地0.1 hm^2，不及世界平均水平的1/2，而且还有进一步减少的趋势；我国水资源的人均占有量是世界的1/4。在我国目前的农业资源禀赋条件下，发展土地密集型的农产品缺乏优势。小麦、棉花、大豆等土地密集型产品在国际农产品贸易竞争中处于劣势。与此相反，由于中国具有丰富劳动力资源，劳动力价格低廉，畜产品、园艺产品等劳动密集型农产品具有较强的出口潜力。"十一五"期间，劳动力密集型农产品出口仍将保持较大的竞争优势。

1. 农业资源多样性优势 中国跨越亚热带和温带，气候条件和自然资源多种多样，能够生产各类农产品，满足世界市场多样化的食品需求。中国正在发挥区域比较优势，重点培育优势农产品和优势产区，

建设优势农产品生产基地。如目前已经或正在形成长江上中游、赣南湘南桂北和浙南闽南粤东柑橘主产区；渤海湾和西北黄土高原苹果生产优势区；中原和东北肉牛优势区；中原、内蒙古、河北、西北、西南肉羊优势区；东北、华北及京津沪牛奶优势区；东南沿海、黄渤海出口水产品优势养殖带。中国大部分地区饲养畜禽、种植蔬菜均具有比较优势。

2. *劳动力资源优势* 研究表明，目前中国农业部门需要劳动力的合理数量为1.96亿人，但2002年农业部门的就业人口达3.25亿，剩余劳动力1.29亿人，农业部测算到“十五计划”期末，农业剩余劳动力将进一步增加到1.8亿人，农村劳动力严重过剩，能够在较长的时期内为出口农产品的生产、加工和服务提供低成本的劳动力供给。上述条件对发展劳动密集型的农产品非常有利。我国的蔬菜、水果、畜产品、水产品，国内价格比国际市场低，具有明显的成本优势和价格竞争力。

3. *市场区位优势* 亚洲是世界农产品贸易最重要、也是最具成长潜力的市场，2004年亚洲市场进口的农产品占世界的23%，日本、韩国、香港、台湾、印度尼西亚、泰国等都是重要的农产品进口国家和地区。由于运距短、运销便捷，我国对亚洲市场出口蔬菜、水果、水产品、肉类等高价值农产品，具有显著的区位优势。

（三）影响中国农产品出口的主要问题

尽管从长期看，中国农产品出口需要逐步调整低成本竞争优势战略，但近期仍然是中国发挥农业比较优势、扩大农产品出口的关键时期。目前还有一系列问题影响中国农产品出口优势的发挥，制约中国农产品的资源优势、比较优势有效转化为竞争优势和出口增长。

1. *出口农产品的质量安全管理仍有待加强* 近年来，我国出口农产品的质量安全水平逐年提高，企业的质量意识不断增强，大部分农产品出口企业已拥有自己的生产基地，实现了标准化生产，并逐步建立起科学、有效的质量监控体系，出口企业质量安全意识提高。但受整体农业生产模式的影响，质量安全水平仍有待提高，质量卫生问题仍是制约我扩大出口的重要因素。

2. *国外技术壁垒将对我国农产品出口形成长期阻碍* 发达国家不断提高进口农产品的技术标准，内容已涉及生态环境、动物福利、知识产权等多个领域。日本、欧盟相继修改食品安全卫生法；日本出台的食品中农业化学品残留“肯定列表制度”大幅提高进口农产品的农药残留检测指标；欧美等发达国家对农产品、食品提出质量可追溯的要求，抬高了我国农产品出口的门槛。

3. *出口的政策支持体系尚未形成* 融资困难成为制约出口企业发展的首要因素，信贷门槛高，贷款困难。一些地方金融机构对农产品出口企业的一年期贷款利率为9%～10%，企业难以承受；土地、山林、农用基础设施等资产无法作为贷款抵押品。出口成本高，影响企业效益。由于发达国家不断提高进口农产品的技术标准，致使我出口农产品检测项目不断增加，加大了出口成本，而在许多发达国家，农产品的检验检疫费用都由政府承担。出口风险防范体系有待加强。出口风险大，企业防范能力弱。目前，我国的农业保险、出口信用保险等制度尚有待健全。农产品出口的风险性高，企业的风险防范能力弱，农产品出口企业参加出口信用保险尚有一定的发展空间。

4. *贸易促进机制还不完善* 农产品出口急需加强信息咨询、交流培训和宣传推广等公共服务，出口营销渠道也有待拓展。由于目前我国农产品出口企业普遍规模较小，进入国际市场的时间不长，缺乏信息收集、处理、分析能力。目前农产品出口信息服务与扩大出口的要求还有较大差距。一是信息资源分散；二是没有建立权威的信息发布机制；三是政府的信息服务机制不够完善。此外，针对农产品出口企业的市场开拓、国际营销、监测预警、技术推广和咨询培训等方面的服务机制尚未形成。

5. *农产品出口企业缺乏国际竞争力，农产品行业组织发展滞后* 近年来，我国农业产业化发展较快，出现了大量具有一定规模和实力的龙头企业。但从总体上说，我国大部分农产品仍以农户生产经营为主，呈现出“小规模、大群体，小生产、大市场”的格局，出口龙头企业少，普遍规模小，实力弱，组织化程度低，抵御出口市场风险和突破技术壁垒的能力不强。

6. *农产品加工程度低，技术创新能力薄弱，缺乏品牌产品* 目前，我国农产品加工业发展水平相对落后，出口农产品中初级产品占60%以上。产品质量和加工水平低，不利于出口企业培育核心竞争力，而且容易引发国外对我国农产品进行反倾销或采取保障措施。我国出口农产品的技术含量低，传统产品多，创新产品少，新品种研发和技术创新能力弱，不适应国际市场消费多样化的需要。目前，我国农产品尚未出现在国际市场上驰名的品牌产品。如何进一步提高农产品深加工程度，不断提高出口产品价值含量，推动农产品出口走品牌发展之路，成为提高农产品出口竞争力的重要课题。

三、农产品出口发展目标

（一）总体目标

根据我国农业发展水平和农业资源禀赋情况，充分发挥农产品出口对优化农业产业结构、促进农民增收的积极作用，适应外贸增长方式转变的要求，借鉴国外促进农产品贸易的先进经验，“十一五”期间农产品出口规划的总体目标：到2010年，农产品出口达到380亿美元，实现年均增长7%的目标。园艺、水海、畜禽产品等优势农产品的质量安全水平全面提升，农产品加工制成品的出口比重显著提高，形成一批具有国际竞争力的出口品种和品牌。加强农产品出口的组织化程度，建立一批具有行业代表性，能充分发挥行业自律和服务职能的农产品行业组织。培育一批具有较强国际竞争能力、带动作用明显的农产品出口重点企业。加强对进口市场法律法规及技术标准研究，加大对出口企业相关法规和技术培训力度，全面提升出口企业质量安全自控能力。发挥不同地区的出口优势，制订区域发展战略，形成梯次发展的农产品出口区域布局。继续巩固、深度开发传统市场，积极开拓新兴市场，逐步形成多元化的农产品出口目标市场格局。

（二）分商品出口目标

1. *水、海产品及制品继续发挥出口优势* 巩固提高在东亚、东南亚地区的市场份额，积极开拓欧美市场。同时，加强对养殖、捕捞的源头管理，建立健全出口基地注册、备案和出口加工企业卫生注册制度，推行良好农业规范（GAP）技术，提高水产养殖和加工企业通过GAP、HACCP等各类国际认证的比例，全面提升产品的质量安全水平。

2. *园艺产品出口力争实现跨越式发展* 提高加工水平，积极开拓欧美市场，分散经营风险，开发适合欧美口味的新品种。积极开发浓缩菜汁、菜脯、婴儿蔬菜食品、大蒜素（油）等高附加值、高营养的深加工产品；生产、加工芦笋、山药等国际市场流行的、公认具有药用保健价值的蔬菜；提高鲜果的保鲜技术，加强市场营销，积极打开浓缩果汁的新市场生产、加工各类食用菌、山野菜等国际市场流行的、公认具有药用保健价值的蔬菜；大力宣传推介有机水果和蔬菜；设法将食用菌、泡菜、豆制品、调味品等东方民族特有的传统食品，打入欧美市场。同时，在出口备案基地中积极推行良好农业规范（GAP）标准化生产，加强对出口加工企业的卫生注册管理，建立质量可追溯体系，提高果蔬、花卉种植企业及加工企业通过GAP、HACCP等国际认证的比例，培育品牌产品，全面提升产品的国际竞争力。

3. *畜禽产品出口努力保持稳定增长* 稳定香港及东南亚市场，扩大对俄罗斯的出口，积极开拓中东、中亚地区牛、羊肉类产品市场。大力发展肉类加工，扩大加工品的出口，严格出口卫生注册制度，推广HACCP体系认证，提高出口企业质量安全自控能力。同时，进一步规范无规定疫病区的监管，积极推广良好农业规范（GAP）标准化生产，加强出口注册、备案养殖场的管理，推广供港澳活畜禽的质量安全管理模式；全面提升产品质量安全。

4. *谷物、豆类及制品出口力争保持传统市场份额* “十一五”期间，根据国内粮食供求关系的变化，在优先保证国内粮食安全的前提下，巩固传统粮食出口市场，鼓励深加工、高附加值的谷物制品出口，同时充分利用国内豆类的品种资源优势、地域生产优势，逐步提高国际市场份额。“十一五”期间，要全面实施技术创新、结构升级战略，努力发展农产品加工品出口，使其出口占农产品出口总额的比重提高到50%以上，农产品加工品出口达到190亿美元。

（三）分市场发展目标

建立多元化的全球农产品市场体系，是“十一五”期间扩大农产品出口的重要目标之一。要稳定和扩大日本、香港、东盟、韩国市场，深度开发欧盟、美国市场，进一步扩大对俄罗斯、加拿大、印度等市场的出口，同时努力开拓拉美、大洋洲、非洲等新兴市场。

1. *继续巩固传统市场*

（1）日本 是世界主要农产品进口国之一，也是我国农产品第一大出口市场，目前中国近1/3的农产品出口输往日本市场，是日本进口农产品的第二大来源国（市场份额占13.8%）。“十一五”期间，在稳定我国目前对日本农产品出口份额的基础上，应继续加大对日出口，特别是扩大加工制成品的出口。

（2）香港 香港本身的农产品需求和转口贸易地位对内地农产品出口具有特殊的重要意义。中国内地是香港鲜活食品的主要供应地，近10年内地农产品在香港市场占有率呈现下降趋势，从1995年的22%下降到2004年的11%，2005年香港下降为中国内地农产品出口的第五大市场（2004年为第二）。内地农产品需进一步提升产品质量，争取逐步恢复市场份额。

（3）韩国 是中国农产品的重要出口市场，在近10年的多数年份是中国的第三大出口市场，两国之间的农产品贸易关系在逐步加强，我国对韩的农产品出口以谷物和水产品为主，其次是蔬菜和油料。我国应进一步发挥区域优势和比较优势，提高中国农产品在韩国的市场份额。

2. *深度开发潜力市场*

(1) 东盟市场　过去20年中，东南亚地区是世界上经济发展最快的地区之一，该地区人口和收入的快速增长也增加了对农产品需求。中国的温带农产品和东盟的热带农产品具有较强的互补性。2002年11月，中国与东盟各国签署了《中国—东盟全面经济合作框架协议》和《农业合作谅解备忘录》。2003年10月在印度尼西亚签署了《关于修订〈中国—东盟全面经济合作框架协议〉的议定书》，确定双方从2004年至2006年，将近600种产品（主要是《税则》第一章至第八章的农产品）的关税逐步削减到零。至2005年4月，中国已与所有东盟国家完成“早期收获”谈判，到2006年，中国与东盟国家的早期收获农产品的关税全部降为零。2004年11月双方签署《货物贸易协议》，中国与东盟老成员国到2010年建成自由贸易区，2015年与东盟新成员国（越南、老挝、缅甸、柬埔寨）建立自由贸易区。届时中国与东盟的绝大多数农产品将实现贸易自由化。“十一五”期间，中国对东盟的农产品出口面临难得的历史性机遇和较为宽松的贸易环境，具有进一步扩大出口的基础。应抓住建立中国—东盟自由贸易区的有利机遇，依托地缘和饮食习惯的优势，加快我国畜产品和加工制成品对东盟的出口。

(2) 欧盟市场　欧盟是世界上最大的农产品市场，消费规模巨大，但同时也是农业保护程度最高的地区之一，进口的关税保护水平较高、技术标准严格。东扩后，欧盟已成为我国农产品出口的第二大市场。“十一五”期间，应制订全面、积极的市场进入展览，拓展和扩大对欧盟的出口，重点发展高质量、高附加值、深加工的畜产品、园艺产品、水产品以及有机、特色农产品的出口。

(3) 美国　美国既是世界最大的农产品出口国，又是主要农产品进口国之一。在中国农产品出口市场排在第三或第四的位置，出口份额在9%～10%。近十年来，中国对美国农产品的出口额增长速度较快，中国农产品具有显著的结构优势和比较优势，具有较大出口潜力。中国向美国出口的主要产品是水产品和园艺产品，尤其是鱼、肉、水果、坚果和蔬菜制成品的出口增长速度比较快。考虑到中美农产品贸易的互补和平衡关系，“十一五”期间，应继续发挥我国农产品的比较优势，积极推动农产品对美国的出口。

3. *大力开拓新兴市场*

近年来，我国对俄罗斯、中东、南美、中亚等新兴市场的农产品出口增长较快。“十一五”期间，应积极建立与新兴市场的稳定贸易渠道，采取灵活贸易方式，帮助企业建立有效的风险防范体制，出口商品以价格优势明显的粮食（如大米）、蔬菜、烟草等农产品为主。应本着贸易互补、农业合作、互利互惠的原则，逐步扩大内地农产品在台湾的市场占有率，出口商品以互补性强的温带农产品及其制品、各地特色农产品为主。

（四）分地区出口目标

1. *东部地区*　我国农产品出口的重点地区在东部地区，东部地区不仅具备资金优势、人力资源优势，而且具备其他地区难以比拟的沿海区位优势。“十一五”期间，东部的山东、广东、浙江、福建、辽宁、北京、江苏、上海等省（直辖市），仍将是我国农产品出口的重点区域，农产品出口额占全国的80%。东部地区要加大国外先进技术引进的力度，继续发挥在水产品、蔬菜、畜产品、水果等农产品方面的出口优势，进一步加大科技投入，开发具有自主知识产权的农产品，培育一批具有辐射带动作用的龙头企业和合作经济组织，提高农业综合素质。优化出口商品结构，立足发展加工食品出口产业，打造名牌产品，促进农产品出口产业的全面升级。鼓励东部地区的农产品出口企业到中西部地区建立出口基地，促进国内农产品加工和出口结构的梯次转移，逐步带动中西部发展农产品出口。

2. *中部地区*　中部大部分地区为我国的传统农区，黑龙江、吉林、河南、湖北、湖南、江西和安徽是我国的粮食主产地，承担着重要的商品粮供应任务。“十一五”期间，这些地区应当进一步调整粮食生产结构，优化品种，提高质量，扩大农产品出口的规模。与此同时，根据中部地区不同的地理环境、气候条件、光热资源和物种特点，发挥地区比较优势，加快产业化经营，实现农业组织形式和机制的创新。面向国外市场，建立各种出口农产品生产基地，进行水产养殖、水果、蔬菜、中药材的生产，利用丘陵、山地、草坡等资源发展草地畜牧业，重点是肉牛和肉羊生产，建成我国优质畜产品的出口基地。

3. *西部地区*　西部地区具有特殊的物种和气候资源优势，园艺产品品种繁多，特色突出，发展潜力大。这些产品大多数为劳动密集型产品，能够大量吸纳农村劳动力就业，增加农民收入。“十一五”期间，西部地区要着力发展特色农产品、有机农产品和原产地标记注册农产品的出口，提高特色农产品的附加值，发展各种地方风味和特色产品的传统技术生产，培育我国农产品出口的新增长点。同时注重发展与周边国家的贸易关系，充分利用与越南、缅甸、印度、蒙古、俄罗斯、阿富汗、巴基斯坦、哈萨克斯坦、塔吉克斯坦等国家和地区毗邻的区位优势，大力发展边境贸易，进一步开拓农产品出口市场。

四、扩大农产品出口的政策措施

（一）强化质量安全管理，提升出口农产品竞争力

1. 强化对出口农产品生产源头的控制　积极推动良好农业规范（GAP）技术应用，推进标准化生产，促进传统生产模式的改进，支持农产品出口企业建立自有种植、养殖基地，推广“公司＋基地”的农产品出口经营模式，建立可追溯体系，实施全程质量控制。充分发挥标准化生产综合示范区的示范带动作用，全面推行标准化生产；对农业投入品的使用进行严格规定，加强对肥料和农药合理使用的监测和管理，严格禁止生产、销售和使用高毒、高残留农药。引导生产基地建立农产品生产记录档案，对生产过程进行严格质量控制。加快推进种植、养殖方式转变，引导各地发展符合防疫条件要求的适度规模的种植、养殖，加强无规定疫病区的建设，全面提高我国动植物疫病监控和防治能力。

2. 强化对农产品出口加工环节的控制　加强对出口食品加工企业的监管和引导。通过国家免检、树立名牌等扶优扶强政策，引导企业自觉提高食品质量，保证食品安全。在出口食品生产企业积极推行良好生产规范（GMP）和危害分析与关键控制点（HACCP）质量管理模式，强化出口食品卫生注册制度，实现食品生产加工全过程的食品安全有效控制；鼓励出口企业获得GAP、GMP、HACCP等与国际要求一致的认证，建立农产品种植、养殖履历和质量可追溯体系，获得国际市场准入通行证。

3. 进一步完善和加强出口农产品的检验检测、安全监测体系　全面加强农产品检验检测基础设施建设，提高出入境检验检疫装备和检测技术水平，加强专业技术人员的业务培训。引导和督促行业组织和出口企业提高自检、预检能力，加强行业、企业实验室建设，培养专业检测人员。鼓励检验检测机构取得实验室国家认可，重点加强和完善出口优势农产品及相关农业投入品的检验检测工作，提高我国农产品的国际竞争力。

（二）优化出口商品结构，实施品牌战略

鼓励企业发展深加工农产品出口，提高农产品附加值。支持和引导农产品出口企业发展自有品牌，在国际市场上形成品牌声誉和固定的消费群体。

1. 推动企业以引进国外先进技术和优良品种与国内自主研发并重的方式，开发自主知识产权产品，提高核心竞争力。制订政策鼓励企业引进国际先进农业生产、加工技术、设备，鼓励进口新品种、新技术以及有助于改善农业生态环境的生物肥、生物农药等农业投入品。

2. 积极推进农产品原产地标记注册制度，对符合出口免检有关规定的原产地标记保护的农产品依法优先予以免检，对信誉良好的原产地标记保护的农产品出口企业实行便捷通关。

3. 建立产品质量的标准体系，积极推广农产品出口行业标准和标识。推广标准化种植、养殖，靠科学技术和对生产的全程监控，稳定产品质量。同时，建立产品质量识别标志，包括标准单位的实际单价、产品基本成分（成分标签）、食品营养质量（营养标签）、产品的新鲜程度（出品日期），使产品能够按质论价。选择园艺、畜禽产品中具备条件的商品品种，鼓励行业组织制订出口行业标准和标识，通过认证方式在出口企业中广泛推广，并在主要出口市场进行重点宣传推介。

4. 制订品牌农产品的海外营销计划。“出口品牌发展资金”优先支持农产品出口品牌建设。对名优农产品出口企业在境外开展自主品牌知识产权保护的费用、为扩大国际市场影响而开展的广告宣传、展览展销和推广活动予以资助；支持品牌出口企业通过进口国（地区）要求的认证、聘请专业机构制订品牌发展战略，开展研发设计活动；帮助品牌企业产品建立国际营销渠道，率先进入跨国采购供应链。

（三）加强培训和信息服务，实施农产品出口促进计划

鼓励农产品出口企业巩固和扩大国际市场份额，通过信息服务、培训咨询和国际会展，帮助企业提高国际营销能力，建立健康、稳定的出口渠道。

1. 建立权威的农产品贸易信息发布系统和敏感商品出口预警体系　有关部门和行业协会要跟踪研究我国出口农产品在主销市场的市场占有比例和竞争情况，及时预警和掌握国外针对我国农产品的贸易调查，建立快速反应机制，充分发挥行业协会的组织协调作用，对反倾销应诉工作进行组织与指导，为企业提供法律援助和技术支持。着手建立技术性贸易措施应对战略和技术性贸易措施预警系统建设方案。建立部门协调、行业主导、企业参与、科技支撑的技术性贸易壁垒预警系统，完善国外技术法规、检疫标准信息收集、处理系统，指导出口企业的技术改造、经营管理和贸易运作。在农产品出口行业建立预警系统，实现快速应对。

2. 提高农产品出口信息服务的水平　加强出口农产品的统计分析工作，跟踪和监测重点出口市场的动态，开展国外农产品市场调研，同时建立有效的国

际农产品信息发布机制。加强部门间协作，整合信息资源；鼓励有条件的地方和行业组织，开展区域性、专业性的农产品出口信息服务，逐步构建多层次、一体化的农产品出口信息服务体系。政府要及时向出口企业通报相关国家的农业、贸易政策法规、疫病疫情、质量卫生标准、检验检疫措施、贸易摩擦、农业谈判等动态。“十一五”期间，要向出口企业陆续发布主要进口国（地区）和我国主要农产品的出口指南，以及重要出口商品的月度报告等公共信息产品。鼓励行业组织、专业咨询机构为农户和农产品出口企业提供出口贸易信息服务和进口国有关技术法规、标准、检验检疫措施等方面的咨询服务。

3. 开展农产品出口培训，提高从业人员素质　制订科学、系统的农产品出口培训计划，积极支持行业组织和地方政府，开展有关国外农产品进口技术标准、企业建立质量监控体系、普及推广出口行业标准、获取国际认证、改进生产、加工技术等方面的培训，重点要加强良好农业规范（GAP）和危害分析与关键控制点（HACCP）的推广，和适应进口国农产品新的技术标准的培训工作 。“十一五”期间，政府要继续加大对农产品出口培训的投入，扩大培训企业范围、提高培训水平。

4. 积极支持企业开展国际市场营销活动　“十一五”期间，重点资助企业和行业组织参加国际博览会、交易会，对中国农产品进行整体宣传，提高我国产品的国际知名度；支持企业和行业组织开展市场调查、广告促销、营销策划、产品推介以及其他市场营销活动；加强与国际认证认可及国际零售商组织的技术交流与合作，推进我国农产品、食品认证的国际互认工作，支持国内认证机构开展符合进口市场要求的认证，资助出口企业通过进口市场要求的认证。

5. 改善出口农产品的物流条件，提高出口效率　加快建设以冷藏和低温仓储运输为主的农产品冷链系统，加快开通整车运输鲜活农产品的绿色通道，减免农产品运输车辆的通行费用，实现省际互通。“十一五”期间，要重点解决好农产品出口重点区域和西部农产品主产区的冷链运输问题，以降低出口成本，突破发展瓶颈。

（四）加强行业组织建设，提高农产品出口组织化程度

1. 提高农业生产的组织化程度　在农产品出口重点区域大力成立农业专业合作组织，在组织执行出口合同、指导农民进行标准化生产方面发挥作用，帮助出口企业降低组织、运营成本，提高产品质量控制的可靠性。发挥提高农业经济实体的生产组织化程度，走规模化、产业化道路，对农业进行市场化的运作和管理，提高农产品的生产效率和突破技术性贸易壁垒的能力。

2. 加强农产品出口行业组织建设　“十一五”期间，应大力发展各类出口农产品的行业商会、协会和中介组织，加快出口农产品的行业组织建设，选择水海、禽肉、蔬菜、水果等重点出口产品建立健全行业组织和商品协会，实行企业自主管理、自我服务和自我监督。充分发挥行业组织的作用，提高行业组织化程度，规范农产品出口秩序，积极应对国际贸易纠纷。充分发挥行业协会在加强合作、行业自律、共同对外方面的积极作用。在加强相互协调和行业自律的同时，代表企业与政府进行对话和谈判，使其在维护企业利益、开拓国际市场、突破技术壁垒和解决贸易争端中发挥重要作用。针对水产品、肉食、蔬菜、花生、水果等大宗出口产品中存在的问题，政府有关部门积极参与行业协会的有关协调活动。

3. 大力扶持和培育农产品出口经营主体　发展农业产业化经营。继续加大对多种所有制、多种经营形式的农业产业化企业的支持力度。鼓励龙头企业以多种利益联结方式，带动基地和农户。“十一五”期间应注重发挥龙头企业和农业专业合作组织的带动作用。在我国具有比较优势的农产品领域培育一批产业关联度大、技术装备水平高、国际竞争力强、出口规模大、效益好、带动农民就业、促进农民明显的农产品出口龙头企业，大力推进农业产业化经营，着重发展农产品加工业，鼓励企业积极引进新技术、新品种、新工艺、新设备，提高农业综合素质。实行“公司+基地”、“公司+基地+农户”、“订单农业”等形式，通过龙头企业或农民专业合作组织，在生产、加工、流通领域全面实施农业标准，引导农产品市场向区域化、规模化、专业化方向发展。

（五）创新扩大农产品出口的政策支持体系

深入研究世贸规则，借鉴国外支持农业发展的成功经验，完善支持农产品出口的政策体系，“十一五”期间，要继续探索建立扩大优势农产品出口的财政、税收、金融、保险机制。

1. 中央外贸发展基金要向支持农产品出口倾斜，提升农产品的国际竞争力　重点支持出口能力强、带动作用明显的产业化龙头企业对其建立健全农产品质量标准体系，通过国际标准认证、建立或整改出口基地、建立农产品种养殖履历和质量可追溯体系、开展技术研发和技术改造予以资助。

2. 对符合信贷条件的农产品出口企业，积极提供信贷支持　“十一五”期间，要加大政策性金融的支持力度，研究制订对农产品出口提供政策性金融扶持的具体办法，针对农产品的特点，加快研究、设计满足农产品出口企业需求的金融产品。拓宽农业发展银行的业务范围，在完善运行机制基础上，加大对农产品出口的信贷支持力度。

3. *继续完善农产品出口政策性保险制度* 探索出口信用保险与农业保险相结合的风险防范机制，扩大农产品出口信用保险的承保范围，提高服务水平，有效提高企业投保比率，增强农产品出口企业的风险防范能力。

4. *完善税收支持政策* 研究规范统一农产品加工品商品代码，调整农产品出口退税率结构，鼓励企业出口深加工农产品。对农产品出口生产企业进口生产加工检测检验设备及企业自用的通用设备，按照国家有关规定，在关税减免等方面给予适当优惠。

5. *减免出口农产品的检验检疫费用，加快通关速度* 改善农产品出口检验检疫设施条件，增加出口检测点。改进检验检疫办法，关口前移，逐步从对产品检测监管向对生产过程监管转变，由主要依靠每批检验向加强基地监管转变，尽可能减少检查批次。“十一五”期间，要参照国外经验，减免出口农产品检验费用，减少企业出口成本。制订分类监管办法，建立出口企业数据库，对通过 HACCP、GMP、GAP、欧盟注册认证、ISO9000、ISO14000 系列等质量体系和环境认证，质量好、守信誉的农产品出口企业，简化检验检疫程序；对符合条件的企业，经有关部门批准，给予免检或委托自检；加快农产品特别是鲜活产品出口的通关速度。

（六）加大对外交涉力度，创造良好国际环境

“十一五”期间，要提高政府部门的快速反应能力，强化部门间信息沟通机制，加大对外交涉的力度：第一，积极参与世界贸易组织新一轮谈判，推进农产品贸易自由化进程，以解决农产品贸易存在的三个主要问题（市场准入、国内支持和出口补贴），减少来自其他国家的不公平竞争，为扩大我国农产品出口创造宽松、公平的竞争环境；第二，加快双边自由贸易协定谈判进程。要推进中国—东盟、中国—澳大利亚等自由贸易协定谈判和与周边国家和地区经贸一体化的进程，扩大和巩固我国农产品出口市场；建立和欧盟、日本、美国、东南亚国家、俄罗斯等重点市场的双边磋商机制，帮助企业开拓国际市场；第三，加强对外交涉力度，最大限度地化解争端和纠纷，为农产品出口创造较好的国际市场环境。同时，积极与各国建立以民间组织为主、官民结合的交流磋商机制。

全国食品工业“十一五”发展纲要

（国家发展和改革委员会等3部委 发改工业［2006］2240号 2006年10月19日）

一、前 言

食品工业是关系国计民生的生命工业，也是一个国家、一个民族经济发展水平和人民生活质量的重要标志。经过改革开放20多年的快速发展，我国食品工业已经成为国民经济的重要产业，在经济社会发展中具有举足轻重的地位和作用。特别是“十五”时期，食品工业呈现出快速发展的势头，成为国民经济发展中增长最快、最具活力的产业之一，对提高城乡居民生活水平、推动相关产业发展、扩大就业、带动农民增收等做出了重要贡献，为“十一五”发展奠定了良好基础。

“十一五”时期是全面建设小康社会的关键时期，也是贯彻落实科学发展观、推进社会主义新农村建设的第一个五年规划期。站在新的历史起点上，食品工业要把握好这个重要的战略机遇期，按照贯彻落实科学发展观的要求，以《国民经济和社会发展第十一个五年规划纲要》为指导，结合食品工业自身发展的现状和趋势，科学制定具有战略性、前瞻性和导向性的《食品工业“十一五”发展纲要》，全面提升食品工业的发展水平，对提高农产品附加值，稳定和发展农业生产，扩大就业，调整经济结构，配合资源枯竭型城市转型，满足人民日益增长的物质需要，提高生活水平，实现全面建设小康社会的宏伟目标都具有重要的意义。

二、"十五"时期食品工业的成就

"十五"时期，我国食品工业依托巨大的市场需求，应对加入世界贸易组织后的新变化，继续保持强劲的增长势头，行业发展总体水平有了较大提高，提前实现"十五"规划确定的主要发展目标。

（一）食品工业持续快速健康发展，经济效益稳步提高

"十五"时期，在市场需求和政策导向的双驱动下，我国食品工业进入新一轮快速增长期。2005 年，全国国有及规模以上非国有食品工业企业实现总产值 20 344.8 亿元，比 2000 年增长 97.2%，年均增长 19.4%；工业增加值 6 300.0 亿元，比 2000 年增长 87.8%，年均增长 17.6%；销售收入 19 900.0 亿元，比 2000 年增长了 101.3%，年均增长 20.3%；利税总额 3 365 亿元，比 2000 年增长 91.9%，年均增长 11.4%。其中，粮油加工、肉类加工、乳制品加工等行业的工业增加值和利润年均增长率均超过 20%。

（二）主要食品产量大幅度增加，产品结构调整取得新进展

2005 年，我国食品工业主要产品的产量分别达到：小麦粉 3 922 万 t、食用植物油 1 612 万 t、肉类总产量 7 743 万 t（其中肉类制品 850 万 t）、乳制品 1 146万 t、啤酒 3 062 万 t、软饮料 3 380 万 t，分别比 2000 年增长了 42.2%、92.6%、26.4%、530%、37.2%和 126.7%（见表 1）。

表 1　2000 年和 2005 年食品工业主要产品的产量

单位：万 t

产　品	2000 年	2005 年	五年累计增长（%）	年均增长率（%）
小麦粉	2 759	3 922	42.2	7.3
食用植物油	837	1 612	92.6	14.0
肉类总产量	6 125	7 743	26.4	4.8
其中：肉类制品	407	850	108.8	15.9
乳制品	208	1 310	5.3 倍	44.5
其中：液体乳	125	1 146	8.2 倍	55.8
方便主食品	250	458	83.2	12.9
罐头	178	360	102.2	15.1
软饮料	1 491	3 380	126.7	17.8
啤酒	2 231	3 062	37.2	6.5
成品糖	700	904	29.1	5.2

食品工业的产品结构趋于优化，有效满足了消费者日益增长的多层次需求。"十五"期末，我国粮食加工业中特等米和标一米占大米总产量的 92%以上，比 2000 年提高了 7 个百分点；特制二等以上精制小麦粉占面粉总产量的 75%，比 2000 年提高了 5 个百分点；全精炼食用植物油占食用植物油总量的比重由 2000 年的 30%提高到 60%以上；精深加工肉制品占肉类总产量的比重上升到 11%，比 2000 年提高了 5 个百分点；液体乳产量占乳制品的产量由 2000 年的 60%提高到 91%以上；软饮料制造业打破过去一直以碳酸饮料为主的局面，形成了包装饮用水、碳酸饮料、果蔬饮料、茶饮料等多元化发展的态势。

（三）产品质量明显改善，食品安全水平稳步提高

"十五"时期，随着卫生部制定的《食品安全行动计划》、国家食品药品监督管理局会同有关部门制定的《食品药品放心工程实施方案》和《食品企业 HACCP 实施指南》等规章，以及一系列以食品安全标准为重点的食品标准的颁布实施，食品企业的主体资格和生产经营行为得到有效规范，生产条件和经营环境更加符合食品安全和卫生要求，产品质量稳中有升，各类产品抽检合格率均呈上升趋势，食品安全水平不断提高。如肉类行业 100 强企业中通过 ISO9000 认证的企业达到 77 家，通过 HACCP 认证的企业有 61 家。

（四）企业组织结构进一步优化，生产集中度逐步提高

"十五"时期，我国食品工业兼并、重组步伐加快，一批具有市场竞争优势的骨干食品企业发展壮大，成长起一批知名企业和名牌产品，名优产品的市场份额明显提高。2005 年，食品工业百强企业完成销售收入 4 987.9 亿元，占全行业的 25.6%；总资产 4 586.3 亿元，占全国食品工业的 28.9%；实现利税总额 1 920.0 亿元，占全国食品行业的 57.1%。部分食品行业的生产集中度达到较高水平，其中：乳制品行业十强企业销售收入占全行业的 54.7%，饮料行业十强企业产量占全行业的 39.5%，制糖行业十强企业产量占全行业的 43.6%，啤酒行业 3 大企业集团的产量合计占全行业的 31.6%。

（五）企业所有制结构呈多元发展态势，民营企业和"三资"企业发展迅速

"十五"期间，我国食品工业利用外资发展迅速。据不完全统计，全世界食品工业 50 强中，已有 30 多家在我国开办合资和独资企业。同时，一批民营食品企业迅速成长，在食品工业中已具有重要地位。2005 年，规模以上国有食品企业 2 039 个，实现销售收入 3 086.7 亿元，占 15.5%；集体企业 1 001 个，实现销售收入 753.4 亿元，占 3.8%；"三资"企业 3 910 个，实现销售收入 5 367.5 亿元，占 27.0%；民营企业（股份合作企业、股份制企业和私营企业）16 497

个，实现销售收入9 664.5亿元，占53.7%，居于主导地位。与2000年相比，国有企业比重降低了近23个百分点，“三资”企业和民营企业分别提高了4个百分点和17个百分点。

（六）食品工业区域布局渐趋合理，企业集群式发展的格局逐渐形成

“十五”时期，围绕稻谷、小麦、玉米、大豆、油菜、甘蔗、果蔬、牛羊肉、奶、水产品等农产品生产基地和食品消费市场，初步形成了一批食品生产企业密集区和多个优势农产品加工产业带，呈现出集群式发展的特色和较为合理的区域布局，如黄淮海地区优质专用小麦加工产业带，东北及内蒙古东部玉米、大豆加工产业带，长江流域优质油菜加工产业带，华东、中南、西南、华北及东北地区猪牛羊禽肉加工产业带，东北、华北、西北地区乳制品加工产业带，广西、云南糖料加工产业带，东南沿海、黄渤海出口水产品加工带等。

（七）食品科学技术较快发展，加工装备水平不断提高

“十五”时期，国家组织实施了一批以食品加工为主的农产品深加工重大科技专项攻关，重点对稻米、小麦、玉米、大豆、马铃薯、苹果、肉制品、奶制品等的重大关键技术与加工设备进行研发，攻克了膜分离、物性修饰、无菌冷灌装、浓缩、冷加工等加工关键技术难题，开发了冷却肉、大豆分离蛋白、浓缩苹果汁、玉米变性淀粉等市场潜力大的新产品，研制出一批包括48 000瓶/h的啤酒灌装生产线、36 000瓶/h不含气饮料塑料灌装生产线、180 000包/班的方便面生产线、4 200袋/h的牛奶无菌包装生产线、工业机器人、高速6色凹印机、双瓶吹瓶机、多层共挤设备、冷冻干燥设备及纸浆模塑机械等技术含量高的食品加工装备，缩短了我国食品加工技术和装备与国际先进水平的差距，部分领域接近国际先进水平，个别领域达到国际领先水平。

（八）食品工业带动能力进一步显现，解决“三农”问题的作用不断增强

“十五”时期，食品工业在扩大农村就业、促进农民增收上的作用越来越明显，带动能力进一步加强。国家通过实施“农产品深加工食品工业专项工程”，对粮油加工、肉类加工、乳制品加工、果蔬加工以及特色资源加工等五大行业的农产品加工项目给予了重点支持。到2005年底，已建成投产143个项目，年加工转化农产品约900万t，直接提供就业岗位17万个，带动农户650万多户，户均增收2 000元左右。

三、食品工业存在的问题

“十五”期间，我国食品工业虽然成效显著，但与世界先进水平相比仍存在较大差距，与全面建设小康社会的新要求相比，还有不小差距。

（一）食品工业转化增值能力较低，整体水平亟待进一步提高

我国食物资源丰富，粮食、油料、蔬菜、水果、肉类和水产品等农产品产量均居世界首位，但是以这些农产品为原料的食品加工、转化增值程度偏低。在加工量方面，目前我国加工食品占消费食品的比重仅为30%，远低于发达国家60%～80%的水平。其中，我国经过商品化处理的蔬菜仅占30%，而欧盟、美国、日本等发达国家占90%以上；我国柑橘加工量仅为10%左右，而美国、巴西达到70%以上；我国肉类工厂化屠宰率仅占上市成交量的25%左右，肉制品产量占肉类总产量只有11%，而欧盟、美国、日本等发达国家已全部实现工厂化屠宰，肉制品占肉类产量的比重达到50%。在产值方面，2005年我国食品工业总产值与农业总产值的比值仅为0.5：1，而发达国家约为2.0～3.7：1。

（二）高附加值产品比例偏低，品种结构不够合理

目前，我国食品工业仍以初加工产品居多，精深加工产品较少。例如，玉米加工产品主要以生产普通淀粉、酒精、白酒和饲料为主，新开发的综合利用产品不多，多元醇、变性淀粉等深加工产品少，市场需求看好的乳酸、聚乳酸产品还处于开发阶段。大豆加工基本上以油脂和饼粕等初级加工产品为主，高附加值的卵磷脂、异黄酮等深加工品少。肉产品结构“四多四少”的现状依然存在，即：白条肉、冷冻肉多，分割肉、冷却肉、小包装肉品种少；生肉制品多，熟肉制品少；高温制品多，低温制品少；粗加工产品多，精深加工产品少。

（三）企业规模偏小，组织结构有待进一步优化

目前，我国稻谷加工达到日生产能力400t及以上合理规模的企业不足1%；大部分油菜籽加工企业年加工能力不足10万t；甘蔗糖厂的平均日榨能力仅为2 500t；规模以上软饮料企业的年均产量只有3万t，10万t以上的企业仅25家；罐头加工企业的平均规模仅为1 000t左右。企业规模小，严重制约了食品行业生产集中度的提高。如我国猪肉加工4强企业的加工能力占规模以上企业加工能力不足10%，而美国猪肉加工4强企业占全国加工能力的50%以上，荷兰猪肉加工3强企业的加工能力占全国的

74%，丹麦最大猪肉加工企业的加工能力高达全国的80%；在饮料制造方面，美国10大饮料公司占全美饮料总产量的96.9%，远高于我国39.5%的水平。

（四）食品工业布局尚不尽合理，区域优势没有充分发挥

一是区域发展不平衡。我国食品工业主要分布在东部发达地区的格局20年来没有发生大的变化。在产品销售收入方面，目前东、中、西三大区域食品工业的比重约为3.2∶1.3∶1；在产品深加工方面，东部地区的食品工业与农业的总产值之比为1.05∶1，中部地区为0.50∶1，西部地区为0.40∶1。中西部地区由于食品工业发展滞后，丰富的原料资源优势没有转化为产业优势。二是食品工业布局与农业生产布局衔接不够紧密。食品生产、加工和销售脱节的问题仍然普遍存在，农业生产与食品加工互为促进的机制尚未建立起来，造成原料供应与食品工业发展的要求不相适应，增加了农产品长途运输的成本和物流过程的损失，导致资源浪费。如我国虽然有300多个小麦品种，但适合加工优质面包和饼干的专用品种缺乏，每年不得不从国外进口1 000多万t加工专用小麦，另外加工啤酒的大麦大量依靠进口。我国95%的柑橘为鲜食品种，适合加工的仅占5%，其中80%仅适合加工成橘瓣罐头，适合加工橙汁的品种很少。

（五）食品工业关键技术与装备水平不高，自主创新能力亟待加强

我国食品工业整体技术和装备水平比发达国家落后20年左右。食品加工装备制造业产品稳定性、可靠性和安全性较低，能耗高，成套性差；整体研发能力不高，关键技术自主创新率低；一些关键领域对外技术依赖度高，不少高技术含量和高附加值产品主要依赖进口，部分重大产业核心技术与装备基本依赖进口；定向分离与物性修饰、非热杀菌、多级浓缩干燥等食品工业技术，以及连续冻干设备、超低温单体冷冻设备等一批共性关键重大技术与大型成套装备亟待突破。

（六）食品安全保障水平仍然较低，总体形势不容乐观

我国的食品安全水平与消费者的期望相比，仍然有较大差距，安全事故时有发生，社会公众对食品卫生仍缺乏安全感，食品安全形势依然严峻。一是食品标准制定方法和体系不能适应食品安全控制的要求，存在标准体系结构、层次不够合理，个别标准之间存在交叉重复，食品安全标准短缺，标准技术水平偏低，标准实施力度不够等一系列的问题。二是食品企业违法生产食品现象不容忽视。少数不法分子违法使用食品添加剂和非食品原料生产加工食品。另外，加工设备落后、卫生保证能力差的手工及家庭加工方式在食品生产加工领域中占较大比例。三是新材料和新工艺不断出现，直接应用于食品及间接与食品接触的化学物质日益增多，带来新的食品安全隐患。四是从农田到餐桌食物链污染情况时有发生，其中源头污染（种植、养殖过程）和环境污染给食品卫生带来较大影响。

四、“十一五”时期食品工业的发展环境分析

“十一五”时期是我国以科学发展观为指导，实施新的国民经济和社会发展规划的重要时期，也是我国经济结束WTO过渡期，加快融入国际经济的关键时期。与“十五”期间所处的国内外环境有所不同，在这个时期，食品工业发展既要符合国家总体规划，满足全面建设小康社会的要求，也要适应全球化过程中更为严峻的国际竞争环境，不断提高竞争力，实现更快更好地发展。新的形势和任务，将对我国食品工业产生重要影响。

（一）食品工业的发展机遇

1. *国民经济持续快速发展和城市化水平的提高，给食品工业发展创造了巨大的需求空间* 根据《国民经济和社会发展第十一个五年规划纲要》的预期目标，“十一五”时期国内生产总值年均增长7.5%，城乡居民人均纯收入分别年均增长5%，城市化率提高到47%，全国总人口控制在13.6亿人。根据有关预测，同期我国城市居民的恩格尔系数预计将由2004年的37.7%下降到2010年的35%，平均生活水平处于富裕型阶段；农村将由2004年的47.2%下降到2010年的41.6%，平均生活水平从小康型向富裕型阶段转变。上述因素的共同作用将对食品消费总量和结构产生重要影响，即：虽然代表食品消费的恩格尔系数将下降，但仍位于居民消费支出比重之首，食品消费总量仍将不断增加，商品性消费日益取代自给型消费，工业化食品比重逐步增长，为食品工业发展提供巨大的市场空间。

2. *农业结构调整和产业化进程加快，为食品工业提供更加丰富的优质原料* “十一五”时期，我国将继续按照农业部颁布的《优势农产品区域布局规划（2003—2007年）》的方案，调整农业产业结构，加强专用农产品原料基地建设，促进农业由生产导向型向市场导向型、加工导向型转变，推动农产品生产专业化、优质化和区域化，为食品工业发展提供优质、专用的加工原料。

3. *西部大开发、振兴东北地区等老工业基地、*

促进中部崛起和建设社会主义新农村等重大发展战略，为食品工业创造了新的发展机遇　东北、中部和西部地区是我国重要的农业主产区，农村人口比重大，拥有丰富的食物资源，发展食品工业不仅潜力巨大，而且也具备了快速发展的基础。“十一五”时期，在上述重大发展战略的共同推动下，这些地区食品工业发展的硬件、软件环境将不断改善，有利于进一步发挥区位优势和农业资源优势，发展成为我国重要的食品工业基地。

4. 国家重视发展循环经济，为食品工业发展营造了良好的宏观环境　食品工业主要利用可再生资源为原料，其生产消费过程产生的废弃物可以再利用或者还田，具有循环经济的特征。在国家大力倡导发展循环经济的背景下，食品工业的发展将更加受到政府和社会的重视，所面临的宏观环境将越来越好。目前，一些省自治区、直辖市已经把加快发展食品工业，作为提高区域竞争力和促进经济发展的重要战略举措。

5. 全球经济和区域经济一体化进程的加快，为我国食品工业在更大范围内配置资源、开拓市场创造了条件　“十一五”时期，随着我国加入WTO过渡期的结束，国内食品工业对外开放程度将进一步加大。这有利于我国食品工业更好地引进国际先进的技术、设备和管理经验，合理利用国外食物资源保障原料供给，进一步拓展食品工业的国际市场。

（二）食品工业面临的挑战

1. 环保要求高，资源消耗量大，食品工业发展成本增加　一方面，我国食品工业企业规模普遍偏小，远没有达到合理的经济规模，一部分企业难以支付污染治理的成本。另一方面，食品工业部分行业的能耗和水资源消耗比较大，不利于资源节约利用。按照建设节约型社会和环境友好型社会的要求，未来食品工业发展面临着加强环保治污和减少资源消耗的双重压力和约束，提高了食品企业的行业准入门槛。

2. 食品工业发展受制于融资难问题　食品工业原料收购季节性强、资金用量大、需求集中，而食品加工企业大多利润率不高，靠自我积累发展的能力不足。目前的融资环境不利于食品生产企业获得金融支持。一是中小企业资产规模小、信用等级低、抵押物少，只有小部分能够获得商业性金融机构的信贷；二是民营企业由于政策的限制，难以得到政策性银行的资金支持；三是农村信用合作社等涉农金融机构的力量有限，远远不能满足食品企业对资金的要求；四是部分大企业因位置远离城市，不动产价值低、变现困难，获得银行贷款的难度较大。

3. 食品市场竞争日趋激烈，食品企业面临严峻挑战　一方面，外国资本进入我国食品工业十分活跃，利用其技术和资金优势，争夺国内市场，提高市场垄断能力，对技术水平相对落后、资金实力不强的国内食品企业造成重大威胁。另一方面，很多国家提高进口食品的检测标准，食品国际贸易的技术门槛和环保要求趋于增强，有的成为保护本国产业的非关税贸易壁垒。涉及产品范围会越来越广，监管措施越来越具体，我国食品出口面临的阻力增大。如欧盟和日本于2006年启动了更加严格的食品检测新标准，对我国食品出口构成不利的影响。

4. 对食品安全的要求提高，食品安全和卫生水平在食品工业中的重要性更加突出　随着人民生活水平的提高，食品安全问题越来越引起全社会的关注。食品加工既可以提高食品的质量，又可能增加不安全的因素。建立从原料生产、采购、贮运、加工到成品包装、销售等各环节的食品安全体系，是食品工业发展面临的重大课题。

五、“十一五”时期食品工业发展的指导思想、原则和目标

（一）指导思想和基本原则

“十一五”时期食品工业发展的指导思想是：按照全面建设小康社会和构建社会主义和谐社会的要求，全面落实科学发展观，走新型工业化道路，以市场需求为导向，以发展农业产业化为契机，依托农业生产，反哺农业生产，继续调整食品工业结构，进一步提升行业发展总体水平；优化区域布局，加强原料基地建设，培育食品加工产业带和企业集群；转变增长方式，促进资源精深加工和综合利用，发展循环经济；增强自主创新能力，推动行业科技进步，促进食品加工装备制造业的发展；加强食品安全体系建设，提高食品营养和安全水平，确保居民放心食用。促进食品工业健康、稳定和可持续发展。

“十一五”时期，食品工业发展的基本原则：一是自主创新，科技先导。瞄准世界食品加工技术与产业发展前沿，推进科技创新和技术进步，增强食品工业原始创新、集成创新和引进消化吸收再创新能力。积极采用高新技术和先进适用技术改造食品工业，加快科技成果推广应用和产业化步伐，提高产品的科技含量。二是培育品牌，做大做强。加快产品结构调整，避免片面追求规模扩张，转变增长方式。加强新产品开发力度，努力打造食品知名商标。对拥有区域性和全国性知名商标的企业要给予必要支持和保护，帮助企业牢固树立商标意识，做好商标宣传，提高产品竞争力。鼓励和推动企业通

过并购、重组、联合等方式，拓展经营规模，做大做强，提高食品工业的生产集中度。扩大开放，鼓励优势企业“走出去”，开拓国际市场和到国外设厂，争创世界食品知名品牌。三是突出优势，集聚发展。遵循经济规律，充分发挥不同区域的比较优势，加快资金、技术、人才等要素向优势产区和优势行业流动，促进产业延伸，培育产业集群，形成特色食品加工产业带（区）。四是注重营养，提高质量。注重以营养科学为指导，注重保存食物原料固有的营养成分，优化食品中营养素配比，维护和提升加工食品的营养品质，满足人民生活水平提高对营养健康的要求。五是标准先行，保障安全。参照国际标准，结合国情，建立国家食品标准和统一、规范的食品认证认可体系，完善食品安全检测和监控系统体系。在加强部门协调的基础上，强化食品工业的市场准入管理，确保食品在原料、加工、包装、运输和食用等全过程中的卫生和安全。六是节约资源，综合利用。全面树立循环经济的理念，提高资源综合利用水平和食物出品率，尽可能做到“吃干榨净”，降低资源消耗，确保资源的合理利用和永续利用。大力发展资源深度加工，延长产业链，促进农产品转化增值，拓宽食品工业发展的空间。

（二）发展目标

1. *食品工业的规模和效益持续快速增长* 2010年，食品工业总产值从2005年的20 345亿元增加到40 900亿元，年均增长15%；利税总额从2005年的3 365亿元增加到6 768亿元以上，年均增长15%；食品工业产值与农业产值之比从2005年的0.5∶1提高到0.8∶1。

2. *基本建立相对完善的食品工业国家科技创新体系，形成重点突出、结构合理的食品科技总体布局和创新平台* 2010年食品工业技术进步贡献率达到40%左右，大中型企业生产装备应用微电子和信息技术的比重达到50%以上，重点行业的关键技术达到国际先进水平。

3. *食品安全体系建设逐步完善，食品安全水平显著提高* 建立起符合我国国情的食品标准体系、食品安全法律法规体系、控制技术和检测技术体系、食品安全认证认可体系，以及比较健全的市场信用体系和食品安全信息体系，显著提高人民群众对食品消费的放心食用程度。

4. *企业组织结构逐步优化* 通过跨国、跨区域、跨行业、跨所有制的资源整合，打造一批具有较强竞争力的大企业、大集团。2010年销售收入100亿元以上的食品工业企业达到20家以上，食品工业百强企业的生产集中度（以销售收入来衡量）超过30%。

5. *深加工和综合利用水平明显提高* 2010年加工食品占食品消费的比重提高到40%以上；食品加工业和食品制造业产值的比重提高到70%以上；粮食加工、食用植物油加工、肉类屠宰加工、果蔬加工等行业的副产品综合利用率大幅度提高。

6. *公众营养状况不断改善* “十一五”期间，食品工业产品的总量和结构要基本满足改善公众营养的需要，逐步消除营养不良、营养失衡等状况，城乡居民膳食结构和营养水平不断改善，人民生活质量和健康状况明显提高。2010年基本达到小康和更加富裕的食物结构和膳食营养要求，全国人均每日摄入能量达到2 300kcal，蛋白质75g，脂肪70g，其中：城市居民人均每日摄入能量2 250kcal，蛋白质75g，脂肪80g；农村居民人均每日摄入能量2 320kcal，蛋白质75g，脂肪65g。

7. *可持续发展能力进一步增强* 食品工业“三废”排放达到国家规定的指标范围。单位产值能耗降低20%，单位工业增加值用水量降低30%，工业固体废物综合利用率达到80%以上，主要污染物排放总量减少10%。

“十一五”时期，食品工业发展的主要目标见表2。

表2 “十一五”时期食品工业发展的主要目标

类别	指标	2005年	2010年	年均增长率（%）	属性
速度和效益	总产值（亿元） 利税（亿元） 食品工业产值与农业产值之比	20 345 3 365 0.5∶1	40 900 6 768 0.8∶1	15 15	预期性
企业结构	销售收入超百亿元的企业（个） 百强企业生产集中度（销售收入,%）	>10 25.6	>20 >30		预期性
科 技	技术进步贡献率（%） 生产装备应用微电子和信息技术的比重（%）		40 50		预期性

（续）

类　别	指　标	2005年	2010年	年均增长率（%）	属性
深加工和综合利用	加工食品占食品消费的比重（%）	35	40	[5]	预期性
	食品加工业与食品制造业产值的比重（%）	68	70	[2]	
公众营养水平	能量摄入量（kcal /d）	2 250	2 300		预期性
	蛋白质摄入量（g/d）	66	75		
	脂肪摄入量（g/d）	76	70		
资源与环境	单位产值能耗降低（%）		20		约束性
	单位工业增加值用水量降低（%）		30		
	工业固体废物综合利用率（%）		＞80		
	主要污染物排放总量减少（%）		＞10		

注：食品工业总产值和利税为2005年价格；带［　］为五年累计数。

六、"十一五"时期食品工业发展的重点行业及区域布局

"十一五"食品工业发展要在统筹规划、全面推进的基础上，按照量大面广、转化农产品数量多、出口增值大、就业容量多、产业关联度高、带动能力强的准则，确定重点行业及其发展方向，择优扶强，实现跨越式发展。依据上述条件，"十一五"食品工业发展的重点行业是：

（一）粮食加工业

"十五"期间，我国粮食加工业取得了长足发展。2005年规模以上粮食加工企业8 700个，实现工业产值3 200亿元；粮食加工技术和装备水平不断提高，初步形成了优势明显的产业布局。"十一五"时期要继续改进粮食加工业企业规模小、粗加工能力过剩、深加工产品少、技术装备相对落后的问题。

1. *发展方向和目标*　重点抓好稻谷、小麦、玉米、大豆和薯类的精深加工与综合利用，兼顾杂粮的开发。小麦、稻谷加工继续以生产高质量、方便化主食食品为主，重点发展专用面粉、营养强化面粉、专用米、营养强化米、方便米面制品、预配粉等，推进传统主食品生产工业化；玉米加工除继续发展高质量的主食食品、休闲食品、方便食品等外，进一步发展应用前景广、市场需求潜力大的淀粉糖、有机酸、聚乳酸、变性淀粉、多元醇等精深加工产品；大豆加工重点发展大豆分离蛋白、大豆功能性蛋白、大豆组织蛋白和其他高附加值产品；薯类加工重点发展淀粉、全粉、变性淀粉、薯条（片）和方便湿粉等产品；杂粮加工重点发展荞麦、燕麦、豌豆、红豆等为原料的方便食品和功能食品。加大粮食综合开发利用力度，提高糠麸、胚芽、稻壳、豆渣、薯渣等副产物的综合利用水平。"十一五"期末，初步建立起现代化粮食加工业体系。到2010年，粮食通过加工增值30%左右，深加工比例由目前的8%提高到15%左右；日处理稻谷100t以上的碾米企业加工量占总加工量的比例由现在的33%增加到45%，日处理小麦200t以上的面粉企业加工量占总加工量的比例由42%增加到50%以上。

2. *区域布局*　发挥粮食主产区的资源优势，以现有骨干企业为依托，通过技术进步和结构调整，达到合理经济规模。同时，发挥主销区的市场优势，重点培育联动作用强、辐射区域广的大型加工企业。在北方、黄淮海等小麦主产区，发展生产面包、面条、饼干等优质专用粉加工企业，形成优质小麦加工产业群。在大中城市和东部沿海等小麦主销区，结合产业结构调整，发展大型企业集团，建立适合城市特点的主食品加工基地，推进面制主食品工业化。通过重组、兼并等形式，在主产区和主销区，培育形成20家以上日处理小麦超过1 000t的大型制粉企业。在东北、华东、华南、华中、西南等稻谷主产区，主要发展稻米的深加工企业，构建稻谷加工产业群，推进米糠、稻壳、碎米等综合利用，建设年处理稻谷15万～30万t的加工企业；在珠江三角洲、长江三角洲以及部分大城市等稻米主销区，建设一批年产2万t的大米主食品生产基地。在东北三省和黄淮海两大玉米主产区，大力发展高油玉米、糯玉米、高直链淀粉玉米等优质专用玉米加工基地，逐步形成玉米深加工的产业群；在西南山地玉米产区、西北灌溉玉米产区和青藏高原玉米产区，重点发展特色玉米食品加工业。利用中西部地区和东北地区的特色农业资源，建立杂粮和薯类加工基地，重点发展西北地区的荞麦、燕麦、大麦、小米、绿豆、蚕豆等加工业及东北、西南地区的马铃薯、甘薯和木薯加工业。

（二）食用植物油加工业

我国是食用植物油生产和消费大国。2005年食用植物油生产总量达到1 612万t，花色品种日益丰富，技术水平与国外差距明显缩小。但是，我国食用

植物油加工业存在产能过剩、油料综合利用水平低、区域布局不够合理等突出矛盾。其中，大豆油加工原料的国际依存度超过50%，加工能力的70%集中在东南沿海地区。

1. *发展方向和目标* 在控制加工总量基础上，整合现有食用油加工资源，调整结构和区域布局，稳步发展花生油、大豆油、菜籽油和棉籽油等食用油，加快发展山茶油、红花油、橄榄油、米糠油、胚芽油等特色食用油，扩大精炼油和专用油的比重，提高油料综合利用程度，开发利用油料蛋白、生物活性物质等产品，同时推进传统豆制品工业化和新兴豆制品加工业的发展。“十一五”期末，初步形成布局合理、发展有序、特色明显的油脂加工业体系。到2010年，食用油脂产量达到2 500万t以上，食用油精加工产品所占比例提高到70%；日处理大宗油料300t以上的油脂加工厂的比例由目前的20%提高到45%；农村一、二级油的消费比例逐步提高。

2. *区域布局* 油料主产区以现有骨干加工企业为依托，优化资源配置，达到合理的规模；主销区重点培植生产规模大、联动作用强的大型企业，提升产品质量和档次，提高精深加工和综合利用水平。在东北和黄淮海等大豆主产区，重点发展非转基因大豆加工业和大豆蛋白、磷脂等新兴大豆制品加工业，鼓励通过兼并、重组形成若干个日加工量1 000t以上的大豆制油企业，逐步形成产业集群；在渤海湾、长江三角洲和珠江三角洲等沿海地区，建成大型食用油深加工基地。在南方油菜籽主产区和黄淮海花生主产区，以现有骨干企业为依托，培育形成若干个日处理油料1 000t及以上的大型菜籽油和浓香花生油加工企业；在东北、西北等葵花籽主产区，重点发展日处理500t的中型葵花籽油精深加工生产线。在新疆、山东、河北、山西等产棉区，重点发展棉籽油、棉籽蛋白和脂肪酸衍生物、甘油、棉酚等产品。在东北、华东、华中等稻谷产区和玉米产区，大力发展米糠油和玉米胚芽油等谷物油；在西北、西南及中南地区，重点发展油茶籽、油橄榄、红花籽、沙棘、葡萄籽、核桃等特种油料加工。

（三）果蔬加工业

我国果蔬资源产量居世界首位，果蔬产业已成为我国仅次于粮食的第二大农业支柱产业。“十五”期间，我国果蔬加工业持续快速发展，形成了环渤海和西北黄土高原两大浓缩苹果汁加工基地、西北番茄酱加工基地，东南沿海脱水蔬菜、罐头和速冻果蔬加工基地。与发达国家相比，我国果蔬产业仍然比较落后，采后损失率达20%～30%以上，果品和蔬菜深加工率不足10%和1%。

1. *发展方向和目标* 果品加工重点发展浓缩果汁、天然果肉原汁、非还原果汁、复合汁、果汁饮料、果酒以及轻糖型和混合型罐头，蔬菜加工重点发展低温脱水蔬菜、速冻菜、蔬菜罐头、切割菜、复合果蔬汁；鼓励农产品批发市场及农产品流通企业建设果蔬预冷、分级、包装、贮运现代物流体系，加快果蔬皮渣综合利用和果蔬流通技术研究，开发果蔬功能产品。“十一五”期末，基本建立我国现代果蔬加工和物流配送体系，形成布局合理、区域特色明显的果蔬加工业产业集群。到2010年，果蔬采后商品化率提高到60%以上，采后损失率降低到10%～15%，果蔬的深加工转化率分别达到10%～15%和3%～5%，果蔬皮渣的综合利用水平大幅度提高，经济效益进一步改善。

2. *区域布局* 在原料主产区重点发展浓缩果蔬汁（浆）、脱水果蔬、速冻果蔬、罐藏果蔬等加工业及贮运保鲜；在大中城市等主销区，重点发展果蔬汁等终端产品。同时，大力培育大型果蔬流通加工企业。在山东、陕西、辽宁等地发展浓缩苹果汁，新疆等西部地区发展番茄酱、浓缩葡萄汁，河北、天津、安徽等地发展桃浆、浓缩梨汁，重庆、湖北等地发展柑橘浓缩汁与非还原柑橘汁，海南和云南等地发展热带果汁。在东北、西北、西南等果蔬主产区及东南沿海发达地区，重点发展脱水果蔬产业和果蔬速冻产业，形成环形产业布局，增强出口能力。

（四）肉类加工业

我国肉类产量位居世界第一。“十五”期间，我国肉类加工业保持了较快的增长势头，肉类总产量年均增长4.8%，涌现出一批具有国际先进水平的大型肉类加工企业。但是，我国肉类生产集中度和工业化程度还比较低，肉类产品质量安全问题仍很突出，品种结构不合理、深加工转化率不高的局面仍未得到根本性的转变。

1. *发展方向和目标* 大力发展冷却肉、分割肉和熟肉制品，扩大低温肉制品、功能性肉制品的生产，积极推进中式肉制品工业化生产步伐；在稳步发展猪肉产品的同时，重点发展牛羊肉、禽肉制品；广泛开展畜禽血液、骨组织、脏器等副产品的综合利用研究，开发生产各种生物制品。继续推行定点屠宰，稳步提高机械化屠宰的比重，完善肉品加工全程质量控制体系，保障肉类食品安全。“十一五”期末，基本建立较为完善的肉类加工业体系，培育一批具有国际竞争力的大型肉类加工企业，企业组织化程度和行业生产集中度明显提高。到2010年，肉类总产量超过8 400万t，其中，猪肉、牛羊肉、禽肉各占60%、20%和20%左右；肉类制品产量超过1 100万t，占肉类总产量的13.1%；上市流通的畜禽工业化屠宰加工产品的比重达到45%～50%左右，大中城市全部实行工厂化、机械化屠宰；大型肉类加工企业的综合利用产值占总产值的比重达到20%以上，规模以上肉类企业通过ISO90001和HACCP体系认证比重达到90%。

2. *区域布局* “十一五”期间，大城市和东部沿海发达地区仍将是我国肉类消费的领先地区，而东北、华北、西北、西南等地区则是肉类生产增长的主要地区。针对这一特点，“十一五”时期，在华东、西南、华北、东北地区，重点建设猪肉及其产品加工业基地；在中原、东北地区，重点建设牛肉及其产品加工业基地；在西北、内蒙古及河北北部、中原和西南地区，重点建设羊肉及其产品加工业基地；在中部和东部的家禽主产区，重点建设禽肉及其产品加工业基地。

(五) 水产加工业

水产品是我国目前最大的食品出口行业之一，2005年我国水产品及制品出口额达71.8亿美元，占食品出口总额的29.5%，居于首位。“十五”时期，我国水产品加工业取得了突破性进展，已经形成冷冻冷藏、调味休闲品、鱼糜与鱼糜制品、海藻化工、海洋保健食品等几十个产业门类。但是，我国水产品加工的比例远低于发达国家的水平，产业集中度不高、加工技术与装备落后、资源再利用程度低。

1. *发展方向和目标* 在巩固和提升传统特色产品的基础上，调整水产加工制品结构，重点发展速冻小包装、冷冻调理食品、即食性熟食水产食品，加大水产品的综合开发力度，探索远洋渔业资源开发与利用，积极推进海洋功能食品的生产。海水产品加工以海洋低值水产品加工为重点，大力开发精制食用鲜鱼浆、风味鱼丸、鱼卷等方便食品，以及人造蟹肉、贝肉、鱼翅等合成水产食品；淡水鱼加工重点发展分割和切片加工，加大鱼糜、鱼片、腌制品、熏制品和调味品等深加工制品的开发力度；贝类加工重点开发贝类调味品、干制品、熏制品、软罐头和动物钙源食品等深加工制品。“十一五”期末，基本建立以面向出口的鱼类、虾蟹、贝类和藻类加工为重点的水产品加工业体系。到2010年，水产品加工量达到2 000万t左右，水产品加工比例达到60%以上，通过HACCP认证的企业达到15%以上。

2. *区域布局* 在东南沿海、环渤海和长江中下游优势水产品养殖区，建设水产品加工产业基地。其中，在浙江、江苏、福建、广东、广西、海南等东南沿海，重点建设鳗鱼、对虾、罗非鱼等产品加工基地；在山东、河北、辽宁等环渤海地区，重点建设对虾、贝类等产品加工业基地及海产品批发市场；在湖南、江西、安徽和江苏等长江中下游地区，重点建设淡水产品加工业基地及水产品批发市场，鼓励水产品产区批发市场完善冷冻功能。

(六) 乳制品加工业

乳及乳制品是最接近于完善的食品。“十五”期间，我国乳制品加工业生产集中度进一步提高，技术装备水平达到或接近世界先进水平，产品产量明显改善。2005年乳制品产量达到1 310万t，实现工业总产值886.7亿元。但是，我国乳制品加工业存在机械化挤奶比例低，产品结构不够合理，企业规模小，自动化程度低的问题。

1. *发展方向和目标* 逐步减少普通奶粉的生产，提高配方奶粉的比例；大幅度提高鲜奶加工量，扩大液体奶生产；城市型乳品企业重点发展巴氏杀菌乳、发酵乳、灭菌乳、功能乳等液体乳制品，基地型乳品企业仍以乳粉为主，重点发展配方乳粉、全脂乳粉、脱脂乳粉、功能乳及超高温灭菌乳等，有市场、有条件的地方，适当发展干酪、乳清和奶油等乳制品。“十一五”期末，基本建立较为完善的乳制品制造业体系，技术装备水平达到或接近世界先进水平。到2010年，乳制品产量达2 190万t，年均增长率15%，其中：固体乳制品产量年均增长率为7%，产量达到210万t；液体乳制品产量年均增率为16%，总产量达到1 980万t。

2. *区域布局* 在东北、华北、西北等传统农牧区的奶源基地，培育乳粉和超高温灭菌乳等乳制品大型加工企业，在北京等大城市和长江三角洲、珠江三角洲等地区，重点发展液体乳和各种乳制品生产企业。

(七) 饮料制造业

饮料制造业是我国食品工业中发展最快的行业之一。“十五”期间，我国饮料制造业产值年均增长18.3%。2005年规模以上饮料生产企业的产量为3 380.4万t，实现工业总产值3 073.5亿元；饮料品种结构渐趋合理，生产集中度进一步提高，果蔬汁出口大幅度上升。饮料制造业存在地区发展不平衡，品种结构不够合理，生产集中度较低，装备主要依赖进口等问题。

1. *发展方向和目标* 继续提高饮料生产总量，进一步调整产品结构，重点发展果蔬汁饮料、植物蛋白饮料和茶饮料等产品，适度发展瓶（罐）装饮用矿泉水，降低碳酸类饮料的比例，发展并规范功能性饮料的生产；鼓励通过兼并、重组、融资等手段，培育大型饮料企业集团，实现产业升级。“十一五”期末，建立一个产品结构更趋合理、产业集中度更高的现代饮料加工体系。到2010年，全国软饮料总产量达到5 700万t，年均增长率约11%。其中，果蔬汁饮料产量达到1 140万t，瓶（罐）装饮用水产量达到2 250万t，碳酸饮料产量达到1 140万t，茶饮料、功能性饮料和蛋白饮料等其他饮料产量达到1 170万t左右。

2. *区域布局* 在果品优势区，重点发展果汁及果汁饮料加工企业；在长江三角洲、珠江三角洲地区以及大城市，重点培育茶饮料、保健饮料、运动功能性饮料以及果汁饮料加工企业；在水源条件优越的西南、中南地区，重点发展天然矿泉水、纯净水、茶饮料等加工企业。

（八）制糖业

我国是世界上主要的食糖生产和消费大国。"十五"期间我国制糖业稳步发展，2004/2005年度制糖期食糖产量达到903万t，实现工业总产值353.6亿元；食糖生产逐步向广西等优势地区转移，企业规模不断扩大。但是，我国制糖行业的整体技术和设备水平还比较落后，生产成本较高，产品质量不稳定，综合利用效率低，污染严重。

1. *发展方向和目标* 按存量调整为主、增量调整为辅的方针，鼓励以大型制糖企业为核心，以资产为纽带，采取联合、收购、兼并、控股等方式组建大型制糖企业集团，促进制糖企业与内外贸企业联合，实现农工贸、内外贸一体化经营；加强制糖企业的技术进步，提高工艺水平和装备的先进性；按照市场需求增加产品花色品种，发展幼糖、单晶冰糖、方糖等精炼糖，推广小包装；鼓励和支持糖厂综合利用产品生产的社会化进程，集中处理制糖企业的蔗渣、甜菜废丝、糖蜜等废弃物；促进甘蔗糖和甜菜糖的协调发展，提高糖料单产和含糖率；有序发展淀粉糖，充分发挥其对平衡食糖需求和调节市场的作用；推进食糖和燃料乙醇联产的战略研究，积极研究开发利用废糖蜜生产化工产品和能源替代产品。"十一五"期末，基本形成产业布局合理、发展有序的制糖工业体系，使我国糖业步入良性发展时期。到2010年，食糖产量达到1 450万t左右，淀粉糖产量达到650万t；精制糖产量占食糖总产量的30%以上；糖料日处理能力由现在的74万t增加到83.3万t，单一企业平均生产规模达到4.5万t/年；甘蔗糖和甜菜糖每百吨原料标准煤耗分别控制在5t和6t以下。

2. *区域布局* 在广西、云南、广东、海南等南方甘蔗产区，新疆、黑龙江等北方甜菜产区支持制糖企业联合、兼并、重组，建立科工贸一体化的大型企业集团，建设南方和北方两大糖料加工产业区（带）；在东北、华北等玉米、甘薯优势产区，建设淀粉糖生产加工基地。

七、"十一五"时期食品工业发展的重点任务

（一）构建食品工业国家科技创新体系

全面提升我国食品工业的自主创新能力，重点突破一批重大、共性关键技术，形成一批技术创新能力强的食品企业和产业集群，建设一批科技创新基地和产业化示范生产线，培育一批食品科技人才队伍，构建科技创新的基础平台，使我国食品工业科技水平达到21世纪初的国际先进水平，为我国食品工业的可持续快速发展提供强有力的科技支撑。

"十一五"时期食品工业重点突破的一批共性关键技术为：

1. 在现代加工技术方面，重点攻克现代高效分离、质构重组与物性修饰技术、清洁生产技术、食品生物工程技术、新型热力杀菌技术、非热力加工技术、无菌冷灌装技术等。

2. 在现代干燥技术方面，重点攻克高效节能干燥技术、连续冷冻干燥技术、特征远红外与微波干燥技术、悬浮干燥技术、超低温冻结技术、高效节能速冻技术等。

3. 在食品质量与安全控制技术方面，重点攻克溯源技术、真伪鉴别技术、在线物性探测技术、快速检测技术、微生物测报技术、食品安全风险性评估技术、食品安全监测预警技术、全程质量与食品安全控制技术、食品安全标准体系等。

4. 在现代物流技术方面，重点攻克数字化和信息化处理技术、数字化存储与智能配送技术、智能分级技术、快速预冷技术与冷链技术、综合保鲜技术等。

"十一五"时期食品工业科技创新基础平台建设为：以大专院校和科研院所为主体，建立3～5个食品技术创新开放实验室，构建包括粮油加工、果蔬加工、畜禽产品加工和水产品加工在内的食品工业科技创新平台。以企业为主，建立3～5个食品技术创新工程中心，构建包括食品科技国际交流与合作在内的食品工业工程技术创新平台。同时，加强食品工业综合竞争力和宏观战略决策能力，构建食品工业发展战略研究平台，重点开展食品工业技术扩散系统研究、食品工业推进系统研究和食品工业未来发展战略研究。

（二）支持食品装备制造业发展

食品装备制造业是为食品工业提供技术装备的重要产业，对提高我国食品工业装备国产化率和整体发

展水平起着举足轻重的作用。“十一五”时期，食品装备制造业要改变自主创新能力弱、技术装备水平低、成套性和稳定性差等的现状，重点加强分离设备、冷冻设备、干燥设备、杀菌设备、罐装设备、包装设备等现代食品加工装备的研发制造。

在节能干燥设备方面，重点开发流化床干燥、微波远红外真空组合干燥、连续真空冷冻干燥等设备。在连续高效分离与浓缩设备方面，重点开发连续离心分离、膜分离与浓缩、工业色谱柱分离和连续萃取、短程分子蒸馏等连续、高效、节能、环保的分离与浓缩装备。在超低温冷冻冷藏设备方面，重点开发远洋捕捞船用超低温急冻冷藏设备和冷链设备。在新型杀菌与包装设备方面，重点开发非热力杀菌设备，同时研究开发无菌灌装、无菌运输等设备，形成连续高效杀菌、无菌灌装一体化生产线。

“十一五”时期食品工业重点行业装备制造业发展方向：

1. 粮食加工　围绕米面制品，重点发展主食加工设备和副产品综合利用设备；围绕玉米的工业化应用，发展深加工设备。

2. 油脂加工　重点发展大型制油高效、节能设备，油脂精炼装备，专用油脂以及大豆蛋白分离和提取设备。

3. 畜禽屠宰加工　重点开发牲畜真空采血、电刺激、畜禽热气隧道式湿烫及连续自动去毛（羽）、多工位扒皮设备，胴体劈半和在线检测设备，高湿雾化冷却排酸设备，大型真空斩拌机、滚揉机和高速灌肠机等肉类深加工设备，以及冷却肉、清真肉制品、低温肉制品、功能性肉制品和发酵肉制品加工设备，实现我国畜禽屠宰加工装备的成套化、国产化。

4. 水产品加工　重点发展去鳞、剖腹、去内脏、分级设备，鱼糜、鱼浆加工设备，贝类净化设备和壳肉分离设备，水产品微冻保鲜设备，鱼虾无水保活运输设备，海洋药物及天然化合物提取设备。

5. 乳制品加工　重点发展液体乳加工和无菌包装设备、干酪加工设备、乳清分离设备、超高温灭菌设备。

6. 果蔬加工　重点开发果蔬预冷和配送设备、果蔬分级包装设备、净菜加工与储运设备、冷打浆设备、大型果汁浓缩设备、柑橘半果榨汁设备。

7. 饮料制造　重点发展无菌冷灌装设备、大型饮料在线检测及自动剔除设备、全自动饮料混合设备、加工前处理装备、高分子材料自动“制瓶—灌装—封口”一体化设备。

8. 包装设备　大力发展纸包装设备、液体包装设备和包装材料制造设备，重点发展5万瓶/h以上的吹瓶机、1.5万瓶/h的PET瓶结晶设备、注拉吹制瓶设备、5万瓶/h以上的饮料冷灌装设备、UHT奶的杀菌灌装设备和ESL（延长鲜奶储存寿命）设备。

（三）建立现代食品物流体系

建立现代市场营销网络和物流中心，对推动食品工业发展、实现食品安全营养要求至关重要。一是鼓励企业建立现代市场营销网络和标准化的物流中心，推广代理制和连锁分销制方式，鼓励企业在各省、自治区、直辖市的大中城市设立总代理、直销店，以营销打品牌，以品牌促营销。二是加快建立现代食品物流配送体系，鼓励食品生产企业应用现代物流管理技术，改造企业内部流程，实行物流外包。支持食品流通企业建设配送中心，鼓励食品专业批发市场进行标准化改造。利用信息化技术和供应链管理技术，推动食品电子商务发展，推进全球采购、营销和售后服务，降低交易成本。三是鼓励举办各种食品博览会、交流会，促进食品流通，推动国内外合作。四是积极开拓农村市场，改善农村消费环境和物流通道，建立符合农村市场特点的食品营销和配送服务体系。

（四）完善食品安全保障体系

尽快完善食品安全保障体系建设，提高食品安全水平，推动食品工业的健康发展。一是继续推行食品市场准入制度，建立比较完善的食品安全控制和管理体系，包括良好流通秩序、良好生产规范（GMP）、危害分析及关键控制点（HACCP）、全面质量管理（TQM）、ISO9001质量认证体系等。二是借鉴国际食品安全管理的先进经验，鼓励食品加工企业建立严格的食品召回制度，支持流通企业建设完善的食品溯源制度。三是加快食品标准制修订步伐，提高标准的有效性，全面提升食品的质量水平。四是加强食品安全教育，提高公众的食品安全意识。五是强化食品企业环保意识，加大环境污染治理的力度。

八、“十一五”时期食品工业发展的政策措施

1. 推进机制和体制创新，加强宏观调控和规划引导　一要建立统一协调的食品工业发展管理机制。由国务院综合部门牵头，会同有关部门，建立全国食品工业发展协调会议机制，对食品工业发展进行宏观指导，负责重大问题的协调和决策。进一步理顺各部门的管理权限，各负其责，相互配合，切实履行好政府主管部门的职责，加强对食品工业的监管和协调。各省（自治区、直辖市）地方政府要建立相应的协调机制，抓好本地区食品工业发展的工作。二要尽快制

订和完善与食品工业相关的法律、法规、条例和规章制度，将食品工业的发展纳入法制管理的轨道，依法监管。

2. 加大对食品工业科技进步的投入，增强发展动力　一要增加食品工业和食品流通的科技投入，在加强食品科技基础研究的基础上，支持一批重大关键技术开发项目和关键设备的研制工作，促进具有自主知识产权的产品研究开发和转化。同时，加速食品工业高新技术成果产业化，充分利用优秀传统工艺技术与高新技术的组装、集成和工程化配套转化，促进食品工业高新技术产业化和行业技术进步。二要加强食品工业领域国家重大科学工程、国家重点实验室、国家工程中心和博士后工作站的建设，培育食品工业科技创新平台和研发基地。特别是要加大对现有食品科研院（所）的改革力度，鼓励和支持大型食品生产企业建立自己的科研开发机构，使企业逐步成为食品科技开发的主体。三要广泛开展食品工业科技的国际合作与交流，把自主研发与引进、消化吸收国外先进技术相结合，充分利用好国际科技资源。四要抓紧实施人才、专利、技术标准战略，营造吸引人才的宏观环境和条件，培育食品工业科技人才。

3. 建设优质专用农产品生产基地，确保食品工业发展的原料需求　根据我国自然条件和食品工业发展的要求，充分发挥区域优势，以工业结构调整促进农业产业化，引导农业生产，发展优质、专用、安全的加工原料基地。一是大力支持食品生产企业发展专业化的加工原料供给基地，逐步实现加工原料的专用化、规模化和标准化。二是加强加工专用品种的引进、选育和推广，为食品工业的发展提供符合加工要求的品种保障。三是鼓励食品生产企业以“公司＋农业专业合作组织”、“公司＋农户”、“公司＋基地”、农民投资入股等产业化经营模式，与农民建立稳定的购销关系和合理的利益分配机制，保证食品工业优质专用原料的有效供给。

4. 加快调整产品结构，努力打造食品工业知名商标　一要结合资源供给状况，运用高新技术，促进资源的深度开发利用和综合利用，开发科技含量高、附加值高的优质新产品，提高精、深加工产品的比重，进一步优化产品结构。二要加强对优秀传统食品商标的挖掘，培育一批在国际市场上具有明显竞争优势的民族特色商标，推动传统食品的工业化生产，提升传统食品的吸引力和竞争力。三要加强名、优、特、新食品的商标注册管理，保护知识产权，创造公平竞争的环境，积极培育和扶持知名商标。四要充分利用《原产地域产品保护规定》，加大对知名商标的保护。

5. 培育和壮大食品工业龙头企业，推动产业结构升级　一要从财政、税收、信贷等政策上扶持优势龙头企业，着力培养一批技术创新能力、现代管理能力和带动能力强的龙头企业，带动整个行业的发展。二要通过联合、兼并、收购等资本运营方式，实现“强强联合”、“强弱联合”，培育和组建一批资本结构多元化、产品科技含量高、市场竞争力强的食品工业龙头企业，提高产业的集中度和核心竞争力。三要积极帮助和支持龙头企业获得产品进出口经营权，促进产品出口。四要对龙头企业在立项、基地建设、原料收购、批发和流通网络建设、科技研发、技术服务、质量标准和信息网络体系建设等方面，给予必要的扶持。

6. 积极实施对外开放战略，不断拓展发展领域　一要积极参与WTO双边和多边谈判，不断提高我国在国际贸易谈判中的地位，争取有利于我国食品工业发展的各项条款和规定，降低技术壁垒的风险，为技术引进和食品出口创造条件。二要鼓励和支持食品出口企业获得国际质量认证、环保认证、安全认证等有关国际权威认证。三要在巩固原有出口市场的基础上，努力开拓美国、欧盟、日本、东盟等市场，加大独联体、东欧、非洲、澳新、拉美等新兴市场的开发力度，增加食品出口份额。四要鼓励和支持有条件的大型食品企业集团到境外设点办厂，开发利用境外原料资源，扩大企业发展空间，实现从单纯出口商品向海外设厂、进行境外投资的转变。五要结合食品各领域发展目标，适时修订《外商投资产业指导目录》，鼓励外商投资食品工业高新技术领域，鼓励外资投向中西部和东北老工业基地的食品工业优势项目，兼并重组老的食品加工企业，促进产业结构调整和区域协调发展。

7. 强化食品标准管理，加大标准实施力度　以促进食品工业发展和提高食品质量安全水平为重点，在已建立的食品标准体系框架的基础上，通过修改、补充、调整，进一步完善标准体系。积极跟踪国际和国外先进标准发展动态，重点研究国际食品法典委员会（CAC）、国际标准化组织（ISO）、美国、欧盟、日本等国际组织和发达国家食品标准，提升我国食品标准的整体水平。开展重要标准的宣贯、人员的培训，提高企业的标准意识和执行标准的自觉性。强化标准的实施工作，加大监督力度，确保食品生产企业能按照标准组织生产，产品质量符合强制性标准的要求。

8. 促进投资主体多元化，多渠道增加对食品工业的投入　一要鼓励多层次、多形式、多种经济成分发展食品工业，促进大型龙头食品企业资本构成多元化，解决中小食品企业融资难的问题。二要继续加大国家及各级地方财政对农产品加工业特别是食品工业的扶持力度，推动食品企业的技术改造和工艺设备更新。三要鼓励有实力的食品企业在国内外资本市场上市融资，发行企业债券。

9. 发挥中介组织的作用，加强食品行业自律 完善食品工业行业协会和其他中介组织的服务职能，充分发挥其在信息统计、行业规划、行业自律、技术咨询、贸易仲裁、反倾销与应诉、法律规范与标准制定、人才培训、技术交流和社会化服务等方面的作用，支持行业协会等中介组织积极开展民间交流，建立与各国同行间的合作伙伴关系。

10. 在资源枯竭型城市转型中，大力扶持食品生产加工业的发展，使之成为吸纳转产人员就业的重要接续产业 国家在财政、税收、资金投入上给予必要的扶持。

农产品加工业“十一五”发展规划

（农业部 农企发［2006］7号 2006年12月20号）

“十一五”时期，是推进社会主义新农村建设、统筹城乡与社会协调发展、加快构建社会主义和谐社会的重要阶段。发展农产品加工业是建设现代农业的重要内容，对于落实中央提出的推进社会主义新农村建设的战略部署，解放和发展农村生产力，促进农村生产发展和农民生活富裕具有重要意义。

本规划根据党中央、国务院编制“十一五”规划的有关要求，从我国农业、农村经济和社会发展的实际出发，按照农产品加工业发展的特点和规律，在全面分析“十五”发展情况的基础上，确定了“十一五”期间以食品工业为主的包括粮油、果蔬、畜产品、水产品和传统农产品等主要农产品加工业发展的指导思想、主要原则和目标，明确了重点领域与相关区域布局，提出一批重点工程和促进农产品加工业发展的政策措施，是“十一五”期间指导全国农产品加工业发展的重要依据。

一、农产品加工业发展现状及趋势

（一）我国农产品加工业发展现状

“十五”以来，我国农产品加工业快速发展，成为国民经济中最具成长活力的产业之一。主要表现在：

1. 农产品加工业总量快速增长，运行态势良好 “十五”期间，农产品加工业产值的年均增长近15%。2005年我国农产品加工业产值达到4.2万亿元，比上年增长16%。全国规模以上的农产品加工企业达7万多家，从业人数近1 800万人，占全部工业从业人员的28%。目前，农产品加工业是我国国民经济的第一大支柱产业，也是发展最快的产业之一。

2. 在繁荣地方经济，促进农民增收和转移农村剩余劳动力等方面的作用日益显现 农产品加工业在地方经济发展中的地位和作用日益增强，逐步成为地区经济发展的重要力量，并在增加农民收入，转移农村剩余劳动力等方面发挥了重要作用。在一些以农业为主的县市，农产品加工业的税收对本级财政的贡献率已达到70%，通过建立“公司＋基地＋农户”、“公司＋中介组织＋农户”、“公司＋村委会＋农户”等多种利益连接机制，增加农民收入。目前，国家级农业产业化龙头企业580多家，带动农户8 726万户，占全国农户总数的35.2%，参与产业化经营的农户比普通农户每户年平均增收1 300多元。

3. 产业和产品结构进一步优化，逐步实现了由初加工向深加工的转变 农产品加工业的产业结构和产品结构逐步调整，形成了以粮油、果蔬、畜产品和水产品加工为主导行业的农产品加工产业格局。其中，食品工业比重上升，2005年食品工业占农产品加工业产值的比重达到50%。产品结构呈现多样化趋势，方便食品、快餐食品、休闲食品、营养保健食品等发展迅速，产品附加值不断提高，主要农产品深加工比例达到30%以上，逐步由初加工向深加工转变。

4. 农产品加工企业规模扩大，核心竞争力不断增强 近年来，国内已涌现出一批起点高、成长快、规模大的农产品加工企业集团，成为农产品加工业的中坚力量。到2005年底，全国年销售收入500万元以上的农产品加工企业7万多家，全国农产品加工业增加值的20%以上是由固定资产5 000万元以上的企业创造的，并有效带动了关联企业的发展。在全国6万多家农业产业化龙头企业中，国家级龙头企业580

多家，省级重点龙头企业3 750多家，一大批农产品加工龙头企业，不仅规模大，效益好，而且带动能力强，辐射面广。

5. 农产品加工向产区和大城市郊区集中，优势产业集群初步形成　各地根据资源禀赋和区位优势，围绕优势农产品和市场需求发展农产品加工业，建设了一批特色鲜明的农产品加工产业带和加工区。在农业部确立13种优势农产品区域布局的基础上，构建了我国农产品加工产业带和以大城市郊区为依托的加工区，带动了龙头企业的集聚和优势产业集群的形成。

(二)“十一五”期间我国农产品加工业发展环境条件

“十一五”是我国全面建设小康社会的关键时期，统筹城乡区域协调发展，发展现代农业，提高农业综合竞争力，促进农民增收，为农产品加工业发展创造了环境条件，具体体现在：

1. 农产品原料丰富　近年来，我国农产品丰年有余，供求基本平衡，粮食、水果、肉类、奶类、水产品等主要农产品产量已位居世界首位，农业开始步入效益农业阶段，通过延长农业产业链，提高附加值，农产品加工业正在成为效益农业的主导产业。

2. 政策环境宽松　新阶段，中央提出推进社会主义新农村建设战略任务和“以工促农、以城带乡”的方针，2004年以来中央连续下发了三个1号文件，国务院编制并下发了《国民经济和社会发展“十一五”规划纲要》，提出了一系列推动农业发展的相关政策措施，为加快农产品加工业的发展进一步指明了方向。

3. 国内市场需求旺盛　目前我国人均GDP已经达到1 700美元，人民生活开始向全面实现小康迈进，食品消费结构进入了加速调整和升级的重要阶段，在农产品直接消费减少的同时，对加工制品出现了数量和质量上的巨大需求，农产品加工业快速发展的市场环境已经形成。

4. 国际贸易环境逐步改善　我国加入WTO，有利于农产品加工业利用国外资源，有利于农产品加工业扩大出口，有利于国外先进技术及管理经验的引进、消化、吸收和再创新，提升技术水平和产业素质，增强我国农产品加工业的综合竞争力。

(三)“十一五”期间我国农产品加工业发展面临的矛盾和问题

在外部环境上，首先是竞争加剧，农产品贸易逆差，跨国企业对国内企业构成巨大挑战；其次是生产成本增加，人民币升值、能源、食糖和用工紧张造成相应价格的持续上涨，导致加工业生产成本快速增加，近10年来，我国农业生产成本以平均每年10%的速度递增，使农产品价格随之提高；再次是城乡之间、地区之间发展不平衡，使产加销一体化的农业整体竞争优势难以形成。

在我国农产品加工业自身发展上，存在许多问题和不足。一是加工规模和整体水平还比较低。总体上看，中小企业和家庭作坊较多，产业集中度不高，处于低水平循环。目前发达国家农产品加工率在90%左右，我国只有45%左右（初加工以上）；发达国家农产品深加工（两次以上加工）占80%，我国只有30%左右；发达国家农产品加工产值与农业产值之比为2～4∶1，我国仅为1.1∶1。二是加工技术装备差距还比较大。我国农产品加工的技术装备80%还处于20世纪70～80年代的世界平均水平，15%左右处于20世纪90年代水平，只有5%左右达到国际先进水平。三是加工标准和质量控制体系不完善。普遍存在标准陈旧，体系不健全，不适应行业发展与国际接轨的需要，甚至有些重要领域存在标准空白现象。四是服务体系建设滞后。农民专业合作经济组织和行业协会发展滞后，公益性社会化服务平台尚未形成。五是管理体制不完善，政策不配套。

二、指导思想、主要原则和目标

(一)“十一五”期间我国农产品加工业发展的指导思想

坚持以邓小平理论和“三个代表”重要思想为指导，以科学发展观为统领，全面贯彻党的十六届三中、四中、五中和六中全会精神，按照“转变、拓展、提升”三大战略的总体部署，围绕现代农业建设、农民就业增收、社会主义新农村建设及农村和谐社会建设，以科学规划为先导，以科技创新为支撑，切实转变经济增长方式，因地制宜、突出特色、合理布局，围绕大宗、优势农产品，重点发展精深加工，增加农民收益，提高农产品附加值，逐步实现由初级加工向精深加工的转变、由数量增长向质量和效益提高转变，促进农产品加工业持续、稳定、健康发展。

(二)“十一五”期间我国农产品加工业发展的主要原则

1. 坚持以人为本的原则　把促进农业发展、农村繁荣、农民富裕作为农产品加工业发展的出发点和落脚点。通过农产品加工业的带动，建设专业化、标准化、规模化原料基地，形成加工企业与农户风险共担、利益均沾的利益连接机制，使农民分享到加工环节利益。

2. 坚持市场导向原则　充分发挥市场对资源配

置的主导作用，通过优化资源配置，提高行业的整体效益；通过研究、开发一批名牌产品，提高市场占有率；通过培育一批农产品加工优势企业和主导产业，提高国际竞争能力。

3. *坚持质量安全原则*　建立和完善农产品加工标准体系，建立"从农田到餐桌"全程质量控制体系。严格执行农产品（食品）卫生标准和产品标准，大力发展无公害食品、绿色食品和有机农产品，确保农产品加工的质量安全。

4. *坚持科技创新原则*　整合科技资源，加强国外先进技术的引进、消化和吸收，加大技术集成和原始创新，加强企业技术创新，全力打造一批农产品加工科技创新基地和产业化示范基地，全面提高我国农产品加工业的自主创新能力，在关键技术领域实现重点突破。

5. *坚持因地制宜原则*　充分发挥资源、经济、市场和技术优势，依托优势农产品生产区域，发展特色农产品加工业，逐步形成农产品生产和加工相协调的现代农业产业带，实现农产品加工与原料基地的有机结合，将资源优势、区位优势转变为经济优势。

6. *坚持可持续发展原则*　实施可持续发展战略，积极发展环境友好型和资源节约型农产品加工业，原料基地建设必须服从生态环境建设的要求，农产品加工的过程要重视清洁生产和循环利用，加强资源的深度开发利用，节能降耗，减少环境污染，走可持续发展之路。

（三）"十一五"期间我国农产品加工业发展的目标

"十一五"期间，农产品加工业发展紧紧抓住农产品加工增值的关键环节，在结构调整和产业不断升级、质量和效益明显提高、显著降低加工能耗的前提下，力争实现年均增长12%的发展速度，2010年农产品加工业产值突破7万亿元，到"十一五"末农产品加工业产值与农业的产值之比超过1.5∶1。具体目标为：

1. *农产品加工水平要有较大提高*　到2010年我国主要农产品加工转化率（初加工以上）达到60%，精深加工比重明显增加。其中粮食加工转化率达到75%，水果超过15%，蔬菜达到5%，肉类达到15%，水产品超过35%；主要农产品深加工比例（两次以上加工的产品占其产量的比例）达到40%以上。

2. *产品质量水平要有较大提升*　建立高效的农产品质量安全监控体系，绿色食品和有机农产品生产得到更快发展，推动农产品加工企业开展各类产品及管理体系认证，全面提升农产品加工业标准化水平。到2010年，力争60%左右的规模以上农产品加工企业通过ISO、HACCP体系认证，培育一批在国内外市场具有较大潜力和市场占有率的名牌产品。

3. *技术与装备水平要有较大提升*　研制一批具有独立自主知识产权的农产品加工关键技术，开发一批先进的农产品加工重大装备。到2010年，农产品加工新技术得到推广和较广泛应用，农产品加工关键装备国产化率达到60%以上，总体技术与装备水平达到21世纪初的国际先进水平，部分领域达到同期国际先进水平。

4. *龙头企业集群要有较大发展*　培育一大批年销售收入超过100亿元和超过50亿元的龙头企业，做大做强一批农产品加工示范企业和国际竞争力强的出口企业。

5. *基地建设布局要更加优化*　根据《农产品优势布局规划》和《特色农产品布局规划》以及农产品出口需要，建设一大批高标准农产品生产和加工基地，带动农户进行标准化生产。

6. *产业化经营带动能力要有较大提升*　扶持发展一批农民专业合作经济组织和中介服务组织，力争使更多农户进入农业产业化经营领域，农户来自产业化经营的收入明显增加。

三、重点领域与相关区域布局

（一）"十一五"期间我国粮油加工业发展重点

1. *玉米加工*　加强高油玉米、蜡质玉米、高直链玉米等加工专用玉米品种的选育，建设优质原料示范基地；发展专用变性淀粉、玉米淀粉糖、多元醇、乳酸和聚乳酸、淀粉基生物材料等精深加工产品，以及玉米胚芽、蛋白粉和玉米纤维等副产物综合利用新技术、新工艺研究与产业化开发；开展玉米主食食品、休闲食品、方便食品和功能食品的产业化开发；研制年产10万t以上玉米变性淀粉生产专用设备，主要包括脱胚磨、针磨、分离机、浓缩机等；开发竞争力强和技术含量高的品牌产品，使玉米的加工转化率（不包括饲料）由12%提高到20%。

在东北三省、内蒙古等北方春播玉米区和河北、山东、河南等黄淮海平原夏播玉米区，调整玉米加工区域布局，增强玉米主产区的加工转化能力；在河北、吉林、山东等玉米淀粉加工主产省，建立加工专用玉米生产基地，为产品加工提供原料保障；在四川、重庆、云南、贵州等西南山地玉米区，甘肃、陕西、新疆等西北灌溉玉米区和青藏高原玉米区重点发展特色玉米食品、玉米深加工产品和饲料工业。

2. *大豆加工*　加强高油、高蛋白和无豆腥味大豆等加工专用品种的选育，建设优质原料生产示范基地；重点发展销路广、市场潜力大的豆奶（粉）、浓缩蛋白、组织蛋白、专用分离蛋白、改性大豆蛋白等新兴大豆食品或食品基料，使总产量得到较大幅度增长；开展传统豆制品工业化生产技术和装备研制与产品开发，提升产品工业化水平；加强大豆加工副产物综合利用技术研究，积极开发大豆磷脂、低聚糖、异黄酮、食用纤维等功能性食品，以及利用油脚、皂脚水解提取脂肪酸、甘油和利用废弃食用油脂生产生物柴油。同时，优化产业和产品结构，提高大豆综合加工利用能力，延伸大豆产业链条，形成一批在国际市场上具有竞争力的龙头企业和名牌产品，使1 000t/d以上制油企业加工量占总加工量的比例提高到70%、大型龙头企业加工量占总加工量的40%。

在广州、深圳、东莞、北海、厦门等珠江三角洲，上海、张家港、宁波等长江三角洲和大连、青岛、烟台、日照等黄渤海等沿岸、沿海地区建设高级调和油、饲用蛋白、脂肪酸、甘油、维生素E、精制磷脂等生产基地和出口基地；在东北和山东、河南、河北、安徽等黄淮海地区发展大豆浓缩蛋白、组织蛋白、分离蛋白和大豆蛋白粉的生产，并丰富生产品种、开发其终端产品；加强非转基因原料基地建设，大力发展传统豆制品生产，带动区域经济发展。

3. 稻米加工　开发具有良好市场前景的发芽糙米、留胚米、蒸谷米，高纯度米蛋白、米淀粉脂肪替代物、米糠多糖、米糠油、稻壳可降解环保餐盒等高附加值产品；开展米饭、米线、营养强化米、营养米粉等传统大米主食品的加工技术与装备的研究开发，发展米制食品工业化生产；建立健全稻谷加工标准体系、全程质量控制体系和快速检测体系。使日处理稻谷100t以上碾米企业加工量占总加工量的比例提高到45%以上，标准一等以上大米占总量的90%，优质品牌化的大米供应量占全国城镇大米年消费总量的20%左右，工业化米制品产量占稻米总产量的20%。

在东北三省和江苏、江西、湖北、湖南等省培育年处理30万t的加工龙头企业，并形成相应规模的碎米、米糠、稻壳综合开发利用能力；在四川、广西、云南、贵州、陕西、甘肃、宁夏等西部地区建设企业规模为年产3万～5万t的营养大米、营养米粉生产基地。

4. 小麦加工　加强面包、饼干、蛋糕、馒头和面条等加工专用小麦品种的选育，建设优质原料生产基地；优先支持发展食品专用粉、营养强化面粉、预配粉，以及重点发展传统面制主食品工业化生产与应用，实现中式配餐、学生营养配餐及大众面制主食品的工业化生产；开展小麦加工副产品综合利用，开发麦胚食品等高附加值产品；培育和发展我国小麦加工业龙头企业，打造名牌产品，提高产业规模效益和集约化程度；实现面制食品手工制法向工业化生产的转变，使小麦专用粉加工量达到面粉总加工量的18%、日处理小麦200t以上的面粉企业加工量占总加工量的比例达到50%、小麦副产品及综合利用率提高到10%。

在河北、山西、江苏、安徽、山东、河南、陕西、甘肃、新疆发展以优质强筋小麦为原料，生产面包、面条、馒头等专用小麦粉为主的加工企业；在江苏、安徽、河南的部分地区和湖北发展以优质弱筋小麦为原料，生产饼干、蛋糕专用小麦粉为主的加工企业；在黑龙江、内蒙古发展以强筋春小麦为主要原料，生产面条、馒头等专用小麦粉为主的加工企业；在小麦主产区培育日处理小麦1 000t以上的大型面粉加工企业，并提高综合利用水平，京津沪、广东发展日处理面粉10万t以上的传统面制品和日产20万包以上的方便面工业化生产。

5. 油菜籽加工　发展高产"双低"、专用高芥酸、高油酸、高硬脂酸等品种，建立加工专用原料基地；开发和推广菜籽干法脱皮、低温冷榨、膨化浸出、低温脱溶、物理精炼等制油新技术、新设备，减少环境污染，提高产品质量，降低能耗；利用菜籽饼粕、皮壳、油脚等副产物，开展综合利用技术研究，开发生物柴油、润滑油、油墨涂料等新产品，使菜籽精炼油年产量增加到600万t，油菜籽加工设备国产化率由70%提高到90%，脱皮、低温压榨、膨化浸出等制油新技术得到推广应用。

在重庆、四川、云南、贵州、青海等长江上游地区，安徽、江西、湖北、湖南及河南信阳等长江中游地区，上海、江苏、浙江等长江下游地区进行加工企业布局。企业布局生产规模要大、中、小相结合，优势产区应重点发展大型加工企业；产品档次要高、中、低相结合，以发展高中档产品为主，油菜籽优势产区应重点发展高档产品。

6. 薯类加工　开展高淀粉型、油炸型、高蛋白型等马铃薯加工专用品种的选育和贮运技术研究，提高加工原料的品质；开展薯类淀粉和变性淀粉技术研究，提高薯类淀粉和变性淀粉加工水平；开展马铃薯条（片、全粉）、甘薯方便湿粉等技术研究与开发，增加薯类食品的品种，提高产品的质量；加强废弃物的综合利用，发展配合饲料生产，解决薯类加工厂废弃物污染问题。使薯类加工转化率提高到25%，深加工转化率提高到10%。薯类淀粉总产量增加到150万t，变性淀粉增加到30万t，薯类食品增加到50万t，薯类加工设备国产化率由70%提高到90%。

马铃薯与甘薯类加工企业主要在河北、山西、内蒙古、辽宁、吉林、黑龙江、福建、山东、湖北、湖南、重庆、四川、云南、贵州、陕西、甘肃、宁夏等地布局；木薯加工企业主要在广西和广东布局。加工企业生产规模要大、中、小相结合，薯类优势产区应重点发展大型企业，产品档次要高、中、低相结合，以发展高中档产品为主，薯类优势产区要重点发展高档产品为主。

7. 特色杂粮加工　加强燕麦、荞麦、啤酒大麦、小米，以及红小豆、绿豆、蚕豆等食用豆类等特色杂粮加工特性研究，建立优质加工专用原料基地；利用新工艺、新技术和新装备，开发和生产适销对路、竞争力强、技术含量高的产品，扩大产品的应用领域；优先发展功能性、营养型早餐类食品，加强传统食品的改造和工业化生产，开展燕麦β-葡聚糖、荞麦黄酮等高附加值成分的研究，开发具有保健功能的特色食品；开发燕麦早餐食品、荞麦传统食品、大麦茶、小米饮料、豆类食品馅料等产品，并拓宽产品的应用范围，满足多样化的市场需求。

杂粮、杂豆加工业的发展也应按照作物优势区域带进行合理布局；生产企业的规模大、中、小相结合，以发展大中型企业为主；优势产区重点发展初中级加工，产品档次高、中、低相结合；经济发达地区加工企业要以发展高档产品为主，面向城市高端消费人群。

（二）“十一五”期间我国果蔬加工业发展重点

1. 果蔬汁加工　加强果蔬汁加工专用品种引进和选育，研究原料预处理技术、高效榨汁技术、膜技术、非热力杀菌技术、无菌包装技术、浓缩汁冷冻贮藏技术以及综合利用技术等；对引进的关键设备与零部件及加工工艺进行消化、吸收，同时引进新型的加工设备，如高压脉冲电场杀菌机等；开发果蔬汁新产品，主要包括NFC果蔬汁、复合汁和果蔬汁主剂；建立既与国际接轨又适合中国国情的果蔬汁加工全程质量安全控制体系，并进行产业化示范和推广。

在加工布局上，原料主产区建立浓缩加工厂，发展浓缩果蔬汁、果蔬浆等半成品，大中城市等消费市场建立灌装加工厂，发展果蔬汁终端产品；辽宁、山东、陕西等地发展浓缩苹果汁；内蒙古、新疆、甘肃、宁夏等西部地区发展番茄酱、浓缩葡萄汁；天津、河北、安徽等地发展桃汁、浓缩梨汁；重庆、湖北等地发展柑橘浓缩汁与NFC柑橘汁；海南和云南等地发展热带果汁；北京、上海、广州等大城市发展直饮型果蔬汁终端产品；形成高端产品与低端产品、半成品与终端产品、出口与内销产品共存的产品结构布局。

2. 果蔬罐头加工　选育适合罐头加工的专用品种，并对其加工特性进行研究；加强去皮技术、电脑程序控制自动杀菌技术、综合利用技术等研究，研发连续化、智能化的加工装备；开发易开罐、软包装、半刚性包装等新型包装容器和材料；重点开发轻糖型、混合型等新型果蔬罐头产品，建立并推广罐头加工全程质量安全控制体系。

立足区域布局和产品布局，考虑原料基地和产品市场两大因素，进行企业的合理布局。在河北、浙江、安徽、福建、山东、湖南、新疆等传统生产省份集中发展果蔬罐头生产；在浙江、湖南、四川、湖北等发展柑橘罐头，河北、辽宁、浙江、山东、安徽等发展桃罐头；在福建、山东、山西等发展芦笋罐头；在浙江、福建等发展竹笋罐头；在新疆等西部地区发展番茄罐头。

3. 脱水果蔬加工　选育适合脱水果蔬加工的专用品种，并建立原料基地；研究冷冻干燥、真空微波干燥、低温膨化干燥、联合干燥、太阳能利用及产品分级等技术，开发新型脱水果蔬产品；开发先进、高效、节能的脱水设备；建立并推广脱水果蔬加工全程质量控制体系。

在果蔬主产地及东南沿海贸易发达地区，如山西、江苏、浙江、福建、山东等地发展脱水果蔬产业，同时向西部地区如甘肃、宁夏、新疆等发展，形成“优势品种、优势产区加工”的“双优”布局。重点发展洋葱、大蒜、南瓜、胡萝卜、姜、辣椒、萝卜条等脱水产品，扩大脱水马铃薯、洋葱、胡萝卜等大品种生产规模。重点在东南沿海出口基地进行加工业布局，同时发展甘肃、宁夏、新疆等西部地区及东北三省的脱水果蔬加工，增强向中亚及俄罗斯等欧洲国家的出口能力。

4. 果蔬速冻加工　选育适合速冻果蔬加工的专用品种，并对其加工特性进行研究；研究快速冻结和快速解冻新技术，开发速冻果蔬新型产品，扩大豌豆、甜玉米、草莓、荔枝、杨梅等产品生产规模；开发生产能力高的连续螺旋式速冻机、超低温液氮和二氧化碳喷淋式速冻机以及配套的果蔬预冷机，并开展速冻包装材料的研发；建立并推广速冻果蔬加工全程质量控制体系。

在果蔬主产地及东南沿海地区，河北、辽宁、江苏、浙江、福建、山东、广东等地发展速冻果蔬产业，同时向东北及云南、新疆等边疆省份发展，形成环形发展产业布局。重点发展芋头、菠菜、豆类等速冻品种，扩大豌豆、甜玉米、马铃薯等大品种生产规模；增加国际市场上交易量可观的速冻水果生产如速冻草莓、杨梅等果品；重点在东南沿海出口基地进行加工业布局，加强云南、新疆等西部地区及东北三省的速冻果蔬企业建设，增强向南亚、中亚及俄罗斯等欧洲国家的出口能力。

5. 果蔬物流　研发果蔬商品化处理技术与设备；研究果蔬贮运保鲜新技术，开发新型果蔬保鲜剂、保鲜材料及保鲜设备；研究果蔬鲜切技术、品质控制及与快速检测技术；建立果蔬冷链储运系统和果蔬物流信息平台；按照国际质量标准和要求建立果蔬物流全程质量控制体系，并进行产业化推广与示范。

立足山东、陕西的苹果产业带、长江中上游的柑橘产业带，以及河北、辽宁、山东等蔬菜主产区进行物流区域布局，重点发展大蒜、洋葱、番茄、芦笋、青椒和辣椒、胡萝卜、萝卜、甘蓝、花椰菜等出口蔬菜和苹果、梨和柑橘等出口果品。在东部沿海地区蔬菜主产地建设大型蔬菜物流企业；在河北、辽宁、浙江、山东、湖南、陕西等果品主产省建设大型果品物流企业。

（三）"十一五"期间我国畜产品加工业发展重点

1. 肉制品加工　加强冷却肉、冰鲜禽肉、发酵肉制品、传统肉制品、功能性肉制品等产品精深加工与物流配送技术研究与开发，增加肉制品加工品种，提高肉品加工能力；加强对畜禽血液、骨组织、畜禽脏器、皮毛绒等的利用；研制开发具有我国自主知识产权的肉品加工先进设备，重点开发自动化智能分级生产设备、自动化肉品加工生产设备、自动化在线或定位检测设备等，提高我国肉品加工关键设备的自给率；开展研究微生物预报预测技术、溯源技术，建立完善的肉制品加工全程质量控制体系，建立动物产品质量安全保障体系，使我国肉品加工率达到10%，设备国产化率达到50%。

在东北及河北、内蒙古、甘肃、青海、宁夏、新疆等牛羊资源丰富地区，重点进行优质牛羊肉的屠宰与加工龙头企业布局，以生产冷却牛羊肉、冷冻小包装牛羊肉、低温肉制品等产品为主；在河北、山东、河南、四川等活猪资源丰富地区，重点进行生猪屠宰和加工龙头企业布局，以生产冷却猪肉、高温火腿肠、发酵肉制品和低温肉制品等产品为主；在西南地区，重点进行中式传统肉制品加工龙头企业布局，以生产腊肠、腊肉、宣威火腿等产品主，兼顾低温肉制品的开发生产；在江浙水禽资源丰富地区，重点进行水禽加工龙头企业布局，以生产水禽低温肉制品和盐水鸭等特色产品为主。

2. 乳制品加工　加强原料奶营养与加工特性研究，建立优质奶源基地；研究干酪、益生菌发酵产品、强化婴儿乳粉、免疫活性肽等新型乳制品加工技术，优化我国乳制品的产品结构；研究并建立菌种资源库，选育出风味独特、性能优良、便于商品化的优良菌种，生产国际先进水平的商品化直投式发酵剂；研究现代乳品质量及安全检验技术，开发质量检验设备，建立乳品加工标准体系和全程质量控制体系，提升乳制品国际竞争力。

在东北及内蒙古东部玉米带及天然草场丰富地区，利用丰富的原料奶优势，建立和发展乳牛养殖和乳品加工龙头企业，主要发展专用乳粉、UHT奶、长保质期巴氏杀菌奶和乳饮料、冰淇淋等制品；在中原、华南、西南、华东及城市周边的奶业区，支持发展大中型乳品企业，主要生产供城市消费的巴氏消毒奶、酸奶和冰淇淋等短效产品；对缺乏原料奶供应的城市以UHT奶、酸奶为主；对于相对落后的农村以奶粉、UHT袋奶为主。因地制宜，结合资源、市场、发展潜力等进行合理布局，将规模优势、资源优势、技术优势和市场优势转化为经济优势，避免过度集中投资，造成局部奶源的紧张和市场的拼争，鼓励中小企业发展酸奶、巴氏消毒奶等短效产品，使企业形成自我生存的特色优势。

3. 蛋制品加工　重点进行消毒包装洁蛋、液态蛋、高特性专用蛋粉等新型蛋制品生产关键技术和设备的研究开发；对溶菌酶、特异性抗体（IgY）因子、清壳素、生物活性钙素、硫酸软骨素等蛋及蛋壳内活性成分的提取及应用进行研究开发，提高蛋品及副产物附加值；对松花皮蛋、咸蛋和糟蛋等中式传统蛋制品现代化生产技术进行研究，提升传统蛋制品的生产技术水平；加强蛋品加工国产化设备的研究与推广；建立禽蛋加工生产操作规程与全程质量控制体系，对蛋禽饲料、蛋禽养殖生产的各个环节进行规范和控制，确保禽蛋原料质量与安全。

在河北、辽宁、吉林、黑龙江、江苏、安徽、山东、河南、湖北、湖南等鸡蛋生产集中的地区，重点发展消毒分级的鲜蛋（洁蛋）、液态蛋、软包装卤蛋以及方便蛋制品生产企业；在洞庭湖、鄱阳湖周围江苏、浙江、江西、湖北、湖南等省水禽蛋资源丰富地区，大力发展水禽蛋品加工企业；在浙江、江西、湖北、湖南等鹌鹑蛋生产集中的地区，重点发展对我国香港、台湾和东南亚、日本、欧洲等地出口鹌鹑皮蛋的加工；在西部的重庆、四川、贵州、陕西四省，主要建立无公害、绿色放养禽蛋生产加工企业。

（四）"十一五"期间我国水产品加工业发展重点

1. 淡水鱼类加工　研究烤鳗、鱼糜制品、鲟鱼子、水产模拟食品等精深加工技术，开发冷冻调理食品、冷藏保鲜鱼制品、即食食品和休闲食品；利用加工废弃物研究开发氨基酸、调味品、营养品、健康饮料、功能食品等；开发淡水鱼加工专用成套设备；建立淡水鱼加工的全程质量控制体系。

在浙江、福建、广东、广西、海南等地区主要进行鳗鱼、鲢鱼、罗非鱼、鲮鱼、鲟鱼等加工开发，发展烤鳗、冻鱼及鱼片、鱼罐头、鱼糜和鱼糜制品、氨基酸调味品、鲟鱼子、腌熏制品、鱼露、模拟食品、方便食品、功能性食品等的加工；在辽宁、江苏、山东等地区主要进行鲢鱼、鳙鱼、鲟鱼等加工开发，发展鱼糜和鱼糜制品、鱼罐头、冻鱼及鱼片、氨基酸调味品、模拟食品、方便食品、功能性食品等的加工；在安徽、江西、湖北、湖南、四川等地区主要进行鲢鱼、鳙鱼、罗非鱼和鲟鱼等加工开发，发展鱼糜及鱼糜制品、冻鱼及鱼片、鱼罐头、腌熏制品等加工。

2. 海水鱼类加工　研究以海水养殖鱼类、远洋捕捞鱼类、海水中上层鱼类的超低温速冻技术、物流保鲜技术、干燥技术、质构重组技术等，开发海水鱼类加工新产品；加强海水鱼类加工副产品的综合开发利用，达到提高经济效益和资源利用率的目的；建立完善的海水鱼类生产、加工、流通和消费的质量安全保障体系。

在海水中上层鱼类主要分布地区，辽宁、浙江、福建、山东、广东等省，主要进行鱼粉和鱼油加工，其次进行腌干制品和鱼糜制品加工；在远洋捕捞鱼类主要分布地区，辽宁、浙江、山东等省，主要进行金枪鱼等深海鱼类加工，开发鱼糜制品、调味制品和保健食品；在海水养殖鱼类主要分布地区，浙江、福建、山东、广东等省，重点进行养殖大黄鱼、鲈鱼加工。

3. 虾、蟹类加工　研究原料虾蟹的质量控制技术、虾蟹新产品的精深加工技术如超低温速冻技术、保鲜技术，开发新型生物保鲜剂及加工成套设备；利用虾蟹加工废弃物开发甲壳质和甲壳胺等精深加工产品。

在山东、广东、广西、海南等对虾加工主要分布地区，应加强对虾养殖过程中渔用兽药使用的监督管理，提高出口对虾的质量安全水平。

4. 贝、藻类加工　研究养殖贝类的生物危害检测技术，贝类的净化、保鲜与保活技术，贝类的活性物质提取技术，开发新型贝类产品；研究藻类危害物脱除与检测技术、活性物质提取技术，开发海藻食品、海藻胶、海藻保健品、海藻化妆品；建立贝、藻类加工标准体系与全程质量控制体系。

在辽宁、福建、山东、广东等贝类主要分布地区，主要开发供应超市的保鲜牡蛎、冷冻牡蛎、裹面包屑的牡蛎产品；浙江主要发展缢蛏精深加工；江苏主要发展文蛤加工；广东主要发展贻贝加工。在辽宁、福建、山东等海带主要分布地区，重点开发海带食品、海带调味品、海带保健食品、海带化工产品；江苏、浙江开展紫菜研发，重点发展紫菜食品、保健品和海藻化工产品；广东省开展江蓠、马尾藻、紫菜、麒麟菜和螺旋藻等研发，优先发展藻类即食食品、藻类保健品、藻类药物；海南应重点发展海洋蔬菜藻类食品和琼脂胶、卡拉胶和海藻胶加工产品。

5. 其他海产品加工　研究鱿鱼质构重组技术与综合利用技术、海参胶原蛋白稳定技术与保鲜技术、海蜇深加工技术与含矾废水污染物控制技术，开发鱿鱼鱼糜制品和调味制品、海参保鲜制品和保健食品、海蜇方便食品等高附加值产品。

在远洋捕捞主要分布地区，辽宁、浙江、山东、天津等省、直辖市，主要进行鱿鱼深加工，开发鱼糜制品、调味鱿鱼制品、鱿鱼废弃物开发保健食品；在海水养殖主要分布地区，山东、辽宁等省，重点进行海参加工。在山东、辽宁、广西、天津等省、自治区、直辖市主要开发海蜇深加工产品和方便食品。

(五)“十一五”期间我国传统农产品加工业发展重点

1. 茶叶加工　开展绿茶清洁加工技术研究，名优茶机械化、标准化加工技术研究和关键设备的研制，以及绿茶连续化、智能化加工的前期工艺技术研究，建立符合现代食品加工要求的绿茶示范生产线；开展新型茶饮料开发及制备新技术研究、袋泡绿茶加工的关键技术研究；开展茶叶天然产物提取与利用研究，主要研究类黄酮化合物、茶多糖、茶氨酸、茶色素等天然产物的提取与利用，开发功能性的高附加值产品。

茶叶初制加工主要在原料主产区布局，茶叶精制加工及深加工主要在中心城市布局；出口茶叶加工主要在沿海城市布局；茶叶初制加工以发展中小规模为主，在原料运输方便的前提下，尽可能扩大加工能力。茶叶加工产品结构，力争传统加工产品比重下降，精深加工产品比重上升。

2. 糖料加工　重点发展精炼糖（精制幼砂糖、单晶冰糖、赤砂糖等）加工业；鼓励开展以低成本糖料为原料生产燃料酒精的研究；支持采用生物膜和基因工程等高新技术，开发精细化工产品等，提高食糖加工副产物综合利用水平，开展甘蔗渣造纸、甜菜废丝利用研究和开发等。

糖料加工主要在原料主产区布局。重点建设南方、北方两大糖料加工业重点产业带，其中，南方重点产业带布局在广西、云南、广东和海南四省、自治区，北方重点产业带主要布局在黑龙江、新疆、内蒙古三省、自治区。支持制糖企业建立科工贸一体化的大型企业集团，充分发挥规模经营效益。

3. *蜂产品加工* 加强蜂产品功能因子研究，重点进行功能因子的提取、合成、分析、检测、功能评价、分离重组等，拓展蜂产品的开发深度和范围，提高蜂产品的附加值；加大蜂蜜果糖的开发，通过深加工提取和转化技术，将商品价值低的次等级蜂蜜加工成蜂蜜果糖，同时添加功能因子，使之成为对糖尿病人和心血管病人有辅助疗效的保健食品；开展蜂花粉开发利用研究，采用高科技手段，对花粉进行破壁，富集核酸，并利用其中的黄酮、维生素等活性物质，开发以抗衰老功能为主的蜂花粉核酸制品。

蜂产品加工主要在北京、上海、江苏、浙江、湖北、广东、四川等省、直辖市布局，以发展蜂蜜、蜂王浆、蜂花粉、蜂胶等深加工保健产品为主，大力发展有机蜂产品、保健蜂产品、传统蜂产品、出口蜂产品等。

4. *食用菌加工* 加强食用菌加工和保鲜技术研究，提高产品质量和档次，增强国际市场竞争力；重点开发食用菌即食食品和保健食品，增加食用菌产品附加值；大力开展食用菌药用成分提取与利用研究，延长产业链，提高食用菌生产的综合效益。

在浙江、福建、山东等食用菌主产区，建立一批食用菌生产加工基地，大力发展无公害、绿色和有机食用菌生产加工，积极推进食用菌即食食品、保健品及药物开发，从根本上提升我国食用菌行业发展水平。初加工主要在主产区进行布局，精深加工主要在中心城市布局。在食用菌加工产品结构中，力争初加工制品比重下降，不超过80%，即食、保健食品和药物制品比重上升，分别达到15%和5%。

四、重点任务

“十一五”期间将通过重点任务的实施，为推进我国农产品加工业发展提供有力的支撑。

（一）农产品加工示范基地建设工程

按照农产品加工业发展规律，结合实施《优势农产品区域布局规划》，根据各地加工业发展的基础和特点，选择资源和市场配套性强、可以形成产业集聚和经济优势的农产品加工区域及大城市郊区，重点建设一批全国农产品加工示范基地。建设的主要内容是：通过推进农产品加工业的产业集聚，进一步整合各种资源和生产要素，改善基础设施条件，为农产品加工业快速发展提供示范样板。示范基地建设要与优势农产品区域布局和商品粮基地建设相协调，布局合理、特色突出，按照促进优势产业带形成与发展、商品粮基地巩固与提高的要求，以市场为导向，依靠科技进步，不断提高农产品综合加工能力，实现由初级加工向精深加工转变，由传统加工工艺向现代高技术转变，由资源消耗型向高效利用型转变，使示范基地成为促进农产品加工业健康发展的推动力量。到2010年，重点培育500个全国农产品加工示范基地。同时，选择一批龙头加工企业作为示范基地的依托单位，加强对科研开发、技术改造、营销服务等方面引导，使其形成与优势农产品生产规模相适应的配套加工能力。

（二）加工专用原料基地建设工程

在《优势农产品区域布局规划》确定的专用小麦、专用玉米、优质水稻、高油大豆、柑橘、苹果、甘蔗、肉牛肉羊、生猪、牛奶、水产品等13种优势农产品、41个优势产区内，按照农产品加工的具体要求，选育加工专用品种，并建立加工专用原料基地，以满足农产品加工业发展的要求。鼓励加工企业直接参与加工专用原料生产，按照国际通行标准建设加工专用原料基地，实现专业化生产、规模化种养、标准化管理，形成安全可靠的加工原料来源。建设的主要内容是：以优势农产品产业带及种、养基地为依托，以加工企业为龙头，建立一批与加工业配套的粮油、蔬菜、果品、畜禽、蛋、奶及水产品专用原料基地。到2010年，依据《优势农产品区域布局规划》，在全国培育50个具有区域特色、示范带动作用大的农产品加工专用原料基地，为农产品加工业健康发展提供原料保障。

（三）农产品加工技术创新工程

通过有效整合大专院校、科研单位和企业的力量，构建农产品加工业技术创新体系，形成农产品加工业技术创新机制。建设的主要内容是：加快农产品加工研发中心建设。加速农产品加工公共资源整合，以中国农业科学院为依托建设国家农产品加工研发中心，以中央或地方大专院校、科研单位为依托重点建设50个专业性的农产品加工研发分中心，解决农产品加工业重大技术创新、技术引进和技术推广问题。推进建立企业技术研发中心。在100家农产品加工骨干企业进行建立技术研发中心的试点，鼓励科研院所、大专院校与企业的产学研对接，组建专业性的农产品加工研发中心或农产品加工企业的技术创新机构，选准科研重点，进行联合攻关，开发一批具有自主知识产权的科技成果，促进建立以加工企业为主体，科研单位、大专院校为依托的自主创新机制。促进科技成果的产业化。用好农产品加工重大关键技术筛选的成果，每年对20～30项农产品加工适用和重大关键技术进行推广示范，通过研究、开发、引进、推广一批农产品加工重大关键技术、工艺和装备，突破农产品精深加工和综合利用方面技术瓶颈的制约，全面提升我国农产品加工业的技术水平，培育一批具有较高市场占有率的名牌产品。国家重点在农产品加工研发中心和骨干企业技术研发中心基础设施建设、农产品加工关键技术引进、开发上给予扶持。

（四）农产品加工质量安全保障工程

通过健全完善农产品加工质量标准和检测体系，加强从原料生产到加工全过程的标准化管理和质量控制，提高农产品加工质量安全水平。建设的主要内容是：制定并发布《"十一五"农产品加工标准制修订指南》。根据农产品加工业发展的特点以及国际国内标准的现状，研究、制定适合我国国情的农产品加工业标准制定（修订）框架指南，有效指导"十一五"期间我国农产品加工业标准的制定（修订）工作。构建农产品加工国际标准跟踪平台。及时收集、掌握和整理CAC、ISO等国际组织以及美国、日本、韩国、欧盟等主要贸易国农产品进出口标准及政策的发展动态，并随时反映国际农产品贸易中出现的新情况、新趋势和新问题，为广大农产品加工企业采取积极的应对措施和制定（修订）我国农产品加工标准以及政府科学决策提供参考依据。加强农产品加工全程质量控制体系建设。加快农产品加工企业推行良好生产操作规范（GMP）、危害分析与关键控制点（HACCP）和ISO9000族系质量管理与控制体系，进一步加强对已通过认证的企业后续监管。同时，完善农产品加工质量安全检测体系，充分发挥现有农产品质检机构的作用，拓展其检测范围，扶持鼓励现有省级质检中心开展农产品加工业质量安全检测工作；大力支持检测新技术的研究，逐步建立起一套完整的快速、便携、精确的检验检测技术体系，全面提高我国农产品加工业检验检测的能力。建立健全农产品加工企业质量安全诚信体系。研究食用农产品安全诚信的评价指标，建立食用农产品安全诚信监控网络，营造"重质量安全，守行业诚信"的氛围。

（五）农产品加工信息化建设工程

通过信息化带动，促进农产品加工业走新型工业化的路子。建设的主要内容是：健全完善农产品加工信息网络。通过对现有的农产品加工信息网的完善和改扩建，整合全国农产品加工信息资源，构筑县、市、省和国家多层次的农产品加工信息网络，为宏观决策、促进产业发展提供丰富的信息资源。推进农产品加工企业信息化。依托农产品加工信息网，建立农产品加工市场信息预警机制，为农产品加工企业经营管理提供重要依据；同时推动农产品加工企业开展电子商务应用，选择100家在电子商务应用方面有一定基础的农产品加工企业进行试点示范。探索建立农产品物流信息化平台。构建农产品加工、生产、运输、销售的物流信息数据库，对农产品物流各环节进行编码标识和信息采集，实现农产品物流的现代化、标准化和信息化，选择50家农产品加工企业开展物流信息化平台建设试点。

（六）农产品加工创业工程

加强对新办中小型农产品加工企业创业的扶持和服务，促进我国农产品加工业形成合理的产业结构和产品结构，扩大农村劳动力就业、增加农民收入，提高农产品加工转化能力。建设的主要内容是：开展创业辅导培训。选择加工业已经具有一定的基础，并对农产品主产区有较强辐射作用的地区，以农民为主要对象，举办农产品加工创业培训。通过系统、规范的创业培训课程学习，了解就业形势和创业环境，了解申办各类经济组织的要求及相关的政策、法规，激发并增强农民，特别是年轻农民自主创办小企业的信心，学习、掌握企业经营管理的必备知识，提高自主创业的综合素质，以及管理运营企业的能力。加强创业孵化服务。鼓励各地在优势农产品产业带、粮食主产区和大城市郊区建设农产品加工业创业辅导基地，依托当地农产品资源和市场资源孵化中小型加工企业，促进农产品就地转化增值和农民就近转移就业。农产品加工创业辅导基地建设要科学规划，合理布局，要有利于农产品原料和加工产品的集散，有利于技术、人才、资金、信息和劳动力等要素资源的集聚，有利于农民的持续增收。"十一五"期间，全国重点培育50个农产品加工创业辅导基地进行试点示范。构建创业服务平台。培训服务平台，用好现有的农业、乡镇企业培训中心，通过评估、认证，确定一批农产品加工创业培训基地。信息服务平台，整合现有的与农产品加工有关的网络、报刊等媒体，建立为中小型农产品加工企业提供创业信息服务的平台。咨询服务平台，广泛发动社会力量，为中小型农产品加工企业提供企业诊断、技术和管理等方面的咨询服务。信用服务平台，建立新办中小型农产品加工企业信用档案，开展信用征集、信用登记评估、信用发布以及诚信活动，规范企业创业行为。

五、促进农产品加工业发展的政策措施

党中央、国务院高度重视农产品加工业的发展，把其作为促进县域经济发展、增加农民收入和提高农业综合生产能力的重要措施之一，"十一五"期间，必须抓住机遇，进一步落实完善各项政策，营造良好环境，有效化解制约发展的矛盾和问题，促进农产品加工业健康发展，为此提出以下政策措施。

（一）加大财政、金融以及税收等方面的扶持力度

继续落实好2004年以来下发的三个中央1号文件、国务院办公厅《关于促进农产品加工业发展的意见》（国办发［2002］62号）等一系列重要文件中关于加快发展农产品加工业的有关要求，加强与有关部门的协调，全面落实相关政策。积极协调财政部门争取设立农产品加工业发展专项资金。加大对农产品加工业的财政支持，加强对重点优势农产品加工业的基础设施建设、关键技术研发、引进和推广的扶持；加强对农产品加工业创业扶持，鼓励农民个人或各类农村合作经济组织，在主要农产品产地新办以吸纳当地农民就业为主的农产品加工企业，争取由财政给予适当补助；增强粮食转化能力，争取通过财政贴息鼓励种粮大户、农民合作组织和粮食加工企业的基本建设、流动基金等生产性投入；加强对农产品加工综合利用的扶持。积极配合税务部门做好农产品加工业增值税改革，争取对农产品加工企业开展综合利用、建设加工专用原料基地的税收优惠政策。积极协调金融部门推行积极的金融政策，拓宽农产品加工企业融资渠道，通过探索仓单质押等办法，不断扩大对企业流动资金的支持；争取政策性银行加大对农产品加工业的支持力度，增加中长期贷款；争取扩大农业政策性保险的试点范围。鼓励和支持农产品加工企业利用资本市场直接融资，鼓励有条件的地方建立专业担保机构，为农产品加工企业提供融资担保。

（二）鼓励探索企业与农户利益连接新机制

积极引导，进一步完善“龙头企业＋农民专业合作经济组织＋农户”、“龙头企业＋农村经纪人＋农户”和“龙头企业＋基地＋农户”等各种企业与农户利益连接模式。在此基础上，探索农民合作组织兴办农产品加工业、农民土地经营权入股或转移、“公司＋中介组织＋农民”形式的股份制合作组织等新型模式和机制，以加强企业和农户间的利益联系，建立利益共享、风险共担、长期稳定的利益连接机制，使农户最大限度地分享农产品加工、流通等环节的利益，建立农民增收的长效机制。鼓励龙头企业参与农业结构调整和农产品标准化生产基地建设，支持以龙头企业为依托，建立大型农产品生产、加工和销售基地，逐步形成专业化、标准化和规模化的农业产业带；鼓励和引导龙头企业按行业进行联合，形成具有较强竞争力的企业集群。

（三）建立健全各类社会化服务

鼓励各类服务机构，围绕农产品加工业的需要，发挥在行业状况调查、产业规划制定、行业诚信体系建设、项目评估、技术咨询、人才培训、质量检测等方面的作用，促进我国农产品加工业的行业管理和服务逐步规范化。鼓励同类型的农产品加工企业之间组建专业协会，加强行业自律，协调解决行业内部矛盾，支持行业协会组织出口企业积极应对国外歧视性反倾销等限制性措施，促进行业健康发展。积极支持从事优势农产品加工、销售的企业，参加国内外的大型展览展销，提高我国优势农产品加工制品的市场知名度和占有率。协调有关部门，在协会的开办、登记、注册等方面提供便利。对有关农产品加工业的创业辅导、融资担保、科技服务、信息传递、政策咨询、人员培训、标准体系建设等公益性服务，要争取各级政府的支持，健全服务网络，强化服务功能。

（四）加快技术创新步伐

积极协调有关部门，加大国家科技支撑计划、跨越计划、农业综合开发、“948”等对农产品加工项目的资助力度，不断提升农产品加工业的原始创新能力和核心竞争力。促进中小型农产品加工企业技术创新，在产品研发、技术引进、标准与信息体系建设、人员培训等方面加强引导和扶持。鼓励大企业增加科研投入，建立技术研发中心，提高企业技术创新能力，开发具有自主知识产权的新技术和新产品。鼓励科研院所、大专院校和加工企业之间强强联合、优势互补，形成以“企业为主体、以科研单位为依托”的技术研发体系，加快农产品加工业的技术创新步伐。

（五）推进重点任务实施

积极协调有关部门，切实加强引导，加快推进六项工程重点任务的实施，争取对六项工程的公共基础设施和公共服务手段、措施的政策扶持。通过重点任务的实施，形成一批优势农产品加工产业集群，优化加工业布局，提升产业的带动力和支撑力；建设一批农产品加工专用原料基地，实现加工原料的标准化、规模化、专业化生产；培育一批具有带动效应和具有成长潜力的中小企业，促进农产品的就地加工增值和农民的就近转移就业；加速构建农产品加工业技术创新体系，形成农产品加工业技术创新机制；健全完善农产品加工质量标准和检测体系，加强从原料生产到加工全过程的标准化管理和质量控制，提高质量控制的整体水平；搭建信息化平台，推进农产品加工业管理和生产的信息化水平。

（六）提高认识，加强领导

各级农业部门必须充分认识大力发展农产品加工业的重大战略意义，要按照中央的要求，切实履行好职责范围内农产品加工业的宏观管理和指导工作。按照农产品加工业的发展规律，转变工作职能，创新工作方式，完善工作机制，提高工作水平。农业部根据国务院赋予的职能，围绕解决好“三农”问题，加强管理职能建设，尽快完善配套措施和保障手段，切实发挥作用，建立统一、协调、高效的工作体系，实施有效指导。地方各级农业部门要积极协调政府及有关部门，尽快整合力量，进一步明确职能，切实落实责任，形成推进农产品加工业发展的工作合力，为农产品加工业创造宽松、有力的发展环境。

第四部分

国内综合统计资料

国内综合统计资料
简 要 说 明

1. 本部分统计资料主要包括农林牧渔业主要产品产量、农产品加工机械拥有量及农产品加工行业固定资产投资情况、按国民经济行业分类统计有关农产品加工业现状、农产品加工业主要产品产量、农产品加工业主要产品出口创汇情况、农产品加工业部分行业与企业排序，以及我国西部地区综合统计等7部分统计数据。

2. 香港和澳门特别行政区的统计是构成国家统计总体的一部分，但根据中华人民共和国《香港特别行政区基本法》和《澳门特别行政区基本法》的有关原则，香港、澳门与内地是相对独立的统计区域，根据各自不同的统计制度和法律规定，独立进行统计工作。本部分中所涉及的统计数据均未包括香港、澳门特别行政区和台湾省。这三部分相关统计数据，另在本年鉴附录中列出。

3. 本部分统计资料数据，除已注明“资料来源”之外，其余均采用国家统计局公布的数据。

4. 本部分采用的统计数据，基本上以2005年数据为主，为了保持与上卷年鉴提供数据的连续性，有一部分统计数据是在上卷基础上，延续列出。

5. 本部分有关表中所示“规模以上非国有企业”是指年产品销售收入500万元以上的非国有企业。

6. 本部分有关表中所示工业产值、工业增加值、工业产品销售产值、利税总额等数据未单独标注者，均按当年价格计算（当年价格既为现行价格）。

7. 本部分统计资料数据所使用的度量单位，均采用国际统一标准计量单位。对有关行业未按国际统一标准计量单位提供的数据，编辑部均按国际统一标准计量单位进行了相应换算。

8. 本部分中同一类、同一行业统计数据，由于管理渠道、统计范围、数据采集方法、时间等略有不同，加之有些行业与相关管理部门交叉较多，因此数据也略有不同。但来自同一系统的数据基本上是一致的。

9. 本部分统计资料中，依据国家统计局、农业部、国家林业局、中国食品工业协会、中国轻工联合会、中国纺织工业协会等部门、行业提供的相关数据，开辟的“我国西部地区综合统计”专栏，由于时间短促，难免有误，请给予批评指正。

10. 本部分统计资料中符号使用说明：“空格”表示该项统计指标数据不详或无该项数据；“*”或“①”表示本表下有注解。

农林牧渔业主要产品产量统计

表 1　我国主要农产品产量（2001—2005 年）　　单位：万 t

年份	粮食						
	合计	谷物				豆类	薯类
		小计	稻谷	小麦	玉米		
2001	45 264	39 648	17 758	9 387	11 409	2 053	3 563
2002	45 706	39 799	17 454	9 029	12 131	2 241	3 666
2003	43 070	37 429	16 066	8 649	11 583	2 128	3 513
2004	46 947	40 133	17 909	9 195	13 029	2 232	3 558
2005	48 402	42 777	18 059	9 745	13 937	2 158	3 468

年份	棉花	油料				麻类	
		小计	花生	油菜籽	芝麻	小计	黄红麻
2001	532.4	2 865	1 442	1 133	80.4	68.1	10.6
2002	491.6	2 897	1 482	1 055	89.5	96.4	15.9
2003	486.0	2 811	1 342	1 142	59.3	85.3	10.0
2004	632.4	3 066	1 434	1 318	70.4	107.4	8.7
2005	571.4	3 077	1 434	1 305	62.5	110.5	8.3

年份	糖料			茶叶	烟叶	
	小计	甘蔗	甜菜		小计	烤烟
2001	8 655	7 566	1 089	70.2	235.0	205
2002	10 293	9 011	1 282	74.5	245.0	214
2003	9 642	9 024	618	76.8	226.0	202
2004	9 571	8 985	586	83.5	240.6	216.3
2005	9 452	8 664	788	93.5	268.3	243.5

年份	水果						蔬菜*
	合计	苹果	柑橘	梨	葡萄	香蕉	
2001	6 658	2 002	1 161	880	368	527	48 422
2002	6 952	1 924	1 199	931	448	556	52 861
2003	14 517	2 110	1 345	980	518	590	54 032
2004	15 341	2 368	1 496	1 064	568	606	55 065
2005	8 836	2 401	1 592	1 132	579	652	56 452

* 从 2003 年起，蔬菜产量中含菜用瓜。

表 2　各地区主要农产品产量（2005 年）　　单位：万 t

地　区	一、粮　食								
	总　产	其中:夏收粮食	1. 谷　物						
			总　产	(1) 稻　谷				(2) 小　麦	
				总产	早稻	中稻	晚稻	总产	其中:春小麦
全国总计	**48 402**	**10 640**	**42 777**	**18 059**	**3 187**	**11 410**	**3 461**	**9 745**	**603**
北　京	94.9	26.8	90.5	0.5		0.5		26.7	
天　津	137.5	47.4	133.1	12.2		12.2		47.4	2.1
河　北	2 598.6	1 166.0	2 452.9	51.6		51.6		1 150.3	2.0
山　西	978.0	205.5	882.1	0.9		0.9		202.3	0.4
内蒙古	1 662.2		1 342.1	62.2		62.2		143.6	143.6
辽　宁	1 745.8	38.8	1 660.3	416.5		416.5		7.9	7.4
吉　林	2 581.2		2 352.5	473.3		473.3		2.7	2.7
黑龙江	3 092.0		2 324.7	1 121.5		1 121.5		94.0	94.0
上　海	105.4	13.9	101.3	85.5		82.2	3.3	9.9	
江　苏	2 834.6	844.4	2 696.9	1 706.7		1 704.9	1.8	728.5	
浙　江	814.7	43.2	705.3	644.8	79.3	453.6	111.9	21.8	
安　徽	2 605.3	865.2	2 385.8	1 250.8	153.1	954.9	142.8	808.1	
福　建	715.2	38.3	544.0	526.6	148.5	175.7	202.4	2.0	
江　西	1 757.0	9.1	1 677.6	1 667.2	666.0	266.5	734.7	2.7	
山　东	3 917.4	1 801.1	3 650.1	95.8		95.8		1 800.5	2.1
河　南	4 582.0	2 609.2	4 277.5	359.8		359.8		2 577.7	
湖　北	2 177.4	302.5	1 956.2	1 535.3	206.9	1 075.4	253.0	208.9	
湖　南	2 678.6	63.4	2 452.7	2 296.2	734.4	723.8	838.0	13.4	
广　东	1 395.0	94.1	1 185.1	1 117.0	538.0		579.0	1.9	
广　西	1 487.3	16.9	1 384.9	1 169.1	572.0	68.7	528.4	1.8	1.8
海　南	153.0	13.3	116.0	110.6	51.4	2.5	56.7		
重　庆	1 168.2	172.9	845.8	521.5	0.2	521.1	0.2	78.6	
四　川	3 211.1	565.0	2 581.4	1 505.7	2.2	1 503.0	0.5	427.4	
贵　州	1 152.1	214.7	901.2	472.8	0.1	472.7		73.0	
云　南	1 514.9	222.3	1 259.2	646.3	35.3	602.3	8.7	106.9	
西　藏	93.4		89.6	0.6		0.6		25.6	8.4
陕　西	1 043.0	436.8	963.9	89.2		89.2		401.2	
甘　肃	836.9	338.0	605.4	4.1		4.1		264.8	122.4
青　海	93.3		49.1					39.3	39.3
宁　夏	299.8	84.6	266.3	61.1		61.1		79.4	65.7
新　疆	876.6	406.5	843.0	53.8		53.8		369.2	111.3

（续）

地区	一、粮食						
	1. 谷物				2. 豆类		
	（3）玉米	（4）谷子	（5）高粱	（6）其他谷物	总产	（1）大豆	（2）杂豆
全国总计	**13 937**	**179**	**255**	**603**	**2 158**	**1 635**	**523**
北京	62.6	0.4	0.2	0.1	2.4	2.3	0.1
天津	73.2	0.1	0.2		3.9	3.8	0.1
河北	1 193.8	43.5	7.4	6.3	51.2	42.4	8.8
山西	616.1	38.2	11.2	13.4	36.7	26.0	10.7
内蒙古	1 066.2	23.4	21.7	25.0	164.1	130.9	33.2
辽宁	1 135.5	27.3	62.8	10.3	43.6	38.4	5.2
吉林	1 800.7	4.1	66.0	5.7	152.8	130.2	22.6
黑龙江	1 042.9	6.8	25.8	33.7	680.0	629.5	50.5
上海	2.8			3.1	3.2	2.1	1.1
江苏	174.8			86.9	82.4	48.7	33.7
浙江	25.9			12.8	47.4	29.4	18.0
安徽	264.9	0.2	1.5	60.3	95.5	88.8	6.7
福建	13.2	0.1	1.1	1.0	24.7	18.2	6.5
江西	6.3		0.5	0.9	24.9	17.9	7.0
山东	1 735.4	10.7	4.9	2.8	68.2	65.1	3.1
河南	1 298.0	11.2	1.9	28.9	74.4	58.1	16.3
湖北	194.9	0.2	1.1	15.8	65.0	43.4	21.6
湖南	134.0		3.1	6.0	56.7	40.0	16.7
广东	61.5	0.1		4.6	24.4	18.9	5.5
广西	212.0	0.5	0.6	0.9	40.3	32.1	8.2
海南	5.4				2.2	1.0	1.2
重庆	233.1		8.0	4.6	42.2	17.7	24.5
四川	580.8		17.7	49.8	131.5	52.6	78.9
贵州	344.3	0.2	4.1	6.8	37.8	16.2	21.6
云南	449.3		0.5	56.2	77.2	17.4	59.8
西藏	1.7			61.7	3.2	0.1	3.1
陕西	459.7	6.5	1.3	6.0	37.1	24.5	12.6
甘肃	248.5	4.3	7.5	76.2	41.7	15.0	26.7
青海	0.9			8.9	11.8		11.8
宁夏	121.4	0.5	0.1	3.8	6.0	1.1	4.9
新疆	376.7	0.2	5.4	10.7	25.4	23.2	2.2

（续）

地区	一、粮食		二、油料						三、棉花
	3. 薯类*		总产	1. 花生	2. 油菜籽	3. 芝麻	4. 胡麻籽	5. 向日葵	总产
	总产	其中:马铃薯							
全国总计	**3 468**	**1 417**	**3 077**	**1 434**	**1 305**	**62.5**	**36.2**	**192.8**	**571.4**
北京	2.0		2.5	2.5		0.009 6		0.021 5	0.21
天津	0.5		1.3	0.8		0.035		0.46	8.35
河北	94.5	32.0	152.7	140.3	4.7	1.46	2.31	3.55	57.70
山西	59.2	46.2	21.3	2.9	0.77	0.43	3.79	10.27	10.29
内蒙古	156.0	150.4	122.2	1.4	28.3	0.86	4.57	85.30	0.177
辽宁	41.9	29.3	36.8	33.0	0.11	0.60		2.73	0.27
吉林	75.9	72.8	54.4	28.7		3.53		16.19	0.17
黑龙江	87.3	85.0	60.6	4.8	0.32	0.79		33.16	
上海	0.9		6.9	0.4	6.5				0.177
江苏	55.3		216.0	55.5	158.7	1.83		0.031	32.27
浙江	62		50.1	4.9	44.7	0.60			2.16
安徽	124	3.1	270.7	79.3	182.3	8.96	0.000 6	0.006	32.46
福建	146.5	29.5	27.4	25.5	1.8	0.12		0.006 4	0.004
江西	54.5	2.1	76.1	31.7	41.7	2.53			8.72
山东	199.1		363.9	359.9	2.98	0.24		0.048 5	84.63
河南	230.1		449.6	338.3	87.7	22.10		1.51	67.70
湖北	156.1	68.1	293.9	60.2	219.1	13.70	0.001 8	0.69	37.50
湖南	169.2	39.2	141.0	31.7	108.2	0.96		0.019 7	19.75
广东	185.5	19.2	77.0	75.9	0.99	0.16			
广西	62.1		63.2	55.1	6.3	0.46			0.089
海南	34.8		8.5	8.3		0.18			
重庆	280.2	101.9	42.7	9.7	31.8	0.69		0.50	0.017
四川	498.2	144.9	232.3	62.0	168.7	0.60		0.31	2.47
贵州	213.1	147.5	84.9	7.3	76.5	0.019	0.006 5	0.64	0.057
云南	178.5	157.9	36.2	5.7	29.0	0.019 5	0.001 2	0.82	0.022
西藏	0.6	0.6	6.1	0.015	6.1				
陕西	42.0	29.7	45.4	7.6	30.3	1.68	0.90	3.97	7.78
甘肃	189.8	189.8	50.3	0.18	26.6		16.19	4.92	11.05
青海	32.4	32.4	31.9		31.6		0.28		
宁夏	27.5	27.5	12.2		0.01		5.77	5.94	
新疆	8.2	8.2	38.9	0.64	9.2	0.018	2.39	21.69	187.40

（续）

地区	四、麻类					五、糖料		
	总　产	1. 黄红麻	2. 苎麻	3. 大麻	4. 亚麻	总　产	1. 甘蔗	2. 甜菜
全国总计	**110.49**	**8.28**	**27.71**	**4.13**	**69.46**	**9 452**	**8 663.8**	**788.11**
北　京								
天　津								
河　北	0.73	0.077		0.002 8		42.66		42.66
山　西	0.003 8			0.003 8		3.96		3.96
内蒙古	2.54			0.010	2.53	138.28		138.28
辽　宁	0.011 4				0.011	6.29		6.29
吉　林	0.61			0.015	0.59	7.35		7.35
黑龙江	36.15			1.58	34.54	155.00		155.00
上　海						14.51	14.51	
江　苏	0.47	0.058	0.41	0.003 6		22.23	22.2	0.026
浙　江	0.12	0.086	0.035			89.97	89.97	
安　徽	3.19	1.94	0.79	0.41		21.32	21.32	
福　建	0.036	0.025	0.011			93.33	93.33	
江　西	1.26	0.15	1.09			78.31	78.31	
山　东	0.21	0.18		0.014				
河　南	3.76	3.69		0.068		25.20	25.19	
湖　北	4.86	0.34	4.45		0.076	42.90	42.90	
湖　南	13.98	0.057	13.07		0.853	100.40	100.40	
广　东	0.14	0.14				1 114.25	1 114.25	
广　西	1.07	0.96	0.11			5 154.69	5 154.69	
海　南	0.088	0.088				278.90	278.90	
重　庆	1.24	0.011	1.19			11.46	11.46	
四　川	6.85	0.423	6.40			133.158	132.89	0.268
贵　州	0.15	0.008 5	0.086	0.018	0.029	67.80	67.76	0.041
云　南	14.10	0.000 6	0.005 5	0.27	13.82	1 415.90	1 415.50	0.39
西　藏								
陕　西	0.094	0.049	0.044	0.000 1		0.295	0.216 7	0.078 3
甘　肃	1.74			1.74		14.54		14.54
青　海	0.001 2			0.001 2		0.044		0.044
宁　夏	0.001 1					0.059		0.059
新　疆	17.90				17.01	419.12		419.12

(续)

地区	六、烟叶		七、蔬菜、瓜类				
	总产	其中：烤烟	总产	1. 蔬菜（含菜用瓜）	2. 瓜类（果用瓜）		
					总产	(1) 西瓜	(2) 甜瓜
全国总计	**268.30**	**243.5**	**63 736.1**	**56 451.5**	**7 284.6**	**5 989.3**	**882.6**
北京	0.000 6		459.7	423.9	35.8	33.8	1.65
天津			583.2	542.7	40.5	32.5	7.85
河北	0.98	0.493	6 947.0	6 467.6	479.4	384.9	38.65
山西	0.63	0.61	970.4	901.5	68.9	57.8	6.95
内蒙古	1.97	1.52	1 165.9	1 009.1	156.8	88.6	43.41
辽宁	3.42	3.17	2 076.8	1 954.8	122.0	57.7	29.89
吉林	5.97	2.49	1 001.7	832.6	169.1	112.8	48.23
黑龙江	7.35	7.35	1 459.9	1 153.5	306.4	213.9	88.33
上海			476.4	409.0	67.4	50.9	13.89
江苏	0.073		4 008.7	3 604.7	404.0	325.7	42.36
浙江	0.398		2 058.9	1 764.6	294.3	255.5	13.42
安徽	2.60	2.47	2 231.1	1 671.2	559.9	492.35	35.75
福建	11.66	11.51	1 482.4	1 402.7	79.7	65.80	9.57
江西	2.12	1.98	1 341.1	1 145.9	195.2	169.4	9.15
山东	7.55	7.34	9 952.4	8 607.0	1 345.4	1 130.8	145.49
河南	28.84	28.06	7 166.7	5 880.2	1 286.5	1 158.4	120.50
湖北	11.14	7.88	3 222.8	2 916.9	305.9	261.2	38.23
湖南	21.29	20.39	2 675.2	2 399.0	276.2	243.4	30.27
广东	6.30	5.06	2 710.8	2 596.0	114.8	84.38	7.82
广西	3.29	1.97	2 325.9	2 130.6	195.3	179.4	15.33
海南	0.003 3	0.003 3	370.0	312.2	57.8	44.37	3.15
重庆	9.02	7.17	916.3	890.5	25.8	23.70	0.50
四川	18.17	13.23	2 825.7	2 714.3	111.4	93.0	2.18
贵州	36.89	34.45	884.4	839.9	44.5	37.66	2.46
云南	79.90	77.22	1 004.0	970.9	33.06	25.80	1.06
西藏			42.92	42.9	0.020 7	0.020 7	
陕西	5.92	5.88	1 010.31	869.9	140.4	117.1	18.03
甘肃	3.38	3.14	975.16	866.9	108.26	89.6	8.86
青海	0.073		85.62	84.5	1.12	1.05	
宁夏	0.075	0.075	221.73	183.6	38.13	33.28	4.02
新疆	0.073	0.032	1 082.85	862.2	220.65	124.1	95.58

* 薯类产量按 5kg 薯折 1kg 粮食计算，下同。

表 3 我国玉米主产区生产情况（2005 年）

地 区	播种面积（khm^2）	单产（kg/hm^2）	产量（万 t）
吉 林	2 775.2	6 489	1 800.7
河 北	2 677.4	4 459	1 193.8
山 东	2 731.4	6 354	1 735.4
河 南	2 508.3	5 175	1 298.0
黑龙江	2 220.2	4 697	1 042.9
内蒙古	1 805.8	5 904	1 066.2
辽 宁	1 792.5	6 335	1 135.5

表 4 各地区水果产量（2005 年） 单位：t

地 区	水 果	其 中					
		苹 果	梨	柑 橘	桃	猕猴桃	葡 萄
全国总计	**88 355 015**	**24 011 081**	**11 323 514**	**15 919 149**	**7 624 207**	**456 819**	**5 794 411**
北 京	761 188	138 447	145 759		306 210	78	50 559
天 津	277 877	66 039	22 553		48 997		93 229
河 北	9 184 789	2 202 273	3 246 220		1 248 910	1 047	863 938
山 西	2 454 962	1 648 413	246 247		132 355	212	119 187
内蒙古	220 332	62 319	77 602				29 119
辽 宁	3 292 674	1 299 595	690 345		346 978		581 711
吉 林	661 950	252 298	134 833		612		109 971
黑龙江	461 974	177 432	48 422				20 720
上 海	336 262	114	18 794	179 908	102 818	178	26 681
江 苏	2 023 426	552 794	556 158	52 026	318 699	1 349	153 021
浙 江	2 836 914		310 375	1 481 053	285 842	7 433	219 942
安 徽	1 517 201	278 143	638 058	12 427	212 186	2 435	173 264
福 建	4 793 578	198	147 755	2 153 154	199 653	3 406	59 066
江 西	1 302 821		74 538	1 098 239	37 292	8 523	3 741
山 东	12 014 767	6 716 634	1 061 389		2 011 740	6 573	831 401
河 南	5 556 928	3 006 245	654 680	35 878	601 029	120 569	412 605
湖 北	2 607 910	12 437	501 856	1 462 596	468 766	8 584	49 671
湖 南	2 432 667		108 417	2 120 228	94 888	25 186	52 255
广 东	8 316 862		42 963	1 826 814	86 860		
广 西	5 715 755		120 741	1 876 759	122 080	1 823	119 135
海 南	1 625 256			19 748			
重 庆	1 288 113	6 094	180 049	909 085	55 554	2 453	20 727
四 川	4 157 550	242 923	684 593	2 137 435	319 039	30 902	160 827
贵 州	514 229	10 230	123 740	172 181	65 468	12 057	21 050
云 南	1 366 290	159 396	197 028	211 091	113 385	1 642	69 734
西 藏	8 671	5 674	836	96	1 412		103
陕 西	7 657 393	5 601 167	621 224	167 573	280 971	240 319	139 372
甘 肃	1 724 459	1 012 568	283 345	2 858	102 261	70	77 506
青 海	14 772	7 316	5 105		412		80
宁 夏	314 818	222 126	12 081		2 913		48 154
新 疆	2 912 627	330 206	367 808		56 877		1 287 642

(续)

地区	其中					
	红枣	柿子	香蕉	菠萝	荔枝	龙眼
全国总计	**2 488 506**	**2 185 041**	**6 518 128**	**848 902**	**1 440 589**	**1 091 485**
北京	6 950	56 781				
天津	24 691	11 402				
河北	807 577	333 382				
山西	196 858	55 169				
内蒙古						
辽宁	71 883					
吉林						
黑龙江						
上海	1 038	2 083				
江苏	9 978	120 952				
浙江		35 973				
安徽	20 166	103 001				
福建	85	160 475	855 398	37 731	160 289	216 452
江西	5 467	9 474				
山东	687 372	138 997				
河南	268 091	258 584				
湖北	20 182	47 699				
湖南	21 567	10 126				
广东		114 772	3 302 250	521 002	862 059	464 025
广西	22 892	441 083	1 173 887	65 385	334 797	381 709
海南			913 257	202 648	70 338	15 654
重庆	1 696	6 409	1 903		186	939
四川	8 261	42 131	17 547	31	6 328	4 685
贵州	1 822	13 652	8 662	3	426	467
云南	4 062	34 067	245 224	22 102	6 166	7 554
西藏						
陕西	188 232	173 881				
甘肃	75 450	14 858				
青海						
宁夏	15 566					
新疆	28 620					

表 5　各地区茶叶产量（2005 年）　　单位：t

地　区	茶　叶	其中				
		红毛茶	绿毛茶	乌龙毛茶	紧压茶原料	其他茶叶
全国总计	**934 857**	**47 941**	**691 020**	**103 820**	**27 653**	**64 423**
北　京						
天　津						
河　北						
山　西						
内蒙古						
辽　宁						
吉　林						
黑龙江						
上　海						
江　苏	12 068	1 335	10 105			628
浙　江	144 370	145	142 926	130	307	862
安　徽	59 619	2 484	54 890			2 245
福　建	184 826	1 652	88 923	85 924	10	8 317
江　西	16 691	2 687	12 503	1 501		
山　东	6 645		6 645			
河　南	16 902		16 902			
湖　北	84 976	6 546	67 221		9 432	1 777
湖　南	71 978	15 399	35 912	625	9 497	10 545
广　东	44 465	1 562	20 686	15 493	6	6 718
广　西	26 181	440	20 695			5 046
海　南	950	1	894			55
重　庆	16 545	3 211	10 215			3 119
四　川	97 941	996	73 817	134	8 199	14 795
贵　州	22 915	61	14 123	1	95	8 635
云　南	115 880	11 422	102 661	12	107	1 678
西　藏	3					3
陕　西	11 382		11 382			
甘　肃	520		520			
青　海						
宁　夏						
新　疆						

表 6 我国农垦系统主要农产品产量（2004—2005 年）

项 目	产 量（万 t）		
	2004 年	2005 年	同比增长（%）
一、粮食	1 666	1 859	11.57
其中：夏收粮食	152	182	19.74
1. 稻谷	839	908	8.22
其中：早稻	27	26.5	－1.85
2. 小麦	197	257	30.46
其中：春小麦	122	149	22.13
3. 玉米	337	389	15.43
4. 谷子	0.87	0.95	9.20
5. 高粱	5.00	6.23	24.60
6. 其他谷物	38.6	53.1	37.56
7. 大豆	202	194	－3.96
8. 薯类（折粮）	22.4	20.4	－8.93
二、棉花	116	125	7.23
其中：长绒棉	7.71	8.17	5.97
三、油料	65.2	67	2.65
其中：花生	8.19	9.06	10.62
油菜籽	30.9	29.7	－3.88
向日葵	16.9	18.2	7.69
四、麻类	26.68	24.49	－8.21
五、糖料	689	668	－3.0
其中：甜菜	171.25	197.34	15.24
甘蔗	517.48	470.18	－9.14
六、烟叶	0.37	0.42	13.51
其中：烤烟	0.28	0.27	－3.57
七、药材	2.84	2.81	－1.06
八、蔬菜、瓜类	876	856	－2.28
九、其他农作物	60.56	67.82	11.99
十、水果	163.13	178.79	9.60
十一、茶叶	3.90	4.64	18.97
十二、干胶	38.99	31.99	－17.95
十三、剑麻（折纤维）	2.37	2.60	9.70

表 7　各地区农垦系统主要农产品产量（2005 年）　　单位：万 t

地区	粮食	棉花	油料	糖料	大豆	干胶	椰子
全国总计	**1 859**	**125**	**67**	**668**	**194.35**	**31.99**	**1 142**
北京	0.19				0.002		
天津	0.79	0.26	0.000 9		0.065		
河北	33.92	2.51	0.098	0.38	0.75		
山西	2.35	0.019	0.043	0.002	0.011		
内蒙古	122.14	0.12	21.12	2.91	21.10		
辽宁	99.47		0.32	0.22	1.46		
吉林	52.72		1.34	0.068	1.25		
黑龙江	1 026.51		11.35	51.60	154.63		
上海	15.89	0.073	0.012		0.008		
江苏	68.70	0.87	0.75		0.35		
浙江	1.22	0.007	0.01		0.07		
安徽	23.35	0.87	0.73		2.25		
福建	7.34		0.38	4.03	0.18		
江西	36.97	0.52	1.65	0.62	0.29		
山东	4.34	0.49	0.031		0.24		
河南	15.89	0.42	1.28		1.67		
湖北	61.38	7.02	9.03	0.56	1.76		
湖南	31.30	4.01	1.60	28.85	0.54		
广东	4.37		0.66	178.49	0.05	2.13	
广西	0.95		0.24	181.52	0.07	0.068	
海南	10.65		0.61	30.50	0.07	16.25	1 107
重庆	0.019		0.001		0.000 4		
四川	0.037		0.002				
贵州	0.59		0.049	3.53	0.004		
云南	3.24		0.023	41.79	0.018	13.43	
西藏							
陕西	4.19	0.73	0.29		0.106		
甘肃	11.76	0.65	0.83	0.12	0.000 2		
青海	0.84		0.82				
宁夏	23.50		0.98	0.058	0.26		
新疆（兵团）	150.84	98.68	9.53	130.85	4.76		
新疆（农业）	22.85	5.65	0.86	4.05	0.29		
新疆（畜牧）	20.08	1.77	2.18	7.42	2.11		
热作两院	0.059		0.0028	0.275		0.11	35
广州							
南京	0.32		0.021		0.0024		
昆明							
哈尔滨	0.21						

表 8 我国农垦系统茶、蚕、果、林生产情况（2004—2005 年）

指 标	单 位	2004 年	2005 年	同比增长（%）
一、年末实有茶园面积	khm^2	30.6	30.3	−1.0
茶叶总产量	万 t	3.9	4.6	19.0
二、年末实有桑园面积	khm^2	2.1	1.6	−22.3
三、年末实有果园面积	khm^2	231.3	241.3	4.3
水果总产量	万 t	163.1	178.8	9.6
其中：苹果	万 t	22.6	25.4	12.4
梨	万 t	24.3	28.7	18.2
柑橘	万 t	22.9	20.6	−10.2
四、年末实有橡胶园面积	khm^2	412.4	424.2	2.9
当年橡胶平均开割面积	khm^2	302.5	312.2	3.2
每公顷产干胶	kg	1 150.0	1 024.5	−10.9
全年干胶总产量	万 t	39.0	32.0	−18.0
五、当年造林面积	khm^2	126.1	84.5	−33.0
用材林	khm^2	31.9	19.6	−38.5
经济林	khm^2	15.1	10.4	−31.0
防护林	khm^2	76.5	51.0	−33.4
薪炭林	khm^2	1.5	3.0	94.8
特种用材林	khm^2	1.1	0.4	−64.7

表 9 我国热带、亚热带作物产量（2005 年）

项 目	单位	总 计	福建	广东	广西	海南	云南
一、橡胶总产量（干胶片）	t	513 618	40	24 784	678	247 775	240 341
二、咖啡豆总产量（干咖啡豆）	t	21 919				283	21 636
三、椰子（按果实计）	万个	23 248		254		22 963	31
四、腰果总产量（干果）	t	390				388	2
五、香料作物（按香料油）	t	1 267	6	15		71	1 175
其中：香茅草（按香料油）	t	1 022	6	15		71	930
六、剑麻（番麻）（按纤维计）	t	55 478	881	23 491	25 475	5 640	21

表 10 我国棉花主产区生产情况（2004—2005 年） 单位：万 hm^2、万 t

地 区	面 积			产 量		
	2004 年	2005 年	同比增减(%)	2004 年	2005 年	同比增减（%）
新 疆	113.7	116.05	2.07	178.3	187.4	5.10
山 东	105.9	84.63	−20.08	109.8	84.6	−22.95
河 南	95.2	78.16	−17.90	66.7	67.7	1.50
河 北	66.9	57.35	−14.28	66.5	57.7	−13.23
湖 北	40.8	39.03	−4.34	39.5	37.5	−5.06
江 苏	40.9	36.83	−9.95	50.3	32.3	−35.79
安 徽	39.9	37.57	−5.84	41.2	32.5	−21.12
湖 南	16.8	15.09	−10.18	20.3	19.8	−2.46
主产区总计	520.1	464.71	−10.65	572.6	519.5	−9.27
全国总计	569.3	506.19	−11.09	632.4	517.4	−9.65
主产区占全国比重（%）	91.36	91.81	0.49	90.54	90.92	0.42

表 11　我国主要蔬菜产量增减情况（2004—2005 年）　　单位：万 t

项　目	2004 年	2005 年	同比增长（%）
蔬菜合计	**55 065**	**56 451**	**2.52**
叶菜类	21 240	21 616.2	1.77
菠菜	1 567	1 617.9	3.25
芹菜	1 919	1 951.3	1.68
大白菜	10 346	10 308.3	−0.36
甘蓝	2 846	2 985.8	4.91
油菜	1 214	1 254.9	3.37
瓜菜类	6 893	7 085.5	2.79
黄瓜	3 655	3 817.1	4.44
块根、块茎类	7 810	8 208.1	5.10
萝卜	3 833	3 935.2	2.67
胡萝卜	1 330	1 331.4	0.11
茄果菜类	7 865	8 051.8	2.38
茄子	2 176	2 263.4	4.02
番茄	3 619	3 556.5	−1.73
葱蒜类	4 685	4 913.3	4.87
大葱	1 892	1 925.0	1.74
大蒜	1 567	1 654.1	5.56
豆类蔬菜	2 753	2 883.1	4.73
四季豆	1 333	1 391.4	4.38
豇豆	757	825.7	9.08
水生菜类	978	996.7	1.91
莲藕	704	707.1	0.44
其他蔬菜		2 696.8	

表 12　我国主要林产品产量（2001—2005 年）　　单位：万 t

年　份	木材（万 m³）	生　漆	油桐籽	油茶籽	松　脂	核　桃	橡　胶
2001	4 552	0.5	40.7	82.5	56.4	25.2	59.9
2002	4 436	0.6	38.9	85.5	56.3	34.0	70.5
2003	4 759	0.9	37.3	77.9	62.6	39.4	79.2
2004	5 200	1.0	38.1	87.5	67.3	43.7	92.3
2005	5 560	1.4	36.9	87.5	76.7	49.9	103.2

表 13　各地区主要林产品产量（2005 年）

单位：t

地　区	生漆	油桐籽	油茶籽	乌桕籽	五倍子	棕片	松脂	竹笋干	核桃	板栗	紫胶（原胶）
全国总计	**14 316**	**368 688**	**875 022**	**30 466**	**20 308**	**60 617**	**767 134**	**463 154**	**499 074**	**1 031 857**	**1 897**
北　京									13 787	21 853	
天　津									442	312	
河　北									47 032	107 079	
山　西									54 432	62	
内蒙古											
辽　宁									25 576	42 326	
吉　林									2 888	288	
黑龙江											
上　海											
江　苏			170	9				686	151	20 535	
浙　江		162	43 361	13		754	1 940	142 267		60 428	
安　徽	220	3 208	9 743	356	5	1 683	5 433	15 865	6 300	68 786	
福　建	892	20 928	72 597	1 145	124	12 162	72 299	153 497	112	49 134	119
江　西	355	16 160	198 020	268	123	5 140	93 164	6 921	3 255	25 706	2
山　东									20 465	218 095	
河　南	955	45 802	8 079	2 557	1 709		266	30	25 339	112 351	
湖　北	4 413	10 315	9 928	10 669	814	1 830	8 334	3 139	9 051	128 099	
湖　南	3 022	42 523	374 516	6 703	10 298	9 282	32 850	20 026	3 761	35 545	101
广　东	29	5 193	30 470	253		1 640	154 593	17 825		8 637	342
广　西	71	60 372	117 363	133	142	2 616	301 943	18 770	339	45 951	
海　南						58	3 836	803			
重　庆	794	20 041	1 991	3 032	1 461	2 735	4 795	5 354	3 272	5 991	
四　川	725	30 314	2 464	1 953	1 152	6 290	2 911	62 190	59 272	14 105	126
贵　州	1 328	81 669	10 558	2 948	1 943	4 733	4 882	9 542	6 840	12 286	54
云　南	404	18 883	4 618	147	153	8 901	79 663	5 555	91 200	21 277	1 135
西　藏									622		
陕　西	1 047	12 577	144	280	2 289	2 761	225	684	63 790	30 778	18
甘　肃	61	541			95	32			29 675	2 209	
青　海									86	24	
宁　夏									627		
新　疆									31 761		

表 14　我国主要牲畜饲养情况（2001—2005 年）　单位：万头（只）

年 份	合 计	大牲畜年底存栏头数				
		牛	马	驴	骡	骆 驼
2001	14 996	12 824	826	882	436	28
2002	15 189	13 085	809	850	419	26
2003	15 500	13 467	790	821	396	27
2004	15 738	13 782	764	792	374	26
2005	15 948	14 158	740	777	360	27

年 份	肉猪出栏头数	牛出栏头数	猪年底存栏头数	羊年底存栏只数		
				合 计	山 羊	绵 羊
2001	54 937	4 118	45 743	29 826	16 129	13 697
2002	56 684	4 401	46 292	31 655	17 276	14 379
2003	59 201	4 703	46 602	34 054	18 321	15 733
2004	61 801	5 019	48 189	36 639	19 551	17 088
2005	66 099	5 288	50 335	37 266	19 876	17 390

表 15　我国主要畜产品产量（2001—2005 年）

年 份	肉类产量（万 t）					奶类产量（万 t）		禽蛋产量（万 t）
	总产量	猪牛羊肉				总 产 量	其中:牛奶	
		小 计	猪 肉	牛 肉	羊 肉			
2001	6 333.9	5 026.0	4 184.5	548.8	292.7	1 122.9	1 025.5	2 336.7
2002	6 586.5	5 227.9	4 326.6	584.6	316.7	1 400.4	1 299.8	2 462.7
2003	6 932.9	5 506.3	4 518.6	630.5	357.2	1 848.6	1 746.3	2 606.7
2004	7 244.8	5 776.8	4 701.6	675.9	399.3	2 368.4	2 260.6	2 723.7
2005	7 741.3	6 157.6	5 010.6	711.5	435.5	2 864.8	2 753.4	2 879.5

年 份	蜂蜜(万 t)	蚕 茧（万 t）		绵羊毛（万 t）			山羊毛总产（t）	羊绒总产（t）
		总 产	其中:桑蚕茧	总 产	细羊毛	半细羊毛		
2001	25.2	66	60	29.8	11.5	8.8	34 241	10 968
2002	26.5	69.8	64.5	30.8	11.2	10.2	35 459	11 765
2003	28.9	66.7	61.1	33.8	12.0	11.0	36 692	13 528
2004	29.3	73.1	67.7	37.4	13.0	12.0	37 727	14 515
2005	29.3	78.0	71.3	39.3	12.8	12.3	36 904	15 435

表 16 各地区奶类产量（2004—2005 年） 单位：万 t

地 区	2004 年		2005 年	
	奶类产量	其中：牛奶	奶类产量	其中：牛奶
全国总计	**2 368.4**	**2 260.6**	**2 864.83**	**2 753.37**
北 京	70.08	70.04	64.22	64.20
天 津	54.24	54.24	63.41	63.41
河 北	276.95	266.46	348.64	340.35
山 西	63.67	61.15	73.75	71.28
内蒙古	502.06	497.85	696.86	691.05
辽 宁	62.28	58.45	78.83	74.88
吉 林	26.00	25.32	30.00	29.40
黑龙江	378.06	374.48	444.22	440.24
上 海	25.20	25.20	23.76	23.76
江 苏	56.90	53.61	57.90	56.62
浙 江	25.95	25.95	26.67	26.67
安 徽	10.19	10.19	11.05	11.02
福 建	21.14	20.80	19.77	19.42
江 西	11.63	11.60	12.52	12.51
山 东	188.68	160.88	220.97	187.07
河 南	78.99	74.50	108.50	104.00
湖 北	11.67	11.67	12.22	12.22
湖 南	6.66	6.66	6.91	6.91
广 东	11.22	10.94	11.94	11.64
广 西	4.87	4.82	5.37	5.35
海 南	0.10	0.10	0.11	0.11
重 庆	8.62	8.51	8.61	8.61
四 川	53.00	52.61	59.03	58.56
贵 州	3.61	3.56	3.75	3.75
云 南	28.34	26.86	32.68	30.91
西 藏	26.20	20.29	26.98	21.21
陕 西	125.52	96.19	141.73	113.34
甘 肃	25.87	25.51	31.69	31.19
青 海	24.10	22.75	25.02	23.62
宁 夏	46.93	46.06	57.85	57.85
新 疆	139.73	133.32	159.83	152.22

表 17 我国农垦系统主要畜产品产量（2004—2005 年） 单位：万 t

项 目	2004 年	2005 年	同比增长（%）
一、肉类总产量	125.33	145.76	16.30
猪肉	74.07	88.22	19.10
牛肉	11.43	14.00	22.48
羊肉	16.71	19.14	14.54
二、牛奶	210.20	245.49	16.79
三、羊毛	2.74	2.92	6.57
四、蜂蜜	0.56	0.65	16.07
五、禽蛋	21.43	22.38	4.43

表 18 我国水产品产量（2001—2005 年）

单位：kt

年份	总产量	1. 海水产品	其中		2. 内陆产品	其中	
			捕捞	养殖		捕捞	养殖
2001	43 813	25 717	14 406	11 311	18 096	2 146	15 950
2002	45 645	26 463	14 335	12 128	19 182	2 252	16 930
2003	47 045	26 857	14 324	12 533	20 188	2 468	17 720
2004	49 018	27 678	14 511	13 167	21 340	2 420	18 920
2005	51 017	28 381	14 533	13 848	22 636	2 551	20 085

表 19 各地区水产品产量（2005 年）

单位：kt

地区	总产量	1. 海水产品	其中		2. 内陆产品	其中	
			捕捞	养殖		捕捞	养殖
全国总计	**51 017**	**28 381**	**14 533**	**13 848**	**22 636**	**2 551**	**20 085**
北京	64.3				64.3		64.3
天津	338	49	38	11	289	12	277
河北	989	572	311	261	418	86	332
山西	38				38	1.4	36.6
内蒙古	83				83	29	54
辽宁	4 253	3 642	1 520	2 122	612	42	570
吉林	119				119	25	94
黑龙江	446				446	51	395
上海	354	150.3	149.6	0.74	203	3.6	199.4
江苏	3 887	1 134	583	551	2 752	329	2 423
浙江	4 838	4 024	3 143	821	814	93	721
安徽	1 776				1 776	379	1 397
福建	6 022	5 319	2 221	3 097	703	85	618
江西	1 684				1 684	244	1 440
山东	7 361	6 261	2 681	3 580	1 100	123	977
河南	517				517	35	482
湖北	3 180				3 180	436	2 744
湖南	1 735				1 735	168	1 567
广东	6 952	3 980	1 720	2 259	2 973	130	2 843
广西	2 839	1 737	843	894	1 102	114	988
海南	1 500	1 271	1 080	191	230	24	206
重庆	251				251	13	238
四川	982				982	69	913
贵州	95				95	12	83
云南	238				238	26	212
西藏	0.55				0.55	0.5	0.05
陕西	76				76	4	72
甘肃	15.6				15.6	1.1	14.5
青海	2.05				2.05	0.07	1.98
宁夏	59				59	0.33	58.67
新疆	80				80	15	65

表 20　我国沿海地区海洋捕捞水产品产量（2005 年）　　单位：kt

地　区	海洋捕捞产量	按捕捞海域分				
		渤　海	黄　海	东　海	南　海	其　他
全国总计*	**14 533**	**1 233**	**3 204**	**4 871**	**3 767**	**1 457**
天　津	38	23	3.2			12
河　北	311	260	47			3.8
辽　宁	1 520	548	664	43.4	2.95	262
上　海	150			34.5		115
江　苏	583		413	149		20
浙　江	3 143	0.27	184	2 723	4.6	231
福　建	2 221			1 792	222	207
山　东	2 681	403	1 893	128	21	236
广　东	1 720				1 594	126
广　西	843				843	
海　南	1 080				1 080	

*　全国产量包括中农发集团的数据。

表 21　我国沿海地区海水养殖水产品产量（2005 年）　　单位：kt

地　区	海水养殖产量	按养殖水域分			集约化养殖方式		
		海上	滩涂	陆基	深水网箱	普通网箱	工厂化
全国总计	**13 848**	**7 163**	**5 426**	**1 259**	**21**	**267**	**78**
天　津	11			11			0.89
河　北	261	152	83	26			4.10
辽　宁	2 121	1 382	620	119	0.15	4.70	
上　海	0.74		0.74				9.59
江　苏	551	73	390	89	0.30	0.35	
浙　江	881	222	408	251	8.50	25	2.6
福　建	3 097	1 826	1 103	168	3.40	107	2.52
山　东	3 580	2 246	1 200	134	5.60	31	47
广　东	2 259	992	982	285	0.64	82	7.66
广　西	894	235	552	108		6.8	2.06
海　南	191	34	89	68	2.13	11	2.14

表 22 各地区农垦系统水产品产量（2005 年） 单位：hm²、t

地 区	水产养殖面积	水产品总产量	其中：养殖产量	对虾养殖面积	对虾产量
全国总计	**283 200**	**794 752**	**672 230**	**19 513**	**24 644**
北 京	18	77	77		
天 津	646	6 877	6 877		
河 北	15 439	68 933	61 000	3 541	6 806
山 西	8	3	3		
内 蒙 古	261	3 681	1 479		
辽 宁	89 987	181 620	105 465	9 593	4 985
吉 林	613	1 308	1 160		
黑 龙 江	19 044	18 984	14 069		
上 海	4 203	11 811	11 811		
江 苏	4 169	24 259	21 363	207	399
浙 江	1 159	5 972	5 970	266	1 197
安 徽	4 500	3 431	2 882		
福 建	1 795	26 133	18 542	193	805
江 西	18 558	23 924	16 997		
山 东	5 074	6 879	2 946	3 600	500
河 南	541	4 053	3 833		
湖 北	38 836	230 686	230 686		
湖 南	24 630	74 828	68 502		
广 东	3 850	21 755	21 755	1 269	166
广 西	1 178	10 351	10 351	76	509
海 南	4 998	34 395	33 720	768	4 277
重 庆	39	209	209		
四 川	86	721	721		
贵 州	127	154	154		
云 南	1 576	4 962	4 962		
西 藏					
陕 西	49	49	49		
甘 肃					
青 海	233	16	16		
宁 夏	3 824	5 366	5 366		
新疆（兵团）	31 908	20 026	18 046		
新疆（农业）	3 127	1 690	1 657		
新疆（畜牧）	2 400	292	292		
热作两院	12	37			
广 州	100	531	531		
南 京	152	659	659		
昆 明					
哈 尔 滨	60	80	80		

表 23 轻工业系统食品工业所需农牧业原料生产量（2003—2004 年）

单位：万 t

产品名称	2003 年	2004 年	同比增长（%）
一、农产品			
粮食	43 069.5	46 946.9	9.00
其中：稻谷	16 065.6	17 908.8	11.47
小麦	8 648.8	9 195.2	6.32
玉米	11 530.0	13 028.7	12.99
豆类	2 127.5	2 232.1	4.92
薯类	3 513.3	3 557.7	1.27
油料	2 811.0	3 065.9	9.07
其中：花生	1 342.0	1 434.2	6.87
油菜籽	1 142.0	1 318.2	15.43
芝麻	59.3	70.4	18.72
甘蔗	9 023.5	8 984.9	－0.43
甜菜	618.2	585.7	－5.26
烟叶	225.7	240.6	6.60
其中：烤烟	201.5	216.3	7.34
茶叶	76.8	83.5	8.72
水果	14 517.4	15 340.9	5.67
其中：苹果	2 110.2	2 367.5	12.19
柑橘	1 345.4	1 495.8	11.18
梨	979.8	1 064.2	8.61
葡萄	517.6	567.5	9.64
香蕉	590.3	605.6	2.59
二、林产品			
其中：油茶籽	78.0	85.5	9.62
核桃	39.4	34.02	－13.65
三、畜产品			
其中：猪肉	4 518.6	4 326.6	－4.25
牛肉	630.4	584.6	－7.27
羊肉	357.2	316.7	－11.34
奶类	1 848.6	1 400.4	－24.25
其中：牛奶	1 746.3	1 299.8	－25.57
禽蛋	2 606.7	2 462.7	－5.52
蜂蜜	28.9	26.46	－8.44
四、水产品	4 704.6	4 564.5	－2.98
海水产品	2 685.7	2 646.3	－1.47
其中：鱼类	2 823.6	1 022.3	－63.79
虾蟹类	437.0	310.6	－28.92
贝类	1 163.7	1 119.3	－3.82
澡类	141.3	133.3	－5.66
淡水产品	2 018.8	1 918.2	－4.98
其中：鱼类	1 795.2	1 710.2	－4.73
虾蟹类	138.8	122.4	－11.82
贝类	54.13	56.7	4.75

表 24　我国各地区主要中药材产量（2005 年）　　单位：t

地区	人参		甘草		枸杞	
	2004 年	2005 年	2004 年	2005 年	2004 年	2005 年
全国总计	**5 879**	**7 296**	**39 558**	**16 554**	**37 088**	**4 394**
北　京						
天　津						
河　北						
山　西	6	5	4 759	4 101	133	102
内蒙古						
辽　宁	4 544	2 477	719	508	71	123
吉　林						
黑龙江	1 020	1 102	5 336	744	102	103
上　海						
江　苏		24		588		106
浙　江						
安　徽	150		15		695	
福　建						
江　西	88	270	424	5 000	8	
山　东				122		797
河　南	36	2	1 828	3 024	154	304
湖　北	11		278		80	
湖　南			450	492	1 800	1 968
广　东				18		147
广　西						
海　南					394	
重　庆			36	39	609	590
四　川	24	38	449	151	41	55
贵　州				522		99
云　南			7		11	
西　藏						
陕　西						
甘　肃			22 392		767	
青　海						
宁　夏		3 378	2 845	1 245	3 222	
新　疆						

表 25　我国按人口平均的主要农畜产品产量（2001—2005 年）单位：kg/人

年份	粮食	棉花	油料	水果	茶叶	猪牛羊肉
2001	356	4.2	22.5	52.3	0.55	39.5
2002	357	3.8	22.6	54.3	0.58	40.8
2003	334	3.8	21.8	112.7	0.60	42.7
2004	362	4.9	23.7	118.4	0.64	44.6
2005	371	4.4	23.6	123.6	0.72	47.2
年份	**禽蛋**	**牛奶**	**水产品**	**糖料**	**烤烟**	**黄红麻**
2001	18.3	8.1	34.4	68.1	1.60	0.08
2002	19.2	10.2	35.6	80.4	1.67	0.12
2003	20.2	13.6	36.5	74.8	1.56	0.08
2004	21.0	17.4	37.8	73.8	1.70	0.10
2005	22.0	21.1	39.2	72.5	1.86	0.063

农产品加工机械拥有量及农产品加工行业固定资产投资情况

表 26　农业部系统农产品加工机械年末拥有量（2005 年）

地　区	农产品加工机械动力		粮食加工机械（万台）	棉花加工机械（万台）	油料加工机械（万台）	饲料粉碎机（万台）
	万台	（万 kW）				
全国总计	**1 004.12**	**7 038.67**	**678.68**	**22.72**	**58.72**	**303.84**
北　京	0.99	6.94	0.75		0.04	0.51
天　津	3.12	25.83	0.74	0.09	0.09	0.44
河　北	93.64	806.72	36.24	3.23	5.30	9.29
山　西	17.27	127.03	11.46	0.40	1.38	4.05
内蒙古	14.04	115.30	8.17		1.38	11.32
辽　宁	15.20	183.90	10.66	0.03	0.32	8.16
吉　林	12.52	110.53	10.11		0.45	5.59
黑龙江	9.88	97.03	4.29		0.70	4.32
上　海	0.43	4.25	0.41		0.02	0.14
江　苏	25.26	230.99	16.17	1.08	2.01	8.96
浙　江	24.07	166.21	12.67	0.99	0.67	1.55
安　徽	35.99	294.88	22.50	2.23	3.87	7.28
福　建	14.42	113.13	10.77		0.92	3.13
江　西	29.58	338.80	20.94	1.19	3.62	4.26
山　东	103.34	917.41	33.68	3.21	6.27	18.46
河　南	73.95	533.22	34.70	4.55	8.21	16.40
湖　北	54.51	334.66	44.23	1.23	3.30	23.88
湖　南	78.22	468.70	62.16	2.56	4.29	16.76
广　东	20.93	178.81	13.74		2.12	6.60
广　西	63.97	381.61	44.81	0.04	1.91	29.75
海　南	1.96	20.17	1.87		0.09	0.46
重　庆	49.97	198.44	53.11	0.08	1.06	20.35
四　川	80.58	437.66	89.82	0.48	4.06	34.71
贵　州	79.91	344.55	77.17	0.11	1.46	30.15
云　南	43.23	286.07	21.41		0.40	11.89
西　藏						
陕　西	27.41	153.40	22.47	0.66	1.24	9.66
甘　肃	22.24	92.06	9.51	0.17	1.85	6.27
青　海	1.49	10.26	0.86		0.48	0.70
宁　夏	2.25	19.28	1.57	0.03	0.55	4.15
新　疆	3.75	40.85	1.70	0.36	0.68	4.66

表 27　我国农产品加工行业固定资产投资情况（2005 年）　单位：亿元

行　业	投资额	新增固定资产	固定资产交付使用率（%）（平均值）
合　计	**4 975.2**	**3 256.7**	**64.6**
农副食品加工业	893.9	594.2	66.5
食品制造业	543.5	355.2	65.3
饮料制造业	348.7	216.1	62.0
烟草制造业	95.5	52.5	55.0
纺织业	1 059.2	681.8	64.4
纺织服装、鞋、帽制造业	384.3	256.0	66.6
皮革、毛皮、羽毛（绒）及其制品业	202.7	129.6	64.0
木材加工及木、竹、藤、棕、草制品业	280.9	187.4	66.7
家具制品业	189.1	115.3	61.0
造纸及纸制品业	549.3	379.5	69.1
印刷业和记录媒介的复制	227.5	164.3	72.2
橡胶制品业	200.6	124.8	62.2

表 28　我国农产品加工行业新增固定资产后主要产品新增生产能力（2004—2005 年）

产品名称	单　位	2004 年	2005 年
胶合板	万 m^3/年	1 947	2 015
轮胎外胎	万 m/年	4 395	3 752
轮胎内胎	万 m/年	2 301	2 244
化学纤维	t/年	3 295 972	2 665 296
棉纺锭	锭	6 741 370	13 486 477
毛纺锭	锭	165 788	163 844
原　盐	万 t/年	368	931
机制糖			
年生产糖	t/年	986 622	696 991
日处理原料	t/年	43 562	53 658
奶　粉	t/年	53 570	164 923
啤　酒	万 t/年	310	384
白　酒	万 t/年	118	316
其他酒	万 t/年	47	48
卷　烟	箱/年	1 168 950	1 551 074
机制纸	万 t/年	717	1 216
机制纸板	万 t/年	338	387
商业冷藏库	万 t	255	492
粮食仓库	万 kg	141 239	139 617
粮食仓库	m^2	316 173	480 412

表 29 我国农产品加工行业 50 万元以上施工、投产项目个数（2005 年）

行业	施工项目		全部建成投产项目（个）	项目建成投产率（%）
	总计	其中：新开工(个)		
合计	**29 597**	**22 936**	**16 671**	**55.24**
农副食品加工业	5 850	4 735	3 534	60.4
食品制造业	3 244	2 489	1 662	51.2
饮料制造业	2 067	1 568	1 194	57.8
烟草制品业	310	158	165	53.2
纺织业	5 310	4 065	2 918	55.0
纺织服装、鞋、帽制造业	2 946	2 238	1 594	54.1
皮革、毛皮、羽毛（绒）及其制品业	1 345	1 008	626	46.5
木材加工及木、竹、藤、棕草制品业	2 480	2 062	1 582	63.8
家具制造业	1 356	1 073	730	53.8
造纸及纸制品业	2 220	1 648	1 294	56.3
印刷业和记录媒介的复制	1 531	1 157	858	56.0
橡胶制品业	938	726	514	54.8

表 30 林业系统森工固定资产投资（2005 年）

项目	2004 年	2005 年	同比增长（%）
一、森工固定资产投资完成额（按构成分）（万元）	129 646	173 847	34.09
基本建筑	55 980	69 678	24.47
更新改造	35 139	72 280	105.70
其他投资	38 527	31 889	−17.23
二、当年新增固定资产	99 376	134 737	35.58

表 31 林业系统各地区森工固定资产投资（2005 年）

单位：万元

地区	合计	基本建设	更新改造	其他投资
全国总计	**173 847**	**69 678**	**72 280**	**31 889**
北京				
天津				
河北				
山西				
内蒙古	16 720	999		15 721
辽宁				
吉林	60 725	31 127	19 083	10 515
黑龙江	16 803	13 200	3 603	
上海				
江苏				
浙江	62	50		12
安徽	1 227	1 207		20
福建	36 864	1 102	33 934	1 828
江西	172	105	55	12
山东				
河南				

（续）

地　区	合　计	基本建设	更新改造	其他投资
湖　北	1 123	834	168	121
湖　南				
广　东				
广　西	11 003	4 881	6 122	
海　南				
重　庆				
四　川	4 594	3 454	334	806
贵　州				
云　南	6 989	5 923	254	812
西　藏				
陕　西	478	478		
甘　肃				
青　海				
宁　夏				
新　疆	231	231		

表 32　我国农垦系统固定资产投资（2004—2005 年）　单位：亿元

项　目	2004 年	2005 年	同比增长（%）
固定资产投资总额	358.12	449.54	25.53
当年新增固定资产	281.94	358.20	27.09

表 33　我国食品工业完成固定资产投资后新增主要产品生产能力（2003—2004 年）

产品名称	单　位	2003 年	2004 年
机制糖			
年生产	万 t	64.3	42
日处理原料	t	2 340	40 551
卷烟	万箱/年		117
酒	万 t/年	42	1 380
糖果	t/年	930	
奶粉	t/年	51 690	49 070
原盐	万 t/年		209

表 34　我国水产行业固定资产投资（2004—2005 年）　单位：万元

名　称	2004 年	2005 年	同比增长（%）
一、投资总额	3 055 697	3 473 448	13.67
捕捞生产	478 950	565 768	18.13
养殖生产	1 292 682	1 370 376	6.01
水产加工	597 099	782 414	31.04
市场流通	128 951	108 734	−15.68
渔业执法	9 351	13 098	40.07

（续）

名　　称	2004 年	2005 年	同比增长（%）
渔港	72 430	104 931	44.87
科研、教育	6 861	10 776	57.06
技术推广	12 126	11 537	−4.86
渔业检测	3 799	7 645	101.24
资源保护	12 191	13 505	10.78
苗种生产	200 192	235 766	17.77
其他	163 562	246 792	50.89
二、本年新增固定资产	1 325 300	1 407 811	6.23

按国民经济行业分类统计
农产品加工业现状

表 35　我国农产品加工业全部国有及规模以上非国有工业企业主要指标（2005 年）

行　　业	单位数（个）	工业总产值（亿元）	工业增加值（亿元）	主营业务收入（亿元）	利润总额（亿元）	从业人员年平均人数（万人）
合　　计	**88 290**	**52 489.42**	**15 843.98**	**51 110.69**	**2 551.45**	**2 049.38**
农副食品加工业	14 575	10 614.95	2 745.96	10 366.49	398.71	222.55
食品制造业	5 553	3 779.39	1 168.32	3 665.75	206.21	121.02
饮料制造业	3 519	3 089.27	1 164.73	3 055.28	221.46	89.00
烟草制品业	190	2 840.74	2 059.99	2 850.84	406.54	19.67
纺织业	22 569	12 671.65	3 240.19	12 374.53	437.13	590.96
纺织服装、鞋、帽制造业	11 865	4 974.63	1 419.86	4 780.00	206.16	346.06
皮革、毛皮、羽毛（绒）及其制品业	6 227	3 462.79	944.38	3 315.94	138.50	228.84
木材加工及竹藤棕草制品业	5 397	1 827.71	510.86	1 749.45	82.43	83.33
家具制造业	3 074	1 427.26	384.87	1 387.39	61.89	71.27
造纸及纸制品业	7 461	4 161.33	1 146.40	4 034.25	194.04	130.14
印刷业、记录媒介的复制	4 826	1 442.96	463.06	1 386.55	93.19	66.90
橡胶制品业	3 034	2 196.74	595.36	2 144.22	105.19	79.64

表 36　我国农产品加工业全部国有及规模以上非国有工业企业主要经济效益指标（2005 年）

行　　业	工业增加值率（%）	总资产贡献率（%）	流动资产周转次数（次/年）	产品销售率（%）	全员劳动生产率 [元/（人·年）]
平　　均　　值	**32.50**	**15.35**	**2.40**	**97.99**	**156 883**
农副食品加工业	25.87	12.24	3.64	98.03	123 385
食品制造业	30.91	12.38	2.41	97.83	96 536
饮料制造业	37.70	16.40	1.90	97.78	130 862
烟草制品业	72.52	57.68	1.43	101.43	1 047 313
纺织业	25.57	9.26	2.47	97.92	54 830

（续）

行　　业	工业增加值率（%）	总资产贡献率（%）	流动资产周转次数（次/年）	产品销售率（%）	全员劳动生产率［元/（人·年）］
纺织服装、鞋、帽制造业	28.54	11.76	2.58	97.48	41 030
皮革、毛皮、羽毛（绒）及其制品业	27.27	12.79	2.83	97.90	41 268
木材加工及竹、藤、棕、草制品业	27.95	12.15	2.91	96.94	61 303
家具制造业	26.97	10.40	2.45	97.97	54 003
造纸及纸制品业	27.55	9.09	2.21	97.64	88 091
印刷业、记录媒介的复制	32.09	9.66	1.68	97.60	69 219
橡胶制品业	27.10	10.39	2.26	97.39	74 758

表 37　我国农产品加工业国有及国有控股工业企业主要指标（2005 年）

行　　业	单位数（个）	工业总产值（亿元）	工业增加值（亿元）	主营业务收入（亿元）	利润总额（亿元）	从业人员年平均人数（万人）
合　　计	**6 003**	**7 721.96**	**3 526.58**	**7 866.33**	**589.90**	**234.44**
农副食品加工业	1 393	1 089.84	248.96	1 173.73	29.48	26.77
食品制造业	595	476.50	161.40	488.98	25.80	16.68
饮料制造业	557	843.68	357.68	843.62	78.90	27.46
烟草制品业	153	2 812.86	2 050.89	2 823.10	404.77	18.51
纺织业	905	923.87	243.67	923.72	−2.22	73.79
纺织服装、鞋、帽制造业	282	110.13	33.80	104.36	1.38	11.58
皮革、毛皮、羽毛（绒）及其制品业	72	24.30	7.20	23.00	0.59	1.88
木材加工及竹、藤、棕、草制品业	243	172.51	51.00	170.36	3.59	10.77
家具制造业	96	53.61	12.95	54.95	3.64	1.78
造纸及纸制品业	374	523.86	151.65	573.56	18.00	15.88
印刷业和记录媒介的复制	1 149	288.11	115.43	283.10	16.18	16.59
橡胶制品业	184	40 269	91.95	403.85	9.79	12.75

表 38　我国农产品加工业国有及国有控股工业企业主要经济效益指标（2005 年）

行　　业	工业增加值率（%）	总资产贡献率（%）	流动资产周转次数（次/年）	产品销售率（%）	全员劳动生产率［元/（人·年）］
平　均　值	**33.69**	**11.53**	**1.63**	**98.60**	**157 173**
农副食品加工业	22.84	8.00	2.92	99.26	93 017
食品制造业	33.87	8.44	1.52	98.96	96 769
饮料制造业	42.40	16.36	1.37	97.74	130 277
烟草制品业	72.91	58.06	1.43	101.46	1 108 076
纺织业	26.38	3.77	1.49	98.80	33 021
纺织服装、鞋、帽制造业	30.69	3.72	1.28	98.31	29 181
皮革、毛皮、羽毛（绒）及其制品业	29.64	4.75	1.17	97.53	37 355
木材加工及竹、藤、棕、草制品业	29.57	4.79	1.51	96.79	47 371
家具制造业	24.15	11.01	2.08	99.03	72 868

（续）

行　　业	工业增加值率（%）	总资产贡献率（%）	流动资产周转次数（次/年）	产品销售率（%）	全员劳动生产率［元/（人·年）］
造纸及纸制品业	28.95	5.78	1.69	98.79	95 469
印刷业和记录媒介的复制	40.06	7.22	1.29	98.37	69 574
橡胶制品业	22.83	6.47	1.79	98.17	72 103

表 39　我国农产品加工业“三资”工业企业主要指标（2005 年）

行　　业	单位数（个）	工业总产值（亿元）	工业增加值（亿元）	主营业务收入（亿元）	利润总额（亿元）	从业人员年平均人数（万人）
合　　计	**21 219**	**16 816.53**	**4 752.15**	**16 473.15**	**761.95**	**715.20**
农副食品加工业	2 130	3 071.71	774.36	3 006.60	114.92	53.75
食品制造业	1 294	1 376.69	461.29	1 358.77	92.66	32.92
饮料制造业	569	1 056.07	403.89	1 104.18	76.84	19.58
烟草制品业	6	6.90	3.70	8.82	1.68	0.41
纺织业	5 007	3 201.80	836.28	3 116.89	116.40	148.11
纺织服装、鞋、帽制造业	5 110	2 290.07	673.10	2 221.19	87.15	178.77
皮革、毛皮、羽毛（绒）及其制品业	2 494	1 827.08	504.90	1 754.72	61.72	146.01
木材加工及竹、藤、棕、草制品业	918	426.84	114.12	408.40	16.99	17.08
家具制造业	1 051	788.09	209.96	768.68	33.31	39.08
造纸及纸制品业	1 234	1 454.58	379.75	1 440.43	75.71	31.19
印刷业和记录媒介的复制	662	467.78	149.46	455.23	43.50	18.16
橡胶制品业	744	848.92	241.34	829.24	41.07	30.14

表 40　我国农产品加工业“三资”工业企业主要经济效益指标（2005 年）

行　　业	工业增加值率（%）	总资产贡献率（%）	流动资产周转次数（次/年）	产品销售率（%）	全员劳动生产率［元/（人·年）］
平　均　值	**31.13**	**11.09**	**2.16**	**100.30**	**92.848**
农副食品加工业	25.21	11.11	3.22	98.38	144 066
食品制造业	33.51	14.35	2.29	98.40	140 125
饮料制造业	38.24	16.96	2.30	98.36	206 257
烟草制品业	53.62	19.04	1.18	127.68	90 329
纺织业	26.12	7.34	2.11	97.58	56 463
纺织服装、鞋、帽制造业	29.39	10.32	2.54	97.73	37 652
皮革、毛皮、羽毛（绒）及其制品业	27.63	9.80	2.51	97.93	34 580
木材加工及竹、藤、棕、草制品业	26.74	8.55	2.16	97.11	66 829
家具制造业	26.64	8.30	2.20	98.29	53 728
造纸及纸制品业	26.11	7.36	1.86	97.03	121 763
印刷业和记录媒介的复制	31.95	11.41	1.52	97.24	82 303
橡胶制品业	28.43	8.56	2.01	97.92	80 077

表 41　我国农产品加工业私营工业企业主要指标（2005 年）

行　　业	单位数（个）	工业总产值（亿元）	工业增加值（亿元）	主营业务收入（亿元）	利润总额（亿元）	从业人员年平均人数（万人）
合　　计	**43 980**	**15 586.62**	**4 122.62**	**14 997.60**	**635.96**	**648.52**
农副食品加工业	7 615	3 435.28	916.53	3 302.19	138.14	77.67
食品制造业	2 307	837.68	241.87	796.39	40.65	34.81
饮料制造业	1 486	465.73	148.93	433.86	23.84	17.72
烟草制品业	2	1.23	0.37	1.13	0.07	0.02
纺织业	12 879	5 035.94	1 220.36	4 903.15	179.12	217.03
纺织服装、鞋、帽制造业	5 053	1 555.77	435.13	1 480.30	58.52	105.68
皮革、毛皮、羽毛（绒）及其制品业	2 758	957.57	257.74	932.94	43.56	52.73
木材加工及竹、藤、棕、草制品业	3 426	932.02	258.66	892.25	47.27	40.87
家具制造业	1 532	468.87	126.07	450.24	22.63	23.04
造纸及纸制品业	3 836	1 140.85	308.97	1 086.02	44.15	44.53
印刷业和记录媒介的复制	1 828	370.13	100.83	353.13	15.35	17.01
橡胶制品业	1 258	385.55	107.16	374.40	22.66	17.41

表 42　我国农产品加工业私营工业企业主要经济效益指标（2005 年）

行　　业	工业增加值率（%）	总资产贡献率（%）	流动资产周转次数（次/年）	产品销售率（%）	全员劳动生产率［元/（人·年）］
平　均　值	**27.83**	**16.37**	**4.00**	**97.61**	**75 666**
农副食品加工业	26.68	15.78	4.55	97.59	118 001
食品制造业	28.87	13.59	3.20	97.18	69 487
饮料制造业	31.98	15.28	2.58	97.16	84 067
烟草制品业	30.40	33.75	12.69	99.55	181 956
纺织业	24.34	11.28	3.00	97.61	56 230
纺织服装、鞋、帽制造业	27.97	14.48	3.06	97.23	41 175
皮革、毛皮、羽毛（绒）及其制品业	26.92	18.70	3.72	97.87	48 876
木材加工及竹、藤、棕、草制品业	27.75	18.83	4.11	97.25	63 292
家具制造业	26.89	15.41	3.06	97.31	54 708
造纸及纸制品业	27.08	12.53	2.81	97.64	69 381
印刷业和记录媒介的复制	27.24	9.86	2.34	97.81	59 270
橡胶制品业	27.79	16.97	2.92	97.07	61 548

表 43　我国农产品加工业大中型工业企业主要指标（2005 年）

行　　业	单位数（个）	工业总产值（亿元）	工业增加值（亿元）	主营业务收入（亿元）	利润总额（亿元）	从业人员年平均人数（万人）
合　　计	**8 437**	**27 629.84**	**9 072.19**	**27 312.53**	**1 656.71**	**929.56**
农副食品加工业	996	4 363.72	1 154.84	4 359.02	196.96	92.25
食品制造业	633	2 244.65	717.47	2 207.95	145.59	63.32
饮料制造业	555	2 123.96	836.57	2 159.42	167.66	55.35
烟草制品业	108	2 722.03	1 976.48	2 803.87	401.79	17.43

（续）

行　　业	单位数（个）	工业总产值（亿元）	工业增加值（亿元）	主营业务收入（亿元）	利润总额（亿元）	从业人员年平均人数（万人）
纺织业	2 635	6 790.01	1 748.74	6 670.73	249.64	302.90
纺织服装、鞋、帽制造业	982	2 167.22	618.79	2 076.79	124.71	112.27
皮革、毛皮、羽毛（绒）及其制品业	650	1 739.89	482.75	1 669.98	76.96	109.83
木材加工及竹、藤、棕、草制品业	234	515.57	142.43	497.78	27.96	20.83
家具制造业	302	674.56	182.13	662.84	32.68	32.25
造纸及纸制品业	641	2 204.08	620.45	2 162.90	111.95	56.44
印刷业和记录媒介的复制	327	584.83	193.69	571.17	49.57	23.67
橡胶制品业	374	1 499.32	397.85	1 470.08	71.24	43.02

表 44　我国农产品加工业大中型工业企业主要经济效益指标（2005 年）

行　　业	工业增加值率（%）	总资产贡献率（%）	流动资产周转次数（次/年）	产品销售率（%）	全员劳动生产率［元/（人·年）］
平　均　值	**32.91**	**15.13**	**2.16**	**97.93**	**174 112**
农副食品加工业	26.46	11.86	3.12	98.52	125 180
食品制造业	31.96	13.56	2.36	97.98	113 301
饮料制造业	39.39	18.27	1.89	98.31	151 153
烟草制品业	72.61	58.86	1.44	101.28	1 133 799
纺织业	25.75	8.69	2.21	98.19	57 733
纺织服装、鞋、帽制造业	28.55	11.72	2.15	96.54	55 115
皮革、毛皮、羽毛（绒）及其制品业	27.75	11.59	2.51	97.82	43 953
木材加工及竹、藤、棕、草制品业	27.62	9.96	2.16	96.48	68 376
家具制造业	27.00	7.77	2.19	98.29	56 480
造纸及纸制品业	28.15	7.70	2.05	97.57	109 933
印刷业和记录媒介的复制	33.12	11.64	1.61	96.86	81 830
橡胶制品业	26.54	9.89	2.22	97.34	92 488

表 45　2005/2006 年制糖期全国制糖行业主要经济技术指标

行业实现销售收入（亿元）	实现利税总额（亿元）	平均含糖分（%）		平均单产（t/hm^2）		平均产糖率（%）	
		甘蔗糖	甜菜糖	甘蔗糖	甜菜糖	甘蔗糖	甜菜糖
407	98.6	13.95	14.35	54	33.6	12.15	12.57

资料来源：表中数据由中国糖业协会提供。

表 46　我国食品和包装机械生产、经营、销售情况（2005 年）

年销售收入（亿元）		进出口总额（亿美元）		其中：进口总额（亿美元）		出口总额（亿美元）	
销售收入	同比增长（%）	总　额	同比增长（%）	出口总额	同比增长（%）	出口总额	同比增长（%）
673.7	20.5	26.07	－19.64	19.99	－28.61	6.07	36.71

资料来源：表中数据由中国食品和包装机械工业协会提供。

表 47 林业系统农产品加工业总产值及销售产值（2004—2005 年）

行业	工业总产值（万元）			工业销售产值（万元）		
	2004 年	2005 年	同比（%）	2004 年	2005 年	同比增长（%）
总计	**3 020 467**	**3 414 624**	**13.05**	**2 734 917**	**2 796 757**	**2.26**
一、非木质林产品加工制造业	31 464	112 540	257.68	28 051	111 400	297.13
二、木材加工及竹藤、棕、草制品业	1 981 002	2 121 113	7.07	1 815 027	1 632 205	－10.07
其中：锯材、木片加工业	254 300	335 152	31.79	237 110	262 261	10.61
人造板制造业	1 212 461	1 370 422	13.03	1 115 508	1 024 366	－8.17
木制品制造业	485 305	362 208	－25.36	437 824	310 882	－28.99
竹藤棕草制品制造业	28 936	53 331	84.31	24 585	34 696	41.13
三、木质、竹、藤家具制造业	143 160	239 337	67.18	122 772	131 153	6.83
四、木、竹、浆造纸及纸制品业	151 521	204 592	35.03	100 179	189 694	89.36
五、林产化学产品制造业	122 287	95 064	－22.26	118 103	91 034	－22.92
六、木、竹、藤工艺品制造业	9 192	18 212	98.13	6 375	16 459	158.18
七、专用设备、仪器仪表制造业	10 414	11 159	7.15	10 111	10 386	2.72

表 48 林业系统各地区农产品加工业总产值（2005 年） 单位：万元

地区	总计	非木质林产品加工制造业	木材加工及竹、藤、棕、草制品业				
			合计	锯材、木片加工业	人造板制造业	木制品制造业	竹、藤、棕、草制品制造业
全国总计	**3 414 624**	**112 540**	**2 121 113**	**335 152**	**1 370 422**	**362 208**	**53 331**
北京	3 462						
天津							
河北	58 988	508	42 487	120	42 325	42	
山西	262		257		257		
内蒙古	69 535		32 213	400	25 675	6 138	
辽宁	115 245	1 088	65 683	16 879	38 537	10 057	210
吉林	300 991	8 280	235 377	25 667	87 879	120 945	886
黑龙江	116 110	2 442	73 819	11 905	29 129	32 475	310
上海	15 170		12 870		1 600	11 270	
江苏	702 099		518 440	45 221	418 848	37 825	16 546
浙江	14 773	668	12 361	1 250	4 000	7 111	
安徽	90 271	1 554	80 943	7 937	65 069	5 097	2 840
福建	167 283		138 465	584	124 448	12 145	1 288
江西	38 257	1 918	19 962	3 249	14 842	994	877
山东	199 287		128 609		124 483	4 126	
河南	72 006	10	49 740	34 279	11 370	2 250	1 841
湖北	226 723	7 619	166 418	19 331	122 993	13 065	11 029
湖南	486 633	53 776	212 402	74 141	103 547	22 973	11 741
广东	81 541	50	45 712	31 717	9 227	3 589	1 179
广西	227 703		102 570	8 141	94 429		
海南	57 661	31 049	19 104	19 104			
重庆	30 670		6 352	1 545	3 271	636	900
四川	97 187		30 687	3 942	2 391	23 452	902
贵州	46 374	3 481	30 323	7 345	16 404	3 975	2 599

（续）

地 区	总 计	非木质林产品加工制造业	木材加工及竹、藤、棕、草制品业				
			合 计	锯材、木片加工业	人造板制造业	木制品制造业	竹、藤、棕、草制品制造业
云 南	41 237	97	12 148	2 048	9 471	446	183
西 藏	2 277		1 156	1 156			
陕 西	18 741		13 322		13 322		
甘 肃	834		725		725		
青 海							
宁 夏							
新 疆							

地 区	木质、竹、藤家具制造业	木、竹、浆造纸及纸制品业	林产化学产品制造业	木、竹、藤工艺品制造业	专用设备、仪器仪表制造业
全国总计	**239 337**	**204 592**	**95 064**	**18 212**	**11 159**
北 京					
天 津					
河 北	26	3 860	1 421		
山 西			5		
内 蒙 古		33 118	898		
辽 宁	19 067	1 702	4		
吉 林	5 218	2 858	12 391		625
黑 龙 江	1 805	95			1 667
上 海					
江 苏	103 434	10 000		1 732	400
浙 江				102	
安 徽	840		251		
福 建			8 449		6 790
江 西	110		368	185	
山 东					
河 南	5 420	7 150		325	
湖 北	7 522	20 979	2 161	7 531	357
湖 南	55 051	12 357	4 221	3 121	720
广 东	6 022		747	216	
广 西		61 900	53 443	5 000	600
海 南	175	190	76		
重 庆	17 984		500		
四 川	2 675	48 010	680		
贵 州	4 386		2 500		
云 南		2 373	3 709		
西 藏					
陕 西			1 623		
甘 肃	109				
青 海					
宁 夏					
新 疆					

表 49 林业系统各地区农产品加工业销售产值（2005 年） 单位：万元

地 区	总 计	非木质林产品加工制造业	木材加工及竹、藤、棕、草制品业				
			合 计	锯材、木片加工业	人造板制造业	木制品制造业	竹、藤、棕、草制品制造业
我国总计	**2 796 757**	**111 400**	**1 632 205**	**262 261**	**1 024 366**	**310 882**	**34 696**
北 京	2 452						
天 津							
河 北	52 724	370	41 593	120	41 435	38	
山 西	110		105		105		
内 蒙 古	70 248		32 557	403	25 846	6 308	
辽 宁	110 007	1 088	63 839	17 379	36 887	9 363	210
吉 林	296 497	8 210	230 452	25 178	85 689	118 719	866
黑 龙 江	113 215	2 379	72 284	11 800	28 525	31 649	310
上 海	8 350		8 350		850	7 500	
江 苏	230 947		104 109	3 521	98 617	1 245	726
浙 江	14 682	681	12 252	1 219	4 000	7 033	
安 徽	86 253	780	79 537	7 706	65 042	3 949	2 840
福 建	164 207		136 257	589	122 970	11 363	1 335
江 西	37 394	1 753	19 923	3 273	14 718	1 096	836
山 东	196 924		129 590		121 809	7 781	
河 南	64 062	37	45 524	32 278	9 698	2 138	1 410
湖 北	216 760	7 643	161 746	16 762	122 499	10 976	11 509
湖 南	436 382	53 776	183 657	56 511	95 478	21 290	10 378
广 东	73 506	50	39 599	27 081	9 060	2 280	1 178
广 西	221 536		98 545	8 303	90 242		
海 南	57 154	31 049	18 503	18 503			
重 庆	22 475		4 407	1 500	2 447	109	351
四 川	90 210		27 240	1 907	1 856	23 457	20
贵 州	46 873	3 481	30 756	7 387	16 762	4 063	2 544
云 南	40 712	103	13 377	1 893	10 826	475	183
西 藏	2 071		1 156	1 156			
陕 西	18 370		12 787		12 787		
甘 肃	885		782		782		
青 海							
宁 夏							
新 疆							

地 区	木质、竹、藤家具制造业	木、竹、浆造纸及纸制品业	林产化学产品制造业	木、竹、藤工艺品制造业	专用设备、仪器仪表制造业
全国总计	**131 153**	**189 694**	**91 034**	**16 459**	**10 380**
北 京					
天 津					
河 北	24	3 650	1 421		
山 西			5		
内 蒙 古		33 027	1 268		
辽 宁	18 424	1 702	4		

（续）

地　区	木质、竹、藤家具制造业	木、竹、浆造纸及纸制品业	林产化学产品制造业	木、竹、藤工艺品制造业	专用设备、仪器仪表制造业
吉　林	5 528	2 861	12 463		625
黑龙江	1 941	120			1 206
上　海					
江　苏	9 580			712	380
浙　江				102	
安　徽	760		251		
福　建			7 805		6 666
江　西	110		348	150	
山　东					
河　南	4 618	6 495		170	
湖　北	3 890	20 675	973	7 531	310
湖　南	50 345	11 472	4 188	2 621	510
广　东	6 022		747	173	
广　西		60 570	52 597	5 000	689
海　南	175	284	76		
重　庆	17 405				
四　川	568	46 597	612		
贵　州	4 386		2 575		
云　南		2 241	3 115		
西　藏					
陕　西			1 738		
甘　肃	103				
青　海					
宁　夏					
新　疆					

表 50　林业系统农产品加工业国有独立核算大中型工业企业主要经济效益指标（2005 年）

指标名称	单　位	2005 年
总资产贡献率	%	5.2
资本保值增值率	%	107.4
资产负债率	%	55.3
流动资产周转率	次/年	1.4
成本费用利润率	%	2.0
全员劳动生产率	元/（人·年）	36 661.0
产品销售率	%	97.1

表 51 林业系统农产品加工业各地区国有独立核算大中型工业企业主要经济效益指标（2005 年）

地区	总资产贡献率（%）	资本增值保值率（%）	资产负债率（%）	流动资产周转率（次/年）	成本费用利润率（%）	全员劳动生产率[元/（人·年）]	产品销售率（%）
全国总计	**5.2**	**107.4**	**55.3**	**1.4**	**2.0**	**36 661**	**97.1**
北京							
天津							
河北							
山西							
内蒙古	10.4	143.5	43.4	1.6	6.1	32 168	100.9
辽宁							
吉林	7.2	96.6	50.2	1.3	4.2	36 633	98.1
黑龙江	−3.1	115.2	41.4	0.3	−31.3	15 785	95.7
上海							
江苏							
浙江							
安徽	6	90.9	53	2.1	0.4	37 581	99.1
福建	5.5	104.5	56.2	2.2	4.5	91 683	95.9
江西							
山东	12.2	123.8	54.4	2.3	7.7	72 245	98.8
河南							
湖北	2.3	77.4	69.3	1	0.4	40 238	80.3
湖南	0.3	119.1	75	0.6	−11.2	5 941	102.2
广东							
广西	6	101.8	73.4	2.3	1.2	122 459	95.5
海南							
重庆							
四川	−0.3	164.5	70.7	0.8	−9.7	6 982	101.9
贵州	−7.9	152.9	147.2	0.6	−30.7	10 799	95.8
云南	0.8	121.8	80.6	0.7	−3.8	1 776	92.3
西藏	10.5	108.6	43	0.9	19.7	20 450	86.7
陕西							
甘肃	−5.1	−115	105.2	0.8	37.5	−3 552	106.1
青海							
宁夏							
新疆							

表 52 我国水产品加工业发展情况（2004—2005 年）

项 目	单 位	2005 年	2004 年	同比增长（%）
一、水产品加工企业	个	9 128	8 745	4.38
水产品加工能力	万 t/年	1 696.2	1 426.6	18.89
二、水产品冷库	座	6 328	5 964	6.10
冻结能力	万 t/日	26.5	25.1	5.22
冷藏能力	万 t/次	256.7	218.2	17.65
制冰能力	万 t/日	12.9	10.2	27.49
冷藏总量	万 t·日	9 903.9	18 240.8	−45.70
制冰总量	万 t	809.4	766	5.68
三、水产品加工总量	万 t	1 195.5	1 032	15.84
其中：淡水加工产品	万 t	112.3	91.9	22.12
（一）水产品冷冻	万 t	725.9	599.3	21.12
其中：冷冻加工品	万 t	293.4	226.8	29.40
（二）鱼糜制品及干腌制品	万 t	194.6	170.4	14.15
其中：鱼糜制品	万 t	44.6	33	35.33
干制品	万 t	76	70.5	7.86
藻类制品	万 t	51.6	44.6	15.49
（三）罐头制品	万 t	17.7	14.4	23.36
（四）饲料	万 t	165.4	168.2	−1.67
其中：鱼粉	万 t	72	65.8	9.39
（五）鱼油制品	万 t	1.8	2.3	−20.49
（六）其他水产加工品	万 t	90	77.3	16.48
其中：助剂和添加剂	万 t	4.5	4	12.53
珍珠	Kg	1 437 320	1 382 164	48.61
四、用于加工的水产品总量	万 t	1 548.70	1 382.3	12.04
其中：淡水产品	万 t	178.70	137.6	29.94

资料来源：表中数据出自 2006 年版《中国渔业年鉴》。

表 53 我国水产品加工业加工能力、产量及产值（2002—2005 年）

年 份	加工企业数（个）	加工能力（万 t/年）	水产品加工总产量		折合水产品原料（万 t）	总产值（亿元）	占水产品总产值比率（%）
			总产量（万 t）	同比增长率（%）			
2002	8 140	1 224.7	704.5	1.97		76.11	25.6
2003	8 287	1 306.3	912.1	29.47		915.44	
2004	8 745	1 427.0	1 032.0	13.20	1 382.30	1 107.60	28.0
2005	9 128	1 696.2	1 195.5	15.84	1 578.74		

表 54　我国沿海省、自治区、直辖市水产品加工业生产情况（2005 年）

单位：万 t

地　区	水产品加工企业		水产品加工品总量	其　　中					
	企业数（个）	加工能力（万 t/年）		冷冻水产品	鱼糜及干腌制品	罐制品	饲料	鱼油制品	其他
全国总计	**9 128**	**1 696.2**	**1 195.5**	**725.9**	**194.6**	**17.7**	**165.4**	**1.84**	**90.0**
天　津	12	9.29	0.213	0.193					0.02
河　北	246	20.9	14.36	4.22	1.21	0.48	8.17	0.015	0.269
辽　宁	717	182.27	111.58	64.07	37.39	0.86	6.99	0.015	2.24
上　海	21	3.47	2.58	0.44					2.14
江　苏	765	192.5	58.31	36.72	2.78	1.08	14.01	0.006 6	3.72
浙　江	1 962	173.5	173.35	136.06	17.87	1.49	15.51	0.09	2.36
福　建	1 475	151.5	176.71	79.27	40.88	1.24	47.13	0.33	7.84
山　东	1 855	583.8	443.19	266.81	52.97	6.79	54.47	1.03	61.12
广　东	1 139	192.99	119.47	81.30	18.69	4.15	8.66	0.25	6.42
广　西	141	31.78	16.04	11.03	2.68	0.01	0.285		2.03
海　南	241	76.52	32.95	25.88	3.42	0.026	2.54	0.09	0.998
11 省区市小计	8 574	1 618.52	1 148.75	705.96	177.89	16.13	157.77	1.83	89.16
11 省区市占全国比率（%）	93.93	95.42	96.09	97.25	91.41	91.13	95.38	99.46	99.06

表 55　我国乡镇集体企业农产品加工业现状（2004 年）

行　　业	企业单位数（个）	平均职工人数（人）	工业总产值（万元）	工业增加值（万元）	工业销售产值（万元）	应缴增值税（万元）
食品加工业	8 578	1 202 176	38 200 550	8 749 136	57 704 789	547 348
食品制造业	3 105	524 517	10 281 418	2 487 087	9 895 096	244 836
饮料制造业	1 693	246 790	5 748 804	1 545 406	5 548 982	197 327
烟草加工业	32	7 771	196 871	51 382	186 354	7 867
纺织业	14 322	2 614 938	57 233 583	12 144 345	55 170 111	1 150 487
服装及其他纤维制品制造业	10 937	2 722 891	32 848 181	7 891 517	34 435 921	663 520
皮革、毛皮、羽绒及其制品业	3 312	740 167	12 562 442	2 767 414	12 101 979	258 272
木材加工及竹、藤、棕、草制品业	3 885	546 269	8 435 696	1 977 812	8 093 596	209 922
家具制造业	2 048	362 676	5 728 574	1 366 853	5 458 028	112 449
造纸及纸制品业	4 538	682 851	14 544 180	3 515 816	13 952 675	402 990
印刷及记录媒介复制业	1 989	225 687	4 179 930	1 097 345	4 048 792	125 382
橡胶制品业	1 151	371 556	4 759 826	1 050 762	4 644 683	85 173
小　　计	**55 954**	**10 248 289**	**194 720 055**	**44 644 875**	**188 241 006**	**4 005 573**

资料来源：表中数据出自 2005 年版《中国乡镇企业年鉴》。

表 56 我国乡镇规模以上农产品加工业企业基本情况（2004—2005 年）

项　目	单　位	2004 年	2005 年	同比增长（%）
企业数	个	54 439	70 297	29.13
从业人员	人	9 876 733	12 793 498	29.53
工业总产值	万元	189 960 229	307 987 194	62.13
工业增加值	万元	43 594 113	71 965 206	65.11
营业收入	万元	183 596 323	292 592 999	59.36
利润总额	万元		14 993 496	

表 57 轻工业系统农产品加工业分行业主要经济指标（2004 年）　单位：亿元

行　业	企业单位数（个）		工业总产值	产品销售收入	利税总额	流动资产年平均余额	固定资产净值年平均余额	出口交货值
	合　计	其中：亏损						
轻工业总计	**67 776**	**11 894**	**37 376**	**35 814**	**1 567**	**15 750**	**9 886**	**9 339**
有关农产品加工行业小计	36 032	6 510	21 021	20 131	897	8 549	6 187	3 465.3
农副食品加工业	12 244	2 015	8 052	7 811	234	2 415	1 598	868
食品制造业	4 950	1 118	2 844	2 689	133	1 262	923	283
饮料制造业	3 332	787	2 557	2 435	170	1 545	1 203	85
制盐	174	33	124	126	22	99	88	5.3
皮革、毛皮、羽毛（绒）及制品业	4 885	736	2 718	2 577	99	977	411	1 427
木、竹、藤、棕草制品业	852	117	186	175	12	59	33	81
家具制造业	2 323	386	947	902	40	398	233	461
造纸及纸制品业	6 086	1 109	3 144	2 988	141	1 489	1 575	206
轻工专用设备制造业	1 186	209	449	428	46	305	123	49

注：表中数据出自 2005 年版《中国轻工业年鉴》。

表 58 轻工业系统食品工业分行业主要经济指标（2004 年）　单位：亿元

行　业	企业单位数（个）		工业总产值	工业增加产值	产品销售收入	利税总额	流动资产年平均余额	固定资产净值年平均余额	从业人员（万人）
	合计	其中：亏损							
一、食品工业合计	**23 304**	**4 982**	**16 280.92**	**5 633.15**	**15 884.87**	**2 762.68**	**7 012.52**	**4 560.05**	**411.2**
农副食品加工业	14 097	2 740	8 344.89	1 966.44	8 136.15	384.80	2 475.56	1 705.36	196.5
谷物磨制	3 143	455	978.64	226.36	951.45	40.52	257.33	195.85	20.6
饲料加工	2 268	484	1 257.36	265.74	1 236.63	43.91	310.77	159.01	19.5
植物油加工	1 752	407	1 838.36	393.06	1 820.22	34.86	613.97	289.51	18.7
其中：食用植物油加工	1 502	393	1 814.53	385.48	1 798.48	33.70	607.05	284.26	18.2
制糖业	329	92	332.82	107.51	316.21	51.17	169.21	191.42	15.3
屠宰及肉类加工	2 439	549	1 652.36	390.38	1 681.03	72.96	439.52	374.47	51.9
水产品加工	1 549	290	1 142.31	287.67	1 042.89	58.42	323.79	200.48	29.8
蔬菜、水果及坚果加工	1 627	247	490.44	134.19	465.20	33.61	179.32	119.40	22.6

（续）

行　业	企业单位数（个）		工业总产值	工业增加产值	产品销售收入	利税总额	流动资产年平均余额	固定资产净值年平均余额	从业人员（万人）
	合计	其中：亏损							
其他农副食品加工	1 170	216	652.61	161.52	622.48	49.36	181.65	175.22	17.9
二、食品制造业	5 528	1 347	2 899.08	873.37	2 782.17	256.53	1 350.50	1 059.89	110.9
焙烤食品制造业	932	211	304.16	92.49	294.40	27.21	122.80	94.82	15.7
糖果、巧克力及蜜饯制造业	416	82	212.36	69.39	201.25	24.74	111.45	67.65	7.9
方便食品制造业	722	63	478.07	136.34	468.53	35.72	253.15	254.39	21.9
液体乳及乳制品制造业	692	219	702.74	208.67	683.79	65.78	234.13	203.43	17.7
罐头制造	676	175	237.84	62.54	217.19	11.08	133.19	80.47	13.5
调味品、发酵制品制造	854	233	460.91	141.94	443.93	41.99	260.37	209.15	17.8
其他食品制造	1 236	261	503.01	161.99	473.08	50.01	235.41	149.98	16.4
三、饮料制造业	3 469	862	2 440.82	910.05	2 393.19	436.17	1 474.88	1 171.88	83.9
酒精制造业	150	50	107.27	28.27	101.76	7.72	43.93	58.68	3.8
酒的制造业	1 839	461	1 363.07	579.76	1 291.07	315.30	965.07	748.44	57.0
软饮料制造业	983	282	882.13	279.73	917.54	279.73	421.13	340.31	19.2
精制茶加工业	497	69	88.44	23.30	82.82	6.46	44.69	24.45	3.9
四、烟草加工业	210	33	2 596.03	1 883.29	2 573.40	1 685.18	1 711.64	622.91	19.9
烟叶复烤	62	9	51.90	24.49	65.07	12.88	63.70	53.77	2.7
卷烟制造	114	12	2 530.85	1 853.42	2 495.14	1 670.30	1 640.52	562.04	16.2
其他烟草制品加工	34	12	13.27	5.37	13.18	2.00	7.42	7.10	0.93

表 59　我国食品工业焙烤糖制食品行业主要经济指标（2004 年）

行　业	产量（万 t）	销售收入（亿元）	利润总额（亿元）	税金总额（亿元）	资产总计（亿元）	负债总计（亿元）	流动资金周转次数（次/年）	销售收入利润率（%）
合　计	**662.16**	**962.49**	**37.66**	**38.29**	**838.72**	**464.28**	**2.37**	**4.03**
糖果业	63.2	165.72	11.54	9.42	153.70	85.38	1.92	6.96
糕点业	34.01	79.1	3.01	3.73	76.36	44.62	2.04	3.81
饼干业	105.46	187.94	6.15	8.52	151.4	82.7	2.5	3.27
方便食品业	364.49	425.21	13.34	14.45	355.17	187.68	2.79	3.14
其中：方便面	276.4	310.54	9.68	10.99	255.1	128.96	2.94	3.00
蜜饯业		46.98	3.60	0.094	43.14	23.35	1.91	7.66
冷冻饮品业	95.06	57.54	0.02	2.08	58.95	40.55	2.49	0.35

表 60　我国饮料行业主要经济指标（2003—2004 年）

项　　目	单　位	2003 年	2004 年	同比增长（%）
企业数	个	3 194	3 469	8.61
其中：亏损企业数	个	815	862	5.77
工业总产值	亿元	2 233.22	2 440.92	9.30
工业增加值	亿元	795.97	910.05	14.33
产品销售收入	亿元	2 117.23	2 393.19	13.03
利润总额	亿元	149 04	155.16	4.11
利税总额	亿元	402.78	436.17	8.29
固定资产值合计	亿元	1 737.23	1 774.04	2.12
流动资产年平均余额	亿元	1 424.04	1 474.82	3.57
固定资产净值年平均余额	亿元	1 149.80	1 171.88	1.92

表 61　我国乳制品行业主要经济指标（2004—2005 年）

指　　标	单　位	2004 年	2005 年	同比增长（%）
企业单位数	个	636	698	9.75
其中：亏损企业数	个		196	
工业总产值	亿元	700.74	891.2	27.18
产品销售收入	亿元	675.27	866.3	28.29
利税总额	亿元	59.52	84.72	42.34
利润总额	亿元		48.16	
全部从业人员平均人数	万人		19.23	
全员劳动生产率	万元/（人·年）		13.80	

资料来源：表中数据由中国乳制品工业协会提供。

表 62　轻工业系统机械行业重点企业分类（涉及农产品加工部分）主要经济指标（2004 年）

产 品 分 类	企业数（个）	工业总产值（万元）	工业销售产值（万元）	出口交货值（万元）	利税总额（万元）
造纸机械	35	238 036	216 295	4 093	15 160
酿酒、饮料、乳品机械	21	129 509	119 614	13 179	11 074
制革、制鞋机械	14	19 295	17 880	2 160	1 421
糖、盐及食品包装机械	35	253 637	223 449	16 583	26 045
织物加工及洗涤机械	11	74 743	74 871	5 509	6 993
其他机械	26	173 108	171 945	31 958	9 572
合　　计	**206**	**1 467 391**	**1 391 624**	**127 156**	**125 238**

表 63　我国烟草工业主要经济指标（2003—2004 年）

指　　标	单　位	2003 年	2004 年	同比增长（%）
企业单位数	个	147	210	42.86
其中：亏损企业	个	22	33	50.00
工业总产值	亿元	2 137.54	2 596.03	21.45
工业增加值	亿元	1 259.78	1 883.29	49.49
产品销售收入	亿元	2 134.55	2 573.40	20.56

（续）

指 标	单 位	2003年	2004年	同比增长（%）
利润总额	亿元	269.45	366.20	35.91
利税总额	亿元		1 685.18	
固定资产原值合计	亿元	1 012.85	1 169.18	15.43
流动资产年平均余额	亿元	1 623.17	1 711.64	5.45
固定资产净值年平均余额	亿元		622.91	

表64 我国纺织工业主要经济指标（2005年）

行 业	企业单位数（个）	工业总产值（亿元）	产品销售收入（亿元）	利润总额（亿元）	出口交货值（亿元）	职工总数（万人）
有关农产品加工行业小计	**35 978**	**20 471**	**19 794**	**690**	**5 737**	**978.3**
纺织业	22 135	12 518	12 148	422	3 234	580.9
棉、化纤纺织及印染精加工业	9 410	6 533	6 351	201	1 207	302.1
毛纺织和染整精加工业	1 271	1 027	992	38	233	34.3
麻纺织业	321	159	146	4.4	24	14.0
丝绢纺织及精加工业	2 087	1 151	1 153	29	255	45.2
纺织制成品制造业	3 520	1 552	1 498	65	537	61.8
绳、索、缆的制造业	184	14	46	1.8	15	2.4
纺织带和帘子布制造业	309	97	178	5.7	33	6.2
无纺布制造业	476	75	156	5.9	34	4.4
针织品、编织品及其制品业	5 526	800	2 009	84	977	123.5
毛针织品及编织品制造业	1 669	261	606	26	299	44.8
丝针织品及编织品制造业	289	39	106	4.8	56	5.9
纺织服装、鞋、帽制造业	11 737	1 524	4 699	198	2 297	340.2
化学纤维制造业	1 302	1 246	2 504	48.5	153	40.8
合成纤维制造业	1 135	1 023	2 216	34	133	31.2
纺织专用设备制造业	804	241	443	21	52	16.5

表65 纺织工业国有及国有控股企业主要经济指标（2005年）

行 业	企业单位数（个）	工业总产值（亿元）	产品销售收入（亿元）	利润总额（亿元）	出口交货值（亿元）	职工总数（万人）
有关农产品加工行业小计	**1 480**	**1 819**	**1 819**	**6.6**	**353**	**117.0**
纺织业	1 013	1 044	1 033	1.4	259	85.05
棉、化纤纺织及印染精加工业	476	687	689	0.84	157	60.0
毛纺织和染整精加工业	93	82.8	77	−1.43	22	5.3
麻纺织业	30	31.7	29.5	−1.00	9.7	4.8
丝绢纺织及精加工业	98	81.9	83.6	1.04	12.2	5.0
纺织制成品制造业	156	70.0	69.7	1.30	24.6	3.56
绳、索、缆的制造业	9	1.13	1.2	0.015	0.11	0.13
纺织带和帘子布制造业	18	16.0	14.8	0.16	3.9	0.53

（续）

行　业	企业单位数（个）	工业总产值（亿元）	产品销售收入（亿元）	利润总额（亿元）	出口交货值（亿元）	职工总数（万人）
无纺布制造业	17	7.55	7.2	0.15	1.8	0.26
针织品、编织品及其制品业	160	90.7	84.6	0.63	33.1	6.40
毛针织品及编织品制造业	39	37.0	29.4	－0.19	13.2	2.39
丝针织品及编织品制造业	9	2.3	2.3	－0.013	1.8	0.19
纺织服装、鞋、帽制造业	300	118	115	1.78	48.7	12.81
化学纤维制造业	90	552	548	－0.29	34.8	13.99
合成纤维制造业	63	367	380	－13.02	22.3	7.53
纺织专用设备制造业	77	105	124	3.77	10.6	5.14

表 66　纺织工业棉纺行业规模以上企业主要经济指标（2005 年）

指　标	单　位	2004 年	2005 年	同比增长（%）
企业个数	个	5 434	7 632.0	40.45
工业总产值	亿元	3 683.17	5 136.1	39.45
工业销售产值	亿元	3 601.32	5 035.1	39.81
产品销售收入	亿元	3 554.83	5 005.5	40.81
出口交货值	亿元	619.69	749.1	20.88
利润总额	亿元	86.33	159.9	85.22
应交增值税	亿元	93.07	137.8	48.06
资产合计	亿元	3 353.80	4 171.4	24.38
流动资产净值年平均余额	亿元	1 487.75	1 854.1	24.62
固定资产净值年平均余额	亿元	1 306.00	1 665.8	27.55
负债合计	亿元	2 208.03	2 637.4	19.45
亏损企业亏损金额	亿元	29.21	24.8	－15.10
职工人数	万人	232.90	258.9	11.16

表 67　纺织工业毛纺行业规模以上企业主要经济指标（2005 年）

指　标	单位	规模以上毛纺织企业		规模以上毛针织企业		规模以上毛制品企业	
		2005 年	同比（%）	2005 年	同比（%）	2005 年	同比（%）
企业单位数	个	1 271	11.43	1 669	35.56	220	78.86
销售产值	亿元	1 008	32.00	626	24.00	114	21.00
产值率	%	98.11	0.03	96.42	1.30	96.48	0.65
出口交货值	亿元	233	19.15	299	19.27	43	17.52
外销比例	%	23		48		37	
完成固定资产投资	亿元	102	45.70	46	70.40	9	23.60

表 68 纺织工业丝绸行业规模以上企业主要经济指标（2005 年）单位：亿元

指标		丝绸工业合计	丝绢及精加工				丝制品	丝针织	全国纺织
			小计	缫丝	绢纺和丝织	丝印染			
企业单位数（个）		2 558	2 087	621	1 231	235	182	289	35 978
亏损数（个）		432	350	94	194	62	28	54	6 008
亏损面（%）		16.89	16.77	15.14	15.76	26.38	15.38	18.69	16.92
产品销售收入	全年	1 322.42	1 153.51	207.24	730.87	214.40	64.18	105.73	19 793.76
	同比（%）	17.55	17.22	30.96	17.75	4.96	31.26	13.82	26.29
利润总额	全年	37.79	29.16	5.33	18.73	5.10	3.84	4.78	689.72
	同比（%）	6.18	4.45	2.39	1.48	0.59	0.63	1.10	181.88
亏损企业亏损总额	全年	5.88	5.15	0.90	2.72	1.53	0.44	0.29	117.84
	同比（%）	−5.62	−7.87	−16.21	16.83	−30.06	123.53	−34.07	3.48
资产合计	全年	1 144.39	1 001.58	142.13	654.99	204.46	60.72	82.09	16 015.38
	同比（%）	12.29	11.49	15.27	10.95	10.69	29.93	10.85	14.39
负债合计	全年	744.01	668.42	96.64	435.68	136.10	33.23	42.36	9 660.16
	同比（%）	11.33	10.48	10.89	10.09	11.45	35.45	9.36	13.44
工业总产值	全年	1 329.80	1 151.31	216.22	718.83	216.56	64.99	113.51	20 470.59
	同比（%）	17.20	16.65	34.15	15.34	6.80	27.47	17.30	25.97
销售产值	全年	1 303.23	1 129.31	211.44	704.25	213.63	63.78	110.14	20 011.29
	同比（%）	16.62	15.94	32.61	14.63	6.65	26.63	18.40	26.09
出口交货值	全年	345.25	255.46	39.98	143.35	72.14	33.53	56.26	5 736.89
	同比（%）	2.17	−1.49	17.63	−0.43	−11.37	16.69	12.87	18.24
从业人员（万人）	全年	53.86	45.16	14.98	23.34	6.84	2.80	5.90	978.34
	同比（%）	3.27	2.40	3.15	1.61	2.68	12.68	5.96	6.36

表 69 纺织工业麻纺织行业主要经济指标（2005 年）

指标	单位	2004 年	2005 年	同比增长（%）
企业单位数	个	327	386.00	18.04
工业总产值	亿元	134.69	177.64	31.89
产品销售产值	亿元	129.83	170.94	31.66
产品销售收入	亿元	127.72	163.62	28.11
出口交货值	亿元	24.75	25.28	2.14
利润总额	亿元	3.52	4.84	37.50
应交增值税	亿元	3.73	4.45	19.30
亏损企业亏损额	亿元	1.16	1.76	51.72
资产合计	亿元	144.67	196.55	35.86
流动资产净值平均余额	亿元	78.50	99.41	26.64
固定资产净值平均余额	亿元	45.23	64.42	42.43
负债合计	亿元	94.44	123.60	30.88
职工人数	万人	13.68	15.25	11.48

表 70 纺织工业印染行业规模以上企业主要经济指标（2005 年）

指 标	单 位	2004 年	2005 年	同比增长（%）
企业单位数	个	1 417	1 778.00	25.48
工业总产值	亿元	1 166.58	1 397.10	19.76
产品销售产值	亿元	1 141.37	1 367.02	19.77
产品销售收入	亿元	1 126.59	1 345.71	19.45
出口交货值	亿元	408.33	457.82	12.12
利润总额	亿元	30.67	41.45	35.13
应交增值税	亿元	20.28	25.43	25.39
资产合计	亿元	999.52	1 134.55	13.51
亏损企业亏损额	亿元	8.72	10.24	1.74
负债合计	亿元	621.46	701.44	12.87
产销率	%	98.33	97.85	−0.49
销售利润率	%	2.99	3.08	2.70
职工人数	万人	40.37	43.13	6.84

表 71 纺织工业针织行业规模以上企业主要经济指标（2005 年）

指 标	单 位	2004 年	2005 年	同比增长（%）
企业单位数	个	2 382	5 526.00	131.99
工业总产值	亿元	1 669.24	2 094.73	25.49
产品销售产值	亿元	1 623.45	2 043.76	25.89
产品销售收入	亿元	1 593.62	2 008.92	26.06
出口交货值	亿元	810.11	977.32	20.64
利润总额	亿元	61.42	83.97	36.71
资产合计	亿元	1 376.24	1 572.08	14.23
负债合计	亿元	800.08	913.29	14.15
亏损企业亏损额	亿元	9.62	9.08	−5.62
产销率	%	97.26	97.57	0.32
销售利润率	%	4.17	4.18	0.33
出口比率	%	48.83	47.81	−2.09
职工人数	万人	116.11	123.52	6.38

表 72 纺织工业服装制造业主要经济指标（2005 年）

指 标	单 位	2004 年	2005 年	同比增长（%）
产品销售收入	亿元	3 718.45	4 699	26.37
产品销售税金及附加	亿元	14.21	20	40.76
应交增值税	亿元	85.71	106	23.67
资产合计	亿元	2 673.34	3 127	16.97
流动资产净值平均余额	亿元	1 505.82	1 810	20.20
固定资产净值平均余额	亿元	707.72	824	16.43
利润总额	亿元	148.77	198	33.09
负债合计	亿元	1 524.32	1 758	15.33
亏损企业亏损额	亿元	20.90	21	0.47
职工人数	万人	316.69	340	7.38

表 73 纺织工业纺机行业主要经济指标（2005 年）

指　　标	单 位	2004 年	2005 年	同比增长（%）
企业单位数	个	606	731.00	20.06
工业总产值	亿 元	380.38	469.47	23.42
产品销售收入	亿 元	369.96	453.65	22.62
利润总额	亿 元	20.44	23.36	14.27
进出口总额	亿美元	52.04	43.16	−17.06
出口总额	亿美元	6.68	8.71	30.34
进口总额	亿美元	45.36	34.45	−24.06
亏损企业亏损额	亿 元	1.28	1.69	32.15
产值利润率	%	5.00	4.98	−0.40

表 74 我国皮革工业经济运行情况（2003—2004 年）

行　　业	单 位	2003 年	2004 年	同比增长（%）
企业单位数	个		4 484	
工业总产值	亿元	2 000.83	2 421	21.00
产品销售收入	亿 元	1 883.61	2 298	22.00
利润总额	亿 元	69.77	90	29.00
利税总额	亿 元	115.87	146	26.00
商品进出口总额	亿美元	243.58	292.3	20.00
其中：出口额	亿美元	183.61	218.5	19.00
进口额	亿美元	60.16	74.0	23.00

注：表中数据来自中国轻工业信息中心，为皮革工业中全部国有及规模上非国有皮革工业企业统计数据。

表 75 我国家具行业经济运行情况（2003—2004 年）

指　　标	单 位	2003 年	2004 年	同比增长（%）
家具总产值	**亿元**	**2 040.00**	**2 730.00**	**33.82**
家具出口金额	亿美元	73.33	103.53	41.18
家具进口金额	亿美元	5.45	7.26	26.26

表 76 我国造纸工业各地区主要经济指标（2004 年）

地　区	工业总产值（万元）	企业单位数（个）	亏损企业数（个）	利润总额（万元）	税金总额（万元）	从业人员（人）
全国总计	**21 025 032**	**3 009**	**577**	**996 343**	**857 704**	**760 167**
北　京	159 980	28	10	28 294	8 583	3 606
天　津	114 758	61	17	1 267	3 954	77 449
河　北	984 938	202	37	36 980	31 519	51 767
山　西	46 422	16	3	3 084	1 743	3 319
内蒙古	55 442	9	1	776	3 353	1 929
辽　宁	207 496	69	21	−6 776	11 686	21 183
吉　林	162 738	25	13	−34 913	8 429	11 928
黑龙江	292 686	44	10	−1 389	17 344	15 671
上　海	375 205	70	25	5 067	17 802	9 379
江　苏	2 300 336	147	17	144 993	86 420	42 295

（续）

地　区	工业总产值（万元）	企业单位数（个）	亏损企业数（个）	利润总额（万元）	税金总额（万元）	从业人员（人）
浙　江	2 714 687	553	85	99 754	123 140	76 305
安　徽	314 964	72	21	8 217	13 258	14 778
福　建	736 564	149	40	7 982	31 162	23 518
江　西	144 247	73	17	27 708	5 304	11 137
山　东	5 880 936	282	23	384 468	248 887	169 899
河　南	1 465 930	287	21	95 863	56 324	76 622
湖　北	470 371	98	20	25 212	22 170	21 745
湖　南	792 242	163	28	41 192	38 041	34 747
广　东	2 407 627	289	56	87 298	68 016	53 953
广　西	257 159	59	2	6 153	12 662	16 014
海　南	4 581	4		28.4	118	228
重　庆	69 532	29	7	−645	3 145	4 414
四　川	463 388	111	22	10 904	19 458	30 990
贵　州	22 825	20	10	−1 580	1 173	228
云　南	167 014	40	20	17 625	8 837	7 216
陕　西	164 499	57	15	780	4 054	21 956
甘　肃	32 839	25	3	491	1 889	5 369
青　海	894	2	1	−21	2.3	335
宁　夏	180 457	17	6	8 189	8 549	13 827
新　疆	34 275	8	4	−655	2 107	3 761

表 77　我国新闻出版业产业基本情况（2004 年）

	类　别	单　位	2003 年	2004 年	同比增长（%）
总计	图书、期刊、报纸	亿印张		2 100.90	
	折合用纸量	万 t	418.59	486.19	16.15
	其中：书籍用纸量	万 t		57.56	
	课本用纸量	万 t		51.68	
	期刊用纸量	万 t		25.96	
	报纸用纸量	万 t		350.69	
	图片用纸量	万 t		0.30	
图书	图书出版总量	种	190 396.7	208 294.00	9.4
	其中：新版图书	种	110 845.0	121 597.00	9.7
	重版重印图书	种	79 611.6	86 697.00	8.9
	总印数	亿期（张）	65.6	63.13	−3.8
	总印张	亿印张	435.1	465.59	0.7
	折合用纸量	万 t		109.52	
	定价金额	亿元	561.9	592.89	5.5
期刊	出版总数	种	9 511.9	9 940.00	4.58
	平均印数	万册	19 912.1	17 208.00	−13.58
	总印数	亿册	29.5	28.35	−3.82
	总印张	亿印张	109.1	110.51	1.27
	折合用纸量	万 t		25.96	
	定价金额	亿元	127.6	129.91	1.81

（续）

类　别		单　位	2003年	2004年	同比增长（%）
报纸	出版种数	种	2 119.1	1 922.00	−9.30
	平均期印数	万份	19 071.5	19 521.63	2.36
	总印数	亿份	192.7	202.40	5.03
	总印张	亿印张	1 235.6	1 524.80	23.41
	折合用纸量	万t		350.69	
	定价金额	亿元	239.9	252.66	5.30
音像制品及电子出版物	出版种数	种	13 332.8	15 406	15.55
	出版数量	亿盒（张）	2.2	2.06	−6.36
	发行数量	亿盒（张）	1.96	1.72	−12.24
	发行金额	亿元	13.2	11.29	−14.79
出版物进出口	出　口				
	图书、期刊、报纸	种次	1 077 884	889 901	−17.43
	出口数量	万册（份）	762.2	767.96	0.75
	出口金额	万美元	2 280.3	2 546.23	11.66
	进　口				
	图书、期刊、报纸	种次	690 663.1	651 986.00	−5.60
	进口数量	万册（份）	1 877.5	1 974.89	5.19
	进口金额	万美元	14 608.5	16 254.93	11.27

表78　我国120个书刊印刷企业（含其他印刷）主要经济指标（2004年）

工业总产值（万元）	工业增加值（万元）	产品销售收入（万元）	胶印印刷		书刊装订		照相制版	
			产量（万对开色令）	产值（万元）	产量（万令）	产值（万元）	产量（四开块）	产值（万元）
687 016	286 401	608 609	7 587.4	194 659.8	2 289.9	54 115	1 389 098	15 289.9

表79　我国120个包装印刷企业主要经济指标（2003—2004年）

年　份	工业总产值（万元）	销售收入（万元）	利税总额（万元）	利润总额（万元）
2003	1 021 000	823 900	114 700	68 900
2004	1 270 300	1 053 100	105 400	71 500
同比增减（%）	24.41	27.82	8.82	3.77

注：参加上述统计的企业、创利税万元以上的106个，占88.33%。其中：500万元以上的28个，占22.68%；1 000万元以上的有20个占16.66%。

表80　我国58个印刷机械企业主要经济指标（2004年）

年份	工业总产值（万元）	工业增加值（万元）	产品销售收入（万元）	实现利税（万元）	平均固定资产净值（万元）	出口交货值（万元）
2004	560 009	204 947	531 996	88 655	243 334	45 709

表 81　我国橡胶工业主要经济指标（2005 年）

指　　标	单　位	2004 年	2005 年	同比增长（%）
企业单位数	个		376.00	
产品销售收入	亿元	829.06	1 028.04	24.00
出口交货值	亿元	211.84	311.70	47.14
橡胶总消耗量	万 t	177.05	198.30	12.00

注：表中数据为我国橡胶工业中 376 个会员企业的统计数据。

表 82　我国橡胶工业全部独立核算工业企业主要经济指标（2001—2003 年）

行　　业	企业单位数（个）			工业总产值（万元）		
	2001 年	2002 年	2003 年	2001 年	2002 年	2003 年
橡胶制品业	1 777	1 822	2 016	8 938 161	10 645 973	13 129 006
其中：轮胎制造业	218	224	235	4 401 953	5 360 183	6 663 770
力车胎制造业	78	82	81	339 079	410 153	683 948
橡胶板管带制造业	379	370	435	997 828	1 087 390	1 387 336
橡胶零件制造业	274	322	355	673 721	839 316	996 922
再生橡胶制造业	88	89	114	172 105	175 124	266 680
橡胶靴鞋制造业	279	286	280	1 227 431	1 433 367	1 397 260
日用橡胶制品业	121	145	166	423 435	582 817	827 755
其他橡胶制品业	293	267	312	652 315	700 850	824 876
橡胶制品翻修业	47	37	38	50 294	56 773	80 458
其中：轮胎翻修业	40	31	38	46 113	47 115	
其他橡胶制品翻修业	7	6		4 181	9 658	
橡胶工业专用设备制造业	54	57	80	191 227	215 977	443 750

行　　业	工业销售产值（万元）			出口交货值（万元）		
	2001 年	2002 年	2003 年	2001 年	2002 年	2003 年
橡胶制品业	8 666 836	10 391 395	12 795 994	1 894 514	2 154 711	2 677 449
其中：轮胎制造业	4 282 975	5 294 741	6 514 830	926 526	1 012 270	1 280 049
力车胎制造业	334 774	409 918	659 646	35 614	62 955	114 127
橡胶板管带制造业	946 692	1 045 344	1 345 340	80 589	90 948	126 150
橡胶零件制造业	654 106	821 296	968 653	146 144	177 371	234 220
再生橡胶制造业	164 397	166 928	256 175	4 976	3 044	13 239
橡胶靴鞋制造业	1 198 943	1 348 617	1 364 780	430 294	520 901	473 349
日用橡胶制品业	406 436	567 370	806 756	111 040	142 296	270 868
其他橡胶制品业	629 541	681 893	799 534	159 331	144 926	156 449
橡胶制品翻修业	48 973	55 290	80 280			
其中：轮胎翻修业	44 934	45 818				
其他橡胶制品翻修业	4 039	9 472				
橡胶工业专用设备制造业	18 164	19 802	40 877	22 182	22 009	39 425

（续）

行　业	利税总额（万元）			全部从业人员平均人数（人）		
	2001 年	2002 年	2003 年	2001 年	2002 年	2003 年
橡胶制品业	711 116	631 694	856 046	616 043	620 762	622 391
其中：轮胎制造业	378 115	335 517	451 775	198 422	196 655	186 448
力车胎制造业	20 627	22 065	38 150	26 241	27 805	32 245
橡胶板管带制造业	73 052	28 843	83 560	101 794	87 976	94 208
橡胶零件制造业	67 457	69 812	112 532	58 064	67 108	69 285
再生橡胶制造业	16 476	13 451	16 680	14 017	12 300	15 508
橡胶靴鞋制造业	56 527	40 568	42 842	138 747	144 786	125 684
日用橡胶制品业	25 719	25 780	41 139	23 721	30 346	44 862
其他橡胶制品业	70 659	53 453	63 882	49 320	50 428	50 763
橡胶制品翻修业	2 484	2 207	5 498	4 717	3 358	3 588
其中：轮胎翻修业	2 169	1 979		4 319	3 059	
其他橡胶制品翻修业	315	228		398	299	
橡胶工业专用设备制造业	785	11 574	28 625	15 047	12 394	16 675

表 83　我国中药行业经济效益情况（2004—2005 年）

年份	行　业	工业总产值（亿元）	工业销售产值（亿元）	产品销售收入（亿元）	实现利润（亿元）
2004	**全国医药工业合计**	**3 641.7**	**3 247.7**	**3 476.0**	**325.4**
	其中：中药工业	957.8	849.2	891.9	90.9
	中成药工业	746.8	759.6	709.4	75.8
	中药饮片工业	211.0	89.6	182.3	15.1
	中药工业占我国医药工业比例（%）	26.3	26	25.7	28
2005	**全国医药工业合计**	**4 562**	**4 363**	**4 424**	**371.4**
	其中：中药工业	1 186	1 091	1 106	104
	中成药工业	1 022	938		
	中药饮片工业	164	153		
	中药工业占我国医药工业比例（%）	26	25	25	28

资料来源：表中数据来自中国中医药协会。

表 84　我国农产品加工业能源消费总量和主要能源品种消费量（2004 年）

行　业	能源消费总量（万 t 标准煤）	煤炭消费量（万 t）	焦炭消费量（万 t）	原油消费量（万 t）	汽油消费量（万 t）	煤油消费量（万 t）	柴油消费量（万 t）	燃料油消费量（万 t）	天然气消费量（亿 m³）	电力消费量（亿 kW·h）
合计	**14 202.75**	**8 389.65**	**26.73**	**2.75**	**96.34**	**7.87**	**246.60**	**174.60**	**4.21**	**1 906.63**
农副食品加工业	1 820.78	1 064.15	5.79	0.14	16.07	0.33	42.96	11.82	0.20	202.03
食品制造业	1 026.11	770.98	3.88	0.20	7.80	0.33	20.95	14.56	1.49	100.05
饮料制造业	848.54	698.13	1.38	0.43	8.05	0.54	13.40	10.03	0.56	66.71
烟草加工业	238.16	126.01			0.93	0.03	6.38	1.07	0.28	31.25
纺织业	4 550.25	1 991.36	2.16	0.20	21.26	2.05	57.55	72.72	0.50	719.32
纺织服装、鞋、帽制造业	472.82	171.20	0.96	0.47	7.95	0.70	28.42	5.49	0.10	72.57
皮革、毛皮、羽毛（绒）及其制品业	279.28	84.41	0.29	0.07	4.05	0.37	18.10	10.83	0.02	45.44

（续）

行　业	能源消费总量（万t标准煤）	煤炭消费量（万t）	焦炭消费量（万t）	原油消费量（万t）	汽油消费量（万t）	煤油消费量（万t）	柴油消费量（万t）	燃料油消费量（万t）	天然气消费量（亿 m^3）	电力消费量（亿kW·h）
木材加工及竹、藤、棕草制品业	552.48	352.69	1.42	0.10	3.43	1.36	9.22	2.30	0.08	61.56
家具制造业	110.94	26.25	1.16	0.04	2.28	0.24	5.72	0.21	0.03	20.59
造纸及纸制品业	3 081.35	2 713.93	6.81	0.38	8.88	0.91	25.70	26.85	0.37	359.33
印刷业和记录媒介复制	338.32	36.21	0.11		5.89	0.74	7.79	1.45	0.20	78.37
橡胶制品业	883.72	354.33	2.77	0.72	9.75	0.27	10.41	17.27	0.38	149.41

农产品加工业主要产品产量

表 85　我国农产品加工业主要产品产量（2004—2005 年）

产品名称	单位	2004 年	2005 年	同比增长（%）
纱	万 t	1 291.34	1 450.54	12.33
布	亿 m	482.10	484.39	0.48
机制纸及纸板	万 t	5 413.27	6 205.42	14.63
原盐	万 t	4 043.44	4 661.06	15.27
成品糖	万 t	1 033.70	912.37	－11.74
卷烟	亿支	18 736.35	19 389.08	3.48
罐头	万 t	533.56	500.32	－6.23
啤酒	万 kL	2 948.59	3 126.05	6.02
精制食用植物油	万 t	1 682.63	2 070.96	23.08
中成药	万 t	146.24	106.48	－27.19
合成橡胶	万 t	184.04	205.13	11.46
橡胶轮胎外胎	万条	32 709.37	34 390.06	5.14

表 86　轻工业系统农产品加工业主要产品产量（2004 年）

产　品	单　位	2003 年	2004 年	同比增长（%）
纸浆	万 t	1 292.83	1 516.23	17.28
机制纸	万 t	2 404.65	2 873.56	19.50
机制纸板	万 t	1 852.72	1 989.64	7.39
纸制品	万 t	1 034.52	1 306.18	26.26
原盐	万 t	3 102.84	3 710.07	19.57
机制糖	万 t	1 040.94	1 017.62	－2.26
方便主食品	万 t	325.41	364.46	12.00
其中：方便面	万 t	253.78	276.42	8.92
乳制品	万 t	717.28	949.18	32.33

（续）

产　品	单　位	2003 年	2004 年	同比增长（%）
其中：液体乳	万 t	616.26	806.74	30.91
罐头	万 t	266.90	313.37	17.41
味精	万 t	111.99	114.92	2.62
饮料酒	万 kL	2 953.40	3 378.39	14.39
其中：白酒（折 65 度）	万 kL	305 63	311.68	1.98
啤酒	万 kL	2 525.43	2 910.05	15.23
葡萄酒	万 kL	32.03	36.76	14.77
软饮料	万 t	2 451.95	2 912.43	18.78
其中：碳酸饮料	万 t	541.86	617.23	13.91
饼干	万 t	97.87	105.47	7.77
羽绒服装	亿件	1.18	1.32	12.28
轻革	亿 m^2	4.37	5.10	16.69
皮鞋	亿双	18.42	21.21	15.14
革皮服装	万件	8 568.13	7 740.45	−9.66
家具	亿件	2.23	2.58	15.55

表 87　我国粮油工业主要产品产量（2003—2004 年）　单位：万 t

产　品	2003 年	2004 年	同比增长（%）
大米	2 131.3	2 257.1	5.90
其中：特等米	667.6	764.2	14.47
标准一等米	1 194.6	1 310.2	9.68
标准二等米	201.2	139.2	−30.82
其他	67.9	43.5	−35.94
小麦粉	2 789.4	2 938.1	5.33
其中：特制一等粉	1 076.8	1 215.3	12.86
特制二等粉	810.7	781.0	−3.66
标准粉	403.8	342.8	−15.11
专用粉	348.1	380.4	9.28
其他	150.0	218.6	45.73
食用植物油	953.1	953.8	0.07
按品种分：大豆油	391.9	527.7	34.65
菜籽油	286.9	230.8	−19.55
花生油	45.4	53.3	17.40
棉籽油	26.6	35.5	33.46
其他	202.3	106.5	−47.36
按等级分：一级油		346.8	
二级油		211.5	
三级油		68.7	
四级油		190.3	

表 88　我国淀粉产量及品种情况（2005 年）　单位：万 t

品　种	2004 年	2005 年	同比增长（%）	占总淀粉（%）
合　计	**933.57**	**1 106.65**	**18.54**	**100.00**
玉米淀粉	826.26	1 016.6	17.90	91.87
木薯淀粉	42.04	54.42	29.44	4.92
马铃薯淀粉	24.47	13.74	−43.85	1.24
甘薯淀粉	4.00	2.30	−42.50	0.21
小麦淀粉	0.78	19.50	大幅增长	1.76

表 89 我国淀粉深加工品产量（2005 年） 单位：万 t

主要品种	2004 年	2005 年	同比增长（%）	占深加工（%）
合计	**416.83**	**476.72**	**43.63**	**100.00**
变性淀粉	32.89	55.86	69.84	11.72
结晶葡萄糖	71.35	112.98	58.35	23.70
液体淀粉糖	227.50	257.76	13.30	54.07
糖醇	39.33	50.12	27.43	10.51

表 90 我国淀粉产量分布及生产规模情况（2005 年）

地区	淀粉产量（万 t）	占淀粉总产量（%）	生产规模情况	
			年产 10 万 t 企业数（个）	企业最大淀粉产量（万 t/年）
合计	**1 106.61**	**100.00**	**24**	
山东	422.41	38.17	7	150.31
河北	194.49	17.58	7	36.47
吉林	189.35	17.11	3	118.96
陕西	52.27	4.72	1	50.00
广西	44.65	4.03		
山西	56.15	5.07	1	20.00
河南	66.09	5.97	3	15.02
其他 13 个省区市	81.20	7.35	2	12.01

注：其他 13 个省、自治区、直辖市为：北京、内蒙古、辽宁、黑龙江、江苏、浙江、四川、贵州、云南、广东、海南、甘肃、新疆。

表 91 我国玉米淀粉生产规模情况（2005 年）

项目	单位	2004 年	2005 年	同比增长（%）
年产 100 万 t 以上的企业	个	1	2	100.00
年产 100 万 t 以上的企业总产量	万 t	126.82	269.27	112.32
占全国玉米淀粉总产量	%	14.71	26.49	80.08
年产 40 万 t 以上的企业	个	5	5	平
年产 40 万 t 以上的企业总产量	万 t	297.86	293.10	−1.60
占全国玉米淀粉总产量	%	34.54	28.83	−16.53
年产 30 万 t 以上的企业	个	5	3	−40.00
年产 30 万 t 以上的企业总产量	万 t	166.20	97.78	−41.17
占全国玉米淀粉总产量	%	19.27	9.62	−50.08
年产 10 万 t 以上的企业	个	10	14	40.00
年产 10 万 t 以上的企业总产量	万 t	139.41	197.57	41.72
占全国玉米淀粉总产量	%	16.17	19.43	20.16

表 92　我国部分淀粉深加工品生产规模情况（2004—2005 年）

类别	项　目	单位	2004 年	2005 年	同比增长（%）
变性淀粉	年产 5 万 t 以上的企业	个	1.00	2.00	100.00
	年产 5 万 t 以上的企业总产量	万 t	5.10	19.69	286.08
	占全国总产量	%	15.51	35.25	127.27
	年产 3 万 t 以上的企业	个	2.00	4.00	100.00
	年产 3 万 t 以上的企业总产量	万 t	7.90	16.88	113.67
	占全国总产量	%	24.02	30.22	25.81
	年产 1 万 t 以上的企业	个	6.00	6.00	平
	年产 1 万 t 以上的企业总产量	万 t	9.83	11.54	17.40
	占全国总产量	%	29.89	20.66	−30.88
结晶葡萄糖	年产 20 万 t 以上的企业	个	0	1.00	100.00
	年产 20 万 t 以上的企业总产量	万 t		21.72	
	占全国总产量	%		19.22	
	年产 10 万 t 以上的企业	个	3.00	4.00	33.33
	年产 10 万 t 以上的企业总产量	万 t	38.20	49.47	29.50
	占全国总产量	%	53.53	43.79	−18.20
	年产 5 万 t 以上的企业	个	3.00	4.00	33.33
	年产 5 万 t 以上的企业总产量	万 t	19.94	30.54	53.16
	占全国总产量	%	27.94	27.03	−3.26
	年产 2 万 t 以上的企业	个	3.00	3.00	平
	年产 2 万 t 以上的企业总产量	万 t	8.00	7.73	−3.37
	占全国总产量	%	11.21	6.84	−38.98
液体淀粉糖	年产 50 万 t 以上的企业	个	1.00	2.00	100.00
	年产 50 万 t 以上的企业总产量	万 t	72.50	130.22	79.61
	占全国总产量	%	31.87	46.88	47.10
	年产 10 万 t 以上的企业	个	7.00	4.00	−42.86
	年产 10 万 t 以上的企业总产量	万 t	93.96	63.70	−32.21
	占全国总产量	%	41.30	22.93	−44.48
	年产 5 万 t 以上的企业	个	4.00	8.00	100.00
	年产 5 万 t 以上的企业总产量	万 t	29.59	54.70	84.86
	占全国总产量	%	13.01	16.69	28.29

表 93　我国食品添加剂主要产品产量（2003—2004 年）　　单位：万 t

产品名称	2003 年	2004 年	同比增长（%）
总　　计	**287.97**	**330.00**	**14.60**
味　精	121.00	116.00	−4.13
柠檬酸及盐	42.00	54.00	28.57
酶制剂	35.00	40.00	14.29
酵　母	7.60	10.00	31.58
食用香精香料	5.00	5.50	10.00
食用着色剂	6.65	8.80	32.33
高倍甜味剂	8.72	9.90	13.53
糖醇类甜味剂	31.00	45.00	45.16
防腐抗氧保鲜剂	9.50	10.50	10.53
增稠乳化剂	5.50	6.50	18.18
品质改良剂	5.00	9.00	80.00
营养强化剂	11.00	12.50	13.64

表 94　我国饮料行业软饮料各地区主要产品产量（2004 年）　　单位：万 t

地　区	软饮料			
	合　计	碳酸饮料	果汁及果汁饮料	瓶（桶）装饮用水
全国总计	**2 912.4**	**671.23**	**500.04**	**1 205.94**
北　京	127.07	47.05	49.72	29.47
天　津	86.29	32.29	1.68	21.13
河　北	155.37	0.49	7.26	37.95
山　西	17.51	7.87	8.92	0.73
内蒙古	5.99	1.04	0.57	3.89
辽　宁	90.59	21.96	5.49	43.52
吉　林	81.62	26.68	2.36	50.53
黑龙江	20.03	8.85	1.39	7.42
上　海	219.91	103.84	6.78	85.52
江　苏	137.19	31.49	25.49	29.57
浙　江	553.96	95.31	49.91	307.35
安　徽	24.01	5.37	5.99	9.79
福　建	90.37	27.88	19.78	12.17
江　西	35.43	6.29	16.09	13.04
山　东	127.64	28.95	46.33	41.58
河　南	95.79	13.43	26.87	24.49
湖　北	103.19	23.78	14.46	45.19
湖　南	35.07		0.19	27.41
广　东	557.14	132.96	105.70	248.85
广　西	36.10	7.48	1.49	23.04
海　南	26.19	6.37	3.07	15.3
重　庆	44.94	11.68	7.19	23.43
四　川	95.92	14.31	31.11	47.75
贵　州	17.68	0.029	1.65	14.75
云　南	31.25	4.71	1.29	20.52
西　藏	0.42			0.40
陕　西	71.01	9.26	53.77	5.47
甘　肃	11.78	1.55	1.23	8.37
青　海	1.02		0.031	0.99
宁　夏				
新　疆	11.94	0.29	4.21	6.32

表 95　我国罐头工业各地区产品产量（2003—2004 年）　单位：万 t

地　区	2003 年	2004 年	同比增长（%）
总　计	**436.38**	**313.37**	**−28.19**
北　京		0.01	
天　津	0.10	0.80	700.00
河　北	25.00	20.27	−18.92
山　西	3.46	3.28	−5.20
内蒙古	0.21	0.11	−47.62
辽　宁	5.15	6.45	25.24
吉　林			
黑龙江	1.39	1.29	−7.19
上　海	4.03	4.51	11.92
江　苏	5.82	5.51	−5.33
浙　江	47.60	48.96	2.86
安　徽	3.38	3.23	−4.44
福　建	47.74	63.31	32.61
江　西	0.86	1.04	20.93
山　东	13.20	18.99	43.86
河　南	2.91	3.32	14.09
湖　北	5.52	8.08	46.38
湖　南	12.22	16.23	32.82
广　东	8.04	10.60	31.84
广　西	7.49	14.29	90.79
海　南	13.13	12.03	8.38
重　庆	2.19	1.69	−22.83
四　川	7.13	6.23	−12.62
贵　州	0.14	0.36	157.14
云　南	0.60	1.02	70.00
西　藏			
陕　西	0.25	0.26	4.00
甘　肃	9.00	0.03	−99.67
青　海			
宁　夏			
新　疆	41.95	61.47	46.53

表 96　我国烟草工业主要产品产量（2002—2004 年）

年　份	烟叶（万 t）	烤烟（万 t）	卷烟（万箱）
2002	244.70	213.50	3 467.08
2003	225.70	201.50	3 580.86
2004	240.60	216.27	18 744.13

表 97　我国酒精工业产品产量（2003—2004 年）　单位：万 kL

地　区	2003 年	2004 年	同比增长（%）
全国总计	**254.19**	**285.96**	**12.50**
山　东	48.99	51.35	4.80
吉　林	21.13	33.11	56.70
黑龙江	32.41	32.47	0.20
河　南	21.84	29.98	37.30
江　苏	20.31	24.54	20.80
广　西	16.94	20.40	20.40
天　津	19.96	19.04	－4.60
云　南	16.09	17.46	8.50
四　川	12.74	11.25	－11.70
安　徽	9.64	10.43	8.20
广　东	6.86	8.01	16.80
河　北	5.55	6.24	12.40
甘　肃	4.96	5.33	7.50
山　西	1.80	3.50	94.40
内蒙古	0.53	2.95	456.60
辽　宁	2.84	2.66	－6.30
新　疆	3.60	2.37	－34.20
海　南	2.81	2.01	－28.50
陕　西	0.92	0.97	5.40
宁　夏	0.61	0.81	32.80
湖　北	0.40	0.56	40.00
贵　州	0.44	0.34	－22.70
江　西	0.05	0.09	80.00
湖　南	0.22	0.07	－68.20

表 98　我国各地区白酒产量（2003—2004 年）　单位：万 kL

地　区	2003 年	2004 年	同比增长（%）
全国总计	**305.59**	**311.70**	**2.00**
北　京	7.48	8.26	10.40
天　津	3.88	3.04	－21.40
河　北	9.79	9.55	2.50
山　西	6.55	6.28	－4.10
内蒙古	7.76	10.54	35.80
辽　宁	16.32	17.64	8.10
吉　林	14.13	12.80	－9.40
黑龙江	4.50	5.72	27.10
上　海	0.66	0.71	7.60
江　苏	20.85	21.98	5.40
浙　江	1.89	2.27	20.10
安　徽	22.15	20.71	－6.50
福　建	0.73	0.82	12.80
江　西	5.91	6.03	2.00

（续）

地　区	2003 年	2004 年	同比增长（%）
山　东	58.87	58.40	－0.80
河　南	17.56	21.71	23.60
湖　北	11.96	14.19	18.60
湖　南	2.28	2.41	5.70
广　东	7.92	7.91	－0.08
广　西	1.23	1.11	－9.80
海　南	1.04	1.23	18.30
重　庆	1.62	4.99	8.00
四　川	51.89	50.64	－2.40
贵　州	9.85	9.22	－6.40
云　南	1.62	2.24	38.30
西　藏		0.12	
陕　西	2.92	3.07	5.10
甘　肃	2.02	2.22	9.90
青　海	1.22	1.18	－3.30
宁　夏	0.63	0.60	－4.80
新　疆	4.15	4.11	－1.00

表 99　我国饲料工业产品产量（2002—2005 年）　单位：万 t

年　份	饲料产量	其中		
		配（混）合饲料	浓缩饲料	预混合饲料
2002	8 319	6 239	1 764	316
2003	8 712	6 428	1 958	326
2004	9 300	6 822	2 080	364
2005	10 700	7 762	2 498	472

资料来源：表中数据由全国饲料工作办公室提供。

表 100　2005/2006 年制糖期糖料与食糖生产情况

单位：万 hm^2、万 t、个

地　区	2005 年糖料种植面积	糖料入榨量	产糖量	开工工厂数
全国合计	**140.50**	**7 231.52**	**881.5**	**289**
甘蔗糖合计	121.44	6 589.69	800.8	251
广　东	12.64	877	92.2	41
其中：湛江	10.53	729.6	76.7	22
广　西	76.67	4 322	537.7	94
云　南	24.49	1 139	141.3	78
海　南	6.00	151.8	17.8	19
福　建	0.55	37.07	3.7	4
四　川	0.57	34.11	3.6	6
其　他	0.53	28.73	4.5	9
甜菜糖合计	19.07	641.83	80.7	38
黑龙江	7.00	151	18.4	12
新　疆	7.80	363	44.1	14
内蒙古	3.47	97.83	12.5	8
其　他	0.80	30	5.7	4

资料来源：表中数据由中国糖业协会提供。

表 101　我国食用菌产量、产值、出口情况（2005 年）

地　区	产　量（t）	产　值（万元）	出口量（t）	创　汇（万美元）	主要品种产量（t）		
					香　菇	平　菇	双孢菇
全国总计	**13 345 994**	**5 854 788**	**628 413**	**96 381.5**	**2 424 845**	**3 705 937**	**1 524 669**
北　京	36 247	23 831			3 365	16 129	1 019
天　津	56 515	24 847			6 000	30 000	
河　北	861 845	410 000			107 059	337 088	39 229
山　西	55 000	41 000			3 479	28 700	3 009
辽　宁	502 080	180 095			134 775	193 069	5 478
吉　林	456 310	210 000			45 000	105 000	2 500
黑龙江	547 737	258 831			13 080	150 000	12
上　海	62 092	43 486			6 578	7 948	14 897
江　苏	1 004 005	234 000			17 640	519 697	187 947
浙　江	620 000	380 000			330 000	100 000	32 000
安　徽	320 224	119 022			31 120	87 695	69 082
福　建	1 783 400	646 300			387 200	139 700	321 800
江　西	420 000	150 000			140 500	170 100	4 345
山　东	1 326 080	544 800			155 100	531 000	262 500
河　南	2 014 281	751 947			333 562	630 589	140 572
湖　北	611 650	244 660			217 000	139 100	37 800
湖　南	580 000	350 000			85 000	110 000	52 000
广　东	455 000	418 000			33 600	107 800	13 350
广　西	341 650	130 200			47 931	23 598	213 309
重　庆	58 911	23 565			26 440	11 057	11 359
四　川	678 000	271 300			40 200	100 900	96 600
云　南	55 690	149 590			8 500	7 000	5 000
陕　西	470 013	235 007			251 406	148 582	6 592
宁　夏	14 084	4 477				7 085	5 619
新　疆	15 180	9 830			310	4 300	1 650

地　区	主　要　品　种　产　量　（t）						
	金针菇	草　菇	黑木耳	毛木耳	银　耳	滑　菇	猴头菇
全国总计	**838 517**	**274 338**	**975 584**	**1 124 845**	**184 130**	**203 746**	**45 348**
北　京	6 782	889	469				
天　津				300			10
河　北	110 981	3 514	15 429	6 500	1 500	52 600	
山　西	3 630	190	4 000		2 030		300
辽　宁	1 093	510	1 499			129 246	45
吉　林	4 000		250 000			6 000	500
黑龙江	23 000		350 000			11 500	15
上　海	13 198	4 613					
江　苏	136 253	15 173	6 495	9 208	13 690		160
浙　江	100 000	3 000	20 000	3 000	100		1 000

（续）

地区	主要品种产量（t）						
	金针菇	草菇	黑木耳	毛木耳	银耳	滑菇	猴头菇
安徽	21 868	40	16 421	71 945	110		18
福建	40 600	31 400	28 000	221 900	161 200	3 600	27 000
江西	7 000	5 500	5 000	8 000			60
山东	95 700	62 500	31 100	2 800	100	800	5 300
河南	61 224	15 017	70 400	517 760	3 820		
湖北	28 900	300	111 600	4 000	80		20
湖南	45 100	4 180	2 320	12 600	1 500		2 000
广东	82 500	124 500		5 850			8 880
广西	10 723	2 912	13 481	4 482			40
重庆	4 382		4 570	1 000			
四川	38 000		3 500	255 200			
云南	850		600	300			
陕西	383	100	40 490				
宁夏	2 350		210				
新疆							

地区	主要品种产量（t）						
	鸡腿菇	白灵菇	杏鲍菇	茶树菇	小平菇	姬菇	袖珍菇
全国总计	**285 100**	**172 727**	**135 943**	**191 346**	**68 038**	**346 426**	**95 762**
北京	197	4 189	1 505	314		640	
天津	150	15 000	30			5 000	
河北	36 191	7 713	11 945			131 243	32
山西	100	2 300	3 200		4 560		
辽宁	2 924	862	756			530	
吉林	1 000	1 000	600		50		
黑龙江	25	10	25				
上海	800	600	535	500		4 483	5 878
江苏	38 629	100	7 754	6 412	4 148		
浙江	2 000	2 000	15 000	2 000	5 000	5 000	2 100
安徽	2 056	3 826	5 031	1 412	230	315	452
福建	17 400	971					
江西	11 000		5 000	50 700	500	300	400
山东	86 600	23 800	21 400	400	5 700	18 500	3 600
河南	55 744	98 726	14 389	7 006		10 215	
湖北	2 640	3 000	10	100	22 000		6 600
湖南	4 200	4 600					
广东	11 500						
广西	1 317						
重庆	103						
四川	5 000						
云南	2 000	100					
陕西	1 864	130					
宁夏	1 660						
新疆		3 800					

（续）

地　区	主　要　品　种　产　量　(t)									
	灰树花	竹荪	姬松茸	松茸	牛肝菌	羊肚菌	灵芝	天麻	茯苓	其他菇
全国总计	**4 675**	**37 464**	**43 607**	**1 695**	**17 086**	**803**	**86 731**	**50 111**	**171 422**	**271 106**
北　京	15						6			728
天　津							25			
河　北	150						600			
山　西	10		58		66	23	135	46	22	
辽　宁				95	620	200	13	480		29 887
吉　林	20		40	100	300		10 000	200		3 000
黑龙江			60				10			
上　海										
江　苏							4 007			
浙　江	2 000	50			100		2 000	1 000	3 000	
安　徽		6					3 041	5 250	300	2
福　建										
江　西		600	100				1 735	100	60	9 000
山　东	50		400		100		17 100	1 500	30	
河　南		130	450				2 989	27 435	3 810	20 074
湖　北		50	500		300	30	6 000	3 600	28 000	20
湖　南										
广　东										
广　西										
重　庆										
四　川										
云　南										
陕　西										
宁　夏										
新　疆										

资料来源：表中数据为25个省、自治区、直辖市统计数据，由中国食用菌协会提供，产量均按鲜品统计（干品折鲜品按1∶10）。

表102　我国农垦系统农产品加工业主要产品产量（2004—2005年）

产　品	单位	2004年	2005年	同比增长（%）
粮食商品量	万t	1 404.40	1 566.72	11.56
粮食商品率	%	84.29	84.28	
食用植物油	万t	71.27	82.06	15.14
机制糖	万t	118.10	115.02	−2.61
乳制品	万t	14.04	15.37	9.47
消毒液体奶	万t	84.24	93.59	11.10
饮料酒	万t	116.08	126.71	9.16
其中：葡萄酒	万t	7.45	5.88	−21.07
混、配合饲料	万t	211.01	213.63	1.24
纱	万t	29.39	26.43	−10.07
布	亿m	3.95	4.88	23.54
机制纸及纸板	万t	90.56	100.44	10.91

表 103　农垦系统各地区农产品加工业主要产品产量（2005 年）

地　区	机制纸及纸板（t）	纱（万 t）	布（万 m）	机制糖（t）	饮料酒（t）	乳制品（t）	食用植物油（t）
全国合计	**1 004 443**	**26**	**48 754**	**1 150 212**	**1 267 148**	**153 708**	**820 589**
北　京	16 796				10	6 858	
天　津	6 877				38 151	2 028	
河　北	607 316		5 249		3 211	20 910	222
山　西							
内蒙古					622	14 547	8 814
辽　宁	6 796				176 809	3 478	1 806
吉　林					3		
黑龙江				16 915	36 466	55 350	493 073
上　海						4 527	
江　苏		1					8 393
浙　江	25 816		16 698		359 053	59	
安　徽		1			3 513	1 473	2 792
福　建	79 011				1 063		250
江　西	53 617	5	577	277	29 355		4 561
山　东					320	900	260
河　南	1 061		38		15 600		25
湖　北	37 270	6	11 915	500	310 902	717	96 024
湖　南	38 951	2	1 457	41 591	2 831	6 560	5 406
广　东	17 910			352 576	1 272		1 424
广　西	20 950			503 748	120	132	339
海　南				31 482	310		30
重　庆						657	
四　川						90	
贵　州					380	893	
云　南				49 942	141		12
西　藏							
陕　西			4 307			68	4 286
甘　肃					141 576		
青　海						208	
宁　夏					105 297		129
新疆（兵团）	66 460	12	8 371	153 181	40 143	10 045	180 693
新疆（农业）			142		223		8 940
新疆（畜牧）					21 100		3 110

表 104　我国森林工业主要产品产量（2004—2005 年）

主 要 产 品	单　位	2004 年	2005 年	同比增长（%）
锯材	万 m^3	1 532.5	1 790.3	16.82
木片	万实积 m^3	2 400.8	1 217.7	−49.28
人造板	万 m^3	5 446.5	6 392.9	17.38
胶合板	万 m^3	2 098.6	2 515.0	19.84
纤维板	万 m^3	1 560.5	2 060.6	32.05
刨花板	万 m^3	642.9	576.1	−10.39
其他人造板	万 m^3	1 144.5	1 241.3	8.46
胶合木	万 m^3	40.8	74.1	81.62
木地板	万 m^2	12 300.5	17 322.8	40.83

（续）

主 要 产 品	单 位	2004 年	2005 年	同比增长（%）
卫生筷子	标准箱	8 183 212.0	11 073 984	35.33
人造板表面装饰板	万 m^2	34 058.8	27 014.1	−20.68
热固性树脂装饰层压板	万 m^2	19.8	1.35	−93.18
单板	万 m^2	371 774.8	291 171.6	−23.68
林产化学产品				
松香类产品	t	537 600	671 571	24.92
松节油类产品	t	86 779	98 440	13.41
樟脑	t	3 852	6 734	74.82
冰片	t	517	568	4.06
栲胶类产品	t	12 853	7 805	−39.27
紫胶类产品	t	1 117	1 318	17.99
木材热解产品				
木炭	t	107 273	145 220	35.37
活性炭	t	98 384	141 612	43.94
软木制品				
软木砖	m^3	1 612	7 382	357.94
软木纸	m^3	12 388	4 296	−65.32

表 105 林业系统森林工业主要产品产量（2004—2005 年）

主要产品	单 位	2004 年	2005 年	同比增长（%）
锯材	万 m^3	204.77	216.18	5.57
木片	万 m^3	243.77	281.21	15.36
人造板	万 m^3	639.42	632.15	1.14
热带材人造板	万 m^3	16.53	20.64	24.86
胶合板	万 m^3	56.40	55.89	−0.90
纤维板	万 m^3	381.11	406.64	6.70
刨花板	万 m^3	148.09	130.45	−11.91
其他人造板	万 m^3	37.29	39.16	5.01
胶合木	万 m^3	9.85	6.59	−33.10
木地板	万 m^2	1 682.08	2 363.23	40.49
卫生筷子	标准箱	5 185 255	4 372 036	−15.68
人造板表面装饰板	万 m^2	1 098.30	930.38	−15.29
热固性树脂装饰层压板	万 m^2			
单板	万 m^2	31 208.38	1 207.26	−96.13
林产化学产品				
松香类产品	t	141 380	134 946	−4.55
松节油类产品	t	18 115	15 213	−16.02
樟脑	t			
冰片	t	16	1	−93.75
栲胶类产品	t	6 172	5 758	−6.71
紫胶类产品	t	245	53	−78.37
木材热解产品				
木炭	t	31 791	15 942	−49.85
活性炭	t	4 030	2 420	−39.95
软木制品				
软木砖	m^3	1 612	1 333	−17.31
软木纸	m^3	9 070	4 041	−55.45

表 106　各地区森林工业主要产品产量（2005 年）

单位：万 m^3、万实积 m^3

地　区	锯材	木材	人　造　板						胶合木	木地板（万 m^2）
			合计	热带材人造板	胶合板	纤维板	刨花板	其他人造板		
全国总计	**1 790.3**	**1 217.7**	**6 392.9**	**152.3**	**2 515**	**2 060.6**	**576.1**	**1 241.3**	**74.05**	**17 322.8**
北　京										
天　津										
河　北	99.8	21.35	902.04		408.90	140.75	112.50	239.89	1.51	45.08
山　西	1.25		0.22		0.03		0.19			
内蒙古	85.01	314.45	48.68		5.08	14.56	24.70	4.35	1.32	0.59
辽　宁	60.04	7.70	84.08		13.89	40.09	17.91	12.20	4.59	983.76
吉　林	114.43	17.95	114.49		27.90	22.11	31.18	33.29	4.50	961.16
黑龙江	58.12	45.26	71.44		5.70	16.85	37.48	11.40	1.47	1 077.60
上　海										
江　苏	70.92	21.29	1 144.57		555.67	248.96	54.03	285.92	1.25	2 157.67
浙　江	279.73	58.96	505.78	49.80	288.14	96.11	5.93	115.60	7.31	5 113.84
安　徽	43.69	17.20	255.72		87.99	98.73	22.18	46.83		1 156.97
福　建	117.93	60.24	358.65		128.33	131.10	19.97	79.25	12.31	890.55
江　西	79.06	27.44	172.60		40.94	64.23	18.49	48.95	3.12	1 018.11
山　东	228.06	90.42	1 209.72		460.65	425.61	129.37	193.77	3.73	137.56
河　南	68.98	49.31	212.11		87.23	62.46	33.15	29.19	9.94	8.81
湖　北	21.21	17.10	146.56	1.00	18.57	90.99	12.17	24.82	0.21	158.96
湖　南	160.51	225.35	221.94		118.00	41.00	7.30	55.56	14.00	950.00
广　东	48.24	81.06	340.05	21.04	58.55	253.53	15.69	4.21	0.09	30.52
广　西	62.10	82.41	339.56	69.08	134.00	166.05	12.28	27.23	0.19	38.04
海　南	11.86	19.99	10.92	10.92	1.57	6.56	2.79			
重　庆	12.69	0.10	9.06		1.64	3.87	0.35			
四　川	35.51	2.75	95.48		20.67	58.66	6.09	10.07	3.27	1 641.26
贵　州	16.39	0.19	54.36		34.79	6.06	4.58	8.92	0.05	58.97
云　南	86.30	27.30	79.35	0.44	14.95	50.10	6.98	7.33	3.65	889.20
西　藏	8.55									
陕　西	0.03	0.01	9.21			8.91		0.30		0.02
甘　肃			0.80			0.80				
青　海										
宁　夏										
新　疆										

（续）

地区	卫生筷子（标准箱）	人造板表面装饰板（万m²）	热固性树脂装饰层压板（万m²）	单板（万m²）	松香类产品（t）	松节油类产品（t）	樟脑（t）	冰片（t）	栲胶类产品（t）	紫胶类产品（t）	木材热解产品（t）		软木制品（m³）	
											木炭	活性炭	软木砖	软木纸
全国总计	**11 073 984**	**27 014.1**	**1.35**	**291 172**	**671 571**	**98 440**	**6 734**	**568**	**7 805**	**1 318**	**145 220**	**141 612**	**7 382**	**4 296**
北京														
天津														
河北	16 320	149.8	0.85	25 678.3							3 506			
山西														
内蒙古	829 114			0.16					1 760		219			
辽宁				0.25							6 451			
吉林	426 842	448.4		821.25							3 668			
黑龙江	1 859 320	192.8		796.45							1 800			
上海														
江苏	6 004	120.01		30 295.4							50			
浙江	601 957	24 118.7	0.50	3 687.7	2 692	4 660					7 167	64 140		
安徽	253 564	215.2		3 874	1 146	361					23 675	1 122		
福建	1 158 458	29.0		15.52	62 170	12 180	5 088	16			1 140	38 528		
江西	916 874	9.15		539.5	69 507	28 537	56				13 023	8 454		
山东	163 475	1 656.6		219 985							15 862	26 002		
河南	262 010	8.37		2 158.9	725	31					772	240	6 049	255
湖北	54 910			827.6	4 934	690					504	200	1 333	
湖南	2 464 150	18.00		1 119.6	25 075	4 169	2	380			16 761	1 836		
广东	420 100			132.9	73 807	11 673	1 569			20	18 124			
广西	2 000	46.03		29.3	360 168	23 590			5 975		100			
海南					3 842	361			70		5 030			
重庆					530									
四川	211 004			257.3	3 367	476				95	200			
贵州	69 360	2.12		1.76	3 393	157					15 588			
云南	89 905			850.2	60 215	11 555	19	171		1 203	11 364			840
西藏														
陕西														3 201
甘肃														
青海														
宁夏														
新疆														

表 107 林业系统各地区森林工业主要产品产量（2005 年）

地区	锯材（万 m^3）	木片（万 m^3）	人造板（万 m^3）						胶合木（万 m^3）	木地板（万 m^2）	卫生筷子标准箱	人造板表面装饰板（万 m^2）
			合计	热带材人造板	胶合板	纤维板	刨花板	其他人造板				
全国总计	**216.2**	**281.2**	**632.2**	**20.64**	**55.89**	**406.64**	**130.45**	**39.16**	**6.59**	**2 363.2**	**4 372 036**	**930.38**
北 京												
天 津												
河 北	0.01		21.08		0.18	20.90						
山 西			0.14				0.14					
内蒙古	8.71	5.90	29.96		0.21	9.22	16.22	4.31	1.32	0.59	808 064	
辽 宁	19.82	0.22	25.76		10.61	12.40		2.75	0.51	76.32		
吉 林	22.21	12.45	60.46		4.25	22.00	31.13	3.08	1.03	894.80	278 331	448.38
黑龙江	56.36	45.26	67.77		5.59	13.30	37.48	11.40	1.47	1 077.60	1 859 320	192.76
上 海												
江 苏	0.58	0.04	0.41		0.23		0.18			7.25	6 000	
浙 江	1.83	2.18	4.00			4.00						
安 徽	5.96	2.12	34.71		1.31	26.04	6.36	1.00				214.21
福 建	3.08	19.18	103.42		7.72	88.56	5.61	1.53		146.00		29.00
江 西	4.82	0.29	9.25		2.56	2.37	2.66	1.66		38.61	89 860	
山 东	0.26		101.75		4.57	88.13	9.05					
河 南	0.29	1.70	13.66		5.39	4.73	1.30	2.24				
湖 北	2.46	0.09	28.06		0.77	16.14	8.01	3.15	0.05	53.86	12 000	
湖 南	42.97	102.32	26.78		6.27	15.30	2.76	2.45	0.59	18.07	37 963	
广 东	7.96	43.68	2.00		0.25	1.30	0.15	0.30				
广 西	2.83	14.10	77.64	20.64	2.65	69.58	5.42			38.04		46.03
海 南	5.37	1.50										
重 庆	0.20		0.54		0.54							
四 川	1.28	0.50	0.44		0.42	0.02			0.07	0.03		
贵 州	3.82	0.04	6.31				3.20	3.12		0.01	4 970	
云 南	2.96	1.81	2.80		0.60	2.14		0.05		8.08		
西 藏	8.55											
陕 西	0.02		8.91			8.91				0.02		
甘 肃			0.80			0.80						
青 海												
宁 夏												
新 疆												

（续）

地区	单板（万 m²）	松香类产品（t）	松节油类产品（t）	樟脑（t）	冰片（t）	栲胶类产品（t）	紫胶类产品（t）	木材热解产品（t）		软木制品（m³）	
								木炭	活性炭	软木砖	软木纸
全国总计	**1 207.3**	**134 946**	**15 213**		**1**	**5 758**	**53**	**15 942**	**2 420**	**1 333**	**4 041**
北　京											
天　津											
河　北											
山　西											
内蒙古	0.13					1 760		219			
辽　宁								1 061			
吉　林	259.10							2 262			
黑龙江	796.45							1 800			
上　海											
江　苏											
浙　江											
安　徽		450	146								
福　建		3 825	894						744		
江　西		6 139	672		1			372	250		
山　东											
河　南	13.06	88	10								
湖　北		1 298	290					500		1 333	
湖　南	2.17	3 582	395					1 003	336		
广　东	0.18	10 173	1 087				20	435			
广　西		97 061	9 642			3 928					
海　南		1 469	252			70		30			
重　庆											
四　川		460	20				13				
贵　州		1 718	132					8 044			
云　南		8 683	1 673				20				840
西　藏											
陕　西											3 201
甘　肃											
青　海											
宁　夏											
新　疆											

表 108　我国水产品加工产品的主要种类与产量（2002—2005 年）

单位：万 t

年　份	冷冻制品	干制品	腌熏制品	鱼糜及其制品	动物蛋白饲料	罐制品	其他
2002	447.8	54.3	23.2	10.2	48.4	4.3	107.1
2003	543.4	68.9	21.1	24.9	129.1	14.5	108.2
2004	599.3	70.5	22.4	32.9	168.2	14.4	77.3
2005		76.0				17.7	90.0

表 109 纺织工业主要产品产量（规模以上企业）（2004—2005 年）

产品名称	单位	2004 年	2005 年	同比增长（%）
化纤用浆粕	万 t	59.71	83.10	39.17
化学纤维	万 t	1 419.78	1 629.20	14.75
粘胶纤维	万 t	97.27	118.00	21.31
合成纤维	万 t	1 313.82	1 500.25	14.19
锦纶纤维	万 t	61.62	71.66	16.29
涤纶纤维	万 t	1 099.13	1 270.16	15.56
腈纶纤维	万 t	79.29	86.53	9.13
维纶纤维	t	37 554.20	41 749.00	11.17
丙纶纤维	万 t	27.67	24.46	−11.60
纱	万 t	1 142.63	1 412.40	23.61
布	亿 m	321.51	377.61	17.45
棉布	亿 m	158.52	196.58	24.01
混纺交织布	亿 m	64.56	70.59	9.34
纯化纤布	亿 m	98.42	110.45	12.22
印染布	亿 m	281.92	326.15	15.69
帘子布	t	312 683.00	317 123.00	1.42
绒线（毛绒）	万 t	36.87	38.70	4.96
呢绒	万 m	27 963.00	32 960.00	17.87
麻袋（混合数）	万条	4 704.00	4 963.00	5.51
苎麻布及亚麻布	万 m	17 841.00	21 568.00	20.89
丝	t	110 872.00	132 536.00	19.54
丝织品	万 m	699 398.00	777 381.00	11.15
针棉织品折用纱线量	万 t	83.69	92.30	10.29
非织造布	万 t	28.97	35.03	20.92
服装	万件	1 266 514.00	1 479 795.00	16.84
梭织服装	万件	603 754.00	709 833.00	17.57
西服及西服套装	万件	42 854.00	49 381.00	15.23
衬衫	万件	83 358.00	91 910.00	10.26
儿童服装	万件	30 823.00	36 615.00	18.79
羽绒服装	万件	12 175.00	15 919.00	30.75
针织服装	万件	67 057.00	766 424.00	16.11
合成纤维单体	万 t	651.03	741.26	13.86
聚酯	万 t	705.73	807.50	14.42
纺织机械	亿元	380.38	469.47	23.42

表 110 纺织工业丝绸行业主要产品产量（2004—2005 年）

主要产品	单位	2004 年	2005 年	同比增长（%）
丝产量	万 t	10.27	11.30	10.00
其中：桑蚕丝	万 t	8.04	8.78	9.20
丝织品（包括化纤绸）	亿 m	69.87	77.70	11.20

表 111　纺织工业麻纺织行业主要产品产量（2004—2005 年）

类别	主要产品	单位	2004 年	2005 年	同比增长（%）
苎麻	苎麻精干麻耗量	万 t	8.68	9.30	7.19
	苎麻纱	万 t	9.95	12.80	28.60
	苎麻布	亿 m	1.81	2.00	10.63
	苎麻夏布	万匹	396.49	2.26	−99.43
	苎麻印染布	亿 m	0.52	0.60	15.94
亚麻	亚麻纤维耗量	万 t	8.55	23.00	169.01
	亚麻纱	万 t	6.40	7.44	16.30
	亚麻布	亿 m	1.37	1.75	27.75
	其中：纯亚麻布	亿 m	0.88	1.09	23.69
	亚麻印染布	亿 m	0.39	0.50	26.98
黄麻	黄麻纱	万 t	9.46	12.70	34.23
	黄麻布	亿 m	1.11	1.60	44.74
	黄麻麻袋	万条	1 375.00	1 360.00	1.10
	黄麻纤维进口量	万 t	6.42	8.22	28.04

表 112　我国皮革行业主要产品产量（2003—2004 年）

主要产品	单位	2003 年	2004 年	同比增长（%）
轻革	亿 m^2	4.36	5.10	17
皮鞋	亿双	18.26	21.00	15
革皮服装	万件	8 600.00	7 740.00	−10

表 113　我国家具工业主要产品产量（2004—2005 年）

单位：万件

年份	产量
2004	30 509
2005	33 990
同比增长（%）	11.41

资料来源：表中数据由中国轻工业信息中心提供。

表 114　我国造纸工业纸浆消耗情况（2003—2004 年）

品种	2003 年		2004 年	
	消耗（万 t）	所占比例（%）	消耗（万 t）	所占比例（%）
纸浆消耗量	**3 910**	**100.0**	**4 455**	**100.0**
一、木浆	820	21.0	970	22.0
其中：国产木浆	217	5.6	238	5.5
进口木浆	603	15.4	732	16.5
二、非木浆	1 170	30.0	1 180	26.0
其中：苇（芒）浆	115	2.9	118	2.6
竹浆	60	1.5	80	1.8
蔗糖浆	50	1.3	45	1.0
禾草浆	830	21.3	820	18.0
棉、麻浆	15	0.4	14	0.3
其他浆	100	2.6	103	2.3
三、废纸浆	1 920	49.0	2 305	52.0
其中：国产废纸浆	1 170	29.9	1 321	30.0
进口废纸浆	750	19.1	984	22.0

表 115　我国各类造纸纤维原料所占比重（2004 年）　单位：万 t

名　称	木　浆	草类纤维	废纸浆	总量
我国造纸纤维原料消耗量	970	1 180	2 305	4 455
在造纸纤维原料所占的比重（%）	22	26	52	100

表 116　我国机制纸及纸板主要品种产量（2003—2004 年）　单位：万 t、%

品　种	2003 年		2004 年	
	产量	比例（%）	产量	比例（%）
纸及纸板合计	**4 300**	**100.00**	**4 950**	**100.00**
一、纸				
1. 新闻纸	207	4.81	300	6.00
2. 印刷书写纸	960	22.32	1 020	20.60
其中：书刊印刷纸	520	12.09	550	11.10
书写纸	250	5.81	280	5.65
3. 涂布纸	240	5.58	300	6.00
其中：铜版纸	210	4.88	250	5.00
4. 生活用纸	347	8.07	384	7.75
5. 包装用纸	480	11.16	470	9.50
二、纸板				
1. 白纸板	550	12.79	670	13.50
其中：涂布白纸板	510	11.86	630	12.70
2. 箱纸板	680	15.81	830	16.80
3. 瓦楞原纸	670	15.58	810	16.40
其中：高强度瓦楞原纸	230	5.35	270	5.50
三、特种纸及纸板	80	1.86	85	1.70
四、其他	86	2.00	81	1.60

表 117　各地区重点纸品产量（2004 年）　单位：万 t

地　区	纸及纸板	机制纸	机制纸板	新闻纸
全国总计	**4 863.2**	**2 873.6**	**1 989.6**	**299.9**
北　京	14.3	7.7	6.5	
天　津	18.5	1.6	16.9	0.93
河　北	313.1	164.2	148.9	19.2
山　西	16.4	12.9	3.5	1.3
内蒙古	18.2	12.2	6.0	
辽　宁	56.3	34.0	22.2	
吉　林	43.9	28.7	15.2	17.3
黑龙江	62.8	48.5	14.3	3.6
上　海	15.9	21.2	14.7	14.1
江　苏	506.3	358.7	147.6	1.9
浙　江	747.9	200.8	547.2	1.5
安　徽	104.8	43.2	61.5	
福　建	165.9	98.4	67.4	36.3

（续）

地　区	纸及纸板	机制纸	机制纸板	新闻纸
江　西	35.5	17.1	18.4	1.9
山　东	997.2	663.9	333.3	91.0
河　南	495.4	257.8	237.6	2.4
湖　北	98.4	69.2	29.4	26.8
湖　南	167.9	142.0	25.9	22.9
广　东	597.7	409.8	187.9	30.4
广　西	88.3	84.6	3.7	14.8
海　南	1.1	0.95	0.15	
重　庆	22.9	5.8	17.10	
四　川	102.8	74.2	28.60	9.3
贵　州	5.7	4.9	0.73	
云　南	20.3	9.3	11.10	
陕　西	52.4	45.4	6.90	3.8
甘　肃	9.0	5.7	3.4	
青　海	0.21	0.21		
宁　夏	44.4	39.6	4.8	
新　疆	19.5	10.8	8.7	

表 118　我国纸和纸板消费结构情况（2003—2004 年）　　单位：万 t

产品名称	2003 年					2004 年				
	生产量	进口量	出口量	消费量	比重（%）	生产量	进口量	出口量	消费量	比重（%）
机制纸及纸板	**4 306**	**634.71**	**128.71**	**4 806**	**100**	**4 950**	**614**	**125**	**5 439**	**100**
一、机制纸										
1. 新闻纸	207	35.13	1.19	241	5.0	300	12	1.74	310.3	5.7
2. 印刷书写纸	960	39.14	25.93	973	20.2	1 020	47	21.73	1 045.3	19.2
印刷书刊纸	520			534	11.1	550			550	10.1
涂布纸	240	101	43.3	298	6.2	300	102	44.24	357.7	6.6
铜版纸	210	52.34	35.3	227	4.7	250	63	38.40	7 746	5.0
书写纸	250			250	5.2	280			280	5.1
3. 包装用纸	480	27.87	3.87	504	10.4	470	29	2.90	496.1	9.1
4. 生活用纸	347	3.64	22.64	328	6.8	384	5	27.58	361.4	6.6
二、纸板										
包装纸板										
其中：白纸板	550	104.26	9.21	645	13.4	670	108	6.44	771.6	14.2
涂布白纸板	510	102.92	9.21	603	12.5	630	107	6.43	730.6	13.4
箱纸板	680	117.18	1.71	796	16.6	830	128	1.53	956.5	17.6
瓦楞原纸	670	134.9	2.90	802	16.7	810	114	2.76	921.2	16.9
其中：高强度瓦楞纸	230	133.5	3.30	362	7.5	270			270.0	5.0

表 119 我国造纸工业主要产品生产及消费情况（2003—2004 年） 单位：万 t

产品名称	生产量			消费量		
	2003 年	2004 年	同比（%）	2003 年	2004 年	同比（%）
总 量	**4 300**	**4 950**	**15.12**	**4 806**	**5 439**	**13.17**
一、新闻纸	207	300	44.93	241	310	28.63
二、未涂布印刷书写纸	960	1 020	6.25	973	1 045	7.40
其中：书刊印刷纸	520	550	5.77	534	575	7.68
书写纸	250	280	12.00	250	280	12.00
三、涂布纸	240	300	25.00	298	358	20.13
其中：铜版纸	210	250	19.05	227	274	20.70
四、生活用纸	347	384	10.66	328	361	10.06
五、包装用纸	480	470	−2.08	504	496	−1.59
六、白纸板	550	670	21.82	645	772	19.69
其中：涂布白纸板	510	630	23.53	603	731	21.23
七、箱纸板	680	830	22.06	796	956	20.10
八、瓦楞原纸	670	810	20.90	802	921	14.84
其中：高强度瓦楞原纸	230	270	17.39	362	381	5.25
九、特种纸及纸板	80	85	6.25	109	114	4.59
十、其他纸及纸板	86	81	−5.81	110	106	−3.64

表 120 我国纸和纸板生产、消费及进口量与人均消费量（2001—2004 年）

年 份	纸和纸板总产量（万 t）	纸和纸板总消费量（万 t）	纸和纸板进口量（万 t）	人均消费量（kg）
2001	3 200	3 683	559	29
2002	3 780	4 332	635	33
2003	4 300	4 806	635	37
2004	4 950	5 439	720	42

表 121 我国 120 个重点书刊印刷（含其他印刷）企业主要产品产量（2004 年）

	书刊排字（万字）	书刊印刷（万令）	胶印印刷（万对开色令）	书刊装订（万令）	照相制版（四开块）
总 计	377 362.9	2 127.5	7 587.4	2 289.9	1 389 098

表 122 我国纸和纸板人均消费量与美国的比较（2001—2004 年）

单位：kg/人、年

年 份	2001	2002	2003	2004
我国人均消费量	29	33	37	42
美国人均消费量	324	314	324	

表 123　我国橡胶工业主要产品产量（2004—2005 年）

产品名称	单位	2004 年	2005 年	同比增长（%）
综合外胎	万条	13 796.4	16 000.00	16.20
1. 子午胎	万条	7 736.3	10 000.00	29.26
2. 全钢胎	万条	1 669.2	2 411.77	44.49
3. 出口轮胎	万条	5 399.3	6 591.43	22.08
4. 出口交货值	亿元	159.5	238.67	49.60
力车胎				
1. 摩托车胎	万条	4 152.2	5 831.00	40.43
2. 手推车胎	万条	932.0	1 124.00	20.60
3. 自行车胎	万条	23 823.9	21 441.50	—0.10
4. 出口交货值	亿元	5.3	6.78	26.80
胶管、胶带				
1. 输送带	万 m^2	6 838.4	8 256.00	20.73
尼龙带	万 m^2	2 702.0	3 665.80	35.67
2. 胶管	万标 m	4 298.1	4 268.00	—0.70
3. 出口交货值	亿元	4.4	5.68	27.66
胶鞋	亿双	4.2	4.40	3.62
1. 出口胶鞋	万双	8 187.9	7 844.00	—4.20
橡胶制品（销售收入）	亿元	25.4	30.28	19.40
出口交货值	亿元	3.9	5.10	30.81
乳胶制品（销售收入）	亿元	14.4	14.68	2.16
1. 安全套	亿只	45.1	36.05	11.84
2. 医用乳胶手套	亿双	1.7	2.17	26.19
3. 家用乳胶手套	亿双	1.1	1.13	5.68
4. 输血胶管	万 m	391.3	417.00	6.58
5. 出口交货值	亿元	4.8	5.60	15.85
炭黑	万 t	95.7	111.60	16.56
出口炭黑	t	56 506.1	69 220.00	22.50
销售收入	亿元	35.6	47.20	32.69

表 124　我国人均主要工农业产品产量（2001—2005 年）

产品名称	单位	2001 年	2002 年	2003 年	2004 年	2005 年
粮食	kg	355.89	356.97	334.29	362.22	371.26
棉花	kg	4.19	3.84	3.77	4.88	4.38
油料	kg	22.53	22.63	21.82	23.66	23.60
糖料	kg	68.05	80.39	74.83	73.84	72.50
茶叶	kg	0.55	0.58	0.60	0.64	0.72
水果	kg	52.35	54.30	112.68	118.36	123.65
猪牛羊肉	kg	39.52	40.83	42.74	44.57	47.20
水产品	kg	34.44	35.64	36.51	37.82	39.20
布	m	22.80	25.18	27.44	37.20	37.15
机制纸及纸板	kg	29.70	36.45	37.64	41.77	47.60
纱	kg	5.98	6.64	7.63	9.96	11.13

农产品加工业主要产品出口创汇情况

表 125　我国海关出口农产品及加工品数量与金额（2004—2005 年）

单位：万美元

产品名称	单位	2004 年		2005 年	
		数量	金额	数量	金额
活猪	万头	197	23 965	176	22 686
活家禽	万只	1 926	3 333	2 502	3 740
鲜冻牛肉	万 t	2	3 033	2	4 150
鲜冻猪肉	万 t	29	45 954	25	40 612
冻鸡	万 t	7	9 245	9	11 145
鲜冻兔肉	t	6 396	1 007	8 925	2 106
水海产品	万 t	176	405 231	176	434 677
鲜蛋	百万个	1 047	4 028	921	4 352
谷物及谷物粉	万 t	473	82 766	1 014	151 856
稻谷和大米	万 t	91	23 944	69	23 234
玉米	万 t	232	32 571	864	110 753
蔬菜	万 t	470	278 114	520	330 200
鲜或冷藏蔬菜	万 t	314	106 263	353	132 755
干豆	万 t	80	33 092	87	38 815
橘、橙	t	333 264	9 745	426 153	12 834
鲜苹果	t	774 131	27 441	824 050	30 631
核桃仁	t	9 894	2 996	12 447	4 611
栗子	t	39 928	6 327	38 896	5 306
松子仁	t	9 542	6 890	11 655	7 632
大豆	万 t	33	14 493	40	16 958
花生及花生仁	万 t	40	29 867	45	31 959
食用植物油（食用棕榈油）	t	65 215	6 327	225 214	17 207
食糖	t	85 191	2 579	358 290	11 077
天然蜂蜜	t	81 325	8 901	88 499	8 763
茶叶	t	280 193	43 685	286 563	48 431
辣椒干	t	73 094	11 437	70 140	10 041
猪肉罐头	t	54 090	7 929	52 059	8 397
蘑菇罐头	t	298 459	29 754	302 747	29 281
啤酒	万 L	14 080	6 849	14 694	6 955
肠衣	t	62 229	50 411	63 094	50 816
填充用羽毛、羽绒	t	37 590	34 776	36 466	35 784
药材	t	169 864	26 639	203 007	28 745
烤烟	t	135 206	22 148	112 128	21 766

（续）

产品名称	单位	2004年		2005年	
		数量	金额	数量	金额
锯材	m^3	474 626	21 755	615 324	278 590
生丝	t	11 288	21 360	10 972	24 455
山羊绒	t	4 159	23 574	3 662	24 765
兔毛	t	2 970	4 387	1 988	3 714
棉花（原棉）	t	9 092	1 574	4 962	791
苎麻	t	1 245	470	1 144	458
中式成药	t	12 194	11 344	12 251	12 532
烟花、爆竹	t	285 395	34 786	325 952	40 229
松香及树脂酸	t	342 893	16 386	347 462	25 453
新的充气橡胶轮胎	万条	19 969	248 675	22 522	378 137
纸及纸板（未切成形）	万t	101	82 115	167	134 403
棉纱线	t	431 031	133 380	469 532	139 995
亚麻及苎麻纱线	t	25 119	11 528	23 440	13 219
丝织物	万m	25 221	58 845	29 017	72 994
棉机织物	万m	530 071	604 472	610 328	699 804
亚麻及苎麻机织物	万m	23 774	39 859	25 093	45 234
合成短纤与棉混纺机织物	万m	219 155	116 259	243 356	142 141
人造纤维短纤机织物	万m	51 397	25 826	68 425	37 987
地毯	万m^2	13 632	77 331	17 505	93 216
棉浴巾	万条	27 390	42 113	40 126	63 482
塑料编织袋（周转袋除外）	万条	235 287	34 259	276 996	45 135
纺织机械及零件			66 677		86 940
家具及零件			1 016 766		1 350 387
服装（针织、钩织的除外）			2 668 198		3 243 219
针织或钩编服装			2 342 531		2 787 777
皮鞋	万双	115 311	631 778	136 046	806 543
橡塑或塑料底布鞋（含球鞋）	万双	93 228	185 833	111 567	235 821
鬃刷	万把	58 966	9 238	57 337	10 395
人造花	t	284 214	57 668	280 101	61 157
竹编织品	t	84 425	16 687	78 409	15 571
藤编织品	t	36 641	9 871	32 561	9 355
草编织品	t	45 942	11 645	53 512	13 907
柳编织品	t	108 780	25 446	104 061	28 134

表 126　我国海关进口农产品及加工品数量与金额（2004—2005 年）

单位：万美元

产品名称	单位	2004 年		2005 年	
		数量	金额	数量	金额
谷物及谷物粉	万 t	974	222 888	627	140 887
小麦	万 t	726	164 961	354	77 287
稻谷和大米	万 t	76	25 345	52	19 945
大豆	万 t	2 023	697 917	2 659	777 879
食用植物油	万 t	676	366 535	621	281 508
其他植物油	万 t	34	22 554	42	28 040
食糖	万 t	121	27 558	139	38 327
配制的动物饲料	万 t	14	12 226	11	12 107
天然橡胶（包括胶乳）	万 t	128	152 427	141	185 466
合成橡胶（包括胶乳）	万 t	109	141 423	109	179 810
原木	万 m^3	2 631	280 432	2 937	324 356
纸浆	万 t	732	356 772	759	372 551
锯材	万 m^3	601	138 256	597	150 779
棉花（原棉）	万 t	191	317 624	257	319 709
羊毛及条	万 t	25	120 715	27	131 797
纺织用合成纤维	万 t	99	137 760	84	138 275
聚酯纤维	万 t	51	53 221	35	42 324
聚丙烯腈纤维	万 t	46	77 681	47	878 823
纸及纸板（未切成形）	万 t	611	384 852	521	354 489
制冷压缩机	万台	1 992	108 823	1 774	101 309

表 127　我国乡镇企业主要农产品加工业产品出口创汇情况（2004—2005 年）

单位：万元

类别		2004 年	2005 年	同比增长（%）
按产品类别分出口交货值	**小　计**	**109 593 679**	**128 781 915**	**17.51**
	轻工类	45 859 467	55 930 655	21.96
	食品类	9 532 826	11 116 924	16.62
	土畜产类	3 070 418	2 848 061	−7.24
	纺织服装类	39 487 527	46 031 744	16.57
	工艺品类	11 643 441	12 854 531	10.40

资料来源：表中数据出自《2005 中国农业统计资料》。

表 128 我国林产品进出口数量（2004—2005 年）

产品名称		贸易	单位	2004 年	2005 年
原木	针叶原木	出口	m^3		742
		进口		16 003 654	18 270 100
	阔叶原木	出口	m^3	6 137	6 185
		进口		10 304 868	11 097 886
	合计	出口	m^3	6 137	6 927
		进口		26 308 522	29 367 986
锯材		出口	m^3	489 331	682 072
		进口		6 051 670	6 054 178
单板		出口	m^3	110 498	104 091
		进口		154 142	151 800
特形材		出口	t	221 247	424 922
		进口		11 962	13 127
刨花板		出口	m^3	130 751	95 035
		进口		652 594	633 972
纤维板		出口	m^3	509 945	1 376 697
		进口		1 377 045	1 137 113
胶合板		出口	m^3	4 305 484	5 583 972
		进口		799 298	589 120
木制品		出口	t	1 983 984	2 009 708
		进口		37 844	39 018
家具		出口	件	175 777 874	211 601 212
		进口		851 909	863 112
木片		出口	t	1 094 162	880 655
		进口		302 680	871 274
木浆		出口	t	1 504	20 456
		进口		7 214 995	7 520 149
废纸		出口	t	163	30
		进口		9 845 481	13 628 936
纸和纸制品		出口	t	576 634	790 907
		进口		5 100 886	4 372 254
木炭		出口	t	68 141	37 497
		进口		31 066	43 013
松香		出口	t	342 888	347 455
		进口		2 152	2 345
水果	柑橘类	出口	t	361 385	465 623
		进口		66 889	61 530
	鲜苹果	出口	t	774 131	824 050
		进口		37 281	33 204
	鲜梨	出口	t	318 218	368 298
		进口		500	81
	鲜葡萄	出口	t	17 800	21 257
		进口		58 887	57 490
	山竹果	出口	t	2	3
		进口		30 811	35 200
	鲜榴莲	出口	t	1	
		进口		85 500	75 371
	鲜龙眼	出口	t	1 547	3 251
		进口		109 418	143 375

（续）

产品名称		贸易	单位	2004年	2005年
坚果	核桃	出口	t	25 805	32 267
		进口		2 687	3 717
	板栗	出口	t	37 581	37 065
		进口		13 503	13 763
	松子仁	出口	t	9 542	11 655
		进口		70	27
	开心果	出口	t	3 572	4 992
		进口		9 473	11 965
干果	梅干及李干	出口	t	1 697	663
		进口		1 101	503
	龙眼干、肉	出口	t	311	250
		进口		55 461	44 385
	柿饼	出口	t	11 067	11 603
		进口		21	59
	红枣	出口	t	15 796	13 808
		进口		26	1
	葡萄干	出口	t	12 122	13 392
		进口		10 772	11 274
果汁	柑橘类果汁	出口	t	3 266	3 848
		进口		48 255	60 814
	苹果汁	出口	t	487 139	648 463
		进口		1 344	461

表129 我国林产品进出口金额（2004—2005年）

单位：千美元

产品名称		贸易	2004年	2005年
总计		**出口**	**16 300 854**	**20 574 172**
		进口	**18 647 755**	**20 715 437**
原木	针叶原木	出口		91
		进口	1 168 493	1 387 979
	阔叶原木	出口	1 959	1 950
		进口	1 635 825	1 855 561
	合计	出口	1 959	2 040
		进口	2 804 318	3 243 540
锯材		出口	219 843	281 431
		进口	1 387 144	1 516 885
单板		出口	120 710	128 529
		进口	109 913	121 181
特形材		出口	278 238	557 133
		进口	15 043	25 099
刨花板		出口	21 394	18 396
		进口	123 197	115 461
纤维板		出口	125 121	396 067
		进口	272 725	229 268
胶合板		出口	1 249 941	1 879 039
		进口	384 280	276 681
木制品		出口	2 934 699	3 139 195
		进口	52 953	49 605
家具		出口	5 229 343	6 843 165
		进口	72 706	87 217
木片		出口	102 486	92 893
		进口	39 929	122 141

（续）

产品名称		贸易	2004年	2005年
木浆		出口 进口	825 3 526 709	10 728 3 694 780
废纸		出口 进口	24 1 381 599	8 1 965 743
纸和纸制品		出口 进口	768 335 3 710 008	1 060 777 3 509 871
木炭		出口 进口	39 067 2 809	22 501 6 070
松香		出口 进口	163 850 4 392	254 515 4 849
水果	柑橘类	出口 进口	105 020 43 433	143 383 44 859
	鲜苹果	出口 进口	274 407 29 417	306 313 25 428
	鲜梨	出口 进口	90 665 234	122 078 52
	鲜葡萄	出口 进口	7 382 67 482	9 982 82 385
	山竹果	出口 进口	10 29 764	1 39 547
	鲜榴莲	出口 进口	1 52 501	 47 863
	鲜龙眼	出口 进口	1 131 69 286	1 348 73 265
坚果	核桃	出口 进口	31 043 2 648	46 112 3 767
	板栗	出口 进口	58 461 21 813	49 803 21 993
	松子仁	出口 进口	68 896 100	76 324 154
	开心果	出口 进口	4 800 17 432	6 403 19 252
干果	梅干及李干	出口 进口	1 568 972	1 073 591
	龙眼干、肉	出口 进口	1 041 28 730	883 26 933
	柿饼	出口 进口	13 210 11	16 314 43
	红枣	出口 进口	10 942 25	11 561 1
	葡萄干	出口 进口	18 397 14 666	21 762 15 747
果汁	柑橘类果汁	出口 进口	3 347 50 443	3 974 62 562
	苹果汁	出口 进口	325 345 1 042	458 169 412
其他		出口 进口	4 029 252 4 325 028	4 612 272 5 282 191

表 130　我国食用菌产品出口情况（2005 年）

产　品　名　称	数量（t）	同比增长（%）	金额（万美元）	同比增长（%）
合　　计	**628 413**	**8.04**	**96 381.5**	**6.81**
蘑菇菌丝	9 091	50.00	236.1	20.00
伞菌属蘑菇	2 761	99.46	827.9	125.31
鲜或冷藏的块菌	1 148	40.07	168.1	−14.32
鲜或冷藏的松茸	1 429	23.58	5 855.7	9.89
鲜或冷藏的香菇	26 412	−18.17	5 590.3	−9.09
鲜或冷藏的金针菇	1 047	1.55	103.5	8.36
鲜或冷藏的草菇	5 229	54.48	65.4	52.43
鲜或冷藏的口蘑	39	−10.11	0.75	9.58
其他鲜或冷藏的蘑菇	6 515	−17.84	1 372.3	3.05
冷冻松茸	658	26.19	1 177.8	18.62
盐水小白蘑菇	15 622	8.52	1 399.3	7.93
盐水的其他伞菌属蘑菇	19 348	13.90	2 273.3	8.45
其他暂时保藏的伞菌属蘑菇	1 400	15.98	137.9	17.25
盐水松茸	350	−39.08	534.6	−21.34
盐水其他蘑菇及块菌	7 035	4.94	931.9	69.56
其他暂时保藏的蘑菇及块菌	16 159	25.87	1 669.2	30.64
干伞菌属蘑菇	700	−53.33	936.7	−55.20
干木耳	7 936	−4.84	3 485.9	15.47
干银耳	2 384	24.60	1 177.9	29.17
干香菇	24 267	−1.84	17 555.9	15.33
干金针菇	20	117.20	7.4	120.18
干草菇	10	−80.65	3.8	−82.92
干口蘑	2	12.20	3.9	321.11
干牛肝菌	1 062		1 668.8	
未列名干蘑菇及块菌	1 877	−3.98	1 948.9	−4.06
冬虫夏草	3.5	−25.90	1 338.3	−14.98
天麻	88	96.50	34.9	13.16
茯苓	5 103	33.03	556.7	3.64
其他制作或保藏的伞菌属蘑菇	4 209	14.09	731.7	6.55
小白蘑菇（洋蘑菇）罐头	276 410	3.52	22 113.8	3.15
其他伞菌属蘑菇罐头	34 894	40.55	5 291.9	−29.64
制作或保藏的块菌	3 911	−69.91	486.7	−58.37
未列名主要用作药物的植物及其他部分	139 020	20.17	14 570.9	20.80
其他蘑菇罐头	11 443	72.26	1 875.7	133.39
其他制作或保藏的蘑菇	828	−26.65	307.2	−30.85

表 131 轻工业系统农产品加工业主要出口产品创汇情况（2004 年）

主要产品名称	单 位	出口产品		同比增长（%）	
		数 量	金 额	数 量	金 额
轻工业产品出口总额	**万美元**		**15 766 730**		**25.09**
有关农产品加工业产品合计	**万美元**		**6 534 125**		**55.76**
制浆	万 t、万美元	1.75	1 615	−30.24	−23.62
纸张	万 t、万美元	140.40	129 226	−60.02	−54.68
香料香精	万 t、万美元	2.19	14 702	18.32	18.60
制盐	万 t、万美元	81.21	3 459	−29.02	−2.69
糖	万 t、万美元	8.52	2 582	−17.42	−12.66
罐头	万 t、万美元	178.64	136 322	11.31	11.61
巧克力食品	万 t、万美元	2.01	4 433	5.74	13.03
味精	万 t、万美元	0.91	855	40.74	36.34
冷冻饮品	万 t、万美元	1.00	1 489	55.00	64.99
酒	万 L、万美元	32 058	26 098	−36.91	−11.16
其他食品	万 t、万美元	883.45	1 268 317	5.34	22.10
饮料	万美元		83 959		38.30
皮革及其制品	万美元		2 541 026		14.04
毛皮及其制品	万美元		200 211		120.04
木制品及其他天然植物制品	万美元		274 081		25.81
家具	万美元		1 035 272		39.30
抽丝刺绣工艺品	万美元		62 932		46.74
地毯	万 m^2、万美元	13 646.2	77 574	40.13	21.24
烟花爆竹	万 t、万美元	28.54	34 786	10.33	10.10
天然植物编织工艺品	万 t、万美元	36.78	79 389	8.34	17.41
刷子	万把、万美元	238 786	36 611	15.26	28.48
轻工机械	万美元		65 469		47.83
纸制品	万 t、万美元	79.79	103 282	30.36	40.02
羽绒制品	万美元		350 435		34.58

表 132 轻工业系统农产品加工业主要进口产品情况（2004 年）

主要产品名称	单 位	进口产品		同比增长（%）	
		数 量	金 额	数 量	金 额
轻工业产品进口总额	**万美元**		**4 903 060**		**25.63**
有关农产品加工业产品合计	**万美元**		**2 632 514**		**76.21**
制浆	万 t、万美元	731.79	356 767	21.28	34.09
纸张	万 t、万美元	615.93	402 505	−3.78	4.14
香料香精	万 t、万美元	1.63	18 737	17.16	26.94
糖	万 t、万美元	121.43	27 558	56.66	58.28
罐头	万 t、万美元	1.14	1 116	25.76	22.66
巧克力食品	万 t、万美元	2.32	7 504	16.99	19.88

（续）

主要产品名称	单 位	进口产品		同比增长（%）	
		数 量	金 额	数 量	金 额
味精	万 t、万美元	0.04	64	−6.29	4.57
冷冻饮品	万 t、万美元	0.16	552	102.28	138.03
酒	万 L、万美元	10 319	24 986	−4.93	39.21
其他食品	万 t、万美元	1 592.59	874 918	22.96	29.55
饮料	万 t、万美元		7 016		−13.05
皮革及其制品	万美元		369 155		19.86
毛皮及其制品	万美元		19 288		39.23
木制品及其他天然植物制品	万美元		4 986		53.03
家具	万美元		72 601		26.28
抽丝刺绣工艺品	万美元		13 921		3.31
地毯	万 m²、万美元	1 049.24	5 880	15.26	25.68
烟花爆竹	万 t、万美元	0.001	14	−20.89	151.85
天然植物编织工艺品	万 t、万美元	0.44	495	−23.92	1.87
刷子	万把、万美元	22 590	3 283	29.49	57.44
轻工机械	万美元		360 673		15.81
纸制品	万 t、万美元	20.48	59 650	−4.63	15.86
羽绒制品	万美元		845		−21.57

表 133 我国乳制品进口情况（2005 年） 单位：万美元、万 t

产 品 名 称	进 口		同比增长（%）	
	数 量	金 额	数 量	金 额
乳制品	**32.00**	**45 900**	**−7.81**	**3.25**
其中：乳粉	10.69	23 275	−26.20	−14.11
乳清粉	18.76	15 764	5.40	31.37
奶油				
干酪	0.717 7		持平	

表 134 我国乳制品出口情况（2005 年） 单位：万 t、万美元

产 品 名 称	出 口		同比增长（%）	
	数 量	金 额	数 量	金 额
乳制品	**7.0**	**8 200**	**16.24**	**45.43**
其中：液体乳	3.6			
乳粉	1.8			
炼乳	1.6			

表 135　我国罐头产品出口情况（2004 年）　　单位：t、万美元

产品名称	出口量	同比增减（%）	出口额	同比增减（%）
全国总计	**1 786 437**	**11.31**	**136 324**	**11.61**
鸡罐头	17 595	91.63	52	327.91
其他家禽肉及杂碎罐头	291	－12.00	46	－11.54
猪肉及杂碎罐头	54 063	3.65	7 927	5.62
牛肉及杂碎罐头	8 084	56.70	1 294	81.23
未列名肉类及杂碎罐头	742	－29.44	115	－21.23
肉类罐头合计	64 940	8.92	9 936	16.25
绞碎制作或保藏的鱼罐头	4 981	73.88	739	69.89
番茄罐头（整个或切片）	4 616	20.46	226	30.64
番茄酱罐头	437 355	9.00	22 237	8.52
小白蘑菇（洋蘑菇）罐头	267 009	17.10	21 437	15.16
其他伞菌属蘑菇罐头	24 828	－17.07	7 520	－18.31
其他蘑菇罐头	6 643	49.19	803	84.60
脱荚豇豆及菜豆罐头	4 814	－4.17	275	0.36
未脱荚豇豆及菜豆罐头	16 066	－25.75	1 084	－19.52
芦笋罐头	97 465	－6.07	9 803	－1.64
清水马蹄罐头	54 878	16.62	3 070	32.27
蚕豆罐头	19 208	33.58	682	30.65
水煮竹笋罐头（每件容积≥8kg）	104 261	7.49	9 196	24.05
其他竹笋罐头	83 084	14.71	5 718	26.81
其他非醋方法制作或保藏的未冷冻蔬菜及什锦蔬菜罐头	81 728	40.36	8 938	－3.60
蔬菜罐头合计	1 201 954	10.58	90 997	11.58
花生米罐头	2 142	8.79	240	14.83
核桃仁罐头	660	－25.31	275	－22.54
其他果仁罐头	10 013	5.09	2 806	－1.85
干果罐头合计	12 815	3.51	3 322	－2.98
菠萝罐头	77 064	39.38	3 666	41.71
柑橘属水果罐头	282 819	12.64	17 035	6.96
其他制作或保藏的柑橘属水果罐头	31	－41.07	2	
烹煮的非柑橘属水果制果酱、果冻、果泥及果膏罐头	19 101	34.61	1 454	26.32
梨罐头	29 808	31.82	1 555	37.13
桃罐头	70 215	－11.59	5 523	－6.41
荔枝罐头	19 484	5.28	1 170	10.69
龙眼罐头	1 639	－7.14	106	－22.06
水果罐头合计	500 160	12.92	30 514	8.40
零售包装的狗食、猫食饲料罐头	1 586	1 169.83	814	2 807.14

表 136　我国罐头产品出口的主要国家或地区（2003—2004 年）

单位：万 t、万美元

其中：猪肉及杂碎罐头出口国家或地区

国家或地区	2003 年			2004 年		
	数　量	金　额	占出口（%）	数　量	金　额	占出口（%）
合　计	**52 161**	**7 506**	**100.00**	**64 644**	**17 258.4**	**100.00**
香　港	14 072	2 209	29.43	14 288	2 767.6	16.04
新加坡	7 864	1 269	16.91	393	168.1	0.97
马来西亚	14 010	1 738	23.15	10	5.3	0.03
菲律宾	6 798	882	11.75	2	2.7	0.02
日　本				49 406	14 130.3	81.87

其中：牛肉及杂碎罐头出口国家或地区

国家或地区	2003 年			2004 年		
	数　量	金　额	占出口（%）	数　量	金　额	占出口（%）
合　计	**5 159**	**714**	**100.00**	**8 804**	**1 294.7**	**100.00**
香　港	759	110	15.37	698	99.5	7.69
马来西亚	1 014	130	18.13	1 292	158.5	12.24
俄罗斯	170	22	3.02			
印度尼西亚	1 098	139	19.52	943	116.9	9.03
哈萨克斯坦	48	3	0.43	192	23.3	1.80
韩　国	1 699	244	34.16	3 662	538.8	41.62

其中：蘑菇罐头出口国家或地区

国家或地区	2003 年			2004 年		
	数　量	金　额	占出口（%）	数　量	金　额	占出口（%）
合　计	**184 064**	**15 192**	**100.00**	**266 949**	**21 427.8**	**100.00**
美　国	6 995	852	5.61	37 370	4 031.2	18.81
加拿大	15 359	1 278	8.41	19 206	1 485.5	6.93
德　国	29 413	2 341	15.41	28 257	2 270.3	10.60
日　本	11 714	1 214	7.99	13 042	1 376.7	6.42
香　港	14 100	1 259	8.29	11 516	966.0	4.51
荷　兰	10 811	891	5.86	12 598	1 080.5	5.04

表 137　我国卷烟出口的主要国家或地区（2003—2004 年）

国家或地区	2003 年			2004 年		
	数量（亿支）	金额（万美元）	占出口（%）	数量（亿支）	金额（万美元）	占出口（%）
合　计	**184.23**	**23 744.1**	**100.00**	**165.31**	**22 146.4**	**100.00**
香　港	41.01	7 884.2	33.20	31.44	6 567.2	29.65
新加坡	12.70	1 208.6	5.09	13.25	1 500.7	6.78
缅　甸	11.20	1 554.4	6.55	0.92	1 148.1	5.18
日　本	5.62	668.4	2.82	7.15	777.2	3.51
马来西亚	7.31	889.7	3.75	7.26	1 044.1	4.71
意大利	1.68	388.4	1.64	1.04	285.2	1.29
加拿大	4.63	1 123.3	4.73	4.63	1 068.7	4.83
美　国	17.69	1 088.3	4.58	12.19	818.4	3.70

表 138　我国进口卷烟的国家或地区（2003—2004 年）

国家或地区	2003 年			2004 年		
	数量（亿支）	金额（万美元）	占出口（%）	数量（亿支）	金额（万美元）	占出口（%）
合　计	**18.78**	**3 808.6**	**100.00**	**25.61**	**5 115.7**	**100.00**
香　港	2.48	325.4	8.54	3.04	419.3	8.20
英　国	9.41	2 044.7	53.69	11.69	2 543.1	49.71
美　国	3.62	738.4	19.39	4.89	998.7	19.52
日　本	0.09	24.9	0.65	0.24	72.6	1.42

表 139　我国蜂蜜生产及出口情况（2002—2005 年）单位：万 t、万美元

年份	世界产量（万 t）	我国产量（万 t）	占世界比例（%）	出口量（万 t）	出口率（%）	出口创汇（万美元）
2002	12.0	25.78	20.30	3.6	13.92	7 794
2003	127.0	26.78	21.80	8.6	32.11	10 300
2004	130.9	27.60	21.08	8.1	29.35	8 894
2005	130.4	29.30	22.47	8.85	30.20	8 762.9

表 140　我国蜂产品出口情况（2004—2005 年）　单位：t、万美元

主要产品	2004 年		2005 年		同比增减（%）	
	数　量	金　额	数　量	金　额	数　量	金　额
蜂蜜	81 325	8 900.83	88 499	8 762.89	8.82	−1.55
鲜蜂王浆	664.92	979.45	794.78	1 224.18	19.53	24.99
蜂王浆冻干粉	205.13	868.63	168.01	733.77	18.10	−15.53
金额总计		10 748.95		10 720.85		−0.26

资料来源：表中数据由中国农业科学院蜜蜂研究所提供。

表 141　我国蜂产品出口的主要国家或地区（2005 年）

蜂蜜出口的主要国家或地区情况					
国家或地区	数量（t）	占出口（%）	金额（万美元）	占出口（%）	单价（美元/kg）
日　本	41 396.9	46.78	4 369.4	49.86	1.055 497
美　国	28 264.5	31.94	2 390.9	27.29	0.845 917
加拿大	3 115.7	3.52	293.8	3.35	0.942 948
西班牙	2 602.9	2.94	272.0	3.10	1.044 901
韩　国	2 101.0	2.37	187.8	2.41	0.893 652
新加坡	1 711.4	1.93	214.3	2.45	1.252 175
英　国	1 268.2	1.43	123.3	1.41	0.971 906
德　国	1 265.5	1.43	133.7	1.53	1.056 309
马来西亚	1 225.6	1.39	125.4	1.43	1.023 210
中国香港	1 060.2	1.20	137.6	1.57	1.297 464
小　计	**88 499**	**100.00**	**8 763**	**100.00**	**0.990 166**

（续）

国家或地区	数量（t）	占出口（%）	金额（万美元）	占出口（%）	单价（美元/kg）
蜂王浆出口的主要国家或地区情况					
日本	505.63	63.62	824.81	67.38	16.313
法国	41.97	5.28	62.17	5.08	14.813
中国香港	42.89	5.40	53.86	4.40	12.558
美国	30.45	3.83	40.36	3.30	13.256
德国	22.31	2.81	35.09	2.87	15.730
土耳其	25.50	3.21	29.71	2.43	11.649
沙特阿拉伯	23.26	2.93	27.32	2.23	11.745
瑞士	14.65	1.84	23.23	1.90	15.585
西班牙	10.53	1.32	16.23	1.33	15.414
韩国	11.60	1.46	15.84	1.29	13.654
小计	**794.78**	**100.00**	**1 224.18**	**100.00**	**15.403**
蜂王浆冻干粉出口的主要国家或地区情况					
国家或地区	数量（t）	占出口（%）	金额（万美元）	占出口（%）	单价（美元/kg）
日本	102.21	60.84	467.67	63.73	45.756
美国	21.47	12.78	80.35	10.95	37.424
澳大利亚	14.42	8.58	58.19	7.93	40.369
瑞士	13.68	8.14	56.95	7.76	41.630
韩国	4.82	2.87	17.56	2.39	36.439
马来西亚	3.87	2.30	20.20	2.75	52.206
中国香港	1.18	0.70	4.40	0.60	37.478
埃及	1.00	0.60	5.06	0.69	50.621
法国	1.00	0.60	4.67	0.64	46.722
沙特阿拉伯	1.00	0.60	3.52	0.48	35.200
小计	**168.01**	**100.00**	**733.77**	**100.00**	**43.675**

资料来源：表中数据由中国农业科学院蜜蜂研究所提供。

表 142 我国水产品进出口贸易情况（2002—2005 年）

年份	出口量（万 t）	出口额（亿美元）	进口量（万 t）	进口额（亿美元）
2002	208.5	46.9	249.1	22.7
2003	210.0	54.9	233.0	24.8
2004	242.1	69.7	298.6	32.3
2005	257.0	78.9	366.0	51.2

注：2005 年水产品进、出口总量达 623 万 t；进出口总额达 121.1 亿美元；实现贸易顺差 37.7 亿美元；出口额继续位居大宗农产品首位，占全国农产品出口总额的 28.6%。按经贸方式划分：国内水产品出口占总额 64%，进口原料再加工出口占总额 34%。按加工方式比较：初级冷冻产品占出口总额的 59%，深加工品占 41%。

表 143 我国食品和包装机械进出口情况（2004—2005 年）

项目	单位	2004 年	2005 年	同比增长（%）
进出口总额	亿美元	32.44	26.07	−19.64
其中：进口总额	亿美元	28.00	19.99	−28.61
出口总额	亿美元	4.44	6.07	36.71
进出口贸易逆差	亿美元	23.56	13.92	−40.92

表 144 纺织工业纺织原料及制品进出口额统计（2005 年）

单位：亿美元、%

类别	全贸易方式		一般贸易		进料加工		来料加工	
	当年	同比	当年	同比	当年	同比	当年	同比
一、出口								
总计	**1 076.57**	**21.28**	**745.41**	**24.56**	**183.04**	**14.21**	**100.46**	**2.24**
丝及丝绸	13.36	25.77	13.07	26.78	0.14	－16.82	0.06	－0.44
毛及毛织品	18.45	7.59	12.14	6.90	5.00	6.43	1.09	21.78
棉及棉织品	74.38	12.87	49.11	14.15	22.83	15.71	1.95	－14.22
麻及麻织品	6.18	11.79	4.32	14.26	1.65	6.13	0.17	13.54
化纤长丝及织品	58.83	14.18	48.77	13.04	8.45	22.26	0.75	－11.46
化纤短纤及织品	43.88	23.42	29.97	28.43	11.01	5.72	1.28	－3.63
絮、毡、无纺布	8.60	44.65	5.19	50.81	2.60	35.86	0.59	31.17
铺地织品	9.32	20.54	7.26	15.88	1.87	38.34	0.09	23.01
特种织物花边	27.09	37.18	23.63	42.35	2.34	17.88	0.84	0.93
涂层布及工业用布	17.55	42.10	12.50	10.16	4.26	49.27	0.30	－5.19
针织布	36.52	21.99	16.94	38.68	17.35	7.71	2.00	34.92
针织服装及附件	308.72	19.65	230.79	20.79	33.56	14.77	26.91	1.35
梭织服装及附件	350.32	20.87	215.65	30.53	55.47	9.66	61.12	1.85
其他纺织织物	103.36	32.78	76.06	28.02	16.51	29.48	3.31	10.75
二、进口								
总计	**234.11**	**1.97**	**55.87**	**4.95**	**94.57**	**－0.06**	**68.33**	**－3.39**
丝及丝绸	1.36	－2.43	0.05	－49.42	0.57	8.36	0.68	－1.90
毛及毛织品	21.47	2.79	8.79	17.16	3.93	－12.48	6.06	－4.99
棉及棉织品	70.78	2.61	17.93	－7.52	32.42	0.41	13.37	－5.14
麻及麻织品	4.77	1.42	1.52	1.93	1.99	4.08	0.95	－7.61
化纤长丝及织品	37.41	－0.47	8.10	6.19	14.37	－1.84	13.90	－3.56
化纤短纤及织品	32.58	－4.80	10.00	1.62	13.05	－5.61	8.17	－9.10
絮、毡、无纺布	7.07	14.27	1.30	25.42	3.11	14.94	2.35	8.75
铺地织品	0.62	6.28	0.41	－3.91	0.16	30.48	0.02	7.34
特种织物花边	8.46	3.45	0.48	50.62	4.16	－0.53	3.71	4.08
涂层布及工业用布	14.50	7.44	2.39	14.87	7.15	10.03	4.28	0.94
针织布	18.78	3.64	0.56	56.40	8.21	3.38	9.81	2.21
针织服装及附件	6.95	8.27	1.61	45.91	2.45	7.27	2.47	－8.36
梭织服装及附件	8.15	2.84	2.28	44.30	2.56	－12.91	2.38	－12.71
其他纺织织物	1.19	34.92	0.45	18.87	0.44	60.63	0.19	37.64

表 145　纺织工业纺织品服装进出口额（2005 年）

单位：亿美元、%

项　目	出口						进口					
	小计		纺织品		服装		小计		纺织品		服装	
	当年	同比	当年	同比	当年	同比	当年	同比	当年	同比	当年	同比
一、贸易方式	1 175.35	20.69	439.69	22.93	735.66	19.40	170.99	1.76	154.90	1.42	16.09	5.08
1. 一般贸易	819.13	24.28	318.44	23.99	500.69	24.46	20.73	20.62	16.49	16.36	4.24	40.64
2. 进料加工	199.59	12.68	96.49	15.26	103.09	10.37	79.07	2.33	73.79	2.84	5.29	−4.36
3. 来料加工	107.09	1.31	12.40	5.67	94.70	0.77	66.37	−3.87	61.26	−3.33	5.11	9.86
4. 其他贸易	49.55	55.22	12.37	128.01	37.18	40.32	4.79	5.74	3.35	−2.62	1.45	31.94
二、主要类型企业												
1. 国有企业	348.66	2.17	123.66	4.87	225.00	0.74	28.31	−16.30	24.48	−16.35	3.83	−16.02
2. 集体企业	103.07	4.88	50.49	7.88	52.58	2.16	6.05	−4.36	5.52	−4.64	0.53	−1.30
3. 三资企业	403.25	20.37	147.33	22.01	255.92	19.44	120.88	3.60	112.30	3.62	8.58	3.39
4. 民营企业	320.38	60.73	118.22	63.65	202.16	59.07	15.74	40.42	12.60	35.44	3.14	64.69
三、主要国家或地区												
1. 亚洲	555.66	3.01	247.60	17.20	308.06	−6.12	155.64	0.45	142.10	0.33	13.54	1.73
中国香港	148.43	−14.59	80.59	5.30	67.84	−30.24	18.56	−6.35	11.71	−9.20	6.85	−1.02
中国澳门	7.75	−16.00	2.31	3.86	5.44	−22.30	1.41	−19.77	0.13	−71.95	1.28	−1.22
中国台湾省	6.30	2.54	2.95	9.69	3.36	−3.02	32.12	−2.61	31.78	−2.59	0.34	−4.41
日本	181.03	5.54	34.48	11.17	146.54	4.29	33.62	−4.12	32.03	3.47	1.59	−15.59
韩国	41.71	−0.35	17.30	22.79	24.41	−12.10	26.31	1.18	25.20	0.53	1.11	18.42
土耳其	6.36	49.09	5.52	50.82	0.84	38.69	0.37	17.49	0.25	5.19	0.11	58.06
东盟	56.40	23.28	36.74	28.66	19.66	14.33	6.86	5.64	6.26	3.23	0.59	40.10
2. 欧洲	280.09	44.37	67.86	38.12	212.22	46.49	10.42	18.60	8.26	14.78	0.16	35.85
欧盟	188.63	55.30	53.00	37.17	135.63	63.76	9.92	18.86	7.95	15.87	1.97	32.93
3. 非洲	49.11	19.82	30.93	21.23	18.18	17.48	0.14	60.36	0.07	29.95	0.07	110.04
4. 大洋洲	26.23	15.26	6.48	11.79	19.76	16.44	0.42	−19.09	0.34	−1.65	0.08	−53.25
澳大利亚	22.33	15.32	5.35	9.46	16.98	17.30	0.38	18.94	0.30	0.77	0.08	−52.85
5. 北美自由贸易区	224.95	56.78	69.10	38.55	155.85	66.50	4.20	17.32	3.99	17.70	0.20	10.30
美国	195.76	66.09	60.10	47.38	135.66	76.00	3.93	20.37	3.76	20.34	0.17	21.07
加拿大	22.27	52.91	5.44	28.55	16.83	62.88	0.17	−17.89	0.16	−18.41	0.01	−10.78
墨西哥	6.92	−37.39	3.56	−26.78	3.36	−45.73	0.10	−7.45	0.08	0.87	0.02	−29.47
6. 欧盟、美国	384.39	60.62	113.10	42.34	1271.29	69.66	13.85	19.31	11.71	17.26	2.14	31.90
7. 非欧盟、美国	790.96	7.68	326.59	17.36	464.37	1.78	157.14	0.45	143.19	0.31	13.95	1.90
四、分原料加工												
1. 棉制产品	411.13	31.66	140.72	19.18	270.41	39.25	53.93	6.64	46.16	4.71	7.77	19.73
2. 毛制产品	56.38	15.38	16.83	4.41	39.56	20.77	9.95	−7.36	8.43	−9.00	1.52	2.90
3. 麻制产品	7.63	20.66	7.63	20.66	0.00	0.00	1.86	−11.64	1.86	−11.64	0.00	0.00
4. 丝制产品	33.60	14.73	11.29	27.73	22.31	9.11	1.76	10.83	1.30	3.29	0.46	40.04
5. 化纤制产品	422.03	19.98	189.53	26.20	232.50	15.34	81.84	0.54	79.02	1.01	2.81	−11.18
6. 未列名其他材料	244.57	8.53	73.69	26.71	170.88	2.21	21.66	0.09	18.13	1.91	3.53	−8.34

表 146　我国纺织品服装进出口贸易情况（2001—2005 年）

年份	项目	进出口（亿美元）	出口（亿美元）	进口（亿美元）	贸易差额（亿美元）	同比增长（%）		
						进出口	出口	进口
2001	全国	5 097.68	2 661.55	2 436.13	225.42	7.50	6.80	8.20
2001	纺织	680.48	543.23	137.25	405.98	1.66	2.41	－1.19
2001	纺织占全国	13.35	20.41	5.63	180.10			
2002	全国	6 207.90	3 255.70	2 952.20	303.50	21.78	21.80	21.20
2002	纺织	773.87	630.18	143.69	486.49	13.72	16.01	4.69
2002	纺织占全国	12.47	19.36	4.87	160.29			
2003	全国	8 512.10	4 383.70	4 128.40	255.30	37.10	34.60	39.90
2003	纺织	960.70	804.84	155.86	648.98	24.15	27.72	8.47
2003	纺织占全国	11.29	18.36	3.78	254.20			
2004	全国	11 547.40	5 933.60	5 613.80	319.80	35.70	35.40	36.00
2004	纺织	1 141.89	973.85	168.04	805.81	18.86	21.01	7.81
2004	纺织占全国	9.89	16.41	2.99	251.97			
2005	全国	14 221.20	7 620.00	6 601.20	1 018.80	23.20	28.40	17.60
2005	纺织	1 346.34	1 175.35	170.99	1 004.36	17.90	20.69	1.76
2005	纺织占全国	9.47	15.42	2.59	98.58			

表 147　纺织工业主要毛纺产品进出口数量比较（2004—2005 年）

主要产品	单位	2004 年	2005 年	同比增长（%）
进口洗净毛	t	38 879	32 491	－16.43
出口洗净毛	t	28 143	30 462	8.24
进口羊毛条	t	38 879	32 491	－16.43
出口羊毛条	t	28 143	30 462	8.24
进口呢绒	亿 m	0.838	0.768	－8.32
出口呢绒	亿 m	1.15	1.16	10.73
出口羊毛毯	万条	104	90	－13.16
出口化纤毛毯	万条	19 556	25 425	30.01
出口毛针织服装	亿件	3.63	2.86	－21.15
其中：羊毛衫出口数量	亿件	1.69	1.16	－3.99
羊绒衫出口数量	亿件	0.14	0.188	30.51
出口毛梭织服装	亿件	0.56	0.675	19.91

表 148 纺织工业针织物及针织服装出口情况（2005 年）

产　品	单位	数量（亿件）	同比（%）	金额（亿美元）	同比（%）
针织物	万 t	92.92	14.95	36.52	21.99
其中：起绒织物	万 t	22.92	22.58	7.61	27.83
经编织物	万 t	6.04	41.88	2.70	42.11
针织服装及附件				308.72	19.65
其中：棉针织服装及附件				135.39	37.92
化纤针织服装及附件				117.68	13.85
针织服装	亿件	145.38	6.15	263.97	18.68
其中：棉针织服装	亿件	76.08	22.59	128.75	37.23
化纤针织服装	亿件	56.77	−6.38	105.77	11.88
其中：男衬衫	亿件	1.23	30.06	3.01	28.93
女衬衫	亿件	1.26	87.13	2.44	68.99
男内衣	亿件	12.89	11.75	7.94	18.87
女内衣	亿件	34.36	−6.30	20.85	8.10
T 恤衫	亿件	34.04	29.22	52.94	35.25
套头衫	亿件	28.93	33.87	94.08	39.30
袜子	亿双、条	66.98	37.07	17.17	39.97
其中：连裤袜	亿条	4.59	8.58	2.29	21.96
长筒袜	亿双	1.50	61.21	3.05	63.34

表 149 纺织工业真丝产品分类出口情况（2005 年）

产品名称		单位	数量	同比（%）	金额（万美元）	同比（%）	单价*	同比（%）
蚕丝类		万 t	3.04	10.91	61 449	28.50	20.19	15.87
其中	桑蚕丝	万 t	1.02	−3.14	22 638	12.95	22.20	16.65
	捻绒丝	万 t	0.39	12.57	9 815	25.80	25.19	11.75
	绢绣丝	万 t	1.28	32.86	24 058	56.38	18.74	17.71
	柞蚕丝	万 t	0.077	2.00	1 817	37.90	23.53	35.20
	废丝	万 t	0.27	11.83	3 121	45.30	11.46	29.93
真丝绸缎		万 m	2.90	15.04	73 281	23.98	2.52	7.77
其中	坯绸	万 m	2.36	14.54	52 130	13.89	2.21	9.59
	印染绸	万 m	0.53	16.16	19 998	19.37	3.80	2.76
真丝服装及制成品		万件（套）	3.80	10.11	240 411	10.53	6.33	0.32
其中	手帕	万条	654	29.42	508	37.49	0.78	6.24
	头巾	万条	3 630	37.46	8 705	29.28	2.40	−5.95
	领带	万条	10 765	18.25	22 827	23.70	2.12	4.60
	服装	万件（套）	20 488	1.04	191 108	6.82	9.33	5.73
	梭织服装	万件（套）	11 218	−0.54	110 003	8.66	9.81	9.26
	针织服装	万件（套）	9 270	3.02	81 105	4.43	8.75	1.36

* 表中单价为美元/kg、美元/m、美元/件套。

表150 纺织工业印染六大类产品进出口情况（2005年）

产　品	进、出口	数量（亿m）	同比（%）	金额（亿美元）	同比（%）	单价（美元/m）
纯棉染色布	进口	5.84	－0.07	8.71	0.08	1.49
纯棉印花布		0.52	－11.48	1.01	－20.14	1.96
棉混纺染色布		1.30	－6.68	2.74	－4.36	2.11
棉混纺印花布		0.13	13.85	0.20	12.44	1.55
合纤长丝织物		20.15	－10.12	20.29	－1.85	1.01
T/C印染布		1.83	－12.64	2.24	－10.94	1.22
小　计		**29.77**	**－8.23**	**35.19**	**－2.79**	**1.18**
纯棉染色布	出口	13.68	13.59	17.21	13.45	1.26
纯棉印花布		9.49	20.04	7.88	20.04	0.83
棉混纺染色布		1.02	3.05	1.35	7.59	1.33
棉混纺印花布		0.68	19.19	0.64	34.02	0.94
合纤长丝织物		61.45	8.98	47.14	7.82	0.77
T/C印染布		17.43	14.87	10.62	25.45	0.61
小　计		**103.75**	**11.48**	**84.84**	**11.82**	**0.82**

表151 纺织工业主要家纺产品出口数量与金额情况（2005年） 单位：万美元

产　品	单　位	数量	同比增长（%）	金额	同比增长（%）
被子	t	52 045	18.61	252 727	23.69
床上用织物制品	条	80 780	45.32	173 160	60.52
毯子及旅行毯子	条	31 185	27.26	125 968	31.20
窗帘	万件	37 024	21.21	116 726	28.05
装饰用织物制品	万件	43 482	13.77	79 817	28.82
刺绣品	t	7 930	105.06	70 081	119.20
浴巾（盥）及厨房用品	万条	40 126	46.46	63 482	50.74
其他棉制毛巾织物	万条	217 050	15.89	61 114	22.77
缝纫线	Kg	14 835	3.05	43 080	7.07
床罩	万件	7 049	29.89	30 138	55.73

表152 纺织工业纺织机械进出口情况（2004—2005年） 单位：亿美元

进出口	产品类别	2004年	2005年	同比增长（%）
进口	针织机械	9.20	7.87	－14.49
	印染后整理机械	7.45	7.30	－2.06
	织机	6.66	6.16	－7.48
	纺纱机械	6.60	4.44	－32.77
	辅助装置及零配件	5.19	4.02	－22.49
	化纤机械	7.73	3.52	－54.49
	织造准备机械	1.70	0.74	－56.48
	非织造机械	0.84	0.41	－51.23
	合　计	**45.36**	**34.45**	**－24.06**
出口	针织机械	1.49	2.48	66.77
	印染后整理机械	1.78	2.25	26.53
	辅助装置及零配件	1.34	1.82	35.44
	纺纱机械	1.51	1.41	－6.53
	化纤机械	0.30	0.33	8.97
	织机	0.18	0.27	52.82
	非织造机械	0.025	0.099	290.41
	织造准备机械	0.063	0.055	－13.20
	合　计	**6.68**	**8.71**	**30.34**

表 153　纺织工业纺织机械产品各类企业出口所占比重（2005 年）

企 业 类 别	出口金额（万美元）	占全部出口比重（%）
合　计	**87 089.36**	**30.34**
国有企业	24 817.35	3.31
集体企业	3 488.49	24.15
合作企业	362.24	－16.39
私营企业	20 900.35	101.97
独资企业	29 834.65	30.18
合资企业	7 498.45	19.80
个体企业	187.85	

表 154　我国皮革工业主要产品进出口情况（2005 年）

单位：万美元

出　口					
主 要 产 品	单位	数量	同比（%）	金额	同比（%）
皮面皮鞋	万双	136 046	18.0	806 543	27.7
旅行用品及箱包		·		731 154	17.2
皮革服装	万件	5 617	－8.3	227 588	－1.3
毛皮服装	kt	9	－0.9	187 249	39.5
皮革手套	万双	85 281	9.5	86 059	0.7
足、排、篮球	万个	13 292	10.5	17 904	10.9
生皮	kt		107.2	229	· 90.5
成品及半成品革	kt	224	－5.8	156 392	11.7
靴鞋零件及类似品	kt	153	－0.7	61 898	7.4
皮革机械	万台	3	58.2	2 344	102.7
总　计				**2 277 360**	**18.6**
进　口					
主 要 产 品	单位	数量	同比（%）	金额	同比（%）
生皮	kt	899	8.6	132 392	6.1
成品及半成品	kt	1 119	3.5	350 281	4.5
靴鞋零件及类似品	kt	37	－6.1	32 630	2.8
皮革及制鞋机械	台	9 956	－22.6	8 855	1.2
皮革机械零件	t	1 116	8.2	684	18.2
旅行用品及箱包				16 330	44.1
皮革服装	万件	8	41.6	1 248	12.8
皮面皮鞋	万双	567	45.1	15 283	41.9
皮革手套	万双	40	－0.7	116	20.2
毛皮衣服	t	9	17.1	268	219.4
足、排、篮球	万个	159	49.1	194	48.5
总　计				**558 282**	**6.4**

资料来源：表中数据由中国皮革工业协会提供。

表 155 我国家具工业主要产品进出口情况（2005 年）

单位：万美元

主要产品	单位	进口			
		数量	同比（%）	金额	同比（%）
家具				68 441.4	6.09
木家具	万件	72.92	4.92	6 874.5	18.07
金属家具	t	4 948.68	49.57	2 554.2	43.20
塑料家具	t	3 448.09	－3.00	2 318.2	1.89
其他家具	t	71 600.08	2.01	53 117.4	－11.08
床垫	万张	2.06	5.10	188	29.83
家具零件	t	18 907.39	－3.44	3 389.1	18.97
		出口			
		数量	同比（%）	金额	同比（%）
家具				1 376 701	32.98
木家具	万件	14 936.99	16.49	465.783.2	26.53
金属家具	t	1 554 227	25.57	197.352.5	42.74
塑料家具	t	153 235.8	20.17	23 928.5	34.88
其他家具	t	931 072	17.32	610 306.5	33.95
床垫	万张	317.95	51.48	8 350.7	34.39
家具零件	t	517 590.9	29.54	70 979.2	43.80

表 156 我国纸浆及废纸进出口情况（2003—2004 年）

单位：万 t、亿美元

产品名称	2003 年				2004 年			
	进口		出口		进口		出口	
	数量	金额	数量	金额	数量	金额	数量	金额
纸浆及废纸合计	**1 541.58**	**38.91**	**2.61**	**0.212**	**1 962**	**52.93**		
一、纸浆	603.40	26.60	2.51	0.21	732	35.67		
1. 机械木浆	8.94	0.32	0.009	0.006	7.57	0.32		
2. 化学溶解浆	26.86	1.70	0.000 1	0.000 1	28.99	2.09		
3. 硫酸盐木浆	493.70	21.40	0.3	0.015	603.40	29.14		
其中：未漂针叶木浆	65.66	2.40	0.016	0.000 6	62.0	2.55		
未漂非针叶木浆	0.34	0.014			0.43	0.02		
漂白针叶木浆	196.36	8.9	0.17	0.008	244.06	13.16		
漂白非针叶木浆	231.32	10.1	0.12	0.007	296.91	13.41		
4. 亚硫酸盐木浆	5.01	0.27	0.064	0.004	6.66	0.38		
其中：未漂针叶木浆	0.26	0.012			0.36	0.02		
未漂非针叶木浆	0.29	0.015	0.003 6	0.003	0.18	0.01		
漂白针叶木浆	2.3	0.12	0.009	0.000 4	4.39	0.24		
漂白非针叶木浆	2.16	0.12	0.019	0.001	1.72	0.10		
5. 半化学木浆	64.35	2.17	0.009	0.000 07	75.14	3.34		
6. 其他纸浆	4.54	0.017	2.1	0.19	10.16	0.41		
二、废纸	938.18	12.3	0.1	0.001 8	1 230	17.26		

表 157 我国纸、纸板、纸浆及废纸进口情况（2001—2004 年） 单位：万 t

项 目	2001 年	2002 年	2003 年	2004 年
进口纸和纸板	558	637	635	614
纸浆	490	526	603	732
废纸	642	687	938	1 230
耗材（亿美元）	64	70	82.33	96.87

表 158 我国印刷机械进出口统计（2004 年）

产品名称	单位	出口		进口	
		数量	金额	数量	金额
一、印前设备					
小计	台、万美元		3 242		4 688
激光照相排版设备	台、万美元				
其他照相排版及排字机器	台、万美元				
其他方法排字的机器、器具及设备	台、万美元	847	108	41	90
铸字机	台、万美元	286	25	38	85
制版机器、器具及设备	台、万美元	751	241	754	2 800
未列明铸字机或制版用的机器、器具及设备	台、万美元	246	25	183	82
铸字、排字或制版机的零件	kg、万美元	110 259	47	40 003	355
活字、印版、滚筒印刷用的版、片、筒等	kg、万美元	6 246 056	2 796	651 660	1 276
二、印刷机					
小计	台、万美元		21 310		156 302
卷曲进料式胶印机	台、万美元	105	2 136	106	16 861
办公室用片取式胶印机	台、万美元	30	3	85	132
平张纸进料式胶印机	台、万美元	386	634	1 052	63 146
未列名胶印机	台、万美元	784	181	142	1 707
卷曲进料式凸版印刷机	台、万美元	49	314	201	2 170
其他凸纸印刷机	台、万美元	248	219	358	1 615
苯胺印刷机	台、万美元	56	233	103	2 988
照相凹版印刷机	台、万美元	460	949	153	4 300
喷墨印刷机	台、万美元	8 592	4 899	11 279	7 090
圆网印刷机	台、万美元	185	318	168	1 789
平网印刷机	台、万美元	554	294	1 874	9 547
其他网式印刷机	台、万美元	463	306	971	4 231
其他未列名印刷机	台、万美元	176 284	6 686	25 466	24 789
印刷用辅助机器	台、万美元	8 114	1 278	2 698	4 853
印刷及印刷用辅助机器零件	kg、万美元	9 734 550	2 860	8 256 506	11 184
三、印后设备					
小计	台、万美元		2 882		13 071
锁线装订机	台、万美元	21 702	59	135	441
胶订机	台、万美元	207	131	252	917
其他书本装订机器	台、万美元	55 646	436	1 264	2 163
书本装订机的零件	kg、万美元	104 485	37	83 296	210
切纸机	台、万美元	876 156	1 850	6 779	8 465
制造包、袋和信封的机器	台、万美元	324	369	206	875
切纸机的零件	kg、万美元				
总计	**万美元**		**27 400**		**174 000**

表 159 我国中药行业进出口情况（2004—2005 年） 单位：亿美元、%

年份	行业	进出口		出口		进口	
		总额	同比增长（%）	总额	同比增长（%）	总额	同比增长（%）
2004	全国医药合计	199	29	107	31	90	26
	中药合计	9.5	15.3	7.25	17.6	2.26	8.6
2005	全国医药合计	256.91	29.1	138.10	29.07	118.81	32.01
	中药合计	10.7	12.62	8.30	14.55	2.40	6.43

表 160 我国橡胶工业制品出口量与出口额（2001—2003 年）

产品名称	单位	2001 年		2002 年		2003 年	
		出口量	出口额	出口量	出口额	出口量	出口额
新的充气橡胶轮胎	万条、万美元	11 072.84	100 261.6	13 390.53	121 837.7	15 778.05	160 764.1
轮胎内胎	万条、万美元	12 478.56	7 726.00	14 610.14	8 838.50	16 431.03	10 047.9
翻新轮胎	万条、万美元	1.44	22.80	2.19	46.70	1.89	43.60
汽车用旧轮胎	万条、万美元	1.68	8.60	34.47	13.90	9.12	11.40
实心或半实心轮胎，胎面及轮胎衬带	万条、万美元	979.06	1 040.70	12 457.14	1 477.80	15 324.75	2 033.20
橡胶输送带、三角带、传送带	t、万美元	26 111.21	6 299.70	28 302.58	6 256.00	37 969.28	8 605.30
橡胶卫生医疗用品	t、万美元	6 203.92	2 173.20		2 274.10	795.67	2 986.80
外科手套及其他手套	万双、万美元	113 329.34	7 718.5	137 044.2	8 791.9	201 481.1	13 086.8
橡胶杂件	t、万美元	88 189.74	22 486.50	113 707.26	27 624.6	146 624.78	34 753.1
橡胶管	t、万美元	13 936.03	2 739.9	14 792.99	3 134.9	19 789.64	4 523.6
橡胶医疗用衣着用品	t、万美元	1 120.98	424	1 315.06	472.9	1 296.41	633.6
未硫化橡胶板、片、带、及制品	t、万美元	13 284.38	1 504.2	61 188.73	6 243.3	22 729.32	2 738.7
硫化橡胶线、绳、板、片、带、及型材	t、万美元	23 067.15	2 553	28 326.59	2 977.8	47 157.82	4 533.9
硬质橡胶及制品		5 935.3	719.2	8 424.76	926	10 351.85	1 317.1
再生胶等	t、万美元	10 933.77	325.8				
胶鞋	万双、万美元	283 663.11	502 613.7	300 906.7	545 389	354 301.14	638 579.2
防水靴鞋		3 504.8	13 294.6	3 613.31	12 306	3 969.40	13 670.3
滑雪靴、防护鞋等		207 327.7	350 979.9	224 644.38	392 457.9	268 486.9	465 398.6
运动鞋、篮球鞋、网球鞋等		72 830.61	138 339.2	72 648.99	140 625.1	81 844.8	159 510.3

表 161 我国橡胶工业制品进口量与进口额（2001—2003 年）

产 品 名 称	单 位	2001 年		2002 年		2003 年	
		进口量	进口额	进口量	进口额	进口量	进口额
新的充气橡胶轮胎	万条、万美元	411.80	3 869.30	310.61	5 660.90	309.29	9 943.20
轮胎内胎	万条、万美元	414.27	231.40	203.89	122.10	140.96	108.20
翻新轮胎	万条、万美元	3.77	9.80	0.11	7.20		10.30
汽车用旧轮胎	万条、万美元	0.05	7.50	0.21	20.83	0.66	30.50
实心或半实心轮胎胎面及轮胎衬带	t、万美元	1 667.20	506.80	1 774.9	505.5	2 926.82	888.0
橡胶输送带、三角带、传动带	t、万美元	7 985.75	6 011.00	9 462.46	6 189.40	14 716.14	10 412.30
橡胶卫生医疗用品	t、万美元	639.47	867.90	862.34	974.10	823.08	913.20
外科手套及其他手套	万双、万美元	18 305.62	573.90	25 359.8	58.10	16 214.2	1 033.10
橡胶杂件	t、万美元	27 171.53	25 851.40	33 108.02	30 298.7	40 518.94	46 692.80
橡胶管	t、万美元	9 978.83	9 452.50	12 950.94	11 597.00	20 970.13	21 486.50
橡胶医疗用衣着用品	t、万美元	309.94	241.70	1 053.48	281.50	41.431.0	407.6
未硫化橡胶板、片、带、及制品	t、万美元	65 100.45	8 575.2	92 125.67	11 953.5	259 910.8	29 196.7
硫化橡胶板、线、绳、片、带、及型材	t、万美元	54 721.76	10 796.50	59 676.33	11 641.8	64 696.19	14 842.0
硬质橡胶及制品	t、万美元	2 287.56	842.4	2 587.21	1 102.6	1 865.46	1 228.80
再生胶等	t、万美元	3 442.46	267.40	8 498.23	461.80	72 734.97	3 556.50
胶鞋	万双、万美元	281.81	998.60	304.34	1 714.10	608.71	3 009.90
防水靴鞋		4.48	22.20	5.72	28.80	8.62	23.40
滑雪靴、防护鞋等		163.66	255.20	238.05	833.10	488.80	1 667.50
运动鞋、网球鞋、篮球鞋等		113.67	721.20	60.57	852.20	111.29	1 319.00

表 162 我国橡胶工业中轮胎细分产品进出口情况（2004 年）

产 品 名 称	进 口		出 口	
	数量（条）	金额（美元）	数量（条）	金额（美元）
机动小客车用新的充气橡胶轮胎	1 512 824	55 733 852	21 423 288	440 066 122
客车或货运机动车辆用新的充气橡胶轮胎	354 073	53 537 153	19 222 259	760 418 810
航空器用新的充气橡胶轮胎	32 643	10 905 807	1 139	446 378
农用车及机器用新人字型或类似胎面充气轮胎	86	25 608	2 685 530	18 095 085
建筑等用新人字型胎面充气轮胎≤61cm	279 697	1 009 467	4 707 802	12 892 501
其他新人字型或类似胎面充气橡胶轮胎	644	485 445	29 416	302 985
建筑等用新人字型胎面充气轮胎＞61cm	1 556	3 860 970	32 350	8 170 163
其他农用车及机器用新的充气橡胶轮胎	2 062	100 632	887 995	2 154 687
其他建筑搬运车辆等用新充气轮胎钢圈≤61cm	2 593	677 297	17 581	415 166
其他建筑搬运车等用新充气轮胎钢圈＞61cm	4 479	4 656 724	3 512	809 990
未列名新的充气橡胶轮胎	64 026	10 203 036	7 765 783	48 746 996
客车、货运机动车辆用橡胶内胎	116 831	593 032	13 581 384	18 895 681
航空器用橡胶内胎	14	1 066	614	24 378
未列名橡胶内胎	205 953	244 255	10 402 491	7 655 461
总 计	**2 577 481**	**142 034 344**	**80 761 144**	**1 319 094 403**

表 163 我国橡胶工业橡胶机械进出口情况（2004 年）

产品	进口		出口	
	数量（万 t）	金额（万美元）	数量（万 t）	金额（万美元）
充气轮胎模塑或翻新及内胎模塑成型机器	112	233.63	207	5 658.00
其他挤出机	1 526	4 129.87	1 755	37 975.94
其他橡胶加工机器	490 273	12 183.76	8 093	84 616.75
合　计	**491 911**	**16 547.26**	**10 055**	**128 250.69**

表 164 我国天然橡胶、合成橡胶进口情况（2001—2003 年）

产品	2001 年		2002 年		2003 年	
	数量（万 t）	金额（万美元）	数量（万 t）	金额（万美元）	数量（万 t）	金额（万美元）
天然橡胶	98	57 231	95.6	69 449.7	120.31	115 510.2
合成橡胶	75	79 411	91.52	93 947.5	100.61	115 247.8

农产品加工业部分行业与企业排序

表 165 2004 年轻工业系统农产品加工业分行业主要经济指标

序号	按工业总产值排序：行业	工业总产值（亿元）	行业占轻工系统比重（%）	序号	按工业销售产值排序：行业	工业销售产值（亿元）	行业占轻工系统比重（%）
	全国轻工行业合计	**37 376.1**	**100**		**全国轻工行业合计**	**36 506.7**	**100**
1	农副食品加工业	8 052.4	21.54	1	农副食品加工业	7 888.3	21.61
2	造纸及制品业	3 143.6	8.41	2	造纸及制品业	3 061.6	8.39
3	食品制造业	2 844.3	7.61	3	食品制造业	2 760.4	7.56
4	皮革、毛皮、羽（绒）及其制品业	2 718.3	7.27	4	皮革、毛皮、羽（绒）及其制品业	2 653.6	7.27
5	饮料制造业	2 557.4	6.84	5	饮料制造业	2 524.5	6.92
6	家具制造业	947.2	2.53	6	家具制造业	929.9	2.55
7	木竹藤棕草制品业	186.4	0.50	7	木竹藤棕草制品业	179.4	0.49
8	制盐	124.5	0.33	8	制盐	126.7	0.35

序号	按利税总额排序：行业	利税总额（亿元）	行业占轻工系统比重（%）	序号	按利润总额排序：行业	利润总额（亿元）	行业占轻工系统比重（%）
	全国轻工行业合计	**2 762.1**	**100**		**全国轻工行业合计**	**1 566.7**	**100**
1	饮料制造业	447.4	16.20	1	饮料制造业	234	14.93
2	农副食品加工业	360.9	13.07	2	农副食品加工业	170.3	10.87
3	造纸及制品业	260.2	9.42	3	造纸及制品业	141.1	9.00
4	食品制造业	241.5	8.74	4	食品制造业	132.6	8.46
5	皮革、毛皮、羽（绒）及其制品业	161.6	5.85	5	皮革、毛皮、羽（绒）及其制品业	99.0	6.32
6	家具制造业	59.7	2.16	6	家具制造业	39.9	2.54
7	制盐	22.1	0.80	7	制盐	7.8	0.50
8	木竹藤棕草制品业	11.9	0.43	8	木竹藤棕草制品业	6.5	0.41

（续）

序号	按出口交货值排序			序号	按产品销售收入排序		
	行业	出口交货值（亿元）	行业占轻工系统比重（%）		行业	产品销售收入（亿元）	行业占轻工系统比重（%）
	全国轻工行业合计	**9 339.4**	**100**		**全国轻工行业合计**	**35 814.1**	**100**
1	皮革、毛皮、羽（绒）及其制品业	1 427.3	15.28	1	饮料制造业	7 810.9	21.81
2	农副食品加工业	868.4	9.30	2	食品加工业	2 988.5	8.34
3	家具制造业	461.3	4.94	3	造纸及制品业	2 688.9	7.51
4	食品制造业	282.6	3.03	4	食品制造业	2 577.2	7.20
5	造纸及制品业	206.3	2.21	5	皮革、毛皮、羽（绒）及其制品业	2 434.6	6.80
6	饮料制造业	84.5	0.90	6	家具制造业	902.2	2.52
7	木竹藤棕草制品业	81.3	0.87	7	木竹藤棕草制品业	174.9	0.49
8	制盐	5.3	0.06	8	制盐	125.9	0.35

序号	按资产总计排序			序号	按全部从业人员平均人数排序		
	行业	资产总计（亿元）	行业占轻工系统比重（%）		行业	从业人员（万人）	行业占轻工系统比重（%）
	全国轻工行业合计	**30 869.8**	**100**		**全国轻工行业合计**	**1 514.7**	**100**
1	农副食品加工业	4 843.2	15.69	1	农副食品加工业	190.9	12.60
2	造纸及制品业	3 728.0	12.08	2	皮革、毛皮、羽（绒）及其制品业	181.9	12.01
3	饮料制造业	3 381.8	10.96	3	造纸及制品业	118.0	7.79
4	食品制造业	2 638.7	8.55	4	食品制造业	106.9	7.06
5	皮革、毛皮、羽（绒）及其制品业	1 669.8	5.41	5	饮料制造业	89.1	5.88
6	家具制造业	769.4	2.49	6	家具制造业	52.8	3.49
7	制盐	255.8	0.83	7	木竹藤棕草制品业	13.4	0.88
8	木竹藤棕草制品业	104.1	0.34	8	制盐	12.3	0.81

表166 2004年轻工业系统农产品加工业分行业进出口总额

序号	按出口总额排序		序号	按进口总额排序	
	行业	出口总额（亿美元）		行业	进口总额（亿美元）
	全国轻工行业合计	**1 576.67**		**全国轻工行业合计**	**490.31**
1	皮革、毛皮及其制品业	274.12	1	食品饮料制造业	94.37
2	食品饮料制造业	152.14	2	制浆造纸业	93.30
3	家具制造业	103.53	3	皮革、毛皮及其制品业	38.84
4	林制品及其他天然植物制品	27.41	4	轻工机械	36.07
5	制浆造纸业	13.14	5	家具制造业	7.26
6	轻工机械	6.55	6	制盐	0.72
7	制盐	0.35	7	林制品及其他天然植物制品	0.50

表 167　2004 年我国白酒制造业销售收入前 10 名企业

单位：亿元

序号	企业名称	销售收入	同比增长（%）
1	四川省宜宾五粮液集团有限公司	138.10	13.96
2	中国贵州茅台酒厂（集团）有限责任公司	32.67	21.20
3	四川剑南春集团有限责任公司	20.26	16.34
4	泸州老窖集团有限责任公司	19.47	17.74
5	山西省杏花村汾酒集团公司	15.15	28.70
6	安徽省古井集团有限责任公司	14.11	26.26
7	四川沱牌集团有限公司	9.23	0.01
8	四川全兴股份有限公司	7.95	－13.72
9	湖北枝江酒业股份有限公司	7.18	11.99
10	安徽口子窖酒业股份有限公司	5.69	16.20

表 168　2004 年我国白酒行业创利税前 10 名企业

单位：亿元

序号	企业名称	利税总额	同比增长（%）
1	四川省宜宾五粮液集团有限公司	38.16	12.04
2	中国贵州茅台酒厂（集团）有限责任公司	24.10	40.99
3	四川剑南春集团有限责任公司	8.76	25.97
4	山西省杏花村汾酒集团公司	4.32	11.88
5	泸州老窖集团有限责任公司	4.12	9.02
6	四川全兴股份有限公司	2.89	848.94
7	北京红星股份有限公司	2.33	－0.40
8	安徽古井集团股份有限公司	2.18	－12.44
9	内蒙古河套酒业集团股份有限公司	2.07	28.15
10	四川沱牌集团有限公司	2.01	－2.49

表 169　2004 年我国白酒行业白酒产量前 10 名企业

序号	企业名称	产量（kL）	同比增长（%）
1	四川省宜宾五粮液集团有限公司	134 487	－27.26
2	四川剑南春集团有限责任公司	58 035	14.57
3	四川沱牌集团有限公司	54 121	4.44
4	湖北枝江酒业股份有限公司	48 622	32.52
5	泸州老窖集团有限责任公司	46 696	－13.52
6	沈阳妈妈街酒业有限公司	42 550	－5.33
7	山东天府集团公司	42 476	36.58
8	山西省杏花村汾酒集团公司	37 936	－1.98
9	北京红星股份有限公司	37 235	－5.61
10	北京顺鑫农业股份有限公司牛栏山酒厂	35 879	35.47

表 170　2004 年我国啤酒企业自产麦芽和专业麦芽企业产品销售情况

序号	企业名称	产品销售收入（万元）	序号	企业名称	产品销售收入（万元）
1	大连中粮麦芽有限公司	253 000	7	山东江海麦芽有限公司	120 000
2	大连兴泽制麦有限公司	188 000	8	烟台市麦芽厂	75 000
3	广州麦芽有限公司	180 000	9	永顺泰（宝定）麦芽有限公司	58 139
4	青岛啤酒股份有限公司麦芽公司	159 561	10	欧麦宝定麦芽有限公司	50 000
5	宁波麦芽有限公司	140 000	11	兰州黄河企业集团公司	34 300
6	北京燕京啤酒集团公司	131 693	12	济南卢堡啤酒有限公司麦芽公司	7 645

表 171　2004 年我国啤酒产量 20 万千升以上企业

序号	企业名称	产量（kL）	序号	企业名称	产量（kL）
1	青岛啤酒集团有限公司	3 691 337	12	三得利啤酒（上海）有限公司	306 766
2	华润雪花啤酒（中国）有限公司	3 128 306	13	山东银表啤酒有限公司	246 070
3	北京燕京啤酒集团公司	2 849 862	14	百威（武汉）国际啤酒有限公司	244 116
4	哈尔滨啤酒有限公司	1 298 781	15	烟台啤酒朝日有限公司	235 817
5	河南金星啤酒集团有限公司	1 225 968	16	四平金士百啤酒有限公司	229 592
6	重庆啤酒（集团）有限责任公司	1 115 966	17	宁波金狮啤酒有限公司	215 231
7	广州市珠江啤酒集团公司	1 057 504	18	浙江石梁啤酒有限公司	213 365
8	福建雪津啤酒有限公司	726 746	19	江苏大富豪啤酒有限公司	211 948
9	金狮啤酒集团有限公司	432 066	20	杭州西湖啤酒朝日有限公司	204 396
10	湖北金龙泉啤酒集团公司	406 935	21	河南维雪啤酒有限公司	200 230
11	深圳金威啤酒有限公司	388 633			

表 172　2004 年我国啤酒销售收入 3 亿元以上企业

序号	企业名称	销售收入（万元）	序号	企业名称	销售收入（万元）
1	青岛啤酒集团有限公司	888 037	14	山东银麦啤酒股份有限公司	54 398
2	北京燕京啤酒集团公司	677 542	15	烟台啤酒朝日有限公司	48 378
3	华润雪花啤酒（中国）有限公司	508 634	16	蓝带集团股份有限公司	47 501
4	广州市珠江啤酒集团公司	270 866	17	宁波金狮啤酒有限公司	38 055
5	重庆啤酒（集团）有限责任公司	234 806	18	浙江石梁啤酒有限公司	37 518
6	金星啤酒集团有限公司	222 268	19	江苏大富豪啤酒有限公司	37 455
7	百威（武汉）国际啤酒有限公司	191 363	20	亚洲太平洋酿酒有限公司	35 567
8	哈尔滨啤酒集团有限公司	190 825	21	杭州西湖啤酒朝日（股份）有限公司	35 394
9	福建雪津啤酒有限公司	151 234	22	兰州黄河嘉酿啤酒有限公司	35 301
10	深圳金威啤酒有限公司	102 431	23	四平金士百啤酒有限公司	35 245
11	三得利啤酒（上海）有限公司	81 283	24	济南卢堡啤酒有限公司	34 283
12	金狮啤酒集团有限公司	76 197	25	河南维雪啤酒有限公司	34 188
13	湖北金龙泉啤酒集团公司	60 513	26	新疆乌苏啤酒有限责任公司	30 204

表 173　2004 年我国啤酒创利税总额亿元以上企业

序号	企业名称	利税总额（万元）	序号	企业名称	利税总额（万元）
1	青岛啤酒集团有限公司	223 149	12	上海三得利啤酒有限公司	20 525
2	北京燕京啤酒集团公司	164 889	13	湖北金龙泉啤酒集团公司	16 468
3	华润雪花啤酒（中国）集团公司	156 844	14	新疆乌苏啤酒有限责任公司	14 465
4	重庆啤酒（集团）有限责任公司	93 296	15	德州克代尔集团有限公司	14 801
5	广州市珠江啤酒集团公司	79 327	16	大连大雪企业集团啤酒有限公司	13 231
6	福建雪津啤酒集团公司	68 399	17	烟台啤酒集团有限公司	13 023
7	金星啤酒集团有限公司	61 586	18	宁波金狮啤酒有限公司	12 042
8	哈尔滨啤酒（集团）有限公司	59 692	19	江苏大富豪啤酒有限公司	11 695
9	百威（武汉）国际啤酒集团公司	53 903	20	浙江石梁啤酒有限公司	10 809
10	深圳金威啤酒有限公司	35 871	21	杭州西湖啤酒朝日（股份）有限公司	10 759
11	金狮啤酒集团有限公司	23 868	22	山东银麦啤酒股份有限公司	10 272

表 174　2004 年我国葡萄酒产量居行业中前 10 名的省、自治区、直辖市

地区	产量（万 kL）	占全国总产量的百分比（%）
山东	15.12	41.5
河北	6.65	18.1
天津	3.44	9.3
新疆	3.01	8.2
吉林	2.24	6.1
北京	1.48	4.0
河南	1.00	2.7
甘肃	0.59	1.6
云南	0.44	1.2
陕西	0.42	1.1

注：2004 年 10 省、自治区、直辖市葡萄酒产量，占全国总产量的 93.8%。

表 175　2004 年我国葡萄酒行业产量、效益名列前茅的省

地区	产量总计（万 kL）	资产总计（亿元）	销售收入（亿元）	利润总额（亿元）	税金总额（亿元）
山东	15.12	39.4	41	5.5	4.4
河北	6.65	22.7	11	0.94	1.7
占全国比例（%）	60	51	70	76	65

表 176　2004 年我国饮料行业按产量排序前 9 名企业

序号	企业名称	序号	企业名称
1	杭州娃哈哈集团有限公司	6	上海梅林正广和（集团）有限公司
2	农夫山泉股份有限公司	7	椰树集团有限公司
3	乐百氏（广东）食品饮料有限公司	8	深圳达能益力泉饮品有限公司
4	北京汇源饮料食品集团有限公司	9	露露集团有限责任公司
5	怡宝食品饮料（深圳）有限公司		

表 177　2005/2006 年度我国纺织工业各行业“企业竞争力”前 10 名企业

企业名称	企业名称
棉纺织	
山东华乐纺织股份有限公司	华芳集团有限公司
山东岱银纺织集团股份有限公司	安徽华茂集团有限公司
山东德棉集团有限公司	河南新野纺织股份有限公司
山东魏桥创业集团有限公司	泰丰纺织集团
天虹纺织集团有限公司	浙江华孚集团有限公司
无锡市第一棉纺织厂	富丽达集团控股有限公司
东营市天信纺织有限公司	鲁泰纺织股份有限公司
兰雁集团股份有限公司	黑牡丹（集团）股份有限公司
宁波百隆纺织有限公司	福建嘉达纺织股份有限公司
石家庄常山纺织集团有限责任公司	襄樊三五四二纺织总厂
毛纺织　毛针织	
上海春竹企业发展有限公司	江苏倪家巷集团有限公司
山东如意科技集团有限公司	江苏振阳集团
内蒙古鄂尔多斯羊绒集团有限责任公司	江苏澳洋实业（集团）有限公司
北京雪莲毛纺织服装集团公司	浙江新澳集团
江苏阳光集团有限公司	维信（内蒙古）羊绒股份有限公司
丝绸	
万事利集团有限公司	达利（中国）有限公司
广东省丝绸（集团）公司	杭州金富春丝绸化纤有限公司
江苏吴江丝绸集团有限公司	浙江喜欣丝绸股份有限公司
江苏富安茧丝绸股份有限公司	深圳华丝企业股份有限公司
江苏新民纺织科技股份有限公司	鑫缘茧丝绸集团股份有限公司
麻纺	
山西绿洲纺织有限责任公司	铜陵华源麻业有限公司
江苏泛佳亚麻纺织厂有限公司	湖北银泉纺织股份有限公司
哈尔滨继佳纺织有限公司	湖南洞庭苎麻纺织印染厂
浙江金达创业股份有限公司	湖南益鑫泰麻业服装实业有限公司
浙江金鹰集团有限公司	新申集团
化纤	
万杰集团有限责任公司	吉林化纤集团有限责任公司
山东海龙股份有限公司	青岛中达化纤有限公司
广东开平春晖股份有限公司	神马实业股份有限公司
广东新会美达锦纶股份有限公司	桐昆集团股份有限公司
中国石化上海石油化工股份有限公司	浙江恒逸集团有限公司

（续）

针织	
企业名称	企业名称
上海三枪集团有限公司	武汉猫人服饰股份有限公司
北京铜牛针织集团有限责任公司	青岛即发集团控股有限公司
宁波申洲针织有限公司	浙江宏达经编股份有限公司
江苏东渡纺织集团有限公司	富润控股集团有限公司
江苏 AB 集团有限责任公司	福建凤竹纺织科技股份有限公司
印染	
企业名称	企业名称
山东大海集团有限公司	浙江大和纺织、印染服装（集团）有限公司
华纺股份有限公司	浙江永通染织集团有限公司
江苏紫荆花纺织科技股份有限公司	浙江美欣达印染集团股份有限公司
佛山南方印染股份有限公司	浙江航民实业集团有限公司
青岛凤凰印染有限公司	浙江稽山印染有限公司
服装	
企业名称	企业名称
伟星集团有限公司	美特斯邦威集团有限公司
庄吉集团有限公司	海澜集团公司
红豆集团有限公司	森马列集团有限公司
报喜鸟集团有限公司	雅戈尔集团股份有限公司
波司登股份有限公司	福建柒牌集团有限公司

资料来源：此名单由中国纺织工业协会及各专业协会于 2006 年 4 月 27 日发布，表中排名不分前后，以汉字笔画为序。

表 178　2005/2006 年度我国纺织工业出口前 100 名企业

排序	企业名称	排序	企业名称
1	福田实业（集团）有限公司	15	内蒙古鄂尔多斯羊绒集团有限责任公司
2	山东魏桥创业集团有限公司	16	维科控股集团股份有限公司
3	中国华源集团有限公司	17	山东如意科技集团有限公司
4	东莞德永佳纺织制衣有限公司	18	浙江嘉欣丝绸股份有限公司
5	浙江永通染织集团有限公司	19	孚日家纺股份有限公司
6	广东省丝绸（集团）公司	20	宁波百隆纺织有限公司
7	宁波申洲针织有限公司	21	上海汉森投资发展有限公司
8	青岛即发集团控股有限公司	22	宜兴乐祺纺织印染集团有限公司
9	互太（番禺）纺织印染有限公司	23	维信（内蒙古）羊绒股份有限公司
10	江苏阳光集团有限公司	24	江苏东渡纺织集团有限公司
11	鲁泰纺织股份有限公司	25	黑牡丹（集团）股份有限公司
12	上海华申国际企业（集团）有限公司	26	雅戈尔集团股份有限公司
13	波司登股份有限公司	27	宁波布利杰针织集团有限公司
14	华芳集团有限公司	28	江苏澳洋实业（集团）有限公司

（续）

排序	企 业 名 称	排序	企 业 名 称
29	宁波太平鸟投资集团有限公司	65	宁波众鑫印染有限公司
30	湖北美尔雅集团有限公司	66	番禺潭州振裕纺织染印有限公司
31	深圳华丝企业股份有限公司	67	杉杉投资股份有限公司
32	天龙控股集团有限公司	68	七海（广东）织染厂有限公司
33	浙江美欣达印染集团股份有限公司	69	山东大海集团股份有限公司
34	浙江华孚集团股份有限公司	70	广东新会美锦纶股份有限公司
35	华纺股份有限公司	71	浙江金达创业股份有限公司
36	浙江湖州大港纺织印染集团有限公司	72	浙江稽山印染有限公司
37	山东亚光纺织集团	73	山东省艺达有限公司
38	红豆集团有限公司	74	浙江新天龙工贸有限公司
39	兰雁集团股份有限公司	75	江苏大生集团股份有限公司
40	恒柏集团有限公司	76	湖北裕波纺织集团股份有限公司
41	江苏梦兰集团公司	77	浙江大和纺织印染服装（集团）有限公司
42	江苏红柳床单集团有限公司	78	淮北印染集团公司
43	内蒙古鹿王羊绒有限公司	79	铜陵华源麻业有限公司
44	江苏老三集团有限公司	80	浙江金鹰集团有限公司
45	湛江纺织企业（集团）公司	81	浙江天马实业股份有限公司
46	邯郸海盛威纺织印染有限公司	82	无锡洛社印染有限公司
47	仪证化纤股份有限公司	83	浙江巴欠领带有限公司
48	达利（中国）有限公司	84	浙江真爱集团有限公司
49	宁波博洋家纺有限公司	85	宁波雅戈尔日中纺织印染有限公司
50	宁波狮丹努集团有限公司	86	泰丰纺织集团
51	烟台北方家用纺织品股份有限公司	87	中山侨光纺织有限公司
52	山东维尔纺织集团股份有限公司	88	浙江芬莉袜业有限公司
53	浙江巨鹰集团股份有限公司	89	浙江袜业有限公司
54	云蝠服饰股份有限公司	90	山东桑莎制衣集团
55	无锡市第一棉纺织厂	91	浙江丝得莉集团有限公司
56	河南新野纺织股份有限公司	92	三元控股集团有限公司
57	辽宁时代集团熊岳印染有限责任公司	93	中国纺织机械（集团）有限公司
58	宁波宏利集团有限公司	94	厦门翔鹭化纤股份有限公司
59	浙江天翔羽绒集团有限公司	95	江苏鹿港毛纺集团限公司
60	江苏联发集团股份有限公司	96	宁波明达针织有限公司
61	山东云龙绣品有限公司	97	山东德棉集团有限公司
62	张家港市纱洲纺织印染进出口有限公司	98	安徽皖维集团有限责任公司
63	喜迎门集团公司	99	新乡白鹭化纤集团有限责任公司
64	青岛凤凰印染有限公司	100	南阳纺织集团有限公司

表179 2005年度我国纺织工业主营业务收入前100名企业

排序	企业名称	排序	企业名称
1	山东魏桥创业集团有限公司	51	广东开平春晖股份有限公司
2	中国石油化工有限公司天津分公司	52	宁波申洲针织有限公司
3	广东省丝绸（集团）公司	53	山东大海集团有限公司
4	雅戈尔集团股份有限公司	54	美特斯邦威集团有限公司
5	中国华源集团有限公司	55	鲁泰纺织股份有限公司
6	江苏阳光集团有限公司	56	福建柒牌集团有限公司
7	仪征化纤股份有限公司	57	互太（番禺）纺织印染有限公司
8	江苏三房巷集团有限公司	58	浙江翔盛集团有限公司
9	红豆集团有限公司	59	山东海龙股份有限公司
10	浙江恒逸集团有限公司	60	喜盈门集团公司
11	华芳集团有限公司	61	江苏虎豹集团公司
12	浙江远东化纤集团	62	恒柏集团有限公司
13	桐昆集团股份有限公司	63	江苏大生集团有限公司
14	中国石化上海石油化工股份有限公司	64	维信（内蒙古）羊绒股份有限公司
15	杉杉投资股份有限公司	65	富丽达控股有限公司
16	中国纺织机械（集团）有限公司	66	神马实业股份有限公司
17	荣盛化纤集团有限公司	67	天龙控股集团有限公司
18	福田实业（集团）有限公司	68	江苏新雅鹿集团有限公司
19	海澜集团公司	69	伟星集团有限公司
20	波司登股份有限公司	70	森马集团有限公司
21	维科控股集团有限公司	71	大扬集团有限公司
22	上海申达（集团）有限公司	72	报喜鸟集团有限公司
23	江苏恒力化纤有限公司	73	泰丰纺织集团
24	江苏梦兰集团	74	河南新野纺织股份有限公司
25	内蒙古鄂尔多斯羊绒集团有限责任公司	75	广东新会美达锦纶股份有限公司
26	万杰集团有限责任公司	76	宁波太平鸟投资集团有限公司
27	宁波百隆纺织有限公司	77	桐乡市凤鸣合纤有限公司
28	浙江赐富化纤集团有限公司	78	山东亚光纺织集团
29	山东如意科技集团有限公司	79	山东岱银纺织集团股份有限公司
30	江苏澳洋实业（集团）有限公司	80	浙江华鼎集团有限责任公司
31	浙江永通染织集团有限公司	81	宁波洛兹集团有限公司
32	青岛即发集团控股有限公司	82	湖南华升工贸进出口（集团）公司
33	浙江华孚集团有限公司	83	浙江湖州大港纺织印染集团有限公司
34	吉林化纤集团有限责任公司	84	新乡白鹭化纤集团有限公司
35	江苏华西集团公司	85	安徽华茂集团有限公司
36	东莞德永佳纺织制衣有限公司	86	宁波博洋家纺有限公司
37	浙江红剑集团有限公司	87	南阳纺织集团有限公司
38	孚日家纺股份有限公司	88	山西三维集团股份有限公司
39	江苏倪家巷集团有限公司	89	浙江嘉欣丝绸股份有限公司
40	石家庄常山纺织集团有限责任公司	90	江西涤纶厂
41	浙江化纤联合集团有限公司	91	浙江金鹰集团有限公司
42	厦门翔鹭化纤股份有限公司	92	江苏老三集团有限公司
43	庄吉代集团有限公司	93	江苏华亚化纤有限公司
44	浙江航民实业集团有限公司	94	三元控股集团有限公司
45	上海华申国际（集团）有限公司	95	张家港市欣欣化纤有限公司
46	江苏吴江丝绸集团有限公司	96	湖北美尔雅集团有限公司
47	天虹纺织集团有限公司	97	兰雁集团股份有限公司
48	山东德棉集团有限公司	98	华纺股份有限公司
49	浙江美欣达印染集团股份有限公司	99	东营市天信纺织有限公司
50	中国石化集团四川维尼轮厂	100	黑牡丹（集团）股份有限公司

表 180　2005 年度我国纺织工业毛纺织毛针织行业主营业务收入前 50 名企业

排序	企业名称	排序	企业名称
1	江苏阳光集团有限公司	26	江苏汇丰羊绒有限公司
2	内蒙古鄂尔多斯集团有限责任公司	27	江苏蝶美集团有限公司
3	山东如意科技集团有限公司	28	常州市毛条厂有限公司
4	江苏澳洋实业（集团）有限公司	29	宁波中鑫毛纺集团公司
5	江西华西集团公司	30	内蒙古双河羊绒集团有限公司
6	江苏倪家巷集团有限公司	31	湖北仙桃毛纺织集团有限公司
7	维信（内蒙古）羊绒股份有限公司	32	肇庆市昆庆毛绒厂有限公司
8	北京雪莲毛纺服装集团公司	33	中山侨光纺织有限公司
9	内蒙古鹿王羊绒（集团）公司	34	无锡协新集团有限公司
10	天宇毛工业（张家港保税区）有限公司	35	江苏灵丰纺织集团有限公司
11	浙江新澳集团	36	山东南山实业股份有限公司
12	嘉兴市兔皇羊绒有限公司	37	广东美雅集团股份有限公司
13	云蝠服饰股份有限公司	38	江苏箭鹿毛纺股份有限公司
14	江苏港洋实业股份有限公司	39	兰州三毛纺织（集团）有限责任公司
15	内蒙古东达羊绒制品有限公司	40	上海瀛春毛纺织有限公司
16	浙江华源兰宝有限公司	41	广东联发毛纺织有限公司
17	江苏振阳集团	42	上海申一毛条有限公司
18	江苏鹿港毛纺集团有限公司	43	宁夏圣雪绒国际企业集团有限公司
19	浙江正兴集团有限公司	44	上海三毛企业集团股份有限公司
20	宁夏马斯特羊绒集团	45	青岛韩一华瑞纺织有限公司
21	浙江真爱集团有限公司	46	上海欣红纺织有限公司
22	上海春竹企业发展有限公司	47	包头富华羊绒衫有限公司
23	常州三毛纺织集团有限公司	48	北京东方叶扬纺织有限公司
24	张家港普坤纺织实业有限公司	49	潍坊名羊毛纺服饰有限责任公司
25	张家港保税区澳丰毛纺有限公司	50	上海华丰寰宇企业发展有限公司

表 181　2005 年度我国纺织工业针织行业主营业务收入前 50 名企业

排序	企业名称	排序	企业名称
1	福田实业（集团）有限公司	15	浙江海利得新材料股份有限公司
2	青岛即发集团控股有限公司	16	浙江芬莉袜业有限公司
3	东莞德永佳纺织制衣有限公司	17	浙江巨鹰集团股份有限公司
4	宁波申州针织有限公司	18	浙江永利经编股份有限公司
5	江苏老三集团有限公司	19	宁波狮丹努集团有限公司
6	宁波市布利杰针织集团有限公司	20	浙江袜业有限公司
7	江苏东渡纺织集团有限公司	21	浪莎针织有限公司
8	上海三枪集团有限公司	22	浙江梦娜针织袜业有限公司
9	浙江加佰利控股集团有限公司	23	武汉猫人服饰股份有限公司
10	北京铜牛针织集团有限责任公司	24	宁波宏利集团有限公司
11	承德帝贤针织集团股份有限公司	25	雄鹰针织品印染（常熟）有限公司
12	富润控股集团有限公司	26	常州市顶呱呱棉服饰有限公司
13	武汉爱帝集团有限公司	27	南京中脉科技发展有限公司
14	江苏 AB 集团有限责任公司	28	宁波康尔针织制衣有限公司

（续）

排序	企业名称	排序	企业名称
29	南通海林集团有限公司	40	海宁德俊织染集团有限公司
30	福建凤竹纺织科技股份有限公司	41	山东滨州春晓针织制衣集团有限公司
31	宁波明达针织有限公司	42	青岛华金染织有限公司
32	上海嘉乐股份有限公司	43	山东青情集团有限公司
33	江苏兰瑞针织有限公司	44	青岛雪达集团有限公司
34	浙江宏达经编股份有限公司	45	山东兰凤针织集团有限公司
35	江苏爱娇集团	46	招远市针织厂有限公司
36	诸暨步人袜业有限公司	47	宁波甬南针织有限公司
37	浙江宝娜斯袜业有限公司	48	常熟凯兰针织有限公司
38	中山华泰纺织有限公司	49	浙江顺时针织服饰有限公司
39	浙江正元集团有限公司	50	宁波富宏针织有限公司

表 182　2005 年度我国纺织工业丝绸行业主营业务收入前 30 名企业

排序	企业名称	排序	企业名称
1	广东省丝绸（集团）有限公司	16	浙江虹绢丝绸集团有限公司
2	江苏吴江丝绸集团有限公司	17	浙江新昌达利发丝绸有限公司
3	浙江嘉欣丝绸股份有限公司	18	四川南充六合（集团）有限责任公司
4	万事利集团有限公司	19	吴江工艺织造厂
5	浙江丝得莉集团有限公司	20	无锡鼎球绢丝纺有限公司
6	鑫缘茧丝绸集团股份有限公司	21	江苏华佳丝绸有限公司
7	江苏新民纺织科技股份有限公司	22	山东天力丝绸有限公司
8	深圳华丝企业股份有限公司	23	江苏泗绢集团有限公司
9	浙江巴贝领带有限公司	24	江苏富安茧丝绸股份有限公司
10	达利（中国）有限公司	25	浙江三环丝绸股份有限公司
11	成都天友发展有限公司	26	浙江恒越绢纺有限公司
12	浙江华源丝业有限公司	27	云南千佛茧丝绸集团有限公司
13	杭州金富春丝绸化纤有限公司	28	四川新世纪丝绸实业有限公司
14	海安县恒源丝绸集团有限公司	29	海宁市海涓纺织有限责任公司
15	浙江天松集团有限公司	30	山东锦冠丝业有限责任公司

表 183　2005 年度我国纺织工业棉纺（色）织行业主营业务收入前 50 名企业

排序	企业名称	排序	企业名称
1	山东魏桥纺织集团有限责任公司	10	鲁泰纺织股份有限公司
2	华芳集团有限公司	11	江苏大生集团有限公司
3	上海申达（集团）有限公司	12	富丽达集团控股有限公司
4	宁波百隆纺织有限公司	13	泰丰纺织集团
5	浙江华孚集团有限公司	14	河南新野纺织集团股份有限公司
6	石家庄常山纺织集团有限责任公司	15	山东岱银纺织集团股份有限公司
7	上海华申国际企业（集团）有限公司	16	安徽华茂集团有限公司
8	天虹纺织集团有限公司	17	南阳纺织集团有限公司
9	山东德棉集团有限公司	18	兰雁集团股份有限公司

（续）

排序	企业名称	排序	企业名称
19	东营市天信纺织有限公司	35	江苏裕纶纺织集团有限公司
20	黑牡丹（集团）股份有限公司	36	北京京棉集团有限责任公司
21	山东华乐纺织股份有限公司	37	太仓利泰纺织厂有限公司
22	无锡市第一棉纺织厂	38	武汉江南实业集团有限公司
23	江苏向阳集团有限公司	39	宁波雅戈尔日中纺织印染有限公司
24	邯郸海盛威纺织印染集团有限公司	40	江苏通裕纺织集团有限公司
25	洛阳白马集团有限责任公司	41	湛江纺织企业（集团）公司
26	湖南东信集团有限公司	42	天津纺织集团天一有限公司
27	江苏联发集团股份有限公司	43	武汉一棉集团有限公司
28	弘生集团	44	帛方纺织有限公司
29	湖北孝棉实业集团有限责任公司	45	河北衡水达大集团有限公司
30	湖北裕波纺织集团股份有限公司	46	江苏双山集团股份有限公司
31	山东樱花纺织集团有限公司	47	开平奔达纺织印染集团有限公司
32	福建南纺股份有限公司	48	邢台方圆纺织印染集团有限公司
33	山东滨州环宇纺织集团有限责任公司	49	柳州立宇集团有限责任公司
34	襄樊三五四二纺织总厂	50	临清三和纺织集团有限公司

表 184　2005 年度我国纺织工业化纤行业主营业务收入前 50 名企业

排序	企业名称	排序	企业名称
1	中国石油化工股份有限公司天津分公司	26	江苏华亚化纤有限公司
2	仪征化纤股份有限公司	27	张家港市欣欣化纤有限公司
3	江苏三房巷集团有限公司	28	安徽皖维集团有限责任公司
4	浙江恒逸集团有限公司	29	山东高密银鹭化纤有限公司
5	浙江远东化纤集团	30	唐山三友集团化纤有限公司
6	桐昆集团股份有限公司	31	浙江大普集团有限公司
7	中国石化上海石油化工股份有限公司	32	烟台氨纶集团有限公司
8	荣盛化纤集团有限公司	33	济南正昊化纤新材料有限公司
9	江苏恒力化纤有限公司	34	黑龙江龙涤集团有限公司
10	万杰集团有限责任公司	35	张家港市中港特种化纤厂
11	浙江赐富化纤集团有限公司	36	东丽合成纤维（南通）有限公司
12	吉林化纤集团有限责任公司	37	秦皇岛奥莱腈纶有限公司
13	浙江红剑集团有限公司	38	南京化纤股份有限公司
14	浙江化纤联合集团有限公司	39	云南云维股份有限公司
15	厦门翔鹭化纤股份有限公司	40	丹东化学纤维股份有限公司
16	中国石化集团四川维尼纶厂	41	湖南省湘维有限公司
17	广东开平春晖股份有限公司	42	福建纺织化纤集团有限公司
18	浙江翔盛集团有限公司	43	江苏金达来集团公司
19	山东海龙股份有限公司	44	湖南金迪化纤有限责任公司
20	神马实业股份有限公司	45	保定天鹅化纤集团有限公司
21	广东新会美达锦纶股份有限公司	46	湖北新丰化纤工业有限公司
22	桐乡市凤鸣合纤有限公司	47	浙江富丽达纤维有限公司
23	新乡白鹭化纤集团有限责任公司	48	岳阳巴陵石化化工化纤有限公司
24	山西三维集团股份有限公司	49	浙江华峰氨纶股份有限公司
25	江西涤纶厂	50	海盐华明化纤有限公司

表 185　2005 年度我国纺织工业麻纺织行业主营业务收入前 30 名企业

排序	企业名称	排序	企业名称
1	湖南华升工贸进出口（集团）公司	16	宜兴市华东亚麻纺织有限公司
2	浙江金鹰集团有限公司	17	浙江绍兴新三江印染有限公司
3	诸城市德利源纺织有限公司	18	黑龙江圆宝纺织股份有限公司
4	浙江金达创业股份有限公司	19	温州汇浩亚麻纺织有限公司
5	铜陵华源麻业有限公司	20	达县智鹏苎麻纺织厂
6	新申集团	21	大竹县金桥麻业有限公司
7	哈尔滨继佳纺织有限公司	22	湖南广源麻业有限公司
8	湖北银泉纺织股份有限公司	23	东平洲际泰亚麻纺织有限公司
9	重庆市涪陵金帝工业集团有限公司	24	浙江海荣布业发展有限公司
10	山东省蒙阴棉纺织有限公司	25	克山金鼎亚麻纺织有限责任公司
11	湖南洞庭苎麻纺织印染厂	26	湖北天化麻业股份有限公司
12	湖北精华纺织集团有限公司	27	湖北阳新远东麻业有限公司
13	曲阜市锦绣纺织有限公司	28	山西绿洲纺织有限责任公司
14	无锡天元实业有限公司	29	江苏泛佳亚麻纺织厂有限公司
15	湖南益鑫泰麻业服装实业有限公司	30	东嘉麻棉（常州）有限公司

表 186　2005 年度我国纺织工业印染行业主营业务收入前 50 名企业

排序	企业名称	排序	企业名称
1	浙江永通染织集团有限公司	26	无锡洛社印染有限公司
2	浙江航民实业集团有限公司	27	福建协盛丰印染实业有限公司
3	浙江美欣达印染集团股份有限公司	28	淮北印染集团公司
4	山东大海集团有限公司	29	常州月夜灯芯绒有限公司
5	互太（番禺）纺织印染有限公司	30	杭州圣山实业有限公司
6	天龙控股集团有限公司	31	浙江同辉染整有限公司
7	浙江湖州大港纺织印染集团有限公司	32	佛山南方印染股份有限公司
8	三元控股集团有限公司	33	昌邑华达织造有限公司
9	华纺股份有限公司	34	杭州中纺印染有限公司
10	宜兴乐旗纺织集团有限公司	35	永新印染厂（深圳）有限公司
11	张家港市纱洲纺织印染进出口有限公司	36	浙江新时代染整有限公司
12	浙江大和纺织印染服装（集团）有限公司	37	深圳海润实业有限公司
13	江阴市康源印染有限公司	38	明石染厂有限公司
14	浙江万亨盛印染有限公司	39	邯郸新维印染股份有限公司
15	浙江天马实业股份有限公司	40	潍坊齐荣纺织有限公司
16	浙江稽山印染有限公司	41	安徽福华皖碳纤维有限公司
17	江苏紫荆花纺织科技股份有限公司	42	福州福华纺织印染有限公司
18	七海（广东）织染厂有限公司	43	深圳中冠纺织印染股份有限公司
19	番禺潭州振裕纺织印染有限公司	44	南通纺织控股集团纺织印染有限公司
20	辽宁时代集团熊岳印染有限责任公司	45	浙江华东纺织印染有限公司
21	浙江亚太特宽幅印染有限公司	46	中山正兴纺织厂有限公司
22	青岛凤凰印染有限公司	47	重庆市三五三三印染服装总厂
23	常州东恒染织集团有限公司	48	香港润成（开平）整染厂
24	宁波众鑫印染有限公司	49	山西彩佳印染有限公司
25	浙江新天龙工贸有限公司	50	国营石家庄第二印染厂

表187　2004年我国被认定为“真皮标志生态皮革”的企业

排序	企业名称	排序	企业名称
1	辛集东明皮革有限公司	10	新乡黑白明亮制革有限公司
2	浙江长森股份有限公司	11	烟台制革有限责任公司
3	佰立特皮业有限公司	12	河南鞋城（集团）总公司
4	辛集腾跃皮革有限公司	13	南海中港皮业有限公司
5	宏四海皮革有限公司	14	成都立申实业有限公司
6	远东皮革有限公司	15	晋江兴业皮革有限公司
7	浙江金鑫皮革有限公司	16	三大久制革有限公司
8	山东茂德皮革集团有限公司	17	成都岚牌实业有限责任公司
9	河南省方圆皮革有限公司	18	山东高密雪龙皮革有限公司

注：经中国皮革协会综合评定，2004年又批准了三大久制革有限公司、成都岚牌实业有限责任公司、山东高密雪龙皮革有限公司为真皮标志生态皮革企业，至此，这类企业已有18家。

表188　2004年我国皮革工业荣获“中国真皮名鞋品牌”与“中国真皮名装品牌”的企业

2004年中国真皮名鞋品牌与生产企业

生产企业	真皮名鞋品牌
意尔康鞋业集团有限公司	意尔康
飞驼鞋业有限公司	飞驼
杰豪鞋业有限公司	杰豪
福建石狮市福盛鞋业有限公司	木林森
青岛孚德鞋业有限公司	孚德
澳伦鞋业有限公司	澳伦
深圳市富丽达鞋业有限公司	富丽达
重庆科尔士实业（集团）有限公司	科尔士
惠特鞋业有限公司	惠特
郑州市双凤鞋业有限公司	双凤
南京万里集团	万里
浙江邦赛鞋业有限公司	邦赛
成都市艾民儿皮制品有限责任公司	艾民儿
成都市卡美多鞋业有限公司	卡美多

2004年中国真皮名装品牌与生产企业

生产企业	真皮名鞋品牌
北京市西比利亚皮货集团	澳妮儿
海宁市三星兄弟皮革制衣有限责任公司	三星
海宁圣尼时装有限公司	圣尼

注：2004年中国真皮名鞋品牌和企业与中国真皮名装品牌与企业，由中国皮革工业协会评定推荐，表中排名不分先后。

表 189 2004 年我国重点造纸企业销售收入排名前 30 名企业

序号	企业名称	销售收入（万元）	序号	企业名称	销售收入（万元）
1	山东晨鸣纸业集团股份有限公司	857 482	16	山东日照森博浆纸有限责任公司	146 929
2	金东纸业（江苏）有限公司	635 133	17	福建省南纸股份有限公司	136 846
3	华泰集团有限公司	510 800	18	山东华金集团有限公司	129 863
4	东莞玖龙纸业有限公司	483 361	19	山东泰山纸业股份有限公司	129 300
5	山东太阳纸业股份有限公司	408 608	20	安徽山鹰纸业股份有限公司	123 230
6	山东博汇集团	390 053	21	青岛海王纸业股份有限公司	115 075
7	山东泉林纸业有限责任公司	319 329	22	浙江永泰纸业集团股份有限公司	112 624
8	泰格林纸集团有限责任公司	300 000	23	金红叶纸业苏州工业园区有限公司	111 517
9	宁波中华纸业有限公司	254 225	24	广东中顺纸业集团有限公司	110 000
10	理文造纸有限公司	230 594	25	苏州紫兴纸业有限公司	105 220
11	山东临清银行纸业集团有限责任公司	214 976	26	山东照东方纸业集团有限公司	94 579
12	芬欧汇川（常熟）有限公司	210 427	27	福建省青山纸业股份有限公司	90 090
13	金华盛纸业苏州工业园区有限公司	208 715	28	民丰集团公司	84 188
14	广州造纸集团有限公司	199 084	29	河南银鸽实业投资集团	80 000
15	珠海经济特区红塔仁恒纸业有限公司	180 638	30	新乡新亚纸业集团股份有限公司	78 000

表 190 2004 年我国重点造纸企业创利税总额排名前 30 名企业

序号	企业名称	利税总额（万元）	序号	企业名称	利税总额（万元）
1	山东晨鸣纸业集团股份有限公司	134 584	16	山东日照森博浆纸有限责任公司	15 330
2	金东纸业（江苏）有限公司	108 516	17	山东华金集团有限公司	14 144
3	华泰集团有限公司	75 000	18	宁波中华纸业有限公司	14 016
4	山东太阳纸业股份有限公司	51 590	19	山东泰山纸业股份有限公司	13 600
5	山东博汇集团	51 003	20	山东照东方纸业集团有限公司	13 089
6	珠海经济特区红塔恒仁纸业有限公司	42 164	21	安徽山鹰纸业股份有限公司	12 091
7	山东泉林纸业有限责任公司	41 571	22	民丰集团公司	11 458
8	泰格林纸集团有限责任公司	36 000	23	河南银鸽实业投资集团	11 000
9	山东临清银河纸业集团有限责任公司	27 189	24	福建省南纸股份有限公司	10 096
10	东莞玖龙纸业有限公司	26 217	25	山东鲁南纸业集团	10 066
11	全华盛纸业苏州工业园区有限公司	21 397	26	宁夏美利纸业股份有限责任公司	10 000
12	广州造纸集团有限公司	19 876	27	维达纸业（江门）有限公司	10 000
13	新乡新亚纸业集团股份有限公司	17 900	28	河南许昌宏伟纸业纸品有限公司	8 700
14	牡丹江恒丰纸业集团有限责任公司	17 071	29	德州沪平永发造纸有限公司	7 722
15	苏州紫兴纸业有限公司	15 931	30	中山联合鸿兴造纸有限公司	6 696

表 191　2004 年我国重点造纸企业产量排名前 30 名企业

序号	企 业 名 称	产 量（万 t）	序号	企 业 名 称	产 量（万 t）
1	东莞玖龙纸业有限公司	169.92	16	新乡新亚纸业集团股份有限公司	33.00
2	山东晨鸣纸业集团股份有限公司	144.00	17	中山联合鸿兴造纸有限公司	30.55
3	金东纸业（江苏）有限公司	130.08	18	福建省南纸股份有限公司	29.32
4	山东太阳纸业股份有限公司	87.90	19	无锡荣成纸业股份有限公司	27.73
5	理文造纸有限公司	87.00	20	浙江景兴纸业股份有限公司	26.80
6	华泰集团有限公司	76.82	21	东莞金洲纸业有限公司	26.00
7	山东博汇集团	60.00	22	山东照东方纸业集团有限公司	24.58
8	泰格林纸集团有限责任公司	55.00	23	山东华金集团有限公司	24.26
9	宁波中华纸业有限公司	53.77	24	福建省青山纸业股份有限公司	24.08
10	广州造纸集团有限公司	45.29	25	河北永新纸业有限公司	23.10
11	安徽山鹰纸业股份有限公司	44.76	26	珠海经济特区红塔仁恒纸业公司	22.73
12	山东（临清）银河纸业集团股份有限公司	37.72	27	山东泰山纸业股份有限公司	22.30
13	芬欧汇川（常熟）有限公司	37.41	28	宁夏美利纸业股份有限责任公司	21.01
14	金华盛纸业（苏州工业园区）有限公司	36.57	29	浙江永泰纸业集团股份有限公司	20.22
15	山东泉林纸业有限责任公司	34.15	30	承德兴业纸业有限公司	20.00

表 192　2002—2004 年我国纸及纸板产量 100 万 t 以上的省

单位：万 t

2002 年		2003 年		2004 年		同比增长（%）
省	产 量	省	产 量	省	产 量	
1. 山东	666	1. 山东	853	1. 山东	997	16.88
2. 浙江	496	2. 浙江	601	2. 浙江	748	24.46
3. 广东	410	3. 广东	543	3. 广东	598	10.13
4. 河南	355	4. 河南	420	4. 江苏	506	49.26
5. 江苏	315	5. 江苏	339	5. 河南	495	17.86
6. 河北	288	6. 河北	275	6. 河北	313	13.82
7. 福建	123	7. 福建	144	7. 湖南	168	34.40
8. 湖北	103	8. 湖南	125	8. 福建	166	15.28
		9. 四川	102	9. 安徽	105	6.06
		10. 安徽	99	10. 四川	103	0.98

表 193　2004 年我国印刷企业实现利税前 20 名企业

序号	企 业 名 称	实现利税（万元）	序号	企 业 名 称	实现利税（万元）
1	北京印刷集团公司	4 772.7	11	天津市新闻出版局	1 693.5
2	湖南印刷集团有限公司	3 897.7	12	南京爱德印刷有限公司	1 635.0
3	新华通讯社印刷厂	3 795.0	13	解放军报印刷厂（2230）	1 642.0
4	人民日报社印刷厂	3 615.0	14	河南第一新华印刷厂	1 255.8
5	辽宁印刷集团有限公司	2 908.0	15	上海中华印刷有限公司	1 251.8
6	上海印刷（集团）公司	2 062.0	16	北京新华印刷厂	1 107.0
7	山西新华印业有限公司	2 049.0	17	河南第二新华印刷厂	1 081.0
8	北京京华印刷总厂	2 038.0	18	河北新华印刷一厂	1 060.0
9	安徽新华印刷股份公司	1 901.0	19	北京中科印刷有限公司	1 036.0
10	浙江印刷集团公司	1 887.0	20	江西新华印刷厂	1 025.0

表 194 2004 年我国印刷企业胶印产量百万以上对开色令企业

单位：万对开色令

序号	企业名称	产量	序号	企业名称	产量
1	上海印刷（集团）公司	574.0	10	江西新华印刷厂	201.9
2	北京印刷集团公司	520.2	11	上海三印时报印刷公司	178.2
3	湖南印刷集团有限公司	486.3	12	北京乾沣印刷公司	153.3
4	利丰雅高长城印刷公司	311.1	13	西安新华印刷厂	151.0
5	中国印刷总公司	302.9	14	浙江印刷集团公司	136.0
6	北京新华印刷厂	285.9	15	山东新华印刷厂临沂厂	129.0
7	上海中华印刷有限公司	238.0	16	河北新华印刷一厂	118.0
8	辽宁印刷集团有限公司	229.0	17	河北新华印刷二厂	109.4
9	山西新华印业有限公司	213.4			

表 195 2004 年我国包装印刷企业销售收入亿元以上的主要企业

序号	企业名称	销售收入（万元）	序号	企业名称	销售收入（万元）
1	中国包装生产基地	181 000	10	宁波三Ａ集团有限公司	21 594
2	浙江广博集团股份有限公司	120 678	11	苏州印刷总厂有限公司	20 461
3	鹤山雅图仕印刷有限公司	100 398	12	浙江爱迪尔包装集团公司	19 315
4	上海界龙实业股份有限公司	78 000	13	浙江曙光印刷有限公司	18 051
5	杭州中粮美特容器有限公司	41 641	14	浙江新雅投资集团有限公司	16 605
6	杭州伟成包装印刷公司	41 406	15	山东鲁烟莱州印务有限公司	13 590
7	湖州天外绿色包装印刷有限公司	37 338	16	北京德宝商三包装印刷有限公司	13 500
8	四川宜宾五粮液精美印务有限公司	35 231	17	浙江东经包装有限公司	10 633
9	浙江立可达包装材料有限公司	23 705			

表 196 2004 年我国包装印刷企业实现利税总额千万元以上前 20 名企业

序号	企业名称	实现利税（万元）	序号	企业名称	实现利税（万元）
1	中国包装生产基地	29 100	11	鹤山雅图仕印刷有限公司	2 216
2	湖州天外绿色包装印刷有限公司	11 123	12	北京京华印刷厂	2 038
3	浙江广博集团股份有限公司	9 796	13	浙江新雅投资集团有限公司	2 160
4	上海界龙实业股份有限公司	8 355	14	温州康尔达印刷器材有限公司	1 729
5	杭州伟成包装印刷公司	6 623	15	昆明彩印有限责任公司	1 674
6	四川宜宾五粮液精美印务有限公司	5 530	16	浙江曙光印刷有限公司	1 640
7	浙江爱迪尔包装集团公司	5 206	17	北京双燕商标彩印有限公司	1 625
8	浙江立可达包装材料有限公司	2 967	18	浙江富康包装印刷有限公司	1 608
9	山东鲁烟莱州印务有限公司	2 480	19	桐乡印刷有限公司	1 594
10	苏州印刷总厂有限公司	2 265	20	杭州中粮美特容器有限公司	1 503

表 197　2004 年我国重点造纸机械企业实现销售收入 5 000 万元以上的企业

序号	企 业 名 称	销售收入（万元）	序号	企 业 名 称	销售收入（万元）
1	山东安丘汶瑞机械制造有限公司	13 073	6	湖北沙市轻工机械有限公司	8 148
2	山东昌华造纸机械有限公司	11 300	7	山东淄博海天纸机公司	8 057
3	山东济宁华一轻工机械有限公司	10 541	8	山东潍坊凯信机械有限公司	5 032
4	山东淄博晨钟轻工机械有限公司	8 807	9	福建省轻工机械有限公司	5 000
5	山东潍坊杨帆机械有限公司	8 300			

表 198　2004 年我国重点造纸机械企业实现利税总额 500 万元以上的企业

序号	企 业 名 称	利税总额（万元）	序号	企 业 名 称	利税总额（万元）
1	山东安丘汶瑞机械制造有限公司	2 160	5	山东潍坊扬帆机械有限公司	950
2	山东济宁华一轻工机械有限公司	1 784	6	山东潍坊凯信机械有限公司	797
3	山东淄博晨钟轻工机械有限公司	1 058	7	山东淄博海天纸机公司	739
4	山东昌华造纸机械有限公司	976	8	福建省轻工机械设备有限公司	650

表 199　2004 年劳动生产率在 10 万元以上的重点造纸机械企业

单位：万元/（人·年）

序号	企 业 名 称	劳动生产率	序号	企 业 名 称	劳动生产率
1	湖北沙市轻工机械有限公司	36.00	5	山东淄博晨钟轻工机械有限公司	19.60
2	山东济宁华一轻工机械有限公司	26.91	6	山东潍坊扬帆机械有限公司	19.30
3	山东潍坊凯信机械制造有限公司	25.00	7	福建省轻工机械设备有限公司	16.67
4	山东安丘汶瑞机械制造有限公司	20.70			

表 200　2003 年我国橡胶工业协会会员企业按销售收入排序

序号	轮胎行业		序号	力车胎行业	
	企 业 名 称	销售收入（万元）		企 业 名 称	销售收入（万元）
1	安徽佳通轮胎公司	397 805	1	厦门正新橡胶有限公司	109 425
2	山东三角集团有限公司	353 664	2	杭州中策橡胶有限公司	84 970.9
3	山东成山轮胎股份公司	351 517	3	天津万达轮胎集团公司	34 781.0
4	杭州中策橡胶有限公司	284 468	4	江苏飞驰股份有限公司	25 535.3
5	青岛双星轮胎有限公司	267 826	5	广州第一橡胶厂	22 690.9
6	上海轮胎橡胶（集团）股份公司	258 654	6	山东锦轮股份有限公司	19 830.9
7	青岛黄海橡胶（集团）公司	250 072	7	山东正兴轮胎公司	17 896.9
8	河南风神轮胎股份公司	210 832	8	红豆集团无锡通用橡胶有限公司	14 430.5
9	贵州轮胎股份公司	189 212	9	山东临沂金宇轮胎有限公司	10 121.7
10	山东玲珑橡胶有限公司	187 847	10	天津飞亚达车胎厂	9 938.0

（续）

胶鞋行业			炭黑行业		
序号	企业名称	销售收入（万元）	序号	企业名称	销售收入（万元）
1	青岛双星集团有限责任公司	97 983.6	1	天津海豚炭黑有限公司	25 480.3
2	浙江荣光集团有限公司	43 541.0	2	江西黑猫炭黑股份有限公司	24 923.9
3	解放军 3537 工厂	25 323.40	3	中橡（马鞍山）化学工业有限公司	24 607.4
4	上海回力鞋业有限公司	16 409.9	4	茂名永业股份有限公司	23 258.8
5	杭州雅加实业有限公司	15 930.0	5	苏州宝化炭黑有限公司	18 318.7
6	解放军 3544 工厂	10 667.90	6	温州三维集团公司	15 037.3
7	常州鸿福鞋业有限公司	9 229.0	7	中橡集团炭黑研究院	13 651.2
8	福祥集团（福建）有限公司	9 156.0	8	沙河炭黑厂	12 870.9
9	沈阳胶鞋总厂	8 523.0	9	大石桥辽滨炭黑厂	12 001.9
10	张家港贝顺橡胶制品有限公司	1 045.9	10	杭州富春江化工有限公司	11 263.9
乳胶行业			橡胶制品行业		
序号	企业名称	销售收入（万元）	序号	企业名称	销售收入（万元）
1	青岛双蝶集团股份有限公司	32 504.80	1	安徽宁国中鼎密封件有限公司	48 002
2	张家港大裕橡胶制品有限公司	12 775.46	2	中国人民解放军第 3517 工厂	37 456
3	桂林南方橡胶（集团）公司	12 530.50	3	铁岭华晨橡塑制品有限公司	18 252
4	广州第十一橡胶厂	11 751.60	4	上海华向橡胶制品有限公司	16 843
5	中橡集团上海乳胶厂	9 929.82	5	贵航股份红阳密封件公司	15 262
6	北京乳胶厂	6 056.00	6	南京新星汽车橡胶厂	13 703
7	大连乳胶厂	5 538.00	7	沈阳第四橡胶厂	13 642
8	安徽中键塑胶制品有限公司	4 165.80	8	西北橡胶总厂	11 437
9	沈阳天地乳胶有限公司	4 102.00	9	中南橡胶集团有限责任公司	10 752
10	北京瑞京乳胶制品有限公司	3 758.40	10	石家庄第一橡胶股份有限公司	10 184

表 201　2004 年我国橡胶机械行业前 20 名企业主要经济指标

企业名称	总产值（亿元）	销售产值（亿元）
江苏双象集团有限公司	6.39	6.31
桂林橡胶机械厂	5.36	5.37
益阳橡胶塑料机械集团有限公司	3.60	3.57
淄博工业搪瓷厂	3.47	3.40
淄博市化工设备厂	3.27	3.21
福建华橡自控技术股份有限公司	3.08	3.09
四川亚西橡塑机器有限公司	2.96	2.96
上海精元机械有限公司	2.65	2.13
淄博太极工业搪瓷有限公司	2.30	2.25
青岛亚东橡机集团有限公司	2.15	2.07
桂林橡胶工业新技术开发实业公司	1.46	1.46
广东省湛江机械厂	1.02	0.94
即墨市宏业橡胶机械厂	1.00	0.95
汕头市远东轻工装备公司	0.95	0.48
南京龙鼎自动化设备研究所	0.71	0.69
南通市新科橡塑机械有限公司	0.69	0.68
江门市蓬江纸厂有限公司	0.56	0.66
淄博华星化工设备厂	0.47	0.46
宁波晃大精密机械有限公司	0.46	0.55
无锡市第一橡塑机械有限公司	0.42	0.41

表 202　2004 年我国中成药独立核算企业按资产总额前 50 名企业

排序	企业名称	排序	企业名称
1	三九医药股份有限公司	26	河南羚锐制药股份有限公司
2	中国北京同仁堂（集团）有限公司	27	河南竹林众生制药股份有限公司
3	天津中新药业集团股份有限公司	28	贵州益佰制药股份有限公司
4	太极集团涪陵制药厂	29	贵州神奇制药有限公司
5	吉林延边敖东集团股份有限公司	30	咸阳步长制药有限公司
6	南京医药产业（集团）有限责任公司	31	株洲千金药业股份有限公司
7	东宝实业集团有限公司	32	桂林三金药业股份有限公司
8	吉林修正药业集团	33	清华紫光古汉生物制药有限公司
9	天津天士力制药股份有限公司	34	黑龙江乌苏里江制药股份有限公司
10	深圳万基药业有限公司	35	成都地奥九鸿制药厂
11	上海雷允上药业有限公司	36	通化茂祥制药有限公司
12	山东东阿阿胶集团有限责任公司	37	甘肃奇正实业集团有限公司
13	九芝堂股份有限公司	38	漳州片仔癀实业股份有限公司
14	成都地奥集团有限公司	39	神威药业有限公司
15	江中药业股份有限公司	40	广州中一药业有限公司
16	通化金马药业集团股份有限公司	41	四川志远广和制药有限公司
17	青岛国风药业股份有限公司	42	成都恩威制药有限公司
18	浙江康恩贝制药股份有限公司	43	内蒙古亿利科技实业股份有限公司药业分公司
19	河南肖宛西制药股份有限公司	44	浙江康莱特药业有限公司
20	云南白药集团股份有限公司	45	通化万通药业股份有限公司
21	江苏康缘药业股份有限公司	46	上海实业联合集团药业有限公司
22	正大青春宝药业有限公司	47	西藏灵芝奇正藏药厂
23	汇仁集团有限公司	48	陕西必康制药有限责任公司
24	河北恒利集团有限公司	49	杭州天目山药业股份有限公司
25	武汉健民药业集团有限公司	50	浙江天皇药业有限公司

表 203　2004 年我国中成药独立核算企业销售收入前 50 名企业

排序	企业名称	排序	企业名称
1	天津天士力集团有限公司	16	吉林敖东集团股份有限公司
2	修正药业集团公司	17	山东东阿阿胶集团有限责任公司
3	汇仁集团有限公司	18	山东鸿洋神水产科技有限公司
4	天津中新药业集团股份有限公司	19	江中药业股份有限公司
5	上海雷允药业有限公司	20	厦门金日制药有限公司
6	南京医药产业（集团）有限公司	21	鲁南制药股份有限公司
7	烟台新时代健康产业有限公司	22	浙江康恩贝制药股份有限公司
8	中国杭州青春宝集团有限公司	23	三九医药股份有限公司
9	深圳万基药业有限公司	24	仁和（集团）发展有限公司
10	诚志股份有限公司	25	神威药业有限公司
11	北京同仁堂科技发展股份公司	26	河南省宛西制药股份有限公司
12	太极集团涪陵制药厂	27	云南白药集团股份有限公司
13	九芝堂股份有限公司	28	连云港康缘集团有限公司
14	成都地奥集团	29	广洲中一药业有限公司
15	北京同仁堂股份有限公司	30	贵州益佰制药股份有限公司

（续）

排序	企业名称	排序	企业名称
31	广西金嗓子有限责任公司	41	诺氏制药（吉林）有限公司
32	石家庄山岭药业股份有限公司	42	河北恒利集团有限公司
33	黑龙江省葵花药业有限公司	43	广州奇星药业有限公司
34	天津天士力制药股份有限公司	44	成都中汇制药有限公司
35	四川蜀中制药有限公司	45	武汉健民药业集团股份有限公司
36	西安绿谷制药有限公司	46	漳州片仔癀药业股份有限公司
37	佛山市顺德区容桂康复来保健品有限公司	47	咸阳步长制药有限公司
38	贵州神奇制药有限公司	48	承德颈复康药业集团
39	贵州神奇药业股份有限公司龙江分厂	49	江西桑海集团有限责任公司
40	广州王老吉药业股份有限公司	50	贵州白灵制药有限公司

表 204　2005 年我国中成药按出口金额前 10 名企业

序号	企业名称	序号	企业名称
1	北京同仁堂股份有限公司	6	天津中新药业集团股份有限公司
2	漳州片仔癀药业股份有限公司	7	美康国际贸易发展公司
3	广州市医药进出口公司	8	兰州佛慈制药股份有限公司
4	上海医药（集团）有限公司	9	灵宝市豫西药业有限责任公司
5	杭州天地保健品有限公司	10	浙江省医药保健品进出口有限公司

注：2005 年我国中成药保健品全年累计出口 14 212.49t，同比增长 2.01%，出口金额 1.53 亿美元，同比增长 10.27%。本表按企业出口金额排序。

我国西部地区综合统计

表 205　我国西部地区主要农产品产量（2004—2005 年）　　单位：万 t

主要农产品	2004 年	2005 年	同比增长（%）
一、粮食作物	12 971.3	13 438.7	3.60
（一）谷物	10 705.5	11 131.7	3.98
稻谷	4 506.7	4 586.3	1.77
小麦	1 983.9	2 037.8	2.72
玉米	3 802.9	4 094.6	7.67
谷子	32.2	35.7	10.87
高粱	63.9	66.9	4.69
（二）豆类	553.6	618.2	11.67
大豆	305.9	230.7	8.11
杂豆	247.7	287.4	16.03
（三）薯类	1 712.3	1 688.9	－1.37
马铃薯	1 008.6	990.9	－1.75
二、油料作物	733.3	766.3	4.50
花生	145.0	149.8	3.31
油菜籽	434.9	444.6	2.23

（续）

主要农产品	2004年	2005年	同比增长（%）
芝麻	4.8	4.3	−10.42
胡麻籽	33.2	30.1	−9.34
向日葵籽	98.4	124.1	26.12
三、棉花	201.8	209.1	3.62
四、麻类	38.8	44.9	15.72
黄红麻	1.5	1.5	
五、糖料	7 373.6	7 355.3	−0.25
甘蔗	6 916.3	6 782.5	−1.93
甜菜	457.4	572.8	25.23
六、烟叶	139.6	158.0	13.18
烤烟	126.2	144.7	14.66
七、茶叶	25.0	29.1	16.40
八、水果	3 322.8	3 664.9	10.30

表206　我国西部地区主要农产品单位面积产量（2004—2005年）

单位：kg/hm²

主要农产品	2004年	2005年	同比增长（%）
一、粮食作物	4 030.9	4 096.3	1.62
（一）谷物	4 606.5	4 703.7	2.11
稻谷	6 143.6	6 244.1	1.64
小麦	3 234.5	3 224.0	0.32
玉米	4 778.3	4 974.5	4.11
谷子	1 354.2	1 596.6	17.90
高粱	3 206.5	3 600.6	12.29
（二）豆类	1 463.3	1 614.9	10.36
大豆	1 496.1	1 579.5	5.57
杂豆	1 424.9	1 657.7	16.34
（三）薯类	3 320.3	3 178.7	−4.26
马铃薯	3 182.2	2 854.1	−10.31
二、油料作物	1 751.4	1 819.3	3.88
花生	2 127.7	2 165.8	1.79
油菜籽	1 701.5	1 725.8	0.89
芝麻	1 000.3	1 045.1	4.88
胡麻籽	1 124.6	1 106.7	−1.59
向日葵籽	2 016.9	2 314.5	14.76
三、棉花	1 514.7	1 574.3	3.93
四、麻类	3 400.1	3 422.3	0.65
黄红麻	2 050.7	1 982.6	−3.32
五、糖料	63 797.2	63 157.6	−1.00
甘蔗	65 592.6	64 494.7	−1.67
甜菜	45 123.2	50 709.6	12.38
六、烟叶	1 843.0	1 918.7	4.11
烤烟	1 835.5	1 914.3	4.29

表 207 我国西部地区茶叶产量（2005 年） 单位：t

地区	茶叶总产量	其中				
		红毛茶	绿毛菜	乌龙毛菜	紧压茶原料	其他茶
全国总计	**934 857**	**47 941**	**691 020**	**103 820**	**27 653**	**64 423**
地区小计	291 367	16 130	237 413	147	8 401	33 276
地区占全国比重（%）	31.17	33.65	34.36	0.14	30.38	51.65
内蒙古						
广西	26 181	440	20 695			5 046
重庆	16 545	3 211	10 215			3 119
四川	97 941	996	73 817	134	8 199	14 795
贵州	22 915	61	14 123	1	95	8 635
云南	115 880	11 422	106 661	12	107	1 678
西藏	3					3
陕西	11 382		11 382			
甘肃	520		520			
青海						
宁夏						
新疆						

表 208 我国西部地区水果产量（2004—2005 年） 单位：kt

品种	2004 年	2005 年	同比增长（%）
全国产量总计	**83 941**	**88 355.00**	**5.26**
地区产量小计	20 779	22 543.10	8.49
地区占全国比重（%）	24.75	25.51	3.07
苹果	7 273	7 660	5.32
甘橘	4 953	5 477.00	10.58
梨	2 465	2 674.00	8.48
香蕉	1 294	1 447.00	11.82
菠萝	89	87.50	−1.69
荔枝	379	348.00	−8.18
龙眼	364	395.00	8.52
桃	967	1 120.00	15.82
猕猴桃	278	289.00	3.96
葡萄	1 818	1 973.00	8.53
红枣	266	346.60	30.30
柿子	633	726.00	14.69

表 209　我国西部地区森林工业主要产品产量（2005 年）

产　　品	单　　位	全国产量	地区产量	占全国比重（%）
锯　材	万 m^3	1 790.3	308.3	17.22
木　片	万 m^3	1 217.7	433.1	35.56
胶合板	万 m^3	2 515.0	211.2	8.40
纤维板	万 m^3	2 060.6	321.4	15.60
刨花板	万 m^3	576.1	71.2	12.36
胶合木	万 m^3	74.1	8.48	11.44
木地板	万 m^2	17 322.8	2 628.1	15.17
卫生筷子	标准箱	11 073 984	2 009 065	18.14
人造板表面装饰板	万元 m^2	27 014.1	48.2	0.18
单　板	万元 m^2	291 171.6	1 138.7	0.39
松香类产品	t	671 571	427 673	63.68
松节油类产品	t	98 440	35 778	36.34
樟　脑	t	6 734		
冰　片	t	568	171	30.11
栲胶类产品	t	7 805	7 735	99.10
紫胶类产品	t	1 318	1 298	98.48
木材热解产品	t			
木　炭	t	145 220	27 690	19.07
活性炭	t	141 612		
软木制品				
软木砖	m^3	7 382		
软木纸	m^3	4 296	4 041	94.06

表 210　我国西部地区热带、亚热带作物面积和产量（2005 年）

项　　目	单　位	全国产量	地区产量	占全国比重（%）
一、橡胶（按干橡片计算）				
收获面积	khm^2	464.8	142.9	30.74
产　　量	t	513 618	241 019	46.93
二、咖啡豆（按干咖啡豆计算）				
收获面积	khm^2	15.5	15.3	98 71
产　　量	t	21 919	21 636	98.71
三、椰子（按果实计算）				
收获面积	khm^2	25.1		
产　　量	万个	23 248	31	0.13
四、腰果				
收获面积	khm^2	1.6	0.1	6.25
产　　量	t	390	2	0.51
五、香料作物				
收获面积	khm^2	8.2	7.7	93.90
产　　量	t	1 267	1 175	92.74
香茅草				
收获面积	khm^2	6.6	6.1	92.42
产　　量	t	1 022	930	91.00
六、剑麻、番麻（折纤维）				
收获面积	khm^2	13.8	6.8	49.28
产　　量	t	55 478	25 496	45.96

表 211　我国西部地区主要畜产品产量（2004—2005 年）

产品名称	单　位	2004 年	2005 年	同比增长（%）	占全国比重（%）
一、肉类总产量	万 t	1 991.6	2 171.6	9.04	28.05
猪　肉	万 t	1 370.9	1 477.5	7.84	29.49
牛　肉	万 t	184.2	203.3	10.37	28.57
羊　肉	万 t	194.5	220.1	13.16	50.54
禽　肉	万 t	197.1	222.3	12.79	15.18
兔　肉	万 t	20.5	23.4	14.15	45.79
二、其他畜产品产量					
奶　类	万 t	988.8	1 249.4	26.36	43.61
牛　奶	万 t	938.4	1 197.7	27.63	43.50
蜂　蜜	万 t	6.8	7.2	5.88	24.57
禽　蛋	万 t	359.7	388.2	7.92	13.48
山羊毛	t	16 999	18 223	7.20	49.38
羊　绒	t	9 825	10 402	5.87	67.39
绵羊毛	t	237 855	253 942	6.76	64.59
细羊毛	t	85 510	86 535	1.20	67.68
半细羊毛	t	52 876	56 100	6.10	45.58

表 212　我国西部地区水产品产量（2004—2005 年）　　单位：kt

产品名称	2004 年	2005 年	同比增长（%）	占全国比重（%）
水产品总产量	**51 076.4**	**4 718.6**	**7.50**	**9.24**
按海水、内陆分				
海水产品产量	28 383.3	1 739.6	7.92	6.13
内陆水产品产量	22 693.1	2 979.0	9.07	13.13
按生产性质分				
捕捞产量	17 123.3	1 130.0	5.87	6.60
养殖产量	33 953.1	3 588.5	8.20	10.57

表 213　我国西部地区人均主要农产品、畜产品、水产品产量（2004—2005 年）

单位：kg/人

产品名称	2004 年	2005 年	同比增长（%）
一、主要农产品			
（一）粮食	350.3	374.7	6.97
1. 谷物	289.1	310.4	7.37
稻谷	121.7	127.9	5.09
小麦	53.6	56.8	5.97
玉米	102.7	114.2	11.20
谷子	0.9	1.0	11.11
高粱	1.7	1.9	11.76
2. 豆类	15.0	17.2	14.67
大豆	8.3	9.2	10.84
杂豆	6.7	8.0	19.40
3. 薯类	46.2	47.1	1.95
马铃薯	27.2	27.6	1.47

（续）

产品名称	2004 年	2005 年	同比增长（%）
（二）油料	19.8	21.4	8.08
花生	3.9	4.2	7.69
油菜籽	11.7	12.4	5.98
芝麻	0.1	0.1	平
胡麻籽	0.9	0.8	—11.11
向日葵	2.7	3.5	29.63
（三）棉花	5.5	5.8	5.45
（四）麻类	1.0	1.3	30.00
黄红麻			
（五）糖料	199.2	205.1	2.96
甘蔗	186.8	189.1	1.23
甜菜	12.4	16.0	29.03
（六）水果	89.7	102.2	13.94
（七）烟叶	3.8	44.4	15.79
烤烟	3.4	4.0	17.65
二、畜产品			
（一）猪牛羊肉	47.2	53.0	12.29
猪　肉	37.0	41.2	11.35
牛　肉	5.0	5.7	14.00
羊　肉	5.3	6.1	15.09
（二）奶类	26.7	34.8	30.34
牛奶	25.3	33.4	32.02
（三）禽蛋	9.7	10.8	11.34
三、水产品	11.8	13.2	11.86
鱼　类	8.6	9.6	11.63
虾蟹类	0.7	0.8	14.29

资料来源：表中数据来自 2006 年《中国农村统计年鉴》。

表 214　我国西部地区农林牧渔业总产值、增加值及构成（2004—2005 年）

名　称	总产值		增加值	
	2004 年	2005 年	2004 年	2005 年
一、绝对数（亿元）				
合　计	8 654.9	9 571.8	5 424.7	5 960.8
1. 农业	4 582.1	5 048.6	3 119.3	3 408.5
2. 林业	365.5	394.4	258.5	282.0
3. 牧业	3 239.6	3 609.1	1 757.0	1 948.1
4. 渔业	267.0	300.5	184.9	208.4
二、构成（%）				
农林牧渔业合计	100.00	100.00	100.00	100.00
1. 农业	52.94	52.75	57.50	57.18
2. 林业	4.22	4.12	4.77	4.73
3. 牧业	37.43	37.71	32.39	32.68
4. 渔业	3.08	3.14	3.41	3.50
三、西部占全国的比重（%）				
农林牧渔业总产值合计	23.88	24.26	25.06	25.84
1. 农业	25.26	25.74	26.37	26.72
2. 林业	27.54	27.67	28.54	28.91
3. 牧业	26.61	27.11	29.51	29.94
4. 渔业	7.40	7.48	8.88	8.95

注：自 2003 年起农林牧渔业总产值执行新国民经济行业分类标准，包括农林牧渔服务业生产总值。

表 215 我国西部地区林业产业总产值（2005 年） 单位：万元

地 区	总 计	第一产业	第二产业	第三产业
全国总计	**84 587 418**	**43 555 608**	**34 865 412**	**6 166 398**
地区小计	18 221 759	12 378 056	4 015 674	1 828 029
占全国比重（%）	21.54	28.42	11.52	29.65
内蒙古	1 126 853	675 974	308 776	142 103
广 西	2 934 454	1 841 467	1 027 113	65 874
重 庆	1 092 656	578 371	193 481	320 804
四 川	4 003 314	2 009 655	1 197 499	796 160
贵 州	984 295	744 352	199 376	40 567
云 南	2 377 919	1 680 672	617 577	79 670
西 藏	139 988	109 223	24 645	6 120
陕 西	1 263 118	1 184 339	58 138	20 641
甘 肃	568 753	520 443	14 049	34 261
青 海	27 074	26 629		445
宁 夏	240 410	239 470	579	361
新 疆	1 799 754	1 571 918	106 420	121 416

注：表中第一产业为农林牧渔业总产值；第二产业为林业制造业、采矿业、电力、煤气、水的生产供应和建筑业；第三产业为交通运输、仓储及邮政业、服务行业等。

表 216 我国西部地区林业系统森林工业固定资产投资（2005 年） 单位：万元

地 区	总 计	其中：基本建设	更新改造	其他投资	本年新增固定资产
全国总计	**173 847**	**69 678**	**72 280**	**31 889**	**134 737**
地区小计	40 015	15 966	6 710	17 339	40 971
占全国比重（%）	23.02	22.91	9.28	59.37	30.41
内蒙古	16 720	999		15 721	26 804
广 西	11 003	4 881	6 122		8 550
重 庆					
四 川	4 594	3 454	334	806	1 861
贵 州					
云 南	6 989	5 923	254	812	2 601
西 藏					
陕 西	478	478			478
甘 肃					
青 海					
宁 夏					
新 疆	231	231			677

表 217　我国西部地区林业系统农产品加工业总产值（2005 年）　单位：万元

地　区	非木质林产品加工制造业	木材加工及竹、藤、棕、草制品业			
		合　计	锯材木片加工业	人造板制造业	木制品制造业
全国总计	**112 540**	**2 121 113**	**335 152**	**1 370 422**	**362 208**
地区小计	3 578	229 496	24 577	165 688	34 647
占全国比重（%）	3.18	10.82	7.33	12.09	9.57
内蒙古		32 213	400	25 675	6 138
广　西		102 570	8 141	94 429	
重　庆		6 352	1 545	3 271	636
四　川		30 687	3 942	2 391	23 452
贵　州	3 481	30 323	7 345	16 404	3 975
云　南	97	12 148	2 048	9 471	446
西　藏		1 156	1 156		
陕　西		13 322		13 322	
甘　肃		725		725	
青　海					
宁　夏					
新　疆					

地　区	竹藤棕草制品业	木质、竹藤家具制造业	木、竹浆造纸及纸制品业	林产化学产品制造业	木、竹藤工艺品制造业	专用设备、仪器、仪表制造业
全国总计	**53 331**	**239 337**	**204 592**	**95 064**	**18 212**	**11 159**
地区小计	4 584	25 154	145 401	63 353	5 000	600
占全国比重（%）	8.6	10.51	71.07	66.64	27.45	5.38
内蒙古			33 118	898		
广　西			61 900	53 443	5 000	600
重　庆	900	17 984		500		
四　川	902	2 675	48 010	680		
贵　州	2 599	4 386		2 500		
云　南	183		2 373	3 709		
西　藏						
陕　西				1 623		
甘　肃		109				
青　海						
宁　夏						
新　疆						

表 218 我国西部地区林业系统农产品加工业销售产值（2005 年）单位：万元

地　区	非木质林产品加工制造业	木材加工及竹、藤、棕、草制品业			
		合　计	锯材木片加工业	人造板制造业	木制品制造业
全国总计	**111 400**	**1 632 205**	**262 261**	**1 024 366**	**310 882**
地区小计	3 584	221 607	22 549	161 548	34 412
占全国比重（%）	3.22	13.58	8.60	15.77	11.07
内蒙古		32 557	403	25 846	6 308
广　西		98 545	8 303	90 242	
重　庆		4 407	1 500	2 447	109
四　川		27 240	1 907	1 856	23 457
贵　州	3 481	30 756	7 387	16 762	4 063
云　南	103	13 377	1 893	10 826	475
西　藏		1 156	1 156		
陕　西		12 787		12 787	
甘　肃		782		782	
青　海					
宁　夏					
新　疆					

地　区	竹藤棕草制品业	木质、竹藤家具制造业	木、竹浆造纸及纸制品业	林产化学产品制造业	木、竹藤工艺品制造业	专用设备、仪器、仪表制造业
我国总计	**34 696**	**131 153**	**189 694**	**91 034**	**16 459**	**10 386**
地区小计	3 098	22 462	142 435	61 905	5 000	689
占全国比重（%）	8.93	17.13	75.09	68.00	30.38	6.63
内蒙古			33 027	1 268		
广　西			60 570	52 597	5 000	689
重　庆	351	17 405				
四　川	20	568	46 597	612		
贵　州	2 544	4 386		2 575		
云　南	183		2 241	3 115		
西　藏						
陕　西				1 738		
甘　肃		103				
青　海						
宁　夏						
新　疆						

表219　我国西部地区林业系统农产品加工业国有独立核算大中型企业主要经济指标（2005年）

地　区	总资产贡献率（%）	资本保值增值率（%）	资产负债率（%）	流动资产周转率（次）	成本费用利润率（%）	全员劳动生产率[元/(人·年)]	产品销售率（%）
我国总计	**5.2**	**107.4**	**55.3**	**1.4**	**2.0**	**36 661**	**97.1**
地区平均值	2.06	96.87	80.5	1.1	0.93	27 285	97.03
内蒙古	10.4	143.5	43.4	1.6	6.1	32 168	100.9
广　西	6.0	101.8	73.4	2.3	1.2	122 459	95.5
重　庆							
四　川	−0.3	164.5	70.7	0.8	−9.7	6 892	101.9
贵　州	−7.9	152.9	147.2	0.6	30.7	10 799	95.8
云　南	0.8	121.8	80.6	0.7	−3.8	1 776	92.3
西　藏	10.5	108.6	43.0	0.9	19.7	20 450	86.7
陕　西							
甘　肃	−5.1	−115	105.2	0.8	−37.5	−3 552	106.1
青　海							
宁　夏							
新　疆							

表220　我国西部地区乡镇规模以上农产品加工企业主要经济指标（2005年）

地　区	企业单位数（个）	平均职工数（人）	工业增加值（万元）	工业总产值（万元）	营业收入（万元）	利润总额（万元）
全国总计	**70 297**	**12 793 498**	**71 965 206**	**307 987 194**	**292 592 999**	**14 993 496**
地区小计	5 396	844 431	5 164 387	19 551 402	18 249 793	953 303
占全国比重（%）	7.68	6.60	7.18	6.35	6.24	6.36
内蒙古	457	101 736	983 027	3 443 964	3 225 742	248 684
广　西	906	90 361	234 317	1 182 373	1 101 751	56 637
重　庆	644	105 932	407 355	1 607 277	1 571 019	59 632
四　川	1 521	255 749	1 929 185	6 622 792	6 210 313	329 625
贵　州	277	47 043	336 240	1 234 344	1 064 857	89 962
云　南	312	56 769	347 177	1 699 947	1 661 566	85 826
西　藏	151	2 593	8 467	20 935		463
陕　西	353	70 869	303 338	1 318 271	1 222 304	48 594
甘　肃	336	52 127	290 838	949 815	832 681	61 387
青　海	21	4 369	15 839	65 233	59 858	5 267
宁　夏	208	28 503	149 407	656 214	615 969	33 640
新　疆	210	28 380	159 197	750 237	683 733	33 586

表 221　我国西部地区食品工业分行业工业总产值（2004 年）　单位：亿元

地　区	食品工业分行业工业总产值				
	合　计	农副食品加工业	食品制造业	饮料制造业	烟草加工业
全国总计	**16 280.92**	**8 344.89**	**2 899.08**	**2 440.92**	**2 596.03**
地区小计	2 922.25	1 075.48	420.30	503.31	923.16
占全国比重（%）	17.95	12.89	14.50	20.62	35.56
内蒙古	366.99	140.82	180.82	30.72	14.63
广　西	389.02	293.19	19.82	29.14	46.87
重　庆	146.44	58.11	22.04	23.97	42.32
四　川	636.65	263.32	62.50	237.79	73.04
贵　州	193.22	24.19	17.18	53.77	98.08
云　南	670.57	86.05	12.38	19.57	552.57
西　藏	2.88	0.61	0.26	2.01	
陕　西	220.28	77.94	39.37	49.98	52.99
甘　肃	120.86	47.28	14.15	25.33	34.10
青　海	10.24	6.22	1.02	3.00	
宁　夏	35.93	12.36	12.79	9.36	1.42
新　疆	129.17	65.39	37.97	18.67	7.14

表 222　我国西部地区纺织工业主要经济指标（2005 年）　单位：亿元

地　区	企业单位数（个）	从业人员（万人）	工　业增加值	工　业总产值	产品销售收　入	利润总额	出　口交货值
全国总计	**35 978**	**978.3**	**20 011.3**	**20 470.6**	**19 793.8**	**689.7**	**5 736.9**
地区小计	1 174	51.9	697.1	713.3	688.0	17.02	109.4
占全国比重（%）	3.26	5.31	3.48	3.48	3.48	2.47	1.91
内蒙古	153	6.78	151.2	155.1	159.0	9.38	38.45
广　西	137	5.05	42.2	43.7	40.3	−0.11	3.58
重　庆	141	4.74	52.3	54.7	52.4	0.61	11.15
四　川	377	14.23	230.2	234.5	219.2	3.84	38.58
贵　州	34	1.01	7.06	7.3	6.5	−0.11	0.68
云　南	28	1.74	17.1	17.5	17.0	2.23	1.89
西　藏	3	0.006	0.007	0.006 2	0.007 6		
陕　西	112	9.27	69.5	71.5	66.6	−1.23	9.08
甘　肃	58	2.13	17.4	18.5	16.1	−0.35	1.31
青　海	12	0.47	5.3	5.6	4.5	0.26	1.37
宁　夏	33	0.73	36.7	35.4	35.7	1.88	0.43
新　疆	86	5.77	68.1	69.5	70.7	0.62	2.86

表 223　我国西部地区纺织工业（国有及国有控股企业）主要经济指标（2005 年）

单位：亿元

地　区	企业单位数（个）	从业人员（万人）	工　业总产值	产品销售收　入	利润总额	出　口交货值
全国总计	**1 480**	**116.99**	**1 818.8**	**1 819.04**	**6.63**	**353.03**
地区小计	203	18.85	183.26	168.46	−1.73	30.49
占全国比重（%）	13.72	16.11	10.08	9.26		8.64
内蒙古	15	1.55	24.28	18.25	−0.458	8.32
广　西	27	1.71	15.60	15.01	−0.432	0.44
重　庆	11	1.66	10.63	10.34	−0.73	2.99
四　川	25	2.63	41.74	37.79	0.20	7.10
贵　州	17	0.48	2.90	2.67	−0.098	0.17
云　南	10	1.23	13.55	13.18	1.98	1.13
西　藏	3	0.006	0.006 2	0.007 6		
陕　西	48	6.54	41.57	40.26	−1.44	7.53
甘　肃	7	0.57	4.84	4.29	−0.27	0.73
青　海	4	0.095	0.65	0.63	0.073	
宁　夏	5	0.089	6.79	5.44	0.148	
新　疆	31	2.29	20.70	20.54	−0.705	2.08

表 224　我国西部地区森林工业主要产品产量（2005 年）

地　区	锯材（万 m^3）	木片（万 m^3）	胶合板（万 m^3）	纤维板（万 m^3）	刨花板（万 m^3）	胶合木（万 m^3）	木地板（万 m^2）	卫生筷子（标准箱）
全国总计	**1 790.3**	**1 217.7**	**2 515**	**2 060.6**	**576.1**	**74.05**	**17 322.8**	**11 073 984**
地区小计	308.32	433.06	211.13	321.43	71.20	8.48	2 628.08	2 009 065
占全国比重(%)	17.22	35.56	8.40	15.60	12.36	11.45	15.17	18.14
内蒙古	85.01	314.45	5.08	14.56	24.70	1.32	0.59	829 114
广　西	62.10	82.41	134.00	166.05	12.28	0.19	38.04	2 000
重　庆	12.69	0.10	1.64	7.07	0.35			
四　川	35.51	2.75	20.67	58.66	6.09	3.27	1 641.26	211 004
贵　州	16.39	0.19	34.79	6.06	4.58	0.05	58.97	69 360
云　南	86.30	27.30	14.95	50.10	6.98	3.65	889.20	89 905
西　藏	8.55							
陕　西	0.03	0.01		8.91			0.02	
甘　肃				0.80				
青　海								
宁　夏								
新　疆								

（续）

地区	人造板表面装饰板（万 m²）	单板（万 m²）	松香类产品（t）	松节油类产品（t）	樟脑（t）	冰片（t）	橡胶类产品（t）	紫胶类产品（t）	木材热解产品（t）		软木制品（m³）	
									木炭	活性炭	软木砖	软木纸
全国总计	**27 014.1**	**291 171.6**	**671 571**	**98 440**	**6 734**	**568**	**7 805**	**1 318**	**145 220**	**141 612**	**7 382**	**4 296**
地区小计	48.15	1 138.65	427 673	35 778	19	171	7 735	1 298	27 471			4 041
占全国比重(%)	0.18	0.39	63.68	36.34	0.28	30.11	99.10	98.48	18.92			94.06
内蒙古		0.16					1 760		219			
广　西	46.03	29.27	360 168	23 590			5 975		100			
重　庆			530									
四　川		257.30	3 367	476				95	200			
贵　州	2.12	1.76	3 393	157					15 588			
云　南		850.16	60 215	11 555	19	171		1 203	11 364			840
西　藏												
陕　西												3 201
甘　肃												
青　海												
宁　夏												
新　疆												

表 225　我国西部地区农垦系统主要农产品加工企业产品产量（2005 年）

地区	纱（万 t）	布（万 m）	机制糖（t）	饮料酒（t）	乳制品（t）	食用植物油（t）	机制纸及纸板（t）
全国总计	**26**	**48 754**	**1 150 212**	**1 267 148**	**153 708**	**820 589**	**1 004 443**
地区小计	12	12 820	706 871	288 279	49 388	206 323	87 410
占全国比重(%)	46.15	26.30	61.46	22.75	32.13	25.14	8.70
内蒙古				622	14 547	8 814	
广　西			503 748	120	132	339	20 950
重　庆					657		
四　川					90		
贵　州				380	893		
云　南			49 942	141		12	
西　藏							
陕　西		4 307			68	4 286	
甘　肃				141 576			
青　海					208		
宁　夏				105 297		129	
新疆（兵团）	12	8 371	153 181	40 143	10 045	180 693	66 460
新疆（农业）		142			223	8 940	
新疆（畜牧）					21 100	3 110	

表 226 我国西部地区轻工业系统农产品加工业产品产量（2004 年）

地 区	纸 浆（万 t）	机制纸（万 t）	机制纸板（万 t）	纸制品（万 t）	原 盐（万 t）	机制糖（万 t）	糖 果（万 t）	方便主食品（万 t）
全国总计	**1 516.23**	**2 873.56**	**1 989.64**	**1 306.18**	**3 710.07**	**1 017.62**	**63.21**	**364.46**
地区小计	144.86	292.71	91.08	131.37	793.07	847.88	1.20	32.60
占全国比重（%）	9.55	10.19	4.58	10.06	21.38	83.32	1.90	8.94
内蒙古	17.32	12.18	6.02	9.79	163.24	10.68		2.20
广 西	38.92	84.63	3.68	14.57	10.05	606.86		2.95
重 庆	1.32	5.84	17.13	20.73	49.41		0.36	4.52
四 川	39.88	74.21	28.58	54.34	353.31	6.57	0.81	5.67
贵 州	3.04	4.94	0.73	2.29		2.04	0.01	2.09
云 南	16.18	9.25	11.09	11.63	60.48	190.46	0.02	3.00
西 藏								
陕 西	0.38	45.39	6.97	8.81	10.00			9.44
甘 肃	3.40	5.69	3.36	1.69	6.09	0.81		0.01
青 海		0.21		0.16	82.63			
宁 夏	2.09	39.62	4.78	0.23				
新 疆	22.33	10.75	8.74	7.13	57.86	30.46		2.72

地区	乳制品（t）	罐头（t）	味精（万 t）	冻饮品（万 t）	液化乳（万 t）	发酵酒精（万 t）	饮料酒（万 kL）	软饮料（万 t）
全国总计	**949.18**	**313.37**	**114.92**	**95.02**	**806.74**	**285.95**	**3 378.39**	**2 912.43**
地区小计	360.17	85.46	7.85	39.94	322.75	61.88	520.32	328.06
占全国比重（%）	37.95	27.27	6.83	42.03	40.00	21.64	15.40	11.26
内蒙古	270.14	0.11			256.35	2.95	61.95	6.00
广 西	3.10	14.29	0.40	36.02	3.10	20.40	48.99	36.10
重 庆	8.97	1.69	2.90	1.04	8.87		51.28	44.94
四 川	7.57	6.23	1.37	0.53	2.95	11.25	166.24	95.92
贵 州	2.42	0.36		1.25	2.38	0.34	23.14	17.68
云 南	12.03	1.02		0.85	11.14	17.46	22.74	31.25
西 藏	0.17			0.06			4.02	0.42
陕 西	25.37	0.26		0.09	11.58	0.97	65.41	71.01
甘 肃	5.00	0.03	0.03	0.06	4.13	5.33	33.22	11.78
青 海	1.06				1.04		1.18	1.02
宁 夏	12.73		2.42	0.02	10.75	0.81	10.40	
新 疆	11.61	61.47	0.73	0.02	10.46	2.37	37.75	11.94

（续）

地区	轻革（万 m²）	皮鞋（万双）	革皮服装（万件）	毛皮服装（万件）	羽绒服装（万件）	家具（万件）	皮包、袋（万个）
全国总计	**51 018.74**	**212 142.14**	**7 740.45**	**537.86**	**13 182.03**	**25 816.55**	**100 402.16**
地区小计	4 337.85	1 572.48	158.46	9.21	34.63	363.40	0.90
占全国比重（%）	8.50	0.74	2.05	1.71	0.26	1.41	0.09
内蒙古	3.43	1.91		0.01	0.65	5.80	
广　西	1 893.30	20.48			2.71	12.22	0.90
重　庆	77.21	1 158.23	16.58		26.72	49.33	
四　川	1 735.31	298.30	133.54		3.15	99.10	
贵　州		2.64				20.77	
云　南	42.39	5.00				8.72	
西　藏		3.06	0.01			0.15	
陕　西	30.00	74.42	0.29			12.11	
甘　肃	12.82	4.38	8.04	9.15	1.40	9.16	
青　海	13.41	4.06		0.01		0.64	
宁　夏						3.00	
新　疆	529.98			0.04		142.40	

表 227　我国西部地区纺织工业纺织品、服装进出口额（2005年）

单位：亿美元

地区	出口			进口		
	小　计	纺织品	服　装	小　计	纺织品	服　装
全国总计	**1 175.35**	**439.69**	**735.66**	**170.99**	**154.88**	**16.11**
地区小计	43.06	16.53	26.53	0.76	0.49	0.27
占全国比重（%）	3.66	3.76	3.61	0.44	0.32	1.68
内蒙古	4.21	1.06	3.15	0.03	0.03	
广　西	2.82	0.86	1.95	0.25	0.22	0.03
重　庆	1.88	1.50	0.39	0.06	0.06	
四　川	9.58	4.84	4.75	0.30	0.08	0.22
贵　州	0.14	0.05	0.09			
云　南	1.37	1.01	0.36	0.05	0.03	0.02
西　藏	0.53	0.15	0.38	0.01	0.01	
陕　西	2.89	1.71	1.18	0.04	0.04	
甘　肃	0.54	0.21	0.33			
青　海	0.53	0.32	0.21			
宁　夏	0.55	0.19	0.36			
新　疆	18.02	4.63	13.39	0.02	0.02	

其 他

表 228 农业部批准的第十二批定点农产品批发市场（2006 年）

序号	市 场 名 称	序号	市 场 名 称
1	北京西沙窝农副产品批发市场	38	安徽省东至县官港茶叶香菇市场
2	天津市隆海葛沽农产品市场	39	安徽省阜南县蔬菜批发市场
3	天津市静海县范庄子蔬菜批发中心	40	安徽省黄山绿色食品城
4	天津市蓟州蔬菜批发市场	41	安徽省太湖县皖西南山货交易市场
5	天津市宝粮农副产品批发市场	42	安徽省滁州乌衣粮油批发市场
6	河南省新乐市花生米市场	43	安徽省凤台县顾桥皖北米面批发市场
7	河北省衡水东明蔬菜果品批发市场	44	福建省泉州市华州水果中心批发市场
8	河南省宣化盛发蔬菜副食市场	45	福建省华安县华仙茶都
9	河北省大名县南李庄花生批发市场	46	福建省莆田市农副产品批发市场
10	河北省霸州市益津蔬菜批发市场	47	福建省福州市海峡茶都
11	山西省运城运达果品贸易有限公司	48	江西省丰城市水禽水产品批发市场
12	山西省祁县肉牛禽蛋交易市场	49	江西省新余市优质农产品批发市场
13	山西省寿阳县平头富山农副产品批发有限公司	50	江西省新干县三湖红桔批发市场
14	内蒙古鄂尔多斯市东胜区富兴蔬菜批发市场	51	山东省德州市南郊岳高铺瓜果蔬菜批发市场
15	内蒙古锡林浩特市交易市场	52	山东省沾化县王尔庄海蜇批发市场
16	内蒙古乌兰察布市察右后旗北方马铃薯批发市场	53	山东省青州高柳蔬菜批发市场
17	内蒙古呼伦贝尔市海拉尔区新桥批发市场	54	山东省济宁蔬菜批发市场
18	内蒙古赤峰市松山区蔬菜批发市场	55	山东省新泰市青龙路市场
19	内蒙古兴安盟森发农林牧产品批发市场	56	山东省济南市堤口路果品批发市场
20	辽宁省鞍山市果品批发市场	57	河南省南阳市华山路蔬菜批发市场
21	辽宁省凌源市四官营子蔬菜批发市场	58	河南省济源市南街集贸市场
22	辽宁省铁岭市银川区贸易城农贸市场	59	河南省荥阳市董村蔬菜批发大市场
23	吉林省榆树市五棵树黄牛交易市场	60	河南省新乡市牧野蔬菜批发大市场
24	吉林省集安市新开河人参中药材产地批发市场	61	河南省中源辣椒城交易中心
25	吉林省洮南市杂粮杂豆市场	62	河南省焦作金土地农贸市场
26	吉林省伊通县营城子镇黄牛市场	63	河南省漯河市南关农副产品批发市场
27	黑龙江北安农贸交易中心	64	湖北省咸丰县仔猪批发市场
28	黑龙江鹤岗市万圃源蔬菜批发市场	65	湖北省潜江市江汉果蔬批发市场
29	黑龙江七台河市合兴蔬菜综合批发市场	66	湖北省罗田县板栗批发市场
30	江苏省苏州市相城区生态农副产品批发市场	67	湖北省襄樊市蔬菜批发市场
31	江苏省邳州市宿羊山镇大蒜市场	68	湖南省娄底市湘中果品蔬菜批发市场
32	江苏省张家港市青草巷农副产品批发市场	69	湖南省邵阳市城步湘城农副产品批发市场
33	江苏省扬州阿波罗花木批发市场	70	湖南省湘潭市蔬菜批发市场
34	浙江省杭州果品有限公司	71	广东省东莞市江南农副产品批市场
35	浙江省嘉兴平湖市农副产品综合批发市场	72	广东省佛山市南海区永利综合批发市场
36	浙江省台州市路桥区蔬菜批发市场	73	广西凭祥市天源水果交易市场
37	浙江（嘉善）农产品批发市场	74	广西荔浦县农副产品综合批发市场

（续）

序号	市场名称	序号	市场名称
75	广西永福县三皇乡果蔬批发市场	94	甘肃省榆中县蒋家营蔬菜批发市场
76	海南奥林昌海果蔬批发市场	95	甘肃省陇兴农产品有限公司
77	重庆市潼南无公害蔬菜批发市场	96	甘肃省兰州市红古农产品批发市场
78	重庆三亚湾水产品综合中交易市场	97	青海省海南藏族自治州恰小恰农畜产品批发市场
79	四川省成都龙泉聚和（国际）果蔬交易市场	98	青海省大通县城关农副产品批发市场
80	四川省达州市塔沱农副产品综合批发市场	99	宁夏石嘴山市百花蔬菜批发市场
81	四川省油江市川西北仔猪交易批市场	100	宁夏中卫市城关批发市场
82	贵州省贵阳市谷丰粮油食品批发市场	101	宁夏固原市原州区蔬菜批发市场
83	贵州省乌当蔬菜产地批发市场	102	新疆昌吉市亚中高城综合批发市场
84	云南省罗平海丰银渔业有限公司	103	新疆乌鲁木齐市新联农贸批发市场
85	云南省泸西县综合交易市场	104	新疆霍城县神农市场
86	云南华宁华奚柑橘批发市场	105	新疆喀什市正大农贸综合市场
87	陕西省咸阳三原惜字恒丰蔬菜交易市场	106	新疆哈密市丰盛农副产品批发市场
88	陕西省西安市高陵县东新街村蔬菜批发市场	107	新疆和田市昆仑农产品批发市场
89	陕西省宝鸡市陈仓区太公庙蔬菜市场	108	新疆乌鲁木齐市华凌新产品综合批发市场
90	陕西省汉中市洋县果菜批发市场	109	新疆兵团农十师北屯军垦农产品交易市场
91	甘肃省渭源县会川马铃薯优质种薯专业批发市场	110	新疆兵团农二师库尔勒市孔雀农副产品综合批发市场
92	甘肃省临洮县现代化综合花卉交易市场	111	新疆兵团农七师一三七团绿衡蔬菜瓜果批发市场
93	甘肃省定西市安定马铃薯综合交易中心	112	新疆兵团农四师六十二团农产品综合批发市场

注：农业部定点市场工作自 1995 年开展以来，已经批准 11 批共 503 个定点市场，表中 112 个市场为农业部批准的第 12 批定点市场。摘自农业部 2006 年 12 月 5 日发布的农市场（2006）22 号《关于批准第十二批农业部定点市场的通知》。

表 229　2004 年度我国食品工业最具成长性民营企业（100 个）

序号	企业名称	序号	企业名称
1	河北五得利集团	18	宁夏香山酒业（集团）有限公司
2	沂水正航食品有限公司	19	广东丰源粮油工业有限公司
3	南通宝港油脂发展有限公司	20	滕州市雪源淀粉有限责任公司
4	河南省淇县永达食业有限公司	21	新民市胜源肉禽有限公司
5	淮安市华茂食品有限公司	22	厦门市同安银祥实业有限公司
6	山西雁门乳业有限责任公司	23	山东新昌肉食有限责任公司
7	福建雅客食品有限公司	24	江西汪氏蜜蜂有限公司
8	山西晋美油脂有限公司	25	江苏汤沟酒业有限公司
9	四川省资阳市四海发展实业有限公司	26	南京桂花鸭（集团）公司
10	山西纪元玉米产业有限公司	27	山东金牌实业有限公司
11	陵县乐悟集团	28	河南省华宝工贸有限公司
12	杭州佳美旅游营养食品有限公司	29	福建金石制油有限公司
13	成都市伍田食品有限公司	30	山东孔府家集团有限公司
14	宁夏香山中宁枸杞制品有限公司	31	广东温氏食品集团有限公司
15	山西省平遥县龙海实业有限公司	32	内蒙古临河市宏发油脂有限责任公司
16	南通顺发面粉有限责任公司	33	河南省天冰冷饮有限公司
17	山东驰中食品有限公司	34	贵阳南阳老干妈风味食品有限责任公司

（续）

序号	企业名称	序号	企业名称
35	四川省福润肉类食品有限公司	68	青岛西苑冷冻食品有限公司
36	卫河酒业有限责任公司	69	黑龙江省飞鹤乳业有限公司
37	江苏双沟曲酒厂	70	山东德州中普食品有限公司
38	上虞市东海食品有限公司	71	通州市银河面粉有限公司
39	浙江李子园牛奶食品有限责任公司	72	青岛尚恩肉食蔬菜有限公司
40	四川省苍溪县鸿宇冷冻食品有限公司	73	蓬莱市红火火食品股份有限公司
41	昌黎县淀粉有限公司	74	江苏阿里山食品有限公司
42	青岛波尼亚食品有限公司	75	浚县王庄乡齐雪淀粉厂
43	四川隆昌四海发展实业有限公司	76	滕州市恒仁淀粉有限责任公司
44	邯郸市东方面粉有限公司	77	山东亚奥特乳业有限公司
45	厦门中盛粮油企业公司	78	西安国维淀粉有限责任公司
46	石家庄市田牛牧业有限公司	79	河南省许昌姚花春酒业集团
47	天津蓬勃油脂有限公司	80	吴江市合兴味精有限公司
48	招远市圆龙华茂食品有限公司	81	内蒙古草原牛妈妈乳业股份有限公司
49	四川和久农业集团有限公司	82	邹平六和畜牧有限公司
50	齐齐哈尔市丰源肉联厂	83	内江山山酒业有限责任公司
51	番禺绿环美食品有限公司	84	自贡市华润肉食品有限公司
52	天津市利康油脂有限公司	85	山东德州双王食品有限公司
53	沪县吉龙食品有限公司	86	郑州金苑面业有限公司
54	辽源市金昌企业集团公司	87	江苏金杨集团公司
55	潍坊汇源实业有限公司	88	浙江华发出口茶厂
56	陕西老牛面粉有限公司	89	临清市东盛食品有限公司
57	宜宾市高金食品有限公司	90	鲁信面粉有限公司
58	巨野县华星油脂有限公司	91	莆田市东南香米业发展有限公司
59	大连华农豆业科技发展有限公司	92	格力特实业有限公司
60	招远市江东食品有限公司	93	临邑县克代尔啤酒有限公司
61	山东高密市商羊神酒业有限公司	94	沭阳县商业肉联厂
62	大丰市佳丰油脂有限责任公司	95	河北省邢台沙河市金沙河面业有限责任公司
63	深圳市博康保健品有限公司	96	青岛凯乐制粉有限公司
64	新疆麦趣尔食品有限公司	97	福建康宏股份有限公司
65	邹平县三星植物油厂	98	隆昌瑞丰有限公司
66	遂宁市高金食品有限公司	99	四川阆中光路冷冻食品有限公司
67	河北省邢台市隆尧县中旺食品集团有限公司	100	辽源市德春米业公司

表 230　2004 年度我国食品工业百强企业

序号	企业名称	序号	企业名称
1	河南省漯河市双汇实业集团有限责任公司	7	内蒙古蒙牛乳业集团股份有限公司
2	四川宜宾五粮液集团有限公司	8	东海粮油（张家港）工业有限公司
3	可口可乐（中国）饮料有限公司	9	内蒙古伊利实业集团股份有限公司
4	天津顶新集团	10	青岛啤酒股份有限公司
5	山东金锣企业集团总公司	11	维维集团
6	杭州娃哈哈集团有限公司	12	华润雪花啤酒（中国）有限公司

（续）

序号	企 业 名 称	序号	企 业 名 称
13	百事可乐（中国）有限公司	58	东莞徐记食品有限公司
14	上海光明乳业股份有限公司	59	黑龙江省完达山乳业股份有限公司
15	北京燕京啤酒股份有限公司	60	福建雪津啤酒有限公司
16	统一企业食品有限公司	61	黑龙江省北大荒米业有限公司
17	长春大成实业集团有限公司	62	北京顺鑫农业股份有限公司
18	诸城市外贸有限责任公司	63	东莞市东糖集团公司
19	石家庄三鹿集团股份有限公司	64	南京喜之郎食品有限公司
20	雀巢中国食品有限公司	65	菱花集团公司
21	秦皇岛金海粮油工业有限公司	66	中国绍兴黄酒集团有限公司
22	南海油脂工业（赤湾）有限公司	67	乐百氏（广东）食品饮料有限公司
23	冠生园（集团）有限公司	68	河北省邢台市隆尧县华龙食品集团有限公司
24	黑龙江省九三油脂有限责任公司	69	佛山市海天调味食品有限公司
25	北京汇源饮料食品集团	70	焦作黄河集团公司
26	大海粮油工业（防城港）有限公司	71	山东香驰粮油有限公司
27	三河汇福粮油食品制作有限公司	72	河南省潢川华英禽业集团总公司
28	吉林德大有限公司	73	山东大洋食品集团有限公司
29	中国贵州茅台酒厂（集团）有限责任公司	74	南宁糖业股份有限公司
30	南通宝港油脂发展有限公司	75	育岛万福集团股份有限公司
31	得利斯集团有限公司	76	河南汇通肉食品股份有限公司
32	河南省莲花味精集团有限公司	77	广东健力宝饮料有限公司
33	山东凤祥有限责任公司	78	海南椰岛股份有限公司
34	烟台张裕集团有限公司	79	黑龙江华润酒精有限公司
35	重庆啤酒集团	80	山东新昌肉食有限责任公司
36	山东九发集团公司	81	露露集团有限责任公司
37	山东渤海油脂工业有限公司	82	黄龙食品工业有限公司
38	北海粮油工业（天津）有限公司	83	河南省科迪食品集团股份有限公司
39	内蒙古草原兴发股份有限公司	84	南京雨润肉食品有限公司
40	哈尔滨啤酒有限公司	85	高唐蓝山集团总公司
41	好当家集团有限公司	86	英特儿营养乳品有限公司
42	河北五得利面粉集团有限公司	87	吉林省长春皓月清真实业股份有限公司
43	广州珠江啤酒股份有限公司	88	上海太太乐调味食品有限公司
44	辽宁富虹油品集团有限公司	89	四川沱牌集团有限公司
45	四川剑南春集团有限责任公司	90	上好佳（中国）有限公司
46	山东龙大企业集团有限公司	91	龙口新龙食油有限公司
47	箭牌口香糖有限公司	92	湖南唐人神集团股份有限公司
48	百威（武汉）国际啤酒有限公司	93	河南大用实业有限公司
49	泸州老窖集团有限责任公司	94	中法合营王朝葡萄酿酒有限公司
50	山东鲁花集团有限公司	95	红牛维他命饮料有限公司
51	爱芬食品（北京）有限公司	96	秦皇岛骊骅淀粉有限公司
52	山西省杏花村汾酒集团公司	97	四川全兴股份有限公司
53	河南省南街村有限公司	98	广东顺德糖厂有限公司
54	青岛九联集团股份有限公司	99	湖北枝江酒业股份有限公司
55	四川蓝剑（集团）有限责任公司	100	河南省淇县永达食业有限公司
56	上海良友海狮油脂实业有限公司		
57	安徽省古井集团有限责任公司		

表 231　我国轻工业系统中列入国家 500 强企业的农产品加工企业（2004 年）

名次	企业名称	地区	营业收入（万元）	实现利润（万元）	收入增长率（%）
	进出口贸易业				
1	中国粮油食品进出口集团有限公司	北　京	11 000 167	92 899	0.27
2	东方国际（集团）有限公司	上　海	2 472 246	12 875	2.19
3	广东省丝绸（集团）公司	广　东	1 347 084	3 953	0.56
4	中国纺织品进出总公司	北　京	1 000 631	12 346	55.77
5	中国纺织工艺品进出总公司	北　京	947 322	−718	9.70
6	广州轻工集团有限公司	广　东	322 045	1 266	22.67
	食品加工与饮料制造业				
1	河南省漯河市双汇实业集团有限责任公司	河　南	1 215 965	64 546	42.99
2	四川省宜宾五粮液集团有限公司	四　川	1 211 882	129 251	20.38
3	杭州娃哈哈集团有限公司	浙　江	1 018 918	136 669	15.39
4	青岛啤酒股份有限公司	山　东	750 796	25 387	8.23
5	内蒙古伊利实业股份有限公司	内蒙古	629 933	19 959	57.09
6	江苏雨润食品产业集团有限公司	江　苏	623 326	27 932	50.09
7	北京燕京啤酒有限公司	北　京	608 102	30 144	27.04
8	光明乳业股份有限公司	上　海	598 108	28 246	19.11
9	上海梅林正广和（集团）有限公司	上　海	538 700	6 429	−4.41
10	石家庄三鹿集团股份有限公司	河　北	530 456	22 122	72.59
11	天津市一轻集团（控股）有限公司	天　津	502 984	18 685	15.12
12	大连华农豆业集团股份有限公司	辽　宁	500 216	30 118	49.21
13	广州珠江啤酒集团有限公司	广　东	335 990	18 320	18.55
	烟草加工业				
1	玉溪红塔烟草（集团）有限责任公司	云　南	2 733 621	262 028	−18.63
2	上海烟草集团公司	上　海	1 617 335	424 437	−0.84
3	云南昆明卷烟厂	云　南	988 493	122 176	20.08
4	湖南长沙卷烟厂	湖　南	909 955	90 196	15.48
5	常德卷烟厂	湖　南	724 756	66 003	19.32
6	杭州卷烟厂	浙　江	710 629	81 448	25.47
7	颐中烟草（集团）有限公司	山　东	593 874	18 135	16.52
8	宁波卷烟厂	浙　江	537 330	46 398	7.34
9	南京卷烟厂	江　苏	474 280	62 635	16.75
10	贵阳卷烟厂	贵　州	418 167	18 376	8.31
11	将军烟草集团有限公司	山　东	418 121	19 897	16.82
12	河南新郑烟草（集团）公司	河　南	378 713	10 600	9.04
13	淮阴卷烟厂	江　苏	360 412	31 000	17.69
	纺织业				
1	上海纺织控股（集团）有限公司	上　海	2 600 298	8 317	22.90
2	山东魏桥创业集团有限公司	山　东	1 142 876	59 648	88.15
3	江苏国泰国际集团有限公司	江　苏	1 038 073	15 135	40.76
4	浙江东方集团控股有限公司	浙　江	968 076	5 073	42.08

（续）

名次	企业名称	地区	营业收入（万元）	实现利润（万元）	收入增长率（%）
5	浙江省丝绸集团有限公司	浙江	468 865	7 777	−4.34
6	宁波维科集团股份有限公司	浙江	465 006	10 861	48.40
7	东莞福安纺织印染有限公司	广东	440 856	8 738	16.19
8	广东省开平涤纶企业集团公司	广东	405 982	10 700	22.59
9	内蒙古鄂尔多斯羊绒集团有限责任公司	内蒙古	397 245	28 982	37.91
10	天津纺织集团有限公司	天津	331 414	7 030	38.20
11	山东省绮丽集团公司	山东	331 342	2 329	29.49
	服装及其他纤维品制造业				
1	雅戈尔集团股份有限公司	浙江	1 001 964	55 511	46.37
2	江苏阳光集团有限公司	江苏	667 008	25 239	10.73
3	海澜集团公司	江苏	532 221	24 844	32.51
4	衫衫集团有限公司	浙江	402 511	17 606	25.38
	木材加工、造纸及纸制品业				
1	山东大王集团有限公司	山东	778 044	66 249	52.83
2	山东晨鸣纸业集团股份有限公司	山东	752 739	67 886	65.57
3	金东纸业（江苏）有限公司	江苏	737 536	76 471	22.67
4	红星家具集团有限公司	江苏	623 000	9 210	49.40
5	上海新高潮（集团）有限公司	上海	588 880	21 390	4.44
	橡胶、塑料制品业				
1	双星集团有限责任公司	山东	579 260	9 132	1.47
2	申达集团有限公司	江苏	396 848	22 123	53.77
3	杭州中策橡胶有限公司	浙江	369 439	13 549	45.60
4	三角集团有限公司	山东	361 528	12 754	16.21
5	浙江大东南集团有限公司	浙江	357 950	21 215	73.93
6	佛山塑料集团股份有限公司	广东	357 838	11 781	42.37
7	山东成山集团有限公司	山东	356 517	9 817	37.11

5

第五部分

各省、自治区、直辖市农产品加工业

北京京郊农产品加工业

北京市乡镇企业局

一、基本情况

截止到2006年6月底，京郊乡镇农产品加工企业664个，同比增加50个，职工7万余人；完成总收入118亿元，同比增长25%。其中规模以上企业329个，同比增加20个；完成总收入51.2亿元，同比增长23%。带动农户约47万户。经农业部批准，北京郊区共有10个全国农产品加工示范基地和19个全国农产品加工示范企业。与2005年比较，北京郊区农产品加工企业增加、规模增大、产品增多、质量提高。京郊农产品加工业蓄势待发，通过政府的引导和政策支持，经企业多年的投入与发展，京郊农产品加工业已具备了向更高层面进军的实力。主要是：主导产业日益突出。食品加工业、食品制造业、饮料制造业和木材及竹藤棕草制造业的规模以上企业职工达到3.9万人，同比增长25.8%；销售收入116亿元，同比增长26.6%；工业增加值22.4亿元，同比增长30.2%。企业规模及数量快速增长，产品质量提高。郊区营业收入超亿元的农产品加工企业达到28个。如：通州蒙牛乳业（北京）有限责任公司2005年实现营业收入10亿元，同比增长56.3%。北京千喜鹤食品有限公司实现销售收入10亿元，同比增长102.8%。郊区已有10多个农产品加工企业通过和获得了国际上公认的食品行业HACCP认证，拿到了通向国际、国内食品市场的通行证。10个全国农产品加工示范基地发展迅速，成为京郊农产品加工业产业集聚、招商引资、农民就业增收的重要载体。通州区潞城镇食品加工基地实现销售收入12.5亿元，同比增长56.3%。蒙牛集团2006年在通州建立了华北生产基地，进一步扩大了生产规模。

二、发展特点

1. 拉动农业，延伸了第一产业链条　据统计，郊区规模以上农产品加工企业带动各类种植基地面积达93.33khm²，占农作物耕地面积的40%。郊区农产品加工业的发展，延伸了农业产业链条，提高了农产品附加值，加快了郊区传统农业向现代农业的转变过程。中旺集团、汇源果汁、丰收葡萄酒，直接拉动了北京、河北、山东的小麦和果树种植业；蒙牛有限公司、天河顺鸭业则拉动了畜牧业的发展。

2. 带动农户致富增收　农产品加工企业在促进农民增收方面效果显著。顺义北郎中村依托种植业优势，以农产品加工业为主发展经济，近几年相继建成了年屠宰加工60万头商品猪的市定点屠宰厂、年产5 000t的肉食制品厂、年加工5 000万kg的面粉厂。这3家企业村民投资入股占企业总股本金的40%，村民每年可获取可观的股金收入。大兴申安食品厂、李记酱菜厂、顺义前鲁鸭场通过给农民下订单，对农民提供给企业的梨、蔬菜、活鸭随行就市，市场价格高就按照市场价收购，当市场价低于企业的订单价格时，就按订单价收购，这种实行最低保护价的方法，使农民心中有了底，提高了种植养殖的积极性，企业也有了稳定的原料来源。北京丰收葡萄酒有限公司在大兴区采育镇建立起600多hm²葡萄种植基地，5 000农户靠种葡萄每公顷地纯收入37 500多元，比种粮收入增加数倍。顺义区北小营镇2 100多农户养鸭，供应该镇前鲁鸭厂、全有鸭厂、潮白鸭厂等十几家专门从事北京鸭屠宰加工、冷冻储藏、运输销售的企业，每个农户靠养鸭年收入可达2万元。

3. 促进农民商品经济意识的转变　“三农”问题的核心是农民问题。农民要想脱贫致富，首先是要经历思想意识、思维方式的转变，才能带来生活方式的转变、生活水平的提高。农产品加工企业通过公司带农户的方式，引导农民由自给自足的小农经济向市场经济、订单农业、有计划种养殖的新生产方式转变。

4. 为乡镇企业找到新的发展空间　一方面北京郊区的农产品加工业在整个农业和乡镇企业中所占的比重还很低，还有很大的发展余地。同时种植业既可为农产品加工业提供可靠的原料保证，又带来了一个副产品，就是郊区出现了众多的旅游村，这些村多以观光采摘为主，适应了城市居民到农村休闲养生的需要，拉动了第三产业的发展。郊区农业观光园已有790个。另外，受郊区面积较小的制约，出现了郊区农产品加工业到周边省发展的情况。例如北京蟹岛种植养殖有限公司到内蒙古建起10.67khm^{2}绿色食品基地；北京御香苑畜牧有限公司与内蒙古、东北合作，开展肉牛饲养加工、餐饮销售；大发正大集团、卓宸畜牧有限公司将产品成功打入国际市场，卓宸一年出口牛肉近万吨，大发正大集团年出口额5亿多元。

5. 立足首都，辐射全国　汇源食品集团将总部设在顺义、中旺投资集团将总部设在朝阳；蟹岛以北京为中心，走进内蒙古谋发展。企业看中的是立足首都，给企业带来的形象展示、信息传递的快捷、交通的便利等，以北京为轴心谋求在全国各地加速发展。

6. 首都大市场吸纳作用明显　北京人均GTP近6 000美元，全市年食品消费额近1 000亿元。巨大的市场吸引企业纷纷来投资设厂。北京汇源食品饮料有限公司将总部迁到北京顺义区北小营镇以后，公司发展步伐加快，销售额10年间增加150多倍。

7. 做精品名品　北京郊区农业种植面积小，不适合形成大的农产品加工生产企业。可是北京是个特大型城市，随着人们生活水平提高，对生活质量要求自然相应提高。“绿色纯天然、有机无污染、安全无毒”是人们对农产品加工产品的要求，也是企业的卖点。众多农产品加工企业的产品可以着力在北京市场打造成知名品牌，北京乡镇企业生产的丰收牌葡萄酒、汇源牌果汁饮料，分别荣获中国名牌称号。

8. 科技推动创新　首都北京人才资源丰富、技术先进，京郊乡镇有14家被农业部乡镇企业局认定的农产品加工技术创新企业，这些企业新产品开发、科企合作进展明显，这将有效地推动农产品加工技术的提升。

三、主要工作

1. 做好引导服务，加速农产品加工产业发展　继2005年成功地举办了中国农产品加工业发展与奥运经济论坛暨北京市农产品加工业投资洽谈会后，2006年8月再次举办中国农产品加工业名品精品展。本次展会有共32个省、自治区、直辖市、计划单列市组团参加；参展单位298个，其中外省市224个，北京市65个，科研院所6个，设备制作商3个；展示面积5 300m^2，参展产品、品种、规格、花色共九大类10 000余种；科研成果34项，推介项目70项。

2. 认真做好本市10个全国农产品加工示范基地和19个全国农产品加工示范企业跟踪服务，使其起到示范带动作用，促进了郊区农产品加工业的良性可持续发展。

3. 通过好中选优和严格的手续，向奥组委有关部门推荐了一批准备供奥运会期间使用的农产品加工产品。

4. 政策扶持　2006年确定对郊区42个农产品加工企业新建、扩建、技术改造的项目给予贴息政策扶持资金，扶持资金额为3 900多万元。这些项目计划总投资41.2亿元，项目竣工达产后，可新增职工2万人，可年新增销售收入69亿元，利税10亿元。

5. 创新工作机制，建立融资平台　为贯彻落实市政府政策支农与金融支农联动的精神，北京市乡镇企业局和北京农村商业银行决定共同支持京郊农产品加工企业发展。市乡镇企业局将汇总的10个区县共34个经济效益好、信誉高的农产品加工企业项目推荐给北京农村商业银行，该行将向符合贷款要求的项目发放信贷支持。

京郊乡镇企业认真贯彻落实科学发展观，坚持走集约、内涵式发展道路，抓住新农村建设机遇，努力创新发展思路，建立新的机制，为新农村建设提供强有力的产业支撑。2008年，奥运会将在北京举办，对农产品加工业来说是巨大的商机。北京现有70多个农产品加工龙头企业，产品质量均通过国家有关部门认证。通过第一、二届全国农产品加工业精品展示会，已向组委会推荐部分精品。奥运经济的诱人商机，有利于刺激企业快速发展，从而带动整个农产品加工业的发展。“好风凭借力，送我上青云”，京郊的农产品加工业借助首都的天时、地利、人和，迎来了黄金发展佳期。

天津市农产品加工业

天津市农村工作委员会

一、发展现状

经过最近几年的调整、发展和提高，天津市农产品加工企业的规模不断扩大，素质明显提升，初步形成了粮食加工、乳制品加工、肉类制品加工、果蔬加工和饮料、酒制品加工等五个规模较大的行业。据对年销售收入500万元以上的郊区农产品加工业和市直属市级重点龙头企业统计，各行业的主要情况如下：

1. *粮油加工*　培育发展了以天津利金粮油股份有限公司为代表的一批粮食加工企业，其产品主要包括面粉、方便面、粉丝、调味品、添加剂、食用油、玉米淀粉。2005年底共有粮油加工企业47个，当年实现营业收入33.6亿元，增加值4.6亿元。

2. *乳制品加工*　培育发展了以天津海河乳业有限公司为代表的一批乳制品加工企业，其产品主要包括巴氏消毒奶、超高温灭菌奶、酸奶、奶饮料和奶粉等。2005年底共有乳制品加工企业12个，当年实现销售收入11.2亿元，增加值1.1亿元。

3. *肉类深加工*　培育发展了以宝迪农业科技股份有限公司、大成万达（天津）有限公司和中敖畜牧集团有限公司为代表的一批肉类加工企业，其产品主要是分割肉、冷冻肉、熟肉制品和深加工系列产品等。2005年底共有肉类屠宰及加工企业35个，当年实现营业收入31.8亿元，增加值5.5亿元。

4. *蔬菜、水果加工*　培育发展了以金钟农副产品有限公司和中法合营王朝葡萄酿酒有限公司为代表的一批蔬菜及水果加工企业，其产品以速冻蔬菜、腌制菜、蔬菜汁、蔬菜罐头、水果汁、水果罐头、葡萄酒等为主。2005年共有加工企业21个，当年实现营业收入13.5亿元，增加值5.5亿元。

5. *糖、酒类和饮料加工*　培育发展了以天津挂月集团有限公司为代表的一批农产品加工企业，其主要产品包括酒精、各类白酒、啤酒、蜜饯、糖果和巧克力等。2005年共有加工企业26个，当年实现营业收入11.1亿元，增加值2.8亿元。

6. *其他农产品加工*　在水产品加工方面，主要是以海产品加工为主，其产品以传统的冷冻品居多，精加工和高科技含量的加工产品相对较少。2005年共有水产品加工企业11个，当年实现营业收入4.2亿元，增加值1.6亿元。在饲料加工方面，其产品主要是畜禽、鱼虾的浓缩料、预混料和颗粒料。2005年共有饲料加工企业25个，当年实现营业收入22.6亿元，增加值约3亿元。

虽然天津市农产品加工业有了较快发展，取得了一定成效。但就总体而言，与天津直辖市的地位，特别是与天津滨海新区加快发展的要求，与农业增效、农民增收的要求仍有一定的差距。主要表现在：一是大型农产品加工龙头企业数量较少、带动能力不强。二是农产品初加工的较多，精深加工的较少，品种和质量有待进一步提高。三是对农产品加工业还缺乏整体科学规划，农产品加工与基地建设还不尽协调，龙头企业与农户的利益联结机制还不尽完善。四是农产品加工业的标准化体系、检测体系、督察体系、技术推广体系、质量认证体系以及信息服务体系还不适应农产品加工业发展的要求。

二、发展重点

1. *乳制品加工*　重点发展巴氏消毒奶、超高温灭菌奶、液体调制奶和酸奶、奶酪、奶油、乳清制品等适销对路的产品。进一步提高超高温消毒奶的产量和质量，重点开发牛奶甜点制品、免疫牛奶、功能牛奶和花色奶等。重点扶持天津海河乳业，宁河的中芬、三鹿、完达山乳业，宝坻的津河、恒康乳业；北辰的光明梦得和武清的娃哈哈等乳制品企业精深加工项目。进一步优化企业和产品结构，形成相对集中、布局合理的产业格局。

2. *蔬菜加工*　围绕西青、东丽、蓟县、静海、宝坻等蔬菜产区，积极发展有机蔬菜产品和绿色蔬菜产品加工，加快发展具有出口潜力的蔬菜罐头、速冻菜、脱水菜、蔬菜汁、蔬菜粉、蔬菜脆片以及膨化蔬菜和保健蔬菜等。新建、扩建和改造一批出口型蔬菜深加工企业，扩大出口创汇规模。

3. *果品加工*　坚持果品采摘后商品化出售与果

品深加工并重，进一步突出区域特色，在蓟县重点发展梨、苹果、桃浓缩果汁和水果罐头加工；在汉沽、蓟县等区县重点发展干红、干白葡萄酒生产；在静海、大港区县突出发展冬枣及冬枣加工业。扩大果品加工基地规模，努力打造果品知名品牌。

4. *水产品加工* 建成全国最大的金枪鱼加工基地，建设占地 17 万 m^2 的金水海洋食品科技园，投产后可年加工金枪鱼制品 1 700t，加工其他海洋水产品 3 800t 以上；积极发展鱼、虾、贝类、海珍品等水产品的精深加工，扩大水产品加工量和加工品种，充分利用闲置冷库开展来料加工和半成品、方便食品、休闲食品、方便菜肴等新的加工品种。

5. *肉类深加工* 进一步提高肉类精深加工的科技水平和生产能力，大力发展冷却肉、分割肉和直接食用的各类熟肉精制品；利用生物技术，搞好畜禽内脏、毛、骨、血等副产品的综合利用，延长产业链条，提高产品附加值。重点扶持宝坻的宝迪、武清的中敖、东丽的国顺、北辰的宝顺和大海、蓟县的利和盛和顺京等一批肉类加工企业，促使其做大做强。

6. *禽蛋加工* 重点开发腌蛋、皮蛋、天然风味蛋和保健功能性产品；深度开发蛋黄精、蛋黄粉、卵磷脂、蛋黄油等一系列广泛应用于医疗、保健、美容、食品等领域的高附加值产品。在蓟县、宝坻等远郊县禽蛋集中产地建设一批禽蛋加工企业，重点扶持太阳食品有限公司等禽蛋精深加工企业，带动家禽养殖业向更高水平发展。

7. *粮食深加工* 以精深加工为重点，实现从粗加工向精加工、从单一品种加工向多品种加工、从简单产品加工向深加工产品转化。重点发展各类专用产品和营养、经济、方便食品。围绕远郊区等粮食产区，重点对现有粮食加工企业进行技术改造，扶持粮食加工龙头企业向更高层次发展，带动产品升级。深度开发玉米淀粉，生产变性淀粉、柠檬酸、淀粉糖等高附加值产品。饲料要向专用化、特种化、保健化和颗粒化方向发展。重点发展销路广、市场潜力大的食用植物油生产，加快研制高质量、高附加值、高效益的具有特殊营养功能的新产品。

三、主要措施

（一）提高认识，加强宏观指导

发展农产品加工业，可以促进优化农业区域布局和优势农产品生产基地建设，延长农业产业链条，提高农业综合效益，推动传统农业向现代化农业转变；发展农产品加工业，实现农业产业化经营，是增加农民就业、带动农民增收的重要途径；发展农产品加工业，是坚持城乡一体化发展，建设社会主义新农村的需要。各级政府要进一步统一思想，提高认识，将此项工作纳入本地区经济和社会发展规划，列入政府工作的重要议程，切实转变政府职能，改进工作方法，加强对农产品加工业的宏观指导和服务。各有关部门要明确职责分工，加强协调与配合，形成推进合力，共同促进农产品加工业的健康发展。

（二）创造政策环境，加快发展步伐

全面落实中央和地方有关农产品加工业发展的财政、信贷、税收、土地等各项扶持政策。按照“工业反哺农业、城市支持农村”和“多予少取放活”的方针，结合当地实际，研究制定切实可行的扶持措施和优惠政策。各级都要选择培育一批农产品加工重点骨干企业给予重点扶持，促其率先发展。

1. *扩大农产品加工总量* 根据建设社会主义新农村的需要，把发展农产品加工业作为破解“三农”问题的重要举措，结合开展“村企互动”活动，鼓励本市农民个人、社会法人和工商企业在农村投资建立农产品加工企业。凡符合国家产业政策，依法登记注册，有良好的经营记录，优先使用本地原料的企业，将给予一定的扶持。

2. *扶持农产品品牌发展* 按照既要加快发展，又要规范运行的要求，鼓励和支持规模化农产品加工企业引进先进的管理理念，打造消费者“信得过”的品牌产品和地方特色产品。抓好农产品加工企业的 ISO9000 认证、ISO14000 认证和 HACCP 认证工作。对年度内通过国际管理体系认证和获得市级名牌、著名商标的农产品加工企业，将给予政策奖励。

3. *扶持龙头企业加快发展* 充分发挥龙头企业技术改造贷款贴息资金的引导作用，重点扶持农产品加工骨干企业实行优质农产品基地建设、科研开发、生产加工、营销服务一体化经营。同时对重点龙头企业给予税收和信贷方面的优惠与支持。

4. *加强服务体系建设* 加强对农产品加工企业的服务和指导。在人才培养、企业家培训、信息服务、企业融资等方面加强服务。把中小型农产品加工企业列为信用担保体系的优先扶持对象；对重点农产品加工企业的人才培训、信息网络建设、科技成果推广、项目论证、企业诊断等给予一定的资助。

（三）抓好项目和园区建设

依据本市资源、技术、区位优势，立足国内、国外两个市场，顺应科技发展趋势，每年都要谋划一批、储备一批、建设一批、投产一批农产品加工项目，年年都有新的增长点。要统筹规划，加大对农产品加工项目建设的管理力度，实行项目建设责任制。

把农产品加工业项目建设与小城镇建设结合起来，在农产品加工业已有一定基础并较为集中的地区，合理规划发展一批农产品加工专业园区，为新建农产品加工项目提供坚实的载体。

（四）加快农产品加工企业的技术创新和管理创新

引导农产品加工龙头企业积极引进国内外先进技术、工艺、设备和管理经验，提升农产品加工企业的技术水平和管理水平。鼓励、支持企业与大专院校一起组建科技研究与开发中心，提高企业引进、吸收先进技术设备和自主进行技术创新的能力。在骨干企业着力推行 ISO9000 质量体系认证和 ISO14000 环境体系认证，加强职工的技能培训，提高企业管理水平和整体素质。

河北省农产品加工业

河北省中小企业局

一、发展现状

到 2005 年底，全省农产品加工企业达到 9.97 万个，从业人员 135.5 万人。其中，规模以上农产品加工企业达到 1 917 个，从业人员 48 万人，完成增加值 321 亿元，出口产品交货值 178 亿元。组织推荐认定全国农产品加工示范企业 24 个，加工示范基地 11 个，优势农产品加工产业集群 20 个，涌现出了一大批农产品加工龙头企业和具有明显特色的优势农产品加工产业集群，已成为河北省国民经济中最具活力的产业之一。主要发展特点是：

1. *农产品加工业规模不断扩大*　到 2005 年底，全省农产品加工企业达到 9.97 万个，比“九五”末增加 5.52 万个；规模以上农产品加工企业达到 1 917 个，比“九五”末增加 1 519 个；实现增加值 763 亿元，比“九五”末增加 663 亿元。

2. *农产品加工产业集群初步形成*　近年来，河北省农产品加工企业开始由过去的“单打独奏”向产业集群发展，各地因地制宜，科学谋划，形成了一批优势农产品加工隆起带和产业集群。如冀中南平原，形成了面粉加工、淀粉加工、方便食品加工等粮食加工优势产业集群；形成了环京津、环省会两大牛奶加工优势产业集群；以唐山、保定、沧州为主的特色果品加工产业集群。2005 年，紧紧围绕畜牧、蔬菜、果品三大主导产业和八大优势农产品基地，进一步优化农产品加工业区域布局，组织筛选了 15 个优势农产品加工产业集群，在政策咨询、科技成果应用、技术信息等方面给予重点指导和服务，提高优势产业的聚集度。利用省中小企业发展专项资金对 5 个优势农产品加工产业集群的技术研发机构给予扶持。2006 年 3 月，为促进全省中小企业产业集群发展，省政府出台了《关于中小企业产业集群发展的意见》，明确提出促进产业集群发展的总体思路、发展目标和具体政策措施，认定了 50 个省级产业集群，其中农产品加工产业集群 20 多个。

3. *农产品加工业示范基地迅速壮大*　“十五”期间，河北省按照“一县一业，一乡一品”的工作思路，积极培育县域特色主导产业、农产品加工基地和专业园区。到 2005 年底，全省拥有年营业收入 5 亿元以上的特色主导产业 167 个，其中农产品加工业优势产业有 50 多个。经县级以上政府批准的乡镇工业园区已发展到 491 个，园区内企业总数 86 858 个，从业人员 132.7 万人，园区内企业完成增加值 734.4 亿元，上缴税金 57.9 亿元，企业出口产品交货值 174.9 亿元。其中，农产品加工产业园区和基地占到全省乡镇工业园区总数的 30%以上，已成为促进农产品加工业发展的重要载体。河北省已拥有全国农产品加工业示范基地 11 个，省级农产品加工示范县（市）20 个。

4. *加工龙头企业带动作用明显增强*　按照农业产业化经营的思路，各地把农产品加工龙头企业作为重点来抓，发展壮大了一批规模大、效益好、带动能力强、辐射面广的农产品加工龙头企业，全省农业产业化龙头企业由“九五”末的 471 个，增加到 2005 年的 908 个，其中国家级龙头企业达到 21 个，省级龙头企业达到 230 个。2005 年，龙头企业实现销售收入 832.6 亿元，比“九五”末增加 564.8 亿元，年均增长 25.4%。龙头企业共带动农户 518 万户，其中，订单农户达到 34.5%，比“九五”末提高 12 个百分点。

5. *招商引资势头强劲*　“十五”期间，全省各地对农产品加工业的招商引资十分重视，坚持把招商引资工作作为发展农产品加工业的切入点，通过抓环境建设、政策扶持和提供优质服务，吸引了一批国内外知名大企业到河北省兴办农产品加工项目，为农产品加工业的发展注入了新的活力。近两年来，先后有内蒙古伊利、蒙牛以及上海均瑶、四川新希望等知名企业来河北省投资农产品加工业。

二、主要做法

1. 狠抓政策落实　积极协调有关部门，认真贯彻落实《国务院办公厅印发关于促进农产品加工业发展意见的通知》精神和《农业部推进农产品加工行动计划》以及《河北省人民政府关于扶持农业产业化经营龙头企业的若干意见》的宣传贯彻，落实好国家及省在税收、财政、金融、出口、投资、用地、用电等方面的扶持政策。为进一步完善政策措施，省局代省政府起草并出台了《河北省人民政府关于加快农产品加工业发展的意见》，明确了农产品加工业发展的总体思路、基本原则、发展目标、发展重点和主要措施，并将国家和省促进农产品加工业发展方面的政策措施进行了汇总，辑印了《农产品加工业发展指南》，免费发给重点龙头企业。

2. 突出抓好农产品加工重点项目建设　把抓好农产品加工项目建设作为促进农业增效、农民增收的重要举措，积极筹备召开了全省农业项目建设工作会议，提出了用抓工业的思路、理念、机制和办法，抓一批带动能力强、有市场前景和发展潜力的以社会投资为主的竞争性项目，重点抓好加工转化、市场建设、基地建设、良种繁育和科技型项目，突出抓好农产品储藏、保鲜、精深加工项目。省政府确定对农业项目建设实行月报和季调度制度，对投资5 000万元以上项目各市汇总后一月一报，对投资亿元以上重点项目一季度召开一次重点项目建设调度会，分析研究解决项目建设中存在的实际问题，推进农业项目建设，提高农业综合竞争力。

3. 大力发展优势产业集群　进一步优化农产品加工业区域布局，突出优势农产品产业和优势产区，实行扶优扶强的非均衡发展战略，做大做强一批优势农产品加工产业带和产业区，以“高、大、外、新”为重点，推动农产品加工传统产业、工艺和技术升级。围绕畜牧、蔬菜、果品三大主导产业，重点培育优势产业集群，利用中小企业发展专项资金扶持五大优势农产品加工产业集群建立和完善技术创新机构，提高农产品加工转化能力和附加值，促进农业增效、农民增收。

4. 扶持壮大龙头企业　按照“扶强龙、育新龙、兴小龙、引外龙”的思路，搜集整理了一批国内外知名农产品加工流通企业的基本情况，辑印成册，印发各市，有针对性地引导农产品加工流通企业与国内外大企业、大集团的合资合作，促进农业项目招商引资。按照省政府《关于加快农产品加工业发展的意见》要求，组织筛选一批省级农产品加工重点示范企业，在技术信息、贷款担保、招商引资、教育培训等方面，给予重点扶持。支持和鼓励民营企业把发展劳动密集型的农产品加工业作为再次创业的突破口，主动延伸产业链条，与基地、农户建立稳固的利益联结机制，形成一批专用、优质、稳定的农产品加工原料生产基地，为龙头企业提供加工原料。

5. 积极推进科技成果转化　近年来，主动与中国农业大学、中国农业科学院等国内10多所农业大专院校和科研单位加强校企、院企合作，推进科技成果转化，组织农产品加工项目对接，收集整理了150多项最新农产品深加工技术成果，辑印成册，举办了全省农产品深加工科技成果暨技术项目对接会，发布了200多项先进适用的技术项目，当场达成校企、院企技术合作项目意向协议100多项。

三、主要措施

1. 强化政策支持　切实抓好国务院《关于促进农产品加工业发展的意见》、省政府《关于加快农产品加工业发展的意见》等政策文件的督导落实，把国家和省扶持农产品加工业发展的各项优惠政策落到实处。加强调查研究，把握全省农产品加工重点行业、重点领域发展动态，及时发现新问题，提出新的政策措施。积极争取各级财政建立农产品加工专项扶持资金，加大对农产品加工业的扶持力度，为农产品加工业发展营造良好的政策环境。

2. 培育产业集群　有重点地培育一批农产品加工产业集群，重点扶持大名面粉加工、隆尧食品加工、赵县淀粉加工、清河羊绒（毛）加工、高阳纺织品加工、蠡县毛纺加工、辛集皮革加工、廊坊肉类加工、枣强皮毛加工、石家庄乳品加工等十大农产品加工优势产业集群，力争到2010年，十大产业集群年销售收入都达到50亿元或100亿元以上。

3. 壮大龙头企业　扶持壮大一批技术创新能力强、产业关联度大、辐射面广、带动力强、具有国际竞争能力的现代化农产品加工龙头企业。一是积极创造条件，改善投资环境，大力吸引工商资本、外来资本、民营资本介入十大国家级农产品加工示范基地建设，谋划一批大型农产品加工项目，提升一批龙头企业档次，加快龙头企业做大做强步伐。二是通过资产兼并、收购等形式整合资源，推进龙头企业实现低成本扩张，重点培育50个全国农产品加工示范企业，提高它们在国内外市场上的竞争能力。三是选择一批大型农产品加工企业，帮助它们与国内外知名农产品加工企业在市场、资金、产品、技术上的对接，建立一批高水平的中外合资合作企业。

4. 推进技术创新　加大对农产品加工业基础研究和应用研究及新产品开发的力度，不断提升农产品加工业的自主创新能力和核心竞争力。技术创新要主攻良种、新产品和加工装备三个方面。加快培育推广专用、优质的品种；加快研发名、特、优、新产品，特别是要围绕市民消费需求，开发方便食品和功能性、保健性食品；采取引进、消化、吸收和自主开发相结合的方式，研发高新农产品加工技术装备。推进产、学、研结合，鼓励科研院所、大专院校和加工企业之间强强联合、优势互补，形成以"企业为主体、以科研单位为技术依托"的技术研发体系。通过举办技术对接会、成果发布会、展览会等形式，加快科研成果转化，引进一批先进的农产品加工技术、设备和工艺，推广应用一批农产品加工先进适用技术，改造提高一批传统的农产品加工企业，提升全省农产品加工企业整体技术水平。

5. 鼓励扶持创业　把农产品加工作为全省中小企业创业辅导基地建设的扶持重点，在专项资金扶持上给予倾斜。同时，积极引导工商资本、民营资本创建农产品加工创业基地，催生一批从事农产品加工的中小企业，并帮助其不断发展壮大。

6. 完善社会服务　把为农产品加工业服务作为中小企业社会化服务体系建设的重点，强化服务手段，不断加大对农产品加工创业扶持和服务。在中国中小企业河北网建立农产品加工信息技术发布平台，及时发布市场信息、产品质量信息和技术项目信息，并为农产品加工企业开展ISO9000、ISO14000、HACCP和GMP等认证，提供高效优质服务。指导全省中小企业担保机构进一步做好对中小型农产品加工企业的融资担保服务，积极引导和鼓励担保机构把农产品加工业作为服务重点，加大担保服务力度，为缓解农产品加工企业融资困难提供有效支持。用好国家中小企业银河培训工程专项培训经费和省、市、县三级中小企业培训经费，每年定向为农产品加工企业免费培训一批技术及管理人员，提高农产品加工企业的管理及技术水平。

7. 实施外向带动　支持农产品加工企业大力开拓国内外市场，大力发展出口创汇产品。引导农产品加工企业扩大出口，鼓励有条件的企业到境外投资办厂，建立原料基地或技术研发中心。积极组织以农产品加工企业为主的境外产品博览、项目招商，促进大企业与国际知名企业的合作。组织省内农产品加工企业积极参加中博会、APEC中小企业博览会、廊交会等国内各类大型商贸洽谈活动，为农产品加工业走向市场搭建平台。

8. 加强组织领导　以农业部乡镇企业局加挂农产品加工局牌子为契机，进一步理顺管理体制。河北省人民政府《关于加快农产品加工业发展的意见》文件中明确提出："省中小企业局负责与国家农产品加工业领导小组办公室及相关机构进行工作联络，牵头组织协调各相关部门研究制定和落实加快农产品加工业发展的政策措施"。省局将组织协调有关部门积极落实文件精神，加强对农产品加工业的宏观指导和服务，建立健全农产品加工业统计、考核指标体系，建立市、县主管领导及相关部门发展农产品加工业责任制及激励机制。通过有效机制整合现有的政策、资金、土地、科技、人才等资源，加强与相关部门的协作，形成合力，共同推进全省农产品加工业快速发展。

山西省农产品加工业

山西省乡镇企业管理局

一、发展现状

近些年，通过各方努力，山西省农产品加工业已经成为新兴产业中发展最快的产业之一，同时也是产业结构调整的一个最主要成果。据统计，到2005年底，全省农产品加工企业共有5 213个，农产品加工业营业收入突破200亿元，5年平均递增15.8%，从业人员18.9万人，占工业从业人员的23.2%，形成固定资产203.5亿元，带动农户131万户。农产品加工业主要分布在粮油加工、果蔬加工、畜禽加工等生产领域，规模以上企业466个，其中销售收入过亿元的企业25个。总体上看，农产品加工业发展速度快，呈现以下几个明显的特点：

1. 形成了龙头带基地、基地连农户的运行机制，呈现出原料基地化的趋势　经过这些年的不断实践，山西省农产品加工企业逐步形成了“龙头＋基地＋农户”、“契约＋农户”等多种运行机制，走出了一条龙头带基地、基地带农户的路子，搭起了农户和农产品走向市场的桥梁。在龙头企业的带动下，全省形成了一批与大企业配套的种植养殖基地，如蔬菜、奶牛、肉鸡、粮食、水果基地。长治市50个龙头企业就联系种植基地200多khm^2，联系养牛基地25万头，养驴基地53万头，养鸡基地780万只，联系农户数达16万户。全省上规模的466个农产品加工企业，基本上都建立了自己的原料基地，已逐步形成了产业加工链条，产业化程度都比较高。

2. 涌现出了一批具有农产品加工特色的产业集群，大大提升了全省的加工水平　分行业看，粮油加工企业占75％，果蔬加工企业占7％，畜禽加工企业占13％，其他类型企业占5％。在畜禽加工企业中乳制品企业194个。已基本形成以古城乳业、康喜奶业、阿牛奶业、恒康乳业为代表的乳制品加工企业群体；以忠民集团、强盛集团、青玉油脂为代表的粮油加工企业群体；以沁州黄集团、绿是金集团、大同荣康为代表的小杂粮加工企业群体；以陈醋集团、四眼井醋业、绿韵食品、榆次聚泉醋业为代表的系列醋产品生产企业群体；以天骄枣业、天渊枣业、特达干果为代表的干果特产加工企业群体；以天龙啤酒、厦普赛尔等企业为代表的饮料企业群体；以新绛维之王、稷山胃乐、朔州辈辈龙为代表的果蔬加工企业群体；以粟海集团、山西宏明、介休聚兴、长治世龙、灵石獭兔、应县长城园肉乳为代表的畜禽加工企业群体等八大群体。这些群体以农业产业化经营为纽带，有力地带动了当地农村经济的发展，使得农产品加工产业化进程大大加快。

3. 形成了一批具有区域特色的产业　从区域空间分布看，农产品加工企业，在地方经济中发挥了十分重要作用。每个地市，大部分县都有一些上规模的农产品加工企业。从发展速度、总量规模和发展水平来看，主要集中在运城、长治、朔州、太原等地市，越是矿产资源贫乏的地区，农产品加工企业发展水平越快；越是龙头企业相对集中的地区，农产品加工企业发展水平越高。从产业分布看，全省已经形成以长治、晋城为代表的晋东南小杂粮等特色农产品加工，以运城、临汾为代表的粮油、果蔬加工，以朔州、忻州为代表的畜产品、乳制品加工，以太原、晋中为代表的醋、酒、饮料加工，以吕梁为代表的枣、核桃等干果加工区域特色产业。

4. 涌现出一批市场占有率较高的绿色名牌产品，代表着山西省农产品加工企业的最高水平　山西省农产品加工企业产品品种很多，有几百种，几乎遍及所有农产品。近些年，各地在培育品牌上狠下工夫，依靠科技进步，不断提升产品质量，涌现出一批名牌产品。其中，山西水塔牌老陈醋等多种产品获得全国驰名商标，古城奶粉等近10种产品获得中国名牌产品称号。全省获得国际、国内、省部级以上各种奖项的产品近300种，初步形成了一定的名优产品品牌优势。同时，各地还大力发展无公害产品，发展绿色产品，一大批产品获得绿色认证。仅长治绿色产品认证数量就达135个，居全国地级市之首。

二、存在的主要问题

近年来，尽管山西省的农产品加工业得到了长足的发展，也取得了可喜的成绩，但与山东等农产品加工业发达的地区相比还有一定的差距，存在着一些问题。主要体现在以下几个方面：

1. 总量少，企业规模小，农产品转化率不高　发达国家的农产品加工业产值与农业产值的比例是3∶1，全国平均是1.3∶1，而山西省是0.4∶1差距很大。全省农产品加工企业中，大部分企业规模小、战线长、转化率低的问题较为明显。多数企业采取分散经营，整体素质不高，品牌杂、小、弱，缺乏市场竞争能力，难以创造知名品牌和形成整体优势。

2. 技术装备落后，农产品附加值低　山西省农产品加工企业多是20世纪90年代的技术装备，普遍存在科技含量低，产品开发能力弱，加工程度浅，精、特、优产品少，产业链条短，市场辐射面小等问题。由此造成资源利用率低、产品附加值低、经济效益低。

3. 融资渠道不畅，资金投入不足　农产品加工业缺乏必要的投资和信贷政策扶持。由于农产品加工业一次性投入大、生产周期较长、资金占用时间长、周转慢，企业普遍缺乏启动和流动资金。各级财政用于农产品加工业的贷款贴息和周转专项资金数额偏小，且现有的扶持资金集中在重点龙头企业，难以惠及到众多中小型农产品加工企业，相对于其他工业，农产品加工业的信贷资金额度规模太小。

4. 产品多，精品少　全省农产品加工的产品有近300种，但真正在全国或全省叫得响的产品很少，即使是已经获得奖项的产品，由于宣传力度不够，营销措施不到位，市场占有率也较低，如永济芦笋，年加工出口量已达2万t以上，虽在国内外市场小有名气，却没有一个品牌产品。

5. 人才缺乏，技术开发不力　企业普遍存在缺乏专业技术人才和企业管理人才。由于农产品加工企业利润薄，职工普遍收入低，福利待遇也比较低，使各类专业技术人才和管理人才聘不到、留不住、养不起。同时，由于资金不足，技术开发难度很大，就连技术引进也受到限制，使农产品加工业整体上科技含量不高，制约了发展。

三、主要措施

1. 认真谋划农产品加工建设项目，积极创造条件，在政策、资金上倾斜，确保农产品建设项目的顺利进行　一是强化项目建设意识，以调产为主线，发展为主导，积极谋划、广泛招商、优化环境、规范运作、精心抓好项目实施。主要是在各级干部中增强发展的忧患意识，进一步增强发展经济的责任感和紧迫感。二是把农产品加工业在占用土地、税收减负、电力保障、利益分配等方面从优从宽安排。通过疏理解决协调各方面关系，帮助办理有关建设手续，解决好项目建设过程中存在的实际困难，突出为农民和有关企业解决水、电、路等配套服务。

2. 积极做好农产品加工业的引导和示范工作，使其真正起到辐射作用，真正成为农民增收的重点　一是立足本省农产品资源特色，以市场导向、区域特色、品种创新、产业延伸为出发点，提出全省农产品加工业的发展方向和重点。二是加强和科研院所的联系合作，积极开发科研推广项目，提升农产品的科技水平。三是强化公司与基地、农户的协调配合，在保障农民收入逐步提高的前提下，保证龙头企业的原料基地建设。

3. 大力扶持龙头企业　一个好的企业，往往能够推动一个产业发展、产业升级，带动一个区域经济发展。增强龙头企业的带动能力和辐射能力，通过资金扶持、科技培植、提高管理水平等手段，培育一大批农产品加工企业，使企业管理上档次、上水平，以质取胜，达到增效共赢的目的。积极培育新的贸工农一体化、产加销一条龙的产业化经营，以促进本省优势农产品区域布局和产业结构调整。

4. 加大财政、金融扶持力度，积极探索多元投入机制　一是调整支农资金安排比例，集中资金用于农产品加工龙头企业项目投入。进一步加大对龙头企业财政贴息范围和力度。二是各级金融部门对调整农业结构，发展高效种植业的农户，放宽政策，简化手续，加大贷款扶持力度。三是加大农产品加工招商引资力度，通过招商引资和项目建设吸引社会资金，非农资金的投入，实现企业投资方式市场化运作，鼓励外来资金兴办农产品加工企业，建设农产品基地，发展农产品加工业。

内蒙古自治区农畜产品加工业

内蒙古自治区农牧业产业化办公室

一、发展现状

1. 经济总量不断扩大　截止到2005年底，全区销售收入百万元以上农畜产品加工企业1 541个，比“九五”期末的526个纯增了1 015个；拥有总资产691亿元，是“九五”期末的3.6倍；实现销售收入874亿元，占到全区工业六大主导产业销售收入的20%以上，是“九五”期末的6.5倍；实现增加值230亿元，是“九五”期末的7.2倍，占全区工业增加值的20.3%，列全区工业六大主导产业的第三位。其中，通辽市、巴彦淖尔市的农畜产品加工业占到当地工业的40%以上。2006年上半年，全区销售收入百万元以上的加工企业达到1 600个，比上年同期增加164个；实现销售收入434.1亿元，比上年同期增长21.3%；完成增加值132.1亿元，比上年同期增长24.9%，继续保持平稳较快增长。

2. 规模企业发展迅速　2005年，全区销售收入500万元以上（规模以上）的加工企业达到927个，比“九五”期末的288个纯增了639个。规模以上企业完成增加值占百万元以上企业完成增加值的98.2%，支撑带动作用十分明显。亿元以上的企业114个，比“九五”期末的18个纯增了96个；10亿元以上的企业9个，比“九五”期末纯增了8个；百亿元企业2个，实现了历史性突破。

3. 品牌建设得到大发展　近年来，内蒙古农畜产品加工业培育了一批优质、高效、安全、生态名牌产品，其中有13个农畜产品加工品牌被评为中国驰名商标。在打造品牌的同时，积极扶持龙头企业做大做强。到2005年，全区共有18个企业成为农业产业化国家重点龙头企业；2006年又新评定了83个自治区级农牧业产业化重点龙头企业。自治区级以上农牧业产业化重点龙头企业数累计达137个。

4. 主导特色产业稳步发展　一是乳制品产业。近年来，全区乳制品产业得到了长足发展，销售收入年均增长速度均在50%以上。2005年，全区乳制品企业完成液态奶产量362.76万t，占全国液态奶产量1 145万t的32%，居全国第一。乳品企业实现销售收入249亿元，其中伊利、蒙牛的销售收入双双突破百亿元，在同行业的领先优势进一步扩大。二是肉类产业。2005年，全区有规模以上肉类加工企业260个，实现销售收入217亿元。加工能力达到180万t，实际加工肉类145万t，综合加工率达到63%。其中牛羊肉加工企业225个，已形成年加工肉羊100万只以上的企业15个，羊肉分割产品形成六大类、100多个花色品种。猪肉加工有15个，禽类加工有20个。肉类加工企业无论从数量还是企业的知名度，都有很大的提高，有些企业处于国内领先水平，近几年是肉类产业发展最快的时期。三是羊绒加工。2005年底，有百万元以上羊绒加工企业171个，综合加工能力超过2万t，区内加工率达到100%，实现销售收入137.6亿元，并且形成了一批知名企业，创建出“鄂尔多斯”、“鹿王”、“维信”三个全国驰名商标。在皮革、皮毛加工方面，逐步引进一批国内外加工企业，形成300万t绵羊皮剪绒制品、100万张服装革和3 000t绵羊毛的加工能力。绒毛产业已经摆脱了原料价格大起大落、加工企业恶性竞争的局面，走上了理性发展的轨道，呈现出逐步提高的发展趋势。四是粮油产业。2005年，全区有百万元以上粮食加工企业306个，实现销售收入81.2亿元；有百万元以上油料加工企业70个，实现销售收入35.9亿元。全区工业加工粮食716万t，加工率为43.1%。玉米加工发展迅猛，以玉米为原料的加工企业达到180个（含饲料加工），2005年工业加工玉米250多万t，初步形成了分别以通辽和呼和浩特市为中心辐射周边盟市的两大玉米加工集中区和加工企业集群，初、深、精加工合理搭配的良性产业格局，成为粮食产业发展的支柱和新亮点。五是蔬菜加工产业。全区有蔬菜加工企业83个，年加工鲜菜200万t，占总产量的20%左右。主要是巴彦淖尔市加工130万t番茄，其余70万t为脱水蔬菜和出口鲜菜精加工。实现年销售收入11亿元。六是马铃薯产业。2005年，全区有百万元以上加工企业42个，实现销售收入7.7亿元。全区加工马铃薯120万t，加工率达到16%。加工产品主要有马铃薯全粉、精淀粉、淀粉和马铃薯片、薯条。七是饲草饲料产业。随着牲畜头数的增加，饲养水平的提高和生态建设的需要，逐步成为本区的大产业。2005年，全区有百万元以上饲草、饲料加工企业96个，生产配混合饲料200万t，实现销售收入45.6亿元。特色产业是内蒙古的一大优势，近年来发展势头很好，加工企业初具规模。2005年，全区销售收入100万元以上特色产业加工企业达到248个，实现销售收入70.4亿元。2006年上半年百万元以上加工企业达到274个，实现销售收入38.7亿元，同比增长96.1%。宇航人的沙棘系列产品开发，东胜天骄沙棘酱油、醋的开发，巴林左旗鹿产品的开发以及二连、满洲里特种养殖毛皮对蒙古、俄罗斯的出口都形成了各自的特色和优势。

5. 经济效益明显提高　2005年，全区销售收入百万元以上加工企业实现利润总额67.6亿元，是“九五”期末的7.2倍。2006年上半年实现利润34.5亿元，比上年同期增长44.4%。

6. 社会贡献越来越大　2005年，全区销售收入百万元以上企业实际上缴税金28.9亿元，占全区地方财政收入的10%左右，是“九五”期末的6倍。2006年上半年上缴税金达到15.5亿元，比上年同期增长27%。2005年，加工企业收购农畜产品资金达264亿元，是“九五”期末的4.6倍。加工企业带动了142万农牧户进入到产业化经营的链条中，是“九五”期末的2.6倍，占到全区总农牧户数的40%。2005年，农牧业产业化为农牧民提供人均纯收入1 000多元，比2004年纯增了180多元，产业化经营为农牧民提供的收入占到农牧民人均纯收入的1/3左右。

在农畜产品加工业取得明显成效的同时，也存在着一些不容忽视的问题。主要是：龙头企业规模小，加工层次不高，市场竞争力弱，带动力不强；基地原料供应在数量和质量安全方面不能适应龙头企业的加工需要，牛羊肉加工企业吃不饱；农牧民合作经济组织运行机制不健全，组织结构松散，对接市场的能力弱，综合实力不强；加工企业与基地农牧户的利益联结机制不健全，农牧民从产业化经营中得到的实惠不多；投入机制不健全，中小企业和农牧户贷款困难，资金短缺的矛盾依然突出。对于这些问题，将高度重视，认真加以解决。

二、主要经验

1. 坚持把加强领导、完善政策，作为推进农畜产品加工业发展的关键　在宏观政策方面，自治区第七次党代会提出了实施工业化、城镇化、农牧业产业化的“三化”互动战略，将农牧业产业化摆上重要议事日程，以此作为农村牧区经济结构调整和农牧民增收的突破口和切入点。自治区党委、政府相继出台了《关于加快农村牧区经济发展，千方百计增加农牧民收入的意见》、《关于进一步推进农牧业产业化经营的意见》，为推动和指导全区农畜产品加工业提供了有力的政策保证。在组织机构建设方面，从自治区到各盟市、旗县都成立了农牧业产业化办公室，建立了自治区产业化联席会议制度，及时研究产业化经营及农畜产品加工业发展的重大问题。在新一轮机构改革中，自治区党委、政府要求全区各级政府把农村牧区一、二、三产业统筹规划，种植业、养殖业和农畜产品加工业统一管理，并且将推进农牧业产业化工作作为对盟市领导班子实绩考核的重要内容，为推动农畜产品加工业的发展提供了强有力的组织保障。经过几年的努力，在全区形成了党委、政府高度重视，有关部门协调配合，上下联动、合力推进的工作局面。

2. 坚持把确立主导产业、理清发展思路，作为推进农畜产品加工业发展的重点　一是在产业定位上，本着市场导向、效益优先、发挥优势的宗旨，自治区确定乳、肉、绒（皮革、皮毛）、粮油、马铃薯（蔬菜、瓜果）、饲料饲草产业（特种生物资源及沙产业）为本区农畜产品加工的六大主导产业。按照自治区的整体布局，各盟市本着有所为、有所不为的发展战略，结合本地区的资源、区位、加工优势，分别确立了各地的主导产业，制定主导产业的发展规划。二是在工作布局上，首先巩固提高目前已在国内市场居领先地位的优势企业，做大做强乳、肉、绒产业和具有知名品牌的龙头企业；其次大力扶持极具发展潜力、成长性好的新兴产业，培育壮大粮油、马铃薯、饲料饲草、皮革皮毛产业。此外，鼓励各地区根据当地的比较优势，加强特色生物资源、沙产业等方面的开发。

3. 坚持把以项目建设为载体、实施专项推进，作为推进农畜产品加工业发展的重要手段　从自治区到盟市、旗县都加强了项目库建设，围绕主导产业，注重策划大项目，明确重点项目，建立了项目库。并根据市场变化的需要，对项目库实行动态管理，力争做到储备一批，开发一批，实施一批。项目库的建设不仅便于各级政府加大对重点行业和地区的支持，也有利于实施招商引资，推动主导产业的开发。近年来，项目工作抓得比较扎实，竣工投产项目较多。2005年，全区1 000万元以上在建项目425个，投资规模346亿元，年内完成投资100亿元。2006年上半年，在建项目407个，投资规模436亿元，已完成投资78亿元。一大批项目的建成投产，为农畜产品加工业发展注入了新的动力。

4. 坚持把创新投资体制、加大投入力度，作为推进农畜产品加工业发展的保障　近年来，自治区不断加大对加工企业和基地建设的投入力度，政府在投入方式上创新思路、创新机制。纵向上打破过去就生产抓生产，就基地抓基地的做法，从基地到龙头按产业化系列进行安排；横向上改变过去各种资金单独分散使用的局面，财政支农、基本建设、农业综合开发、扶贫等资金按照总体规划，集中投向重点龙头企业和重点基地。在政府统一协调下，充分发挥各职能部门的作用，对重大项目采取“拼盘”投资的办法，渠道不变，各计其功，形成合力，达到最佳的资金使用效益。

此外，近年来各地还积极拓宽融资渠道，加大招商引资力度，先后引进河南双汇、上海光明乳业、河北梅花味精、新疆屯河等一批区内外国家级重点龙头企业在内蒙古建设加工厂，世界500强之一的雀巢集团也在自治区内落户，为农畜产品加工业增添了力量。

三、主要措施

1. 推进行业整合，做大做强加工企业　坚持培育和引进相结合，通过市场引导、政策扶持和项目带动，重点支持一批大型龙头企业以优势产业为依托，以资本运营为纽带，实施联合、兼并重组，大范围整合资源和生产要素，进一步做大做强，推进产业集聚，提升产业层次，打造优势企业集群，提高市场竞争力。

2. 加强基地建设，推进规模化、标准化、专业化生产　紧紧围绕主导产业，推进基地的规模化、标准化、专业化生产，发展集约化经营，做大做强一批优势农畜产品产业带和生产基地，不断提高农畜产品的产量和质量。加快专业化小区建设，充分利用本区农牧业环境污染较轻的资源条件，发挥后发优势，生产优质、绿色、无公害的农畜产品，发展生态农牧业。积极培养种植和养殖大户，利用重点户的示范和带动作用促进基地建设。

3. 实施品牌战略，提高市场竞争力　鼓励和支持国家和自治区级龙头企业率先采用国际国内先进标准，实施品牌战略，以品牌整合资源、开拓市场、扩张规模、壮大实力，不断增强农畜产品的品牌优势和市场竞争力。重点培育乌珠穆沁羊肉、苏尼特羊肉、河套番茄酱等一批有一定市场基础和品牌优势的农畜产品品牌和产品成为驰名商标和名牌产品。

4. 发展精深加工，提升产业层次　以科技为先导，依托大专院校、科研单位和重点骨干加工企业，建设一批自治区级各类农畜产品加工研究中心和工程技术中心，着力提升产业技术层次和工艺装备水平。培植农畜产品加工示范企业，大力发展乳、肉、绒、玉米等产品的精深加工，不断提高加工档次，增加花色品种，提升产品科技含量和附加值，发展循环经济，延伸产业链条，促进农牧业资源综合利用，实现加工增值提效。

5. 发展专业合作经济组织，提高农牧民组织化程度　按照“引导不参与，支持不干预，服务不包办”的要求，围绕主导产业和特色产品，大力培育多层次、多形式、多领域的专业合作经济组织。加强指导、服务和政策扶持，抓好典型示范，促进专业合作经济组织完善组织制度和运作模式，提高经营管理水平，为农牧民参与产业化经营和进入市场发挥好中介服务功能。

6. 拓展融资渠道，加大招商引资工作力度　一是继续加大对农畜产品加工业的扶持力度，认真总结经验，改进工作，进一步安排、落实好扶持项目和投资计划，提高扶持资金的使用效益。二是在加强项目库建设的基础上，精心筛选和策划一批重点项目，加强与有关金融机构的业务对接，做好项目推介工作。三是开展多层次的招商引资活动，组织更多的企业家走出去，积极参加由农业部等国家有关部门主办的各类经贸洽谈会、博览会、招商会，向区内外推荐重点项目，并做好后续跟踪服务工作，切实落实好已引进和对接的项目，不断提高招商引资的成功率。

辽宁省农产品加工业

辽宁省农产品加工行业发展推进小组办公室

一、发展现状

（一）农产品加工业已成为辽宁省支柱产业之一

到2005年底，辽宁省规模以上农产品加工企业达2 427个，实现销售收入1 248.0亿元，占规模以上全部工业企业销售收入的11.8%，居全省工业行业的第四位，同比增长幅度高出全省规模以上工业企业18.3个百分点，拉动全省工业经济增长4.1个百分点，比“九五”期末增加1.4倍，年均增长19.3%。年销售收入超亿元的农产品加工企业达到198个，实现销售收入610.7亿元。

1. 食品工业　规模以上食品加工企业1 063个，总资产528亿元，实现销售收入698.6亿元，占全省规模以上农产品加工企业销售收入的55.9%，占全国食品行业销售收入的3.5%，居全国第10位，比“九五”期末增长176.4%，年均增长22.6%。在农产品加工行业，食品工业发展速度最快，所占比重最大。其中水产品加工160万t，居全国第3位；白酒26万t，居全国第4位；啤酒188万t，居全国第6位；乳制品47.2万t，居全国第6位；食用植物油98万t，居全国第6位；软饮料90万t，居全国第12位。全省涌现了一批具有较强牵动作用的大中型食品加工企业，打造了一些全国、省内的知名品牌。如2005年，“鸡宝宝”牌鸡肉产品实现销售收入9亿元，在全国同行业排名第1位；“富虹”牌色拉油实现销售收入28亿元，同行业排名第4位；“红梅”牌味精实现销售收入3.5亿元，同行业排名第8位。

2. 纺织工业　规模以上纺织品企业742个，总资产330亿元，实现销售收入302.7亿元，占全省规模以上农产品加工业销售收入的25.9%，占全国纺织行业销售收入的1.5%，居全国第10位。

3. 其他农产品加工业　包括以农产品为原料的制药、造纸、木材加工、家具、工艺美术品等行业，规模以上其他农产品加工企业622个，实现销售收入246.7亿元，占规模以上农产品加工业销售收入的19.8%，“十五”期间年均增长16.7%。

（二）农产品加工业已成为县域经济的重要组成部分

省委、省政府提出以发展县域经济为载体、推进社会主义新农村建设的战略方针，做出了发展壮大县域经济的一系列重要部署，并指出要走“以现代农业为基础，以工业化为主导，以城镇化为支撑”的发展路子。省委领导强调，农产品加工业关联农村工业化和农业现代化两方面，既是县域经济的重要支撑，也是实现农业现代化的核心产业。要把农产品精深加工、综合利用和全面升值放到突出位置，切实增强加快农产品加工业发展的紧迫感和责任感，努力把全省农产品加工业提高到一个新的水平。全省规模以上农业产业化加工龙头企业数、销售收入、利税、出口创汇分别占全部规模以上农业产业化龙头企业（包括加工型龙头企业、流通型龙头企业、生产型龙头企业）的80.9%、64.6%、83.3%和71%，农产品加工业推动了农业（原料）生产的集约化、标准化和工厂化，促进了产业的发展和人口的集聚，加速了现代农业和农村城镇化进程。例如，农产品加工业已成为阜新市经济转型中的重要主导产业，2005年其实现产值占全部工业产值的比重由2000年的12.7%增加到30%以上，成为全市工业中的第二大行业。沈阳辉山农业高新区在不到4年的时间内，引进打造加工龙头企业200多个，2005年规模以上企业工业总产值实现70.4亿元（农产品加工业占主体），财政收入实现4亿元，拉动就业10.6万人。

（三）农产品加工业促进了农业增效和农民增收

农产品通过多层次加工，提升了附加值，提高了农业综合利用水平，给农民带来更多的实惠。大连庄河市近几年崛起了100多个以海产品加工为主的企业，2005年，规模以上农产品加工企业产值突破25亿元（其中加工型水产企业78个，年加工量20万t，产值16亿元），占该市工业产值的34%，促进地方财政收入实现5.6亿元，拉动就业1.98万人，带动15万户农民实现人均纯收入达5 138元。全省以农产品加工企业为主体的规模以上农业产业化龙头企业带动农民310万户，农民人均从产业化链条内获得纯收入达1 100元，比上年增长27.9%，占当年农民人均纯收入的29.8%。同时，农产品加工企业的发展，促进了农村剩余劳动力就近就地转移，推动了经济社会和谐发展和社会主义新农村建设，“十五”期间，全省规模以上农产品加工企业转移农村劳动力达20万人。

（四）农产品加工业已成为农业和农村经济结构战略性调整的重要带动力量

辽宁省农产品加工业已从被动发展的“工业依附型”向主动发展的“市场主导型”现代加工业转变。农产品加工业引领着农业结构调整的方向，促进了农产品区域化布局、标准化生产、规模化经营，催生了与农民利益密切关联的企业、农民经纪人及农民专业合作组织，推进了农业产业化、农村工业化和城镇化。2002年以来，大连市采取了从“北三市”开发资金中安排5亿多元，对在北部山区兴办农产品加工企业和收购农产品实行政策补贴；在市支农资金中安排1.7亿元，对80个固定资产投资额在1 000万元以上的农产品加工重点龙头企业实行投资政策补贴等激励政策，使全市“十五”期间规模以上农产品加工企业新增223个，达420个；销售收入新增169亿元，达321亿元；发展农民专业合作经济组织207个，培育年销售农产品500t以上的农民经纪人600个，带动全市65%的农户进入农业产业化链条。

二、存在的主要问题

尽管“十五”期间以食品工业为主体的辽宁省农产品加工业得到了快速发展，奠定了较好基础，但与其他沿海发达地区相比还有较大差距，加快发展的任务还相当艰巨。主要存在以下问题：

1. *农产品加工结构不合理* 全省农产品综合加工率虽在50%以上，但大多为初级加工，而精深加工比例较小。以玉米加工为例，玉米是辽宁第一大粮食作物，2005年产量达1 069万t，加工比例占40%，但绝大部分集中于加工饲料和普通淀粉，而变性淀粉、燃料酒精、医用材料、玉米纤维等高端产品刚刚起步，有的甚至是空白；大豆加工仍以榨油为主，大豆蛋白、磷脂产品、油脂的深度开发还是雏形；制粉、碾米工业的副产品基本没有加工；蔬菜深加工也只是起步。农产品深加工率只有20%左右，低于山东、江苏、浙江等发达省份。

2. *农产品加工龙头企业竞争力弱* 辽宁省现有农产品加工企业产品结构单一、技术创新能力不足、精深加工水平低、品牌产品少、市场占有率低，造成加工龙头企业规模偏小，竞争实力不强。虽然年销售收入亿元以上的加工企业近200个，但几乎没有称雄全国的大企业，全省最大的农产品加工企业年销售收入为50亿元左右。

3. *加工业对农业的拉动作用有限* 由于加工龙

头企业缺乏强势竞争力，加之企业与原料基地时有脱节、农企利益联结机制不紧密、服务体系不健全等种种原因，辽宁省农产品加工业对农业的拉动作用不强，缺少能够带动一个地区经济发展、促进农民增收、实现产业经济良性循环的企业典型。

4. 宏观发展环境亟待进一步改善　一是经济管理理念转变滞后。一些职能部门仍习惯于计划经济的思维方式和管理模式，缺乏主动提供服务和规范管理理念。二是发展支持理念转变滞后。习惯于对实力型、成熟型、传统型企业的扶持，忽视对起步型、成长型、创新型企业的扶持。三是对农产品加工业的政策扶持缺乏统筹。支持政策和资金投入缺乏合力，资金分散在各个部门。省里没有支持农产品加工业的专项资金。四是中介服务组织发展跟不上。加工龙头企业和农户之间缺乏中介桥梁，多数加工行业没有协会性组织。五是涉及农产品加工的管理体制和运行机制不顺。

三、主要措施

1. 围绕五大分区，打造加工基地　引导、促进各市县做好地区优势这篇文章，构建区域优势鲜明的主导产业基地，搞好“第一车间”建设，大力发展优质特色农产品加工业。在辽东重点发展特产品加工业，开发绿色加工食品、中药材制成品、保健品和柞蚕纺织品，规范发展木制品加工业；在辽西重点发展适应半干旱地区的农业资源加工业，推进草业生态化和产业化，打造牛羊等草食畜牧业、多样性干鲜果品、薯类、优质杂粮等农产品加工业；在辽北重点发展粮牧并举加工业，打造专用玉米、优质大豆、生猪、肉牛等粮食和畜产加工企业，突出综合利用和精深加工；在中部充分利用城市群的各种有利条件，打造精品农业基地，发展综合型农产品加工业，建设中部平原农业加工密集区；在南部沿海充分利用开放条件，打造水产、水果等出口型农产品加工业，建设沿海农业加工密集区。

2. 强化创新、开放，促进产业升级　农产品生产和加工的发展对科技创新的依赖性很强。国家和省推进科技创新大政方针已经明确。要在鼓励科技创新中，调整科技支出结构，加大对农产品加工科技开发的投入，研究建立农产品加工科技开发风险基金，推进自主创新成果的转化和产业化进程，尤其要加速推进生物能源、生物化工、生物制药等高新产业的发展。按照省委、省政府提出的大力发展沿海经济带、打造“五点一线”的战略构想，贯彻落实《辽宁省人民政府关于鼓励沿海重点发展区域扩大对外开放的若干政策意见》，紧紧抓住中国成为世界投资热点和东北老工业基地振兴、国际产业转移、外资瞩目辽宁、南资北扩的历史机遇，创造优越环境，提供优质服务，吸引境外、域外、民间的资金、技术、人才投入，积极培育农产品加工密集区和农产品工业园区，发挥产业集聚作用，形成沿海牵动、中部辐射、全局互动的农产品加工业开放、发展新格局。

3. 整合财力资源，发挥资金效能　紧紧围绕推进“全国重要的优质特色农产品加工和生产基地”建设，采取积极措施，整合政府财力资源，捆绑使用，集中投放，最大限度地发挥资金的使用效益，支持农产品加工业快速发展。建立协调机制，在不改变资金管理渠道的前提下，整合资金形成投资合力，达到对原料生产基地的投入与对龙头企业的扶持相“对称”。

4. 培育加工“龙头”，打造企业品牌　一是打造一批“旗舰”式加工龙头。选择一批实力雄厚、带动力强、市场前景好、发展潜力大的重点龙头企业，实行重点培育，促进同行业企业间的联合、并购、重组和参股，走集团化、连锁化经营之路，发挥其对地区经济和农民增收的带动作用。到2010年，争取100亿元以上的企业发展1～2个，50亿元的企业发展2～4个，培育12个农产品加工产业集群，并以加工产业集群为核心，构筑农产品加工产业新格局。二是扶持中小型龙头企业做大做强。选择一批市场前景好、与农户联结紧密、有资源优势、科技含量大、管理水平高、发展后劲强的中小型龙头企业，在财政支持、金融融资政策等方面实行倾斜措施，使这类企业快速做强做大。三是培育精深加工龙头。通过自主创新、引进消化、联合开发等途径，培育一批精深加工龙头企业，带动粮食、水果、蔬菜、畜产、水产等辽宁优势产业的精深加工。到2010年，农产品精深加工产品比重由20%提高到35%。四是加快培育加工企业品牌。分行业确定一批重点打造、培育的对象，选出几个市场占有率高、影响大、有前景的品牌作为辽宁省农产品加工业的标志性品牌进行培育，促进品牌向名牌、省内名牌向全国名牌转化。制定鼓励品牌做大做响的政策，抓好品牌商标的国内外注册，建立农产品名牌评定、发布制度，营造有利于名牌发展的氛围。对已获国家驰名商标、省著名商标和国家、省名牌产品称号的企业产品，优先列入技术改造、新产品开发等计划。

5. 发展中介组织，提高带动能力　加强农民专业合作经济组织、农产品加工行业协会和其他为农服务的中介组织建设，鼓励各类农业、农民中介服务组织参与农业产业化经营和直接创办加工龙头企业。大力发展“加工龙头＋中介服务组织＋基地＋农户”的农业产业化链条模式，充分发挥各类农村中介合作组织在推进农产品加工、发展农业产业化经营中的桥梁、纽带作用，提高农民的组织化程度。

吉林省农产品加工业

吉林省农业委员会

一、发展势头强劲，成效显著

近年来，吉林省农产品加工业以资源优势为依托，在市场和政策驱动下得到了整合扩张，在迅速发展的同时，对地方经济的拉动作用日趋明显。

1. *总量不断扩张，规模实力增强* 近年来，吉林省农产品加工业进入了快速发展阶段，实现了由小到大、由弱到强，超常规、跨越式发展。2004 年，农产品加工业销售收入达到 670 亿元，比 2000 年翻了一番。2005 年，龙头企业粮食加工量达到 1 100 万 t，比上年增长 16.2%；肉猪加工量达到 950 万头，比上年增长 42.6%；肉牛加工量达到 140 万头，比上年增长 41.4%。农产品加工业销售收入实现 1 002.9亿元，比上年增长 49.5%，比 2000 年增加 3 倍多，农产品加工业已成为吉林省经济发展的最具希望、最具潜力的支柱产业。这一期间，在各级党委、政府的扶持下，通过兼并、重组、扩建、技改等形式，大成、皓月、吉粮、德大、华正等一大批大型农产品加工龙头企业迅速壮大，同时辐射带动一大批中小企业快速兴起。长春大成工业区已形成了 300 万 t 玉米加工能力，遍布近 20 个县（市）的原料玉米种植基地，带动了百万户农民增收致富，已经成为世界第二大玉米深加工基地。

2. *农产品加工系列不断壮大，区域布局不断优化* 在市场和政策的双重作用下，优势资源不断向优势产业集中，优势产业不断向优势区域集聚，依托粮食、畜牧业、长白山特产资源和良好的环境资源，在全省已形成了三大产业十大系列农产品加工龙头企业群，对全省国民经济发展起到了强有力的推动作用，从而使农产品加工业成为全省三大支柱产业之一。

3. *组织方式不断创新，利益联结机制日益完善* 在龙头企业和基地农民之间建立完善的利益联结机制，是发展农产品加工业的重要环节。多年来，全省各地围绕提高企业对农户的带动功能，不断创新组织模式，在巩固发展“公司＋农户”的基本联结模式基础上，又进一步探索了“公司＋合作社＋农户”、“公司＋协会＋农户”等新的模式。联结模式的不断创新、完善，为龙头企业加强生产基地建设、充分发挥带动作用创造了条件。2006 年，龙头企业与农户签订粮食作物订单面积达到 1 966.7khm^2，畜产品订单达到 2.6 亿头（只）。通过产销订单、股份合作、委托协议等多种有效形式，使公司与农户之间的利益联结更加体现出自愿、平等、互惠和双赢。

4. *注重研发创新，产品科技含量不断提升* 依托高校、科研单位联合开发、合作攻关，已成为龙头企业普遍采取的手段，产加研一体化步伐明显加快，一批具有自主知识产权的新产品相继投产，科技已成为龙头企业加速发展、提高经济效益的重要支撑。据统计，省级重点加工型龙头企业的技术创新投入占销售收入的比重达到 0.93%。大成集团玉米化工醇的研究与开发、皓月集团利用牛内脏研发的 73 种生化制品、辽源金昌集团利用牛血提炼的口服 SOD 等一些具有自主知识产权的核心技术，在世界都处于领先地位，使企业在提高市场竞争力的同时获得了巨大的经济效益。

5. *农产品加工业基地不断壮大，产业集群迅速发展* 在农业部组织实施的“农产品加工推进行动”的推动下，吉林省农产品加工业基地建设发展迅速，规模不断扩大，功能不断增强，结构不断优化，集群优势开始显现，规模效益和带动能力明显提高，已经成为本省农产品加工业和区域经济发展新的增长点和工业反哺农业的基地。通过推行标准化生产规程，主要粮食的优质品率超过 90%，733.3 khm^2 水稻，533.3 khm^2 大豆实现了优质专用，按照加工与市场需求生产的专用特用玉米达到 1 333.3 khm^2。其中，

10个农产品加工业基地被农业部命名为全国农产品加工业示范基地。

二、科学谋划，全力推进

1. 坚持做大做强龙头企业，不断提升带动功能 龙头企业的发展水平是农产品加工业发展水平的重要标志。多年来，省委、省政府始终把龙头企业建设作为推进农产品加工发展的重中之重，实施产业带动、项目拉动战略，先后启动了重点农产品加工转化“213”工程（20个已建项目、10个在建项目和30个拟建项目）、农产品加工龙头企业工程和“粮变肉”工程等，通过这些有效措施，发展壮大了一批大型龙头企业，逐步使资源优势转变为经济优势，以粮食、畜产品、特产品为原料的产业链条不断拉长，产品附加值不断增加，市场占有率不断提升，基地生产水平不断提高，农业竞争力明显增强。

2. 坚持高标准建设基地，为龙头企业提供基础保障 基地是龙头企业生产的第一生产车间，是农产品加工的基础，基地供给的原料直接关系着龙头企业的产品质量和市场信誉。近些年来，根据龙头企业的实际需求，结合不同区域的资源特色和生产基础，规划建设了一批具有一定规模和水平的标准化、专业化的农产品生产基地，实现了区域化布局，标准化生产、规模化经营，使粮食、畜产品、特产品的品质不断提高。

3. 坚持实施名牌战略，加大市场开拓力度 品牌是企业的形象，象征着企业经营管理的整体水平。吉林省的粮食、畜产品等主要农产品人均占有量、商品量、调出量多年居全国前列，深加工产品主要销往省外、国外市场。培育具有吉林特色的农产品知名品牌，对开拓市场，搞活流通，推动农产品加工业快速发展至关重要。近年来，通过展会宣传品牌，联合重组整合品牌，开拓市场推介品牌等多种有效措施，培植了大成赖氨酸、德大鸡肉、皓月牛肉、华正猪肉和敖东中药等一批在国内外有较高知名度和影响力的品牌企业和名牌产品，在市场开拓中发挥了重要作用。

4. 坚持科技创新，增强发展的内在动力 科技是企业生存、发展的第一要素，特别是核心技术已成为龙头企业在市场竞争中的制胜法宝。多年来，吉林省采取鼓励、支持、引导相结合的办法，支持企业成立研发中心或与大专院校、科研单位联办科研机构，提升科技创新能力，开发具有自主知识产权新技术、新产品，并引导龙头企业坚持高起点建设，特别是2006年农业部乡企局推出了农产品加工精深加工技术，吉林省积极在龙头企业推广，已取得明显成效。

5. 加强政策扶持，营造发展氛围 农产品加工业的发展过程就是各种要素向农业流动的过程，加快完成这个过程，不仅要依靠市场配置资源，而且还要依靠优化发展环境，为各种要素的有序流动提供重要保障。多年来，吉林省创造性地贯彻国家有关政策，为龙头企业发展壮大提供有力的政策支持。2005年，省委、省政府先后出台了《关于进一步促进乡镇企业快速高效发展的若干意见》和《关于进一步促进农业产业化经营的若干政策意见》两个文件，在财政、税收、土地用水、用电等方面，对农产品加工业给予了有力的扶持。2006年，在财力比较紧张的情况下，省里又在2005年5 000万元专项资金基础上安排了11 500万元，支持农产品加工业建设与发展。同时，省委、省政府主要领导和分管领导经常深入到龙头企业进行现场办公，解决企业发展中遇到的实际问题。经过全省上下的共同努力，农产品加工业逐步成为省内外、国内外企业集团投资合作的热点，民营企业、个体工商业户也积极投资农产品加工业。

三、抓住历史机遇，进一步做大做强农产品加工业

吉林省的农产品加工业虽然取得了可喜的成绩，但仍然存在着产业链条短、附加值低、融资渠道狭窄、资金不足等实际困难和问题，需要在今后工作中重点加以解决。“十一五”期间，是吉林省农产品加工业发展的重要战略机遇期，关键是用活政策，形成合力，加快发展，将农产品加工业做大做强。

1. 总体思路 紧紧围绕龙头企业建设，充分利用市场调节和政策扶持，加快建立促进农业产业化经营的多元投入机制、资源整合机制、技术创新机制和企业家成长机制，实现资本、资源、技术、人才各种要素向优势区域、优势产业、优势企业快速集聚，推动全省农产品加工业走上区域联合、集群发展、多极增长、群体推进的路子，在建设社会主义新农村的进程中，实现更快更好地发展。

2. 发展目标 经过5年的努力，形成与优势农产品产业带相适应的加工业布局，建成一批农产品加工骨干企业和示范基地；建立农产品加工业的技术创新体系，健全农产品生产及加工制品质

量安全标准；农产品加工业增加值占国内生产总值和工业增加值的比重有较大提高。具体目标是：到2010年，农产品加工业销售收入达到3 000亿元，利税达到300亿元。粮食加工能力达到150亿kg以上。围绕实现这一目标，全省农产品加工业重点抓好粮食加工、畜产品加工业和特产品加工的三大产业，包括玉米、大豆、水稻、生猪、肉牛、禽类、乳业、蔬菜（包括山野菜和食用菌）、中草药和林特产品十大系列。同时，围绕资源优势建立100个优质农产品生产基地。

黑龙江省农产品加工业

黑龙江省乡镇企业局

一、发展现状及特点

“十五”以来，黑龙江省乡镇企业农产品加工业总产值年均增长17.6％，2005年，全省乡镇企业农产品加工业总产值达792.8亿元，增加值244.3亿元，分别占全省工业总产值、增加值的11.6％、8.7％；实现税收32.1亿元，占规模以上工业企业税收的8.7％；从业人员18.4万人，占全部工业从业人员的9.8％。2005年，规模以上农产品加工企业已有627个，其中超亿元的企业达74个。实现工业总产值419.2亿元，占全部农产品加工业总产值的79.4％。主要特点是：

1. *在全省农产品加工业中占据主体地位*　在全省23个国家级和187个省级农业产业化重点龙头企业中，乡镇企业约占90％左右。

2. *骨干企业经济实力增强*　经过“十五”以来的发展，农产品加工企业的组织结构进一步优化，涌现出了一批经济实力较强、装备较先进、技术水平较高的大型农产品加工龙头企业和企业集团。例如，哈尔滨五常绿风优质米开发有限公司、黑龙江阳霖油脂集团、黑龙江翔宇实业集团有限责任公司、黑龙江沃华马铃薯制品有限公司、北奇神绿色产业集团、黑河爱辉区山珍产品有限责任公司等等。

3. *成为农民增收和扩大就业的重要渠道*　农产品加工业的发展，扩大了农产品的销售市场，带动了农产品基地建设，吸纳了农村剩余劳动力，增加了农民收入。2005年，城乡直接就业25万个，间接就业78万个，拉动相关产业增加收入50亿元，直接带动农户约120万户，每户年平均增收1 700元。

4. *区域特色日益明显*　黑龙江省是农业资源大省，发展农产品加工业有着得天独厚的条件，各地因地制宜，积极发展有明显优势和突出特色的农产品加工业，形成了一批各具特色的农产品加工优势区域。如兰西县充分利用亚麻市场看好的机遇，依托亚麻基地的保障优势，积极构建亚麻产业集群，重点发展了一批亚麻原料、纺纱、编织企业。肇东宋站乳品产业，在伊利、绿洲两个龙头企业的带动下，形成了有上千个养牛户，近百个鲜奶采集、收购点为一体的产业集群。牡丹江的东宁县是我国最大的黑木耳集散中心，是全国唯一无公害黑木耳生产示范基地县。2005年销售木耳2万t，实现销售额6亿多元。随着绥阳黑木耳批发市场的发展，黑木耳产业中生产、收购、加工、运输、销售、市场服务等环节逐步健全完善，已经形成了独具特色的产业集群。

5. *培育了一批名牌产品和具有竞争力的名特优产品*　黑龙江省乡镇企业农产品加工业坚持以市场为导向，围绕资源优势，以产品创新和技术创新为手段，形成了一批具有竞争力的名特优新产品。“十五”期间，获国家和省名牌产品121项，获国家绿色食品证书350项。“梧桐”、“北大荒”、“五常绿风”牌大米，“完达山”、“龙丹”、“金星”、“摇篮”、“飞鹤”牌乳制品，“大众”、“希波”、“义利”“里道斯”牌肉制品，“港进”、“丽雪”牌粉丝，“龙江春”、“北大仓”、“宾州”、“桂花”牌白酒，“哈尔滨”、“佳凤”、“北国”、“泉雪”牌啤酒等产品享誉国内外。

二、存在的主要问题

黑龙江省乡镇企业农产品加工业虽然有了一定的发展，但仍处于起步阶段，与发达国家和先进省市相比，还有很大差距。主要表现为：

1. *农产品加工总体水平低*　全省乡镇企业农产品加工业增加值仅占乡镇企业经济的13.4％，而且总体竞争力较弱，企业规模较小，缺少牵动力强的大型龙头企业。

2. 科技含量低，企业创新能力弱　全省乡镇企业农产品加工企业的设备和工艺落后，多数企业仍处于粗加工阶段，没有形成高附加值的农产品加工产业链。自主开发能力不强，新工艺、新材料、新技术在农产品加工方面的应用程度低，农产品加工的技术攻关对产业发展支持弱。企业技术人才和管理人才缺乏，缺少具备创新、开拓进取精神的企业家。

3. 投资不足，影响了加工业整体水平的提高　资金短缺依然是影响乡镇企业农产品加工业发展的瓶颈问题。由于农产品加工业一次性投入大，原料收购时间集中，资金需求量大，农产品加工企业普遍存在缺乏流动资金，尤其是大宗农产品加工企业资金短缺问题更加突出，大部分企业难以扩大规模，一些企业改扩建项目工程不能及时配套、完善，生产能力不能充分发挥。

4. 缺乏总体规划，支持政策不到位　一些地方还存在布局不合理、无序竞争和运输难的问题等，还未形成良好的农产品加工业发展环境和有效的管理体系。

5. 管理体制亟待理顺，服务体系有待健全　农产品加工企业门类很多，涉及多个部门，管理体制亟待理顺，农产品加工业标准化体系、检测体系、食品安全体系、技术推广体系、质量保证体系以及信息网络体系的建立有待加强。

三、主要措施

1. 进一步明确认识，加大对农产品加工业的扶持力度　一是政策扶持。省里陆续出台了一系列为加快企业发展的政策，已初步形成了内容比较完善、措施比较配套、门类比较齐全的促进非公有制经济发展的政策体系。二是资金的支持。建议各级政府要加大对农产品加工业的资金扶持力度，设立民营企业发展专项资金，重点向农产品加工企业倾斜。三是逐步建立融资平台。与各银行、担保公司等金融机构合作，开展银企对接活动，召开企业贷款现场推进会，向金融机构推荐信用度高、管理规范、有发展潜力的农产品加工企业。四是为企业引进人才搭建平台。为使企业引进人才，省乡镇企业局与省有关部门联合举办人才招聘洽谈会，并设立了省级中小企业培训基地，使中小企业教育培训向多门类、多形式、规模化发展。

2. 加快龙头企业和农产品加工示范基地建设，推进农业产业化经营　企业规模小，产品档次低，竞争能力弱，是本省农产品加工业的突出问题。为此，要在加快龙头企业和基地建设上下工夫。一是引导和推进企业联合重组。重点引导和支持机制好、竞争力强、辐射带动面广、与农民利益关系密切的农产品加工龙头企业和有条件的龙头企业进行技术改造和资产的优化重组，通过参股、控股、兼并、合并、租赁等形式，扩大规模，增强实力，发展成为大型龙头企业集团。二是加快品牌整合。农产品的竞争实质上就是质量和品牌的竞争，要采取各种政策措施，培育品牌、整合品牌、扩张品牌、保护品牌，引导品牌集中，抱团开拓市场，合力打响品牌，不断提升黑龙江省农产品加工企业的知名度和市场竞争力。三是搞好各级龙头企业和基地的联结。积极扶持龙头企业建设专业化、规模化、标准化的农产品生产基地。支持龙头企业为基地农户提供信息、技术、营销服务。遵循产业发展规律，引导龙头企业和基地农户通过合同连接、服务连接和资产连接等多种形式，结成经济利益共同体，建立起有效的利益分配机制，构建市场牵龙头、龙头带基地、基地连农户的产业化格局，提高产业整体效益，真正实现农业产业化经营。

3. 扩大对外开放，加快发展外向型农产品加工业　首先，努力扩大农产品出口。积极招商引资，扶持一批外向型龙头企业、大型营销组织和中介服务组织，加快培育农产品出口的市场主体。其次，推进对俄农业合作战略升级。加快对俄农产品基地建设，在加强境内基地建设的同时，在俄远东地区和新西伯利亚等地区建立生产基地。发展对俄出口创汇型龙头企业，支持企业技术改造、研发产品、培育品牌，增强出口创汇能力。

4. 推进加工园区建设，促进农产品加工业产业集群发展　全省已初步形成了粮食、畜产品、林产品、乳产品、山产品等产业集群和“一乡一业”、“一村一品”的块状经济格局，要在此基础上，以中小企业工业园区为载体，引导企业向园区聚集，不断推进农产品加工业向产业集群发展。在园区建设中，要坚持科学规划，合理布局，要突出产业特色，突破行政区划限制，与全省的农产品加工业发展规划相衔接。力求做到高起点，高标准，一次规划，分步实施。逐步吸引农产品加工及其配套企业向园区聚集，形成一批特色明显、产品知名、竞争力较强的农产品加工产业集群。

5. 推进技术创新和产品创新　第一，要引导企业加大科技投入。鼓励企业设立技术开发基金，提高新产品开发经费和风险调节基金的提取比重，增强企业自主开发、自主创新能力。第二，要加快研发机构建设。引导和鼓励企业培养一支自己的研发队伍，建立科技开发机构，开发具有自主知识产权的技术和产品，不断提高企业技术创新能力。第三，要走产学研相结合的路子。鼓励农产品加工骨干企业与大专院校、科研院所联合组建科学技术研究与开发中心，建立健全“政、产、学、研、金、介”相结合的农产品加工业创新支撑体系。第四，要引进推广新技术。要积极为企业搭建信息平台，及时提供技术装备、工艺、成果和政策信息，鼓励企业大力引进、消化、吸收省外国外先进、成熟、实用的技术装备，并大力推广，尽快缩短本省农产品加工装备与国外先进水平的差距，努力把全省农产品加工业推向新阶段，提到新水平。

上海市农产品加工业

上海市农业委员会

一、发展现状

上海郊区现有农产品加工企业 4 322 个，从业人员 61 万人。2005 年，农产品加工领域完成增加值 305 亿元，实现销售收入 1 396 亿元。根据上海市委、市政府提出的建设农业科技强市的要求，上海农产品加工业以提高质量水平和竞争能力为重点，形成了“抓产后加工、带产中生产和服务全国”的工作思路。通过抓科技兴农，组织跨部门、跨学科的科技力量，开展技术攻关，进行自主创新；引进国外先进的加工设备，开展消化吸收进行二次创新；组织对相关技术进行组合，开展集成创新。培育了一批农产品深加工企业，使这批企业的农产品加工关键设备和技术达到当今国际先进水平，通过抓提高农民组织化程度，形成了一批“企业＋生产基地＋农户”的农产品加工企业。在上海农产品加工企业中，涌现了一批在全国行业内具有较大影响的企业，如光明乳业是乳产品加工业的企业，上海高榕食品公司是蔬菜加工出口企业，上海大山合集团是香菇生产、加工和出口贸易企业，上海汉德食品有限公司是水产品加工企业。这些具有行业领先地位企业的形成，不仅提高了上海在农产品加工领域的地位，而且也为今后上海的农产品与食品加工业在更大范围内整合产业资源、形成国内国际竞争优势、扩大市场覆盖等方面，奠定了良好的基础和条件。

随着国民经济的高速增长和人民生活水平的迅速提高，近几年，上海农产品加工在冻干果蔬、保鲜切片（丝）蔬菜、冷冻水产品、流态化速冻蔬菜、低温油炸膨化食品、果汁果酒、免淘大米、畜禽蛋品加工等方面已开展了一定的研究和开发。主要产品有：

1. 一滴奶　上海的乳业企业中，龙头企业是光明乳业股份公司。该公司主要从事乳和乳制品的开发、生产和销售，奶牛和公牛的饲养、培育，物流配送、营养保健食品的开发、生产和销售。形成了消毒奶、保鲜奶、酸奶、超高温灭菌奶、奶粉、黄油干酪、果汁饮料等系列产品，是国内最大规模的乳制品生产、销售企业之一。光明乳业在全国布局近 20 个工厂、9 个大类近 200 个品种，资产达 35 亿元。2005 年实现主营业务收入 69 亿元，净利润 3.2 亿元。

2. 一粒米　在上海现有米业企业中，上海海丰米业有限公司是一个集产加销、农工贸于一体的米业专营公司。公司自营生产基地 16.7khm^2，年销售海丰牌优质大米 4 万 t 以上。公司主导产品海丰牌优质大米自 1997 年率先获得国家 A 级绿色食品认证后，先后被评为上海市名牌产品和全国首批放心米。其稻米的加工生产通过 ISO9002 国际质量体系认证。

为适应现代人生活节奏快、生活质量要求高的新情况，上海海丰米业有限公司引进了国际上最先进的 NTWP50B 免淘米精加工流水线。经该套流水线加工后的米粒大小均匀、整齐，减少了碎米率，免淘米比精米增加白度 8%，米饭的美味度增加 4%；由于真正免淘洗，因此避免了多种营养物质的流失；NTWP 加工米的副产品米糠可制取生物保健品脂多糖，其经济效益是原料米的 30～40 倍。设备引进后，海丰米业新增生产能力 3 万 t/年，新增产值 800 万元/年，新增利润 200 万元/年。公司已在上海崇明、江苏苏州等地建立了产业基地，带动农民 2.5 万人，人均可增收 70～80 元/年。

3. 一只蛋　在上海的蛋品企业中，上海南汇汇绿蛋品有限公司是一个集蛋鸡饲养、蛋品生产、禽蛋加工、销售为一体的专业性蛋品公司。公司与南汇全区的蛋鸡场所、崇明、奉贤、东海农场以及浙江磐安和江苏盐城、海安等蛋鸡场以“统一供种、统一防疫、统一供料、统一收购”形式建立供销关系。但由于出口鸡蛋在分级、加工、包装上有严格要求，如每枚蛋的重量差异不允许超过5g。而手工分级、包装所造成的损耗很大，这成为提高鸡蛋质量、发展出口的瓶颈。2002年10月引进了鸡蛋分级包装流水线，生产能力大大提高，分别为上海华联、良友、宝钢、二军大、空军政治学院等超市和单位提供蛋品，其中，仅华联超市每天就要销售阿强鸡蛋500箱，平均每天出口1个集装箱的鸡蛋。

4. 一棵菜　上海九田食品公司位于松江现代农业园区五库示范区内。公司占地16 600m^2，总建筑面积4 000 m^2。为使加工产品符合进口国的各项技术指标，2002年引进了单体流态化速冻设备，全自动、智能化制冷设备以及蔬菜洗涤机、金属选别机2台。公司开展了HACCP认证和员工培训，在松江区建设200 hm^2 基地，种植荷兰豆、青刀豆等4个种植品种，还联系了外地特约供货基地，年加工产品2 000 t。公司投产后吸纳工人300名，带动2 000户农户从事出口蔬菜生产。

5. 一只虾　上海汉德食品有限公司注册于上海奉贤现代农业园区。公司主要从事水产品及肉类加工销售。2004年生产水产品8 000t，其中70%出口，全年水产产值达3.5亿元，出口创汇3 500万美元，解决农业人口就业1 000余人，带动淡水养殖农户3 000多户。并通过了上海市出入境商品检验检疫局HACCP体系认证，也是上海唯一一家可以出口欧盟的水产注册企业。

虾产品历来是我国水产品出口的优势产品。以上海杭州湾板块的淡水养殖面积不断扩大，尤其是南美白对虾的产量不断增加，使生产的季节性和市场的均衡性矛盾凸现出来。为此，通过从丹麦、瑞典、德国、美国引进虾类深加工关键设备，根据欧美市场的不同需求，可加工带头（无头）整虾的生虾制品、熟虾制品及综合调味虾食品和熟虾浅开背虾仁等。汉德公司充分利用当地资源，采用“公司＋基地＋农户”的产业公司模式，带动的农户水养面积从2003年的6.7 khm^2 扩大到2004年的43.3 khm^2。除本市外，苏北、安徽的大量养殖户是最直接的受益者。

6. 绿色食品、冻干食品　上海星辉蔬菜有限公司生产的蔬果休闲食品能保持原色泽、原风味和原营养，受到市场欢迎。该公司引进日本、美国的蔬菜深加工设备，可加工蔬菜类和水果类的各种产品。设备能完成清洗杀菌、切分、低温高真空度油炸，使油炸的时间缩短，保持原色、原味、原营养，投放市场后非常受欢迎，大型超市家乐福主动联系生产企业，表示进场费减半，并在超市的显眼处摆放。上海星辉蔬菜有限公司年加工不同风味的蔬果膨化休闲食品1 200t，销售收入4 800万元；加工净菜6 000t，销售收入2 400万元。带动上海郊区3 000个农户，创造近600个就业岗位。

7. 桑果　桑果（椹）被誉为“既是食品又是药品”的果实，药用历史悠久，又是春季的时令鲜果。上海崇明县地理位置非常适合桑树的种植，农民种植桑树的积极性很高，在崇明种有1.3 khm^2 桑果树。由于桑果的鲜果货架期很短，收果期前后只有1个月。上海松外松实业有限公司为促进当地资源优势向产业优势转移，对桑果进行综合开发，采用国际先进的加工设备，确保了产品安全卫生、生产过程环保。生产优质的桑椹饮料、桑椹酒等，附加值大大提高，既解决了桑椹的出路，又丰富了市场。农民种植桑树，养蚕、摘果两相宜，经济效益很可观。

二、主要做法

1. 大力扶持龙头企业，开展技术创新　上海市委、市政府十分重视农产品加工业的发展，2002年，市政府决定从中小企业贷款信用担保资金中划出2亿元，为农业产业化龙头企业提供贷款信用担保；从科技攻关专项资金及创新基金中安排一定比例的资金，专项用于支持现代农业技术创新及产业化。2004年，共落实市农业产业化重点扶持项目24个，市财政扶持资金安排5 318万元，农业产业化专项贷款贴息资金2 078万元，扶持农民专业合作社1 400万元，行业协会专项补贴资金200万元。据初步统计，市财政用于重点项目的5 318万元扶持资金，带动社会资本投入27 316万元，是公共财政投入的5.13倍。这批重点扶持项目完成后可新建各类生产及配套用房近10万m^2，新增各类生产设备近百套（台），较大地改善了农业产业化龙头企业的形象，提高了能力和产品质量，提高了农产品的科技含量，增强了上海农产品在国内和国际市场的竞争力，发挥了农业产业化龙头企业的辐射和带动作用。

2. 加强与科研机构的合作力度，加大自主创新技术力度　上海新成食品有限公司依托科研优势，不断开发新产品，与市食品学会、交通大学农学院等科研机构、大专院校建立了协作关系，以咨询、论证、科技服务等多种形式，聘请专家、教授、高级工程师给予帮助，开展小包装、洁净蔬菜、脱水、腌渍蔬菜产品的开发工作，同时指导农户种养生产，形成“公司+科研+农户”模式。既拓展了国内外市场，又带动了农户增收。2004年，公司销售收入超过1.75亿元，带动农户2 300多户。

3. 以标准化为抓手，促进农产品品牌建设 全市注册品牌的农产品118个，55个企业的107个产品通过市安全优质卫生农产品认证。据统计，在全年销售额1亿元以上的23个龙头企业中，有近80%的企业建立了产品质量检测体系，1/3的企业通过了ISO9000系列或国家绿色食品、市安全卫生优质农产品认证，有的还在申报HACCP认证。同时，还涌现了光明乳业、新成名厨、大瀛鸭鸭、海丰米业、阿强蛋品、一只鼎食品、爱森肉食品、良元食品、淀山湖蛋品、小农夫玉米、宝杨黄瓜、伟国肉鸭等80多个具有一定市场知名度的农产品品牌。其中，光明乳业、一只鼎系列、海丰米业、大瀛鸭鸭、淀山湖蛋品荣获2004年上海市名牌产品称号。

4. 组织龙头企业到国内外参展，不断拓宽发展思路 近几年来，每年组织30多个农产品出口企业到国外参展，已先后到马来西亚、捷克、英国、澳大利亚、日本等国参展，每次都有数十位企业人员和200多种农产品参展。既学到国外先进的农产品加工技术、包装理念，又在开拓国际市场方面取得显著成效。据不完全统计，每次参展都获得了数额可观的订单。

三、存在的主要问题

上海农产品加工产业经过多年的努力，取得了一定的成绩，但是进一步发展还存在着制约因素，主要是：

1. 大多数农产品加工企业的规模较小，与农业原料基地的产业链还未真正形成。加工农产品生产基地建设相对滞后，原料产品供应不稳定。带动当地农业发展、农民增收能力有限，也影响了农产品加工企业规模的扩大。

2. 装备水平仍较低，技术相对落后，能耗高，加工成本高，原料利用率低，终端产品的内外质量均有待提高。

3. 标准化和质量检测、社会化服务配套跟不上。少数企业标准化意识和质量检测手段落后，影响了加工企业质量的提高。名牌产品和规模化龙头企业不多，加工产品内销较多，出口总量还有待进一步拓展。

四、工作重点

上海农产品加工业的总体目标是认真贯彻“科教兴市”主战略，通过“三个创新”（自主创新、集成创新、引进消化吸收再创新）来提高郊区农产品精深加工的水平，使农产品加工向安全化、多样化、功能化、方便化、国际化方向发展，形成一批在国际市场上具有较强竞争力的龙头企业和名牌产品。主要措施：

1. 改造传统加工技术 引进具有国际先进水平的农产品采后加工装备，进行二次创新。

2. 构建农产品加工业原料保障体系 根据农产品加工发展的需要，建设专业化、标准化、优质化和布局合理、专用、安全、稳定的优势农产品原料生产基地，逐步形成原料基地和加工企业、加工企业和销售市场之间布局合理、畅通便捷的储藏运输网络。

3. 加快与国际标准接轨，不断完善农产品加工产品标准 在中国加入WTO的新形势下，为了提高农产品国际竞争力，必须加快建设农产品安全标准与检测体系，使外来农产品和沪产农产品安全进入流通市场。在农产品加工企业中进一步完善经过国际权威认证机构认证的HACCP、SQF、ISO体系，使质量安全监控体系从田头到餐桌全覆盖。

4. 加强农业的国际合作交流 加大吸引先进技术力度，优化农产品加工工艺，形成技术特色，开发新产品，提高产品质量和档次。积极发展技术密集型、技术含量高和附加值高的农产品，并提高其在加工产品结构中的比重。

5. 坚持农产品加工业的可持续发展 把农产品加工业的发展与环境保护紧密结合起来，合理解决农产品加工过程中废弃物的排放，推进农产品加工业的清洁生产，提高农产品的综合利用水平，同时加强农产品原料基地的环境监管，促使农产品加工业的可持续发展。

6. 培育一批现代化的农产品加工龙头企业 统筹规划、布局合理、各具特色，培育一批现代化的农产品加工龙头企业，提升上海农产品加工水平，吸纳农村劳动力，带动农民增收。

江苏省农产品加工业

江苏省农林厅

一、快速发展，农产品加工业已成为现代农业的重要组成部分

近年来，在省委、省政府的正确领导和农业部的大力支持下，全省各地围绕农业增效、农民增收，大力推进农业产业化经营，不断提高农产品加工转化水平，全省农产品加工业稳步发展，形成了具有一定规模的农产品加工业体系。“十五”期间，农产品加工业产值年增长率保持在10%～15%之间，以农产品为直接原料的加工企业已达到 7 281 个，从业人员 155 万人，产值 4 697.1 亿元，增加值 1 187.8 亿元，利税 265.6 亿元。主要发展特点是：

1. 产业门类齐全　江苏省农产品加工业涉及国家统计分类上的农产品加工业 12 大类的所有方面，其中与农产品加工直接相关的五类加工业中，稻米加工能力超过 2 000 万 t；面粉加工能力约占全国的 1/10左右；油料加工能力全国第一，东海粮油工业（张家港）有限公司加工能力亚洲最大；棉花加工方面，全国纺织看江苏；畜产品加工发展较快，规模化企业正在崛起；茶叶加工方面，名特茶机械加工率已达 70% 以上，国内领先；林产品加工以木材加工、名特优经济林木加工为主，逐步形成了“小林业、大产业”的发展格局。

2. 区域特色明显　各地立足资源禀赋，大力发展农业特色产业和特色产品加工业，全省涌现出一大批农产品加工业的特色产品，如徐州维维豆奶、南通长寿食品、南京桂花盐水鸭、雨润肉制品、镇江香醋、无锡酱排骨、苏州碧螺春茶叶等，在全国都具有较高知名度。全省有 2 658 个农产品通过国家无公害农产品认证；有 504 家企业的 1 331 个产品有效使用绿色食品标志，累计开发绿色食品产品 1 616 个；有 104 家企业的 232 个产品通过有机食品认证；有 130 个农产品有效使用江苏名牌产品标志。

3. 出口快速增长　农产品加工企业积极开拓国际市场，农产品及其加工品出口品种越来越多，数量越来越大，出口的国家和地区越来越广。2005 年，全省农产品出口 10.4 亿美元，同比增长 19.2%；2006 年上半年出口 5.83 亿元，增幅 28.9%。鑫缘茧丝绸集团股份有限公司和富安茧丝绸股份有限公司的 5A 级以上高品质白茧丝出口量已占全国的 20%。灌南大盛板业有限公司从英国引进 4 条农作物秸秆人造板生产线，利用丰富的麦草资源生产均质板，产品实现零甲醛释放，符合欧洲 Super E0 标准，全部出口到日本和欧洲。

4. 带动能力增强　全省初步形成一批规模大、科技含量高、市场竞争力强、带动作用明显的农产品加工企业群，成为带动农产品加工业发展的领头羊。2006 年上半年，全省 28 个农业产业化国家重点龙头企业实现销售收入 231 亿元，同比增长 18%；利税总额 10.9 亿元，增长 16%；新开发产品 105 个。南京雨润集团 38 个子（分）公司遍布 10 多个省、自治区、直辖市，低温肉制品市场占有率位居全国第一，2006 年上半年实现销售收入 62.5 亿元。镇江恒顺醋业集团公司已兼并、控股、收购山西、四川、安徽等地 5 家规模较大的农产品加工企业，近期与新加坡合作投资 7 500 万美元建设 20 万 t 香醋扩建项目，集聚国际资本打造醋业航母。

二、整体谋划，强势推进农产品加工业发展

近年来，省农林厅把促进农产品加工业发展作为农业和农村经济的重点工作，结合农业产业化经营，从产业基础抓起，从规划入手，确定目标，理清思路，突出重点，加强指导，全力推进。重点抓了以下几个方面的工作：

1. 制定农产品加工业发展规划　在充分调研和论证的基础上，省农林厅编制了《2005—2010 年沿江、沿海、沿东陇海线、沿运河农产品加工产业带发展规划》，并对各区域农产品加工业发展战略进行了定位。沿江农产品加工产业带主要是立足全省，接轨长三角和国际市场，重点发展农产品精深加工；沿海农产品加工产业带主要是发挥资源优势，大力发展超市农业、绿色农业和品牌农业；沿东陇海线农产品加工产业带主要是立足淮北，成为全省农产品加工密集

区、淮海农业产业化示范区和苏北工业化支撑点；沿运河农产品加工产业带主要是发挥传统品牌优势，引入先进加工工艺和技术，提升品牌知名度和竞争力等。全省各地正按照省里规划并结合实际，进一步明确农产品加工业重点发展的项目、重点建设的基地、重点培育的企业，全面推进农产品加工“一群（农产品加工龙头企业群）四带”建设。

2. *大力发展优势农产品产业* 安全、优质、丰富的农产品是农产品加工业发展的基础。大力推进农业结构调整，重点在全省发展优质稻米、特色蔬菜、优质瘦肉型猪、特色林业等16个优势农产品产业和地区性特色农业产业，农产品的标准化生产、区域化布局、产业化开发水平不断提高。全省优质稻米、专用小麦、优质油菜、高品质棉比重分别达60%、52%、95%和23%；优质瘦肉型猪、优质地方家禽、波杂山羊比重分别达52%、51%和28%；特色蔬菜、优质水果、名特茶比重分别达70%、67%、40%；生猪、蛋禽、肉禽、奶牛规模养殖比重分别达到33%、59%、48%和63%。

3. *大力培育农产品加工业龙头企业* 发展农产品加工业，关键是培育和壮大农产品加工龙头企业。从2003年开始，结合推进农业产业化经营，省农林厅从优化发展环境、加大资金支持、引导科技创新等各个角度，积极培育农产品加工业龙头企业。全省共有南京奶业集团等322个企业被评为全国大中型农产品加工流通企业，南京远望富硒农产品有限责任公司等20家企业被评为第一批全国农产品加工业示范企业，维维集团股份有限公司等14家企业的技术创新机构被认定为全国农产品加工业企业技术创新机构，大丰市优质棉花生产加工示范基地等8个基地被评为全国农产品加工业示范基地。

4. *积极引导“三资”投入农产品加工业* 为推进农业招商引资，解决农业内部资金缺乏的问题，省农林厅专门成立了农业招商引资工作指导小组，积极引导民间资本、工商资本、外商资本（以下简称“三资”）投入农业和农产品加工业。近4年来，全省“三资”投入农业总额超过600亿元，其中70%以上投入到农产品加工业。2005年，全省“三资”投入农业规模以上项目（工商资本、民间资本500万元以上、外商资本50万美元以上）投资额为261亿元，2006年上半年投资额达153.1亿元。“三资”成为农产品加工业资金投入的重要来源，解决了农业产业化和农产品加工业发展的资金瓶颈，更带来了先进的理念、全新的机制和广阔的市场。同时，各地举办的睢宁山羊节、高邮鸭蛋节、盱眙龙虾节、淮安稻米节、高淳螃蟹节等形式多样、丰富多彩的展会，也为“三资”投入农产品加工业搭建了平台，取得了明显效果。

5. *培育农产品加工业集群* 为探索农产品加工业发展与节约用地相结合的新路子，培育产业集群，省农林厅鼓励各地建立不同形式的农产品加工业园区，用工业园区的成功经验开发农产品加工业园区。2006年上半年，会同省外经贸厅批复设立江苏省兴化市农副产品加工园区。加工园区发展势头良好，原有企业产销两旺，在建企业、签约企业的投资大，起点高，成为全市农产品加工业发展的“引擎”。区内拥有投资1 000万元以上的农产品加工企业16个，协议投资总额11.3亿元，现实际到位3.5亿元，主要涉及脱水蔬菜、饲料加工、纺织、麦芽、水产品加工、调味品、精炼油、肉制品生产加工等领域。昆山市现代农业示范区成立以来已引进内外资企业45个，合同利用外资1亿多美元，内资3亿多美元，形成了一个农产品精深加工和研发集群。

三、突出重点，加大农产品加工工作力度

下一步，将按照农业部农业产业化和农产品加工推进行动方案的要求，紧紧围绕高效农业规模化、农业产业化和现代农业建设，以市场为导向，以科技为支撑，以加工企业为龙头，因地制宜，完善规划，合理布局，加大投入，推进农产品加工原料生产基地化、加工制品精深化、产加销经营一体化，促进农产品加工业持续健康发展。

1. *围绕高效农业规模化，大力发展农产品精深加工* 为提高农业经济效益，省委、省政府提出“十一五”期间要大力推进高效农业规模化，并将之列为江苏新农村建设十大工程之首，要求到“十一五”末期，全省每公顷平均效益30 000元以上的种植面积占耕地总面积的1/3；畜牧业规模养殖比重每年提高5个百分点；农产品加工业产值与农林牧渔业总产值之比达到1∶1。围绕这一目标，省农林厅将把发展农产品精深加工作为推进高效农业规模化的重要途径，促进农产品由卖原料向卖产品、由初加工向深加工、由粗加工向精加工方向发展。根据本省农产品生产及加工的比较优势，粮油产品重点发展专用、优质、营养、经济、方便、多样化的精深加工产品及其制品；蔬菜园艺产品重点发展冻干脱水蔬菜、冷冻菜、保鲜菜和果品精深加工；奶业重点发展配方奶粉、液态奶、酸奶等奶制品，加快发展干酪、奶油、干酪素等深加工产品；肉类重点发展分割肉及其深加工制品；禽蛋类重点开发天然、保健、功能性产品，

深度开发蛋黄精粉、卵磷脂等医药、保健产品。

2. 围绕农业产业化，培育壮大农产品加工企业集群　打造产业集群的核心是形成企业集群。省农林厅将进一步推进优势区域、优势产业、优势企业的集聚，在全省建成以农业产业化国家和省级重点龙头企业为首，有品位、有规模、有档次、强带动的农产品加工企业群。重点是提高农产品加工企业的“四个能力”：一是以优化产业布局、扩大加工规模为突破口，提高对当地农产品资源的消化能力；二是以加强利益联结、完善“行业协会＋龙头企业＋专业合作组织＋农户”的产业化模式为突破口，提高对农户的带动能力；三是以建立研发机构、开发自主知识产权新产品为突破口，提高自主创新能力；四是以完善质量管理体系、打造名牌产品为突破口，提高在国内外市场上的竞争能力。

3. 围绕现代农业建设，引导“三资”投入农产品加工业　按照中央要求，立足省情，江苏省建设社会主义新农村的基本思路是实施“三化”战略，即以工业化致富农民、以城市化带动农村、以产业化提升农业；建设现代农业的路径是“以工投农、以工改农、以工带农”。这为实现农产品加工业跨越式发展提供了前所未有的机遇。下一步，将继续坚持以工业理念发展农业的思路，以现代农业建设推动农产品加工业发展，以农产品加工业发展促进现代农业建设。一是引导“三资”投入农产品加工业，解决农产品加工业发展的资金瓶颈；二是用现代科学技术和管理方式改造农产品加工业，从整体上提高农产品加工企业的素质；三是推进“一乡一品”、“一县一业”和村企互动，实现原料、劳动力和资本的有效配置，构建高效农业经济板块。

浙江省农产品加工业

浙江省乡镇企业局

一、主要发展特点

1. 集聚发展的特色明显　以“一乡一品”、“一县一业”为特征的同类产业集聚生产方式，构成了浙江经济最大的特色和优势。近年来，浙江省农产品加工业产业集聚区呈现出数量扩张、质量稳步提高的良好发展态势，已形成初具规模的农产品加工基地300多个。如安吉的竹制品，临安的水煮笋，黄岩的水果罐头，遂昌的竹炭，桐乡的羊毛衫，海宁的皮革，诸暨的珍珠，舟山、温岭、玉环的水产品，萧山的羽绒羽毛、蔬菜加工等，都在全国市场占据很大的份额。云和县的木制玩具企业达到了561个，从业人员2万多人，品种1万多个，产值占全国的50%，占全球木制玩具市场份额的6%。

2. 龙头企业发展迅速　涌现了一批辐射力强、带动作用明显的农产品加工龙头企业，如海通食品公司、德华木业集团、山下湖珍珠集团、欣欣饲料公司、康鑫食品公司、爱斯曼食品公司等。截至2005年底，全省农产品加工业500万元以上规模企业达到了12 110个，比2000年增加7 162个；实现销售收入5 278.59亿元，比2000年增长220.61%；实现利润215.7亿元，比2000年增长189.91%。

3. 品牌战略初见成效　全省各地农产品加工企业品牌意识逐渐提高，商标注册大幅增长，并涌现了一批名牌产品。拥有“五芳斋”、“李子园”、“不老神”、“养生堂”等中国驰名商标40个，“雪舫蒋”火腿、“祐康”食品、“兴业”鱼糜、“国泰”和“铜钱桥”酱腌菜、“TOYOSHIMA”水果罐头、“艾莱依”羽绒制品、“金鹰牌”桑蚕绢丝、“阮仕牌”和“千足牌”及“佳丽牌”珍珠首饰等中国名牌产品92个。在1 039个浙江省级名牌产品中，农产品加工产品占40%以上。

4. 出口持续快速增长　“十五”期间，全省农产品加工业出口呈现快速增长的良好势头，每年平均以19.2%的速度增长，2005年出口额53.39亿美元，相当于全省农林牧渔业总产值的30.25%，占全省出口贸易总额的6.95%，来自农产品出口的收入已占农民全部收入的10%强。绿茶出口量和创汇额均占全国50%以上，列全国第一；柑橘产量连续多年名列全国第一，以柑橘为原料的橘瓣罐头出口量占全国2/3以上，占世界的1/2；蜂王浆产量和出口量已占全球贸易总量的近1/2；淡水珍珠产量占世界的60%以上。外向型农产品加工发展较好的慈溪市，在农产品加工出口企业中就业的农村劳动力人数已达到93 635人，占全市农村劳动力的15.65%。

5. *产加销一体化经营步伐不断加快*　据不完全统计，实行产加销一体化经营的企业已超万家。这些企业与基地（农户）形成了较为稳定的利益共同关系，既保证了企业自身的经济效益，又增加了农民的收入。以丽水市为例，到2005年底，全市农民专业合作经济组织已发展到289个，带动农户29.92万户，联结基地31.8khm²，极大地提高了农产品生产经营的集约化和组织化程度。

二、主要工作举措

1. *把发展农产品加工业作为发展农村经济的重要抓手*　浙江省政府在指导农村经济发展的过程中，一直把发展农产品加工业作为解决“三农”问题的重要环节来抓，切实加强领导，实行政策扶持。1998年，省委、省政府出台了《关于积极发展农业产业化经营的若干意见》，2002年省政府又出台了《关于加快发展农产品加工业的通知》，提出多形式、多渠道、多层次发展农产品加工的路子和相应扶持的政策措施，从而为推进全省农产品加工业的大发展创造了良好的氛围。各地党委、政府对农产品加工业也非常重视，纷纷制定相关政策扶持农产品加工业的发展。温州市在充分调研的基础上，出台了《温州市农产品加工规划》（2002—2010年），从资金等多方面给予大力扶持。全省各级乡镇企业、经贸、科技、农业、林业、财政、金融等部门，对于发展农产品加工业的思想十分统一，形成了上下配合，相互协作，合力推进农产品加工业发展的良好氛围。

2. *注重发挥农产品加工示范企业的典型引路作用*　全省有规划、有重点、有措施地扶持一批生产规模较大、发展前景良好、带动力强的农产品加工示范企业，通过典型的引导和示范，把农产品加工工作引向深入。省乡镇企业局积极行使引导、服务职能，从2000年起着重抓了省级农产品加工示范企业的培育、扶持工作，每年从省乡镇企业中小企业专项资金中拨出一块来扶持省级农产品加工示范企业，及时发现和总结推广示范企业的成功经验，并于2004年召开了全省促进农产品加工业发展的经验交流大会，效果十分明显。全省绝大部分市县对农产品加工龙头企业实行了多予少取政策，增强了龙头企业的发展后劲。

3. *高度重视农产品加工业技术支撑体系建设*　针对农产品加工业面广量大，自主创新能力不足的状况。一是抓了农产品加工共性技术服务中心建设。全省已建立浙西蜂业科技创新服务中心、舟山市水产加工技术中心、艾莱依羽绒制品研发技术服务中心等12个省级农产品加工共性技术服务平台和25家省农产品加工企业技术创新机构，市县级技术服务平台已有100多个。农业部命名的第一批农产品加工企业技术创新机构中浙江就占了19个，名列前茅。二是鼓励农产品加工企业设立企业技术创新机构，这些机构对解决农产品加工企业中的关键技术，提高企业的技术创新能力起到了重要的作用，效果十分显著。

4. *广泛开展农产品加工业质量体系认证*　获取质量认证是接轨国际市场必备的通行证，也是企业提高质量水平、提高盈利水平的金钥匙。为了把质量认证真正落到实处，全省各地普遍加大了农产品加工企业质量安全重要意义的宣传，选择了一批有资质的认证机构，上门为企业服务，开展ISO9001认证、ISO14001、HACCP、绿色产品认证、有机产品认证。同时，引导企业根据市场需求，大力开发生产无公害产品、绿色产品、有机农产品投放市场。到2005年，全省有247个企业的558种产品获得了国家级绿色食品证书，30个企业的55种产品获得有机食品认证。

5. *积极搭建面向农产品加工业的服务平台*　一是搭建农产品加工信息服务平台，如在省乡镇企业局门户网站上开通了浙江农产品加工专栏，设立了政策导向、市场行情、企业简介、名特优产品介绍和企业家风采等栏目。二是搭建农产品加工培训服务平台，每年举办农产品加工质量安全培训班，由政府买单，邀请资深专家作专题讲座。各市县也根据企业的需求，因地制宜开展农产品加工企业职工的技能培训。通过上下联动，全省每年培训员工在50万人次以上。三是搭建农产品市场营销服务平台，每年选择一批企业参加各种展览展销会、经贸洽谈会。

三、“十一五”总体思路

“十一五”期间，浙江省农产品加工业总的发展思路是以科学发展观为统领，按照科技创新战略、品牌名牌战略、质量安全战略，实现农产品加工业由初级加工向精深加工转变，由传统加工工艺向采用先进适用技术转变，由小批量加工向规模化加工转变，由粗放型加工向资源综合利用型加工转变。

1. *培育农产品加工龙头企业，增强农产品加工业的整体实力*　对具有区域特色、加工规模较大、符合国家产业导向政策、联结农户较为密切的农产品加工企业，要在资金、税收等方面给予倾斜，鼓励做大做优做强，并鼓励企业通过联合、兼并、资产重组、股票上市等途径，提高市场开拓能力和技术创新能力，提高规模效益、品牌效益。各级政府要建立或增加农产品加工业发展专项资金，培育和扶持一批竞争优势明显和带动力强的集团型农产品加工企业，争取在国内同行业中具有领先地位。

2. 建立健全自主创新激励机制，强化农产品加工业的研发功能　一是积极鼓励、引导农产品加工企业注重科技投入、人才引进，走技术创新促企业发展之路。二是鼓励有条件的企业积极设立企业技术中心，以提高企业技术创新能力。三是切实抓好农产品加工企业的品牌建设，引导企业树立品牌意识，培育品牌、提升品牌、经营品牌、延伸品牌，做到“无牌贴牌变有牌，有牌变名牌”，引导和支持更多产品进入全省、全国著名商标和名牌产品行列。

3. 加大质量体系认证力度，全面推行农产品加工企业的标准化生产　引导企业切实加强质量管理，建立和完善产品质量体系认证，把质量监测贯穿于企业生产经营的每一个环节，努力提高产品质量。着重抓好农产品的质量认证、无公害产品认证、绿色产品认证、有机产品认证工作，实现农产品加工企业的标准化、产业化、规模化。

4. 构建全方位多功能服务平台，提高对农产品加工业的服务水平　以强化服务功能为支撑，构建四个平台。一要构建和完善农产品加工信息服务平台，加大信息量，提高信息质量。二要构建和完善农产品市场开拓服务平台，加大对本省农产品的市场推介力度，组织、鼓励企业参加各种农产品展览会。三要构建和完善农产品加工培训服务平台，充分利用农业部蓝色证书工程、国家发改委中小企业司银河培训工程等载体，为农产品加工企业创造培训机会。四要构建和完善农产品加工技术服务平台。从提高农产品加工技术含量入手，有步骤、有重点地引进、研发和推广一批农产品重大关键技术。同时，积极参与农业部的农产品加工实用技术对接推广活动。

5. 培育农产品加工基地，形成一大批具有特色的农产品加工区域　指导和扶持农产品加工基地进一步完善综合功能和要素集约配置，减轻基地农产品加工企业生产成本，引导有科技型、成长型等发展前景大的农产品加工企业进入基地创业，优化农产品加工业布局。

安徽省农产品加工业

安徽省农业委员会

一、发展特点

安徽省农产品加工业历史悠久，有许多优势产业和亮点，在国民经济中占有一席之地。农产品加工企业数量最多的是农副食品加工业，其次是纺织业；产品销售收入排列前 3 位的是纺织业、农副食品加工业、烟草制品业；利润总额排列前 3 位的是烟草制品业、橡胶制品业和食品制造业；税金总额排列前 3 位的是烟草制品业、饮料制造业和纺织业。总结近年来全省农产品加工业的发展情况，主要有以下特点：

1. 一批优势产业的形成，为农产品加工业发展奠定了良好基础　一是“皖烟”。安徽省与周边发达省份在制烟产业上差距不大，具有一定的实力和竞争力。二是“皖酒”。本省大部分县都有酒厂，有些酒厂规模较大、各具特色，安徽的白酒在华东乃至全国都有声誉、有实力、有竞争力，如“古井贡”、“口子酒”等。三是“皖茶”。茶叶种植遍及黄山、安庆、六安、池州、宣城等市，是安徽的重要特色农产品，历史悠久，享誉中外。此外，安徽羽绒制品加工、柳编业、食品加工中的山核桃、徽派炒货等，近年发展势头很好，在全国名列前茅。

2. 一批骨干企业的快速成长，为农产品加工业发展提供了有力支撑　经过多年的培植，特别是近几年的大力发展，已形成一批农产品加工骨干企业，如丰原、古井、华茂等。很多产业以骨干企业支撑，形成了产业催生骨干企业，骨干企业促进产业发展的局面。如柳编业中的庆发湖、华安达两大企业，产值都过亿元，有力地促进了沿淮地区柳编产业的发展。全省销售额过亿元的企业 100 多个，这些企业是安徽省农产品加工业发展的骨干和支柱。

3. 一批特色农产品加工制品品牌的打造，为农产品加工业发展争得了市场知名度　如粮油工业中的皖王面粉、丰大面条、家乐大米、大平色拉油等；皖茶中的“黄山毛峰”、“六安瓜片”等；徽派炒货中的

"洽洽瓜子"、"小刘瓜子"等；皖酒行业中的"古井贡酒"、"口子酒"、"迎驾贡酒"、"文王贡酒"等。此外，如百春牌洋槐蜜、露仙牌酱菜、天方牌茶叶、黄池牌茶干、义门牌苔干、刘老二牌符离集烧鸡、云海牌白厂丝、鸿润牌羽绒系列制品等品牌都具有很高的知名度和市场占有率，深受广大消费者的欢迎。大平牌色拉油、鸿润牌羽绒于2005年被认定为中国名牌产品。

4. *民间及省外、境外资本的注入，为农产品加工业发展注入了新的活力* 合肥华泰食品有限责任公司是民营农产品加工龙头企业，年营销收入超10亿元，成为本省最大的食品制造企业。花园油脂、大平油脂等一大批民营企业成为本省农产品加工企业的支柱。近年来，南京雨润、广东锦丰、山东九发、上海通洋、蒙牛乳业、伊利乳业、山东鲁王等一批省外大企业落户安徽，担当"龙头"办企业，建基地，推进了全省农产品加工业的蓬勃发展。

5. *农业产业化的积极推进，有力地促进了农产品加工业发展* 农产品加工与农业产业化紧密结合，既有利于农产品加工业的发展，又有利于农业产业化龙头企业的壮大、原料生产基地的建设和农民收入的增加。在全省4 000多个农业产业化龙头组织中，从事农产品加工的龙头企业占多数；在全省313个国家级和省级农业产业化龙头企业中，农产品加工业占九成。这些企业在为当地农村经济发展做出重要贡献的同时，自己也得到了快速发展。

6. *农产品加工龙头企业的发展，促进了地方经济的发展* 各地在推进农业产业化经营中，把培育和壮大农产品加工龙头企业作为重中之重，大力发展农产品加工业，大力引进国内外大型农产品加工企业，成为县域经济发展的支柱产业，促进了当地经济发展、农业结构调整、区域经济形成和农民收入增加。据不完全统计，2004年，全省17个市农产品加工龙头企业3 457个，创产值445.19亿元。其中，年产值500万元以上的1 332个，创产值389.38亿元。部分市龙头企业加工产值占全市工业产值的比重已超过或接近半壁江山，如蚌埠市达69.8%，巢湖、亳州、六安分别达46.4%、46.2%、44.7%。

二、主要差距

安徽省农产品加工业发展总体水平不高，表现为加工企业规模小，加工层次低，与拥有的丰富资源比，与农业大省的地位比，与农村经济发展的要求还有很大差距。一是农产品加工转化率低。主要农产品加工转化率约为20%左右，比全国低。二是新型食品加工业发展起步慢。肉、奶、蔬菜、水产品等新型食品加工明显落后，本省市场基本由省外加工产品主导。三是企业规模偏小。规模以上农产品加工企业销售收入居华东末位。四是加工技术水平较低，产品档次低。全省农产品加工业的科技贡献率只有35%左右；在加工档次上，以一般农产品粗加工为主，精深加工不足，全省粮棉油等大宗农产品初加工比重占90%。五是适应农产品加工的优质原料基地建设滞后。小麦、稻谷、玉米、花生、大豆、棉花等农产品原料的品质、品种难以适应标准化加工要求，加工专用农产品缺乏，直接制约了加工产品质量和市场竞争力。六是农产品加工企业与基地农户间利益联结关系不够紧密。在全省农业产业化龙头组织中，与农户利益联结关系密切的仅占总数的较小比率，大多缺少紧密的利益机制。七是各地发展不平衡。有的市规模以上农产品加工业上百个，而有的市仅有十几个。八是农产品加工业发展的规划工作薄弱。

三、主要措施

1. *规划先行，加快优势产业的培育和发展* 要尽快组织力量，根据《全国主要农产品加工业发展规划》，落实和完善相应规划的编制，并指导各地抓紧农产品加工规划的编制工作，协调地区之间的产业和产品分工，选准各地的主导产业，集中力量支持优势产业更快的发展。

2. *扶持农产品加工重点企业* 支持农产品加工骨干企业实行优质农产品基地建设、科研开发、生产加工、营销服务一体化经营。重点培植有自主知识产权、产业关联度大、带动能力强、有国际竞争力的大中型农产品加工龙头企业，确定一批农产品加工优强企业，纳入省重要骨干企业进行管理。

3. *充分发挥民营经济在发展农产品加工业的重要作用* 国有资本要加大改制改组力度，从这些不占优势的行业中退出和收缩；通过股份制、股份合作制、出售、租赁、独资、承包等多种方式，加快农产品加工企业产权制度改革步伐，促进生产要素向优势企业、优势产品和优秀经营者集聚；为民营企业进入农产品加工业提供政策保证和市场许可。今后主要依靠民营力量推进本省农产品加工业的发展。

4. *加大招商引资力度* 今后要抓住和利用上海及长三角地区产业梯度转移和资本对外扩张的机遇，落实省委、省政府"东向发展战略"，充分发挥安徽省劳动力资源、土地资源、生态资源以及丰富的农产品资源，采取走出去、请进来的方式，吸引长三角及其他发达地区和国内外知名企业，以其资金、技术、品牌、市场等优势，来安徽省建基地、办加工，或与安徽的农产品加工企业嫁接，发挥后发优势，实现全省农产品加工业的跨越式发展。

5. 依靠科技进步，用好人才　依靠科技进步关键在人才，要加强对农产品加工企业负责人的培养和引导，培训、引进、用好各类人才，树立正确的企业发展观，依靠科技进步，提升技术装备、生产手段、产品研发能力、质量保证体系和深加工能力等的水平。

6. 充分发挥“小企业、大群体”的作用　“铺天盖地”发展，才能有“顶天立地”产生。小企业是实现资本原始积累，培养民营企业家的摇篮，是发展之星、希望之光。要关心、爱护、扶持小企业，帮助他们克服“小”的缺陷，实现“大”的发展。

7. 充分利用农业品种资源丰富的优势发展板块经济　要突出区域特色和区位优势，形成合理的区域分工，把基地布局在最佳区域内，做到自然适宜、经济合理、技术可行、生态平衡、可持续发展。各地要扬长避短，实施错位竞争和板块经济发展，实现农产品加工业区域基地的巩固和扩大。

8. 加强领导，进一步发挥政策的推动作用　要实现既定的目标任务，在目前的体制下必须统筹有关各方，形成合力，计划、经贸、农业、财政、科技、卫生、质检、工商、税务等行政主管部门，各司其责，加强协作，进一步制定、完善和落实相关政策，引导、激励和推动全省农产品加工业的持续健康发展。

福建省农产品加工业

福建省农业厅

一、发展现状

1. 规模扩张比较迅速，主导产业基本形成　从20世纪90年代开始，福建省农产品加工业保持较快的增长速度，成为带动农村经济发展的重要产业和推动农业结构优化升级的重要因素。随着农业的持续发展和温饱问题的逐步解决，农产品加工业得以迅猛发展，农产品加工业成为最具活力的行业之一。2005年，全省农产品加工业增加值889.46亿元，占全省GDP的13.5%，高于全国8%的水平。年末企业总数达19 001个，从业人员182.16万人，实现产值2 851.92亿元，比上年增长26.5%；比全省工业平均水平高9.5个百分点；出口交货值836.54亿元，比上年增长6.3%；实现利润130.30亿元，比上年增长36.8%，高于全省工业平均水平13.0个百分点。全省农产品加工企业产值在1亿元以上的企业510个，在5 000万元以上的企业1 054个，占全部的5.5%。全省规模以上农产品加工业产值为2 513.51亿元，比2000年年均递增25.5%；食品加工业产值为637.86亿元，比2000年年均递增24.6%。农产品加工业已经成为促进福建省国民经济发展的重要产业之一，2005年全省规模以上农产品加工业和食品加工业产值分别位居全国31个省、自治区、直辖市第5位和9位，农产品加工业占全省规模以上工业总产值的30.9%。全省规模以上农副食品加工业、食品制造业、饮料制造业产值分别为372.3亿元、167.05亿元和98.51亿元，分别占食品加工业的58.37%、26.19%和15.44%。此外，粮油加工业产值为169.65亿元，占食品加工业的30.1%；茶叶加工产值为41.50亿元，占食品加工业的7.4%；畜禽加工产值为25.76亿元，占食品加工业的4.6%；蔬菜加工产值为39.00亿元，占食品加工业的6.9%；水果加工产值为25.41亿元，占食品加工业的4.5%；食用菌加工产值为17.54亿元，占食品加工业的3.1%。

2. 龙头企业快速成长，形成鲜明产业集群和品牌　随着农产品加工业的快速发展，福建省农业产业化龙头企业迅速形成。自1997年省里首次确定重点扶持100个省级农业产业化龙头企业以来，到2005年已发展到农业产业化国家重点龙头企业23个，省级龙头企业131个，市级龙头企业达614个。优势资源不断向优势产业集中，优势产业不断向优势区域集聚，农业产业化龙头企业生产经营规模不断扩大，产业链逐步延伸，辐射、带动能力明显增强，有力地推动全省农业产业化进程。一批有特色的农产品加工产业带和农产品加工基地形成，初步形成了具有本省特色的农产品加工集群和龙头企业带动型的生产基地。2005年，17个国家级农业产业化龙头（不含笋和水产品）加工企业从业人员达1.61万人，占全省食品加工业（不含笋和水产品，下同）的8.4%，产值46.14亿元，占全省食品加工业的8.2%；55个省级农业产业化龙头（农牧业）加工企业从业人员达1.82万人，占全省食品加工业的9.5%；加工业产值68.08亿元，占全省食品加工业的12.1%。各地发挥资源优势，选准项目，基本形成了粮油、食用菌、茶叶、畜禽、果蔬等区域明显的特色农产品加工产业体系的产业集群，福州、泉州、漳州粮油加工产值占全省的58.7%，宁德、漳州、福州食用菌加工产值占全省的91.3%，泉州、福州、宁德精制茶加工产值占全省的71.1%，漳州水果和蔬菜加工产值分别占全省的66.4%和48.8%，厦门、南平、漳州畜禽加工产值分别占全省的30.3%、20%和14.7%。企业总体实力不断增强，涌现了一批规模化、集团化的现代化加工企业和知名品牌。厦门罐头厂、福建紫山集团有限公司、厦门银鹭集团有限公司进入中国罐头行业十强，其产量及出口量在本省处于领先位置，主要产品在国内外市场具有较高的占有率。银鹭、惠尔康、达利园、金冠、雅客、蜡笔小新、福马、古龙、安记、雪津、惠泉等11个品牌的农牧产品获中国名牌，其中银鹭、惠尔康获中国驰名商标。部分农牧加工产品出口具有较强的竞争力，2005年出口千万美元以上的农牧产品有加工蔬菜、蘑菇罐头、茶叶和猪肉罐头，出口额分别为39 849万美元、15 437万美元、4 435万美元和1 129万美元，出口增幅除猪肉罐头比上年下降6.6%外，蔬菜、蘑菇罐头、茶叶分别比上年增长14.4%、15.8%和25.1%。

3. 农产品加工业结构优化，特色农产品加工向高附加值精深加工转变 福建省资源、区位优势显著，适宜茶叶、水果、食用菌、畜禽等特色农牧业生产，其产量位居全国前茅，发展特色农产品加工业的基础较好。近年来，通过提高科技含量培育特色农牧品种，大力开展特色农产品的深加工技术攻关和加快开发引进推广新技术、新工艺、新设备，促进特色农产品由初级加工向高附加值精深加工转变，并根据市场多元化的需求，发展不同档次的特色农产品加工品，增加特色农产品的内在价值和附加值。2005年，全省深加工食品工业产值367.17亿元，比上年增长16.5%，占全部食品工业的65%。如粮食加工业开发了各种等级专用粉、免淘米、珠光清洁米；植物油厂已经不是单纯的榨油，而是通过精炼开发了精炼油、色拉油和人造奶油等多种专用油脂，并且对副产品植物蛋白也进行了加工利用。肉制品加工由原来中低档的白条肉、冷冻肉、高温肉向高档优质的冷却肉、低温肉、小包装肉方向发展。荔枝加工不仅充分利用省内资源，而且还充分利用省外资源加工成速冻荔枝，产品附加值大为提高。

4. 市场辐射带动日益体现，经济社会实现双赢 随着农产品加工业的发展，农产品及其加工品的竞争力和市场占有率也进一步提高。调查表明，2004年福建省农副食品加工业和食品制造业省外市场占有率分别为17.7%和37.6%，境外市场占有率分别为30%和28.5%，对经济社会发展具有明显的辐射带动作用。不但拉动农业增产，而且在增加农民收入方面显示出了巨大威力。大量农业企业的兴办，增加了农民的就业机会，直接提高了务工收入，而且带动广大农户按照企业需求组织农产品生产，提高了农业生产经营效益。2005年，国家级龙头农产品加工企业自带生产基地的占69.7%。仅龙海市在蔬菜加工中引进流态单体速冻和低温真空脱水加工技术，带动了全省蔬菜产业化的发展，该市就有10多个此类加工企业，带动全市蔬菜种植面积达14khm^2，加工出口12多万t，成为龙海市农村支柱产业；龙海市台资企业带动6.8万农户参与生产经营，发展了13.3khm^{2}的订单农业生产基地，转移农村劳动力4.2万人，农民人均增收1 600多元。

5. 闽台农业加工合作全面拓展，全方位交流合作新格局形成 福建省已经成为祖国大陆对台农业引进合作的密集区，农业利用台资总额在内地各省（自治区、直辖市）中位居第一。在福建省兴办的许多台资农业企业，外接国际市场、内联生产基地和农户，具有雄厚的资金、先进的技术设备和完善的市场营销网络，成为农业产业化的龙头企业。台湾省农业良种的引进带动了福建种养业的发展，种养业的兴起促进了农产品加工业的发展，农产品加工业的发展带动了罐头、包装、保鲜、运输、销售等相关产业的发展，延伸了农业产业链。2005年，闽台以农产品为原料加工企业达2 599个，实现产值955.15亿元，同比增长23.2%。其中农副食品加工业134个，食品制造业115个，饮料制造业78个。这些农产品加工企业主要分布在福州、厦门、泉州、漳州沿海一带，近几年还形成了以漳州漳浦、龙海为中心的闽台合作农产品加工示范区。闽台合作农产品加工业正从合资、合作向整体引进发展，成为带动全省农产品加工产业升级的重要力量。漳州已成为台商投资农业的密集区和首选地，农业利用台资占全省一半以上，是内地各

省市农业利用台资最多的设区市。

二、存在的主要问题

1. *农产品加工业转化和增值能力不强，结构性矛盾比较突出* 福建省农产品加工水平虽然位居全国前10位，但加工转化和增值能力不强。2005年，全省农产品加工增值率达到51%，但远低于发达国家80%～90%的水平，农产品加工产值是农林牧渔业总产值的1.8倍，与发达国家3倍以上的水平还有较大差距。农产品资源的有效利用较低，水果加工率仅为12.6%。同时结构性矛盾也比较突出。农产品初级加工产品仍占绝大比例，精深加工比重不大，2005年农产品精深加工食品工业产值占农产品加工业产值比为12.9%，比上年下降0.7个百分点；出口创汇能力不足，出口交货值占全部农产品加工的29.3%，仍低于全省工业2.8个百分点。

2. *企业研发能力弱，技术水平较低* 一是企业加工设备与技术较为落后，创新能力不强。由于设备的简陋和技术的落后，科研人才缺乏，导致农产品加工损耗率较高，精深加工不充分，多层次开发的产品少，产品档次低，市场竞争力不强，不能适应快速发展的消费市场的需求。2005年，全省农产品加工企业研发经费投入仅占全部农产品加工产值的0.14%，远低于全省工业0.56%的水平。二是农产品品质不适应加工业的发展。农业科技投入不足，先进科技工具和手段运用偏少。三是农业科研成果转化率低。据省政府发展研究中心测算，福建省农业科研成果虽名列全国第12位，但转化为现实农业生产力的却仅为第26位。

3. *加工企业偏小，规模经济效益低* 2005年，全省农产品加工企业产值在1亿元以上的仅占2.7%，户均利润68.58万元，比全省工业低17.14万元。全省规模以下食品加工企业3 013个，占食品加工企业的76.8%；全省食品加工企业年产值上亿元的企业仅105个，占全部加工企业的2.6%；户均利润48.36万元，比全省工业低37.0万元。个体食品加工业6.58万户，占全部食品工业单位的93%。户均产值仅21.31万元，比全部个体工业户均产值低35.45万元。占绝大多数的小型农产品加工企业，缺乏市场竞争力。2005年全省规模以上食品加工业户均产值5 396.45万元，居全国第19位，比全国平均水平低27.0%。

4. *流动资金不足，企业投资意愿不强* 2005年全省规模以上食品加工企业应收账款净额和产成品库存资金为79.44亿元，比上年增长29.6%；占流动资产平均余额的35.4%，比上年提高1.7个百分点。加之农产品加工行业，企业自身积累少，资金来源渠道主要靠银行贷款，银行对规模小的企业农产品加工企业因抵押物不足，几乎不愿授信。据调查，全省仅有3家国家级和7家省级农业产业化龙头企业获得农发行政策性贷款。因此，许多产品质量好、发展前景大的企业，因资金问题而不能扩大生产。据对全省204个农产品加工企业调查表明，由于受资金的瓶颈制约，34.3%的企业投资意愿不强。

5. *企业与原材料生产基地连接不紧密，辐射带动作用不强* 调查表明省级龙头企业自带生产基地只占42.4%，大部分的农产品加工企业没有固定的原材料供应基地，农产品的质量和数量供应没有保障。另据对我省19个省级农业龙头企业调查情况看，企业的辐射带动能力仍偏弱，带动农户规模不够、作用不强，每个调查企业平均带动农户数仅1.08万户，这与目前国家级重点龙头企业平均带动农户7.6万户相比，差距很大。调查中还发现，有些龙头企业经营规模较大，但生产原料和基地建在省外，对当地农民的直接带动作用不大。

6. *管理分散，宏观调控能力低* 福建省农产品加工业分属多个部门管理，企业管理体制尚未理顺，宏观调控能力不足，导致农产品加工业的标准化体系、检测体系、食品安全体系、技术推广服务体系、质量认证体系以及信息网络体系不健全。同时长期以来对农产品加工业的发展重视不够，政策环境尚待进一步优化。

7. *食品企业结构和地区布局不合理，区域性农产品加工优势不显著* 受现有行政区划和部门管理体制的影响，农产品加工业区域布局不合理的问题也十分突出，区域特色和比较优势发挥不够。福建省90%以上的食品加工企业集中在东南沿海地区，与农产品原料产地丰富的山区相分离，而既有原料又有市场潜力的闽中西北部地区农产品加工企业则为数不多，失衡的区域布局使农产品加工业总体优势不能发挥，整个行业的效率和效益难以提高。

三、主要做法

1. *认真贯彻农业部工作方针，部署福建省农产品加工工作* 认真贯彻落实农业部农产品加工业推进行动，建设开放合作、安全高效、可持续发展的海峡两岸现代农业。省里把发展农产品加工业作为增加农民收入、调整农村经济结构、提高农业国际竞争力的有效途径，高度重视农产品加工业的发展，采取一系列切实有效的措施，加大对农产品加工工作的支持力度。在2003年，国务院办公厅出台了《关于促进农产品加工业发展的意见》后，省委、省政府及省级有关部门就相继出台了《中共福建省委福建省人民政府关于加快农业产业化经营的意见》、《福建省财政扶持农业产业化省级部门龙头企业贷款贴息资金管理暂行办法》、《福建省农牧业产业化龙头企业认定和运行监测管理暂行办法》等政策措施，从多方面扶持农产品加工业的发展。省农业厅根据国务院、省委省政府有关文件和农业部《全国主要农产品加工业发展规划》、《农产品加工业发展行动计划》主要精神，组织编制了《福建省特色农产品深加工产业发展专项规划》(2005—2010)，明确了本省特色农产品深加工产业发展的指导思想、基本原则、总体目标和布局，确定了发展方向、重点，并提出了促进全省特色农产品深加工产业发展的对策建议。2005年9月，省农业厅成立了福建省农产品加工推广总站，专职负责全省农产品加工工作。2006年，省农业厅把农产品加工业列为做强“三大产业”（即园艺产业、畜牧产业和农产品加工业）重点产业之一。在2006年的“三重点一突破”的重点工作中，又把农产品加工业作为省厅“一突破”的重要工作来抓。

各地党委、政府对农产品加工业也非常重视，纷纷制定相关政策扶持农产品加工业的发展。如龙岩市政策先行强化服务，逐步健全市、县联动抓加工产业的机制，落实“三个制度”（项目挂钩制度、绩效考评制度和产业工作月报制度），产业工作渐入正轨。出台了《龙岩市鼓励支持发展农产品加工产业优惠政策》，从供地、用电、用水、税费、贷款、服务等方面为加工企业提供全方位的优质服务和优惠政策，营造产业发展良好环境。其中，对各地建立的加工园区由市财政按每公顷75 000元标准给予补助。福州市本级财政（农业部门）投入近3 000万元资金，扶持示范基地建设。

2. *转变观念，以工业化理念谋划加工型农业* 农产品加工企业是从农业生产发展而来的存在着深厚的农业生产的痕迹，与现代企业发展相比存在很大差距，生产粗放。福建省从观念入手，跳出农业抓农业，用工业化思路发展农业，用产业的办法提升加工业、创造良好环境，帮助企业以优势资源为基础，以市场为导向，以技术为支撑，以经济效益为中心，以发展主导产品、争创农业品牌为依托，大力发展特色鲜明的农业产业集群，使农产品产业集中度得到提高，产业的集聚力得到加强，优势产业带动作用更加有力，为加快产业集群建设提供了有力的产业支撑。

3. *重点抓加工型基地建设，打造加工产业“块状经济”* 按照“全面规划、分步实施、总体布局、重点推进”的思路，明确农业结构调整的主攻目标，抓紧实施优势农产品区域布局规划，充分发挥农业的比较优势，积极推广“龙头带基地、基地连农户”的发展模式，各设区市根据当地资源优势和传统特色，充分挖掘产业发展潜力，优化布局，加大对优势农产品生产基地建设的投入，大力培育、发展有市场开拓能力、辐射面广、带动农户能力强、高标准的大型农产品加工企业，带动建设区域化、标准化的生产基地和专业乡、专业村，实现原料生产的基地化，初步形成了各具特色的产业块。

4. *着力扶持特色农产品加工业，打造优势产业集群* 注重发挥各大宗特色农产品资源的比较优势，充分挖掘产业发展潜力，积极引导农产品加工企业和项目向园区集聚，在布局上依托优势特色农产品所在乡镇，规划建设农产品特色工业园区，把企业发展与区域特色农业，原料基地建设、特色工业园区和小城镇建设有机结合起来，整体协调发展，初步形成了各具特色的产业集群。如龙岩市高度重视农产品加工产业集群工作，成立了专门的工作班子，财政、金融、税收、土地等方面加大对农产品加工产业集群的扶持力度，出台了系列优惠政策，进一步加快了园区建设进度。连城县出台了《连城县红心食品加工区鼓励投资的实施方案》，除了低价提供“三通一平”的熟地外，还设立了食品加工鼓励基金，补助投资者建设甘薯和其他低污染食品加工企业；长汀县远山食品加工园区对入驻企业可享受该县针织、轻纺产业的优惠政策。

5. *狠抓项目突出招商，扎实推进产业集聚* 项目是推进加工产业发展的重要抓手。2005年，各地突出当地特色，围绕当地农产品加工产业的发展，积极开发项目、策划项目、储备项目、推介项目，形成集聚效应，并把招商引资作为促进区域农业经济发展的重要推动力，作为弥补投入资金、增加资本总量的主要途径。通过资本注入、项目带动，加快农产品加工产业的发展。

6. *培育特色农产品加工示范企业，促进“一村一品”的发展* 为大力发展优势特色农产品加工业，扶持壮大成长型农产品加工中小企业，发挥农产品加工业在提高农业综合效益，加快农业增长方式转变，发展现代农业，建设社会主义新农村等方面的重要作用，省农业厅围绕本省《三条特色农业产业带、四大主导产业和九个重点特色农产品发展区域布局规划》，2006年重点对水果、蔬菜、茶叶、畜禽、食用菌、粮油等特色产品加工，特别是适宜发展“一村一品”，在连接农户，增加就业，解决当地农产品销售、增值等方面具有显著带动作用的中小型农产品加工企业进行扶持，已评选出第一批15个省级农产品加工示范企业，在全省各地发挥了很好的示范效应，促进了当地“一村一品”的发展。

7. 加强合作，积极发展闽台农产品加工业 充分利用与台湾省地缘相近、血缘相亲、文缘相承、商缘相连、法缘相循的“五缘”密切关系，积极开展对台农产品加工业交流与合作，自1981年第一家注册的台资农业企业在漳州落户至2006年6月底，全省累计批办农业台资项目1 903个，合同利用台资23.4亿美元，实际到资13.3亿美元；累计从台湾省引进农产品生产、加工设备5 000多台套，引进栽培、养殖和加工等先进实用技术800多项，为来闽台商的再创业提供了新天地，已经成为内地对台农业引进合作的密集区。不少企业取得丰厚的回报，不断增资扩厂，投资合作规模呈加速发展态势。

江西省农产品加工业

江西省农业厅

一、发展现状

2005年，江西省粮食产量为1 757万t，同比增长5.65%；棉花产量为9万t，同比增长2.81%；油料产量为76万t，同比增长2.14%；水果产量为130万t，同比增长27.26%；蔬菜产量为1 146万t，同比增长2.43%；茶叶产量2万t，同比增长24.09；肉类产量237万t，同比增长8%；禽蛋产量42万t，同比增长6%；奶类产量13万t，同比增长18%；水产品产量168万t，同比增长7.69%。

1. 粮油加工业 2005年，全省粮油加工企业1 708个，包括大米加工企业1 689个，油脂加工企业19个。其中，国有粮食加工企业211个（油脂3个，大米208个），占12.4%。全省粮油加工年综合生产能力2 388万t（国有粮食加工企业为406万t），其中大米2 331万t，面粉24万t，食用植物油加工油料25万t，精炼7.5万t。粮食加工业资产总计34.5亿元，其中大米加工业33亿元，食用植物油加工业为1.2亿元。销售收入88.2亿元（国有粮食加工企业11.6亿元，占13%），其中大米加工业87.5亿元，占99%。粮食加工实现利润总额1.4亿元（国有粮食加工企业127万元），其中大米加工业1.37亿元，占97.8%，食用油加工573万元。主要产品产量大米358万t，小麦粉3.8万t，食用植物油0.6万t。

2. 畜禽产品加工业 2005年，全省畜牧小区新增300多个，总数达到1 000个；畜禽规模养殖户新增3.68万户，生猪出栏突破2 500万头大关，达到2 502万头，比上年增长13.5%，肉、蛋、奶产量和生猪出栏分别比2000年增长33.2%、52.8%、247.3%和20%，均高于全国增长水平，增幅位于全国前茅。围绕加快畜产品加工业的发展，各地纷纷出台了推进畜产品加工企业发展的优惠政策，通过结合工业企业结构的调整、乡镇企业的转制和私营企业的发展，积极鼓励和支持多种经济成分参与兴办畜产品加工企业。各地通过建立和完善畜禽良种繁育体系，向畜禽产品生产基地、养殖场和养殖专业户、大户提供稳定优质的加工原料。各级政府通过政策引导、合理布局、重点扶持等措施，建立多元化的投入机制，加大了对龙头企业的扶持力度。省畜牧兽医局制定与国际市场接轨的有关畜产品质量标准和检验标准，不断缩小与发达国家的差距，提高了畜产品的出口水平。

3. 水产品加工业 2005年，全省水产品加工企业数量达到100多个，单班加工能力6万多t，加工品总产量达到9万t，用于加工的水产品达到13万t，水产品加工率达到10%左右。已建立水产养殖、加工、流通等各类产业化组织（企业）205个，其中省级农业产业化龙头企业13个。全省水产品人均占有量为39.5kg，比2000年增加9kg。全省水产品出口创汇额达8 000万美元，较2000年增加2.96倍，为全省大宗农产品出口之首，也连续6年居全国内陆省份水产品出口之首。水产品出口创汇中，100%来自加工企业。

4. 农产品市场流通 2005年，全省共拥有各类农产品市场2 260个，各类农产品批发市场185个，年农产品交易总额在140亿元以上。全省现有农业部定点农产品批发市场15个，省定点农产品批发市场26个。全省各地各级大小各类农产品协（合）作组织有3 000余个，通过各类民间农产品流通组织带动了全省50余万农民参与了农产品流通，其中专门从事各类农产品贩运的人数达到10余万人。2005年5月，还成立了江西省农产品市场流通协会，民间流通组织的活跃极大地推动了农业生产的发展。省农业厅利用江西农业信息网现有的资源，建立了全省统一的农产品流通、交易信息发布系统，在网络上及时发布各地农产品交易信息，为农产品生产者、经销商和运输人员提供了一个极好的信息获取渠道。同时，在全省开通了农产品绿色通道，据统计，全省已发放“绿色”通道通行证5万余张。按照农业部等部委的要求，2005年10月，“哈尔滨—海口”的全国“绿色通道”江西段正式开通，对于在这条通道上装载运输鲜活农产品的省内外车辆一律予以减半收取通行费，这是江西省第一次对外省运载农产品车辆实行优惠政策，标志着全省农业对外开放达到了一个新的水平。

5. 农产品质量安全 2005年3月，省农业厅印发了《关于开展2005年全省农产品质量安全例行监测和预警工作的通知》，决定从2005年起全面建立全省农产品质量安全例行监测和初级农产品农药残留、兽药残留等检测信息发布制度。6月，省农业厅印发的《江西省农业厅农产品质量安全信息发布工作方案》，又进一步明确了本省农产品质量安全信息发布程序。2005年，省厅开展了三次农产品质量安全例行监测，检测结果都及时对外发布。全省各级农业部门参与和组织制定了250余项省级农业地方标准，64项市、县农业地方标准技术规范，458项农产品企业标准。全省已建各类农产品生产标准化示范基地297个，生产规模达96.7khm^2。并成功地创建了8个全国无公害农产品标准化生产示范县、7个全国农产品标准化生产综合示范区。制定了《江西省农业标准化生产示范区管理办法》，开展了标准化知识培训，打造了一支农产品标准化推广工作队伍。到2005年，全省认定无公害农产品产地430个，其中种植业产地256个，生产规模164.7khm^2；畜牧业产地94个，养殖规模6 270万头（只、羽）；渔业产地80个，养殖规模127.3khm^2；通过农业部全国无公害农产品统一认证的产品达230个，其中种植业163个，认证实物产量101万t；畜牧业产品27个，认证实物产量7.4万t；渔业产品40个，认证实物产量4.7万t。

此外，2005年全省农业部门引进内资项目704个，合同金额82.9亿元；实际到位资金52.1亿元，同比增长18.4%。其中，引进外资项目35个，合同金额1亿美元，实际引进外资6 000万美元，是上年的2倍。合同金额5 000万元以上的项目有30多个。农产品出口创汇2亿美元，同比增长17.6%，其中出口额较大的有水产业的烤鳗，经济作物中的棉麻制品、蔬菜制品和畜牧业的皮革制品等。农业产业化经营加大了对省级农业产业化龙头企业运营情况的监测，重新认定了191个省级以上龙头企业。初步形成了以191个省级以上龙头企业为骨干，600余个市级龙头企业为网络、一大批县乡产业化组织为基础的发展态势。

二、发展重点

当前和今后一段时期内，江西省农产品加工业的发展要以建立农业产业化经营为基础，认真组织实施《江西省优质农产品生产加工基地建设规划》，充分发挥本省良好的生态环境和资源优势，打好绿色牌、生态牌，采取“因地制宜、一地一品、规模化生产、产业化经营”的策略，着力培植具有比较优势的主导产业，形成一批具有浓郁地方特色的产业化基地。

1. 粮油加工 进一步调优粮油产品结构，大力发展优质、专用、绿色产品，扩大优质早稻、高档晚稻、优质加工专用稻、“双低”优质油菜的种植面积，抓好粮油优质品种的更换和农产品加工关键技术的开发利用，从品种开发、生产、储运、加工、技术装备等面进行整体研究，引导企业开发各类无公害食品、绿色食品、特色食品、保健食品和出口创汇食品。

2. 畜禽加工 结合本省资源优势，畜禽业发展的重点是加大对草山、草坡、草洲资源的开发利用和冬季农田种草养畜禽的开发力度，大力发展草食动物养殖。畜禽加工业要以骨干肉类食品加工企业为龙头，带动畜禽业向养殖、加工、销售一条龙方向发展，引导鲜肉制品向小包装、细分割、便携带方向发展；熟肉制品向多品种、系列化、小包装、易储存方向发展；生产设备逐步向连续化、自动化、大批量和无菌加工技术方向发展；积极开发研制具有江西传统风味的酱、卤、腊肉制品工业化生产的工艺和设备。奶制品主要解决奶源问题，扩大奶畜数量，提高奶品质量，扩大机械化挤奶。

3. 果蔬加工 果业继续按照“南橘北梨”的发展思路，抓好赣南脐橙、南丰蜜橘等特色水果的开发，加快“三北”地区梨业的大发展。大力发展鲜果保鲜储藏和精深加工，提高分级筛选、清洗、打蜡、包装等商品化水平。有步骤地扩大浓缩果汁、天然果肉原汁加工能力，开发具有特色的果汁果肉饮料、果蔬混合饮料、果酒等深加工。蔬菜生产要扩大无公害蔬菜种植规模，引导菜农严格按照“无公害生产技术规程”操作，抓好施肥、使用农药等关键环节；大力推行净菜上市，提高蔬菜采后清洗、分级、包装等商品化处理水平。

4. 茶叶加工　茶叶是江西省传统优势农产品，有一大批名优产品享誉市场，具有良好的发展基础，今后，重点是运用新技术、新工艺，加快制茶技术和设备的改造，提高产品质量和包装档次；在产品开发和生产上，以名优茶叶为重点，向保质、保鲜、保特色方向发展，大力发展有机茶、保健茶等系列产品。

5. 水产品加工　按照“一保鲜、二保活、三加工”的原则，以鲜、活产品销售为主，大力发展以名优水产品为重点的保鲜运输业，扩大暂养面积，推广集装箱保鲜、气体置换保鲜、冷冻保鲜等新技术，形成生产、暂养、保活保鲜运输一条龙。

6. 市场建设　依托优质农产品基地，重点抓好粮食、生猪、水产、水果、茶叶、花卉、蔬菜、药材、竹木等一批农产品批发交易市场的开发和建设，包括产地批发市场和销地批发市场，把市场建设与原料基地建设有机结合起来，提高流通效率，降低交易成本。

三、政策措施

1. 制定和完善优惠政策　为把江西省建成沿海优质农产品供应基地，推进农产品加工业的发展，各级政府要在土地、产业投资、税收及科研开发等方面制定一系列优惠政策，增加对农产品生产、加工和市场体系建设的投入，推进农业产业化经营的发展，大力实施“品牌”战略。

2. 加大资金投入　各级政府要对优良品种的引进、推广、农产品生产基地建设、加工企业的技术改造及技术创新给予重点支持；通过财政贴息、以奖代补等手段，对高新技术成果和农产品著名品牌进行扶持。各金融部门，特别是农村信用社和农业银行要在严格执行信贷管理规定的基础上，加大对农产品加工企业的扶持力度，增加有效信贷投入，同时，改进金融服务，督促企业及时到人民银行办理贷款证登记，为企业结算提供优质服务。鼓励利用资本市场筹集发展资金，可采取民营、股份合作、买断经营权、租赁、承包、转让等形式搞活企业，吸引民间资本、国有资本、国外资本投资农产品加工业，实现投资主体多元化。

3. 提高科技水平　针对江西省农产品加工企业技术储备不足和开发能力较低的现状，各级政府要抓紧制定科技发展规划，建立健全科技开发机构和技术推广体系，鼓励科技部门和涉农科研院所积极开展农产品加工、转化、增值项目的引进、研发、服务工作，加快科研成果的转化。为龙头企业提供有价值的新技术、新工艺、新发明。研究和制定相关政策，鼓励科研院所、大专院校与企业加强合作，提高企业的技术水平和新产品开发能力，促进全省农产品加工业的快速发展。

4. 完善市场体系　一是促进生产要素市场的形成和完善。加快农业生产要素交易市场建设，促进生产要素的市场配置。在巩固和完善农村土地承包经营关系的基础上，切实制定有利于山地、水面、果园等农业生产要素流转的政策，推进农业规模经营。二是切实加强农产品基地建设。充分调动农户、龙头企业和社区的积极性，走“小规模、大群体”的路子，不断增强经济实力。政府各部门要做好协调工作，引导龙头企业通过与农户签订产销合同，实行保护价收购，同时，鼓励农户以土地、劳力入股等方式，结成风险共担，利益共沾的经济利益共同体。三是引进现代营销方式和流通组织形式，发展农产品配送和连锁经营，放手发展中介组织、合作组织和经纪人队伍，形成完善的农产品流通体系。

5. 加快结构调整　在农业结构战略性调整中，要以市场为导向，按照农产品加工标准化、优质化的要求，调整和优化农产品生产结构。各地要树立“一乡一品”、“一县一业”的思路，集中优势资源和生产要素，大力培育具有区域优势的产业或产业带，实现工厂化加工、规模化生产，形成一批“赣”牌特色农产品，以特色占领市场。大力培育和发展龙头骨干企业，加快农业产业化的发展，按照《江西省农业产业化经营省级龙头企业发展规划》提出农产品加工项目建设的五项要求（即带动力强、辐射面宽、发展潜力大、受益农户多、能起龙头带动作用），建立起省、设区市、县三级农产品加工业扶持体系，集中力量扶持100个市场知名度较高，享有较好声誉的龙头企业，力争这100个企业到2010年销售收入达到500亿元以上，年交易额300亿元以上，利税50亿元以上，带动农户达到全省1/3左右。

6. 建立服务体系　一是建立和完善技术推广、良种繁育、职业培训、农产品检测、中介服务等社会化服务体系，为品牌农产品发展提供产前、产中、产后服务。重点加快完善江西省农产品信息网络，拓宽信息的收集和发布渠道，为农产品加工企业和农户提供及时、准确的信息服务；改革现有农业技术推广体系，走农业技术服务社会化、市场化的路子，逐步建立起多种所有制并存、机制灵活高效的技术服务体系，建立信用担保体系，财政部门、税务部门要在资金、政策等方面予以支持。二是要积极引进和采用国际标准，重点推广国家、行业和江西省现有的农产品质量标准和技术操作规程，加强地方标准的制定，尽快建立和完善产品质量卫生安全的强制性标准，相应地建立和完善农产品产地环境标准、产品加工包装标准、产品储运标准、动植物检疫标准、检验检测方法及相关的技术规范，健全本省农产品质量认证和标识制度。三是健全质量安全体系，进一步完善农产品加工制品质量检验检测手段，加强对农产品加工质量安全的监督、检测和检查，完善有关法规，并严格执法。四是加大帮扶力度。各级工商行政管理部门、质量技术监督部门要在注册商标、申报品牌、保护名牌等方面予以支持；各级政府要通过组织形式多样的名优农产品展销、订货、招商等活动，扩大江西农产品的知名度。

（注：本文为编辑部根据该省相关资料编辑整理）

山东省农产品加工业

山东省农业厅

一、发展现状

据不完全统计，到2005年底，全省规模以上农产品加工龙头企业达到5 868个，其中销售收入过亿元的884个，10亿元以上的61个，20亿元以上的12个，30亿元以上的4个，50亿元以上的2个，100亿元以上的2个。规模以上农产品加工龙头企业实现销售收入4 489.38亿元，出口创汇81.93亿美元，上缴税金125.46亿元，实现利润240.62亿元。山东省农产品加工业的发展，主要呈现出如下特点：

1. *东部地区整体水平不断提高，中西部地区快速跟进* 潍坊、烟台、青岛和威海4市规模以上农产品加工龙头企业的数量、销售收入分别占全省总数的32.53%和38.64%，过亿元、外向型、省重点及国家重点农产品加工龙头企业分别达到全省总数的36.20%、40.75%、36.21%和57.78%。内陆地区的临沂、济宁、滨州和德州4市，近几年跟进速度较快，规模以上农产品加工龙头企业数量、销售收入已分别占全省总数的38.85%和37.85%。随着东西结合步伐的加快，聊城、菏泽2市农产品加工龙头企业也进入快速发展的轨道，规模以上农产品加工龙头企业已达到619个，实现销售收入400.67亿元。

2. *经营领域不断拓宽，主导产业优势区域逐渐形成* 全省规模以上农产品加工龙头企业主要集中在粮食、棉花、蔬菜、肉类、油料、果品、水产等产业，企业数量分别达到1 266个、896个、873个、565个、371个、342个、282个，在龙头企业的带动下，形成了潍坊蔬菜、威海水产、烟台果品等各具特色的专业经济区和产业经济带。

3. *多元化发展格局已经形成，民营企业成为主要力量* 到2005年底，全省规模以上农产品加工龙头企业群体中，民营成分龙头企业（包括集体企业、股份制企业、私营企业）达到5 273个，占总数的89.86%；销售收入达到3 749.64亿元，占总数的83.52%。

4. *经营链条不断拉长，农产品转化增值能力提高* 许多地方凭借自身优势，围绕主导产业发展农产品加工龙头企业，上中下游龙头企业协调发展，区域内配套成龙，大大提高了农产品转化增值能力。据测算，龙头企业农产品加工增值率已达65%。

5. *龙头企业集团化趋势明显，市场竞争力增强* 一些农产品加工龙头企业利用自己的资金优势、品牌优势和市场优势，实行低成本扩张、多渠道联合、多层次发展，形成了大龙带小龙、小龙带农户的可喜局面。西王集团始由小作坊式的油棉厂发展成为职工3 100余人，总资产16.7亿元，辖有16个子公司的全国工业大型企业集团。企业现年加工玉米能力50万t，年产30万t玉米淀粉、20万t结晶葡萄糖、8万t麦芽糊精、10万t玉米色拉油、10万t高蛋白玉米纤维饲料、1万t酵母。淀粉系列产品、结晶葡萄糖、麦芽糊精、玉米色拉油先后打入国际市场，远销亚、欧、非、大洋洲的十几个国家和地区。

二、主要做法

多年来，山东省把发展农产品加工龙头企业作为提升农业产业化经营水平、建设现代农业的关键措施来抓，主要做了以下几方面的工作：

1. *多形式建设农产品加工龙头企业，壮大龙头企业群体* 国有、集体一起上，独资、合资、合作一齐上，调动社会各方面力量参与龙头企业建设。许多国有大中型企业把生产经营触角延伸到农业领域，凭借其雄厚的人才、资金、设备优势，逐步发展成为农业产业化经营的重要推动力量。据不完全统计，全省投资农业产业化开发的大中型国有工商企业已达1 000多个。外商投资农产品加工龙头企业数量达到677家，资产总额达448.53亿元，固定资产为216.81亿元，实现销售收入638.20亿元，出口创汇32.05亿美元，税后利润36.10亿元，上缴税金18.14亿元，分别占全省总数的8.06%、15.47%、9.99%、39.12%、15.00%、14.46%。莱阳市积极引导社会资本进入农产品加工领域，打造出了一支整体实力比较强的“农字号联合舰队”。到2005年底，全市规模以上农产品加工龙头企业共有95个，资产达到85.03亿元，实现销售收入123.29亿元，形成了以龙大、鲁花、天府、吉龙、春雪等具有一定规模企业为代表的龙头企业群体。以这批龙头企业为依托，在莱阳城区东部已建成一个在全国颇具影响力的食品加工城。

2. *外延扩张与内涵挖潜并举，增强农产品加工龙头企业的规模优势* 为了加快农产品加工龙头企业的技改步伐，省政府专门制定了大中型龙头企业改造规划，引导龙头企业由单一经营向多种经营转变，拓展经营领域，发挥综合经营优势。诸城市外贸集团经过十多年的发展，围绕肉鸡、淀粉、色素、包装等主导产品形成了肉鸡良种繁育、饲料生产、产品包装、宰杀加工、熟食品生产、淀粉生产、色素提炼、热电联产等支柱产业。其中肉鸡一体化生产体系形成年产父母代种鸡200万套、商品代雏鸡1亿只、饲料50万t、加工冻鸡15万t、分割出口5万t、加工熟食品8万t的规模，是全国最大的肉鸡出口生产基地之一；玉米淀粉年产能力160万t，居全国同行业前列；色素提炼形成年加工色素2亿克的能力，带动基地13.3khm^2，是全球最大的饲料级天然色素出口生产基地。

3. *推行“三改一加强”，提高农产品加工龙头企业的整体素质* 全省国有、集体性质的龙头企业有90%以上实行了公司制、股份制、股份合作制改造。谷神公司通过产权改革，引进外资，创立民营合资的谷神集团，使企业焕发出勃勃生机和充沛活力。有的放矢的引进人才、信息、资金、设备、技术等资源，使企业规模扶摇直上。同时开展了用人制度、分配制度、管理机构、营销体制等多方面的改革，增强了企业凝聚力和竞争力，达到了年加工饲料14.4万t、籽棉500t、大豆20万t、养殖种猪3 000头、出栏育肥猪5 000头的规模。

4. *实行标准化生产，积极参与国际市场的竞争* 鼓励农产品加工龙头企业积极引进国外资金、技术、设备、人才和管理经验，建立各类农产品出口生产基地，并按照国际规范标准加强对农产品及其加工企业的标准质量认证，努力实现与国际市场的全方位接轨。到2005年底，全省规模以上农产品加工龙头企业建立质检机构的有5 151个，占总数的61.38%；实行现代管理制度的有5 246个，占总数的62.5%；通过ISO体系认证的有1 817个，占总数的21.65%；通过ISO14000体系认证的有1 099个，占总数的13.1%；通过HACCP体系认证的有904个，占总数的10.7%。龙大集团不断加大投资规模，加快发展步伐。在兴建多个国际一流水准的大型全封闭无菌加工工场的基础上，建有总容量达8万多t的恒温库、低温库和气调库；按国际标准建立了规模化的PIC种猪繁育、养殖、屠宰和加工基地；与日商合资，新建了国内大型的一流的调理食品专业加工场、国内最先进的水产品加工出口专业化企业，以及真空冷冻干燥制品项目。生产加工保鲜果蔬、冷冻蔬菜、调理食品、FD（真空冷冻干燥）制品、水产品、粮油制品、肉类食品、调味品共八大系列400多个品种，出口日、韩、美、德、俄等国家。

5. *加大科技创新力度，促进企业的快速健康发展* 引导各地相继建起了一批规模较大、科技含量较高的高起点龙头企业，并在此基础上，鼓励龙头企业建立自己的科研机构，加强同大专院校、科研院所的协作，实行产学研结合。截止到2005年底，全省规模以上农产品加工龙头企业拥有研发机构1 937个，专职研发人员2.15万名。2005年度投入研发经费23.23亿元，获得国家级科研成果166项，省级科研成果414项，获得发明专利718项。经过几年努力，烟台龙大集团、青岛六和集团等龙头企业，都已发展成为层次较高、规模较大的龙头企业集团。临沂市三维油脂股份有限公司，加大科研投资力度，在稳定发展豆油、花生油、高级烹调油等10多个品种的基础上，又确定研究开发粉末油脂、食用磷脂、卵磷脂、大豆异黄酮以及生物肥、生物农药等高新技术产品。

6. *加强政策扶持，为龙头企业创造良好的发展环境* 自1994开始，省委、省政府陆续出台了多项关于扶持龙头企业、鼓励招商引资、支持个体私营经济和农村合作经济发展的政策措施，并在项目审批、资金投放、税费减免等方面给予倾斜扶持，调动各方面参与产业化经营的积极性。2002年4月29日，省委、省政府在潍坊召开了全省农业产业化工作会议，会议确定继续加大对产业化经营的扶持力度。从2002年起连续五年，省财政每年安排不少于5 000万元专项资金，与银行信贷资金捆绑滚动使用，支持龙头企业发展；省财政2006年安排5 000万元资金，用于农业标准和检测体系建设；农业综合开发和扶贫资金的安排使用，要与推进农业产业化经营结合起来，从多种经营资金中每年安排不少于5 000万元，直接用于扶持农业龙头企业；省高新技术产业贴息专项资金和科技型中小企业创新专项资金，每年安排一定比例用于扶持农业龙头企业；对农业龙头企业申报国家扶持的高新技术产业化推进项目、农产品深加工项目和技改贴息项目，省有关部门优先推荐上报。另外，在税收、信贷、用地、用电等各方面，也要在国家政策允许的范围内予以倾斜和优惠，提供更加优质高效的服务。

三、存在的主要问题

1. *农产品加工龙头企业规模偏小*　据统计，2005年全省规模以上农产品加工龙头企业的销售收入平均为7 649万元，销售收入过亿元的企业只占总数的11.5%。

2. *加工层次偏低，创汇能力较弱*　农产品加工龙头企业多数以初加工为主，出口创汇产品也以原料型的居多。

3. *出口市场过于集中，受国际市场的波动影响大*　出口创汇企业的市场过于集中，主要集中在日本和韩国，日韩市场稍有风吹草动，都会对企业造成很大的影响。

4. *质量监督监测体系不健全，受国外非关税壁垒制约严重*　山东省农产品质量监督监测体系，尤其是畜产品的检疫防疫体系，远远不能适应加入WTO的需要，农产品的出口受到很大的限制。

四、主要措施

1. *制定科学的发展规划，加快构建农产品加工业体系*　尽快制定山东省农产品加工业发展规划。在布局上，突出各地、各传统产业经济带的农产品资源、市场资源、地理位置及经济发展等方面的优势。在形式上，打破所有制、行业和行政区域界限，坚持国有、集体、民营、合作、外资、混合所有制一齐上，调动社会各方面的力量参与农产品加工业发展。鼓励工商企业换业、转产、兼营，兴办农产品加工项目，努力形成农产品加工企业多元化发展的局面。在结构上，重点培植一批规模大、层次高、市场竞争力强的大型农产品加工龙头企业，大力发展以加工转化优势农产品、特色农产品、吸纳农村剩余劳动力的中小型劳动密集型企业，大力支持发展外向度高、科技含量高、附加值高的农产品加工企业。通过强化政策措施，改善农产品加工企业发展环境，尽快构建起与农产品生产、市场需求相配套的农产品加工业体系。

2. *加强农产品基地建设，为农产品加工业提供原料保障*　在现有农业商品基地的基础上，新建、扩建一批市场潜力大、加工增值高的原料型农产品生产基地。要通过大力推行农业标准化，规范基地的生产与管理，提高基地的生产能力和产品质量；通过实施品牌、名牌战略，加快发展无公害、绿色食品等优质产品原料开发与生产，尽快形成与农产品加工企业配套发展的专用、优质、稳定的农产品生产基地。鼓励农产品加工企业建设自己的原料生产基地，或通过定向投入、定向服务、定向收购等方式与基地农民建立稳定的合同购销关系。

3. *加快标准体系和检测体系建设，提高农产品加工业质量安全水平*　参照国际标准，抓紧制（修）订农产品及加工制品的质量安全标准和技术规范，并逐步与国际标准接轨；加强农业质量检测机构建设，提高检测水平和检测能力；加强质量认证工作，逐步建立产品质量等级标识制度；完善有关法规，建立产品质量监督制度，加强对农产品加工业的质量检测、检查和监督。农产品加工企业必须依照国家强制性标准建立相应的质量控制体系，确保产品质量。鼓励农产品加工企业采用国外先进标准，或按照市场需求，采用高于山东省现行标准的外埠标准组织生产。

4. *加快经营机制创新，促进农产品加工业的健康发展*　要进一步深化企业改革，建立现代企业制度，为农产品加工业发展创造良好的体制条件；鼓励农产品加工企业采用先进的管理方式，提高企业的管理水平；支持农产品加工企业实行产品研发、基地建设、生产加工、营销服务一体化经营，与基地农民建立效益联结机制，形成利益共同体，共同发展农业产业化经营。同时，加强农产品加工业行业协会、专业协会等中介服务组织建设，发挥其在社会化服务、开展行业自律、防止无序竞争、协调解决贸易争端等方面的作用。

5. *加大科技创新力度，推动农产品加工企业走新型工业化道路*　抓紧制定农产品加工业技术发展的政策措施，加快农业科技创新，加快农产品加工科技成果转化和先进适用技术的推广，为农产品加工业发展提供技术支持。当前的重点是加快开发与推广农产品精深加工工艺、技术和装备。积极扶持鼓励农产品加工业实施产学研对接工程，提高自主创新能力，并采用引进、合作开发等形式不断提高技术与装备水平。培育一批拥有自主知识产权、产业关联度大、带动能力强的科技型农产品加工龙头企业。

6. 努力开拓国外市场，着力提高农产品加工业的外向度 实行全方位、多层次、宽领域的对外开放，充分利用两种资源、两个市场，加快发展农产品加工业，提高农产品加工业的外向化水平。引导和鼓励农产品加工企业积极开展对外交流合作，大力引进国外资本、优良品种、先进技术、管理方法和高级人才，转变生产经营方式。支持农产品加工企业加快建立健全国际市场营销体系和网络，开展多种形式的营销活动，积极开拓多元化国际市场，扩大农产品出口创汇。鼓励有条件的农产品加工企业"走出去"，输出技术、劳务、品牌和资金，到境外投资创办生产基地，发展加工项目，不断提高农产品在国际市场上的占有率。

河南省农产品加工业

河南省乡镇企业管理局

一、基本情况

2005年，河南省粮食总产量达4 582万t，其中夏粮总产量2 609.21万t，秋粮总产量1 972.79万t；油料总产量449.6万t，其中花生仁335.1万t，油菜籽87.7万t，芝麻26.8万t；棉花总产量67.7万t；蔬菜总产量5 880.25万t；水果、烟叶、黄红麻、茶叶产量分别达到580万t、28.84万t、4万t和1.5万t。养殖小区达到3 295个，生猪、蛋鸡、肉鸡规模饲养比重分别达到49%、64%和94%。肉类总产量达到689万t，其中猪牛羊肉产量375.3万t。禽蛋产量达到375万t，牛奶产量达到104万t。水产品产量达到51.68万t。全省第一产业增加值达到1 843.04亿元，占全省生产总值的17.49%。

2005年，全省农产品加工企业达到4万多个，农产品加工业总产值近3 000亿元，从业人员达到210万人，实现增加值750亿元，占全省生产总值的7.5%。其中，全省规模以上农产品加工企业达到3 111个，产值876.67亿元，销售收入858.07亿元，利润70.84亿元。全省粮食加工能力达到3 200万t，加工产量达1 876万t，其中年产小麦粉1 300万t，味精22.1万t，糖10万t；油料的加工能力达到825万t，年产花生油、菜籽油、芝麻油、大豆油、棉清油等505万t；猪牛羊肉的加工能力达到390万t；棉纺锭1 000万锭，年产棉纱138.8万t，棉布16亿m；软饮料210万t，啤酒300万t，速冻米面食品100万t，畜肉制品100万t，白酒25万t；机制纸及纸板750万t，皮革2 500万m^2。主要特点是：

1. 形成了一批市场占有率高的名牌产品 河南省的肉制品、方便面、速冻食品、面粉等均为全国销量第一，火腿肠、速冻食品、方便面、饼干、浓缩果汁、味精等优势产品的国内市场占有率分别达到70%、60%、60%、25%、21%和20%。涌现出"三全"、"思念"、"科迪"牌速冻食品，"众品"、"永达"、"大用"、"邦杰"、"汇通"牌肉制品，"神象"、"金苑"牌面粉，"白象"、"斯美特"、"南街村"牌方便面，"金丝猴"牌奶糖，"十三香"牌调味品，"金星"、"奥克"牌啤酒等知名品牌。

2. 农产品加工业产业集中度提高，产业集群发展迅速，区域特色初步形成 全省有农产品加工业产业集群40个，其中食品加工产业集群有27个。郑州的速冻食品、啤酒，许昌的粮食加工，漯河的方便食品、冻鲜肉和肉制品，信阳的毛尖茶、华英鸭，固始的柳编，鹤壁的鸡肉，商丘、驻马店、新乡的面粉，长垣的卫生材料，三门峡的果品加工，安阳的纺织，周口的皮革及制品等，都已形成了特色鲜明的产业体系和产业集群。许昌市农产品加工基地，有各种类型的农产品加工企业998个，其中农业产业化国家重点龙头企业2个，国家级农产品加工业示范企业2个，省级农业产业化龙头企业7个，市级农业产业化龙头企业50个，中国名牌产品1个，河南省著名商标6个，带动农户100户以上的产业化经营组织205个，带动64万农户从事订单农业；从业人员8.6万人；已形成了大豆加工、小麦加工、中药材加工、甘薯加工、畜产品加工、蔬菜加工、板材加工、棉花及棉短绒加工、造纸及纸制品、花木种植等优势行业，年加工大豆63万t，小麦168万t，三粉（甘薯淀粉、粉条、粉皮）85万t，畜产品300万头，蔬菜5.6万t，中药10万t，烟草复烤5万t，蜂产品1.8万t，各种花木6 000万株；年销售收入近235亿元，税利31.2亿元。

3. *龙头企业辐射带动作用增强*　全省有省以上农业产业化龙头企业129个，其中农产品加工企业119个，年产值665.41亿元，完成销售收入624.91亿元，实现利润23.97亿元，上缴税金23.29亿元，带动农户390万户。这些大型农产品加工企业不仅规模大、效益好，而且带动能力强，辐射面广，围绕龙头企业的产业链不断加长。如商丘市虞城县利民工业园，以河南科迪（集团）为龙头，带动了96个企业发展种植、养殖和食品加工业，年生产方便面10万t，速冻甜玉米3万t，乳品15万t，安排1.1万人就业；年销售收入达到16.3亿元，利润1.6亿元，集群内农民人均年收入达到9 960元。漯河市的肉类加工业，在龙头企业双汇集团的带动下，派生出“汇通”、“豫汇”、“金运”、“汇东”等一批肉类加工企业，这些企业吸纳“双汇”的技术、管理、营销理念和模式，提高了企业的生产管理水平，带动了整个地区产业素质的提高，还形成拥有500多部冷藏车和数千辆生猪运输车的运输产业，上千人的生猪收购队伍和数十万人的禽畜饲养队伍，带动了服务业和养殖业的发展。

4. *促进了外向型经济的发展*　2005年，全省农产品加工业出口产品200多个品种，远销50多个国家和地区，出口创汇15亿美元。如许昌的发制品加工产业集群出口创汇3亿美元，漯河的肉类加工产业集群出口创汇1.8亿美元，南阳的地毯、丝毯产业集群出口创汇7 800万美元，孟州桑坡的毛皮加工产业集群出口创汇7 000万美元，固始县三尖河乡柳编产业集群出口创汇2 600万美元。全省已形成了221个特色鲜明的农产品加工出口基地，如鹤壁、信阳等地的禽肉，漯河、周口、许昌等地的肉类，郑州的食品加工，驻马店、周口的芝麻，三门峡的苹果汁等。这些农产品出口基地与龙头企业和农户相结合，采取“公司＋基地”、“公司＋协会＋农户”等生产经营模式，进行一体化、规模化、标准化生产，不但带动了当地农民增收，也增强了他们抵御国际市场风险的能力。

二、存在的主要问题

1. *加工总量不足，精深加工程度较低，科技投入严重不足*　河南省农产品加工业产值与农林牧渔业总产值之比仅为0.5：1，农产品加工程度只有45%，初加工与精深加工的比例仅为1：0.8，农产品加工增值比例仅33%。2005年，全省规模以上农产品企业的研发投入16.65亿元，仅占销售收入的1.94%。开发投入不足，导致农产品加工业装备和工艺水平落后，产品开发和科技创新能力弱，科技成果转化率低。

2. *技术装备落后，企业规模较小*　河南省农产品加工企业的技术装备水平处于20世纪80年代的世界平均水平，15%左右处于90年代水平，只有5%左右达到目前国际先进水平。企业规模普遍偏小，到2005年底，全省日处理小麦200t以上的企业不到100个，占粮食加工企业总量的3.2%。由于技术装备水平落后和企业规模小，在一定程度上造成了资源浪费，企业自主开发新产品的能力较低。此外，在产品质量、卫生标准、环境保护等方面也存在着一些不容忽视的问题。

3. *利益机制不完善，产加销脱节*　多数粮食加工企业与农户还是一种松散的买卖关系，企业与农户之间没有形成利益共同体，也没有产加销一体化经营；签订的合同缺乏履行保证机制。同时，企业和农户获得的市场信息不足，市场营销渠道不畅。此外，一些边远山区由于交通不便，信息不灵，资源优势很难转化为产业优势。

4. *发展资金严重不足*　农产品加工企业普遍缺乏启动资金和流动资金。

三、几点建议

1. *制定和创造有利于农产品加工业发展的政策环境*　一是要加大国家、省基本建设和财政支农资金对农产品加工业的投资力度。二是按照农产品加工业发展的要求调整贷款结构，增加对农产品加工业的贷款总量，特别要加大农产品加工龙头企业和示范企业的扶持力度，国家应拿出一定量的资金对农产品加工龙头企业、示范企业的贷款给予贴息。三是积极拓宽融资渠道，加快符合上市条件的大型粮食加工企业上市融资。四是在税收政策上给予农产品加工企业一定的优惠。

2. *加快完善农产品加工业社会化服务体系*　应积极扶持和发展协会、商会和各种中介组织，建立健全技术推广、职业培训、信息网络等社会化服务体系，使粮食的生产、加工、销售紧密地联系起来。

3. *大力推进农产品加工业的科技进步和创新能力*　国家应出台促进农产品加工业发展的技术政策，增加对农产品生产和加工科研开发的投入。鼓励科研单位、大专院校与企业加强合作，深入开展农产品精深加工的工艺、技术、品种等方面的开发与创新研究，加快科研成果的转化，全面提升企业的技术水平和研发能力，提高产品的质量和效益。

4. 大力培植农产品加工业龙头企业的发展，促进规模化经营　采取以拳头产品为龙头，以骨干企业为核心，以资产为纽带，大力培植和组建一批经营规模大、技术含量高、辐射带动作用强，集生产经营、科研开发为一体的农产品加工企业集团，增加企业在国内外市场的竞争力。国家要加大对重点龙头企业的政策倾斜和扶持力度，使之真正起到振兴农业农村经济的龙头作用。

湖北省农产品加工业

湖北省农业厅

一、发展现状

1. 发展迅速并成长为全省国民经济的支柱产业　湖北省农产品加工业门类齐全，涵盖了农产品加工的12个子行业。其中，纺织业、食品加工业、烟草制品业比重最大，其次是饮料制造业、造纸业及食品制造业。据统计，2004年，全省规模以上农产品加工企业2 056个，占全部工业企业数的33%；实收资本247.06亿元，占10.9%；实现销售收入876.88亿元，占18.2%；从业人员50.55万人，占28.6%。"十五"以来，全省农产品加工业产值年均增长8%，2004年，农产品加工业产值926.57亿元，占全省工业总产值的18.9%。以农产品为原料的轻工业已成为全省工业的重要组成部分、国民经济的重要支柱产业。

2. 企业实力增强且农业产业化稳步发展　近年来，一大批农产品加工企业产值、利润和税金年年翻番，成长很快。2004年，全省规模以上农产品加工企业平均资产、产值分别为4 251万元和4 506万元，其中食品加工企业平均资产、产值分别为1 911万元和3 127万元；农业产业化龙头企业发展到3 500个，其中国家级重点龙头企业22个、省级重点龙头企业179个。2004年，省级重点龙头企业固定资产总额90.7亿元，销售收入263.7亿元，创利润14.4亿元，上缴税金10.4亿元，创汇1.7亿元。产业化龙头企业与基地（农户）形成了相对稳定的利益联结关系，既降低了企业的交易成本，又能确保农民获得稳定收益，带动农民持续增收。

3. 专业化生产区域逐步形成且特色鲜明　2004年，全省纳入农业产业化经营的种植面积2 818 khm^2，占全省农作物播种面积的39%；水产养殖基地面积412.7khm^2，占全省淡水养殖面积的62%。江汉平原的生猪、水产养殖和粮、棉、油、林木加工，鄂北岗地的粮食、饲料加工，鄂东南和鄂东北的楠竹、苎麻、茧丝、板栗，鄂西山区的茶叶、烟叶、水果、药材，武汉等大中城市郊区的蔬菜、奶业、花卉、时令水果，已形成区域特色。

4. 投资主体多元化且非国有经济比重扩大　投资主体多元化和非国有经济占主体地位，是湖北省以农产品为原料的轻工业经济构成的一个突出特点。从投资主体看，除国有资本外，还有集体资本、私营资本、外商资本和港澳台资本，投资主体多元化的特征十分明显。从经济构成看，非国有经济的主体地位日益突出。2004年，在以农产品为原料的轻工业中，国有及国有控股企业有企业单位数301个，实收资本70.01亿元，产值267.74亿元，利税76.66亿元，分别占总数的4.8%、3.1%、28.9%和13.7%，国有经济的比重已显著降低。

5. 吸纳农村富余劳动力能力提高且带动农民增收效果显著　近几年，农产品加工业从业人员一直保持增长态势，乡镇农产品加工企业仍然是吸纳农村富余劳动力的主体。2004年，平均每个规模以上农产品加工企业拥有职工245人，比1997年增加74人。在以农产品加工企业为主体的龙头企业带动下，产业化龙头企业实行产加销一体化经营，与基地（农户）形成了较为稳定的利益共同关系，带动了当地农业和农村经济的健康发展，全省以不同形式参与农业产业化经营的农户546万户，占总农户的一半以上，2004年参与产业化经营的农户户均增收1 229元。

二、存在的主要问题

1. 农产品加工转化整体水平低，产业和产品结构不合理　全省农产品加工率只有40%，深加工率不到20%，农林牧渔业总产值与农产品加工业产值之比仅为1∶0.7，在居民食品消费中，工业食品比重仅为30%左右。

2. 企业生产规模小、名牌少，市场竞争能力弱　2004年，全省年销售收入过5亿元的加工型龙头企业只有2个，没有一个过10亿元的龙头企业，近年来，省内虽然出现了一些优质、特色产品，但还没有享誉国内国际市场的知名品牌。

3. 技术装备和科技含量水平低，企业创新发展能力不足　多数企业缺乏产品自主开发能力，新工艺、新材料、新技术的应用程度低，科技人才数量短缺，水平不高。

4. 原料基地不配套，加工业发展受到制约　多数农产品品质不能满足加工需要，区域性、专业化的大基地不但数量少，而且存在区域间结构雷同、低水平重复建设的问题。

5. 社会化服务体系不健全　农产品加工业的标准化体系、检测体系、食品安全体系、技术推广体系、质量认证体系以及信息服务体系还不适应农产品加工业发展的要求，农产品加工业从原料生产到加工的产品质量和安全问题还比较突出。

三、主要措施

1. 统一思想认识，加强规划引导和政策指导　一是各地和有关部门要根据《湖北省优势农产品加工业发展规划（2004—2010年）》，制定本地区、本行业的农产品加工业发展规划，明确发展目标，突出发展重点。二是要充分发挥规划对产业发展的引导和指导作用，充分调动社会各界参与和支持农产品加工业发展的积极性，开拓发展空间，创新发展机制。三是扎实推进规划的组织实施，各地、各部门要在资金、技术、人才、政策、环境等多方面为农产品加工业发展创造条件，特别要在落实扶持政策方面加大检查和督办力度，促进农产品加工业的持续稳定发展。

2. 调整结构，建立稳定的原料基地　把农业结构战略性调整和发展农产品加工业结合起来，按照区域化布局、专业化生产、标准化管理的发展思路，突出地方特色，充分发挥区域比较优势，以农产品加工企业为龙头，建立一批与加工企业相配套的粮油、蔬菜、果品、畜禽、蛋奶和水产品原料基地，促进农产品加工业发展。大力提倡发展有机农业和绿色农业，按照讲究营养、保证卫生、注重特色、符合保健、崇尚美味、回归自然的要求，生产无公害农产品，为农产品加工企业提供安全、优质的加工原料。鼓励农户、专业合作经济组织与农产品加工企业形成稳定的利益联结关系，降低农民的违约率，为企业提供稳定的原料来源。

3. 加快市场主体培育和产业资源整合，壮大龙头企业　一是积极引进龙头企业。把引进农业产业化龙头企业作为招商引资的重要内容，改善软硬环境，特别要注重引进国内外知名企业，发挥其示范带动作用，提高全省农产品加工业的整体素质和综合实力。二是引导和鼓励中小加工企业实行联合、改组、改造，通过体制和技术创新，提高市场竞争力。三是结合原料基地建设，按照区域化布局、专业化生产、标准化管理、产业化经营和社会化服务的发展思路，在原料集中产区建立专业性或综合性的加工小区，发挥群体优势和规模效应。

4. 加快科技进步，提高企业技术水平和产品的档次　一是鼓励企业设立科技发展基金，加速折旧。鼓励企业设立科技发展基金，鼓励企业加速折旧，提高新产品开发费用和风险调节基金的提取比例，增强企业技术创新能力，开发具有自主知识产权的技术和产品。二是帮助企业与科研单位建立紧密的合作关系。大专院校和科研单位要根据企业的技术需要，开发新技术、新工艺、新设备、新产品，通过技术入股、专利转让等方式，加速科技成果转化。三是鼓励企业引进先进技术、工艺、设备、人才和管理方式。在重视“硬件”引进的同时，注重“软件”引进，以此推动农产品加工企业的技术进步和管理水平的提高。特别是利用本省的教育资源优势，加强农村职业技术教育，培养和造就一支熟练掌握先进实用技术的专业队伍，为农产品加工业的可持续发展提供重要的要素支撑。四是鼓励有条件的龙头企业建立产品研发中心，开展超前研究，储备科技成果，不断增强农产品加工业的核心竞争力。

5. 建立严格的市场准入制度，完善质量安全体系　一是各级有关部门要加强农产品质量监督检验检测体系建设，逐步建立全过程动植物检疫、农药（兽药）残留检测、环境质量监测和产品质量控制，确保加工业原料的质量安全。二是加强产品生产、储运、销售全过程的质量和卫生安全监督，严格执行质量和卫生标准。三是把推行农产品及其加工产品的质量标准与建设各类农产品加工基地结合起来，逐步建立标明产成品的产地、质量、标准的等级标识制度。

6. 扶持现代物流企业发展，着力开拓销售市场　一是加强市场建设。在农产品加工区建设一批现代化的产地批发市场，完善市场交易、检测检验和信息服务等设施，增强服务功能，扩大辐射范围。二是推广新的市场营销方式。建立现代流通设施，充分运用拍卖、连锁经营、统一配送和电子商务等现代交易方式，不断扩大流通区域，提高流通效率。建立功能齐全、反应敏捷的进出口预警系统，及时提供原料供应及产品贸易信息。三是积极组织企业参加优质产品的交易、评比等活动，广泛宣传名优产品，树立“金字”品牌。对在开发名牌中成绩突出的企业和个人给予奖励，同时要注重保护名牌产品的声誉，严厉打击假冒伪劣行为。

7. 落实优惠政策，加快产业发展　一是落实农产品加工业税收优惠政策。在所得税方面，落实财政部、国家税务总局《关于国有农口企事业单位征收企业所得税问题的通知》规定，对经过全国农业产业化联席会议审查认定为重点农产品加工龙头企业从事种植业、养殖业和农林产品初加工取得的所得，暂免征收企业所得税。落实财政部、国家税务总局《关于促进技术进步有关财务税收问题的通知》和国家税务总局《关于促进技术进步有关税收问题的补充通知》规定，企业研究开发新产品、新技术、新工艺所发生的各项费用在企业所得税前扣除；在增值税方面，将农产品加工企业进项抵扣率由10%提高到13%，减轻农产品加工企业的增值税税赋。落实《国务院关于调整进口设备税收政策的通知》精神，对符合国家高新技术目录并经国家有关部门批准引进的项目，进口国内不能生产的农产品加工设备和先进技术，免征进口关税和进口环节增值税。落实《国务院办公厅印发关于促进农产品加工业发展意见的通知》中关于对农产品出口实行与法定退税率一致的退税政策，对出口退税率尚未达到法定征税率的农产品，优先考虑适当提高出口退税率。二是改进对农产品加工企业的信贷服务。要在防范金融风险、保证信贷资金安全的前提下，做好对农产品加工企业的信贷支持工作。商业银行要通过资质评估，对一批实力强、资信好、资产负债率低和发展前景良好的农产品加工企业，核定一定的授信额度。在确定对农产品加工企业贷款时，要以企业授信等级为主要标准，不受银行对地区授信等级的限制。对于农产品加工企业季节性收购农产品所需流动资金，商业银行要及时核发。对于农产品加工企业申请固定资产贷款，商业银行要适当放宽抵押担保条件，简化审批手续。要继续扩大农业发展银行对龙头企业的农产品收购资金贷款的范围。三是拓宽农产品加工企业融资渠道。鼓励和支持农产品加工企业利用资本市场筹集发展资金。在同等条件下，证券机构要优先受理符合上市条件的重点农产品加工企业上市，并在配股和增发新股方面给予优先安排。农产品加工企业还可以通过股份制、股份合作制、出售、独资、租赁、承包等多种形式，吸引城乡个体私营资本、集体资本、国有资本、金融资本和国外资本投资农产品加工业，实现投资主体和产权主体多元化。加大招商引资力度，鼓励农产品加工企业积极、有效地利用外资。四是加大对农产品加工业的财政支持。各级政府要进一步调整投资结构，增加对农产品加工业的扶持。投资重点用于为农产品加工企业服务的基础性项目，包括技术引进和推广、市场建设、产品质量检测和环境保护等方面。省级财政每年要安排一定数量的资金，用于重要农产品加工业的技术改造贷款贴息。五是降低重点龙头企业成立进出口公司的条件，并适当放宽经营范围。对出口配额的分配实行市场化运作，公开竞争，为农产品加工企业积极参与国际竞争创造条件。

湖南省农产品加工业

湖南省乡镇企业局

一、发展现状

经过近几年的不断发展，全省农产品加工业发展已进入了结构不断优化、质量不断提高的新阶段，呈现出以下显著特点：

1. 农产品加工规模不断壮大，逐步形成了有较强竞争实力的龙头企业　全省注册登记的农产品加工企业已发展到了2.6万个，总资产448亿元，主要涉及粮油、棉麻、果蔬、茶叶、畜禽、生猪、水产品、乳制品、竹木林纸、中药材、皮革加工等20多个行业，基本上涵盖了全省农业发展的优势产业和特色产业，形成了门类十分齐全、产品种类众多的农产品加工体系。全省规模以上农产品加工企业1 722个，其中年销售收入500万～1 000万元的756个，1 000万～5 000万元的673个，5 000万～

1亿元的155个，1亿元以上的138个。全省有国家级、省级重点龙头企业166个，其中国家级24个，省级142个。2005年166个国家级、省级龙头企业完成销售收入413亿元，实现利润18.2亿元，出口创汇3.5亿美元，分别比上年增长15.1%、13.7%和13%。全省还涌现出了泰格林纸、正虹科技、唐人神集团等一批发展快、规模大、在全国有一定影响力的龙头企业。

2. 农产品基地建设不断优化，逐步形成了按区域化布局的优势农业产业带　各地按照市场需求，立足资源优势，以农产品加工业为依托，打破趋同格局，推动农业生产要素优化组合，促进了全省农产品优势产业带的发展。在龙头企业的带动下，全省在最具优势的集中产地建设了100多个优质农产品基地县和200多个重点生产基地，使生态优质食用大米、高支棉花、"双低"油菜、柑橘、优质绿茶、苎麻、外销生猪、肉牛（羊）、牛奶、加工出口淡水产品等10个按区域化布局的优势农业产业带建设初见成效。如粮食以金健米业、盛湘米业等龙头企业为依托，在湘西北等主产区建设了35个优质稻基地县；生猪以唐人神、正虹科技、新五丰等龙头企业为依托，在京珠高速沿线建设了35个生猪基地县；水果以熙可食品、洞庭食品等龙头企业为依托，在湘南南岭山区、湘中雪峰山区和湘西武陵山区建设了18个柑橘基地县。通过抓优势产业带建设，全省不仅带动形成了一批特色产业，而且有力地促进了水稻、生猪、水果、茶叶等传统产业的不断发展。比如生猪产业，1999年全省年出栏还只有5 000多万头，2005年已发展到了年出栏7 000多万头，年产值600多亿元。加上饲料、肉类加工、皮革加工等相关产业，年综合产值达到了800多亿元，是湖南农业经济中最大的支柱产业之一。优势产业带的发展还带动了农产品优质率的提高，全省优质稻基地面积占水稻播种面积的比重达到了50%以上；油菜、棉花优质率都在90%以上；三元杂交瘦肉型生猪比重提高到了55%。全省农产品综合优质率达到了60%以上。

3. 农产品科技质量水平不断提高，逐步形成了有市场影响力的名牌产品　针对本省农产品品牌多而杂，缺乏市场竞争力的状况，各地不断加大品牌创建力度，组织实施名牌战略，取得了较好成效。全省农产品加工企业中已有中国驰名商标5个，中国名牌3个，湖南省著名商标116个，湖南省名牌120个。名牌战略的实施有力地提升了龙头企业的市场竞争力，进一步增强了湖南农产品在国内外市场的开拓能力。加加集团致力于打造企业品牌，在狠抓科技开发，注重产品质量的同时，先后投入2.5亿元资金用于企业品牌的宣传推广，过硬的产品质量，强势的媒体宣传，使"加加"品牌的市场知名度不断提高，企业规模不断发展壮大，先后获得"中国食品行业突出贡献奖"、"国家食品工业重点企业"、"国家免检产品"、"湖南省纳税大户"等殊荣。省茶业有限公司针对国际市场对有机茶需求旺盛的良好势头，每年投入400多万元，开展有机茶生产加工质量攻关，打造出了五大系列、100多个"君山银针"品牌系列产品，畅销日本、美国、俄罗斯、德国等20多个国家和地区。

4. 农产品市场销售领域不断拓展，逐步形成了功能不断完善的市场流通体系　全省已形成各类农产品市场1 100多个，其中年交易额过亿元的专业批发市场49个，有14个规模较大、起点较高的的农产品批发市场被农业部门确定为定点市场。长沙红星农产品大市场以大批发、大流通为宗旨，根据市场流通导向，云集全国各地农产品资源，再根据市场需求将产品配送到全国各地，为湖南省农产品的销售提供了一个宽阔平台，市场现有经营户4 000多个，农产品物流贸易辐射到了全国1个省、自治区、直辖市的2 000多个县市。长沙马王堆农产品批发大市场以农产品的批发、储藏、加工和配送为主，年成交量30亿kg，成交额突破了50亿元，被评为"全国蔬菜行业50强市场"。各地还支持农产品加工企业加强营销网络建设，大多数龙头企业都建起了以直销连锁经营为主要形式的营销网络。随着营销网络的发展，湘米、茶叶、柑橘、肉类、水产品等已从传统的广东市场扩大到了全国和世界各地。金健米业近几年共建立直销网点近万家，形成了覆盖全国25个省级城市、150个地级城市、85%以上大中城市市场的网络销售体系。同时，各地在发展营销协会，鼓励农民特别是鼓励农民营销大户进入市场流通方面也做了大量工作。全省农产品市场流通体系开始向多渠道、多层次、多元化方向发展。

5. 农产品加工企业与农民的利益联结机制不断完善，逐步形成了带动农民增收致富的经营格局　龙头企业在不断发展的进程中，积极探索与市场农业相适应的组织形式，创造出了"公司＋基地＋农户"、"公司＋协会＋农户"以及订单农业等多种利益联结模式，使农产品加工企业与基地农户的利益结合日趋紧密。湘潭市伟鸿食品有限公司采取"公司＋协会＋农户"的产业化经营模式，以协会为中介对农户实行"七统一"的服务，即统一购销、统一引种、统一防疫、统一培训、统一饲料、统一结算和统一贷款，先后带动了65个基地村、16个大型养猪场和9 000多农户养猪，每年通过协会收购

生猪120万头，入会农民每年增收7 000多万元，户均增收1 000多元。洞庭水殖公司通过“公司＋基地＋农户”的产业化经营模式，在省内外建立了27.3khm²水产品养殖基地，使2 600多养殖户进入了公司的产业链，农民户均增收超过了2 000元。湖南银利来公司与永州市208个行政村的8万多农户签订了水稻产销合同，落实订单生产面积26khm²，全部以高于市场10%～25%的价格分品种收购，每年为当地农民增收6 000多万元。

湖南省农产品加工业发展虽然取得了长足发展，但与发达地区相比，仍存在很大差距。一是经济总量还不多。2005年，全省农产品加工业销售收入虽然达到了1 100多亿元，但远远不及山东等农业发达地区。二是企业规模还不大。山东、内蒙古、黑龙江、河南等省、自治区都涌现出了一批产值过100亿元的龙头企业，而湖南省还没有过50亿元的龙头企业。三是加工能力还不强。黑龙江北大荒米业集团2004年的粮食加工能力就达到了300多万t，而湖南作为产粮大省，还没有过20万t的加工企业。四是科研开发还较弱。相当一部分企业缺少自主研发的技术和产品，不具备持续发展能力。五是产业结构还不优。一些地方区域性特色经济发展不够，部分地区龙头企业低水平重复建设和拼资源、拼消耗、拼环境等问题比较突出。

二、主要做法

1. *加大了政策支持力度* 近几年，国家对农产品加工业发展十分重视，先后出台了一系列扶持政策，支持龙头企业发展。为使这些政策落到实处，省乡镇企业局积极争取有关部门，加大政策执行力度，洞庭水殖、隆平高科等一批国家级龙头企业每年税费的减免都达到了1 000万元以上。为支持省级农产品加工龙头企业的发展，在充分调研的基础上，省政府出台了《关于加快农业五大产业链建设推进农业产业化经营》文件，从财政扶持、税收扶持、收费减免、信贷等方面对龙头企业发展制定了一系列扶持政策。长沙、岳阳、永州、常德等市州也制定了一系列切实可行的扶持政策。还加大对市州农产品加工业发展的考评，每年都设立奖项对农产品加工业发展工作突出的先进市县、龙头企业和先进个人进行了表彰奖励，营造了农产品加工业发展的良好氛围。

2. *加大了资金扶持力度* 为了支持农产品加工龙头企业发展，省乡镇企业局将省财政扶持乡镇企业的资金转到了主要扶持农产品加工业发展，每年用于龙头企业贷款贴息的资金有1 000多万元。省直部门掌握的资金也正在捆绑使用，重点支持龙头企业发展。各市州也加大了财政支持力度，长沙市2006年对农产品加工业固定资产投资2 000万元以上的新项目和年内技术改造投资500万元以上的项目，安排了3 000万元的农产品加工专项扶持资金。积极争取银行信贷支持，省农业发展银行2005年一般贷款由2004年的10亿元增加到20亿元，“十一五”期间将向湖南省以农产品加工为主的农业产业化项目提供600亿元政策性金融贷款。长沙市、怀化市、株洲市、湘潭市政府已分别与农业发展银行湖南省分行签订了总额210亿元的信贷合作协议，一批资金已经落实到了企业。省政府每年还组织龙头企业参加银企合作洽谈，帮助企业解决技改和流动资金问题，全省已有7个市州成立了14家信用担保公司，农产品加工业已逐步成为信贷资金投放的热点。

3. *加大了科技创新力度* 把科技进步作为推进农产品加工业发展的重头戏来抓，不断加大工作力度。一是狠抓了龙头企业科企对接。2005年12月17日，省农业产业化办公室和中国农业科学院、省科技厅、省农业科学院联合举办了湖南省农业产业化龙头企业科企合作对接会，会上有60个国家级、省级龙头企业与中国农业科学院、中国科学院等一批科研院所签订了科企项目合作协议，有10个企业与科研院所联合成立了科企研发中心。2006年4月份，长沙市也举办了科企对接会，共签订了24个农产品加工科技合作项目，预计可为企业年增加产值85亿元。二是狠抓了龙头企业自主科技创新。全省龙头企业已自主组建研发中心51个。正虹公司组建了国内一流的科研中心和实验基地，每年提取公司总利润的5%用于企业科研中心的研发，被科技部认定为“国家火炬计划重点高新技术企业”。金健米业、亚华种业、隆平高科、正清集团、盛湘集团等龙头企业还启动了“博士后流动站”，吸纳海内外高科技人才为本企业的产品创新、工艺创新和管理创新服务。三是狠抓了龙头企业人才培训。结合农业部“蓝色证书工程”，大力开展龙头企业人才培训，重点开展了职业技能培训，每年开设培训工种20多个，培训人员10多万多人。

4. *加大了标准化生产力度* 为了从源头上控制农产品质量，各地狠抓农产品基地的标准化生产，全省无公害农作物面积由2001年不到333.3khm²增加到1 933.3khm²，绿色、有机农产品基地面积也在不断增多。一些龙头企业还通过建立自己的农产品原料基地，不断提高加工原料的质量水平。据初步统计，全省仅国家级、省级龙头企业就联结基地面积

800khm²，带动农户达到了490万户。各地还狠抓农产品质量检测体系建设，已有12个市州建立了农产品质量检测中心，10个市州建立了畜禽水产品质量检测中心，30多个县市建立了检测机构。为了进一步提高龙头企业国际国内市场的开拓能力，各地狠抓龙头企业质量认证体系建设，全省获得国内产品质量认证的龙头企业产品已有300多个，获得国外产品质量认证的100多个。按照省人大的要求，积极参与“三湘农产品质量安全行活动”，每年都集中开展农产品质量安全专项整治行动，通过集中整治，全省农产品质量安全水平有了明显提高。

5. *加大了招商引资力度* 近年来，组织龙头企业参加了一系列的招商引资活动，取得了较好成效，2005年以来全省共签订以农产品加工为主的农业招商引资合同项目1 100多个，实际到位外资2.39亿美元、内资130多亿元。还把引进战略投资伙伴作为加快推进农产品加工业发展的重要工作来抓，引导龙头企业坚持把引资与引智结合起来，引进与开发结合起来，许多龙头企业通过引进战略投资伙伴，实现了企业的跨越式发展。如湖南熙可食品公司原是永州市的一家民营企业，通过引进英国EJ公司作为战略合作伙伴后，不到5年时间，企业固定资产由150万元增加到了6 000多万元，出口额由不足50万美元，增加到了1 389万美元。

三、基本思路和工作重点

当前和今后一个时期，全省农产品加工业发展总的要求是：龙头企业集群要有大发展，农产品加工业水平要有大提高，农产品品牌建设要有大突破，农产品加工带动能力要有大提升，农产品加工业发展环境要有大改善。为实现上述目标，必须抓住关键，突出重点，切实做好以下工作：

1. *要主攻产业集群发展* 围绕粮棉油、果蔬菜、肉蛋禽、竹木林纸、烟草五大农业产业链的发展，规划建设一批与大基地、大龙头、大市场相联结的农产品加工业项目，形成产业聚群，推动农产品加工业发挥优势，提升规模，提高质量，提升效益，到2010年，全省农产品加工业销售收入达到3 000亿元，农产品及加工品出口额达到10亿美元左右，农产品商品率达到70%以上。

2. *要主攻龙头企业规模壮大* 按照“扶优、扶强、扶大”的原则，紧紧围绕实施好“131”工程，着力培育壮大一批起点高、规模大、带动力强的大型农产品加工骨干龙头企业。特别是要充分利用本省大宗农产品的资源优势，以资本运营为纽带，整合资源，通过联合与兼并，重点在粮食、水果、生猪三大产业上培育一批产值在30亿元、50亿元、甚至过100亿元的企业集团，争取在龙头企业发展规模上追赶国内先进省份。

3. *要主攻基地标准化生产* 积极发展有机农业和绿色农业，以农产品加工企业为龙头，按照区域化布局、专业化生产、标准化管理、产业化经营和社会化服务的发展思路，高标准建设好生态优质食用大米、高支棉花、“双低”油菜、柑橘、优质绿茶、外销生猪等优势农产品产业带。大力引导龙头企业通过定向投入、定向服务、定向收购，建立稳定的农产品原料基地，形成一批与加工企业相配套、示范效应大、质量安全好、带动面广的现代化农产品原料基地，力争“十一五”末，全省优势农产品基地面积要达到2 667khm²以上，龙头企业从基地采购量占加工量的比重达到70%以上。

4. *要主攻产品档次提高* 重点是抓好龙头企业与科研院所的科技对接，通过产品科技含量的不断提高，提升产品档次。要引导龙头企业通过购买科研院所的新产品、新技术、新工艺，加快科研院所科技成果向现实生产力的转化进程；要通过企业出课题，龙头企业和科研院所共同攻关或共同建立科研中心的形式，不断提高企业自主科研开发水平；要通过科企业合作，加快企业科技人才的引进和培训。要进一步加大工作力度，力争省级、国家级重点龙头企业都能与科研究院所开展合作。

5. *要主攻名优品牌发展* 帮助和支持龙头企业创建一批省级、国家级的名优名牌。重点支持进入“131”工程的龙头企业提升技术，强化标准，加强管理，争取使这140个企业的产品首先成为国家级或省级名牌产品。力争到“十一五”末，全省农产品“中国驰名商标”和“中国名牌”产品达到20个以上，省级“著名商标”和“湖南名牌”达到300个以上。

6. *要主攻市场网络建设* 加快农产品专业批发市场建设，重点培育一批年交易额50亿元以上、辐射全国的农产品专业批发市场。加快龙头企业连锁直销经营体系建设，重点扶持100个龙头企业形成自己的控制到终端的大营销网络。抓好农产品物流服务体系建设，逐步在农产品重要集散地和交通枢纽建立集加工、保鲜、流通为一体的大型农产品物流配送中心。积极支持农民组建农产品流通专业协会，大力发展农村各类中介组织和经纪人队伍。

7. *要主攻招商引资发展* 充分利用国际资本看好中国市场和沿海企业向内地梯度转移的机遇，加大招商力度。突出产业招商、专业招商，把招商引资的重点放在世界强势农产品加工企业和国内优势企业上。精心选择一批吸引力大、竞争力强、发展潜力大的项目，建立湖南农产品加工招商项目库，做好项目包装、策划和推介工作。积极参与组织龙头企业国内外农业招商活动，认真筹办各种农业展销活动。

广东省农产品加工业

广东省乡镇企业局

一、发展现状

1. *农产品加工业已经发展成为广东的主要产业之一* 据不完全统计，2005 年全省规模以上农产品加工企业有 7 495 个，总产值达 2 443.67 亿元，占全省规模以上乡镇工业企业总产值 7 448.89 亿元的 32.81%，实现增加值 562.89 亿元，占全省乡镇企业当年规模以上工业增加值 170 515 亿元的 33%；实现营业收入 2 295.50 亿元，占全省规模以上乡镇工业营业收入 7 045.52 亿元的 32.58%；利润总额 86.50 亿元，占全省规模以上乡镇工业利润总额 285 亿元的 30.35%。农产品加工业的发展为解决广东"三农"问题、推动广东农产品加工业发展发挥了重要作用。

2. *农产品加工体系已初步形成* 在农产品加工业 12 大类别中，广东的农产品加工企业涵盖了全部类别，形成了以纺织服装及其他纤维制造业、皮革（毛皮、羽绒）及其制品、食品、饮料制造等行业为主、各业并举的产业格局。主要分布在以下十大加工行业：农副产品加工业；食品制造业；饮料制造业；烟草制造业；纺织业；纺织服装、鞋、帽制造业；皮革、毛皮、羽毛（绒）及其制品业；印刷及记录媒介复制业；木材加工及木、竹、藤、棕、草制品业；家具制造业；造纸及纸制品业；橡胶制品业。

3. *成为解决"三农"问题的主要渠道之一* 农产品加工企业大多是劳动密集型企业，对从业人员的专业技术水平要求不高，企业大都围绕农产品原产地区域就近发展，因此成为农民就业、增加收入和繁荣农村经济的便利渠道。2005 年，全省规模以上农产品加工企业的从业人员达 159.39 万人，占全省规模以上工业企业职工年平均数 425.46 万人的 37.46%，成为广东吸纳社会就业的重要渠道之一。其中仅服装、皮革、纺织 3 个行业吸纳就业人员就达 120.72 万人，占全省规模以上工业企业职工年平均数的 28.37%。

4. *服装、纺织、皮革制造等行业得到充分发展* 广东农产品加工业各行业发展差异比较大，规模比较大的主要是服装及其他纤维制造业、纺织业、皮（毛）及其制成品制造业 3 个行业。2005 年，上述 3 个行业规模以上农产品加工企业总数为 4 832 家，占全省农产品加工企业总数的 65.47%，产值达 1 563.96亿元，占全省规模以上农产品加工企业总产值的 64%。

5. *农产品加工企业逐步向集团化、规模化经营方向发展* 企业建设农业生产基地和产业化经营的步伐不断加快，对品牌建设日益重视，涌现了一批辐射力强、带动作用明显的龙头企业和知名度较高的名牌产品。到 2005 年底止，广东已经有广东温氏集团等国家级农业龙头企业 19 个，河源市万绿宝食品有限公司等省级农业龙头企业 101 个，其大部分都是农产品加工企业。同时，涌现了一批名牌产品，如"佳宝牌""康辉牌"凉果、"汾煌牌""百事可乐牌"饮料、"香雪牌"抗病毒口服液、"挂绿牌"丝苗米等等。

二、主要做法

1. *领导重视，把发展农产品加工业摆上重要位置* 省委、省政府在指导农村经济发展的过程中，一直把发展农产品加工业作为解决"三农"问题的重要环节来抓，切实加强领导，实行政策扶持。2000 年 3 月省委、省政府在湛江市召开了全省农业结构调整暨农产品加工流通工作现场会议，认真总结和部署了全省农业结构调整和农产品力加工流通工作。2001 年 7 月，省委举行八届七次全会专门深入分析研究全省农业和农村工作的新情况新问题，审议并通过了《中共广东省委关于大力推进农业产业化经营的决定》，确定在"十五"时期农产品加工要实现较大突破，争取到 2005 年全省农产品加工率达到 40%左右。中共中央政治局委员、省委书记张德江到广东后高度重视发展民营经济，在 2003 年初召开了高规格的全省民营经济工作会议，出台了《中共广东省委、广东省人民政府关于加快民营经济发展的决定》及12个配套文件，其中专门制定了扶持农产品加工业发展的《广东省关于扶持民营农产品加工企业发展的实施办法》，从多方面扶持农产品加工业的发展。

各地党委、政府对农产品加工业也非常重视，纷纷制定相关政策扶持农产品加工业的发展。汕头市委、市政府邀请国内外专家，以三级干部会议的形式召开了汕头市发展农业大商品经济研讨会，提出多形式、多渠道、多层次发展农产品加工的路子和相应扶持的政策措施，从而为推进该市乡镇企业农产品加工业的大发展创造了良好的氛围；茂名市委、市政府出台了《关于发展特色产业促进工业脱颖而出的决定》、《关于鼓励我市农副产品扩大出口的通知》，并与小城镇发展战略相结合，调整农产品工业布局；广州市在充分调研的基础上，以市政府名义出台了《关于促进广州农产品加工业发展的意见》，从资金等多方面给予大力扶持。

2. 因地制宜，坚持多形式、多渠道和外向带动的发展路子 各地根据本地实际，充分发挥各自资源和人才、劳力的优势，发展各具特色的农产品加工业。湛江市充分发挥本地南亚热带农作物和农产品及海产品资源丰富的优势，不断调整农业布局，优化产品结构，全市建立了海水养殖、林业、水果、畜牧、北运菜等五大门类21个生产基地；茂名市立足资源优势，以特色产品为依托，采取国有、集体、私营、股份合作等多轮驱动的形式，大力创办农产品加工企业。全市已形成了粮油食品加工、果蔬加工、皮革手套加工、竹木工艺品加工、药品加工、羽绒加工、巢丝加工、海产品加工、橡胶制品加工等系列产品的加工企业近3 000个，年产值50多亿元。其中产值超亿元的企业9个，产值超千万元的企业40多个；汕头市坚持“四个轮子”一起转的方针，充分发挥侨资、民资、民力的优势发展农产品加工业，有效地提高初级农产品的附加值，延伸农业产业链，提高农业的整体效益。

3. 抓大带小，充分发挥龙头企业的龙头作用和示范效应 各地有规划、有重点、有措施地扶持一批基础较好、生产规模较大、有发展前景的农产品加工企业，以品牌、销路、技术为纽带，并以此为龙头把千家万户的初级加工企业联结起来，不断地推动农产品加工业向高层次发展，逐步形成龙头连基地带农户，集种养加一体化、产供销一条龙的产业化经营新格局。如地处粤东山区的梅州市，近年来实行“高起点规划、高标准建设、高效能管理”的办法建设一批上规模的农产品加工龙头企业，有效地推动了全市农产品加工业的发展。到2005年全市年销售额1亿元以上的农产品加工企业有大埔西岩茶叶集团公司、丰顺威华食品罐头厂2个，3 000万～1亿元的有梅县梅雁蓝藻公司等10个，1 000万～3 000万元大埔县顺兴养殖饲料等4个。该市的梅雁企业集团是一家上市公司，近年来在发展农产品加工过程中，充分发挥公司的资金、人才、管理优势，充分利用丰富的农产品资源，开发科技含量高的新产品，其下属的梅县蓝藻有限公司，近年来投资5 000多万元建成我国最大的螺旋藻生产基地之一，公司对螺旋藻养殖场生产的螺旋干粉进行深加工螺旋藻片。同时，利用丰富的金柏资源，开发提取柏黄酮和生产金柏含片。新产品项目开发为梅州农村经济发展增添了活力。

三、存在的主要问题

1. 企业规模普遍偏小，实力不强，龙头企业不多，辐射效应不明显 从销售收入来看，由于广东省农产品加工企业主要以家庭作坊为基础发展起来的，集约化程度低、规模小，企业销售收入大部分在千万元左右，辐射效应不明显。即使是销售收入排前几名、较大型的农产品加工企业也无法与国内外大型农产品加工企业相媲美。从从业人员规模上看，大部分农产品加工企业从业人员在几十人到几百人之间，超1 000人的企业也很少。

2. 加工技术落后，品种单一，档次较低 大多数农产品加工企业设备简陋、工艺落后、机械化、自动化程度较低，技术人才缺乏，以初（粗）加工为主，附加值不高，极少企业采用先进机械装备和工艺技术，小型企业中相当部分为家庭手工作坊式，设备简单陈旧，以手工操作为主。

3. 企业经营管理水平不高，经营理念落后 广东省农产品加工企业从发展上看可分为以下几类：第一类是从家庭作坊发展起来的，比重占多数。这类企业的所有权与经营权合一，停留在“家族式”和“经验型”的管理水平上。第二类是部分在市场经济的搏杀中积累了一定资金的创业者，比重其次。他们有一定的创新意识和进取精神，技术水平总体比第一类企业高，产品质量也相对稳定。但大多数也停留在“家族式”管理水平上。第三类是在原有或集体企业基础上发展起来的，比重不大。体制上有些已转为股份制，有些改为国有民营，有些仍保持过去的经营管理方式。这类企业在市场、技术、人才、资源等方面都有比较好的基础和优势，但大多数企业不同程度存在历史包袱沉重、管理低效、机制不灵活等问题。第四类是外商投资的农产品加工企业，但数量极少。

4. 行业秩序和市场秩序不规范　一是质量安全管理体系不完善。从原材料生产、加工到销售都没有形成完整的管理体系，产品质量安全存在隐患。二是超市经营秩序不规范。合法经营企业的农产品进入超市时存在障碍，进入超市门槛障碍。三是其他零售市场秩序混乱。由于把关不严，监控不力，一些不符合国家质量安全标准的产品未经检测就进入市场，出现市场排斥合格产品或优质产品的奇怪现象。

5. 贷款难度大，资金紧缺　由于农产品加工业大都是中小企业，经济基础较薄弱，加工季节性强，又缺乏担保机制，很难从银行获得贷款，企业资金短缺，严重影响了加工业的发展。一些好的项目和新项目，因缺乏必要的启动资金得不到发展。

6. 交叉管理，“合力”不足　农产品加工企业大多扎根农村，基本属乡镇企业范畴，理应由乡镇企业行政主管部门管理。然而，在现实中又涉及到许多相关部门的管理职能和利益，使农产品加工业处于交叉管理状况，难以形成有效的“合力”。

四、主要措施

1. 科学规划，分类指导　根据《全国主要农产品加工业发展规划》和《全国优势农产品区域布局规划》，结合本省实际，发展重点领域。主要发展果品、肉食品、海产品、蔬菜加工业和木材、皮革、服装制造业，使之成为具有现代化水平的农产品加工制造业。

2. 抓好农业部农产品加工业示范基地、示范企业和技术创新机构的建设，充分发挥其示范带动作用　广东省获农业部认定的农产品加工业示范基地有两批共6个，示范企业22个，技术创新机构7个。要加强对这些基地、企业和机构的跟踪管理、指导和服务，并在现有政策上给予倾斜扶持，使其充分发挥示范带动作用。

3. 大力发展农产品加工龙头企业　引导和支持个体生产、加工、运销专业大户和民营企业创办农产品加工企业，或以资金、技术参股等多种方式，联合其他经济实体组建多种形式的加工型龙头企业。支持农业研究机构进行机制转型，发展成为科技含量较高的农产品加工企业。促进龙头企业与高等院校、科研院所合作。鼓励、支持科研单位和高等院校以技术合作、项目合作等形式与龙头企业联办或自办农产品加工企业。鼓励外商投资创建加工型龙头企业，支持生产型农业龙头企业与外商合资兴建符合国际质量安全标准的大型农产品深加工企业。鼓励外资农产品加工企业增资扩产，增强辐射带动能力。鼓励中心镇以项目为依托，积极引进外资组建高科技、外向型的农产品加工企业。同时，支持重组联合组建农产品加工型龙头企业。支持经营同类产品、规模偏小的加工企业，依照市场规则，通过多种方式，组建大型加工企业集团，提升实力，做大规模，快速发展。支持乡镇企业在调整产业、产品结构中发展成为加工型龙头企业。

4. 建立农产品加工园区，促进产业集聚　按照“政府引导、企业参与、多元投入、要素集聚、市场运作、加快发展”的思路，建设若干个农产品加工园区。首先以调整工业园区为契机，使农产品加工企业聚集发展。在已形成特色种养业产业带或加工企业群聚的地方，建立农产品加工产业园。同时，降低企业入园门槛，积极引导农产品加工企业向园区集聚。其次依托加工园区，建立原料基地。以园区为依托，以企业为主体，以订单为纽带，引导农民按照有关质量标准和要求，调整优化种养结构，建设规模化的农产品原料基地，建立和扩大无公害农产品生产基地，提高原材料质量，实现加工企业与原料生产基地的良性互动。

5. 推动技术进步和科技创新，实现农产品精深加工的目标　鼓励科研院所优先解决农产品加工中的紧迫性技术问题。对部分关键技术的研究，可由政府出资或政府与企业联合出资，面向国内外科研机构公开招标，通过攻关予以解决。鼓励企业建立技术研发中心开展研发活动，加大科技人才培养与引进力度。同时，鼓励农产品加工企业加快设备更新和技术改造，提高农产品精深加工水平。鼓励企业加快引进国内外先进技术、设备和工艺，改造农产品加工企业；引导企业加强对引进技术的消化吸收，支持企业采用高新技术和先进技术改造农产品加工企业，增加技改投入，支持加工型龙头企业积极争取列入国家级和省级重点技改项目。

6. 积极推动名牌战略　首先以扶持加工型农业龙头企业为契机，培育知名企业和名牌产品。对国家、省和市确认的农业龙头企业，给予资金扶持，使其做强做大，作为知名企业和名牌产品的“苗子”给予培育和扶持。其次引导企业重视产品质量管理，以优质助推品牌建设。引导企业建立完善的质量管理体系，包括ISO 9000质量认证等国际上通行的质量管理认证体系，提高产品质量档次。再次运用城市发展规划、产业政策引导和扶持相关产业和企业做大做强，实现企业集群、产业集聚和规模化经营，产生规模效应，扩大相关产业和企业的知名度，不断推动名牌产品战略。通过举办农产品加工成品中名、优、特、新产品的博览会、展销会、交易会等活动，展示广东农产品加工品的特色和优势。同时，促进既有名牌巩固、升级。建立部门领导联系制度，密切注意已获“著名商标”和“名牌产品”企业的发展状况，加强管理、扩大宣传，不断提高企业和产品的知名度，缩短市级“著名商标”向省级“著名商标”、省级“著名商标”向国家级“驰名商标”的升级过程，不断推动国产名牌向国际名牌发展。引导企业将企业名、商品名、品牌名统一起来，帮助企业塑造良好的企业形象，以良好的企业形象创造名牌、扩展市场。

7. 建立和完善质量安全标准体系　加快制定农产品加工业的质量安全标准体系。按照全面规划、突出重点、分步推进、与国际接轨的原则，从主要农产品生产加工的标准化入手，积极引进和采用国际标准，加快制定符合国际惯例、国家标准和本省实际的农产品加工质量安全标准，尽快形成完善的农产品加工业的产品标准体系和质量保证体系。建立对农产品加工成品国际标准、特别是主要贸易国农产品加工成品质量标准动态跟踪制度。同时，把推行农产品加工质量安全标准体系与各类农产品生产基地的建设结合起来，逐步建立标明产品的产地、质量、标准等级的标识制度，并建立起严格的农产品市场准入制度。

8. 尽快建立和完善农业保险机制　为避免农产品价格波动过大，支持和保护农业和农产品加工业的发展，必须尽快建立和完善适应本省实际的农业保险机制。首先加强农业保险立法。可在行政规章方面先行一步，建立政策性农业保险，探索建设农业保险机制的新路子。其次，建立适用的农业保险形式。一是成立政策性的农业保险公司；二是政府资本和民营资本共建农业保险；三是实行强制与自愿相结合的保险形式。

9. 完善社会化服务体系建设　建立广东农产品加工业信息网，鼓励各市、县农产品市场信息网络和农产品加工企业上网。加强农产品加工信息的综合利用，充分发挥媒体作用，以开放共享的形式提供国内外最新信息。另外，要切实抓好中介组织和行业协会建设。积极配合有关部门，认真抓好农产品加工业的中介组织、行业协会及各类专业协会的建设。充分发挥各类行业协会和中介组织的作用，加强管理和服务，维护农产品生产加工贸易中各个方面的利益。

广西壮族自治区农产品加工业

广西壮族自治区乡镇企业局

一、发展现状

近年来，广西农产品加工业一直保持良好的发展势头。2005 年，广西乡镇企业中农产品加工业继续稳步增长，农产品加工企业已达近 7.5 万个，从业人员 46 多万人，农产品加工业总产值达 592 亿元，增加值达 193 亿元，分别比上年增长 0.5%和 4.32%。其中，规模以上农产品加工业总产值为 74 亿元，同比增长 2.8%，占规模以上乡镇工业总产值的 24%；增加值 16 亿元，同比增长 6.67%，占规模以上乡镇工业总产值的 24%。2006 年 1～6 月份，全区乡镇企业规模以上农产品加工企业 8 000 多户，从业人数 12 万人，增加值达 19 亿元，营业收入 71 亿元，实现利润 4 亿元，上缴税金 3 亿元。这表明，广西农产品加工业在总量稳步上升的同时，农产品加工水平和经济效益保持同步增长。初步形成了蔗糖、木薯、桑蚕、粮油、畜水产品、林木、果蔬、花茶香料、烟草、现代中药等为主导产业的农产品加工业，农产品加工业的快速发展为扩大农产品市场、推动农业和农村经济整体效益的提高发挥了重大作用。

1. 加工体系初步形成，加工领域不断拓宽，发展势头良好　“十五”期间，北京汇源集团桂林生态果业有限公司、香港华锦集团、杭州娃哈哈集团、防城港大海粮油等一批国内知名企业集团相继进入广西农产品加工业领域，同时广西本土如广西卷烟总厂、南宁糖业、桂林漓泉等企业的发展壮大，使广西农产品加工企业的发展实力显著增强，加工体系初步形成，加工领域不断拓宽。广西农产品加工龙头企业如广西黑五类食品集团有限责任公司、贵港扬翔饲料有限公司、桂林市力源粮油食品有限公司、广西凤翔集团畜禽食品有限公司、广西皇氏生物工程乳业有限公司、北海国发海洋生物产业股份有限公司等一批经济实力较强、装备较先进、技术水平较高的大型农产品加工龙头企业和企业集团，以及广西凤糖生化股份有限公司甘蔗加工示范基地、广西农垦糖业集团蔗糖加工示范基地、南宁糖业甘蔗加工示范基地的发展实力显著增强。桂林市2005年农产品加工业年产值超千万元的企业有128个，其中年销售收入1 000万～5 000万元的企业有91个，5 000万～1亿元的企业有16个，超亿元的企业有21个；2001—2005年，全市农产品加工龙头企业产值、销售收入、利润年均增长分别为17.5%、16.6%、22.9%。初步形成了以粮食、肉类、果蔬、竹木、中草药为主的加工体系，产品涉及食品、竹木制品、罐头饮料、中成药、纸制品、竹胶合板、乳制品、冷藏保鲜、生物制品、植物提取、特色产品等59个品种。南宁市2005年规模以上农产品加工企业有212个，从业人员达5.88万人，带动农户约90万户。其中，被确定为国家级龙头企业3个，被确定为自治区级龙头企业18个，被确定为南宁市级龙头企业46个。2005年，南宁市规模以上农产品加工企业实现工业总产值143.05亿元，增加值56.81亿元，税收总额18.88亿元，利润总额8.37亿元，分别占全市规模以上企业实现数的38.69%、46.95%、68.18%、62.46%，对全市工业总产值增长的贡献率达27.1%。

2. *地域分工格局粗具雏形，带动能力明显增强* 广西农产品加工业以优势资源、优势产业为依托，经过多年的发展，基本形成了各具特色的地域加工分工格局。如桂北罗汉果、银杏加工业；桂南剑麻加工业；桂西北特色酒业；桂西北山野蔬菜深加工；桂西南及桂东苦丁茶、高档茶叶加工；桂东南竹藤棕草编加工；桂西巴马、凤山等少数民族地区保健长寿食品加工；鹿寨、合浦、蒙山、宜州、环江、宾阳、横县、上林、忻城、柳城等县市蚕丝加工业；武鸣、横县、扶绥、蒙山、崇左、马山、贺州等地的木薯淀粉加工业；南宁、桂林、柳州、贵港、玉林等主要城市的优质谷精深加工企业；防城港及钦州港的大型粮油加工企业；防城、藤县、凤山、岑溪、德保、那坡、容县等地八角、玉桂、茴油、茴香醇、茴香精等食用、烟用、医用和化妆品用香料香精加工企业；南糖、贵糖、凤糖、迁糖、农垦糖业等重点制糖企业集团的制糖业；北海、钦州、防城港三市的海水产品加工业；南宁、桂林、百色、贺州、玉林、钦州、梧州等市果蔬深加工业；南宁、桂林、百色、贺州、玉林、柳州、梧州的现代中药业；环江和巴马香猪、梧州腊味、荔浦芋头、合浦鹅肥肝等各具特色的地域加工分工格局，有效地带动了县域经济的发展。

3. *提升农产品加工水平、不断延伸产业链* 随着农产品加工龙头企业的不断发展壮大，企业产业链逐步延伸。如桂林力源粮油饲料有限责任公司最初只生产饲料，随着养殖业规模化、集约化的发展，现已形成饲料加工—鸡苗孵化—肉鸡饲养—肉鸡加工—鸡产品销售的肉鸡生产产业链；桂林莱茵生物有限公司等企业除加工生产中成药、植物提取物等产品外，还建立了原料供应种植基地，形成了“公司+基地+农户”的产业化经营模式。广西农产品加工龙头企业通过“龙头企业+合作组织+农户”、“公司+基地+农户”以及订单农业的发展模式，有效地延伸了产业链。形成了一批特色产品和知名品牌，如中草药加工业的“三金”系列、“天和”系列都是全国知名品牌，而南药集团生产的青蒿琥酯联合用药被世界卫生组织批准为全球唯一供应商。“百事”、“汇源”、“福润”等著名品牌的落户也为广西农产品加工业增色不少。

近年来，通过科技攻关，广西农产品加工的科技含量和附加值不断提高。罗汉果甜甙提取技术、天然植物有效成分提取技术、竹产品加工技术等方面达到了国内领先水平。桂林莱茵生物科技股份有限公司“从罗汉果中提取罗汉果甜甙的方法”、“分离提取松树皮低聚体原花青素的方法”、桂林集琦实力天然物科技有限公司从天然植物中提取分离食品功能因子的生化技术、广西千方药业有限公司采用分子变形法高新技术提取和精制芦丁，其技术均达到了国内领先水平。农产品加工龙头企业科技水平的提高，为企业的壮大积蓄了发展后劲。

二、主要做法

近年来，广西认真执行国家八部委关于扶持农业产业化重点龙头企业的税收优惠等政策，自治区人民政府出台了《关于贯彻落实国务院西部大开发政策若干规定的通知》、《广西壮族自治区关于加快工业发展的若干规定》等政策文件，对采用新工艺、新技术，利用广西农业资源生产的新产品或进行资源综合利用以及为农产品加工生产、流通服务的行业进一步鼓励其发展。

1. *统一思想，加强领导* 各地党委、政府切实把发展农业产业化龙头企业提到重要的议事日程抓紧抓好，市、县区结合资源特点、发挥比较优势，按照“一县几品”或“一乡一品”的农产品加工工作思路，以点带面，以点促面，把工作的重点放在培植、壮大农产品加工龙头企业方面上来。同时，切实加强领导，实行领导挂钩联系制度，每一个龙头企业由一名市、县区四家班子领导联系，帮助企业发展生产。一是建立机构，市、县（区）相应成立了农业产业化工作领导小组等领导协调机构，由分管副市长、副县长分别兼任领导小组组长，经委及相关部门为成员单位。二是制定政策，加大扶持力度。柳州市下发了

《柳州市农业产业化重点龙头企业实施方案》、《关于促进农业和农村经济发展保持农民收入稳定增长若干问题的意见》、《关于加快工业经济发展的若干意见》等文件，市财政每年安排500万元专项贴息和补助资金重点扶持农业龙头企业的发展，有力地扶持和支持了农产品加工业的发展。三是做好服务，为民办实事。紧紧围绕农业产业化经营工作，突出“重点”为主题，强化了服务、宣传和接受监督，制作了“服务卡”，写上了服务范围和联系电话，便于联系，贴近了企业。

2. *加大招商引资力度，增加对农产品加工的投入*　加大招商引资力度，是克服资金、人才、技术短缺，经营管理落后等困难，加快工业发展的首选途径。广西一直把项目招商引资作为发展农产品加工业的重要工作来抓，先后组织有关部门和企业到广东、江浙、东南亚等地区和国家进行招商引资活动。各地不断改善投资软硬环境，加强项目建设的统筹协调，主动协助业主做好项目建设的前期工作，把工作着重点放到加快推进项目开工建设上来。通过招商引资、引进嫁接等方式，吸引国内外企业来投资落户，加快优势资源开发和优势产业的形成。一批国内知名企业集团相继进入广西农产品加工业领域。2005年，桂林市永福县新引进50万元以上项目62个，计划总投资9.7亿元，全县50万元以上的各类在建项目有105个，计划总投资47.28亿元。河池市的宜州市采取积极有效措施，克服困难，迎难而上，认真落实招商引资责任制，全市引进工业项目65个，合同总投资额7.5亿元，实际到位资金4.2亿元，完成投资3.1亿元，竣工投产项目49个。

还通过组织参加中国中小企业博览会等各种活动，为民营企业牵线搭桥，促进本区民营企业的对外经济技术合作与交流，推动民营企业的产品走出广西。2005年，在广州举办的第二届中国中小企业博览会中，组织了广西区14个市、36个企业参展参会，展位24个，参展产品达254种，签订投资合同（协议）11个，总投资5.5亿元；签订供销合同（协议）22个，成交金额6.4亿元。近期，自治区经委发挥自身优势，积极组织协调进行广深合作，组织全区工业园区到深圳进行大规模的招商引资活动，并派出精干人员到深圳进行“挂职招商”，同时组织大批深圳企业家到广西各地考察，寻求进一步合作的商机。

3. *调整和优化结构，产业化稳步推进*　注重从结构调整、优化农产品加工入手，利用本地丰富农林资源，发展农产品加工业，实现农产品加工增值。重视并加强培植龙头企业的工作，实行产、加、销一条龙和农、工、贸一体化，延长产业链，积极推进农业产业化进程，取得了一定的效果。崇左市的龙州、宁明等县利用自己特有的丰富土特产资源优势，开发中草药生产和绿色保健食品，成立了中草药购销公司，集种植、加工、销售于一体。大新、天等县充分利用丰富的苦丁茶资源招商引资，引来了海南老板成立的广西万承苦丁茶发展有限公司（大新）和广西天等桂仙苦丁茶有限公司，从事苦丁茶产品的综合加工与开发，基本上消化了大新、天等两县的苦丁茶鲜叶，苦丁茶青的收购价格也从原来的每千克7元上升到每千克16元，农民增加了收入，带动了两县苦丁茶种植业的发展等，成为乡镇企业新的亮点。

三、今后工作重点

“十一五”期间，继续保持农产品加工业的快速增长，农产品加工业增加值年均增长15%，占全区国内生产总值和工业增加值的比重有大幅度提高；基本形成以水果、蔗糖、蔬菜、畜禽、水产品、烟草为主的食品工业，以林纸、林板、林化为主的林产工业以及现代中药加工等为支撑的农产品加工产业体系，初步形成合理的农产品加工区域布局，培育出一批大型骨干加工企业和名牌产品。使农产品加工业成为新的重要经济增长点、农民增收和财政收入的重要来源。坚持科学的发展观，坚持以市场为导向，以提高农业效益和农民收入为突破点，围绕广西“资源、特色、绿色农产品”优势，因地制宜，科学规划，依靠科技进步，大力发展农产品加工业，形成“一县一品，几乡一品”的特色经济发展格局，建设广西绿色农产品工业基地。深入实施经济发展战略，促进农产品加工业持续、快速、健康发展。

1. *坚持以人为本，促进农产品加工业的协调发展*　以扩大农民就业、增加农民收入，以农业和农民作为立足之本；发挥本地资源优势，大力发展农产品加工业，带动农村经济的发展。

2. *以培育龙头企业为核心*　运用现代工业的观念、思路、机制和办法及国外同行业成功经验来做大做强一批农产品加工龙头企业，按照产业化经营模式与基地农户形成利益共同体，激励技术创新提升加工水平，运用现代营销方式开辟产品市场，引入多渠道融资方式增加投入，实行科学化管理，增强企业活力和竞争力。

3. *增强可持续发展的观念*　要解放思想，更新观念，切实转变增长方式，变粗放型增长为集约型增长。把农产品的精深加工作为产业提升的主攻方向，大力发展循环经济，不断提高农产品及其加工副产品的综合利用水平和效率。

4. *发挥区域优势* 结合本地资源和区域比较优势，加强适合加工的农产品新品种研发和标准化、规模化生产，发展有优势和有特色的农产品加工业，逐步形成适合不同区域的农产品生产和加工产业带。

5. *增强开拓市场的观念* 要以提高农产品市场竞争力为出发点和落脚点，不但要考虑国内市场的拓展，还要考虑国际市场的扩大，通过多种方式开拓国外市场。

6. *建立健全农产品加工业的质量标准体系和社会化服务体系* 开展产品地理标志认证和原种保护工作。

7. *推进科技进步和科技创新* 通过推进科技进步和科技创新，研究和开发新产品，使广西农产品加工业逐步摆脱个体手工作坊模式，发展成科技含量高的规模企业。

8. *培育知名品牌* 知名品牌是提高自主创新能力的标志，是一个企业、一个城市乃至一个国家经济实力和科技水平的体现，也是打入国内外市场的通行证，紧紧围绕“资源、特色、绿色”优势，坚持把产品质量放在首位，推进技术创新，产品创新，培育一批区内外、国内外知名度高、质量优良、具有特色优势的知名品牌。

9. *加大财政资金的投入和金融信贷的支持力度* 加快建立各级中小企业投融资担保机构，贯彻落实自治区人民政府办公厅《关于加快我区中小企业信用担保体系建设的意见》精神，进一步发挥现有的中小企业投融资担保机构的作用，通过担保贷款的方式，为符合条件的中小企业、民营企业提供支持，并针对县域工业企业的特点和要求，积极探索和发展新的担保方式，加大对发展县域工业的支持力度。同时积极探索建立和完善多层次、多元化、多形式非公有制企业信用担保体系的路子，支持鼓励有条件的民营企业建立股份制或会员制等形式的担保机构和风险投资机构。争取大部分市成立中小企业信用担保机构，鼓励有条件的县成立中小企业信用担保机构。

10. *加快农产品加工业信息化建设步伐* 发挥政府的职能，引导企业积极发展农产品加工信息化体系建设，促进农产品加工业的有序地快速发展。

海南省农产品加工业

海南省乡镇企业管理局

一、发展现状

农产品加工业是农业产业链延伸的最高层次，在农村经济发展中具有牵动全局的作用。加工业上不去，种植业就搞不活，畜牧业也难以有大的发展，农产品的出口创汇将受到限制，农业增效、农民增收和社会主义新农村建设的目标就难以实现。

1. *开辟农民增收渠道，提高农民收入水平* 彻底解决农民收入低的问题，必须超越农业、农村、农民的范畴加以思考。农民靠出售原始产品或原料产品很难大幅度提高收入，只有通过农产品的精深加工，延长农业产业链，实现农产品在生产、流通、加工各环节的增值，使农民分享各环节的利润，才能更快地提高收入。文昌市农民围绕椰子系列加工做文章，创办了椰子加工企业 300 多个，完成加工产值近 10 亿元，不但实现了椰子加工增值 5～10 倍，还促进了椰子生产的迅速发展，出现了椰果供不应求、价格稳中有升的局面。同时也使参与加工业经营的农民获取了更多的利润分红、承包金、租赁金、工资等非农收入。文昌天际食品有限公司是一家农民股份合作制企业，主要利用当地椰子等农产品加工各种糖果、饼干等特色食品，品种近 200 个，实现年加工产值 3 000 多万元，出口创汇 50 多万美元，除大量收购农产品原料和招收当地农民工，增加农民收入外，所有股东每年都得到 8 万～10 万元的利润分红。企业与农民之间这种“共赢”合作，不仅壮大了企业，也富了农民。文昌的成功经验充分证明，新阶段的农业增效和农民增收，必须大力发展农产品加工业。

2. *转移农村富余劳动力，拓宽了农民的就业渠道* 农产品加工业的发展，将带动农村相关产业的发展，如商业、包装、储运、服务等第三产业的发展，这些产业都是劳动密集型产业，在延伸农业产业链的同时，有效地延长了农村劳动力的就业链，为农民就业开辟了多种渠道，提供更多的就业机会，使农村劳动力从农业中转移出来，从事加工业及第三产业，拓展就业门路，开辟新的收入来源。海口市琼山区龙塘镇有服装加工业和为服装加工服务的第三产业企业

754个，从业人员6 912人，占全镇总劳动力的52.4%，全镇农民人均纯收入3 843元，比全省平均水平高837元。其中从事服装加工的职工人均纯收入5 208元，比全镇农民人均纯收入增加1 365元，服装加工业提供给农民的人均纯收入达1 227元，占全镇农民人均纯收入的32%。服装加工业的发展，不但使全镇50%的农村劳动力向第二、三产业转移，也为邻近市县的剩余劳动力创造了就业机会。每年的生产旺季，都要从临近的乡镇和市县招收近千名农民进厂打工，为解决农民就业和加速农村劳动力转移做出了积极的贡献。

3. 加快农业结构调整，推进了产业化经营 发展农产品加工业是推进农业产业化经营、加快农业和农村经济结构调整的有效带动力量。加工企业一头连接市场，一头连接农户，是农业产业化经营的中心环节，也是关键环节。通过发展农产品加工业，把农产品生产、加工和销售联为一体，向农民传递及时、准确的市场信息，指导农民做好生产季节和品种安排，及时调整生产和产业结构，促进农业生产向规模化、多样化、优质化发展。海南万昌有限公司在澄迈县美亭镇创办了苦丁茶生产和加工基地，在创办生产基地初期是办基地、搞示范，做给农民看；在发展加工销售期是出技术、找销路，带着农民干；在发展壮大时期是出品牌、做广告，领着农民赚。2005年，该公司采取“公司+基地+农户”的经营模式，带动当地600多户农民发展苦丁茶种植333.3多hm^2，改变了当地长期以种植木薯、甘薯等低效农作物为主的产业结构，推动了产业升级，增加了农民收入。该镇农民种植苦丁茶每公顷年均收入37 500多元，比种植传统的木薯、甘薯等低效作物每公顷增加31 500元。

4. 提高农产品附加值，增强了市场竞争能力 我国加入世贸组织后，农业面临的竞争已不是初级农产品和单个生产环节的竞争，而是包括产前、产中和产后诸环节的整个产业体系的竞争。农产品加工，不仅可以提高附加值，增加农民收入，而且可以通过延伸农业链，把生产、加工、包装、储运、销售等纳入农业经营的内容，要跳出农业抓农业，使农业摆脱仅仅提供食物和原料的不利地位，形成“从田头到餐桌”的完整产业链，不断提升产品档次、质量和附加值，提高整体效益，延长农产品的销售时间和销售半径，规避农产品季节性集中上市产丰价贱的风险，增强市场竞争力。海南泉溢食品有限公司采取“公司+农户”的经营模式，在海口市美兰区演丰镇创办了一家水产品出口加工厂，对农民生产的鱼虾实行合同保护价收购，带动养殖业规模化发展，保证了加工原料的充足供应，增强出口创汇能力，提高经济和社会效益。2005年该镇农民共发展优质罗非鱼养殖200多hm^2，优质海虾养殖133.3多hm^2，确保农民收入稳定增加。同时也增强了加工创汇能力，该公司已创造了年加工出口罗非鱼片6 000多t、海虾1 600多t，创汇1 380万美元的骄人成绩，产品远销日本、美国及欧洲等国际市场。

5. 促进小城镇建设，统筹了城乡经济发展 农村是否繁荣，关键要看农村工业化、城镇化和现代化的建设水平，农产品加工业的发展在推进农村工业化的同时，有力地推进农村城镇化建设，加快农村劳动力向二、三产业和中小城镇转移，带动农村和小城镇的商业、交通、运输、饮食、旅游等第三产业的发展，缩小城乡差别，促进城乡经济统筹发展。农民向二、三产业和小城镇转移的过程，实质上就是减少农民和推进农村城镇化的过程。农产品加工业是小城镇建设的重要载体，它不仅聚集社会资源，带动小城镇的基础设施和公共事业建设，而且也拉动社会需求和消费，加速城镇化进程。调查显示，海口市的龙塘镇、东山镇，文昌市的会文镇，澄迈县的永发镇，琼海市的加积镇，儋州市的那大镇等农产品加工业较发达的地区，不仅带动城镇人口的增加，也促进地方财政的快速增长。上述各镇的财政收入的50%都来源于农产品加工业。不少乡镇正是靠一个产品、一个产业，带动了一方经济，致富了一方农民。海口市东山镇，共有服装加工企业60多家，年加工各类服装500多万件，实现产值2亿元，转移农村劳动力4 270人，服装加工业已成为该镇的支柱产业和财政收入的重要来源。文昌市会文镇积极引导加工向和小城镇集中，创办了加工企业一条街，带动各类加工业及相关第三产业发展到400多个，为农村提供就业岗位4 000多个，由于各类加工业的集中连片，为小城镇建设提供了产业支撑，带动了各项基础设施和公共事业的蓬勃发展，大大加速了城镇化建设进程。

二、存在的主要问题

近年来，海南省农产品加工业得到了新发展，但是原料供给不稳定、企业规模小、技术设备落后、加工转化率低、资金投入不足等问题十分突出，严重制约着农产品加工业的快速发展。

1. 管理体系未理顺，机构不健全 长期以来，农产品加工业没有相对统一的管理机构，造成生产、加工相脱节，扶持、监督相分离，致使种养、加工和流通各环节之间的管理不顺，协调不够和信息不灵，出现了重复建设，内耗资源的尴尬局面。

2. 财政金融的支持力度不够 由于农产品加工

企业大多数是中小企业，在财政及金融支持上，只有少数的龙头企业能够享受到，而绝大多数成长型的加工企业难以得到政府或金融部门的支持，企业融资能力较弱、融资渠道窄，融资难度大，严重制约了加工企业的快速发展和壮大。

3. 技术装备落后，结构性矛盾突出　本省绝大多数加工企业为劳动密集型企业，企业规模较小，设备简陋，一些传统产品仍停留在手工作坊式的水平，生产管理成本高。从产品结构上看，粗加工产品多，精深加工产品少，产品档次较低，很难适应市场需求和变化。从区域布局上看，70%的农产品加工企业都集中在沿海地区，中部山区的自然资源和劳力资源没有得到充分利用。

4. 企业与农户之间的利益连接机制不完善　多数加工企业与农户的联系基本上还是一种松散的买卖关系，而不是一种固定的契约关系或利益共同体。即使是一些加工型的龙头企业也是如此，未能形成产加销一体化经营。交替出现了季节性的“买难”和“卖难”现象，削弱了企业和农户双方抵御市场风险能力。

5. 加工专用原料基地建设滞后　农产品加工专用品种不足是制约本省农产品加工业发展的重要因素。一方面是多数特色农产品的政策和技术偏重于追求高产高效，忽视加工业对农产品的品质和品种要求。另一方面是专用原料基地建设滞后，多数原料来源基本上从分散经营的农户收购，影响加工质量和效益。

6. 行业标准和质量控制体系不健全　一是原料生产的质量保证体系不健全，直接影响加工产品的质量提高。二是农产品加工安全保障体系建设滞后，存在着缺标、没标或执行标准不细、不严等问题。三是质量检测控制体系不健全，质检机构的技术、设备和手段落后，不能适应产品开发和市场开拓的需要。

三、主要对策

1. 坚持规划先行，明确重点和方向，在优化产业结构和产品布局上下工夫　加快农产品加工业发展，首先要制订符合海南省产业结构和特点的加工业发展规划，按照优化布局的原则，结合资源特色和区域比较优势，认真搞好“十一五”农产品加工业发展规划和行动计划，明确发展方向和重点，合理规划区域布局，优先发展特色食品加工业，防止重复建设。积极引导农产品加工业向小城镇和主要工业园区集中，节省公共基础设施投入。发挥企业聚集和分工合作效应。努力实现农产品由初级加工向高新科技含量和高附加值的精深加工转变；由资源消耗型向高效利用和节约型转变；由传统加工工艺向先进适用技术转变，不断提高加工综合效益和产品质量，增强市场竞争力。

2. 坚持项目推进，扶持主导产业，在发挥龙头带动和政策导向上下工夫　按照优势农产品区域布局规划、产业政策和资源配置原则，着重发展一批具有市场优势和潜力，对农业结构调整和提升农业综合竞争能力有较大影响的农产品加工示范项目。示范项目要在优势农产品区域内选择，并在原料和加工基地建设、先进技术研发、技术改造、市场开拓等方面给予重点扶持，使其形成种养加一条龙、产加销一体化的具有较强带动辐射能力的产业化加工企业新龙头。根据本省的资源优势和特色产业，近期要重点建设畜禽、椰子、胡椒、槟榔、菠萝、芒果、香蕉、橡胶等主要农产品的加工示范项目。注重发展一批果菜冷藏保鲜项目，集中建设一批地头式冷库，提高鲜活农产品的冷藏保鲜能力。力争“十一五”期间全省冷藏保鲜规模达到10万t，经过冷藏保鲜处理的出岛瓜果菜达60%以上。积极组织一批具有区域比较优势、有地方特色和市场前景好的示范项目，采取多种形式进行对外招商。通过项目招商，引进先进技术装备、资金和人才，带动农产品加工业向规模化、集约化和专业化方向发展。

3. 坚持集中连片开发，推进城镇化建设，在发展加工业园区和城镇化上下工夫　通过连片开发和集中建设，引导农产品加工业从零星分散向集中连片发展，充分发挥加工业对工业园区和小城镇建设的带动作用。集中连片开发，既可以节约土地，方便区域布局规划和减少公共设施投入，节约社会资源，降低企业成本，又可以充分发挥企业和产业相互配套、相互依存的聚集效应，促进商贸、交通、饮食、旅游等服务产业的发展，加速资金、技术、劳力和物流的区域性转移和流动，促进工业园区和小城镇的规模化发展。在集中连片开发中，要注重抓好几方面工作：一是科学规划，合理布局。按照区位优势、资源条件和人口规模进行规划，选择企业比较集中、人口相对密集、基础设施较好，便于工业“三废”综合治理的中心城镇优先布局。二是完善基础设施建设。加工园区要逐步实现通水、通路、通电、通讯和平整土地，避免基础设施重复建设和浪费。三是落实配套政策，完善管理体制。要在土地使用、企业登记、户籍改革、税收、信贷等方面给予政策倾斜。加强投资环境建设，建立健全管理服务机构，完善管理体制和运行机制，组织相关部门共同研究，协调解决企业用地、用工、水电供应和社会治安保障问题，消除企业的后顾之忧。近期要重点抓好定安塔岭农产品加工示范基地建设，为全省农产品加工园区建设提供示范和借鉴。

4. 坚持产业化经营，拉长农业产业链，在扶持农产品加工龙头企业上下工夫　扶持农产品加工龙头企业就是扶持农业产业化经营。由于海南省农民的组织化程度低，生产经营能力差，缺乏市场竞争的组织应变能力。而农产品加工龙头企业，不仅拥有雄厚的资金技术力量，而且在连接市场和农户、掌握市场信息和参与市场竞争方面都具有绝对优势。因此，扶持培育和发展壮大加工龙头企业，是推进产业化经营，解决广大农民分散经营与统一大市场对接的最现实、最有效的办法。当前我国已进入以工促农、以城带乡的历史新阶段，要鼓励引导大型工业企业参与农产品加工业的投资与合作，通过投资入股、合作兼并等形式，扶持农产品加工龙头企业的发展与壮大，努力培育一批种养加一条龙、科工贸一条线、产供销一体化的骨干加工龙头企业，促进加工龙头上规模、上档次、上水平。

5. 坚持创新发展，依靠科技进步，在发展农产品精深加工上下工夫　科技是第一生产力，科技创新是促进产业优化升级的源动力。发展现代农业要靠科技创新，发展现代农产品加工业更要依靠技术创新。因此，在加快农产品加工业发展进程中，既要鼓励发展农产品的分级、包装、储藏、保鲜等初加工和半成品加工，又要大力发展农产品的精深加工，把初级农产品转化为高技术含量和高附加值的品牌产品，达到加工增值增效的目的。一是要抓好热作产品的深加工。重点抓好椰子、胡椒、槟榔、咖啡、橡胶等优势产品的精深加工和综合利用。积极引进新技术、新工艺、新设备，开发系列新产品，扩大加工规模和总量，提高质量和档次。二是发展畜禽产品深加工。充分利用无疫区的品牌优势，积极引进大型肉制品加工企业，引导肉制品加工业向细分割、急冷冻、便携带、系列化、精包装、便食用的精深方向发展，争取畜禽加工产品进入国际市场，真正把海南省建设成为全国的畜禽产品加工出口基地。三是继续发展水产品深加工。突出抓好海淡水对虾、鲍鱼、罗非鱼的深加工，力争在藻类、贝类加工和出口方面取得新突破。

6. 坚持因地制宜，建设原料基地，在发展标准化原料生产上下工夫　海南省农产品的专用化程度不高，原料产品的品种改良和均衡供给能力差。要保障农产品加工业持续快速发展，必须做好原料生产和均衡供应的文章。在搞好原料生产的区域布局基础上，积极抓好一批标准化原料生产示范基地建设，建立专业化、标准化、优质化的农产品原料生产和供应体系。要立足现有农产品生产基地，加强加工专用型的品种选育、改造和推广，加大原料基地改造的基础设施建设和技术投入力度，逐步形成布局合理、专用、优质、稳定的标准化加工原料基地。基地建设要采取产业化的运作模式，鼓励加工企业通过定向投入、定向服务、定向收购等方式，与基地经营农户和周边种养农民建立稳定的合同契约关系，或采取土地入股等形式与农民结成利益共同体，确保原料的稳定均衡供给，带动农民增加收入。

7. 坚持统一思想，切实加强领导，在强化规范管理上下工夫　加快农产品加工业发展，是省委、省政府作出的重大战略部署，各级政府和有关部门要进一步统一思想，提高认识，真正把发展农产品加工业作为繁荣农村经济、增加农民收入和建设社会主义新农村的重点工作来抓，把它纳入经济社会发展规划，摆上重要工作议事日程。在各级农业部门的牵头协调下，成立统一的协调管理机构，负责对本地区农产品加工业进行规划、指导、协调、管理和服务，改变农业生产、加工、销售相分离的不利局面，推进产加销一体化经营。对不同地区、不同特点的农产品加工业，要实行分类指导，注重实效，防止盲目发展和重复建设。各级发展与改革、财政、商贸、海洋渔业、农垦、林业、国土资源、环保、科技、金融、卫生、税务、工商、质检等行政主管部门要各负其责，各司其职，加强协作，转变职能，改善服务，形成合力，共同推动我省农产品加工业协调快速发展。

重庆市农产品加工业

重庆市乡镇企业局

一、发展现状

1. 农产品加工业已成为重庆一大支柱产业　“十五”期间农产品加工业快速发展，产值年均增长速度达到20%，增加值年均增长速度达到16%，高于本市同期生产总值的增长速度。到2005年，全市农产品加工企业达1.7万多个，其中重点企业2 100

多个，市级以上农产品加工龙头企业149个；实现产值达831亿元，占整个工业产值的19.3%，与同期农林牧渔业总产值比高出10%，比2000年提高了31个百分点；工业增加值达到232.3亿元，占整个工业生产总值的19.57%，相当于农业生产总值的42.84%。农产品加工业的快速发展对本市经济发展产生了巨大的拉动作用，已成为区县经济的重要支撑。

2. 农产品加工业是推动农业产业化和规模化经营的重要力量 农产品加工业的发展，对农产品生产的品种、品质、生产数量、生产集中度提出了更高的要求，极大地推进了农业结构调整。随着农业"三百"工程的实施，促进了一批优势农业产业带的形成。到2005年，全市共建设各类优质农产品生产基地866.7khm²，其中农业产业化百万工程基地建设666.7 khm²，年产优质蚕茧3.1万t，出栏优质瘦肉型生猪310万头，出栏优质肉牛21万头，优质肉羊220万只，优质肉兔700万只。初步形成了柑橘、优质中药材、草食牲畜、榨菜、优质蚕茧、优质花椒和优质生猪、笋竹等产业带。涪陵榨菜加工和荣昌夏布加工被农业部确定为全国农产品加工示范基地。在种、养、加、销各个环节培育和壮大了一批龙头企业。

3. 农产品加工业是促进农工互动的关键环节 农产品加工业的发展，推动了农业产业化的快速发展。全市农产品商品率由2001年的50.7%提高到了2005年的56.7%。全市龙头企业发展到2 100多个，比2000年增加1 500个，其中，市级龙头企业达到159个，国家级重点龙头企业19个；固定资产总值达150亿元，比2000年增加1倍多；销售收入250亿元，比2000年增加3倍多。龙头企业的快速成长，对相关产业的发展形成了有力支撑，并在一些产业形成了企业集群，优化了农业区域布局和农村产业结构。同时，农业产业化也有力地推动了加工业的提升，吸引了一批城市工商企业、外来企业向农产品加工业投资。全市已形成了一批产加销一体化、以产业化利益机制为纽带，与基地结为较为稳定利益共同关系的产业化经营企业，促进了企业规模、产品多元化和企业集群的发展。农产品加工企业的集中联片发展，促进了工业园区的建设和发展，极大地推动了小集镇的建设。农产品加工业和农业产业化的相互促进、共同发展，是农工互动、建立和谐社会的真正体现。

4. 农产品加工业是农民就业、增收的重要载体 近年来，由于农产品加工业的发展，其从业人员一直保持增长态势。乡镇农产品加工企业是吸纳农村富余劳动力的主体，农民从产中环节向产前环节和产后环节延伸，从事农产品加工和运销，从而获取了农业的后续利润，增加了农民的收入。至2005年，全市农产品加工业吸纳就业人员62.9万人，其中乡镇企业农产品加工业吸纳农民就业29.1万人，占乡镇工业企业从业人员的25.5%。此外，城乡个体农产品加工户还吸纳了大量农民就业。农产品加工业已成为农民增收、扩大就业的重要渠道，农民家庭经营收入保持稳定增长，2005年全市农民家庭经营收入达到1 541元，比1997年增长52%。

5. 农产品加工业是扩大出口的新生力量 农产品加工的大量深精产品，不但为人们的生活提供了丰富的食品和用品，而且为繁荣市场做出了突出贡献，同时已逐步发展成为重庆市出口创汇的新生力量。全市共有农产品出口企业152个，2005年农产品出口创汇2.79亿美元，占全市出口总额的11.1%。其中，乡镇企业农产品出口1.43亿美元，占全市农产品出口创汇总额的51.3%。主要出口农产品有桑蚕丝及机织物、苎麻及机织物、冻猪肉、肉罐头、肠衣、猪鬃、茶叶、菌类、复合肥等，涌现出了重庆粮油食品进出口公司、重庆嘉泰丝绸公司、涪陵金帝公司、永川金凤丝绸公司、祥飞石柱丝绸公司、万州蓝希络公司等一批出口规模较大的企业。

二、主要做法

1. 政策推动 近年来，市委、市政府相继出台了《关于进一步加快乡镇企业发展的决定》和《全市乡镇企业结构调整的意见》、《关于加快民营企业发展的决定》，成为当前和今后一个时期全市中小企业、乡镇企业发展和结构调整的纲领性文件，对推动乡镇企业发展具有十分重要的指导意义。文件明确了抓好农产品加工业的原则、政策、措施等，提出"乡镇企业要因地制宜发展农产品加工业；乡镇企业的发展要与推进农业产业化经营相结合，促进农业资源的深度开发利用；到'十五'期末要扶持100个农业产业化龙头企业。农产品加工业的产值占乡镇工业总产值的比重提高到30%以上；经县以上农业产业化办公室认可的农产品加工龙头企业，报经重庆市地税局批准，可给予一定时期的减免所得税"。为农产品加工业的发展创造了一个良好的环境。

2. 规划引导 重庆市乡镇企业局在制定《重庆市乡镇企业"十五"计划及2015年远景目标规划》中也把发展农产品加工业作为了"十五"到2015年乡镇企业发展的重点，提出要着力突出农业产业化发展，大力提升、改造传统产业，加大产品结构调整力

度，提高农产品附加值，2005年又制定了《“十一五”重庆市农产品加工业发展规划》明确了发展重点和产业布局，有力地引导了本市农产品加工业的发展。

3. 投资拉动　近年来，各区县（市）通过土地使用权的流转，投资合作等形式，吸纳原有企业，社会单位，工商企业私营业主等社会资本与农业产业化，农产品加工项目合作。“十五”期间，每年全市农产品加工、农业产业化经营投资500万元以上的项目达50多个，年投资额近10亿元，为推动农产品加工业发展增添了后劲。

4. 财政扶持　在资金、项目等方面重点向农产品加工业倾斜。近几年，市农业产业化资金、市乡镇企业发展资金等农发资金重点用于扶持农产品加工业的发展，从2000年起，在乡镇企业发展资金安排上，明确要求农产品加工业企业，农业产业化企业要占70%以上，每年要安排近1 000万元财政资金扶持农产品加工业的发展。在乡镇企业发展资金的有偿使用方面，也注重了农产品加工项目的安排，对缓解企业资金压力起到了导向和四两拨千斤的作用。

5. 强化服务　在为全市乡镇企业加强指导和提供服务的工作中，加强了融资、创业、培训、法律、市场、技术、质量、信息等八大服务平台建设，为农产品加工业发展提供全方位和多层次的服务。重点开展了融资、创业培训、市场开拓等服务。切实帮助解决企业在生产经营中遇到的困难和问题，促进了企业的发展。

三、存在的主要问题

1. 加工深度不够　重庆市农产品加工业发展水平偏低，农产品加工转化率、深加工（两次以上加工）率、加工制造食品占食物消耗总量分别只有25%、15%、20%，均低于全国总体水平。

2. 原料品种结构不适应农产品加工的需要　一是农产品品种品质不能满足精深加工需要，缺乏农产品加工业发展需要的专用、优质原料。二是原料生产分散、规模化程度低，使农产品加工企业的发展规模受影响。三是由于农产品加工企业与农户之间的利益联结机制不够完善，履行合同的信用度较差，致使农产品加工业发展缺乏稳定可靠的原料基地。

3. 品牌培养不够　农产品加工仍然存在着“小、散、弱”小企业偏多，龙头企业和规模企业偏少；粗加工企业偏多，精深加工企业偏少，传统产品偏多，科技含量高的产品偏少（创新产品更少），一般产品偏多，名牌产品偏少。另外市内地区发展不平衡。

4. 标准体系不够健全　部分加工产品存在着标准不适应现实发展需要或与国际接轨有差距。比较突出的是农产品加工业从原料生产到加工过程管理分散，还未形成完整有效的管理体系和质量安全标准体系，产品质量、食品安全、加工管理仍存在一些问题。

四、主要措施

“十一五”期间要认真贯彻国务院办公厅印发的《关于促进农产品加工业发展的意见》，加大工作力度，实施好《“十一五”重庆市农产品加工业发展规划》，以促进农产品加工业加快发展。主要措施有：

1. 加强领导，创造宽松的发展环境　一是进一步加强对农产品加工业的指导服务工作。农产品加工业的发展，涉及工业、农业、商业等多个部门，要通力合作，为农产品加工业的发展创造宽松的外部环境。市乡镇企业局要加强对全市非公有制经济、中小企业、乡镇企业农产品加工企业的管理、指导和服务；农产品生产、加工、流通领域的管理部门要加强协调，共同做好农业产业化、农产品加工业结构调整以及农产品产加销、贸工农一体化工作，促进农产品加工业的健康发展。二是制定相关法规和政策。结合本市实际，研究制定农产品加工业发展的地方性法规，同时尽快建立食品安全技术法规体系，逐步将农产品加工业的发展纳入法制管理的轨道，实行依法监管。制定《加快农产品加工业发展的意见》等相关措施，加大对农产品加工业的扶持力度，努力提高农产品加工业发展水平。三是加强考核和评价工作。建立农产品加工业发展工作机制，加大考核评价的力度。将农产品加工业发展目标任务纳入对市级有关部门和区县政府的年度工作考核评价内容，以促进全市农产品加工业的发展。

2. 优化结构，建设好原料基地　在农业结构战略性调整中，要以市场为导向，按照农产品加工业对原料的需求和优势农产品区域化布局的要求，调整和优化农产品结构；按照农产品加工业标准化、优质化要求，调整和优化农产品生产结构，实现由“生产、加工、市场”向“市场、加工、生产”的转变。遵循区域化布局、专业化生产、标准化管理、产业化经营和社会化服务的发展思路，突出地方特色，充分发挥区域比较优势，以农产品加工企业为龙头，以分散的农户为配套服务，建立一批与加工企业相配套的粮油、果品、蔬菜、畜禽、水产和特色农产品原料基地，促进农产品加工业的发展。在种植业方面，大力发展优质水稻、“双低一高”油菜、耐储存的优质水果、优质蔬菜以及各种名、特、优、稀且适宜深度加工的农产品；在畜牧、水产方面，大力发展草食牲畜、瘦肉型猪、优质肉牛和高附加值的水产品，发展适应市场需求和满足加工要求的优质专用品种。要大力提倡发展有机农业和绿色农业，按照讲求营养、保证卫生、注重特色、符合保健、崇尚美味、回归自然的要求，生产无公害农产品，为农产品加工企业提供安全、优质的加工原料。农产品加工基地建设，要在农户家庭经营的基础上，走“小规模、大群体”的路子，鼓励农户、专业合作经济组织与农产品加工企业通过合同、合作等方式，形成稳定的利益联结关系。提倡农产品加工企业主要通过定向投入、定向服务、定向收购等方式，兴办稳定的农产品原料基地。

3. 争创品牌，培育企业集团　一是引导企业提高企业管理水平。要以打造核心竞争力为出发点，从体制改造、机制健全、组织完善等方面引导企业努力提高管理水平，推进信息化在企业中的运用，大力推广先进的质量管理方法，建立面向竞争、面向客户的企业管理模式。二是引导企业树立品牌意识。使企业实现由商品生产经营向品牌生产经营的转变，尽快形成一批具有自主知识产权的驰名商标，并做好注册商标、驰名商标、原产地域、名牌产品的申报和保护，提高名牌产品市场占有率，促进农产品加工业上规模、上档次、上水平。三是培育一批企业集团。要积极扶持一批基础好、生产规模较大、有发展前景的加工龙头企业，组建跨地区、跨行业、跨所有制，集贸、工、农一体化的大型企业集团，充分发挥企业集团的龙头作用和示范效应。并培育一批与农民利益关系密切的专业化龙头企业、科技先导型龙头企业、外向型加工龙头企业，拓展发展空间。四是鼓励企业做大做强。围绕主导产业发展，积极鼓励有竞争力的农产品加工企业利用资金、技术、品牌、市场等优势，通过联合、兼并、资产重组、股票上市等途径，提高企业规模化经营、专业化生产和网络化销售的水平，促进企业由初加工向精深加工方向发展。支持企业通过吸纳员工入股、外来参股、中外合资等方式改变单一的产权结构，构建开发型、多元化的混合所有制企业，不断增强企业的发展活力。

4. 加大投入，完善投融资机制　一是稳定并统筹协调市财政资金对农产品加工业的扶持和导向投入；二是继续引导商业银行对农产品加工企业的信贷服务；三是不断壮大已经推行的贷款担保业务；四是引导社会资金投入。

5. 转变职能，逐步完善服务体系　一是完善融资服务平台，通过推进多种形式的信用担保体系引导开发银行、商业银行、信用社等金融机构的金融服务。二是争取新建重庆市农产品加工服务中心，其功能为人员培训、产品研发、科技孵化、技能鉴定，国内外产品展示。三是完善培训服务平台，做好人才的委培、代培、自培（依靠乡镇企业干校、电大企业管理学院）等方面的定向培养。四是完善创业服务平台。充分利用各种社会资源组织创业辅导和创业培训，为创业者开辟道路。五是完善信息服务平台。在现有网络的基础上打造多层次、多渠道覆盖面广的农产品加工信息公共服务平台。六是完善市场服务平台，充分发挥好市中小企业产品推介中心、市中小企业国际经贸促进中心的作用。七是完善质量服务平台，帮助企业建立和完善质量检验管理制度。八是完善法律服务平台。充分发挥好法律服务中心、维权投诉中心的作用，为农产品加工企业维权提供服务。

四川省农产品加工业

四川省乡镇企业局

一、发展现状

四川省是农产品资源十分丰富的大省，主要农产品产量均居全国前列。2005 年粮食总产量 3 409 万 t，出栏生猪 8 764 万头，肉类总产量 949 万 t，水果总产量 540 万 t，蔬菜产量 2 704 万 t，为农产品加工业的发展提供了丰富的生产原料。改革开放以来，特别是“十五”以来，四川省农产品加工业进入了崭新的发展阶段，农产品加工业有了高速发展。据统计，到 2004 年底，全省从事农产品加工业的企业达 12 172 个，从业人员 62.03 万人，实现营业收入 1 158.68 亿元。其中，规模以上企业 1 851 个，从业人员 38.29 万人，实现销售收入 802.48 亿元，完成工业增加值 253.84 亿元，利税总额 135.82 亿元，成为四川省国民经济中最具活力的产业之一。农产品加工业在助农增效、助农就业，助农增收，推动农村经济社会发展上发挥了十分重要的作用，也是构建和谐社会，繁荣农村经济、增加农民收入，推进社会主义新农村建设不可替代的生力军。经过20多年的发展，全省乡镇、中小企业中农产品加工业初步形成以下特点：

1. 农产品加工门类齐全，区域特色初步显现 全省农产品加工门类基本涵盖了本省的主要农产品，形成了粮食、油料、饲料、肉类、果蔬、水产、木材、酒类、饮料、中药材、皮毛羽绒、竹藤棕草等20余类农产品加工企业。各地区以本地生产的大宗农产品为依托，初步形成了区域性农产品加工体系。以成都为中心的成都平原及周边是四川的粮食、油料、生猪的主要生产基地，依托农产品资源上的优势，现已发展为四川省的主要粮油猪加工区；乐山、雅安以茶叶生产基地为依托，发展茶叶及精深加工业；宜宾、泸州及崇州、大邑、邛崃是四川省的优质酿酒带，现已形成了四川省最大的两个白酒生产基地；以中藏药材生产为依托，成都形成了药业中心，辐射带动了周边地区的中藏药材加工产业。还有达州的苎麻加工业，眉山的制浆、造纸业，成都新繁、龙泉的蔬菜加工业等各具区域特色的农产品加工业集群。

2. 涌现了大批规模企业，实力不断增强 全省现有24个国家级的龙头企业，150个省级龙头企业，2005年实现销售总收入518亿元。龙头企业的发展推动了农产品加工业规模化生产进程，辐射带动作用强，效益好，成为全省农产品加工业的中坚力量。

3. 在增加农民收入、转移农村剩余劳动力中发挥了重要作用 近年来，四川省农产品加工企业一直保持较快发展态势，加工企业通过推行“公司＋基地＋农户”等经营模式，使主要农产品加工品种不断丰富，品质不断提高，从业人员不断扩大，农民收入不断增加。一大批龙头加工企业的成长，不仅直接推动了农产品加工业的发展，而且带动了加工原料的基地化生产和千家万户的种养，催生了新的营销组织和营销方式。据对全省152户省以上重点农产品加工龙头企业的调查，辐射带动农户218万户，农民人均收入增收300元。

4. 建立了一批优质农产品加工原料生产基地 随着人们生活水平的不断提高和环保意识的日益增强，无公害、绿色、有机食品将成为21世纪主要消费食品。在龙头企业的辐射带动下，各地区依托现有优势农产品生产区域，扶持建立优质农产品加工原料生产基地，发挥山区绿色生态优势，实现特色农产品加工与原料基地的有机结合，逐步形成了大批各具特色的农产品加工原料生产基地和产业带。

5. 农产品加工业对经济增长的贡献度显著提高 农产品加工业在地方经济发展中的地位和作用日益增强，逐步成为地区经济发展的主导力量，全省农产品加工业产值占工业总产值比重逐年提高。在有的县市，农产品加工业已成为财政收入中的主体。农产品加工企业在原料收购、为农村剩余劳动力提供就业岗位、增加农民工资性收入等环节表明，通过发展农产品加工业，提高了农产品综合利用水平，扩大了县域经济总量，增加了农民收入和财政收入，吸纳了农村剩余劳动力。

二、存在的主要问题

1. 农产品加工率低，生产与加工脱节现象严重 四川省农产品加工业总产值大致接近农林牧渔业总产值的一半。加工与种植的比率不到0.2∶1，与发达国家和全国平均水平还有很大的差距。

2. 精深加工能力弱，资源利用率差 四川省农产品加工企业总体还处于起步阶段，表现在初级加工、粗加工产品多，精加工、二次以上深加工产品少，资源利用率低。农产品加工产品多数是只经过简单的初加工就投入市场，进行深加工的数量比重较小，综合开发的产品为数不多，副产物综合利用水平更差。农产品加工副产品大多被作为废弃物处理，不仅造成浪费，而且带来环境污染。这种低水平加工，资源的低水平利用减少了农产品增值的机会，加大资源浪费程度。

3. 企业规模偏小，技术水平，设备装备普遍落后，自身发展能力不强 农产品加工企业总体上规模偏小，生产和加工集约化程度低，大多数加工设备简陋、加工工艺落后，技术人才缺乏，采用先进设备加工工艺少，生产的机械化程度远远底于发达国家水平。还有相当一部分是家庭作坊。由于企业规模小，创新能力弱，缺乏产品自主开发能力，新工艺、新技术、新材料的应用程度低。

4. 技术和管理人才匮乏，质量标准与质量控制体系建设滞后 除了少数规模较大的农产品加工企业外，大多农产品加工企业专业技术人员相对较少。管理经营人员不少是企业所有者自身及其家族成员和一些乡土能人，经营管理水平不高。对企业战略运营中的品牌建设、专业化、多元化和国际化等各种问题缺乏深入长远的规划。不少企业没有取得ISO 9000认证、HACCP认证。

5. 资金投入严重不足 由于企业规模偏小，难以得到省里扶持龙头企业的财政贴息款。农产品加工企业资金不足，制约了加工企业的扩大、技改和宣传。有的企业通过技改后，生产规模扩大，产品畅销，但由于流动资金不足，难以贷到款，而无法和农民履行收购合同，对企业生产经营造成严重影响。

三、主要措施

1. *重点培育和发展农产品加工骨干企业* 围绕特色农业，以市场为导向，大力开发和培育以农产品加工为主的龙头企业，创造出产品更新、效益更高、竞争力更强的企业规模结构，形成下游产品企业带动上游产品企业，大企业辐射小企业，企业带动农业生产的良好发展态势。在培育和发展农产品加工龙头企业的过程中，一是创新组织形式、经营机制。大力推广订单农业、合同契约、合同加服务、股份合作、资产入股等经营方式，使企业和农民建立稳定的利益连接机制，形成真正的利益共享、风险共担的经济共同体。二是组建企业集团。积极鼓励和引进投资农产品加工项目，以资产为纽带，以拳头产品为龙头，以骨干企业为核心，实行改组、兼并、联合，加快培植和组建一批生产经营规模大、技术含量高、辐射带动作用强，集生产经营、科研开发于一体的跨行业、跨地区、跨所有制的农工贸一体化加工集团。三是面向国内外两个市场，建立完善市场营销、服务、信息收集处理机制。

2. *提高农产品加工的技术水平和科技创新能力* 一是利用互联网建立技术信息发布的平台，筛选并推广一批先进、成熟的农产品加工实用技术。二是鼓励加工企业与科研单位、大专院校加强联合与合作，增强农产品精深加工工艺技术、品种和功能等方面的创新研究与开发生产的能力。三是用好乡镇企业技改资金，扶持农产品加工企业的技术创新和新产品开发。四是通过各种方式、多种渠道，为农产品加工企业培训人才，全面提高员工的素质与管理水平。

3. *大力推进农产品加工企业对外的交流与合作* 积极引进省外，特别是沿海民营企业、外资企业及其他法人合资、合作，解决资金短缺问题；树立国际经营战略思想，有实力的企业要把战略重点从国内向国际转移，参与国际产业链分工。加快企业信息化建设，逐步实现生产营销、融资、人才以及研发的国际化，在世界范围内进行资源的最优配置。企业还可以采取与国际大型跨国公司之间竞争与合作和相结合的策略，通过与国外的战略合作，引进新的管理经验、建立新的管理模式，迅速获得技术优势、市场优势和品牌优势等，提高企业的国际竞争力。

4. *加快农产品加工业的质量标准体系建设* 按照“统筹规划、合理布局、突出重点、分步实施”的原则，加快农产品加工质量安全检验检测机构的建设，提高质检人员素质，充实质检设备，完善质检手段，增强质检能力。研究制定符合本省实际并能够与国际接轨的农产品原料和加工业制品质量安全标准、技术规程和合格评定标准。积极开展残留和转基因等加工品的质量安全检验检测，逐步将质量安全检验检测工作纳入规范化和法制化轨道。

5. *加强对农产品加工业的扶持力度* 在资金支持上，各级财政要继续扶持重点骨干龙头企业，引导农产品加工企业的技术改造、基地建设和新产品开发等。农产品加工企业要充分利用市场机制，拓宽融资渠道，实现投资主体和产权主体多元化。在信贷支持上，积极开展银企间沟通与合作，商业银行对实力强、资信程度高、发展前景良好的农产品加工企业，通过资质评估，核定一定的授信额度，重点给予支持，尤其是对收购季节性农产品所需流动资金予以优先安排。在税收减免上，根据现行政策和实际发展情况，对新办农产品加工企业五年内免征所得税。农产品加工企业从事初级加工产品取得的收入，暂免征所得税等。在外向型经济发展上，对具有自营进出口权条件的农产品加工企业，在出口许可证和对外贸易发展资金上予以重点支持。

贵州省农产品加工业

贵州省乡镇企业局

一、发展现状

1. *农产品加工业已成为贵州省农村经济发展新的增长点* “十五”期间，全省规模以上农产品加工业总产值年均增长 13.37%，增加值年均增长 17.27%。2005 年，规模以上农产品加工业总产值 331.28 亿元，增加值 176.89 亿元。其中，除烟草加工业外的农产品加工业总产值 217.04 亿元，增加值 91.97 亿元，分别占全省规模以上工业总产值、增加值的 12.84%和 15.70%；实现利税总额 49.09 亿元，占全省规模以上工业企业利税总额的 21.11%。农产品加工业已成为全省工业经济中增长较快、后发优势突出并极具发展活力的重要产业之一。

2. 形成一批具有相对优势的龙头企业　经过多年发展，贵州农产品加工业涌现出了贵阳南明老干妈风味食品有限公司、贵州益佰制药股份有限公司、贵州永红食品有限公司、贵州康星油脂（集团）有限公司等一批经济实力较强的具有相对优势的农产品加工龙头企业和企业集团。据不完全统计，全省规模以上农产品加工企业超过 500 个，其中年产值亿元以上的有 36 个。

3. 形成一批名特优产品、优质原料基地和农产品交易市场　贵州省农产品加工企业，通过技术创新，形成了一批名特优产品和优质原料基地。截止 2005 年，累计有 31 个企业的 216 个产品获绿色食品标志证书，"陶华碧老干妈"牌系列调味品等一批农产品加工产品已成为市场占有率较高的名牌产品；累计建有绿色食品生产基地 32 个、65.3khm^2；建优质油菜基地 366.7 khm^2，优质水稻基地 370 khm^2，辣椒基地 66.7 khm^2，竹基地 46.7 khm^2；启动实施了 90 个优质畜牧产品基地建设项目，发展了 1 200 多个生态养殖示范小区，规模养殖场达 5 309 个，畜业增加值占农林牧渔业增加值的比重上升到 33.13%，在农民纯收入中来自畜牧业的收入比 2000 年增长 15.28%；建成农产品批发市场 199 个，年成交额 2 亿元以上的有 6 个，1 000 万元以上的有 28 个。为农产品加工业发展奠定了较好的基础。

4. 农产品加工业已成为农民增收和扩大就业的重要途径　据不完全统计，2005 年，各类农产品加工企业从业人员共 8.25 万人，人均年收入 7 000 余元。同时，农产品加工业的发展带动了农业结构的调整和农业效益的提高，进一步促进了农民收入的稳定增长。

二、存在的主要问题

1. 农业生产整体水平不高　多年来，贵州省农业得到很大发展，但由于农业基础薄弱以及投入农业基础设施、新技术推广、劳动力培训等方面资金不足，农村经济相对落后，农业生产整体水平不高，影响农产品加工业发展。

2. 农产品原料生产与加工需求矛盾突出　原料基地建设滞后是贵州省农产品加工业的薄弱环节。农产品加工业发展需要的专用、优质原料缺乏，原料生产分散，规模化生产程度低，主要农产品品质不能满足加工需要，影响农产品加工业发展。

3. 农产品市场建设薄弱　大多数农产品市场设施简陋，同时缺乏统一规划和布局，交易方式陈旧，市场化组织程度低，农村经纪人队伍的发展不适应市场需要，农民进入市场渠道不畅，抗御市场风险能力弱。

4. 农产品加工业规模小、科技含量低、创新能力弱　多数农产品加工企业专业技术人才缺乏，企业规模小，实力弱。许多农产品加工企业设备落后，劳动生产率低。科技创新能力弱，多数企业缺乏产品自主开发能力，新工艺、新材料、新技术的应用程度低，产品档次不高，市场竞争力不强。

5. 资金投入短缺　资金投入不足是制约贵州省农产品加工业发展的重要因素，如 2005 年，全省农产品加工业固定资产投入仅 23.28 亿元，占全社会固定资产投入的 2.29%，无力更新先进的技术装备和加工工艺。农产品加工企业大多数是小企业，可抵押物少，担保难、融资难，加之农产品加工原料收购季节性强，正常周转流动资金量较大，资金供需矛盾突出，难以满足正常生产需要。

三、政策措施

1. 多渠道筹集、进一步加大资金投入　发展农产品加工业，要按照市场经济的规律培育经营投资主体，激活各项资本的投入，多渠道筹集农产品加工业发展资金。省财政每年预算安排的乡镇企业发展资金、农业产业化发展资金、农业综合开发配套资金、中小企业发展资金等专项资金要调整支出结构，通过贷款贴息等形式，吸引更多的金融资金和社会资金投入农产品加工业。对年营业收入在 1 亿元以上，实现税收在 800 万元以上，资产负债率小于 50%，所使用原料 60%以上为省内提供的农产品加工龙头企业和农业品加工制品获得全国驰名商标的企业，予以重点扶持。对农产品加工龙头企业申报国家扶持的高新技术产业化推进项目、农产品深加工项目和技改贴息项目，省有关部门应优先推荐上报。要支持有条件的农产品加工企业建立现代企业制度，推动资本经营。对符合条件的重点龙头企业，实行规范的公司制后，要支持企业申请发行股票和上市。

2. 积极争取金融部门的扶持　商业银行要把扶持农产品加工业作为信贷工作的重要内容，在资金安排上给予积极支持。对农产品加工龙头企业，要依据企业正常生产周期和贷款用途，合理确定贷款期限和利率，原则上不上浮利率。农村信用社（合作银行）要积极开展农户信用评级建设，推行农户小额信用贷款和农户联保贷款方式，扩大基地农户贷款的发放，支持农产品加工企业发展。各地已建立的各类信用担保机构要优先安排农产品加工企业的贷款担保。鼓励有条件的农产品加工骨干企业和农民专业合作经济组织组建形式多样的农业贷款担保机构，建立“银、企、农”风险共担机制。

3. *落实税收支持政策* 各地要认真落实《国务院办公厅印发关于促进农产品加工业发展意见的通知》中确定的税收优惠政策。农产品加工企业研究开发新产品、新技术、新工艺所发生的各项费用，在缴纳企业所得税前扣除。农产品加工企业引进技术和进口农产品加工设备，符合国家有关税收政策规定的，免征关税和进口环节增值税。对重点农产品加工骨干企业从事种植业、养殖业和农产品初加工所得，要落实免征3～5年企业所得税的政策。

4. *建立农产品加工质量标准体系和监督体系* 全面实行农产品加工QS生产许可认证，进一步引导和支持企业开展ISO 9000族质量管理体系、ISO 14000环境管理体系、ISO 18000职业健康安全管理体系和HACCP食品安全管理体系等认证工作。借鉴国内外先进质量监管模式，建立贵州省农产品加工业从原料到成品加工的一系列质量监督体系，有效控制农产品加工产品质量，保证食品安全，提高农产品加工企业市场竞争力。

5. *其他配套措施* 鼓励支持国有、集体农产品加工企业的转制、重组。以技术作价入股出资注册的农产品加工企业，允许农产品加工专业技术人员科技成果入股金可占注册资本的35%。国土部门在编制土地利用总体规划和计划时，要对农产品加工企业用地进行统筹考虑，合理安排。电力部门要保证对农产品加工企业的供电。加强对企业的政策宣传、培训，提高企业学习、理解、运用政策的能力。积极开展农产品加工企业的展销推优工作。通过组织企业参加各种展示、展销、推介活动，利用电视、广播、报纸、网络等媒体，推介品牌、宣传品牌，扩大品牌企业的知名度，将品牌优势转化为市场优势，实现品牌效益。对促进农产品加工业发展有重大贡献的企业及专业技术人员和管理人员，给予表彰和奖励。

云南省农产品加工业

云南省乡镇企业局

一、发展现状

“十五”以来，云南省农产品加工企业发展迅猛，除烟草加工、蔗糖加工外，茶叶加工、野生食用菌加工、花卉、生物产业得以长足发展和突显。“十五”期间，全省乡镇农产品加工企业67 600户，从业人员306 731人，农产品加工企业完成总产值、增加值、上缴税金分别为253.8亿元、54.8亿元、6.1亿元，分别占全部乡镇工业的21.1%、21.2%、15.5%。主要发展特点是：

1. *立足资源优势，不断壮大农产品加工实力* 伴随着种养殖业规模化生产发展，一批以规模农产品、绿色生物资源基地为依托的农特产品加工业应运而生，逐渐成为云南省经济发展颇具活力的增长点。初步形成了粮油、蔗糖、茶叶、畜禽、乳品、蔬菜、果品、饮料、调味品、食用菌、薯类、麻丝、林竹、橡胶和生物制药15个具有加工潜力的重点产业。农产品加工业通过调整产业布局，逐步围绕优势农产品资源富集区、交通带、小城镇及各类特色园区建成了一系列农特产品加工聚集区，进一步提升全省农产品加工业发展水平，形成了曲靖马铃薯加工、思茅茶叶加工、大理野生菌出口加工、西双版纳天然橡胶加工、宣威特色畜产品加工、元谋无公害特色蔬菜加工、呈贡鲜切花加工、文山三七深加工、砚山辣椒加工、楚雄生物制药加工、大理乳业加工、临沧蔗糖加工、德宏柠檬咖啡加工等十多个农特产品加工业基地和产业聚集区，农产品加工业产值占全省农产品加工业产值65%以上，其中云南元谋无公害特色蔬菜加工基地等6个基地被农业部确定为“全国农产品加工示范基地”；云南丰瑞油脂公司等14个企业被农业部命名为“全国农产品加工示范企业”；盘龙云海药业公司、元江万绿生物（集团）公司、宏斌绿色食品公司等12个企业被农业部认定为“农产品加工技术创新机构”企业；一批企业与大专院校、科研院所建立了长期稳定的合作关系；产品加工质量大幅提升，

190多个企业通过ISO9000等体系认证，31个农产品加工企业的63种产品通过绿色食品认证，5个企业的16种产品获得有机食品认证；26个企业的27个产品被评为云南省名牌产品。这些企业成为全省农产品加工产业的中坚力量，为把云南省建成全国重要的生物资源开发创新基地和绿色农产品加工出口基地打下了良好基础。

2. 围绕资源调整结构，实现经济可持续发展 云南素有有色金属王国和植物王国之称。长期以来，云南乡镇企业的发展主要围绕矿产开采和冶炼加工业为主，通过不断调整和完善，本省丰富的生物和农特产品可再生资源优势得到逐步开发，乡镇企业产业结构不断提升，逐步向发展绿色经济可持续发展产业迈进。烟、糖、茶、胶等云南传统农产品加工业产品产量大幅增长，其中，卷烟产量由2000年的612.7万箱发展到2005年的631.47万箱；茶叶产量由7.9万t发展到11.59万t；橡胶产量由17.00万t发展到24.03万t，烟、糖、茶、胶已经发展成全国重要的加工业基地，工业基础得到进一步巩固。另外，林产品、麻丝、植物药加工等一批新成长起来的产业发展较快。人造板产量由2000年的44.80万m^3发展到2005年的78.00万m^3；机制纸及纸板由22.30万t发展到28.88万t；中成药由5 175t发展到8 664t。农产品加工业的发展，对提高农产品转化增值水平，增加农民就业和农民收入起到关键性作用。2005年，全省农产品加工业实现总产值349亿元，占全部工业总产值的16%；增加值91.5亿元，占全部工业增加值的9.47%；实缴税金4.53亿元，占工业税收的1.4%；农产品加工转化率33.87%。以农产品加工为龙头的生物产业迅猛发展，农产品加工企业占全省工业企业总数的49.9%，从业人员占全省乡镇企业从业人员的24.4%，完成增加值、总产值、上缴增值税，分别占全省乡镇工业总数的22.9%、23.2%、20.8%。

二、主要做法和经验

1. 规划引导，整体推进 农产品加工业要快速、协调发展，必须统筹规划全行业发展。云南省乡镇企业局根据农业部乡镇企业局和省政府有关要求，组织编制了《云南省“十一五”农产品加工业发展规划》，通过市场供需状况、资源优势情况，规划、引导，制定发展规划和政策，明确产业发展方向，确定发展的目标，打破行政区划限制，加强地区合作，形成合理产业布局，推进产业的科学化、集约化、可持续化发展。根据《中共云南省委、云南省人民政府关于加快县域经济发展的决定》，制定了实施意见，组织编制了《云南省县域工业特色产业发展规划》。还组织制定了《云南省乡镇企业“十一五”发展规划》、《云南省“十一五”丝麻产业发展规划》，根据新型工业化发展要求特编制了2005—2020年《云南省新型工业化烟草及配套产业发展规划》、《云南省新型工业化医药产业发展规划》、《云南新型工业化农特产品加工业发展规划》、《云南省新型工业化造纸工业发展规划》、《云南省生物能源——燃料乙醇发展规划》，确定了本省农产品加工业不同时期发展目标和重点，明确了产业发展的思路，布局发展方向。对各主要产业，分别从重点发展方向、重点产品、重点项目等方面进行了细化，打破行政区划界线，综合各地优势，提出了相应发展要求和指导意见。

2. 措施到位，推进发展 为推进云南省农产品加工业的发展，根据农业部《农产品加工推进行动》，省局组织制定和实施了“云南省优势农产品加工推进工程”，年初下发了《2006年云南省农产品加工工作指导意见》，全面部署和落实了本省2006年农产品加工工作的任务；为进一步推进6个国家农产品加工基地发展，省局印发了《云南省农产品加工示范基地规划要点》，指导基地科学规划，完善措施；为培育重点骨干企业，印发了《云南省加快县域工业特色产业重点企业发展指导意见》，组织评定了“云南100户重点农产品加工企业”，围绕重点企业发展，加大了对重点骨干企业的扶持力度；为及时了解本省农产品加工业发展情况，开始了对本省116个重点农产品加工企业进行直报监测统计工作。

3. 聚集发展，效果显著 农产品加工业的聚集发展，能充分发挥基地和园区的聚集效应，农特产品加工企业的集约化经营水平将得以有效提高。云南省通过优化重组现有较分散的乡镇企业园区和各类特色园区，使各类产业集聚区逐步形成科技企业孵化区、新型产业成长区和农村富余劳动力容纳区。通过引导和发展各加工园区技术进步投入不断加大，生物资源开发创新和农产品加工业技术进步投资占全省乡镇企业固定资产投资的20%以上，盘龙云海药业公司、元江万绿生物（集团）公司、宏斌绿色食品公司等12个企业被农业部认定为“农产品加工技术创新机构”企业，永胜映华植物化工（集团）有限公司技术中心等技术中心通过了省级认定；一批企业与大专院校、科研院所与产业集聚园区建立了长期稳定的合作关系。园区和加工基地中的企业总体上产品质量大幅提升，有31个农产品加工企业的63种产品通过绿色食品认证，5个企业的16种产品获得有机食品认证。元谋县生物创新科技园区内共有36个农产品加工企业，其中有21个企业25个产品获得无公害农产品认证、3个无公害蔬菜品种获得“云南名牌产品”称号，36个企业共创产值3.5亿元，占全县工业总产值7.4亿元的47.3%；上缴税金343万元，占全县工业税收2 118万元的16.2%；带动5万农户种植果蔬10khm²，支付农产品原料款2.5亿元。思茅市有世界闻名的大叶种普洱茶，在充分利用当地种植规模优势基础上，大力地促进了茶叶加工基地建设，2005年底全市拥有茶园面积72 khm²，茶叶年产量达3.8万t，总产值达10.2亿元，20.4万农户106万农民种茶，人均茶叶收入660.4元，被农业部确定为全国农产品加工业示范基地。祥云县刘厂镇充分利用交通区位优势和本地充裕的廉价劳动力，大力发展野生食用菌加工业。经过多年的努力，以野生食用菌加工为主的农产品加工业有了较快的发展，初步实现了由家庭作坊式加工向连接国际市场的规模化加工企业的跨越式发展，成为云南省最大的野生食用菌收购、加工、出口的集散地，被农业部确定为“野生食用菌加工示范基地”。镇内集聚野生食用菌加工企业、加工贸易户150多个，对省内各地采集的野生食用菌进行收购，并在镇内集中加工，已逐步形成了野生食用菌加工产业集群。成功开发出100多种野生食用菌加工技术，对松茸、牛肝菌、木耳、羊肚菌、鸡油菌及杂菌等50多种珍贵可口的美味野生食用菌进行批量加工。2005年加工野生食用菌7 050t，产值1.7亿元，产品远销日本、泰国、法国、美国、荷兰、意大利、德国、加拿大等10多个国家，直接出口创汇近1 000万美元，加工园区每年吸纳农村富余劳动力上万人，增加农民收入5 000多万元，极大地拓展了农村富余劳动力就业空间，通过产业集聚发展，在当地形成了一个集野生食用菌产供销一条龙的生产加工销售基地，有力地促进了全镇经济社会的快速、协调发展。

4. *整合资源、做大做强* 先后编制了糖、茶、胶三大行业整合方案。糖业整合方案经省政府批准后，实施推进工作较快，效果也比较好，新组建的英茂股份公司、云南力量生物制品公司和双江糖业三大公司产量超过全省糖产量的50%，企业数由78个整合到40个左右，仅云南力量生物制品公司下属企业数由过去的3个扩大到15个；在橡胶整合上，云南天然橡胶集团公司完成了云南农垦系统橡胶的整合工作；在乳制品行业，云南较有名气的蝶泉、雪兰等品牌被新希望集团整合；在制药、食品、茶叶等行业也进行了一批企业的整合。通过行业整合提高了产业的集中度，提升了品牌价值，企业优势得到互补、资源得到充分利用，整个行业正逐步走上良性循环轨道。

三、存在的主要问题

1. *科技水平低，产业链条短* 云南省农产品加工企业普遍存在着新产品开发能力弱、技术装备落后的突出问题。农产品加工业中除烟草和制药产业技术水平相对较高外，包括食糖、茶叶、橡胶、淀粉、果蔬加工在内的大部分农产工业品仍处于粗加工阶段，由于产品的科技含量低，产品的内在质量、包装、卫生水平等质量要求与国外同类产品相比存在差距，加工制品科技含量低，精深加工品种少，产品市场竞争力弱。另外，缺乏适应农产品加工业发展的科研储备和技术支撑，企业发展后劲不足。

2. *龙头企业少，带动能力弱* 2005年，全省规模以上农产品加工企业只有500个，由于规模小，先进技术推广、产品开发、市场营销和企业管理方面都存在许多差距，龙头企业对整个产业的带动力弱。在许多企业生产系统的环节中没有形成与协会和农户的有效连接机制，造成产业的紧密度不高，价格不稳定，原料得不到保障等问题，影响了整个产业的发展，龙头企业对产业带动力弱，龙头企业优势没有得到充分发挥。

3. *流动资金缺乏，影响到企业正常生产* 由于农产品加工季节性较强，原料收购期企业流动资金需求量大，而农产品加工企业大多地处县乡，受银行营业网点收缩影响，企业流动资金贷款十分困难，有的企业有巨额订单，而无法保证生产情况十分突出。

4. *人才短缺，制约企业做大做强* 由于大部分农产品加工企业地处边远农村，企业急需的技术人才及管理人才招聘较为困难，尤其是技术创新技术人才、企业生产经营管理人才及市场营销人才严重缺乏，直接影响农产品加工企业发展水平提高。

5. *产业外向度低，产品出口量小* 包括卷烟产品在内的大部分农产加工品出口量不大，国际贸易额比重低，在现有的农产加工企业中“三资”企业少，本地企业“走出去”从事营销或者经营农产品加工的不多，国外资金、技术、人才和管理在云南省农产品加工企业中份额小。

四、主要措施

1. *壮大规模，推进农产品加工业发展* 一是要依靠科技进步和加强管理提升现有企业的市场竞争力，做大做强一批龙头骨干企业，规模以上企业户数要比“十五”末提高8～10个百分点、企业综合效益提高15个百分点。二是加快培育一批拉动能力大、辐射范围广、市场竞争能力强的重点骨干企业。三是突出大（规模大）、高（技术水平高、附加值高）、外（外向型）、多（多种所有制、多形式）、新（新产品）。采用多种经营模式，使龙头企业与广大农户之间结成风险共担、利益均沾的经济共同体。

2. 优化结构，推进农产品精深加工　一是要围绕《云南省优势农产品区域布局规划》，重点加快畜产品、马铃薯、蚕桑、橡胶、麻类、林产品等18类优势农产品加工业发展，到2010年乡镇企业农产品加工业产值力争突破1 000亿元，年均增长16%；优势农产品加工转化率达到55%以上。二是依靠优势资源和已经形成的加工能力，在重点加工业产区（带）培植200个重点骨干乡镇企业，建立15个具有相当规模和水平的农产品加工示范基地，培植和扶持一批上亿元的骨干龙头企业。三是注重提高加工产品的档次和附加值，引导加工企业在深加工和精加工上下功夫，广泛运用新技术、新工艺、新设备，提高质量和效益。特别是要抓好产品质量安全管理，实行标准化生产和名牌带动，大力开发名特优新产品，提高产品市场竞争力。

3. 大力发展各类中介组织，优化农业产业化组织结构，提高农民组织化程度　一是积极发展各种形式的农产品行业协会。二是加强监督管理，使各类中介组织真正成为连接农户与龙头企业、农户与市场的桥梁与纽带。三是抓紧制定农民专业合作经济组织管理法规，明确合作组织的法人地位，制定相应的扶持政策。四是加强对农户的产前、产中、产后服务，发挥桥梁与纽带以及龙头带动作用。

4. 加快建立推进农产品加工企业投融资新机制，增强龙头企业发展后劲　一是按照农产品加工业发展的客观要求，优化融资环境，建立“企业和农户投入为主体、社会投入为补充，政府投入为导向”的投资新机制。二是充分发挥企业的投资主体作用，引导各类社会资金，向农产品加工产业聚集。三是做好银政、银企合作工作，加强企业信誉建设，改善金融服务。

5. 全面开放，加大招商引资力度　凡是国家产业政策允许的项目和领域，允许各种资本包括国外资本进入，鼓励跨地区或者跨国进行原料基地建设，鼓励非农产品加工企业通过独资、参股、控股等形式进入农产品加工领域，鼓励跨地区之间的兼并、联合与重组，继续推进产业整合工作，支持有条件的企业大胆“走出去”闯市场，加大招商引资力度，实现全方位的对外开放，全面提高云南省农产品加工业的外向水平。

6. 树立品牌，加大特色产品开发　继续加大云南地方特色产品的开发力度，从资源、示范区布局以及产品设计和品牌宣传上从云南特色出发，同时大力引进国外先进技术和工艺设备，提高产品档次。对于15个农产品加工示范区的布局和产业定位也要突出区位优势，避免低水平重复建设。县域经济的发展也要突出地方特色，通过特色产品占领市场份额，树立云南品牌形象。

西藏自治区农畜产品加工业

西藏自治区乡镇企业局

一、发展现状

2005年，全区农畜产品加工企业总产值约9亿元，销售收入8.4亿元，利税总额2.9亿元。据2003年全区农畜产品加工业调查的统计表明，全区共有资产总额在50万元以上的企业66个，从业人员3 499人，企业总产值达4.12亿元。根据资产规模分类，有总资产上亿元的企业1个，上千万元的企业22个，百万元的企业32个，50万～100万元的企业11个；根据经济成分分类，有国有企业14个，股份制企业18个，集体企业21个，民营企业13个；根据产业分类，有粮油（蔬菜）加工（流通）企业26个、畜产品加工（流通）企业34个、饮品加工企业6个。“十五”以来，在中央第四次西藏工作座谈会精神的指导下，在自治区党委和政府的正确领导下，全区农畜产品加工业取得了良好的发展成就。

1. 农畜产品加工企业经济效益稳步提高　2003年与2000年相比，农畜产品加工企业产值增长36%，销售收入增长43%，利税增长47%。

2. 加工企业规模扩大，实力增强　2002年至

2005年，自治区先后认定自治区级农业产业化龙头企业13个，其中农畜产品加工企业达7个。7个企业固定资产总额达10亿元，产值达3亿元，分别占全区农畜产品加工企业固定资产和产值总额的38%和40%。

3. 以特色资源为依托的农畜产品加工企业发展迅速　近年来，依托特色资源、推进产品加工、创建特色竞争优势，成为农畜产品加工企业发展的主要趋势。高原之宝牦牛乳业股份有限公司、银河股份有限公司、曲登尼玛矿泉水厂等企业，无一不是靠特色产业起家、靠特色产品开辟市场。

4. 农畜产品加工企业的所有制结构发生明显变化　民营企业开始成为农畜产品加工业发展的重要力量，涌现出了达氏集团、龙湖工贸有限公司、阳光生物有限公司等一批具有较雄厚的经济实力和较强竞争能力的龙头企业。

5. 农畜产品加工业对推动农牧业和农牧区经济结构调整，增加农牧民收入的作用初步显现　高原之宝牦牛乳业股份有限公司与城关区400个奶牛养殖户签订了长期购奶合同，保证敞开收购牛奶，投产以来已向奶牛养殖户支付购奶款160多万元，平均每户近4 000元；龙湖工贸有限公司与农户签订了12 590t的优质粮食收购合同，达氏集团与农户签订了3 900余t的优质油菜收购合同；银河科技发展股份有限公司与堆龙德庆、尼木、江孜等县签订了800t青稞收购协议，每吨青稞收购价达1 660元，为农民增收249万元。通过农畜产品加工企业的带动，紧密了生产与市场的衔接，解决了农畜产品“卖难”问题，拓宽了农牧民的增收渠道。

二、存在的主要问题

西藏农畜产品加工业与全国水平相比差距较大。农畜产品加工率还不到10 %；农畜产品加工业产值与农林牧渔业总产值的比例只有0.1∶1。总体上讲，农畜产品加工业还处在起步阶段，存在不少问题和困难。主要表现在：

1. 缺乏具有较强经济实力和带动能力的龙头企业　农畜产品加工企业绝大多数规模较小，主体上处在传统手工和家庭作坊式的经营水平，企业实力不强，对农牧民增收和地方经济发展的带动能力十分有限。全区66个规模农畜产品加工企业连接基地80khm^2，辐射连接农户10万户，企业户均销售收入仅有467万元。

2. 企业技术装备落后，科技基础薄弱，创新发展的后劲不足　现有的绝大多数企业，主要为内地的深加工企业提供初级产品，设备简陋，劳动生产率低下。企业缺乏产品自主开发能力，新工艺、新技术、新材料的应用程度低，加工标准和质量控制体系不健全。企业职工素质较低，技术人才严重短缺，个别企业引进的先进设备亦因人员素质问题，无法高效运转甚至闲置，影响了企业经济效益的提高。

3. 对农畜产品加工业的投资不足，扶持力度有待进一步加强　“十五”头两年，以农畜产品加工业为主的轻工业固定资产投资仅1.98亿元，仅占全社会固定资产投资的1%左右。在投资、信贷、税收等方面，对农畜产品加工业的扶持政策较少，从事农畜产品加工的企业与从事其他产品生产的企业相比没有明显的政策优势，影响了投资者的积极性。

4. 缺乏统一规划和统一指导　农畜产品加工业从原料生产到加工管理分散，尚未形成完整有效的管理体系，没有明确的行政主管部门，造成管理体制不顺，产前、产中、产后脱节。对农畜产品加工企业缺乏必要的宏观指导和信息服务，致使一些产品滞后于市场需求和消费结构的变化，一些企业在低水平上盲目扩张，出现较大的亏损。

5. 缺乏基地的有力支撑，产业化带动面窄　农畜产品加工业与农牧业原料基地连接不紧密，企业与农牧户之间没有建立稳定的产销关系，未确立利益共享、风险共担的机制。分散的农牧业生产提供的原料，在品种、品质、规格等方面不适应企业的要求，原料生产规模化、专业化、标准化程度低，农畜产品加工业发展缺乏稳定可靠的原料保障。

三、政策措施

1. 提高认识，统一思想　农畜产品加工业是拉动国民经济发展的重要产业，是农牧业结构调整的重要带动力量，是增加农牧民收入的有效手段，是实现传统农牧业向现代农牧业转变的突破口，是促进农村工业化、城镇化和现代化的重要途径。各级各部门要牢固树立发展农畜产品加工业就是发展农牧业和农牧区经济，扶持农畜产品加工业就是扶持农牧民的观念，切实把农畜产品加工业摆在重要位置，加大工作力度，实现加快发展。

2. 理顺和强化职能，搞好指导服务　针对本区农畜产品加工业工作职能不明确，缺少宏观管理部门的实际，要抓紧成立全区农畜产品加工业发展领导小组，在自治区行政主管部门组织专人设立领导小组办公室。领导小组及办公室全面负责农畜产品加工业发展的组织领导、协调指导、制定政策、招商引资、经营监管、信息服务等工作。

3. 制定规划，明确目标　农畜产品加工业列入自治区“十一五”经济社会发展总体规划，并作为重大支柱产业进行研究和部署。同时，根据新形势发展要求，认真研究制定农畜产品加工业发展规划，明确工作思路、发展目标、区域布局、重点行业及对策措施，加大规划的落实力度，充分发挥农畜产品加工业在推进农牧区经济结构战略性调整、增加农牧民收入、实现农牧业现代化等方面的重大作用。

4. 制定政策，优化环境　认真抓好现有支持农业产业化龙头企业和农畜产品加工企业的政策落实，确保各项政策落实到位。特别是针对本区农畜产品加工企业的原料是从农户手中收购，企业因无法取得增值税发票而不能享受抵扣进项税的情况，税收部门应根据企业实际收购农畜产品及价格在企业缴纳增值税时按规定予以抵扣进项税。要在防范金融风险、保证信贷安全的前提下，加强对农畜产品加工企业的信贷支持工作，实行企业授信等级制度，适当放宽抵押担保条件，简化审批手续。拓宽农畜产品加工企业融资渠道，鼓励和支持农畜产品加工企业利用资本市场筹集发展资金。

陕西省农产品加工业

陕西省乡镇企业局

一、发展现状

2005年，全省乡镇企业实现营业收入2 774.5亿元，增加值735.8亿元，工业增加值396.4亿元，利润总额156.3亿元，实缴税金49.8亿元，出口交货值16.3亿元，从业人员达到418.2万人，支付工资总额210.1亿元。乡镇企业中的农产品加工业也得到了发展壮大。据2005年统计，全省乡镇企业农产品加工企业11.44万个，从业人员62万人，实现营业收入502.7亿元。农产品加工业实现营业收入、从业人员分别占到全省乡镇工业企业的36.1%和37.8%。主要特点是：

1. 形成了一批农产品加工骨干行业　全省乡镇企业农产品加工业涉及20多个行业，粮油及饲料加工、乳品制造业、果汁加工、纺织、竹藤、棕草制品、造纸等行业成为乡镇企业农产品加工业最大的行业。其中粮油及饲料加工业营业收入均超过100亿元。在这些骨干行业中，果汁、乳品业优势较大。果汁加工企业39个，从业人员2 168人，年产果汁20.8万t，转化果类产量150万t；乳品加工企业178个，从业人员9 944多人，年转化鲜奶量200多万t。

2. 培育了一大批龙头企业和名牌产品　近年来，农产品加工业逐步发展壮大，涌现了一批在省内外有一定影响力的骨干龙头企业和名牌产品。2005年，全省规模以上农产品加工乡镇企业达到315个。乡镇企业中有农业产业化国家重点龙头企业11个，省级农业产业化重点龙头企业60个。乳品、果汁、造纸、饲料等7个产品被评为陕西省名牌产品，西安银桥股份有限公司生产的奶粉被评为中国名牌产品和中国驰名商标。

3. 发挥区域优势，建设农产品加工基地　关中地区依托粮食、果业、畜牧等优势资源，建设关中农产品加工基地，粮食加工、饲料加工、乳品加工、果汁加工等在全省占绝对优势，果汁占全省96.3%，饲料加工占全省的77.1%，乳制品占全省的95.4%。陕南地区依托生物资源，形成了中药材、茶叶、蚕桑加工、食用菌等加工基地。陕北地区依托红枣、杂粮、薯类等优势资源，形成了豆制品、粉条、小杂粮精深加工基地。

4. 农产品加工业外向化趋势明显　2005年，全省乡镇企业农产品加工业出口创汇企业27个，完成出口交货值3.3亿元，占全省乡镇企业出口交货值的20.2%。2005年，全省乡镇企业招商引资项目162个，合同或协议引进资金70亿元，其中农产品加工企业分别占到48%和56%。

5. 加快了农产品资源的转化，促进了农民增收　据测算，2005年全省乡镇企业粮食加工量占全省粮食总量的80%，生产食用油转化油料占全省油料总量60%，加工乳品转化奶类量占全省奶类总量的68%，加工果汁量占到全省果汁总量的71%。通过加工转化，解决了农民“卖难”问题。全省农民人均从乡镇企业农产品中得到的工资性收入，占到全省农民人均纯收入的11%。一些发展快的乡村，农民人均纯收入的50%以上来自乡镇企业农产品加工业的贡献。

6. *农产品加工示范基地快速发展，起到了示范引导作用*　2005年，农业部农产品加工业领导小组确认于陕西扶风、兴平、三原等3个基地为全国农产品加工业示范基地，2005年3个基地内农产品加工企业实现营业收入48.9亿元，完成利税12.8亿元，分别比2004年增长21%、18.5%。同时，各基地加大了基础设施的建设力度，水、电、路、通信均直通企业，强化服务意识，为入园农产品加工企业提供优质高效的服务，为全省农产品加工基地的发展，树立了典型，起到了示范引导作用。

二、主要做法

1. *积极引导农民创办农产品加工企业*　近两年来，经过深入调研，提出加快催生小企业，推进农民工业化创业行动，引导农民充分利用和发挥本省农产品数量多、品种多、原料供应丰富、深度加工潜力巨大的优势，把发展农产品加工业作为农民工业化创业的一项紧迫任务。2005年，全省新增乡镇企业3.38万个，其中新增农产品加工企业6 000多个。

2. *抓好农产品加工业重点项目建设*　每年在各市申报的基础上，筛选确定50个投资在1 000万元以上的农产品加工建设项目，作为全省乡镇企业的重点建设项目，实行逐级领导包抓责任制，落实专人负责跟踪服务，协调解决项目建设中的有关问题，促进项目尽快建成投产。2005年，有38个农产品加工项目建成投产，进一步壮大了全省乡镇企业农产品加工业的实力。

3. *缓解农产品加工企业融资难问题*　近年来，先后与人民银行西安分行共同组织了“金融专家乡镇企业行”等活动，邀请金融机构的专家重点考察农产品加工企业，使银企面对面进行沟通与了解，金融机构加深了对乡镇企业农产品加工业的了解，增强了投贷的信心，为构建新型银企关系做了有益探索。2005年4月份，与人民银行西安分行又共同组织金融机构与乡镇企业座谈及项目推介活动，进一步加强了银企双方的了解与合作，其中有23个农产品加工项目与银行进行接触洽谈，达成协议贷款1亿多元，解决了部分企业资金短缺问题。

4. *大力开展对外合作与交流*　2003年以来，先后组织各级主管部门和农产品加工企业，约350多人次去东北、西北、东部沿海等地寻求项目合作，开拓市场；组织150多人次赴俄罗斯、东南亚、南非等国家和地区开展国际交流，寻求发展商机。2005年6月，组织企业到新加坡举办经贸洽谈会，促成了农业产业化国家重点龙头企业、西部最大的浓缩苹果汁加工企业——陕西恒兴果汁饮料有限公司与新加坡佳福公司的合作。不但引进了外资，使恒兴的浓缩果汁加工主业得到了巩固和加强，而且双方将在果渣饲料加工和果糖提取方面开展合作，进一步提高陕西省苹果的综合加工利用能力。

5. *建立农产品加工企业联系制度*　结合新时期新形势下农产品加工业的发展需要，转变工作职能，落实服务责任，建立企业联系制度。2004年以来，实施局机关各处室联系地市，干部联系重点农产品加工企业的包联制度，确定领导挂帅，处室包干，责任到人，定期联系沟通，协调解决问题。在陕西省乡镇企业（中小企业）信息网上设立了专栏，为农产品加工企业提供项目咨询、政策导向、产品推介等服务。

6. *加大财政扶持力度*　为了调动农产品加工企业的发展积极性，充分发挥财政资金的政策导向作用，近年来，每年从全省乡镇企业发展专项资金中拿出300余万元，用于农产品加工企业流动资金贷款和技术改造项目贷款贴息，初步统计，“十五”期间，支持了100多个农产品加工企业，累计贴息达1 600多万元，有力地支持了全省乡镇企业农产品加工业的发展。同时，积极协助农产品加工企业争取西部外经贸发展资金、中小企业市场开拓资金和中小企业专项扶持资金等中央和省级财政扶持，使企业最大限度地享受到各级财政对农产品加工业的支持政策。

三、存在的主要问题

1. *由于各地经济发展水平上的差异，基地建设的规模和档次有着明显的差距*　在一些经济发展较快、农产品加工基地建设起步较早的地方，从思想认识、发展思路、品牌和市场意识等方面都已经形成良性循环，规模扩大，主导产业明显。而经济欠发达、基地建设起步迟的地方，基地示范带动性不强，尚处于摸索阶段。

2. *农产品深度开发和加工滞后，基地建设产业化水平有待提高*　一是龙头企业规模偏小，技术落后，农产品深加工滞后，导致加工增值能力低，带动辐射能力不够强。二是农民组织化程度还不高，企业与农户关系还不够紧密。相当一部分农业企业与基地农户之间的关系是松散型的，没有形成紧密的经济利益共同体，运作不规范。

3. 农产品加工基地建设的扶持政策没有完全到位 一是土地问题。各地都在积极探索土地流转机制，但因缺乏有效的法律和政策依托，制约了土地的合理流转。二是信贷问题。农产品加工基地建设需要大量的资金支持，但农户和龙头企业的融资环境较差，企业贷款困难依然比较普遍，一些农产品的加工转化项目苦于缺乏资金而不能实施。三是扶持问题。近年来，各级财政对农产品加工龙头企业的支持较多，但对农产品加工基地的支持较少，造成了各地建设农产品加工基地的积极性不高，建设资金短缺等问题。

4. 行业管理不适应市场形势发展要求 管理体制不顺，缺乏统一规划和组织协调，造成企业盲目布点，阻碍了农产品加工业的发展。

四、主要措施

1. 以项目建设为着力点，加快发展一批农产品加工小企业 发挥本省农产品资源优势，以项目为载体，以创办小企业、增加新岗位、促进农民增收为重点，加强创业培训，帮助农民掌握创业知识，更新就业观念，增强创业本领，同时鼓励农民外出打工、返乡创业，积极投身创业大潮，提高创业成功率，创办一批具有地域特色优势的农产品加工小企业，推进农产品加工企业总量扩张，实现农产品加工业跨越式发展。

2. 典型引路，发展培育一大批农产品加工示范企业 引导乡镇企业采取多种形式，加快发展，实现扩张，发挥龙头带动作用。年内将组织召开一次农产品加工现场会议，学习先进，推广经验。同时，围绕县域经济发展和农业产业化的要求，树立一批典型，抓好一批以农产品加工业为主导产业的示范村、镇，努力打造具有陕西区域特色的“一村一品”；命名百强农产品加工龙头企业。

3. 落实扶持政策，加大资金投入 在现有财政扶持资金的基础上，今后每年再新增100万元，用于农产品加工企业的政策性贴息。同时在引导企业采取多种形式增加资金投入的同时，积极争取信贷支持。将与人民银行西安分行、省农业银行等金融机构联合，着力推荐一批农产品加工项目，争取农产品加工基地建设资金。

4. 大力发展农产品加工业基地 着力围绕粮食、油料、果品、肉类、蛋奶、蔬菜、土特产品等优势资源，引导企业引进新技术、新工艺，进行深精加工、系列开发，提升农产品加工业发展水平。依托果汁、乳品、面粉、淀粉、方便面、食用油、饲料、中药材等优势产业，培育一批省级农业产业化重点龙头企业和农产品加工业示范企业。选择与资源和市场需求配套，已初步形成产业集聚和经济优势的农产品加工区域，建设一批农产品加工示范基地。

5. 加强对外交流合作，提升农产品加工水平 2006年，组织农产品加工龙头企业的负责人去国外或外省考察学习，拓展视野，寻找商机，以优势资源和潜力项目吸引更多的外商到陕西投资农产品加工业。

甘肃省农产品加工业

甘肃省乡镇企业局

一、发展现状

近年来，甘肃省乡镇企业农产品加工业紧紧围绕农产品加工、贮藏、保鲜、运销和基础设施配套等重点，加大工作力度，加强扶持引导，在促进农业产业化经营、推动地方工业发展、带动农村小城镇建设和拓宽农民增收渠道等方面发挥了积极作用。截止到2005年底，全省乡镇企业农产品加工企业已发展到4.3万个，从业人员26万人，当年完成增加值60.8亿元，总产值247.6亿元，利润总额14.4亿元，上缴税金3.8亿元，完成出口交货值11亿元，农产品加工业增加值已占到全省乡镇企业工业增加值的37.8%，占全省农业增加值的17%。全省规模以上农产品加工企业317个，主要集中在粮食、畜产品、蔬菜加工、马铃薯及玉米淀粉加工、酒类及饲料加工等领域，企业年实际加工量约760多万t，农产品加工转化率达到34.8%。农产品加工业已成为本省国民经济新的增长点。农产品加工企业的迅速发展，推动了地方特色产业发展和农村经济结构调整，形成了一些有特色、有优势的产业集群，如黄羊镇面粉产业，张掖、酒泉的草产业、制种产业和果蔬加工产业，定西的马铃薯产业，河西地区及白银的啤酒原料产业等，都形成了一定的群体规模，部分骨干企业正在向规模化、集约化经营发展，总体呈现出良好的发展势头，初步形成了具有地方特色的区域产业带，成为推动区域经济发展的新的增长点，在县域经济和农村经济发展中的带动作用日益凸显。主要特点是：

1. **坚持项目带动，在扩大产业规模、促进产业集聚上求突破** 近年来，把发展以农产品加工为主的农业产业化龙头企业作为乡镇企业发展的主攻方向，使农产品加工项目和农产品的储藏、保鲜和营销项目成为乡镇企业项目建设的重点。全省各类农产品加工企业加工能力达到 1 100 万 t。仅 2005 年，全省共有 708 个农产品加工项目开工建设，实际完成投资 33.5 亿元，这两项指标都占全省乡镇企业项目建设数和实际完成投资额的 30%以上，有 495 个项目建成投产。

2. **坚持开放开发，在招商引资和发展外向型经济上求突破** 为了切实解决上项目缺资金这一困扰乡镇企业发展的瓶颈问题，积极组织企业走出去、请进来，坚持以开放促发展。在省委、省政府和农业部的重视和支持下，2001 年以来，在兰州、天水、武威、酒泉、白银先后成功举办了五届全国乡镇企业贸洽会，并每年都组团参加全国性的经贸洽谈活动，取得了丰硕成果。特别是五届贸洽会，每届都有大批合作项目签约，成为甘肃省乡镇企业开放开发和招商引资的重要平台。2006 年，白银全国乡镇企业贸洽会签约项目达到 620 个，总投资 355 亿元，其中农产品加工项目 181 个，占到 29%，农产品加工项目总投资 55 亿元，占到 16%。“十五”期间，全省乡镇企业共引进资金 116.9 亿元，其中相当大的部分投入到了农产品加工业。引进资金已经成为农产品加工业的重要资金来源。2005 年，全省农产品出口 1.58 亿美元，占全省出口总值的 14%，比 2004 年增长 43%。庆阳市白瓜子产品占全国出口总量的 70%、占全球市场份额的 40%。

3. **坚持农业产业化经营，在培植龙头企业发展上求突破** “十五”期间，把乡镇企业的发展与农业产业化相结合，着重扶持和引导农产品加工龙头企业的发展，取得了较好的成效，使上规模、上水平、上档次的农产品加工企业不断增多。到 2005 年底，全省乡镇企业中，规模以上农产品加工企业发展到 317 个。兰州黄河企业集团公司和甘肃荣华实业集团公司 2 个企业成功上市，有 7 个企业被列入农业产业化国家重点龙头企业，占到全省农业产业化国家重点企业总数 13 个的一半以上，56 个乡镇企业被列入省级农业产业化重点龙头企业，占到总数的 2/3，有 13 个企业被农业部命名为第一批全国农产品加工业示范企业，初步形成了乡镇企业与农业产业化相互促进、共同发展的良好格局。

4. **坚持政策推动和正确引导，在促进农产品加工业稳步发展上求突破** 在省委、省人大、省政府、省政协的重视、支持和省乡镇企业局的积极争取下，全省基本完成了乡镇企业、中小企业、非公经济管理职能的整合和机构调整工作，在省局机关设立了农业产业处，理顺了管理体制，加强了宏观引导。省政府办公厅批转了《甘肃省乡镇企业 2005—2007 农产品加工业发展规划》，省中小企业、乡镇企业局制定了《甘肃省乡镇企业、中小企业农产品示范基地（园区）命名及管理办法》、《甘肃省乡镇企业、中小企业农产品示范企业命名及管理办法》，通过规范引导，强化服务，夯实基础，促进农产品加工企业不断提高发展水平和质量。

在认真总结本省乡镇企业农产品加工业取得的成绩的同时，还应看到存在的一些不容忽视的困难和问题。一是农产品加工企业的整体素质还不高。绝大多数农产品加工企业规模小，技术水平低，产业链条短，市场竞争能力不强。二是企业与农户之间的利益连接机制还不够完善。多数企业和农户之间没有形成真正意义上的利益共同体。原料生产的品种品质结构不适应加工要求，缺乏农产品加工业发展需要的专用、优质原料，使农产品加工企业的发展规模受到影响。三是融资渠道不畅，资金严重不足。多数农产品加工企业自有资金不足和季节性收购原料所需流动资金多、资金占用时间长之间的矛盾突出。四是缺乏完善的中介服务机构。服务体系不健全，没有充分发挥各种行业协会、商会、中介机构等社会化服务组织的服务作用，缺少资产评估、项目咨询、人才培训、信息网络、产品检测、物流配送等服务组织，现有的中介组织的服务水平和服务质量满足不了发展的需要。

二、发展重点

1. **小麦加工业** 小麦加工业要以河西地区、沿黄地区、陇东地区、陇南（包括天水）旱塬和水川区等小麦主产区为布局优势区域，大力发展从专用小麦种植到小麦系列产品深加工的产业化经营。要对现有面粉加工企业进行技术改造和资产重组，扩大生产规模，提高产品技术含量；对出粉率低、能耗高的小型面粉厂适当控制发展，避免低水平重复建设；做大做强武威市黄羊红太阳面业集团等现有龙头企业，加大张掖市甘州区金鹰面粉加工厂20万t优质面粉生产线等10个重点项目的建设力度。3年内力争将武威市黄羊镇建成西部地区有影响的食品工业城。

2. 玉米加工业　要以河西地区、沿黄地区、城郊区、水川区以及天水、陇南、平凉、庆阳等玉米主产区为布局优势区域，加大高油玉米、优质蛋白玉米等新品种的培育与开发力度，开发多样化的玉米食品、多用途的工业原料及高附加值产品。做大做强甘肃荣华实业（集团）股份有限公司等现有龙头企业，加大甘肃新茂实业有限公司3万t异麦芽低聚糖生产线等8个重点项目的建设力度。3年内力争将武威市凉州区建成西北地区最大的以玉米为基本原料的生物化工基地。

3. 瓜果蔬菜加工业　以河西走廊、沿黄灌区、泾渭河流域、徽成盆地为主的蔬菜主产区，以河西和中部为主的瓜类主产区，以庆阳、平凉、天水为主的水果主产区，以天水、陇南为主的优质干果主产区为布局优势区域，逐步建立科学的采前管理、采后处理、贮运保鲜、加工、销售一条龙的瓜果蔬菜产业体系。依靠科技进步，发展无公害、无污染的绿色瓜果蔬菜基地，努力提高瓜果蔬菜品质。通过引进国外瓜果蔬菜商品化处理设备和技术，大力发展瓜果蔬菜精深加工和综合利用，重点发展瓜果汁及瓜果汁饮料、果酱、果粉、果酒、果蔬萃取保健食品以及具有出口潜力的果蔬罐头、速冻菜、脱水菜、蔬菜汁、蔬菜粉、蔬菜脆片、膨化蔬菜和保健蔬菜等。加快高档食用菌种、培养材料的研发，发展高档食用菌加工系列产品。3年内年销售收入5 000万元以上的瓜果蔬菜贮藏、保鲜、加工龙头企业力争达到8个。

4. 优质牧草加工业　紧紧围绕“草业大省，牧业强省”的总体构想，以河西地区、中部干旱地区以及陇东塬区为布局优势区域，大力发展优质牧草加工业，以满足新形势下养殖业发展的需要。优质牧草饲料加工业要向专用化、特种化、保健化和颗粒化方向发展。要引导乡镇企业充分利用本省丰富廉价的农作物秸秆资源，大力发展秸秆饲料加工业，努力提高农产品综合利用价值。3年内年销售收入2 000万元以上的优质牧草加工龙头企业力争达到3个。

5. 肉牛肉羊加工业　以河西地区及白银、平凉、庆阳、临夏、甘南等牛羊主产区为优势区域，大力发展牛羊系列产品深加工。肉类加工要向机械化屠宰、深加工、冷藏和综合开发利用的方向发展。鼓励肉食品加工企业进入食品配送领域，通过超市、连锁方式销售加工肉制品。注重骨、毛等废弃物的综合利用，减少环境污染，提高经济效益。3年内年销售收入5 000万元以上的牛羊肉加工龙头企业力争达到4个。

6. 啤酒原料加工业　以河西地区及白银、兰州为布局优势区域，依托兰州黄河啤酒集团公司等啤酒制造企业，发展啤酒原料产业，促进啤酒原料工业与啤酒制造业协调发展。做大做强甘肃莫高股份金昌啤酒原料分公司、白银华惠麦芽公司等现有啤酒原料加工龙头企业。3年内全省乡镇企业新增啤酒麦芽生产能力20万t，新增啤酒花生产能力1万t，力争将甘肃建成全国啤酒原料工业基地。

7. 马铃薯加工业　以定西、白银、兰州、天水、陇南等市（州）的马铃薯主产县（区）为布局优势区域，充分发挥已形成的脱毒种薯繁育体系作用，建成一批专用马铃薯加工原料基地，大力发展薯类淀粉、变性淀粉、马铃薯全粉、马铃薯复合薯片和速冻薯条等产品，实现多次加工转化增值，发展产业化经营。3年内力争将甘肃建成全国最大的马铃薯脱毒种薯基地、商品薯生产基地和马铃薯加工基地，构筑甘肃马铃薯产业发展新格局。

8. 中药材加工业　以定西、陇南、张掖、平凉等中药材主产区为布局优势区域，引导中药材的规范化与标准化种植，建设一批中药材种植基地，做好中药材系列保健品的研制和开发工作，加快实现中药提取物及中药饮片、浓缩颗粒的产业化，推进超临界二氧化碳萃取等先进技术在中药生产中的应用，发展高效、速效、长效和剂量小、毒性小、副作用小、使用方便的新型中药。3年内力争把甘肃建成全国有影响的中药材生产、加工、集散基地。

9. 乳产品产业　以兰州、临夏、甘南、酒泉、张掖、武威等地为优势区域，大力调整产品结构，狠抓鲜奶和乳品质量，开发适合不同消费群体的多层次、多样化的新产品。结合国家改善营养行动计划，科学引导消费，加快实施“学生饮用奶”计划等，使奶类、乳制品及其延伸制品进入广大农村居民的饮食范围，提高人均消费水平和生活质量。3年内年销售收入5 000万元以上的乳制品加工龙头企业力争达到5个。

在抓好以上九大产业的同时，对有一定基础，具有区域特色发展优势，发展前景广阔的皮革产业、制种产业、花卉产业也要加大扶持力度。

三、主要措施

1. 加强服务引导，夯实发展基础　根据甘肃省农产品加工业发展的实际和现状，当前和今后一个时期，重点在引导做好优势农产品产业布局的同时，进一步修订和完善产业发展规划，通过加大结构调整，充分发挥市场配置资源的作用，做大做强一批农产品加工企业，促进农产品加工产业带和示范基地的形成和发展。下一步省里还将协同有关部门陆续出台有关加强农产品加工质量安全、提高自主创新和研发能力等一系列的意见和办法，通过加强规范化管理和规划引导，进一步明确农产品加工业的目标、任务和发展方向，进一步加大对农产品加工企业的服务措施，引导促进全省农产品加工业的健康发展。

2. 加大扶持力度，做大做强农产品龙头企业 要进一步加大对农产品加工龙头企业的扶持力度，培植一批产业关联度大、带动能力强、市场竞争力强的大中型农产品加工龙头企业。要鼓励有条件的龙头企业进行技术改造和资产的优化重组，通过参股、控股、兼并、合并、租赁等形式，扩大规模，增强实力，发展成大型龙头企业集团。鼓励农产品加工骨干企业实行优质农产品基地建设、科研开发、生产加工、营销服务一体化经营。要按照“扶优、扶强、扶大”的原则，重点支持机制好、有竞争优势、辐射带动面广、与农户利益关系密切的龙头企业。各地要以当地的优势农产品加工企业为重点，采取推行项目建设责任制等一些行之有效的办法和措施，强化跟踪协调和服务，重点进行扶持和培育，使其尽快做大做强。

3. 拓宽融资渠道，增加资金投入 积极探索建立以企业投入为主体，财政、信贷、引资、农户和社会各方共同投入的多元化投入机制，加大对龙头企业的融资力度，拓宽融资渠道。一是加大招商引资力度。要进一步改善投资环境，积极组织具有特色的优势项目参与全国、全省各地举办的招商引资活动，积极引进域外资本。二是鼓励吸收社会闲散资金。通过项目推介，提供必要的政策和技术服务，引导民间资本运用股份合作制方式，把钱用在投资办企业上。支持农民以土地或集资入股，采取合资、合作、合伙等多种形式直接投资办企业。三是争取信贷、财政部门的资金支持。协调银行、信用社等金融组织按照“区别对待，择优扶持，效益优先”的原则，积极支持农产品加工龙头企业发展。四是鼓励有条件的企业通过股票上市进行融资。五是用足用活国家和省里有关扶持农产品加工业发展的信贷、财政、税收等各项优惠政策，向政策要资金。

4. 加快科技进步，提高农产品加工业科技含量 积极引进先进适用技术、现代加工设备、工艺流程和先进管理方法，不断提高产品的市场竞争力和企业经济效益。大力发展品牌农产品。要充分发挥科研院所、大专院校和农业服务体系的科技优势，搞好产、学、研结合，鼓励全省广大科技人员积极参与农产品加工业的各项工作，不断提高乡镇企业农产品加工业的整体素质。坚持把大力推进技术创新、千方百计增强自主创新能力作为结构调整的中心环节，用信息化带动工业化，不断提高特色产业发展的科技含量。坚持节约发展、清洁发展、安全发展，实现持续发展，发展循环经济，保护生态环境，依法淘汰落后工艺技术，关闭破坏资源、污染环境和不具备安全生产条件的企业，加快建设资源节约型、环境友好型社会。

5. 加强农产品加工服务体系建设 坚持社会化、专业化、市场化的原则，加强与有关部门的协作与配合，充分利用社会资源，依靠全社会的力量，建立为农产品加工企业服务的各类中介组织和社会化服务组织，重点围绕信用担保，投资融资，创业辅导，技术支持，信息服务，管理咨询，市场开拓，经营管理，国际合作等领域，培育社会化的服务体系，积极引导协调农产品加工企业按市场经济规律组织一批同一行业、同一产业和以经济利益为纽带的集团和行业协会，加强社会化协作，提高市场竞争能力，规范企业行为，加强行业自律，维护企业合法权益和公平竞争的环境。通过“公司＋农户”、“协会＋农户”等各种组织形式和产业化经营方式，促进龙头企业带动农产品生产者按照市场需求调整农产品品种布局和结构，提高农产品生产的规模化和组织化程度，为农产品龙头企业提供可靠、安全的原料生产基地。

6. 加强园区建设，构筑农产品加工产业集聚平台 园区建设是产业集聚的载体和平台，加快园区建设，对于促进和加快农产品加工业的产业集聚度，提升企业的群体规模优势，促进产业布局和产品布局调整都有重要的作用，要通过加强园区的基础设施建设，优化投资环境，加强农产品产业集群的发展规划和引导，依托各地的比较优势和资源禀赋，下大力气培育一批农产品加工特色优势产业。要根据主导产业发展方向和产业政策，规划建设一批农产品加工业示范园区。实行优惠的市场准入政策，鼓励广大农产品加工企业向示范园区进行集聚。要有目标地吸引那些具备产业带动优势和有产业关联效应或配套协作功能的农产品加工项目进入区内，以企业集群带动产业集群的发展。加大对园区内农产品加工重点项目、循环经济试点项目、清洁生产项目，以及优势农产品加工企业技改扩建项目的资金扶持和服务力度，通过加强园区建设，构筑甘肃省农产品加工产业集聚的平台，促进农产品加工业向规模化、现代化方向发展。

青海省农畜产品加工业

青海省农牧厅产业化办公室

一、发展现状

1. 区域特色初步显现 初步建设了以小麦、油料为主的粮油加工业，以马铃薯、蚕豆为主的薯类加工和流通业，以牛羊肉及其副产品为主的肉食品加工业，以毛绒皮为主的纺织、服装加工业，以青稞、水果为主的酒制品和饮料加工业，以辣椒为主的蔬菜加工业，以枸杞、甘草、大黄、藏茵陈、黄芪、红景天、党参为主的中藏药加工业。农畜产品初级加工开始向多样化方向发展，农畜产品加工业的链条不断延伸，原料综合利用率不断提高。

2. 基地建设稳定发展 按照“因地制宜、突出特色、适度规模、集中连片”的原则，以市场为导向，以产业化龙头企业和农畜产品加工企业为载体，建设了一批具有比较优势、适应市场需求的特色优势农畜产品生产基地。全省初步形成了以互助、湟中、民和、乐都、大通为主的马铃薯基地，全省马铃薯种植面积比上年增长15.59%；以湟中、互助、大通为主的蚕豆基地，种植面积增长3.14%；以湟中、互助、大通、平安、贵德、门源为主的油菜基地，种植面积增长1.4%；以西宁市城西区、城北区为主的花卉基地，种植面积增长0.15%；以循化为主的辣椒基地，种植面积增长44%。2005年，全省马铃薯、油菜、蚕豆、花卉、药材的种植面积不断增加，占总种植面积的比重由上年的52.38%上升到59.06%。畜产品逐步向川水奶牛、浅垴山良种肉牛、农区瘦型猪，西宁及海东良种肉羊、青南与环湖藏羊、牦牛以及柴达绒山羊7个优势产业带推进，良种畜比例有了明显增加，母畜比例达到49%。

3. 农畜产品加工龙头企业不断发展壮大 40个生产经营规模较大、技术含量较高、经营机制较活、辐射带动作用较强的企业成为省级农畜产品加工龙头企业。各地结合实际，亦相应确定了本地的龙头企业。这些龙头企业的培育和发展，推动了农畜产品加工业实施名牌战略的进程，其中“雪舟”、“互助”牌商标已成为“中国驰名商标”，率先开创了青海省无驰名商标的先河；涌现出了一些特级、一级信用和诚信守法先进企业；培养、招聘了一些科技人才。综合竞争能力不断增强，成为推动农畜产品加工业发展的中坚力量。

4. 促进了农牧业增效、农牧民增收 近几年，农畜产品加工业一直保持较快的发展态势，加工企业尤其是龙头企业通过“公司+基地+农户”等经营模式，使主要农畜产品的品种不断丰富，品质不断提高，附加值不断增加，从业人员不断扩大，农牧民收入不断增加。据对全省重点农畜产品加工龙头企业的调查，2005年，40个重点企业订单面积达33.3khm²，辐射带动农户35万个约60万人。

二、存在的主要问题

1. 原材料与加工需求不相适应 一些农畜产品生产分散，布局不合理，品质不高，标准化、规模化程度低，农畜产品加工业的发展规模受到影响。而且农畜产品加工企业与农牧户之间利益联结机制不完善，履行合同的信用程度较低，农畜产品加工业发展缺乏稳定可靠的原料基地保障。

2. 科技基础薄弱 农畜产品加工企业的技术水平、设备装备普遍滞后，有的还停留在初加工、粗加工阶段，科技含量低，缺乏高附加值产品，难以形成规模效应。许多企业自我创新不够，缺乏产品自主开发能力，新工艺、新材料、新技术的应用程度低。质量标准与质量控制体系建设滞后，技术推广和信息服务不适应加工业的发展需求。企业技术人才匮乏，影响了企业的良性发展。

3. 资金投入严重不足 农畜产品加工企业主要以中小型企业为主，产品经营方式是季节性收购、加工、销售，流动资金贷款难度大，许多传统农畜产品未能及时收购，仅加工几个月就没有原料。加之贷款难度增大，招商引资不力，制约着农畜产品加工业的发展和壮大。

4. 部分龙头企业发挥产品优势和打造高原知名

品牌意识淡薄 青海独特的自然环境、地理条件，蕴藏着丰富而独特的高原特色农畜产品，吸引诸多国内外客商和企业投资。而企业的无序竞争，形成恶性循环，资源成为低廉的原材料在市场销售，使一些产品难以发挥优势，高原知名品牌少，对企业开拓国内外市场的竞争力受到影响。

三、主要措施

1. **重点培育和发展农畜产品加工骨干企业** 积极围绕高原特色资源，以市场为导向，大力开发和培育以农畜产品加工、储藏、保鲜、销售、运输为主的骨干龙头企业，创造出产品更新、效益更高、竞争力更强的企业规模结构，形成下游产品企业带动上游产品企业，大企业辐射小企业，企业联动农牧业资源开发的良好发展态势。在培育和发展农畜产品加工龙头企业的过程中，一是创新组织形式、经营机制。大力推广订单农牧业、合同契约、合同加服务、股份合作、资产入股等经营方式，使农畜产品加工企业和农牧民建立稳定的利益连接机制，形成真正的利益共享、风险共担的经济实体。鼓励农畜产品加工企业通过定向投入、定向服务、定向收购等方式，建立“小规模大群体”的种养格局，同时兴办农畜产品原料基地，保证获得稳定的和规格、质量符合标准的加工原料。二是组建企业集团。积极鼓励和引进“老板”投资农畜产品加工项目，以资产为纽带，以拳头产品为龙头，以骨干企业为核心，实行改组、兼并、联合，加快培植和组建一批生产经营规模大、技术含量高、辐射带动作用强，集生产经营、科研开发于一体的跨行业、跨地区、跨所有制的农工贸一体化的加工集团。三是面向国内外两个市场，建立完善市场营销、服务、信息收集处理机制。通过市场牵龙头带基地，基地联农户，使千家万户独立经营的小生产有组织地走向千变万化的大市场。

2. **加快基地建设** 重点建设8个农畜产品加工基地：一是牛羊肉基地。以青藏高原绿色肉食品有限公司、青海绿草原肉食品公司为龙头，建立6万t牛羊肉加工基地，辐射带动农牧户10万户。同时，培育和引进省内外经营牛羊肉的公司或经纪人，在省外建立3～5个相对稳定的经销点（窗口），年外销牛羊肉达到4万t。二是绒毛基地。以雪舟三绒集团公司、青海藏羊集团为龙头，建立牦牛绒、山羊绒和羊毛加工基地，年加工牦牛绒500t、山羊绒150t、羊毛5 000t，分别辐射带动农牧户5万户和0.5万户，转移安置全省农村牧区剩余劳动力8 000人，年出口创汇3 000万美元。三是马铃薯基地。以威思顿生物工程公司、绿原实业有限公司、嘉宝农业有限公司、祥源开发公司为龙头，在互助、湟中、大通、民和、乐都建立高原4号、下寨65、青薯2号以及小白花马铃薯种植加工基地9.3 khm^2，辐射带动农户5万户；大力培育农产品经销公司、中介组织和经纪人队伍，形成省内外联手的马铃薯经销网络，建立马铃薯购销基地，签订马铃薯种植、购销订单6.7khm^2，带动农户约3万户。四是油菜基地。以大通昶财、湟中弘大、通发、平安芳谱、互助金丰等油料加工企业为龙头，建立50个万亩集中连片杂交油菜种植基地33.3khm^2，全省杂交油菜种植总面积达到100 khm^2，辐射带动农户15万户。进一步稳定油籽收购价，遏制油籽经营商的无序竞争，让农民获得更多的实惠。五是蚕豆基地。以青海兴源、湟中外贸公司为龙头，建立30个533.3 hm^2集中连片蚕豆基地16 khm^2，生产蚕豆5 000t，打造青海蚕豆的品牌，并在积累资金的基础上，逐步向蚕豆加工增值上迈进。六是牛奶基地。以天露乳业公司为龙头，配合省里实施引进良种奶牛繁育基地建设项目，不断加快奶牛基地建设，天露乳业公司在西宁周边半径100km范围内建立奶源基地，年收购鲜奶3万t，辐射带动农户1万户，重点解决奶源不足、农牧户养牛价格偏低或不稳定、鲜奶保鲜保质设施滞后的问题。七是花卉基地。以农发、卉源花卉公司为龙头，重点在西宁市城西区建立花卉基地266.7 hm^2，实行专业化、规模化、科技化种植，辐射带动农户1 300户。八是蔬菜基地。以各地蔬菜批发市场为龙头，继续加大蔬菜日光节能温棚设施建设，巩固提高海东、西宁、格尔木“三点一线”连贯德的蔬菜基地的规模和科技含量，持续发展常规蔬菜和季节性蔬菜的生产，引进扩大反季节和新特优蔬菜的生产。在重点蔬菜产地建设20t蔬菜保鲜库10座，减少蔬菜产后损失，实现蔬菜增值，适应市场对反季节蔬菜的需求。抓紧实施西宁市百绿园珍稀名特优蔬菜引进种植示范推广及蔬菜保鲜库建设项目。

3. **提高农畜产品加工业科技创新的能力和水平** 一是加大对农畜产品生产和加工投入，进一步推动农畜产品加工业发展的进程。二是鼓励科研单位、大专院校与加工企业加强联合与合作，增强农畜产品精深加工工艺技术、品种和功能等方面的创新研究和开发生产的能力。三是加快提高企业技术创新研究和开发能力。重点骨干农畜产品加工企业要积极建立科研开发中心，培育加工技术创新体系，探索建立健全技术、设备工程化、专业化、标准化体系，大力引进国内外先进技术、工艺、设备和管理，积极开展质量体系认证或产品质量认证，加快与国内外先进标准和国际标准接轨，努力培育一批具有一定实力的生产型、科技型农畜产品加工企业，开发一批具有自主知识产权的技术和产品。加快推进实施名牌战略的进程。四是坚持可持续发展。新上项目一开始就要做到高起点、高水平，顺应市场需求，重视“绿色”和“特色”，突出高原无污染，坚决防止低水平重复建设。五是通过各种方式、多种渠道，积极推行学历文凭和职业培训资格证书并重的劳动用工制度，进一步加强培养熟悉农畜产品加工业相关行业的技术、管理、贸易、应对国际贸易争端的各类专业人才，建设一支稳定的、创新能力强的高水平人才队伍。

4. 加大政策扶持　按照“企业投入为主体，社会投入为补充，政府投入为导向”的投资新体制，认真贯彻落实中央1号文件精神和省委、省政府《关于加快发展农牧业产业化经营的决定》精神，努力营造加快发展农畜产品加工业的良好氛围。

宁夏回族自治区农产品加工业

宁夏回族自治区农牧厅

一、发展现状

2005年，宁夏回族自治区粮食产量为299.8万t，同比增长3.20%；油料产量为12.2万t，同比增长−11.54%；水果产量为31.5万t，同比增长37.76%；蔬菜产量为183.6万t，同比增长10.34%；肉类产量为26.2万t，同比增长7.38%；奶类产量为57.8万t，同比增长23.24%；水产品产量为5.9万t，同比增长4.22%。初步形成了牛奶、枸杞、清真牛羊肉和马铃薯四大战略性支柱产业带，以及酿酒葡萄、蔬菜、淡水鱼、优质牧草饲料、优质水稻、玉米等六大区域特色优势产业带。初步建立起了以优势特色农产品为依托的农业产业化发展平台，形成了卫宁、清水河流域和贺兰山东麓的枸杞产业带；盐同灵的滩羊、引黄灌区的肉羊、肉牛改良和六盘山的肉牛等清真牛羊肉产业带；吴忠、银川市的奶产业带；南部山区的马铃薯产业带；引黄灌区的优质粮食、水产品、蔬菜产业带和贺兰山东麓的葡萄产业带。全区农产品加工企业已达3 100多个，规模以上企业136个，销售收入1 000万元的企业66个，过亿元的企业已有6个，已培育出“夏进”牛奶、“宁夏红”枸杞酒、“西夏王”葡萄酒、“圣雪绒”羊绒、“塞北雪”面粉、“夏绿”脱水菜等知名品牌。优势农产品产业化加工格局基本形成。例如，银川市重点扶持液态奶、清真牛羊肉等农产品加工企业，已发展龙头企业18个，吸纳农村劳动力16万人，促进了农业结构调整，提高了农产品附加值，增加了农民收入。吴忠市在夏进等企业的带动下，农民近一半的收入来自奶产业。石嘴山市特色农产品生产企业以订单、租赁土地、农资赊销、技术指导服务等方式与农户加强联系，建立原料生产基地，企业有了比较稳定的原料基地，农民有了稳定的收入渠道。中宁县农民从枸杞产业得到的现金收入人均可达1 320元，占农民人均纯收入的1/3以上。固原市草畜、马铃薯和劳务产业已成为农民增收的重要渠道，农民人均草畜、马铃薯和劳务产业的收入总和占农民人均纯收入的55%以上。全区40%的大米、40%的肉类、80%的奶产品、90%的枸杞、80%的水产品销往区外市场。自治区党委、政府启动实施《宁夏优势特色农产品区域布局和发展规划》以来，优势特色产业呈现出区域化布局、规模化生产、产业化经营的发展态势。优势产业发展情况如下：

1. 枸杞加工业　枸杞是宁夏在全国最赋有特色的农产品，自治区政府把枸杞产业作为全区农业发展的战略主导产业，从政策上、资金上给予扶持。各地特别是枸杞主产区充分发挥枸杞产业的品牌、科技、种植、加工和市场优势，采取有效措施，大力发展枸杞产业。在“宁夏红”等品牌的带动下，2005年，全区加工干枸杞产量为5万t，约占全国总产量的50%；年产值达15亿元。其中原果收入6亿元，加工产值9亿元。出口量约占全国出口量的60%，出口创汇达500多万美元。全区枸杞加工、营销企业为100多个，其中枸杞规模加工流通企业52个，形成了以宁夏红、杞浓、圣杞乐、早康等为主体的枸杞酒、枸杞籽油、果汁、叶茶等10大类

40多种产品，枸杞加工转化率达到了总产量的15%。主产区中宁县已成为全国枸杞的集散地，在全国136个大中城市建立了稳固的枸杞产品销售渠道和网点，从事枸杞营销的人员达1万余人。2005年，有40多万人加入了枸杞种植和深加工领域，有近20万劳动力从事枸杞采摘，使主产区和周边邻县的农村剩余劳动力实现了就地就近转移，增加了他们的收入。中宁县农民收入1/3以上来自枸杞产业，惠农、原州、同心等发展重点县（区）枸杞集中乡镇或村农民来自枸杞的收入为40%～80%。全区有10万农户依靠枸杞产业增收致富，全区农民纯收入中枸杞收入人均380元。

2. *奶产品加工业* 2005年，全区奶牛存栏22.4万头，鲜奶产量55万t。宁夏奶牛存栏约占全国的2%，在全国排名第15位，在西部地区排名第7位；牛奶产量约占全国的2%，在全国排名第14位，在西部地区排名第5位。全区人均鲜奶占有量已由2003年的68kg增加到2005年92kg，是全国人均占有量的5倍。到2005年底，全区已建成奶牛养殖园区230个，进入奶牛养殖园区的奶牛8.2万头，占全区奶牛存栏总数的36.6%。与没有进入园区的散养殖户相比，每头奶牛最低可增加收益400元，多的达到1 500元。全区已形成吴忠和银川市两个奶牛相对集中的银吴平原奶牛带，这两个地区奶牛存栏数和产奶量已分别占全区总数的95.3%和97.3%。奶牛养殖户发展到14 680户，从业人员5.1万人。银吴奶业主产区农民人均收入的45%以上来自于奶牛养殖收入。吴忠市奶产业产值占到牧业产值的68.5%，养殖奶牛对畜牧业纯收入的贡献率平均达到38.3%。全区乳品加工企业31个，规模以上加工企业（日处理鲜奶50t以上）9个，日处理鲜奶1 800～2 000t。其中，夏进乳业、维维北塔属国家级龙头企业，金河乳业和北方乳业属自治区级龙头企业。夏进乳业是全区最大的液态奶生产企业，已进入“中国乳业20强企业”，带动奶牛养殖户15 000多户，仅2003—2005年三年累计给奶农发放奶款达到5.2亿元。据不完全统计，2005年7、8、9三个月全区乳品龙头企业共收购鲜奶142 846t，同比多收41 969t，同比增长37.2%。全区液态奶产量居全国第八位，2005年全区乳业产值8.5亿元。奶产品销售辐射全国26个省、自治区，充分发挥了龙头企业的带动作用，保证了奶产业持续、平稳、健康的发展。

3. *清真牛羊肉加工业* 2005年，全区牛羊肉产量达到12万t，占肉类总产量的46%，比2003年提高6个百分点；肉牛饲养量突破了百万头大关，达到110万头；肉羊饲养量突破千万只大关，达到1 053万只；牛羊肉产值达到18亿元，占全区牧业产值的39.1%，占农林牧渔业总产值的13%；全区农民从牛羊肉生产中的收入人均达到474元，占农民人均家庭经营收入的14.8%。全区清真牛羊肉加工企业已达70多个，形成固定资产2亿元，加工能力达到8万t。宁夏贺兰山肉羊产业集团形成了3万t的生产能力，并在国外建立了销售窗口；甘肃中汇牛羊集团落户泾源县，对原泾河清真肉联厂进行了兼并改造，形成了屠宰2万头的加工能力；宁夏金福来羊产业集团年屠宰加工能力100万只，生产优质羔羊肉1.5万t。清真牛羊肉产品已经进入北京、上海、广州等各大城市，正在逐步开拓中东地区、东南亚以及香港等国家和地区市场，清真牛羊肉产业已成为代表宁夏民族品牌的优势产业。宁夏已建成牛羊定点屠宰厂22个，家禽定点屠宰厂13个。其中，有7个屠宰厂达到了出口肉品屠宰加工标准，有5个屠宰厂屠宰加工环境符合国内标准；有10个牛羊定点屠宰厂、10个家禽定点屠宰厂是为本地服务型的企业。全区牛羊进点屠宰率达到85%，家禽进点屠宰率达到70%。已注册了贺兰山、金福来、涝河桥、泾河、沙漠王子、纳氏肥牛、金伯爵等多个清真肉品品牌。每年全区清真肉品屠宰加工量达到10.3万t，行业可实现产值15.7亿元。清真肉品区外销量占总产量的近1/3。

2005年，全区已经形成各类综合交易市场100多个，集散功能逐步增强。宁夏涝河桥清真牛羊肉交易批发市场年交易和屠宰肉牛4万头、肉羊60万只，交易额达3亿多元，客流量达1 000多人次/日，与陕、京、沪等10多个省、自治区、直辖市建立了长期稳定的购销网络。平罗县宝丰牛羊肉交易专业市场，年交易量达到50多万头（只），交易额达到1.5亿多元。西吉县单家集牛羊肉交易市场，年贩运肉牛5万头，肉羊3万只，屠宰肉牛3.2万头、肉羊1.5万只。随着牛羊肉生产加工数量的扩长和质量的提升，涌现出了一批区域性行业协会和流通服务组织，为提高农民组织化程度发挥了重要作用。固原市牛羊产业协会辐射全市5个县（区），会员已经发展到1万多户。盐池县众联滩羊养殖合作社，入社会员已达到2 000多户，滩羊饲养量达到53万只。平罗县宝丰羊产业协会，成功地走出了一条自繁自育、流通贩运、快速育肥、定点屠宰的路子。

4. *马铃薯加工业* 宁夏种植马铃薯历史悠久，主要集中在南部山区和中部干旱带。随着消费趋向的改变和加工业的逐步发展，马铃薯作为工业原料和绿色食品走俏市场，在农民增收致富中发挥了积极作用。近年来，宁夏马铃薯产业有了长足发展，种植区域优势和分工逐步显现，产业优势和链条业已形成，加工企业发展迅速。截止到2005年底，全区共有马铃薯加工企业3 138个，马铃薯加工率达到40%。其中，固原市有马铃薯加工企业3 100个，年转化加工鲜薯100万t，淀粉系列产品销售量达到10万t，其中出口5 000t，主要销往国内17个省、自治区、直辖市。以马铃薯加工为主的淀粉业已经占固原市工业总产值的23%以上，成为当地经济发展的重要支柱。全市已基本形成了以加工企业为骨干，千家万户为补充的马铃薯产业化雏形。2005年，马铃薯产业总产值约9.7亿元，真正成为农业发展的区域主导产业。

5. 葡萄加工业　葡萄产业是宁夏具有区域优势的特色产业之一，自治区党委、政府十分重视发展葡萄产业，出台了《关于加快葡萄产业发展的实施意见》，将葡萄产业确定为宁夏农业发展的优势产业之一，列入了农业产业化发展纲要。2005年，自治区财政厅、农牧厅、林业局等部门联合印发了《推进特色优势产业发展的政策意见》和《加快农产品龙头企业发展的若干政策意见》，将葡萄产业列为重点产业进行扶持，对新建园的葡萄基地实行了“以奖代补”政策。由于措施得力，葡萄产业发展较快。2005年，全区葡萄产量达到6万t，其中酿酒葡萄达到3万t；鲜食葡萄达到3万t。葡萄产值达到3.5亿元。形成了“西夏王”和“御马”、“杞浓”等葡萄酒地方品牌。有效带动了农民增收，成为促进产业良性发展的新亮点。2005年，全区葡萄加工能力进一步增强，葡萄酒生产加工企业已达14个，年加工能力5.23万t，年产葡萄酒近2万t，占全国40万t的近5%。西夏王、御马等龙头企业的酿酒设备及工艺达到了国内先进水平，培育了西夏王、御马、杞浓等品牌，基本形成了区域化布局、规模化经营、专业化生产的产业化发展格局。宁夏贺兰山东麓是生态条件最佳的酿酒葡萄种植区域。2005年已建成葡萄基地9.3khm²，其中酿酒葡萄基地5.3 khm²，总产量3万t左右，已有葡萄酒生产企业6个，设计加工能力5万t。

6. 绒毛加工业　2005年，全区有绒毛加工企业为89个，其中规模以上的企业30个。在89个企业中，粗加工企业83个，纺织企业6个。全区羊绒产量253t，羊毛产量9 455t，从业人员达17 000多人，总产值达到41.35亿元。形成了圣雪绒集团、中银绒业、马斯特集团等骨干企业，产生了“圣雪绒”国家级名牌，绒产品出口欧美十几个国家。全区已形成年分梳绒5 500t、羊绒纱900t、羊绒衫155万件的生产能力。2005年，全区羊绒加工业呈现产销两旺、效益提高、出口强劲的好势头。规模以上22个羊绒企业完成工业总产值35.85亿元，同比增长40.09%，绒毛产业总计完成工业总产值41.35亿元；实现销售收入37.7亿元，同比增长45%；利税总额2.38亿元，同比增长52.13%；出口创汇7 361万美元（不含转手出口的3 000万美元）。绒毛产业主要集中在同心、灵武，现已成为两县市的主导产业，有力地促进了当地县域经济发展。灵武市羊绒企业的各项经济指标快速增长，开始向规模化、产业化方向发展，现有羊绒加工企业40个，从业人员3 000余人，2005年分梳无毛绒2 000t，羊绒衫36万件，产值达到15亿元。同心县现有绒毛加工企业43个，拥有梳绒机660台（套），2005收购原绒4 800t，生产无毛绒1 200t，产值达61 000万元，销售收入12亿元，利润6 437万元，从业人员12 000多人。2005年，灵武市市级财政收入1.15亿元，羊绒产业的贡献占1/4；同心县2005年县级财政收入3 243万元，羊绒产业的贡献占1/3。因此，羊绒产业成为拉动农民增收和县域经济的重要产业。

二、主要做法

1. 制定发展规划，加大政策引导　围绕“农产品竞争力增强、农业增效和农民增收”的目标，用工业理念来经营农业，抓龙头，建基地，连农户，通过制定规划措施和扶持政策，推动农产品加工业发展。自治区党委、政府高度重视和支持产业化工作，先后制定了《关于扶持农业产业化经营重点龙头企业发展的意见》、《关于大力扶持农产品加工业发展的意见》、《关于宁夏农业产业化重点龙头企业振兴工程实施方案》、《宁夏优势特色农产品区域布局及发展规划》、《关于引导和扶持农村专业合作组织发展的意见》等，构筑了农产品加工业发展的新格局。自治区党委、政府召开了农村专业合作组织工作会、现场经验交流会和农产品加工业工作会议。通过政策引导，措施带动，有力地推动了农产品加工业发展的进程。

2. 培育市场主体，发展龙头企业和专业合作组织　为实现农产品加工业的产业化经营，自治区农牧厅把建设龙头企业和大力发展农村专业合作组织作为培育市场主体的关键环节来抓。自治区每年整合2 000万元左右的资金，对规模龙头企业重点扶持；针对本区经济欠发达、资金缺乏的现状，鼓励乡镇企业的发展，在一些产业上形成了小规模、大群体的企业发展模式，仅石嘴山市就有脱水蔬菜企业118个，从业职工6 000多人，年出口创汇350万美元。为加强企业与基地联系、开展行业自律，组织企业成立了脱水蔬菜、乳制品、马铃薯淀粉、枸杞、亚麻、粮食等农产品加工企业协会，做了许多有益的工作。乳制品工业协会为推动奶产业发展，在鲜奶市场波动时，开展建设诚信企业活动，稳定价格，扩大产量，保护了奶农的利益；召开了宁夏农村经济与奶产业发展高峰论坛，邀请国内知名专家来宁，帮助研究分析问题，破解发展难题。自治区农牧厅把为企业和中介组织服务作为工作重点，帮助企业开拓市场、实施品牌战略，组织本区的国家级龙头企业和绿色食品生产企业参加中国农产品交易会，召开宁夏优势特色农产品推介会，将政府形象和企业品牌结合。在50多家农产品加工企业中开展ISO 9000认证，帮助企业建立质量保证体系。帮助企业与合作组织开展培训，推行“蓝色证书”，开展职业技能鉴定，提高职工社员素质。

3. *纵向整体推进，拉紧产业链条* 按照《宁夏优势特色农产品区域布局及发展规划》的目标，重点建设四大战略性主导产业、六个区域性优势产业，对每个产业从市场销售、企业产品、原料基地、企业和农户的利益连接等方面分析研究，针对薄弱环节采取措施，拉紧产业链条。特别关注那些影响产业发展的瓶颈环节、企业和农户利益连接的环节，力求从整体上推动农产品产业的发展。为落实自治区“重振宁夏大米雄风”的要求，实施了“优质米产业化工程”，从解决本区水稻整精米率低、品牌不统一等问题入手，进一步加大了优质稻品种引育、推广力度，使优质稻种植面积达到60%，引进了一批先进的收割脱粒机械，狠抓了适时收获，开展绿色食品认证，统一产地品牌，使宁夏大米的产量、质量和市场竞争得到了全面提升，精米加工和区外销售量增长较快。

4. *加大科技推广力度，建设优质原料基地* 一是创建科技示范园，加快科技成果的组装配套与综合示范推广步伐。建立自治区级科技示范园区14个，各类区域优势特色农产品科技示范园区100多个。二是大力实施“良种工程”，努力提高农产品的优质化率。重点在全区进行了高产奶牛冷配改良、肉牛肉羊杂交改良、马铃薯专用脱毒种薯、玉米专用品种引进推广等。全区农作物良种覆盖率达90%以上，畜禽良种覆盖率达75%以上，其中奶牛在90%以上，鸡达到了99%。三是充分发挥龙头企业在科技创新中的主体作用，积极引导龙头企业参与科技推广。石嘴山市脱水菜企业协会积极参与脱水甜椒病毒攻关，三年来与农技部门密切配合，取得显著成效；同心、固原的马铃薯加工流通企业和专业合作组织积极参与专用种薯的推广种植，形成了“政府+脱毒中心+企业+农户”“四位一体”的新型良种产业化推广模式。四是积极扶持各类农业产业化组织开展绿色食品、无公害产品产地认定和产品认证工作，全面提高农产品品质。全区已有绿色食品60个，无公害产品133个，无公害产地167个。标准化无公害生产的全面推行，有效地提升了农产品的市场竞争能力。

三、存在的主要问题

1. *产业优势尚不突出* 宁夏的优势特色产业虽然有了长足的发展，但优势资源与优势产业的关联度还不高，还没有形成一大批优势产业基地，产业“优”而无“势”、产品“特”而不“强”的状况较为普遍，有些产业还没有真正成为支撑区域经济发展的主导产业。产业基地的专业化程度小，有些较为分散，还没有形成集约化、规模化生产的组织能力和经营能力。如蔬菜生产基地和奶牛养殖基地过于分散，且以家庭经营为主，规模化程度不高，产品档次低，难以形成规模优势。

2. *特色产业链条短* 宁夏的特色产业大都是根据当地的自然条件和资源优势发展起来的，产业内部产加销、贸工农之间衔接不够紧密，产品多为初级加工，科技含量较低。尤其是特色农产品，主要分布在不同的县域内，大多是小打小闹，变卖初级产品，没有形成带动区域经济发展的优势产业。有特色的农产品因产业“断链”而难成规模，无法形成竞争优势。

3. *特色品牌培育滞后* 宁夏打出的主导产业和地方特色产业品牌，虽然名目多，但能真正立足市场的品牌却很少。尤其是同类产品的品牌，各地各自为政，称谓不一，不适应农产品加工业发展的形势，不便于向外推介，不易做大做强产业。

4. *支持特色产业发展的融资渠道少* 虽然自治区对特色产业发展给予了很大的扶持，但从产业的发展形势来讲还很不够，特色优势产业的发展资金严重不足，需要更多的社会资金和信贷资金的支持。

四、主要扶持措施

（一）财税政策

凡新办农产品加工企业和农业部等部委认定的农业产业化国家重点龙头企业，除享受国家现行的税收优惠政策之外，同时享受自治区人民政府《宁夏回族自治区招商引资的若干政策规定》的各项优惠政策。根据自治区人民政府《推进我区工业化进程，加强财源建设奖励办法（试行）》有关规定，对财源建设先进企业给予鼓励。根据自治区党委、人民政府《关于大力扶持农产品加工工业发展的意见》有关规定，继续鼓励各地结合实际建设农产品加工专业园区。新建的农产品加工企业原则上都要进入园区。各级国土资源部门对农产品加工专业园区和企业所需用地，要优先安排，优先审批，其农用地转用、土地征（占）用各项费用按国家重点项目用地标准低限执行。基地农户占用基本农田以外的耕地建简易饲养场和农作物晾晒场，未破坏土壤耕作层或轻度破坏易于恢复的，不视为改变用途。对重点农产品加工龙头企业生产用电要优先安排，电力部门要保证对农产品加工企业的供电，电价应以大宗工业电价相同的标准收取。对农产品加工企业运销鲜活农产品常年开通“绿色通道”，经过有关部门批准的“绿色通道”，减半收费。

（二）投资参股经营

1. *投资参股经营项目扶持的原则*　财政投资只参股、不控股；自愿申报、平等竞争、择优扶持；谁投资、谁受益、谁承担风险；政企分开、委托监管；规范操作、稳步推进、适时退出。

2. *扶持的对象和重点*　扶持的对象是国家级和自治区级农业产业化龙头企业（含自治区级农发机构审定的龙头企业）；主要扶持粮食等主要农产品的加工转化以及对当地主导产业建设起积极促进作用的其他产业化经营项目。

3. *立项条件*　第一，符合国家产业化经营项目的扶持范围，资源丰富独特、技术优势明显，市场销售顺畅，投入产出率高，项目辐射面广，带动农民增收明显，项目建设符合环保和农业可持续发展要求，项目建设用地落实，原材料供应有保障，加工所需的原材料70%以上来自农户，自筹资金来源有保障，项目采用技术路线先进合理，技术依托可靠，产品具有较强的市场竞争能力，项目投资经济合理，有较强的抗风险能力，能够实现国有资产保值增值。第二，扶持项目实施单位，必须是依法注册、具有独立公司法人的股份或有限责任公司，产权明晰、管理规范、经营期两年以上，总资产规模5 000万元以上，固定资产规模不低于2 500万元，实收资本不低于1 500万元，年销售收入6 500万元以上，近两年连续盈利，发展前景良好，有较强的自筹资金能力，资产负债率低于60%，银行信用等级AA级以上（含AA级），企业法人信誉良好，具备完成项目建设和经营相适应的经营管理能力。

4. *项目申报及审批*　按照属地管理和自下而上的原则逐级申报，投资参股项目由自治区财政部门最终评审确定。

（三）以奖代补扶持

1. 对产业关联度大、带动基地、农户能力强、辐射面广、规模大、产品有市场、经济效益好的农产品龙头企业，通过以奖代补方式进行扶持。一是战略性主导产业。清真牛羊肉加工年销售收入达到1 000万元，马铃薯淀粉加工年销售收入800万元，乳品加工年销售收入1 500万元，枸杞加工年销售收入1 000万元、转化鲜枸杞5 000t以上的企业，当销售收入每超过上年100万元，给予以奖代补资金5万元奖励；马铃薯、枸杞流通企业年销售收入2 000万元以上，当年销售收入每超过上年200万元，给予以奖代补资金5万元奖励。二是牧草及秸秆饲料、果品、蔬菜产业。年销售收入达到500万元以上的加工企业，当年销售收入每超过上年100万元，给予以奖代补资金5万元奖励；销售企业销售额达到1 000万元以上，淡水渔业流通企业销售额达到1 500万元以上，当年销售收入每超过上年200万元，给予以奖代补资金5万元奖励。三是粮油、玉米淀粉、葡萄产业。年加工销售收入达到2 000万元以上的企业，当年销售收入每超过上年200万元，给予以奖代补资金5万元奖励。

2. 为了提高农产品加工的技术水平，对积极开展研发创新，开发新产品引进新技术，创建品牌，培育人才等方面将给予奖励和补助。一是对龙头企业建立科技研发机构、自主或与科研单位合作开发具有自主知识产权的新工艺、新技术、新产品的，科技开发经费投入不低于销售收入3%的，将给予以奖代补资金5万～20万元奖励。二是大力推进名牌战略，帮助和支持具有宁夏原产地和品质特色的名牌产品发展，争创一批关联度大、带动力强、辐射面广的优质农产品加工名牌产品，对获得中国驰名商标、证明商标和创国家名牌产品的企业，给予以奖代补资金50万元奖励；创自治区名牌产品的企业，给予以奖代补资金20万元奖励。三是对使用贷款或引进资金进行技术改造的企业，给予贴息补助或奖励。四是积极推进农产品加工企业的质量体系认证，对企业开展GMP（良好操作规范）、HACCP（危害分析与关键控制点）、ISO 9001、ISO 14000系列质量体系认证的，给予补助。

3. 鼓励支持企业、行业协会开展厂长经理培训、招商引资、开拓市场、打造品牌、产品展销、实施节能降耗、环保治污、开展诚信活动等。

4. 鼓励企业围绕优势特色农产品，创建专业农产品产地批发市场，对农产品批发市场基础设施功能建设、提升改造贷款给予贴息；凡通过农业部农产品流通标准化、规范化管理验收的农产品专业批发市场，每个给予以奖代补资金15万元奖励。鼓励支持企业发展农产品配送、产销直挂、连锁经营等现代物流方式。

（四）鼓励金融部门放贷农产品加工业流通企业

1. 根据自治区财政厅、人民银行银川市中心支行《关于下发鼓励我区金融机构发放贷款财政奖励政策的通知》规定，凡在宁夏注册的国有银行自治区分行、银川市商业银行、自治区农村信用联合社和石嘴山市城市信用社，对农业优势特色产业的加工流通企业贷款余额当年余额超过上年余额的部分，每增加1亿元，由自治区财政厅奖励8万元，增加余额不足1亿元的部分，按实际数额同比例计算奖励额。财政奖励资金专向用于补偿当年贷款过程增加的服务成本或对有突出贡献人员的奖励。

2. 建立特色产业农产品加工与流通企业贷款担保机制。鼓励各级中小企业担保机构为特色产业农产品加工与流通企业进行贷款担保。担保资金额（出资）500万元，鼓励担保机构2万元。担保资金额（出资）每增加200万元多给予以奖代补资金1万元奖励。

（注：本文为编辑部根据该自治区相关资料编辑整理）

新疆维吾尔自治区农产品加工业

新疆维吾尔自治区乡镇企业管理局

一、发展现状

近年来，新疆依托丰富的农产品资源优势，大力发展农产品加工业，取得了较好的成绩。以农产品为原料的加工、保鲜、贮藏、运销业已成为新疆农村经济的重要组成部分。据不完全统计，到2005年，全区乡及乡以上农产品加工企业1 774个，实现总产值234.24亿元，比上年增长8.7%。其中，销售收入在500万元以上的规模农产品加工企业479个，工业总产值217亿元，比上年增长22.39%；工业增加值56.8亿元，增长17.11%；销售收入201.4亿元，增长19.31%。企业类型涉及粮油加工、乳制品、饮料酒、纺织业、造纸等行业。自治区已命名的121个农业产业化重点龙头企业中，乡镇企业占到了37个。已初步形成了以棉花为代表的白色产业，以红花、番茄、枸杞、胡萝卜、红辣椒等为代表的红色产业，以吐鲁番葡萄、哈密瓜及库尔勒香梨、杏、石榴等为代表的特色优质瓜果园艺业和以牛羊肉、奶、蛋、禽等为代表的畜牧产业的发展格局，为发展农产品加工业提供了良好的资源优势。农产品加工业的发展，促进了农业产业化经营，为推进新疆农村工业化进程、为农村富余劳动力的转移、农牧民收入的增加以及民族团结和社会进步做出了积极的贡献。

二、主要收获

1. *加强了领导，形成了良好的发展氛围* 改革开放以来，在自治区党委、政府的正确领导下，各地政府和乡镇企业管理部门把推进农产品加工业作为调整农牧业结构、加快农村牧区经济发展、增加农牧民收入、实现兴区富民奔小康的突破口和重要途径。积极采取措施，制定了新疆“十一五”农产品加工业发展规划，重点扶持30个农产品加工一体化科技示范项目和10个重点乡镇工业园区，并把发展乡镇工业园区作为推动农产品加工业的一项主要措施，把重点工业园区的基础设施建设纳入全疆小城镇建设总体规划，对园区中的重点农产品加工企业在贷款贴息上予以支持。各地也充分认识到加快农产品加工业发展的重要性、紧迫性，从过去挂在口头上的重视转变为落实在行动上的重视，切实加强对发展农产品加工业的宏观指导，形成了全疆大力发展农产品加工业的良好氛围。如巴音郭楞蒙古自治州实施“2333”工程，即培育23个有一定规模、有特色资源优势和实力的农产品加工企业，用3～5年的时间，使其年销售收入过2亿元，利税过2 000万元；选择33个成长型、有潜力的中小企业予以重点扶持，争取用3年左右的时间，使其成长为年产值过亿元或千万元，利税达千万元或百万元的“小巨人”企业。培育一批起点高、成长快、科技含量高、市场前景好、辐射带动能力强的农产品加工企业。从选定的22个重点扶持大企业来看，其中农产品加工企业11个，占总户数的50%；销售收入14.75亿元，占总收入105亿元的14%；利税总额1.29亿元，占总利税28.72亿元的4.5%。从选定的27个“小巨人”企业来看，其中农产品加工企业10个，占总户数的37%；营业收入2.10亿元，占总收入6.58亿元的31%；利税总额2 657万元，占总利税9 175万元的28.7%。

2. *拓展了农民就业渠道，增加了农民收入* 近年来，新疆大力发展农产品加工、保鲜、储运和其他服务，发展农业产业化经营，培育带动力强的龙头企业，健全企业与农户利益共享、风险共担的机制等，延长了农业产业链条，为农民提供了稳定的就业岗位和独特的社会保障，造就了一大批新型产业工人，培育了一大批农村企业家，改变了农民的生产生活方式，缩小了城乡和工农差距。“十五”期间，全区新增小企业5.03万个，新增农民就业14.8万人，转移划转乌鲁木齐市区3.58万职工。全区农产品加工业的工资收入由“九五”末的35.33亿元增加到57.35亿元，年均增长10.17%。农民人均从农产品加工业中获得的工资收入由“九五”末的382元上升到585元，昌吉、巴州等一些地区达到千元以上，成为农民增加收入的重要来源。

3. *提升了农业产业化水平，加快了现代农业的发展* 农产品加工业脱胎于农业，反过来又承担反哺农业的责任，改善了农业的基础条件，扩大了农业的规模效应，有效地推动了农业现代化的建设。“十五”期间，农产品加工业发展迅猛，全区农产品加工企业达到1 774个，逐步形成以粮油、棉纺、肉制品、乳制品、番茄、葡萄酒、林果园艺产品和药材等为主的优势产业，实现销售收入234.24亿元，增加值69亿元。其中，479个规模以上农产品加工企业实现增加值57亿元。新疆康尤美粮油集团公司等8个企业被农业部确定为全国农产品加工业示范企业，乌鲁木齐北园春集团公司等9个企业被农业部确定为全国大中型农产品加工流通企业。

4. *优化了农村产业布局，加速了农村城镇化进程* 新疆农产品加工业坚持把农产品加工园区建设作为提升工业化、加快城镇化的有效载体，紧紧围绕提高园区的承载力、吸引力、辐射力做文章，“以园带镇，以镇兴园”，互为依托，注重营造小城镇建设的新环境，催生相关的运输、餐饮、服务业等第三产业的发展，促进了产业集聚、人口集聚、资源集聚，使大量农村富余劳动力向二、三产业和小城镇转移，加速农村城镇化进程。全区已建成具有一定规模的农产品加工工业园区51个。入园企业1.29万个，累计固定资产投资36.71亿元，从业人员9.65万人，占全区乡镇企业从业人员的10.11%；实现营业收入116.87亿元，占全区乡镇企业总量的22.63%；工业增加值30.85亿元，占全区乡镇企业的47.08%；上缴税金2.86亿元，占全区乡镇企业的17.40%。聚集在小城镇及工业园区中的乡镇企业已占全区乡镇企业总数的20%以上，巴州西尼尔等4个工业园区被农业部确定为全国农产品加工业示范基地，为改善新疆农村面貌、发展农村基础设施和公共事业等方面做出了许多贡献。

5. *壮大了县域经济，加快了新农村建设步伐* “十五”末，全区农产品加工业达到36.86万个，与“九五”末相比增加5.04万个，其中营业收入100万元以上企业1 182个，500万元以上规模企业493个，1 000万元以上的325个，5 000万元以上的68个，过亿元的23个。农产品加工业固定资产原值达到228.72亿元，比“九五”末的126.61亿元翻了近一番，年均递增12.56%；农产品加工业增加值131.8亿元，比“九五”末的74.57亿元净增57.24亿元，年均递增12.06%；农产品加工企业全员劳动生产率达到54 112元/人·年，比“九五”末净增16 635元/人·年；人均利税5 574元，比“九五”末净增1 951元；农产品加工业累计上缴税金69.02亿元，支援农业和农村各项社会事业建设资金近6 000万元，对农业的反哺能力不断增强。

三、存在的主要问题

1. *农产品加工业促进社会主义新农村建设的长效机制不健全不到位* 一是基地建设滞后，企业与农户利益连接机制还没有真正形成。原料生产分散，规模化、标准化程度低，部分优质、专用品种原料供应不足，影响到农产品加工企业快速发展。企业与农户的利益机制不完善，真正形成“风险共担，利益共享”的经济共同体的较少，农民没有真正得到流通与加工环节的利益。二是在转移吸收农村富余劳动力方面，重使用，轻培养，特别是一些初创型小企业，由于自身实力所限，用于提高务工农民素质的投入不足、力度不强，按规定应当提取的职工教育经费没有提够留足、落实到位，致使务工农民的技能与现代化大生产的需求不尽适应。三是在解决务工农民老有所养、医有所保方面，一些企业由于实力不强，积累不多，能纳入统筹的资金很少，致使扩大社保面举步维艰。

2. *企业规模小、数量少，对社会主义新农村建设服务能力不足* 从全疆情况来看，一是拥有各类农业产业化组织1 000多个，带动全区60%以上的农户，但销售收入过亿元的龙头企业只有40个，仅占4%。真正上规模、上档次、上水平的企业很少，经济力量薄弱，缺乏带动区域经济发展的强大实力。企业规模小、数量少，对农副产品的加工转化总量不足，精深加工程度较低，产品档次不高。二是加工转化品种单一、层次低。粮食主要加工成面粉，棉花主要加工成棉纱，油料主要加工成食用油。初级产品多，中高档产品少；附加值低，效益不高。有相当一部分龙头企业设备陈旧，工艺落后，精深加工程度较低，辐射带动能力弱，反哺农业的能力弱。

3. 资金筹措困难，农产品加工业资金投入不足 资金问题是长期制约农产品加工业发展的瓶颈。金融体制改革后，金融部门上收贷款权限，企业贷款难、担保难的现象十分突出，信贷资金逐年减少。由于资金投入不足，一些市场好、潜力大、扶农支农效果好的农产品加工业项目不能及时开工建设，企业技术改造工作进展缓慢，部分企业装备和工艺水平落后，产品开发和科技创新能力弱，科技成果转化率低等。这些都严重影响到新疆农产品加工业的健康发展。

4. 农产品加工业发展缺乏有效的政策扶持 自治区内尚未有一个部门专门管理农产品加工业，多头管理，政出多门，与建立完整的农业产业体系的要求极不适应。农产品加工业中扶农支农各种要素整合比较薄弱，未能形成合力；企业在创业辅导、融资担保、信息服务、人员培训、技术推广、质量检测与标准体系建立等方面难以得到有力支持，尚没有形成一个公平、公开的社会化服务平台，使新疆本来具有优势和特色的农产品加工业没有发挥应有作用。

四、主要措施

1. 从建设社会主义新农村的高度，充分认识发展农产品加工业的重要性 在新的形势下发展农产品加工业，其实质就是发展农村的二、三产业、发展农村的非农产业、积极推进农村工业化和建设“生产发展，生活宽裕，乡风文明，村容整洁，管理民主”的社会主义新农村。就是要把贯彻落实中央、自治区两个1号文件精神变为具体的行动。这就要求把发展农产品加工业要与全区社会和经济发展的总体目标相结合，与构建和谐新疆、建立节约型社会相结合，与推进新型工业化相结合，与建设社会主义新农村相结合，与农业和农村经济结构战略性调整相结合。总之，要找准切入点，走出优势突出、特色鲜明、竞争力不断增强的发展路子，为新疆经济和社会发展做出更大的贡献。

2. 健全服务体系、加大指导力度 一是按照市场经济规律的要求，从当地资源条件和生产力发展水平的实际出发，根据国家和自治区产业政策，科学规划，合理布局，充分利用现有的加工企业示范项目，通过技术改造，扩大生产加工能力，防止盲目发展和重复建设，加强对农产品加工业的宏观指导，建立和完善农产品加工业项目库。二是切实加快建立健全农产品加工业的质量安全标准体系，强化服务功能。把推行农产品质量标准与建设各类农产品加工基地和相关的科技示范园区结合起来，建立标明产成品产地、质量、实施标准的等级标识制度。健全农产品质量监督检验检测体系。积极推进农产品加工品质特别是食品等质量认证进程，尽快建立危害分析与关键控制点（HACCP）、良好操作规范（GMP）、有机食品、绿色食品等多种内容的质量认证体系。完善覆盖面宽、时效性强的农产品市场信息网络，为农产品加工企业和农户提供及时、准确的信息服务。建立多层次、多元化市场体系，扶持和发展各种中介组织，建立健全技术推广、职业培训等社会化服务体系。切实加强对农产品加工业的服务，为农产品加工业的健康发展奠定坚实的基础。三是大力培植龙头企业，加强经济合作。围绕支柱产业的关键环节和关键产品，以市场为导向，不断壮大龙头企业。把龙头企业示范项目建设与优化农业产业结构结合起来，把营造规模优势与发展“小而强”、“小而精”、“小而专”、“小而特”企业结合起来。鼓励个体私营企业、股份合作企业扩大规模，促使企业技术上档次，产品上质量，经营上水平，成为龙头企业，提高市场竞争力，真正成为农户通向市场的桥梁。

3. 加快建立稳定的农产品专用原料基地，为加工业提供基础保障 在农业结构战略性调整中，围绕自治区党委、政府提出“建设五大基地、十大类支柱产业和百个名牌产品”的农业产业产品结构调整思路，按照农产品加工业标准化、优质化的要求，调整和优化农产品生产结构。按照区域化布局、专业化生产、标准化管理、产业化经营和社会化服务的发展思路，突出地方特色，充分发挥区域比较优势，以农产品加工企业为龙头，建立一批与加工企业相配套的原料基地，促进农产品加工业发展。大力提倡发展有机农业和绿色农业，按照讲究营养、保证卫生、注重特色、符合保健、崇尚美味、回归自然的要求，生产无公害绿色和有机农产品，为农产品加工企业提供安全、优质的加工原料。农产品加工基地建设，要在农户家庭经营的基础上，坚持走“小规模、大群体”的路子，鼓励农户、专业合作经济组织与农产品加工企业通过合同、合作等方式，形成稳定的利益联结关系，通过定向投入、定向服务、定向收购等方式，兴办稳定的农产品原料基地。

4. *大力发展农产品加工园区，提高产业集聚度* 大力发展农产品加工园区，充分发挥工业园区对于实现工业合理布局、产业优化升级和加快工业化和城镇化进程的巨大推动作用。一是制定鼓励工业园区发展的相关政策，强化规划引导和规范管理。要保证所有工业园区高起点规划、高标准实施，以完善的设施、齐全的功能、合理的布局、优质的服务，吸引资金、技术和项目入园，提高产业积聚度，推进经济结构调整和产业优化升级，创建具有新疆特色的农产品加工经济发展新格局。二是以现有工业园区为依托，以名优产品为龙头，以优势产业为支撑，以骨干农产品加工企业为载体，大力引进资金、项目和技术，提升产品档次，加速农产品加工产业集聚，使农产品加工园区成为工业经济发展的新亮点。

5. *加快技术进步，提高企业素质* 一是提高企业的科技创新能力。农业产业化龙头企业应设立科技发展基金，建立科技开发中心，加大技术改造力度，加强现代信息技术的应用，开发具有自主知识产权的技术和产品，不断提高企业技术创新的能力。二是积极与有关大专院校和科研单位加强合作，加大农产品加工技术研究和新产品开发的力度。特别应加强现代生物技术、微电子、新材料等技术在农产品加工业中的应用研究。运用直接开发、技术入股、转让等多种方式，尽快实现技术的商品化。三是加大引进国外先进的技术、工艺、设备和管理，在重视引进“硬件”的同时，更应注意“软件”的引进，推动农产品加工企业的科技进步和管理水平的提高。扩大与国内外的交流与合作，引进人才和技术，形成一批推进农产品加工业发展的骨干力量。四是加强农产品加工业职工队伍的教育培训。大力开展学历教育、继续教育和工人技术等级考核等多形式、多内容的培训活动，规范工人技术操作规程，提高专业技术人员的技术水平。同时对基地农民进行有针对性的培训，培养和造就一批高素质的职工队伍。

6. *深化企业改革，增强企业活力* 通过深化企业改革，建立起一整套适合市场经济体制要求的、适合企业自身特点的现代企业制度。在巩固已有改革成果的基础上，进一步明晰产权、转变机制、完善管理，着力解决法人治理结构、激励动力机制和约束制衡机制等方面存在的问题，增强企业发展的活力。一是深化企业内部劳动、人事、分配制度方面的改革。二是健全质量责任制，完善售后服务体系。三是严格贯彻执行《安全生产法》，明确和落实安全生产责任制，建立健全安全生产规章制度，使企业真正成为自主经营、自负盈亏、自我发展、自我约束的法人实体和市场竞争主体，为企业参与国际、国内市场竞争创造条件。四是实施品牌战略，发展拳头产品，提升农产品加工业知名度。通过建立品牌建设组织协调机制，加大知识产权保护力度，加快诚信体系建设，为品牌发展构筑服务平台，发挥舆论宣传和监督作用，提高企业和社会的品牌意识。

7. *大力推进对内对外开放，促进外向型农产品加工业发展* 实施“走出去、引进来”并举，加大对农产品加工项目的招商引资力度，鼓励和支持农产品加工企业与国内外知名企业、知名品牌开展合作。在抓好现有江苏维维集团、娃哈哈、康师傅、草原兴发等国内外知名企业在新疆投资的同时，进一步拓展视野，瞄准国内外其他农产品加工领域的大企业、大集团，广泛开展合作，吸引更多的知名企业来自治区投资办厂，建立生产基地，利用其资本、技术、管理、品牌、市场优势，加快全区农产品加工业发展步伐。各地尤其是外贸部门应加大对农产品加工制品出口的支持和协调服务。按照中央外贸发展基金使用方向和使用条件，对农产品及其加工品出口项目融资予以贴息。国有商业银行要在流动资金贷款方面优先保证农产品加工企业出口所需，对资信好的农产品加工出口企业，核定一定的授信额度，用于对外出具投标、履约和预付金担保函。外经贸、商检、海关、质检、税务等部门应进一步简化审批手续，放宽审批条件，支持具备条件的农产品加工企业尽快获得进出口自营权，并认真落实出口配额、出口退税方面的优惠政策。有关部门应认真分析研究国际市场需求信息，帮助农产品加工龙头企业制定切实可行的国际市场营销战略，通过扩大出口，带动农产品加工业发展。支持和鼓励有条件的农产品加工企业到国外建立办事处或建厂，直接参与国际市场竞争。

8. *推动农产品加工企业文化建设向高层次发展* 各地农产品加工企业要深刻认识到企业文化是一个企业在发展过程中形成的以企业精神和经营管理理念为核心，凝聚、激励企业各级经营管理者和员工归属感、积极性、创造性的人本管理理论，是企业的灵魂和精神支柱。只有注重塑造企业精髓，培育企业精神，建设优秀的企业文化，才能促进企业长久发展，才能真正实现以人为本的管理，实现与社会、自然的和谐发展。各地要把企业文化建设作为今后的一项重要工作来抓，积极指导企业根据自身的实际和特点，在科学分析企业现有文化特色和个性的基础上，开展形式多样的企业文化创建活动，提炼新的企业文化，同时，注重企业文化建设和企业制度改革相结合，重视企业文化的理论提升、加强企业文化与相关管理方式的综合运用，促进企业文化发展，不断增强企业的凝聚力和向心力，提高企业竞争力。

6 第六部分

标准、专利

农产品加工业部分国家标准（2006年）

标　准　号	标　准　名　称	代　替　标　准
GB 317—2006	白砂糖	GB 317—1998
GB/T 5719—2006	橡胶密封制品　词汇	GB/T 5719—1995
GB/T 6038—2006	橡胶试验胶料　配料、混炼和硫化设备及操作程序	GB/T 6038—1993
GB/T 6433—2006	饲料中粗脂肪的测定	GB/T 6433—1994
GB/T 6434—2006	饲料中粗纤维的含量测定　过滤法	GB/T 6434—1994
GB/T 7294—2006	饲料添加剂　维生素 K_3（亚硫酸氢钠甲萘醌）	GB 7294—1987
GB/T 7303—2006	饲料添加剂　维生素C（L-抗坏血酸）	
GB/T 7740—2006	天然肠衣	GB/T 7740—1987
GB/T 8269—2006	柠檬酸	GB/T 8269—1998
GB/T 8622—2006	饲料用大豆制品中尿素酶活性的测定	GB/T 8622—1988
GB/T 9176—2006	桑蚕干茧	GB 9176—1988
GB/T 9841—2006	饲料添加剂　维生素 B_{12}（氰钴胺）粉剂	GB 9841—1988
GB/T 9840—2006	饲料添加剂　维生素 D_3 微粒	GB/T 9840—1988
GB/T 10893.2—2006	压缩空气干燥器　第2部分：性能参数	
GB/T 10784—2006	罐头食品分类	GB/T 10784—1989
GB/T 11603—2006	羊毛纤维平均直径测定法　气流法	GB/T 11603—1989
GB/T 12728—2006	食用菌术语	GB/T 12728—1991
GB 13078.1—2006	饲料卫生标准　饲料中亚硝酸盐允许量	
GB 13078.2—2006	饲料卫生标准　饲料中赭曲霉毒素A和玉米赤霉烯酮的允许量	
GB/T 13088—2006	饲料中铬的测定	GB/T 13088—1991
GB/T 13092—2006	饲料中霉菌总数的测定	GB/T 13092—1991
GB/T 13213—2006	猪肉糜类罐头	GB/T 13213—1991
GB/T 13214—2006	咸牛肉、咸羊肉罐头	GB/T 13214—1991
GB/T 14151—2006	蘑菇罐头	GB/T 14151—1999
GB 15108—2006	原糖	GB/T 15108—1994
GB 16568—2006	奶牛场卫生规范	GB 16568—1996
GB/T 17593.1—2006	纺织品　重金属的测定　第1部分：原子吸收分光光度法	GB/T 17593.1—1998
GB/T 17593.3—2006	纺织品　重金属的测定　第3部分：六价铬　分光光度法	
GB/T 17593.4—2006	纺织品　重金属的测定　第4部分：砷、汞原子荧光分光光度法	
GB/T 17695—2006	印刷品用公共信息图形标志	GB/T 17695—1999
GB/T 18412.1—2006	纺织品　农药残留量的测定　第1部分：77种农药	GB/T 18412—2001
GB/T 18412.2—2006	纺织品　农药残留量的测定　第2部分：有机氯农药	
GB/T 18412.3—2006	纺织品　农药残留量的测定　第3部分：有机磷农药	
GB/T 18412.4—2006	纺织品　农药残留量的测定　第4部分：拟除虫菊酯农药	
GB/T 18412.6—2006	纺织品　农药残留量的测定　第6部分：苯氧羧酸类农药	
GB/T 18412.7—2006	纺织品　农药残留量的测定　第7部分：毒杀酚	

（续）

标 准 号	标 准 名 称	代 替 标 准
GB/T 18414.1—2006	纺织品　含氯苯酚的测定　第1部分：气相色谱-质谱法	GB/T 18414.1—2001
GB/T 18414.2—2006	纺织品　含氯苯酚的测定　第2部分：气相色谱法	GB/T 18414.2—2001
GB/T 18738—2006	速溶豆粉和豆奶粉	GB/T 18738—2002
GB/T 20103—2006	膜分离技术　术语	
GB/T 20188—2006	小麦粉中溴酸盐的测定　离子色谱法	
GB/T 20189—2006	饲料中莱克多巴胺的测定　高效液相色谱法	
GB/T 20193—2006	饲料用骨粉及肉骨粉	
GB/T 20194—2006	饲料中淀粉含量的测定　旋光法	
GB/T 20195—2006	动物饲料　试样的制备	
GB/T 20196—2006	饲料中盐霉素的测定	
GB/T 20293—2006	油辣椒	
GB/T 20362—2006	鸡蛋中氯羟吡啶残留量的检测方法　高效液相色谱法	
GB/T 20363—2006	饲料中苯巴比妥的测定	
GB/T 20369—2006	啤酒花制品	
GB/T 20371—2006	食品工业用大豆蛋白	
GB/T 20372—2006	花椰菜　冷藏和冷藏运输指南	
GB/T 20373—2006	变性淀粉中乙酰基含量的测定　酶法	
GB/T 20374—2006	变性淀粉　氧化淀粉羧基含量的测定	
GB/T 20375—2006	变性淀粉　羧甲基淀粉中羧甲基含量的测定	
GB/T 20376—2006	变性淀粉中羟丙基含量的测定　质子核磁共振波谱法	
GB/T 20378—2006	原淀粉　淀粉含量的测定　旋光法	
GB/T 20382—2006	纺织品　致癌染料的测定	
GB/T 20383—2006	纺织品　致敏性分散染料的测定	
GB/T 20384—2006	纺织品　氯化苯和氯化甲苯残留量的测定	
GB/T 20385—2006	纺织品　有机锡化合物的测定	
GB/T 20386—2006	纺织品　邻苯基苯酚的测定	
GB/T 20387—2006	纺织品　多氯联苯的测定	
GB/T 20392—2006	HVI棉纤维物理性能试验方法	
GB/T 20393—2006	天然彩色棉制品及含天然彩色棉制品通用技术要求	
GB/T 20411—2006	饲料用大豆	
GB 20415—2006	橡胶涂覆织物　绝缘带	
GB/T 20439—2006	印刷技术　印前数据交换　用于四色印刷特征描述的输入数据	
GB/T 20444—2006	猪组织中四环素族抗生素残留量检测方法　微生物学检测方法	
GB/T 20452—2006	仁用杏杏仁质量等级	
GB/T 20453—2006	柿子产品质量等级	
GB/T 20460—2006	橡胶配合剂　天然碳酸钙　试验方法	

（续）

标准号	标准名称	代替标准
GB/T 20502—2006	膜组件及装置型号命名	
GB/T 20551—2006	畜禽屠宰 HACCP 应用规范	
GB 20554—2006	海带	
GB/T 20569—2006	稻谷储存品质判定规则	
GB/T 20570—2006	玉米储存品质判定规则	
GB/T 20571—2006	小麦储存品质判定规则	
GB/T 22000—2006	食品安全管理体系　食品链中各类组织的要求	
NY/T 224—2006	双孢蘑菇	NY/T 224—1994
NY/T 230—2006	椰子油	NY/T 230—1994
NY/T 419—2006	绿色食品　大米	NY/Y　419—2000
NY/T 422—2006	绿色食品　食用糖	NY/T 422—2000
NY/T 468—2006	动物组织中盐酸克伦特罗的测定　气相色谱/质谱法	NY/T 468—2001
NY/T 472—2006	绿色食品　兽药使用准则	NY/T 472—2001
NY/T 604—2006	生咖啡	NY/T 604—2002
NY/T 605—2006	焙炒咖啡	NY/T 605—2002
NY/T 751—2006	绿色食品　食用植物油	NY/T 751—2003
NY/T 930—2006	饲料级甲酸	NY 930－2005
NY/T 940—2006	番茄等级规格	
NY/T 941—2006	青花菜等级规格	
NY/T 942—2006	茎用莴苣等级规格	
NY/T 943—2006	大白菜等级规格	
NY/T 944—2006	辣椒等级规格	
NY/T 945—2006	蒜薹等级规格	
NY/T 946—2006	蒜薹、青椒、柑橘、葡萄中仲丁胺残留量的测定	
NY/T 948—2006	香蕉脆片	
NY/T 949—2006	木菠萝干	
NY/T 950—2006	番荔枝	
NY/T 952—2006	速冻菠菜	
NY/T 954—2006	小粒黄豆	
NY/T 955—2006	莱阳梨	
NY/T 956—2006	番茄酱	
NY/T 957—2006	番茄粉	
NY/T 958—2006	花生酱	
NY/T 959—2006	脱水蔬菜　根菜类	
NY/T 960—2006	脱水蔬菜　叶菜类	
NY/T 961—2006	宽皮柑橘	

（续）

标 准 号	标 准 名 称	代 替 标 准
NY/T 962—2006	花椰菜	
NY/T 963—2006	苦瓜	
NY/T 964—2006	菠菜	
NY/T 965—2006	豇豆	
NY/T 966—2006	白瓜子	
NY/T 967—2006	农作物品种审定规范　小麦	
NY/T 976—2006	浙南—闽西—粤东宽皮柑橘生产技术规程	
NY/T 977—2006	赣南—湘南—桂北脐橙生产技术规程	
NY/T 980—2006	罐装甜玉米加工技术规范	
NY/T 981—2006	沙棘汁加工技术规范	
NY/T 982—2006	甘薯粉丝加工技术规范	
NY/T 983—2006	苹果贮运技术规范	
NY/T 988—2006	稻谷干燥机械　作业质量	
NY/T 994—2006	花生剥壳机　作业质量	
NY/T 995—2006	谷物（小麦）联合收获机械　作业质量	
NY/T 1005—2006	移动式粮食干燥机质量评价技术规范	
NY/T 1010—2006	大豆品质同质性评价技术规范	
NY/T 1014—2006	脱粒机　质量评价技术规范	
NY/T 1016—2006	水果蔬菜中乙烯利残留量的测定　气相色谱法	
NY/T 1017—2006	秸秆气化装置和系统测试方法	
NY/T 1018—2006	蔬菜及其制品中磷的测定	
NY/T 1019—2006	家禽脱羽设备	
NY/T 1020—2006	家禽浸烫设备	
NY/T 1021—2006	生猪浸烫设备	
NY/T 1022—2006	生猪刮毛设备	
NY/T 1023—2006	饲料加工成套设备　质量评价技术规范	
NY/T 1024—2006	饲料混合机质量评价技术规范	
NY/T 1025—2006	青饲料切碎机安全使用技术条件	
NY/T 1028—2006	饲料添加剂　左旋肉碱	
NY/T 1029—2006	仔猪、生长肥育猪维生素预混合饲料	
NY/T 1030—2006	饲料中沙丁胺醇的测定　气相色谱/质谱法	
NY/T 1031—2006	饲料安全性评价　亚急性毒性试验	
NY/T 1032—2006	饲料中胆固醇的测定　气相色谱法	
NY/T 1033—2006	饲料中西马特罗的测定　气相色谱/质谱法	
NY/T 1037—2006	天然胶乳　表观黏度的测定　旋转黏度计法	
NY/T 1038—2006	天然生胶初加工原料　凝胶　验收方法	

（续）

标准号	标准名称	代替标准
NY/T 1039—2006	绿色食品　淀粉及淀粉制品	
NY/T 1040—2006	绿色食品　食用盐	
NY/T 1041—2006	绿色食品　干果	
NY/T 1042—2006	绿色食品　坚果	
NY/T 1043—2006	绿色食品　人参和西洋参	
NY/T 1044—2006	绿色食品　藕及其制品	
NY/T 1045—2006	绿色食品　脱水蔬菜	
NY/T 1046—2006	绿色食品　焙烤食品	
NY/T 1047—2006	绿色食品　水果、蔬菜罐头	
NY/T 1048—2006	绿色食品　笋及笋制品	
NY/T 1049—2006	绿色食品　薯芋类蔬菜	
NY/T 1050—2006	绿色食品　龟鳖类	
NY/T 1051—2006	绿色食品　枸杞	
NY/T 1052—2006	绿色食品　豆制品	
NY/T 1053—2006	绿色食品　味精	
NY/T 1054—2006	绿色食品　产地环境调查、监测与评价导则	
NY/T 1055—2006	绿色食品　产品检验规则	
NY/T 1056—2006	绿色食品　贮藏运输准则	
NY/T 1057—2006	棉种过量式稀硫酸脱绒技术规范	
NY/T 1061—2006	香菇等级规格	
NY/T 1062—2006	菜豆等级规格	
NY/T 1063—2006	荷兰豆等级规格	
NY/T 1064—2006	芥蓝等级规格	
NY/T 1065—2006	山药等级规格	
NY/T 1066—2006	马铃薯等级规格	
NY/T 1067—2006	食用花生	
NY/T 1068—2006	油用花生	
NY/T 1069—2006	速冻马蹄片	
NY/T 1070—2006	辣椒酱	
NY/T 1071—2006	洋葱	
NY/T 1072—2006	加工用苹果	
NY/T 1073—2006	脱水姜片和姜粉	
NY/T 1075—2006	红富士苹果	
NY/T 1076—2006	南果梨	
NY/T 1077—2006	黄花梨	
NY/T 1078—2006	鸭梨	

（续）

标 准 号	标 准 名 称	代 替 标 准
NY/T 1079—2006	荔浦芋	
NY/T 1080—2006	荸荠	
NY/T 1081—2006	脱水蔬菜原料通用技术规范	
NY/T 1082—2006	黄土高原苹果生产技术规程	
NY/T 1083—2006	渤海湾地区苹果生产技术规程	
NY/T 1084—2006	红富士苹果生产技术规程	
NY/T 1087—2006	油菜籽干燥与储藏技术规程	
NY/T 1090—2006	农作物品种审定规范　稻	
NY/T 1094.1—2006	小麦实验制粉　第1部分：设备、样品制备和润麦	
NY/T 1094.2—2006	小麦实验制粉　第2部分：布勒氏法　用于硬麦	
NY/T 1094.3—2006	小麦实验制粉　第3部分：布勒氏法　用于软麦低提取率	
NY/T 1094.4—2006	小麦实验制粉　第4部分：布勒氏法　用于软麦统粉	
NY/T 1094.5—2006	小麦实验制粉　第5部分：实验磨法	
NY/T 1095—2006	小麦沉淀值测定　Zeleny法	
NY/T 1096—2006	食品中草甘膦残留量测定	
NY/T 1097—2006	食用菌菌种真实性鉴定　酯酶同工酶电泳法	
NY/T 1098—2006	食用菌品种描述技术规范	
NY/T 1099—2006	稻米中总砷的测定　原子荧光光谱法	
NY/T 1100—2006	稻米中铅、镉的测定　石墨炉原子吸收光谱法	
NY/T 1101—2006	转基因植物及其产品食用安全性评价导则	
NY/T 1102—2006	转基因植物及其产品食用安全检测　大鼠90天喂养试验	
NY/T 1123—2006	带式穿流干燥机	
NY/T 1124—2006	魔芋精粉机	
NY/T 1127—2006	螺旋挤压式薯类粉丝机	
NY/T 1129—2006	豆类精选机	
NY/T 1131—2006	浓缩天然胶乳包装容器　钢桶	
NY/T 1132—2006	隧道窑式蔬果干燥机　技术条件	
NY/T 1136—2006	挤搓式玉米种子脱粒机　技术条件	
NY/T 1141—2006	稻麦割脱机　质量评价技术规范	
NY/T 1142—2006	种子加工成套设备质量评价技术规范	
NY/T 1144—2006	畜禽粪便干燥机质量评价技术规范	
NY/T 1158—2006	动物性食品中甲硝唑残留的检测方法　高效液相色谱法	
NY/T 1162—2006	鹿茸片	
NY/T 1163—2006	仙居鸡　肉用系	
NY/T 1164—2006	裘皮　蓝狐皮	
NY 1165—2006	羔羊肉	

（续）

标准号	标准名称	代替标准
NY/T 1167—2006	畜禽场环境质量及卫生控制规范	
NY/T 1168—2006	畜禽粪便无害化处理技术规范	
NY/T 1169—2006	畜禽场环境污染控制技术规范	
NY/T 1170—2006	苜蓿干草捆质量	
NY/T 1172—2006	生鲜牛乳质量管理规范	
NY/T 1173—2006	动物毛皮检验技术规范	
NY/T 1174—2006	肉鸡屠宰质量管理规范	
NY/T 1179—2006	茸鹿生产性能测定技术规范	
NY/T 1180—2006	肉嫩度的测定　剪切力测定法	
NY/T 1189—2006	柑橘贮藏	
NY/T 1190—2006	柑橘等级规格	
NY/T 1191—2006	砀山酥梨	
NY/T 1192—2006	肥城桃	
NY/T 1193—2006	姜	
NY/T 1196—2006	农作物品种审定规范　稻	
NY/T 1197—2006	农作物品种审定规范　玉米	
NY/T 1198—2006	梨贮运技术规范	
NY/T 1199—2006	葡萄保鲜技术规范	
NY/T 1201—2006	蔬菜及其制品中铜、铁、锌的测定	
NY/T 1202—2006	豆类蔬菜贮藏保鲜技术规程	
NY/T 1203—2006	茄果类蔬菜贮藏保鲜技术规程	
NY/T 1204—2006	食用菌热风脱水加工技术规范	
NY/T 1205—2006	大豆水溶性蛋白含量的测定	
NY/T 1206—2006	茶叶辐照杀菌工艺	
NY/T 1207—2006	辐照香辛料及脱水蔬菜热释光鉴定方法	
NY/T 1208—2006	葱蒜热风脱水加工技术规范	
NY/T 1209—2006	农作物品种试验技术规程　玉米	
NY/T 1218—2006	黄淮海地区强筋白硬冬小麦	
NY/T 1219—2006	浓缩天然胶乳初加工原料　鲜胶乳	
NY/T 1230—2006	饲料粉碎机　筛片和锤片质量评价技术规范	
NY/T 1241—2006	蜂产品加工技术管理规范	
NY/T 1242—2006	奶牛场 HACCP 饲养管理规范	
NY/T 1243—2006	蜂蜜中农药残留限量（一）	
NY/T 1245—2006	奶牛用精饲料	
NY/T 1246—2006	饲料添加剂　维生素 D_3（胆钙化醇）油	
NY/T 1251—2006	蚕茧干燥设备	

（续）

标准号	标准名称	代替标准
NY/T 1252—2006	大豆异黄酮	
NY/T 1256—2006	冷冻水产品辐照杀菌工艺	
NY/T 5022—2006	无公害食品　香蕉生产技术规程	NY/T 5022—2001
NY 5058—2006	无公害食品　海水虾	NY 5058—2001
NY 5066—2006	无公害食品　龟鳖	NY 5066—2001
NY 5073—2006	无公害食品　水产品中有毒有害物质限量	NY 5073—2001
NY 5152—2006	无公害食品　鲆鲽鳎	NY 5152—2002
NY 5160—2006	无公害食品　鲑鳟鲟	NY 5160—2002
NY/T 5183—2006	无公害食品　杨桃生产技术规程	NY/T 5183—2002
NY 5288—2006	无公害食品　蛤	NY 5288—2004
NY 5305—2006	无公害食品　小杂粮	NY 5305—2005
NY 5316—2006	无公害食品　可食用花卉	
NY 5317—2006	无公害食品　芽类蔬菜	
NY 5318—2006	无公害食品　参类	
NY 5319—2006	无公害食品　瓜子	
NY 5320—2006	无公害食品　甜叶菊	
NY 5321—2006	无公害食品　荚果	
NY 5322—2006	无公害食品　仁果类水果	
NY 5323—2006	无公害食品　香辛料	
NY 5324—2006	无公害食品　（常绿果树）坚（壳）果	
NY 5325—2006	无公害食品　螺	
NY 5326—2006	无公害食品　头足类水产品	
NY 5327—2006	无公害食品　鲻科、鲹科、军曹鱼科海水鱼	
NY 5328—2006	无公害食品　海参	
NY 5329—2006	无公害食品　海捕鱼	
NY 5330—2006	无公害食品　食用菌	
NY 5331—2006	无公害食品　水生蔬菜产地环境条件	
NY 5332—2006	无公害食品　大田作物产地环境条件	
NY/T 5333—2006	无公害食品　食用菌生产技术规范	
NY/T 5334—2006	无公害食品　小麦粉加工技术规范	
NY/T 5335—2006	无公害食品　产地环境质量调查规范	
NY/T 5336—2006	无公害食品　粮食生产管理规范	
NY/T 5337—2006	无公害食品　茶叶生产管理规范	
NY/T 5338—2006	无公害食品　家禽屠宰加工生产管理规范	
NY/T 5339—2006	无公害食品　畜禽饲养兽医防疫准则	
NY/T 5340—2006	无公害食品　产品检验规范	

（续）

标 准 号	标 准 名 称	代 替 标 准
NY/T 5341—2006	无公害食品　认定认证现场检查规范	
NY/T 5342—2006	无公害食品　产品认证准则	
NY/T 5343—2006	无公害食品　产地认定规范	
NY/T 5344.1—2006	无公害食品　产品抽样规范　第1部分：通则	
NY/T 5344.2—2006	无公害食品　产品抽样规范　第2部分：粮油	
NY/T 5344.3—2006	无公害食品　产品抽样规范　第3部分：蔬菜	
NY/T 5344.4—2006	无公害食品　产品抽样规范　第4部分：水果	
NY/T 5344.5—2006	无公害食品　产品抽样规范　第5部分：茶叶	
NY/T 5344.6—2006	无公害食品　产品抽样规范　第6部分：畜禽产品	
NY/T 5344.7—2006	无公害食品　产品抽样规范　第7部分：水产品	

农产品加工业机械行业标准（2006年）

标 准 号	标 准 名 称	代 替 标 准
JB/T 7220—2006	刮刀卸料离心机	JB/T 7220—1994
JB/T 7658.1—2006	氨制冷装置用辅助设备　第1部分：淋水式冷凝器	JB/T 7658.1—1995
JB/T 7658.2—2006	氨制冷装置用辅助设备　第2部分：油分离器	JB/T 7658.2—1995
JB/T 7658.3—2006	氨制冷装置用辅助设备　第3部分：立式蒸发器	JB/T 7658.3—1995
JB/T 7658.4—2006	氨制冷装置用辅助设备　第4部分：卧式蒸发器	JB/T 7658.4—1995
JB/T 7658.5—2006	氨制冷装置用辅助设备　第5部分：蒸发式冷凝器	JB/T 7658.5—1995
JB/T 7658.6—2006	氨制冷装置用辅助设备　第6部分：空气冷却器	JB/T 7658.6—1995
JB/T 7658.7—2006	氨制冷装置用辅助设备　第7部分：搅拌机	JB/T 7658.7—1995
JB/T 7658.8—2006	氨制冷装置用辅助设备　第8部分：贮液器	JB/T 7658.8—1995
JB/T 7658.9—2006	氨制冷装置用辅助设备　第9部分：低压循环桶	JB/T 7658.9—1995
JB/T 7658.10—2006	氨制冷装置用辅助设备　第10部分：集油器	JB/T 7658.10—1995
JB/T 7658.11—2006	氨制冷装置用辅助设备　第11部分：中间冷却器	JB/T 7658.11—1995
JB/T 7658.12—2006	氨制冷装置用辅助设备　第12部分：紧急泄氨器	JB/T 7658.12—1995
JB/T 7658.13—2006	氨制冷装置用辅助设备　第13部分：空气分离器	JB/T 7658.13—1995
JB/T 7658.14—2006	氨制冷装置用辅助设备　第14部分：氨液分离器	JB/T 7658.14—1995
JB/T 7658.15—2006	氨制冷装置用辅助设备　第15部分：氨气过滤器	JB/T 7658.15—1995
JB/T 7658.16—2006	氨制冷装置用辅助设备　第16部分：氨液过滤器	JB/T 7658.16—1995
JB/T 7658.17—2006	氨制冷装置用辅助设备　第17部分：立式冷凝器	JB/T 7658.17—1995
JB/T 7658.18—2006	氨制冷装置用辅助设备　第18部分：卧式冷凝器	JB/T 7658.18—1995
JB/T 8653—2006	水平带式真空过滤机	JB/T 8653—1997
JB/T 10550—2006	真空技术　真空烧结炉	
JB/T 10639—2006	不干胶贴标机	
JB/T 10640—2006	多功能装盒机	
JB/T 10641—2006	软双铝包装机	
JB/T 10642—2006	旋开盖真空封口机	JB/T 7549.2—1994
JB/T 20083—2006	小型动态提取浓缩机组	
JB/T 20084—2006	热泵外加热式双效浓缩器	
JB/T 20085—2006	隧道式微波干燥灭菌机	
JB/T 20090—2006	旋料式切片机	

农产品加工业轻工行业标准（2006年）

标准号	标准名称	代替标准
QB/T 1016—2006	鸡皮纸	QB/T1016—1991
QB/T 1017—2006	仿羊皮纸	QB/T1017—1991
QB/T 1178—2006	工业用缝纫机　振动的测试方法	QB/T1178—1991
QB/T 1460—2006	伸性纸袋纸	QB/T1460—1992
QB/T 1599—2006	书画纸	QB/T1599—1992
QB/T 1697—2006	纸浆泵	QB/T1697—1993
QB/T 1698—2006	纸浆泵　试验方法	QB/T1698—1993
QB/T 1700—2006	高压均质泵	QB/T1700—2001
QB/T 1706—2006	条纹牛皮纸	QB/T1706—1993
QB/T 1709—2006	工业羊皮纸	QB/T1709—1993
QB/T 1926—2006	夹层锅	QB/T1926—1993
QB/T 2151—2006	工业用缝纫机　电脑控制刺绣机	QB/T2151—1995
QB/T 2256—2006	工业用缝纫机　高速平缝缝纫机机头	QB/T2256—1996
QB/T 2294—2006	纸杯	QB/T2294—1997
QB/T 2300—2006	植物蛋白饮料　椰子汁及复原椰子汁	QB/T2300—1997
QB/T 2342—2006	复印纸	QB/T2342—1997
QB/T 2429—2006	晒图原纸	QB/T2429—1999
QB/T 2438—2006	植物蛋白饮料　杏仁露	QB/T2438—1999
QB/T 2469—2006	甜菜颗粒粕	QB/T2469—2000
QB/T 2762—2006	复合麦片	
QB/T 2766—2006	矿物油型造纸机循环润滑系统润滑油	
QB/T 2767—2006	合成型造纸机循环润滑系统润滑油	
QB/T 2768—2006	造纸机循环润滑系统冲洗油	
QB/T 2779—2006	鞋面用聚氯乙烯人造革	
QB/T 2780—2006	鞋面用聚氨酯人造革	
QB/T 2784—2006	咸牛肉罐头	GB/T 13214—1991
QB/T 2785—2006	咸羊肉罐头	GB/T 13215—1991
QB/T 2786—2006	清蒸猪肉罐头	GB/T 13512—1992
QB/T 2787—2006	原汁猪肉罐头	GB/T 13513—1992
QB/T 2788—2006	清蒸牛肉罐头	GB/T 13514—1992
QB/T 2793—2006	食品添加剂　乙酸芳樟酯	GB 10348—1989
QB/T 2794—2006	食品添加剂　苯甲醇	GB 10354—1989
QB/T 2795—2006	食品添加剂　广藿香油	GB 11961—1989
QB/T 2796—2006	食品添加剂　丁酸	GB 11962—1989
QB/T 2797—2006	食品添加剂　己酸	GB 11963—1989
QB/T 2798—2006	食品添加剂　杭白菊浸膏	GB 15559—1995
QB/T 2799—2006	皮革　透气性测定方法	GB/T4689.22—1996
QB/T 2800—2006	皮革成品部位的区分	GB/T 4690—1984
QB/T 2801—2006	皮革成品验收规则	GB/T 4693—1984
QB/T 2802—2006	皮革成品的包装、标志、运输和保管	GB/T 4694—1984
QB/T 2804—2006	纸和纸板白度测定法　45/0定向反射法	GB/T 8940.1—1988

（续）

标 准 号	标 准 名 称	代 替 标 准
QB/T 2805—2006	纸和纸板表面吸收速度的测定	GB/T 461.2—2002
QB/T 2807—2006	扑克牌纸板	QB/T3501—1999
QB/T 2808—2006	口罩纸	
QB/T 2809—2006	轻型印刷纸	
QB/T 2810—2006	吸尘器集尘袋外层纸	
QB/T 2811—2006	造纸研磨碳酸钙	
QB/T 2812—2006	纸张定量、水分的在线测定（近红外法）	
QB/T 2815—2006	工业用缝纫机　高速曲折缝纫机机头	
QB/T 2816—2006	工业用缝纫机　单（双）针下送料立柱式平缝机机头	
QB/T 2817—2006	食品添加剂　迷迭香提取物	
QB/T 2822—2006	毛皮服装	
QB/T 2830—2006	榨菜盐	
QB/T 2831—2006	运动营养食品　能量补充食品	
QB/T 2832—2006	运动营养食品　蛋白质补充食品	
QB/T 2833—2006	运动营养食品　能量控制食品	
QB/T 2834—2006	运动营养食品　食用肌酸	
QB/T 2839—2006	果蔬脆片成套设备	

农产品加工业纺织行业标准（2006 年）

标 准 号	标 准 名 称	代 替 标 准
FZ/T 01096—2006	纺织品耐光色牢度试验方法：碳弧	GB/T 8428—1987
FZ/T 01097—2006	织物光泽测试方法	GB/T 8686—1988
FZ/T 01098—2006	纺织品　耐氧化氮和烟熏色牢度试验用控制标样和褪色标准	GB/T 13766—1992
FZ/T 10001—2006	气流纱捻度的测定退捻加捻法	FZ/T 10001—1992
FZ/T 12001—2006	气流纺棉本色纱	FZ/T 12001—1992
FZ/T 12002—2006	精梳棉本色缝纫专用纱线	FZ/T 12002—1993
FZ/T 12003—2006	粘胶纤维本色纱线	FZ/T 12003—1995
FZ/T 12004—2006	涤粘混纺本色纱线	FZ/T 12004—1995
FZ/T 12014—2006	针织用棉色纺纱	
FZ/T 12015—2006	精梳天然彩色棉纱线	
FZ/T 12016—2006	涤与棉混纺色纺纱	
FZ/T 12017—2006	天然彩色棉气流纺纱	
FZ/T 13004—2006	粘胶纤维本色布	FZ/T 13004—1995
FZ/T 13006—2006	涤粘混纺本色布	FZ/T 13006—1995
FZ/T 13012—2006	普梳涤与棉混纺本色布	FZ/T 13012—1998
FZ/T 14004—2006	粘胶纤维印染布	FZ/T 14004—1995
FZ/T 14005—2006	涤粘混纺印染布	FZ/T 14005—1995
FZ/T 14010—2006	普梳涤与棉混纺印染布	
FZ/T 20011—2006	毛针织成衣扭斜角试验方法	FZ/T 20011—1995
FZ/T 20016—2006	毛条、洗净毛疵点及重量试验方法	FZ/T 20016—1999
FZ/T 20019—2006	毛机织物脱缝程度试验方法	FZ/T 20019—1999

（续）

标 准 号	标 准 名 称	代 替 标 准
FZ/T 20023—2006	毛机织物经汽蒸后尺寸变化率的测定　霍夫曼法	
FZ/T 22003—2006	机织雪尼尔本色线	
FZ/T 22004—2006	环锭纺及空芯锭圈圈线	
FZ/T 24002—2006	精梳毛织品	FZ/T 24002—1993
FZ/T 24003—2006	粗梳毛织品	FZ/T 24003—1993
FZ/T 51002—2006	粘胶纤维用竹浆粕	
FZ/T 52006—2006	竹材粘胶短纤维	
FZ/T 52007—2006	热熔法用丙纶短纤维	GB/T 17687—1999
FZ/T 61001—2006	纯毛、毛混纺毛毯	FZ/T 61001—1991
FZ/T 61002—2006	化纤仿毛毛毯	FZ/T 61002—1991
FZ/T 61004—2006	拉舍尔毯	FZ/T 61004—1991
FZ/T 61005—2006	线毯	FZ/T 61005—1999
FZ/T 61006—2006	纬编腈纶毛毯	
FZ/T 62003—2006	手帕	FZ/T 62003—1991
FZ/T 63001—2006	涤纶本色缝纫用纱线	FZ/T 63001—1992
FZ/T 70005—2006	毛纺织品伸长和回复性试验方法	FZ/T 70005—1992
FZ/T 70010—2006	针织物平方米干燥重量试验的测定	
FZ/T 70011—2006	针织保暖内衣标志	
FZ/T 71005—2006	针织用棉本色纱	FZ/T 71005—1994
FZ/T 72002—2006	毛条喂入式针织人造毛皮	FZ/T 72002—1993
FZ/T 72005—2006	羊毛针织人造毛皮	
FZ/T 72006—2006	割圈法针织人造毛皮	
FZ/T 72007—2006	经编人造毛皮	
FZ/T 72003—2006	针织天鹅绒面料	FZ/T 72003—1998
FZ/T 72008—2006	针织牛仔布	
FZ/T 73023—2006	抗菌针织品	
FZ/T 73024—2006	化纤针织内衣	
FZ/T 73025—2006	婴幼儿针织服饰	
FZ/T 73026—2006	针织裙套	
FZ/T 80004—2006	服装产品出厂检验规则	FZ/T 80004—1998
FZ/T 80007.1—2006	使用粘合衬服装剥离强力试验方法	FZ/T 80007.1—1999
FZ/T 80007.2—2006	使用粘合衬服装耐水洗测试方法	FZ/T 80007.2—1999
FZ/T 80007.3—2006	使用粘合衬服装耐干洗测试方法	FZ/T 80007.3—1999
FZ/T 80010—2006	服装人体头围测量方法与帽子尺寸代号	GB/T 17837—1999
FZ/T 81005—2006	绗缝制品	FZ/T 81005—1991
FZ/T 81012—2006	围巾、披肩	
FZ/T 90001—2006	纺织机械产品包装	FZ 90001—1991
FZ/T 92029—2006	梳棉机　盖板骨架	FZ/T 92029—1995
FZ/T 92033—2006	粗纱悬锭锭翼	FZ/T 92033—1995
FZ/T 93034—2006	棉纺悬锭粗纱机	FZ/T 92034—1995
FZ/T 93064—2006	棉粗纱机牵伸下罗拉	
FZ/T 94049—2006	分批整经机	

农产品加工业水产行业标准（2006 年）

标 准 号	标 准 名 称	代 替 标 准
SC/T 0003—2006	水产企业 HACCP 管理体系认证指南	
SC 1071—2006	欧洲鳗鲡	SC/T 1071—2006
SC/T 1072—2006	长吻鮠配合饲料	
SC 1090—2006	怀头鲇	
SC/T 2024—2006	种海带	
SC 2032—2006	虾夷扇贝	SC/T 2032—2006
SC 2035—2006	文蛤	
SC/T 2037—2006	刺参配合饲料	SC 2037—2006
SC/T 2053—2006	鲍配合饲料	
SC 2055—2006	凡纳滨对虾	
SC 2056—2006	青蛤	
SC/T 3025—2006	水产品中甲醛的测定	
SC/T 3026—2006	冻虾仁加工技术规范	
SC/T 3027—2006	冻烤鳗加工技术规范	
SC/T 3028—2006	水产品中噁喹酸残留量的测定　液相色谱法	
SC/T 3029—2006	水产品中甲基睾酮残留量的测定　液相色谱法	
SC/T 3030—2006	水产品中五氯苯酚及其钠盐残留量的测定　气相色谱法	
SC/T 3031—2006	水产品中挥发酚残留量的测定　分光光度法	
SC/T 3034—2006	水产品中三唑磷残留量的测定　气相色谱法	
SC/T 3036—2006	水产品中硝基苯残留量的测定　气相色谱法	
SC/T 3037—2006	冻罗非鱼片加工技术规范	
SC/T 3038—2006	咸鱼加工技术规范	
SC/T 3111—2006	冻扇贝	SC/T 3111—1996
SC/T 3115—2006	冻章鱼	
SC/T 3116—2006	冻淡水鱼片	
SC/T 3117—2006	生食金枪鱼	
SC/T 3118—2006	冻裹面包屑虾	
SC/T 3214—2006	干鲨鱼翅	
SC/T 3216—2006	半干淡盐黄鱼	
SC/T 3504—2006	饲料用鱼油	
SC/T 3505—2006	鱼油微胶囊	
SC/T 4019—2006	聚乙烯—聚乙烯醇网线　混捻型	
SC/T 5029—2006	高强度聚乙烯渔网线	
SC/T 5031—2006	聚乙烯网片　绞捻型	
SC/T 7201.1—2006	鱼类细菌病检疫技术规程　第 1 部分：通用技术	
SC/T 9011.1—2006	冻结装置试验方法　第 1 部分：总则	
SC/T 9011.2—2006	冻结装置试验方法　第 2 部分：平板冻结装置试验方法	
SC/T 9011.3—2006	冻结装置试验方法　第 3 部分：隧道冻结装置试验方法	
SC/T 9011.4—2006	冻结装置试验方法　第 4 部分：流态冻结装置试验方法	
SC/T 9020—2006	水产品低温冷藏设备和低温运输设备技术条件	

农产品加工业烟草行业标准（2006 年）

标准号	标准名称	代替标准
YC/T 9—2006	卷烟厂设计规范	YC0009—93
YC/T 85.1—2006	烟草机械　振动式输送机　第 1 部分：型式与基本参数	YC/T 85.1—1996
YC/T 85.2—2006	烟草机械　振动式输送机　第 2 部分：技术条件	YC/T 85.2—1996
YC/T 86.1—2006	烟草机械　带式输送机　第 1 部分：型式与基本参数	YC/T 86.1—1996
YC/T 86.2—2006	烟草机械　带式输送机　第 2 部分：技术条件	YC/T 86.2—1996
YC/T 87.1—2006	烟草机械　贮柜　第 1 部分：型式与基本参数	YC/T 87.1—1996
YC/T 87.2—2006	烟草机械　贮柜　第 2 部分：技术条件	YC/T 87.2—1996
YC/T 88.1—2006	烟草机械　喂料机　第 1 部分：型式与基本参数	YC/T 88.1—1996
YC/T 88.2—2006	烟草机械　喂料机　第 2 部分：技术条件	YC/T 88.2—1996
YC/T 89.1—2006	烟草机械　振动式筛分机　第 1 部分：型式与基本参数	YC/T 89.1—1996
YC/T 89.2—2006	烟草机械　振动式筛分机　第 2 部分：技术条件	YC/T 89.2—1996
YC/T 205—2006	烟草及烟草制品　仓库　设计规范	
YC/T 206—2006	卷烟销售网络业务规范	
YC/T 208—2006	滤棒成形纸	
YC/T 209.1—2006	烟用材料编码　第 1 部分：烟用材料分类代码与产品代码	
YC/T 210.1—2006	烟叶代码　第 1 部分：烟叶分类与代码	
YC/T 210.2—2006	烟叶代码　第 2 部分：烟叶形态代码	
YC/T 210.3—2006	烟叶代码　第 3 部分：烟草品种代码	
YC/T 210.4—2006	烟叶代码　第 4 部分：烟叶部位代码	
YC/T 210.5—2006	烟叶代码　第 5 部分：烟叶颜色代码	
YC/T 210.6—2006	烟叶代码　第 6 部分：烟叶等级代码	
YC/T 213.1—2006	烟草机械产品用物料　分类和编码　第 1 部分：总则	
YC/T 213.2—2006	烟草机械产品用物料　分类和编码　第 2 部分：专用件	
YC/T 213.3—2006	烟草机械产品用物料　分类和编码　第 3 部分：机械外购件	
YC/T 213.5—2006	烟草机械产品用物料　分类和编码　第 5 部分：电气元器件	
YC/T 213.6—2006	烟草机械产品用物料　分类和编码　第 6 部分：原、辅材料	
YC/T 214.1—2006	烟草机械　二氧化碳膨胀叶丝生产线　第 1 部分：设计导则	
YC/T 214.3—2006	烟草机械　二氧化碳膨胀叶丝生产线　第 3 部分：验收导则	

农产品加工业包装行业标准（2006 年）

标准号	标准名称	代替标准
BB/T 0016—2006	包装材料　蜂窝纸板	BB/T 0016—1999
BB/T 0031—2006	电化铝烫印箔	GB/T 10456—1989
BB/T 0032—2006	纸管	GB/T 12124—2003
BB/T 0033—2006	气雾剂产品的分类及术语	GB/T 14448—1993
BB/T 0034—2006	包装容器　扭断式铝防盗瓶盖	GB/T 14803—1993
BB/T 0035—2006	家用电冰箱包装	GB/T 16268—1996
BB/T 0036—2006	缝纫机包装	GB/T 16469—1996
BB/T 0037—2006	双面涂覆聚氯乙烯阻燃防水布、篷布	GB/T 16741—1997
BB/T 0038—2006	包装容器　$1m^3$ 金属中型散装箱	GB/T 18456—2001
BB/T 0039—2006	商品零售包装袋	GB/T 18893—2002

农产品加工业发明专利（2005 年）

［2005 年农产品加工业（含加工制品、加工技术与设备）部分专利选摘］

申请或批准号	发明名称	申请人	通讯地址	发明人
200510009974.7	尾部变速吸风回收脱粒机	林道永	(157100) 黑龙江省海林市朝鲜族实验小学农具厂	林道永
200520003592.9	移动式玉米脱粒机	曲贺林	(136500) 吉林省梨树县小城子镇宏兴机械厂	曲贺林
200520009448.6	微型脱粒机	郭继强	(401543) 重庆市合川市钱塘镇华新街 54 号	郭继强
200520020153.9	单轴流式脱粒滚筒	徐长海	(154002) 黑龙江省佳木斯市红旗路 207 号长水汽车配件商店	徐长海
200520020763.9	螺旋筋式脱粒机滚筒	林道永	(157100) 黑龙江省海林市朝鲜族实验小学农具厂	林道永
200520021007.8	脱粒机的分离复脱组合式装置	石玉升	(152300) 黑龙江省海伦市建设路立新小学对过海伦市农具厂	石玉升、柏连鹏等
200520022449.4	多功能脱粒粉碎机	胡雪峰	(652200) 云南省昆明市石林县板桥乡大官庄 202 号	胡雪峰
200520022559.0	多功能脱粒机	毛如全	(652100) 云南省昆明市宜良县蓬莱乡汝全农机修造厂	毛如全、何有能等
200520029892.4	振动式高效粉碎机	蒋海宾	(450103) 河南省荥阳市广武镇广武村 1263 号	蒋海宾
200520029993.1	穗株种子脱粒机	张文凯	(453100) 河南省卫辉市保险东一路 44 号	张文凯
200520032855.9	切碎脱粒组合机	李云安	(629300) 四川省大英县蓬莱镇江南东路 179 号	李云安
200520032856.3	半分离式脱粒机	李云安	(629300) 四川省大英县蓬莱镇江南东路 179 号	李云安
200520033373.5	稻麦两用脱粒机	任清志	(617000) 四川省攀枝花市仁和区仁和镇田坝村公所	任清志
200520033766.6	玉米脱粒机自动调间隙装置	郭 旭	(629001) 四川省遂宁市船山区工业园区天福机器厂	郭 旭
200520034487.1	轻便式稻麦脱粒机	欧春生	(638661) 四川省华蓥市阳和镇阳和村 1 组 17 号	欧春生
200520035177.1	自动筛选脱粒机	宾荣海	(542408) 广西壮族自治区桂林市平乐县青龙乡平地村委上宾村	宾荣海
200520035664.8	带风扇的水稻脱粒机	邱广初	(546601) 广西壮族自治区荔浦县马岭镇永宁街 126 号	邱广初
200520051882.0	一种脱粒机	陈立永	(417700) 湖南省双峰县永丰镇城东为民机械厂	陈立永
200520055159.X	脱粒机筛床装置	冯文雄	(525000) 广东省茂名市茂南区金塘镇州村 8 组	冯文雄
200520082825.9	稻麦脱粒机二次回收装置	李树新	(271604) 山东省肥城市安庄镇西肥城泰峰机械有限公司	李树新、梁曰才等
200520089591.0	双滚筒脱粒机	郎忠良	(113201) 辽宁省新宾县北四平乡北旺清村	郎忠良

（续）

申请或批准号	发明名称	申请人	通讯地址	发明人
200520096356.6	可调式动力振动筛稻谷脱粒机	刘文虎	（545100）广西壮族自治区柳江县拉堡第一工业区远东路9号	刘文虎
200520104377.8	水稻脱粒机	温英德	（530500）广西壮族自治区上林县里丹云莫136号上林县里丹脱粒机厂	温英德
200520110916.9	改进的粮食清选机	侯国义、赵清海等	（831800）新疆维吾尔自治区奇台县东关街108号	侯国义、赵清海等
200510007640.6	发酵牧草饲料及其制备方法	杨　静	（100022）北京市朝阳区建国路88号现代城D座1911	杨　静
200510016802.2	糖化纤维饲料及其制备方法	石晓岭	（136000）吉林省四平市铁西区条子河村四平市磷脂厂	石晓岭
200510042544.5	一种混合饲料	周凤山	（252400）山东省聊城市莘县魏庄乡东八庙村养殖场	周凤山
200510044747.8	一种啤酒糟生产富酶蛋白饲料的方法	李军训	（271000）山东省泰安市凤台村山东宝来利来生物工程股份有限公司	李军训、杜金华等
200510066479.X	一种蛋白饲料	陶燕铎、邵赟等	（810001）青海省西宁市西关大街59号	陶燕铎
200510119735.7	一种蛋白饲料及其加工方法	韩福山	（116033）辽宁省大连市甘井子区椒北路34号楼5-3-2号	韩福山
200510063039.9	植物秸秆饲料产业化产品及其制备方法	单德章	（261500）山东省高密市民营科技园天达采禾动物保健品有限公司	单德章
200520002564.5	多功能铡草粉碎机	杨学仁	（835503）新疆维吾尔自治区特克斯县乔拉克铁热克乡供销社	杨学仁
200520003222.5	秸秆粉碎机	马曙光	（057450）河北省邱县发起农机修造厂	马曙光、石书龙等
200520012032.X	高效铡草粉碎机	杨学仁	（835503）新疆维吾尔自治区特克斯县乔拉克铁热克乡学仁农机制造厂	杨学仁
200520022222.X	半自动青饲料切碎机	陈春连	（651700）云南省昆明市嵩明县嵩阳镇昆明市嵩明云春机械配件厂	陈春连
200520022407.0	双刀安全型青饲料切碎机	黄高勇	（650041）云南省昆明市东郊贵昆路3号（省冶金进出口公司仓库内）	黄高勇
200520022566.0	平衡式饲料粉碎机	张云华	（652115）云南省昆明市宜良县马街乡马街办事处	张云华
200520022693.0	高效切削饲料粉碎机	张　新	（652100）云南省昆明市宜良县兴营农机修造厂（天力大酒店旁）	张　新、罗富昌等
200520022791.4	粗饲料加工机	时玉珠	（102205）北京市昌平区阳坊镇西马坊村中北街49号	时玉珠
200520029113.0	干湿饲料粉碎机	孙金库	（132416）吉林省桦甸市榆木桥子镇寿山村暖木屯	孙金库
200520034917.X	脱粒切碎两用机	王新明	（610036）四川省成都市金牛区银沙北街88号四川省农机鉴定站	王新明
200520035526.X	饲料粉碎机	廖世奇	（643119）四川省荣县观山镇四村9组	廖世奇
200520051342.2	青饲料切碎磨浆机	刘　刚	（417106）湖南省涟源市龙塘乡马头村	刘　刚

（续）

申请或批准号	发明名称	申请人	通讯地址	发明人
200520085482.1	动力秸秆粉碎机	郭宝瑞	(250014) 山东省济南市历下区解放路79号	郭宝瑞
200520091322.8	复合秸秆揉丝机	孙维良	(110015) 辽宁省沈阳市东陵区泉园3路84号	孙维良、王大睿等
200510018450.4	紫苏籽脱皮、低温压榨制油工艺	武汉工业学院	(430023) 湖北省武汉市汉口常青花园中环西路特1号	刘大川、李江平等
200510098585.6	一种熟制松籽的加工方法	胡桂红	(325406) 浙江省平阳县山门镇平西路193号	胡桂红
200510105791.5	一种葵花籽的加工方法	胡亦攀	(325406) 浙江省平阳县山门镇平西路191号	胡亦攀
200520012183.5	直连式碾米粉碎机	徐献军	(613100) 四川省井研县研城镇东门新村	徐献军
200520013496.2	碾米机进料装置	杨水芳	(311811) 浙江省诸暨市枫桥镇工业开发区浙江齐鲤机械有限公司	马丙春、杨 勇等
200520033128.4	全自动免调节自控碾米机	李绵军	(642350) 四川省安岳县岳阳镇外南街温家巷7号附1号	李绵军
200520034816.2	全封闭结构柜式碾米粉碎组合机	邹益平	(614800) 四川省乐山市五通桥区桥沟镇十字街	邹益平
200520034952.1	碾米粉碎组合机	钟得文	(629015) 四川省遂宁市船山区新桥镇四川省钟声机电设备制造有限公司	钟得文
200520035740.5	稻谷出糙精米一体机	李仲之	(621100) 四川省三台县潼川镇环城路62号附4号	李仲之
200520050552.X	全自动槟榔加工制作设备	胡 斌	(411100) 湖南省湘潭市雨湖区解放北路江麓机械厂互助村7栋306号	胡 斌
200520052130.6	圆弧丝杠推进式莲子脱壳机	李 俊	(417000) 湖南省娄底市乐坪西街华达机械厂保卫处	张建国、李 俊等
200520058698.9	成套碾米设备	陈伯诚	(512529) 广东省韶关市始兴县顿岗中学路口百成粮机制造有限公司	陈伯诚
200520058702.1	大米抛光机	陈伯诚	(512529) 广东省韶关市始兴县顿岗中学路口百成粮机制造有限公司	陈伯诚
200520067909.5	花生的脱衣装置	叶永灿	(528000) 广东省佛山市同济路34号506室	叶永灿
200520085804.2	双风道碾米机	李恩义	(276500) 山东省日照市莒县城阳镇土门首日照日兴机械厂	李恩义
200520089345.5	磨磋式原粮脱皮机	董洪林	(113305) 辽宁省抚顺市大孤家镇半拉山村4组	董洪林
200520104854.0	砻谷机进料装置	杨水芳	(311811) 浙江省诸暨市枫桥镇工业开发区浙江齐鲤机械有限公司	杨文根
200510002011.4	“无菌”面粉的生产方法	苏凤歧	(015000) 内蒙古自治区巴彦淖尔市团结北路恒丰小区6单元301	苏凤歧
200510009720.5	富蛋白小麦粉及其生产方法	赵维山	(150036) 黑龙江省哈尔滨市香坊区衡山路18号北大荒麦业有限公司	张显明、赵维山等

（续）

申请或批准号	发明名称	申请人	通讯地址	发明人
200510017449.X	复合营养平衡面粉	张银涛	(451100) 河南省新郑市人民路7号药厂家属院	张银涛
200510023827.5	粉碎机	樊静贤	(201900) 上海市宝山宝林九村1号102	樊静贤
200510038850.1	红薯全粉的加工方法	何贤用	(224200) 江苏省东台市弶港镇浪港路1号	何贤用、沈寒等
200510040524.4	完全蛋白质面粉及用其制作的食品	何伟荣	(230031) 安徽省合肥市解放军电子工程学院71幢303室	何伟荣
200510041188.5	旋转式蒸汽去皮机	何贤用	(224200) 江苏省东台市弶港镇浪港路1号	何贤用、高云根等
200510059622.2	一种利用马铃薯资源进行深加工的方法	华中科技大学	(430074) 湖北省武汉市洪山区珞瑜路1037号华中科技大学	张晓昱、孙敏等
200510060030.2	一种采用有机富硒小麦开发强化营养面粉的方法	王雅各	(453059) 河南省新乡市6号信箱西区5号楼三单元7号	李晓抒、王靖等
200510090992.2	一种发芽玉米营养高筋面粉	杜成杰、杜丹松等	(102600) 北京市大兴区金惠园二里1号楼8单元201号	杜成杰、杜丹松等
200520010104.7	多级式气流超细粉碎装置	杜陵敏	(400020) 重庆市江北区建北2支路8号24-12	杜陵敏
200520024443.0	超微磨粉机	施德昱	(730000) 甘肃省兰州市润城花园7单元301室	施德昱
200520031181.0	磨面机	王春茂	(463900) 河南省西平县人和乡北王店村	王春茂
200520050955.4	剪切式破碎机	李晓阳	(412000) 湖南省株洲市芦淞区贺家土电厂宿舍31栋208号	李晓阳
200520073759.9	风力分选破碎机	倪明、马国安等	(243000) 安徽省马鞍山市花山区城建村7栋102号	倪明、马国安等
200520083681.9	小麦破粒机	王文山	(261500) 山东省高密市密水街办碾头居委会227号	王文山
200520086931.4	一种面食加工机械的熟化成型装置	李庆鑫	(271000) 山东省泰安市上高乡宁家村3-2A	李庆鑫
200510003050.6	一种保健方便粉条的制作方法	李笃华	(550001) 贵州省贵阳市云岩区扁井西巷66号费玉兰转	李笃华
200510006615.6	一种烤饼及其制作方法	邵秋明、邵康华等	(350001) 福建省福州市古楼区沙帽井1号新4号楼101室	邵秋明、邵康华等
200510018171.8	一种鱼面及其生产方法	陈洪林、徐金良等	(430060) 湖北省武汉市武昌区徐东大道316号	陈洪林、徐金良等
200510017345.9	胶原蛋白食品的生产方法	荣衍真、郁昌虎等	(450003) 河南省郑州市金水区群办路3号附43号	荣衍真、郁昌虎等
200510016852.0	一种速冻饺子及制备方法	朴光日	(133000) 吉林省延吉市小营信用社崔云学转	朴光日
200510018845.4	一种香酥馅饼及其加工工艺	李延兵	(448000) 湖北省荆门市工商街9号	李延兵
200510021510.8	面包及其制备方法	吴微	(618300) 四川省广汉市三星镇星盛街11号	吴微

（续）

申请或批准号	发明名称	申请人	通讯地址	发明人
200510020707.X	赖氨酸玉米挂面及制备方法	陈瑕	(614500) 四川省乐至县城前进街22号	陈　瑕
200510037741.8	一种自然发酵酸面包及其制备方法	江南大学	(214036) 江苏省无锡市惠河路170号(江南大学食品学院)	黄卫宁、杨秀琴等
200510038696.8	冷冻面团专用流态起酥油及其制造方法	江南大学	(214036) 江苏省无锡市惠河路170号(江南大学食品学院)	黄卫宁、张忠慧等
200510040425.6	一种微波冷冻海绵蛋糕面团及其制造方法	江南大学	(214036) 江苏省无锡市惠河路170号(江南大学食品学院)	黄卫宁、袁永利等
200510040429.4	一种微波冷冻休闲脆饼面团及其制造方法	江南大学	(214036) 江苏省无锡市惠河路170号(江南大学食品学院)	黄卫宁、段立等
200510040834.6	夹层式冷冻面团搅拌机	江南大学	(214036) 江苏省无锡市惠河路170号(江南大学食品学院)	黄卫宁、贾春利等
200510041171.X	一种功能性烘焙食品无面筋面包及其生产方法	江南大学	(214036) 江苏省无锡市惠河路170号江南大学食品学院	黄卫宁、杨秀琴等
200510042477.7	玉米煎饼及其制作方法	李凤光	(262200) 山东省诸城市瞬王街道办事处箭口村	李凤光
200510049938.3	山药薏米糕及其制作工艺	汝　源	(314100) 浙江省嘉善县魏塘镇下塘街34号楼3梯402室	汝　源
200510050459.3	百合绿豆糕及其制作工艺	汝　源	(314100) 浙江省嘉善县魏塘镇下塘街34号楼3梯402室	汝　源
200510051017.0	连续盒式糕饼食品气调保鲜包装机	苏明智	(510507) 广东省广州市天河区粤垦路161号瑞心苑心茗阁1304室	苏明智、朱振国等
200510052239.4	芝麻胡桃仁糕及其制作工艺	杨　敏	(314102) 浙江省嘉善县西塘镇钟介福宿舍北幢西梯602室	杨　敏
200510053330.8	肉制膨化面及其生产方法	林庆坚	(310000) 浙江省杭州市天成路95号万家花园万和苑19-2-302室	林庆坚
200510065444.4	方便面片及其加工工艺	李宝华	(154625) 黑龙江省七台河市北兴农场鹿场	李宝华
200510073623.2	一种红参保健面条	王浩贵	(321200) 浙江省武义县城东路24号	王浩贵
200510073624.7	一种固阴止汗保健面条	王浩贵	(321200) 浙江省武义县城东路24号	王浩贵
200510078202.9	全质蔬菜面及其生产方法	徐功林	(236300) 安徽省阜南县王店乡政府	徐功林
200510088959.6	仙人掌面条	向云辉	(629000) 四川省遂宁市安居区中心镇新寨子村5社3号	向云辉
200510098431.7	营养冷面的加工方法	陈晓梅	(118002) 辽宁省丹东市振兴区春二路十号楼二单元206室	陈晓梅
200520021805.0	新型液压面条机	高俊岭	(157011) 黑龙江省牡丹江市爱民区北安乡金龙村	刘洪吉、高俊岭等
200520031671.0	用于粉条加工的揉面机	薛胜国	(467542) 河南省汝州市庙下乡薛庄村5组	薛胜国
200520113769.0	自动蛋糕机	赵锡亭	(265600) 山东省莱州市三山岛西由同发草业有限公司	赵锡亭
200510039237.1	铁强化饼干及生产方法	季庆云、胡伟佳等	(226000) 江苏省南通市濠西园80-206室	季庆云、胡伟佳等

（续）

申请或批准号	发明名称	申请人	通讯地址	发明人
200510041358.X	银杏饼干、米饼及其制作方法	殷年国	(225400) 江苏省泰兴市西城公寓 14 号楼 101 室	殷年国
200520043853.X	一种有馅饼干的制作装置	陈玉熙	(200093) 上海市杨浦区内江路 384 弄 12 号 303 室	陈玉熙、唐美丽等
200520061699.9	饼干夹心机的搅拌机构	卢礼权	(528300) 广东省佛山市顺德区勒流镇江义工业区日成机械厂	卢礼权
200510013285.3	淀粉组合物植物胶囊及制备方法	天津大学	(300072) 天津市南开区卫津路 92 号天津大学	高建平、陈静远等
200510023654.7	奶类液体米饭制造的改进方法	王永明	(200050) 上海市长宁区华阳街道愚园路 1355 弄 23 号 305 室	王永明
200510042256.X	一种花生食品的生产方法	刘昌水	(257091) 山东省东营市胶洲路 97 号东营市人民医院	刘昌水
200510048308.4	方便饭菜的生产储运方法及储运装置	喻跃海	(315400) 浙江省余姚市泗门镇明朗新村（原朗霞镇镇西新村）6 号	喻志明、喻跃海等
200510053212.7	马铃薯淀粉废水中提取蛋白质的设备及技术	陶德录	(756000) 宁夏回族自治区固原市试验区长丰路 106 号	陶德录
200510022141.4	酿酒冷却水循环利用方法及其装置	魏华海	(618200) 四川省绵竹市剑南镇玉妃路二段 440 号	魏华海
200510038044.4	啤酒大麦的制麦新工艺	扬州大学	(225001) 江苏省扬州市大学南路 88 号	汪志君、方维明等
200510040487.7	一种反渗透生产无醇啤酒的方法	江南大学	(214036) 江苏省无锡市惠河路 170 号	陆健、冯凌蕾等
200510094061.X	一种啤酒制备方法	邓灵童	(225323) 江苏省泰州市刁铺镇环溪路 19 号	邓灵童
200510106656.2	一种黄酒酒脚的利用方法	朱乙彬	(312030) 浙江省绍兴县柯桥街道笛扬商苑二期 3 幢 405 室	朱乙彬
200510114261.7	一种营养红葡萄酒及其制备方法	孙天民	(100088) 北京市海淀区学院路蓟门里东五楼 907 号	孙天民
200510123464.2	一种冰冻葡萄酒及其制备方法	马玉祥、彭新全等	(066600) 河北省昌黎县十里堡乡苓芝顶	马玉祥、彭新全等
200520007816.3	液态发酵酿酒蒸馏装置	叶界平	(323000) 浙江省丽水市寿尔福路 609 号	叶界平
200520032872.2	白酒蒸馏冷凝装置	刘强生	(610000) 四川省成都市青羊区德盛路 75 号 9 单元 24 号	刘强生
200520087910.4	白酒卧式过滤机	马彰原	(030600) 山西省晋中市榆次区窑新街 37 号	马彰原、马昆等
200520087911.9	立式白酒除浊过滤机	马彰原	(030600) 山西省晋中市榆次区窑新街 37 号	马彰原、马昆等
200520091134.5	高效节能酿造蒸馏器	王镇	(110013) 辽宁省沈阳市沈河区乐郊路 5-1-363	王镇
200510005199.8	无糖无脂冰淇淋粉	熊旭华	(100035) 北京市海淀区西三环北路 72 号世纪经贸大厦 2061	熊旭华

（续）

申请或批准号	发明名称	申请人	通讯地址	发明人
200510009714.X	玉米肽饮料及其加工方法	田玉忠	（150080）黑龙江省哈尔滨市南岗区哈平路160号	田玉忠
200510012386.9	一种葡萄汁饮料及其生产方法	山西大学	（030006）山西省太原市坞城路36号	张丽增、张福增等
200510020525.2	青梅饮料及其制备方法	李协鼎	（650000）云南省大理州洱源县茈碧乡大庄村	李协鼎、李学海等
200510042528.6	一种复合蔬菜汁及其制备方法	谢兆坤	（273411）山东省临沂市费县探沂镇费县腾达新型建材有限公司	谢兆坤
200510043308.5	一种粉丝蛋白饮料的生产方法	赵 昱	（265400）山东省招远市迎宾路32号	赵 昱
200510046242.5	大豆植物蛋白冰淇淋的制备方法	黄作庆	（116001）辽宁省大连市中山区宏大路18号万达大厦2104房间	黄作庆
200510009753.X	用杜香的嫩叶制作保健茶的方法	潘兰宝	（145000）黑龙江省塔河县塔河镇新建街十一委五组	潘兰宝
200510009762.9	刺五加茶水及其制备方法	郑 滨、周华等	（150086）黑龙江省哈尔滨市南岗区学府路287号（省外贸冷库）	郑滨；周华等
200510009763.3	银杏叶茶水及其制造方法	郑 滨、周华等	（150086）黑龙江省哈尔滨市南岗区学府路287号（省外贸冷库）	郑 滨、周华等
200510010675.5	一种普洱保健茶及其制备方法	王乐观	（665000）云南省思茅市环城西路247号	王乐观
200510010740.4	一种补肾益髓食品茶及其制备方法	钟传贵	（650000）云南省昆明市环城南路816号9幢102号	钟传贵
200510010741.9	一种适宜女性饮用的食品茶及其制备方法	钟传贵	（650000）云南省昆明市环城南路816号9幢102号	钟传贵
200510017547.3	一种袋泡茶	孔德忠	（453100）河南省卫辉市前曹街33号	孔德忠
200510049062.2	一种鲜果蔬冰茶的制备方法	刘志强、刘晓晔等	（310029）浙江省杭州市江干区秋涛路景芳二区47-2-302	刘志强、刘晓晔等
200510049125.4	一种保健茶及制备方法	鲁汝协	（325404）浙江省平阳县腾蛟镇莱场街49号	鲁汝协
200510065873.1	一种含有金花茶的保健制品	黄扶民	（536000）广西壮族自治区北海市西藏路新开泰小区7巷7号	黄扶民
200510073004.3	松针茶的制备方法及其制备的松针茶	吉 玲、成江等	（100021）北京市朝阳区华威南路华辉苑3号楼1808室	吉 玲、成江等
200510038143.2	全自动干式大蒜脱皮机	程慎言	（221700）江苏省徐州市丰县县城农业银行	程慎言、程秀玲等
200510043543.2	蜂胶枣及其制作方法	张其润	（252000）山东省聊城市兴华西路77号	张其润
200510044363.6	一种从蜂花粉中提取脂肪类化合物的方法	山东师范大学	（250014）山东省济南市历下区文化东路88号	耿 越、张 健等
200510046839.X	一种复合蜂花粉及生产工艺	周云川	（110025）辽宁省沈阳市和平区太原南街220号圣野蜂王浆有限公司	周云川
200510049745.8	纳米蜂胶制品的制备方法	浙江大学	（310027）浙江省杭州市西湖区浙大路38号	胡福良、李英华等

（续）

申请或批准号	发明名称	申请人	通讯地址	发明人
200510078725.3	一种蜂王浆与蜂蜜制品的配方及其制备方法	孙民富	(264006) 山东省烟台市开发区珠江路32号3号厂房E区131室	孙民富
200520068978.8	一种搓压式大蒜分瓣机	程慎言	(227000) 江苏省徐州市丰县县城农业银行	程慎言
200510005478.4	油料作物脱脂后整粒复原的方法	裴丹平	(462000) 河南省漯河市自由贸易区东京路144号	裴丹平
200510012358.7	一种五香酱油及其加工方法	李进喜	(030021) 山西省太原市太原工贸学校	李进喜、李凌云等
200510017415.0	一种棉籽胚片的处理工艺	王建设	(450051) 河南省郑州市嵩山路140号	王建设、王 琳
200510018477.3	一种茶油加工新工艺	朱少新	(200125) 上海市临沂路181弄32号401室	朱少新
200510031458.4	微波萃取油脂的方法	万绍平	(330029) 江西省南昌市二七北路82号三单元401室	万绍平、郑小非等
200510032262.7	从柑橘类果皮中提取橘子油和果胶的方法	中南大学	(410083) 湖南省长沙市岳麓区麓山南路154号	郭学益、刘海涵等
200510033271.8	高环氧值植物油及其制备方法与应用	华南理工大学	(510640) 广东省广州市天河区五山路381号	瞿金清、陈焕钦等
200510036855.0	用微波和溶剂提取小麦胚芽油的方法	广州大学	(510405) 广东省广州市广园中路248号	樊亚鸣、陈永亨等
200510040602.0	煎炸油净化处理方法	许庆华	(211700) 江苏省淮安市盱眙县盱城镇沙岗村石桥路5-1号	许庆华
200510045043.2	原生态花生油及饼粕生产工艺	李长东	(253100) 山东省平原县王杲铺镇菜市场	李长东
200510045672.5	颗粒状大豆蜡的制取方法及其成型设备	王 全	(116021) 辽宁省大连市沙河口区龙江路50号1-2-1	王 全
200510049888.9	一种柑橘皮精油的提取工艺	浙江大学	(310027) 浙江省杭州市玉古路20号	叶兴乾、刘东红等
200510053450.8	一种提取大蒜油的方法	中国农业大学	(100094) 北京市海淀区圆明园西路2号	倪元颖、李景明等
200510054604.5	食用油连续过滤精炼方法	王朝阳	(830026) 新疆维吾尔自治区乌鲁木齐市经济技术开发区科技园路7号	王朝阳
200510071543.3	超临界枸杞渣粕萃取物及其生产方法	全亚平	(750004) 宁夏回族自治区银川市上海路水产巷12号楼2单元501室	全亚平
200510096437.0	一种高浓度天然香精的生产方法	朱 江	(710077) 陕西省西安市莲湖区民洁路热电小区9栋1单元5楼南户	朱 江、李元瑞等
200510098730.0	一种玉米皮提取玉米纤维油的方法	尤 新	(100045) 北京市西城区三里河一区3号院2号楼1102室	尤 新、茹 杰等
200510107468.1	油料脱色吸附剂再生方法	刘 聪	(201411) 上海市奉贤区奉城镇洪庙东大村D区6幢21号501室	刘 聪
200510115180.9	一种提取南瓜籽油及南瓜籽蛋白的方法	中国农业大学	(100094) 北京市海淀区圆明园西路2号	李全宏

（续）

申请或批准号	发 明 名 称	申请人	通 讯 地 址	发明人
200510117264.6	一种提取含植物甾醇油脂的方法	尤 新	(100045) 北京市西城区三里河一区3号院2号楼1102室	尤 新、茹 杰等
200520011128.4	节能式食用油自动净化装置	张廷杰	(100028) 北京市朝阳区西坝河西里1号楼1403室	张廷杰
200520030999.0	螺旋压榨装置	陈向华	(472000) 河南省三门峡市湖滨区建设路七街坊39号楼3-7号	陈向华
200520078223.6	脱皮菜籽仁低温调质装置	张建新	(724200) 陕西省勉县贾旗路中段陕西建兴农业科技有限公司	宋建民
200520095096.0	小型榨油专用连续进出料炒锅	荔同训	(448000) 湖北省荆门市五里铺刘集乡刘集卫生所转	荔同训
200510010806.X	集成膜循环提取工艺	戴 群	(650224) 云南省昆明市金星小区金福园512幢商务底层太空水工程公司	戴 群
200510027955.7	循环冷凝固相微萃取装置	上海交通大学	(200240) 上海市闵行区东川路800号	贾金平、廖黎燕等
200510032156.9	物料分选装置	郝志刚	(410007) 湖南省长沙市雨花区广济桥鸿园小区3栋402室	郝志刚、徐毅茹等
200510036210.7	一种黄粉虫食品及其制备方法	李 政	(518000) 广东省深圳市深南中路红岭大厦B座九楼吉林省政府驻深办	李 政
200510036965.7	蜗牛保健制品及其制造方法	宋兆华	(518000) 广东省深圳市南山区南山大道西海明珠大厦1615	宋兆华
200510038285.9	一种酶法综合利用虾加工下脚料的方法	江南大学	(214036) 江苏省无锡市惠河路170号	夏文水、姜启兴等
200510049041.0	一种酸辣苦笋加工方法	余学军	(311300) 浙江省临安市锦城镇人民广场东侧科技大楼胡学明转	余学军
200510056749.9	中式菜肴的工业化生产方法	尹家君	(100011) 北京市朝阳区安贞西里1区甲1号江苏油田联络处6033室	尹家君
200510064301.1	一种压滤机的过滤脱水方法	宋家骏、赵鸿才等	(100037) 北京市海淀区增光路16号1号楼913号	宋家骏、赵鸿才等
200510095733.9	一种改进的固相微萃取方法	南京大学	(210093) 江苏省南京市汉口路22号	于红霞、沈 敏等
200510096917.7	一种鱼粉蛋白水解物与制备方法及其应用	厦门大学	(361005) 福建省厦门市思明南路422号	杨 剑、卢昌义等
200510122844.4	一种同时生产低钠无糖牛奶和乳糖的方法	方雅悯	(225300) 江苏省泰州市鼓楼南路348号科技中心	方存林、陈 奔等
200520017149.7	复合式三相分离器	王 鹏	(163711) 黑龙江省大庆市龙凤区龙凤镇商埠街龙宝路13号	王 鹏
200520022863.5	一种分子蒸馏器	郭春寅	(101300) 北京市顺义后沙峪泗上北京市泽龙生物制品厂	郭春寅
200520031404.3	真空蒸发塔	冯长祯、王性仁等	(454450) 河南省博爱县清华镇八街月贵巷3号	冯长祯、王性仁等
200520034517.9	一种蒸馏冷凝装置	孙 海	(610081) 四川省成都市金牛区一环路北三段南玻商厦B座505室	孙 海

（续）

申请或批准号	发 明 名 称	申请人	通 讯 地 址	发明人
200520052221.X	螺旋管冷凝冷却器	罗茂华	（425006）湖南省永州市零陵区潇湘西路36号	罗茂华；郑仕华
200520058378.3	一种简易萃取分离装置	吴伦祥	（526200）广东省四会市凤山路68号七座12号	吴伦祥
200520060960.3	低温微波萃取装置	广州大学	（510405）广东省广州市广园中路248号	樊亚鸣、陈永亨等
200520067002.9	固相萃取装置	陈 忠	（510660）广东省广州市大观南路中海康城花园蝴蝶南街29栋1504	陈 忠
200520076273.0	逆流夹层式蒸发器	南京师范大学	（210097）江苏省南京市宁海路122号	顾正桂、林 军等
200520091933.2	变频调速管式高速分离机	薛晓光	（116033）辽宁省大连市甘井子区砬子山新村4号	薛晓光、邱会模等
200520109092.3	新型卧式离心机	柳英爱、洪光成等	（256100）山东省淄博市沂源县沂河路10号	柳英爱、洪光成等
200520110085.5	一种卧式离心机	洪光成、柳英爱等	（256100）山东省淄博市沂源县沂河路10号	洪光成、柳英爱等
200520114739.1	一种固相萃取装置	王璟琳	（046011）山西省长治市城北东街73号长治学院化学系	王璟琳
200510012522.4	食用醋的生产方法及其设备	明克宽	（030027）山西省太原市万柏林区东社村西街1巷3号	明克宽、明艳梅等
200510016688.3	醋饮料及其制备方法	李亚军	（138001）吉林省松原市宁江区文化街10委	李亚军
200510016736.9	大豆粉醋疗食品及其制备方法	张 术	（130021）吉林省长春市自由大路506号	张术、张跃红等
200510018782.2	大蒜复合汁及其制备方法	徐福梅	（430070）湖北省武汉市洪山区狮子山街西苑区3栋9门7号	徐福梅
200510041834.8	全料谷子米醋及其酿造方法	张孟祥	（715403）陕西省韩城市昝村镇昝村醋房	张孟祥
200510056607.2	一种甘薯醋	王浩贵	（321200）浙江省武义县城东路24号	王浩贵
200510056609.1	一种胡萝卜醋	王浩贵	（321200）浙江省武义县城东路24号	王浩贵
200510060614.X	固体醋的制备方法	浙江大学	（310029）浙江省杭州市西湖区延安路浙大湖滨校区医学院	朱海红、周林福等
200510061040.8	大蒜素解毒醋及其制作方法	浙江大学	（310031）浙江省杭州市延安路353号浙江大学湖滨校区	刘慧刚、徐立红等
200510090829.6	一种山楂果醋饮料及其生产工艺	闫 斌	（068150）河北省隆化县苔山路59号	闫 斌
200510129837.7	一种营养保健醋及其制备方法	宋学军	（025150）内蒙古自治区赤峰市巴林右旗大板镇山丹食品有限责任公司	宋学军
200510003043.6	玫瑰糖及制作方法	黄菊声	（550025）贵州省贵阳市花溪区青岩镇北街112号	黄菊声、黄林声等
200510010644.X	豆末糖及制作工艺	普 绩	（652700）云南省通海县文献里28号斯贝佳食品有限公司	普 绩

（续）

申请或批准号	发明名称	申请人	通讯地址	发明人
200510020628.9	一种活性甜茶糖及其制造方法	陈显刚	（541004）广西壮族自治区桂林市施家园26幢601室	陈显刚
200510035131.4	一种由甘蔗直接制造高品质白糖的工艺	霍汉镇	（510180）广东省广州市东风西路医国街源溢里2号701室	霍汉镇
200510048132.2	利用一砂再溶糖浆生产精品糖的方法	凌建新	（030001）山西省太原市新建南路15号	凌建新、吴英等
200510050674.3	一种纤维素转化左旋葡聚糖装置	浙江大学	（310027）浙江省杭州市西湖区浙大路38号	王树荣、骆仲泱等
200510104764.6	流体糖浆的生产工艺	韩景银	（257091）山东省东营市胶洲路97号人民医院	韩景银
200510106039.2	甜高粱秆榨汁生产高果糖浆	新疆大学	（830046）新疆维吾尔自治区乌鲁木齐市胜利路14号	计巧灵、马雪娟等
200510120909.1	一种大蒜低聚果糖的生产方法	暨南大学	（510632）广东省广州市天河区黄埔大道西601号	黄雪松
200510006003.7	一种提取秸秆纤维的方法	徐莉莉	（325608）浙江省乐清市淡溪镇马岙村	徐莉莉、徐静静等
200510007524.4	真皮纤维绒的加工工艺及其产品	苏立暖	（325208）浙江省瑞安市马屿镇工业园区	苏立暖
200510050391.9	一种制浆造纸方法	俞祖勋	（310012）浙江省杭州市灵隐路117医院60幢3-302	俞祖勋
200510091822.6	零排放无污染的生态纸浆组合生产工艺	葛文宇	（116011）辽宁省大连市西岗区北岗街27号	葛文宇
200510014902.1	高剪切纤维离解机	天津科技大学	（300222）天津市河西区大沽路1038号	侯庆喜、卢晓江等
200510016940.0	一种用葵花籽皮制造浆粕的方法	赵义民	（135000）吉林省梅河口市飞跃小区5号楼1门301号	才景志
200510032640.1	一种用植物茎秆生产纤维的方法	陈建旭	（528420）广东省中山市沙溪镇剑龙新村3巷11号	陈建旭、王来云等
200510034200.X	棉秆皮纤维纱线及其加工方法	刘 磊、金石永等	（510630）广东省广州市天河区骏景花园（中山大道190号）骏茵轩B1001	刘 磊、金石永等
200510034201.4	棉秆皮纤维及其加工方法	刘 磊、金石永等	（510630）广东省广州市天河区骏景花园（中山大道190号）骏茵轩B1001	刘 磊、金石永等
200510036778.9	一种胶原纤维填料制品及其加工方法	张立文	（510800）广东省广州市花都区新华镇莲塘新庄社	张立文
200510054007.2	一种提取秸秆纤维及附着组织的方法	徐莉莉	（325608）浙江省乐清市淡溪镇马岙村	徐莉莉、徐静静等
200510064299.8	制革生产用的新型助剂	张壮斗	（476000）河南省商丘市梁园区白银路北段218号	张壮斗
200520007984.2	棉花加工除尘二次回绒装置	郑小龙	（830000）新疆维吾尔自治区乌鲁木齐市南昌路新疆农业大学药学院	郑吉善、郑小龙等
200520008820.1	双效点触式采棉机	孙子安	（831400）新疆维吾尔自治区吐鲁番市西环南路百泉民用锅炉厂转	孙子安

（续）

申请或批准号	发明名称	申请人	通讯地址	发明人
200520020462.6	剥麻机	肖　方	(150111) 黑龙江省双城市新城区计生委家属楼3单元602室	肖方、肖元等
200520021306.1	双滚轮式皮革刻层机	林　青	(150030) 黑龙江省阿城市和平街九如胡同18号	林　青
200520024008.8	手提式棉花试轧机	李玉生	(061600) 河北省东光县信用合作联合社王清国转	李玉生
200520024255.8	棉柴粉碎机	殷佃丰	(256402) 山东省淄博市桓台县田庄镇大庞村	李孝华、胡庆鸾等
200520024256.2	棉柴折断机	殷佃丰	(256402) 山东省淄博市桓台县田庄镇大庞村	李孝华、胡庆鸾等
200420051848.9	棉桃脱壳机	王志城、王一平等	(233000) 安徽省蚌埠市吴湾路453号涂山新技术开发部	王志城、王一平等
200520077484.6	双皮辊高效轧花机	王剑松	(221000) 安徽省萧县龙城镇淮海路305号	王剑松
200520087308.0	电动棉花桃剥壳机	李宝贵	(251900) 山东省滨州市无棣县信阳乡车里西村	李宝贵
200520087498.6	一种棉籽剥绒锯片	宋淑玲	(257017) 山东省东营市商河路85号胜利油田钻井工艺研究院	宋淑玲
200520096434.2	环保纤维机	张荣斌	(431700) 湖北省天门市竟陵镇四牌楼街农机大院	张荣斌
200520108019.4	转笼式籽棉除杂烘干机	夏　强	(832208) 新疆维吾尔自治区玛纳斯县新疆玛纳斯新湖总厂工业科	夏　强
200520125644.X	一种小型棉花加工机	杨荣田	(257342) 山东省东营市广饶县石村镇三里村广饶晶宇新型材料有限公司	杨荣田、吕振洪等
200520132239.0	棉花剥花机	梅小坤、黄小周等	(570314) 海南省海口市港澳大道26号	梅小坤、黄小周等
200510003206.0	米面粉肠衣肉肠切分及切面收紧方法和设备	吴再盛	(550018) 贵州省贵阳市云岩区余家巷64号2单元15号	吴再盛
200510010820.X	一种竹筒肉肠及其制备工艺	刘嘉凝	(650051) 云南省昆明市北京路632号龙腾大酒店13层	刘嘉凝
200510012778.5	一种蛋白肠衣及其生产方法	张　桥	(050091) 河北省石家庄市桥西区滨河街18号41-2-101	张　桥
200510017526.1	一种鱼刺分离装置及其分离方法	关　健	(450003) 河南省郑州市金水区沈庄前街45号院3号楼1单元1号	关　健
200510038290.X	低胆固醇稀奶油的加工方法及用途	扬州大学	(225009) 江苏省扬州市大学南路88号	顾瑞霞、生庆海等
200510043368.7	沸腾（水煮）酥骨鱼生产线	冯家彪	(264000) 山东省烟台市芝罘区新安街3-7号	冯家彪
200510053464.X	鱼虾火腿肠的配料方法	段经磊	(233500) 安徽省蒙城县三义镇白桥村段庄	段经磊
200510060015.8	方便松花蛋生产方法	叶明伟	(311400) 浙江省富阳市鹳山路22号	叶明伟
200510072323.2	一种熟肉制品包裹的新工艺	梁世剑、梁永恒等	(066200) 河北省秦皇岛市山海关区石河镇沟渠寨村	梁世剑、梁永恒等

（续）

申请或批准号	发 明 名 称	申请人	通 讯 地 址	发明人
200520029518.4	打毛机打脱的禽体与羽毛分离装置	王锦光	（130300）吉林省德惠市红旗街	王锦光
200520056843.X	虾剖腹机	殷小春	（524038）广东省湛江市赤坎区南方六横路4号	殷小春
200520059827.6	新型剥鱼皮机	殷小春	（524038）广东省湛江市赤坎区南方六横路4号	殷小春
200520068198.3	虾类清洗装置	彭德权	（524200）广东省雷州市西湖大道95号	彭德权
200520081916.0	肉糜棒挤出机	侯冰洁	（255000）山东省淄博市张店区人民西路25-3号宏程名座A座606室	侯冰洁
200520093642.7	离心式真空制冷斩拌机	杜文武	（111000）辽宁省辽阳市太子河区小祁家镇方双5组	杜文武
200520118593.8	一种家禽类开生制胚清洗处理系统	王 富	（102601）北京市大兴县庞各庄镇常各庄	王 富
200510021139.5	卷烟膨胀梗颗粒填充料的制备方法	周 川	（614007）四川省乐山市西南核物院内成都市宏普科技有限公司	刘朝辉、刘 毅等
200510031248.5	烟丝烘丝工艺及装置	长沙卷烟厂	（410007）湖南省长沙市劳动中路426号	陈 俭、周海林等
200510037813.9	一种烟梗回潮的方法及设备	王训明	（221000）江苏省徐州市湖滨新村五期38号楼301室	李世勇、董顺德等
200510048606.3	一种用于烤烟房的红外辐射涂料及其制备方法	翁 宇	（650302）云南省安宁市昆明钢铁公司投资经营部	翁 宇
200520022580.0	再造烟片抄造成形装置	陶性田	（650225）云南省昆明市王旗营路静园小区7幢2单元202室	陶性田、刘长战等
200520050276.7	卷烟薄片烘干装置	长沙卷烟厂	（410007）湖南省长沙市劳动中路426号	黎 明、尹大锋等
200520069236.7	烟梗回潮设备	王训明	（221000）江苏省徐州市湖滨新村38号楼301室	李世勇、董顺德等
200520090449.8	一种烤烟智能化烤房	朴海平	（110035）辽宁省沈阳市皇姑区昆山西路116号	朴海平
200520099892.1	烟叶烘烤湿度平衡调节器	程迎辉	（672100）云南省祥云县祥城镇环城南路143号县烟草公司	程迎辉、全昀曦等

第七部分

大 事 记

1 月

7日 在农业部办公厅的指导和支持下，由农业部乡镇企业局、农业部农产品加工领导小组办公室联合首都新闻媒体共同组织推举评选的“2005年中国农产品加工业十大新闻和十大新闻人物”暨“第三届中国农村十大致富带头人”揭晓仪式在北京人民大会堂隆重举行。九届全国人大常委会副委员长布赫、九届全国政协副主席王文元、农业部副部长范小建出席揭晓仪式并作了重要讲话。出席会议的还有国务院原副秘书长安成信及农业部、科技部、财政部、国家发展和改革委员会等相关部委领导。农业部乡镇企业局局长、农业部农产品加工领导小组办公室主任甘士明主持了揭晓仪式。新华社、人民日报社、光明日报社、中央人民广播电台、中央电视台、经济日报、农民日报、搜狐网、中国工商时报、中国农村杂志社、中国乡镇企业报、农业部中国国家农产品加工信息网、中国农业产业化协作网等首都各大新闻单位的领导和记者参加了揭晓仪式。参加揭晓仪式的还有来自地方的新闻媒体、各地政府领导和社会各界的知名人士。

12日 由中国纺织工业协会主办的全国纺织工业发展与改革工作会议在北京召开。此次会议旨在贯彻中央经济工作会议精神，研究我国纺织工业“十一五”发展大计以及2006年工作思路。会上，国家发改委副主任欧新黔、商务部部长助理傅自应、中国纺织工业协会会长杜钰洲相继讲话和作会议报告。杜钰洲会长首先回顾了“十五”期间我国纺织工业的发展情况和取得的成绩，深刻分析了当前我国纺织工业发展面临的形势，提出了我国“十一五”期间纺织工业发展的目标、任务和工作重点，明确了2006年工作的基本思路。“第二批全国纺织企业家创业奖表彰”、“第四批纺织特色城镇、产业集群试点地区授牌”以及“2005年中国纺织行业年度创新人物颁奖典礼”等活动同期举行。全国政协副主席郝建秀出席大会，全国政协原副主席、中国企业家协会会长陈锦华为获奖代表颁奖、授牌并发表讲话。

12～13日 全国食品药品监督管理工作会议在北京召开，这是食品药品监管系统在“十一五”规划开局之年召开的一次重要会议。其主要任务是以邓小平理论和“三个代表”重要思想为指导，认真贯彻党的十六大、十六届五中全会和中央经济工作会议精神，以科学发展观统领食品药品监管工作全局，树立科学监管理念，回顾总结2005年工作，明确“十一五”工作的总体思路，部署2006年重点工作。中共中央政治局委员、国务院副总理吴仪专门就此次会议做出重要批示，对2006年的食品药品监管工作提出十分重要的指导意见。国家食品药品监督管理局党组书记、局长邵明立在大会开幕式上作了工作报告。邵明立要求2006年做好六项重点工作：一是加强基础设施建设，改善监管条件；二是创新机制，加强食品安全综合监督；三是推进农村“两网”建设向纵深发展，促进社会主义新农村建设；四是进一步整顿和规范药品生产流通秩序，确保药品安全有效；五是以制度建设为重点，规范医疗器械管理；六是继续做好防控人感染高致病性禽流感相关工作。国家食品药品监督管理局党组成员、副局长惠鲁生做了会议总结，对贯彻会议精神提出了明确要求。

14日 2006年全国烟草工作会议在北京召开。主要任务是认真贯彻落实中央经济工作会议精神，紧密联系行业实际，全面贯彻落实科学发展观，总结2005年工作情况，安排2006年工作任务，重点研究部署当前和今后一个时期行业改革与发展需要着力做好的几方面工作，明确任务，努力推动行业持续稳定协调健康发展。国家发改委副主任欧新黔出席会议并作重要讲话。国家烟草专卖局党组书记局长姜成康，党组成员副局长张保振、何泽华、李克明、张辉以及中国烟草学会理事长杨传德出席会议。姜成康局长向与会代表传达了国务院领导同志近期对烟草工作的重要批示，并作了题为《完善体制机制，优化资源配置，增强竞争实力，全面提升水平，推动烟草行业持续稳定协调健康发展》的工作报告。报告中，姜成康局长认真总结了2005年行业各项工作的完成情况，进一步分析了行业今后继续保持平稳发展所面临的严峻挑战，提出了当前和今后一个时期烟草行业改革与发展的总体思路，姜成康局长在报告中并对2006年烟草行业主要工作进行了安排。

2 月

15～16日 2006年度绿色食品产品抽检工作会议在广州召开，农业部蔬菜品质监督检验测试中心（广州）等16个绿色食品产品定点委托监测机构的负责人、业务骨干参加了会议。会议通报了2005年度绿色食品产品抽检情况，安排布置了2006年的绿色食品产品抽检工作。2005年，中心抽检绿色食品产品1 043个，抽检完成率为90.7%；不合格产品18个，抽检合格率为98.3%。其中，因卫生安全指标不合格被取消绿色食品标志商标使用许可的产品有14个。近几年，绿色食品产品抽检工作日益规范，产品抽检完成率和产品抽检合格率呈稳步提高趋势，表明绿色食品产品质量的可靠性和抽检工作的有效性均在提高。2006 年，计划安排绿色食品抽检产品 1 182个，由 16 个检测机构承担抽检工作。为确保绿色食品产品质量，2006 年的产品抽检计划中加大了对质量风险高、老百姓普遍关注的稻米、蔬菜、乳制品等产品的抽检力度。会议对 2006 年绿色食品产品抽检和申报检验工作提出了具体要求。各承检机构在 2006 年的产品抽检工作中要严格按照《绿色食品产品抽样准则》规范抽样，确保抽样的真实性和代表性，对未抽到样品的企业，要深入调查，摸清情况；对有意逃避抽检和拒绝抽检的企业，要及时报告，将按有关规定进行严肃处理；各承检机构要加强与各地绿办的沟通和联系，采取灵活多样的抽样方式，降低成本，提高效率。要在做好监督检验工作的同时，把好认证申报检验关，发现问题，及时解决。与会代表还对“绿色食品产品质量抽检项目判定依据及相关标准”进行了修改、完善，并对做好 2006 年绿色食品产品质量抽检工作提出了意见和建议。

24 日 由中国标准化研究院与法国贝尔国际验证机构承办的 ISO 22000 食品安全管理系列标准国际研讨会在北京举行。本次研讨会是国家标准委与法国标准协会（AFNOR）之间加强交流与合作的一次重要活动。来自国家标准委、国家认监委、农业部畜牧局、认证机构国家认可委、商务部屠宰技术鉴定中心等单位的中外专家参加会议。此次研讨会的主要内容是介绍食品安全管理体系国际标准的主要内容、进展以及我国的转化应用情况，并探讨国内外食品安全管理体系国际标准的实施与应用。为满足确保整个食品链安全以及全球开展认证认可的迫切需要，ISO 22000《食品安全管理体系食品链中各组织的要求》于 2005 年 9 月正式颁布，得到了全球的广泛关注，许多国家已经或正在转化此国际标准为本国的国家标准。我国已于 2005 年 10 月正式将 ISO 22000 转化为国家标准，这对完善我国的食品安全标准体系，提高食品企业的食品安全管理水平，推动认证认可工作，并加速与国际接轨具有极其重要的意义。本次研讨会是 ISO 22000 国际标准起草组与中国国家标准转化组之间一次难得的交流机会，进一步加深了中国标准转化组对 ISO 22000 的认识，这对中国国家标准的宣贯、实施与应用必将产生积极的影响。

25 日 在举行的十届全国人大常委会第二十次会议上，对农产品质量安全法草案进行了第二次审议。全国人大法律委员会副主任委员李重庵汇报草案修改情况时说，针对原草案所称“农产品质量安全”的含义不够清楚的问题，有些常委会委员和地方、部门提出，农产品质量既包括涉及人的健康、安全的质量要求，也包括涉及产品的营养成分、口感、色香味等非安全性质量指标。需要由法律规范、监管、保障的，应是农产品质量中的安全性要求。二审稿增加规定：“本法所称农产品质量安全，是指农产品质量符合保障人的健康、安全的要求”。

3 月

2 日 中国纺织工业协会在北京举行新闻发布会，中国纺织工业协会新闻中心主任孙淮滨在会上向媒体公布 2006 年纺织行业的主要经济工作。按照国家经济工作的统一部署和产业发展的总体要求，2006 年纺织行业将着力增强自主创新能力，着力转变经济增长方式，着力提高经济运行的质量和效益，力争实现纺织行业“十一五”发展的良好开局。2006 年，中国纺织工业协会拟在全行业重点开展以下五项工作：一是以贯彻科学发展观统领纺织行业发展全局，认真做好“十一五”规划。科学地判断新时期纺织行业面临国内外发展机遇和挑战，科学地评价纺织行业在市场经济中的发展和进步，科学地辨别市场配置资源的积极作用和可能带来的负面影响，科学地分析行业经济粗放型增长的现实表现和隐藏的危机，科学地制定未来五年行业发展的指导思想、目标与重点、政策与措施。在此基础上形成并开始实施的“十一五”发展规划。二是全面提高行业自主创新能力，加快纺织先进生产力建设。主要包括“三大创新”：包括科技创新、经营管理创新和产业链整合创新。三是规范企业社会责任，推广中国纺织企业社会责任管理体系，在全行业树立以人为本建设和谐社会的历史责任感。四是进一步提高行业性中介服务的效率和水平，着力开展与当前行业发展与提升大局紧密相关的中介服务。五是继续开展国际合作与交流，进一步加强行业经济与民间外交，贯彻合作共赢的对外方针，扩大与发展中国家和发达国家同行和相关产业各种形式的合作。

17 日 国家发改委经济运行局、国家统计局工业交通统计司、中国食品工业协会联合在四川成都举办 2005 年度白酒工业经济运行发布会。有关部门、新闻单位、部分省、直辖市食品工业协会、部分重点企业的 400 多位代表参加了会议。国家发改委经济运行局副局长牛建国发布了“2005 年度全国白酒工业经济运行情况”，并作了《落实科学发展观促进白酒工业健康发展》的讲话；国家统计局工业交通统计司副司长耿勤发布了“2005 年度国民经济运行情况及 2006 年展望”，并与中国食品工业协会联合发布白酒百强企业生产经营情况。发布会得到了全国白酒生产经营骨干企业的广泛参与和支持。

21 日 国家发改委经济运行局、中国轻工业联合会、中国皮革协会在北京联合举办 2005 年度皮革行业经济运行暨真皮标志品牌发布会。全国政协常委、中国轻工业联合会副会长潘蓓蕾出席，国务院研究室、商务部、国家工商行政管理总局、国有资产监督管理委员会等有关部门、皮革行业骨干企业及中央电视台、新华社、人民日报、经济日报等新闻单位的 200 余名代表参加了发布会。国家发改委经济运行局副局长牛建国发表了《2005 年度皮革工业经济运行及 2006 年工作展望》的讲话；中国皮革协会常务副理事长张淑华作了题为《以科学发展观为指导开创我国皮革行业品牌工作新局面》的情况介绍；中国轻工业联合会副会长王世成宣读了《关于授予佩挂真皮标志皮鞋、皮革服装、裘皮服装排头产品和箱包排头产品 2006 年荣誉称号的决定》；企业代表宣读了由皮革行业骨干企业共同倡议并提出的《中国皮革行业品牌宣言》。

4 月

10～11 日 中国粮食行业协会在山东济南召开全国放心粮油进农村工作会议。国家粮食局局长聂振邦、中国粮食行业协会会长白美清出席会议并作了重要讲话，山东省政府副省长张昭福、国家粮食局副局长张桂凤等有关领导出席了会议，商务部等有关单位也派员参加，全国各省、直辖市粮食行业协会和放心粮油进农村先进单位的代表共 260 多人。会议要求，粮食行业要按照建设社会主义新农村的部署，继续推进“放心粮油工程”，积极开展“放心粮油进农村”活动，提高放心粮油的普及率和市场占有率，力争放心粮油占领城市市场 90％以上，农村市场 55％～60％以上。会议部署了 2006 年“放心粮油进农村”活动的主要工作；表彰了山东半球集团等 56 家“放心粮油进农村”先进单位，并颁发了“全国放心粮油进农村先进单位”证书和标牌。会上，山东省粮食行业协会等有关单位作了典型经验交流。

12 日 国务院总理温家宝主持召开国务院常务会议，审议并原则通过《国务院关于完善粮食流通体制改革政策措施的意见》。会议指出，随着粮食流通体制改革的推进，也出现了一些新的情况和问题，主要是国有粮食购销企业改革进展不够平衡，促进粮食稳定增产和农民持续增收的有效机制尚未建立，粮食宏观调控和流通监管体制有待健全。必须进一步加大改革力度，完善政策措施，健全体制机制，确保粮食流通体制改革的顺利推进。当前要着力做好以下几个方面的工作：一是加快推进国有粮食购销企业改革，切实转换企业经营机制，使国有粮食购销企业真正成为市场主体。二是加快清理和剥离国有粮食企业财务挂账，继续做好国有粮食企业分流职工再就业和社会保障工作，抓紧库存陈化粮的定向销售，妥善解决企业历史包袱。三是积极培育和规范粮食市场，加快建立全国统一开放、竞争有序的粮食市场体系。进一步培育和规范多种粮食市场主体，健全粮食收购市场准入制度，加强粮食市场监管执法，完善粮食市场体系建设，维护正常流通秩序。四是加强粮食产销衔接，逐步建立产销区之间的利益协调机制。大力发展长期稳定的粮食产销合作关系，建立有利于产销区协作发展的支持体系，支持和引导产区与销区优势互补。五是切实加强和改善粮食宏观调控，确保国家粮食安全。完善粮食直补和最低收购价政策，加大对主产区和种粮农民的支持力度，进一步加强和充实地方粮食储备，完善中央储备粮管理体系，探索建立中长期粮食供求总量和品种结构的平衡机制，保证市场粮食的有效供应。

19 日 国家发改委经济运行局、国家统计局工业交通统计司、中国食品工业协会联合在人民大会堂举办 2005 年度食品工业经济运行发布会。有关部委、新闻单位、部分省、直辖市食品工业协会、部分重点企业的 300 多位代表参加了会议。国家发改委经济运行局副局长牛建国发布了“2005 年度全国食品工业经济运行情况及 2006 年工作展望”；国家统计局工业交通统计司副司长耿勤介绍了“2005 年度国民经济运行情况”并与中国食品工业协会联合发布了“食品百强企业生产经营情况”；中国食品工业协会会长王文哲就“食品工业分行业生产情况”作了介绍；海关总署综合统计司张炳政就“2005 年度食品进出口贸易情况”作了介绍；参会的企业代表作了典型经验发言。

26～27 日 全国绿色食品工作座谈会在杭州召开。会议的主要任务，是按照农业部农产品质量安全工作的总体部署，围绕“全面加快发展、全力打造品牌”的中心任务，结合当前面临的新情况和新问题，研究绿色食品工作的思路、对策和措施。目的是通过制度、机制改革创新，加强体系队伍能力建设，进一步发挥工作系统的职能作用和整体优势，全面提升工作运行质量，推动绿色食品又快又好地发展。全国 42 个绿色食品管理机构和 30 个绿色食品定点委托监测机构的负责人共 110 余人参加了会议。中国绿色食品发展中心马爱国主任在会上作了题为《齐心协力开拓创新 推动绿色食品事业持续健康地加快发展》的讲话。会议全面总结了绿色食品事业取得的进展与成效。总体上看，绿色食品事业保持了良好的发展势头，产品总量规模继续扩大，品牌效应不断增强，实现了速度、质量、效益的同步增长。会议要求，整个绿色食品工作系统要把握机遇，扎实工作，不断推动绿色食品事业持续健康地加快发展，为推进社会主义新农村和现代农业建设做出更大的贡献。

5 月

18 日 农业部乡镇企业局举办的农产品加工重大技术推介活动在湖南省湘西土家族苗族自治州吉首市举办。农业部乡镇企业局甘士明局长、湖南省乡镇企业局龙新平局长、湘西自治州胡章胜副州长出席会议并讲话，农业部乡镇企业局副局长王秀忠参加会议。开幕式由湘西自治州委王承荣副书记主持。甘士明在讲话中指出，通过举办农产品加工重大技术推介活动，加快山区农产品加工快速发展，一是促进实现山区农业由产品农业向产业农业的转变，做大做强做优农业，并形成产业化经营，从根本上改变“背篓”、“提篮”农业的制约，促进农业升级提质。二是促进山区农业在产业空间上实现跨越，延长产业链，提高附加值，从根本上改变初级农产品受“剥削”的地位，拓展农业的增值空间。三是促进山区实现农业产业经营的一体化，改变分散的农户与市场对接难的状况，实现农业的规模经营、集约经营。甘士明指出，关于农产品加工今后发展的着力点，“十五”期间我国农产品加工业年均增长 17%，比工业增长率高 6 个百分点，已进入产业升级的阶段。农产品加工企业必须着眼于工艺技术打造，提高自主创新能力；必须着眼于提高产业集中度，改变加工过度分散的状况；必须着眼于农产品精深加工，提高综合利用水平。此次推介活动，主要是从技术入手，增强山区农产品加工企业的创新能力，提高精深加工率、附加值和市场占有率。甘士明强调指出：加强大专院校、科研单位与企业的互动，实现科技人员、科研成果与企业的有效对接，是企业寻求技术支撑的需要，也是加速科研成果产业化的重要举措。他要求参加推介活动的代表认真向专家学习，真正做到学有所获，获有所用，用有所效。来自湘西、恩施两自治州，湖南省怀化、张家界等地市的 120 人参加了农产品加工重大技术推介活动，农业部第四批扶贫联络组成员参加了推介活动的开幕式。农产品加工重大技术推介活动得到了代表的好评，认为推介活动为农产品加工企业指明了方向，提供了技术支撑，对于促进农产品加工业的持续快速健康发展、促进技术成果向现实生产力的转变具有积极作用。

19 日 全国烟草科学技术大会在北京隆重开幕。国家烟草专卖局局长姜成康、副局长张保振等和中国烟草学会理事长杨传德出席会议。会议由国家烟草专卖局副局长李克明主持。会上，姜成康局长发表了题为《全面增强自主创新能力 为建设创新型行业而努力奋斗》的重要讲话，张保振副局长发表了题为《统筹制订规划 实施项目带动 努力提升我国烟草科技自主创新水平》的讲话。姜成康局长在讲话中指出，烟草行业的科技发展，要认真贯彻中央提出的“自主创新、重点跨越、支撑发展、引领未来”的科技发展指导方针，紧密结合烟草行业实际，努力做到“坚持方向、突出重点、持续创新、支撑发展”。继续坚持中式卷烟的发展方向，坚定不移地走中式卷烟的发展道路，把发展中式卷烟作为烟草科技发展的主要任务。进一步突出重点，力求在重要领域和关键技术上取得重大突破，带动行业科技水平全面提升。要坚持有所为、有所不为，明确主攻方向，集中力量攻关，力求取得实效。努力实现持续创新，把持续创新作为企业发展的战略重点，促进企业持续健康发展。把行业发展真正转移到依靠科技进步、自主创新的轨道上来，使科技进步、自主创新真正成为推动行业发展的强大支撑。切实转变增长方式，提高资源利用率，努力实现节约发展、清洁发展、安全发展、可持续发展。张保振副局长在讲话中指出，围绕烟草行业当前和今后一个时期科技发展的总体目标，国家烟草专卖局在统筹规划的基础上制定了《烟草行业中长期科技发展规划纲要（2006－2020 年）》。他要求全行业准确把握行业科技发展的总体思路，切实明确行业科技发展的重点领域、重大专项，认真落实推进科技发展的政策措施，大力推进科技体制改革，实施重大项目带动战略，进一步加大科技投入，加强科技人才队伍建设，建立健全激励机制，实施知识产权与技术标准战略，并在思想认识上把握好信心勇气与脚踏实地的关系，自主创新与对外开放的关系，科研单位与企业院校的关系，体制创新与科技创新的关系，成果、专利、标准、品牌之间的关系等几个重大关系。

29～30 日 国家质检总局在北京召开全国食品生产监管工作会议，国家质检总局局长李传卿、副局长蒲长城出席会议并讲话。李传卿在讲话中指出，下一步食品安全监管工作要狠抓落实，突出重点，从六个方面狠抓落实。一要在全面整顿食品生产加工业方面抓好落实。继续开展全面普查，摸清底数；继续实施全面整顿，加快实施市场准入步伐；加快实行分类监管，严格落实三个责任制。二要在查处滥用添加剂和非食品原料方面抓好落实。打假执法以端黑窝点为主，加强对生产加工企业原料监督；加强对企业使用添加剂情况的跟踪力度，加快添加剂限量标准的制定。三要在加强小作坊的监管方面抓好落实。重点要放在农村和城乡接合部，关键要抓好落实区域监管责任制；要加大对无证查处的力度，保持端黑窝点的高压态势，引导小作坊走合作、联合、做大做强的路。四要在培育扶持一批三优食品方面抓好落实。要加快扶持树立一批优秀的食品生产加工企业，把质量管理基础打牢。要引导优质食品进入中国产品质量电子监管网，加大监管力度。五要在应对突发事件方面抓好落实。建立预警制度，制定应急预案，有效应对、妥善处置突发事件，正确引导媒体的舆论监督。六要在建立健全食品安全监管长效机制方面抓好落实。加快推进食品安全法规体系、食品安全标准体系和食品安全检测体系的建设，不断提高质检系统依法行政的能力和水平。蒲长城在讲话中指出，各级质检部门必须对当前形势进行冷静的分析，统一思想，提高认识，在食品安全监管工作中全面落实科学发展观。要让食品安全监管工作在维护人民群众切身利益，建立和谐社会方面发挥重要作用，在促进地方经济健康发展方面发挥重要作用；在体现政府执政能力方面发挥重要作用。各级质检部门要理清思路，抓住重点，努力实现食品安全监管工作新突破。

6 月

8 日 2006 年全国蜂胶工作会议在浙江桐庐召开，来自全国 19 个省、自治区、直辖市的 200 余名代表参加会议。本次会议由中国蜂产品协会蜂胶专业委员会、科技工作委员会、蜂产品医疗保健专业委员会联合主办，桐庐县人民政府、杭州天厨保健品有限公司承办。大会开幕式由中国蜂产品协会会长助理、蜂胶专业委员会秘书长吕泽田主持，中国蜂产品协会顾问罗梦传、副会长王振山、楼云、潘建国等领导出席大会并讲话。会上，罗梦传作了题为《大力推进自主创新，构建创新性蜂业，提高我国蜂业企业国际竞争力》的主题发言。王振山致开幕词，他强调当前我国蜂胶市场最重要的问题就是质量安全问题，自主创新的基础、市场规范的基础就是质量安全问题，中国蜂胶产业健康发展的基础也是质量安全问题。尽管近几年我国蜂胶产业取得了很大的成就，但在自主创新方面总体水平还较低，基本处于低水平重复生产。真正称得上具有知识产权的蜂胶产品屈指可数，企业之间恶性模仿他人知识产权的现象、打击别人抬高自己的不道德行为时有发生。中国蜂胶产业经历了独特的发展历程，希望大家能够共同努力，创造蜂胶产业的新局面。

16 日 2006 中国农产品质量安全国际论坛在哈尔滨市召开。本次论坛由黑龙江省人民政府、联合国粮农组织、美国食品安全联合会、加拿大阿尔伯达省农业与农村发展部主办，由黑龙江省农委承办。农业部农产品质量安全中心罗斌副主任应邀出席并作了题为《中国农产品质量安全认证的发展》专题报告，就中国农产品质量安全认证发展的现状、基本模式及无公害农产品、绿色食品、有机食品（以下简称“三品”）发展前景等问题做了较为全面的阐述。报告从无公害农产品、绿色食品和有机食品三者的共性、区别及相互关系的角度，解析了中国农产品认证的基本类型。报告认为，中国农业正朝着高产、优质、高效、生态、安全的方向加快发展，城乡居民对安全优质农产品的消费需求呈快速增长态势，无公害农产品、绿色食品、有机食品等安全优质农产品具有广阔的发展前景和市场空间，应立足现实、着眼未来，从宏观层面把握好三个关键：一要因势利导，把握农产品质量安全认证发展方向。根据农产品质量安全工作阶段性目标和任务要求，中国农产品质量安全认证仍将继续以产品认证为主，体系认证为辅。产品认证应当坚持以无公害农产品为重点、绿色食品为先导、有机食品为补充的发展思路。二要围绕中心，以农业和农村经济中心工作为重心，推动“三品”加快发展。发展无公害农产品、绿色食品和有机食品，要立足“三农”，做好“四个结合”，即与农业结构调整相结合、与农业产业化发展相结合、与农民增收相结合、与农产品出口相结合。三要加强监管，保障“三品”健康发展。一是在坚持模式特色的前提下，遵循国际通行做法，进一步规范和完善农产品认证管理的制度安排、体制构架和运行机制，保证认证工作的有效性、公正性和规范性，做到“规范运作、严格管理、确保质量、提高水平”。二是进一步建立和完善监管制度，全面落实各项监管措施，加强对获证产品的质量管理和标志管理，确保认证农产品生产和流通有序地发展。三是增强为企业和农户服务的意识，把监管融入服务之中。同时，在新的形势下，切实加强农产品质量安全认证工作体系建设，不断优化工作运行机制，提高队伍的整体素质，全面提升自身竞争力，推动农产品质量安全认证管理工作的质量和效率迈上一个新的水平。

29～30 日 全国烟草行业现代物流建设工作会议在重庆召开。国家烟草专卖局副局长何泽华出席会议并发表重要讲话，就行业卷烟物流建设工作提出了明确要求。他指出，现在行业物流建设工作越来越受到行业各级领导的高度重视，运行水平有了较大程度的提高，基础设施建设大大加强；优化流程、科学规划和精细管理为卷烟物流建设积累了宝贵经验。但从整体上看，行业物流工作“硬件水平不低，运行水平不高”，还处在起步和探索阶段，行业上下应客观看待成绩，正确面对差距。何泽华副局长就如何开展当前和今后一个时期的卷烟物流建设工作提出了明确要求。他指出，卷烟物流建设工作要在国家烟草专卖局统一管理、统一组织的前提下，以企业为主体，先省内、后省外，先卷烟、后物资，以省为单位，规划先行、流程优先，系统整合资源，建设与管理并重。全行业各级单位要进一步深化对行业现代物流的认识，从提升行业整体实力、转变经济增长方式和提升经营管理水平的高度来认识现代物流的重要性，克服“重装备、轻信息，重建设、轻管理”的思想，牢牢把握卷烟现代物流“服务、高效、低成本”的核心本质，处理好“现代与现实、水平与速度、硬件与软件、建设与管理”的关系，坚持统筹协调，合理规划，建设适应行业改革发展的现代物流体系。国家烟草专卖局经济运行司司长王平、法规司司长刘敬如、中烟电子商务公司总经理李宝忠分别就行业物流建设等有关方面工作进行了具体部署。国家烟草专卖局有关部门领导和行业各直属单位的代表共150余人参加了会议。

7 月

24 日 由中国肉类协会主办的2006中国国际肉类大会在北京召开。商务部姜增伟副部长、国家食品药品监督管理局惠鲁生副局长、世界肉类组织主席帕屈克·摩尔、秘书长劳伦斯·瑞克森及来自世界30多个国家的肉类行业组织官员、肉类企业代表、经济学家等700多人参加会议，就肉类工业品牌发展战略进行了深入的探讨和交流。会间，国家政府主管部门对中国肉类工业品牌发展与创新提出了指导性意见，世界肉类组织分析了肉类发达国家创建肉类品牌的成功经验供与会的肉类企业决策者们分享和借鉴，同时知名企业代表在会上做了精彩的发言。世界肉类组织在本次大会上向部分企业颁发了《世界肉类组织会员证书》，中国肉类协会发布了“2005—2006中国肉类工业影响力品牌”及“为发展中国肉类工业做出特殊贡献的企业”。

25 日 由世界肉类组织和中国肉类协会共同主办的第四届中国国际肉类工业展览会和首届中国肉类食品文化节在北京开幕。全国政协副主席孙孚凌、国家食品药品监督管理局副局长惠鲁生、世界肉类组织主席帕屈克·摩尔、秘书长劳伦斯·瑞克森、中国肉类协会会长李水龙及国家相关部门领导、肉类企业代表共同出席了开幕式，孙孚凌副主席为展览会揭幕。第四届中国国际肉类工业展览会得到了澳洲肉类及畜牧业协会、爱尔兰食品局、美国肉类出口协会的大力协办。本届展览会的展出面积3万m^2，来自中国、美国、英国、德国、爱尔兰、意大利、瑞典、丹麦、瑞士、新西兰、马耳他、荷兰、日本、印度、韩国等30多个国家的近600个参展企业同台展示和交易，展览范围涉及肉类食品加工、肉类机械设备、肉类食品添加剂及配料、肉类食品包装物料、肉类加工技术等，展出内容涵盖了肉类食品产业链。参展企业在展览会期间组织的多场技术交流讲座和新技术发布推广活动，为企业和客户提供了更广阔的学习交流空间。第四届中国国际肉类工业展览会较之前三届展览会凸现出以下特点：一是规模增大，新企业增多；二是参展企业展位设计更具品位，更具有市场化；三是参展企业对展览会更加重视，参加本届展览会的部门既有市场部、企划部，还有生产部、技术部，企业主要负责人也来到了展览会现场亲自与客户沟通洽谈；四是专业观众数量创历届最高，据统计在为期三天的展览期间，来自国内外的5万名专业观众和采购商到展览会现场进行洽谈采购、考察参观。

26～27 日 农业部在山东济南召开了全国饲料工作会议。农业部副部长张宝文，山东省人民政府副省长贾万志出席会议，农业部畜牧业司、全国畜牧总站、中国饲料工业协会、山东省农业厅、山东省畜牧办以及来自全国各省畜牧饲料主管部门、各省饲料工作（业）办公室等单位领导共150多人参加了会议。这次会议以总结“十五”饲料工作的成绩和经验，表彰全国秸秆养畜十佳示范县，分析当前饲料业面临的新形势，明确“十一五”饲料业的发展思路和目标，研究部署“十一五”促进饲料业发展的工作重点，推进我国由饲料大国向饲料强国转变。会上，张宝文副部长以《开拓创新，扎实工作，努力把我国建设成为饲料强国》为题作了重要讲话。他充分肯定了“十五”时期饲料业发展和饲料工作取得的显著成绩，全面阐述了饲料业在建设社会主义新农村中的重要意义。他强调，要客观分析当前饲料业发展面临的挑战和机遇，充分认识饲料工作的新形势和新任务。“十一五”期间，发展饲料业必须着眼于推动种植业和支持养殖业，着眼于发展畜牧业生产和增加农民收入，着眼于社会主义新农村建设。通过实施“大原料、大安全、大企业、大市场”战略，实现饲料业从数量速度型向质量效益型转变，从粗放经营向集约经营转变，从资源消耗型向资源节约型转变，从依靠粮食向依靠各类农副产品转变的饲料业发展新路子，全面增强我国饲料业的国际市场竞争力，最终实现由饲料大国向饲料强国的转变。张宝文副部长指出，“十一五”

饲料业发展的目标是，逐步实现安全、优质、高效、协调发展，确保饲料产品供求平衡和质量安全；实现饲料业结构进一步优化；提高科技对饲料业的贡献率，饲料企业的国际竞争能力显著增强；进一步健全和完善饲料业生产与经营的法律体系，保障饲料业持续、健康发展，为养殖业持续健康发展提供有力保障，为建设现代农业、增加农民收入、推进社会主义新农村建设做出新的贡献。会上，与会代表从不同角度交流了当地饲料业发展和饲料工作的经验，农业部畜牧业司宗锦耀副司长对会议进行了总结。

8 月

20～22 日 中国乳制品工业协会第 12 次年会暨第 6 次乳品技术精品展示会在哈尔滨市举行，全国乳制品行业的企业家、专家、教授以及同乳制品行业密切相关的企业代表 2 000 余人出席了会议。大会开幕式由协会常务副理事长牟静君主持，宋昆冈理事长致辞并就本年度我国乳业发展的情况及问题作主旨讲话。本次会议首次设立“技术大讲堂”，有 15 位中外专家作了技术报告。本次年会特设“企业家论坛”，有 11 位企业家专家就行业发展问题及建议发表了演讲。本次年会还同期举办了第 6 次乳品技术精品展示会，共有近 200 余个国际国内知名企业参加展出，展出面积 10 000m^2，展出展位近 400 个。展出产品包括乳品机械设备、包装材料及印刷、乳制品添加剂及配料、企业管理技术等方面。这是一次乳品加工技术的总汇展示，所展出的产品都是经过筛选的精品，代表着国内外先进技术水平，代表着行业生产技术发展方向，参展的企业都是在国内外具有较高知名度、有着良好信誉的企业。在本次展示会上，一个显著的特点就是展示了一些国际先进技术国产化的成果。展示会还举办了多场新产品、新技术推介会，有 31 个中外企业的专家作了专题讲座。其中法国参展团举办了专场技术讲座。

23～25 日 由农业部农产品加工领导小组办公室与北京市农村工作委员会主办、北京市乡镇企业局承办、顺鑫农业股份有限公司协办的第二届中国农产品加工业名品精品展在北京举办。本次展会共有 32 个省、自治区、直辖市、计划单列市组团参加；参展单位 298 个；展示面积 5 300m^2，参展产品、品种、规格、花色共九大类 1 万余种；科研成果 34 项，推介项目 70 项。北京市副市长牛有成、农业部总经济师薛亮等领导出席展览会。这次展览会以全国农产品加工业示范企业、农业产业化国家重点龙头企业、中国名牌产品、中国驰名商标、中华老字号、全国食品工业优秀龙头企业为主，参展各界人士达到 4.5 万人。总体上看，第二届中国农产品加工业名品精品展的成功举办，反映了当前中国农产品加工业发展的成果；进一步引起了各方面对发展农产品加工业、延伸农业产业链、繁荣首都消费品市场、发展奥运经济、促进农民非农就业增收的重视；取得了一大批合作意向及销售成果。展会达到了预期的目的，取得了圆满成功。据农业部农产品加工业领导小组办公室不完全统计，参展企业签订订单近 1 000 个，现场销售与协议金额 3.5 亿元，获得合作意向 1 500 多个。北京市共有参展企业 65 个，展示农产品加工名品、精品、新品 1 122 种，通过本次展览会共获得订单 128 个，现场销售与协议金额 1.5 亿元，达成合作意向 224 个。

31 日 全国粮食科学技术大会在北京召开。这次会议以落实国家科技发展纲要，增强自主创新能力，推动粮食科技工作，开创粮食科技新局面为主题。会议的主要任务是：认真学习贯彻全国科学技术大会精神和《国家中长期科学和技术发展规划纲要》，总结“十五”粮食科技工作，研究落实《“十一五”粮食科技发展指导意见》，全面部署“十一五”及当前粮食科技各项工作。国家粮食局局长聂振邦在会上作了题为《认真贯彻落实全国科学技术大会精神 大力推进粮食行业科技进步》的重要讲话，副局长郄建伟在会上作了《全面建设小康社会 保障国家粮食安全 加快推进粮食科技创新体系建设》的工作报告。会议全面总结了“十五”期间粮食科技取得的显著成绩，充分肯定了粮食科技进步对推动粮食流通现代化，促进粮食产业发展，保护广大种粮农民利益，满足城乡居民日益增长的需求，保障国家粮食安全起到的重要支撑作用。会议认为，粮食科技进步是保障国家粮食安全的根本措施和实现粮食流通现代化的基础，是建设社会主义新农村的迫切需要，也是粮食产业健康持续发展的主要支撑。会议要求，要把推动粮食科技进步作为“十一五”粮食工作的一项重大战略任务，以科学发展观为统领，以国家粮食安全和市场需求为导向，以可持续发展为重点，坚持“自主创新，重点跨越，支撑发展，引领未来”的指导方针，坚持创新引领、统筹协调、优化机制的原则，建立符合建设社会主义新农村和构建资源节约型、环境友好型社会要求的，安全、环保、节约和高效的粮食流通技术体系。会议确定了“十一五”期间我国粮食科技发展的重点领域，科技部农村科技司司长杜占元做了题为《当前农村科技工作发展情况报告》的专题报告，国家粮食局副局长郄建伟在闭幕式上作了总结讲话。国家粮食局党组全体成员出席了会议。各省、自治区、直辖市、计划单列市及新疆生产建设兵团粮食局有关负责人，国务院有关部委相关司负责人，中国储备粮管理总公司、中国粮油食品（集团）有限公司、中国华粮物流集团公司和中谷粮油集团公司的有关负责人等出席了会议。

9 月

1～3日 中国奶业协会第五届会员代表大会在北京召开。本次会议的主要任务是学习贯彻落实回良玉副总理对奶业发展和中国奶业协会工作的重要批示精神。回良玉在此次会议召开前夕，对奶业发展和中国奶业协会的工作作了重要批示："建设现代奶业，致富农户，繁荣农村；推进奶业发展，扩大消费需求，增强人民体质。真挚希望中国奶业协会更好地发挥'协调、服务、维权、自律'的职能，更好更多地为全国奶业发展办实事做贡献"。会议认为，回良玉副总理的批示，进一步明确了我国奶业发展的方向，吹响了我国奶业由传统型向现代奶业进军的号角；进一步明确了推进奶业发展的指导思想；对中国奶业协会给予了殷切希望，并提出了更高的要求。农业部副部长张宝文在致辞时说，我国奶业市场潜力巨大，是一个新型的前景广阔的朝阳产业。加快奶业发展，对于增加农民收入，改善城乡居民膳食结构、提高全民身体素质，促进农村产业结构调整和带动相关产业发展，乃至建设社会主义新农村，都具有十分重要的意义。2006年是实施奶业"十一五"发展规划和2020年远景目标规划的第一年，要起好步，开好头，扎扎实实把规划的各项要求落到实处。会上，中国奶业协会常务副理事长兼秘书长魏克佳汇报了第四届中国奶业协会的工作，并建议新一届协会要抓好六件实事：一是继续推进奶牛养殖基础工作，为奶农服务。二是充分发挥龙头企业对产业发展的带动作用，为乳品企业服务。三是加强市场形势分析和饮奶公益宣传，为培育开拓市场服务。四是做好技术培训，为会员服务。五是扩大国际合作与交流，为融入世界奶业服务。六是加强自身建设，提高服务质量。会上经民主选举，产生了第五届中国奶业协会的理事、常务理事、理事长、副理事长和秘书长。刘成果当选为理事长，魏克佳当选为常务副理事长兼秘书长。会议期间，还举办了第四届中国国际奶业展览会，有来自荷兰、韩国、瑞典、德国、日本等10多个国家的130家企业参展。

3～5日 由中国皮革协会主办的中国皮革协会第五届理事会第四次扩大会议在上海召开。会议的中心议题是调整结构，转变增长方式，携手推进皮革行业"十一五"良好开局。会议邀请了国家有关部委和中国轻工业联合会领导，以及来自全国各地皮革行业生产、经营、管理、科研院校及皮革生产基地的代表等，共300余人出席了会议。会议重点邀请了包括制革、制鞋、皮衣、皮件、毛皮、皮机、皮化等主体和配套行业的企业家代表，以及生产基地、科研院所的负责人，研讨了对《中国皮革行业"十一五"发展规划》的意见和建议，统一了思想，形成了共识，有利于以科学发展观统领皮革行业发展全局，有利于加快结构调整和增长方式转变，有利于推进皮革产业的全面、协调、可持续发展。会上，中国轻工业联合会副会长做重要讲话；中国轻工业联合会副会长、中国皮革协会理事长徐永以《落实"十一五"规划精神，开创皮革行业发展新局面》为题，对皮革行业的"十一五"发展规划进行了解读；中国皮革协会常务副理事长张淑华提出了《2007年中国皮革协会工作计划建议》，除按常规提出各项任务及要求外，根据当前面临的新形势，提出了2007年协会工作新的增长点；中国皮革协会秘书长苏超英汇报了《2006年中国皮革协会工作总结》；中国皮革协会副理事长、康奈集团董事长郑秀康宣读了《关于增加奖学金额度以及继续资助参与国际科技活动的决定》；中国皮革协会副理事长、河南省皮革行业协会理事长朱岩宣读了《中国皮革行业社会责任指南》；中国皮革协会副理事长杨祥娣宣布了《2006年增补中国皮革协会常务理事、理事单位名单》；中国皮革协会副理事长、四川省皮革行业协会理事长李开华宣读了《2006"真皮标志杯"中国鞋类设计大奖赛获奖名单》，并举行了颁奖仪式。会后，全体代表参观了2006年中国国际皮革展、中国国际鞋类展、国际时装及时尚配饰展。

23日 中国纺织工业协会第二届会员代表大会在北京召开。本届大会是一次换届大会，也是一次承前启后的大会，杜钰洲会长代表第一届理事会在会上作了工作报告，会议选举产生了第二届理事会、常务理事会和协会领导班子。全国人大常委会副委员长顾秀莲，全国政协副主席中国企业联合会会长陈锦华应邀出席了会议，出席会议的还有各相关协会负责人、国资委行业协会联系办公室负责人，以及各省市协会、产业集群地代表、企业代表等近200人。杜钰洲会长对第一届理事会的工作做了全面回顾与总结。他说，过去的五年，正是中国纺织工业协会在中国工业经济撤销专业行政部门、深化市场化改革的大背景下、肩负产业社会化大生产的历史重任、走上中国和全球化大市场的五年。中国纺织工业协会坚持高举邓小平理论和"三个代表"重要思想的伟大旗帜，始终遵循党中央、国务院的大政方针，在国内外新的机遇和挑战中发挥产业服务与自律、纽带与桥梁的作用，引导全体会员和全行业为早日建成现代化纺织强国奋力拼搏，探索前进，做出了应有的贡献。杜钰洲会长还对第二届理事会工作作了全面部署。他说，2006年是纺织工业第十一个五年计划的开局之年。落实“十一五”规划纲要，是纺织工业协会第二届理事会的重要历史使命。按照行业“十一五”规划纲要的基本要求，第二届理事会工作的总体思路是：坚持科学发展观，走新型工业化发展道路，以提高创新能力为中心，促进科技进步和培育自主品牌，加快纺织产业升级，转变增长方式，实现纺织工业全面、协调、可持续发展，全面实现纺织工业“十一五”发展规划目标，为在2020年前早日建成现代化纺织强国打下坚实的基础。

10 月

16～20日 第四届中国国际农产品交易会（简称农交会）在北京举办。此届农交会由农业部主办，由国家发改委、财政部、商务部、海关总署、国家质检总局、北京市人民政府、中国国际贸易促进委员会等多部委协办。本届农交会紧紧围绕“新农村、新农业、新生活”的时代主题，重点展示了党中央、国务院做出建设社会主义新农村的重大战略决策开局之年，农业和农村工作取得的新成就、新进展。参加此次展会的企业有农业产业化国家重点龙头企业，产品获无公害农产品认证、绿色食品认证、有机食品认证的企业，大中型农产品出口贸易流通企业，优秀种植、水产、畜牧等生产企业，农产品和食品包装企业，外资合资企业及境外知名企业等；参展产品包括农业高新技术、成果及产品，无公害农产品，绿色食品，有机食品，台湾省农产品及加工品，农产品及食品包装设备等。通过举办农产品的国际性展会，为我国的优质农产品提供了更加充分和广泛的展示平台，较大地推动了农产品的国内外贸易、产销衔接和农业的国际交流、区域交流和贸易、科技交流，构筑了中外企业交流空间，促进了我国农产品出口，进一步扩大了我国农业的开放领域，推动了我国农产品品质的不断提高和市场竞争力的持续增强。中共中央政治局委员、国务院副总理回良玉出席了本届农交会开幕式并讲话，他指出，刚刚闭幕的党的十六届六中全会对构建社会主义和谐社会做出了战略部署。要认真贯彻六中全会精神，坚持以发展农村经济为中心，坚持农村基本经营制度，加快建设现代农业，加强农业基础设施建设，强化农业科技支撑，优化农业和农村经济结构，扎实推进社会主义新农村建设，促进农业不断增效、农村加快发展、农民持续增收，使农业安全稳固、农村安定繁荣、农民安居乐业，为构建社会主义和谐社会打下坚实基础。回良玉副总理提出，中国国际农产品交易会是展示我国农业和农村经济发展成果的重要窗口，在推动国际间、地区间农业合作与交流中发挥着重要作用，要坚持办下去，而且要越办越好，办出特色，创出品牌，努力办成国际一流的农产品交易会。全国人大常委会副委员长乌云其木格、全国政协副主席白立忱也出席了开幕式并参观了交易会展厅，全国政协副主席王忠禹参观了农交会。

26日 国家发改委、农业部、科技部和中国轻工业联合会在北京联合召开宣传贯彻食品工业“十一五”发展纲要会议。会议发布的《食品工业“十一五”发展纲要》（以下简称《发展纲要》），是国家指导“十一五”食品工业发展的纲领性文件，对加快转变经济增长方式，促进食品工业实现全面、协调和可持续发展，推动结构调整和产业升级具有重要意义。《发展纲要》全面回顾了“十五”食品工业发展取得的成就，对行业发展的重大问题、未来发展的机遇和挑战进行了深入分析，从全局和战略的高度对我国食品工业未来五年的发展进行了总体部署，明确了“十一五”期间食品工业发展的指导思想、原则、重点行业和主要任务。“十一五”食品工业发展的重点行业包括粮食加工业、食用植物油加工业、果蔬加工业、肉类加工业、水产加工业、乳制品加工业、饮料制造业、制糖工业等8个行业。主要任务是构建食品工业科技创新体系、加快发展食品装备制造业、建立现代食品物流体系和完善食品安全保障体系。《发展纲要》同时也提出了相应的对策措施。一是推进机制和体制创新，加强宏观调控和规划引导。二是推动食品工业科技进步，增强发展动力。三是建设优质专用农产品生产基地，确保食品工业发展对原料的需求。四是加快调整产品结构，努力打造食品工业知名商标。五是培育和壮大食品工业龙头企业，推动产业结构升级。六是积极实施对外开放战略，不断拓展发展领域。七是促进投资主体多元化，多渠道增加对食品工业的投入。八是发挥中介组织的作用，加强食品工业行业自律。会议最后指出未来5年是我国食品工业发展的战略机遇期，既面临着重大机遇，也存在严峻挑战。要站在新的历史起点上，各有关部门、地方政府、企业和单位要按照科学发展观的要求，以高度的历史责任感、强烈的忧患意识和宽广的世界眼光，认真贯彻落实《发展纲要》，紧紧抓住发展机遇，积极应对各种挑战，确保食品工业健康、稳定和可持续发展，为全面建设小康社会做出应有的贡献。

31日 农业部在青岛召开全国农产品加工业工

作会议，会期两天。会议总结了“十五”期间我国农产品加工业发展的成效和经验，提出了“十一五”期间农产品加工业发展目标，即在结构调整和产业不断升级、质量和效益明显提高、加工能耗显著降低的前提下，力争实现年均增长12%的发展速度，到2010年，农产品加工业产值突破7万亿元，农产品加工业总产值与农林牧渔业总产值之比超过1.5∶1。农业部副部长危朝安在会议上指出，“十一五”期间，农产品加工业要围绕现代农业建设、农民就业增收、社会主义新农村建设和农村和谐社会建设，以科学规划为先导，以科技创新为支撑，切实转变经济增长方式，重点发展精深加工，逐步实现由初级加工向精深加工的转变、由数量增长向质量和效益提高转变。各级农业部门必须统筹规划，抓住关键，突出重点：要进一步完善和落实扶持政策，积极争取财政等部门的支持。要认真组织实施《农产品加工业“十一五”规划》，结合实际制订本地区的农产品加工发展规划，各地要加强重点工程建设，加快农产品加工示范基地、加工专用原料基地、农产品加工技术创新、农产品加工质量安全保障、农产品加工信息化、农产品加工创业六大工程建设；要建立和完善社会化服务体系，包括技术创新服务、质量标准服务、信息服务、人才培训服务、指导行业协会服务体系。危朝安强调，各级农业部门要切实履行起对职责范围内农产品加工业的宏观管理和指导工作，要力争做到组织领导到位，整合各种要素落实到位，环境创造落实到位，合力推进落实到位。形成推进农产品加工业发展的工作合力，促进农产品加工业又快又好地发展，为社会主义新农村建设提供强有力的产业支撑。

11 月

2～4日 国家粮食局召开首届粮食储藏技术与管理论坛。这次论坛由国家粮食局主办，浙江省粮食局承办，中国储备粮管理总公司、国家粮食局科学研究院、成都粮食储藏科学研究所协办。国家粮食局局长聂振邦在开幕式上作了重要讲话，国家粮食局副局长郄建伟主持了论坛开幕式，并在闭幕式上讲话。来自国内外的专家学者、企业代表和粮食行政管理部门的负责人共200余人出席了论坛。中国储备粮管理总公司副总经理姚瑞坤，浙江省粮食局李林访，以及来自北京、河北、黑龙江、上海、江苏、河南、湖南、广东、四川、甘肃、青海、宁夏等15个省、自治区、直辖市的粮食局长也出席了论坛。围绕“绿色储粮技术和储备粮仓储管理”的主题，共有30位专家从地方储备粮管理机制建设、粮食仓储企业管理、国内外绿色储粮技术的最新进展、粮食防护剂现状与发展趋势、低温储粮技术、机械通风技术、气调储粮技术、电子辐照技术等方面进行了广泛讨论，同时对浅层地能、自然冷源的利用、通风和制冷节能技术进行了研讨。聂振邦在致词中提出，各级粮食行政管理部门、仓储企业、粮食科技工作者和粮食职工要共同做好以下工作：第一，进一步完善粮食储备制度，提高粮食保障能力。第二，加强对粮食仓储行业指导，实现“藏粮于管理”。第三，重视农户储粮工作，支持社会主义新农村建设。第四，加强粮食储藏技术研究，为食品安全提供技术支持。第五，继续深化和完善粮食购销体制改革，建立现代企业制度。第六，加强人才培养，建设一支有战斗力的粮食仓储队伍。郄建伟在闭幕式讲话中指出，我国是粮食生产、消费和储藏大国，粮食管理部门和粮食企业担负着确保粮食储藏安全的重任。要从粮食储藏技术与管理入手，加强粮食仓储法律法规体系建设，加强粮食储藏技术标准体系建设，加强行政法规和技术标准执行体系建设，切实做好粮食仓储行业管理和企业管理。粮食科研单位要坚持“自主创新、重点跨越、支撑发展、引领未来”的指导方针，潜心研究粮食储藏技术，为逐渐形成有中国特色、符合中国国情的粮食绿色储粮技术体系，为建设资源节约型和环境友好型社会做出积极贡献。

22日 农业部在北京召开全国农产品质量安全监管工作视频会议，农业部部长杜青林强调，要充分认识加强农产品质量安全监管工作的重要性和紧迫性，进一步加大执法力度，加强组织领导，认真落实农产品质量安全监管措施，全面提高农产品质量安全监管工作水平。杜青林说，在党中央、国务院的高度重视下，国家先后出台了《农业法》、《畜牧法》、《渔业法》、《动物防疫法》、《农药管理条例》、《兽药管理条例》、《饲料和饲料添加剂管理条例》等法律法规，特别是《农产品质量安全法》的颁布实施，标志着我国农产品质量安全工作正进入新的发展阶段。按照党中央、国务院部署，在各级党委政府领导下，各级农业部门认真贯彻农产品质量安全法律法规，狠抓农产品产地环境、生产过程、市场准入等关键环节，积极推动全程监控，已初步形成“政府重视、部门协作、全社会参与”的农产品质量安全监管机制。据农业部监测，2006年37城市蔬菜农药残留超标率、22城市畜产品和8城市水产品兽药残留超标率及违禁药物检出率明显下降，农产品质量安全总体水平呈持续稳步提高态势。农业部副部长尹成杰等部领导出席会议，牛盾副部长主持会议。中宣部、卫生部、国家工商总局、国家质检总局、国家食品药品监管局有关负责人出席了会议。

29日 商务部在北京举办2006年农产品出口信息发布会暨惠农政策研讨会。商务部副部长易小准、中央农村工作领导小组办公室副主任唐仁建共同启动了商务部“农产品贸易专题”新网址，并发布了农产品出口信息服务的标识（Logo）。发布会通过多媒体演示，系统介绍了商务部农产品出口信息服务体系。发布会后，农业部、商务部、国家质检总局、认监委、食品土畜进出口商会、信保公司等部门负责人向参会代表系统介绍了国家推进农业产业化、农产品出口的检验检疫、良好农业规范等方面的惠农、支农政策。来自各地商务主管部门、农产品重点出口企业、出口行业组织及专家学者150多人参加了会议。易小准副部长在致辞中表示，“三农”问题是关系我国现代化建设全局的根本性问题，中央明确提出要把解决好“三农”问题作为全党工作的重中之重。长期以来，农产品出口对增加农民收入、带动农村就业、促进农业产业结构调整、推进现代农业建设发挥了重要作用，对解决“三农”问题意义重大。商务部高度重视农产品出口，近年来围绕扩大农产品出口做了大量的工作，制定了《农产品出口“十一五”发展规划》，成为“十一五”期间指导我国农产品出口的指导性文件；积极加强与各相关政府部门之间的沟通和协作，形成推进农产品出口的部门合力；推动农产品出口信用保险，主动防范市场风险，农产品出口信用保险的规模快速增长；加大对外交涉力度，积极应对国外技术壁垒，并取得积极成效；针对农产品出口企业融资难的问题，积极争取为农产品出口提供信贷支持。

12 月

4～5日 在中国科技部、美国农业部的支持下，由中美农业科技合作联合工作组主办、南京农业大学承办的中美食品安全研讨会在南京举行。来自中国科技部和国家质检总局的官员、美国农业部的食品安全专家、中国疾病控制中心、南京农业大学等单位的专家学者及雨润集团等部分企业界人士参加会议，针对中美食品安全现状及对应措施、技术发展及合作意向进行了深入的分析和积极的讨论。科技部农村科技司贾敬敦副司长在欢迎词中，回顾了自2002年中美双方签署《中国科技部与美国农业部农业科技合作议定书》以来，双方联合工作组在食品安全方面所开展的主要活动和取得的进展，希望中美科学家进一步加强合作，积极开拓合作领域和方式，并就建立中美肉品质量安全研究中心提出建议。美国肉用动物研究中心主任Mohammad Koohmaraie博士代表美国农业部表示，非常高兴来到南京参加中美食品安全研讨会。他简要介绍了美国农业部农业研究服务局的机构设置及职能，表示非常愿意与中国同行就双方所共同关注的食品安全问题展开深层次讨论，分享两国在食品安全研究领域的技术和经验。鲍俊凯副司长代表国家质检总局，就中国食品安全卫生管理体制及食品安全卫生现状做了主题发言。中美双方10多位专家在南京农业大学做了专题报告，内容涉及食品安全现状、食品安全检测和控制技术及食品安全管理等研究热点和热门话题。最后，Mohammad Koohmaraie博士和贾敬敦副司长进行了总结发言。Mohammad Koohmaraie博士表示非常愿意和中国科技部和科学家开展合作，并全权代表美国农业部开展与中国食品安全与质量进行合作。贾司长在总结发言中说，随着经济全球化进程的加快，食品全球化生产、流通和消费的趋势已经越来越明显。加强食品安全领域的国际交流与合作是保障食品安全的一个重要途径。中国科技部非常重视与美国农业部建立起来的农业科技合作平台，希望中美食品安全与质量联合工作组通过此平台，就业已确定的领域以及中心的建立迅速开展实质性合作，最终达到合作共赢的目的。

12日 中国纺织工业协会在北京召开首届中国纺织服装社会责任年会，年会以“构建负责任的供应链”为主题并邀请了供应链利益相关各方代表开展了对话与交流。国家发改委副主任欧新黔、中华全国总工会副主席苏立清、中国纺织工业协会会长杜钰洲发表讲话；中国纺织工业协会副会长兼社会责任建设推广办公室主任孙瑞哲作了“构建负责任的供应链”的主题发言，会议由中国纺织工业协会副会长陈树津主持。中国纺织工业协会杜钰洲会长在发言中指出，自觉履行社会责任是中国纺织工业实现行业结构调整和产业升级的重要基础，是落实科学发展观、构建和谐社会的必然要求。面对全球经济一体化的新形势，中国纺织工业必须积极应对新挑战并把握新的历史机遇。中国要走从纺织大国向纺织强国迈进之路，不仅要完成从量的增长向质的提高转变、从制造向创造的提升，还要尽快摆脱目前在全球供应链中的低端微利地位，更重要的是以文明的生产方式，自律的行业规范，建立对人、社会、环境负责任的行业可持续发展机制。杜钰洲会长强调，我们的目标是通过构建和谐企业、和谐产业集群、和谐行业、和谐全球供应链，为构建中国社会主义和谐社会乃至和谐世界做出积极贡献。国家发改委副主任欧新黔在讲话中指出，国家发改委重视企业社会责任在纺织行业结构调整和产业升级中的积极作用，将其作为指导纺织工业贯彻落实科学发展观、实现健康可持续发展的重点工作。中国纺织工业协会率先推出中国纺织企业社会责任管理体系（CSC9000T），为促进行业经济增长方式转变探索了新路，中国纺织工业协会的做法值得其他行业借鉴。中华全国总工会副主席苏立清在大会上的发言中表示，坚持以人为本，建立维权机制，切实维护职工合法权益，实现双赢，是建立纺织企业社会责任管理体系的目标，也是中国工会围绕党和国家工作大局开展工作的重要任务。

17日 机械工业食品机械标准化技术委员会（简称食品机械标委会）成立大会在北京召开，来自全国食品机械行业的科研单位、大专院校、行业机构以及有关重点骨干企业的标委会委员出席了会议，会议由中国包装和食品机械总公司副总经理、食品机械标委会秘书长赵有斌主持。中国机械工业联合会标准工作部谭湘宁处长、中国农业机械化科学研究院副院长李树君出席了会议并作重要讲话。秘书长赵有斌首先介绍了食品机械标委会筹备工作情况，中国包装和食品机械总公司总经理、食品机械标委会副主任委员刘文秀传达了中国机械工业联合会《关于成立机械工业食品机械标准化技术委员会的批复》，批复“机械工业食品机械标准化技术委员会”由33名委员组成，李树君为主任委员；刘文秀、吴建国、谢祖琪、代元忠为副主任委员；赵有斌为委员兼秘书长；王国扣为委员兼副秘书长。食品机械标委会秘书处设在中国农业机械化科学研究院，主要负责食品机械等技术领域国家及行业标准制修订工作。会上，中国机械工业联合会标准工作部谭湘宁处长介绍了我国标准化工作现状、管理体制、运行机制、重点任务和发展趋势，结合我国食品机械标准化工作提出了指导性意见。中国农业机械化科学研究院副院长、食品机械标委会主任李树君介绍了我国食品机械行业发展现状、标准化工作情况，提出了食品机械标委会自身建设和今后开展工作的建议。会议期间，举办了标准制修订技术讲座，邀请中国机械工业标准化技术协会常务副秘书长于美梅讲授了标准制修订工作程序、标准编写审查基本要求等相关基础技术知识。

8
第八部分
附　录

附录简要说明

1. 本部分统计资料数据主要包括：香港、澳门特别行政区和台湾省相关统计数据；世界和部分国家主要农产品收获面积、单产和总产量；禽畜产品产量；主要国家农业与农产品加工业生产指数；农产品加工业主要经济指标；世界主要国家农、林、畜、禽产品进、出口情况；按营业额排序的世界最大500家企业中农产品加工业企业。

2. 本部分统计资料数据主要来源于国家统计局、农业部、2005年联合国粮农组织数据库、2005年联合国工发组织出版的《国际工业统计年鉴》、2005年版《国际统计年鉴》、世界银行统计数据。未注明“资料来源”的数据，均采用国家统计局公布的数据。

3. 本部分统计资料中符号使用说明：“空格”表示该项统计指标数据不详或无该项数据；“*”、“①”、“△”表示本表下面有注解。

表 1 部分国家（地区）农业生产指数（2005 年）

（1999—2001＝100） 单位：%

国家或地区	农 业	种植业	畜牧业	食 品	非食品
世界总计	**111.3**	**111.2**	**111.1**	**111.3**	**114.3**
埃 及	116.8	114.6	117.0	118.9	110.8
南 非	111.1	111.1	112.0	111.3	79.4
加拿大	106.9	108.5	106.9	108.0	109.2
美 国	106.4	106.9	105.9	104.3	118.4
巴 西	126.1	124.0	124.8	123.6	145.8
中 国	129.1	122.2	139.7		
印 度	106.2	102.8	105.5	114.1	120.4
日 本	96.8	94.8	96.8	98.8	94.2
韩 国	95.7	94.1	96.3	102.6	58.2
法 国	97.2	97.4	97.2	98.9	99.2
德 国	97.1	96.6	97.2	100.2	83.2
意大利	101.2	105.1	101.4	96.7	105.8
俄罗斯	111.9	123.4	111.9	103.7	122.4
英 国	97.1	98.4	97.2	97.5	87.2
澳大利亚	92.4	92.4	95.2	93.4	70.5

表 2 我国台湾省农业生产指数（2002—2004 年）

（2001＝100）

年 份	总指数	种植业	林 业	畜牧业	渔 业
2002	104.1	105.5	111.6	98.1	108.1
2003	104.3	102.7	117.1	96.2	115.8
2004	99.9	97.6	121.3	96.1	107.5

表 3 部分国家（地区）主要粮食收获面积、单产、总产量（2005 年）

国家或地区	小 麦			稻 谷		
	收获面积（khm^2）	单产（kg/hm^2）	总产量（kt）	收获面积（khm^2）	单产（kg/hm^2）	总产量（kt）
世界总计	**215 615**	**2 913**	**628 101**	**153 784**	**4 022**	**618 535**
埃 及	1 255	6 488	8 141	650	9 539	6 200
南 非	801	2 541	2 034	1.4	2 286	3.2
加拿大	9 831	2 599	25 547			
美 国	20 226	2 823	57 106	1 353	7 401	10 012
巴 西	2 374	2 191	5 201	3 936	3 339	13 141
中 国	22 500	4 282	96 340	29 300	6 330	185 454
印 度	26 300	2 738	72 000	43 000	3 000	129 000
日 本	215	3 954	850	1 680	6 541	10 989
韩 国	2	3 500	7	980	6 549	6 418
法 国	5 288	6 982	36 922	18	5 722	103
德 国	3 188	7 396	23 578			

（续）

国家或地区	小麦			稻谷		
	收获面积（khm^2）	单产（kg/hm^2）	总产量（kt）	收获面积（khm^2）	单产（kg/hm^2）	总产量（kt）
意大利	2 128	3 539	7 530	222	6 171	1 370
俄罗斯	23 045	2 066	47 608	125	4 576	572
英　国	1 870	7 995	14 950			
澳大利亚	11 359	2 119	24 067	50	8 600	430

国家或地区	玉米			谷子			高粱		
	收获面积（khm^2）	单产（kg/hm^2）	总产量（kt）	收获面积（khm^2）	单产（kg/hm^2）	总产量（kt）	收获面积（khm^2）	单产（kg/hm^2）	总产量（kt）
世界总计	**147 171**	**4 720**	**694 576**	**35 718**	**769**	**27 388**	**44 704**	**1 311**	**58 621**
埃　及	840	8 095	6 800				160	5 938	950
南　非	3 343	3 589	11 996	21	571	12	98	3 608	354
加拿大	1 084	7 743	8 392						
美　国	30 082	9 316	280 228	200	1 400	280	2 301	4 279	9 848
巴　西	11 469	3 040	34 860				758	2 017	1 530
中　国	26 222	5 059	132 645	1 070	1 963	2 101	673	3 855	2 593
印　度	7 400	1 960	14 500	12 000	750	9 000	9 400	851	8 000
日　本	0.06	2 500	0.15	0.3	1 000	0.3			
韩　国	15	4 200	63				2	1 333	2
法　国	1 633	8 099	13 226	5	5 600	28	51	5 255	268
德　国	443	8 597	3 811						
意大利	1 056	10 064	10 622				35	6 393	221
俄罗斯	885	3 592	3 179	650	703	457	27	741	20
英　国									
澳大利亚	75	4 160	312	35	1 000	35	659	2 653	1 748

表4　部分国家（地区）马铃薯收获面积、单产、总产量（2005年）

国家或地区	收获面积（khm^2）	单产（kg/hm^2）	总产量（kt）
世界总计	**18 640**	**17 225**	**321 061**
波　兰	594	18 525	11 009
德　国	276	40 382	11 158
俄罗斯	3 140	11 592	36 400
法　国	147	43 177	6 347
荷　兰	161	42 460	6 836
加拿大	165	29 394	4 850
美　国	439	43 552	19 111
乌克兰	1 514	12 867	19 480
中　国	4 402	16 594	73 037
印　度	1 400	17 857	25 000
日　本	88	32 955	2 900
意大利	72.	25 086	1 810
英　国	140	45 000	6 300

表 5　部分国家（地区）甘薯收获面积、单产、总产量（2005 年）

国家或地区	收获面积（khm^2）	单产（kg/hm^2）	总产量（kt）
世界总计	**8 751**	**14 788**	**129 404**
巴布亚新几内亚	104	5 000	520
布隆迪	125	6 675	834
菲律宾	120	4 542	545
卢旺达	149	5 963	886
美　国	36	19 271	698
尼日利亚	516	4 876	2 516
日　本	41	25 610	1 050
坦桑尼亚	500	1 940	970
乌干达	602	4 402	2 650
中　国	5 008	21 400	107 176
印　度	100	9 000	900
印度尼西亚	177	10 406	1 840
越　南	205	7 561	1 550

表 6　部分国家（地区）木薯收获面积、单产、总产量（2005 年）

国家或地区	收获面积（khm^2）	单产（kg/hm^2）	总产量（kt）
世界总计	**18 696**	**10 876**	**303 341**
中　国	251	16 809	4 216
印　度	240	27 917	6 700
越　南	390	14 615	5 700
菲律宾	204	7 990	1 630
泰　国	986	17 180	16 938
印度尼西亚	1 224	15 903	19 459
巴　西	1 933	13 783	26 645
坦桑尼亚	670	10 448	7 000
加　纳	784	12 424	9 739
乌干达	407	13 514	5 500
卢旺达	116	6 756	782
巴拉圭	310	15 839	4 910
莫桑比克	1 050	5 857	6 150
尼日利亚	4 118	9 271	38 179

表 7　部分国家（地区）主要油料收获面积、单产、总产量（2005 年）

国家或地区	大豆			花生		
	收获面积（khm^2）	单产（kg/hm^2）	总产量（kt）	收获面积（khm^2）	单产（kg/hm^2）	总产量（kt）
世界总计	**91 299**	**2 300**	**209 976**	**25 214**	**1 424**	**35 908**
埃　及	14	3 071	43	61	3 115	190
南　非	150	1 847	277	43	2 000	85
加拿大	1 158	2 589	2 999			
美　国	28 842	2 872	82 820	650	3 249	2 113
巴　西	22 895	2 192	50 195	125	2 327	292
中　国	9 500	1 779	16 900	4 872	2 958	14 409
印　度	6 900	957	6 600	6 600	894	5 900
日　本	150	1 533	230	9	2 222	20
韩　国	86	1 454	125	3.4	2 059	7
法　国	56	2 589	145			
德　国	1	1 000	1			
意大利	148	3 969	588			
俄罗斯	690	851	587			
英　国	148	3 969	588			
澳大利亚	34	2 912	99	25	1 600	40

国家或地区	芝麻			油菜籽			向日葵		
	收获面积（khm^2）	单产（kg/hm^2）	总产量（kt）	收获面积（khm^2）	单产（kg/hm^2）	总产量（kt）	收获面积（khm^2）	单产（kg/hm^2）	总产量（kt）
世界总计	**7 561**	**439**	**3 321**	**26 951**	**1 722**	**46 410**	**23 398**	**1 328**	**31 066**
埃　及	30	1 233	37				15.7	2 300	36
南　非							460	1 502	691
加拿大				5 154	1 639	8 447	67	1 358	91
美　国				456	1 491	680	1 045	1 681	1 756
巴　西	24.5	633	15.5	35	1 700	60	126	1 587	200
中　国	661	1 098	725	7 220	1 808	13 050	1 085	1 705	1 850
印　度	1 850	368	680	6 800	941	6 400	3 000	617	1 850
日　本				0.3	2 167	0.65			
韩　国	30	600	18	1.15	871	1			
法　国				1 211	3 649	4 419	644	2 252	1 450
德　国				1 345	3 463	4 659	28	2 381	66
意大利	0.17	11 765	2	3.4	1 798	6	128	2 353	301
俄罗斯				260	1 096	285	5 320	1 181	6 280
英　国				603	3 174	1 914			
澳大利亚				1 080	1 042	1 125	53	1 302	69

表 8 部分国家（地区）籽棉、黄麻收获面积、单产、总产量（2005 年）

国家或地区	籽棉			黄麻		
	收获面积（khm^2）	单产（kg/hm^2）	总产量（kt）	收获面积（khm^2）	单产（kg/hm^2）	总产量（kt）
世界总计	**35 086**	**1 919**	**67 335**	**1 352**	**2 117**	**2 862**
埃及	315	2 603	820	0.95	2 316	2.2
南非	23.4	2 232	52			
孟加拉国	20	2 250	45	437	1 831	800
美国	5 533	2 272	12 574			
巴西	1 254	2 972	3 727	1.4	1 264	1.8
中国	5 060	3 379	17 100	36	1 889	68
印度	9 100	824	7 500	820	2 317	1 900
缅甸	300	600	180	31	849	26
巴基斯坦	3 193	2 280	7 279	0.02	1 100	0.022
泰国	11	1 273	14	3.4	1 471	5
土库曼斯坦	600	1 667	1 000			
土耳其	600	3 817	2 290			
哈萨克斯坦	288	1 910	550			
伊朗	194	2 320	450			
澳大利亚	285	4 133	1 178			

表 9 部分国家（地区）烟叶、茶叶收获面积、单产、总产量（2005 年）

国家或地区	烟叶			茶叶		
	收获面积（khm^2）	单产（kg/hm^2）	总产量（kt）	收获面积（khm^2）	单产（kg/hm^2）	总产量（kt）
世界总计	**3 981**	**1 649**	**6 565**	**2 561**	**1 335**	**3 419**
印度尼西亚	145	972	141	116	1 475	171
南非	10.50	2 261	24	5.8	1 897	11
加拿大	16	2 688	43			
美国	124	2 335	290	3.85		
巴西	493	1 783	879	953	2 104	8.1
中国	1 402	1 915	2 686	500	987	941
印度	438	1 365	598	49	1 661	831
日本	19.40	2 520	49	1.4	2 041	100
韩国	18	1 981	36		1 071	1.5
法国	8.60	2 326	20			
德国	5	2 400	12			
意大利	38	2 895	110			
土耳其	190	741	141	100	2 020	202
伊朗	20	1 050	21	32	1 625	52
巴基斯坦	45	1 871	84			

表 10 部分国家（地区）甘蔗、甜菜收获面积、单产、总产量（2005 年）

国家或地区	甘蔗			甜菜		
	收获面积（khm²）	单产（kg/hm²）	总产量（kt）	收获面积（khm²）	单产（kg/hm²）	总产量（kt）
世界总计	**19 705**	**65 458**	**1 289 820**	**5 508**	**44 049**	**242 621**
埃　及	135	121 000	16 335	70	48 781	3 430
南　非	312	69 632	21 725			
加拿大				13.8	52 174	720
美　国	387	66 634	25 804	501	49 298	24 724
巴　西	5 767	72 847	420 121			
中　国	1 340	66 216	88 730	234	33 803	7 910
印　度	3 750	61 952	232 320			
日　本	24	56 250	1 350	68	61 765	4 200
韩　国						
法　国				379	77 317	29 303
德　国				428	59 395	25 427
意大利				248	48 387	12 000
俄罗斯				780	27 590	21 520
英　国				128	58 594	7 500
澳大利亚	420	91 062	38 246			

表 11 部分国家（地区）蔬菜、水果和坚果产量（2005 年） 单位：kt

国家或地区	蔬菜和瓜类	水　果	坚　果
世界总计	**883 145**	**509 110**	**8 711**
埃　及	16 140	8 196	34
南　非	2 471	5 447	12
加拿大	2 620	692	
美　国	39 185	25 873	1 296
巴　西	7 503	35 423	284
中　国	435 024	87 056	1 363
印　度	80 529	47 031	492
日　本	11 594	3 623	24
韩　国	12 160	2 487	64
法　国	8 185	10 339	57
德　国	3 737	4 248	17
意大利	16 687	19 203	307
俄罗斯	15 201	4 019	65
英　国	2 660	281	
澳大利亚	1 909	3 509	50

表 12 部分国家（地区）甘蓝、番茄收获面积、单产、总产量（2005 年）

国家或地区	甘蓝			番茄		
	收获面积（khm^2）	单产（kg/hm^2）	总产量（kt）	收获面积（khm^2）	单产（kg/hm^2）	总产量（kt）
世界总计	**3 219**	**21 679**	**69 782**	**4 551**	**27 472**	**125 016**
埃及	19	28 947	550	195	38 974	7 600
南非	2.72	64 012	174	6.5	76 253	494
加拿大	9.58	21 192	203	8.9	96 848	862
美国	86.5	24 918	2 156	173	73 873	12 766
巴西				58	56 582	3 304
中国	1 719	19 833	34 101	1 305	24 247	31 644
印度	280	21 429	6 000	540	14 074	7 600
日本	55	40 000	2 200	13	58 462	760
韩国	52	63 462	3 300	6	66 667	400
法国	9.8	22 449	220	2.9	217 448	631
德国	21.6	45 139	975	0.45	124 444	56
意大利	13	22 366	287	141	55 324	7 815
俄罗斯	168	23 720	3 985	146	13 562	1 980
英国	9	28 889	260	0.19	410 995	79
澳大利亚	2	40 000	80	8.5	56 054	474

表 13 部分国家（地区）茄子、青辣椒和青胡椒收获面积、单产、总产量（2005 年）

国家或地区	茄子			青辣椒和青胡椒		
	收获面积（khm^2）	单产（kg/hm^2）	总产量（kt）	收获面积（khm^2）	单产（kg/hm^2）	总产量（kt）
世界总计	**1 765**	**17 293**	**30 524**	**1 697**	**14 742**	**25 015**
埃及	43	23 256	1 000	29	15 862	460
墨西哥	2	28 000	56	141	13 175	1 854
加拿大				2.1	20 894	43.5
美国	2.1	29 078	61	34.4	28 423	978
荷兰	0.08	500 000	40	1.2	262 500	315
中国	952	17 896	17 030	613	20 449	12 531
印度	510	16 078	8 200	5.5	9 182	51
日本	12	32 917	395	3.7	41 892	155
韩国	0.3	16 667	5	70	6 000	420
法国	0.45	43 333	19.5	0.65	41 539	27
印度尼西亚	43	5 864	252	174	5 012	871
意大利	12.6	29 609	374	14	26 898	378
以色列	0.65	72 308	47	2.3	51 304	118
英国				0.055	247 273	13.6
澳大利亚				2.8	19 845	56

表 14 部分国家（地区）西葫芦和南瓜、黄瓜收获面积、单产、总产量（2005 年）

国家或地区	西葫芦和南瓜			黄瓜		
	收获面积（khm^2）	单产（kg/hm^2）	总产量（kt）	收获面积（khm^2）	单产（kg/hm^2）	总产量（kt）
世界总计	**1 542**	**12 648**	**19 504**	**2 483**	**16 836**	**41 808**
埃及	39	17 602	690	28	21 429	600
南非	19	19 999	379	1.2	14 478	17.4
加拿大	5.2	12 878	68	4.1	42 652	174
美国	40	20 340	804	69	14 119	969
墨西哥	39	14 359	560	17	27 941	475
中国	308	18 714	5 768	1 553	17 101	26 560
印度	360	9 722	3 500	18	6 667	120
日本	16.5	13 939	230	14.5	46 897	680
韩国	10	31 000	310	6	66 667	400
法国	4.8	40 729	196	0.54	234 935	127
德国				2.7	42 654	117
意大利	16	30 999	50 557	2	38 000	76
俄罗斯				87	14 943	1 300
英国				0.13	473 077	61.5
澳大利亚	6	16 039	95	1.1	15 455	17

表 15 部分国家（地区）干洋葱、大蒜收获面积、单产、总产量（2005 年）

国家或地区	干洋葱			大蒜		
	收获面积（khm^2）	单产（kg/hm^2）	总产量（kt）	收获面积（khm^2）	单产（kg/hm^2）	总产量（kt）
世界总计	**3 181**	**18 207**	**57 910**	**1 439**	**10 148**	**14 603**
埃及	42.6	30 567	1 302	8.35	22 500	187.83
南非	16	26 488	426			
加拿大	6.1	33 850	207			
美国	67.4	54 412	3 670	12.79	18.53	236.96
巴西	56.6	18 710	1 059	10.52	8.13	85.60
中国	901	21 144	19 047	774	21 371	16 541
印度	530	10 377	5 500	120	4 170	500
日本	23	52 174	1 200			
韩国	16	62 500	1 000	30.24	11 830	357.74
法国	9.85	43 858	432	3.66	7 720	28.26
德国	8.46	47 293	400			
意大利	12.6	30 106	379	3	8 920	26.81
俄罗斯	125	13 120	1 640	30.61	7 720	236.17
英国	11	32 451	363			
澳大利亚	5.6	41 985	23 335			

表16 部分国家（地区）西瓜、胡萝卜收获面积、单产、总产量（2005年）

国家或地区	西瓜			胡萝卜		
	收获面积（khm^2）	单产（kg/hm^2）	总产量（kt）	收获面积（khm^2）	单产（kg/hm^2）	总产量（kt）
世界总计	**3 604**	**26 910**	**96 982**	**1 132**	**21 912**	**24 804**
埃及	63.51	25 010	1 588.4	5.55	27 370	151.9
南非	4.50	14 420	64.9	4.50	29 530	132.9
加拿大	0.20	21 200	4.2	8.82	33 300	293.7
美国	57.14	29 230	1 670.2	39.81	40 200	1 600.4
巴西	80.89	21 260	1 719.7			
中国	1 707.50	35 077	59 894.0	402.40	33 086	13 313.8
印度	20.00	12 750	255.0	24.00	14 580	349.9
日本	15.00	30 270	454.1	21.00	29 210	613.4
韩国	21.65	38 040	823.6	2.17	36 920	80.1
法国	0.20	34 800	7.0	15.89	44 800	711.9
德国				10.50	52 740	553.8
意大利	14.52	38 780	563.1	13.69	44 340	607.0
俄罗斯	113.40	8 120	920.8	89.20	19 750	1 761.7
英国				8.44	80 190	676.8
澳大利亚	3.74	33 960	127.0	7.20	42 050	302.8

表17 部分国家（地区）樱桃、葡萄收获面积、单产、总产量（2005年）

国家或地区	樱桃			葡萄		
	收获面积（khm^2）	单产（kg/hm^2）	总产量（kt）	收获面积（khm^2）	单产（kg/hm^2）	总产量（kt）
世界总计	**603.90**	**5 080**	**3 068.00**	**7 326.00**	**8 633**	**63 243.00**
埃及				58.19	21 910	1 274.94
南非	0.15	3 190	0.48	120.80	13 930	1 682.74
加拿大	2.04	6 100	12.44	9.46	8 260	78.14
美国	46.63	7 560	352.52	377.57	14 990	5 659.77
巴西				71.64	18 030	1 291.67
中国	4.00	3 750	15.00	408.10	12 630	5 154.30
印度	1.70	4 710	8.01	60.00	20 000	1 200.00
日本	4.18	3 920	16.39	19.20	10 710	205.63
韩国				22.91	16 060	367.93
法国	12.18	5 060	61.63	851.97	8 880	7 565.49
德国	46.40	4 310	199.98	98.00	11 430	1 120.14
意大利	29.97	3 180	95.30	839.72	10 350	8 691.10
俄罗斯	86.00	3 780	325.08	56.80	5 600	318.08
英国	0.38	2 630	1.00	0.75	1 600	1.20
澳大利亚	1.40	5 840	8.18	150.56	13 380	2 014.49

表 18 部分国家（地区）橙、柑果等产量（2005 年） 单位：kt

国家或地区	橙	柑 橘	柠檬、酸橙	芒 果	菠 萝	香 蕉
世界总计	**59 713**	**23 736**	**12 694**	**28 525**	**17 571**	**72 034**
埃 及	1 850	661	338	375		875
南 非	1 154	113	215	77	162	280
墨西哥	3 977	360	1 988	1 573	721	2 100
美 国	11 677	476	732	3	195	8
巴 西	18 271	1 163	986	950	1 477	6 584
中 国	2 547	11 044	623	3 582	1 404	6 518
印 度	3 100		1 420	10 800	1 300	16 820
日 本	89	1 060			11	1
韩 国		584			1	
泰 国	350	668	80	1 700	1 997	2 000
印度尼西亚	2 071			1 438	710	4 874
马来西亚	12		4	20	330	530
法 国	1	24	0.6			
意大利	2 105	611	583			
澳大利亚	395	101	28	37	110	257

表 19 部分国家（地区）苹果、草莓等产量（2005 年） 单位：kt

国家或地区	苹 果	梨	桃、油桃	草 莓	栗 子	核 桃
世界总计	**74 094**	**19 542**	**15 562**	**3 664**	**1 120**	**1 653**
埃 及	546	38	361	105		27
南 非	708	309	226	9		
加拿大	370	15	30	25		
美 国	4 740	796	1 430	1 004		295
巴 西	973	21	236	3		2
中 国	23 681	10 851	5 829	12	805	415
印 度	1 470	200	150			34
日 本	755	352	152	198	24	
韩 国	357	452	201		55	1
法 国	2 191	263	397	54	12	26
德 国	1 592	398	13	119		17
意大利	2 136	878	1 710	168	50	15
俄罗斯	2 030	102	50	215	18	14
英 国	205	23		48		
澳大利亚	255	139	100	20		

表 20 部分国家（地区）生咖啡、可可豆收获面积、单产、总产量（2005 年）

国家或地区	生咖啡			可可豆		
	收获面积（khm^2）	单产（kg/hm^2）	总产量（kt）	收获面积（khm^2）	单产（kg/hm^2）	总产量（kt）
世界总计	**9 566**	**759**	**7 263**	**6 873**	**547**	**3 759**
尼日利亚	4	910	4	1 062	340	631
墨西哥	744	420	312	83	580	48
利比里亚	16	200	3	15	170	3
美国	2	1 080	3			
巴西	2 368	1 040	2 463	639	310	198
中国	16	1 560	25			
印度	328	820	269	18	440	8
越南	492	1 700	836			
印度尼西亚	1 398	500	699	500	1 200	600
泰国	67	920	62	1	500	
缅甸	6	530	3			
马来西亚	52	750	39	42	800	33
菲律宾	131	770	101	11	520	6
古巴	62	210	13	6	320	2
加纳	8	230	2	2 000	370	740

表 21 我国台湾省主要农产品产量（2002—2004 年） 单位：万 t

年份	稻谷	槟榔	菠萝	芒果	甘蔗	茶叶	花生	香蕉
2002	146.1	16.2	41.6	21.3	197.3	2.0	7.7	22.7
2003	133.8	16.0	44.8	22.1	169.6	2.1	7.3	22.3
2004	116.5	14.3	45.8	18.2	112.9	2.0	6.8	19.0

表 22 部分国家（地区）肉类产量（2004—2005 年） 单位：kt

国家或地区	2004 年	2005 年	同比增长（%）
世界总计	**259 368**	**265 240**	**2.26**
埃及	1 494	1 440	−3.61
南非	1 853	1 890	1.99
加拿大	4 533	4 680	3.24
美国	38 852	39 560	1.82
巴西	19 919	19 920	0.005
中国	72 448	77 430	6.88
印度	6 032	6 300	4.44
日本	3 006	3 000	−0.20
韩国	218	250	14.68

（续）

国家或地区	2004 年	2005 年	同比增长（%）
法　国	6 319	6 180	－2.20
德　国	6 758	6 880	1.81
意大利	4 132	4 100	－0.77
俄罗斯	5 138	4 890	－4.83
英　国	3 212	3 340	3.99
澳大利亚	3 751	3 950	5.31

表 23　部分国家（地区）牛奶产量（2004—2005 年）　单位：kt

国家或地区	2004 年	2005 年	同比增长（%）
世界总计	**523 230**	**530 720**	**1.43**
埃　及	2 130	2 300	7.98
南　非	2 550	2 550	
加拿大	8 000	8 100	1.25
美　国	77 480	80 150	3.45
巴　西	23 320	23 320	
中　国	22 610	27 530	21.76
印　度	37 500	38 500	2.67
日　本	8 330	8 260	－0.84
韩　国	90	90	
法　国	24 360	25 280	3.78
德　国	28 120	27 600	－1.85
意大利	9 970	10 500	5.32
俄罗斯	31 660	30 600	－3.35
英　国	14 560	14 580	0.14
澳大利亚	10 130	10 150	0.20

表 24　部分国家（地区）鸡蛋产量（2004—2005 年）　单位：kt

国家或地区	2004 年	2005 年	同比增长（%）
世界总计	**58 060**	**59 250**	**2.05**
埃　及	240	240	
南　非	340	340	
加拿大	380	380	
美　国	5 280	5 330	0.95
巴　西	1 560	1 560	
中　国	24 326	24 350	0.10

（续）

国家或地区	2004年	2005年	同比增长（%）
印 度	2 460	2 490	1.22
日 本	2 480	2 470	−0.40
韩 国	570	570	
法 国	1 040	1 050	0.96
德 国	800	800	
意大利	710	700	−1.41
俄罗斯	1 990	2 050	3.02
英 国	550	550	
澳大利亚	170	170	

表25 部分国家（地区）蜂蜜产量（2004—2005年） 单位：t

国家或地区	2004年	2005年	同比增长（%）
世界总计	**1 286 620**	**1 304 290**	**1.37**
中 国	298 000	298 000	
埃塞俄比亚	38 100	38 100	
安哥拉	23 000	23 000	
澳大利亚	16 000	16 000	
巴 西	32 290	24 500	−24.13
德 国	25 580	21 230	−17.01
法 国	15 000	15 000	
俄罗斯	52 670	52 130	−1.03
韩 国	28 000	29 000	3.57
加拿大	34 240	36 110	5.46
肯尼亚	21 500	21 500	
罗马尼亚	19 150	19 200	2.33
美 国	83 270	79 220	−4.86
墨西哥	56 810	50 630	−10.88
坦桑尼亚	27 000	27 000	
土耳其	73 930	82 340	11.38
乌克兰	58 000	71 460	23.21
西班牙	36 700	37 000	0.82
希 腊	16 720	15 640	−6.50
匈牙利	19 500	19 710	1.08
伊 朗	35 000	36 000	2.86
印 度	52 000	52 000	

表 26 部分国家（地区）羊毛产量（2004—2005 年） 单位：kt

国家或地区	2004 年	2005 年	同比增长（%）
世界总计	**2 166**	**2 203**	**1.71**
埃　及	7.6	7.6	
南　非	44.2	44.2	
加拿大	1.5	1.5	
美　国	17.1	17.1	
巴　西	11.4	11.4	
中　国	373.9	393.2	5.16
印　度	51.4	51.4	
日　本			
韩　国			
法　国	22.0	22.0	
德　国	15.0	15.0	
意大利	10.1	11.0	8.91
俄罗斯	45.6	46.0	0.88
英　国	60.0	60.0	
澳大利亚	508.8	508.8	

表 27 部分国家（地区）人均每天食物热值、蛋白质和脂肪含量（2003 年）

国家或地区	食物热值（J）	蛋白质（g）	脂肪含量（g）
世界平均	**11 746.8**	**75.7**	**79.6**
埃　及	14 034.8	94.0	59.5
南　非	12 387.9	77.4	77.6
加拿大	15 075.7	104.8	148.4
美　国	15 698.0	114.7	155.2
巴　西	13 155.3	85.3	95.4
中　国	12 295.9	81.8	96.3
印　度	10 340.0	58.8	53.3
日　本	11 574.9	91.5	86.2
韩　国	12 693.2	89.6	83.1
法　国	15 152.2	117.2	168.3
德　国	14 569.7	100.3	141.9
意大利	15 368.0	113.5	156.1
俄罗斯	13 039.1	92.0	85.7
英　国	14 426.6	105.5	134.7
澳大利亚	13 108.9	111.3	132.3
荷　兰	14 615.7	105.0	139.6
丹　麦	14 521.2	108.9	138.5
墨西哥	13 259.9	90.5	89.1
瑞　典	13 416.7	108.2	126.6
匈牙利	14 854.5	95.6	151.8

资料来源：表中数据出自 2005 年版《国际统计年鉴》。

表 28　我国农业主要产品产量居世界位次（1949—2005）

项　目	1949 年	2003 年	2004 年	2005 年
谷　物		1	1	1
肉　类	3	1	1	1
棉　花	4	1	1	1
大　豆	2	4	4	4
花　生	2	1	1	1
油菜籽	2	1	1	1
甘　蔗		3	3	3
茶　叶	3	2	1	1
水　果		1	1	1

表 29　世界主要国家天然橡胶生产情况（2003—2005 年）

国别与项目		2003 年	2004 年	2005 年
泰　国	植胶面积（万 hm^2）	188	208	214
	单产水平（t/hm^2）	1.52	1.52	1.52
	总产量（万 t）	286	316	326
印度尼西亚	植胶面积（万 hm^2）	267.5	291	320
	单产水平（t/hm^2）	0.67	0.67	0.67
	总产量（万 t）	179	195	224.5
马来西亚	植胶面积（万 hm^2）	118	140.8	142.8
	单产水平（t/hm^2）	0.59	0.85	0.85
	总产量（万 t）	70	120	121.4
印　度	植胶面积（万 hm^2）	43.5	46.3	50
	单产水平（t/hm^2）	1.63	1.63	1.63
	总产量（万 t）	71	75.5	78
中　国	植胶面积（万 hm^2）	66.7	66.7	66.7
	单产水平（t/hm^2）	0.85	0.90	0.95
	总产量（万 t）	56.5	60	63.4
越　南	植胶面积（万 hm^2）	45	47	50
	单产水平（t/hm^2）	1.03	1.03	1.03
	总产量（万 t）	46.3	48.4	51.5

资料来源：表中数据来自联合国粮农组织的统计和预测。

表 30　世界主要农畜产品最大生产国（2005 年）

农畜产品	第一位国家	产量（kt）	第二位国家	产量（kt）	第三位国家	产量（kt）
谷物	中国	427 760	美国	364 020	印度	233 960
小麦	中国	97 445	印度	72 000	美国	57 110
稻谷	中国	180 588	印度	129 000	印度尼西亚	53 980
玉米	美国	280 230	中国	139 365	巴西	34 860
谷子	印度	9 400	尼日利亚	6 282	尼日尔	2 100

（续）

农畜产品	第一位国家	产量（kt）	第二位国家	产量（kt）	第三位国家	产量（kt）
高粱	美国	11 555	尼日利亚	8 028	印度	7 700
马铃薯	中国	73 037	俄罗斯	36 400	印度	25 000
甘薯	中国	107 176	乌干达	2 650	尼日利亚	2 516
木薯	尼日利亚	38 179	巴西	26 645	印度尼西亚	19 459
大豆	美国	82 820	巴西	50 200	阿根廷	38 300
甘蔗	巴西	420 120	印度	232 320	中国	86 638
甜菜	法国	29 300	德国	25 430	美国	24 720
可可豆	科特迪瓦	1 331	加纳	737	印度尼西亚	601
茶叶	中国	935	印度	650	斯里兰卡	310
烟叶	中国	2 683	巴西	880	印度	600
籽棉	中国	17 100	美国	12 574	印度	7 500
肉类	中国	77 430	美国	39 560	巴西	19 920
鸡蛋	中国	24 350	美国	5 330	印度	2 490
奶类	印度	91 000	美国	77 520	俄罗斯	31 933
鸡肉	美国	15 514	中国	9 945	巴西	8 668

表 31　香港特别行政区工业生产指数（2002—2005 年）

（2000 年＝100）

工业组别/组别内选定工业	2002 年	2003 年	2004 年	2005 年
所有制造行业	86.2	78.3	80.6	82.6
食品、饮品及烟草制品业	106.4	94.1	99.4	100.5
服装制品业（服装除外）	93.3	95.1	94.7	84.2
纺织制品业（包括针织）	92.5	82.6	79.1	82.5
纸品及印刷业	98.6	98.2	95.9	95.9

表 32　我国台湾省农产品加工业主要产品产量（2001—2005 年）

年　份	食品（万 t）	饮料（万 L）	饲料（万 t）	各种成衣（万打）	纸板（万 t）	人造纤维（万 t）	轮胎（万条）
2001	37.1	44 224.1	545.6	2 188.5	259.1	314.9	1 679.0
2002	38.4	43 499.8	523.3	1 858.1	323.5	335.8	1 932.6
2003	37.4	44 741.7	510.8	1 597.8	340.4	333.3	2 261.9
2004	36.8	39 974.5	482.9	1 743.1	355.5	334.2	2 399.3
2005	41.9	40 399.9	483.2	1 134.9	337.8	289.7	

表 33 美国农产品加工业主要经济指标（2000—2001 年）

按国际标准产业分类（第三版分类）	雇员数（千人）		产 值（百万美元）		增加值（百万美元）		固定资本形成（百万美元）	
	2000 年	2001 年	2000 年	2001 年	2000 年	2001 年	2000 年	2001 年
制造业合计								
肉类、鱼类、水果蔬菜、油类等	677	681	184 003	193 180	61 796	66 279	4 255	3 947
乳制品	132	132	60 780	65 512	20 073	20 832	1 463	1 684
谷物、淀粉及制品牲畜精饲料	108	108	55 830	58 555	23 957	25 861	2 093	1 934
其他食品	593	589	134 622	134 222	79 393	80 558	4 320	4 006
饮料	143	147	64 843	67 406	30 226	31 807	2 673	2 582
烟草制品	28	27	48 509	53 098	41 438	46 092	214	227
纺织品	255	220	38 921	34 224	15 664	13 768	1 254	1 088
服装	442	384	52 770	47 761	24 294	21 626	760	591
皮革制品	39	34	5 886	5 323	2 812	2 506	115	55
木材制品	352	339	50 632	48 145	22 134	20 755	1 732	1 623
纸及纸制品	541	523	163 434	154 093	77 440	72 319	7 340	6 750
印刷业	830	799	104 396	100 792	63 173	60 483	4 417	4 064
橡胶制品	209	194	36 072	33 441	18 819	17 083	1 553	1 141

资料来源：表中数据出自联合国工发组织编制的 2005 年版《国际工业统计年鉴》。

表 34 日本农产品加工业主要经济指标（2001 年）

按国际标准产业分类（第三版分类）	机构数（个）	雇员数（千人）	产 值（十亿日元）	增加值（十亿日元）	固定资本形成*（十亿日元）
制造业合计	**316 207**	**8 477**	**286 609**	**103 268**	**11 301**
肉类、鱼类、水果蔬菜、油类等	12 610	320	7 235	2 267	132
乳制品	728	40	2 248	705	89
谷物、淀粉及制品牲畜精饲料	1 649	31	2 340	538	37
其他食品	24 502	747	13 092	5 880	364
饮料	3 054	74	6 560	2 399	229
烟草制品	31	6	2 951	613	40
纺织品	7 356	115	1 785	811	43
服装	10 868	189	1 372	713	11
毛皮制品	57	1	11	5	
皮革制品	1 926	21	384	150	7
木材制品	10 989	121	2 262	908	36
纸及纸制品	8 998	225	7 554	2 870	355
印刷	20 697	373	7 757	3 574	194
橡胶制品	3 114	109	2 742	1 283	131

* 为 2000 年数据。

资料来源：表中数据来自联合国工发组织编制的 2004 年版《国际工业统计年鉴》。

表 35 德国农产品加工业主要经济指标（2000 年）

按国际标准产业分类（第三版分类）	机构数（个）	雇员数（千人）	产 值（百万欧元）	增加值（百万欧元）	固定资本形成（百万欧元）
制造业合计	**232 954**	**7 520**	**1 301 702**	**414 051**	**57 400**
肉类、鱼类、水果、蔬菜、油类等	19 308	268.7	38 521	8 041	1 145
乳制品	325	41.1	18 797	2 674	431
谷物、淀粉及制品 牲畜精饲料	1 003	25.8	8 155	1 876	307
其他食品	21 629	448.6	40 687	13 177	1 564
饮料	1 802	80.5	19 555	5 431	1381
烟草制品	37	12.7	14 432	1 843	166
纺织品	1 197	54.6	6 465	2 188	304
服装	5 586	77.2	10 563	2 829	158
毛皮制品	808	2.1	111	34	3
皮革制品	920	11.3	1 271	380	52
木材制品	13 654	148.5	15 926	5 657	1 008
纸及纸制品	1 589	155.2	30 951	9 645	2 103
印刷	13 585	196.5	21 263	9 744	1 741
橡胶制品	625	78.2	10 283	4 206	513

资料来源：表中数据出自联合国工发组织编制的 2004 年版《国际工业统计年鉴》。

表 36 英国农产品加工业主要经济指标（2000 年）

按国际标准产业分类（第三版分类）	机构数（个）	雇员数（千人）	产 值（百万英镑）	增加值（百万英镑）	固定资本形成（百万英镑）
制造业合计	**167 476**	**4 020.2**	**439 350**	**148 499**	**19 631.4**
肉类、鱼类、水果、蔬菜、油类等	2 222	189.5	17 620	5 003	645.4
乳制品	609	36. 3	5 978	1 296	223.3
谷物、淀粉及制品牲畜精饲料	723	31.6	6 429	1 609	298.4
其他食品	3 581	203.0	17 609	7 113	809.5
饮料	747	56.9	12 444	4 046	567.1
烟草制品	27	6.4	8 130	1 266	86.2
纺织品	1 412	41.3	2 690	993	93.2
服装	6 326	121.3	5 063	2 021	80.4
毛皮制品	29	0.5	28	8	0.4
皮革制品	628	9.4	634	243	11.4
木材制品	7 414	65.2	4 782	1 851	219.1
纸及纸制品	2 735	98.3	11 344	3 987	573.4
印刷	18 933	190.8	14 223	6 972	1 026.8
橡胶制品	745	41.2	2 973	1 313	175.4

资料来源：表中数据出自联合国工发组织编制的 2004 年版《国际工业统计年鉴》。

表37 法国农产品加工业主要经济指标（2000年）

按国际标准产业分类（第三版分类）	机构数（个）	雇员数（千人）	产 值（百万欧元）	增加值（百万欧元）	固定资本形成（百万欧元）
制造业合计	**21 150**	**2 715**	**622 006**	**162 856**	**24 699**
纺织品	639	46.6	7 221.6	1 806	208
服装	1 165	77.8	9 353.5	2 555	140.4
毛皮制品	10	0.285	64.9	14.8	0.274
皮革制品	172	14.7	1 450.4	666.3	38.4
木材制品	583	41	6 124.4	1 695.7	385.5
纸及纸制品	636	85.5	1 858.08	4 845	998.6
印刷	1 190	73.4	9 097.7	3 249.7	450.3
橡胶制品	171	69.4	8 456.7	3 374.7	466.5

资料来源：表中数据出自联合国工发组织编制的2004年版《国际工业统计年鉴》。

表38 意大利农产品加工业主要经济指标（1999—2000年）

按国际标准产业分类（第三版分类）	机构数（个）		雇员数（千人）		总产值（百万欧元）		增加值（百万欧元）		固定资本形成（百万欧元）	
	1999年	2000年	1999年	2000年	1999年	2000年	1999年	2000年	1999年	2000年
制造业合计	**559 406**	**560 956**	**3 975.4**	**4 017**	**686 995.7**	**783 262.4**	**187 785**	**204 184.1**	**34 165.4**	**38 724.3**
肉类、鱼类、水果、蔬菜、油类等	10 987	10 927	87.1	85.4	25 370.8	25 353.7	4 224.5	3 922.4	1 131.8	1 107.7
乳制品	4 285	4 228	48.9	49.0	14 275.6	14 092.3	2 652.1	2 635.4	796.1	585.1
谷物、淀粉及制品、牲畜精饲料	2 797	2 674	17.4	16.3	8 678.5	8 717.8	1 217.8	1 051.7	317.0	411.7
其他食品	47 673	47 853	142.8	136.6	22 947.1	23 385.5	7 182.0	6 929.7	1 482.9	1 216.8
饮料	3 190	3 225	33.3	33.3	12 140.3	11 916.5	2 237.8	2 484.1	828.6	650.0
烟草制品	78	67	9.8	8.5	1 098.5	1 127.0	339.1	408.4	69.5	43.3
纺织品	10 806	10 307	149.3	145.8	21 121.3	20 823.7	6 375.1	6 528.2	924.3	1 014.6
服装	46 359	45 646	252.0	240.0	25 281.8	27 855.1	7 231.5	8 166.5	724.5	668.5
毛皮制品	2 466	2 378	3.4	3.1	495.9	384.0	136.2	123.9	9.4	14.1
皮革制品	9 992	10 024	49.1	52.2	9 601.6	11 711.1	2 038.1	2 312.8	275.6	353.1
木材制品	45 078	44 434	92.7	96.4	11 528.7	13 269.5	3 728.3	4 147.4	972.3	1 004.2
纸及纸制品	4 700	4 733	75.4	76.2	14 534.4	18 072.0	4 056.2	4 474.6	930.2	994.2
印刷	20 174	20 400	91.8	99.1	11 159.5	13 092.9	4 326.2	4 644.0	833.4	910.8
橡胶制品	1 709	1 701	45.9	46.8	6 631.5	6 947.8	2 209.0	2 316.3	269.7	417.1

资料来源：表中数据出自联合国工发组织编制的2004年版《国际工业统计年鉴》。

表 39 加拿大农产品加工业主要经济指标（2000—2001 年）

按国际标准产业分类（第三版分类）	机构数（个）		雇员数（千人）		产值（百万加元）		增加值（百万加元）	
	2000 年	2001 年	2000 年	2001 年	2000 年	2001 年	2000 年	2001 年
制造业合计	**53 399**	**54 031**	**1 958**	**1 976**	**600 735**	**580 613**	**234 854**	**222 404**
肉类、鱼类、水果蔬菜、油类等	1 899	1 880	106*	129	29 396*	33 819	8 304*	8 867
乳制品	440	434	20	20	10 454	11 525	2 949	3 374
谷物、淀粉及制品牲畜精饲料	758	777	18*	22	9 261*	9 587	3 229*	3 191
其他食品	2 436	2 454	66	66	12 166	12 999	6 078	6 394
饮料	472	490	27	26	9 275	9 478	5 425	5 497
烟草制品	23	23	3	3	3 106	3 068	2 173	2 201
纺织品	433	416	17	18	2 929	2 805	1 136	1 230
服装	2 454	2 437	82	87	7 570	7 346	3 815	3 763
毛皮制品	203	194	3	3	371	278	236	119
皮革制品	236	246	4	4	429	410	158	153
木材制品	1 830	1 789	51	52	10 975	10 735	4 839	4 522
纸及纸制品	872	850	99	100	39 473	37 188	18 253	16 193
印刷	4 748	4 788	78	81	11 692	12 186	6 408	6 874
橡胶制品	363	367	24	27	5 299	5 412	2 259	2 367

* 1999 年的数据。

资料来源：表中数据出自联合国工发组织编制的 2004 年版《国际工业统计年鉴》。

表 40 澳大利亚农产品加工业主要经济指标（2001 年）

按国际标准产业分类（第三版分类）	机构数（个）	雇员数（人）	产 值（百万欧元）	增加值（百万欧元）	固定资本形成（百万欧元）
制造业合计					
肉类、鱼类、水果蔬菜、油类等	1 099	76 467	20 413	8 063	705
乳制品	168	19 399	8 087	2 898	395
谷物、淀粉及制品牲畜精饲料	385	14 248	5 424	2 205	166
其他食品					
饮料	551	22 329	10 034	5 185	480
烟草制品	2	2 305	1 342	824	16
纺织品	454	9 765	1 909	943	49
服装	2 759	20 931	2 469	1 270	18
毛皮制品	94	2 787	843	261	20
皮革制品					
木材制品					
纸及纸制品					
印刷					
橡胶制品	285	8 118	1 488	771	5

资料来源：表中数据出自联合国工发组织编制的 2004 年版《国际工业统计年鉴》。

表 41 印度农产品加工业主要经济指标（2001 年）

按国际标准产业分类（第三版分类）	机构数（个）	雇员数（千人）	产 值（百万卢比）	增加值（百万卢比）	固定资本形成（百万卢比）
制造业合计	**118 370**	**7 512.7**	**9 344 405**	**1 791 376**	**688 848**
肉类、鱼类、水果蔬菜、油类等	3 454	134.9	370 436	29 200	9 471
乳制品	865	83.6	191 545	23 773	4 068
谷物、淀粉及制品牲畜精饲料	12 429	312.2	398 692	26 546	5 903
其他食品	5 688	693.9	462 380	92 809	20 638
饮料	1 048	82.1	100 991	24 507	5 742
烟草制品		493.3	98 507	40 817	2 329
纺织品	9 152	1 019.5	706 011	125 719	27 815
服装	3 273	316.2	144 790	32 704	5 258
毛皮制品	10	0.9	885	104	7
皮革制品	1 199	53.9	43 564	5 237	886
木材制品	1 784	41.6	29 898	3 872	1 009
纸及纸制品	3 378	168.3	171 541	36 785	46 162
印刷	2 208	56.2	33 887	8 958	2 935
橡胶制品	1 927	105.0	127 947	30 316	3 174

资料来源：表中数据出自联合国工发组织编制的 2005 年版《国际工业统计年鉴》。

表 42 韩国农产品加工业主要经济指标（2000—2001 年）

按国际标准产业分类（第三版分类）	机构数（个）		雇员数（千人）		产 值（十亿韩元）		增加值（十亿韩元）		固定资本形成（十亿韩元）	
	2000 年	2001 年	2000 年	2001 年	2000 年	2001 年	2000 年	2001 年	2000 年	2001 年
制造业合计	**98 110**	**105 873**	**2 573.4**	**2 561.4**	**564 834**	**583 793**	**219 425**	**221 860**	**48 579**	**37 245**
肉类、鱼类、水果蔬菜、油类等	2 080	2 300	60.8	63.2	8 121	8 807	2 814	2 887	398	489
乳制品	103	103	8.8	9.3	3 439	4 079	1 375	1 483	133	149
谷物、淀粉及制品牲畜精饲料	896	982	15.9	15.9	8 524	9 237	2 255	2 138	342	331
其他食品	2 912	3 162	69.3	69.0	11 260	11 792	5 590	5 605	710	734
饮料	430	438	17.0	16.8	6 090	5 936	3 712	3 434	507	268
烟草制品	13	12	3.1	2.7	3 696	3 642	2 372	2 403	47	110
纺织品	4 776	5 110	150.9	136.9	17 664	16 332	7 614	4 801	1 547	775
服装	8 493	9 016	139.1	132.4	9 146	10 752	4 343	4 832	249	260
毛皮制品	136	130	2.3	1.7	312	299	117	92	15	4
皮革制品	999	957	18.5	16.2	3 197	3 348	1 055	985	89	61
木材制品	1 144	1 233	17.6	17.3	2 269	2 340	926	896	210	139
纸及纸制品	2 673	2 826	54.4	56.2	13 410	13 418	4 899	4 994	1 194	845
印刷	3 171	3 667	34.4	36.9	3 030	3 343	1 489	1 685	208	234
橡胶制品	986	1 012	35.5	34.3	5 313	5 352	2 474	2 542	539	627

资料来源：表中数据出自联合国工发组织编制的 2004 年版《国际工业统计年鉴》。

表 43 我国台湾省出口与进口商品分类（2002—2005 年） 单位：亿美元

年 份	出口				进口			
	出口额	农产品	农产加工品	工业产品	进口额	原材料	资本设备	消费品
2002	1 306.0	3.5	17.0	1 285.5	1 125.3	761.7	259.2	104.3
2003	1 441.8	3.8	17.7	1 420.3	1 272.5	896.7	260.3	115.5
2004	1 740.1	3.8	20.8	1 715.5	1 678.9	1 181.5	359.9	137.5
2005	1 984.3	3.8	21.1	1 959.5	1 826.2	1 307.9	360.5	157.7

表 44 部分国家（地区）农产品进口额和出口额（2002—2003 年）

单位：亿美元

国家或地区	进口额		出口额	
	2002 年	2003 年	2002 年	2003 年
世界总计	**4 646.3**	**5 485.5**	**4 424.1**	**5 221.8**
埃 及	34.4	26.8	7.7	9.4
南 非	14.9	19.2	24.0	30.5
加拿大	127.1	142.1	164.7	176.0
美 国	450.3	534.8	555.9	623.0
巴 西	32.4	36.0	167.3	209.1
中 国①	161.1	234.5	144.7	168.8
印 度	40.2	49.0	55.2	65.0
日 本	336.3	369.9	16.2	17.0
韩 国	89.6	96.6	16.8	19.0
法 国	252.6	306.6	348.4	420.5
德 国	368.6	455.9	263.5	328.5
意大利	221.9	268.3	174.5	206.5
俄罗斯	93.9	110.3	18.4	23.4
英 国	291.5	350.5	146.6	171.9
澳大利亚	32.3	38.9	160.2	150.0

注：①数据出自联合国粮农组织数据库。
资料来源：表中数据出自 2005 年版《国际统计年鉴》。

表 45 部分国家（地区）牛肉、绵羊肉、猪肉进出口数量（2004 年） 单位：kt

国家或地区	牛肉		绵羊肉		猪肉	
	进口数量	出口数量	进口数量	出口数量	进口数量	出口数量
埃 及	90.62	0.84	0.22	0.07	0.66	
印度尼西亚	12.46	6.21	0.69	0.01	3.45	9.32
加拿大	136.66	630.81	17.38	0.26	128.63	1 004.96
美 国	842.48	1 425.53	78.40	7.36	486.13	1 855.11
巴 西	32.03	875.09	3.66		1.70	462.29
中 国	1 175.28	70.67	86.27	30.23	903.32	418 51
印 度	1.21	245.77	0.01	13.72	0.28	6.77
日 本	387.99	2.48	36.42		785.80	4.66
荷 兰	250.91	333.87	8.58	4.82	327.05	892.66

（续）

国家或地区	牛肉		绵羊肉		猪肉	
	进口数量	出口数量	进口数量	出口数量	进口数量	出口数量
法国	282.38	435.28	139.31	9.58	421.58	773.93
德国	194.37	409.71	32.13	5.02	906.19	930.13
意大利	443.07	177.69	23.73	1.01	814.83	182.72
俄罗斯	421.66	33.69	4.03		526.68	36.27
英国	388.46	111.45	115.87	76.49	610.25	212.74
澳大利亚	7.54	1 543.55	0.37	270.45	83.80	266.70

表 46 部分国家（地区）牛肉、绵羊肉、猪肉进出口金额（2004 年）

单位：百万美元

国家或地区	牛肉		绵羊肉		猪肉	
	进口金额	出口金额	进口金额	出口金额	进口金额	出口金额
埃及	182.75	0.69	0.38	0.06	0.18	
印度尼西亚	27.97	1.05	2.01	0.01	3.28	3.09
加拿大	302.43	1 482.56	76.37	0.43	331.90	1 970.25
美国	3 795.45	741.25	452.45	12.43	1 431.67	2 268.12
巴西	74.79	2 438.60	6.17		1.74	805.27
中国	503.96	118.99	134.26	42.55	666.78	862.95
印度	0.31	365.74	0.03	17.52	0.52	3.3
日本	1 926.97	10.24	131.82		5 230.85	5.93
荷兰	878.95	1 734.17	70.00	37.26	650.02	2 220.81
法国	1 155.72	1 029.33	647.95	72.18	1 269.52	1 374.86
德国	843.56	1 441.83	227.44	32.25	2 383.03	2 232.78
意大利	1 981.49	446.38	133.60	5.73	1 990.25	965.84
俄罗斯	697.86	15.14	5.04	0.01	688.25	25.44
英国	1 482.13	96.70	519.18	344.35	2 430.44	353.14
澳大利亚	20.33	3 552.63	1.39	830.31	191.87	173.73

表 47 部分国家（地区）鸡肉、鸭肉、火鸡肉进出口数量（2004 年）单位：kt

国家或地区	鸡肉		鸭肉		火鸡肉	
	进口数量	出口数量	进口数量	出口数量	进口数量	出口数量
埃及	0.36	0.47		0.05		
印度尼西亚	1.42	0.12	0.06	0.02	0.07	
加拿大	150.71	78.49	2.03	2.88	4.27	17.48
美国	33.93	2 440.10	2.29	4.50	2.24	179.33
巴西	0.34	2 477.89		0.61	0.12	134.34
中国	763.26	396.70	32.68	24.70	35.08	4.60
印度		1.53		0.26		
日本	613.73	1.35	5.07		0.91	
荷兰	411.21	694.71	0.86	7.40	25.19	48.25

（续）

国家或地区	鸡肉		鸭肉		火鸡肉	
	进口数量	出口数量	进口数量	出口数量	进口数量	出口数量
法　国	201.71	678.96	4.83	14.71	15.73	237.58
德　国	417.84	388.29	31.56	5.04	84.45	77.92
意大利	45.87	87.13	1.47	0.10	25.36	63.50
俄罗斯	1 054.80	0.76	1.63	0.01	98.35	
英　国	566.03	284.45	9.84	4.96	34.79	49.98
澳大利亚	0.51	16.92	0.05	0.22		3.64

表 48　部分国家（地区）鸡肉、鸭肉、火鸡肉进出口金额（2004 年）

单位：百万美元

国家或地区	鸡肉		鸭肉		火鸡肉	
	进口金额	出口金额	进口金额	出口金额	进口金额	出口金额
埃　及	0.40	0.53		0.05		
印度尼西亚	1.05	0.21	0.13		0.13	
加拿大	342.06	134.72	5.05	10.05	14.74	13.42
美　国	116.28	1 944.39	9.42	10.77	5.32	255.75
巴　西	0.47	2 599.51	0.05	1.17		212.43
中　国	676.25	708.14	52.61	32.59	35.66	2.87
印　度	0.02	1.65		0.25		
日　本	1 486.76	3.08	50.03		2.31	
荷　兰	673.81	1 299.24	5.98	18.82	40.22	44.30
法　国	455.39	880.03	64.05	99.80	29.58	439.66
德　国	993.46	595.48	111.58	12.18	229.28	135.00
意大利	92.54	129.95	5.85	0.38	63.69	155.18
俄罗斯	625.98	0.86	1.24	0.02	58.39	0.01
英　国	1 791.46	425.99	36.95	14.37	113.91	59.82
澳大利亚	1.68	12.83	0.16	0.71		2.60

表 49　我国纺织服装出口到各国和地区贸易额前 10 名国家和地区（2005 年）

位　次	出口国家和地区	出口金额（亿美元）	同比增长（%）
1	日　本	146.54	4.29
2	美　国	135.66	76.00
3	中国香港	67.84	−30.24
4	俄罗斯	53.14	31.85
5	德　国	30.69	74.44
6	韩　国	24.41	−12.10
7	英　国	21.22	87.26
8	意大利	17.95	70.05
9	澳大利亚	16.98	17.30
10	加拿大	16.83	62.88

表 50 世界和中国纺织纤维产量（含 PP 纤维）（2002—2004 年） 单位：万 t

年份	世界纤维产量				中国纤维产量			
	总计	天然纤维	化学纤维		总计	天然纤维	化学纤维	
			小计	其中合纤			小计	其中合纤
2002	5 750.0	2 157.2	3 592.8	3 381.0	1 552.3	561.1	991.2	915.1
2003	6 092.8	2 301.1	3 791.7	3 565.7	1 809.0	563.3	1 245.7	1 147.2
2004	6 912.3	2 855.8	4 056.5	3 799.2	2 146.8	674.6	1 472.2	1 355.6

表 51 世界主要国家（地区）合成纤维产量（含 PP 纤维）（2002—2004 年）

单位：万 t

年份	全球	中国	美国	欧盟（15）	中国台湾	韩国	日本	印度	中国占（%）
2002	3 381.0	915.1	466.5	349.3	324.2	244.8	129.3	169.0	27.1
2003	3 565.7	1 147.2	402.7	356.5	321.0	227.1	119.8	179.2	32.2
2004	3 799.2	1 355.6	418.0	331.5	313.4	231.6	115.9	191.4	36.7

表 52 世界主要国家（地区）棉花产量（2002—2004 年） 单位：万 t

年份	全球	中国	美国	印度	巴基斯坦	土耳其	中国占（%）
2002	1 915.5	492.0	374.4	230.7	169.8	89.2	25.7
2003	2 060.7	486.9	397.4	300.8	173.4	90.0	23.6
2004	2 620.0	631.9	506.1	407.9	248.2	90.0	24.1

表 53 世界主要国家棉花耗用量（2002—2004 年） 单位：万 t

国家	耗用量	2002 年	2003 年	2004 年
全球	耗用量	2 070.8	2 133.8	2 339.6
	占总（%）	100.0	100.0	100.0
中国	耗用量	559.9	709.9	819.9
	占总（%）	27.0	33.3	35.0
美国	耗用量	177.4	141.3	136.1
	占总（%）	8.6	6.6	5.8
印度	耗用量	296.5	294.9	330.0
	占总（%）	14.3	13.8	14.1
巴基斯坦	耗用量	194.3	210.0	230.0
	占总（%）	9.4	9.8	9.8
土耳其	耗用量	140.0	132.5	155.0
	占总（%）	6.8	6.2	6.6
日本	耗用量	21.7	17.7	16.5
	占总（%）	1.0	0.8	0.7
巴西	耗用量	87.5	80.0	93.5
	占总（%）	4.2	3.7	4.0

表 54　全球人均纤维消费量（1990—2004 年）　单位：kg/（人·年）

名　称	年　份	1990	1995	2002	2004
全球平均		7.7	8.5	8.5	8.6
发达国家	平均	20.9	25.6	25.6	26.4
	美国	25.9	30.9	33.0	33.9
	欧盟（15）	18.0	23.0	23.0	23.5
	其他欧盟国家	13.8	14.2	14.2	15.8
	日本	21.8	26.2	26.2	27.0
	其他发达国家	14.6	18.8	18.8	19.8
东　欧	平均	14.1	10.5	10.5	11.0
	前 USSR	14.8	10.0	10.0	10.5
	其他东欧国家	11.6	12.0	12.0	12.5
发展中国家（地区）	平均	4.1	4.9	4.9	5.0
	中国	5.5	6.5	6.5	6.6
	拉丁美洲	5.7	6.4	6.4	6.4
	南亚	2.7	3.1	3.1	3.2
	东南亚	4.7	6.3	6.3	6.7
	其他发展中国家	3.0	3.6	3.6	3.7

表 55　世界纸浆分类产量（2003—2004 年）　单位：万 t

类　别	2003 年	2004 年	同比增长（%）
纸浆总产量	18 282.8	18 849.6	3.1
其中：化学制浆	12 682.3	13 138.9	3.6
机械制浆	3 190.1	3 273.0	2.6
其他浆	**2 410.4**	**2 437.7**	**1.13**

表 56　世界与中国纸浆、纸及纸板生产与消费情况（2002—2004 年）

单位：万 t

	项　目	2002 年	2003 年	2004 年
世界	纸浆总产量	18 200	18 516.5	18 849.6
	纸浆总消费量	18 265	18 442.3	18 775.4
	纸和纸板总产量	33 070	33 881.5	35 959.9
	纸和纸板总消费量	33 076	33 912.5	35 752.7
	纸和纸板人均年消费量/kg	53.7	51.7	55.6
中国	纸浆总产量	2 944	3 309	3 723
	纸浆总消费量	3 470	3 310	4 455
	纸和纸板总产量	3 780	4 300	4 950
	纸和纸板总消费量	4 332	4 806	5 439
	纸和纸板人均年消费量/kg	33	37	42

资料来源：PPI 杂志《中国统计年鉴》。

表 57　我国台湾省主要纸品产销量情况（2004 年）

单位：t

主要产品	产　量	同比增长（%）	销售量	同比增长（%）	内销量	同比增长（%）	外销量	同比增长（%）
一、纸张总计	1 277 465	2.7	1 269 166	1.7	1 059 057	−0.7	210 109	15.4
印刷书写纸	733 176	0.3	725 881	−1.1	571 528	−3.7	154 353	10.0
其中：铜版纸	361 357	0.7	357 910	−0.7	245 260	−5.5	112 650	11.8
道林纸	269 945	4.0	266 770	2.7	236 815	1.2	29 955	15.9
模造纸	68 153	−11.9	68 136	−12.5	56 395	−12.3	11 741	−13.6
新闻纸	3 333	−23.9	2 770	−54.8	2 770	−54.8		
生活用纸	217 641	9.0	216 937	7.4	214 692	7.0	2 245	68.9
二、纸板总计	3 523 622	3.2	3 527 520	3.6	2 455 953	−0.9	1 071 567	15.7
纸箱用纸板	2 611 806	4.3	2 618 194	5.1	1 897 790	0.5	720 404	19.5
其中：牛皮纸板	1 282 951	6.6	1 288 256	7.4	956 281		331 975	36.2
瓦楞原纸	1 235 172	2.4	1 238 818	3.4	854 080	1.3	384 738	8.3
白纸板	654 505		653 049	−0.7	325 198	−9.6	327 851	10.0
纸与纸板总计	**4 801 087**	**3.1**	**4 796 686**	**3.1**	**3 515 010**	**−0.8**	**1 281 676**	**15.6**

表 58　我国台湾省纸业在全球的地位（2004 年）

项　目	中国台湾			全　球		亚洲
	数量	同比增长（%）	排序	数量	同比增长（%）	数量
纸与纸板产量（万 t）	453.3	3.2	18	33 881.5	2.8	11 064.5
年消费量（万 t）	491.9	6.1	15	33 912.5	2.9	12 100.6
人均消费量［kg/（人·年）］	216.2		13	53.3		31.3

表 59　世界纸和纸板产量排名前 10 名的国家（2004 年）

排　序	国　家	产量（万 t）
1	美　国	8 340.1
2	中　国	4 950.0
3	日　本	3 088.9
4	加拿大	2 046.1
5	德　国	2 039.2
6	芬　兰	1 403.6
7	瑞　典	1 158.9
8	韩　国	1 051.1
9	法　国	1 024.9
10	意大利	966.5

表 60 世界纸和纸浆产量排名前 10 名的国家（2004 年）

排 序	国 家	产量（万 t）
1	美 国	5 358.5
2	加拿大	2 640.6
3	中 国	1 418.0
4	芬 兰	1 261.9
5	瑞 典	1 210.6
6	日 本	1 072.0
7	巴 西	972.8
8	俄罗斯	736.1
9	印度尼西亚	520.9
10	智 利	340.9

表 61 世界纸浆主要净进口和净出口前 5 名的国家（2004 年） 单位：万 t

纸浆主要净进口国			纸浆主要净出口国		
排 序	国 家	净进口量	排 序	国 家	净出口量
1	中 国	732.0	1	加拿大	1 055.4
2	德 国	411.7	2	巴 西	464.9
3	意大利	325.2	3	瑞 典	310.9
4	韩 国	258.3	4	智 利	253.1
5	日 本	231.9	5	芬 兰	218.7

表 62 世界纸和纸板消费量与人均消费量前 5 名的国家（2004 年）

纸和纸板消费量			纸和纸板人均消费量		
排 序	国 家	消费量（万 t）	排 序	国 家	人均消费量（kg/人）
1	美 国	9 225.70	1	卢森堡	345.70
2	中 国	5 439.21	2	比利时	337.9.
3	日 本	3 142.60	3	美 国	312.00
4	德 国	1 944.20	4	芬 兰	285.10
5	英 国	1 267.80	5	摩纳哥	277.70

表 63 世界纸和纸板产品三大净进口国（2002—2004 年） 单位：万 t

国 家	2002 年	2003 年	2004 年
美 国	729.2	793	885.7
英 国	622.2	624	643.8
中 国	551.47	506	489.22

表 64 世界天然橡胶和合成橡胶产量、消费量（2001—2004 年） 单位：kt

年 份	天然橡胶		合成橡胶	
	产 量	消费量	产 量	消费量
2001	7 240	7 030	10 530	10 360
2002	7 340	7 520	10 930	10 790
2003	7 970	7 880	11 540	11 320
2004	8 250	8 090	11 870	11 832

表 65 世界主要国家（地区）合成橡胶产量（2002—2004 年） 单位：万 t

国家或地区	2002 年	2003 年	2004 年
世界总计	**1 093**	**1 135**	**1 189**
加拿大	15	14.8	15.6
美 国	215	211.3	222.5
巴 西	38.4	40.5	43.6
中 国	113.3	127.2	145.6
中国台湾	52.3	52.9	54.8
印 度	7.8	8.6	9.5
日 本	152.2	157.7	155.0
韩 国	67.8	70.0	72.0
法 国	68.1	71.0	72.5
德 国	86.9	88.8	93.1
意大利	25.0	24.4	23.5
俄罗斯	91.9	107.0	112.0
英 国	33.7	32.8	33.4
澳大利亚	0.8	1.0	1.0
荷 兰	17.6	17.6	18.1

表 66 世界主要国家（地区）天然橡胶产量（2002—2004） 单位：万 t

国家或地区	2002 年	2003 年	2004 年
世界总计	**774**	**806**	**825**
泰 国	216.5	287.3	290.0
印度尼西亚	163.0	179.2	185.1
马来西亚	89.0	98.6	100.0
印 度	64.0	70.7	74.0
中 国	46.8	47.8	48.1
越 南	37.3	38.4	40.5
科特迪瓦	12.0	12.7	13.5
利比亚	10.9	11.0	11.2
巴 西	8.9	9.4	10.0
斯里兰卡	9.1	9.2	9.4

（续）

国家或地区	2002 年	2003 年	2004 年
菲律宾	7.6	8.4	8.8
喀麦隆	5.7	5.1	6.0
柬埔寨	4.7	4.7	4.8
尼日利亚	4.5	4.6	4.6
危地马拉	4.0	4.1	4.1
缅　甸	3.0	3.0	3.1

表 67　我国台湾省天然橡胶和合成橡胶消费量（2001—2003 年）　单位：万 t

名　称	2001 年	2002 年	2003 年
合　计	**30.9**	**35.5**	**40.6**
天然橡胶	9.1	10.5	11.5
合成橡胶	21.8	25	29.1

表 68　世界橡胶机械生产厂商前 10 名排序（2003 年）　单位：百万欧元

排序	企业名称	国别	销售量
1	克虏伯	德　国	163.6
2	贝尔斯托夫（Berstorff）	德　国	126.3
3	神户制钢	日　本	100.0
4	三菱重工	日　本	80.0
5	德斯玛（Des ma）	德　国	53.0
6	桂林橡胶机械厂	中　国	52.7
7	Rep	法　国	49.9
8	天津赛象	中　国	46.3
9	Itw 机械公司	美　国	40.0
10	三明华橡自控公司	中　国	39.8

注：在世界橡胶机械生产企业前 36 名排序中，我国青岛高校软控股份有限公司、北京敬业机械设备有限公司、大连诚信橡塑机械有限公司、桂林橡胶设计院实业公司、四川亚西橡塑机器有限公司、北京轮胎设备公司等均已进入世界橡胶机械制造企业 36 强中。

表 69　按营业额排序的世界最大 500 家企业中相关农产品加工企业（2004 年）

企业名称	国家或地区	营业额名次	营业额（百万美元）
食品业			
雀巢	瑞士	43	69 826
阿彻—丹尼尔斯—米德兰公司	美国	131	36 151
泰森食品公司	美国	201	26 441
麦当劳	美国	314	19 065
康尼格拉	美国	332	18 179
达能集团	法国	351	17 040
中国粮油食品进出口公司	中国	434	14 189
饮料业			
百事公司	美国	172	29 261

（续）

企业名称	国家或地区	营业额名次	营业额（百万美元）
可口可乐公司	美国	257	21 962
可口可乐企业	美国	334	18 158
安霍伊泽—布什公司	美国	411	14 934
造纸和纸制品			
国际造纸公司	美国	198	26 722
惠好公司	美国	246	22 665
斯达拉恩索	芬兰	392	15 417
金佰利—克拉克有限公司	美国	394	15 401
出版和印刷业			
大日本印刷公司	日本	467	13 259
凸版印刷公司	日本	471	13 153
橡胶和塑料制品业			
布里奇斯通轮胎公司	日本	250	22 350
米其林公司	法国	294	20 148
固特异轮胎和橡胶	美国	330	18 370
烟草业			
菲利普·莫里斯	美国	50	64 440
英美烟草公司	英国	220	24 201
日本烟草公司	日本	320	18 739
肥皂与化妆品业			
宝洁	美国	77	51 407
欧莱雅	法国	336	18 077
综合			
沃尔玛公司	美国	1	287 989
家乐福	法国	22	90 382
伊藤洋华堂	日本	145	33 632
联合利华	英国/荷兰	81	49 961

图书在版编目（CIP）数据

中国农产品加工业年鉴．2006/科学技术部农村科技司，中国农业机械化科学研究院，中国包装和食品机械总公司编．—北京：中国农业出版社，2007.8
ISBN 978-7-109-11780-8

Ⅰ.中… Ⅱ.①科…②中…③中… Ⅲ.农产品加工—加工工业—中国—2006—年鉴 Ⅳ.F326.5-54

中国版本图书馆 CIP 数据核字（2007）第 111717 号

中国农业出版社出版
（北京市朝阳区农展馆北路 2 号）
（邮政编码 100026）
责任编辑 孟令洋

中国农业出版社印刷厂印刷 新华书店北京发行所发行
2007 年 8 月第 1 版 2007 年 8 月北京第 1 次印刷

开本：787mm×1092mm 1/16 印张：33.25
字数：1065 千字
定价：240.00 元